**CONNECT®**

**|ANTHROPOLOGY**

## Students Get Results with Connect® Anthropology

**McGraw-Hill Connect** strengthens the link between faculty, students, and coursework, helping everyone accomplish more in less time. Innovative, adaptive technology engages students in the course content so they are better prepared, are more active in discussion, and achieve better results.

**14.** award:
10.00 points Problems? Adjust credit for all students.

People often use culture to fulfill psychological needs, such as:

- ○ Friendship, companionship, and approval.
- ○ Learning new table manners.
- ○ Developing new genetic traits.
- ○ Learning new technological skills, such as understanding social networking sites.
- ○ Learning a new language.

People often use culture to fulfill psychological needs, such as friendship, compan...

report a content issue

**CONNECT** INSIGHT™

## Instructors Get Results with Connect Insight™

The first and only analytics tool of its kind, **Connect Insight** is a series of visual data displays, each framed by an intuitive question —(How are my students doing? How is my section doing?)—that provides at-a-glance information regarding how your class is doing. **Connect Insight** is accessible at a moment's notice from your tablet device or desktop.

# anthropology APPRECIATING HUMAN DIVERSITY

## SIXTEENTH EDITION

### Conrad Phillip Kottak
University of Michigan

Mc
Graw
Hill
Education

*To my mother, Mariana Kottak Roberts*

ANTHROPOLOGY: APPRECIATING HUMAN DIVERSITY, SIXTEENTH EDITION
Published by McGraw-Hill Education, 2 Penn Plaza, New York, NY 10121. Copyright © 2015 by McGraw-Hill
Education. All rights reserved. Printed in the United States of America. Previous editions © 2013, 2011, and 2009. No
part of this publication may be reproduced or distributed in any form or by any means, or stored in a database or retrieval
system, without the prior written consent of McGraw-Hill Education, including, but not limited to, in any network or
other electronic storage or transmission, or broadcast for distance learning.

Some ancillaries, including electronic and print components, may not be available to customers outside the United States.

This book is printed on acid-free paper.

4 5 6 7 8 9 0   RMN   21 20 19 18 17 16

ISBN      978-0-07-786154-4
MHID      0-07-786154-X

Senior Vice President, Products & Markets: *Kurt L. Strand*
Vice President, General Manager, Products & Markets: *Michael J. Ryan*
Vice President, Content Production & Technology Services: *Kimberly Meriwether David*
Managing Director: *Gina Boedeker*
Brand Manager: *Courtney Austermehle*
Lead Product Developer: *Rhona Robbin*
Development Editor: *Barbara A. Heinssen*
Digital Development Editor: *Emily Pecora*
Digital Product Analyst: *John Brady*
Brand Coordinator: *Diane Grayson*
Marketing Manager: *Philip Weaver*
Director, Content Production: *Terri Schiesl*
Content Project Manager, Core: *Angela Norris*
Buyer: *Susan K. Culbertson*
Design: *Tara McDermott*
Cover Image: *Steve Vidler/Corbis*
Lead Content Licensing Specialist: *Keri Johnson*
Content Project Manager, Assessment: *Katie Klochan*
Content Project Manager, OLC: *Judi David*
Typeface: *Times Lt Std 10/12*
Compositor: *Aptara®, Inc.*
Printer: *R. R. Donnelley*

All credits appearing on page or at the end of the book are considered to be an extension of the copyright page.

### Library of Congress Cataloging-in-Publication Data

Kottak, Conrad Phillip.
  Anthropology : appreciating human diversity / Conrad Phillip Kottak, University of Michigan. — Sixteenth edition.
    p. cm.
  Includes bibliographical references and index.
  ISBN 978-0-07-786154-4 (alk. paper)—ISBN 0-07-786154-X (alk. paper) 1. Ethnology. 2. Anthropology. I. Title.
GN316.K638 2014
306—dc23

                                                                                          2014011594

The Internet addresses listed in the text were accurate at the time of publication. The inclusion of a website does not
indicate an endorsement by the authors or McGraw-Hill Education, and McGraw-Hill Education does not guarantee
the accuracy of the information presented at these sites.

# contents in brief

v

# contents

# 2 Culture 20

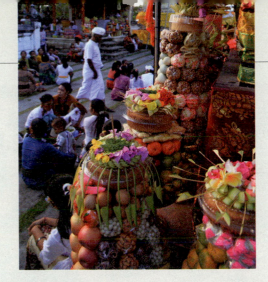

# 3 Applying Anthropology 39

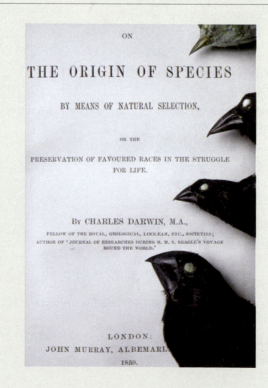

## 6 Human Variation and Adaptation *93*

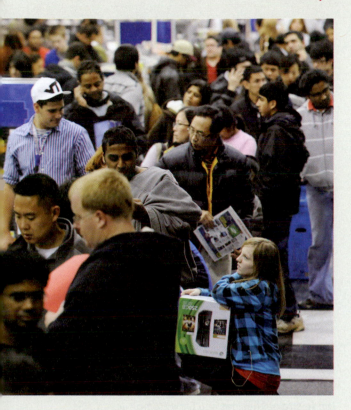

## 7 The Primates *108*

## 8  Early  Hominins   *127*

## 11 The First Farmers  186

## 12 The First Cities and States  207

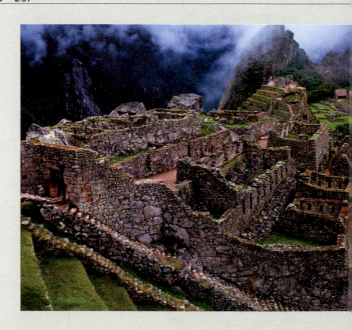

# 13 Method and Theory in Cultural Anthropology *229*

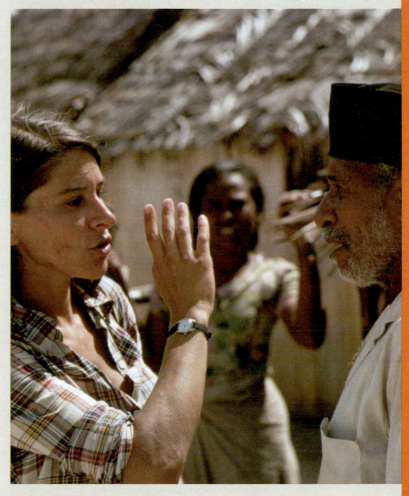

PART 3 APPRECIATING CULTURAL DIVERSITY

# 14 Language and Communication 253

# 15 Ethnicity and Race 274

## 18 Gender  340

## 19 Families, Kinship, and Descent  360

# 20 Marriage 378

# 21 Religion 397

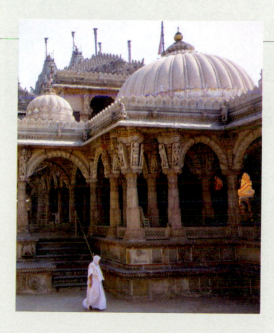

# 22 Arts, Media, and Sports  416

# list of boxes

## appreciating ANTHROPOLOGY

## appreciating DIVERSITY

focus on
**GLOBALIZATION**

## RECAP

# about the author

**Conrad Phillip Kottak**

Conrad Phillip Kottak (A.B. Columbia College, Ph.D. Columbia University) is the Julian H. Steward Collegiate Professor Emeritus of Anthropology at the University of Michigan, where he served as anthropology department chair from 1996 to 2006. He has been honored for his undergraduate teaching by the university and the state of Michigan and by the American Anthropological Association. He is an elected member of the American Academy of Arts and Sciences and the National Academy of Sciences, where he chaired Section 51, Anthropology from 2010 to 2013.

Professor Kottak has done ethnographic fieldwork in Brazil, Madagascar, and the United States. His general interests are in the processes by which local cultures are incorporated—and resist incorporation—into larger systems. This interest links his earlier work on ecology and state formation in Africa and Madagascar to his more recent research on globalization, national and international culture, and the mass media, including new media.

Kottak's popular case study *Assault on Paradise: The Globalization of a Little Community in Brazil* (2006) describes his long-term and continuing fieldwork in Arembepe, Bahia, Brazil. His book *Prime-Time Society: An Anthropological Analysis of Television and Culture* (2009) is a comparative study of the nature and impact of television in Brazil and the United States.

Kottak's other books include *The Past in the Present: History, Ecology and Cultural Variation in Highland Madagascar; Researching American Culture: A Guide for Student Anthropologists;* and *Madagascar: Society and History.* The most recent editions (16th) of his texts *Anthropology: Appreciating Human Diversity* (this book)

and *Cultural Anthropology: Appreciating Cultural Diversity* were published by McGraw-Hill in 2015. He also is the author of *Mirror for Humanity: A Concise Introduction to Cultural Anthropology* (9th ed., McGraw-Hill, 2014) and *Window on Humanity: A Concise Introduction to Anthropology* (6th ed., McGraw-Hill, 2014). With Kathryn A. Kozaitis, he wrote *On Being Different: Diversity and Multiculturalism in the North American Mainstream* (4th ed., McGraw-Hill, 2012).

Conrad Kottak's articles have appeared in academic journals, including *American Anthropologist, Journal of Anthropological Research, American Ethnologist, Ethnology, Human Organization,* and *Luso-Brazilian Review.* He also has written for popular journals, including *Transaction/SOCIETY, Natural History, Psychology Today,* and *General Anthropology.*

Kottak and his colleagues have researched television's impact in Brazil, environmental risk perception in Brazil, deforestation and biodiversity conservation in Madagascar, and economic development planning in northeastern Brazil. More recently, Kottak and his colleague Lara Descartes investigated how middle-class American families use various media in planning, managing, and evaluating the competing demands of work and family. That research is the basis of their book *Media and Middle Class Moms: Images and Realities of Work and Family* (Descartes and Kottak 2009). Professor Kottak currently is collaborating with Professor Richard Pace of Middle Tennessee State University and several graduate students on research investigating "The Evolution of Media Impact: A Longitudinal and Multi-Site Study of Television and New Electronic/Digital Media in Brazil."

Conrad Kottak appreciates comments about his books from professors and students. He can be reached by e-mail at the following Internet address: **ckottak@bellsouth.net.**

# a letter from the author

**Welcome to the 16th Edition of *Anthropology: Appreciating Human Diversity*!**

I wrote the first edition of this book during a time of rapid change in my favorite academic discipline—anthropology. My colleagues and I were excited about new discoveries and directions in all four of anthropology's subfields—biological anthropology, anthropological archaeology, sociocultural anthropology, and linguistic anthropology. My goal was to write a book that would capture that excitement, that would address key changes in anthropology, while providing a solid foundation of core concepts and the basics.

Just as anthropology is a dynamic discipline that explores new discoveries and the profound changes that affect people and societies, this edition of *Anthropology* has kept pace with changes in the way students read and learn core content today through the digital program called **Connect Anthropology.** This program includes assignable and assessable quizzes, exercises, and interactive activities, organized around course-specific learning objectives. In addition, **Connect** includes an interactive eBook, **LearnSmart,** an adaptive testing program, and **SmartBook,** the first and only adaptive reading experience. The tools and resources provided in **Connect Anthropology** are designed to engage students and enable them to improve their performance in the course.

While any competent text must present anthropology's core, it also must demonstrate anthropology's relevance to the 21st-century world we inhabit. Accordingly, several "Focus on Globalization" essays in this book examine topics as diverse as travel and tourism in the ancient and modern worlds, disease pandemics, world sports events (including the Olympics and the World Cup), and the expansion of international finance and branding. In addition, discussions of new media, including social media, have been added to several chapters.

Each chapter begins with a discussion titled "Understanding Ourselves." These introductions, along with examples from popular culture throughout the book, show how anthropology relates to students' everyday lives. My overarching goal for this textbook is to help students appreciate the field of anthropology and the various kinds of diversity it studies. How do anthropologists think and work? Where do we go, and how do we interpret what we see? How do we step back, compare, and analyze? How does anthropology contribute to our understanding of the world? To answer these questions, chapters contain boxed sections titled "Appreciating Anthropology," which focus on the value and usefulness of anthropological research and approaches. Other boxes, titled "Appreciating Diversity," focus on various forms and expressions of human biological and cultural diversity.

Most students who read this book will not go on to become anthropologists, or even anthropology majors. For those who do, this book should provide a solid foundation to build on. For those who don't—that is, for most of my readers—my goal is to instill a sense of appreciation: of human diversity, of anthropology as a field, and of how anthropology can build on, and help make sense of, the experience that students bring to the classroom. May this course and this text help students think differently about, and achieve greater understanding of, their own culture and its place within our globalizing world.

**Conrad Phillip Kottak**

# Highlights of the 16th Edition

Anthropology is an ever-evolving field, reflecting a constant stream of new discoveries, analyses, and interpretations, as well as the rapidly changing world it studies. It is vital to provide new and up-to-date content to enrich, for both students and instructors, the appreciation of anthropology's subject matter, intrinsic interest, and contemporary relevance. In this edition you will find some entirely new discussions and subject matter—in particular, an attempt to delve more deeply into the everyday lives of ancient hominins, as well as systematic attention to the key role of the Internet and social media in today's globalizing world.

## CHAPTER 1: WHAT IS ANTHROPOLOGY?
- New discussion of culturally specific syndromes, including the cultural construction of anorexia in China
- Rewritten section on the scientific method

## CHAPTER 2: CULTURE
- New information on the Internet and social media
- Revised section on globalization

## CHAPTER 3: APPLYING ANTHROPOLOGY
- New section on "Public and Applied Anthropology"
- New "Appreciating Anthropology" box, "Afghanistan: What the Anthropologists Say"

## CHAPTER 4: DOING ARCHAEOLOGY AND BIOLOGICAL ANTHROPOLOGY
- New "Appreciating Diversity" box, "All This from a Finger Bone?", about the reconstruction of the Denisovan genome
- New "Appreciating Anthropology" box, "A Biocultural Approach to Health in the Bolivian Amazon"

## CHAPTER 5: EVOLUTION AND GENETICS
- Two new figures illustrating the geographic distribution of the sickle-cell allele in relation to that of falciparum malaria

## CHAPTER 6: HUMAN VARIATION AND ADAPTATION
- Updated and reorganized content with a new discussion of the CCR5-Δ32 (delta 32) allele and resistance to HIV/AIDS

## CHAPTER 7: THE PRIMATES
- New art and discussions of recent discoveries of early primate fossils in China (the earliest known primate) and East Africa (the earliest known Old World monkeys and protoapes)

## CHAPTER 8: EARLY HOMININS
- New section titled "Oldowan Hominins at the Kanjera Site"
- New "Appreciating Anthropology" box, "*Au. sediba:* Ancestor or Fascinating Sideline?"

## CHAPTER 9: ARCHAIC *HOMO*
Substantially revised, this chapter now includes
- New information on recent *H. rudolfensis* discoveries
- New section titled "Life as a Neandertal"
- New section, "The Denisovans"

## CHAPTER 10: THE ORIGIN AND SPREAD OF MODERN HUMANS
Substantially revised with these additions:
- New section on China's Red Deer Cave people
- New "Appreciating Anthropology" box titled "In with the Old: The Evolutionary Importance of Grandparents"
- Discussion of recent discoveries involving the settlement of the New World, including Oregon's Paisley Caves and California's Channel Islands

## CHAPTER 11: THE FIRST FARMERS
Substantially revised; specific changes include
- New information on the recent discovery of the world's oldest pottery, in China, and recent discoveries about Jomon culture
- New introduction to the "Neolithic Revolution"
- New information on pre-Neolithic herd management in the Middle East and the spread of the Neolithic to Europe
- New sections, "The Neolithic in Europe" and "The Neolithic in Asia"
- New "Appreciating Anthropology" box on how global climate change and other threats are affecting archaeological sites

## CHAPTER 12: THE FIRST CITIES AND STATES
- Significantly revised throughout, including completely rewritten introductory sections and new information on early urbanism in Syria and state formation in the Americas

## CHAPTER 13: METHOD AND THEORY IN CULTURAL ANTHROPOLOGY
- Revised with clearer subheads and an updated section on ethics
- New section, "Online Ethnography"

## CHAPTER 14: LANGUAGE AND COMMUNICATION
- Updated with a new "Appreciating Anthropology" box on California accents
- New section titled "Language, Culture, and History," featuring new information on Proto-Indo-European (PIE)

## CHAPTER 15: ETHNICITY AND RACE
- Updated with the latest demographic data from the United States and Canada
- New sections titled "Minority Groups and Stratification" and "Changing Demographics"
- Revised and updated section on multiculturalism

## CHAPTER 16: MAKING A LIVING
Major revision and rewrite with specific changes, including the following:
- New introduction clarifying the huge importance and transformational nature of food-producing (Neolithic) economies
- New material on foragers in South Asia
- New hunter-gatherer distribution map

## CHAPTER 17: POLITICAL SYSTEMS
- New section titled "Resistance via Social Media"
- New "Appreciating Diversity" box on political mobilizations in rural Thailand

## CHAPTER 18: GENDER
- New discussion of Margaret Mead's pioneering work on gender
- Updated section on gender in industrial societies
- Revised material on transgender and gender identity (as distinguished from sexual orientation)

## CHAPTER 19: FAMILIES, KINSHIP, AND DESCENT
- Informative new "Appreciating Anthropology" box on American family life in the 21st century
- All charts, figures, and statistics have been updated.

## CHAPTER 20: MARRIAGE

Thoroughly updated, the chapter now contains a major new section titled "The Online Marriage Market."

## CHAPTER 21: RELIGION

Substantially revised, the chapter now includes

- Major new section, "Religion and Cultural Globalization," whose subsections are titled "Evangelical Protestantism and Pentecostalism," "Homogenization, Indigenization, or Hybridization?", "Antimodernism and Fundamentalism," and "The Spread of Islam"
- Substantially updated and revised section on world religions
- New "Appreciating Diversity" box, "Hinduism Takes Back Yoga"

## CHAPTER 22: ARTS, MEDIA, AND SPORTS

Significantly revised chapter includes two major new sections titled "Networking and Sociability On- and Offline" and "The Fall from Grace: Golf and the Celebrity Scandal"

## CHAPTER 23: THE WORLD SYSTEM AND COLONIALISM

- Major new section titled "NAFTA's Economic Refugees"
- Expanded discussion of skewed wealth distribution in the contemporary United States (including the Occupy movement)

## CHAPTER 24: ANTHROPOLOGY'S ROLE IN A GLOBALIZING WORLD

A substantially revised section on globalization begins this chapter, which has been updated throughout.

- Section on energy consumption and industrial degradation moved here from the previous chapter
- Major new section on emerging diseases
- Substantially revised sections on global climate change, environmental anthropology, and cultural imperialism and indigenization
- New concluding discussion of anthropology's key lessons

# Improve Student Performance with

McGraw-Hill LearnSmart guides students to an understanding of core concepts by helping them identify knowledge gaps and by providing key content at specific intervals to ensure mastery and long-term knowledge retention. **LearnSmart** continuously adapts as students answer questions, building an optimal learning path, so that students spend less time on concepts they already know and more time focused on those they don't. Reports provide valuable information about individual and class performance.

**Fueled by the Proven and Adaptive LearnSmart Engine**

More students earn A's and B's when they use LearnSmart.

# Offer your students a more personalized reading experience with SMARTBOOK™

**SmartBook** creates a personalized reading experience by highlighting the most important concepts a student needs to learn at a given moment in time. This ensures that every minute spent with **SmartBook** is returned to the student as the most value-added minute possible. The reading experience continuously adapts by highlighting content based on what the student knows and doesn't know.

# Help your Students Succeed with

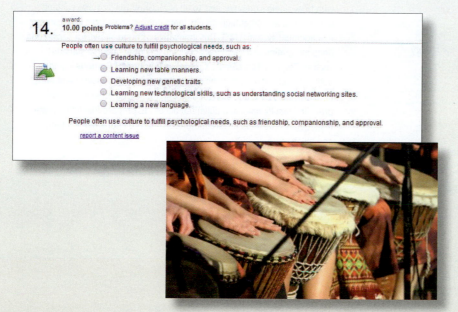

**McGraw-Hill Connect Anthropology**
includes assignable and assessable quizzes, exercises, and interactive activities, organized around course-specific learning objectives. Interactive quizzes and assessments engage students and help them to review and master core content. In addition, **Connect** includes an interactive eBook, LearnSmart, an adaptive testing program, and SmartBook, the first and only adaptive reading experience. The tools and resources provided in **Connect Anthropology** are designed to engage students and enable them to improve their performance in the course. Printable, exportable reports show how well each student (or section) is performing on each course segment.

# Assess Student and Class Performance with

The first and only analytics tool of its kind, **McGraw-Hill Connect Insight** is a series of visual data displays, each framed by an intuitive question (How are my students doing? How is my section doing?) that provides at-a-glance information regarding how your class is doing. **Connect Insight**™ is accessible at a moment's notice from your tablet device.

# Teaching Resources

## |ANTHROPOLOGY

The following instructor resources can be accessed through the Library tab in **Connect Anthropology:**

- Instructor's manual
- PowerPoint lecture slides
- Computerized test bank
- Word version of the test bank
- Links to professional resources and career-related information
- "Beyond the Classroom" essays
- Supplementary content on the following topics: anthropological theories, ethics, and popular culture

**MH Campus**® is the first-of-its-kind institutional service providing faculty with true, single sign-on access to all of McGraw-Hill's course content, digital tools, and other high-quality learning resources from any learning management system (LMS). This innovative offering allows for secure and deep integration and seamless access to any of our course solutions such as Connect, LearnSmart, Create, or Tegrity. **MH Campus** includes access to our entire content library, including eBooks, assessment tools, presentation slides, and multimedia content, among other resources, providing faculty open and unlimited access to prepare for class, create tests/quizzes, develop lecture material, integrate interactive content, and much more.

### Learn Smart. Choose Smart.

**CourseSmart** offers thousands of the most commonly adopted textbooks across hundreds of courses from a wide variety of higher education publishers. It is the only place for faculty to review and compare the full text of a textbook online, providing immediate access without the environmental impact of requesting a printed exam copy. At **CourseSmart,** students can save up to 50% off the cost of a printed book, reduce their impact on the environment, and gain access to powerful Web tools for learning, including full text search, notes and highlighting, and e-mail tools for sharing notes among classmates. Learn more at **www.coursesmart.com.**

With **McGraw-Hill Create** at **www.mcgrawhillcreate.com,** you can design your own course materials. You can rearrange or omit chapters, combine material from other sources, and/or upload your syllabus or any other content you have written to make the perfect resources for your students. You can search thousands of leading McGraw-Hill textbooks to find the best content for your students, and then arrange it to fit your teaching style. You can even personalize your book's appearance by selecting the cover and adding your name, school, and course information. When you order a Create book, you receive a complimentary review copy. Get a printed copy in 3 to 5 business days or an electronic copy (eComp) via e-mail in about an hour. Register today at **www.mcgrawhillcreate.com** and craft your course resources to match the way you teach.

# Acknowledgments

As always, I'm grateful to many colleagues at McGraw-Hill. Thanks to Gina Boedeker, McGraw-Hill's Managing Director for Anthropology, and Courtney Austermehle, Brand Manager. Thanks as well to Diane Grayson, Brand Coordinator for anthropology, and to Rhona Robbin, Lead Product Developer, and Emily Pecora, who has managed the development of Connect Anthropology. It's been a real pleasure to work closely with Development Editor Barbara Heinssen, whom I thank for her excellent ideas, skillful editing, and hard work putting this manuscript—text and visual—into production. I thank Marketing Manager Philip Weaver and McGraw-Hill's entire team of sales reps and regional managers for the work they do in helping professors and students gain access to my books.

I'm truly grateful as well for the superb work of the following: K4 specialist Christine Demma Foushi, Core Content Project Manager Angela Norris, Designer Tara McDermott, Image Content Licensing Specialist Keri Johnson, Text Content Licensing Specialist Wesley Hall, Assessment Content Project Manager Katie Klochan, and OLC Content Project Manager Judi David. I offer special thanks as well to Charlotte Goldman, Freelance Photo Researcher; Deb DeBord, Copyeditor; and Margaret Moore, proofreader. Thanks as well to Scott Lukas, Lake Tahoe Community College, who created the content for the Connect products for this book. I'm grateful also to Richard Pace, who drafted the section on social media in Brazil in Chapter 17.

I'm especially indebted to the reviewers who evaluated the 15th edition of this book:

Maria Altemara, West Virginia University, Robert Morris University

Timi Lynne Barone, University of Nebraska, Omaha

Renée M. Bonzani, University of Kentucky

Christopher A. Brooks, Virginia Commonwealth University

Holly Peters-Golden, University of Michigan

Kevin Keating, Broward College

Richard A. Sattler, University of Montana

Heather Walder, University of Wisconsin—La Crosse

I'm also grateful to the valued reviewers of previous editions of this book and of my *Cultural Anthropology* text. Their names are as follows:

Julianna Acheson, Green Mountain College

Stephanie W. Alemán, Iowa State University

Mohammad Al-Madani, Seattle Central Community College

Douglas J. Anderson, Front Range Community College

E. F. Aranyosi, University of Washington

Robert Bee, University of Connecticut

Joy A. Bilharz, SUNY at Fredonia

James R. Bindon, University of Alabama

Kira Blaisdell-Sloan, Louisiana State University

Kathleen T. Blue, Minnesota State University

Daniel Boxberger, Western Washington University

Vicki Bradley, University of Houston

Lisa Kaye Brandt, North Dakota State University

Ethan M. Braunstein, Northern Arizona University

Ned Breschel, Morehead State University

Peter J. Brown, Emory University

Margaret S. Bruchez, Blinn College

Vaughn M. Bryant, Texas A&M University

Andrew Buckser, Purdue University

Richard H. Buonforte, Brigham Young University

Karen Burns, University of Georgia

Richard Burns, Arkansas State University

Mary Cameron, Auburn University

Joseph L. Chartkoff , Michigan State University

Dianne Chidester, University of South Dakota

Stephen Childs, Valdosta State University

Inne Choi, California Polytechnic State University—San Luis Obispo

Wanda Clark, South Plains College

Jeffrey Cohen, Penn State University

Fred Conquest, Community College of Southern Nevada

Barbara Cook, California Polytechnic State University—San Luis Obispo

Maia Greenwell Cunningham, Citrus College

Sean M. Daley, Johnson County Community College

Karen Dalke, University of Wisconsin—Green Bay

Norbert Dannhaeuser, Texas A&M University

Michael Davis, Truman State University

Hillary Delprete, Wagner College

Paul Demers, University of Nebraska—Lincoln

Darryl de Ruiter, Texas A&M University

Robert Dirks, Illinois State University

William W. Donner, Kutztown University

Mary Durocher, Wayne State University

Paul Durrenberger, Pennsylvania State University

George Esber, Miami University of Ohio

Les W. Field, University of New Mexico

Grace Fraser, Plymouth State College

Todd Jeffrey French, University of New Hampshire, Durham

Richard H. Furlow, College of DuPage

Vance Geiger, University of Central Florida

Laurie Godfrey, University of Massachusetts—Amherst

Bob Goodby, Franklin Pierce College

Gloria Gozdzik, West Virginia University

Tom Greaves, Bucknell University

Mark Grey, University of Northern Iowa

Sharon Gursky, Texas A&M University

John Dwight Hines, University of California, Santa Barbara

Brian A. Hoey, Marshall University

Homes Hogue, Mississippi State University

Kara C. Hoover, Georgia State University

Charles W. Houck, University of North Carolina—Charlotte

Stevan R. Jackson, Virginia Tech

Alice James, Shippensburg University of Pennsylvania

Cara Roure Johnson, University of Connecticut

Richard King, Drake University

Christine Kray, Rochester Institute of Technology

Eric Lassiter, Ball State University

Jill Leonard, University of Illinois—Urbana-Champaign

Kenneth Lewis, Michigan State University

David Lipset, University of Minnesota

Walter E. Little, University at Albany, SUNY

Jon K. Loessin, Wharton County Junior College

Brian Malley, University of Michigan

Jonathan Marks, University of North Carolina–Charlotte

H. Lyn Miles, University of Tennessee at Chattanooga

Barbara Miller, George Washington University

Richard G. Milo, Chicago State University

John Nass, Jr., California University of Pennsylvania

Frank Ng, California State University–Fresno

Constanza Ocampo-Raeder, University of Maine (Orono)

Divinity B. O'Connor DLR-Roberts, Des Moines Area Community College

Martin Ottenheimer, Kansas State University

De Ann Pendry, University of Tennessee–Knoxville

Leonard Plotnicov, University of Pittsburgh

Janet Pollak, William Paterson University

Christina Nicole Pomianek, University of Missouri–Columbia

Geoffrey G. Pope, William Paterson University

Howard Prince, CUNY–Borough of Manhattan Community College

Frances E. Purifoy, University of Louisville

Asa Randall, University of Florida

Mark A. Rees, University of Louisiana at Lafayette

Bruce D. Roberts, Minnesota State University Moorhead

Rita C. Rodabaugh, Central Piedmont Community College

Steven Rubenstein, Ohio University

Robert Rubinstein, Syracuse University

Richard A. Sattler, University of Montana

Richard Scaglion, University of Pittsburgh

Mary Scott, San Francisco State University

James Sewastynowicz, Jacksonville State University

Brian Siegel, Furman University

Michael Simonton, Northern Kentucky University

Megan Sinnott, University of Colorado–Boulder

Esther Skirboll, Slippery Rock University of Pennsylvania

Alexia Smith, University of Connecticut

Gregory Starrett, University of North Carolina–Charlotte

Karl Steinen, University of West Georgia

Noelle Stout, Foothill and Skyline Colleges

Merrily Stover, University of Maryland–University College

Elizabeth A. Throop, Eastern Kentucky University

Ruth Toulson, Brigham Young University

Susan Trencher, George Mason University

Mark Tromans, Broward Community College

Christina Turner, Virginia Commonwealth University

Donald Tyler, University of Idaho

Daniel Varisco, Hofstra University

Albert Wahrhaftig, Sonoma State University

Joe Watkins, University of New Mexico

David Webb, Kutztown University of Pennsylvania

George Westermark, Santa Clara University

Donald A. Whatley, Blinn College

Nancy White, University of South Florida

Katharine Wiegele, Northern Illinois University

Mary S. Willis, University of Nebraska–Lincoln

Brent Woodfill, University of Louisiana at Lafayette

Other professors and many students regularly share their insights about this and my other texts via e-mail and so have contributed to this book. I'm especially grateful to my Michigan colleagues who use my books and have suggested ways of making them better. Thanks especially to a 101 team that includes Tom Fricke, Stuart Kirsch, Holly Peters-Golden, and Andrew Shryock. Special thanks as well to Joyce Marcus and Kent Flannery for continuing to nurture the archaeologist in me. By now, I've benefited from the knowledge, help, and advice of so many friends, colleagues, teaching assistants, graduate student instructors, and students that I can no longer fit their names into a short preface. I hope they know who they are and accept my thanks.

As usual, my family has offered me understanding, support, and inspiration during the preparation of this book. Dr. Nicholas Kottak, who, like me, holds a doctorate in anthropology, regularly shares his insights with me, as does my daughter, Dr. Juliet Kottak Mavromatis, and my wife, Isabel Wagley Kottak. Isabel has been my companion in the field and in life during my entire career in anthropology, and I can't imagine being without her. I renew my dedication of this book to the memory of my mother, Mariana Kottak Roberts, who kindled my interest in the human condition and provided many insights about people and society.

Over my many years of teaching anthropology, feedback from students has kept me up to date on the interests and needs of my readers, as does my ongoing participation in workshops on the teaching of anthropology. I hope this product of my experience will be helpful to others.

**Conrad Phillip Kottak**
**Seabrook Island, SC,**
**and Decatur, Georgia**
**ckottak@bellsouth.net**

# What Is Anthropology?

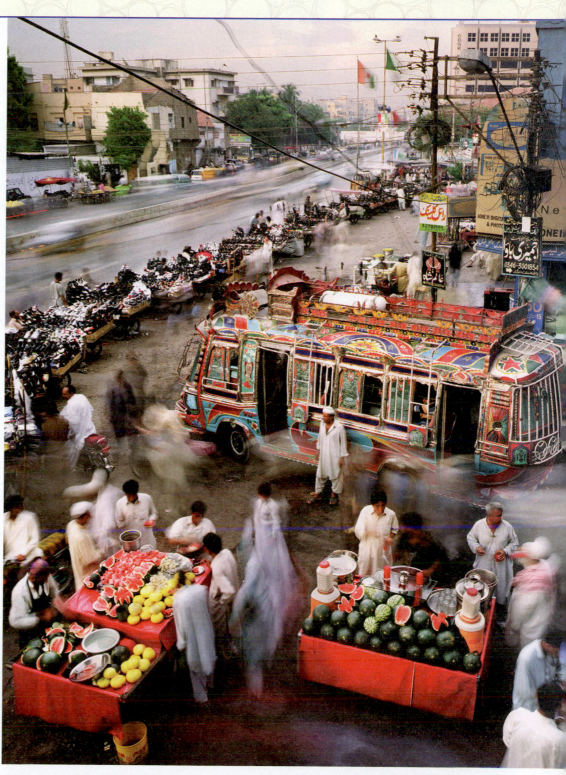

▸ What distinguishes anthropology from other fields that study human beings?

▸ How do anthropologists study human diversity in time and space?

▸ Why is anthropology both scientific and humanistic?

In Karachi, Pakistan, a bus gathers passengers next to watermelon stalls at the edge of a roadside market.

# understanding OURSELVES

When you grew up, which sport did you appreciate the most—soccer, swimming, football, baseball, tennis, golf, or some other sport (or perhaps none at all)? Is this because of "who you are" or because of the opportunities you had as a child to practice and participate in this particular activity? Think about the phrases and sentences you would use to describe yourself in a personal ad or on a networking site—your likes and dislikes, hobbies, and habits. How many of these descriptors would be the same if you had been born in a different place or time?

When you were young, your parents might have told you that drinking milk and eating vegetables would help you grow up "big and strong." They probably didn't as readily recognize the role that *culture* plays in shaping bodies, personalities, and personal health. If nutrition matters in growth, so, too, do cultural guidelines. What is proper behavior for boys and girls? What kinds of work should men and women do? Where should people live? What are proper uses of their leisure time? What role should religion play? How should people relate to their family, friends, and neighbors? Although our genetic attributes provide a foundation for our growth and development, human biology is fairly plastic—that is, it is malleable. Culture is an environmental force that affects our development as much as do nutrition, heat, cold, and altitude. Culture also guides our emotional and cognitive growth and helps determine the kinds of personalities we have as adults.

Among scholarly disciplines, anthropology stands out as the field that provides the cross-cultural test. How much would we know about human behavior, thought, and feeling if we studied only our own kind? What if our entire understanding of human behavior were based on analysis of questionnaires filled out by college students in Oregon? That is a radical question, but one that should make you think about the basis for statements about what humans are like, individually or as a group. A primary reason anthropology can uncover so much about what it means to be human is that the discipline is based on the cross-cultural perspective. One culture can't tell us everything we need to know about what it means to be human. Often culture is "invisible" (assumed to be normal, or just the way things are) until it is placed in comparison to another culture. For example, to appreciate how watching television affects us, as human beings, we need to study not just North America today but some other place—and perhaps some other time (such as Brazil in the 1980s; see Kottak 1990*b,* 2009). The cross-cultural test is fundamental to the anthropological approach, which orients this textbook.

## HUMAN DIVERSITY

Anthropologists study human beings and their products wherever and whenever they find them—in rural Kenya, a Turkish café, a Mesopotamian tomb, or a North American shopping mall. Anthropology explores human diversity across time and space, seeking to understand as much as possible about the human condition. Of particular interest is the diversity that comes through human adaptability.

Humans are among the world's most adaptable animals. In the Andes of South America, people wake up in villages 16,000 feet above sea level and then trek 1,500 feet higher to work in tin mines. Tribes in the Australian desert worship animals and discuss philosophy. People survive malaria in the tropics. Men have walked on the moon. The model of the USS *Enterprise* in Washington's Smithsonian Institution symbolizes the desire to "seek out new life and civilizations, to boldly go where no one has gone before." Wishes to know the unknown, control the uncontrollable, and create order out of chaos find expression among all peoples. Creativity, adaptability, and flexibility are basic human attributes, and human diversity is the subject matter of anthropology.

Students often are surprised by the breadth of **anthropology,** which is the study of the human species and its immediate ancestors. Anthropology is a uniquely comparative and **holistic** science. *Holism* refers to the study of the whole of the human condition: past, present, and future; biology, society, language, and culture. Most people think that anthropologists study fossils and nonindustrial, non-Western cultures, and many of them do. But anthropology is much more than the study of nonindustrial peoples: It is a comparative field that examines all societies, ancient and modern, simple and complex, local and global. The other social sciences tend to focus on a single society, usually an industrial nation like the United States or Canada. Anthropology, however, offers a unique cross-cultural perspective by constantly comparing the customs of one society with those of others.

People share society—organized life in groups—with other animals, including baboons, wolves, mole rats, and even ants. Culture, however, is more distinctly human. **Cultures** are traditions and customs, transmitted through learning, that form and guide the beliefs and behavior of the people exposed to them. Children learn such a tradition by growing up in a particular society, through a process called enculturation. Cultural traditions include customs and opinions, developed over the generations, about proper and improper behavior. These traditions answer such questions as these: How should we do things? How do we make sense of the world? How do we tell right from wrong? What is right, and what is wrong? A culture produces a degree of consistency in behavior and thought among the people who live in a particular society. (This chapter's "Appreciating Diversity" on pp. 4–5 discusses how attitudes about displays of affection, which are transmitted culturally, can also change.)

The most critical element of cultural traditions is their transmission through learning rather than through biological inheritance. Culture is not itself biological, but it rests on certain features of human biology. For more than a million years, humans have possessed at least some of the biological capacities on which culture depends. These abilities are to learn, to think symbolically, to use language, and to make and use tools.

Anthropology confronts and ponders major questions about past and present human existence. By examining ancient bones and tools, we unravel the mysteries of human origins. When did our ancestors separate from those of the apes? Where and when did *Homo sapiens* originate? How has our species changed? What are we now, and where are we going? How have changes in culture and society influenced biological change? Our genus, *Homo,* has been changing for more than one million years. Humans continue to adapt and change both biologically and culturally.

## Adaptation, Variation, and Change

*Adaptation* refers to the processes by which organisms cope with environmental forces and stresses. How do organisms change to fit their environments, such as dry climates or high mountain altitudes? Like other animals, humans have biological means of adaptation. But humans also habitually rely on cultural means of adaptation. Recap 1.1 summarizes the cultural and biological means that humans use to adapt to high altitudes.

Mountainous terrains pose particular challenges, those associated with altitude and oxygen deprivation. Consider four ways (one cultural and three biological) in which humans may cope with low oxygen

**anthropology**
The study of the human species and its immediate ancestors.

**holistic**
Encompassing past, present, and future; biology, society, language, and culture.

**culture**
Traditions and customs transmitted through learning.

| RECAP 1.1 | Forms of Cultural and Biological Adaptation (to High Altitude) | |
|---|---|---|
| **FORM OF ADAPTATION** | **TYPE OF ADAPTATION** | **EXAMPLE** |
| Technology | Cultural | Pressurized airplane cabin with oxygen masks |
| Genetic adaptation (occurs over generations) | Biological | Larger "barrel chests" of native highlanders |
| Long-term physiological adaptation (occurs during growth and development of the individual organism) | Biological | More efficient respiratory system, to extract oxygen from "thin air" |
| Short-term physiological adaptation (occurs spontaneously when the individual organism enters a new environment) | Biological | Increased heart rate, hyperventilation |

# appreciating DIVERSITY

## "Give Me a Hug"

A few years ago I created and taught a course called "Experiencing Culture" to American college students in Italy. Students wrote biweekly journals reflecting on the cultural differences they observed between Europeans and Americans. One thing that really impressed them was the greater frequency and intensity of PDAs—public displays of affection—between romantic couples in Italy, compared with the U.S.

The world's nations and cultures have strikingly different notions about displays of affection and personal space. Cocktail parties in international meeting places such as the United Nations can resemble an elaborate insect mating ritual as diplomats from different countries advance, withdraw, and sidestep. When Americans talk, walk, and dance, they maintain a certain distance from others. Italians or Brazilians, who need less personal space, may interpret such "standoffishness" as a sign of coldness. In conversational pairs, the Italian or Brazilian typically moves in, while the American "instinctively" retreats from a "close talker."

Such bodily movements illustrate not instinct, but culture—behavior programmed by years of exposure to a particular cultural tradition. Culture, however, is not static, as is suggested by this recent account of hugging behavior in American schools. Appreciate as

well that any nation usually contains diverse and even conflicting cultural values. One example is generational diversity, which the famed anthropologist Margaret Mead, one of my teachers, referred to as "the generation gap." Americans (in this case parents and school officials versus teenagers) exhibit generational differences involving the propriety of PDAs and concerns about sexual harassment.

There is so much hugging at Pascack Hills High School in Montvale, N.J., that students have broken down the hugs by type:

There is the basic friend hug, probably the most popular, and the bear hug, of course.

But now there is also the bear claw, when a boy embraces a girl awkwardly with his elbows poking out.

There is the hug that starts with a high-five, then moves into a fist bump, followed by a slap on the back and an embrace.

There's the shake and lean; the hug from behind; and, the newest addition, the triple—any combination of three girls and boys hugging at once.

"We're not afraid, we just get in and hug," said Danny Schneider, a junior at the school, where hallway hugging began shortly after 7 A.M. on a recent morning as students arrived. "The guy friends, we don't care. You just get right in there and jump in."

There are romantic hugs, too, but that is not what these teenagers are talking about.

Girls embracing girls, girls embracing boys, boys embracing each other—the hug has become

Does high school hugging as described in this news story seem strange to you?

pressure at high altitudes. Illustrating cultural (technological) adaptation would be a pressurized airplane cabin equipped with oxygen masks. There are three ways of adapting biologically to high altitudes: genetic adaptation, long-term physiological adaptation, and short-term physiological adaptation. First, native populations of high-altitude areas, such as the Andes of Peru and the Himalayas of Tibet and Nepal, seem to have acquired certain genetic advantages for life at very high altitudes. The Andean tendency to develop a voluminous chest and lungs probably has a genetic basis. Second, regardless of their genes, people who grow up at a high altitude become physiologically more efficient there than genetically similar people who have grown up at sea

level would be. This illustrates long-term physiological adaptation during the body's growth and development. Third, humans also have the capacity for short-term or immediate physiological adaptation. Thus, when lowlanders arrive in the highlands, they immediately increase their breathing and heart rates. Hyperventilation increases the oxygen in their lungs and arteries. As the pulse also increases, blood reaches their tissues more rapidly. These varied adaptive responses—cultural and biological—all fulfill the need to supply an adequate amount of oxygen to the body.

As human history has unfolded, the social and cultural means of adaptation have become increasingly important. In this process, humans have the favorite social greeting when teenagers meet or part these days. . . .

A measure of how rapidly the ritual is spreading is that some students complain of peer pressure to hug to fit in. And schools from Hillsdale, N.J., to Bend, Ore., wary in a litigious era about sexual harassment or improper touching—or citing hallway clogging and late arrivals to class—have banned hugging or imposed a three-second rule.

Parents, who grew up in a generation more likely to use the handshake, the low-five or the high-five, are often baffled by the close physical contact. "It's a wordless custom, from what I've observed," wrote Beth J. Harpaz, the mother of two boys, 11 and 16, and a parenting columnist for The Associated Press, in a new book, "13 Is the New 18." . . .

"Witnessing this interaction always makes me feel like I am a tourist in a country where I do not know the customs and cannot speak the language." For teenagers, though, hugging is hip. And not hugging?

"If somebody were to not hug someone, to never hug anybody, people might be just a little wary of them and think they are weird or peculiar," said Gabrielle Brown, a freshman at Fiorello H. LaGuardia High School in Manhattan.

Comforting as the hug may be, principals across the country have clamped down.

"Touching and physical contact is very dangerous territory," said Noreen Hajinlian, the principal of George G. White School, a junior high school in Hillsdale, N.J., who banned hugging two years ago. . . .

Schools that have limited hugging invoked longstanding rules against public displays of affection, meant to maintain an atmosphere of academic seriousness and prevent unwanted touching, or even groping.

But pro-hugging students say it is not a romantic or sexual gesture, simply the "hello" of their generation. . . .

Amy L. Best, a sociologist at George Mason University, said the teenage embrace is more a reflection of the overall evolution of the American greeting, which has become less formal since the 1970s. "Without question, the boundaries of touch have changed in American culture," she said. "We display bodies more readily, there are fewer rules governing body touch and a lot more permissible access to other people's bodies."

Hugging appears to be a grassroots phenomenon and not an imitation of a character or custom on TV or in movies. The prevalence of boys' nonromantic hugging (especially of other boys) is most striking to adults. Experts say that over the last generation, boys have become more comfortable expressing emotion, as embodied by the MTV show "Bromance," which is now a widely used term for affection between straight male friends. . . .

African American boys and men have been hugging as part of their greeting for decades, using the word "dap" to describe a ritual involving handshakes, slaps on the shoulders and, more recently, a hug, also sometimes called the gangsta hug among urban youth. . . .

Some parents find it paradoxical that a generation so steeped in hands-off virtual communication would be so eager to hug.

"Maybe it's because all these kids do is text and go on Facebook so they don't even have human contact anymore," said Dona Eichner, the mother of freshman and junior girls at the high school in Montvale. . . .

Carrie Osbourne, a sixth-grade teacher at Claire Lilienthal Alternative School, said hugging was a powerful and positive sign that children are inclined to nurture one another, breaking down barriers. "And it gets to that core that every person wants to feel cared for, regardless of your age or how cool you are or how cool you think you are," she said.

As much as hugging is a physical gesture, it has migrated online as well. Facebook applications allowing friends to send hugs have tens of thousands of fans.

devised diverse ways of coping with the range of environments they have occupied in time and space. The rate of cultural adaptation and change has accelerated, particularly during the last 10,000 years. For millions of years, hunting and gathering of nature's bounty—*foraging*—was the sole basis of human subsistence. However, it took only a few thousand years for **food production** (the cultivation of plants and domestication of animals), which originated some 12,000–10,000 years ago, to replace foraging in most areas. Between 6000 and 5000 B.P. (before the present), the first civilizations arose. These were large, powerful, and complex societies, such as ancient Egypt, that conquered and governed large geographic areas.

Much more recently, the spread of industrial production has profoundly affected human life. Throughout human history, major innovations have spread at the expense of earlier ones. Each economic revolution has had social and cultural repercussions. Today's global economy and communications link all contemporary people, directly or indirectly, in the modern world system. Nowadays, even remote villagers experience world forces and events. (See "Focus on Globalization" on p. 8.) The study of how local people adapt to global forces poses new challenges for anthropology: "The cultures of world peoples need to be constantly rediscovered as these people reinvent them in changing historical circumstances" (Marcus and Fischer 1986, p. 24).

**food production**
An economy based on plant cultivation and/or animal domestication.

# GENERAL ANTHROPOLOGY

**general anthropology**
Anthropology as a whole: cultural, archaeological, biological, and linguistic anthropology.

The academic discipline of anthropology, also known as **general anthropology** or "four-field" anthropology, includes four main subdisciplines or subfields. They are sociocultural, archaeological, biological, and linguistic anthropology. (From here on, the shorter term *cultural anthropology* will be used as a synonym for "sociocultural anthropology.") Cultural anthropology focuses on societies of the present and recent past. Anthropological archaeology reconstructs lifeways of ancient and more recent societies through analysis of material remains. Biological anthropology studies human biological variation through time and across geographic space. Linguistic anthropology examines language in its social and cultural contexts. Of the four subfields, cultural anthropology has the largest membership. Most departments of anthropology teach courses in all four subfields. (Note that general anthropology did not develop as a comparable field of study in most European countries, where the subdisciplines tend to exist separately.)

There are historical reasons for the inclusion of the four subfields in a single discipline in North America. The origin of anthropology as a scientific field, and of American anthropology in particular, can be traced back to the 19th century. Early American anthropologists were concerned especially with the history and cultures of the native peoples of North America. Interest in the origins and diversity of Native Americans brought together studies of customs, social life, language, and physical traits. Anthropologists still are pondering such questions as these: Where did Native Americans come from? How many waves of migration brought them to the New World? What are the linguistic, cultural, and biological links among Native Americans and between them and Asia?

**biocultural**
Combining biological and cultural approaches to a given problem.

There also are logical reasons for including anthropology's four subfields in the same academic discipline. Answers to key questions in anthropology often require an understanding of both human biology and culture and of both the past and the present. Each subfield considers variation in time and space (that is, in different geographic areas). Cultural and archaeological anthropologists study (among many other topics) changes in social life and customs. Archaeologists have used studies of living societies and behavior patterns to imagine what life might have been like in the past. Biological anthropologists examine evolutionary changes in physical form, for example, anatomical changes that might have

Early American anthropology was especially concerned with the history and cultures of Native North Americans. Ely S. Parker, or Ha-sa-noan-da, was a Seneca Indian who made important contributions to early anthropology. Parker also served as Commissioner of Indian Affairs for the United States.

been associated with the origin of tool use or language. Linguistic anthropologists may reconstruct the basics of ancient languages by studying modern ones.

The subdisciplines influence each other as members of the different subfields talk to each other, share books and journals, and associate in departments and at professional meetings. General anthropology explores the basics of human biology, society, and culture and considers their interrelations. Anthropologists share certain key assumptions. Perhaps the most fundamental is the idea that sound conclusions about "human nature" cannot be derived from studying a single nation, society, or cultural tradition. A comparative, cross-cultural approach is essential.

## Cultural Forces Shape Human Biology

Anthropology's comparative, biocultural perspective recognizes that cultural forces constantly mold human biology. (**Biocultural** refers to using and combining both biological and cultural perspectives and approaches to analyze and understand a particular issue or problem.) As we saw in "Understanding Ourselves," culture is a key environmental force in determining how human bodies grow and develop. Cultural traditions promote certain activities and abilities, discourage others, and set standards of physical well-being and attractiveness. Physical activities, including sports, which are influenced by culture, help build the body. For example, North American girls are encouraged to pursue, and therefore do well in, competition involving figure skating, gymnastics, track and field, swimming, diving, and many other sports. Brazilian girls, although excelling in the team sports of basketball and volleyball, haven't fared nearly as well in individual sports as have their American and Canadian counterparts. Why are people encouraged to excel as athletes in some nations but not others? Why do people in some countries invest so much time and effort in competitive sports that their bodies change significantly as a result?

Cultural standards of attractiveness and propriety influence participation and achievement in sports. Americans run or swim not just to compete but to keep trim and fit. Brazil's beauty standards traditionally have accepted more fat, especially in female buttocks and hips. Brazilian men have had significant international success in swimming and running, but Brazil

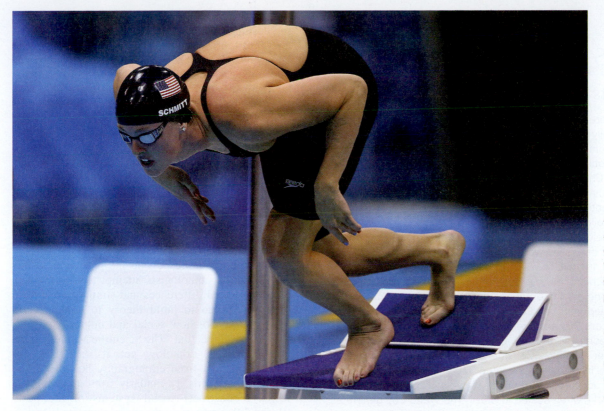

American swimmer Allison Schmitt takes off in the final of the Women's 200-meter freestyle at the 2012 London Olympics. Schmitt won the event and a gold medal, setting an Olympic record. How might years of competitive swimming affect the human body?

rarely sends female swimmers or runners to the Olympics. One reason Brazilian women avoid competitive swimming in particular may be that sport's effects on the body. Years of swimming sculpt a distinctive physique: an enlarged upper torso, a massive neck, and powerful shoulders and back. Successful female swimmers tend to be big, strong, and bulky. The countries that have produced them most consistently are the United States, Canada, Australia, Germany, the Scandinavian nations, the Netherlands, and the former Soviet Union, where this body type isn't as stigmatized as it is in Latin countries. For women, Brazilian culture prefers ample hips and buttocks to a muscled upper body. Many young female swimmers in Brazil choose to abandon the sport rather than their culture's "feminine" body ideal.

## THE SUBDISCIPLINES OF ANTHROPOLOGY

### Cultural Anthropology

**Cultural anthropology,** the study of human society and culture, is the subfield that describes, analyzes, interprets, and explains social and cultural similarities and differences. To study and interpret cultural diversity, cultural anthropologists engage in two kinds of activity: ethnography (based on fieldwork) and ethnology (based on cross-cultural comparison). **Ethnography** provides an account of a particular group, community, society, or culture. During ethnographic fieldwork, the ethnographer gathers data that he or she organizes, describes, analyzes, and interprets to build and present that account, which may be in the form of a book, an article, or a film. Traditionally, ethnographers lived in small communities, where they studied local behavior, beliefs, customs, social life, economic activities, politics, and religion. Today, any ethnographer will recognize that such settings are increasingly exposed to and influenced by external forces and events.

An anthropological perspective derived from ethnographic fieldwork often differs radically from that of economics or political science. Those fields focus on national and official organizations and policies and often on elites. However, the groups that anthropologists traditionally have studied usually have been relatively poor and powerless. Ethnographers often observe discriminatory practices directed toward such people, who experience food and water shortages, dietary deficiencies, and other aspects of poverty. Political scientists tend to study programs that national planners develop, while anthropologists discover how these programs work on the local level.

Communities and cultures are less isolated today than ever before. In fact, as the anthropologist Franz Boas noted many years ago (1966, orig. 1940), contact between neighboring tribes has always existed

**ethnography**
Fieldwork in a particular cultural setting.

**cultural anthropology**
The comparative, cross-cultural study of human society and culture.

# focus on GLOBALIZATION

## World Events

People everywhere—even remote villagers—now participate in world events, especially through the mass media. The study of global-local linkages is a prominent part of modern anthropology. What kinds of events generate global interest? Disasters provide one example. Think of Bhopal, Chernobyl, Chilean miners, and the earthquakes and tsunamis that have ravaged Thailand, Indonesia, and Japan. And there has been space—the final frontier: As many as 600 million people may have watched the first (Apollo 11) moon landing in 1969—a huge audience in the early days of global television. And consider the British royal family, especially the photogenic ones. The wedding of Prince William and Catherine Middleton attracted 161 million viewers—twice the population of the United Kingdom. The birth, public presentation, and naming of their newborn son in 2013 generated international interest. A generation earlier, millions of people had watched Lady Diana Spencer marry England's Prince Charles. Princess Diana's funeral also attracted a global audience.

And, of course, sports: Billions of people watched at least some of the 2012 London Summer Olympics. Consider the FIFA World Cup (soccer), held every four years. In 2006, an estimated 320 million people tuned in; this figure more than doubled to 700 million viewers in 2010 and may well exceed 2 billion in 2014, when hosted in Brazil. The World Cup generates huge global interest because it truly is a "world series," with 32 countries and five continents competing. Similarly, the Cricket World Cup, held every four years (most recently in 2011), is the world's third most watched event: Only the Summer Olympics and the FIFA World Cup exceed it. The Cricket World Cup is televised in over 200 countries, to over 2.2 billion viewers.

Isn't it arrogant to call American baseball's ultimate championship "The World Series" when only one non-U.S. team, the Toronto Blue Jays, can play in it? (The title dates back to 1903, a time of less globalization and more American provincialism.) Baseball is popular in the United States (including Puerto Rico), Canada, Japan, Cuba, Mexico, Venezuela, and the Dominican Republic. South Korea, Taiwan, and China have professional leagues. Elsewhere the sport has little mass appeal.

On the other hand, when we focus on the players in American baseball we see a multiethnic world in miniature. With its prominent Latino and Japanese players, American baseball appears to be more ethnically diverse than American football or basketball. Consider the finalists for the 2012 American League MVP (Most Valuable Player) award, won by Venezuelan Miguel Cabrera of the Detroit Tigers. In second place was New Jersey–born and non-Hispanic Mike Trout (Los Angeles Angels). Third and fourth were two more Latinos, Adrian Beltré (Texas Rangers) and Robinson Cano (New York Yankees). In fifth place came Josh Hamilton, a North Carolinian playing that year for Texas. The previous year's top five included Jacoby Ellsbury, a registered Native American, and Curtis Granderson, an African American New York Yankee. Can you think of a sport as ethnically diverse as baseball? What's the last world event that drew your attention?

and has extended over enormous areas. "Human populations construct their cultures in interaction with one another, and not in isolation" (Wolf 1982, p. ix). Villagers increasingly participate in regional, national, and world events. Exposure to external forces comes through the mass media, migration,

and modern transportation. City, nation, and world increasingly invade local communities with the arrival of tourists, development agents, government and religious officials, and political candidates. Such linkages are prominent components of regional, national, and global systems of politics, economics, and information. These larger systems increasingly affect the people and places anthropology traditionally has studied. The study of such linkages and systems is part of the subject matter of modern anthropology. (See "Focus on Globalization: World Events" for a discussion of world events familiar to millions of people.)

**Ethnology** examines, interprets, and analyzes the results of ethnography—the data gathered in different societies. It uses such data to compare and contrast and to make generalizations about society and culture. Looking beyond the particular to the more general, ethnologists attempt to identify and explain cultural differences and similarities, to test hypotheses, and to build theory to enhance our understanding of how social and cultural systems work. (See the section "The Scientific Method" later in this chapter.) Ethnology gets its data for comparison not just from ethnography but also from the other subfields, particularly from archaeology, which reconstructs social systems of the past. (Recap 1.2 summarizes the main contrasts between ethnography and ethnology.)

## Anthropological Archaeology

**Anthropological archaeology** (also known as archaeological anthropology or, most simply, "archaeology") reconstructs, describes, and interprets human behavior and cultural patterns through material remains. At sites where people live or have lived, archaeologists find artifacts, material items that humans have made, used, or modified, such as tools, weapons, campsites, buildings, and garbage. Plant and animal remains and garbage tell stories about consumption and activities. Wild and domesticated grains have different characteristics, which allow archaeologists to distinguish between the gathering and the cultivation of plants. Animal bones reveal the age and sex of slaughtered animals, providing other information useful in determining whether species were wild or domesticated.

Analyzing such data, archaeologists answer several questions about ancient economies. Did the group get its meat from hunting, or did it domesticate and breed animals, killing only those of a certain age and sex? Did plant food come from wild plants or from sowing, tending, and harvesting crops? Did the residents make, trade for, or buy particular items? Were raw materials available locally? If not, where did they come from? From such information, archaeologists reconstruct patterns of production, trade, and consumption.

Archaeologists have spent much time studying potsherds, fragments of earthenware. Potsherds are

| ETHNOGRAPHY | ETHNOLOGY |
| --- | --- |
| Requires fieldwork to collect data | Uses data collected by a series of researchers |
| Often descriptive | Usually synthetic |
| Group/community specific | Comparative/cross-cultural |

more durable than many other artifacts, such as textiles and wood. The quantity of pottery fragments allows estimates of population size and density. The discovery that potters used materials unavailable locally suggests systems of trade. Similarities in manufacture and decoration at different sites may be proof of cultural connections. Groups with similar pots might be historically related. Perhaps they shared common cultural ancestors, traded with each other, or belonged to the same political system.

Many archaeologists examine paleoecology. *Ecology* is the study of interrelations among living things in an environment. The organisms and environment together constitute an ecosystem, a patterned arrangement of energy flows and exchanges. Human ecology studies ecosystems that include people, focusing on the ways in which human use "of nature influences and is influenced by social organization and cultural values" (Bennett 1969, pp. 10–11). *Paleoecology* looks at the ecosystems of the past.

In addition to reconstructing ecological patterns, archaeologists may infer cultural transformations, for example, by observing changes in the size and type of sites and the distance between them. A city develops in a region where only towns, villages, and hamlets existed a few centuries earlier. The number of settlement levels (city, town, village, hamlet) in a society is a measure of social complexity. Buildings offer clues about political and religious features. Temples and pyramids suggest that an ancient society had an authority structure capable of marshaling the labor needed to build such monuments. The presence or absence of certain structures, like the pyramids of ancient Egypt and Mexico, reveals differences in function between settlements. For example, some towns were places where people came to attend ceremonies. Others were burial sites; still others were farming communities.

Archaeologists also reconstruct behavior patterns and lifestyles of the past by excavating. This involves digging through a succession of levels at a particular site. In a given area, through time, settlements may change in form and purpose, as may the connections between settlements. Excavation can document changes in economic, social, and political activities.

Although archaeologists are best known for studying prehistory, that is, the period before the invention of writing, they also study the cultures of historical and even living peoples. Studying sunken ships off the Florida coast, underwater archaeologists have been able to verify the living conditions on the vessels that brought ancestral African Americans to the New World as enslaved people. In a research project begun in 1973 in Tucson, Arizona, archaeologist William Rathje has learned about contemporary life by studying modern garbage. The value of "garbology," as Rathje calls it, is that it provides "evidence of what people did, not what they think they did, what they think they should have done, or what the interviewer thinks they should have done" (Harrison, Rathje, and Hughes 1994, p. 108). What people report may contrast strongly with their real behavior as revealed by garbology. For example, the garbologists discovered that the three Tucson neighborhoods that reported the lowest beer consumption actually had the highest number of discarded beer cans per household (Podolefsky and Brown 1992, p. 100)! Findings from garbology also have challenged common misconceptions about the kinds and quantities of trash found in landfills: While most people thought that fast-food containers and disposable diapers were major waste problems, they were actually relatively insignificant compared with paper (Rathje and Murphy 2001; Zimring 2012).

# Biological, or Physical, Anthropology

The subject matter of **biological,** or **physical, anthropology** is human biological diversity in time and space. A common interest in biological variation unites five specialties within biological anthropology:

1. Human evolution as revealed by the fossil record (paleoanthropology).

2. Human genetics.

3. Human growth and development.

4. Human biological plasticity (the living body's ability to change as it copes with stresses, such as heat, cold, and altitude).

5. Primatology (the biology, evolution, behavior, and social life of monkeys, apes, and other nonhuman primates).

These interests link biological anthropology to other fields: biology, zoology, geology, anatomy, physiology, medicine, and public health. Osteology—the study of bones—helps paleoanthropologists,

**ethnology**
The study of sociocultural differences and similarities.

**anthropological archaeology**
The study of human behavior through material remains.

**biological anthropology**
The study of human biological variation in time and space.

**physical anthropology**
Same as biological anthropology.

Anthropological archaeologists from the University of Pennsylvania work to stabilize the original plaster at an Anasazi (Native American) site in Colorado's Mesa Verde National Park.

**linguistic anthropology**
The study of language and linguistic diversity in time, space, and society.

who examine skulls, teeth, and bones, to identify human ancestors and to chart changes in anatomy over time. A paleontologist is a scientist who studies fossils. A paleoanthropologist is one sort of paleontologist, one who studies the fossil record of human evolution. Paleoanthropologists often collaborate with archaeologists, who study artifacts, in reconstructing biological and cultural aspects of human evolution. Fossils and tools often are found together. Different types of tools provide information about the habits, customs, and lifestyles of the ancestral humans who used them.

More than a century ago, Charles Darwin noticed that the variety that exists within any population permits some individuals (those with the favored characteristics) to do better than others at surviving and reproducing. Genetics, which developed later, enlightens us about the causes and transmission of this variety. However, it isn't just genes that cause variety. During any individual's lifetime, the environment works along with heredity to determine biological features. For example, people with a genetic tendency to be tall will be shorter if they are poorly nourished during childhood. Thus, biological anthropology also investigates the influence of environment on the body as it grows and matures. Among the environmental factors that influence the body as it develops are nutrition, altitude, temperature, and disease, as well as cultural factors, such as the standards of attractiveness that were discussed previously.

Biological anthropology (along with zoology) also includes primatology. The primates include our closest relatives—apes and monkeys. Primatologists study their biology, evolution, behavior, and social life, often in their natural environments. Primatology assists paleoanthropology, because primate behavior may shed light on early human behavior and human nature.

## Linguistic Anthropology

We don't know (and probably never will know) when our ancestors started speaking, although biological anthropologists have looked to the anatomy of the face and the skull to speculate about the origin of language. As well, primatologists have described the communication systems of monkeys and apes. We do know that well-developed, grammatically complex languages have existed for thousands of years. Linguistic anthropology offers further illustration of anthropology's interest in comparison, variation, and change. **Linguistic anthropology** studies language in its social and cultural context, across space and over time. Some linguistic anthropologists also make inferences about universal features of language, linked perhaps to uniformities in the human brain. Others reconstruct ancient languages by comparing their contemporary descendants and in so doing make discoveries about history. Still others study linguistic differences to discover varied perceptions and patterns of thought in different cultures.

Historical linguistics considers variation over time, such as the changes in sounds, grammar, and vocabulary between Middle English (spoken from approximately 1050 to 1550 c.e.) and modern English. **Sociolinguistics** investigates relationships between social and linguistic variation. No language is a homogeneous system in which everyone speaks just like everyone else. How do different speakers use a given language? How do linguistic features correlate with social factors, including class and gender differences? One reason for variation is geography, as in regional dialects and accents. Linguistic variation also is expressed in the bilingualism of ethnic groups. Linguistic and cultural anthropologists collaborate in studying links between language and many other aspects of culture, such as how people reckon kinship and how they perceive and classify colors.

## ANTHROPOLOGY AND OTHER ACADEMIC FIELDS

As mentioned previously, one of the main differences between anthropology and the other fields that study people is holism, anthropology's unique blend of biological, social, cultural, linguistic, historical, and contemporary perspectives. Paradoxically, while distinguishing anthropology, this breadth also is what links it to many other disciplines. Techniques used to date fossils and artifacts have come to anthropology from physics, chemistry, and geology. Because plant and animal remains often are found with human bones and artifacts, anthropologists collaborate with botanists, zoologists, and paleontologists.

Anthropology is a **science**—a "systematic field of study or body of knowledge that aims, through experiment, observation, and deduction, to produce reliable explanations of phenomena, with reference to the material and physical world" (*Webster's New World Encyclopedia* 1993, p. 937). This book presents anthropology as a *humanistic science* devoted to discovering, describing, understanding, appreciating, and explaining similarities and differences in time and space among humans and our ancestors. Clyde Kluckhohn (1944) described anthropology as "the science of human similarities and differences" (p. 9). His statement of the need for such a field still stands: "Anthropology provides a scientific basis for dealing with the crucial dilemma of the world today: how can peoples of different appearance, mutually unintelligible languages, and dissimilar ways of life get along peaceably together?" (p. 9). Anthropology has compiled an impressive body of knowledge, which this textbook attempts to encapsulate.

Besides its links to the natural sciences (e.g., geology, zoology) and social sciences (e.g., sociology, psychology), anthropology also has strong links to the humanities. The humanities include English, comparative literature, classics, folklore, philosophy, and the arts. These fields study languages, texts, philosophies, arts, music, performances, and other forms of creative expression. Ethnomusicology, which studies forms of musical expression on a worldwide basis, is especially closely related to anthropology. Also linked is folklore, the systematic study of tales, myths, and legends from a variety of cultures. Anthropology, it may be argued, is one of the most humanistic of all academic fields because of its fundamental respect for human diversity. Anthropologists listen to, record, and represent voices from a multitude of nations, cultures, times, and places. Anthropology values local knowledge, diverse worldviews, and alternative philosophies. Cultural anthropology and linguistic anthropology in particular bring a comparative and nonelitist perspective to forms of creative expression, including language, art, narratives, music, and dance, viewed in their social and cultural context.

## Cultural Anthropology and Sociology

Cultural anthropology and sociology share an interest in social relations, organization, and behavior. However, important differences between these disciplines arose from the kinds of societies each traditionally studied. Initially sociologists focused on the industrial West; anthropologists, on nonindustrial societies. Different methods of data collection and analysis emerged to deal with those different kinds of societies. To study large-scale, complex nations, sociologists came to rely on surveys and other means of gathering masses of quantifiable data. Sampling and statistical techniques are fundamental in sociology, whereas statistical training has been less common in anthropology (although this is changing as anthropologists increasingly work in modern nations).

Traditional ethnographers studied small and nonliterate (without writing) populations and relied on methods appropriate to that context. "Ethnography is a research process in which the anthropologist closely observes, records, and engages in the daily life of another culture—an experience labeled as the fieldwork method—and then writes accounts of this culture, emphasizing descriptive detail" (Marcus and Fischer 1986, p. 18). One key method described in this quote is participant observation—taking part in the events one is observing, describing, and analyzing.

In many areas and topics, anthropology and sociology are converging. Sociologists now do research in developing countries and other places that used to be mainly within the anthropological orbit. As industrialization spreads, many anthropologists now work in industrial nations, where they study diverse topics, including rural decline, inner-city life, and the role of the mass media in creating national cultural patterns.

## Anthropology and Psychology

Psychologists, like sociologists, typically do their research in only one—their own—society. Anthropologists know, however, that statements

**sociolinguistics**
The study of language in society.

**science**
Field of study that seeks reliable explanations, with reference to the material and physical world.

about "human" psychology can't rely solely on observations made in a single society. Cross-cultural comparison suggests that certain psychological patterns may indeed be universal. Others are merely found in some but not all societies, while still others are confined to one or very few cultures. *Psychological anthropology* studies cross-cultural similarities and differences in psychological traits and conditions (see LeVine 2010). During the 1920s, 1930s, and 1940s several prominent anthropologists, including Bronislaw Malinowski (1927) and Margaret Mead (1935/1950; 1928/1961) described how particular cultures create distinctive adult personality types by inculcating in their children specific values, beliefs, and behavior patterns (see also Montgomery 2008). Anthropologists have provided needed cross-cultural perspectives on aspects of developmental and cognitive psychology (Kronenfeld et al. 2011; Shore 1996), psychoanalytic propositions (Gijswijt-Hofstra et al. 2005; Paul 1989), and psychiatric conditions (Gijswijt-Hofstra et al. 2005; Kleinman 1991).

Anthropologists are familiar, for example, with an array of *culturally specific syndromes*. These are patterns of unusual, aberrant, or abnormal behavior confined to a single culture or a group of related cultures (see Goleman 1995). One example is *koro*, the East Asian term for intense anxiety arising from the fear that one's sexual organs will recede into one's body and cause death. A distinctive Latin American syndrome is *susto*, or soul loss, whose symptoms are extreme sadness, lethargy, and listlessness. The victim typically falls prey to susto after experiencing a personal tragedy, such as the death of a loved one. A milder malady is *mal de ojo* ("evil eye"), most typically found in Mediterranean countries. Symptoms of evil eye, which mainly affects children, include fitful sleep, crying, sickness, and fever (Goleman 1995). Western cultures, too, have distinctive psychiatric syndromes, some of which appear now to be spreading internationally as a result of globalization. One such syndrome is anorexia nervosa (food refusal or extreme dieting, resulting in self-starvation), which originated in Western industrialized societies, where it once was as culturally confined and specific as susto is to Latin America (Banks 1992).

As ethnic diversity increases within the United States and other Western nations, so, too, does the proportion of psychiatric patients with varied, including non-Western, cultural backgrounds. How has American psychiatry (sometimes informed by anthropological knowledge) reacted to this diversity? The influential *Diagnostic and Statistical Manual of Mental Disorders* (2013), published by the American Psychiatric Association, now recognizes "culture-bound syndromes," another term for the culturally specific syndromes just described. Guidelines published by the *American Journal of Psychiatry* now direct attention to patients' cultural-ethnic backgrounds and fit diagnoses and treatments accordingly (Munoz et al. 2007).

Globalization has also been spreading Western psychological concepts, and even Western psychiatric maladies, across national borders (Watters 2010). Characteristic Western disorders, including post-traumatic stress and anorexia, are spreading transnationally, and Western symptom clusters are replacing indigenous forms and expressions of mental illness. The following case illustrates how a characteristic Western condition, including its distinctive symptoms, is displacing indigenous patterns.

In the late 1980s and early 1990s (as reported by Watters 2010), Dr. Sing Lee, a Hong Kong–based psychiatrist and researcher, documented what was, at that time, a culturally specific, and very rare, form of anorexia nervosa in Hong Kong. Unlike American anorexics, Lee's patients weren't worried about getting fat. Instead, they reduced their food intake in an attempt to fend off unwanted bodily symptoms—most frequently, bloated stomachs. Just as Lee started publishing his findings, however, the understanding of anorexia in Hong Kong suddenly shifted, after a teenage anorexic girl collapsed and died on a busy downtown street. Her death was featured prominently in local newspapers, with such headlines as "Anorexia Made Her All Skin and Bones."

In interpreting the girl's symptoms, many local reporters simply copied from American diagnostic manuals, thus spreading the idea that anorexia in Hong Kong was the same disorder that existed in the United States and Europe. As the general public became familiar with the American diagnosis of anorexia, Lee's patients started mimicking the American symptoms, and the incidence of anorexia increased. Lee's anorexic patient load rose rapidly, from two to three per year to two to three per month. Occurring throughout Hong Kong, that increase sparked another series of media reports, such as "Children as Young as 10 Starving Themselves as Eating Ailments Rise." By the year 2000, Lee concluded, between 3 and 10 percent of young women in Hong Kong had eating disorders. Unlike Lee's earlier patients, these women now cited a fear of getting fat as the key reason for their food refusal. By 2007, about 90 percent of Lee's anorexic patients were reporting a fat phobia (Watters 2010).

Disorders, both physical and mental, and their symptom clusters, easily cross national borders in today's globalized and socially networked world. The *Diagnostic and Statistical Manual of Mental Disorders*, whose fifth edition was published in 2013, serves as an increasingly transnational reference and standard. Imagine as well the role of social media, available through computers, tablets, and cell phones, in transmitting news and images of various conditions that affect, or might affect, their users. The Western form of anorexia surely wouldn't have spread so quickly in Hong Kong without

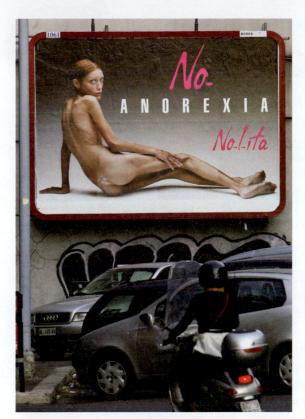

In Rome, a poster featuring an emaciated woman (in an advertisement for an Italian fashion house) bears the headline "No anorexia." How does anorexia illustrate a culturally specific syndrome?

(2) practicing, or **applied, anthropology.** The latter refers to the application of anthropological data, perspectives, theory, and methods to identify, assess, and solve contemporary social problems. As Erve Chambers (1987, p. 309) has stated, applied anthropology is "concerned with the relationships between anthropological knowledge and the uses of that knowledge in the world beyond anthropology." More and more anthropologists from the four subfields now work in such "applied" areas as public health, family planning, business, market research, economic development, and cultural resource management. (This chapter's "Appreciating Anthropology" on pp. 14–15 discusses the career of President Barack Obama's mother, a sociocultural and applied anthropologist.)

Because of anthropology's breadth, applied anthropology has many applications. For example, applied medical anthropologists consider both the sociocultural and the biological contexts and implications of disease and illness. Perceptions of good and bad health, along with actual health threats and problems, differ among societies. Various ethnic groups recognize different illnesses, symptoms, and causes and have developed different health care systems and treatment strategies.

Applied archaeology, usually called *public archaeology,* includes such activities as cultural resource management, contract archaeology, public educational programs, and historic preservation. An important role for public archaeology has been created by legislation requiring evaluation of sites threatened by dams, highways, and other construction activities. To decide what needs saving, and to preserve significant information about the past when sites cannot be saved, is the work of **cultural resource management** (CRM). CRM involves not only preserving sites but also allowing their destruction if they are not significant. The "management" part of the term refers to the evaluation and decision-making process. Cultural resource managers work for federal, state, and county agencies and other clients. Applied cultural anthropologists sometimes work with the public archaeologists, assessing the human problems generated by the proposed change and determining how they can be reduced.

**applied anthropology**
Using anthropology to solve contemporary problems.

**cultural resource management**
Deciding what needs saving when entire archaeological sites cannot be saved.

modern media. After all, it took more than a half century for Western mental health professionals to name, codify, and establish their definition of anorexia. By contrast, after one widely reported death on a busy downtown street, it took just hours for the people of Hong Kong to learn about anorexia and its "Western" symptoms (Watters 2010). Like any other cultural anthropologist working in the 21st century, the student of psychological anthropology must recognize how local, indigenous patterns (psychological-psychiatric in this case) interact with the forces of globalization, including the concepts and conditions it is spreading.

## APPLIED ANTHROPOLOGY

What sort of man or woman do you envision when you hear the word "anthropologist"? Although anthropologists have been portrayed as quirky and eccentric, bearded and bespectacled, anthropology is not a science of the exotic carried on by quaint scholars in ivory towers. Rather, anthropology has a lot to tell the public. Anthropology's foremost professional organization, the American Anthropological Association (AAA), has formally acknowledged a public service role by recognizing that anthropology has two dimensions: (1) academic anthropology and

## THE SCIENTIFIC METHOD

Anthropology, remember, is a science, although a very humanistic one. Within sociocultural anthropology, ethnology is the comparative science that attempts to identify and explain cultural differences and similarities, test hypotheses, and build theory to enhance our understanding of how social and cultural systems work. The data for ethnology come from societies located in various times and places. Ethnologists compare, contrast, and make generalizations about societies and cultures.

## His Mother, the Anthropologist

It is widely known that President Barack Obama is the son of a Kenyan father and a white American mother. Less recognized is the fact that the 44th president of the United States is the son of an anthropologist—Dr. Stanley Ann Dunham Soetoro (usually called simply Ann Dunham). This account focuses on her life and her appreciation of human diversity, which led her to a career in anthropology. A sociocultural anthropologist by training, Dunham focused her attention on issues of microfinance and socioeconomic problems faced by Indonesian women. She used her knowledge to identify and solve contemporary problems. She was both a cultural and an applied anthropologist. A fuller account of Dr. Dunham's life appears in Janny Scott's book *A Singular Woman: The Untold Story of Barack Obama's Mother* (2011).

Anthropologists study humanity in varied times and places and in a rapidly changing world. By virtue of his parentage, his enculturation, and his experience abroad, Barack Obama provides an excellent symbol of the diversity and interconnections that characterize such a world.

In the capsule version of the Barack Obama story, his mother is simply the white woman from Kansas. . . . On the campaign trail, he has called her his "single mom." But neither description begins to capture the unconventional life of Stanley Ann Dunham Soetoro, the parent who most shaped Mr. Obama. . . .

In Hawaii, she married an African student at age 18. Then she married an Indonesian, moved to Jakarta, became an anthropologist, wrote an 800-page dissertation on peasant blacksmithing in Java, worked for the Ford Foundation, championed women's work and helped bring microcredit to the world's poor.

She had high expectations for her children. In Indonesia, she would wake her son at 4 A.M. for correspondence courses in English before school; she brought home recordings of Mahalia Jackson, speeches by the Rev. Dr. Martin Luther King Jr., and when Mr. Obama asked to stay in Hawaii for high school rather than return to Asia, she accepted living apart—a decision her daughter says was one of the hardest in Ms. Soetoro's life.

"She felt that somehow, wandering through uncharted territory, we might stumble upon something that will, in an instant, seem to represent who we are at the core," said Maya Soetoro-Ng, Mr. Obama's half-sister. "That was very much her philosophy of life—to not be limited by fear or narrow definitions, to not build walls around ourselves and to do our best to find kinship and beauty in unexpected places." . . .

Mr. Obama . . . barely saw his father after the age of 2. Though it is impossible to pinpoint the imprint of a parent on the life of a grown child, people who knew Ms. Soetoro well say they see her influence unmistakably in Mr. Obama. . . .

"She was a very, very big thinker," said Nancy Barry, a former president of Women's World Banking, an international network of microfinance providers, where Ms. Soetoro worked in New York City in the early 1990s. . . .

In a Russian class at the University of Hawaii, she met the college's first African student, Barack Obama. They married and had a son in August 1961, in an era when interracial marriage was rare in the United States. . . .

The marriage was brief. In 1963, Mr. Obama left for Harvard, leaving his wife and child. She then married Lolo Soetoro, an Indonesian student. When he was summoned home in 1966 after the turmoil surrounding the rise of Suharto, Ms. Soetoro and Barack followed. . . .

Her second marriage faded, too, in the 1970s. Ms. Soetoro wanted to work, one friend said, and Mr. Soetoro wanted more children. He became more American, she once said, as she became more Javanese. "There's a Javanese belief that if you're married to someone and it doesn't work, it

---

**hypothesis**
A suggested but as yet unverified explanation.

**association**
An observed relationship between two or more variables.

**theory**
A set of ideas formulated to explain something.

## Theories, Associations, and Explanations

Any science aims for reliable explanations that *predict* future occurrences. Accurate predictions stand up to tests designed to disprove (falsify) them. Scientific explanations rely on data, which can come from experiments, observation, and other systematic procedures. Scientific causes are material, physical, or natural (e.g., viruses) rather than supernatural (e.g., ghosts).

In their 1997 article "Science in Anthropology," Melvin Ember and Carol R. Ember describe how scientists strive to improve our understanding of the world by testing **hypotheses**—suggested but as yet unverified explanations. An *explanation* must show how and why the thing to be explained (the *dependent variable*) is caused by, related to, or associated with something else, a *predictor* variable. An **association** is an observed relationship of *covariation* between two or more variables: When one variable changes, the other one changes as well. Theories provide explanations for associations (Ember and Ember 1997). A **theory** is a set of logically connected ideas formulated to explain something. An effective theory offers an explanatory framework that can be applied to multiple cases.

will make you sick," said Alice G. Dewey, an anthropologist and friend. "It's just stupid to stay married." . . .

By 1974, Ms. Soetoro was back in Honolulu, a graduate student and raising Barack and Maya, nine years younger. . . . When Ms. Soetoro decided to return to Indonesia three years later for her fieldwork, Barack chose not to go. . . .

Fluent in Indonesian, Ms. Soetoro moved with Maya first to Yogyakarta, the center of Javanese handicrafts. A weaver in college, she was fascinated with what Ms. Soetoro-Ng calls "life's gorgeous minutiae." That interest inspired her study of village industries, which became the basis of her 1992 doctoral dissertation.

"She loved living in Java," said Dr. Dewey, who recalled accompanying Ms. Soetoro to a metalworking village. "People said: 'Hi! How are you?' She said: 'How's your wife? Did your daughter have the baby?' They were friends. Then she'd whip out her notebook and she'd say: 'How many of you have electricity? Are you having trouble getting iron?'"

She became a consultant for the United States Agency for International Development on setting up a village credit program, then a Ford Foundation program officer in Jakarta specializing in women's work. Later, she was a consultant in Pakistan, then joined Indonesia's oldest bank to work on what is described as the world's largest sustainable microfinance program, creating services like credit and savings for the poor.

President Barack Obama and his mother, Ann Dunham, who was a cultural and applied anthropologist, in an undated photo from the 1960s. Dunham met Obama's father, Barack Obama Sr. from Kenya, when both were students at the University of Hawaii at Manoa; they married in 1960.

Visitors flowed constantly through her Ford Foundation office in downtown Jakarta and through her house in a neighborhood to the south, where papaya and banana trees grew in the front yard and Javanese dishes . . . were served for dinner. Her guests were leaders in the Indonesian human rights movement, people from women's organizations, representatives of community groups doing grass-roots development. . . .

Ms. Soetoro-Ng . . . remembers conversations with her mother about philosophy or politics, books, esoteric Indonesian woodworking motifs. . . .

"She gave us a very broad understanding of the world," her daughter said. "She hated bigotry. She was very determined to be remembered for a life of service and thought that service was really the true measure of a life." Many of her friends see her legacy in Mr. Obama—in his self-assurance and drive, his boundary bridging, even his apparent comfort with strong women.

She died in November 1995, as Mr. Obama was starting his first campaign for public office. After a memorial service at the University of Hawaii, one friend said, a small group of friends drove to the South Shore in Oahu. With the wind whipping the waves onto the rocks, Mr. Obama and Ms. Soetoro-Ng placed their mother's ashes in the Pacific, sending them off in the direction of Indonesia.

One explanation for the occurrence of an association is that it illustrates a general principle. Thus, "water freezes at 32°F" states an association between two variables: the state of the water and the air temperature. The truth of the statement is confirmed by repeated observations of freezing and the fact that water does not solidify at higher temperatures. Such general relationships are called *laws*. Explanations based on such laws allow us to understand the past and predict the future. Yesterday ice formed at 32°F, and tomorrow it will still form at 32°F.

In the social sciences, associations usually are probable, rather than absolute. The variables of interest *tend* to be associated in a predictable way, but there are exceptions (Ember and Ember 1997). For example, we can hypothesize that cross-culturally (that is, in most societies) there is an association between gender and hunting, such that men are much more likely than women to hunt animals. We expect, however, to find exceptions, that is, societies in which women hunt.

One classic cross-cultural study revealed a strong (but not 100 percent) association, or correlation, between a sexual custom and a type of diet. A long postpartum sex taboo (a ban on sexual intercourse between husband and wife for a year or more after the birth of a child) tended to be found in societies where the diet was low in protein (Whiting 1964).

The name *kwashiorkor*, for a condition caused by severe protein deficiency, comes from a West African word meaning "one–two." Some cultures abruptly wean one infant when a second one is born. In today's world, refugees from civil wars, including the Angolan girl shown here, are among the most common victims of malnutrition.

This association was confirmed by cross-cultural data (ethnographic information from a randomly chosen sample of several societies). How might one explain why the dependent variable (the thing to be explained, in this case the postpartum sex taboo) is related to the predictor variable (a low-protein diet). A likely explanation is that, when there is too little protein in their diets, babies can develop and die from a protein-deficiency disease called kwashiorkor. If the mother delays her next pregnancy, her current baby gets to breast-feed longer, thereby ingesting protein from the mother and enhancing its survival chances. Having another baby too soon—forcing early weaning—would jeopardize the survival of the previous one. The postpartum taboo thus enhances infant survival. When the taboo becomes institutionalized as a cultural expectation, people are more likely to comply, and less likely to succumb to momentary temptation.

Theories suggest patterns and relationships, and they generate additional hypotheses. Based, for example, on the theory that the postpartum taboo exists because it reduces infant mortality when the diet is low in protein, one could hypothesize that changes in the conditions that favor the taboo might cause it to disappear. By adopting birth control, for instance, families could space births without avoiding intercourse. So, too, could the taboo disappear if babies started receiving protein supplements, which would reduce the threat of kwashiorkor.

Recap 1.3 summarizes the main steps in using the scientific method. In hypothesis testing, the relevant variables should be clearly defined (e.g., "height in centimeters" or "weight in kilograms" rather than "body size") and measured reliably. The strength and significance of the results should be evaluated using legitimate statistical methods (Bernard 2011). Scholars should be careful to avoid a common mistake in generalizing—citing only cases that confirm their hypothesis, while ignoring negative ones. The best procedure is random selection of cases from a wide sample of societies, not all of which are likely to fit the hypothesis.

| RECAP 1.3 | Steps in the Scientific Method |
|---|---|
| **Have a research question.** | Why do some societies have long postpartum taboos? |
| **Construct a hypothesis.** | Delaying marital sex reduces infant mortality when diets are low in protein. |
| **Posit a mechanism.** | Babies get more protein when they nurse longer; nursing is not a reliable method of contraception. |
| **Get data to test your hypothesis.** | Use a (random) sample of cross-cultural data (data from several societies; such data sets exist for cross-cultural research). |
| **Devise a way of measuring.** | Code societies 1 when they have a postpartum taboo of one year or longer, 0 when they do not; code 1 when diet is low in protein, 0 when it is not. |
| **Analyze your data.** | Notice patterns in the data: Long postpartum taboos generally are found in societies with low-protein diets, whereas societies with better diets tend to lack those taboos. Use appropriate statistical methods to evaluate the strength of these associations. |
| **Draw a conclusion.** | In most cases, the hypothesis is confirmed. |
| **Derive implications.** | Such taboos tend to disappear when diets get better or new reproductive technologies become available. |
| **Contribute to larger theory.** | Cultural practices can have adaptive value by enhancing the survival of offspring. |

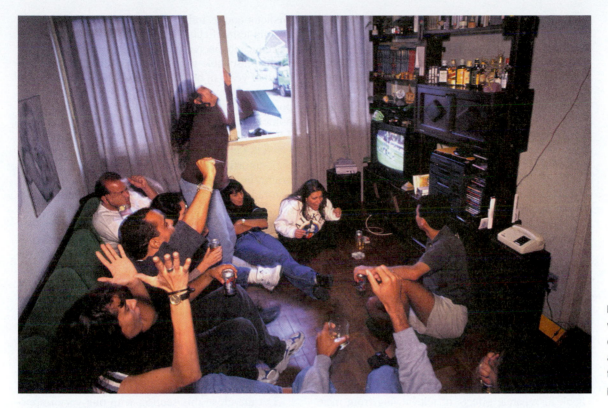

Family and friends watching a soccer game on TV in Brazil. Soccer and telenovelas are key features of Brazilian popular culture.

## When Multiple Variables Predict

The scientific method, as shown in Recap 1.3, is not limited to ethnology but also applies to any anthropological endeavor that formulates research questions and gathers or uses systematic data to test hypotheses. Nor does there have to be a single research question. Often anthropologists gather data that enable them to pose and test a number of separate hypotheses about attitudes and behavior. For example, in our research in Brazil, my colleagues and I have used a combination of methods to study media effects in that country (see Kottak 2009).

Our most general research question is this one: How has variable exposure to media affected Brazilians? Originally, starting in the 1980s, we focused on the effects of television. Our current research has expanded to include all new media. Twice, first in the mid-1980s and again in 2013, we gathered data from more than 1,000 Brazilians living in several communities to explore media effects.

Our research design permitted us to distinguish between *two key measures of individual exposure to television.* First was current viewing level (average daily hours spent watching TV). Such a measure is used routinely to assess the impact of television in the United States. Our second, and far more significant, variable was *length of home TV exposure.* Unlike us, researchers in the United States tend to rely almost solely on current viewing level to measure TV's influence, because there is little variation in length of home exposure, except for variation based on age. Americans aged 70 and younger never have known a world without TV.

Having gathered detailed quantitative data, we could use a statistical method that measures the separate (as well as the combined) effects of several "potential predictors" on a series of dependent variables. To use a more general example, to predict "risk of heart attack" (the dependent variable), potential predictors would include sex (gender), age, family history, weight, blood pressure, cholesterol level, exercise, and cigarette smoking. Each one would make a separate contribution, and some would have more impact than others. However, someone with many "risk factors" (particularly the most significant ones) would have a greater risk of heart attack than someone with few predictors.

Returning to television in Brazil, we used a standard set of nine potential predictor variables and examined their effects on hundreds of dependent variables (Kottak 2009). Our potential predictors included gender, age, skin color, social class, education, income, religious involvement, years of home TV exposure, and current televiewing level. We could measure the separate (as well as the combined) influence of each predictor on each dependent variable.

One of our strongest statistical measures of television's impact on attitudes was the association between TV exposure and liberal views on sex-gender issues. TV exposure had a stronger effect on sex-gender views than did such other predictor variables as gender, education, and income. The heavier and longer-exposed viewers were strikingly more liberal—less traditional in their opinions on such matters as whether women "belong at home," should work when their husbands have good incomes, should work when pregnant, should go to bars, should leave a husband when they no longer love him, and should pursue men they like; whether men should cook and wash clothes; and whether parents should talk to their children about sex. All these questions produced TV-biased answers, in that Brazilian television depicts an urban-modern society in which sex-gender roles are less traditional than in small communities.

Are these effects or just correlations? That is, does Brazilian TV make people more liberal, or do already liberal people, seeking reinforcement for their views, simply watch more television? Do they look to TV and its urban-elite world for moral options that are missing, suppressed, or disapproved of in their own, more traditional towns? We concluded that this liberalization is both a correlation and an effect. There is a strong *correlation* between liberal social views and *current* viewing hours. Liberal small-town Brazilians appear to watch more TV to validate personal views that the local setting discourages or suppresses. However, confirming that long-term TV exposure also has an *effect* on Brazilians' attitudes, there is an even stronger correlation between years of home viewing by individuals and their liberal social views. It is difficult to separate effects of televiewing from mere correlations when we use current viewing level as a predictor variable. Questions like the following always arise: Does television create fears about the outside world—or do already fearful people tend to stay home and watch more TV? *Effects* are clearer when length of home exposure can be measured. Logically, we can compare this predictor and its influence over time to education and its long-term effects. If the cumulative effects of formal education increase with years of schooling, then it seems reasonable to assume a similar influence as a result of years of home exposure to television.

Heavy viewers in Brazil probably are predisposed to liberal views. However, content, entering homes each day, reinforces those views over time. TV-biased and TV-reinforced attitudes spread as viewers take courage from the daily validation of their unorthodox (local) views in (national) programming. More and more townsfolk encounter nontraditional views and come to see them as normal. In this case, we measured and confirmed an association and then offered explanations for why that association is an effect as well as a correlation. Our original study suggested hypotheses for future research on how people use television and how it affects them in other ways, places, and times. Indeed, recent research in a Michigan town (Descartes and Kottak 2009) has revealed forms of use and impact similar to those we discovered in Brazil. Think about how these findings might apply to the political views of contemporary Americans who habitually watch either Fox News or MSNBC.

Let me close this section with one very important caveat. Science is one way—an excellent way—of understanding the world, but it certainly isn't the only way. The work of many prominent anthropologists has more in common with the humanities than with a strictly scientific approach. It is not unusual, for example, for cultural anthropologists to prefer to analyze and interpret, rather than to explain scientifically, aspects of culture. Anthropological approaches that are interpretive, qualitative, and humanistic are considered in this book along with those that are more quantitative and scientific.

## for REVIEW

## summary

1. Anthropology is the holistic and comparative study of humanity. It is the systematic exploration of human biological and cultural diversity. Examining the origins of, and changes in, human biology and culture, anthropology provides explanations for similarities and differences. The four subfields of general anthropology are sociocultural, archaeological, biological, and linguistic. All consider variation in time and space. Each also examines adaptation—the process by which organisms cope with environmental stresses.

2. Cultural forces mold human biology, including our body types and images. Societies have particular standards of physical attractiveness. They also have specific ideas about what activities—for example, various sports—are appropriate for males and females.

3. Cultural anthropology explores the cultural diversity of the present and the recent past. Archaeology reconstructs cultural patterns, often of prehistoric populations. Biological anthropology documents diversity, involving fossils, genetics, growth and development, bodily responses, and nonhuman primates. Linguistic anthropology considers diversity among languages. It also studies how speech changes in social situations and over time.

4. Concerns with biology, society, culture, and language link anthropology to many other fields—sciences and humanities. Anthropologists study art, music, and literature across cultures. But their concern is more with the creative expressions of common people than with arts designed for elites. Anthropologists examine creators and products in their social context. Sociologists traditionally study urban and industrial populations, whereas anthropologists have focused on rural, nonindustrial peoples. Psychological anthropology views human psychology in the context of social and cultural variation.

5. Anthropology has two dimensions: academic and applied. Applied anthropology is the use of anthropological data, perspectives, theory, and methods to identify, assess, and solve contemporary social problems.

6. Ethnologists attempt to identify and explain cultural differences and similarities and to build theories about how social and cultural systems work. Scientists strive to improve understanding by testing hypotheses—suggested explanations. Explanations rely on associations and theories. An association is an observed relationship between variables. A theory is more general, suggesting or implying associations and attempting to explain them. The scientific method characterizes any anthropological endeavor that formulates research questions and gathers or uses systematic data to test hypotheses. Often anthropologists gather data that enable them to pose and test a number of separate hypotheses.

**key terms**

anthropological archaeology 8
anthropology 3
applied anthropology 13
association 14
biocultural 6
biological anthropology 9
cultural anthropology 7
cultural resource management 13
culture 3
ethnography 7

ethnology 8
food production 5
general anthropology 6
holistic 3
hypothesis 14
linguistic anthropology 10
physical anthropology 9
science 11
sociolinguistics 11
theory 14

**critical thinking**

1. What is culture? How is it distinct from what this chapter describes as a biocultural approach? How do these concepts help us understand the complex ways that human populations adapt to their environments?

2. What themes and interests unify the subdisciplines of anthropology? In your answer, refer to historical reasons for the unity of anthropology. Are these historical reasons similar in all places where anthropology developed as a discipline?

3. If, as Franz Boas illustrated early on in American anthropology, cultures are not isolated, how can ethnography provide an account of a particular community, society, or culture? Note: There is no easy answer to this question! Anthropologists continue to deal with it as they define their research questions and projects.

4. The American Anthropological Association has formally acknowledged a public service role by recognizing that anthropology has two dimensions: (1) academic anthropology and (2) practicing, or applied, anthropology. What is applied anthropology? Based on your reading of this chapter, identify examples from current events where an anthropologist could help identify, assess, and solve contemporary social problems.

5. In this chapter, we learn that anthropology is a science, although a very humanistic one. What do you think this means? What role does hypothesis testing play in structuring anthropological research? What are the differences between theories, laws, and hypotheses?

## CHAPTER 2

# Culture

▶ What is culture and why do we study it?

▶ What is the relation between culture and the individual?

▶ How does culture change—especially with globalization?

Offerings at a temple in Bali, Indonesia. People learn and share beliefs and behavior as members of cultural groups.

# understanding OURSELVES

How special are you? To what extent are you "your own person" and to what extent are you a product of your particular culture? How much does, and should, your cultural background influence your actions and decisions? Americans may not fully appreciate the power of culture because of the value their culture places on "the *individual*." Americans like to regard everyone as unique in some way. Yet individualism itself is a distinctive *shared* value, a feature of American culture, transmitted constantly in our daily lives. In the media, count how many stories focus on individuals versus groups. From the late Mr. (Fred) Rogers of daytime TV to "real-life" parents, grandparents, and teachers, our enculturative agents insist we all are "someone special." That we are individuals first and members of groups second is the opposite of this chapter's lesson about culture. Certainly we have distinctive features because we are individuals, but we have other distinct attributes because we belong to cultural groups.

For example, as we saw in "Appreciating Diversity" in Chapter 1 (pp. 4–5), a comparison of the United States with Brazil, Italy, or virtually any Latin nation reveals striking contrasts between a national culture (American) that discourages physical affection and national cultures in which the opposite is true. Brazilians touch, embrace, and kiss one another much more frequently than North Americans do. Such behavior reflects years of exposure to particular cultural traditions. Middle-class Brazilians teach their kids—both boys and girls—to kiss (on the cheek, two or three times, coming and going) every adult relative they see. Given the size of Brazilian extended families, this can mean hundreds of people. Women continue kissing all those people throughout their lives. Until they are adolescents, boys kiss all adult relatives. Men typically continue to kiss female relatives and friends, as well as their fathers and uncles, throughout their lives.

Do you kiss your father? Your uncle? Your grandfather? How about your mother, aunt, or grandmother? The answers to these questions may differ between men and women, and for male and female relatives. Culture can help us to make sense of these differences. In America, a cultural homophobia (fear of homosexuality) may prevent American men from engaging in displays of affection with other men; similarly, American girls typically are encouraged to show affection, while American boys typically aren't. It's important to note that these cultural explanations rely upon example and expectation, and that no cultural trait exists because it is natural or right. *Ethnocentrism* is the error of viewing one's own culture as superior and applying one's own cultural values in judging people from other cultures. How easy is it for you to see beyond the ethnocentric blinders of your own experience? Do you have an ethnocentric position regarding displays of affection?

## WHAT IS CULTURE?

The concept of culture is fundamental in anthropology. Well over a century ago, in his book *Primitive Culture*, the British anthropologist Sir Edward Tylor proposed that cultures—systems of human behavior and thought—obey natural laws and therefore can be studied scientifically. Tylor's definition of culture still offers an overview of the subject matter of anthropology and is widely quoted: "Culture . . . is that complex whole which includes knowledge, belief, arts, morals, law, custom, and any other capabilities and habits acquired by man as a member of society" (Tylor 1871/1958, p. 1). The crucial phrase here is "acquired . . . as a member of society." Tylor's definition focuses on attributes that people acquire not through biological inheritance but by growing up in a particular society where they are exposed to a specific cultural tradition. **Enculturation** is the process by which a child learns his or her culture.

## Culture Is Learned

The ease with which children absorb any cultural tradition rests on the uniquely elaborated human capacity to learn. Other animals may learn from experience; for example, they avoid fire after discovering that it hurts. Social animals also learn from other members of their group. Wolves, for instance, learn hunting strategies from other pack members. Such social learning is particularly important among monkeys and apes, our closest biological relatives. But our own *cultural learning* depends on the uniquely developed human capacity to use **symbols,** signs that have no necessary or natural connection to the things they signify or for which they stand.

On the basis of cultural learning, people create, remember, and deal with ideas. They grasp and apply specific systems of symbolic meaning. Anthropologist Clifford Geertz defines culture as ideas based on cultural learning and symbols. Cultures have been characterized as sets of "control mechanisms—plans, recipes, rules, instructions, what computer engineers call programs for the governing of behavior" (Geertz 1973, p. 44). These programs are absorbed by people through enculturation in particular traditions. People gradually internalize a previously established system of meanings and symbols. They use this cultural system to define their world, express their feelings, and make their judgments. This system helps guide their behavior and perceptions throughout their lives.

Every person begins immediately, through a process of conscious and unconscious learning and interaction with others, to internalize, or incorporate, a cultural tradition through the process of enculturation. Sometimes culture is taught directly, as when parents tell their children to say "thank you" when someone gives them something or does them a favor.

Culture also is transmitted through observation. Children pay attention to the things that go on around them. They modify their behavior not just because other people tell them to but as a result of their own observations and growing awareness of what their culture considers right and wrong. Culture also is absorbed unconsciously. North Americans acquire their culture's notions about how far apart people should stand when they talk not by being told directly to maintain a certain distance but through a gradual process of observation, experience, and conscious and unconscious behavior modification. No one tells Latins to stand closer together than North Americans do, but they learn to do so anyway as part of their cultural tradition.

Anthropologists agree that cultural learning is uniquely elaborated among humans and that all humans have culture. Anthropologists also accept a doctrine named in the 19th century as "the psychic unity of man." This means that although *individuals* differ in their emotional and intellectual tendencies and capacities, all human *populations* have equivalent capacities for culture. Regardless of their genes or their physical appearance, people can learn any cultural tradition.

To understand this point, consider that contemporary Americans and Canadians are the genetically mixed descendants of people from all over the world. Our ancestors were biologically varied, lived in different countries and continents, and participated in hundreds of cultural traditions. However, early colonists, later immigrants, and their descendants have all become active participants in American and Canadian life. All now share a national culture.

## Culture Is Symbolic

Symbolic thought is unique and crucial to humans and to cultural learning. Anthropologist Leslie White defined culture as

> dependent upon symbolling. . . . Culture consists of tools, implements, utensils, clothing, ornaments, customs, institutions, beliefs, rituals, games, works of art, language, etc. (White 1959, p. 3)

For White, culture originated when our ancestors acquired the ability to use symbols, that is, to originate and bestow meaning on a thing or an event, and, correspondingly, to grasp and appreciate such meanings (White 1959, p. 3).

A symbol is something verbal or nonverbal, within a particular language or culture, that comes to stand for something else. There is no obvious, natural, or necessary connection between the symbol and what it symbolizes. A pet that barks is no more naturally a *dog* than a *chien, Hund,* or *mbwa,* to use the words for the animal we call "dog" in French, German, and Swahili. Language is one of the distinctive possessions of *Homo sapiens.* No other animal has developed anything approaching the complexity of language.

Symbols are usually linguistic. But there are also nonverbal symbols, such as flags, that stand for countries, as arches do for a hamburger chain. Holy water is a potent symbol in Roman Catholicism. As is true of all symbols, the association between a symbol (water) and what is symbolized (holiness) is arbitrary and conventional. Water is not intrinsically holier than milk, blood, or other natural liquids. Nor is holy water chemically different from ordinary water. Holy water is a symbol within Roman Catholicism, which is part of an international cultural system. A natural thing has been

Some symbols are linguistic. Others are nonverbal, such as flags, which stand for countries. Here, colorful flags of several nations wave in front of the United Nations building in New York City.

arbitrarily associated with a particular meaning for Catholics, who share common beliefs and experiences that are based on learning and that are transmitted across the generations.

For hundreds of thousands of years, humans have possessed the abilities on which culture rests. These abilities are to learn, to think symbolically, to manipulate language, and to use tools and other cultural products in organizing their lives and coping with their environments. Every contemporary human population has the ability to use symbols and thus to create and maintain culture. Our nearest relatives—chimpanzees and gorillas—have rudimentary cultural abilities. No other animal, however, has elaborated cultural abilities—to learn, to communicate, and to store, process, and use information—to the extent that *Homo* has.

## Culture Is Shared

Culture is an attribute not of individuals per se but of individuals as members of *groups*. Culture is transmitted in society. Don't we learn our culture by observing, listening, talking, and interacting with many other people? Shared beliefs, values, memories, and expectations link people who grow up in the same culture. Enculturation unifies people by providing us with common experiences.

Today's parents were yesterday's children. If they grew up in North America, they absorbed certain values and beliefs transmitted over the generations. People become agents in the enculturation of their children, just as their parents were for them. Although a culture constantly changes, certain fundamental beliefs, values, worldviews, and child-rearing practices endure. Consider a simple American example of enduring shared enculturation. As children, when we didn't finish a meal, our parents may have reminded us of starving children in some foreign country, just as our grandparents might have done a generation earlier. The specific locale changes (China, India, Bangladesh, Ethiopia, Somalia, Darfur—what was it in your home?). Still, American culture goes on transmitting the idea that by eating all our brussels sprouts or broccoli we can justify our own good fortune, compared to a hungry child in an impoverished or war-ravaged country.

Despite characteristic American notions that people should "make up their own minds" and "have a right to their opinion," little of what we think is original or unique. We share our opinions and beliefs with many other people—nowadays not just in person but also via new media. Think about how often (and with whom) you share information or an opinion via texting, Facebook, and Twitter. Illustrating the power of shared cultural background, we are most likely to agree with and feel comfortable with people who are socially, economically, and culturally similar to ourselves. This is one reason Americans abroad tend to socialize with each other, just as French and British colonials did in their overseas empires. Birds of a feather flock together, but for people, the familiar plumage is culture.

## Culture and Nature

Culture takes the natural biological urges we share with other animals and teaches us how to express them in particular ways. People have to eat, but culture teaches us what, when, and how. In many cultures people have their main meal at noon, but most North Americans prefer a large dinner. English people may eat fish for breakfast, while North Americans may prefer hot cakes and cold cereals. Brazilians put hot milk into strong coffee, whereas North Americans pour cold milk into a weaker brew. Midwesterners dine at 5 or 6 P.M., Spaniards at 10 P.M.

Culture molds "human nature" in many directions. People have to eliminate wastes from their bodies. But some cultures teach people to defecate

squatting, while others tell them to do it sitting down. A generation ago, in Paris and other French cities, it was customary for men to urinate almost publicly, and seemingly without embarrassment, in barely shielded *pissoirs* located on city streets. Our "bathroom" habits, including waste elimination, bathing, and dental care, are parts of cultural traditions that have converted natural acts into cultural customs.

Our culture—and cultural changes—affect the ways in which we perceive nature, human nature, and "the natural." Through science, invention, and discovery, cultural advances have overcome many "natural" limitations. We prevent and cure diseases, such as polio and smallpox, that felled our ancestors. We use Viagra to restore and enhance sexual potency. Through cloning, scientists have altered the way we think about biological identity and the meaning of life itself. Culture, of course, has not freed us from natural threats. Hurricanes, floods, earthquakes, and other natural forces regularly challenge our wishes to modify the environment through building, development, and expansion. Can you think of other ways in which nature strikes back at people and their products?

## Culture Is All-Encompassing

For anthropologists, culture includes much more than refinement, taste, sophistication, education, and appreciation of the fine arts. Not only college graduates but all people are "cultured." The most interesting and significant cultural forces are those that affect people every day of their lives, particularly those that influence children during enculturation. *Culture,* as defined anthropologically, encompasses features that are sometimes regarded as trivial or unworthy of serious study, such as "popular" culture. To understand contemporary North American culture, we must consider social media, cell phones, the Internet, television, fast-food restaurants, sports, and games. As a cultural manifestation, a rock star may be as interesting as a symphony conductor, a comic book as significant as a book-award winner.

## Culture Is Integrated

Cultures are not haphazard collections of customs and beliefs. Cultures are integrated, patterned systems. If one part of the system (e.g., the economy) changes, other parts change as well. For example, during the 1950s, most American women planned domestic careers as homemakers and mothers. Most of today's college women, by contrast, expect to get paid jobs when they graduate.

Economic changes have social repercussions. Attitudes and behavior about marriage, family, and children have changed. Late marriage, "living together," and divorce have become commonplace. Work competes with marriage and family responsibilities and reduces the time available to invest in child care.

Cultures are integrated systems, so that when one behavior pattern changes, others also change. During the 1950s, most American women expected to have careers as wives, mothers, and domestic managers. As millions of women entered the workforce, attitudes toward work and family changed. Compare the 1950s mom and kids doing dishes with the contemporary physician entering data on a laptop computer. What do you imagine the physician will do when she gets home?

Cultures are integrated not simply by their dominant economic activities and related social patterns but also by sets of values, ideas, symbols, and judgments. Cultures train their individual members to share certain personality traits. A set of **core values** (key, basic, or central values) integrates each culture and helps distinguish it from others. For instance, the work ethic and individualism are core values that have integrated American culture for generations. Different sets of dominant values exist in other cultures.

## Culture Is Instrumental, Adaptive, and Maladaptive

Culture is the main reason for human adaptability and success. Other animals rely on biological means of adaptation (such as fur or blubber, which are adaptations to cold). Humans also adapt biologically—for example, by shivering when we get cold or sweating when we get hot. But people also have cultural ways of adapting. To cope with environmental stresses we habitually use technology, or tools. We hunt cold-adapted animals and use their fur coats as our own. We turn the thermostat up in the winter and down in the summer. Or we plan action to increase our comfort. We have a cold drink, jump in a pool, or travel to someplace cooler in the summer or warmer in the winter. People use culture instrumentally, that is, to fulfill their basic biological needs for food, drink, shelter, comfort, and reproduction.

People also use culture to fulfill psychological and emotional needs, such as friendship, companionship, approval, and sexual desirability. People seek informal support—help from people who care about them—as well as formal support from associations and institutions. To these ends, individuals cultivate ties with others on the basis of common experiences, political interests, aesthetic sensibilities, or personal attraction. Increasingly, such Internet platforms as Facebook, Google +, and LinkedIn are used to create and maintain social or professional connections.

On one level, cultural traits (e.g., air conditioning) may be called adaptive if they help individuals cope with environmental stresses. But on a different level, such traits can also be *maladaptive*. For example, emissions from our machines have environmental effects that can harm humans and other life. Many modern cultural patterns may be maladaptive in the long run. Examples of maladaptive aspects of culture include policies that encourage overpopulation, poor food-distribution systems, overconsumption, and industrial pollution.

## CULTURE'S EVOLUTIONARY BASIS

The human capacity for culture has an evolutionary basis that extends back at least 2.6 million years—to early toolmakers whose products survive in the archaeological record (and most probably even farther back, based on observation of tool use and manufacture by apes).

Similarities between humans and apes, our closest relatives, are evident in anatomy, brain structure, genetics, and biochemistry. Most closely related to us are the African great apes: chimpanzees and gorillas. *Hominidae* is the zoological family that includes fossil and living humans. Also included as **hominids** are chimps and gorillas. The term **hominins** is used for the group that leads to humans but not to chimps and gorillas and that encompasses all the human species that ever have existed.

Many human traits reflect the fact that our primate ancestors lived in the trees. These traits include grasping ability and manual dexterity (especially opposable thumbs), depth and color vision, learning ability based on a large brain, substantial parental investment in a limited number of offspring, and tendencies toward sociality and cooperation. Like other primates, humans have flexible, five-fingered hands and *opposable thumbs:* Each thumb can touch all the other fingers on the same hand. Like monkeys and apes, humans also have excellent depth and color vision. Our eyes are placed forward in the skull and look directly ahead, so that their fields of vision overlap. Depth perception, impossible without overlapping visual fields, proved adaptive—for judging distance, for example—in the trees. Having color and depth vision also facilitates the identification of various food sources, as well as mutual grooming, picking out burrs, insects, and other small objects from hair. Such grooming is one way of forming and maintaining social bonds.

The combination of manual dexterity and depth perception allows monkeys, apes, and humans to pick up small objects, hold them in front of their eyes, and appraise them. Our ability to thread a needle reflects an intricate interplay of hands and eyes that took millions of years of primate evolution to achieve. Such dexterity, including the opposable thumb, confers a tremendous advantage in manipulating objects and is essential to a major human adaptive capacity: toolmaking. In primates, and especially in humans, the ratio of brain size to body size exceeds that of most mammals. Even more important, the brain's outer layer—concerned with memory, association, and integration—is relatively larger. Monkeys, apes, and humans store an array of images in their memories, which permits them to learn more. Such a capacity for learning is a tremendous adaptive advantage. Like most other primates, humans usually give birth to a single offspring rather than a litter. Receiving more parental attention, that one infant has enhanced learning opportunities. The need for longer and more attentive care of offspring places a selective value on support by a social group. Humans have developed considerably the primate tendency to be social

**core values**
Key, basic, or central values that integrate a culture.

**hominid**
Member of hominid family; any fossil or living human, chimp, or gorilla.

**hominins**
Hominids excluding the African apes; all the human species that ever have existed.

animals, living and interacting regularly with other members of their species.

## What We Share with Other Primates

There is a substantial gap between primate *society* (organized life in groups) and fully developed human *culture,* which is based on symbolic thought. Nevertheless, studies of nonhuman primates reveal many similarities with humans, such as the ability to learn from experience and change behavior as a result. Apes and monkeys, like humans, learn throughout their lives. In one group of Japanese macaques (land-dwelling monkeys), for example, a 3-year-old female started washing sweet potatoes before she ate them. First her mother, then her age peers, and finally the entire troop began washing sweet potatoes as well. The ability to benefit from experience confers a tremendous adaptive advantage, permitting the avoidance of fatal mistakes. Faced with environmental change, humans and other primates don't have to wait for a genetic or physiological response. They can modify learned behavior and social patterns instead.

Although humans do employ tools much more than any other animal does, tool use also turns up among several nonhuman species, including birds, beavers, sea otters, and especially apes (see Campbell 2011; Mayell 2003). Nor are humans the only animals that make tools with a specific purpose in mind. Chimpanzees living in the Tai forest of Ivory Coast make and use stone tools to break open hard, golf-ball-sized nuts (Mercader, Panger, and Boesch 2002). At specific sites, the chimps gather nuts, place them on stumps or flat rocks, which are used as anvils, and pound the nuts with heavy stones. The chimps must select hammer stones suited to smashing the nuts and carry them to where the nut trees grow. Nut cracking is a learned skill, with mothers showing their young how to do it.

In 1960, Jane Goodall (1996) began observing wild chimps—including their tool use and hunting behavior—at Gombe Stream National Park in Tanzania, East Africa. The most studied form of ape toolmaking involves "termiting," in which chimps make tools to probe termite hills. They choose twigs, which they modify by removing leaves and peeling off bark to expose the sticky surface beneath. They carry the twigs to termite hills, dig holes with their fingers, and insert the twigs. Finally, they pull out the twigs and dine on termites that were attracted to the sticky surface. Given what is known about ape tool use and manufacture, it is almost certain that early hominins shared this ability, although the first evidence for hominin stone toolmaking dates back only 2.6 million years. Upright bipedalism would have permitted the carrying and use of tools and weapons against predators and competitors.

The apes have other abilities essential to culture. Wild chimps and orangs aim and throw objects. Gorillas build nests, and they throw branches, grass, vines, and other objects. Hominins have elaborated the capacity to aim and throw, without which we never would have developed projectile technology and weaponry—or baseball.

Like toolmaking, hunting once was cited as a distinctive human activity not shared with the apes. Again, however, primate research shows that other primates, especially chimpanzees, are habitual hunters. For example, in Uganda's Kibale National Park chimps form large hunting parties, including an average of 26 individuals (almost always adult and adolescent males). Most hunts (78 percent) result in at least one prey item's being caught—a much higher success rate than that among lions (26 percent), hyenas (34 percent), or cheetahs (30 percent). Chimps' favored prey there is the red colobus monkey (Mitani and Watts 1999; Mitani et al. 2012).

Archaeological evidence suggests that humans were hunting by at least 2.6 million years ago, based on stone meat-cutting tools found at Olduvai Gorge in Tanzania. Given our current understanding of chimp hunting and toolmaking, we can infer that hominids may have been hunting much earlier than the first archaeological evidence attests. Because chimps typically devour the monkeys they kill, leaving few remains, we may never find archaeological evidence for the first hominin hunt, especially if it was done without stone tools.

## How We Differ from Other Primates

Although chimps often share meat from a hunt, apes and monkeys (except for nursing infants) tend to feed themselves individually. Cooperation and sharing are much more developed among humans. Until fairly recently (12,000 to 10,000 years ago), all humans were hunter-gatherers who lived in small groups called bands. In some world areas, the hunter-gatherer way of life persisted into recent times, permitting study by ethnographers. In such societies, men and women take resources back to the camp and share them. Everyone shares the meat from a large animal. Nourished and protected by younger band members, elders live past reproductive age and are respected for their knowledge and

Primates have five-digited feet and hands, well suited for grasping. Flexible hands and feet that could encircle branches were important features in the early primates' arboreal life. In adapting to bipedal (two-footed) locomotion, hominids eliminated most of the foot's grasping ability—illustrated here by the chimpanzee.

These two photos show different forms of tool use by chimps. Liberian chimps, like the one on the left, use hammer stones to crack palm nuts. On the right, chimps used prepared twigs to "fish" for termites from an ant hill.

experience. Humans are among the most cooperative of the primates—in the food quest and other social activities. In addition, the amount of information stored in a human band is far greater than that in any other primate group.

Another difference between humans and other primates involves mating. Among baboons and chimps, most mating occurs when females enter estrus, during which they ovulate. In estrus, the vaginal area swells and reddens, and receptive females form temporary bonds with, and mate with, males. Human females, by contrast, lack a visible estrus cycle, and their ovulation is concealed. Not knowing when ovulation is occurring, humans maximize their reproductive success by mating throughout the year. Human pair bonds for mating are more exclusive and more durable than are those of chimps. Related to our more constant sexuality, all human societies have some form of marriage. Marriage gives mating a reliable basis and grants to each spouse special, though not always exclusive, sexual rights to the other.

Marriage creates another major contrast between humans and nonhuman primates: exogamy and kinship systems. Most cultures have rules of exogamy requiring marriage outside one's kin or local group. Coupled with the recognition of kinship, exogamy confers adaptive advantages. It creates ties between the spouses' different groups of origin. Their children have relatives, and therefore allies, in two kin groups rather than just one. The key point here is that ties of affection and mutual support between members of different local groups tend to be absent among primates other than *Homo*. Other primates tend to disperse at adolescence. Among chimps and gorillas, females tend to migrate, seeking mates in other groups. Humans also choose mates from outside the natal group, and usually at least one spouse moves. However, *humans maintain lifelong ties with sons and daughters*. The systems of kinship and marriage that preserve these links provide a major contrast between humans and other primates.

# UNIVERSALITY, GENERALITY, AND PARTICULARITY

In studying human diversity in time and space, anthropologists distinguish among the universal, the generalized, and the particular. Certain biological, psychological, social, and cultural features are **universal,** found in every culture. Others are merely **generalities,** common to several but not all human groups. Still other traits are **particularities,** unique to certain cultural traditions.

## Universals and Generalities

Biologically based universals include a long period of infant dependency, year-round (rather than seasonal) sexuality, and a complex brain that enables us to use symbols, languages, and tools. Among the social universals is life in groups and in some kind of family (see Brown 1991). Generalities occur in certain times and places but not in all cultures. They may be widespread, but they are not universal. One cultural generality that is present in many but not all societies is the nuclear family, a kinship group consisting of parents and children. Although many middle-class Americans ethnocentrically view the nuclear family as a proper and "natural" group, it is not universal. It was absent, for example, among the Nayars, who live on the Malabar Coast of India. Traditionally, the Nayars lived in female-headed households, and husbands and wives did not live together. In many other societies, the nuclear family is submerged in larger kin groups, such as extended families, lineages, and clans.

Societies can share the same beliefs and customs because of borrowing or through (cultural) inheritance from a common cultural ancestor. Speaking English is a generality shared by North Americans and Australians because both countries had English settlers. Another reason for generalities is domination, as in colonial rule, when customs and

**universal**
Something that exists in every culture.

**generality**
Culture pattern or trait that exists in some but not all societies.

**particularity**
Distinctive or unique culture trait, pattern, or integration.

procedures are imposed on one culture by another one that is more powerful. In many countries, use of the English language reflects colonial history. More recently, English has spread through diffusion (cultural borrowing) to many other countries, as it has become the world's foremost language for business, travel, and the Internet.

## Particularity: Patterns of Culture

A cultural particularity is a trait or feature of culture that is not generalized or widespread; rather, it is confined to a single place, culture, or society. Yet because of cultural borrowing and exchanges, which have accelerated with globalization, traits that once were limited in their distribution have become more widespread. Traits that are useful, that have the capacity to please large audiences, and that don't clash with the cultural values of potential adopters are more likely to spread than others are. Still, certain cultural particularities persist. One example is a particular food dish (e.g., pork barbeque with a mustard-based sauce available in South Carolina, or the pastie—beef stew baked in pie dough—characteristic of Michigan's upper peninsula). Besides diffusion, which, for example, has spread McDonald's food outlets, once confined to San Bernardino, California, across the globe, there are other reasons cultural particularities are increasingly rare. Many cultural traits are shared as cultural universals and as a result of independent invention. Facing similar problems, people in different places have come up with similar solutions. Again and again, similar cultural causes have produced similar cultural results.

At the level of the individual cultural trait or element (e.g., bow and arrow, hot dog, MTV), particularities may be getting rarer. But at a higher level, particularity is more obvious. Different cultures emphasize different things. *Cultures are integrated and patterned differently and display tremendous variation and diversity*. When cultural traits are borrowed, they are modified to fit the culture that adopts them. They are reintegrated—patterned anew—to fit their new setting. MTV in Germany or Brazil isn't at all the same thing as MTV in the United States. As was stated in the earlier section "Culture Is Integrated," patterned beliefs, customs, and practices lend distinctiveness to particular cultural traditions.

Consider universal life-cycle events, such as birth, puberty, marriage, parenthood, and death, which many cultures observe and celebrate. The occasions (e.g., marriage, death) may be the same and universal, but the patterns of ceremonial observance may be dramatically different. Cultures vary in just which events merit special celebration. Americans, for example, regard expensive weddings as more socially appropriate than lavish funerals. However, the Betsileo of Madagascar take the opposite view. The marriage ceremony there is a minor event that brings together just the couple and a few close relatives. However, a funeral is a measure of the deceased person's social position and lifetime achievement, and it may attract a thousand people. Why use money on a house, the Betsileo say, when one can use it on the tomb where one will spend eternity in the company of dead relatives? How unlike contemporary Americans' dreams of home ownership and preference for quick and inexpensive funerals. Cremation, an increasingly common option in the United States (see Sack 2011), would horrify the Betsileo, for whom ancestral bones and relics are important ritual objects.

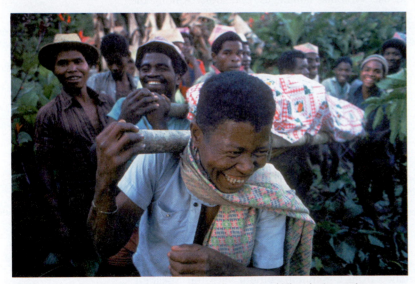

Cultures use rituals to mark such universal life-cycle events as birth, puberty, marriage, parenthood, and death. But particular cultures differ as to which events merit special celebration and in the emotions expressed during their rituals. Compare the wedding party (top) in Bali, Indonesia, with the funeral (bottom) among the Tanala of eastern Madagascar. How would you describe the emotions suggested by the photos?

Cultures vary tremendously in their beliefs, practices, integration, and patterning. By focusing on and trying to explain alternative customs, anthropology forces us to reappraise our familiar ways of thinking. In a world full of cultural diversity, contemporary American culture is just one cultural variant, more powerful perhaps, but no more natural, than the others.

## CULTURE AND THE INDIVIDUAL: AGENCY AND PRACTICE

Generations of anthropologists have theorized about the relationship between the "system," on the one hand, and the "person" or "individual," on the other. The "system" can refer to various concepts, including culture, society, social relations, and social structure. Individual human beings always make up, or constitute, the system. But, living within that system, humans also are constrained (to some extent, at least) by its rules and by the actions of other individuals. Cultural rules provide guidance about what to do and how to do it, but people don't always do what the rules say should be done. People use their culture actively and creatively, rather than blindly following its dictates. Humans aren't passive beings who are doomed to follow their cultural traditions like programmed robots. Instead, people learn, interpret, and manipulate the same rules in different ways—or they emphasize different rules that better suit their interests. Culture is *contested:* Different groups in society struggle with one another over whose ideas, values, goals, and beliefs will prevail. Even common symbols may have radically different *meanings* to different individuals and groups in the same culture. Golden arches may cause one person to salivate, while another person plots a vegetarian protest. The same flag may be waved to support or oppose a given war.

Even when they agree about what should and shouldn't be done, people don't always do as their culture directs or as other people expect. Many rules are violated, some very often (e.g., automobile speed limits). Some anthropologists find it useful to distinguish between ideal culture and real culture. The *ideal culture* consists of what people say they should do and what they say they do. *Real culture* refers to their actual behavior as observed by the anthropologist.

Culture is both public and individual, both in the world and in people's minds. Anthropologists are interested not only in public and collective behavior but also in how *individuals* think, feel, and act. As Roy D'Andrade (1984) has noted, the individual and culture are linked because human social life is a process in which individuals internalize the meanings of *public* (i.e., cultural) messages. Then, alone and in groups, people influence culture by converting their private (and often divergent) understandings into public expressions.

Conventionally, culture has been seen as social glue transmitted across the generations, binding people through their common past, rather than as something being continually created and reworked in the present. The tendency to view culture as an entity rather than a process is changing. Contemporary anthropologists now emphasize how day-to-day action, practice, or resistance can make and remake culture (Gupta and Ferguson 1997b). *Agency* refers to the actions that individuals take, both alone and in groups, in forming and transforming cultural identities.

The approach to culture known as *practice theory* (Ortner 1984) recognizes that individuals within a society or culture have diverse motives and intentions and different degrees of power and influence. Such contrasts may be associated with gender, age, ethnicity, class, and other social variables. Practice theory focuses on how such varied individuals—through their ordinary and extraordinary actions and practices—manage to influence, create, and transform the world they live in. Practice theory appropriately recognizes a reciprocal relation between culture (the system—see above) and the individual. The system shapes the way individuals experience and respond to external events, but individuals also play an active role in the way society functions and changes. Practice theory recognizes both constraints on individuals and the flexibility and changeability of cultures and social systems.

## Levels of Culture

We can distinguish levels of culture, which vary in their membership and geographic extent. **National culture** refers to those beliefs, learned behavior patterns, values, and institutions that are shared by citizens of the same nation. **International culture** is the term for cultural traditions that extend beyond and across national boundaries. Because culture is transmitted through learning rather than genetically, cultural traits can spread through borrowing, or *diffusion,* from one group to another.

Many cultural traits and patterns have become international in scope. For example, Roman Catholics in many different countries share beliefs, symbols, experiences, and values transmitted by their church. The contemporary United States, Canada, Great Britain, and Australia share cultural traits they have inherited from their common linguistic and cultural ancestors in Great Britain. The World Cup is an international cultural event, as people in many countries know the rules of, play, and follow soccer.

Cultures also can be smaller than nations (see Jenks 2005). Although people who live in the same country partake in a national cultural tradition, all nations also contain diversity. Individuals, families, communities, regions, classes, and other groups within a culture have different learning experiences as well as shared ones. **Subcultures** are different

**national culture**
Cultural features shared by citizens of the same nation.

**international culture**
Cultural traditions that extend beyond national boundaries.

**subcultures**
Different cultural traditions associated with subgroups in the same complex society.

Illustrating the international level of culture, Roman Catholics in different nations share knowledge, symbols, beliefs, and behavior associated with their religion. Shown here, Chinese Catholics at an Easter mass in Beijing. In China, worship is allowed only in government-controlled churches, but an estimated 12 million Chinese Catholics belong to unofficial congregations loyal to Rome.

subculture. Soccer and basketball are played internationally. Monster-truck rallies are held throughout the United States. Bocci is a bowling-like sport from Italy still played in some Italian American neighborhoods.

Nowadays, many anthropologists are reluctant to use the term *subculture*. They feel that the prefix "sub-" is offensive because it means "below." "Subcultures" may thus be perceived as "less than" or somehow inferior to a dominant, elite, or national culture. In this discussion of levels of culture, I intend no such implication. My point is simply that nations may contain many different culturally defined groups. As mentioned earlier, culture is contested. Various groups may strive to promote the correctness and value of their own practices, values, and beliefs in comparison with those of other groups or of the nation as a whole. (This chapter's "Appreciating Diversity" on pp. 32–33 demonstrates how contemporary indigenous groups have to grapple with multiple levels of culture, contestation, and political regulation.)

**ethnocentrism**
Judging other cultures using one's own cultural standards.

symbol-based patterns and traditions associated with particular groups in the same complex society. In a large nation like the United States or Canada, subcultures originate in region, ethnicity, language, class, and religion. The backgrounds of Christians, Jews, and Muslims—and the diverse branches of those religions, create subcultural differences among them. While sharing a common national culture, U.S. northerners and southerners also differ in aspects of their beliefs, values, and customary behavior. French-speaking Canadians contrast with English-speaking people in the same country. Italian Americans have ethnic traditions different from those of Irish, Polish, and African Americans. Using sports and foods, Table 2.1 gives some examples of international culture, national culture, and

## Ethnocentrism, Cultural Relativism, and Human Rights

**Ethnocentrism** is the tendency to view one's own culture as superior and to use one's own standards and values in judging outsiders. We witness ethnocentrism when people consider their own cultural beliefs to be truer, more proper, or more moral than those of other groups. However, fundamental to anthropology, as the study of human diversity, is the fact that what is alien (even disgusting) to us may be normal, proper, and prized elsewhere (see the previous discussion of cultural particularities, including burial customs). The fact of cultural diversity calls ethnocentrism into question, as anthropologists have shown all kinds of reasons for unfamiliar practices. During a course like this, anthropology students often reexamine their own ethnocentric beliefs. Sometimes as the strange becomes familiar, the familiar seems a bit stranger and less comfortable. One goal of anthropology is to show the value in the lives of others. But how far is too far? What happens when cultural practices, values, and rights come into conflict with human rights?

Several societies in Africa and the Middle East have customs requiring female genital modification. *Clitoridectomy* is the removal of a girl's clitoris. *Infibulation* involves sewing the lips (labia) of the vagina to constrict the vaginal opening. Both procedures reduce female sexual pleasure and, it is believed in some societies, the likelihood of adultery. Although traditional in the societies where they

**TABLE 2.1** Levels of Culture, with Examples from Sports and Foods

| LEVEL OF CULTURE | SPORTS EXAMPLES | FOOD EXAMPLES |
|---|---|---|
| International | Soccer, basketball | Pizza |
| National | Monster-truck rallies | Apple pie |
| Subculture | Bocci | Big Joe Pork Barbeque (South Carolina) |

occur, such practices, characterized as female genital mutilation (FGM), have been opposed by human rights advocates, especially women's rights groups. The idea is that the custom infringes on a basic human right: disposition over one's body and one's sexuality. Indeed, such practices are fading as a result of worldwide attention to the problem and changing sex/gender roles. Some African countries have banned or otherwise discouraged the procedures, as have Western nations that receive immigration from such cultures. Similar issues arise with circumcision and other male genital operations. Is it right to require adolescent boys to undergo collective circumcision to fulfill cultural traditions, as has been done traditionally in parts of Africa and Australia? Is it right for a baby boy to be circumcised without his permission, as has been done routinely in the United States and as is customary among Jews and Muslims? (A 2011 initiative aimed at banning circumcision in San Francisco, California, failed to make it to the ballot.)

According to an idea known as **cultural relativism,** it is inappropriate to use outside standards to judge behavior in a given society; such behavior should be evaluated in the context of the culture in which it occurs. Anthropologists employ cultural relativism not as a moral belief but as a methodological position: In order to understand another culture fully, we must try to understand how the people in that culture see things. What motivates them—what are they thinking—when they do those things? Such an approach does not preclude making moral judgments. In the FGM example, one can understand the motivations for the practice only by looking at things from the point of view of the people who engage in it. Having done this, one then faces the moral question of what, if anything, to do about it.

We also should recognize that different people and groups within the same society—for example, women versus men or old versus young—can have very different opinions about what is proper, necessary, and moral. When there are power differentials in a society, a particular practice may be supported by some people more than others (e.g., old men versus young women). In trying to understand the meaning of a practice or belief within any cultural context, we should ask who is relatively advantaged and disadvantaged by that custom.

The idea of **human rights** invokes a realm of justice and morality beyond and superior to particular countries, cultures, and religions. Human rights, usually seen as vested in individuals, include the right to speak freely, to hold religious beliefs without persecution, and not to be murdered, injured, enslaved, or imprisoned without charge. These rights are not ordinary laws that particular governments make and enforce. Human rights are seen as *inalienable* (nations cannot abridge or terminate them) and international (larger than and superior to individual nations and cultures). Four

United Nations documents describe nearly all the human rights that have been internationally recognized. Those documents are the UN Charter; the Universal Declaration of Human Rights; the Covenant on Economic, Social and Cultural Rights; and the Covenant on Civil and Political Rights.

Alongside the human rights movement has arisen an awareness of the need to preserve cultural rights. Unlike human rights, **cultural rights** are vested not in individuals but in groups, including indigenous peoples and religious and ethnic minorities. Cultural rights include a group's ability to raise its children in the ways of its forebears, to continue its language, and not to be deprived of its economic base by the nation in which it is located (Greaves 1995). Many countries have signed pacts endorsing, for cultural minorities within nations, such rights as self-determination; some degree of home rule; and the right to practice the group's religion, culture, and language. The related notion of indigenous intellectual property rights (**IPR**) has arisen in an attempt to conserve each society's cultural base—its core beliefs and principles. IPR are claimed as a cultural right, allowing indigenous groups to control who may know and use their collective knowledge and its applications. Much traditional cultural knowledge has commercial value. Examples include ethnomedicine (traditional medical knowledge and techniques), cosmetics, cultivated plants, foods, folklore, arts, crafts, songs, dances, costumes, and rituals. According to the IPR concept, a particular group may determine how its indigenous knowledge and the products of that knowledge are used and distributed, and the level of compensation required. (This chapter's "Appreciating Diversity" discusses how notions of human, cultural, and animal rights may come into conflict.)

The notion of cultural rights recalls the previous discussion of cultural relativism, and the issue raised there arises again. What does one do about cultural rights that interfere with human rights? I believe that anthropology, as the scientific study of human diversity, should strive to present accurate accounts and explanations of cultural phenomena. Most ethnographers try to be objective, accurate, and sensitive in their accounts of other cultures. However, objectivity, sensitivity, and a cross-cultural perspective don't mean that anthropologists have to ignore international standards of justice and morality. The anthropologist doesn't have to approve customs such as infanticide, cannibalism, and torture to recognize their existence and determine their causes and the motivations behind them. Each anthropologist has a choice about where he or she will do fieldwork. Some anthropologists choose not to study a particular culture because they discover in advance or early in fieldwork that behavior they consider morally repugnant is practiced there. When confronted with such behavior, each anthropologist must make a judgment about what, if anything, to do about it. What do you think?

**cultural rights**
Rights vested in religious and ethnic minorities and indigenous societies.

**cultural relativism**
Idea that behavior should be evaluated not by outside standards but in the context of the culture in which it occurs.

**IPR**
Intellectual property rights; an indigenous group's collective knowledge and its applications.

**human rights**
Rights based on justice and morality beyond and superior to particular countries, cultures, and religions.

# appreciating DIVERSITY

## Culture Clash: Makah Seek Return to Whaling Past

Cultures are diverse but not isolated. Throughout human history links between groups have been provided by cultural practices such as marriage, kinship, religion, trade, travel, exploration, and conquest. For centuries, indigenous peoples have been exposed to a world system. Contemporary forces and events make even the illusion of autonomy hard to maintain. Nowadays, as is described here, members of local cultures and communities must heed not only their own customs but also agencies, laws, and lawsuits operating at the national and international levels.

As you read this account and this chapter on culture, pay attention to the various kinds of rights being asserted—animal rights, cultural rights, economic rights, legal rights, and human rights—and how those rights might clash. Also consider the different levels of culture and of political representation (local, regional, national, and global) that determine how contemporary people such as the Makah live their lives and maintain their traditions. Think, too, about the minimal impact on whale populations of the Makah hunt compared with commercial whaling. Today, cultural connections come increasingly through the Internet, as indigenous groups, including the Makah, maintain their own websites—forums for discussions of whaling and other issues of interest to them. Check out http://www.makah.com for the latest on the issues discussed here.

The whaling canoes are stored in a wooden shed, idle for [several] years. They were last used when the Makah Indians were allowed to take their harpoons and a .50-caliber rifle and set out on their first whale hunt since the late 1920s.

There were eight young men in a canoe with a red hummingbird, a symbol of speed, painted on the tip. There were motorboats ferrying other hunters, news helicopters, and animal rights activists in speedboats and even a submarine.

On May 17, 1999, a week into the hunt, the Makah killed a 30-ton gray whale, striking it with harpoons and then killing it with a gunshot to the back of the head.

That rainy spring day remains etched in the minds of many Makah as a defining moment in their efforts to reach back to their cultural and historical roots. It was their first kill in seven decades, and it was their last since they were stopped by court rulings. They have asked the federal government for permission to resume hunting. . . .

The Makah, a tribe of about 1,500 near the mouth of the Strait of Juan de Fuca on the Olympic Peninsula, see themselves as whalers and continue to identify themselves spiritually with whales.

"Everybody felt like it was a part of making history," Micah L. McCarty, a tribal council member, said of the 1999 hunt. "It's inspired a cultural renaissance, so to speak. It inspired a lot of people to learn artwork and become more active in building canoes; the younger generation took a more keen interest in singing and dancing."

The Makah, a tribe of mostly fishermen that faces serious poverty and high unemployment, were guaranteed the right to hunt whales in an 1855 treaty with the United States, the only tribe with such a treaty provision. Whaling had been the tribe's mainstay for thousands of years.

But the tribe decided to stop hunting whales early in the 20th century, when commercial harvesting had depleted the species. Whale hunting was later strictly regulated nationally and internationally, and the United States listed the Northern Pacific gray whale, the one most available to the Makah, as endangered.

The protections helped the whales rebound, and they were taken off the endangered list in 1994. Several years later, the Makah won permission to hunt again, along with a $100,000 federal grant to set up a whaling commission.

By the time they were ready, none of the Makah had witnessed a whale hunt or even tasted the meat, hearing only stories passed down through the generations. They learned that the whale was a touchstone of Makah culture—the tribe's logo today pictures an eagle perched on a whale—and that the tribe's economy was built around the lucrative trade with Europeans in whale oil, used for heating and lighting, during the 18th and early 19th centuries.

For a year before the 1999 hunt, the new Makah whale hunters prepared for their sacramental pursuit, training in canoes on the cold and choppy waters of the Pacific Ocean, praying on the beach in the mornings and at the dock in the evenings.

Animal rights groups were preparing, too. When the hunt began, the small reservation and its surrounding waters were teeming with news helicopters and protest groups. On that May afternoon, when the protesters were somewhere off the reservation, the Makah killed their whale. They held a huge celebration on the beach, where 15 men were waiting to butcher the animal, its meat later kippered and stewed.

But the protests and the television cameras "took a lot of the spirituality out of it," said Dave Sones, vice chairman of the tribal council.

Mr. McCarty said, "I equate it with interrupting High Mass."

The Makah went whale hunting, largely unnoticed, again in 2000, paddling out on a 32-foot cedar whaling canoe, but they did not catch anything. Soon after, animal rights groups, including the Humane Society of the United States, sued to stop the hunting. In 2002, an appeals court declared the hunting illegal, saying the National Oceanic and Atmospheric Administration had not adequately studied the impact of Makah hunting on the survival of the whale species.

Despite the strict national and international regulations on whale hunting, several tribes of Alaska Natives, subsistence whale hunters for centuries, are exempt from provisions of the 1972 Marine Mammal Protection Act, allowing them to hunt the bowhead whale. That species, unlike the

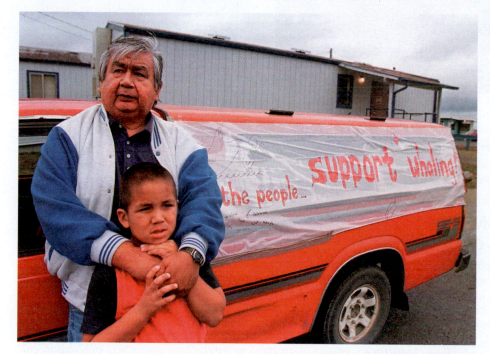

gray whale, is listed as endangered, said Brian Gorman, a spokesman for the oceanic agency.

Despite their treaty rights, the Makah were not granted an exemption under the 1972 act. The tribe [has requested] a waiver that would grant them permanent rights to kill up to 20 gray whales in any five-year period, which they insist they already have under their 1855 treaty.

The Makah's request is "setting a dangerous precedent," said Naomi Rose, a marine mammal scientist for the Humane Society.

The Alaska hunting, Ms. Rose said, "is a true subsistence hunt," whereas the Makah . . . are pursuing "cultural whaling" that is not essential to their diet. . . .

The Makah "have a treaty right, but we're asking them not to exercise it," she said. But other environmental groups, including Greenpeace, which is adamantly opposed to the commercial harvesting of whales, have remained neutral on the Makah's quest.

"No indigenous hunt has ever destroyed whale populations," said John Hocevar, an oceans specialist with Greenpeace. "And looking at the enormous other threats to whales and putting the Makah whaling in context, it's pretty different."

Mr. Gorman, of the federal fisheries agency, said: "They have a treaty right that the U.S. government signed. It doesn't take an international lawyer to figure out that they do have this treaty."

**2014 Update: The situation remains unresolved. The Makah petition to resume whaling continues to be considered by the Marine Fisheries division of NOAA—the National Oceanic and Atmospheric Administration. For the latest on the Makah see www.makah.com.**

Dewey Johnson and his son Michael (top) show their support for fellow Makah tribe members at Neah Bay, Washington, in their quest to hunt gray whales for the first time in 70 years. *Sea Shepherd* captain Paul Watson stands at Neah Bay beside a 25-foot submarine painted to look like an orca whale (below). This ship emits orca sounds that can scare away gray whales. Watson leads the opposition against Makah whaling, which was declared illegal in 2002.

The notion of indigenous property rights has arisen in an attempt to conserve each society's cultural base, including its medicinal plants. The hoodia plant, shown on the left in Botswana, is a Kalahari Desert cactus traditionally used by the San people to stave off hunger. On the right we see HoodiaThin, a commercial appetite suppressant made from imported hoodia and distributed by Los Angeles–based Prime Life Nutritionals. Hoodia is grown today on a few commercial farms in southern Africa (including the San-owned farm on the left).

## MECHANISMS OF CULTURAL CHANGE

**diffusion**
Borrowing of cultural traits between societies.

**independent invention**
The independent development of a cultural feature in different societies.

**acculturation**
An exchange of cultural features between groups in firsthand contact.

**globalization**
The accelerating interdependence of nations in the world system today.

Why and how do cultures change? One way is **diffusion,** or the borrowing of traits between cultures. Such exchange of information and products has gone on throughout human history because cultures never have been truly isolated. Contact between neighboring groups has always existed and has extended over vast areas (Boas 1940/1966). Diffusion is *direct* when two cultures trade, intermarry, or wage war on one another. Diffusion is *forced* when one culture subjugates another and imposes its customs on the dominated group. Diffusion is *indirect* when items move from group A to group C via group B without any firsthand contact between A and C. In this case, group B might consist of traders or merchants who take products from a variety of places to new markets. Or group B might be geographically situated between A and C, so that what it gets from A eventually winds up in C, and vice versa. In today's world, much transnational diffusion is due to the spread of the mass media and advanced information technology.

**Acculturation,** a second mechanism of cultural change, is the exchange of cultural features that results when groups have continuous firsthand contact. The cultures of either group or both groups may be changed by this contact (Redfield, Linton, and Herskovits 1936). With acculturation, parts of the cultures change, but each group remains distinct. In situations of continuous contact, cultures may exchange and blend foods, recipes, music, dances, clothing, tools, technologies, and languages.

One example of acculturation is a *pidgin,* a mixed language that develops to ease communication between members of different societies in contact. This usually happens in situations of trade or colonialism. Pidgin English, for example, is a simplified form of English.

It blends English grammar with the grammar of a native language. Pidgin English was first used for commerce in Chinese ports. Similar pidgins developed later in Papua New Guinea and West Africa.

**Independent invention**—the process by which humans innovate, creatively finding solutions to problems—is a third mechanism of cultural change. Faced with comparable problems and challenges, people in different societies have innovated and changed in similar ways, which is one reason cultural generalities exist. One example is the independent invention of agriculture in the Middle East and Mexico. Over the course of human history, major innovations have spread at the expense of earlier ones. Often a major invention, such as agriculture, triggers a series of subsequent interrelated changes. These economic revolutions have social and cultural repercussions. Thus, in both Mexico and the Middle East, agriculture led to many social, political, and legal changes, including notions of property and distinctions in wealth, class, and power.

## GLOBALIZATION

The term **globalization** encompasses a series of processes that work transnationally to promote change in a world in which nations and people are increasingly interlinked and mutually dependent. Promoting globalization are economic and political forces, along with modern systems of transportation and digital communication. The forces of globalization include international commerce and finance, travel and tourism, transnational migration, and the media—including the Internet and other high-tech information flows (see Appadurai, 2001; Friedman and Friedman 2008; Haugerud, Stone, and Little 2011; Kjaerulff 2010; Scholte 2000). New economic unions (which have met considerable resistance in their member nations) have been created through the

World Trade Organization (WTO), the International Monetary Fund (IMF), and the European Union (EU).

The media, including the Internet and satellite and digital transmissions, play a key role in globalization. Long-distance communication is faster and easier than ever, and now it covers most of the globe. I can now e-mail, call, or Facebook friends in Arembepe, Brazil, which lacked phones and even postal service when I first began to study the community. Information about Arembepe, including YouTube videos made by locals, is now available to anyone, including potential tourists, on hundreds of websites. Anything can be googled. The media help propel a transnational culture of consumption, as they spread information about products, services, rights, institutions, lifestyles, and the perceived costs and benefits of globalization. Emigrants transmit information and resources transnationally, as they maintain their ties with home (phoning, Skyping, Facebooking and -timing, tweeting, videoconferencing, texting, e-mailing, visiting, sending money). In a sense such people live multilocally—in different places and cultures at once. They learn to play various social roles and to change behavior and identity depending on the situation and context (see Cresswell 2006).

The effects of globalization are broad and not always welcome. Local people must deal increasingly with forces generated by larger systems—region, nation, and world. An army of outsiders and potential change agents now intrudes on people everywhere. Tourism has become the world's number one industry (see Holden 2005). Economic development agents and the media promote the idea that work should be for cash rather than mainly for subsistence. Indigenous peoples and traditional societies have devised various strategies to deal with threats to their autonomy, identity, and livelihood (Maybury-Lewis 2002). New forms of cultural expression and political mobilization, including the rights movements discussed previously, are emerging from the interplay of local, regional, national, and international cultural forces (see Ong and Collier 2005).

## Globalization: Its Meaning and Its Nature

Mark Smith and Michele Doyle (2002) distinguish between two meanings of globalization:

1. Globalization as fact: the spread and connectedness of production, communication, and technologies across the world. This is the principal meaning for this book.

2. Globalization as ideology and policy: efforts by the International Monetary Fund (IMF),

Globalization in its current form would not exist without the Internet. Shown here, Chinese youth in an Internet café in Beijing. Using cameras and ID card scanners, the Chinese government monitors activity in each of Beijing's more than 1,500 Internet cafés. Users must be 18 or older. Who monitors Internet use in your country?

the World Bank, and other international financial powers to create a global free market for goods and services. In this second sense, for its advocates, globalization is the way the world should go. For their opponents, it's the way the world should not go (Lewellen 2010).

The first meaning is more neutral. Globalization as systemic connectedness reflects the relentless and ongoing growth of the world system. In its current form, that system, which has existed for centuries, has some radical new aspects. Especially noteworthy are the speed of global communication, the scale (size and complexity) of global networks, and the volume of international transactions.

The fall of the Soviet Empire (in 1989–1990) allowed a truly global economy to emerge (Lewellen 2010). Consider three key features of this new economy: (1) It is based on knowledge and information; (2) its networks are transnational; and (3) its core activities, no matter where they take place, can proceed as a unit in real time (Castells 2001).

The Internet and cell phones have made possible the very rapid global transmission of money, resources, and information. Tasks that are spatially dispersed can now be coordinated in real time. Transactions that once involved face-to-face contact are now processed across vast distances. For example, when you order something from the Internet, the only human being you might speak to is the delivery driver (Smith and Doyle 2002). The computers that process your order from Amazon can be on different continents, and the products you order can come from a warehouse anywhere. The average

Advertising Coca-Cola, a powerful global brand, in Xi'an, China. Savvy branders try to "get them young."

nation-state (see Lugo 1997). Examples of such "multiplaced" people include business and intellectual leaders, development workers, and members of multinational corporations, as well as migratory domestic, agricultural, and construction workers (see Lewellen 2010).

Multinational corporations move their operations to places where labor and materials are cheap. This globalization of labor creates unemployment "back home" as industries relocate and outsource abroad. Multinationals also seek out new markets. They strive to create new needs among specific target groups, especially young people, who increasingly construct their identities around consumption, especially of brand-name products. Successful multinationals, including Nike, Apple, Coca-Cola, and Hugo Boss, invest huge sums in promoting their brands. The goal is to make a particular brand an integral part of the way people see themselves. Savvy branders try to "get them young" (Klein 2000; Smith and Doyle 2002).

Multinational corporations ally themselves with, and influence, politicians and government officials, especially those who are most concerned with world trade. Financial globalization means that nations have less control over their own economies. Such institutions as the World Bank, the International Monetary Fund, the European Union, and the European Central Bank routinely constrain and dictate the national economic policies of countries like Greece and Spain.

food product now travels 1,300 miles and changes hands a dozen times before it reaches an American consumer (Lewellen 2010).

In such a world, Michael Burawoy suggests that anthropologists should shift "from studying 'sites' to studying 'fields,' that is, the relations between sites" (Burawoy 2000, p. xii). People increasingly live their lives across borders, maintaining social, financial, cultural, and political connections with more than one

As capitalism has spread globally, the gap between rich and poor has widened both within and between nations. David Landes (1999) calculated the difference in per capita income between the world's richest and poorest nations (Switzerland and Mozambique at that time) as 400 to 1, versus around 5 to 1 when the Industrial Revolution began about 250 years ago. The key role of knowledge in today's global economy has accelerated this gap, because knowledge tends to be concentrated in industrial nations and certain regions within them. Knowledge has commercial value, as new ideas are converted into the products and services that consumers want (Leadbeater 1999).

for REVIEW

## summary

1. Culture, which is distinctive to humanity, refers to customary behavior and beliefs that are passed on through enculturation. Culture rests on the human capacity for cultural learning. Culture encompasses rules for conduct internalized in human beings, which lead them to think and act in characteristic ways.

2. Although other animals learn, only humans have cultural learning, dependent on symbols. Humans

think symbolically—arbitrarily bestowing meaning on things and events. By convention, a symbol stands for something with which it has no necessary or natural relation. Symbols have special meaning for people who share memories, values, and beliefs because of common enculturation. People absorb cultural lessons consciously and unconsciously.

3. Cultural traditions mold biologically based desires and needs in particular directions. Everyone is cultured, not just people with elite educations. Cultures may be integrated and patterned through economic and social forces, key symbols, and core values. Cultural rules don't rigidly dictate our behavior. There is room for creativity, flexibility, diversity, and disagreement within societies. Cultural means of adaptation have been crucial in human evolution. Aspects of culture also can be maladaptive.

4. The human capacity for culture has an evolutionary basis that extends back at least 2.6 million years—to early toolmakers whose products survive in the archaeological record (and most probably even farther back—based on observation of tool use and manufacture by apes). Humans share with monkeys and apes such traits as manual dexterity (especially opposable thumbs), depth and color vision, learning ability based on a large brain, substantial parental investment in a limited number of offspring, and tendencies toward sociality and cooperation.

5. Many hominin traits are foreshadowed in other primates, particularly in the African apes, which, like us, belong to the hominid family. The ability to learn, basic to culture, is an adaptive advantage available to monkeys and apes. Chimpanzees make tools for several purposes. They also hunt and share meat. Sharing and cooperation are more developed among humans than among the apes, and only humans have systems of kinship and marriage that permit us to maintain lifelong ties with relatives in different local groups.

6. Using a comparative perspective, anthropology examines biological, psychological, social, and cultural universals and generalities. There also are unique and distinctive aspects of the human condition (cultural particularities). North American cultural traditions are no more natural than any others. Levels of culture can be larger or smaller than a nation. Cultural traits may be shared across national boundaries. Nations also include cultural differences associated with ethnicity, region, and social class.

7. Ethnocentrism describes judging other cultures by using one's own cultural standards. Cultural relativism, which anthropologists may use as a methodological position rather than a moral stance, is the idea of avoiding the use of outside standards to judge behavior in a given society. Human rights are those based on justice and morality beyond and superior to particular countries, cultures, and religions. Cultural rights are vested in religious and ethnic minorities and indigenous societies, and IPR, or intellectual property rights, apply to an indigenous group's collective knowledge and its applications.

8. Diffusion, migration, and colonialism have carried cultural traits and patterns to different world areas. Mechanisms of cultural change include diffusion, acculturation, and independent invention.

9. Globalization describes a series of processes that promote change in a world in which nations and people are interlinked and mutually dependent. There is a distinction between globalization as fact (the primary meaning of globalization in this book) and globalization as contested ideology and policy (international efforts to create a global free market for goods and services).

## key terms

acculturation 34

core values 25

cultural relativism 31

cultural rights 31

diffusion 34

enculturation 22

ethnocentrism 30

generality 27

globalization 34

hominid 25

hominins 25

human rights 31

independent invention 34

international culture 29

IPR 31

national culture 29

particularity 27

subcultures 29

symbol 22

universal 27

## critical thinking

1. This chapter includes various authors' definitions of culture (e.g., those of Tylor, Geertz, and Kottak). How are these definitions similar? How are they different? How has reading this chapter altered your own understanding of what culture is?

2. Our culture—and cultural changes—affects how we perceive nature, human nature, and "the natural." This theme continues to fascinate science fiction writers. Recall a recent science fiction book, movie, or TV program

that creatively explores the boundaries between nature and culture. How does the story develop the tension between nature and culture to craft a plot?

3. In American culture today, the term *diversity* is used in many contexts, usually referring to some positive attribute of our human experience, something to appreciate, to maintain, and even to increase. In what contexts have you heard the term used? To what precisely does the term refer?

4. What are some issues about which you find it hard to be culturally relativistic? If you were an anthropologist with the task of investigating these issues in real life, can you think of a series of steps that you would take to design a project that would, to the best of your ability, practice methodological cultural relativism? (You may want to review the use of the scientific method in an anthropological project presented in Chapter 1.)

5. What are the mechanisms of cultural change described in this chapter? Can you come up with additional examples of each mechanism? Also, recall the relationship between culture and the individual. Can individuals be agents of cultural change?

## CHAPTER 3

# Applying Anthropology

▶ Can change be bad and, if so, how?

▶ How can anthropology be applied to medicine, education, and business?

▶ How does the study of anthropology fit into a career path?

Shown here is Dr. Morgan Gerard, VP and Chief Resident Anthropologist at Idea Couture, a global firm based in Toronto, Canada. In a project for Kraft Foods, Gerard guided research designed to suggest future consumption patterns (see http://www.ideacouture.com/leadership-team/morgan-gerard).

# understanding OURSELVES

Can change be bad? The idea that innovation is desirable is almost axiomatic and unquestioned in American culture—especially in advertising. "New and improved" is a slogan we hear all the time—a lot more often than "old reliable." Which do you think is best—change or the status quo?

That "new" isn't always "improved" is a painful lesson learned by the Coca-Cola Company (TCCC) in 1985 when it changed the formula of its premier soft drink and introduced "New Coke." After a national brouhaha, with hordes of customers protesting, TCCC brought back old, familiar, reliable Coke under the name "Coca-Cola Classic," which thrives today. New Coke, now history, offers a classic case of how not to treat consumers. TCCC tried a *top-down change* (a change initiated at the top of a hierarchy rather than inspired by the people most affected by the change). Customers didn't ask TCCC to change its product; executives made that decision.

Business executives, like public policy makers, run organizations that provide goods and services to people. The field of market research, which employs a good number of anthropologists, is based on the need to appreciate what actual and potential customers do, think, and want. Smart planners study and listen to people to try to determine *locally based demand*. In general, what's working well (assuming it's not discriminatory or illegal) should be maintained, encouraged, tweaked, and strengthened. If something's wrong, how can it best be fixed? What changes do the people—and which people—want? How can conflicting wishes and needs be accommodated? Applied anthropologists help answer these questions, which are crucial in understanding whether change is needed, and how it will work.

Innovation succeeds best when it is culturally appropriate. This axiom of applied anthropology could guide the international spread of programs aimed at social and economic change as well as of businesses. Each time an organization expands to a new nation, it must devise a culturally appropriate strategy for fitting into the new setting. In their international expansion, companies as diverse as McDonald's, Starbucks, and Ford have learned that more money can be made by fitting in with, rather than trying to Americanize, local habits.

Anthropology has two dimensions: academic and applied. **Applied anthropology** is the use of anthropological data, perspectives, theory, and methods to identify, assess, and solve contemporary problems (see Ervin 2005; Pelto 2013; Wasson, Butler, and Copeland-Carson 2012). Applied anthropologists help make anthropology relevant and useful to the world beyond anthropology (see Beck and Maida 2013). Medical anthropologists, for example, have worked as cultural interpreters in public health programs, helping such programs fit into local culture. Development anthropologists work for or with international development agencies, such as the World Bank and the U.S. Agency for International Development (USAID). The findings of garbology, the archaeological study of waste, are relevant to the Environmental Protection Agency, the paper industry, and packaging and trade associations. Archaeology also is applied in cultural resource management and historic preservation. Biological anthropologists apply their expertise in programs aimed at public health, nutrition, genetic counseling, aging, substance abuse, and mental health. Forensic anthropologists work with the police, medical examiners, the courts, and

| ANTHROPOLOGY'S SUBFIELDS (ACADEMIC ANTHROPOLOGY) | EXAMPLES OF APPLICATION (APPLIED ANTHROPOLOGY) |
|---|---|
| Cultural anthropology | Development anthropology |
| Archaeological anthropology | Cultural resource management (CRM) |
| Biological, or physical, anthropology | Forensic anthropology |
| Linguistic anthropology | Study of linguistic diversity in classrooms |

Like other forensic anthropologists, Dr. Kathy Reichs (shown here) and her alter ego, Temperance Brennan (played on the TV show *Bones* by Emily Deschanel), work with the police, medical examiners, the courts, and international organizations to identify victims of crimes, accidents, wars, terrorism, and genocide.

international organizations to identify victims of crimes, accidents, wars, and terrorism. Linguistic anthropologists have studied physician–patient speech interactions and have shown how dialect differences influence classroom learning. Most applied anthropologists seek humane and effective ways of helping local people. See Recap 3.1 for examples of applied anthropology in the four subdisciplines.

The ethnographic method is a particularly valuable tool in applying anthropology. Remember that ethnographers study societies firsthand, living with, observing, and learning from ordinary people. Non-anthropologists working in social-change programs often are content to converse with officials, read reports, and copy statistics. However, the applied anthropologist's likely early request is some variant of "take me to the local people." Anthropologists know that people must play an active role in the changes that affect them and that "the people" have information that "the experts" lack.

Anthropological theory, the body of findings and generalizations of the four subfields, also guides applied anthropology. Just as theory aids practice, application fuels theory (see Rylko-Bauer, Singer, and Van Willigen 2006). As we compare social-change programs, our understanding of cause and effect increases. We add new generalizations about culture change to those discovered in traditional and ancient cultures.

## THE ROLE OF THE APPLIED ANTHROPOLOGIST

### Early Applications

Application was a central concern of early anthropology in Great Britain (in the context of colonialism) and the United States (in the context of Native American policy). Before turning to the new, we should consider some deficiencies and dangers of the old. For the British empire, specifically its African colonies, Bronislaw Malinowski (1929) proposed that "practical anthropology" (his term for colonial applied anthropology) should focus on Westernization, the diffusion of European culture into tribal societies. Malinowski questioned neither the legitimacy of colonialism nor the anthropologist's role in making it work. He saw nothing wrong with aiding colonial regimes by studying land tenure and land use, to recommend how much of their land local people should be allowed to keep and how much Europeans should be permitted to take. Malinowski's views exemplify a historical association between early anthropology, particularly in Europe (especially England, France, and Portugal), and colonialism (see also Duffield and Hewitt 2009; Lange 2009; Maquet 1964; Rylko-Bauer et al. 2006).

During World War II, American anthropologists studied Japanese and German "culture at a distance" in an attempt to predict the behavior of the enemies of the United States. Margaret Mead (1977) estimated that during the 1940s, 95 percent of U.S. anthropologists were engaged in the war effort. After that war, applied anthropologists worked on Pacific islands to promote local-level cooperation

**applied anthropology**
Using anthropology to solve contemporary problems.

with American policies in various trust territories. The American Anthropological Association (AAA) has raised strong ethical objections to applying anthropology in war zones and for military intelligence. Such concerns were voiced during the Vietnam War. More recently they have emerged in criticisms of anthropologists' gathering sociocultural information for the military in Iraq and Afghanistan. Anthropological research should not be applied to the potential detriment of the people anthropologists study.

## Academic and Applied Anthropology

After World War II, the baby boom, which began in 1946 and peaked in 1957, fueled a tremendous expansion of the American educational system. New junior, community, and four-year colleges opened, and anthropology became a standard part of the college curriculum. During the 1950s and 1960s, most American anthropologists were college professors, although some still worked in agencies and museums.

Most anthropologists still worked in colleges and museums during the 1970s and 1980s. However, an increasing number of anthropologists were employed by international organizations, governments, businesses, hospitals, and schools. Today, applied anthropologists work in extremely varied contexts, including large development organizations, communities and cultural groups, public institutions, government agencies, NGOs and nonprofit organizations, international policy bodies, and private entities, such as unions, social movements, and increasingly corporations (Rylko-Bauer et al. 2006). The AAA estimates that well over half of anthropology PhDs today seek nonacademic employment. This shift toward application has benefited the profession. It has forced anthropologists to consider the wider social value and implications of their research.

## Applied Anthropology Today

Most contemporary applied anthropologists see their work as radically removed from the colonial enterprise. Applied anthropology today usually is seen as a helping profession, devoted to assisting local people. According to Barbara Rylko-Bauer, Merrill Singer, and John van Willigen (2006), modern applied anthropology uses theories, concepts, and methods from anthropology to confront human problems that often contribute to profound social suffering.

However, applied anthropologists also have clients who are neither poor nor powerless. An applied anthropologist working as a market researcher may be concerned with discovering how to increase sales of a particular product. Such commercial goals can pose ethical dilemmas, as can work in cultural resource management (CRM). The CRM anthropologist helps decide how to preserve significant remains when sites are threatened by development or public works. A CRM firm typically is hired by someone seeking to build a road or a factory. That

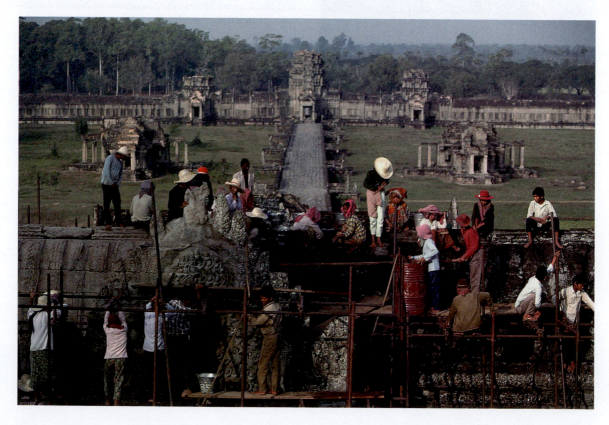

Supervised by archaeologists from India, with funding from the United Nations, these workers are cleaning and restoring the front facade of Cambodia's historic Angkor Wat temple. To decide what needs saving, and to preserve significant information about the past even when sites cannot be saved, is the work of cultural resource management (CRM).

client may have a strong interest in an outcome in which no sites are found that need protecting. Even if they don't work for colonial powers or the military, applied anthropologists still face ethical questions: To whom does the researcher owe loyalty? What problems are involved in holding firm to the truth? What happens when applied anthropologists don't make the policies they have to implement? How does one criticize programs in which one has participated? Anthropology's professional organizations have addressed such questions by establishing codes of ethics and ethics committees. As Karen Tice (1997) has noted, attention to ethical issues has become paramount in the teaching of applied anthropology.

Anthropologists are experts on human problems and social change who study, understand, and respect diverse cultural values. Given this background, anthropologists are highly qualified to suggest, plan, and implement policies affecting people. Proper roles for applied anthropologists include (1) identifying needs for change that local people perceive, (2) collaborating with those people to design culturally appropriate and socially sensitive change, and (3) working to protect local people from harmful policies and projects that may threaten them.

For decades applied anthropologists have collaborated directly with communities to achieve community-directed change (Rylko-Bauer et al. 2006). Applied anthropologists not only work collaboratively with local people but may even be hired by such communities in order to advocate on their behalf. One example is Barbara Rose Johnston's (2005) research commissioned by communities that were adversely affected by the construction of the Chixoy Dam in Guatemala. Johnston's reports document the dam's long-term impact on these communities. She also offered recommendations and a plan for reparations.

# DEVELOPMENT ANTHROPOLOGY

**Development anthropology** is the branch of applied anthropology that focuses on social issues in, and the cultural dimension of, economic development. Development anthropologists don't just carry out development policies planned by others; they also plan and guide policy. (For more detailed discussions of issues in development anthropology, see Crewe and Axelby 2013; Edelman and Haugerud 2005; Mosse 2011; Nolan 2002.)

Still, ethical dilemmas often confront development anthropologists (Escobar 1991, 1995; Venkatesan and Yarrow 2012). Foreign aid, including funds for economic development, usually doesn't go where need and suffering are greatest. Rather, such funds are spent on political, economic, and strategic priorities as international donors, political leaders, and powerful interest groups perceive them. Planners' interests don't always coincide with the best interests of the

local people. Although the stated aim of most development projects is to enhance the quality of life, living standards often decline in the affected area.

## Equity

A commonly stated goal of recent development policy is to promote equity. **Increased equity** means reduced poverty and a more even distribution of wealth. However, if projects are to increase equity, they must have the support of reform-minded governments. Wealthy and powerful people typically resist projects that threaten their vested interests.

Some development projects actually widen wealth disparities; that is, they have a negative equity impact. An initial uneven distribution of resources often becomes the basis for even greater socioeconomic inequality after the project. In Bahia, Brazil (Kottak 2006), for example, sailboat owners (but not nonowners) got loans to buy motors for their boats. To repay the loans, the owners increased the percentage of the catch they took from the men who fished in their boats. Over the years, they used their rising profits to buy larger and more expensive boats. The result was stratification—the creation of a group of wealthy people within a formerly more egalitarian community. These events hampered individual initiative and interfered with further development of the fishing industry. New boats became so expensive that ambitious young men, who once would have sought careers in fishing, no longer could afford to buy a boat of their own. They sought wage labor on land instead. To avoid such results, credit-granting agencies must seek out and invest in enterprising young fishers, rather than giving loans only to owners and established businesspeople.

**increased equity**
Reduction in absolute poverty, with a more even distribution of wealth.

**development anthropology**
Field that examines the sociocultural dimensions of economic development.

A mix of boats harbored in Pucasana, a fishing village in Peru. A boat owner gets a loan to buy a motor. To repay it, he increases the share of the catch he takes from his crew. Later, he uses his rising profits to buy a more expensive boat and takes even more from his crew. Can a more equitable solution be found?

## Afghanistan: What the Anthropologists Say

Anthropologists have a lot to say about the history and culture of, and even recent events in, Afghanistan. This anthropological knowledge has important applications. One is that successful social outcomes are created with the resources at hand, not from on high or far away. Another is the suggestion that innovation should be tried first in urban areas, where it is most likely to be welcome; after that it can spread to the countryside once prejudices against change have waned. Other lessons from the anthropological studies reviewed here include the value of understanding local culture and politics and the dangers of imposing foreign models, and of overreliance on the state and central authority.

Ten years after the Taliban's leaders fled their country in apparent defeat, the U.S. war in Afghanistan has become what one observer calls "a perpetually escalating stalemate." As in Iraq, the United States military has responded . . . with counterinsurgency: eliminate troublemakers in the dark of night, with the most lethal arts, and befriend tribal elders by day, with cultural sensitivity and expertise. The Army has gone so far as to embed credentialed social scientists with front-line troops in "Human Terrain Teams" that engage in "rapid ethnographic assessment," conducting in-

terviews and administering surveys, learning about land disputes, social networks and how to "operationalize" the Pashtun tribal code.

The military, in short, demands local knowledge. . . . Though the chief purveyors of such insight, academic ethnographers, have balked at working with the military. . . they have not ignored the country. Noah Coburn's *Bazaar Politics* is the first extended study of an Afghan community to appear since the Taliban fell. It follows an ambitious history of Afghanistan by the Boston University anthropologist Thomas Barfield. . . .

Anthropologists who studied Afghanistan before the Soviet invasion of 1979 described a complex country at the crossroads of Persian, Indian and Central Asian civilizations where nomads, farmers and traders of disparate cultures jostled against one another. . . . While anthropologists like Fredrik Barth and Charles Lindholm stressed the chronic instability and feuding among Pashtun mountain clans, they also noted the strong value placed on equality among all male members of a tribe; indeed, the Pakistani scholar Akbar Ahmed suggested that the Pashtuns opposed the British Empire on certain occasions because it attempted to introduce unwanted ranks and titles.

In wartime Afghanistan of the 1980s and '90s, anthropologists were scarce. But with the Taliban's fall, a few returned. . . . Arriving in 2006

as a Boston University graduate student, Coburn conducted his anthropological fieldwork in Istalif, a predominantly Tajik village 20 miles north of Kabul that was hostile to the Taliban and relatively safe for foreigners. . . . Istalif was peaceful and stable despite having been razed to the ground by the Taliban in the late 1990s. . . . The continuing stability, in Coburn's view, owed little to the Afghan state or to the presence of international forces; it resulted from a wary equilibrium among rivals who feared disturbing the status quo. . . .

No one was truly in charge. Local power brokers might possess wealth, honor, a reputation for piety, abundant weaponry or powerful allies, but they lacked the means or the will to convert those gifts into decisive authority. The maliks, or elders, made a big show of representing their communities' interests in meetings with outsiders and serving their followers generous meals. . . . But for all their public visibility, the maliks were only as strong as their communities allowed them to be; they were . . . anxious agents of the professions or neighborhoods or clans they served. . . . The mullahs, for their part, had little ability to intervene outside the mosque. . . .

As for the state's representatives, their authority was what Coburn calls a "useful fiction." The district governor wielded his connections to Kabul as best he could, but did not possess

## STRATEGIES FOR INNOVATION

Development anthropologists should work collaboratively with local people to assess, and help them realize, their own wishes and needs for change. Too many true local needs cry out for a solution to waste money funding projects in area A that are inappropriate there but needed in area B, or that are unnecessary anywhere. Development anthropology can help sort out the needs of the As and Bs and fit projects accordingly. Projects that put people first by consulting with them and responding to their expressed needs must be identified (Cernea 1991).

To maximize social and economic benefits, projects must (1) be culturally compatible, (2) respond to locally perceived needs, (3) involve men and women in planning and carrying out the changes that affect them, (4) harness traditional organizations, and (5) be flexible (see Kottak 1990b, 1991).

Consider a recent example of a development initiative that failed because it ignored local culture. Working in Afghanistan after the fall of the Taliban, ethnographer Noah Coburn (2011) studied Istalif, a village of potters. During his fieldwork there Coburn discovered that an NGO had spent $20,000 on an electric kiln that could have greatly enhanced the productivity of local potters. The only problem was great influence, in part because . . . government aid was mainly distributed by locally elected committees. . . .

[Coburn] watched in disbelief as [local leaders] rejected a proposal to pave the main road connecting Istalif with the nearby highway leading to Kabul. The new road would have benefited the entire village . . . ; but one malik objected that its construction would disproportionately assist another malik's sector of the town, and the proposal was quietly tabled. In other words, to disturb the existing distribution of power was to risk reigniting too many local conflicts. . . . The quiet the town has enjoyed since the end of the Taliban regime is . . . largely the result of tacit agreements among bitter rivals over what to forget and ignore. Whatever the fragility of such an arrangement, Coburn implies that it is preferable to the modernizing plans of even the most thoughtful state-builders. The attempt to create impersonal, merit-oriented bureaucracies and to spread liberal beliefs about gender, religion or criminal punishment is as likely to exacerbate conflict as to resolve it. Stability is created with the resources at hand, not from on high or far away. . . .

In his skepticism of centralizers, modernizers and humanitarians, Coburn echoes other anthropologically minded writers. Thomas Barfield's *Afghanistan: A Cultural and Political History* insists that Western powers made a serious error by installing Karzai in a presidency with quasi-monarchical powers. They "attempted to restore a

Afghan schoolgirls walk through Istalif, a predominantly Tajik village of artisans located about 20 miles north of Kabul and studied by ethnographer Noah Coburn.

system designed for autocrats in a land where autocracy was no longer politically sustainable." Similarly, Barfield suggests that asking rural Afghans to rethink their beliefs about religion or women's rights is sure to fail. . . . A better course of action, the record shows, was to pursue "policies of social change in urban areas where they were welcome, and then let them spread to the countryside only after prejudices against them had waned."

Coburn further asserts that "a decrease in the amount of money being spent in the country, and a drawdown of international troops, seem likely to reduce violence because these measures will remove a significant source of political tension." . . . Quite soon . . . those anthropologists who favor a diminished Western presence are likely to get their wish.

SOURCE: Alexander Star, "Afghanistan: What the Anthropologists Say." From *The New York Times* Book Reviews, November 20, 2011. © 2011 The New York Times. All rights reserved. Used by permission and protected by the Copyright Laws of the United States. The printing, copying, redistribution, or retransmission of this Content without express written permission is prohibited. www.nytimes.com

that the kiln was donated to a women's center that men could not enter. The misguided donors ignored the fact that Istalif's men did the work—pot-making and firing—that a kiln could facilitate. Women's role in pottery came later—in glazing and decorating (see this chapter's "Appreciating Anthropology" for more on Afghanistan).

## Overinnovation

Development projects are most likely to succeed when they avoid the fallacy of **overinnovation** (too much change). People usually are willing to change just enough to maintain, or slightly improve on,

what they already have. Motives for modifying behavior come from the traditional culture and the small concerns of ordinary life. Peasants' values are not such abstract ones as "learning a better way," "progressing," "increasing technical know-how," "improving efficiency," or "adopting modern techniques." Rather, their objectives are down-to-earth and specific. People want to guarantee the productivity of their crops, amass resources for a ceremony, get a child through school, or have enough cash to pay bills. The goals and values of subsistence producers differ from those of people who work for cash, just as they differ from those of development planners.

**overinnovation**
Trying to achieve too much change.

Development projects that fail usually are either economically or culturally incompatible (or both). For example, one South Asian project promoted the cultivation of onions and peppers, expecting this practice to fit into a preexisting labor-intensive system of rice growing. Cultivation of these cash crops wasn't traditional in the area. It conflicted with existing crop priorities and other interests of farmers. Also, the labor peaks for pepper and onion production coincided with those for rice, to which the farmers gave priority (see Kottak 1990*b*, 1991).

## Underdifferentiation

The fallacy of **underdifferentiation** is planners' tendency to view "the less-developed countries" (LDCs) as more alike than they are. Often development agencies have ignored huge cultural contrasts (e.g., between Brazil and Burundi) and adopted a uniform approach to deal with very different societies. Planners often try to impose incompatible property concepts and social units. Most often, the faulty social design assumes either (1) units of production that are privately owned by an individual or a couple and worked by a nuclear family or (2) cooperatives that are at least partially based on models from the former Eastern bloc and Socialist countries.

One example of using an inappropriate First World model (the individual and the nuclear family) was a West African project designed for an area where the extended family was the basic social unit. The project succeeded despite its faulty social design because the participants used their traditional extended family networks to attract additional settlers. Eventually, twice as many people as planned

benefited as extended family members flocked to the project area. Here, settlers modified the project design that had been imposed on them by following the principles of their traditional society.

The second dubious foreign social model that is common in development planning is the cooperative. In a comparative study of rural development projects, new cooperatives tended to succeed only when they harnessed preexisting local-level communal institutions. This is a corollary of a more general rule: Participants' groups are most effective when they are based on traditional social organization or on a socioeconomic similarity among members (Kottak 1990*b*, 1991).

An alternative to such foreign models is needed: greater use of indigenous social models in economic development. These are traditional social units, such as the clans, lineages, and other extended kin groups of Africa, Oceania, and many other nations, with their communally held estates and resources. The most humane and productive strategy for change is to base the social design for innovation on traditional social forms in each target area.

## Indigenous Models

Many governments are not genuinely, or realistically, committed to improving the lives of their citizens. Interference by major powers also has kept governments from enacting needed reforms. Occasionally, however, a government does act as an agent of and for its people. One historic example is Madagascar, whose people, the Malagasy, were organized into descent groups prior to indigenous state formation in the 18th century. The Merina, creators of the major precolonial state of Madagascar, wove descent groups into its structure, making members of important groups advisers to the king and thus giving them authority in government. The Merina state made provisions for the people it ruled. It collected taxes and organized labor for public works projects. In return, it redistributed resources to peasants in need. It also granted them some protection against war and slave raids and allowed them to cultivate their rice fields in peace. The government maintained the water works for rice cultivation. It opened to ambitious peasant boys the chance of becoming, through hard work and study, state bureaucrats.

Throughout the history of the Merina state—and continuing to some extent in postcolonial Madagascar—there have been strong relationships between the individual, the descent group, and the state. Local Malagasy communities, where residence is based on descent, are more cohesive and homogeneous than are communities in Latin America or North

In rural Bangladesh, NGOs (nongovernmental organizations) are working to "empower" local people and to improve their livelihoods and incomes. Shown here, an NGO-sponsored women's cooperative credit group meets to discuss the distribution of profits.

America. Madagascar gained political independence from France in 1960. Its new government had an economic development policy aimed at increasing the ability of the Malagasy to feed themselves. Government policy emphasized increased production of rice, a subsistence crop, rather than cash crops. Furthermore, local communities, with their traditional cooperative patterns and solidarity based on kinship and descent, were treated as partners in, not obstacles to, the development process.

In a sense, the descent group is preadapted to equitable national development. In Madagascar, descent groups pooled their resources to educate their most ambitious members. Once educated, these men and women gained economically secure positions in the nation. They then shared the advantages of their new positions with their kin. For example, they gave room and board to rural cousins attending school and helped them find jobs.

This Madagascar example suggests that when government officials are of "the people" (rather than the elites) and have strong personal ties to common folk, they are more likely to promote democratic economic development. In Latin America, by contrast, leaders and followers too often have been from different socioeconomic strata, with no connections based on kinship, descent, marriage, or common background. When elites rule, elites usually prosper. Recently, however, Latin America has elected some nonelite leaders. Brazil's lower class (indeed the entire nation) benefited socioeconomically when one of its own was elected president. Luiz Inácio da Silva, aka Lula, a former factory worker with only a fourth-grade education, served two terms (ending in 2011) as one of the Western Hemisphere's most popular leaders.

Realistic development policies promote change but not overinnovation. Many changes are possible if the aim is to preserve things while making them work better. Successful economic development projects respect, or at least don't attack, local cultural patterns. Effective development draws on indigenous cultural practices and social structures. As nations become more tied to the world capitalist economy, it is not inevitable that indigenous forms of social organization will break down into nuclear family organization, impersonality, and alienation. Descent groups, with their traditional communalism and solidarity, have important roles to play in economic development.

## ANTHROPOLOGY AND EDUCATION

Attention to culture also is fundamental to **anthropology and education,** a field whose research extends from classrooms into homes, neighborhoods, and communities (see Anderson-Levitt 2012; Levinson and Pollock 2011; Spindler and Hammond 2006). In classrooms, anthropologists have observed interactions among teachers, students, parents, and visitors. Jules Henry's classic account of the American elementary school classroom (1955) shows how students learn to conform to and compete with their peers. Anthropologists view children as total cultural creatures whose enculturation and attitudes toward education belong to a context that includes family and peers.

Sociolinguists and cultural anthropologists have worked side by side in education research. In one classic study of Puerto Rican seventh-graders in the urban Midwest (Hill-Burnett 1978), anthropologists uncovered some key misconceptions held by teachers. The teachers mistakenly had assumed that Puerto Rican parents valued education less than did non-Hispanics, but in-depth interviews revealed that the Puerto Rican parents valued it more. The anthropologists also identified certain practices that were preventing Hispanics from being adequately educated. For example, the teachers' union and the board of education had agreed to teach "English as a foreign language." However, they had provided no bilingual teachers to work with Spanish-speaking students. The school was assigning all students (including

**anthropology and education**
Study of students in the context of their family, peers, and enculturation.

A teacher displays flashcards to students in a Spanish language class. In educational anthropology, fieldwork occurs not only in schools and classrooms but also in communities. Educational anthropologists study the backgrounds, behavior, beliefs, and attitudes of teachers, students, parents, and families in their cultural context.

non-Hispanics) with low reading scores and behavior problems to the English-as-a-foreign-language classroom. This educational disaster brought together in the classroom a teacher who spoke no Spanish, children who barely spoke English, and a group of English-speaking students with reading and behavior problems. The Spanish speakers were falling behind not just in reading but in all subjects. They could at least have kept up in the other subjects if a Spanish speaker had been teaching them science, social studies, and math until they were ready for English-language instruction in those areas.

# URBAN ANTHROPOLOGY

For centuries, cities have been influenced by global forces. Today, media-transmitted images and information play an important role in attracting people to cities. People migrate partly for economic reasons, but also to be where the action is. Rural Brazilians routinely cite *movimento*, urban activity and excitement, as something to be valued. International migrants tend to settle in large cities, where a lot is going on and where they can feel at home in ethnic enclaves. For example, 71 percent of immigrants to Canada settle in Toronto, Vancouver, or Montreal. Nearly half of Toronto's citizens were born outside Canada.

The percentage of the world's population living in cities surpassed 50 percent for the first time in 2008 and is projected to rise to 70 percent by 2050 (Handwerk 2008). Only about 3 percent of people were city dwellers in 1800, compared with 13 percent in 1900, 40 percent in 1980, and over 50 percent today (see Handwerk 2008). The degree of urbanization (29.2 percent) in the less-developed countries (LDCs) is well below the world average (50.5 percent). By 2030, however, the percentage of city dwellers in the LDCs is projected to rise to 41 percent. The urbanization growth rate is actually much faster in the LDCs. In Africa and Asia alone, a million people a week migrate to cities (Handwerk 2008). The world had only 16 cities with more than a million people in 1900, versus over 400 such cities today.

Over one billion people live in urban slums, mostly without reliable water, sanitation, public services, and legal security (Handwerk 2008; Vidal 2003). If current trends continue, urban population increase and the concentration of people in slums will continue to be accompanied by rising rates of crime, along with water, air, and noise pollution (see Dürr and Jaffe 2010). These problems will be most severe in the LDCs.

As industrialization and urbanization spread globally, anthropologists increasingly study these processes and the social problems they create. **Urban anthropology,** which has theoretical (basic research) and applied dimensions, is the cross-cultural and ethnographic study of urbanization and life in cities (see Gmelch, Kemper, and Zenner 2010; Pardo and Prato 2012). The United States and Canada have become popular arenas for urban anthropological research on topics such as immigration, ethnicity, poverty, class, and urban violence (Vigil 2010).

## Urban versus Rural

In any nation, urban and rural represent different social systems. However, cultural diffusion, or borrowing, occurs as people, products, images, and messages move from one to the other. Migrants bring rural practices and beliefs to cities and take urban patterns back home (see this chapter's "Appreciating Anthropology"). The experiences and social forms of the rural area affect adaptation to city life. City folk also develop new institutions to meet specific urban needs.

An applied anthropology approach to urban planning starts by identifying key social groups in *specific* urban contexts—avoiding the fallacy of underdifferentiation. After identifying those groups, the anthropologist might elicit their wishes for change, convey those needs to funding agencies, and work with agencies and local people to realize those goals. In Africa relevant groups might include ethnic associations, occupational groups, social clubs, religious groups, and burial societies. Through membership in such groups, urban Africans maintain wide networks of personal contacts and support. The groups provide cash support and urban lodging for their rural relatives. Members may call one another "brother" and "sister." As in an extended family, richer members help their poorer relatives. A member's improper behavior, however, can lead to expulsion—an unhappy fate for a migrant in a large, ethnically heterogeneous city.

One role for the urban applied anthropologist is to help people deal with urban institutions, such as legal and social services, with which recent migrants may be unfamiliar. In certain North American cities, as in Africa, ethnic associations are relevant urban groups. One example comes from Los Angeles, which has the largest Samoan immigrant community in the United States (over 50,000 people). Samoans in Los Angeles draw on their traditional system of matai (matai means "chief"; the matai system now refers to respect for elders) to deal with modern urban problems. One example is a white police officer once shot and killed two unarmed Samoan brothers. When a judge dismissed charges against the officer, local leaders used the matai system to calm angry youths (who have formed gangs, like other ethnic groups in the Los Angeles area). Clan leaders and elders organized a well-attended community meeting, in which they urged young members to be patient. The Samoans then used the American judicial system. They brought a civil case against the officer in question and pressed the U.S. Justice Department to initiate a civil rights case in the matter (Mydans 1992*b*). Not all conflicts involving gangs and law enforcement end so peacefully.

James Vigil (2003, 2010) examines gang violence in the context of large-scale immigrant adaptation to American cities. He notes that most gangs prior to the

1970s were located in white ethnic enclaves in eastern and midwestern cities. Back then, gang incidents typically were brawls involving fists, sticks, and knives. Today, gangs more often are composed of non-white ethnic groups, and handguns have replaced less lethal weapons. Gangs still consist mostly of male adolescents who have grown up together, usually in a low-income neighborhood, where it's estimated that about 10 percent of young men join gangs. Female gang members are much rarer. With gangs organized hierarchically by age, older members push younger ones (usually 14- to 18-year-olds) to carry out violent acts against rivals (Singer 2008; Vigil 2003, 2010). How might an applied anthropologist approach the problem of urban violence? Which groups would have to be involved in the study (see Vigil 2010)?

## MEDICAL ANTHROPOLOGY

**Medical anthropology** is the comparative, biocultural study of disease, health problems, and health care systems (see Wiley and Allen 2013). Both academic and applied, medical anthropology includes anthropologists from all four subfields (see Brown and Barrett 2010; Joralemon 2010; Singer and Baer 2012; Trevathan, Smith, and McKenna 2008). Medical anthropology emerged out of applied work done in public health and international development (Foster and Anderson 1978). Current medical anthropology continues to have clear policy applications, partly because it so often deals with pressing human problems that cry out for solutions (Rylko-Bauer et al. 2006). Medical anthropologists examine such questions as which diseases and health conditions affect particular populations (and why) and how illness is socially constructed, diagnosed, managed, and treated in various societies (Lupton 2012; Singer and Erickson 2011).

**Disease** refers to a scientifically identified health threat caused genetically or by a bacterium, virus, fungus, parasite, or other pathogen. **Illness** is a condition of poor health perceived or felt by an individual within a particular culture. Various cultures and ethnic groups recognize different illnesses, symptoms, and causes and have developed different health care systems and treatment strategies.

The incidence and severity of disease vary as well (see Baer, Singer, and Susser 2013; Barnes 2005). Group differences are evident in the United States. Consider, for example, health status indicators in relation to U.S. census categories: white, black, Hispanic, American Indian or Alaska Native, and Asian or Pacific Islander. Black Americans' rates for six indicators (total mortality, heart disease, lung cancer, breast cancer, stroke, and homicide) range from 2.5 to 10 times greater than those of the other groups (Keppel, Pearch, and Wagener 2002). Other ethnic groups have higher rates for suicide (white Americans) and motor vehicle accidents (American Indians and Alaskan Natives). Overall, Asians have the longest lifespans (see Dressler, Oths, and Gravlee, 2005).

Anthropologists have noted the significance of urban youth groups, including gangs, which now have transnational scope. This 29-year-old man, lodged in the Denver County jail, was one of several jailed gang members who discussed their lives on a 2010 History Channel special. Members look to gangs for social support and physical protection. How might this man's tattoos have social significance?

Hurtado and her colleagues (2005) note very high rates of early mortality among South America's indigenous populations, whose life expectancy at birth is at least 20 years shorter than that of other South Americans (Hurtado et al. 2005). How can applied anthropologists help improve the health of indigenous peoples? Hurtado and colleagues (2005) suggest three steps: (1) Identify their most pressing health problems; (2) gather information on possible solutions; and (3) implement solutions in partnership with the agencies that are in charge of public health programs for indigenous populations.

In many areas, the world system and colonialism worsened the health of indigenous peoples by spreading diseases, warfare, servitude, and other stressors. Traditionally and in ancient times, hunter-gatherers, because of their small numbers, mobility, and relative isolation from other groups, lacked most of the epidemic infectious diseases that affect agrarian and urban societies (Cohen and Armelagos 1984; Inhorn and Brown 1990). Epidemic diseases such as cholera, typhoid, and bubonic plague thrive in dense populations, and thus among farmers and city dwellers. The spread of malaria has been linked to population growth and deforestation associated with food production.

Certain diseases, and physical conditions such as obesity, have spread with economic development and globalization (Inhorn and Wentzell 2012; Ulijaszek and Lofink 2006). Schistosomiasis, or bilharzia (liver flukes), is probably the fastest-spreading and most dangerous parasitic infection now known. It is propagated by snails that live in ponds, lakes, and waterways, usually ones created by irrigation projects. The applied anthropology approach to reducing such diseases is to see if local people perceive a connection between the vector (e.g., snails in

**medical anthropology**
The comparative, biocultural study of disease, health problems, and health care systems.

**disease**
A scientifically identified health threat caused by a known pathogen.

**illness**
A condition of poor health perceived or felt by an individual.

## The Deadliest Global Pandemic of Our Time

A pandemic is an infectious disease that crosses national boundaries and affects millions. In the case of HIV/AIDS, the pandemic has been global. HIV is the virus that causes the disease known as AIDS, which has killed about 25 million people since its discovery in 1981. Globally the number of people living with HIV has risen from about 8 million in 1990 to over 33 million today. In many countries, however, the number of new HIV infections and AIDS cases has declined because millions of people now take antiretroviral drugs. (HIV is classified as a retrovirus—a virus whose genes are encoded in RNA instead of DNA.) As Bono of U2 fame, a prominent campaigner against AIDS, notes, it's amazing what a difference "two little pills a day" can make (see Bono 2011).

Although HIV/AIDS is a global threat, some world areas are more infected than others are. About 68 percent of all HIV infections are in Africa, especially southern Africa. The following indicate the percentages of adults (ages 15–49) living with HIV in the nine contiguous southern Africa countries of Swaziland (26.1 percent), Botswana (23.9), Lesotho (23.2), South Africa (18.1), Namibia (15.3), Zimbabwe (15.3), Zambia (15.2), Mozambique (12.5), and Malawi (11.9). These are the highest rates in the world; in no other country does the figure rise above 10 percent. In these countries, HIV has spread through prostitution (mainly involving female sex workers and their clients). The infection rate is especially high among truckers, miners, and young rural men seeking wage work in cities and labor camps. Returning to their villages, these men infect their wives and the babies they bear.

Overall in Africa the adult infection rate is 5 percent. This is significantly higher than the rates of 1 percent in the Caribbean; 0.8 percent in Eastern Europe; 0.5 percent in North, Central, and South America; and 0.2 percent in Western and Central Europe, North Africa, and the Middle East. The rate in East Asia is minuscule—less than 0.1 percent. The HIV infection rates are below 1 percent in these populous countries: United States, 0.6 percent; Brazil, 0.4 percent; India, 0.3 percent; and China, 0.1 percent (Avert.org 2010).

American foreign aid has been instrumental in slowing the AIDS pandemic. Progress against HIV/AIDS is considered a signature accomplishment of the George W. Bush administration (2001–2009). In 2003, President Bush launched a five-year program aimed at fighting HIV/AIDS (and tuberculosis) in 15 high-risk countries. Congress extended the program in 2008, and it has continued under President Obama. American funding for HIV/AIDS increased from $2.3 billion in 2003 to $6 billion in 2008, and to $6.8 billion in 2011 (Ezekiel 2011). Although the United States was spending only 12 percent more on fighting HIV in 2011 than in 2008, twice as many people were benefiting because of reduced drug costs and streamlined program management (Ezekiel 2011).

Cultural practices play a clear role in HIV transmission. Sexual abstinence and condom use slow the spread of HIV. Infection rates are lower when men are circumcised (as is customary among Muslims) and there is little prostitution. It's estimated that male circumcision cuts HIV transmission by 60 percent. Since 2007, a million men worldwide have been circumcised; three-fourths of those procedures were paid for by the U.S. government.

This tapestry by South African artist Jane Makhubele promotes condom use as a method of AIDS prevention.

the water) and the disease. If not, such information may be provided by enlisting active local groups, schools, and the media.

The highest global rates of HIV infection and AIDS-related deaths are in Africa, especially southern Africa (Mazzeo, Rödlach, and Brenton 2011). As it kills productive adults, AIDS leaves behind dependent children and seniors (Baro and Deubel 2006). Sexually transmitted diseases (STDs) are spread through prostitution as young men from rural areas seek wage work in cities, labor camps, and mines. When the men return home, they infect their wives (see Baer et al. 2013). Cultural factors affect the spread of HIV, which is less likely to be transmitted when men are circumcised. (For more on the AIDS pandemic, see this chapter's "Focus on Globalization.")

The kinds and incidence of disease vary among societies, and cultures perceive and treat illness differently (see Lupton 2012). Still, all societies have what George Foster and Barbara Anderson call "disease-theory systems" to identify, classify, and explain illness. Foster and Anderson (1978) identified three basic theories about the causes of illness: personalistic, naturalistic, and emotionalistic. Personalistic disease theories blame illness on agents, such as sorcerers, witches, ghosts, or ancestral spirits.

Naturalistic disease theories explain illness in impersonal terms. One example is Western medicine, or biomedicine, which aims to link illness to scientifically demonstrated agents that bear no personal malice toward their victims. Thus, Western medicine attributes illness to organisms (e.g., bacteria, viruses, fungi, or parasites), accidents, toxic materials, or genes. Other naturalistic systems blame poor health on unbalanced body fluids. Many Latin cultures classify food, drink, and environmental conditions as "hot" or "cold." People believe their health suffers when they eat or drink hot or cold substances together or under inappropriate conditions. For example, one shouldn't drink something cold after a hot bath or eat a pineapple (a "cold" fruit) when one is menstruating (a "hot" condition).

Emotionalistic disease theories assume that emotional experiences cause illness. For example, Latin Americans may develop *susto*, an illness brought on by anxiety, fright, or tragic news. Its symptoms (lethargy, vagueness, distraction) are similar to those of "soul loss," a diagnosis of similar symptoms made by people in Madagascar.

All societies have **health care systems** consisting of beliefs, customs, specialists, and techniques aimed at ensuring health and diagnosing and curing illness. A society's illness-causation theory is important for treatment. When illness has a personalistic cause, magicoreligious specialists may be effective curers. They draw on varied techniques (occult and practical), which constitute their special expertise. A shaman may cure soul loss by enticing the spirit back into the body. Shamans may ease difficult childbirths by asking spirits to travel up the birth canal to guide the baby out (Lévi-Strauss 1967). A shaman may cure a cough by counteracting a curse or removing a substance introduced by a sorcerer.

If there is a "world's oldest profession" besides hunter and gatherer, it is **curer,** often a shaman. The curer's role has some universal features (Foster and Anderson 1978). Thus, a curer emerges through a culturally defined process of selection (parental prodding, inheritance of the role, visions, dream instructions) and training (apprentice shamanship, medical school). Eventually, the curer is certified by older practitioners and acquires a professional image. Patients believe in the skills of the curer, whom they consult and compensate.

We should not lose sight, ethnocentrically, of the difference between **scientific medicine** and Western medicine per se. To be sure, there have been scientific advances in technology, genomics, molecular biology, pathology, surgery, diagnostics, and applications. However, many Western medical procedures have little justification in science, logic, or fact. Overprescription of drugs, unnecessary surgeries, and the impersonality and inequality of the physician–patient

Merina women plant paddy rice in the highlands south of Antsirabe, Madagascar. Schistosomiasis, of which all known varieties are found in Madagascar, is among the fastest-spreading and most dangerous parasitic infections now known. It is propagated by snails that live in ponds, lakes, and waterways (often ones created by irrigation systems, such as those associated with paddy rice cultivation).

relationship are among the questionable features of Western medical systems (see Briggs 2005). Also, overuse of antibiotics seems to be triggering an explosion of resistant microorganisms.

Still, biomedicine surpasses tribal treatment in many ways. Although medicines such as quinine, coca, opium, ephedrine, and rauwolfia were discovered in nonindustrial societies, thousands of effective drugs are available today to treat myriad diseases. Today's surgical procedures are much safer and more effective than those of traditional societies.

But industrialization and globalization have spawned their own health problems. Modern stressors include poor nutrition, dangerous machinery, impersonal work, isolation, poverty, homelessness, substance abuse, and noise, air, and water pollution (see McElroy and Townsend 2009). Health problems in industrial nations may be caused as much by economic, social, political, and cultural factors as by pathogens. Poverty contributes to many illnesses, including arthritis, heart conditions, back problems, and hearing and vision impairment.

In the United States and other developed countries, good health has become something of an ethical imperative (Foucault 1990). Individuals are expected to regulate their behavior and shape themselves in keeping with new medical knowledge. Those who do so acquire the status of sanitary citizens—people with modern understanding of the body, health, and illness. Such citizens practice hygiene and look to health care professionals when they are sick. People who act differently (e.g., smokers, overeaters, those who avoid doctors) are

**health care systems**
Beliefs, customs, and specialists concerned with preventing and curing illness.

**curer**
One who diagnoses and treats illness.

**scientific medicine**
A health care system based on scientific knowledge and procedures.

At a market in Yangshuo, China, a woman undergoes a moxibustion treatment, in which mugwort, a small, spongy herb, is burned to facilitate healing.

stigmatized as unsanitary and blamed for their own health problems (Briggs 2005; Foucault 1990).

Even getting an epidemic disease such as cholera may be interpreted today as a moral failure. It's assumed that people who act rationally can avoid "preventable" diseases. Individuals are expected to follow scientifically based imperatives (e.g., "boil water," "don't smoke"). People (e.g., gay men, smokers, veterans) can become objects of avoidance and discrimination simply by belonging to a group seen as having a greater risk of poor health (Briggs 2005).

Health interventions always have to fit into local cultures. When Western medicine is introduced, people usually preserve many of their old methods while also accepting new ones. Native curers may go on treating certain conditions (spirit possession), while physicians deal with others. The native curer may get as much credit as the physician for a cure.

More personal treatment strategies that emulate the non-Western curer–patient–community relationship might benefit Western systems. Western medicine tends to draw a rigid line between biomedical and psychological causation. Non-Western theories usually lack this sharp distinction, recognizing that

poor health has intertwined physical, emotional, and social causes (see also Brown and Barrett 2010; Helman 2007; Joralemon 2010; Strathern and Stewart 2010).

Medical anthropology also considers the impact of new scientific and medical techniques on ideas about life, death, and personhood (what it means to be a person). For decades, disagreements about personhood—such as about when life begins and ends—have been part of political and religious discussions of contraception, abortion, and assisted suicide. More recent additions to such discussions include stem cells, "harvested" embryos, assisted reproduction, genetic screening, cloning, and life-prolonging medical treatments.

Kaufman and Morgan (2005) emphasize the contrast between what they call low-tech and high-tech births and deaths. A desperately poor young mother dies of AIDS in Africa, while half a world away an American child of privilege is born as the result of a $50,000 in vitro fertilization procedure. Medical anthropologists increasingly are concerned with how the boundaries of life and death are being questioned and negotiated in the 21st century.

## ANTHROPOLOGY AND BUSINESS

As David Price (2000) has noted, activities encompassed under the label "applied anthropology" are extremely diverse, ranging from research for activist NGOs to producing ethnographies and time-allocation studies of workplaces commissioned by and for management. For decades anthropologists have used ethnography to understand corporate settings and business (Arensberg 1987; Jordan 2013). Ethnographic research in a factory, for example, may view workers, managers, and executives as different social categories participating in a common system. Each group has characteristic attitudes and behavior patterns. These are transmitted through *microenculturation*, the process by which people learn particular roles within a limited social system. The free-ranging nature of ethnography can take the anthropologist back and forth from worker to executive. Each employee is both an individual with a personal viewpoint and a cultural creature whose perspective is, to some extent, shared with other members of his or her group. Applied anthropologists have acted as "cultural brokers," translating managers' goals or workers' concerns to the other group (see Ferraro 2010).

Carol Taylor (1987) has stressed the value of an "anthropologist-in-residence" in a large, complex organization, such as a hospital or corporation. A free-ranging ethnographer can be a perceptive oddball when information and decisions typically move through a rigid hierarchy. If allowed to observe and converse freely with all types and levels of personnel, the anthropologist may acquire a unique perspective on organizational conditions and problems (see Caulkins and Jordan 2013; Cefkin 2009).

Business anthropologist Crysta Metcalf, right, and her team demonstrate a new (in 2008) technology at Motorola in Schaumburg, Illinois. The technology allows people in different locations to communicate while watching the same televised show or event.

# appreciating DIVERSITY

## Culturally Appropriate Marketing

Innovation succeeds best when it is culturally appropriate. This axiom of applied anthropology could guide the international spread not only of development projects but also of businesses, including fast food. Each time McDonald's or Burger King expands to a new nation, it must devise a culturally appropriate strategy for fitting into the new setting.

McDonald's has been very successful internationally. Over 60 percent of its current annual revenue comes from sales outside the United States. One place where McDonald's has expanded successfully is Brazil, where 90 million middle-class people, most living in densely packed cities, provide a concentrated market for a fast-food chain. Still, it took McDonald's some time to find the right marketing strategy for Brazil.

In 1980 when I visited Brazil after a seven-year absence, I first noticed, as a manifestation of Brazil's growing participation in the world economy, the appearance of two McDonald's restaurants in Rio de Janeiro. There wasn't much difference between Brazilian and North American McDonald's. The restaurants looked alike. The menus were more or less the same, as was the taste of the quarter-pounders. I picked up an artifact, a white paper bag with yellow lettering, exactly like the take-out bags then used in American McDonald's. An advertising device, it carried several messages about how Brazilians could bring McDonald's into their lives. However, it seemed to me that McDonald's Brazilian ad campaign was missing some important points about how fast food should be marketed in a culture that values large, leisurely lunches.

The bag proclaimed, "You're going to enjoy the [McDonald's] difference," and listed several "favorite places where you can enjoy McDonald's products." This list confirmed that the marketing people were trying to adapt to Brazilian middle-class culture, but they were making some mistakes. "When you go out in the car with the kids" transferred the uniquely developed North American cultural combination of highways, affordable cars, and suburban living to the very different context of urban Brazil. A similar suggestion was "traveling to the country place." Even Brazilians who owned country places could not find McDonald's, still confined to the cities, on the road. The ad creator had apparently never attempted to drive up to a fast-food restaurant in a neighborhood with no parking spaces.

Several other suggestions pointed customers toward the beach, where *cariocas* (Rio natives) do spend much of their leisure time. One could eat McDonald's products "after a dip in the ocean," "at a picnic at the beach," or "watching the surfers." These suggestions ignored the Brazilian custom of consuming cold things, such as beer, soft drinks, ice cream, and ham and cheese sandwiches, at the beach. Brazilians don't consider a hot, greasy hamburger proper beach food. They view the sea as "cold" and hamburgers as "hot"; they avoid "hot" foods at the beach. Also culturally dubious was the suggestion to eat McDonald's hamburgers "lunching at the office." Brazilians prefer their main meal at midday, often eating at a leisurely pace with business associates. Many firms serve ample lunches to their employees. Other workers take advantage of a two-hour lunch break to go home to eat with the spouse and children. Nor did it make sense to suggest that children should eat hamburgers for lunch, since most kids attend school for half-day sessions and have lunch at home. Two other suggestions—"waiting for the bus" and "in the beauty parlor"—did describe common aspects of daily life in a Brazilian city. However, these settings have not proved especially inviting to hamburgers or fish filets.

The homes of Brazilians who can afford McDonald's products have cooks and maids to do many of the things that fast-food restaurants do in the United States. The suggestion that McDonald's products be eaten "while watching your favorite television program" is culturally appropriate, because Brazilians watch TV a lot. However, Brazil's consuming classes can ask the cook to make a snack when hunger strikes. Indeed, much tele-viewing occurs during the light dinner served when the husband gets home from the office.

Most appropriate to the Brazilian lifestyle was the suggestion to enjoy McDonald's "on the cook's day off." Throughout Brazil, Sunday is that day. The Sunday pattern for middle-class families who live on the coast is a trip to the beach, liters of beer, a full midday meal around 3 P.M., and a light evening snack. McDonald's found its niche in the Sunday evening meal, when families flock to the fast-food restaurant.

McDonald's has expanded rapidly in Brazil, where, as in North America, teenage appetites have fueled the fast-food explosion. As McDonald's outlets appeared in urban neighborhoods, Brazilian teenagers used them for after-school snacks, while families had evening meals there. As an anthropologist could have predicted, the fast-food industry has not revolutionized Brazilian food and meal customs. Rather, McDonald's is succeeding because it has adapted to preexisting Brazilian cultural patterns.

The main contrast with North America is that the Brazilian evening meal is lighter. McDonald's now caters to the evening meal rather than to lunch. Once McDonald's realized that more money could be made by fitting in with, rather than trying to Americanize, Brazilian meal habits, it started aiming its advertising at that goal.

---

Xerox, IBM, and Apple are among the companies that employ anthropologists. Closely observing how people actually use IT products, anthropologists have worked with engineers to design products that are more user friendly.

Key features of anthropology that are of value to business include (1) ethnography and observation as ways of gathering data, (2) a focus on diversity, and (3) cross-cultural expertise (see this chapter's "Appreciating Diversity"). Businesses have heard that anthropologists are specialists on cultural diversity and the observation of behavior. Hallmark Cards has hired anthropologists to observe parties, holidays, and celebrations of ethnic groups to improve its ability to design cards for targeted audiences. Applied anthropologists routinely go into people's homes to see how they actually use products (see Sunderland and Denny 2007).

## PUBLIC AND APPLIED ANTHROPOLOGY

Many academic anthropologists, myself included, occasionally work as applied anthropologists. Most typically, we are asked to advise and consult about the direction of change in nations, regions, and communities where we originally did "academic" research. In my case, this has meant policy-relevant work on environmental preservation in Madagascar and poverty reduction in northeastern Brazil.

Other academics, while not doing applied anthropology per se, have urged the field of anthropology as a whole to engage more in what they call **public anthropology** (Borofsky 2000) or *public interest anthropology* (Sanday 2003). Suggested ways of making anthropology more visible and relevant to the public include nonacademic publishing, testifying at government hearings, consulting, acting as an expert witness, and engaging in citizen activism, electoral campaigns, and political administrations (Sanjek 2004). The stated goals of public anthropology are to engage with public issues by opposing policies that promote injustice and by working to reframe discussions of key social issues in the media and by public officials. As Rylko-Bauer and her colleagues (2006) point out, there is, as well, a long tradition of work guided by such goals in applied anthropology.

New media are helping to disseminate anthropological knowledge to a wider public. The complete world of cyberspace, including the blogosphere, constantly grows richer in the resources and communication opportunities available to anthropologists. Some of the most widely read anthropological blogs include:

Savage Minds, a group blog
http://savageminds.org

Living Anthropologically, by Jason Antrosio
http://www.livinganthropologically.com

Neuroanthropology, by Greg Downey and Daniel Lende
http://blogs.plos.org/neuroanthropology/

Also see this detailed list of anthropology blogs, as updated for 2013:

http://anthropologyreport.com/anthropology-blogs-2013-list/

**public anthropology**
Efforts to extend anthropology's visibility beyond academia and to demonstrate its public policy relevance.

Anthropologists participate as well in various listservs and networking groups (e.g., on LinkedIn and Research Gate). A bit of googling on your part will take you to anthropologists' personal websites, as well as research project websites.

## CAREERS AND ANTHROPOLOGY

Many college students find anthropology interesting and consider majoring in it. However, their parents or friends may discourage them by asking, "What kind of job are you going to get with an anthropology degree?" The first step in answering that question is to consider the more general question "What do you do with any college major?" The answer is "Not much, without a good bit of effort, thought, and planning." A survey of graduates of the University of Michigan's literary college showed that few had jobs that were clearly linked to their majors. Most professions, including medicine and law, require advanced degrees. Although many colleges offer bachelor's degrees in engineering, business, accounting, and social work, master's degrees often are needed to get the best jobs in those fields. Anthropologists, too, need an advanced degree, almost always a PhD, to find gainful employment.

A broad college education, and even a major in anthropology, can be an excellent foundation for success in many fields (see Stephens 2002). One survey of women executives showed that most had majored not in business but in the social sciences or humanities. Only after graduating from college did they study business, leading to an MBA, a master's degree in business administration. These executives felt that the breadth of their college educations had contributed to their business careers. Anthropology majors go on to medical, law, and business schools and find success in many professions that often have little explicit connection to anthropology.

Anthropology's breadth provides knowledge and an outlook on the world that are useful in many kinds of work. For example, an anthropology major combined with a master's degree in business is excellent preparation for work in international business. Breadth is anthropology's hallmark. Anthropologists study people biologically, culturally, socially, and linguistically, across time and space, in various countries, in simple and complex settings. Most colleges offer anthropology courses that compare cultures, along with others that focus on particular world areas, such as Latin America, Asia, and Native North America. The knowledge of foreign areas acquired in such courses can be useful in many jobs. Anthropology's comparative outlook and its focus on diverse lifestyles combine to provide an excellent foundation for overseas employment (see Omohundro 2001; Stephens 2002).

For work in modern North America, anthropology's focus on culture is increasingly relevant. Every day we hear about cultural differences and about problems whose solutions require a multicultural viewpoint—an ability to recognize and reconcile ethnic differences. Government, schools, hospitals, and businesses constantly deal with people from different social classes, ethnic groups, and cultural backgrounds. Physicians, attorneys, social workers, police officers, judges, teachers, and students can all do a better job if they understand cultural differences in a nation that is one of the most ethnically diverse in history.

Knowledge of the traditions and beliefs of the groups that make up a modern nation is important in planning and carrying out programs that affect those groups. Experience in planned social change—whether community organization in North America or economic development overseas—shows that a proper social study should be done before a project or policy is implemented. When local people want the change and it fits their lifestyle and traditions, it has a better chance of being successful, beneficial, and cost effective.

People with anthropology backgrounds do well in many fields. Even if one's job has little or nothing to do with anthropology in a formal or obvious sense, a background in anthropology provides a useful orientation when we work with our fellow human beings. For most of us, this means every day of our lives.

# for REVIEW

## summary

1. Anthropology has two dimensions: academic and applied. Applied anthropology uses anthropological perspectives, theory, methods, and data to identify, assess, and solve problems. Applied anthropologists have a range of employers. Examples are government agencies; development organizations; NGOs; tribal, ethnic, and interest groups; businesses; social service and educational agencies. Applied anthropologists come from all four subfields. Ethnography is one of applied anthropology's most valuable research tools.

2. Development anthropology focuses on social issues in, and the cultural dimension of, economic development. Development projects typically promote cash employment and new technology at the expense of subsistence economies. Not all governments seek to increase equality and end poverty. Resistance by elites to reform is typical and hard to combat. At the same time, local people rarely cooperate with projects requiring major and risky changes in their daily lives. Many projects seek to impose inappropriate property notions and incompatible social units on their intended beneficiaries. The best strategy for change is to base the social design for innovation on traditional social forms in each target area.

3. Anthropology and education researchers work in classrooms, homes, and other settings relevant to education. Such studies may lead to policy recommendations. Both academic and applied anthropologists study migration from rural areas to cities and across national boundaries. North America has become a popular arena for urban anthropological research on migration, ethnicity, poverty, and related topics. Although rural and urban are different social systems, there is cultural diffusion from one to the other.

4. Medical anthropology is the cross-cultural, biocultural study of health problems and conditions, disease, illness, disease theories, and health care systems. Medical anthropology includes anthropologists from all four subfields and has theoretical (academic) and applied dimensions. In a given setting, the characteristic diseases reflect diet, population density, the economy, and social complexity. Native theories of illness may be personalistic, naturalistic, or emotionalistic. In applying anthropology to business, the key features are (1) ethnography and observation as ways of gathering data, (2) cross-cultural expertise, and (3) a focus on cultural diversity. Public anthropology describes efforts to extend anthropological knowledge of social problems and issues to a wider and more influential audience.

5. A broad college education, including anthropology and foreign-area courses, offers excellent background for many fields. Anthropology's comparative outlook and cultural relativism provide an excellent basis for overseas employment. Even for work in North America, a focus on culture and cultural diversity is valuable. Anthropology majors attend medical, law, and business schools and succeed in many fields, some of which have little explicit connection with anthropology.

## critical thinking

1. This chapter uses the association between early anthropology and colonialism to illustrate some of the dangers of early applied anthropology. We also learn how American anthropologists studied Japanese and German "culture at a distance" in an attempt to predict the behavior of the enemies of the United States during World War II. Political and military conflicts with other nations and cultures continue today. What role, if any, could and/or should applied anthropologists play in these conflicts?

2. What roles could applied anthropologists play in the design and implementation of development projects? Based on past experience and research on this topic, what could an applied anthropologist focus on avoiding and/or promoting?

3. This chapter describes some of the applications of anthropology in educational settings. Think back to your grade school or high school classroom. Were there any social issues that might have interested an anthropologist? Were there any problems that an applied anthropologist might have been able to solve? How so?

4. Our culture—and cultural changes—affects how we perceive nature, human nature, and the "natural." Give examples of how medical anthropologists examine the shifting boundaries between culture and nature.

5. Indicate your career plans, if known, and describe how you might apply the knowledge learned through introductory anthropology in your future vocation. If you have not yet chosen a career, pick one of the following: economist, engineer, diplomat, architect, or elementary schoolteacher. Why is it important to understand the culture and social organization of the people who will be affected by your work?

# Doing Archaeology and Biological Anthropology

▸ How do biological anthropologists and archaeologists study the past?

▸ How do anthropologists determine the dates of sites, remains, and evolutionary events?

▸ What ethical concerns and issues affect biological anthropology and archaeology?

Excavations at Gran Dolina, Atapuerca, Spain, where hominin fossils and stone tools date back 800,000 years. Biological anthropologists and archaeologists often collaborate as members of the same field team.

# understanding OURSELVES

Consider Facebook and other *social* networking websites. In how many such sites do you participate? For what do you use them? Do they extend or restrict your social network? Long before the Internet, all humans belonged to social networks. Anthropology studies people as members of groups—networks, societies, and cultures. Compared with our primate relatives, humans are unusually social. Even chimpanzees, our closest relatives, don't cooperate nearly as much as we do. There's reason to believe that our urge to cooperate emerged early in human evolution.

We'll never know all the causes of human sociality, and there is substantial cross-cultural variation in preferences for social contact versus solitude. In some societies sick people say, "I want to be alone," while in others it's "Please don't leave me." Which would it be for you?

Regardless of cultural variation, a human appreciation of the social appears to be based in features of human anatomy—from the brain to the pelvis. Consider the female pelvis, whose evolution has been guided by these facts: (1) Humans walk upright; (2) babies are born with big brains; and (3) babies have to negotiate a complicated birth canal during childbirth. There are striking contrasts between humans and other primates in anatomy and in the birthing process. Nonhuman primates aren't bipedal; they use four limbs rather than two to move about. Compared with humans, they have smaller brains, simpler birth canals, and more independent infants.

Human babies, in moving through the birth canal, must make several turns. Their heads and shoulders, the two body parts with the largest dimensions, must be aligned consistently with the widest parts of that canal. Monkeys and apes don't have this problem; their birth canals have a constant shape. Also, the primate infant emerges facing forward. The mother can grasp it, even pull it straight to her nipple. Human babies are born facing backward, away from the mother, so she has trouble assisting in the birth. The presence of someone else (e.g., a midwife or doctor) to help with delivery reduces the mortality risk for human infants and their mothers.

Birthing assistance is almost universal among human societies. The characteristic human wish to have supportive, familiar people around at childbirth probably goes way back. Based on pelvic openings and estimated infant skull sizes of fossilized human precursors, anthropologists Karen Rosenberg and Wenda Trevathan (2001) surmise that such assistance may date back millions of years. Nonhuman primate mothers seek seclusion when they give birth and act as their own midwives in the birthing process. Not so humans, who are as social as ever. Midwives, obstetricians, and baby showers are all manifestations of human sociality. The next time you encounter one, appreciate that such manifestations of human sociality have deep evolutionary roots.

"Been on any digs lately?" Ask your professor how many times she or he has been asked this question. Then ask how often he or she actually has been on a dig. Remember that anthropology has four subfields, only two of which (archaeology and biological anthropology) require much digging—in the ground, at least. Even among biological anthropologists it's mainly paleoanthropologists (those concerned with the hominin fossil record) who must dig. Students of primate behavior in the wild, such as Jane Goodall, don't do it. Nor, most of the time, is it done by forensic anthropologists, such as the title character in the TV series *Bones*.

Before this course, did you know the names of any anthropologists? If so, which ones—real or fictional? For the general public, biological anthropologists and archaeologists tend to be better known than cultural anthropologists because of what they study and discover—making them attractive subjects for the Discovery Channel. You're more likely to have watched *Bones* or seen a film of Jane Goodall with chimps or a paleoanthropologist holding a skull than to have seen a linguistic or cultural anthropologist at work. Archaeologists occasionally appear in the media to describe a new discovery or to debunk pseudo-archaeological arguments about how visitors from space have left traces on Earth.

This chapter is about what anthropologists do, focusing on archaeology and biological anthropology. Given space limitations, however, only some of the diverse methods and techniques employed by anthropological archaeologists and biological anthropologists can be covered here.

# RESEARCH METHODS IN ARCHAEOLOGY AND BIOLOGICAL ANTHROPOLOGY

Archaeology and biological, or physical, anthropology are two of anthropology's four subfields. Archaeologists tend to study material culture; biological anthropologists tend to study biological remains. Anthropological archaeology reconstructs human behavior, social patterns, and cultural features through the analysis of material remains (and other sources, including written records, if available). Biological anthropologists study living and recent humans (e.g., their genetics, growth, development, and physiological adaptation) and primates (e.g., their behavior and social organization) as well as deceased and ancient ones. Paleoanthropologists study human evolution through skeletal material and related material remains, such as biological traces

(e.g., pollens, animal bones). Doing so, and as they attempt to date ancient human remains, biological anthropologists share many research interests and techniques with archaeologists. Members of both subfields must collaborate with many other kinds of scientists to do their work effectively.

## Multidisciplinary Approaches

Scientists from diverse fields—for example, soil science and **paleontology** (the study of ancient life through the fossil record)—collaborate with archaeologists and biological anthropologists in the study of ancient sites. *Palynology,* the study of ancient plants through pollen samples, can be used to determine a site's environment at the time of occupation. Physicists and chemists help anthropologists with dating techniques. *Bioarchaeologists* may form a picture of ancient life at a particular site by examining human skeletons to reconstruct their physical traits, health status, and diet (Buikstra and Beck 2006; Larsen 2000; Martin, Harrod, and Perez 2013; Stodder and Palkovich 2012). Evidence for social status can endure in hard materials—bones, jewels, buildings— through the ages. During life, bone growth and stature are influenced by diet. Genetic differences aside, taller people often are that way because they eat better than shorter people do. Differences in the chemical composition of groups of bones at a site may help distinguish privileged nobles from less fortunate commoners.

To reconstruct ancient human biological and cultural features, anthropologists analyze material remains, including bones, teeth, and artifacts (manufactured items). Visible remains found at archaeological sites include animal and human bones, charcoal from ancient fires, remains in burials and storage pits, and worked stone and bone. Archaeologists today also draw on microscopic evidence, such as fossil pollen, phytoliths (plant crystals), and starch grains. After artifacts are collected from a site, they are sent to a lab, where, under sterile conditions, they are examined for microscopic traces of plant starch grains, phytoliths, and fossil pollen. These microscopic particles, which can be attached to almost any artifact, can offer valuable clues about

**paleontology**
Study of ancient life through the fossil record.

These photos illustrate three kinds of microscopic evidence of plant characteristics, including domestication. The photo on the left shows a phytolith (plant stone) from domesticated squash, dated to 10,000 B.P., found in the soil at Ecuador's Vegas site. The middle photo shows reserve starch grains from the root of a modern manioc plant. The photo on the right shows a maize pollen grain dated to 5,000 B.P. from the Kob site in Belize.

ancient lifeways, especially diet and food preparation patterns (see Bryant 2013).

A phytolith ("plant stone") is a microscopic crystal found in many plants, including wheat, maize, rice, beans, squash, manioc (cassava), and other early domesticates. Because phytoliths are inorganic and don't decay, they can reveal which plants were present at a given site even when no other plant remains survive. Phytoliths trapped in the plaque of fossilized teeth have revealed, for example, that a recently discovered ancient hominin, *Australopithecus sediba,* had a diet that included fruit, leaves, and bark. Unlike other members of its genus, which fed in open grasslands, *Au. sediba* sought food in woodland areas, much like modern-day chimps and gorillas (Than 2012).

**remote sensing**
Use of aerial photos and satellite images to locate sites on the ground.

Starch grain analysis, another useful technique, recovers microfossils of food plants from the stone tools used to process them. Starch grains preserve well in areas—for example, the humid tropics— where other organic remains typically decay. These grains have been recovered from stone tools, pottery fragments, and basketry, and in human coprolites (ancient feces) (Bryant 2003, 2007*a,* 2007*b,* 2013). Vaughn Bryant (2007*b*) presents a strong case for the importance of such microscopic evidence in studying the past. As one example, he cites Bonnie Williamson's analysis of Middle to Late Stone Age tools from a cave site in South Africa. Examining hundreds of stone tools, Williamson found that many still had residues stuck to their cutting edges. Contradicting the prevailing assumption that such tools were used mainly to hunt and butcher game animals, Williamson found that over 50 percent of all the residues were from plants. Williamson's analysis suggested an important role for women (in gathering and processing plant foods) in early cultures.

Anthropologists also work with geologists, geographers, and other scientists in using satellite images to find ancient footpaths, roads, canals, and irrigation systems, which can then be investigated on the ground. Aerial photos (taken from airplanes) and satellite images are forms of **remote sensing** used in site location. For example, remote sensing enabled archaeologists to discover and study ancient footpaths in Costa Rica around a volcano called Arenal (Scott 2002). Volcanic ash, sediment, and vegetation had hidden the paths, which were up to 2,500 years old. A NASA aircraft discovered them using instruments that could "see" in a spectrum invisible to the naked human eye. The ancient trails showed up as thin red lines, reflecting the dense vegetation growing over them. The paths were dated on the basis of the stratigraphy (layers of geological deposits) formed by multiple eruptions of the nearby Arenal volcano.

Village life arose in this area about 4,000 years ago and lasted through the Spanish Conquest around 500 years ago. Villagers periodically fled volcanic eruptions, returning when it was safe to resume farming in the rich volcanic soil. According to team leader Payson Sheets of the University of Colorado, "they inhabited a very large region and seemed to avoid conflict, conquest and serious disease. . . . They led comfortable lives, relying on an abundance of natural resources and a stable culture" (quoted in Scott 2002). When archaeologists excavated the footpaths, they found stone tools, pottery, and floors of ancient houses. The paths once connected a cemetery, a spring, and quarries where construction stone was mined. A goal of Sheets's field team was to understand ancient activities at the cemetery, where bodies were buried in stone coffins. Ceramics, vessels, and cooking stones confirmed that people had camped, cooked, and feasted at the cemetery (Scott 2002; Sheets 2006).

Anthropologists and other scientists also can use remote sensing to discover and understand events of the more recent past. Satellite images reveal, for example, patterns and sites of flooding and deforestation. By comparing a time series of satellite

Many archaeological sites are visible from the air. Shown here, El Candelabro (the candelabra) is a giant ground drawing within the Paracas National Reserve, Peru. This drawing, located on the coast, can be seen from 12 miles out at sea. El Candelabro has been compared to Peru's Nazca lines, visible only from the air.

images of forest cover, scientists can identify regions where deforestation has been especially severe. Anthropologists can then travel to these areas to see what is happening on the ground—where people and biodiversity (including nonhuman primates) may be at risk. Working with anthropologist Lisa Gezon and geologist Glen Green, I did just this to understand the causes of deforestation in Madagascar (see Green and Sussman 1990; Kottak 1999*b*; Kottak, Gezon, and Green 1994).

## Studying the Past

Archaeologists and biological anthropologists share interests and techniques that enable them to reconstruct the human past. Paleoanthropologists continue to compile the fossil record of human evolution. **Fossils** are remains (e.g., bones), traces, or impressions (e.g., footprints) of ancient life forms. Typically, a team composed of scientists, students, and local workers participates in a paleoanthropological or archaeological study. Such teams may include biological anthropologists, archaeologists, paleontologists, geologists, palynologists, paleoecologists, physicists, and chemists. Paleontologists help locate fossil beds containing remains of animals that can be dated and that are known to have coexisted with hominins at various time periods. Good preservation of faunal (animal) remains may suggest that hominin fossils have survived as well. Sometimes it's impossible to date the hominin fossils and artifacts found at a given site by using the most accurate and direct (radiometric) methods. In this case, comparison of the faunal remains at that site with similar, but more securely dated, fauna at another site may suggest a date for those animal fossils and the hominins and artifacts associated with them (see Gugliotta 2005).

Once potential sites have been identified, more intensive surveying begins (see Watzman 2006). If a site is shown to be a hominin site, much more concentrated work begins. Financial support may come from private donations and government agencies. Working under a lead anthropologist, the field crew will continue to survey and map the area and start searching carefully for bones and artifacts eroding out of the soil. Also, they will take pollen and soil samples for ecological analysis and rock samples for use in various dating techniques.

Consideration of the animal habitats suggested by the site (e.g., forest, woodland, or open country) will assist in the reconstruction of the paleoecological settings in which the hominins lived. Pollen samples help reveal diet. Sediments and other geological samples will suggest climatic conditions at the time of deposition. Sometimes fossils are embedded in rock, from which they must be extracted carefully. Once recovered and cleaned, fossils may be made into casts to permit wider study.

## Survey and Excavation

Archaeologists typically work in teams and across time and space—adopting both local (e.g., excavation) and regional (e.g., survey) perspectives. The most common local approach is to excavate, or dig, through layers in a site. Regional approaches include remote sensing—for example, the discovery of ancient Costa Rican footpaths from space, as described earlier, and systematic survey on the ground. Archaeologists recognize that sites aren't usually discrete and isolated but are parts of larger (regional) social systems. One example of such systems might be a series of villages that offered tribute to the same chief. Another example might be a few bands of hunter-gatherers that got together for annual ceremonies at a particular place. Let's examine some of the main techniques that archaeologists use to study patterns of behavior in ancient societies, based on their material remains.

### Systematic Survey

Archaeologists have two key fieldwork strategies: systematic survey and excavation. **Systematic survey** provides a regional perspective by gathering information on settlement patterns over a large area. *Settlement pattern* refers to the distribution of sites within a region—how people grouped themselves and interacted spatially. Regional surveys reconstruct settlement patterns by addressing several questions: Where were sites located? How big were they? What kinds of buildings did they have? How old are the sites? Ideally, a systematic survey involves walking over the entire survey area and recording the location and size of all sites. From artifacts found on the surface, the surveyor estimates when each site was occupied. A full-coverage survey isn't always possible. The ground cover may be impenetrable (e.g., thick jungle); certain parts of the survey area may be inaccessible. Landowners may deny permission to survey on their property. Archaeologists may have to rely on remote sensing to help locate and map sites.

With regional data, archaeologists can address many questions about the prehistoric communities that lived in a given area. Archaeologists use settlement pattern information to make population estimates and to assess levels of social complexity. Among hunter-gatherers and simple farmers, there are generally low numbers of people living in small campsites or hamlets with little variation in the architecture. Such sites are scattered fairly evenly across the landscape. With increasing social complexity, the settlement patterns become more elaborate. Population levels rise. Such social factors as trade and warfare have played a more important role in determining the location of sites (on hilltops, waterways, trade routes). In complex societies, a settlement hierarchy of sites emerges. Certain sites are larger than others, with greater architectural differentiation. Large sites with specialized architecture (elite residences,

**fossils**
Remains of ancient life.

**systematic survey**
Study of settlement patterns over a large area.

temples, administrative buildings, meeting places) are generally interpreted as regional centers that exerted control over the smaller sites with less architectural differentiation.

## Excavation

During an **excavation,** scientists dig through the layers of deposits that make up a site. These layers, or *strata,* are used to establish the time order of materials. This relative chronology is based on the principle of *superposition*: In an undisturbed sequence of strata, the oldest layer is on the bottom. Each successive layer above is younger than the one below. Thus, remains from lower strata are older than those recovered from higher strata in the same deposit. This relative time ordering of material remains lies at the heart of archaeological, paleoanthropological, and paleontological research.

The archaeological and fossil records are so rich, and excavation is so labor-intensive and expensive, that nobody digs a site without a good reason. Sites are excavated because they are endangered, or because they answer specific research questions (see Sabloff 2008). Cultural resource management (CRM) focuses on managing the preservation of archaeological sites that are threatened by modern development. Many countries require archaeological impact studies before construction can take place. If a site is at risk and the development cannot be stopped, CRM archaeologists are called in to salvage what information they can from the site (see King 2011).

Another reason for choosing a particular site to excavate is that it is well suited to answer specific research questions. An archaeologist studying the origins of agriculture wouldn't want to excavate a large, fortified hilltop city with a series of buildings dating to a period well after the first appearance of farming communities. Rather, he or she would look for a small, hamlet-size site located near good farmland and a water source. Such a site would have evidence of an early occupation dating to the period when farming communities first appeared in that region.

Before a site is excavated, it is surface collected and mapped, so that the researchers can make an informed decision about where exactly to dig. The collecting of surface materials at a given site is similar to what is done over a much larger area in a regional survey. A grid is drawn to subdivide the site. Then collection units, which are equal-size sections of the grid, are marked off on the actual site (see photo below). This grid enables the researchers to record the exact location of any artifact, fossil, or feature found at the site. By examining all the materials on the surface of the site, archaeologists can direct their excavations toward those areas of the site most likely to yield information that will address their research interests. Once an area is selected, digging begins, and the location of every artifact or feature is recorded in three dimensions.

Digging may be done according to arbitrary levels. Thus, starting from the surface, consistent amounts of soil (usually 4 to 8 feet [1.2 to 2.4 meters]) are removed systematically from the excavation unit. This technique of excavation is a quick way of digging, since everything within a certain depth is removed at once. This kind of excavation usually is done in test pits, which are used to determine how deep the deposits of a site go and to establish a rough chronology for that site.

A more labor-intensive and refined way of excavating is to dig through the stratigraphy one layer at a time. The strata, which are separated by differences in color and texture, are studied one by one. This technique provides more information about the context of the artifacts, fossils, or features because the scientist works more slowly and in meaningful layers. A given 4-foot (1.2-meter) level may include within it a series of successive house floors, each with artifacts. If this deposit is excavated according to arbitrary levels, all the artifacts are mixed together. But if it is excavated according to the natural stratigraphy, with each house floor excavated separately, the resulting picture is much more detailed. The procedure here is for the archaeologist to remove and bag all the artifacts from each house floor before proceeding to the level below that one.

Any excavation recovers varied material remains, such as ceramics, stone artifacts

An archaeologist drives in another stake for a large grid at an excavation site in Teotihuacán, Mexico. Such a grid enables the researchers to record the exact location of any artifact or feature found at the site.

(lithics), human and animal bones, and plant remains. Such remains may be small and fragmented. To increase the likelihood that small remains will be recovered, the soil is passed through screens. To recover very small remains, such as fish bones and carbonized plant remains, archaeologists use a technique called *flotation*. Soil samples are sorted using water and a series of very fine meshes. When the water dissolves the soil, the carbonized plant remains float to the top. The fish bones and other heavier remains sink to the bottom. Flotation requires considerable time and labor. This makes it inappropriate to use on all the soil that is excavated from a site. Flotation samples are taken from a limited number of deposits, such as house floors, trash pits, and hearths.

This diver holds a ceramic vessel uncovered from a ship wrecked in 1025 C.E. in Turkey's Serce Liman Bay, Mugla province. Graduate degrees in underwater, or nautical, archaeology are available at East Carolina University, Florida State University, and Texas A&M University. This growing field of study investigates submerged sites, most often shipwrecks.

## KINDS OF ARCHAEOLOGY

Archaeologists pursue diverse research topics, using a wide variety of methods (see Renfrew and Bahn 2005). Experimental archaeologists try to replicate ancient techniques and processes (e.g., toolmaking) under controlled conditions. Historical archaeologists use written records as guides and supplements to archaeological research. They work with remains more recent—often much more recent—than the advent of writing. Colonial archaeologists are historical archaeologists who use written records as guides to locate and excavate postcontact sites in North and South America, and to verify or question the written accounts. Classical archaeologists usually are affiliated with university departments of classics or the history of art, rather than with anthropology departments. These classical scholars tend to focus on the literate civilizations of the Old World, such as Greece, Rome, and Egypt. Classical archaeologists often are more interested in styles of architecture and sculpture than in the social, economic, and political features that typically interest anthropological archaeologists. Underwater archaeology is a growing field that investigates submerged sites, most often shipwrecks. Special techniques, including remotely operated vehicles, are used, but divers also do underwater survey and excavation.

Cultural resource management (CRM) is a type of applied anthropology in which archaeological techniques are used to assess sites that are threatened by development, public works, and road building. Some CRM archaeologists are contract archaeologists, who typically negotiate specific contracts (rather than applying for research grants) for their studies. CRM often must be done rapidly, for example, when an immediate threat to archaeological materials becomes known. Based on a membership study done for the Society of American Archaeology, Melinda Zeder (1997) found that 40 percent of the respondents worked as contract archaeologists. Their employers included firms in the private sector, state and federal agencies, and educational institutions. An equivalent 40 percent held academic positions.

## DATING THE PAST

The archaeological record hasn't revealed every ancient society that has existed on Earth; nor is the fossil record a representative sample of all the plants and animals that ever have lived. Some species and body parts are better represented than others are, for many reasons. Hard parts, such as bones and teeth, preserve better than do soft parts, such as flesh and skin. The chances of fossilization increase when remains are buried in silt, gravel, or sand. Good places for bone preservation include swamps, floodplains, river deltas, lakes, and caves. The species that live in such areas have a better chance to be preserved than do animals that live in other habitats. Fossilization also is favored in areas with volcanic ash. Once remains do get buried, chemical conditions must be right for fossilization to occur. If the sediment is too acidic, even bones and teeth will dissolve. The study of the processes that affect the remains of dead animals is called **taphonomy,** from the Greek *taphos,* which means "tomb." Such processes include scattering by carnivores and scavengers, distortion by various forces, and the possible fossilization of the remains.

The conditions under which fossils are found also influence the fossil record. For example, fossils are more likely to be uncovered through erosion in arid areas than in wet areas. Sparse vegetation allows wind to scour the landscape and uncover fossils. The fossil record has been

**taphonomy**
Study of processes affecting remains of dead animals.

accumulating longer and is more extensive in Europe than in Africa because civil engineering projects and fossil hunting have been going on longer in Europe than in Africa. A world map showing where fossils have been found does not indicate the true range of ancient animals. Such a map tells us more about ancient geological activity, modern erosion, or recent human activity—such as paleontological research or road building. For the primate and hominin fossil records, for example, certain areas provide more abundant fossil evidence for particular time periods. This doesn't necessarily mean that primates or hominins were living only in that area at that time. Nor does failure to find a fossil species in a particular place always mean the species didn't live there. In the words of paleoanthropologist Christopher Stringer, "absence of evidence does not necessarily prove evidence of absence" (quoted in Gugliotta 2005).

We've seen that paleontology is the study of ancient life through the fossil record and that **paleoanthropology** is the study of ancient humans and their immediate ancestors. These fields have established a time frame, or chronology, for the evolution of life. Scientists use several techniques to date fossils. These methods offer different degrees of precision and are applicable to different periods of the past.

## Relative Dating

Chronology is established by assigning dates to geological layers (strata) and to the material remains—the fossils and artifacts—within them. Dating may be relative or absolute. **Relative dating** establishes a time frame in relation to other strata or materials rather than absolute dates in numbers. Many dating methods are based on the geological study of

stratigraphy, the science that examines the ways in which earth sediments accumulate in strata (singular, *stratum*). As was noted previously, in an undisturbed sequence of strata, age increases with depth. Soil that erodes from a hillside into a valley covers, and is younger than, the soil deposited there previously.

Stratigraphy permits relative dating. That is, the fossils in a given stratum are younger than those in the layers below and older than those in the layers above. We may not know the exact or absolute dates of the fossils, but we can place them in time relative to remains in other layers. Changing environmental forces, such as volcanic eruptions, or the alternation of land and sea, cause different materials to be deposited in a given sequence of strata; this allows scientists to distinguish between the strata.

Remains of animals and plants that lived at the same time are found in the same stratum. When fossils are found within a stratigraphic sequence, scientists know their dates relative to fossils in other strata; this is relative dating. When fossils are found in a particular stratum, the associated geological features (such as frost patterning) and remains of particular plants and animals offer clues about the climate at the time of deposition.

Besides stratigraphic placement, another technique of relative dating is fluorine absorption analysis. Bones fossilizing in the same ground for the same length of time absorb the same proportion of fluorine from the local groundwater. Fluorine analysis uncovered a famous hoax involving the so-called Piltdown man, once considered an unusual and perplexing human ancestor (Stringer 2012*b*; Weiner 2003). The Piltdown "find," from England, turned out to be the jaw of a young orangutan attached to the skull of a modern human. Fluorine analysis showed the association to be false. The skull had much more fluorine than the jaw—impossible if they had come from the same individual and had been deposited in the same place at the same time. Someone had fabricated Piltdown man in an attempt to muddle the interpretation of the fossil record. (The attempt was partially successful—it did fool some scientists.)

## Absolute Dating: Radiometric Techniques

Fossils can be dated more precisely, with dates in numbers (**absolute dating**), by using several methods. For example, the $^{14}C$, or carbon-14, technique is used to date organic remains. This is a radiometric technique (so called because it measures radioactive decay). $^{14}C$ is an unstable radioactive isotope of normal carbon, $^{12}C$. Cosmic radiation entering the Earth's atmosphere produces $^{14}C$, and plants take in $^{14}C$ as they absorb carbon dioxide. $^{14}C$ moves up the food chain as animals eat plants and as predators eat other animals.

Many dating methods rely on stratigraphy, the science that studies how sediments accumulate in layers, or strata. Labels make the strata evident as Professor Christopher Henshilwood excavates the south section of Blombos Cave, South Africa.

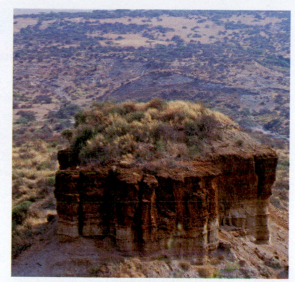

Early hominin fossils abound in Africa's Great Rift Valley, a vista of which is shown on the left. Past volcanic activity permits K/A dating in the valley, including at Olduvai Gorge, Tanzania, whose centerpiece is the rock formation on the right. Note the stratigraphy in the rock formation.

With death, the absorption of $^{14}C$ stops. This unstable isotope starts to break down into nitrogen ($^{14}N$). It takes 5,730 years for half the $^{14}C$ to change to nitrogen; this is the half-life of $^{14}C$. After another 5,730 years, only one-quarter of the original $^{14}C$ will remain. After yet another 5,730 years, only one-eighth will be left. By measuring the proportion of $^{14}C$ in organic material, scientists can determine a fossil's date of death, or the date of an ancient campfire. However, because the half-life of $^{14}C$ is short, this dating technique is less dependable for specimens older than 40,000 years than it is for more recent remains.

Fortunately, other radiometric dating techniques are available for earlier periods. One of the most widely used is the potassium–argon (K/A) technique. $^{40}K$ is a radioactive isotope of potassium that breaks down into argon-40, a gas. The half-life of $^{40}K$ is far longer than that of $^{14}C$—1.3 billion years. With this method, the older the specimen, the more reliable the dating. Furthermore, whereas $^{14}C$ dating can be done only on organic remains, K/A dating can be used only for inorganic substances: rocks and minerals. $^{40}K$ in rocks gradually breaks down into argon-40. That gas is trapped in the rock until the rock is heated intensely (as with volcanic activity), at which point it may escape. When the rock cools, the breakdown of potassium into argon resumes. Dating is done by reheating the rock and measuring the escaping gas.

In Africa's Great Rift Valley, which runs down eastern Africa and in which early hominin fossils abound, past volcanic activity permits K/A dating. In studies of strata containing fossils, scientists find out how much argon has accumulated in rocks since they were last heated. They then determine, using the standard $^{40}K$ deterioration rate (half-life), the date of that heating. Considering volcanic rocks at the top of a stratum with fossil remains, scientists establish that the fossils are older than, say, 1.8 million years. By dating the volcanic rocks below the fossil remains, they determine that the fossils are younger than, say, two million years. Thus, the age of the fossils is set at between two million and 1.8 million years. Note that absolute dating is that in name only; it may give ranges of numbers rather than exact dates.

Many fossils were discovered before the advent of modern stratigraphy. Often we can no longer determine their original stratigraphic placement. Furthermore, fossils aren't always discovered in volcanic layers. Like $^{14}C$ dating, the K/A technique applies to a limited period of the fossil record. Because the half-life of $^{40}K$ is so long, the technique cannot be used with materials less than 500,000 years old.

Other radiometric dating techniques can be used to cross-check K/A dates, again by using minerals surrounding the fossils. One such method, uranium series dating, measures fission tracks produced during the decay of radioactive uranium ($^{238}U$) into lead. Two other radiometric techniques are especially useful for fossils that can't be dated by $^{14}C$ (up to 40,000 before the present, or B.P.) or $^{40}K$ (more than 500,000 B.P.). These methods are thermoluminescence (TL) and electron spin resonance (ESR). Both TL and ESR measure the electrons that are constantly being trapped in rocks and minerals. Once a date is obtained for a rock found associated with a fossil, that date also can be applied to that fossil. The time spans for which the various absolute dating techniques are applicable are summarized in Recap 4.1.

## Absolute Dating: Dendrochronology

**Dendrochronology,** or tree-ring dating, is a method of absolute dating based on the study and comparison of patterns of tree-ring growth. Because trees grow by adding one ring every year, counting the

**dendrochronology**
Tree-ring dating; a form of absolute dating.

| TECHNIQUE | ABBREVIATION | MATERIALS DATED | EFFECTIVE TIME RANGE |
|---|---|---|---|
| Carbon-14 | $^{14}C$ | Organic materials | Up to 40,000 years |
| Potassium–argon | K/A and $^{40}K$ | Volcanic rock | Older than 500,000 years |
| Uranium series | $^{238}U$ | Minerals | Between 1,000 and 1,000,000 years |
| Thermoluminescence | TL | Rocks and minerals | Between 5,000 and 1,000,000 years |
| Electron spin resonance | ESR | Rocks and minerals | Between 1,000 and 1,000,000 years |
| Dendrochronology | Dendro | Wood and charcoal | Up to 11,000 years |

rings reveals the age of a tree. Around 1920, A. E. Douglass of the University of Arizona noticed that wide rings grew during wet years, while narrow rings grew during dry years. Climatic variation, for example, moisture, cold, or drought, produces a distinctive year-by-year ring pattern—observable in all the trees that have grown over the same time period in the same region. Ring patterns of trees can be compared and matched ring for ring. Charting such patterns back through time, scientists can compare wood from ancient buildings to known tree-ring chronologies, match the ring patterns, and determine precisely—to the year—the age of the wood used by the historic or prehistoric builder (see Schweingruber 2007; Speer 2010; Stoffel 2010).

Crossdating is the process of matching ring patterns among trees and assigning rings to specific calendar years. Both visual and statistical techniques are used to make the matches. Wood or charcoal samples from buildings and archaeological sites are crossdated with each other and with wood from living trees to extend the tree-ring chronology beyond the date of the oldest ring of the oldest living tree in the region.

**molecular anthropology**

DNA comparisons used to determine evolutionary links and distances.

Tree-ring dating was first used in the southwestern United States for Native American communities and historical settlements. The bristlecone pine chronology of the American Southwest now exceeds 8,500 years (see Miller 2004). A northern European chronology based on the study of oak and pine is over 11,000 years long. The objective of Cornell University's Aegean dendrochronology project (www.arts.cornell.edu/dendro/), directed by Peter Kuniholm, is to build a master chronology for the region of the Aegean Sea and the Middle East. So far this project has established over 6,000 years of tree-ring chronologies covering much of the period back to about 9,500 years ago. The project encompasses portions of the Aegean, the Balkans, and the Middle East, including Turkey, Cyprus, Greece, parts of Bulgaria and the former Yugoslavia, and some of Italy. (There is one major gap, for which matches have not yet been made, between about 1,500 and 2,500 years ago.) Scientists hope eventually to extend the chronology back to the period in which prehistoric peoples first started using significant amounts of wood in construction (Kuniholm 2004).

Dendrochronology is limited to certain tree species—those growing in a climate with marked seasons. The technique works with oak, pine, juniper, fir, boxwood, yew, spruce, and occasionally chestnut. The trees always have to come from the same region—thus having been exposed to the same environmental patterns—and long ring sequences are needed. Some charcoal fragments from the Neolithic site of Çatalhöyük in Turkey, where dendrochronology has established a 700-year sequence, have as many as 250 rings preserved (Özdoğan, Başgelen, and Kuniholm 2011). Not only do tree rings permit absolute dating; they also provide information about climatic patterns in specific regions.

## Molecular Anthropology

**Molecular anthropology** uses genetic analysis (of DNA sequences) to estimate evolutionary relationships. Molecular studies have been used to assess and date the origins of modern humans and to examine their relation to extinct hominin groups (see this chapter's "Appreciating Diversity" for the role of DNA analysis in discovering an entirely new ancient hominin group—the Denisovans.)

Dr. Tom Sweatnam of the University of Arizona displays tree samples from a giant sequoia. What kinds of information can you get from studying tree rings?

# appreciating DIVERSITY

## All This from a Finger Bone?

Archaeologists and paleoanthropologists increasingly draw on genomics, including reconstructions of ancient DNA, to unravel the mysteries of hominin evolution, including its diverse branches. Their analysis of discovered fossils, no matter how miniscule, can often lead to significant findings. All that is known of an ancient hominin group called Denisovans comes from a tiny finger bone and two very large molar teeth found between 2008 and 2010 in Siberian caves. Neandertals and their cousins, the Denisovans, shared the world with anatomically modern humans. During their overlap in time, modern humans lived mainly in Africa, while Neandertals inhabited Europe and the Middle East; the Denisovans, Asia. Pay attention to the methodological advances described in this account. Such advances have transformed our understanding of hominin evolution.

In the Altay Mountains of southern Siberia . . . there is a cave called Denisova. . . . It was there that a young Russian archaeologist named Alexander Tsybankov was digging one day in July 2008, in deposits believed to be 30,000 to 50,000 years old, when he came upon a tiny piece of bone . . . about the size and shape of a pebble. . . .

Anatoly Derevianko, leader of the Altay excavations, . . . thought the bone might belong to . . . Homo sapiens. Sophisticated artifacts that could only be the work of modern humans, including a beautiful bracelet of polished green stone, had previously been found in the same deposits. But DNA from a fossil found earlier in a nearby cave had proved to be Neanderthal, so it was possible this bone was Neanderthal as well.

Derevianko . . . sent . . . [the bone] to Svante Pääbo, an evolutionary geneticist at the Max Planck Institute for Evolutionary Anthropology in Leipzig, Germany. . . .

When Pääbo received the package . . . , his team was hard at work producing the first sequence of the entire Neanderthal genome. . . . So it wasn't until late 2009 that the little Russian finger bone drew the attention of Johannes Krause, at the time a senior member of Pääbo's team. . . .

The tiny chip of a finger bone, it seemed, was not from a modern human at all. But it wasn't from a Neanderthal either. It belonged to a new kind of human being, never before seen [and thereafter called "Denisovan"]. . . .

DNA degrades over time, so usually very little remains in a bone tens of thousands of years old. Moreover, the DNA from the bone itself, called endogenous DNA, is typically just a tiny fraction of the total DNA in a specimen, most of which comes from soil bacteria and other contaminants. None of the Neanderthal fossils Pääbo and his colleagues had ever tested contained even 5 percent endogenous DNA. . . . To their amazement, the DNA in the finger bone was some 70 percent endogenous. Apparently, the cold cave had preserved it well.

Given so much DNA, the scientists easily ascertained that there was no sign of a male Y chromosome in the specimen. The fingertip had belonged to a little girl who had died in or near Denisova cave tens of thousands of years before. . . .

For a while they thought they might have her toe too. In the summer of 2010 a human toe bone had emerged. . . . The toe bone . . . turned out to be Neanderthal, deepening the mystery of the place.

The green stone bracelet found earlier . . . had almost surely been made by modern humans. The toe bone was Neanderthal. And the finger bone was something else entirely. One cave, three kinds of human being. . . .

When the researchers compared the Denisovan genome with those of various modern human populations, they found no trace of it in Russia or nearby China, or anywhere else, for that matter, except in the genomes of New Guineans, other people from islands in Melanesia, and Australian Aborigines. On average their genomes are about 5 percent Denisovan. . . .

In 2012 Pääbo's group published a new version of the finger bone's genome—astonishingly, one that in accuracy and completeness rivals any living human's genome that has been sequenced. The breakthrough came from a German postdoc in Pääbo's lab named Matthias Meyer. DNA consists of two interlocking strands, the familiar double helix. Previous methods for retrieving DNA from fossil bone could read out sequences only when both strands were preserved. Meyer had developed a technique for recovering short, single-stranded fragments of DNA as well, greatly increasing the amount of raw material to work with. The method produced a version of the Denisovan girl's genome so precise that the team could discriminate between genetic information inherited from her mother and that from her father. In effect, they now had two highly accurate Denisovan genomes, one from each parent. . . .

But what of the little girl herself? . . . She probably had dark hair, dark eyes, and dark skin. It isn't much, but at least it sketches in broad strokes what she looked like. . . .

SOURCE: Jamie Shreeve, "The Case of the Missing Ancestor: DNA from a Cave in Russia Adds a Mysterious New Member to the Human Family," *National Geographic*, July, 2013. http://nationalgeographic.com. Copyright © 2013 National Geographic Society. Reprinted with permission.

Molecular anthropologists examine relationships among ancient and contemporary populations and among species. It's well established, for example, that humans and chimpanzees have more than 98 percent of their DNA in common. Molecular anthropologists also reconstruct waves and patterns of migration and settlement. A *haplogroup* is a biological lineage (a large group of related people) defined by a specific cluster of genetic traits that occur together. Native Americans have at least three major haplogroups, which also are linked to East Asia. Molecular anthropologists also use "genetic clocks" to estimate divergence time (date of most recent common ancestry) among species (e.g., humans, chimps, and gorillas—6–10 million years ago) and of various human groups (e.g., Neandertals and modern humans).

## KINDS OF BIOLOGICAL ANTHROPOLOGY

The past grades into the present when archaeologists do garbology—using garbage to interpret behavior among contemporary humans—or when biological anthropologists study patterns of movement or growth and development among living people. The interests of biological anthropologists are varied and encompass recent and living as well as ancient and deceased humans and other primates. Described in this chapter are many, but far from all, of the topics and methods within contemporary biological anthropology.

### Bone Biology

Central to biological anthropology is **bone biology** (skeletal biology)—the study of bone as a biological

A color-enhanced image of bone affected by osteoporosis (brittle bone disease).

tissue, including its genetics; cell structure; growth, development, and decay; and patterns of movement (biomechanics) (White, Black, and Folkens 2012). Bone biologists study skeletal characteristics of living and deceased humans and hominins. Any scientific interpretation of fossil remains relies on understanding the structure and function of the skeleton. **Paleopathology** is the study of disease and injury in skeletons from archaeological sites (see Cohen and Armelagos 2013). Some forms of cancer leave evidence in the bone. Breast cancer, for example, may spread (metastasize) skeletally, leaving holes or lesions in bones and skull. Certain infectious diseases (e.g., syphilis and tuberculosis) also mark bone, as do injuries and nutritional deficiencies (e.g., rickets, a vitamin D deficiency that deforms the bones).

In forensic anthropology, biological anthropologists work in a legal context, assisting coroners, medical examiners, and law enforcement agencies in recovering, analyzing, and identifying human remains and determining the cause of death (Byers 2011; Stefoff 2011; Tersigni-Tarrant and Shirley 2012). The television series *Bones* offers a view of such work. The creator of *Bones* (books and TV series) is biological/forensic anthropologist Kathy Reichs.

### Anthropometry

Biological anthropologists use various techniques to study nutrition, growth, and development. **Anthropometry** is the measurement of human body parts and dimensions, including skeletal parts (osteometry). Anthropometry is done on living people as well as on skeletal remains from sites. Body mass and composition provide measures of nutritional status in living people. Body mass is calculated from height and weight. The body mass index ($kg/m^2$) is the ratio of weight in kilograms divided by height in meters squared. An adult body mass above 30 is considered at risk of overweight, while one below 18 is at risk of underweight or malnutrition.

### Primatology

Primatology is considered a subfield of biological anthropology. Primate studies are useful to paleoanthropologists who are attempting to understand the behavior and social life of ancient hominins. Primatology also links with sociocultural anthropology (especially ethnography) through its focus on behavior and social life. Primate behavior has been observed in zoos (e.g., de Waal 1998) and through experimentation (e.g., Harlow 1971; Ottaviani and Meconis 2007), but the most significant studies have been done in natural settings, among free-ranging apes, monkeys, and lemurs. Since the 1950s, when primatologists began their shift from zoos to natural settings, numerous studies have been done of apes

**paleopathology**
Study of disease and injury in skeletons from archaeological sites.

**anthropometry**
Measurement of human body parts and dimensions.

**bone biology**
Study of bone as a biological tissue.

(chimps, gorillas, orangutans, and gibbons), monkeys (e.g., baboons, macaques), and lemurs (e.g., Madagascar's indri, sifaka, and ring-tailed lemurs). Arboreal primates (those that spend most of their time in the trees) are difficult to see and follow, but they typically make a lot of noise. Their howls and calls can be studied and teach us about how primates communicate. Studies of primate social systems and behavior, including their mating patterns, infant care, and patterns of contact and dispersal, suggest hypotheses about behavior that humans do or do not share with our nearest relatives—as well as with our hominin ancestors.

## DOING ANTHROPOLOGY RIGHT AND WRONG: ETHICAL ISSUES

Science exists in society and in the context of law and ethics. Anthropologists can't study things simply because they might be scientifically interesting. Ethical issues must be considered as well. Anthropologists typically have worked abroad, outside their own society. In the context of international contacts, different ethical codes and value systems will meet, and often compete.

Archaeologists and biological anthropologists, in particular, often work as members of multinational teams (see Dalton 2006). Some team members will be from the host country—the place (e.g., Ethiopia) where the research takes place. Anthropologists must inform officials and colleagues in the host country about the purpose, funding, and likely results, products, and impacts of their research. They need to negotiate the matter of where the materials produced by the research will be analyzed and stored—in the host country or in the anthropologists' country—and for how long. To whom do research materials such as bones, artifacts, and blood samples belong? What kinds of restrictions will apply to their use?

Contemporary anthropologists recognize that **informed consent** (agreement to take part in the research—after having been informed about its nature, procedures, and possible impacts) should be obtained from anyone who provides information or who might be affected by the research. Although nonhuman primates can't give informed consent, primatologists still must take steps to ensure that their research doesn't endanger the animals they study. Either government agencies or nongovernmental organizations (NGOs) may be entrusted with protecting primates. If this is the case, the anthropologist will need their permission and informed consent to conduct research.

With living humans, informed consent is a necessity, not only in gathering information but especially in obtaining biological samples such as blood or urine (see this chapter's "Appreciating Anthropology" on

Anthropometry, being done here by a French anthropologist, is the measurement of human body parts and dimensions, including skulls and skeletal parts. Anthropometry is done on remains from sites as well as on living people. Has anyone done anthropometry on you?

pp. 70–71). The research subjects must be told how the samples will be collected, used, and identified, and about the potential costs and benefits to them. Informed consent is needed from anyone providing data or information, owning materials being studied, or otherwise having an interest that might be affected by the research.

It is appropriate for North American anthropologists working in another country to (1) include host country colleagues in their research planning and requests for funding, (2) establish truly collaborative relationships with those colleagues and their institutions before, during, and after fieldwork, (3) include host country colleagues in dissemination, including publication, of the research results, and (4) ensure that something is "given back" to host country colleagues. For example, research equipment and technology are allowed to remain in the host country. Or funding is provided for host country colleagues to do research, attend international meetings, or visit foreign institutions—especially those where their international collaborators work.

Even with broad efforts to respect diverse value systems and acknowledge the contributions of the host country and its colleagues, ethical issues continue to arise. Lawsuits against museums by groups seeking the repatriation of remains and artifacts have become common (see Rothstein 2006). Peru, for instance, sued Yale University to recover objects removed during the exploration of Machu Picchu (an important Peruvian archaeological and tourist site) by Yale explorer Hiram Bingham in 1912. Native Australians have argued that images of native Australian fauna, such as the emu and kangaroo, belong exclusively to the Aboriginal people (Brown 2003). Michael F.

**informed consent**
Agreement to take part in research, after being fully informed about it.

# appreciating ANTHROPOLOGY

## A Biocultural Approach to Health in the Bolivian Amazon

This account describes ongoing interdisciplinary research initiated by anthropologists among Bolivia's indigenous Tsimane people. This study provides an excellent example of the biocultural field of medical anthropology, which includes both cultural and biological anthropologists. Also illustrated here is a proper concern with ethical issues in research. Informed consent is obtained prior to participation. The researchers repeatedly explain what they are doing, including showing patients a video about where their blood goes for testing.

SANTA MARÍA, Bolivia—There seems to be little that distinguishes the indigenous Tsimane of northern Bolivia from dozens of other native Amazonian peoples. They still live in small communities, fishing daily, hunting and relying on subsistence farming. They remain relatively isolated from the outside world. They still have large families and fall victim to parasites, worms and infectious diseases. And until a decade ago, few had contact with doctors. Yet since 2002, when the Tsimane Health and Life History Project was founded, the Tsimane (pronounced chee-MAH-nay) have become arguably the most intensely studied

indigenous people in the Western Hemisphere, and perhaps the world.

More than 50 Bolivian and American researchers, doctors and students have participated in the health project, generating an array of landmark studies. The population of 13,000, which stretches along the Maniqui River, has become the scientific community's 21st-century "traditional man."

Research on the Tsimane led to the finding in 2009 that cardiovascular disease is probably an ill of modern societies. Studies of the group also provided the most conclusive data supporting the idea that high levels of physical activity drastically reduce the risk of diabetes, obesity and hypertension. . . .

There have been 42 studies with results published, and at least 33 more are under way. "This is the most productive research site in anthropology today," Ray Hames, an anthropologist at the University of Nebraska–Lincoln, said. . . .

Michael Gurven, an anthropologist at University of California, Santa Barbara, who is a founder and a director of the project, said the primary focus of the Tsimane studies was aging. "We look at what's different and what's similar between Tsimane and Western populations," he said. The

Tsimane were chosen because of their numbers; of all Amazonian indigenous groups still living relatively traditionally, the Tsimane are one of the most numerous. . . .

The Tsimane also have the advantage of variety within that population, said Hillard Kaplan, an anthropologist at the University of New Mexico and the project's other founder and director. A small number of the Tsimane live in or around San Borja, the area's only town; they own motorcycles and use cellphones. The farther up the Maniqui River from San Borja you go, the more traditional the way of life.

In Puerto Yucumo, a village of thatched huts in plantain groves, women sit in groups at midday, their legs outstretched, attending to babies (the average family has nine children), cooking or weaving. They chatter in their native tongue; few speak Spanish and fewer have finished primary school. . . . The infiltration of doctors and anthropologists has had some effect on the culture, the researchers acknowledge, but not as much as might be expected.

"The world is changing around the Tsimane, and they are changing with it, regardless of our presence," said Dr. Kaplan. He said the Tsimane lifestyle

Brown (2003) describes efforts by Hopi Indians to control and restrict historic photos of secret religious ceremonies.

Many anthropologists have worked to represent or assist indigenous groups, for example, when disasters strike or when disputes arise with external agents. Sometimes, however, issues involving access to, or ownership of, physical and archaeological remains place anthropologists and indigenous people in opposed camps. The Native American Graves Protection and Repatriation Act (NAGPRA) gives ownership of Native American remains to Native Americans. Hundreds of thousands of Native American remains are said to be in American museums. NAGPRA requires museums to return remains

and artifacts to any tribe that requests them and can prove a "cultural affiliation" between itself and the remains or artifact.

The 1996 discovery in Washington State (on federal land) of a skeleton dubbed "Kennewick Man" led to a legal case between anthropologists and five Native American tribes (nations) with ancestral homelands in the area where Kennewick Man was discovered. The anthropologists wanted to conduct a thorough scientific study of the 9,000-year-old skeleton—one of the oldest and best preserved human remains ever discovered in North America. What might its anatomy and DNA reveal about the early settlement of the Americas? The Umatilla Indians and their allies in four other Native American was altered much more by government stipends for the children and the elderly, altering the subsistence economy. Nevertheless, the researchers had a threshold moment as they began the study. Could they, in good conscience, send doctors into the villages to study the population without also providing the Tsimane with basic medical care?

They decided they could not. "The depth of our science and the depth of our helping are two sides of the same coin," Dr. Kaplan said. His field team offers basic medical exams for anyone who shows up, provides free medicine for common ailments like stomach parasites, and does on-the-spot analysis of blood, urine and fecal samples.

"It would be unethical not to do this," Jane Lancaster, editor of the journal *Human Nature*, said. "If you are performing research and bothering these people, the least you can do is provide medical care."

Still, officials at one of the project's supporters, the National Science Foundation, wondered: How can you study health conditions while simultaneously altering them? Dr. Kaplan and Dr. Gurven said they convinced the foundation and others that the kind of medical care they administer—sporadic treatment for parasites, ibuprofen for headaches, stitches for machete wounds—does not taint data on chronic, long-term disease. . . .

Researchers study the Tsimane in the Bolivian Amazon.

About 4 to 6 percent of the Tsimane die before age 1, according to the project's unpublished estimates. (That's down from 12 percent in 2002, when Dr. Kaplan and Dr. Gurven began their work; reductions in child and maternal mortality have been the team's most notable public health contribution.) About 15 percent die before age 5. . . .

Dr. Gurven said the researchers repeatedly explain what they are doing. Every patient must give oral consent, and all are shown a video about where their blood goes for testing. . . .

nations believe they have always occupied the region where the skeleton was found. In their view, Kennewick Man was an ancestor, whom they wanted to rebury with dignity and without contamination from scientific testing.

In 2002, U.S. Magistrate Judge John Jelderks ruled that the Kennewick remains could be subjected to scientific study. The judge found little evidence linking the Kennewick find to any identifiable contemporary group or culture. He suggested that the culture to which Kennewick belonged may have ended thousands of years ago. The ruling, later backed by a federal appeals court, cleared the way for the scientists to begin their ongoing study (see Burke et al. 2008; Egan 2005; Walker and Owsley 2012).

## The Code of Ethics

To guide its members in making decisions involving ethics and values, the American Anthropological Association (AAA) offers a Code of Ethics (http://aaanet.org/coe/Code_of_Ethics.pdf.) The most recent code, approved in 2012, points out that anthropologists have obligations to their scholarly field, to the wider society and culture, and to the human species, other species, and the environment. Like physicians who take the Hippocratic oath, the anthropologist's first concern should be to do no harm to the people, animals, or artifacts being studied. The stated aim of the AAA code is to offer guidelines and to promote discussion and education, rather than to investigate possible misconduct. The code addresses several contexts in which

A four-stage reconstruction of "Kennewick Man," whose 9,300-year-old remains, discovered in 1996, represent one of the oldest and most complete skeletons ever found in North America.

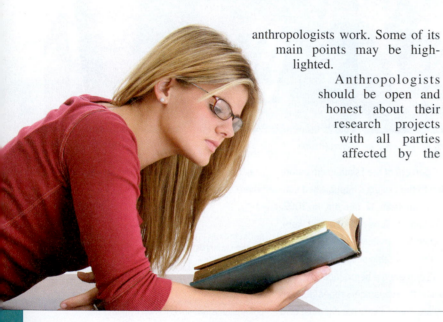

anthropologists work. Some of its main points may be highlighted.

Anthropologists should be open and honest about their research projects with all parties affected by the research. These parties should be informed about the nature, procedures, purpose(s), potential impacts, and source(s) of support for the research. Researchers should pay attention to proper relations between themselves as guests and the host nations and communities where they work. The AAA does not advise anthropologists to avoid taking stands on issues. Indeed, seeking to shape actions and policies may be as ethically justifiable as inaction.

## for REVIEW

## summary

1. As they study the past, archaeologists and biological anthropologists may share research topics and methods, as well as work together in multidisciplinary teams. Remote sensing may be used to locate ancient footpaths, roads, canals, and irrigation systems, which can then be investigated on the ground. Archaeologists combine both local (excavation) and regional (systematic survey) perspectives. Sites are excavated because they are in danger of being destroyed or because they address specific research interests. There are many kinds of archaeology, such as historical, classical, and underwater archaeology.

2. The fossil record is not a representative sample of all the plants and animals that have ever lived. Hard parts, such as bones and teeth, preserve better than soft parts, such as flesh and skin. Stratigraphy and radiometric techniques are used to date fossils.

Carbon-14 ($^{14}$C) dating is most effective with fossils less than 40,000 years old. Potassium–argon (K/A) dating can be used for fossils older than 500,000 years. Dendrochronology provides absolute dates by counting and matching tree rings. Molecular anthropology uses genetic analysis (of DNA sequences) to assess and date evolutionary relationships.

3. Within biological anthropology, bone biology is the study of bone genetics; cell structure; growth, development, and decay; and patterns of movement. Paleopathology is the study of disease and injury in skeletons from archaeological sites. Anthropometry, the measurement of human body parts and dimensions, is done on living people and on skeletal remains from sites. Studies of primates suggest hypotheses about behavior that humans do or do not share with our nearest relatives—as well as with our hominid ancestors.

4. Because science exists in society, and in the context of law and ethics, anthropologists can't study things simply because they happen to be interesting or of scientific value. Anthropologists have obligations to their scholarly field, to the wider society and culture (including that of the host country), and to the human species, other species, and the environment. The AAA Code of Ethics offers ethical guidelines for anthropologists.

## critical thinking

1. Imagine yourself to be an archaeologist researching early farming communities somewhere in the world. What guidelines might you use in choosing sites to investigate? What methods and techniques might you use in your study? What kinds of problems might you encounter during your research?

2. Imagine yourself to be a biological anthropologist working as part of an international team at an African site where early human fossils have been found. What other academic disciplines might be represented on your team? What kinds of jobs would there be for team members, and where would the members be recruited? What might happen to the fossils and other materials that were recovered? Who would be the authors of the scientific papers describing any discovery made by the team?

3. How can fossils be dated when radiometric dating is impossible?

4. This chapter is about how biological anthropologists and archaeologists conduct scientific studies of the past. Science, however, exists in society as well as in the context of law, values, and ethics. What are some examples of how this fact affects the work of biological anthropologists and archaeologists?

5. As this chapter illustrates, many of the ethical issues that affect the work of anthropologists have some legal dimension, whether in their own country, in another country, or even among several nations. Have you thought about law as a possible future career? (If not, think of a friend who has!) Write a convincing argument about why anthropology could be a valuable tool for a lawyer.

# Evolution and Genetics

ON

# THE ORIGIN OF SPECIES

BY MEANS OF NATURAL SELECTION,

OR THE

PRESERVATION OF FAVOURED RACES IN THE STRUGGLE
FOR LIFE.

BY CHARLES DARWIN, M.A.,

FELLOW OF THE ROYAL, GEOLOGICAL, LINNÆAN, ETC., SOCIETIES;
AUTHOR OF 'JOURNAL OF RESEARCHES DURING H. M. S. BEAGLE'S VOYAGE
ROUND THE WORLD.'

LONDON:
JOHN MURRAY, ALBEMARL[E]
1859.

▶ What is evolution,
and how does it
occur?

▶ How does heredity
work, and how is it
studied?

▶ What forces
contribute to genetic
evolution?

Darwin's finches (whose variable beak form suggested natural selection) and the title page of the first edition of
*The Origin of Species.*

# understanding OURSELVES

"Hey, it's all in the genes." We routinely use assumptions about genetic determination to explain, say, why tall parents have tall kids or why obesity runs in families. But just how much do genes really influence our bodies? The genetics behind some physical traits (e.g., blood types) are clear, but the genetic roots of other traits are less so. For example, can you crease or fold your tongue by raising its sides? (See the photo below.) Some people easily can; some people never can; some people who never thought they could can after practicing. An apparent genetic limitation turns out to be more plastic.

Human biology is plastic, but only to a degree. If you're born with blood group O, you've got it for life. The same is true for hemophilia and sickle-cell anemia. Fortunately, cultural (medical) solutions now exist for many genetic disorders. Can you appreciate in yourself or your family any genetic condition for which there has been a cultural (e.g., medical) intervention? Although modern medical advances usually are viewed favorably, some people worry that culture may be intervening too much with intrinsic biological features. Some members of the hearing-impaired community, for example, spurn cochlear implants, viewing them as a threat to a deaf subculture that they hold dear. Plastic surgery, genetic screening, and the possibility of genetic engineering of infants (e.g., "designer babies") concern those who imagine a future in which physical "perfection" might reduce human diversity and increase socioeconomic inequality.

Even as our culture struggles with issues of medically manipulated biological plasticity, many people still question the long-term plasticity of the human genome, a process known as evolution. Most basically, evolution is the idea that all living organisms come from ancestors that were different in some way. The oft-heard statement "evolution is only a theory" suggests to the nonscientist that evolution hasn't been proven. Scientists, however, use the term *theory*

Tongue rolling—a genetic trait, at least partially, which this dad has transmitted to his son.

differently—to refer to an interpretive framework that helps us understand the natural world. In science, evolution is both a theory and a fact. As a *scientific theory*, evolution is a central organizing principle of modern biology and anthropology. Evolution also is a fact. The following are examples of evolutionary facts: (1) All living forms come from older or previous living forms. (2) Birds arose from nonbirds; humans arose from nonhumans; and neither birds nor humans existed 250 million years ago. (3) Major ancient life forms (e.g., dinosaurs) are no longer around. (4) New life forms, such as viruses, are evolving right now. (5) Natural processes help us understand the origins and history of plants and animals, including humans and diseases.

What alternatives to evolution have you heard about? Are those scientific theories? Should they be taught in science classes? Do viruses mutate? Should people who reject evolution still get flu shots?

## EVOLUTION

Compared with other animals, humans have uniquely varied ways—cultural and biological—of adapting to environmental stresses. Exemplifying cultural adaptation, we manipulate our artifacts and behavior in response to environmental conditions. Contemporary North Americans turn up thermostats or travel to Florida in the winter. We turn on fire hydrants, swim, or ride in air-conditioned cars from New York City to Maine to escape the summer's heat. Although such reliance on culture has increased in the course of human evolution, people haven't stopped adapting biologically. As in other species, human populations adapt genetically in response to environmental forces, and individuals react physiologically to stresses. Thus, when we work in the midday sun, sweating occurs spontaneously, cooling the skin and reducing the temperature of subsurface blood vessels.

We are ready now for a more detailed look at the principles that determine human biological adaptation, variation, and change.

During the 18th century, many scholars became interested in biological diversity, human origins, and our position within the classification of plants and animals. At that time, the commonly accepted explanation for the origin of species came from Genesis, the first book of the Bible: God had created all life during six days of Creation. According to *creationism*, biological similarities and differences originated at the Creation. Characteristics of life forms were seen as immutable; they could not change. Through calculations based on genealogies in the Bible, the biblical scholars James Ussher and John Lightfoot even claimed to trace the Creation to a very specific time: October 23, 4004 B.C., at 9 A.M.

Carolus Linnaeus (1707–1778) developed the first comprehensive and still influential classification, or taxonomy, of plants and animals. He grouped life forms on the basis of similarities and differences in their physical characteristics. He used traits such as the presence of a backbone to distinguish vertebrates from invertebrates and the presence of mammary glands to distinguish mammals from birds. Linnaeus viewed the differences between life forms as part of the Creator's orderly plan. Biological similarities and differences, he thought, had been established at the time of Creation and had not changed.

Fossil discoveries during the 18th and 19th centuries raised doubts about creationism. Fossils showed that different kinds of life had once existed. If all life had originated at the same time, why weren't ancient species still around? Why weren't contemporary plants and animals found in the fossil record? A modified explanation combining creationism with *catastrophism* arose to replace the original doctrine. In this view, fires, floods, and other catastrophes, including the biblical flood involving Noah's ark, had destroyed ancient species. After each destructive event, God had created again, leading to contemporary species. How did the catastrophists explain certain clear similarities between fossils and modern animals? They argued that some

According to creationism, all life originated during the six days of Creation described in the Bible. Catastrophism proposed that fires and floods, including the biblical deluge involving Noah's ark (depicted in this painting by the American artist Edward Hicks), destroyed certain species. Note that creationism is not a scientific theory.

ancient species had managed to survive in isolated areas. For example, after the biblical flood, the progeny of the animals saved on Noah's ark spread throughout the world. (This chapter's "Appreciating Diversity" on p. 79 discusses a recent approach called "intelligent design," which has been judged to be a secular repackaging of old-time "creationism.")

## Theory and Fact

The alternative to creationism and catastrophism was *transformism,* also called **evolution.** Evolutionists believe that species arise from others through a long and gradual process of transformation, or descent with modification. Charles Darwin became the best known of the evolutionists. However, he was influenced by earlier scholars, including his own grandfather. In a book called *Zoonomia* published in 1794, Erasmus Darwin had proclaimed the common ancestry of all animal species.

Charles Darwin also was influenced by Sir Charles Lyell, the father of geology (see Eldredge and Pearson 2010). During Darwin's famous voyage to South America aboard the *Beagle,* he read Lyell's influential book *Principles of Geology* (1837/1969), which exposed him to Lyell's principle of **uniformitarianism.** Uniformitarianism states that the present is the key to the past. Explanations for past events should be sought in the long-term action of ordinary forces that still operate today. Thus, natural forces (rainfall, soil deposition, earthquakes, and volcanic action) gradually have built and modified geological features such as mountain ranges. The Earth's structure has been transformed gradually through natural forces operating for millions of years.

Uniformitarianism was a necessary building block for evolutionary theory. It cast serious doubt on the belief that the world was only 6,000 years old. It would take much longer than that for such ordinary forces as rain and wind to produce major geological changes. The longer time span also allowed enough time for the biological changes that fossil discoveries were revealing. Darwin applied the ideas of uniformitarianism and long-term transformation to living things. He argued that all life forms are related and that the number of species has increased over time.

Charles Darwin provided a theoretical framework for understanding evolution. He offered natural selection as a powerful evolutionary mechanism that could explain the origin of species, biological diversity, and similarities among related life forms. Darwin proposed a *theory of evolution* in the strict sense. A *theory* is a set of ideas formulated (by reasoning from known facts) to explain something. The main value of a theory is to promote new understanding. A theory suggests patterns, connections, and relationships that may be confirmed by new research. The *fact* of evolution (that evolution has occurred) was known earlier, for example, by Erasmus Darwin. The *theory* of evolution, through

natural selection (*how* evolution occurred), was Darwin's major contribution. Actually, natural selection wasn't Darwin's unique discovery. Working independently, the naturalist Alfred Russel Wallace had reached a similar conclusion (Shermer 2011; Smith and Beccaloni 2010)). In a joint paper read to London's Linnaean Society in 1858, Darwin and Wallace made their discovery public. Darwin's book *On the Origin of Species* (1859/2009) offered much fuller documentation.

**Natural selection** is the process by which the forms most fit to survive and reproduce in a given environment do so in greater numbers than others in the same population. Natural selection operates when there is competition among members of the population for strategic resources (those necessary for life) such as food and space. Individuals also compete for mates. More than survival of the fittest, natural selection is differential reproductive success. You can win the competition for food and space, but without a mate you have no impact on the future of the species.

For natural selection to work on a particular population, there must be variety within that population, as there always is. The giraffe's neck can illustrate how natural selection works on variety within a population. In any group of giraffes, there always is variation in neck length. When food is adequate, the animals have no problem feeding themselves. But when there is pressure on strategic resources, so that dietary foliage is not as abundant as usual, giraffes with longer necks have an advantage. They can feed off the higher branches. If this ability permits longer-necked giraffes to survive and reproduce even slightly more effectively than shorter-necked ones, giraffes with longer necks will transmit more of their genetic material to future generations than will giraffes with shorter necks.

An incorrect alternative to this (Darwinian) explanation would be the *inheritance of acquired characteristics.* That is the idea that in each generation, individual giraffes strain their necks to reach just a bit higher. This straining somehow modifies their genetic material. Over generations of strain, the average neck gradually gets longer through the accumulation of small increments of neck length acquired during the lifetime of each generation of giraffes. This is not how evolution works. If it did work in this way, weight lifters could expect to produce especially muscular babies. Workouts that promise no gain without the pain apply to the physical development of individuals, not species. Instead, evolution works as the process of natural selection takes advantage of the variety that is already present in a population. That's how giraffes got their necks.

Evolution through natural selection continues today. For example, in human populations there is differential resistance to disease, as we'll see in the later discussion of sickle-cell anemia. One classic recent example of natural selection is the peppered moth, which can be light or dark (in either case with

**natural selection**
Selection of favored forms through differential reproductive success.

**evolution**
Transformation of species; descent with modification.

**uniformitarianism**
Belief that natural forces at work today also explain past events.

Contrast the speckled (peppered) moth on the left with the darker one on the right. Which environment would favor each of these variants?

black speckles, thus the name "peppered"). A change in this species illustrates recent natural selection (in our own industrial age) through what has been called *industrial melanism*. Great Britain's industrialization changed the environment to favor darker moths (those with more melanin) rather than the lighter-colored ones that were favored previously. During the 1800s industrial pollution increased; soot coated buildings and trees, turning them a darker color. The previously typical peppered moth, which had a light color, now stood out against the dark backgrounds of sooty buildings and trees. Such light-colored moths were easily visible to their predators. Through mutations a new strain of peppered moth, with a darker phenotype, was favored. Because these darker moths were fitter—that is, harder to detect—in polluted environments, they survived and reproduced in greater numbers than lighter moths did. We see how natural selection may favor darker moths in polluted environments and lighter-colored moths in nonindustrial or less polluted environments because of their variant abilities to merge in with their environmental colors and thus avoid predators.

The goal of science is to increase understanding by *explaining* things. A scientific explanation shows how and why the thing (or class of things) to be understood (e.g., the variation within and among species) depends on other things. Explanations rely on associations and theories. An association is an observed relationship between two or more variables, such as the length of a giraffe's neck and the number of its offspring, or an increase in the frequency of dark moths as industrial pollution spreads. A theory is more general, suggesting or implying associations and attempting to explain them. A thing or an event—for example, the giraffe's long neck—is explained if it illustrates a general principle or association, such as the concept of adaptive advantage. The truth of a scientific statement (e.g., evolution

occurs because of differential reproductive success due to variation within the population) is confirmed by repeated observations. (See "Appreciating Diversity" for a discussion of differences between evolutionary theory and intelligent design.)

## GENETICS

Charles Darwin recognized that for natural selection to operate, there must be variety in the population undergoing selection. Documenting and explaining such variety among humans—human biological diversity—is one of anthropology's major concerns (see Relethford 2013). Genetics, a science that emerged after Darwin, helps us understand the causes of biological variation. We now know that DNA (deoxyribonucleic acid) molecules make up genes and chromosomes, which are basic hereditary units. Biochemical changes (mutations) in DNA provide much of the variety on which natural selection operates. Through sexual reproduction, recombination of the genetic traits of mother and father in each generation leads to new arrangements of the hereditary units received from each parent. Such genetic recombination also adds variety on which natural selection may operate.

*Mendelian genetics* studies the ways in which chromosomes transmit genes across the generations. *Biochemical genetics* examines structure, function, and changes in DNA. **Population genetics** investigates natural selection and other causes of genetic variation, stability, and change in breeding populations.

### Mendel's Experiments

In 1856, in a monastery garden, the Austrian monk Gregor Mendel began a series of experiments that were to reveal the basic principles of genetics. Mendel studied the inheritance of seven contrasting

**population genetics**
Field that studies genetics of breeding populations.

# appreciating DIVERSITY

## Intelligent Design versus Evolutionary Theory

Evolutionary theory is basic to understanding and appreciating human diversity. Contemporary humans, members of the species *Homo sapiens,* represent one branch in the tree of life. Scientists, who seek natural rather than supernatural explanations, use evolutionary theory to explain how humans evolved from ancestors that were not human. Evolutionary theory also is used to explain biological diversity among contemporary and recent human beings. One proposed alternative to evolution, known as "intelligent design (ID)," is not a scientific theory. In a 2005 ruling (the most recent definitive one on this issue), a federal district judge ruled that ID no longer could be taught in biology classes in Pennsylvania's Dover public school district. The judge found that Dover school board members had violated the U.S. Constitution by requiring their schools' biology curriculum to include the notion that life on Earth was produced by an unspecified intelligent designer. Before this ruling, administrators had been required to read a statement in biology classes asserting that evolution was a theory, not a fact; that the evidence for evolution had gaps; and that ID offered an alternative explanation laid out in a book (purchased by church funds) in the school library. According to the judge (a Republican appointed by President George W. Bush), that statement amounted to an endorsement of religion. It could cause students to doubt a well-established scientific theory by presenting a religious alternative masquerading as a scientific theory (see *New York Times* 2005, p. A32).

The Dover school board policy, adopted in October 2004, was believed to have been the first of its kind in the United States. The school board's attorneys claimed that board members were seeking to improve science education by exposing students to alternatives to Charles Darwin's theory that evolution occurs through natural selection. ID proponents argued that evolutionary theory can't fully explain complex life forms. Their opponents contended that ID amounts to a secular repackaging of creationism, which courts have ruled cannot be taught in public schools. The Pennsylvania judge agreed: The secular purposes claimed by the board were a pretext for the board's real purpose—to promote religion in public schools.

ID advocates have since been voted off the Dover school board. Although the new board planned to remove ID from science classes, interested students could still learn about ID in an elective course on comparative religion. ID did not belong in the *science* curriculum, the judge ruled, because it is "a religious view, a mere relabeling of creationism and not a scientific theory" (*New York Times* 2005, p. A32).

The ID movement asserts that life forms are too complex to have been formed by natural processes and must have been created by a higher intelligence. The fundamental claim of intelligent design proponents, such as William A. Dembski, is that "there are natural systems that cannot be adequately explained in terms of undirected natural forces and that exhibit features which in any other circumstance we would attribute to intelligence" (Dembski 2004). The source of this intelligence never is identified officially. But since the naturalness of the design is denied, its supernaturalness would seem to be assumed. By injecting ID into the science curriculum, the judge ruled, Dover's board was unconstitutionally endorsing a religious view that advances "a particular version of Christianity" (*New York Times* 2005, p. A32).

The Pennsylvania court case thoroughly examined the claim that ID was science. After a six-week trial featuring hours of expert testimony, that claim was rejected. Echoing the overwhelming majority of scientists, the judge found that ID violated the ground rules of science. It relied on supernatural, rather than natural, causation and made assertions that could not be tested or proved wrong (falsified).

Evolution as a *scientific theory* (as defined in the text) is a central organizing principle of modern biology and anthropology. Evolution also is a *fact.* There is absolutely no doubt that biological evolution has occurred and still occurs. To be sure, biologists and anthropologists do debate details involving evolutionary processes and the relative importance of different evolutionary mechanisms. But they accept certain facts: "It is a *fact* that the earth with liquid water is more than 3.6 billion years old. It is a *fact* that cellular life has been around for at least half of that period and that organized multicellular life is at least 800 million years old. It is a *fact* that major life forms now on earth were not at all represented in the past. There were no birds or mammals 250 million years ago. It is a *fact* that major life forms of the past are no longer living. There used to be dinosaurs . . . and there are none now. It is a *fact* that all living forms come from previous living forms. Therefore, all present forms of life arose from ancestral forms that were different. Birds arose from nonbirds and humans from nonhumans. No person who pretends to any understanding of the natural world can deny these facts any more than she or he can deny that the earth is round, rotates on its axis, and revolves around the sun" (Lewontin 1981, quoted in Moran 1993).

One key feature of science is to recognize the tentativeness and uncertainty of knowledge and understanding, which scientists try to improve. As they work to refine theories and to provide accurate explanations, scientists strive for objectivity and impartiality (trying to reduce the influence of the scientist, including his or her personal beliefs and actions). Science has many limitations and is not the only way we have of understanding things. Certainly, the study of religion is another path to understanding. But the goals of objectivity and impartiality do help distinguish science from ways of knowing that are more biased, more rigid, and more dogmatic.

Charles Darwin (1809–1882), the English naturalist made famous by his theory of evolution by means of natural selection.

Alfred Russel Wallace (1823–1913), the Welsh-born British naturalist who independently arrived at a theory of evolution similar to that of Charles Darwin.

**dominant**
Term describing an allele that masks another allele in a heterozygote.

**recessive**
Term describing a genetic trait masked by a dominant trait.

**chromosomes**
Paired lengths of DNA, composed of multiple genes.

**gene**
Place (locus) on a chromosome that determines a particular trait.

Gregor Mendel, the father of genetics.

traits in pea plants. For each trait there were only two forms. For example, plants were either tall (6 to 7 feet [1.8 to 2.1 meters]) or short (9 to 18 inches [23 to 46 centimeters]), with no intermediate forms. The ripe seeds could be either smooth and round, or wrinkled. The peas could be either yellow or green, again with no intermediate colors.

When Mendel began his experiments, one of the prevailing beliefs about heredity was what has been called the "paint-pot" theory. According to this theory, the traits of the two parents blended in their children much as two pigments are blended in a can of paint. Children were therefore a unique mixture of their parents, and when these children married and reproduced, their traits would inextricably blend with those of their mates. However, prevailing notions about heredity also recognized that occasionally the traits of one parent might swamp those of the other. If children looked far more like their mother than their father, people might say that her "blood" was stronger than his. Occasionally, too, there

would be a "throwback," a child who was the image of his or her grandparent or who possessed a distinctive chin or nose characteristic of a whole line of descent.

Through his experiments with pea plants, Mendel discovered that heredity is determined by discrete particles, or units. Although traits could disappear in one generation, they reemerged in their original form in later generations. For example, Mendel crossbred pure strains of tall and short plants. Their offspring were all tall. This was the first descending, or first filial, generation, designated $F_1$. Mendel then interbred the plants of the $F_1$ generation to produce a generation of grandchildren, the $F_2$ generation (Figure 5.1). In this generation, short plants reappeared. Among thousands of plants in the $F_2$ generation, there was approximately one short plant for every three tall ones.

From similar results with the other six traits, Mendel concluded that although a **dominant** form could mask the other form in *hybrid,* or mixed, individuals, the dominated trait—the **recessive**—was not destroyed; it wasn't even changed. Recessive traits would appear in unaltered form in later generations because genetic traits were inherited as discrete units.

| Trait Exhibited by F₁ Hybrids | F₂ Generation (produced by crossbreeding F₁ hybrids) | |
|---|---|---|
| | Exhibit Dominant Trait | Exhibit Recessive Trait |
| Smooth seed shape | Smooth | Wrinkled |
| | 3 + | : 1 |
| Yellow seed interior | Yellow | Green |
| | 3 + | : 1 |
| Gray seed coat | Gray | White |
| | 3 + | : 1 |
| Inflated pod | Inflated | Pinched |
| | 3 + | : 1 |
| Green pod | Green | Yellow |
| | 3 + | : 1 |
| Axial pod | Axial | Terminal |
| | 3 + | : 1 |
| Tall stem | Tall | Short |
| | 3 + | : 1 |
| | Offspring exhibit dominant or recessive traits in ratio of 3:1. | |

**FIGURE 5.1** Mendel's Second Set of Experiments with Pea Plants.
Dominant colors are shown unless otherwise indicated.

**FIGURE 5.2** Simplified Representation of a Normal Chromosome Pair.
Letters indicate genes; superscripts indicate alleles.

| | F₁ | | F₂ | |
|---|---|---|---|---|
| | t | t | T | t |
| T | Tt | Tt | TT | Tt |
| t | Tt | Tt | tT | tt |
| Genotypic ratio | 0:4:0 | | 1:2:1 | |
| Phenotypic ratio | 4:0 | | 3:1 | |

**FIGURE 5.3** Punnett Squares of a Homozygous Cross and a Heterozygous Cross.
These squares show how phenotypic ratios of the F₁ and F₂ generations are generated. Colors show genotypes.

These basic genetic units that Mendel described were factors (now called genes or alleles) located on **chromosomes.** Chromosomes are arranged in matching (homologous) pairs. Humans have 46 chromosomes, arranged in 23 pairs, one in each pair from the father and the other from the mother.

For simplicity, a chromosome may be pictured as a surface (see Figure 5.2) with several positions, to each of which we assign a lowercase letter. Each position is a **gene.** Each gene determines, wholly or partially, a particular biological trait, such as whether one's blood is A, B, or O. **Alleles** (for example, $b^1$ and $b^2$ in Figure 5.2) are biochemically different forms of a given gene. In humans, A, B, AB, and O blood types reflect different combinations of alleles of a particular gene.

In Mendel's experiments, the seven contrasting traits were determined by genes on seven different pairs of chromosomes. The gene for height occurred in one of the seven pairs. When Mendel crossbred pure tall and pure short plants to produce his F₁ generation, each of the offspring received an allele for tallness (T) from one parent and one for shortness (t)

from the other. These offspring were mixed, or **heterozygous,** with respect to height; each had two dissimilar alleles of that gene. Their parents, in contrast, had been **homozygous,** possessing two identical alleles of that gene (see Hartl 2014).

In the next generation (F₂), after the mixed plants were interbred, short plants reappeared in the ratio of one short to three talls. Because shorts only produced shorts, Mendel knew they were genetically pure. Another fourth of the F₂ plants produced only talls. The remaining half, like the F₁ generation, were heterozygous; when interbred, they produced three talls for each short. (See Figure 5.3.)

Dominance produces a distinction between **genotype,** or hereditary makeup, and **phenotype,** or expressed physical characteristics. Genotype is what you really are genetically; phenotype is what you appear as. Mendel's peas had three genotypes—TT, Tt, and tt—but only two phenotypes—tall and short. Because of dominance, the heterozygous plants were just as tall as the genetically pure tall ones. How do Mendel's discoveries apply to humans? Although

**allele**
A variant of a particular gene.

**heterozygous**
Having dissimilar alleles of a given gene.

**homozygous**
Having identical alleles of a given gene.

**genotype**
An organism's hereditary makeup.

**phenotype**
An organism's evident biological traits.

Parent I

| | A | B | O |
|---|---|---|---|
| **A** | AA(A) | AB(AB) | AO(A) |
| **B** | AB(AB) | BB(B) | BO(B) |
| **O** | AO(A) | BO(B) | OO(O) |

Parent II

**FIGURE 5.4** Determinants of Phenotypes (Blood Groups) in the ABO System.
The four phenotypes—A, B, AB, and O—are indicated in parentheses and by color.

some of our genetic traits follow Mendelian laws, with only two forms—dominant and recessive—other traits are determined differently. For instance, three alleles determine whether our blood type is A, B, AB, or O. People with two alleles for type O have that blood type. However, if they receive a gene for either A or B from one parent and one for O from the other, they will have blood type A or B. In other words, A and B are both dominant over O. A and B are said to be *codominant*. If people inherit a gene for A from one parent and one for B from the other, they will have type AB blood, which is chemically different from the other varieties, A, B, and O.

These three alleles produce four phenotypes—A, B, AB, and O—and six different genotypes—OO, AO, BO, AA, BB, and AB (Figure 5.4). There are fewer phenotypes than genotypes because O is recessive to both A and B.

## Independent Assortment and Recombination

Through additional experiments, Mendel also formulated his law of **independent assortment.** He discovered that traits are inherited independently of one another. For example, he bred pure round yellow peas with pure wrinkled green ones. All the $F_1$ generation peas were round and yellow, the dominant forms. But when Mendel interbred the $F_1$ generation to produce the $F_2$, four phenotypes turned up. Round greens and wrinkled yellows had been added to the original round yellows and wrinkled greens.

The independent assortment and recombination of genetic traits provide one of the main ways by which variety is produced in any population. *Recombination* is important in biological evolution because it creates new types on which natural selection can operate.

## BIOCHEMICAL, OR MOLECULAR, GENETICS

If, as in Mendel's experiments, the same genetic traits always appeared in predictable ratios across the generations, there would be continuity rather than

change. There would be no evolution. Various kinds of mutations produce the variety on which natural selection depends. Since Mendel's time, scientists have learned about **mutations**—changes in the DNA molecules of which genes and chromosomes are built. Mendel demonstrated that variety is produced by genetic recombination. Mutation, however, is even more important as a source of new biochemical forms on which natural selection may operate.

DNA does several things basic to life. DNA can copy itself, forming new cells, replacing old ones, and producing the sex cells, or *gametes,* that make new generations. DNA's chemical structure also guides the body's production of proteins—enzymes, antigens, antibodies, hormones, and hundreds of others.

The DNA molecule is a double helix (Crick 1962/1968; Watson 1970). Imagine it as a small rubber ladder that you can twist into a spiral. Its sides are held together by chemical bonds between four bases: thymine (T), adenine (A), cytosine (C), and guanine (G). DNA's duplication leads to ordinary cell division, as shown in Figure 5.5.

In protein building, another molecule, RNA, carries DNA's message from the cell's nucleus to its *cytoplasm* (outer area). The structure of RNA, with paired bases, matches that of DNA. This permits

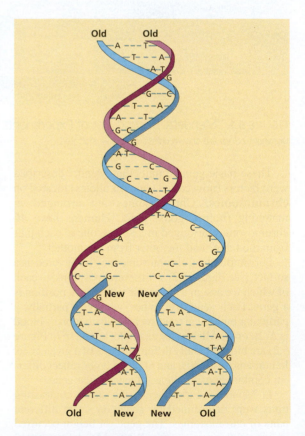

**FIGURE 5.5** DNA Replication.
A double-stranded DNA molecule "unzips," and a new strand forms on each of the old ones, producing two molecules, and eventually two cells, each identical to the first.

RNA to carry a message from DNA in the cell nucleus to guide the construction of proteins in the cytoplasm. A protein, which is a chain of amino acids, is constructed by "reading" a length of RNA. RNA's bases are read as three-letter "words," called *triplets*—for example, AAG. (Because DNA and RNA have four bases, which can occur anywhere in the "word," there are $4 \times 4 \times 4 = 64$ possible triplets.) Each triplet "calls" a particular amino acid, although there is some redundancy; for example, AAA and AAG both call for the amino acid lysine. A protein is made as amino acids are assembled in the proper sequence.

Thus, proteins are built following instructions sent by DNA, with RNA's assistance. In this way, DNA, the basic *hereditary* material, also initiates and guides the construction of hundreds of proteins necessary for bodily growth, maintenance, and repair (see Strachan and Read 2011; Sudbery and Sudbery 2009).

## Cell Division

An organism develops from a fertilized egg, or *zygote,* created by the union of two sex cells (gametes), a sperm from the father and an egg (ovum) from the mother. The zygote grows rapidly through **mitosis,** or ordinary cell division, which continues as the organism grows. Mistakes in this process of cell division, including chromosomal breaks and rearrangements, can cause diseases such as cancer.

The special process by which sex cells are produced is called **meiosis.** Unlike ordinary cell division, in which two cells emerge from one, in meiosis four cells are produced from one. Each has half the genetic material of the original cell. In human meiosis, four cells, each with 23 individual chromosomes, are produced from an original cell with 23 pairs.

A computer image of X and Y chromosomes. Which one is longer?

With fertilization of egg by sperm, the father's 23 chromosomes combine with the mother's 23 to re-create the pairs in every generation. However, the chromosomes sort independently, so that a child's genotype is a random combination of the DNA of its four grandparents. It is conceivable that one grandparent will contribute very little to his or her grandchild's heredity. Independent assortment of chromosomes is a major source of variety, because the parents' genotypes can be assorted in $2^{23}$, or more than eight million, different ways.

## Crossing Over

Another source of variety is **crossing over.** Before fertilization, early in meiosis, as a sperm or an egg is being formed, paired chromosomes temporarily intertwine as they duplicate themselves. As they do this, they often exchange lengths of their DNA (Figure 5.6). Crossovers are the sites where homologous chromosomes have exchanged segments by breakage and reattachment.

Because of crossing over, each new chromosome is partially different from either member of the original pair. As a person produces sex cells, replacing, say, part of a chromosome one has received from

**mitosis**
Ordinary cell division.

**meiosis**
Process by which sex cells are produced.

**crossing over**
Homologous chromosomes intertwine and exchange DNA.

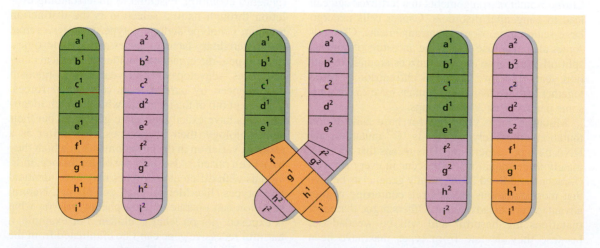

**FIGURE 5.6** Crossing Over.
In the first phase of meiosis, homologous chromosomes intertwine as they duplicate themselves. As they do this, they often exchange lengths of their DNA, as shown here. This is known as crossing over. Note that the lower lengths of the original pair now differ. Each chromosome is therefore chemically different from either member of the original pair.

one's mother with a corresponding section of the homologous chromosome from one's father, crossing over partially contradicts Mendel's law of independent assortment and makes a new combination of genetic material available to the offspring. Because crossing over can occur with any chromosome pair, it is an important source of variety.

## Mutation

Mutations are the most important source of variety on which natural selection depends and operates. The simplest mutation results from substitution of just one base in a triplet by another. (This is called a *base substitution mutation.*) If such a mutation occurs in a sex cell that joins with another in a fertilized egg, the new organism will carry the mutation in every cell. As DNA directs protein building, a protein different from that produced by the nonmutant parent *may* be produced in the child. The child's protein building will differ from the parent's only if the new base codes for a different amino acid. Because the same amino acid can be coded by more than one triplet, a base substitution mutation doesn't always produce a different protein. However, the abnormal protein associated with the hereditary disease sickle-cell anemia is caused by just such a difference in a single base between normal individuals and those afflicted with the disease.

Another form of mutation is *chromosomal rearrangement.* Pieces of a chromosome can break off, turn around and reattach, or migrate someplace else on that chromosome. This can occur in the sex cell, or in the fertilized egg or the growing organism, during mitosis. A mismatch of chromosomes resulting from rearrangement can lead to speciation (the formation of new species). Scientists often find that separate but closely related species living in overlapping ranges cannot interbreed because their chromosomes, due to rearrangement, no longer match. Chromosomal rearrangements in a fertilized egg can lead to congenital disorders. Cancer cells undergo large-scale chromosomal rearrangements. Chromosomes also may fuse. When the ancestors of humans split off from those of chimpanzees around six million years ago, two ancestral chromosomes fused together in the human line. Humans have 23 chromosome pairs, versus 24 for chimps.

Mutation rates vary, but for base substitution mutations, the likely average is $10^{29}$ mutations per DNA base per generation. This means that approximately three mutations will occur in every sex cell (Strachan and Read 2011). Many geneticists believe that most mutations are neutral, conferring neither advantage nor disadvantage. Others argue that most mutations are harmful and will be weeded out because they deviate from types that have been selected over the generations. However, if the selective forces affecting a population change, mutations in its gene pool may acquire an adaptive advantage they lacked in the old environment.

Evolution depends on mutations as a major source of genetically transmitted variety, raw material on which natural selection can work. (Crossing over, independent assortment, and chromosomal recombination are other sources.) Alterations in genes and chromosomes may result in entirely new types of organisms, which may demonstrate some new selective advantage. Variants produced through mutation can be especially significant if there is a change in the environment. They may prove to have an advantage they lacked in the old environment. The spread of the allele that determines sickle-cell anemia provides one example.

## POPULATION GENETICS AND MECHANISMS OF GENETIC EVOLUTION

Population genetics studies the stable and changing populations in which most breeding normally takes place (see Gillespie 2004; Hamilton 2009; Hartl 2014). The term **gene pool** refers to all the alleles, genes, chromosomes, and genotypes within a breeding population—the "pool" of genetic material available. When population geneticists use the term *evolution,* they have a more specific definition in mind than the one given earlier ("descent with modification over the generations"). For geneticists, **genetic evolution** is defined as a change in gene frequency—that is, in the frequency of alleles in a breeding population from generation to generation. Any factor that contributes to such a change can be considered a mechanism of genetic evolution. Those mechanisms include natural selection, mutation (already examined), random genetic drift, and gene flow (see Mayr 2001; Relethford 2012).

## Natural Selection

Natural selection remains the best explanation for (genetic) evolution. Essential to understanding evolution through natural selection is the distinction between genotype and phenotype. *Genotype* refers just to hereditary factors—genes and chromosomes. Phenotype—the organism's evident biological characteristics—develops over the years as the organism is influenced by particular environmental forces. (See the photo of the identical twins on p. 85. Identical twins have exactly the same genotype, but their actual biology, their phenotypes, may differ as a result of variation in the environments in which they have been raised.) Also, because of dominance, individuals with different genotypes may have identical phenotypes (like Mendel's tall pea plants). Natural selection can operate only on phenotype—on what is exposed, not on what is hidden. For example, a harmful recessive gene can't be eliminated from the gene pool if it is masked by a favored dominant.

Phenotype includes not only outward physical appearance but also internal organs, tissues and cells, and physiological processes and systems. Many

(See the photo of the identical twins on p. 85.

**gene pool**
All the genetic material in a breeding population.

**genetic evolution**
Change in gene (allele) frequency in a breeding population.

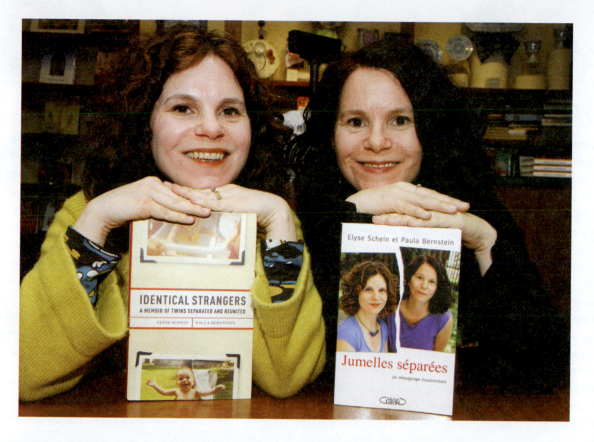

Paula Bernstein and Elyse Schein, authors of *Identical Strangers: A Memoir of Twins Separated and Reunited.* These identical twins, adopted by different middle-class families in the 1960s, were the victims of a New York adoption agency's theory that identical twins would flourish if raised separately. Schein and Bernstein were reunited in 2004.

biological reactions to foods, disease, heat, cold, sunlight, and other environmental factors are not automatic, genetically programmed responses but the product of years of exposure to particular environmental stresses. Human biology is not set at birth but has considerable *plasticity.* That is, it is changeable, being affected by the environmental forces, such as diet and altitude, that we experience as we grow up (see Bogin 2001).

The environment works on the genotype to build the phenotype, and certain phenotypes do better in some environments than other phenotypes do. However, remember that favored phenotypes can be produced by different genotypes. Because natural selection works only on genes that are expressed, maladaptive recessives can be removed only when they occur in homozygous form. When a heterozygote carries a maladaptive recessive, its effects are masked by the favored dominant. The process of perfecting the fit between organisms and their environment is gradual.

## Directional Selection

After several generations of selection, gene frequencies will change. Adaptation through natural selection will have occurred. Once that happens, those traits that have proved to be the most **adaptive** (favored by natural selection) in that environment will be selected again and again from generation to generation. Given such *directional selection,* or long-term selection of the same trait(s), maladaptive recessive alleles will be removed from the gene pool.

Directional selection will continue as long as environmental forces stay the same. However, if the environment changes, new selective forces start working, favoring different phenotypes. This also happens when part of the population colonizes a new environment. Selection in the changed, or new, environment continues until a new equilibrium is reached. Then there is directional selection until another environmental change or migration takes place. Over millions of years, such a process of successive adaptation to a series of environments has led to biological modification and branching. The process of natural selection has led to the tremendous array of plant and animal forms found in the world today.

Selection operates *only* on traits that are present in a population. A favorable mutation *may* occur, but a population doesn't normally come up with a new genotype or phenotype just because one is needed or desirable. Many species have become extinct because they weren't sufficiently varied to adapt to environmental shifts.

There also are differences in the amount of environmental stress that organisms' genetic potential enables them to tolerate. Some species are adapted to a narrow range of environments. They are especially endangered by environmental fluctuation. Others—*Homo sapiens* among them—tolerate much more environmental variation because their genetic potential permits many adaptive possibilities. Humans can adapt rapidly to changing conditions by modifying both biological responses and learned behavior. We don't have to delay adaptation until a favorable mutation appears.

**adaptive**
Favored by natural selection.

# appreciating ANTHROPOLOGY

## H1N1, Anyone?

Anthropology is noteworthy for its holistic and biocultural approaches and its relevance to understanding historic as well as contemporary processes and events. The anthropologists described below view the evolution of disease not just biologically but also in the context of social and political history.

Known to us as a dreaded venereal—sexually transmitted—disease (STD), syphilis apparently originated in the Americas as a nonvenereal bacterium. After it reached Europe, the bacterium mutated into venereal syphilis, which became a major killer during the Renaissance. The same evolutionary principles and mechanisms (e.g., adaptation to new environments and mutation) that operate in the evolution of life in general also apply specifically to the evolution of pathogens that cause disease.

Globalization is an important factor in the spread and mutation of diseases in today's world. The title above suggests one example, the H1N1 virus, which gained attention as a pandemic in 2009–2010, and which continues to mutate today. Also known as swine flu, the virus illustrates the spread of pathogens from animals to humans (and vice versa). Such transmission became much more common after humans domesticated animals and began to live in close proximity to such animals as pigs, poultry, sheep, and cattle.

Columbus, it seems, made another discovery of something that he was not looking for. In a comprehensive genetic study, scientists have found what they say is the strongest evidence yet linking the first European explorers of the New World to the origin of sexually transmitted syphilis. The research, they say, supports the hypothesis that returning explorers introduced organisms leading, in probably modified forms, to the first recorded syphilis epidemic, beginning in Europe in 1493. Earlier traces of syphilis or related diseases had been few and inconclusive in Europe. Yet nonvenereal forms of the diseases were widespread in the American tropics.

Leaders of the new study said the most telling results were that the bacterium causing sexually transmitted syphilis arose relatively recently in humans and was closely related to a strain responsible for the nonvenereal infection known as yaws. The similarity was especially evident, the researchers said, in a variation of the yaws pathogen isolated recently among afflicted children in a remote region of Guyana in South America. . . . The findings suggested Columbus and his men could have carried the nonvenereal tropical bacteria home, where the organisms may have mutated into a more deadly form in the different conditions of Europe.

In the New World, the infecting organisms for nonvenereal syphilis, known as bejel, and yaws were transmitted by skin-to-skin and oral contact, more often in children. The symptoms are lesions primarily on the legs, not on or near the genitals. Kristin N. Harper, a researcher in molecular genetics at Emory University who was the principal investigator in the study, said the findings supported "the hypothesis that syphilis, or some progenitor, came from the New World.". . . Her co-authors included George J. Armelagos, an Emory anthropologist who has studied the origins of syphilis for more than 30 years, and Dr. Michael S. Silverman, a Canadian infectious diseases physician who collected and tested specimens from yaws lesions in Guyana, the only known site today of yaws infections in the Western Hemisphere. The researchers said their study "represents the first attempt to address the problem of the origin of syphilis using molecular genetics, as well as the first source of information regarding the genetic makeup of nonvenereal strains from the Western Hemisphere."

They applied phylogenetics, the study of evolutionary relationships between organisms, in examining 26 geographically disparate strains in the family of Treponema bacteria. Treponema subspecies pallidum is the agent for the scourge of venereal syphilis. The subspecies endemicum causes bejel, usually in hot, arid climates. . . .

John W. Verano, an anthropologist at Tulane, said the findings would "probably not settle the debate" over the origins of venereal syphilis, though most scientists had become convinced that the disease was not transmitted sexually before Europeans made contact with the New World.

---

**sexual selection**
Selection of traits that enhance mating success.

## Sexual Selection

Selection also operates through competition for mates in a breeding population. Males may openly compete for females, or females may choose to mate with particular males because they have desirable traits. Obviously, such traits vary from species to species. Familiar examples include color in birds; male birds, such as cardinals, tend to be more brightly colored than females are. Colorful males have a selective advantage because females like them better. As, over the generations, females have opted for colorful mates, the alleles responsible for

**balanced polymorphism**
Alleles maintain a constant frequency in a population over time.

color have built up in the species. **Sexual selection,** based on differential success in mating, is the term for this process in which certain traits of one sex are selected because of advantages they confer in winning mates.

## Stabilizing Selection

We have seen that natural selection reduces variety in a population through directional selection—by favoring one trait or allele over another. Selective forces also can work to *maintain* variety through *stabilizing selection,* by favoring a **balanced polymorphism,** in

Donald J. Ortner, an anthropologist at the Smithsonian Institution, questioned whether the organisms causing the first European epidemic were actually distinct from others in the treponemal family. "What we are seeing is an organism with a long history, and it is very adaptable to different modes of transmission that produce different manifestations," Dr. Ortner said. . . .

Paleopathologists . . . have for years analyzed skeletons for the bone scars from lesions produced by treponemal diseases, except for the mild form called pinta. In this way, they traced the existence of these infections in the New World back at least 7,000 years. But it has often been difficult to determine the age of the bones and distinguish the different diseases that share symptoms but have different modes of transmission. . . . In her investigation, Ms. Harper studied 22 human Treponemal pallidum strains. The DNA in their genes was sequenced in nearly all cases, examined for changes and eventually used in constructing phylogenetic trees incorporating all variations in the strains.

An Old World yaws subspecies was found to occupy the base of the tree, indicating its ancestral position in the treponemal family, she said. The terminal position of the venereal syphilis subspecies on the tree showed it had diverged most recently from the rest of the bacterial family.

Specimens from two Guyana yaws cases were included in the study, after they were collected and processed by Dr. Silverman. Genetic analysis showed that this yaws strain was the closest known relative to venereal syphilis.

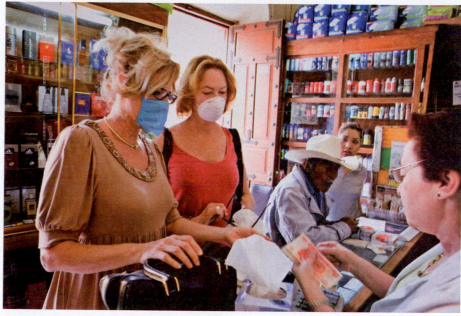

Like earlier diseases, the HINI virus spread (rapidly) within the world system. In spring-summer 2009, people in Mexico bought masks and used hand sanitizers to fend off the flu. About 8,000 foreigners live in the Mexican town of San Miguel Allende, shown here. In this photo two expatriate women carefully purchase items in a local pharmacy. What precautions do they appear to be taking?

If this seemed to solidify the Columbus hypothesis, the researchers cautioned that a "transfer agent between humans and nonhuman primates cannot be ruled out." Dr. Armelagos said research into the origins of syphilis would continue, because "understanding its evolution is important not just for biology, but for understanding social and political history."

Noting that the disease was a major killer in Renaissance Europe, he said, "It could be argued that syphilis is one of the important early examples of globalization and disease, and globalization remains an important factor in emerging diseases."

which the frequencies of two or more alleles of a gene remain constant from generation to generation. This may be because the phenotypes they produce are neutral, or equally favored, or equally opposed by selective forces. Sometimes a particular force favors (or opposes) one allele while a different but equally effective force favors (or opposes) the other allele.

One well-studied example of a balanced polymorphism involves two alleles, $Hb^A$ and $Hb^S$, that affect the production of the beta strain (Hb) of human hemoglobin. Hemoglobin, which is located in our red blood cells, carries oxygen from the lungs to the rest of the body via the circulatory system. The allele that produces normal hemoglobin is $Hb^A$. Another allele, $Hb^S$, produces a different hemoglobin. Individuals who are homozygous for $Hb^S$ suffer from *sickle-cell anemia.* Such anemia, in which the red blood cells are shaped like crescents or sickles (see photo on p. 88), is associated with a disease that usually is fatal. This condition interferes with the blood's ability to store oxygen. It increases the heart's burden by clogging the small blood vessels.

Given the fatal disease associated with $Hb^S$, geneticists were surprised to discover that certain

Sickle cells, magnified 7,400 times. Sickle-cell anemia is a painful disease that affects the red blood cells. The heterozygous phenotype resists both anemia and malaria.

populations in Africa, India, and the Mediterranean had very high frequencies of Hb$^S$. In some West African populations, that frequency is around 20 percent. Researchers eventually discovered that both Hb$^A$ and Hb$^S$ are maintained because selective forces in certain environments favor the heterozygote over either homozygote.

Initially, scientists wondered why, if most Hb$^S$ homozygotes died before they reached reproductive age, the harmful allele hadn't been eliminated. Why was its frequency so high? The answer turned out to lie in the *heterozygote's* greater fitness. Only people who were homozygous for Hb$^S$ died from sickle-cell anemia. Heterozygotes suffered very mild anemia, if

any. On the other hand, although people homozygous for Hb$^A$ did not suffer from anemia, they were much more susceptible to *malaria*—a killer disease that continues to plague *Homo sapiens* in the tropics.

The heterozygote, with one sickle-cell allele and one normal one, was the fittest phenotype for a malarial environment. Heterozygotes have enough abnormal hemoglobin, in which malaria parasites cannot thrive, to protect against malaria. They also have enough normal hemoglobin to fend off sickle-cell anemia. The Hb$^S$ allele has been maintained in these populations because the heterozygotes survived and reproduced in greater numbers than did people with any other phenotype.

The example of the sickle-cell allele demonstrates the relativity of evolution through natural selection: Adaptation and fitness are in relation to specific environments. Traits are not adaptive or maladaptive for all times and places. Even harmful alleles can be selected if heterozygotes have an advantage. Moreover, as the environment changes, favored phenotypes and gene frequencies can change. In malaria-free environments, normal-hemoglobin homozygotes reproduce more effectively than heterozygotes do. With no malaria, the frequency of Hb$^S$ declines because Hb$^S$ homozygotes can't compete in survival and reproduction with the other types. This has happened in areas of West Africa where malaria has been reduced through drainage programs and insecticides. Selection against Hb$^S$ also has occurred in the United States among Americans descended from West Africans. (Compare Figures 5.7 and 5.8 to see the overlap between the geographic distributions of the sickle-call allele and of malaria.)

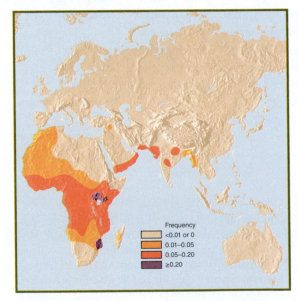

| Frequency | |
|---|---|
| | <0.01 or 0 |
| | 0.01–0.05 |
| | 0.05–0.20 |
| | ≥0.20 |

**FIGURE 5.7**  Geographic Distribution of the Sickle-Cell Allele.

Compare with Figure 5.8.

SOURCE: From Agustín Fuentes, *Biological Anthropology: Concepts and Connections,* 2nd ed., p. 318. Copyright © 2012 by McGraw-Hill Education, LLC. Reprinted with permission.

**FIGURE 5.8**  Regions of the Old World Where Malaria Is Endemic.

Compare Figures 5.7 and 5.8.

SOURCE: From Agustín Fuentes, *Biological Anthropology: Concepts and Connections,* 2nd ed., p. 319. Copyright © 2012 by McGraw-Hill Education, LLC. Reprinted with permission.

# Random Genetic Drift

A second mechanism of genetic evolution is **random genetic drift.** This is a change in allele frequency that results not from natural selection but from chance. To understand why, compare the sorting of alleles to a game involving a bag of 12 marbles, 6 red and 6 blue. In step 1, you draw 6 marbles from the bag. Statistically, your chances of drawing 3 reds and 3 blues are less than those of getting 4 of one color and 2 of the other. Step 2 is to fill a new bag with 12 marbles on the basis of the ratio of marbles you drew in step 1. Assume that you drew 4 reds and 2 blues: The new bag will have 8 red marbles and 4 blue ones. Step 3 is to draw 6 marbles from the new bag. Your chances of drawing blues in step 3 are lower than they were in step 1, and the probability of drawing all reds increases. If you do draw all reds, the next bag (step 4) will have only red marbles.

This game is analogous to random genetic drift operating over the generations. The blue marbles were lost purely by chance. Alleles, too, can be lost by chance rather than because of any disadvantage they confer. Lost alleles can reappear in a gene pool only through mutation.

Although genetic drift can operate in any population, large or small, *fixation* due to drift is more rapid in small populations. *Fixation* refers to the total replacement of blue marbles by red marbles—or, to use a human example, of blue eyes by brown eyes. The history of the human line is characterized by a series of small populations, migrations, and fixation due to genetic drift. One cannot understand human origins, human genetic variation, and a host of other important anthropological topics without recognizing the importance of genetic drift.

# Gene Flow

A third mechanism of genetic evolution is **gene flow,** the exchange of genetic material between populations of the same species. Gene flow, like mutation, works in conjunction with natural selection by providing variety on which selection can work. Gene flow may consist of direct interbreeding between formerly separated populations of the same species (e.g., Europeans, Africans, and Native Americans in the United States), or it may be indirect.

Consider the following hypothetical case (Figure 5.9). In a certain part of the world live six local populations of a certain species. $P_1$ is the westernmost of these populations. $P_2$, which interbreeds with $P_1$, is located 50 miles to the east. $P_2$ also interbreeds with $P_3$, located 50 miles east of $P_2$. Assume that each population interbreeds with, and only with, the adjacent populations. $P_6$ is located 250 miles from $P_1$ and does not directly interbreed with $P_1$, but it is tied to $P_1$ through the chain of interbreeding that ultimately links all six populations.

Assume further that an allele exists in $P_1$ that isn't particularly advantageous in its environment.

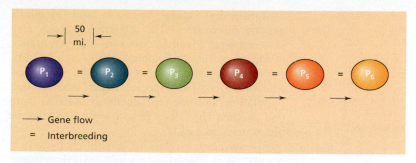

**FIGURE 5.9** *Gene Flow between Local Populations.*
$P_1$–$P_6$ are six local populations of the same species. Each interbreeds (=) only with its neighbor(s). Although members of $P_6$ never interbreed with $P_1$, $P_6$ and $P_1$ are linked through gene flow. Genetic material that originates in $P_1$ eventually will reach $P_6$, and vice versa, as it is passed from one neighboring population to the next. Because they share genetic material in this way, $P_1$–$P_6$ remain members of the same species. In many species, local populations distributed throughout a larger territory than the 250 miles depicted here are linked through gene flow.

Because of gene flow, this allele may be passed on to $P_2$, by it to $P_3$, and so on, until it eventually reaches $P_6$. In $P_6$ or along the way, the allele may encounter an environment in which it does have a selective advantage. If this happens, it may serve, like a new mutation, as raw material on which natural selection can operate.

Alleles are spread through gene flow even when selection is not operating on the allele. In the long run, natural selection works on the variety within a population, whatever its source. Selection and gene flow have worked together to spread the $Hb^S$ allele in Central Africa. Frequencies of $Hb^S$ in Africa reflect not only the intensity of malaria but also the length of time gene flow has been going on (Livingstone 1969).

Gene flow is important in the study of the origin of species. A **species** is a group of related organisms whose members can interbreed to produce offspring that can live and reproduce. A species has to be able to reproduce itself through time. We know that horses and donkeys belong to different species because their offspring cannot meet the test of long-term survival. A horse and a donkey may breed to produce a mule, but mules are sterile. So are the offspring of lions with tigers. Gene flow tends to prevent **speciation**—the formation of new species—unless subgroups of the same species are separated for a sufficient length of time.

When gene flow is interrupted, and isolated subgroups are maintained, new species may arise. Imagine that an environmental barrier arises between $P_3$ and $P_4$, so that they no longer interbreed. If over time, as a result of isolation, $P_1$, $P_2$, and $P_3$ become incapable of interbreeding with the other three populations, speciation will have occurred.

## THE MODERN SYNTHESIS

The currently accepted view of evolution is known as the "modern synthesis." This refers to the synthesis or combination of Darwin's theory of

**random genetic drift**
Genetic change due to chance.

**species**
Population whose members can interbreed to produce offspring that can live and reproduce.

**gene flow**
Exchange of genetic material through interbreeding.

**speciation**
Formation of new species.

**punctuated equilibrium**
Long periods of stability, with occasional evolutionary leaps.

evolution by natural selection and Mendel's genetic discoveries. The modern synthesis also explains what Mendel could not—the inheritance of multifactorial, or complex, traits (e.g., height). According to the modern synthesis, speciation (the formation of new species) occurs when related populations become reproductively isolated from one another. How does genetic evolution lead, or not, to new species?

*Microevolution* refers to genetic changes in a population or species over a few, several, or many generations, but without speciation. *Macroevolution* refers to larger-scale or more significant genetic changes in a population or species, usually over a longer time period, which result in speciation. Indeed, macroevolution is defined as speciation, the divergence of one ancestral species into two (or more) descendant species. Most biologists assume that species develop gradually as successive mutations accumulate in isolated populations, so that eventually the populations are too different to interbreed. But the time and the number of generations required for microevolution to become macroevolution are highly variable.

Modern-day creationists sometimes use a misunderstanding of the contrast between microevolution and macroevolution to comment on evolution. They may say they accept microevolution, such as a change in a species' size or coloring, or as demonstrated in the laboratory or through studies of such traits as the sickle-cell allele. Macroevolution, they claim, by contrast, can't be demonstrated, only inferred from the fossil record.

Note, however, that no degree of phenotypical difference is implied by the term *macroevolution*. A simple chromosomal rearrangement can be sufficient to separate two closely related species whose ranges overlap. They belong to different species not because they are isolated from each other in space but because they cannot hybridize. Although no phenotypic difference is visible between these reproductively isolated species, this is a case of macroevolution rather than microevolution.

To exaggerate the contrast between microevolution and macroevolution would imply, incorrectly, that there are two fundamentally distinct evolutionary processes. Scientists see no such contrast: Microevolution and macroevolution happen in the same way and for the same reasons, reflecting the mechanisms of genetic evolution discussed in this chapter. The modern synthesis recognizes that microevolutionary processes are sufficient to explain macroevolution.

## Punctuated Equilibrium

Charles Darwin saw species as arising from others over time, in a gradual and orderly fashion. Microevolutionary changes would accumulate over the generations to eventually produce macroevolution.

In other words, minor alterations in the gene pool, accumulating generation after generation, would add up to major changes, including speciation, after thousands of years.

The **punctuated equilibrium** model of evolution (see Eldredge 1985; Gould 2007) points to the fact that long periods of stasis (stability), during which species change little, may be interrupted (punctuated) by evolutionary leaps. One reason for such apparent jumps (which are revealed by the fossil record) may be the extinction of one species followed by invasion by a closely related species. For example, a sea species may die out when a shallow body of water dries up, while a closely related species survives in deeper waters. Later, when the sea reinvades the first locale, the protected species extends its range to the first area. Another possibility is that when barriers are removed, a group may replace, rather than succeed, a related one because it has a trait that makes it adaptively fitter in the environment they now share.

When there is a sudden environmental change, rather than such extinction and replacement, another possibility is for the pace of evolution to speed up. Some highly significant mutation(s) or combination of genetic changes may permit the survival of a radically altered species in a new and very different environmental niche. Many scientists believe that the evolution of our hominin ancestors was marked by one or more such evolutionary leaps.

Although species can survive radical environmental shifts, a more common fate is extinction. The Earth has witnessed several mass extinctions—worldwide catastrophes affecting multiple species. The biggest one divided the era of "ancient life" (the Paleozoic) from the era of "middle life" (the Mesozoic). This mass extinction occurred 245 million years ago, when 4.5 million of the Earth's estimated 5 million species (mostly invertebrates) were wiped out. The second-biggest extinction, around 65 million years ago, destroyed the dinosaurs. One explanation for the extinction of the dinosaurs is that a massive, long-lasting cloud of gas and dust arose from the impact of a giant meteorite at the end of the Mesozoic. The cloud blocked solar radiation and therefore photosynthesis, ultimately destroying most plants and the chain of animals that fed on them.

From the fossil record, including the hominin fossil record, we know there are periods of more intense evolutionary change. At the end of the Mesozoic, the extinction of the dinosaurs was accompanied by the rapid spread and speciation of mammals and birds. Speciation responds to many factors, including the rate of environmental change, the speed with which geographic barriers rise or fall, the degree of competition with other species, and the effectiveness of the group's adaptive response.

1. In the 18th century, Carolus Linnaeus developed biological taxonomy. He viewed differences and similarities among organisms as part of God's orderly plan rather than as evidence for evolution. Charles Darwin and Alfred Russel Wallace proposed that natural selection could explain the origin of species, biological diversity, and similarities among related life forms. Natural selection requires variety in the population undergoing selection.

2. Through breeding experiments with peas in 1856, Gregor Mendel discovered that genetic traits pass on as units. These are now known to be chromosomes, which occur in homologous pairs. Alleles, some dominant, some recessive, are the chemically different forms that occur at a given genetic locus. Mendel also formulated the law of independent assortment. Each of the seven traits he studied in peas was inherited independently of all the others. Independent assortment of chromosomes and their recombination provide some of the variety needed for natural selection. But the major source of such variety is mutation, an alteration in the DNA molecules of which genes are made.

3. Biochemical, or molecular, genetics studies structure, function, and changes in genetic material—DNA. Genetic changes that provide variety within a population include base substitution mutations, chromosomal rearrangements, and genetic recombination. Population genetics studies gene frequencies in stable and changing populations. Natural selection is the most important mechanism of evolutionary change. Others include random genetic drift and gene flow. Natural selection works with traits already present in the population. If variety is insufficient to permit adaptation to environmental change, extinction is likely. New types don't appear just because they are needed.

4. One well-documented case of natural selection in contemporary human populations is that of the sickle-cell allele. In homozygous form, the sickle-cell allele, $Hb^S$, produces an abnormal hemoglobin. This clogs the small blood vessels, impairing the blood's capacity to store oxygen. The result is sickle-cell anemia, which usually is fatal. The distribution of $Hb^S$ has been linked to that of malaria. Homozygotes for normal hemoglobin are susceptible to malaria and die in great numbers. Homozygotes for the sickle-cell allele die from anemia. Heterozygotes get only mild anemia and are resistant to malaria. In a malarial environment, the heterozygote has the advantage. This explains why an apparently maladaptive allele is preserved. The preservation of $Hb^A$ and $Hb^S$ alleles within a breeding population is an example of a balanced polymorphism, in which the heterozygote has greater fitness than does either homozygote.

5. Other mechanisms of genetic evolution complement natural selection. Random genetic drift operates most obviously in small populations, where pure chance can easily change allele frequencies. Gene flow and interbreeding keep subgroups of the same species genetically connected and thus impede speciation.

6. The modern synthetic theory of evolution (the modern synthesis) blends the Darwin and Wallace theory of evolution through natural selection with Mendel's discovery of the gene. Microevolution and macroevolution are two ends (short-term and long-term) of a continuum of evolutionary change in which gradually changing allele frequencies in a population eventually can lead to the formation of new species. Punctuated equilibrium theory states that long periods of stasis (stability), during which species change little, are interrupted (punctuated) by evolutionary leaps.

## key terms

adaptive  85

allele  81

balanced polymorphism  87

chromosomes  81

crossing over  83

dominant  80

evolution  77

gene  81

gene flow  89

gene pool  84

genetic evolution  84

genotype  81

heterozygous  81

homozygous  81

independent assortment  82

meiosis  83

mitosis  83

mutation  82

natural selection  77

phenotype  81

population genetics  78

punctuated equilibrium  90

random genetic drift  89

recessive  80

sexual selection  86

speciation  89

species  89

uniformitarianism  77

## critical thinking

1. During the 18th century, many scholars became interested in biological diversity, human origins, and our position within the classification of plants and animals. Why do you think that this interest arose at this time, at least in Europe? Think of historical events that led to the realization that the world is much larger and much more diverse than previously thought.

2. In the context of understanding evolution, why is it important to distinguish between a theory and a fact?

3. Also in the context of understanding evolution, why is it important to distinguish between phenotype and genotype?

4. The strange consequences of mutations have been featured in science fiction books and movies. What is a mutation? What role do they play in evolution? Are they always bad?

# Human Variation and Adaptation

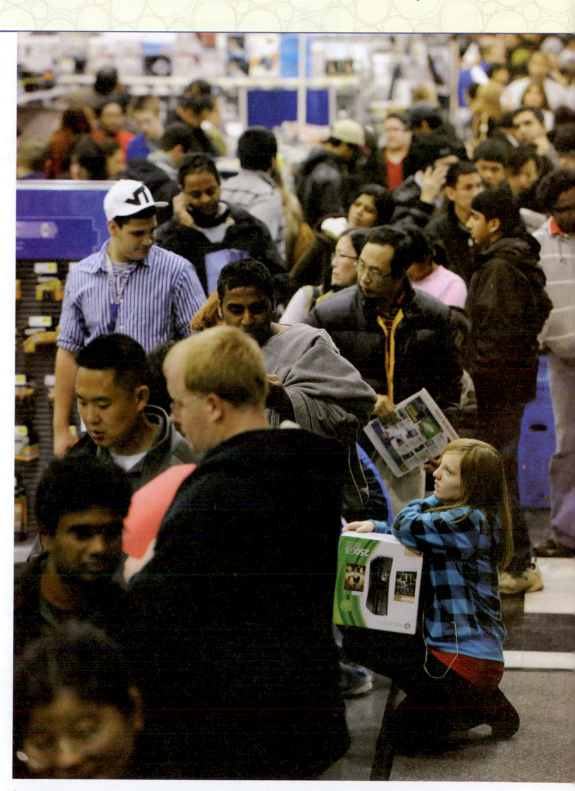

▶ What is the race concept, and why have anthropologists rejected it?

▶ How does natural selection work on contemporary and recent human populations?

▶ Does biological adaptation occur during an individual's lifetime?

Diversity at the mall. Black Friday shoppers wait in line at a Best Buy store in Fairfax, Virginia.

# understanding OURSELVES

How do you imagine human "diversity"? Maybe you associate that word with "race" or "ethnicity." Perhaps you think of differences in skin or eye color, or something like height, which can be observed by the naked eye. In fact, human biological diversity encompasses much more than observable physical differences. It includes our abilities to digest various foods. It also includes our innate resistance or susceptibility to particular diseases. Consider smallpox, a virus that once plagued humankind. When I was a child, everyone was vaccinated against smallpox. Were you? Probably not, because smallpox has been eradicated in nature since 1979. The virus is preserved only in labs. The smallpox vaccine turned out to be highly effective but potentially lethal. At one time, when smallpox was nearing extinction, more people were dying from the vaccine than from the disease. Anthropologists know that people with certain blood types seem to be more at risk from smallpox and its vaccine than are people with other blood types. This type of knowledge about biological diversity can help us make important decisions about public policy and public safety in a society as diverse as our own.

Contemporary North America is strikingly rich in human biological diversity. The photos in this chapter and throughout this book illustrate just a fraction of the world's biological variation. Additional illustration comes from your own experience. Look around you in your classroom or at the mall or multiplex. Inevitably you'll see people whose ancestors lived in many lands. The first (Native) Americans had to cross a land bridge that once linked Siberia to North America. For later immigrants, perhaps including your own parents or grandparents, the voyage may have been across the sea, or overland from nations to the south. They came for many reasons; some came voluntarily, while others were brought in chains. The scale of migration in today's world is so vast that millions of people routinely cross national borders or live far from the homelands of their grandparents. Now meeting every day are diverse human beings whose biological features reflect adaptation to a wide range of environments other than the ones they now inhabit. Physical contrasts are evident to anyone. Anthropology's job is to explain them.

## RACE: A DISCREDITED CONCEPT IN BIOLOGY

Historically, scientists have approached the study of human biological diversity in two main ways: (1) racial classification (now largely abandoned) versus (2) the current explanatory approach, which focuses on understanding specific differences. First we'll consider problems with **racial classification** (the attempt to assign humans to discrete categories [purportedly] based on common ancestry). Then we'll offer some explanations for specific aspects of human biological diversity. *Biological differences are real, important, and apparent to us all.* Modern scientists find it most productive to seek explanations for this diversity, rather than trying to pigeonhole people into categories called races (see Tattersall and DeSalle 2011). Certainly, human groups do vary biologically—for example, in their genetic attributes. But often we observe gradual, rather than abrupt, shifts in gene frequencies between neighboring groups. Such gradual genetic shifts are called **clines,** and they are incompatible with discrete races (see Edgar and Hunley 2009; Mukhopadhyay, Henze, and Moses 2007).

The photos in this chapter illustrate only a small part of the range of human biological diversity. Shown here is a Bai minority woman from Shapin, in China's Yunnan province.

What is race, anyway? In theory, a biological race would be a geographically isolated subdivision of a species. Such a *subspecies* would be capable of interbreeding with other subspecies of the same species, but it would not actually do so because of its geographic isolation. Some biologists also use "race" to refer to "breeds," as of dogs or roses. Thus, a pit bull and a chihuahua would be different races of dogs. Such domesticated "races" have been bred by humans for generations. Humanity (*Homo sapiens*) lacks such races because human populations have not been isolated enough from one another to develop into such discrete groups. Nor have humans experienced controlled breeding like that which has created the various kinds of dogs and roses.

A race is supposed to reflect shared genetic material (inherited from a common ancestor), but early scholars instead used phenotypical traits (such as skin color and facial features) for racial classification. *Phenotype* refers to an organism's evident traits, its "manifest biology"—anatomy and physiology. Humans display hundreds of evident (detectable) physical traits. They range from skin color, hair form, eye color, and facial features (which are visible) to blood groups, color blindness, and enzyme production (which become evident through testing).

Racial classifications based on phenotype raise the problem of deciding which trait(s) should be primary. Should races be defined by height, weight, body shape, facial features, teeth, skull form, or skin color? Like their fellow citizens, early European and American scientists gave priority to skin color. Many schoolbooks and encyclopedias still proclaim the existence of three great races: the white, the black, and the yellow. This overly simplistic classification was compatible with the political use of race during the colonial period of the late 19th and early 20th centuries (see Gravlee 2009). Such a tripartite scheme kept white Europeans neatly separate from their African, Asian, and Native American subjects. Colonial empires began to break up, and scientists began to question established racial categories, after World War II (see Tattersall and DeSalle 2011).

## Races Are Not Biologically Distinct

History and politics aside, one obvious problem with "color-based" racial labels is that the terms don't accurately describe skin color. "White" people are more pink, beige, or tan than white. "Black" people are various shades of brown, and "yellow" people are tan or beige. But these terms have been dignified by more scientific-*sounding* synonyms: Caucasoid, Negroid, and Mongoloid.

Another problem with the tripartite scheme is that many populations don't fit neatly into any one of the three "great races." For example, where would one put the Polynesians? *Polynesia* is a triangle of South Pacific islands formed by Hawaii to the north, Easter Island to the east, and New Zealand to the southwest. Does the "bronze" skin color of Polynesians connect them to the Caucasoids or to the Mongoloids? Some scientists, recognizing this

A Quechua woman in Macha, Bolivia.

A boy at the Pushkar livestock fair, Rajasthan, India.

A young man from the Marquesas Islands in Polynesia.

problem, enlarged the original tripartite scheme to include the Polynesian "race." Native Americans presented a similar problem. Were they red or yellow? Some scientists added a fifth race—the "red," or Amerindian—to the major racial groups.

Many people in southern India have dark skins, but scientists have been reluctant to classify them with "black" Africans because of their Caucasoid facial features and hair form. Some, therefore, have created a separate race for these people. What about the Australian aborigines, hunters and gatherers native to what has been, throughout human history, the most isolated continent? By skin color, one might place some Native Australians in the same race as tropical Africans. However, similarities to Europeans in hair color (light or reddish) and facial features have led some scientists to classify them as Caucasoids. But there is no evidence that Australians are closer genetically to either of these groups than they are to Asians. Recognizing this problem, scientists often regard Native Australians as a separate race.

Finally, consider the *San* ("Bushmen") of the Kalahari Desert in southern Africa. Scientists have perceived their skin color as varying from brown to yellow. Some who regard San skin as "yellow" have placed them in the same category as Asians. In theory, people of the same race share more recent common ancestry with each other than they do with anyone else. But there is no evidence for recent common ancestry between San and Asians. Somewhat more reasonably, some scholars assign the San to the Capoid race (from the Cape of Good Hope), which is seen as being different from other groups inhabiting tropical Africa.

Similar problems arise when any single trait is used for racial classification. An attempt to use facial features, height, weight, or any other phenotypical trait is fraught with difficulties. For example, consider the *Nilotes,* natives of the upper Nile region of Uganda and South Sudan. Nilotes tend to be tall and to have long, narrow noses. Certain Scandinavians also are tall, with similar noses. Given the distance between their homelands, however, there is no reason to assume that Nilotes and Scandinavians are more closely related to each other than either is to shorter and nearer populations with different kinds of noses.

Would it be better to base racial classifications on a combination of physical traits? This would avoid some of the problems just mentioned, but others would arise. First, skin color, stature, skull form, and facial features (nose form, eye shape, lip thickness) don't go together as a unit. For example, people with dark skin may be tall or short and have hair ranging from straight to very curly. Dark-haired populations may have light or dark skin, along with various skull forms, facial features, and body sizes and shapes. The number of combinations is very large, and the amount that heredity (versus environment) contributes to such phenotypical traits is often unclear (see also Anemone 2011).

## Genetic Markers Don't Correlate with Phenotype

The analysis of human DNA indicates that fully 94 percent of human genetic variation occurs within so-called races. Considering conventional geographic "racial" groupings such as Africans, Asians, and Europeans, there is only about 6 percent variation in genes from one group to the other. In other words, there is much greater variation within each of the traditional "races" than between them. Humans are much more alike genetically than are other hominoids (the living apes). This suggests a recently shared common ancestor (perhaps as recent as 70,000 to 50,000 years) for all members of modern *Homo sapiens*. Sampling the mitochondrial DNA (mtDNA) of various populations, Rebecca Cann, Mark Stoneking, and Allan C. Wilson (1987) concluded that humans are genetically uniform overall, suggesting recent common ancestry. The fact that African populations are the most diverse genetically provides evidence that Africa was the site where the human diaspora originated.

An Afghan refugee returning to Afghanistan.

Contemporary work in genomics has allowed scientists to construct regional and global phylogenetic trees based on shared genetic markers. Such trees can be based on mitochondrial DNA (mtDNA) (sampling females) and the Y chromosome (sampling males). As the human genome becomes better known, molecular anthropologists refine their models of genetic relationships among humans and how they dispersed. A **haplogroup** is a lineage or branch of such a genetic tree marked by one or more specific genetic mutations. For example, the global mtDNA tree includes branches known as M and N (among others). The Y chromosome tree includes branches known as C and F (among others). Those four branches (either M or N for mtDNA and either C or F for the Y chromosome) are known to be associated with the spread of modern humans out of Africa between 70,000 and 50,000 B.P. Because Native Australians share those four branches, they are known to be part of that diaspora. The Americas were settled (from Asia) much later than Australia by multiple haplogroups, which reached North America at different times and came by different routes.

Although long-term genetic markers do exist, they don't correlate neatly with phenotype. Phenotypical similarities and differences aren't precisely or even necessarily correlated with genetic relationships. Because of changes in the environment that affect individuals during growth and development, the range of phenotypes characteristic of a population may change without any genetic change whatsoever. There are several examples. In the early 20th century, the anthropologist Franz Boas (1940/1966) described changes in skull form (e.g., toward

rounder heads) among the children of Europeans who had migrated to North America. The reason for this was not a change in genes, for the European immigrants tended to marry among themselves. Also, some of their children had been born in Europe and merely raised in the United States. Something in the environment, probably in the diet, was producing this change. From observations in the Americas, Europe, and Japan, we know now that changes in average height and weight produced by dietary differences in a few generations are common and may have nothing to do with "race" or genetics.

## The AAA RACE Project

To broaden public understanding of human diversity, the American Anthropological Association (AAA) offers its RACE Project, which includes an award-winning public education program titled RACE Are We So Different? This program, which is geared toward middle school–aged children through adults, includes an interactive website and a traveling museum exhibit. You can visit the interactive website right now at www.understandingrace.org/home.html. The museum exhibit may be showing somewhere near you. For its touring schedule visit this website: http://www.understandingrace.org/about/tour.html.

RACE Are We So Different? examines the race concept through the eyes of history, science, and lived experience (see Goodman et al. 2013 for a collection of essays related to the project). It explains how human variation differs from race, when and why the idea of race was invented, and how race and racism affect our everyday lives. The program's three key messages are that (1) race is a recent human invention, (2) race is about culture, not biology, and (3) race and racism are embedded in institutions and everyday life (see also Gravlee 2009; Hartigan 2013).

## HUMAN BIOLOGICAL ADAPTATION

Traditional racial classification assumed that biological characteristics such as skin color were determined by heredity and that they were stable (immutable) over many generations. We now know that a biological similarity doesn't necessarily indicate recent common ancestry. Dark skin color, for

**haplogroup**
Lineage or branch of a genetic tree marked by one or more specific genetic mutations.

example, can be shared by tropical Africans and southern Indians for reasons other than common heredity. Scientists have made considerable progress in explaining variation in human skin color, along with many other features of human biological diversity (see Relethford 2009). We shift now from racial classification to explanation, in which natural selection plays a key role.

## Explaining Skin Color

Natural selection, remember, is the process by which the forms most fit to survive and reproduce in a given environment do so. Over the generations, the less fit organisms die out, and the favored types survive by producing more offspring. The role of natural selection in producing variation in skin color will illustrate the explanatory approach to human biological diversity. Explanations for many other aspects of human biological variation will be examined later in this chapter.

Skin color is a complex biological trait—influenced by several genes (see Jablonski 2006, 2012). Just how many genes is not known. **Melanin,** the primary determinant of human skin color, is a chemical substance manufactured in the epidermis, or outer skin layer. The melanin cells of darker-skinned people produce more and larger granules of melanin than do those of lighter-skinned people. By screening out ultraviolet (UV) radiation from the sun, melanin offers protection against a variety of maladies, including sunburn and skin cancer.

Before the 16th century, most of the world's very dark-skinned peoples lived in the **tropics,** a belt extending about 23 degrees north and south of the equator, between the Tropic of Cancer and the Tropic of Capricorn. The association between dark skin color and a tropical habitat existed throughout the Old World, where humans and their ancestors have lived for millions of years. The darkest populations of Africa evolved not in shady equatorial forests but in sunny open grassland, or savanna, country.

Outside the tropics, skin color tends to be lighter. Moving north in Africa, for example, there is a gradual transition from dark brown to medium brown. Average skin color continues to lighten as one moves through the Middle East, into southern Europe, through central Europe, and to the north. South of the tropics skin color also is lighter. In the Americas, by contrast, tropical populations don't have very dark skin. This is true because the settlement of the New World by light-skinned Asian ancestors of Native Americans was relatively recent, probably dating back no more than 20,000 years.

How, aside from migrations, can we explain the geographic distribution of human skin color? Natural selection provides an answer. In the tropics, intense UV radiation poses a series of threats, including severe sunburn, that make light skin color an adaptive disadvantage (Recap 6.1 summarizes

**melanin**
"Natural sunscreen" produced by skin cells responsible for pigmentation.

**tropics**
Zone between 23 degrees north (Tropic of Cancer) and 23 degrees south (Tropic of Capricorn) of the equator.

Before the 16th century, almost all the very dark-skinned populations of the world lived in the tropics, as does this Samburu woman from Kenya.

Princess Madeleine of Sweden at the wedding of Sweden's Crown Princess Victoria and Daniel Westling at the Stockholm Cathedral. Very light skin color, illustrated in this photo, maximizes absorption of ultraviolet radiation by those few parts of the body exposed to direct sunlight during northern winters.

those threats). By damaging sweat glands, sunburn reduces the body's ability to perspire and thus to regulate its own temperature (thermoregulation). Sunburn also can increase susceptibility to disease. Melanin, nature's own sunscreen, confers a selective

*Also shown are cultural alternatives that can make up for biological disadvantages and examples of natural selection (NS) operating today in relation to skin color.*

| | | CULTURAL ALTERNATIVES | NS IN ACTION TODAY |
|---|---|---|---|
| **DARK SKIN COLOR** | Melanin is natural sunscreen. | | |
| Advantage | In tropics: screens out UV radiation | | |
| | Reduces susceptibility to folate destruction and thus to neural tube defects (NTDs), including spina bifida | | |
| | Prevents sunburn and thus enhances sweating and thermoregulation | | |
| | Reduces disease susceptibility | | |
| | Reduces risk of skin cancer | | |
| Disadvantage | Outside tropics: reduces UV absorption | | |
| | Increases susceptibility to rickets, osteoporosis | Foods, vitamin D supplements | East Asians in northern UK Inuit with modern diets |
| **LIGHT SKIN COLOR** | No natural sunscreen | | |
| Advantage | Outside tropics: admits UV | | |
| | Body manufactures vitamin D and thus prevents rickets and osteoporosis. | | |
| Disadvantage | Increases susceptibility to folate destruction and thus to NTDs, including spina bifida | Folic acid/folate supplements | Whites still have more NTDs |
| | Impaired spermatogenesis | | |
| | Increases susceptibility to sunburn and thus to impaired sweating and poor thermoregulation | Shelter, sunscreens, lotions, etc. | |
| | Increases disease susceptibility | | |
| | Increases susceptibility to skin cancer | | |

advantage (i.e., a better chance to survive and reproduce) on darker-skinned people living in the tropics. (Today, light-skinned people manage to survive in the tropics by staying indoors and by using cultural products, such as umbrellas and lotions, to screen sunlight.) Yet another disadvantage of having light skin color in the tropics is that exposure to UV radiation can cause skin cancer (Blum 1961).

Many years ago, W. F. Loomis (1967) focused on the role of UV radiation in stimulating the manufacture (synthesis) of vitamin D by the human body. The unclothed human body can produce its own vitamin D when exposed to sufficient sunlight. However, in a cloudy environment that also is so cold that people have to clothe themselves much of the year (such as northern Europe, where very light skin color evolved), clothing interferes with the body's manufacture of vitamin D. The ensuing shortage of vitamin D diminishes the absorption of calcium in the intestines. A nutritional disease known as **rickets,** which softens and deforms the bones, may develop. In women, deformation of the pelvic bones from rickets can interfere with childbirth. In cold northern areas, light skin color

maximizes the absorption of UV radiation and the synthesis of vitamin D by the few parts of the body that are exposed to direct sunlight during northern winters. There has been selection against dark skin color in northern areas because melanin screens out UV radiation.

This natural selection continues today: East Asians who have migrated recently from India and Pakistan to northern areas of the United Kingdom have a higher incidence of rickets and osteoporosis (also related to vitamin D and calcium deficiency) than the general British population. A related illustration involves Eskimos (Inuit) and other indigenous inhabitants of northern Alaska and northern Canada. According to Nina Jablonski (quoted in Iqbal 2002), "Looking at Alaska, one would think that the native people should be pale as ghosts." One reason they aren't is that they haven't inhabited this region very long in terms of geological time. Even more important, their traditional diet, rich in fish oils, supplied sufficient vitamin D so as to make a reduction in pigmentation unnecessary. However, and again illustrating natural selection at work today, "when these people don't eat their aboriginal

**rickets**
Vitamin D deficiency marked by bone deformation.

diets of fish and marine mammals, they suffer tremendously high rates of vitamin D–deficiency diseases such as rickets in children and osteoporosis in adults" (Jablonski quoted in Iqbal 2002). Far from being immutable, skin color can become an evolutionary liability very quickly.

According to Jablonski and George Chaplin (2000; see also Jablonski 2006, 2012), another key factor explaining the geographic distribution of skin color involves the effects of UV on folate, an essential nutrient that the human body manufactures from folic acid. Folate is needed for cell division and the production of new DNA. Pregnant women require large amounts of folate to support rapid cell division in the embryo, and there is a direct connection between folate and individual reproductive success. Folate deficiency causes neural tube defects (NTDs) in human embryos. NTDs are marked by the incomplete closure of the neural tube, so the spine and spinal cord fail to develop completely. One NTD, anencephaly (with the brain an exposed mass), results in stillbirth or death soon after delivery. With spina bifida, another NTD, survival rates are higher, but babies have severe disabilities, including paralysis. NTDs are the second most common human birth defect after cardiac abnormalities.

Dark skin color, as we have seen, is adaptive in the tropics because it protects against such UV hazards as sunburn and its consequences. UV radiation also destroys folate in the human body. Preventing this destruction, melanin has the additional adaptive advantage of conserving folate and thus protecting against NTDs, which are much more common in light-skinned than in darker-skinned populations (Jablonski and Chaplin 2000). Africans and African Americans rarely experience severe folate deficiency. Folate also plays a role in another process that is central to reproduction, spermatogenesis—the production of sperm. In mice and rats, folate deficiency can cause male sterility; it may well play a similar role in humans.

Today, of course, cultural alternatives to biological adaptation permit light-skinned people to survive in the tropics and darker-skinned people to live in the far north. People can clothe themselves and seek shelter from the sun; they can use artificial sunscreens if they lack the natural protection that melanin provides. Dark-skinned people living in the north can, indeed must, get vitamin D from their diet or take supplements. Today, pregnant women are routinely advised to take folic acid or folate supplements as a hedge against NTDs. Even so, light skin color still is correlated with a higher incidence of spina bifida.

Jablonski and Chaplin (2000) explain variation in human skin color as resulting from a balancing act between the evolutionary needs to (1) protect against all UV hazards (thus favoring dark skin in the tropics) and (2) have an adequate supply of vitamin D (thus favoring lighter skin outside the tropics). This discussion of skin color shows that common ancestry, the presumed basis of race, is not the only reason for biological similarities. Natural selection, still at work today, makes a major contribution to variations in human skin color.

## Facial Features

Natural selection also affects facial features. For instance, long noses seem to be adaptive in arid areas (Brace 2005; Weiner 1954), because membranes and blood vessels inside the nose moisten the air as it is breathed in. Long noses also are adaptive in cold environments, because blood vessels warm the air as it is breathed in. This form of nose distances the brain, which is sensitive to bitter cold, from raw outer air. These were adaptive biological features for humans who lived in cold climates before the invention of central heating.

The association between nose form and temperature is recognized as **Thomson's nose rule** (Thomson and Buxton 1923), which shows up statistically. In plotting the geographic distribution of nose length among human populations who have lived for many generations in the areas they now inhabit, the average nose tends to be longer in areas with lower mean annual temperatures.

Other facial features also illustrate adaptation to selective forces. Among contemporary humans, average tooth size is largest among Native Australian hunters and gatherers, for whom large teeth had an

**Thomson's nose rule**
Average nose length increases in cold areas.

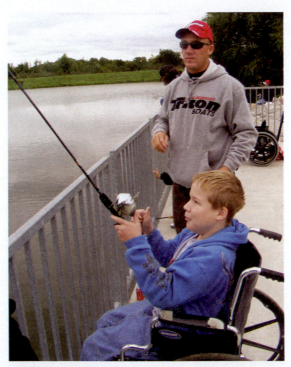

Spina bifida, a congenital (birth) disorder that leaves a portion of the spinal cord exposed, can be treated with surgery and physiotherapy. Shown here is an outing, including fishing, for children with spina bifida in Lee's Summit, Missouri. Why is light skin color correlated with a higher incidence of spina bifida?

adaptive advantage, given a diet based on foods with a considerable amount of sand and grit. People with small teeth—if false teeth and sand-free foods are unavailable—can't feed themselves as effectively as people with more massive dentition can (see Brace 2005).

## Size and Body Build

Certain body types have adaptive advantages for particular environments. In 1847, the German biologist Karl Christian Bergmann observed that within the same species of warm-blooded animals, populations with smaller individuals are more often found in warm climates, while those with greater bulk, or mass, are found in colder regions. The relation between body weight and temperature is summarized in **Bergmann's rule:** The smaller of two bodies similar in shape has more surface area per unit of weight. Therefore, it sheds heat more efficiently. (Heat loss occurs on the body's surface—the skin perspires.) Average body size tends to increase in cold areas and to decrease in hot ones because big bodies hold heat better than small ones do. To be more precise, in a study of a large sample of native populations, average adult male weight increased by 0.66 pound (0.3 kilogram) for every 1 degree Fahrenheit fall in mean annual temperature (Roberts 1953; Steegman 1975).

The Maasai (or Masai) are a Nilotic ethnic group of seminomadic people located in Kenya and northern Tanzania.

In Nunavut, Canada, on the western shore of Hudson Bay, this Inuit couple wear traditional arctic attire in front of a caribou hide tent.

The "pygmies" and the San, who live in hot climates and weigh only 90 pounds on the average, illustrate this relation in reverse.

Body shape differences also reflect adaptation to temperature through natural selection. The relationship between temperature and body shape in animals and birds was first recognized in 1877 by the zoologist J. A. Allen. **Allen's rule** states that the relative size of protruding body parts—ears, tails, bills, fingers, toes, limbs, and so on—increases with temperature. Among humans, slender bodies with long digits and limbs are advantageous in tropical climates. Such bodies increase body surface relative to mass and allow for more efficient heat dissipation. Among the cold-adapted Eskimos or Inuit, the opposite phenotype is found. Short limbs and stocky bodies conserve heat. Cold-area populations tend to have larger chests and shorter arms than do people from warm areas (Roberts 1953).

This discussion of adaptive relationships between climate and body size and shape illustrates that natural selection may achieve the same effect in different ways. East African Nilotes, who live in a hot area, have tall, linear bodies with elongated extremities that increase surface area relative to mass and thus maximize heat dissipation (illustrating Allen's rule). Among the "pygmies," the reduction of body size achieves the same result (illustrating Bergmann's rule). Similarly, the large bodies of northern Europeans and the compact stockiness of the Inuit serve the same function of heat conservation.

Similarly, as we see in "Appreciating Anthropology" on pp. 102–103, human populations use different, but equally effective, biological means of adapting to the environmental stresses associated with high altitudes.

## Genes and Disease

The remainder of this chapter examines additional examples of human biological diversity that reflect adaptation to environmental stresses, including disease, diet, and climate. There is abundant evidence for human genetic adaptation and thus for evolution (change in gene frequency) through selection working in specific environments. One example is the adaptive value of the $Hb^S$ heterozygote in malarial environments. Adaptation and evolution go on in specific environments. There is no generally or ideally adaptive allele and no perfect phenotype. Nor can an allele be assumed to be maladaptive for all times and all places. We've seen that even $Hb^S$, which produces a lethal anemia, has a selective advantage in the heterozygous form in malarial environments. Also, alleles that once were maladaptive can lose their disadvantage if the environment shifts. Today's environment includes medical techniques that allow people with many genetic disorders to live fairly normal lives.

As farming and herding spread about 10,000 years ago, infectious diseases posed a mounting risk. Cultivation supports larger, denser populations

**Allen's rule**
Protruding body parts are bigger in warmer areas.

**Bergmann's rule**
Larger bodies are found in colder areas and smaller bodies in warmer ones.

## Adapting to Thin Air

Anthropologists study the varied ways in which humans adapt, biologically and culturally, to environmental stresses, including disease, temperature, humidity, sunlight, and altitude—as described here. This account describes how anthropologists are studying the dramatically different ways in which three populations have adapted to high altitudes. Working with these populations, in Tibet, Ethiopia, and the Andes, anthropologists follow many lines of evidence— archaeological, biological, and climatological— to answer questions about social, cultural, and biological adaptations. Anthropologists know that the biological diversity we observe among contemporary and prehistoric humans has many causes. This chapter examines those causes, while rejecting attempts to pigeonhole humans into discrete biological categories called races.

Prehistoric and contemporary human populations living at altitudes of at least 8,000 feet (2,500 meters) above sea level may provide unique insights into human evolution, reports an interdisciplinary group of scientists.

Indigenous highlanders living in the Andean Altiplano in South America, in the Tibetan Plateau in Asia, and at the highest elevations of the Ethiopian Highlands in east Africa have evolved three distinctly different biological adaptations for surviving in the oxygen-thin air found at high altitude.

"To have examples of three geographically dispersed populations adapting in different ways to the same stress is very unusual," said Cynthia Beall, a physical anthropologist at Case Western Reserve University in Cleveland, Ohio. "From an evolutionary standpoint the question becomes, Why do these differences exist? . . ."

"High-altitude populations offer a unique natural lab that allows us to follow [many] lines of evidence— archaeological, biological, climatological—to answer intriguing questions about social, cultural, and biological adaptations," said Mark Aldenderfer, an archaeologist at the University of California, Santa Barbara. . . .

The Andean and Tibetan plateaus rise some 13,000 feet (4 kilometers) above sea level. As prehistoric hunter-gatherers moved into these environments, they . . . likely suffered acute hypoxia, a condition created by a diminished supply of oxygen to body tissues. At high altitudes the air is much thinner than at sea level. As a result, a person inhales fewer oxygen molecules with each breath. Symptoms of hypoxia, sometimes known as mountain sickness, include headaches, vomiting, sleeplessness, impaired thinking, and an inability to sustain long periods of physical activity. At elevations above 25,000 feet (7,600 meters), hypoxia can kill.

The Andeans adapted to the thin air by developing an ability to carry more oxygen in each red blood cell. That is: They breathe at the same rate as people who live at sea level, but the Andeans have the ability to deliver oxygen throughout their bodies more effectively than people at sea level do.

"Andeans counter having less oxygen in every breath by having higher hemoglobin concentrations in their blood," Beall said. Hemoglobin is the protein in red blood cells that ferries oxygen through the blood system. Having more hemoglobin to carry oxygen through the blood system than people at sea level counterbalances the effects of hypoxia.

Tibetans compensate for low oxygen content much differently. They increase their oxygen intake by taking more breaths per minute than people who live at sea level.

"Andeans go the hematological route, Tibetans the respiratory route," Beall said.

In addition, Tibetans may have a second biological adaptation, which expands their blood vessels, allowing them to deliver oxygen throughout their bodies more effectively than sea-level people do.

Tibetans' lungs synthesize larger amounts of a gas called nitric oxide from the air they breathe. "One effect of nitric oxide is to increase the

and a more sedentary lifestyle than does hunting and gathering. People live closer to each other and to their own wastes, making it easier for microbes to survive and to find hosts. Domesticated animals also transmit diseases to people.

Until 1979, when the last case was reported, smallpox had been a major threat to humans and a determinant of blood group frequencies (Diamond 1990, 1997). The smallpox virus is a mutation from one of the pox viruses that plague such domesticated animals as cows, sheep, goats, horses, and pigs. Smallpox appeared in human beings after people and animals started living together. Smallpox epidemics have played important roles in world history, often killing one-fourth to one-half of the affected populations. Smallpox contributed to Sparta's defeat of Athens in 430 B.C.E. and to the decline of the Roman empire after C.E. 160.

The ABO blood groups have figured in human resistance to smallpox. Blood is typed according to the protein and sugar compounds on the surface of the red blood cells. Different substances (compounds) distinguish between type A and type B blood. Type A cells trigger the production of *antibodies* in B blood, so that A cells clot in B blood. The different substances work like chemical passwords; they help us distinguish our own cells from invading cells, including microbes we diameter of blood vessels, which suggests that Tibetans may offset low oxygen content in their blood with increased blood flow," Beall said.

A pilot study Beall conducted of Ethiopian highlanders living at 11,580 feet (3,530 meters) suggests that—unlike the Tibetans—they don't breathe more rapidly than people at sea level and aren't able to more effectively synthesize nitric oxide. Nor do the Ethiopians have higher hemoglobin counts than sea-level people, as the Andeans do.

Yet despite living at elevations with low oxygen content, "the Ethiopian highlanders were hardly hypoxic at all," Beall said. "I was genuinely surprised."

So what adaptation have the Ethiopian highlanders' bodies evolved to survive at high altitude? "Right now we have no clue how they do it," Beall said. . . .

Knowing how long the populations have been living at the top of the world is crucial to answering the evolutionary question of whether these adaptations are the result of differences in the founding populations, random genetic mutations, or the passage of time.

Archaeologists, paleontologists, and climatologists are pooling their knowledge to pinpoint when some of these early migrations to the high plateaus occurred.

Aldenderfer . . . says cultural adaptations would have to occur first.

Natives of the Himalayas, like this man (a Nepalese Sherpa), adapt biologically to their high altitude by breathing more rapidly than people who live at sea level. In addition, their lungs synthesize larger amounts of nitric oxide from the air they breathe, which increases the diameter of their blood vessels. People have lived in the Himalayas for more than 20,000 years.

"The ability to survive in such harsh environments required control of fire, an expanded tool kit that included bone needles to make complicated clothing that protected the body in a significant way, and the cultural flexibility to change subsistence practices," he said. . . .

What motivated prehistoric people to move into the harsh and challenging conditions presented by high altitude?

"The highlands offered an attractive option with a landscape that was open and pristine," Aldenderfer said. "People probably started out moving up and down for short terms, and then gradually settled at the higher elevations." . . .

SOURCE: Hillary Mayell, "Three High-Altitude Peoples, Three Adaptations to Thin Air," *National Geographic News,* February 25, 2004. http://news.nationalgeographic.com. © 2004 National Geographic Society. Reprinted with permission.

ought to destroy. The surfaces of some microbes have substances similar to ABO blood group substances. We don't produce antibodies to substances similar to those on our own blood cells. We can think of this as a clever evolutionary trick by the microbes to deceive their hosts, because we don't normally develop antibodies against our own biochemistry.

People with A or AB blood are more susceptible to smallpox than are people with type B or type O. Presumably this is because a substance on the smallpox virus mimics the type A substance, permitting the virus to slip by the defenses of a type A individual. By contrast, type B and type O individuals produce antibodies against smallpox because they recognize it as a foreign substance.

The relation between type A blood and susceptibility to smallpox was first suggested by the low frequencies of the A allele in areas of India and Africa where smallpox had been endemic. A comparative study done in rural India during a virulent smallpox epidemic did much to confirm this relationship. Drs. F. Vogel and M. R. Chakravartti analyzed blood samples from smallpox victims and their uninfected siblings (Diamond 1990). The researchers focused on 415 infected children, none ever vaccinated against smallpox. All but eight of these children had an uninfected (also unvaccinated) sibling.

In most human populations, the O allele is more common than A and B combined. A is most common in Europe; B frequencies are highest in Asia. Since smallpox was once widespread in the Old World, we might wonder why natural selection didn't eliminate the A allele entirely. The answer appears to be this: Other diseases spared the type A people and penalized those with other blood groups.

For example, type O people seem to be especially susceptible to bubonic plague. Type O people also are more likely to get cholera, which has killed as many people in India as smallpox has. On the other hand, the O allele may protect against syphilis, which originated in the New World. Frequencies of type O blood are very high among the native populations of Central and South America. The distribution of human blood groups appears to represent a compromise among the selective effects of many diseases.

In the case of diseases for which there are no known cures, genetic resistance maintains its significance (see Hartigan 2013). There is genetic variation in susceptibility to the HIV virus, for example. Longitudinal studies have shown that people exposed to HIV vary in their risk of developing AIDS and in the rate at which the disease progresses.

As an interesting case of what we might call fortuitous preadaptation or preselection, consider the *CCR5* gene. This gene, which codes for a chemical receptor protein on the surface of white blood cells, is involved in the human immune system. The viral infection HIV uses the *CCR5* receptor to invade and infect cells. But individuals who are homozygous for an allele known as *CCR5-Δ32* (*delta 32*) are resistant to this invasion. This HIV immunity illustrates preadaptation or preselection, because the original selection for the allele had nothing to do with HIV. The allele was adaptive and spread because of the resistance it offered against deadly epidemics that occurred much earlier in European history.

The *CCR5-Δ32* allele is found in between 3 and 14 percent of Europeans, but it is absent in Africans, East Asians, and Native Americans. Among Europeans, the allele is most common in Scandinavia and Russia and least common near the Mediterranean. Susan Scott and Christopher Duncan (2004) argue that most of the lethal epidemics that ravaged Europe between 1347 and 1660 were not bubonic plague (a bacterial infection), as is commonly thought. Instead, they involved a lethal, viral, hemorrhagic fever that used the *CCR5* receptor gene to invade (and usually kill) its human hosts. Hemorrhagic fever disappeared from England after London's Great Plague of 1665–1666, but it continued through 1800 in Sweden, Denmark, Russia, Poland, and Hungary. Given the persistent hemorrhagic plague threat, selection for *CCR5-Δ32* continued in those countries, where it

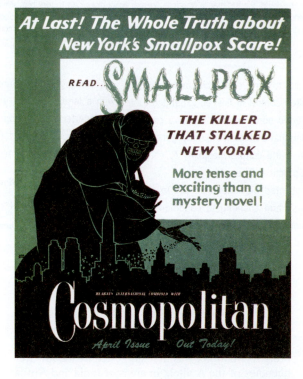

In New York City in 1947, the appearance of nine cases of smallpox, including two deaths, spurred a very successful mass vaccination program. Shown here, lines of people wait to be vaccinated at the New York Health Department on April 14, 1947. The threat made the cover of *Cosmopolitan* magazine.

**phenotypical adaptation**
Adaptive biological changes during an individual's lifetime.

The results of the study were clear: Susceptibility to smallpox varied with ABO type. Of the 415 infected children, 261 had the A allele; 154 lacked it. Among their 407 uninfected siblings, the ratio was reversed. Only 80 had the A allele; 327 lacked it. The researchers calculated that a type A or type AB person had a seven times greater chance of getting smallpox than did an O or B person.

has its highest frequencies (see Relethford 2013, p. 368). Others have suggested a link between the spread of *CCR5-Δ32* and resistance to smallpox. Whatever the disease may have been that favored this allele to begin with, it is clear that it is merely by lucky chance that *CCR5-Δ32* also confers resistance to HIV and AIDS.

Genetic variation no doubt will help determine differential resistance and susceptibility to microbes that may emerge or mutate in the future. (This chapter's "Focus on Globalization" discusses the global spread of infectious diseases.)

## Lactose Tolerance

Many biological traits that illustrate human adaptation are not under simple genetic control. Genetic determination of such traits may be only partial, or several genes may work or interact to influence the trait in question. Sometimes there is a known genetic component but the trait also responds to stresses encountered during growth. We speak of **phenotypical adaptation** when adaptive changes occur during an individual's lifetime. Phenotypical adaptation is made possible by biological plasticity— our ability to change in response to the environments we encounter as we grow (see Bogin 2001; Frisancho 1993).

One genetically determined biochemical difference among human groups involves the ability to digest large amounts of milk—an adaptive advantage when other foods are scarce and milk is available, as it is in dairying societies. All milk, whatever its source, contains a complex sugar called *lactose*. The digestion of milk depends on an enzyme called *lactase*, which works in the small intestine. Among all mammals except humans and some of their pets, lactase production ceases after weaning, so that these animals can no longer digest milk.

Lactase production and the ability to tolerate milk vary between populations. About 90 percent of northern Europeans and their descendants are lactose tolerant; they can digest several glasses of milk with no difficulty. Similarly, about 80 percent of two African populations, the Tutsi of Rwanda and Burundi in East Africa and the Fulani of Nigeria in West Africa, produce lactase and digest milk easily. Both of these groups traditionally have been herders. However, such nonherders as the Yoruba and the Igbo in Nigeria, the Baganda in Uganda, the Japanese and other Asians, Inuit, South American Indians, and many Israelis cannot digest lactose (Kretchmer 1972/1975).

Recent genetic studies have helped clarify when and how humans developed lactose tolerance (see Mielke, Konigsberg, and Relethford 2011). An allele known to favor adult lactose tolerance existed, but still was uncommon, in central and eastern Europe as recently as 3,800 years ago (Burger et al. 2007). Sarah Tishkoff and her associates found that

# focus on GLOBALIZATION

## A Devastating Encounter in the Columbian Exchange

The Columbian exchange (named for Christopher Columbus) was a key early form of globalization, because it forever linked our globe's Western and Eastern Hemispheres. The term refers to the exchange of products, populations, and pathogens between the Old World and the New World that occurred after Columbus reached the Americas in 1492.

One devastating aspect of the Columbian exchange was the global spread of diseases previously confined to the Old World. Having lived with these pathogens for generations, Old World populations had developed various forms of immunity to many of them. Native Americans had no such resistance to Old World diseases, which included smallpox, chicken pox, measles, malaria, yellow fever, cholera, typhoid, bubonic plague, influenza, and the common cold. Only syphilis moved the other way—from the New World to the Old.

By debilitating and decimating the Aztecs of Mexico and the Inca of Peru, severe smallpox epidemics helped the Spanish conquer those peoples and their territories. Up to 90 percent of the population of the New World may have perished from Old World pathogens between 1500 and 1650 (Nunn and Qian 2010).

The African slave trade emerged in the context of Native American depopulation and the demand for human labor to produce commodities on New World plantations. Plantation economies outside the southern United States (where cotton was a New World domesticate) were based mainly on Old World crops (especially sugar and tobacco) introduced to the Americas and the Caribbean as part of the Columbian exchange. About 12 million human beings were involuntarily transported from Africa to the New World during the centuries of the Atlantic slave trade—the 16th through the 19th centuries.

Europeans from Spain, Portugal, the Netherlands, England, and France extended their colonial empires from the Americas to Africa and Asia. Europeans had a degree of genetic resistance to many Old World pathogens, but not to malaria—the scourge of the tropics. Quinine was a New World product that—again through the Columbian exchange—eventually offered Europeans a degree of protection against malaria. Europeans might never have been able to maintain colonial empires in the tropics of Africa, Asia, and South America without quinine (Nunn and Qian 2010). This is yet another way in which western expansion, and ultimately the formation of the modern world system, depended on the Columbian exchange.

Globalization remains an important factor in the spread of diseases today, as anyone knows who has seen the movie *World War Z* or *Contagion*. The spread of pathogens, such as H1N1, or swine flu, from animals (such as pigs, or swine) to humans became more common after people began living in close proximity to domesticated pigs, poultry, sheep, and cattle. These animals, originally domesticated in the Old World, now have a global distribution. How have humans adapted to the diseases their animals transmit?

the alleles behind lactose tolerance in East Africans differ from those of lactose-tolerant Europeans. Her genetic studies of 43 East African groups suggested that three different mutations favoring lactose tolerance arose in Africa between 6,800 and 2,700 years ago (Tishkoff et al. 2007). Again we see that the same phenotype—in this case, lactose tolerance—can be produced by different genotypes. As with the high-altitude adaptations described in "Appreciating Anthropology," natural selection has resulted in different selective solutions to the same environmental challenge. It also should be noted that the variable human ability to digest milk seems to be a difference of degree. Some populations can tolerate very little or no milk, but others are able to metabolize much greater quantities. People who move from no-milk or low-milk diets to high-milk diets can increase their lactose tolerance; this suggests some phenotypical adaptation.

Human biology changes constantly, even without genetic change. In this chapter we've considered several ways in which humans adapt biologically to their environments, and the effects of such adaptation on human biological diversity. Modern biological anthropology seeks to explain specific aspects of human biological variation. The explanatory framework encompasses the same mechanisms—selection, mutation, drift, gene flow, and plasticity—that govern adaptation, variation, and evolution among other life forms (see Mayr 2001).

## for REVIEW

**summary**

1. Humans have access to varied ways—biological and cultural—of adapting to environmental stresses, such as disease, heat, cold, humidity, sunlight, and altitude. Biological diversity among contemporary and prehistoric humans has many causes. This chapter examines those causes, while rejecting attempts to pigeonhole humans into discrete biological categories called races.

2. How do scientists approach the study of human biological diversity? Because of a range of problems involved in classifying humans into racial categories, contemporary biologists focus on specific differences and try to explain them. Because of extensive gene flow and interbreeding, *Homo sapiens* has not evolved subspecies, or distinct races. The genetic breaks that do exist among human populations have not led to the formation of discrete races.

3. Biological similarities between groups may reflect—rather than common ancestry—similar but independent adaptations to similar natural selective forces, such as degrees of ultraviolet radiation from the sun in the case of skin color.

4. Differential resistance to infectious diseases such as smallpox has influenced the distribution of human blood groups. There are genetic antimalarials, such as the sickle-cell allele. Natural selection also has operated on facial features and body size and shape.

5. *Phenotypical adaptation* refers to adaptive changes that occur in an individual's lifetime in response to the environment the organism encounters as it grows. Biological similarities between geographically distant populations may be due to similar but independent genetic changes, rather than to common ancestry. Or they may reflect similar physiological responses to common stresses during growth. Also, human populations have developed different but equally effective ways of adapting to environmental conditions such as heat, cold, and high altitudes.

1. Describe three problems with human racial classification.
2. What explains skin color in humans? Are the processes that determined skin color in humans still continuing today? If so, what are some examples of this?
3. Read the "American Anthropological Association Statement on 'Race'" (http://www.aaanet.org/stmts/racepp. htm). What is its main argument? Why was such a public statement by this institution necessary?
4. If "race" is a discredited concept when applied to humans, what has replaced it?
5. Choose five people in your classroom who illustrate a range of phenotypical diversity. Which of their features vary most evidently? How do you explain this variation? Is some of the variation due to culture rather than to biology?

# The Primates

An infant mountain gorilla shows affection to a silverback male. Apes fascinate us because of their humanlike qualities. Zoo gorillas are especially popular when they are displayed in "family" groups.

▶ How closely are the main primate groups related to one another and to humans?

▶ Why should the study of monkeys and apes be of interest to anthropologists?

▶ When, where, and how did the first primates, monkeys, apes, and hominins evolve?

# understanding OURSELVES

Think about our senses—vision, hearing, touch, taste, and smell. Which are you using right now? Which do you most depend upon to navigate the world? Like almost all other anthropoids—a group that includes monkeys, humans, and apes—humans are diurnal, active during the day. As animals, we are programmed to rise at dawn and to sleep when the sun goes down. As cultural creatures, we venture into the night with torches, lanterns, and flashlights and shut the dark out of our dwellings with artificial light. If we were night animals, we'd sense things differently. Our eyes might be bigger, like those of an owl or a tarsier. Maybe we'd have biological radar systems, as bats do. Perhaps we'd develop a more acute sense of hearing or smell to penetrate the dark.

Many animals rely upon scents and odors to help them interpret the world. Humans, by contrast, use an array of products to cover up or eliminate even the faint odors our limited olfactory apparatus permits us to smell. *Blindness* and *deafness* are common words that indicate the senses whose loss we deem most significant. The rarity of the word *anosmia,* the inability to smell, tells us something about our senses and our values. The sensory shifts that occurred in primate evolution, especially the one from smell to sight, explain something fundamental about ourselves.

How different are we from other primates? No human looks much like a lemur or a tarsier. That's understandable; our ancestries diverged more than 50 million years ago. We're much more closely related to, and look more like, our fellow anthropoids—monkeys and apes. Within this group, we are much more similar to apes than to monkeys. Likewise, apes are more similar to humans than to monkeys. Still, in the popular imagination, humans associate apes with monkeys, rather than with themselves. At zoos, human parents say to their kids, "Look at the monkey," when they are seeing a chimp, a gorilla, or an orangutan. The national tabloids use phrases like "monkeying around" or "monkey see, monkey do" when reporting on stories that involve apes. We easily appreciate the monkey in the ape but not the ape in ourselves.

Still, the apes do fascinate us to some degree because of their humanlike qualities. Zoo gorillas are especially popular when they are displayed in "family" groups. The antics of orangutans and especially of chimps have been featured in movies and TV shows. The *Planet of the Apes* movies recognize both that apes are not monkeys and that apes are quite similar to us. Imagine a live-action film called *Planet of the Monkeys.* Where could a director find human actors who could locomote on four legs for an entire movie?

**Primatology** is the study of nonhuman primates—fossil and living apes, monkeys, and prosimians—including behavior and social life (see Campbell 2011). Fascinating in itself, primatology also helps anthropologists make inferences about the early social organization of *hominids* (members of the family that includes fossil and living humans). Of particular relevance are two kinds of primates:

1. Those whose ecological adaptations are similar to our own: **terrestrial** monkeys and apes—that is, primates that live on the ground rather than in the trees.

2. Those that are most closely related to us: the great apes, specifically the chimpanzees and gorillas.

**primatology**
The study of apes, monkeys, and prosimians.

**terrestrial**
Ground-dwelling.

**taxonomy**
Classification scheme; assignment to categories (*taxa*; singular, *taxon*).

**homologies**
Traits inherited from a common ancestor.

# OUR PLACE AMONG PRIMATES

Similarities between humans and apes are evident in anatomy, brain structure, genetics, and biochemistry. The physical similarities between humans and apes are recognized in zoological **taxonomy**—the assignment of organisms to categories (*taxa*; singular, *taxon*) according to their relationship and resemblance. Many similarities between organisms reflect their common *phylogeny*—their genetic relatedness based on common ancestry. In other words, organisms share features they have inherited from the same ancestor. Humans and apes belong to the same taxonomic superfamily Hominoidea (hominoids). Monkeys are placed in two others (Ceboidea and Cercopithecoidea). This means that humans and apes are more closely related to each other than either is to monkeys.

Figure 7.1 summarizes the various levels of classification used in zoological taxonomy. Each lower-level unit belongs to the higher-level unit above it. Thus, toward the bottom of Figure 7.1, similar species belong to the same genus (plural, *genera*). Similar genera make up the same family, and so on through the top of Figure 7.1, where similar phyla (plural of *phylum*) are included in the same kingdom. The highest (most inclusive) taxonomic level is the *kingdom*. At that level, animals are distinguished from plants.

At the lowest level of taxonomy, a species may have subspecies. These are its more or less—but not yet totally—isolated subgroups. Subspecies can coexist in time and space. For example, the Neandertals, who lived between 130,000 and

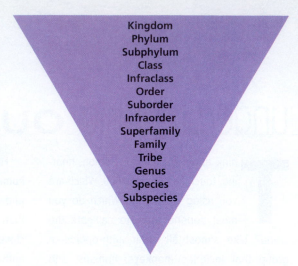

**FIGURE 7.1** The Principal Classificatory Units of Zoological Taxonomy.
Moving down the figure, the classificatory units become more exclusive, so that "Kingdom" at the top is the most inclusive unit and "Subspecies" at the bottom is the most exclusive.

28,000 years ago, may have belonged not to a separate species but merely to a different subspecies of *Homo sapiens*. Just one subspecies of *Homo sapiens* survives today.

The similarities used to assign organisms to the same taxon are called **homologies,** similarities they have jointly inherited from a common ancestor. Table 7.1 summarizes the place of humans in zoological taxonomy. We see in Table 7.1 that we are mammals, members of the class Mammalia. This is

**TABLE 7.1**  The Place of Humans (*Homo sapiens*) in Zoological Taxonomy

*Homo sapiens is an Animal, Chordate, Vertebrate, Mammal, Eutherian, Primate, Anthropoid, Catarrhine, Hominoid, Hominid, and Hominin. (Table 7.2 shows the taxonomic placement of the other primates.)*

| TAXON | SCIENTIFIC (LATIN) NAME | COMMON (ENGLISH) NAME |
|---|---|---|
| Kingdom | Animalia | Animals |
| Phylum | Chordata | Chordates |
| Subphylum | Vertebrata | Vertebrates |
| Class | Mammalia | Mammals |
| Infraclass | Eutheria | Eutherians |
| Order | Primates | Primates |
| Suborder | Anthropoidea | Anthropoids |
| Infraorder | Catarrhini | Catarrhines |
| Superfamily | Hominoidea | Hominoids |
| Family | Hominidae | Hominids |
| Tribe | Hominini | Hominins |
| Genus | *Homo* | Humans |
| Species | *Homo sapiens* | Recent humans |
| Subspecies | *Homo sapiens sapiens* | Anatomically modern humans |

a major subdivision of the kingdom Animalia. Mammals share certain traits, including mammary glands, that set them apart from other taxa, such as birds, reptiles, amphibians, and insects. Mammalian homologies indicate that all mammals share more recent common ancestry with each other than they do with any bird, reptile, or insect.

Humans are mammals that, at a lower taxonomic level, belong to the *order* Primates. Another mammalian order is Carnivora: the carnivores (dogs, cats, foxes, wolves, badgers, weasels). Rodentia (rats, mice, beavers, squirrels) form yet another mammalian order. The primates share structural and biochemical homologies that distinguish them from other mammals. These resemblances were inherited from their common early primate ancestors after those early primates became reproductively isolated from the ancestors of the other mammals.

# HOMOLOGIES AND ANALOGIES

Organisms should be assigned to the same taxon on the basis of homologies. The extensive biochemical homologies between apes and humans confirm our common ancestry and support our traditional joint classification as hominoids (see Table 7.2). For example, it is estimated that humans, chimpanzees, and gorillas have more than 98 percent of their DNA in common.

However, common ancestry isn't the only reason for similarities between species. Similar traits also can arise if species experience similar selective forces and adapt to them in similar ways. We call such similarities **analogies.** The process by which analogies are produced is called **convergent evolution.** For example, fish and porpoises share many analogies resulting from convergent evolution to life in the water. Like fish, porpoises, which are mammals, have fins. They also are hairless and streamlined for efficient locomotion. Analogies between birds and bats (wings, small size, light bones) illustrate convergent evolution to flying.

In theory, only homologies should be used in taxonomy. With reference to the hominoids, there is no doubt that humans, gorillas, and chimpanzees are more closely related to each other than any of the three is to orangutans, which are Asiatic apes. *Hominidae* is the name of the zoological family that includes hominids—fossil and living humans. Because chimps and gorillas share a more recent common ancestor with humans than they do with the orangutan, many scientists now also place gorillas and chimps in the hominid family. *Hominid,* then, refers to the zoological family that includes fossil and living humans, chimpanzees, gorillas, and their common ancestors. This leaves the orangutan (genus *Pongo*) as the only member of the pongid family (*Pongidae*). If chimps and gorillas are classified as hominids, what do we call the group that leads to humans but not to chimps and gorillas? For

**analogies**
Adaptive traits due to convergent evolution.

**convergent evolution**
Similar selective forces produce similar adaptive traits.

**TABLE 7.2**  Primate Taxonomy

*Major subdivisions of the two primate suborders: Prosimii and Anthropoidea. Humans are anthropoids who belong to the superfamily Hominoidea, along with the apes.*

| SUBORDER | INFRAORDER | SUPERFAMILY | FAMILY |
|---|---|---|---|
| Prosimii (prosimians) | Lemuriformes (lemurs) | Lemuroidea | Daubentoniidae (aye-ayes), Indridae (indri), Lemuridae (lemurs) |
| | Lorisiformes (lorises) | Lorisoidea | Lorisidae |
| | Tarsiiformes (tarsiers) | Tarsioidea | Tarsiidae |
| Anthropoidea (anthropoids) | Platyrrhini (platyrrhines—New World monkeys) | Ceboidea | Callitrichidae (tamarins and marmosets), Cebidae |
| | Catarrhini (catarrhines—Old World monkeys, apes, and humans) | Cercopithecoidea | Cercopithecidae (Old World monkeys) |
| | | Hominoidea (hominoids) | Hylobatidae (gibbons and siamangs), Pongidae (pongids—orangutans), Hominidae (hominids—gorillas, chimpanzees, and humans) |

SOURCE: Adapted from Robert Martin, "Classification of Primates," in Steve Jones, Robert Martin, and David Pilbeam, eds., *The Cambridge Encyclopedia of Human Evolution,* pp. 20–21. © Cambridge University Press, 1992. Reprinted with permission of Cambridge University Press.

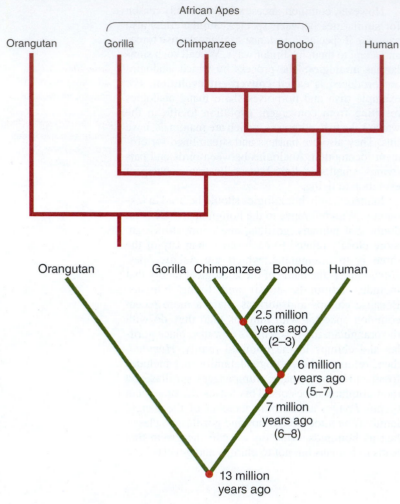

**FIGURE 7.2** Humans and the Apes.

The top drawing shows the evolutionary (phylogenetic) relationships among the living great apes and humans. Note that humans and the African apes are more closely related to each other (as hominids) than either is to the orangutan (a pongid). The bottom drawing shows the same phylogeny, along with estimated dates of divergence and last common ancestor (represented by dots). It is based on the extent of shared DNA among these groups.

SOURCE: From John Relethford, *The Human Species: An Introduction to Biological Anthropology,* 9th ed., (top) p. 134 and (bottom) p. 232. Copyright © 2013 by McGraw-Hill Education, LLC. Reprinted with permission.

**arboreal**
Living in the trees.

**anthropoids**
Monkeys, apes, and humans.

**prosimians**
The primate suborder that includes lemurs, lorises, and tarsiers.

**opposable thumb**
A thumb that can touch all the other fingers.

**bipedal**
Two-footed; upright locomotion (of hominins).

that, some scientists insert a taxonomic level called *tribe* between family and genus. The tribe *hominini* describes all the human species that ever have existed (including the extinct ones) and excludes chimps and gorillas. When scientists use the word *hominin* today, they mean pretty much the same thing as when they used the word *hominid* 20 years ago (Greiner 2003). Table 7.2 summarizes primate taxonomy, and Figure 7.2 illustrates our degree of relatedness to the living great apes.

## PRIMATE TENDENCIES

Primates are varied because they have adapted to diverse ecological niches. Some primates are active during the day; others, at night. Some eat insects; others, fruits; others, shoots, leaves, and bulk vegetation;

and others, seeds or roots. Some primates live on the ground, others live in trees, and there are intermediate adaptations. However, because the earliest primates were tree dwellers, modern primates share homologies reflecting their common **arboreal** heritage (see also Nystrom and Ashmore 2008).

Many trends in primate evolution are best exemplified by the **anthropoids:** monkeys, apes, and humans, which constitute the suborder *Anthropoidea.* The other primate suborder, *Prosimii,* includes lemurs, lorises, and tarsiers. These **prosimians** are more distant relatives of humans than are monkeys and apes. The primate trends—most developed in the anthropoids—can be summarized briefly. Together they constitute an anthropoid heritage that humans share with monkeys and apes.

1. **Grasping.** Primates have five-digited feet and hands that are suited for grasping. Certain features of hands and feet that were originally adaptive for arboreal life have been transmitted across the generations to contemporary primates. Flexible hands and feet that could encircle branches were important features in the early primates' arboreal life. Thumb opposability might have been favored by the inclusion of insects in the early primate diet. Manual dexterity makes it easier to catch insects attracted to abundant arboreal flowers and fruits. Humans and many other primates have **opposable thumbs:** The thumb can touch the other fingers. Some primates also have grasping feet. However, in adapting to **bipedal** (two-footed) locomotion, humans eliminated most of the foot's grasping ability.

2. **Smell to sight.** Several anatomical changes reflect the shift from smell to sight as the primates' most important means of obtaining information. Monkeys, apes, and humans have excellent *stereoscopic* (able to see in depth) and color vision. The portion of the brain devoted to vision expanded, while the area concerned with smell shrank.

3. **Nose to hand.** Sensations of touch, conveyed by *tactile organs,* also provide information. The tactile skin on a dog's or cat's nose transmits information. Cats' tactile hairs, or whiskers, also serve this function. In primates, however, the main touch organ is the hand, specifically the sensitive pads of the "fingerprint" region.

4. **Brain complexity.** The proportion of brain tissue concerned with memory, thought, and association has increased in primates. The primate ratio of brain size to body size exceeds that of most mammals.

5. **Parental investment.** Most primates give birth to a single offspring rather than a litter. Because of this, growing primates receive

more attention and have more learning opportunities than do other mammals. Learned behavior is an important part of primate adaptation.

6. **Sociality.** Primates tend to be social animals that live with others of their species. The need for longer and more attentive care of offspring places a selective value on support by a social group.

## PROSIMIANS

The primate order has two suborders: prosimians and anthropoids. The early history of the primates is limited to prosimian-like animals known through the fossil record. The first anthropoids, ancestral to monkeys, apes, and humans, appeared perhaps 50 million years ago. Some prosimians managed to survive in Africa and Asia because they were adapted to nocturnal life. As such, they did not compete with anthropoids, which are active during the day. Prosimians (lemurs) in Madagascar had no anthropoid competitors until people arrived on that island around 2,000 years ago.

In their behavior and biology, Madagascar's *lemurs*, which include some 50 species, show adaptations to an array of environments, or ecological niches. Their diets and times of activity differ. Lemurs eat fruits, other plant foods, eggs, and insects. Some are nocturnal; others are active during the day. Some are totally arboreal; others spend some time in the trees and some on the ground. Another kind of prosimian is the *tarsier*, today confined to Indonesia, Malaysia, and the Philippines. From the fossil record, we know that after 55 million years ago, several genera of tarsierlike prosimians lived in Asia, North America, and Europe, which were much warmer then than they are now. The one genus of tarsier that survived is totally nocturnal. Active at night, tarsiers don't directly compete with anthropoids, which are active during the day. *Lorises* are other nocturnal prosimians found in Africa and Asia.

## MONKEYS

All anthropoids share resemblances that can be considered trends in primate evolution in the sense that these traits are fully developed neither in the fossils of primates that lived prior to 50 million years ago nor among contemporary prosimians.

The anthropoid suborder has two infraorders: *platyrrhines* (New World monkeys) and *catarrhines* (Old World monkeys, apes, and humans). The catarrhines (sharp-nosed) and platyrrhines (flat-nosed) take their names from Latin terms that describe the placement of the nostrils (see Figure 7.3). Old World monkeys, apes, and humans are all catarrhines. Being placed in the same taxon (infraorder, in this

Compare this line drawing reconstruction of Shoshonius, a tarsierlike Eocene primate, with a modern tarsier from Mindanao in the Philippines. What similarities and differences do you notice?

case) means that Old World monkeys, apes, and humans are more closely related to each other than to New World monkeys. In other words, one kind of monkey (Old World) is more like a human than it is like another kind of monkey (New World). The New World monkeys were reproductively isolated from the catarrhines before the latter diverged into the Old World monkeys, apes, and humans. This is why New World monkeys are assigned to a different infraorder.

All New World monkeys and many Old World monkeys are arboreal. Whether in the trees or on the ground, however, monkeys move differently than apes and humans. Their arms and legs move parallel to one another, as dogs' legs do. This contrasts with the tendency toward *orthograde posture,* the straight and upright stance of apes and humans. Unlike apes, which have longer arms than legs, and humans, who have longer legs than arms, monkeys have arms and legs of about the same length. Most monkeys also have tails, which help them maintain balance in the

**FIGURE 7.3** Nostril Structure of Catarrhines and Platyrrhines.

Above: narrow septum and "sharp nose" of a guenon, a catarrhine (Old World monkey). Below: broad septum and "flat nose" of Humboldt's woolly monkey, a platyrrhine (New World monkey). Which nose is more like your own? What does that similarity suggest?

A woolly spider monkey, or muriqui, from Monte Clares, Brazil. The long arms and elongated prehensile tail create a spiderlike image for this New World monkey.

trees. Apes and humans lack tails. The apes' tendency toward orthograde posture is most evident when they sit down. When they move about, chimps, gorillas, and orangutans habitually use all four limbs.

## New World Monkeys

New World monkeys live in the forests of Central and South America. Unlike Old World monkeys, many New World monkeys have *prehensile,* or grasping, tails. Sometimes the prehensile tail has tactile skin, which permits it to work like a hand, for instance, in conveying food to the mouth. Old World monkeys, however, have developed their own characteristic anatomical specializations. They have rough patches of skin on the buttocks, adapted to sitting on hard, rocky ground and rough branches. If the primate you see in the zoo has such patches, it's from the Old World. If it has a prehensile tail, it's a New World monkey. Among the anthropoids, there's only one nocturnal animal, a New World

monkey called the night monkey or owl monkey. All other monkeys and apes, and humans, too, of course, are diurnal—active during the day.

## Old World Monkeys

The Old World monkeys have both terrestrial and arboreal species. Baboons and many macaques are terrestrial monkeys. Certain traits differentiate terrestrial and arboreal primates. Arboreal primates tend to be smaller. Smaller animals can reach a greater variety of foods in shrubs and trees, where the most abundant foods are located at the ends of branches. Arboreal monkeys typically are lithe and agile. They escape from the few predators in their environment—snakes and monkey-eating eagles—through alertness and speed. Large size, by contrast, is advantageous for terrestrial primates in dealing with their predators, which are more numerous on the ground.

Another contrast between arboreal and terrestrial primates is in **sexual dimorphism**—marked differences in male and female anatomy and temperament. Sexual dimorphism tends to be more marked in terrestrial than in arboreal species. Baboon and macaque males are larger and fiercer than are females of the same species. However, it's hard to tell, without close inspection, the sex of an arboreal monkey.

Of the terrestrial monkeys, the baboons of Africa and the (mainly Asiatic) macaques have been the subjects of many studies. Terrestrial monkeys have specializations in anatomy, psychology, and social

**sexual dimorphism**
Marked differences in male and female anatomy and temperament.

Mandrills (*Papio sphinx*) are terrestrial Old World monkeys. Related to baboons, mandrills live in groups consisting of an adult male, several females, and their young. What kind of sexual dimorphism is shown in this photo?

behavior that enable them to cope with terrestrial life. Adult male baboons, for example, are fierce-looking animals that can weigh 100 pounds (45 kilograms). They display their long, projecting canines to intimidate predators and when confronting other baboons. Faced with a predator, a male baboon can puff up his ample mane of shoulder hair, so that the would-be aggressor perceives the baboon as larger than he actually is.

Longitudinal field research shows that, near the time of puberty, baboon and macaque males typically leave their home troop for another. Because males move in and out, females form the stable core of the terrestrial monkey troop (Cheney and Seyfarth 1990). By contrast, among chimpanzees and gorillas, females are more likely to emigrate and seek mates outside their natal social groups (Bradley et al. 2004; Matsuzawa 2011; Nishida 2012; Wilson and Wrangham 2003). Among terrestrial

monkeys, then, the core group consists of females; among apes it is made up of males.

## APES

The Old World monkeys have their own separate superfamily (Cercopithecoidea), while humans and the apes together compose the hominoid superfamily (Hominoidea). Among the hominoids, the so-called great apes are orangutans, gorillas, and chimpanzees (see Raffaele 2010). Humans could be included here, too; sometimes we are called "the third African ape." The lesser (smaller) apes are the gibbons and siamangs of Southeast Asia and Indonesia.

Several traits are shared by apes (and humans) as distinct from monkeys and other primates. Body size tends to be larger. The life span is longer. There is a longer interval between births of infants, which depend longer on their parent(s). There is a tendency toward upright posture, although habitual upright bipedalism is characteristic only of hominins. The brain is larger, the muzzle or face is shorter and less projecting, and no hominoid has a tail.

Apes live in forests and woodlands, and almost all apes are threatened or endangered today because of human encroachment (see "Appreciating Diversity" on p. 116). The light and agile **gibbons,** which are skilled brachiators, are completely arboreal. (**Brachiation** is hand-over-hand movement through the trees.) The heavier gorillas, chimpanzees, and adult male orangutans spend considerable time on the ground. Nevertheless, ape behavior and anatomy reveal past and present adaptation to arboreal life. For example, apes still build nests to sleep in trees. Apes have longer arms than legs, which is adaptive for brachiation (see Figure 7.4).

**gibbons**
Small, arboreal, Asiatic apes.

**brachiation**
Under-the-branch swinging.

**FIGURE 7.4**   The Limb Ratio of the Arboreal Gibbon and Terrestrial *Homo.*
How does this anatomical difference fit the modes of locomotion used by gibbons and humans?

# appreciating DIVERSITY

## A Planet without Apes

In the past—and continuing today on a global scale—human activity has threatened and reduced diversity among primates. My colleague John Mitani, a professor of anthropology at the University of Michigan, writes here about global threats to the (barely) surviving apes. He appeals to the U.S. Congress to reauthorize the Great Apes Conservation Fund, which can help preserve the diversity represented by our closest relatives. As of this writing (2014), congressional reauthorization appears unlikely.

VIEWERS of . . . [the 2011 film] "Rise of the Planet of the Apes" may be surprised to learn that before our earliest ancestors arrived on the scene roughly seven million years ago, apes really did rule the planet. As many as 40 kinds roamed Eurasia and Africa between 10 and 25 million years ago. Only five types remain. Two live in Asia, the gibbon and orangutan; another three, the chimpanzee, bonobo and gorilla, dwell in Africa. All five are endangered, several critically so. All may face extinction.

A decade ago, Congress stepped forward with a relatively cheap but vitally important effort to protect these apes through innovative conservation programs. . . . But attempts to reauthorize the Great Apes Conservation Fund have gotten stuck in Congress and may become a victim of the larger debate over the national debt.

Hollywood's depiction of apes as cunning—if not conniving—creatures comes close to reality. Fifty years ago, Jane Goodall's observations of chimpanzees' using tools and eating meat demonstrated just how similar apes are to humans. Subsequent fieldwork has underscored this point. . . .

Orangutans fashion tools to extract seeds that are otherwise difficult to obtain. Gorillas engage in conversational vocal exchanges. Bonobos appear to have sex not only to reproduce but also to relieve stress. Male chimpanzees form coalitions to kill their neighbors and take over their territory. . . .

Apes . . . are prime attractions at zoos, and scientists from disciplines ranging from anthropology to biology and psychology study them closely in captivity and in the wild. As our first cousins in the primate family, apes help us to understand what makes us human.

I have been lucky to study all five kinds of apes during 33 years of fieldwork in Africa and Asia. When I look into the eyes of an ape, something stares back at me that seems familiar. Perhaps it is a shock of recognition, or a thoughtfulness not seen in the eyes of a frog, bird or cat. The penetrating stare makes me wonder, "What is this individual thinking?" But as the human population expands, ape numbers continue to dwindle. In previous versions of the "Planet of the Apes" films, greed and consumption by humanlike apes threatened the world. In reality, it is these all-too-human traits that imperil apes.

Habitat destruction because of human activity, including logging, oil exploration and subsistence farming, is the biggest concern. Hunting is another major problem, especially in West and Central Africa, where a thriving "bush meat" trade severely threatens African apes. Poachers are now entering once-impenetrable forests on roads built for loggers and miners. Recently, periodic outbreaks of deadly diseases that can infect humans and apes, like Ebola, have begun to ravage populations of chimpanzees and gorillas.

The Great Apes Conservation Act, enacted in 2000, authorized the spending of $5 million annually over five years to help protect apes in the wild. The act was re-authorized in 2005 for another five years. The program matches public with private dollars to maximize the impact. Since 2006, for example, $21 million in federal dollars spent by the Great Ape Conservation Fund generated an additional $25 million in private grants and support from other governments. . . . The money pays for protecting habitat, battling poachers and educating local populations about the importance of these apes.

For instance, in Indonesia . . . money has been earmarked to block the conversion of forests to commercial oil palm and rubber plantations. In Congo, home to the extremely rare mountain gorilla, alternative fuels have been introduced to discourage the cutting of forests for charcoal production. In Gabon, the program has paid for law enforcement training for park rangers battling poachers. . . . In all, [in 2010], the Great Apes Conservation Fund helped to underwrite more than 50 programs in 7 Asian and 12 African countries. . . .

A planet without apes is not sci-fi fantasy. If we do not take action [to reauthorize] now, sometime in the future . . . our children and our children's children will ask with wonder, and perhaps a certain amount of anger, why we stood by idly while these remarkable creatures were driven to extinction.

SOURCE: John C. Mitani, "Fearing a Planet without Apes." From *The New York Times*, August 20, 2011.

---

The structure of the shoulder and clavicle (collarbone) of the apes and humans suggests that we had a brachiating ancestor. In fact, young apes still do brachiate. Adult apes tend to be too heavy to brachiate safely. Their weight is more than many branches can withstand. Gorillas and chimps now use the long arms they have inherited from their more arboreal ancestors for life on the ground. The terrestrial locomotion of chimps and gorillas is called *knuckle-walking*. In it, long arms and callused knuckles support the trunk as the apes amble around, leaning forward.

## Gibbons

Gibbons are found in the forests of Southeast Asia, especially in Malaysia. Smallest of the apes, male and female gibbons have about the same average height (3 feet, or 1 meter) and weight (12–25 pounds, or 5–10 kilograms). Gibbons spend most of their time just below the forest canopy (treetops). For efficient brachiation, gibbons have long arms and fingers, with short thumbs. Slenderly built, gibbons are the most agile apes. They use their long arms for balance when they occasionally walk erect on the ground or along a branch. Gibbons are the preeminent arboreal specialists among the apes. They subsist on a diet mainly of fruits, with occasional insects and small animals. Gibbons and siamangs, their slightly larger relatives, tend to live in *primary groups,* which are composed of a permanently bonded male and female and their preadolescent offspring.

## Orangutans

There are two existing species of orangutan, Asiatic apes that belong to the genus *Pongo.* Highly endangered, contemporary orangs are confined to two Indonesian islands—Borneo and Sumatra. Orangutans once were found throughout Southeast Asia, but today 90 percent of them live in Indonesia. Borneo has between 40,000 and 50,000 orangutans, while a mere 7,000 survive on Sumatra (Isaacson 2012).

The degree of sexual dimorphism in orangs is striking. Adult males weigh more than twice as much as females. The orangutan male, like his human counterpart, is intermediate in size between chimps and gorillas. Orang males can weigh up to 300 pounds (135 kilograms), but usually they weigh around 200 pounds (90 kilograms). Less bulky than gorillas, male orangs can be more arboreal, although they typically climb, rather than swing through, the trees. The smaller size of females and young permits them to make fuller use of the trees. Orangutans have a varied diet of fruit, bark, leaves, and insects. Because orangutans live in jungles and feed in trees, they are especially difficult to study. However, field reports about orangutans in their natural setting (Schaik 2004) have clarified their behavior and social organization. Orangs are the least sociable of the great apes (see Isaacson 2012; Schaik 2004). Often they are solitary, with their tightest social units formed by females and preadolescent young, and males foraging alone.

With long arms and fingers, the gibbon is the most agile of the apes. As we see here, gibbons occasionally walk upright on the ground, using their long arms as balancers.

Dr. Biruté Galdikas has studied orangutans in Indonesia for decades. Here she carries an orangutan named Isabel, soon to be released (from a rehabilitation center) into the wild at Tanjung Puting National Park on the Indonesian island of Borneo.

Since 1971 Biruté Mary Galdikas has studied wild orangutans in central Borneo. She is one of three prominent primatologists—all women—encouraged by famed paleoanthropologist Louis B. Leakey to study and protect the great apes. The others are Jane Goodall (working with chimpanzees) and the late Dian Fossey (who worked with mountain gorillas). As Galdikas (2007) reports, economic globalization has fueled worldwide demand for pulp, paper, palm oil, and precious metals, leading to the destruction of Indonesia's tropical forests and endangering the orang. About 80 percent of the orang habitat has been either depopulated or totally destroyed (Galdikas 2007). Galdikas has urged Indonesia to impose a tax on multinational companies that profit from rain forest destruction and to use the revenues for forest and orangutan conservation. Indonesia, however, is a large, populous country with millions of poor people. The temptation to exploit natural resources to feed people, and to expand the economy, is great. Is there a realistic chance that the orangutan will survive?

## Gorillas

With just one species, *Gorilla gorilla,* there are three subspecies of gorillas. The western lowland gorilla is the animal you normally see in zoos. This, the smallest subspecies of gorilla, lives mainly in forests in the Central African Republic, Congo, Cameroon, Gabon, Nigeria, and Equatorial Guinea (see Matsuzawa 2011). The eastern lowland gorilla, of which there are only four in captivity, is slightly larger and lives in eastern Congo. There are no mountain gorillas, the third subspecies, in captivity, and it's estimated that no more than 650 of these animals survive in the wild. These are the largest gorillas, with the longest hair (to keep them warm in their mountainous habitat). They also are the rarest gorillas, which Dian Fossey (1983) and other scientists have studied in Rwanda, Uganda, and eastern Congo.

Full-grown male gorillas may weigh 400 pounds (180 kilograms) and stand 6 feet tall (183 centimeters). Like most terrestrial primates, gorillas show marked sexual dimorphism. The average adult female weighs half as much as the male. Gorillas spend little time in the trees. It's hard for an adult male to move his bulk about in a tree. When gorillas sleep in trees, they build nests, which usually are no more than 10 feet (3 meters) off the ground. By contrast, the nests of chimps and female orangs may be 100 feet (30 meters) above the ground.

Most of the gorilla's day is spent feeding. Gorillas move through jungle undergrowth eating ground plants, leaves, bark, fruits, and other vegetation (see Rothman, Raubenheimer, and Chapman 2011). Like most primates, gorillas live in social groups. The *troop* is a common unit of primate social organization, consisting of multiple males and females

Mountain gorillas are the rarest and most endangered kind of gorilla. Dian Fossey (shown here) and other scientists have studied them in Rwanda, Uganda, and eastern Congo. Here, Fossey (now deceased) observes a young gorilla in Rwanda's Virunga Mountains.

Chimpanzees live mainly in tropical rain forests but also in woodlands and mixed forest–woodland–grassland areas, such as the Gombe Stream National Park, Tanzania, where Jane Goodall began to study them in 1960. Shown here 30 years after her first visit to Gombe, Goodall continues her lifelong commitment to these endangered animals.

and their offspring. Although troops with up to 30 gorillas have been observed, most gorillas live in groups of from 10 to 20. Gorilla troops tend to have fairly stable memberships, with little shifting between troops (Fossey 1983). Each troop has a silverback male, so designated because of the strip of white hair that extends down his back. This is the physical sign of full maturity among male gorillas. The silverback is usually the only breeding male in the troop, which is why gorilla troops are sometimes called "one-male groups." However, a few younger, subordinate males may also adhere to such a one-male group.

## Chimpanzees

Chimpanzees belong to the genus *Pan*, which has two species: *Pan troglodytes* (the common chimpanzee) and *Pan paniscus* (the bonobo, or "pygmy," chimpanzee). Like humans, chimps are closely related to the gorilla, although there are some obvious differences. Like gorillas, chimps live in tropical Africa, but they range over a larger area and more varied environments than gorillas do. The common chimp, *Pan troglodytes,* lives in western central Africa (Gabon, Congo, Cameroon), as well as in western Africa (Ivory Coast, Sierra Leone, Liberia, Gambia) and eastern Africa (Congo, Uganda, and Tanzania). Bonobos live in remote and densely forested areas of just one country—the Democratic Republic of Congo (DRC). Common chimps live mainly in tropical

rain forests but also in woodlands and mixed forest–woodland–grassland areas, such as the Gombe Stream National Park, Tanzania, where Jane Goodall and other researchers began to study them in 1960 (see Goodall 2009, 2010).

There are dietary differences between chimps and gorillas. Gorillas eat large quantities of green bulk vegetation, but chimps, like orangutans and gibbons, prefer fruits. Chimps actually are omnivorous, adding animal protein to their diet by capturing small mammals, birds' eggs, and insects.

Chimps are lighter and more arboreal than gorillas are. The adult male's weight—between 100 and 200 pounds (45–90 kilograms)—is about a third of that of the male gorilla. There is much less sexual dimorphism among chimps than among gorillas. Females approximate 88 percent of the average male height. This is similar to the ratio of sexual dimorphism in *Homo sapiens.*

Several scientists have studied wild chimps, and we know more about the full range of their behavior and social organization than we do about the other apes (see Goodall 2009; Matsuzawa 2011; Nishida 2012). The long-term research of Jane Goodall (2010) and others at Gombe provides especially useful information. Approximately 150 chimpanzees range over Gombe's 30 square miles (80 square kilometers). Goodall (2009, 2010) has described communities of about 50 chimps, all of which know one another and interact from time to time. Communities regularly split up into smaller groups: a mother and her offspring; a few males; males,

This photo was taken at a bonobo sanctuary in the Democratic Republic of Congo. Are bonobos (pygmy chimpanzees) smaller than chimps?

**behavioral ecology**
Study of the evolutionary basis of social behavior.

subspecies of common chimpanzee—95 pounds (43 kilograms) for males and 73 pounds (33 kilograms) for females.

Although much smaller than the males, female bonobos seem to rule. de Waal (1995, 1997) characterizes bonobo communities as female-centered, peace-loving, and egalitarian. The strongest social bonds are among females, although females also bond with males. The male bonobo's status reflects that of his mother, to which he remains closely bonded for life.

The frequency with which bonobos have sex—and use it to avoid conflict—makes them exceptional among the primates (de Waal 1997). Despite frequent sex, the bonobo reproductive rate doesn't exceed that of the chimpanzee. A female bonobo gives birth every 5 or 6 years. Then, like chimps, female bonobos nurse and carry around their young for up to 5 years. Bonobos reach adolescence around 7 years of age. Females, which first give birth at age 13 or 14, are full grown by 15 years.

## BEHAVIORAL ECOLOGY AND FITNESS

According to evolutionary theory, when the environment changes, natural selection starts to modify the *population*'s pool of genetic material. Natural selection has another key feature: the differential reproductive success of *individuals* within the population. **Behavioral ecology** studies the evolutionary basis of social behavior. It assumes that the genetic features of any species reflect a long history of differential reproductive success (that is, natural selection). In other words, biological traits of contemporary organisms have been transmitted across the generations because those traits enabled their ancestors to survive and reproduce more effectively than their competition.

Natural selection is based on *differential* reproduction. Members of the same species may compete to maximize their reproductive fitness—their genetic contribution to future generations. *Individual fitness* is measured by the number of direct descendants an individual has. Illustrating a primate strategy that may enhance individual fitness are cases in which male monkeys kill infants after entering a new troop. Destroying the offspring of other males, they clear a place for their own progeny (Hausfater and Hrdy 2008).

Besides competition, one's genetic contribution to future generations also can be enhanced by cooperation, sharing, and other apparently unselfish behavior. This is because of *inclusive fitness*—reproductive success measured by the genes one shares with relatives. By sacrificing for their kin—even if this means limiting their own direct reproduction—individuals actually may increase their genetic contributions (their shared genes) to the future. Inclusive fitness helps us understand why a female might

females, and young; and occasionally solitary animals. The social networks of males are more closed than are those of females, which are more likely to migrate and mate outside their natal group than males are (Wrangham et al. 1994).

When chimps, which are very vocal, meet, they greet one another with gestures, facial expressions, and calls. They hoot to maintain contact during their daily rounds. Like baboons and macaques, chimps exhibit dominance relationships through attacks and displacement. Some adult females outrank younger males, although females do not display as strong dominance relationships among themselves as males do. Males occasionally cooperate in hunting parties (see Nishida 2012).

### Bonobos

Ancestral chimps, and especially hominins, eventually spread out of the forests and into woodlands and more open habitats (see Choi 2011). Bonobos, which belong to the species *Pan paniscus,* apparently never left the protection of the trees. Up to 10,000 bonobos survive in the humid forests south of the Zaire River, in the Democratic Republic of Congo (see Furuichi and Thompson 2008). Despite their common name of *pygmy* chimpanzee, bonobos aren't necessarily smaller than chimps. Bonobos are about the same size as members of the smallest invest in her sister's offspring, or why a male might risk his life to defend his brothers. If self-sacrifice perpetuates more of their genes than direct reproduction does, it makes sense in terms of behavioral ecology. Such a view can help us understand aspects of primate behavior and social organization (for application to humans see Chapais 2008 and Hill et al. 2011).

Maternal care always makes sense in terms of reproductive fitness theory, because females know their offspring are their own. But it's harder for males to be sure about paternity. Inclusive fitness theory predicts that males will invest most in offspring when they are surest the offspring are theirs. Gibbons, for example, have strict male–female pair bonding, which makes it almost certain that the offspring are those of both members of the pair. Thus, we expect male gibbons to offer care and protection to their young, and they do. However, among species and in situations in which a male can't be sure about his paternity, it may make more sense to invest in a sister's offspring than in a mate's, because the niece or nephew definitely shares some of that male's genes.

## PRIMATE EVOLUTION

The fossil record offers evidence for no more than 5 percent of extinct types of primates. Such small numbers provide the merest glimpse of the diverse bioforms—living beings—that have existed on Earth.

With reference to the primate fossil record, we'll see that different geographic areas provide more abundant fossil evidence for different time periods. This doesn't necessarily mean that primates were not living elsewhere at the same time. Discussions of primate and human evolution must be tentative, because the fossil record is limited and spotty (see Ciochon and Fleagle 2012). Much is subject to change as knowledge increases. A key feature of science is to recognize the tentativeness and uncertainty of knowledge. Scientists, including fossil hunters, constantly seek out new evidence and devise new methods, such as DNA comparison, to improve their understanding, in this case of primate and human evolution.

## CHRONOLOGY

Based on fossils found in stratigraphic sequences, the history of vertebrate life has been divided into three main eras. The *Paleozoic* (544–245 **m.y.a.**—million years ago) was the era of ancient life—fishes, amphibians, and primitive reptiles. The *Mesozoic* (245–65 m.y.a.) was the era of middle life—reptiles, including the dinosaurs. The *Cenozoic* (65 m.y.a.–present) is the era of recent life—birds and mammals. Each era is divided into periods; the periods, into epochs.

Anthropologists are concerned with the Cenozoic *era* (Figure 7.5), which includes two *periods:* Tertiary and Quaternary. Each of these periods is subdivided into *epochs.* The Tertiary had five epochs: Paleocene, Eocene, Oligocene, Miocene, and

**m.y.a.**
Million years ago.

| Era | Period | Epoch | Climate and Life Forms |
|---|---|---|---|
| Cenozoic | Quaternary | Holocene<br>10,000 B.P. | Transition to agriculture; emergence of states |
| | | Pleistocene<br>2 m.y.a. | Climatic fluctuations, glaciation; spread of *Homo*, extinction of (hyper)robust australopithecines |
| | Tertiary | Pliocene<br>5 m.y.a. | *Au. africanus, Au. afarensis, Au. anamensis, Ardipithecus* |
| | | Miocene<br>23 m.y.a. | Cooler and drier grasslands spread in middle latitudes; Africa collides with Eurasia (16 m.y.a.) |
| | | Oligocene<br>34 m.y.a. | Cooler and drier in the north; anthropoids in Africa (Fayum); separation of catarrhines and platyrrhines; separation of hylobatids (gibbons) from pongids and hominids |
| | | Eocene<br>54 m.y.a | Warm tropical climates become widespread; modern orders of mammals appear; prosimian-like primates are abundant; anthropoids appear |
| | | Paleocene<br>65 m.y.a | First major mammal radiation |

**FIGURE 7.5** Periods and Epochs of the Cenozoic Era.
The geological time scale is based on stratigraphy. Eras are subdivided into periods, and periods into epochs. In what era, period, and epoch did *Homo* originate?

Pliocene. The Quaternary includes just two epochs: Pleistocene and Holocene, or Recent. Figure 7.5 gives the approximate dates of these epochs. Sediments from the Paleocene epoch (65–54 m.y.a.) have yielded fossil remains of diverse small mammals, including, by the late Paleocene, the earliest known primate. Prosimian-like fossils abound in strata dating from the Eocene (54–34 m.y.a.). Anthropoid fossils date to the Eocene and become more abundant in the ensuing Oligocene (34–23 m.y.a.). Hominoids became widespread during the Miocene (23–5 m.y.a.). Hominins first appeared in the late Miocene, just before the Pliocene (5–2 m.y.a.).

# EARLY PRIMATES

When the Mesozoic era ended, and the Cenozoic era began, around 65 million years ago, North America was connected to Europe but not to South America. (The Americas joined around 20 million years ago.) Over millions of years, the continents have "drifted" to their present locations, carried along by the gradually shifting plates of the Earth's surface (Figure 7.6).

During the Cenozoic, most landmasses had tropical or subtropical climates. The Mesozoic era had ended with a massive worldwide extinction of plants and animals, including the dinosaurs. Thereafter, mammals eventually replaced reptiles as the dominant large land animals. Trees and flowering plants soon proliferated, supplying arboreal foods for the primates that eventually evolved to fill the new niches.

According to the *arboreal theory,* primates became primates by adapting to arboreal life. The primate traits and trends discussed previously developed as adaptations to life high up in the trees. A key feature was the importance of sight over smell. Changes in the visual apparatus were adaptive in the trees, where depth perception facilitated leaping. Grasping hands and feet were used to crawl along slender branches. Grasping feet anchored the body as the primate reached for foods at the ends of branches. Early primates probably had omnivorous diets based on foods available in the trees, such as flowers, fruits, berries, gums, leaves, and insects. The early Cenozoic era witnessed a proliferation of flowering plants, attracting insects that were to figure prominently in many primate diets.

## Early Cenozoic Primates

A tiny, complete skeleton from China, first described in 2013, represents the earliest known primate. The creature was smaller than today's smallest primate—the pygmy mouse lemur of Madagascar. Named *Archicebus achilles* because of its prominent (and monkeylike) ankle and heel, the animal has been tentatively assigned to the tarsier lineage, but very close to the time when the ancestors of tarsiers separated from those of the anthropoids. *Archicebus achilles* weighed no more than 1 ounce, and it had a 5-inch tail that was longer than its 4-inch body. It lived 55 million years ago, when Earth was a natural greenhouse, with rain forests everywhere and palm trees growing in what is now Alaska.

This finding supports the view that the first primates evolved in Asia—not too long after the dinosaurs went extinct (66 million years ago). Somehow primates crossed open water to reach Africa by 38 million years ago (Africa remained an island continent until 16 million years ago). *Archicebus achilles* had the feet of a small monkey; the arms, legs, and teeth of a very primitive primate; and a primitive skull with very small eyes. If it was indeed an early tarsier, its heel and ankle still suggest a close connection to anthropoids. Unlike today's tarsiers, *Archicebus achilles* was not nocturnal. Being so small and metabolically active, it probably spent its days frantically leaping around in the humid tropical forest it inhabited (Ni et al. 2013; Wilford 2013).

*Archicebus achilles* lived late in the Paleocene (65–54 m.y.a.), the first epoch of the Cenozoic era. A diversified group of primates inhabited Europe and North America during the Cenozoic's second epoch, the Eocene (54–34 m.y.a.). In primate evolution, the Eocene was the age of the prosimians, with at least 60 genera in two main families. They lived in Asia, North America, and Europe,

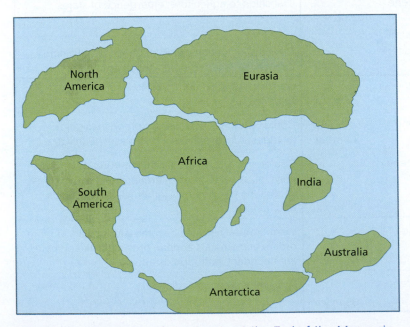

**FIGURE 7.6** Placement of Continents at the End of the Mesozoic.
When the Mesozoic era ended and the Cenozoic began, some 65 million years ago, North America was connected to Europe but not to South America.

*Smilodectes* was a lemurlike primate that lived during the Eocene. Compare the painting reconstructing a *Smilodectes* from Wyoming (left) with this pair of modern black lemurs (*Eulemur macaco*) from Madagascar.

reaching Africa by the late Eocene. By the end of the Eocene, ancestral lemurs had reached Madagascar. They must have traveled from East Africa across the Mozambique Channel—narrower then than now—on thick mats of vegetation. Such naturally formed "rafts" have been observed forming in East African rivers, then floating out to sea.

Early in the Eocene, ancestral anthropoids branched off from the tarsiers and other prosimians. These protomonkeys were diurnal (active during the day) (see Schultz, Opie, and Atkinson 2011). In this diurnal niche, vision was favored over smell. The eyes and brain got bigger, and the snout was reduced. Anthropoid eyes are rotated more forward than are those of prosimians. Also, anthropoids have a fully enclosed bony eye socket, which lemurs and lorises lack. And unlike lemurs and lorises, anthropoids lack a rhinarium, a moist nose continuous with the upper lip. Anthropoids have a dry nose, separate from the upper lip. By the end of the Eocene, many prosimian species had become extinct, reflecting competition from the first anthropoids.

## Oligocene Anthropoids

During the Oligocene epoch (34–23 m.y.a.), anthropoids became the most numerous primates. Most of our knowledge of early anthropoids is based on fossils from Egypt's Fayum deposits. This area is a desert today, but 34–31 million years ago it was a tropical rain forest.

The anthropoids of the Fayum lived in trees and ate fruits and seeds. Compared with prosimians, they had fewer teeth, reduced snouts, larger brains, and increasingly forward-looking eyes. Of the Fayum anthropoid fossils, one group is the more primitive and perhaps is ancestral to the New World monkeys. These protomonkeys were small (2–3 pounds, 0.9–1.4 kilograms), with similarities to living marmosets and tamarins, small South American monkeys.

Another Fayum group seems ancestral to the catarrhines—Old World monkeys, apes, and humans. This group shares with the later catarrhines a distinctive dental formula, 2.1.2.3, meaning two incisors, one canine, two premolars, and three molars. (The formula is based on one-fourth of the mouth, either the right or left side of the upper or lower jaw.) The more primitive primate dental formula is 2.1.3.3. Most other primates, including prosimians and New World monkeys, have the second formula, with three premolars instead of two. Besides the Fayum, Oligocene deposits with primate bones have been found in North and West Africa, southern Arabia, China, Southeast Asia, and North and South America.

In 2013, researchers working in Tanzania's Rukwa Rift Basin reported their discovery of two finds that may be the oldest known fossils from two major primate groups—hominoids (apes and humans) and Old

World monkeys. Geological dating shows the fossils to be 25.2 million years old, several million years older than any other confirmed example of an ancient ape or Old World monkey. Molecular dating based on DNA comparisons previously had suggested that the apes and Old World monkeys diverged 25–30 million years ago. Because these new finds represent individuals that lived 25.2 m.y.a., the split must have occurred earlier than that, perhaps around 30 m.y.a. The ape fossil from Tanzania is a lower right jaw with teeth, and the second find, classified as an Old World monkey, is a jaw fragment with a single tooth. These primates lived during the late Oligocene (Bower 2013; Stevens et al. 2013).

The Oligocene was a time of major geological and climatic change: The Great Rift Valley system of East Africa formed; India drifted into Asia; and a cooling trend began, especially in the Northern Hemisphere, where primates disappeared.

## MIOCENE HOMINOIDS

Hominoid fossils become abundant during the Miocene epoch (23–5 m.y.a.), which is divided into three parts: lower, middle, and upper or late. The early Miocene (23–16 m.y.a.) was a warm and wet period, when forests covered East Africa. Recall that Hominoidea is the superfamily that includes fossil and living apes and humans. For simplicity's sake, the earliest **hominoids** are here called *protoapes,* or simply *apes*. Although some of these may be ancestral to living apes, none is identical, or often even very similar, to modern apes.

*Proconsul* is the name for a group (three known species) of early Miocene protoapes. These ancient apes, which lived in Africa, had teeth with similarities to those of living apes. Below the neck, however, their skeleton was more monkeylike. The *Proconsul* species ranged in size from that of a small monkey to that of a chimpanzee, usually with marked sexual dimorphism. Their dentition suggests they ate fruits and leaves. By the middle Miocene, *Proconsul* had been replaced by other apes.

## Later Miocene Apes

During the early Miocene (23–16 m.y.a.), Africa had been cut off by water from Europe and Asia. But during the middle Miocene, Arabia drifted into Eurasia, providing a land connection between Africa, Europe, and Asia. Migrating both ways—out of and into Africa—after 16 m.y.a. were various animals, including hominoids. Protoapes were the most common primates of the middle Miocene (16–10 m.y.a.). Over 20 species have been discovered in Europe, Africa, and Asia.

The most remarkable Miocene ape was *Gigantopithecus*—almost certainly the largest primate that ever lived. Confined to Asia, it persisted for millions of years, from the Miocene until

400,000 years ago, when it coexisted with members of our own genus, *Homo erectus*. Some people think *Gigantopithecus* is not extinct yet, that we know it today as the yeti and Bigfoot (Sasquatch).

With a fossil record consisting of nothing more than jawbones and teeth, it is difficult to say for sure just how big *Gigantopithecus* was. Based on ratios of jaw and tooth size to body size in other apes, various reconstructions have been made. One has *Gigantopithecus* weighing 1,200 pounds (544 kilograms) and standing 10 feet (3 meters) tall (Ciochon, Olsen, and James 1990). Another puts the height at 9 feet (2.7 meters) and cuts the weight in half (Simons and Ettel 1970). All reconstructions agree, however, that *Gigantopithecus* was the largest ape that ever lived. There were at least two species of *Gigantopithecus:* One coexisted with *H. erectus* in China and Vietnam, and the other, much earlier (5 m.y.a.), lived in northern India.

### *Pierolapithecus catalaunicus*

In 2004, Spanish anthropologists announced their discovery of what may (or may not) be the last common ancestor of humans, chimpanzees, gorillas, and orangutans (Moyá-Solá et al. 2004). This ape

A reconstruction of *Gigantopithecus* by Russell Ciochon and Bill Munns. Munns is shown here with "Giganto." What would be the likely environmental effects of a population of such large apes?

**hominoid**
Zoological superfamily that includes extinct and living apes and hominins.

*Pierolapithecus catalaunicus.* The *Pierolapithecus* bones discovered so far include much of the skull, hand and foot bones, including toe and finger fragments, three vertebrae, two complete ribs, and large pieces of a dozen others. This Miocene ape, first described in 2004, may be the last common ancestor of all the world's living great apes, including the human family.

species, named *Pierolapithecus catalaunicus*, lived around 13 million years ago, during the middle Miocene. The find comes from a rich fossil site near the village of Hostalets de Pierola in Catalonia, Spain. The name *Pierolapithecus* combines part of the village's name with the Greek word for "ape," while *catalaunicus* commemorates Catalonia, the province where both the village and Barcelona are located.

The *Pierolapithecus* bones include much of the skull, hand and foot bones, three vertebrae, two complete ribs, and large pieces of a dozen others. The find appears to represent a single adult male that weighed about 75 pounds (34 kilograms). Like chimps and gorillas, *Pierolapithecus* was well adapted for tree climbing and knuckle-walking on the ground. Based on the shape of the single surviving tooth, it probably was a fruit eater. Several features distinguished *Pierolapithecus* from the lesser apes (gibbons and siamangs) and monkeys. Its rib cage, lower spine, and wrist suggest it climbed the way modern great apes do. The ape's chest, or thorax, is wider and flatter than that of monkeys and is the earliest modern apelike thorax yet found in the fossil record.

In the current timetable of primate evolution, the lineage of Old World monkeys had split off from ancestral apes by some 25 m.y.a. The ancestors of the lesser apes separated from those of the great apes some 16–14 m.y.a. Then, by 11–10 m.y.a., the orangutan line had diverged from that leading to the African apes and humans. Yet another split took place when the gorilla line branched off from the line leading to chimpanzees and hominins. Around 7–6 m.y.a., another split in the lineage led to the various early hominins. Some intriguing fossils dating from that critical time period have been discovered recently.

# for REVIEW

## summary

1. Humans, apes, monkeys, and prosimians are primates. The primate order is subdivided into suborders, superfamilies, families, tribes, genera, species, and subspecies. Organisms in any subdivision (taxon) of a taxonomy are assumed to share more recent ancestry with each other than they do with organisms in other taxa. But it's sometimes hard to tell the difference between homologies, which reflect common ancestry, and analogies, biological similarities that develop through convergent evolution.

2. Prosimians are the older of the two primate suborders. Around 50 million years ago, anthropoids (the other suborder) arose by adapting to a diurnal (daytime) ecological niche. Tarsiers and lorises are prosimians that survived by adapting to nocturnal life. Lemurs survived on the island of Madagascar.

3. Anthropoids include humans, apes, and monkeys. All share fully developed primate trends, such as depth and color vision. Other anthropoid traits include a shift in tactile areas to the fingers. All New World monkeys are arboreal. Old World monkeys include both terrestrial species (e.g., baboons and macaques) and arboreal ones. The great apes are orangutans, gorillas, chimpanzees, and bonobos. The lesser apes are gibbons and siamangs.

4. Gibbons and siamangs live in Southeast Asian forests. These apes are slight, arboreal animals whose mode of locomotion is brachiation. Sexual dimorphism, slight among gibbons, is marked among orangutans, which are confined to two Indonesian islands. Sexually dimorphic gorillas, the most terrestrial apes, are vegetarians confined to equatorial Africa. Two species of chimpanzees live in the forests and woodlands of tropical Africa. Chimps are less sexually dimorphic, more numerous, and more omnivorous than gorillas.

5. From the perspective of behavioral ecology, individuals in a population compete to increase their genetic contribution to future generations. Maternal care makes sense from this perspective, because females can be sure their offspring are their own. Because it's harder for males to be sure about paternity, evolutionary theory predicts they will invest most in offspring when they are surest the offspring are theirs.

6. Primates have lived during the past 65 million years, the Cenozoic era, with seven epochs: Paleocene, Eocene, Oligocene, Miocene, Pliocene, Pleistocene, and Holocene, or Recent. The arboreal theory states that primates evolved by adapting to life high up in the trees.

7. The earliest known primate, discovered in China, dates to the late Paleocene epoch (65–54 m.y.a.). Thereafter, prosimian-like primates proliferated during the Eocene (54–34 m.y.a.). During the Oligocene (34–23 m.y.a.), anthropoids became the most numerous primates. The split between ancestral platyrrhines (New World monkeys) and catarrhines (Old World monkeys, apes, and humans) occurred during the Oligocene.

8. The earliest known hominoid (protoape) dates to 25.2 m.y.a., just before the Miocene (23–5 m.y.a.). Protoapes proliferated during the middle and late Miocene. Since the middle Miocene (16–10 m.y.a.), Africa, Europe, and Asia have been connected. Protoapes spread to all three continents and became the most common primates of the middle Miocene. Asia's *Gigantopithecus,* the largest primate ever to live, persisted for millions of years, finally coexisting with *Homo erectus. Pierolapithecus catalaunicus,* which lived around 13 million years ago, could be the last common ancestor of humans, chimpanzees, gorillas, and orangutans.

## key terms

| | |
|---|---|
| analogies 111 | homologies 110 |
| anthropoids 112 | m.y.a. 121 |
| arboreal 112 | opposable thumb 112 |
| behavioral ecology 120 | primatology 109 |
| bipedal 112 | prosimians 112 |
| brachiation 115 | sexual dimorphism 114 |
| convergent evolution 111 | taxonomy 110 |
| gibbons 115 | terrestrial 109 |
| hominoid 124 | |

## critical thinking

1. How does social organization vary among primates?

2. What is behavioral ecology? How would a behavioral ecologist explain parental investment in offspring? Can you think of any other theoretical frameworks that could be used to explain these cases?

3. What are some unanswered questions about early primate evolution? What kinds of information would help provide answers? What are some of the difficulties that investigators face in solving these questions?

4. There have been reported sightings of "Bigfoot" in the Pacific Northwest of North America and of the yeti (abominable snowman) in the Himalayas. What facts about apes lead you to question such reports?

5. Our cultural background affects the ways in which we perceive nature, human nature, and "the natural." Can you think of aspects of your culture that have affected the way you think about humans' relationship to other primates?

# Early Hominins

- ▶ What key traits make us human, and when and how are they revealed in the fossil record?

- ▶ Who were the australopithecines, and what role did they play in human evolution?

- ▶ When and where did hominins first make tools?

South African paleoanthropologist Phillip Tobias, who died in 2012 at the age of 86. Tobias was well known for his excavations at Sterkfontein, which yielded significant australopithecine remains.

# understanding OURSELVES

**D**o you remember the "monkey bars" in your playground? How did you use them? It sure wasn't like a monkey. The human shoulder bone, like that of the apes, is adapted for brachiation—swinging hand over hand through the trees. Monkeys, by contrast, move about on four limbs. Apes can stand and walk on two feet, as humans habitually do, but in the trees, and otherwise when climbing, apes and humans don't leap around as monkeys do. In climbing we extend our arms and pull up. When we use "monkey bars," we hang and move hand over hand rather than getting on top and running across, as a monkey would do. For most contemporary humans, the ability to use "monkey bars" declines long before our ability to walk. Humans have the shoulder of a brachiator because we share a distant brachiating ancestor with the apes. Bipedal locomotion, on the other hand, is the most ancient trait that makes us truly human. Only when we lose it do we fully appreciate the supreme significance of bipedalism. I know this from personal experience.

On the day before her 99th birthday, my mother broke her hip. She survived a hip replacement operation, spent a week in the hospital, then entered a rehab center, where she had to rely on staff for much of what previously she had done on her own. She couldn't climb in and out of bed, nor could she bathe herself or attend to personal functions.

Watching my mother endure weeks of indignity, I became acutely aware of what bipedalism means to humans. Younger people with greater upper body strength often can move about independently without using their legs. Not so a very old woman who over the years had developed osteoporosis and suffered several fractures (along with arthritis) affecting wrists, arms, and shoulders. All those had been painful reminders of the aging process. None, however, was as devastating as her hip break. Unable to walk and debilitated by an infection she picked up in the hospital, my mother gradually lost her will to live. She stopped following the news, abandoning TV and any attempt to read. Her rehabilitation wasn't succeeding; she hated relying on others for her personal functions. She died less than two months after her fall. My mother's longevity illustrates how cultural advances (e.g., medicine, nutrition, operations) have extended the human lifespan—but only to a point. Certainly no ancient hominin lived for a century; however, humans today are no less bipedal than our ancestors were five million years ago. Bipedalism is an integral and enduring feature of human adaptation.

## WHAT MAKES US HUMAN?

In trying to determine whether a fossil is a human ancestor, should we look for traits that make us human today? Sometimes yes; sometimes no. We do look for similarities in DNA, including mutations shared by certain lineages but not others. But what about such key human attributes as bipedal locomotion, a long period of childhood dependency, big brains, and the use of tools and language? Some of these key markers of humanity are fairly recent—or have origins that are impossible to date. And ironically, some of the physical markers that have led scientists to identify certain fossils as early hominins rather than apes are features that have receded during subsequent human evolution.

Recall that the term *hominin* is used to designate the human line after its split from ancestral chimps. *Hominid* refers to the taxonomic family that includes humans and the African apes and their immediate ancestors. In this book, *hominid* is used when there is doubt about the hominin status of the fossil.

## Bipedalism

As is true of all subsequent hominins, postcranial material from **Ardipithecus,** the earliest widely accepted hominin genus (5.8–4.4 m.y.a.), indicates a capacity—albeit an imperfect one—for upright bipedal locomotion. The *Ardipithecus* pelvis appears to be transitional between one suited for arboreal climbing and one modified for bipedalism. Reliance on *bipedalism*—upright, two-legged locomotion—is the key feature differentiating early hominins from the apes. This way of moving around eventually led to the distinctive hominin way of life. Based on African fossil discoveries, such as Ethiopia's *Ardipithecus,* hominin bipedalism is more than five million years old. Some scientists see even earlier evidence of bipedalism in two other fossil finds, described below—one from Chad (*Sahelanthropus tchadensis*) and one from Kenya (*Orrorin tugenensis*).

Bipedalism traditionally has been viewed as an adaptation to open grassland or savanna country, although *Ardipithecus* lived in a humid woodland habitat. Perhaps bipedalism developed in the woodlands but became even more adaptive in a savanna habitat (see Choi 2011). Scientists have suggested several advantages of bipedalism: the abilities to see over long grass and scrub, to carry items back to a home base, and to reduce the body's exposure to solar radiation. Quadrupedalism exposes the body to 60 percent more solar radiation than does bipedalism. The fossil and archaeological records confirm that upright, bipedal locomotion preceded stone tool manufacture and the expansion of the hominin brain. However, although early hominins could move bipedally on the ground, they also preserved enough of an apelike anatomy to make them good climbers (see the description of *Ardipithecus* on pp. 132–134). They could take to the trees to sleep and to escape terrestrial predators.

## Brains, Skulls, and Childhood Dependency

Compared with contemporary humans, early hominins had very small brains. *Australopithecus afarensis,* a bipedal hominin that lived more than three million years ago, had a cranial capacity (430 cm$^3$—cubic centimeters) that barely surpassed the chimp average (390 cm$^3$). The form of the *afarensis* skull also is like that of the chimpanzee, although the brain-to-body size ratio may have been larger. Brain size has increased during hominin evolution, especially with the advent of the genus *Homo.* But this increase had to overcome some obstacles.

Reconstruction of *Australopithecus* running bipedally with a pebble tool in hand. Along with tool use and manufacture, bipedalism is a key part of being human.

Compared with the young of other primates, human children have a long period of childhood dependency, during which their brains and skulls grow dramatically. Larger skulls demand larger birth canals, but the requirements of upright bipedalism impose limits on the expansion of the human pelvic opening. If the opening is too large, the pelvis doesn't provide sufficient support for the trunk. Locomotion suffers, and posture problems develop. If, by contrast, the birth canal is too narrow, mother and child (without the modern option of Caesarean section) may die. Natural selection has struck a balance between the structural demands of upright posture and the tendency toward increased brain size—the birth of immature and dependent children whose brains and skulls grow dramatically after birth.

## Tools

Given what is known about tool use and manufacture by the great apes, it is likely that early hominins shared this ability as a homology with the apes. We'll see later that the first evidence for hominin stone tool manufacture is dated to 2.6 m.y.a. Upright bipedalism would have facilitated the use of tools and weapons. Bipedal locomotion also allowed early hominins to carry things, including scavenged parts of carnivore kills, back to a home base (see Ferraro et al. 2013). We know that primates have generalized abilities to adapt through learning. Early

**Ardipithecus**
Earliest recognized hominin genus (5.8–4.4 m.y.a.), Ethiopia.

hominins surely had greater cultural abilities than those of modern apes.

## Teeth

One example of an early hominin trait that has been reduced during subsequent human evolution is big back teeth. (Indeed, a pattern of overall dental reduction characterizes human evolution.) Once they adapted to the savanna, with its gritty, tough, and fibrous vegetation, it was adaptively advantageous for early hominins to have large back teeth and thick tooth enamel. This permitted thorough chewing and mixture with salivary enzymes to permit digestion of foods that otherwise would not have been digestible. The churning, rotary motion associated with such chewing also favored reduction of the canines and first premolars (bicuspids). These front teeth are much sharper and longer in the apes than in early hominins. The apes use their sharp, self-honing teeth to pierce fruits. Males also flash their big, sharp canines to intimidate and impress others, including potential mates. Although bipedalism seems to have characterized the human lineage since it split from the line leading to the African apes, many other "human" features came later. Yet other early hominin features, such as large back teeth and thick enamel—which are much less characteristic now—offer clues about who was a human ancestor back then.

## CHRONOLOGY OF HOMININ EVOLUTION

Although recent fossil discoveries have pushed the hominin lineage back to almost six million years ago, humans actually haven't been around too long when the age of the Earth is considered. If we compare Earth's history to a 24-hour day (with one second equaling 50,000 years),

> Earth originated at midnight.
>
> The earliest fossils were deposited at 5:45 A.M.
>
> The first vertebrates appeared at 9:02 P.M.
>
> The earliest mammals, at 10:45 P.M.
>
> The earliest primates, at 11:42 P.M.
>
> The earliest hominins, at 11:56 P.M.
>
> And *Homo sapiens* arrived 36 seconds before midnight. (Wolpoff 1999, p. 10)

Although the first hominins appeared late in the Miocene epoch, for the study of hominin evolution, the Pliocene (5–2 m.y.a.), Pleistocene (2 m.y.a.–10,000 B.P.), and Recent (10,000 B.P.–present) epochs are most important. Until the end of the Pliocene, the main hominin genus was *Australopithecus,* which lived in sub-Saharan Africa. By the start of the Pleistocene, *Australopithecus* had evolved into *Homo.*

## WHO WERE THE EARLIEST HOMININS?

Recent discoveries of fossils and tools have increased our knowledge of hominid and hominin evolution. The most significant recent discoveries have been made in Africa—Kenya, Tanzania, Ethiopia, South Africa, and Chad. These finds come from different sites and may be the remains of individuals that lived hundreds of thousands of years apart. Furthermore, geological processes operating over thousands or millions of years inevitably distort fossil remains. Table 8.1 summarizes the major events in hominid and hominin evolution. You should consult it throughout this chapter and the next one.

### *Sahelanthropus tchadensis*

In July 2001 anthropologists working in Central Africa—in northern Chad's Djurab Desert—unearthed the six- to seven-million-year-old skull of the oldest possible human ancestor yet found. This discovery consists of a nearly complete skull, two lower jaw fragments, and three teeth. It dates to the time period when humans and chimps would have been diverging from a common ancestor. The discovery was made by a 40-member multinational team led by the French paleoanthropologist Michel Brunet. The actual discoverer was the university undergraduate Ahounta Djimdoumalbaye, who spied the skull embedded in sandstone. The new fossil was dubbed *Sahelanthropus tchadensis,* referring to the northern Sahel region of Chad, where it was found. The fossil also is known as "Toumai," a local name meaning "hope of life."

The discovery team identified the skull as that of an adult male with a chimp-sized brain (320–380 cm$^3$), heavy brow ridges, and a relatively flat, humanlike face. Toumai's habitat included savanna, forests, rivers, and lakes—and abundant animal life such as elephants, antelope, horses, giraffes, hyenas, hippopotamuses, wild boars, crocodiles, fish, and rodents. The associated animal species enabled the team to date the site where Toumai was found (by comparison with radiometrically dated sites with similar fauna).

The discovery of Toumai moves scientists close to the time when humans and the African apes diverged from a common ancestor (see Weiss 2005; Wood 2011). As we would expect in a fossil so close to the common ancestor, Toumai blends apelike and human characteristics. Although the brain was chimp-sized, the tooth enamel was thicker than a chimp's enamel, suggesting a diet that included not just fruits but also tougher vegetation of a sort typically found in the savanna. Also, Toumai's snout did not protrude as far as a chimp's, making it more humanlike, and the canine tooth was shorter than that of other apes. "The fossil is showing the first glimmerings of evolution in our direction," according to University of California at

**TABLE 8.1** Dates and Geographic Distribution of Major Hominoid, Hominid, and Hominin Fossil Groups

| FOSSIL GROUP | DATES, m.y.a. | KNOWN DISTRIBUTION |
|---|---|---|
| Hominoid | | |
| *Pierolapithecus catalaunicus* | 13 | Spain |
| Hominid | | |
| Common ancestor of hominids | 8? | East Africa |
| *Sahelanthropus tchadensis* | 7–6 | Chad |
| *Orrorin tugenensis* | 6 | Kenya |
| Hominins | | |
| *Ardipithecus kadabba* | 5.8–5.5 | Ethiopia |
| *Ardipithecus ramidus* | 4.4 | Ethiopia |
| *Kenyanthropus platyops* | 3.5 | Kenya |
| Australopithecines | | |
| Au. anamensis | 4.2–3.9 | Kenya |
| Au. afarensis | 3.8–3.0 | East Africa (Laetoli, Hadar) |
| Au. garhi | 2.6–2.5 | Ethiopia |
| Au. sediba | 1.98–1.78 | South Africa |
| Robusts | 2.6–1.2 | East and South Africa |
| Au. robustus (*Paranthropus*) | 2.0?–1.0? | South Africa |
| Au. boisei | 2.6?–1.2 | East Africa |
| Graciles | | |
| Au. africanus | 3.0?–2.0? | South Africa |
| *Homo* | | |
| H. habilis/H. rudolfensis | 2.4?–1.4? | East Africa |
| H. erectus | 1.9?–0.3? | Africa, Asia, Europe |
| Homo sapiens | 0.3–present | |
| Archaic H. sapiens | 0.3–0.28 (300,000?–28,000) | Africa, Asia, Europe |
| Neandertals | 0.13–0.28 (130,000–28,000) | Europe, Middle East, North Africa |
| Anatomically modern humans (AMHs) | 0.15?–present (150,000–present) | Worldwide (after 20,000 B.P.) |

A skull found in 2001 in northern Chad, dated at six to seven million years old, officially named *Sahelanthropus tchadensis,* more commonly called "Toumai," may or may not be the earliest hominin yet known. On the left, French paleontologist Michel Brunet holds Toumai's skull, a cast of which is shown on the right.

In October 2009, a newly reported *Ardipithecus* find—a fairly complete skeleton of *Ardipithecus ramidus,* dubbed "Ardi," was heralded throughout the media.

Berkeley anthropologist Tim White (quoted in Gugliotta 2002).

Toumai is a nearly complete, although distorted, skull. The placement of its *foramen magnum* (the "big hole" through which the spinal cord joins the brain) farther forward than in apes suggests that *Sahelanthropus* moved bipedally. Its discovery in Chad indicates that early hominin evolution was not confined to East Africa's Rift Valley. The Rift Valley's abundant fossil record may well reflect geology, preservation, and modern exposure of fossils rather than the actual geographic distribution of species in the past. If *Sahelanthropus* was indeed a hominin, its discovery in Chad is the first proof of a more widespread distribution of early hominins.

## *Orrorin tugenensis*

In January 2001 Brigitte Senut, Martin Pickford, and others reported the discovery, near the village of Tugen in Kenya's Baringo district, of possible early hominin fossils they called *Orrorin tugenensis* (Aiello and Collard 2001; Senut et al. 2001). The find consisted of 13 fossils from at least five individuals. The fossils include pieces of jaw with teeth, isolated upper and lower teeth, arm bones, and a finger bone. *Orrorin* appears to have been a chimp-sized creature that climbed easily and walked on two legs when on the ground. Its date of six million years ago is close to the time of the common ancestor of humans and chimps. The fossilized left femur (thigh bone) suggests upright bipedalism, while the thick right humerus (upper arm bone) suggests tree-climbing skills. Animal fossils found in the same rocks indicate *Orrorin* lived in a wooded environment.

*Orrorin*'s upper incisor, upper canine, and lower premolar are more like the teeth of a female chimpanzee than like human teeth. But other dental and skeletal features, especially bipedalism, led the discoverers to assign *Orrorin* to the hominin lineage. *Orrorin* lived after *Sahelanthropus tchadensis* but before *Ardipithecus kadabba,* discovered in Ethiopia, also in 2001, and dated to 5.8–5.5 m.y.a. The hominin status of *Ardipithecus* is more generally accepted than is that of either *Sahelanthropus tchadensis* or *Orrorin tugenensis.*

## *Ardipithecus*

Early hominins assigned to *Ardipithecus kadabba* lived during the late Miocene, between 5.8 and 5.5 million years ago. *Ardipithecus* (*ramidus*) fossils were first discovered in 1992–1994 at Aramis in Ethiopia by Berhane Asfaw, Gen Suwa, and Tim White. Dating to 4.4 m.y.a., these *Ardipithecus ramidus* fossils consisted of the remains of some 17 individuals, with cranial, facial, dental, and upper limb bones. Subsequently, much older *Ardipithecus* (*kadabba*) fossils, dating back to 5.8 m.y.a., were found in Ethiopia. The *kadabba* find consists of 11 specimens, including a jawbone with teeth, hand and foot bones, fragments of arm bones, and a piece of collarbone. At least five individuals are represented. These creatures were apelike in size and anatomy. Their habitat was a mixture of woods and grasslands, and they had ample access to water in springs and lakes. As of this writing, because of its probable bipedalism, *Ardipithecus kadabba* is recognized as the earliest known hominin, with the *Sahelanthropus tchadensis* find from Chad, dated to

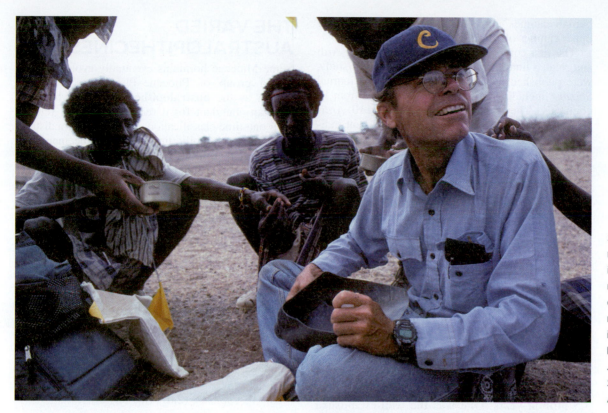

Shown here are three members of the international team responsible for Ardi's discovery and reconstruction. Above is American Tim White. Below are Ethiopians Johannes Haile-Selassie and Berhane Asfaw.

7–6 m.y.a., and *Orrorin tugenensis* from Kenya, dated to 6 m.y.a., as possibly even older hominins.

In October 2009, a newly reported *Ardipithecus* find—a fairly complete skeleton of *Ardipithecus ramidus,* dubbed "Ardi"—was heralded on the front page of the *New York Times* and throughout the media (Wilford 2009a). Ardi (4.4 m.y.a.) replaces Lucy (3.2 m.y.a.—see below) as the earliest known hominin skeleton. The Ethiopian discovery site lies on what is now an arid floodplain of the Awash River, 45 miles south of Hadar, where Lucy was found. Scientists infer that Ardi was female, based on its small and lightly built (gracile) skull and its small canine teeth compared with others at the site. At 4 feet tall and 120 pounds, Ardi stood about a foot taller than and weighed twice as much as Lucy.

The *Ardipithecus* pelvis appears to be transitional between one suited for arboreal climbing and one modified for bipedal locomotion. The pelvis of later hominins such as Lucy shows nearly all the adaptations needed for full bipedalism. Although Ardi's lower pelvis remains primitive, the structure of her upper pelvis allowed her to walk on two legs with a straightened hip. Still, she probably could neither walk nor run as well as later hominins. Her feet lacked the archlike structure of later hominin feet (see Ward, Kimbel, and Johanson 2011). Ardi's apelike lower pelvis indicates retention of powerful hamstring muscles for climbing. Her hands, very long arms, and short legs all recall those of extinct apes, and her brain was no larger than that of a modern chimp.

Based on associated animal and plant remains, *Ardipithecus* lived in a humid woodland habitat. In this environment, *ramidus* did not need, or have, the heavy chewing specializations of later *Australopithecus* species. The size, shape, and wear patterns of *ramidus* teeth suggest an omnivorous diet of plants, nuts, and small mammals. Although *Ardipithecus* probably fed both in trees and on the ground, the canines suggest less of a fruit diet than is characteristic of living apes. With reduced sexual dimorphism, *Ardipithecus* canines resemble modern human canines more than the tusklike, piercing upper canines of chimps and gorillas.

The first comprehensive reports describing Ardi and related findings, the result of 17 years of study, were published on October 2, 2009, in the journal *Science*, including 11 papers by 47 authors from 10 countries. They analyzed more than 110 *Ardipithecus* specimens from at least 36 different individuals, including Ardi. The ancestral relationship of *Ardipithecus* to *Australopithecus* has not been determined, but Ardi has been called a plausible ancestor for *Australopithecus* (see Wilford 2009*a*).

### Kenyanthropus

Complicating the picture is another discovery, which Maeve Leakey has named *Kenyanthropus platyops,* or flat-faced "man" of Kenya. (Actually, the sex hasn't been determined.) This 1999 fossil find—of a nearly complete skull and partial jawbone—was made by a research team led by Leakey, excavating on the western side of Lake Turkana in northern Kenya. They consider this 3.5-million-year-old find to represent an entirely new branch of the early human family tree.

Leakey views *Kenyanthropus* as showing that at least two hominin lineages existed as far back as 3.5 million years. One was the well-established fossil species *Australopithecus afarensis* (see below), best known from the celebrated Lucy skeleton. With the discovery of *Kenyanthropus* it would seem that Lucy and her kind weren't alone on the African plain. The hominin family tree, once drawn with a straight trunk, now looks more like a bush, with branches leading in many directions (Wilford 2001*a*). (Such bushlike, rather than straight-line, evolutionary trees tend to be the rule in nature.)

**australopithecines**
Common term for all members of the genus *Australopithecus*.

***Au. anamensis***
Earliest known *Australopithecus* species (4.2–3.9 m.y.a.), Kenya.

Maeve Leakey and *Kenyanthropus platyops*, which she discovered in 1999 by Lake Turkana.

## THE VARIED AUSTRALOPITHECINES

Some Miocene hominins eventually evolved into a varied group of Pliocene–Pleistocene hominins known as the **australopithecines**—for which we have an abundant fossil record. This term reflects their one-time classification as members of a distinct taxonomic subfamily, the "Australopithecinae." We now know that the various species of *Australopithecus* discussed in this chapter do not form a distinct subfamily within the order Primates, but the name "australopithecine" has stuck to describe them. Today the distinction between the australopithecines and later hominins is made on the genus level. The australopithecines are assigned to the genus *Australopithecus (Au.);* later humans, to *Homo (H.).*

In the scheme followed here, *Australopithecus* had at least seven species:

1. *Au. anamensis* (4.2–3.9 m.y.a.)
2. *Au. afarensis* (3.8–3.0 m.y.a.)
3. *Au. africanus* (3.0?–2.0? m.y.a.)
4. *Au. garhi* (2.6–2.5 m.y.a.)
5. *Au. robustus* (2.0?–1.0? m.y.a.)
6. *Au. boisei* (2.6?–1.2 m.y.a.)
7. *Au. sediba* (1.98–1.78 m.y.a.)

The date ranges given for these species are approximate, because an organism isn't a member of one species one day and a member of another species the next day. Nor could the same dating techniques be used for all the finds. The earliest South African australopithecine fossils (*Au. africanus* and *Au. robustus*), for example, come from a nonvolcanic area where radiometric dating could not be done. Dating of those fossils has been based mainly on stratigraphy. The hominin fossils from the volcanic regions of East Africa usually have radiometric dates.

### Australopithecus anamensis

*Ardipithecus ramidus* may (or may not) have evolved into *Au. anamensis,* a bipedal hominin from northern Kenya, whose fossil remains were reported first by Maeve Leakey and Alan Walker in 1995 (Leakey et al. 1995; Rice 2002). ***Au. anamensis*** consists of 78 fragments from two sites: Kanapoi and Allia Bay. The fossils include upper and lower jaws, cranial fragments, and the upper and lower parts of a leg bone (tibia, or shinbone). The Kanapoi fossils date to 4.2 m.y.a., and those at Allia Bay to 3.9 m.y.a. Members of this species had apelike canines, along with strong jaws and heavily enameled teeth, suggesting they may at times have eaten hard, abrasive foods. They probably preferred the fruits and nuts available in their environment—one of lakes surrounded by forests and woodlands. Based on the tibia, *anamensis* weighed about 110 pounds (50 kg). This would have made it larger than either the earlier *Ardipithecus* or the later *Au. afarensis*. Because of its date and its location in the East African Rift Valley, *Au. anamensis* may be ancestral to *Au. afarensis* (3.8–3.0 m.y.a.), which usually is considered ancestral to all the later australopithecines, as well as to *Homo* (Figure 8.1).

## Australopithecus afarensis

The hominin species known as **Au. afarensis** includes fossils found at two sites, Laetoli in northern Tanzania and Hadar in the Afar region of Ethiopia. Laetoli is earlier (3.8–3.6 m.y.a.). The Hadar fossils probably date to between 3.3 and 3.0 m.y.a. Thus, based on the current evidence, *Au. afarensis* lived between about 3.8 and 3.0 m.y.a. Research directed by Mary Leakey (Maeve's mother-in-law) was responsible for the Laetoli finds. The Hadar discoveries resulted from an international expedition directed by D. C. Johanson and M. Taieb. The two sites have yielded significant samples of early hominin fossils. From Laetoli we have two dozen specimens; and from Hadar, between 35 and 65 individuals. The Laetoli remains are mainly teeth and jaw fragments, along with some very informative fossilized footprints. The Hadar sample includes skull fragments and postcranial material, most notably 40 percent of the complete skeleton of a tiny hominin female, dubbed "Lucy," who lived around 3 m.y.a.

Although the hominin remains at Laetoli and Hadar were deposited half a million years apart, their many resemblances explain their placement in the same species, *Au. afarensis*. The discovery of these fossils forced a reinterpretation of the early hominin fossil record. *Au. afarensis,* although clearly a hominin, was so similar in many ways to chimps and gorillas that our common ancestry with the African apes had to be very recent, probably no more than 8 m.y.a. *Ardipithecus* and *Au. anamensis* are even more apelike.

From the same general area of northern Ethiopia as Lucy comes another important member of *Au. afarensis* (Owen 2006, 2012). This toddler, the world's oldest fossil child, soon was dubbed "Lucy's Baby"—despite having lived a hundred thousand years before Lucy (3.3 m.y.a. for the child versus 3.2 for Lucy). The child is an amazingly complete find, with a more intact skull and much more skeletal material than exists for Lucy. Not surprisingly, given what we already know about *Au. afarensis,* the skull and upper body are apelike, while the lower body confirms bipedalism. Despite bipedalism, the skeleton's upper body includes two complete shoulder blades similar to a gorilla's, so it probably was better at climbing than humans are (see Owen 2012).

Unearthed in 2000, the child probably was female and about 3 years old when she died. The remains include a well-preserved skull, baby teeth, tiny fingers, a torso, a foot, and a kneecap. Although Lucy doesn't have much of a head, her "baby" has a

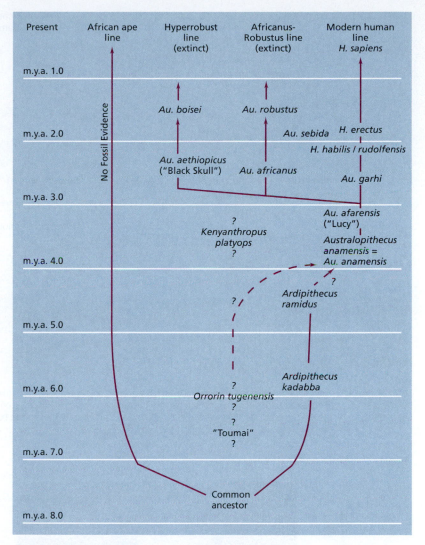

**FIGURE 8.1** Phylogenetic Tree for African Apes, Hominids, and Hominins.

The presumed divergence date for ancestral chimps and hominins was between 6 and 8 m.y.a. Branching in later hominin evolution is also shown. For more exact dates, see the text and Table 8.1.

complete skull, a mandible (jawbone), and a monkey-sized face with a smooth brow.

If Lucy's baby had lived, she would have developed rapidly, reaching adulthood earlier than modern humans, and her lifespan would have been much shorter than ours. The *afarensis* growth cycle was more similar to the chimpanzee pattern than to the modern human pattern. The shorter growth period would have allowed less time for guidance and socialization.

Discussion of hominin fossils requires a brief review of dentition. Moving from front to back, on either side of the upper or lower jaw, humans (and apes) have two incisors, one canine, two premolars, and three molars. Our dental formula is 2.1.2.3, for a total of eight teeth on each side, upper and lower—32 teeth in all—if we have all

**Au. afarensis**
Early *Australopithecus* species (3.8–3.0 m.y.a.), Ethiopia ("Lucy"), Tanzania.

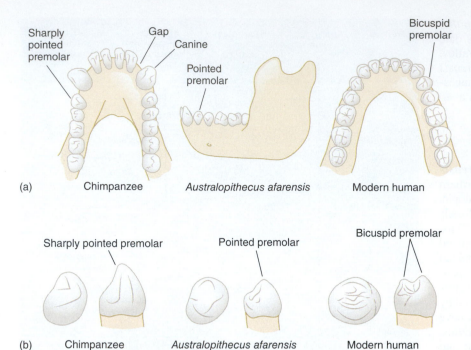

Sharply pointed premolar / Gap / Canine / Pointed premolar / Bicuspid premolar

(a) Chimpanzee — *Australopithecus afarensis* — Modern human

Sharply pointed premolar — Pointed premolar — Bicuspid premolar

(b) Chimpanzee — *Australopithecus afarensis* — Modern human

**FIGURE 8.2** Comparison of Dentition in Ape, Human, and *Au. afarensis* Palates.

Teeth of chimpanzee, *Australopithecus afarensis,* and modern human. In (a), note the parallel tooth rows in the chimpanzee, as compared to those of the modern human. In (b), note the sharply pointed premolar of the chimpanzee, the pointed premolar of *Au. afarensis,* and the bicuspid premolar of the modern human.

SOURCE: From John H. Relethford, *The Human Species: An Introduction to Biological Anthropology,* 9th ed., p. 202. Copyright © 2013 by McGraw-Hill Education, LLC. Reprinted with permission.

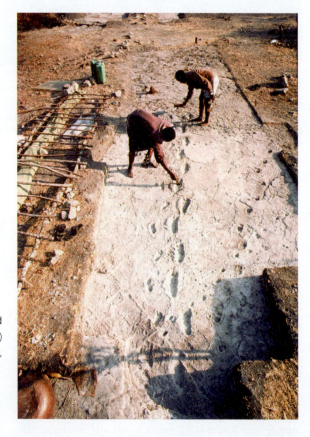

An ancient trail of hominin footprints fossilized in volcanic ash. Mary Leakey found this 230-foot (70-meter) trail at Laetoli, Tanzania, in 1979. It dates from 3.6 m.y.a. and confirms that *Au. afarensis* was a striding biped.

our "wisdom teeth" (our third molars). Now back to the australopithecines.

Compared with *Homo, Au. afarensis* had larger and sharper canine teeth that projected beyond the other teeth. The canines, however, were reduced compared with an ape's tusklike canines. The *afarensis* lower premolar was pointed and projecting to sharpen the upper canine. It had one long cusp and one tiny bump that hints at the bicuspid premolar that eventually developed in hominin evolution (see Figure 8.2).

Their mainly vegetarian diet included leaves, seeds, fruits, and nuts. As well, they probably ate insects, and small vertebrates, such as lizards. Dental microwear studies show that *afarensis* ate soft, sugar-rich foods (such as fruits), but their tooth size and shape confirm that they also could process hard, brittle foods. These may have been fallback foods, which they ate during seasons or years when more desirable foods were unavailable.

When the hard, gritty, fibrous vegetation of grasslands and semidesert enters the diet, the back teeth change to accommodate heavy chewing stresses. Massive back teeth, jaws, and facial and cranial structures suggest a diet demanding extensive grinding and powerful crushing. *Au. afarensis* molars are large. The lower jaw (mandible) is thick and is buttressed with a bony ridge behind the front teeth. The cheekbones are large and flare out to the side for the attachment of powerful chewing muscles.

The *Au. afarensis* skull contrasts with those of later hominins. Its cranial capacity ($430 \, \text{cm}^3$) barely surpasses the chimp average ($390 \, \text{cm}^3$). Below the neck, however, *Au. afarensis* was unquestionably human. Early evidence of striding bipedalism comes from Laetoli, where volcanic ash, which can be directly dated by the K/A (potassium/argon) technique, covered a trail of footprints of two or three hominins walking to a water hole. These prints leave no doubt that a small, striding biped lived in Tanzania by 3.6 m.y.a. The structure of the pelvic, hip, leg, and foot bones also confirms that upright bipedalism was *Au. afarensis*'s mode of locomotion (see Choi 2012; Ward et al. 2011).

Although bidepal, *Au. afarensis* still contrasts in many ways with later hominins. Sexual dimorphism is especially marked. *Au. afarensis* females, such as Lucy, stood between 3 and 4 feet (0.9 and 1.2 meters) tall; males might have reached 5 feet (1.5 meters). Adult males weighed perhaps twice as much as the females did (Wolpoff 1999). Recap 8.1 summarizes data on the various australopithecines, including mid-sex body weight and brain size. Mid-sex means midway between the male average and the female average.

| SPECIES | DATES (m.y.a.) | KNOWN DISTRIBUTION | IMPORTANT SITES | BODY WEIGHT (MID-SEX) | BRAIN SIZE (MID-SEX) (cm³) |
|---|---|---|---|---|---|
| Anatomically modern humans (AMHs) | 195,000– present | | | 132 lb/60 kg | 1,350 |
| *Pan troglodytes* (chimpanzee) | Modern | | | 93 lb/42 kg | 390 |
| *Au. sediba* | 1.98–1.78 | S. Africa | Malapa | Insufficient data | 420 |
| *Au. boisei* | 2.6?–1.2 | E. Africa | Olduvai, East Turkana | 86 lb/39 kg | 490 |
| *Au. robustus* | 2.0?–1.0? | S. Africa | Kromdraai, Swartkrans | 81 lb/37 kg | 540 |
| *Au. africanus* | 3.0?–2.0? | S. Africa | Taung, Sterkfontein, Makapansqat | 79 lb/36 kg | 490 |
| *Au. afarensis* | 3.8–3.0 | E. Africa | Hadar, Laetoli | 77 lb/35 kg | 430 |
| *Au. anamensis* | 4.2–3.9 | Kenya | Kanapoi, Allia Bay | Insufficient data | No published skulls |
| *Ardipithecus* | 5.8–4.4 | Ethiopia | Aramis | Insufficient data | No published skulls |

Lucy and her kind were far from dainty. Her muscle-engraved bones are much more robust than ours are. With only rudimentary tools and weapons, early hominins needed powerful and resistant bones and muscles. Lucy's apelike arms are longer relative to her legs than are those of later hominins; she probably spent some of her time in the trees. Adaptations for living both in the trees and on the ground helped *Au. afarensis* survive for almost a million years.

The *Au. afarensis* fossils show that as recently as 3 m.y.a., our ancestors had a mixture of apelike and hominin features. Canines, premolars, and skulls were more apelike than most scholars had imagined would exist in such a recent ancestor. On the other hand, the molars, chewing apparatus, and cheekbones foreshadowed later hominin trends, and the pelvic and limb bones were indisputably hominin (Figure 8.3 on p. 138). The hominin pattern was being built from the ground up.

The pelvis, the lower spine, the hip joint, and the thigh bone changed in accordance with the stresses of bipedal locomotion. Australopithecine pelvises are much more similar to *Homo*'s than to apes' and show adaptation to bipedalism (Figure 8.4). The blades of the australopithecine pelvis (iliac blades) are shorter and broader than are those of the ape. The sacrum, which anchors the pelvis's two side bones, is larger, as in *Homo*. With bipedalism, the pelvis forms a sort of basket that balances the weight of the trunk and supports this weight with less stress. The australopithecine spine had the lower spine (lumbar) curve characteristic of *Homo*. This curvature helps

Illustration of female *Australopithecus afarensis* "Lucy," discovered in Ethiopia's Omo Valley in 1974.

transmit the weight of the upper body to the pelvis and the legs. Placement of the *foramen magnum* (the "big hole" through which the spinal cord joins the brain) farther forward in *Australopithecus* and *Homo*

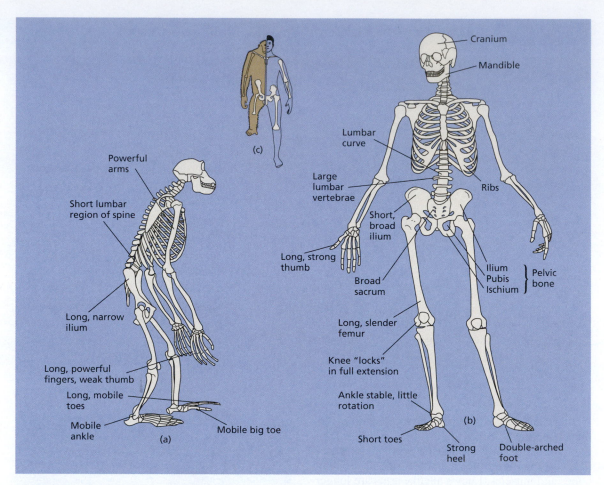

**FIGURE 8.3** *Comparison of* Homo sapiens *and* Pan troglodytes *(the Common Chimp).*
(a) Skeleton of chimpanzee in bipedal position; (b) skeleton of modern human; (c) chimpanzee and human "bisected" and drawn to the same trunk length for comparison of limb proportions. The contrast in leg length is largely responsible for the proportional difference between humans and apes.

**FIGURE 8.4** A Comparison of Human and Chimpanzee Pelvises.
The human pelvis has been modified to meet the demands of upright bipedalism. The blades (*ilia*; singular, *ilium*) of the human pelvis are shorter and broader than those of the ape. The sacrum, which anchors the side bones, is wider. The australopithecine pelvis is far more similar to that of *Homo* than to that of the chimpanzee, as we would expect in an upright biped.

than in the ape also represents an adaptation to upright bipedalism (Figure 8.5).

In apes, the thigh bone (femur) extends straight down from the hip to the knees. In *Australopithecus* and *Homo,* however, the thigh bone angles into the hip, permitting the space between the knees to be narrower than the pelvis during walking. The pelvises of the australopithecines were similar but not identical to those of *Homo.* The most significant contrast is a narrower australopithecine birth canal (Tague and Lovejoy 1986).

Expansion of the birth canal is a trend in hominin evolution. The width of the birth canal is related to the size of the skull and brain. *Au. afarensis* had a small cranial capacity. Even in later australopithecines, brain size did not exceed 600 cm$^3$. Undoubtedly, the australopithecine skull grew after birth to accommodate a growing brain, as it does (much more) in *Homo.* However, the brains of the australopithecines expanded less than ours do. In the australopithecines, the cranial sutures (the lines where the

**FIGURE 8.5** A Comparison of the Skull and Dentition (Upper Jaw) of *Homo* and the Chimpanzee.
The foramen magnum, through which the spinal cord joins the brain, is located farther forward in *Homo* than in the ape. This permits the head to balance atop the spine with upright bipedalism. The molars and premolars of the ape form parallel rows. Human teeth, by contrast, are arranged in rounded, parabolic form. What differences do you note between human and ape canines? Canine reduction has been an important trend in hominin evolution.

bones of the skull eventually come together) fused relatively earlier in life.

Young australopithecines must have depended on their parents and kin for nurturance and protection. Those years of childhood dependency would have provided time for observation, teaching, and learning. This may provide indirect evidence for a rudimentary cultural life.

## Gracile and Robust Australopithecines

In 1924, the anatomist Raymond Dart coined the term *Australopithecus africanus* to describe the first fossil representative of this species, the skull of a juvenile that was found accidentally in a quarry at Taung, South Africa. Radiometric dates are lacking for this nonvolcanic region, but the fossil hominins found at five main South African sites appear (from stratigraphy) to have lived between 3 and 1 m.y.a. The most recent South African *Australopithecus* find, *Au. sediba*, described in this chapter's "Appreciating Anthropology" on pp. 140–141, has been dated more precisely, to 1.98 m.y.a.

The South African australopithecines fall into two groups: **gracile** (*Au. africanus*) and **robust** (*Au. robustus*). "Gracile" indicates that members of *Au. africanus* were smaller and slighter, less robust, than were members of *Au. robustus.* In addition, very robust—*hyperrobust*—australopithecines have been found in East Africa. In the classification scheme followed here, the hyperrobust australopiothecines are assigned to *Au. boisei.* However, some scholars consider *Au. robustus* and *Au. boisei*

to be regional variants of just one species, usually called *Au. robustus* (sometimes given its own genus name as well—*Paranthropus robustus*).

The relationship between the graciles and the robusts has been debated for generations. Graciles and robusts probably descend from *Au. afarensis,* which itself was gracile in form, or from a South African version of *Au. afarensis.* Some scholars have argued that the graciles lived before (3?–2? m.y.a.) and were ancestral to the robusts (2?–1? m.y.a.). Others contend that the graciles and the robusts were separate species that may have overlapped in time. (Classifying them as members of different species implies they were reproductively isolated from each other in time or space.)

The trend toward enlarged back teeth, chewing muscles, and facial buttressing, which already is noticeable in *Au. afarensis,* continues in the South African australopithecines. However, the canines are reduced, and the premolars are fully bicuspid. Dental form and function changed as dietary needs shifted from cutting and slashing to chewing and grinding.

The mainstay of the australopithecine diet was the vegetation of the savanna, although these early hominins also might have hunted small and slow-moving game. As well, they may have scavenged, bringing home parts of kills made by large cats and other carnivores. The ability to hunt large animals was probably an achievement of *Homo* and is discussed in the next chapter.

Living in open savanna country, *africanus* no doubt sought safety (and companionship) in groups—probably with multiple adult males and

**Au. (Australopithecus) africanus**
Gracile *Australopithecus* species (3.0?–2.0? m.y.a.), South Africa.

**gracile**
e.g., *Au. africanus;* less robust, i.e., smaller and slighter than *Au. robustus.*

**robust**
e.g., *Au. robustus* and *Au. boisei;* having large, strong, sturdy bones, muscles, and teeth.

**Au. robustus**
*Paranthropus;* robust *Australopithecus* species (2.0?–1.0? m.y.a.), South Africa.

**Au. boisei**
Late, hyperrobust *Australopithecus* species (2.6?–1.2 m.y.a.), East Africa.

# appreciating ANTHROPOLOGY

## *Au. sediba:* Ancestor or Fascinating Sideline?

Named by *Smithsonian* magazine as the number one hominid (and hominin) fossil discovery of 2011, *Australopithecus sediba* (actually discovered between 2008 and 2010 but described in 2011) has generated a new debate about human origins. The original find is an almost complete skull and partial skeleton of an 11- to 12-year-old boy who stood 4′3″ (1.3 m.) tall. Is this australopithecine a plausible human ancestor, as is claimed by its discoverer, paleoanthropologist Lee Berger? Most experts are skeptical about that claim, while appreciating the fossil for its unique blend of hominin features.

With long arms . . . and powerful fingers, the ancient creatures were built for climbing trees. But they also had long lower limbs, flat feet and a flexible lumbar spine that [allowed them to] . . . cover long distances by walking upright on two legs.

After four years of intense analysis, a team of paleoanthropologists is making its most detailed case yet that a pair of ancient skeletons discovered in a grassy South African valley could represent the direct evolutionary link between modern humans and the family of human ancestors that includes the *Australopithecus* known as Lucy.

In a series of papers published in . . . the journal *Science* [on April 12, 2013], the researchers argue that the "mosaic nature" of the *Australopithecus sediba* specimens makes them a strong candidate to be the . . . "branch of *Australopithecus* that ultimately gave rise to the genus *Homo*, which includes *Homo sapiens*."

The skeleton fossils have so many human-like features "across the whole of the body that it must be considered, at the very least, a possible ancestor," said Lee R. Berger, a paleoanthropologist at the University of Witwatersrand in Johannesburg, South Africa, who discovered the fossils in 2008. . . . But not everyone accepts this view. Critics say the skeletons are not old enough to be the precursors to *Homo*. Others say the similarities can be chalked up to the diversity of early hominids.

At a minimum, the new details . . . are causing scientists to revise . . . some long-held assumptions about the anatomical makeup of our extended evolutionary family. For example, though it was long believed that Australopiths had six lower vertebrae, "one more than humans and at least two more than apes," it is now clear that they had the same number as humans: five. The ape-like boy and older woman who tumbled through a sinkhole and lay buried in a deep underground cave for nearly 2 million years have also given scientists a better view of how our early relatives walked. . . .

By examining bone grooves and muscle attachments in the kneecap, thigh and lower leg bones and comparing them with those in humans and apes, the scientists were able to figure out that the roughly 4-foot-tall [female] walked upright. But she probably did so with a peculiar gait marked by an inward rotation of the knee and hip, causing her narrow-heeled feet to twist slightly. . . . The team wrote that it would need to examine more fossils before it could say whether the entire species walked the same way. Berger said that if modern humans were to observe an *Au. sediba* walking by, their attention would probably not be

females and their young. Like other primates, they maintained social bonds through play and mutual grooming. Their environment included large cats, and there is fossil evidence that these early hominins may have been as much the hunted as the hunters.

The skulls, jaws, and teeth of the australopithecines leave no doubt that their diet was mainly vegetarian. Natural selection modifies the teeth to conform to the stresses associated with a particular diet. Massive back teeth, jaws, and associated facial and cranial structures confirm that the australopithecine diet required extensive grinding and powerful crushing.

In the South African australopithecines, both deciduous ("baby") and permanent molars and premolars are massive, with multiple cusps. The later australopithecines had bigger back teeth than did the earlier ones. However, this evolutionary trend ended with early *Homo,* which had much smaller back teeth, reflecting a dietary change that will be described later.

Although contrasts with *Homo* in the front teeth are less marked, there was just as much canine sexual dimorphism (smaller teeth of females) in *Au. africanus* as there had been in *Au. afarensis* (Wolpoff 1999). Sexual dimorphism in general was much more pronounced among early hominins than in *Homo sapiens. Au. africanus* females were about 4 feet (1.2 meters), and males 5 feet (1.5 meters), tall. The average female probably had no more than 60 percent the weight of the average male. (That figure contrasts with today's average female-to-male weight ratio of about 88 percent.)

In the australopithecines, a massive face housed large upper teeth and provided a base for the attachment of powerful chewing muscles. The cheekbones were elongated, massive structures (Figure 8.6) that anchored large chewing muscles running up the jaw. Another set of robust chewing muscles extended from the back of the jaw to the sides of the skull.

In the more robust australopithecines (*Au. robustus* in South Africa and *Au. boisei* in East Africa), drawn to its legs. "What would be a great difference would be how it swung its long upper limbs during that walk and the shrugged-shoulder appearance of its upper body," he said. The researchers speculated that the animals spent their lives both in trees and walking on the ground. In other aspects of the research, scientists reported that these specimens had jaws and teeth that are recognizably human. In earlier studies, researchers concluded too that the creature's hands were capable of precise gripping. The presence of several human-like features has led Berger and others to suggest that *Au. sediba*, which lived an estimated 1.78 million to 1.95 million years ago, may have been the species that evolved into the earliest members of the *Homo* genus. But other paleoanthropologists have pointed out several problems with that thesis.

Donald Johanson, the Arizona State University paleoanthropologist who discovered Lucy in 1974, said the first *Homo* species appeared 2.4 million years ago in eastern Africa. Instead of giving rise to the genus *Homo*, *Au. sediba* would have been a contemporary. "Sediba abundantly demonstrates a unique set of anatomical features of an

Lee Berger with his son, Matthew, and fossils of *Australopithecus sediba*. Matthew found one of the fossils while chasing his dog.

*Australopithecus* species that was most likely a dead-end branch on our tree," said Johanson, who was not involved in the new studies. . . .

SOURCE: Monte Morin, "Evidence Points toward Solving Evolutionary 'Missing Link.'" *Los Angeles Times*, April 11, 2013. Copyright © 2013 Los Angeles Times. Reprinted with permission.

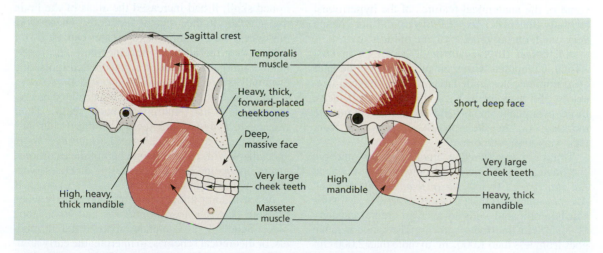

**FIGURE 8.6** Skulls of Robust (Left) and Gracile (Right) Australopithecines, Showing Chewing Muscles.

Flaring cheek arches and, in some robusts, a sagittal crest supported this massive musculature. The early hominin diet—coarse, gritty vegetation of the savanna—demanded such structures. These features were most pronounced in *Au. boisei*.

(Left) Profile view of an *Au. boisei* skull—Olduvai Hominid (OH) 5, originally called *Zinjanthropus boisei*. This skull of a young male, discovered by Mary Leakey in 1959 at Olduvai Gorge, Tanzania, dates back 1.8 million years. (Right) Profile view of an *Au. africanus* (gracile) skull (Sterkfontein 5). The cranium, discovered by Dr. Robert Broom and J. T. Robinson in April 1947, dates back to 2.4–2.9 m.y.a.

these muscles were strong enough to produce a *sagittal crest*, a bony ridge on the top of the skull. Such a crest forms as the bone grows. It develops from the pull of the chewing muscles as they meet at the midline of the skull.

In 1985, the paleoanthropologist Alan Walker made a significant find near Lake Turkana in northern Kenya. It is commonly called the "black skull" because of the blue-black sheen it bore from the minerals surrounding it. The jaw was apelike and the brain was small (as in *Au. afarensis*), but there was a massive bony crest atop the skull (as in *Au. boisei*). Walker and Richard Leakey (Maeve's husband, and Walker's associate on the 1985 expedition) view the black skull (dated to 2.6 m.y.a.) as a very early hyperrobust *Au. boisei*. Others (e.g., Jolly and White 1995) assign the black skull to its own species, *Au. aethiopicus*. The black skull shows that some of the anatomical features of the hyperrobust australopithecines (2.6?–1.0 m.y.a.) did not change very much during more than one million years.

*Au. boisei* survived through 1.2 m.y.a in East Africa. Compared with their predecessors, the later australopithecines tended to have larger overall size, skulls, and back teeth. They also had thicker faces, more prominent crests, and more rugged muscle markings on the skeleton. By contrast, the front teeth stayed the same size.

Brain size (measured as cranial capacity, in cubic centimeters—cm$^3$) increased only slightly between *Au. afarensis* (430 cm$^3$), *Au. africanus* (490 cm$^3$), and *Au. robustus* (540 cm$^3$) (Wolpoff 1999). These figures can be compared with an average cranial capacity of 1,350 cm$^3$ in *Homo sapiens*. The modern range goes from less than 1,000 cm$^3$ to more than 2,000 cm$^3$ in normal adults. The cranial capacity of chimps (*Pan troglodytes*) averages 390 cm$^3$ (see Recap 8.1). The brains of gorillas *(Gorilla gorilla)* average around 500 cm$^3$, which is within the australopithecine range, but gorilla body size is much greater.

## THE AUSTRALOPITHECINES AND EARLY *HOMO*

By 2 m.y.a., the ancestors of *Homo* had become reproductively isolated from the later australopithecines, such as *Au. robustus* and *Au. boisei*. By 2 m.y.a. the fossil sample of hominin teeth from East Africa has two clearly different sizes. One set is huge, the largest molars and premolars in hominin evolution; those teeth belonged to *Au. boisei*. The other group of (smaller) teeth belonged to members of the genus *Homo*. The status of a recent find, *Au. sediba,* as a possible human ancestor is debated in this chapter's "Appreciating Anthropology."

By 1.9 m.y.a., there is clear fossil evidence that different hominin groups occupied different ecological niches in Africa. One of them, *Homo*—by then *Homo erectus*—had a larger brain and a reproportioned skull; it had increased the areas of the brain that regulate higher mental functions. These were our ancestors, hominins with greater capacities for culture than the australopithecines had. *H. erectus* hunted and gathered, made sophisticated tools, and eventually displaced its cousin species, *Au. boisei*.

*Au. boisei* of East Africa, the hyperrobust australopithecines, had mammoth back teeth. Their females had bigger back teeth than did earlier australopithecine males. *Au. boisei* became ever more specialized with respect to one part of the traditional australopithecine diet, concentrating on coarse vegetation with a high grit content.

We still don't know why, how, and exactly when the split between *Australopithecus* and *Homo* took place. Scholars have defended many different models, or theoretical schemes, to interpret the early hominin fossil record. Because new finds so often have forced reappraisals, most scientists are willing to modify their interpretation when given new evidence.

The model of Johanson and White (1979), who coined the term *Au. afarensis,* proposes that

*Au. afarensis* split into two groups. One group, the ancestors of *Homo,* became reproductively isolated from the australopithecines between 3 and 2 m.y.a. This group eventually gave rise to **Homo habilis,** a term coined by L. S. B. and Mary Leakey (Richard's parents) to describe early members of the genus *Homo.* Another form of early *Homo* was *H. erectus,* which appears to have lived contemporaneously with *H. habilis* between around 1.9 and 1.4 m.y.a. (Spoor et al. 2007; Wood 2011). Other members of *Au. afarensis* evolved into the various kinds of later australopithecines (*Au. africanus, Au. robustus,* and hyperrobust *Au. boisei,* the last member to become extinct). Figure 8.7 is a drawing of the skulls of four species of *Australopithecus.*

There is good fossil evidence that *Homo* and *Au. boisei* coexisted in East Africa. *Au. boisei* seems to have lived in very arid areas, feeding on harder-to-chew vegetation than had any previous hominin.

This diet would explain the hyperrobusts' huge back teeth, jaws, and associated areas of the face and skull.

## OLDOWAN TOOLS

The simplest obviously manufactured tools were discovered in 1931 by L. S. B. and Mary Leakey at Olduvai Gorge, Tanzania. That locale gave the tools their name—Oldowan pebble tools. The oldest tools from Olduvai are about 1.8 million years old. Still older (2.6–2.0 m.y.a.) Oldowan implements have been found in Congo, Ethiopia, Kenya, and Malawi.

Stone tools consist of flakes and cores. The *core* is the piece of rock, in the Oldowan case about the size of a tennis ball, from which flakes are struck. Once flakes are removed, the core can become a

**Homo habilis**
Earliest (2.4?–1.4? m.y.a.) member of genus *Homo.*

Au. afarensis        Au. africanus        Au. robustus        Au. boisei

**FIGURE 8.7**   Four Types of Australopithecine.
What are the main differences you notice among these four types of early hominins?

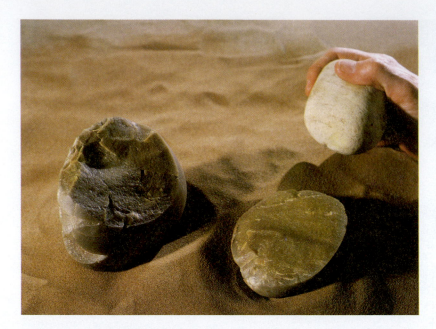

A modern human hand holds a rock to demonstrate how Oldowan stone tools were made. Oldowan chopper tools were rounded rocks sharpened by blows that detached a flake. The sharp flakes that were detached actually make up the bulk of the Oldowan tool industry.

**Oldowan**
Earliest (2.6–1.2 m.y.a.) stone tools; sharp flakes struck from cores (choppers).

**Au. garhi**
Toolmaking *Australopithecus* species (2.6–2.5 m.y.a.), Ethiopia.

tool itself. A *chopper* is a tool made by flaking the edge of such a core on one side and thus forming a cutting edge.

**Oldowan** pebble tools represent the world's oldest formally recognized stone tools. Core tools are not the most common Oldowan tools; flakes are. The purpose of flaking stone in the Oldowan tradition was not to create pebble tools or choppers but to create the sharp stone flakes that made up the mainstay of the Oldowan tool kit (Toth 1985). Choppers were a convenient by-product of flaking and were used as well. However, hominins most likely did not have a preconceived tool form in mind while making them.

Oldowan choppers could have been used for food processing—by pounding, breaking, or bashing. Flakes probably were used mainly as cutters, for example, to dismember game carcasses. Crushed fossil animal bones indicate that stones were used to break open marrow cavities. Also, Oldowan deposits include pieces of bone or horn with scratch marks suggesting they were used to dig up tubers or insects. Oldowan core and flake tools are shown in the photos on this page. The flake tool in the lower photo is made of chert. Most Oldowan tools at Olduvai Gorge were made from basalt, which is locally more common and coarser.

For decades anthropologists have debated the identity of the earliest stone toolmakers. The first *Homo habilis* find got its name (*habilis* is Latin for "able"—to make tools) for its presumed status as the first hominin toolmaker. Recently, the story has grown more complicated, with a discovery making it very likely that at least one kind of australopithecine also made and habitually used stone tools.

## *Au. garhi* and Early Stone Tools

In 1999 an international team reported the discovery, in Ethiopia, of a new species of hominin, along with the earliest traces of animal butchery (Asfaw, White, and Lovejoy 1999). These new fossils, dating to 2.6–2.5 m.y.a., may be the remains of a direct human ancestor and an evolutionary link between *Australopithecus* and the genus *Homo*. At the same site was evidence that antelopes and horses had been butchered with the world's earliest stone tools. When scientists excavated these hominin fossils, they were shocked to find a combination of unforeseen skeletal and dental features. They named the specimen *Australopithecus garhi* (**Au. garhi**). The word *garhi* means "surprise" in the Afar language.

Tim White, coleader of the research team, viewed the discoveries as important for three reasons. First, they add a new potential ancestor to the human family tree. Second, they show that the thigh bone (femur) had elongated by 2.6–2.5 million years ago, a million years before the forearm shortened—to create our current human limb proportions. Third, evidence that large mammals were being butchered shows that early stone technologies were aimed at getting meat and marrow from big game. This may signal the beginning of a dietary revolution that eventually led to the occupation of new habitats and continents (*Berkeleyan* 1999).

In 1997 the Ethiopian archaeologist Sileshi Semaw announced he had found the world's earliest stone tools, dating to 2.6 m.y.a., at the nearby Ethiopian site of Gona. But which human ancestor had made these tools, he wondered, and what were they used for? The 1999 discoveries by Asfaw, White, and their colleagues provided answers, identifying *Au. garhi* as the best candidate for toolmaker (*Berkeleyan* 1999).

The association, in the same area at the same time, of *Au. garhi,* animal butchery, and the earliest stone tools suggests that the australopithecines were toolmakers, with some capacity for culture. Nevertheless, cultural abilities developed exponentially with *Homo*'s appearance and expansion. With increasing reliance on hunting, toolmaking, and other cultural abilities, *Homo* eventually became the most efficient exploiter of the savanna niche. The last surviving members of *Au. boisei* may have been forced into ever-more-marginal areas. They eventually became extinct. By 1 m.y.a., a single species of hominin, *H. erectus,* not only had rendered other hominin forms extinct but also had expanded the hominin range to Asia and Europe. An essentially human strategy of adaptation, incorporating hunting as a fundamental ingredient of a generalized foraging economy, had emerged. Despite regional variation, it was to be the basic economy for our genus until 11,000 years ago. The next chapter describes the fossils, tools, and life patterns of the various forms of *Homo*.

## Oldowan Hominins at the Kanjera Site

Comparisons with chimps and bonobos suggest that hominins always have lived in social groups composed of multiple males and females. Our closest relatives, chimps and bonobos, lack *pair bonding;* a chimp female in estrus will mate with multiple males, and males mate with multiple females. Hominins, which are even more social than chimps and bonobos, have continued to live in groups with multiple adult males and females. At some point in their evolution, however, hominins developed pair bonding (Lukas and Clutton-Brock 2013; Opie et al. 2013; Zimmer 2013). A male and a female would pair off, bond, and mate exclusively or mainly with each other for a significant period of time. Such a bond would increase the likelihood that the offspring of the female were also those of the male. Both parents would do all they could to ensure the child's survival and well-being. At some point, especially as hominins became dependent on hunting, a gender-based division of labor developed. Men who hunted took meat home to share with their mates, their children, and other members of their social group.

Anthropologists have found excellent evidence for hunting around two million years ago at a very rich site in Kenya—the Kanjera South, or KJS, site, located on the shores of Lake Victoria (Ferraro et al. 2013). The archaeologists analyzed thousands of tools and animal bones (many showing marks of cutting or cracking) from the site. Using Oldowan stone tools, the ancient hominins who occupied the site were acquiring and processing meat—from hunting and scavenging. The animal bones at the site reveal that these Oldowan hominins hunted and butchered numerous small antelopes. The archaeologists could tell this because bones of the entire animal were present at the site—indicating that carcasses had been brought back whole. Cut marks show that hominins used their simple stone tools to remove animal flesh. They also used fist-sized stones to crack open animal bones to get at the marrow. The Oldowan hominins ate larger antelopes as well, but these typically were scavenged rather than hunted. Again the bones tell the story: The larger animals were represented by only part of the skeleton and skull, suggesting that hominins brought back remainders from the kills of other predators, which could not as easily get at the brains and bone marrow of their prey.

The Kanjera site provides the earliest, and very complete, evidence for what the anthropologists call "persistent" reliance on meat within the hominin diet. We don't know the genus or species of these hominins, but we do know the significance of a meat-laden diet. Meat supported population increase and territorial expansion among hominins. We hear so much today about the dangers of too much red meat that we forget that meat is an excellent and concentrated source of calories and protein. Its inclusion in the ancient hominin diet supported an increase in the size of the human body and brain, which is a very expensive organ in terms of its energy needs. To summarize, a regular diet of red meat was a key factor allowing the growth of the hominin body and brain and the spread of hominins within and beyond Africa. Among the likely social changes associated with the new diet were pair bonding, increased parental (especially male) investment in children, and a gender-based division of labor.

# for REVIEW

## summary

1. A skull found in 2001 in northern Chad, dated at 6–7 million years old, officially named *Sahelanthropus tchadensis,* more commonly called "Toumai," may or may not be the earliest hominin yet known, as may the somewhat less ancient *Orrorin tugenensis,* found in Kenya in 2001.

2. Hominins lived during the late Miocene, Pliocene (5.0–2.0 m.y.a.), and Pleistocene (2.0 m.y.a–10,000 B.P.) epochs. The australopithecines had appeared by 4.2 m.y.a. The seven species of *Australopithecus* were *Au. anamensis* (4.2–3.9 m.y.a.), *Au. afarensis* (3.8–3.0 m.y.a.), *Au. africanus* (3.0?–2.0? m.y.a.), *Au. garhi* (2.6–2.5 m.y.a.), *Au. robustus* (2.0?–1.0? m.y.a.), *Au. boisei* (2.6?–1.2 m.y.a.), and *Au. sediba* (1.98–1.78 m.y.a.). The earliest definite hominin remains, from Ethiopia, are classified as *Ardipithecus kadabba* (5.8–5.5 m.y.a.) and *ramidus* (4.4 m.y.a.). Next comes *Au. anamensis,* then a group of fossils from Hadar, Ethiopia, and Laetoli, Tanzania, classified as *Au. afarensis.*

3. These earliest hominins shared many primitive features, including slashing canines; elongated pre-molars; a small, apelike skull; and marked sexual dimorphism. Still, *Au. afarensis* and its recently discovered predecessors were definite hominins. In *Au. afarensis* this is confirmed by large molars and, more important, by skeletal evidence (e.g., in Lucy) for upright bipedalism.

4. Remains of two later groups, *Au. africanus* (graciles) and *Au. robustus* (robusts), were found in South Africa. Both groups show the australopithecine trend toward a powerful chewing apparatus. They had large molars and premolars and large and robust faces, skulls, and muscle markings. All these features are more pronounced in the robusts than they are in the graciles. The basis of the australopithecine diet was savanna vegetation.

5. By 2.0 m.y.a. there is ample evidence for two distinct hominin groups: early *Homo* and *Au. boisei,* the hyperrobust australopithecines. The latter eventually became extinct around 1.2 m.y.a. *Au. boisei* became increasingly specialized, dependent on tough, coarse, gritty, fibrous savanna vegetation. The australopithecine trend toward dental, facial, and cranial robustness continued with *Au. boisei,* but these structures were reduced in *H. habilis* (2.4?–1.4? m.y.a.) and *H. erectus* (1.9?–0.3? m.y.a).

6. Pebble tools dating to between 2.6 and 2.0 m.y.a. have been found in Kenya, Ethiopia, Congo, and Malawi. Scientists have disagreed about their maker, some arguing that only early *Homo* could have made them. Evidence has been presented that *Au. garhi* made pebble tools around 2.6–2.5 m.y.a. Cultural abilities developed exponentially with *Homo*'s appearance and evolution. A regular diet of red meat was a key factor allowing the growth of the hominin body and brain and the spread of hominins within and beyond Africa. Among the likely social changes associated with the new diet were pair bonding, increased parental (especially male) investment in children, and a gender-based division of labor.

## key terms

Ardipithecus 129

*Au. afarensis* 135

*Au. africanus* 139

*Au. anamensis* 134

*Au. boisei* 139

*Au. garhi* 144

*Au. robustus* 139

australopithecines 134

gracile 139

*Homo habilis* 143

Oldowan 144

robust 139

## critical thinking

1. If you found a new hominid fossil in East Africa, dated to five million years ago, would it most likely be an ape ancestor or a human ancestor? How would you tell the difference?

2. In trying to determine whether a fossil is a human ancestor, researchers sometimes look for traits that have receded during subsequent human evolution. What is an example of this? How could humans come to lose or reduce a trait that is used to determine ancestry in the past?

3. In human evolution, what is the relationship between brains, skulls, and childhood dependency? Thinking back to Chapter 1, how does the study of this relationship illustrate anthropology's biocultural approach?

4. What new light did the fossil known as "Ardi" shed on the understanding of human evolution?

5. The fossil remains found in Laetoli and Hadar forced a reinterpretation of the early hominin record. How so? What does this reinterpretation suggest about hominins' relation to apes?

# Archaic *Homo*

▶ What were the earliest forms of *Homo,* and where did they originate and eventually migrate?

▶ What were the major toolmaking traditions and adaptive strategies of archaic *Homo*?

▶ What were the Neandertals like, and how did they differ from earlier and later forms of *Homo*?

A Neandertal skeleton (right) and a modern human skeleton (left and behind) displayed at New York's American Museum of Natural History. The Neandertal skeleton, reconstructed from casts of more than 200 fossil bones, was part of an exhibit titled "The First Europeans: Treasures from the Hills of Atapuerca" (Spain).

# understanding OURSELVES

**F**red Flintstone was the only caveman (the only cave person, for that matter) to appear on a VH1 list of the "200 Greatest Pop Culture Icons." He ranked number 42, between Cher and Martha Stewart. The Flintstones and their neighbors, the Rubbles, don't look much like Neanderthals (which anthropologists spell Neandertal, without the *h*). Real Neandertals had heavy brow ridges and slanting foreheads, and they lacked chins. *The Flintstones* transposed a 20th-century American blue-collar lifestyle back to prehistoric times—Fred and Barney worked in factories, "drove" stone cars, and used dinosaurs as construction cranes and can openers. While it is clearly ridiculous to imagine that Neandertals used dinosaurs as tools, it is equally outlandish to think that dinosaurs and Neandertals might have coexisted. Dinosaurs were extinct long before humans, hominins, or hominids ever walked the Earth. Just as American popular culture never tires of calling apes "monkeys," it can't seem to resist mixing dinosaurs and cave people.

Decades after Fred first appeared on TV, Geico commercials introduced new cavemen, along with the slogan "So easy a caveman can do it." The 21st-century world of Geico's cavemen included cell phones, airports, and tennis courts. Geico's cavemen shared another modern trait—a sense of outrage over the insult implied in their sponsor's slogan. Should it be insulting to call someone a "caveman" or a "Neandertal"? Consider that the average Neandertal brain was larger than the average human brain, although what that says about intelligence isn't clear. One fossil in particular helped create the enduring popular stereotype of the slouching, inferior Neandertal caveman. This was a skeleton discovered a century ago at La Chapelle-aux-Saints in southwestern France. The original assessment of this fossil created an inaccurate image of Neandertals as apelike brutes who had trouble walking upright. Closer analysis revealed that La Chapelle was an aging man with arthritic bones. This illustrates the danger of attempting to reach broad conclusions based upon a small sample size.

Actually, as one would expect, Neandertals were a variable population. Some fossil hominins even combine Neandertal robustness with modern features. For example, the remains of a 4-year-old boy found in Portugal, dating back some 24,000 years, show mixed Neandertal and modern features. This find and others have raised the question as to whether Neandertals and anatomically modern humans could have mated. Another modern activity in which the Geico cavemen engage is dating anatomically modern women. The extent to which similar attractions are part of history is one more subject for scientific debate.

## EARLY *HOMO*

By two million years ago, there is African evidence for two distinct hominin groups: early *Homo* and *Au. boisei*, the hyperrobust australopithecines, which became extinct around 1.2 m.y.a. The australopithecine trend toward dental, facial, and cranial robustness continued through *Au. boisei*. However, these structures were reduced as early forms of *Homo* evolved into early *H. erectus* by 1.9 m.y.a. By that date *Homo* was hunting large animals to supplement the gathering of vegetation and scavenging.

Meet two kinds of early *Homo:* on the left, KNM-ER 1813; on the right, KNM-ER 1470. The latter (1470) has been classified as *H. rudolfensis.* What's the classification of 1813?

## H. rudolfensis and H. habilis

In 1972, in an expedition led by Richard Leakey, Bernard Ngeneo unearthed a skull designated KNM-ER 1470. The name comes from its catalog number in the Kenya National Museum (KNM) and its discovery location (East Rudolph—ER)—east of Lake Rudolph, at a site called Koobi Fora, in Kenya. The 1470 skull attracted immediate attention because of its unusual combination of a large brain (775 cm³) and very large molars. Its brain size was more human than that of the australopithecines, but its molars recalled those of the hyperrobust australopithecines. Some paleoanthropologists attributed the large skull and teeth to a very large body, assuming that this had been one *really big* hominin. But no postcranial remains were found with 1470, nor have they been found with any later discovery of a 1470-like specimen.

How to interpret 1470 when its brain size argued for *Homo,* while its back teeth said *Australopithecus?* Dating estimates ranged from 1.8 m.y.a. to as far back as 2.4 m.y.a. In 1986, it received its own species name, *H. rudolfensis,* from the lake near which it was found. This label has stuck. Note the contrasts in the two skulls in the photo above. KNM-ER 1813, on the left, is considered *H. habilis;* KNM-ER 1470, on the right, is *H. rudolfensis.* The *habilis* skull has a more marked brow ridge and a depression behind it, whereas 1470 has a less pronounced brow ridge and a longer, flatter face.

For almost 40 years after finding 1470, the Leakey family and others scoured deposits near Lake Turkana for similar fossils. Between 2007 and 2009 they found them (see Gibbons 2012; Leakey et al. 2012). In 2012 Maeve Leakey and her associates announced the discovery at Koobi Fora of a face and two jawbones, showing that 1470 was not unique.

These new fossils, dating to 2.03–1.78 m.y.a., confirmed that *H. rudolfensis* lived in the same area and at the same time as at least two other species of *Homo—habilis* and *erectus.*

The face of the newly discovered *H. rudolfensis* skull—that of a juvenile—was well preserved and included upper teeth. It was a smaller version of the 1470 skull, both featuring an unusually flat face that contrasts with the more jutting upper jaw of *H. habilis.* The lower jawbones, one of which was remarkably complete, gave new information, because the 1470 fossil had no lower jaw. The new jaw and face showed that *H. rudolfensis* had an unusual U-shaped palate, with canines facing the front of the jaw rather than placed on the sides in a V-shaped palate, as in *H. habilis.* The new jaws also had smaller molars than expected, based on those of 1470. The new fossils were found within 10 kilometers of the 1470 discovery site, and within the same region where fossils of *H. habilis* and *H. erectus* have been discovered.

## H. habilis and H. erectus

A team headed by L. S. B. and Mary Leakey (parents of Richard) discovered the first representative of *Homo habilis* (OH7—Olduvai Hominid 7) at Olduvai Gorge in Tanzania in 1960. Olduvai's oldest layer, Bed I, dates to 1.8 m.y.a. This layer has yielded both small-brained *Au. boisei* fossils (average 490 cm³) and *H. habilis* skulls, with cranial capacities between 600 and 700 cm³.

Another important *habilis* find is OH62, the partial skeleton of a female *H. habilis* from Olduvai Bed I. This was the first find of an *H. habilis* skull with a significant amount of skeletal material. OH62, dating to 1.8 m.y.a., consists of parts of the skull, the right arm, and both legs. The fossil, found by Tim White in 1986, was surprising because of its small size and apelike limb bones. Not only was OH62 just as tiny as Lucy (3 feet, or 0.9 meter), its arms were longer than expected. The limb proportions suggested greater tree-climbing ability, compared with later hominins. *H. habilis* may still have sought occasional refuge in the trees.

The small size and primitive proportions of *H. habilis* were unexpected, given what was known about early *H. erectus* in East Africa. In deposits near Lake Turkana, Kenya, Richard Leakey had uncovered two *H. erectus* skulls dating to 1.6 m.y.a. By that date, *H. erectus* (males, at least) had already attained a cranial capacity of 900 cm$^3$, along with a modern body shape and height. An amazingly complete young male *H. erectus* fossil (WT15,000) found at West Turkana in 1984 by Kimoya Kimeu, a collaborator of the Leakeys, has confirmed this. WT15,000, also known as the Nariokotome boy, was a 12-year-old male who had already reached 5 feet 5 inches (1.67 meters). He might have grown to 6 feet had he lived.

### Sister Species

Two recent hominin fossil finds from Ileret, Kenya (east of Lake Turkana), are very significant, mainly for two reasons: They show that (1) *H. habilis* and *H. erectus* overlapped in time rather than being ancestor and descendant, as had been thought, and (2) sexual dimorphism in *H. erectus* was much greater than expected (see Spoor et al. 2007; Wilford 2007a).

One of these finds (KNM-ER 42703) is the upper jawbone of a 1.44 million-year-old *H. habilis*. The other (KNM-ER 42700) is the almost complete but faceless skull of a 1.55 million-year-old *H. erectus*. These finds negated the conventional view (held since the Leakeys described the first *habilis* in 1960) that *habilis* and then *erectus* evolved, one after the other. Instead, they apparently split from a common ancestor prior to 2 m.y.a. Then they lived side by side in eastern Africa for perhaps half a million years. According to Maeve Leakey, one of the authors of the report (Spoor et al. 2007), the fact that they remained separate species for so long "suggests that they had their own ecological niche, thus avoiding direct competition" (quoted in Wilford 2007a, p. A6). They coexisted in the same general area (an ancient lake basin), much as gorillas and chimpanzees do today.

Given these finds, the fossil record for early *Homo* in East Africa must be revised as follows: *H. rudolfensis* (2.03–1.78 m.y.a.), *H. habilis* (1.9–1.44 m.y.a), and *H. erectus* (1.9–0.3? m.y.a). The oldest definite *H. habilis* (OH24) dates to 1.9 m.y.a., as does the oldest *erectus*.

What about sexual dimorphism in *H. erectus*? As the smallest *erectus* find ever, KNM-ER 42700 also may be the first female *erectus* yet found, most probably a young adult or late subadult. Its small skull suggests that the range in overall body size among *H. erectus* was much greater than previously thought, with greater sexual dimorphism than among chimps or contemporary humans. Another possibility is that the (as yet undiscovered) *H. erectus* males that lived in this area along with the female also were smaller than the typical *erectus* male.

### The Significance of Hunting

The ecological niche that separated *H. erectus* from both *H. habilis* and *Au. boisei* involved greater reliance on hunting, along with improved cultural means of adaptation, including better tools. Significant changes in technology occurred during the 200,000-year period between Bed I (1.8 m.y.a.) and Lower Bed II (1.6 m.y.a) at Olduvai. Toolmaking got more sophisticated soon after the advent of *H. erectus*. Out of the crude tools in Bed I evolved better-made and more varied tools. The earliest (1.76 m.y.a.) tools of the *Acheulean* type (see the following section) associated with *H. erectus* come from the site of Kokiselei near Lake Turkana in Kenya (Wilford 2011c). These tools show signs of symmetry, uniformity, and planning. Edges are straighter than with Oldowan tools, and differences in form suggest functional differentiation. The tools were being made and used for different jobs, such as smashing bones or digging for tubers. This new technology made it possible for *Homo* not only to acquire meat more reliably but also to dig and process tubers, roots, nuts, and seeds more efficiently. New tools that could batter, crush, and pulp coarse vegetation also reduced chewing demands.

*Au. boisei* (left) and *H. habilis* (right). Both OH5 (L) and OH24 (R) were found in Bed I at Olduvai Gorge, Tanzania, and were probable contemporaries.

Dietary changes eased the burden on the chewing apparatus, so that chewing muscles developed less. Supporting structures, such as jaws and cranial crests, also were reduced. Smaller jaws had less room to fit large teeth. The size of teeth, which form before they erupt, is under stricter genetic control than jaw size and bone size are (see von Cramon-Taubadel 2011). Natural selection began to operate against the genes that produced large teeth, which now caused dental crowding, impaction, pain, sickness, fever, and sometimes death (there were no dentists). *H. erectus* back teeth are smaller, and the front teeth are relatively larger, than australopithecine teeth. *H. erectus* used its front teeth to pull, twist, and grip objects. A massive ridge over the eyebrows (a superorbital torus) provided buttressing against the forces exerted in these activities. It also provided protection, as we see in "Appreciating Diversity" on p. 152.

As hunting became more important, encounters with large prey animals increased. Individuals with stronger skulls had better-protected brains and better survival rates. Natural selection favored the thickening of certain areas for better protection against blows and falls. The base of the skull expanded dramatically, with a ridge of spongy bone (an occipital bun) across the back. Finally, average cranial capacity expanded from about 500 cm$^3$ in the australopithecines to 1,000 cm$^3$ in *H. erectus,* which is within the modern range of variation.

## OUT OF AFRICA I: *H. ERECTUS*

Hominins migrated out of Africa in multiple waves. First to expand was *H. erectus,* whose spread occurred between 2 and 1 m.y.a. Did the ancestors of the Neandertals and Denisovans (see later in this chapter) branch off in, and then leave, Africa, perhaps as early as 800,000 years ago? Or did they evolve from *H. erectus* ancestors in Asia or Europe? Populations of anatomically modern humans (**AMHs**) certainly left Africa, maybe more than once, as early perhaps as 110,000 B.P., but mainly around and after 70,000 B.P. That last wave included the ancestors of all humans on Earth today.

*H. erectus* initiated the expansion of hominins beyond Africa—to Asia and Europe. Small groups broke off from larger ones and moved a few miles away. They foraged new tracts of edible vegetation and carved out new hunting territories. Through population growth and dispersal, *H. erectus* gradually spread and changed. Fueling this expansion was commitment to an essentially human lifestyle based on hunting and gathering. This basic pattern survived until recently in certain parts of the world, although it now is fading rapidly. We focus in this chapter on the biological and cultural changes that led from early *Homo,* through intermediate forms, to anatomically modern humans.

This photo shows the early (1.6 m.y.a.) *Homo erectus* WT15,000, or Nariokotome boy, found in 1984 near Lake Turkana, Kenya. This is the most complete *Homo erectus* ever found.

## Paleolithic Tools

The stone toolmaking techniques that evolved out of the Oldowan tradition, and that lasted until about 15,000 years ago, are described by the term **Paleolithic** (from Greek roots meaning "old" and "stone"). The Paleolithic, or Old Stone Age, has three divisions: Lower (early), Middle, and Upper (late). Each part is associated with a particular stage in human evolution. The Lower Paleolithic is roughly associated with *H. erectus;* the Middle Paleolithic, with archaic *H. sapiens,* including the Neandertals of western Europe and the Middle East; and the Upper Paleolithic, with anatomically modern humans.

The best stone tools are made from rocks, such as flint, that fracture sharply and in predictable ways when hammered. Quartz, quartzite, chert, and obsidian also are suitable. Each of the three main divisions of the Paleolithic had its typical *toolmaking traditions*—coherent patterns of tool manufacture. The main Lower Paleolithic toolmaking tradition used by *H. erectus* was the **Acheulean,** named after the French village of St. Acheul, where it was first identified. Recent finds in Kenya date the oldest Acheulean hand axes to 1.76 m.y.a.

In Oldowan tools, flaking wasn't done to make choppers (according to a predetermined form). It was done simply to produce sharp flakes. A fundamental difference shows up in the Acheulean tradition, which involved chipping the core bilaterally and symmetrically. The core was converted from a round piece of rock into a flattish, oval hand ax about 6 inches

**Paleolithic**
Old Stone Age, including Lower (early), Middle, and Upper (late).

**AMHs**
Anatomically modern humans.

**Acheulean**
Lower Paleolithic tool tradition associated with *H. erectus.*

## Headstrong Hominins

On the evolutionary timeline of hominin biological diversity, the anatomical contrasts between *Homo erectus* and modern humans are clear. There must have been behavioral differences as well. How did anatomy and behavior fit together in *H. erectus* populations? Noel Boaz and Russell Ciochon (2004) proposed that several protective features of the *H. erectus* skull evolved in response to behavior, specifically interpersonal violence—fighting among those thick-skulled hominins. Ever since the discovery of the first *H. erectus* skull, scholars have been struck by the unusual cranial anatomy. The top and sides of the skull have thick, bony walls (see the photos). The *H. erectus* skullcap resembles a cyclist's helmet—low and streamlined, so as to protect the brain, ears, and eyes from impact. "In contrast, we modern humans hold our enormous, easily injured, semiliquid brains in relatively thin-walled bony globes. We have to buy our bicycle helmets" (Boaz and Ciochon 2004, p. 29). In other words, a cultural adaptation (plastic) has replaced a biological one (bone).

Based on these and other cranial features, Boaz and Ciochon speculate that *H. erectus* needed sturdy anatomical headgear to protect against life-threatening breaks. Even today, with modern medicine, skull fractures can be fatal. An apparently minor fracture can rip blood vessels inside the skull. Blood builds up under the skull. Such a hematoma pushing on the brain can cause a coma and, eventually, death.

For *H. erectus* this bleeding would have been much more problematic than for people with access to modern medicine. The neurological damage caused by such a hematoma can lead to partial paralysis, locomotion problems, poor hand-eye coordination, difficulties in speaking, and cognitive disruptions. Boaz and Ciochon note that "any traits that reduced the chances of cranial fracture would have given a substantial evolutionary advantage to the individuals who possessed them" (Boaz and Ciochon 2004, p. 30).

The authors contend that the blows delivered in a fight are more likely to land at eye level than on the top of the head. Although modern human skulls have some degree of eye-level bony armor, the thicker ring of bone in the *H. erectus* skull would have provided much more protection. The thick brow ridge protected the eye sockets, while bony bulges on each side of the skull shielded the sinus where blood flows into the internal jugular vein. This buttressing also protected the ear region. Finally, the bony ridge at the back of the skull protected several sinuses that carried blood within the rearmost brain lobes.

The thick jaws of *H. erectus* also would have been adaptive. Today, a broken jaw makes it painful, difficult, and sometimes impossible to chew. Surgical wiring of the broken sections is required. For *H. erectus*, such a break could have been life-threatening. There was an inside thickening of the jaw, just behind the chin, to protect against breaks.

Among the dozens of *H. erectus* fossils found near Beijing, China, the anthropologist/anatomist Franz Weidenreich detected several fractures that had subsequently healed. The fact that the trauma victims survived offers confirmation of the protective value of their skulls. Boaz and Ciochon believe that the thick skulls and healed fractures of *H. erectus* provide a record of violence within the species.

This defensive armor—the anatomical headgear—was reduced once *H. sapiens* evolved a larger, more globular, thin-walled skull. Although human violence didn't end, other means of protection, avoidance of conflict, or both evolved among the descendants of *H. erectus*. Boaz and Ciochon think those new protective mechanisms belong to the realm of cultural rather than biological diversity.

*Homo erectus* skullcaps have been likened to bicycle helmets because of their protective properties. These three skulls show dramatic similarities despite different ages. The skull shown at the left is a cast of Skull XII from the "Peking Man" collection and dates to 670,000–410,000 years ago. The two other skulls are much older. Sangiran 2 from Java (middle photo) may be as old as 1.6 m.y.a., while OH9 from Olduvai Gorge, Tanzania (right), may date back 1.4 million years. What similarities do you note among the three skulls?

(15 centimeters) long. Its cutting edge was far superior to that of the Oldowan chopper (see Figure 9.1). The Acheulean hand ax embodies a predetermined shape created from a template in the toolmaker's mind. Archaeological evidence for tools illustrating such a mental template confirms a cognitive leap between earlier hominins and *H. erectus*.

Analysis of their wear patterns suggests that Acheulean hand axes were versatile tools used for many tasks, from butchering and cutting to woodworking and vegetable preparation. Cleavers—core tools with a straight edge at one end—were used for heavy chopping and hacking at the sinews of larger animals. Stone picks probably were used for digging. Acheulean toolmakers also used flakes, with finer edges, for light-duty tools—to make incisions and for finer work. Flakes became progressively more important in human evolution, particularly in Middle and Upper Paleolithic toolmaking.

Dating back at least 1.76 m.y.a., the Acheulean tradition illustrates trends in the evolution of technology: greater efficiency, the manufacture of tools with predetermined forms and for specific tasks, and an increasingly complex technology. These trends became even more obvious with the advent of *H. sapiens*.

## Adaptive Strategies of *H. erectus*

Interrelated changes in biology and culture have increased human adaptability—the capacity to live in and modify an ever-wider range of environments. Improved tools helped *H. erectus* increase its range. Biological changes also increased hunting efficiency. *H. erectus* had a rugged but essentially modern skeleton that permitted long-distance stalking and endurance during the hunt. The *H. erectus* body was much larger and longer-legged than those of previous hominins, permitting longer-distance hunting of large prey. There is archaeological evidence of *H. erectus*'s success in hunting elephants, horses, rhinos, and giant baboons.

Increased cranial capacity has been a trend in human evolution. The average *H. erectus* brain (about 1,000 cm³) doubled the australopithecine average. The capacities of *H. erectus* skulls range from 800 to 1,250 cm³, well above the modern minimum.

*H. erectus* had an essentially modern, though very robust, skeleton with a brain and body closer in size to *H. sapiens* than to *Australopithecus*. Still, several anatomical contrasts, particularly in the cranium, do distinguish *H. erectus* from modern humans. *H. erectus* had a lower and more sloping forehead accentuated by a large brow ridge above the eyes (see "Appreciating Diversity" on p. 152). Skull bones were thicker, and the braincase was lower and flatter than in *H. sapiens*, with spongy bone development at the lower rear of the skull. Seen from behind, the *H. erectus* skull has been compared to a half-inflated football and to a hamburger bun. The face, teeth, and jaws were larger than those of contemporary humans but smaller than

**FIGURE 9.1** Evolution in Toolmaking.
Finds at Olduvai Gorge and elsewhere show how pebble tools (the first tool at the left) evolved into the Acheulean hand ax of *H. erectus*. This drawing begins with an Oldowan pebble tool and moves through crude hand axes to fully developed Acheulean tools associated with *H. erectus*.

those of *Australopithecus*. The front teeth were especially large, but molar size was well below the australopithecine average.

Archaeologists have found and studied several sites of *H. erectus* activity, including cooperative hunting. Hearths at various sites confirm that fire was part of the adaptive kit controlled by *H. erectus*. Evidence for human control over fire has been found in Israel, dating back to almost 800,000 years ago. The newest evidence of fire, dated at 1 m.y.a., comes from Wonderwerk Cave (South Africa), where microscopic plant ashes and burned bits of bone have been found in soil that previously yielded dozens of stone tools (Berna et al. 2012). However, no remains of a hearth or campfire area, where fires would have been lit repeatedly, have been found in Wonderwerk

An Acheulean hand ax from Gesher Benot Ya'aqov, Israel, Jordan River. This site, shown here under excavation, dates back to 750,000 B.P. Which hominin might have made the ax?

Cave. The first hearths date back only 400,000 years (Rice 2012). Fire provided protection against cave bears and saber-toothed tigers. It permitted *H. erectus* to occupy cave sites, including Zhoukoudian, near Beijing, China, which has yielded the remains of more than 40 specimens of *H. erectus*. Fire widened the range of climates open to human colonization. Its warmth enabled people to survive winter cold in temperate regions. Cooking breaks down vegetable fibers and tenderizes meat. Cooking also kills parasites and makes meat more digestible, thus reducing strain on the chewing apparatus.

Could language (fireside chats, perhaps) have been an additional advantage available to *H. erectus*? Archaeological evidence confirms the cooperative hunting of large animals and the manufacture of complicated tools. These activities may well have been too complex to proceed without some kind of language. Speech would have aided coordination, cooperation, and the learning of traditions. Words, of course, aren't preserved until the advent of writing. However, given the fact that even apes have been shown to have some potential for language-based communication, and given the brain size within the low *H. sapiens* range, it seems plausible to assume that *H. erectus* had rudimentary speech.

## The Evolution and Expansion of *H. erectus*

Let's review now some of the fossil data, whose geographic distribution is mapped in Figure 9.2. The most important early out-of-Africa site is Dmanisi in the former Soviet Republic of Georgia. Discoveries there include one fairly complete skull, one large mandible, and two partial skulls—one of a young adult male (780 cm$^3$) and one of an adolescent female (650 cm$^3$). These hominin fossils are dated

**FIGURE 9.2** Location of Some Major *Homo erectus* Sites.

SOURCE: From John Relethford, *The Human Species: An Introduction to Biological Anthropology*, 9th ed., p. 273. Copyright © 2013 by McGraw-Hill Education, LLC. Reprinted with permission.

to 1.77–1.7 m.y.a. There are notable similarities between the two partial skulls and that of the Nariokotome boy from Kenya (1.6 m.y.a.). Tools of comparable age associated with the Kenyan and Georgian fossils also are similar (see Vekua, Lordkipanidze, and Rightmire 2002). The Dmanisi finds suggest a rapid spread, by 1.77 m.y.a., of early *Homo* out of Africa and into Eurasia.

The Dmanisi fossils are the most ancient undisputed hominin finds outside Africa. How did they get to Georgia? The most probable answer is "in pursuit of meat." As hominins became more carnivorous, they expanded their home ranges in accordance with those of the animals they hunted. Meat-rich diets provided higher-quality protein as fuel. Once hominins developed stronger bodies and high-protein meat diets, they could—indeed had to—spread out. They ranged farther to find meat, and this expansion eventually led them out of Africa, into Eurasia (Georgia) and eventually Asia (see Wilford 2000). More recent skeletal finds from Dmanisi suggest how this expansion might have taken place (Wilford 2007*b*). (Previously only skulls had been found there.) Four new fossil skeletons reveal an advanced spine and lower limbs that would have facilitated mobility.

In 1891, the Indonesian island of Java yielded the first (although not the most ancient) *H. erectus* fossil find, popularly known as "Java man." Eugene Dubois, a Dutch army surgeon, had gone there specifically to discover a transitional form between apes and humans. Of course, we now know that the transition to hominin had taken place much earlier than the *H. erectus* period and occurred in Africa. However, Dubois's good luck did lead him to the most ancient human fossils then known—parts of an *H. erectus* skull and a thigh bone. Later excavations in Java uncovered additional remains. The various Indonesian *H. erectus* fossils date back at least 700,000, and perhaps as much as 1.6 million, years. The four-stage photo spread at the right shows a reconstruction of *H. erectus* based on the Javanese find Sangiran 17, the most complete *H. erectus* skull from Indonesia.

Fragments of a skull and a lower jaw found in northern China at Lantian may be as old as the oldest Indonesian fossils. Other *H. erectus* remains, of uncertain date, have been found in Algeria and Morocco in North Africa. *H. erectus* remains also have been found in Upper Bed II at Olduvai, Tanzania, in association with Acheulean tools. In "Appreciating Diversity" on p. 152, you will find a photo of one such find, OH9, which dates back perhaps 1.4 million years, along with a photo of a Javanese find, Sangiran 2, which may be a bit older. African *H. erectus* fossils also have been found in Ethiopia, Eritrea, and South Africa (in addition to Kenya and Tanzania). The time span of *H. erectus* in East Africa was long. Later *H. erectus* fossils have been found in Bed IV at Olduvai, dating to 500,000 B.P., about the same age as the Beijing fossils, described below as well as in "Appreciating Diversity."

The largest group of *H. erectus* fossils was found in the Zhoukoudian cave in China. The Zhoukoudian ("Peking"—now Beijing—"man") site, excavated from the late 1920s to the late 1930s, was a major find for the human fossil record. Zhoukoudian yielded remains of tools, hearths, animal bones, and more than 40 hominins, including five skulls. One of these Beijing fossils, Skull XII, is shown in "Appreciating Diversity" on p. 152. The Zhoukoudian group lived between 670,000 and 410,000 years ago, when the Chinese climate was colder and moister than it is today—based on animal remains found with the human fossils. The people at Zhoukoudian ate venison; seed and plant remains show they gathered as well as hunted.

What about Europe? A cranial fragment found at Ceprano, near Rome, Italy, in 1994 has been assigned a date of 400,000 B.P. (see Mounier, Condemi, and Manzi 2011). Other possible *H. erectus* remains have been found in Europe, but their dates are uncertain. They usually are classified as late *H. erectus* or transitional between *H. erectus* and early *H. sapiens*.

## ARCHAIC H. SAPIENS

Africa, which was center stage during the australopithecine period, is joined by Asia and Europe during the *H. erectus* and *H. sapiens* periods of hominin evolution. European fossils and tools have contributed disproportionately to our knowledge and interpretation of early (archaic) *H. sapiens*. This doesn't mean that *H. sapiens* evolved in Europe or that most early *H. sapiens* lived in Europe. Indeed, the fossil evidence confirms that *H. sapiens*, like *H. erectus* before it, originated in Africa. Anatomically modern *H. sapiens* (abbreviated AMHs, for "anatomically modern humans") lived in Africa for more than 100,000 years before reaching Europe around 45,000 years ago (Benazzi et al. 2011; Higham et al. 2011). There probably were many more AMHs in the tropics than in Europe during the ice ages. We merely *know more* about recent human evolution in Europe because archaeology and fossil hunting—not human evolution—have been going on longer there than in Africa and Asia.

(a)

(b)

(c)

(d)

Meet *Homo erectus*. Sangiran 17 is the most complete *H. erectus* skull from Java. In this process of reconstruction, a cast of the fossil (a) was rounded out with teeth, lower jaw, and chewing muscles (b). Additional soft tissues (c) and then the skin (d) were added. Given the robust features of this fossil, it is assumed to be male.

*Fossil representatives of the genus* Homo, *compared with anatomically modern humans (AMHs) and chimps (Pan troglodytes).*

| SPECIES | DATES | KNOWN DISTRIBUTION | IMPORTANT SITES | BRAIN SIZE (cm³) |
|---|---|---|---|---|
| Anatomically modern humans (AMHs) | 195,000 B.P. to present | Worldwide | Omo Kibish, Herto, Border Cave, Klasies River, Skhūl, Qafzeh, Cro-Magnon | 1,350 |
| Neandertals | 130,000 to 28,000 B.P. | Europe, southwestern Asia | La Chapelle-aux-Saints | 1,430 |
| Archaic *Homo sapiens* | 300,000? to 28,000 B.P. | Africa, Europe, Asia | Kabwe, Arago, Dali, Mount Carmel caves | 1,135 |
| *Homo erectus* | 1.9 m.y.a. to 300,000 B.P. | Africa, Asia, Europe | East, West Turkana, Olduvai, Ileret, Dmanisi, Zhoukoudian, Java, Ceprano | 900 |
| *Pan troglodytes* | Modern | Central Africa | Gombe, Mahale | 390 |

**archaic *H. sapiens***
Early *H. sapiens* (300,000 to 28,000 B.P.); includes Neandertals.

**Neandertals**
Archaic *H. sapiens* group inhabiting Europe and the Middle East from 130,000 to 28,000 B.P.

**Pleistocene**
Main epoch (2 m.y.a.–10,000 B.P.) of evolution of *Homo*.

**glacials**
Major advances of continental ice sheets in Europe and North America.

**interglacials**
Extended warm periods between glacials.

Recent discoveries, along with reinterpretation of the dating and the anatomical relevance of some earlier finds, are filling in the gap between *H. erectus* and archaic *H. sapiens*. **Archaic *H. sapiens*** (300,000? to perhaps as late as 28,000 B.P.) encompasses the earliest members of our species, along with the **Neandertals** (*H. sapiens neanderthalensis*—130,000–28,000 B.P.) of Europe and the Middle East and their Neandertal-like contemporaries in Africa and Asia. (See Recap 9.1 and Figure 9.3 for a summary and timeline of species within the genus *Homo*.) Brain size in archaic *H. sapiens* was within the modern human range. (The modern average, remember, is about 1,350 cm³.) A rounding out of the braincase was associated with the increased brain size. As Jolly and White (1995) put it, evolution was pumping more brain into the *H. sapiens* cranium—like filling a football with air.

## Ice Ages of the Pleistocene

Traditionally and correctly, the geological epoch known as the **Pleistocene** has been considered the epoch of early human life. Its subdivisions are the Lower Pleistocene (2–1 m.y.a.), the Middle Pleistocene (1 m.y.a.–130,000 B.P.), and the Upper Pleistocene (130,000–10,000 B.P.). These subdivisions refer to the placement of geological strata containing, respectively, older, intermediate, and younger fossils. The Lower Pleistocene extends from the start of the Pleistocene to the advent of the ice ages in the Northern Hemisphere around one million years ago.

Each subdivision of the Pleistocene is associated with a particular group of hominins. Late *Australopithecus* and early *Homo* lived during the Lower Pleistocene. *Homo erectus* spanned most of the Middle Pleistocene. *Homo sapiens* appeared late in the Middle Pleistocene and was the sole hominin of the Upper Pleistocene.

During the second million years of the Pleistocene, there were several ice ages, or **glacials,** major advances of continental ice sheets in Europe and North America. These periods were separated by **interglacials,** long warm periods between the major glacials. (Scientists used to think there were four main glacial advances, but the picture has grown more complex.) With each advance, the world climate cooled and continental ice sheets—massive glaciers—covered the northern parts of

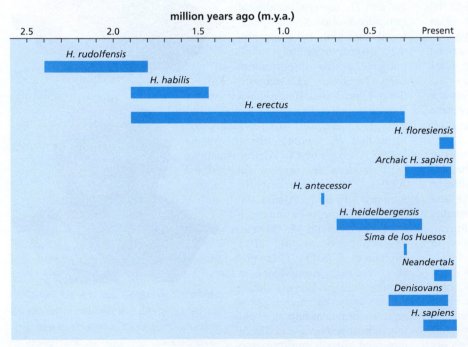

**FIGURE 9.3**    Timeline of Species within the Genus *Homo* in Increments of 100,000 Years, from 2.5 m.y.a. through the Present.

Some scientists (as in this book) include *H. heidelbergensis* and the Neandertals within archaic *H. sapiens*.

Europe and North America. Climates that are temperate today were arctic during the glacials.

The ice sheets advanced and receded several times during the last glacial, the *Würm* (75,000–12,000 B.P.). Brief periods of relative warmth during the Würm (and other glacials) are called *interstadials,* in contrast to the longer interglacials. Hominin fossils found in association with animals known to occur in cold or warm climates, respectively, permit us to date them to glacial or interglacial (or interstadial) periods.

## *H. antecessor* and *H. heidelbergensis*

In northern Spain's Atapuerca Mountains, the site of Gran Dolina has yielded the remains of 780,000-year-old hominins that Spanish researchers call *H. antecessor* and see as a possible common ancestor of the Neandertals and anatomically modern humans. The nearby cave of Sima de los Huesos has yielded thousands of fossils representing at least 33 hominins. Almost 300,000 years old, they may represent an early stage of Neandertal evolution (Lemonick and Dorfman 1999).

A massive hominin jaw was discovered in 1907 in a gravel pit at Mauer near Heidelberg, Germany. Originally called "Heidelberg man," or *Homo heidelbergensis,* the jaw appears to be around 500,000 years old. The deposits that yielded this jaw also contained fossil remains of several animals, including bear, bison, deer, elephant, horse, and rhinoceros. Some anthropologists have revived the species name *H. heidelbergensis* to refer to a group of fossil hominins, including the Ceprano

fragment described on p. 155, that in this text are described as either late *H. erectus* or archaic *H. sapiens.* This group would include hominins dated (very roughly) between 700,000 and 200,000 years ago and found in Europe, Africa, and Asia. Such fossils, here assigned to either *H. erectus* or archaic *H. sapiens,* would be transitional between *H. erectus* and later hominin forms such as the Neandertals and anatomically modern humans (see Mounier et al. 2011).

Besides the hominin *fossils* found in Europe, there is archaeological—including abundant stone tool—evidence for the presence and behavior of late *H. erectus* and then archaic *H. sapiens.* A chance discovery on England's Suffolk seacoast shows that humans had reached northern Europe by 700,000 years ago (Gugliotta 2005). Several stone flakes were recovered from seashore sediment bordering the North Sea. These archaic humans colonized northern Europe more than 200,000 years earlier than previously imagined—during an interglacial period. At that time, the fertile lowlands they inhabited were part of a land bridge connecting what is now Britain to the rest of Europe. They lived in a large delta with several rivers and a dry, mild Mediterranean climate. Various animals were among its abundant resources. It is not known whether the descendants of these settlers remained in England. The next glacial period may have been too extreme for human habitation so far back.

At the site of Terra Amata, overlooking Nice in southern France, archaeologists have documented human activity dating back 300,000 years. Small

Reconstruction of a hut made from saplings about 300,000 years ago at the Terra Amata site in Nice, France. The Terra Amata Museum, whose diorama is shown here, was built on the archaeological site, which was visited annually by ancient foragers. What foods did they eat?

bands of hunter-gatherers (15–25 people) made annual visits, during late spring–early summer, to Terra Amata, then a sandy cove on the Mediterranean coast. There is evidence for 21 such visits. Four groups camped on a sand bar, six on the beach, and 11 on a sand dune. Archaeologists surmise that the 11 dune sites represent that number of annual visits by the same band (deLumley 1969/1976).

From a camp atop the dune, these people looked down on a river valley where animals were abundant. Bones found at Terra Amata show that their diet included red deer, young elephants, wild boars, wild mountain goats, an extinct variety of rhinoceros, and wild oxen. The Terra Amata people also hunted turtles and birds, fished, and collected oysters and mussels. The arrangement of postholes shows that these people used saplings to support temporary huts. There were hearths within the shelters. Tools were made from locally available rocks and beach pebbles. Thus, at Terra Amata, hundreds of thousands of years ago, people were already

pursuing a lifestyle that survived in certain coastal regions until very recently.

Archaic *H. sapiens* lived during the last part of the *Middle Pleistocene*—during the *Mindel* (second) glacial, the interglacial that followed it, and the following *Riss* (third) glacial. The distribution of the fossils and tools of archaic *H. sapiens,* which have been found in Europe, Africa, and Asia, shows that *Homo*'s tolerance of environmental diversity had increased. For example, the Neandertals and their immediate ancestors managed to survive extreme cold in Europe. Archaic *H. sapiens* occupied the Arago cave in southeastern France at a time when Europe was bitterly cold. The only Riss glacial site with facial material, Arago, was excavated in 1971. It produced a partially intact skull, two jawbones, and teeth from a dozen individuals. With an apparent date of about 200,000 B.P., the Arago fossils have mixed features that seem transitional between *H. erectus* and the Neandertals. Figure 9.4 maps sites of archaic *Homo,* including the Neandertals.

**FIGURE 9.4** Archaic Human Sites: Discovery Sites for Archaic *Homo,* Including the Neandertals.

SOURCE: From Agustin Fuentes, *Biological Anthropology: Concepts and Connections,* 2nd ed., p. 262. Copyright © 2012 by McGraw-Hill Education, LLC. Reprinted with permission.

# THE NEANDERTALS

Neandertals were first discovered in western Europe. The first one was found in 1856 in a German valley called Neander Valley—*tal* is the German word for "valley." Scientists had trouble interpreting the discovery. It was clearly human, yet different enough from modern Europeans to be considered strange and abnormal. This was, after all, 35 years before Dubois found the first *H. erectus* fossils in Java and almost 70 years before the first australopithecine was found in South Africa. Darwin's *On the Origin of Species,* published in 1859, had not yet appeared to offer a theory of evolution through natural selection. There was no framework for understanding human evolution. Over time, the fossil record filled in, along with evolutionary theory. There have been numerous subsequent discoveries of Neandertals in Europe and the Middle East and of archaic human fossils with similar features in Africa and Asia.

Fossils that are not Neandertals but that have similar features (such as large faces and brow ridges) have been found in Africa and Asia. The Kabwe skull from Zambia (130,000 B.P.) is an archaic *H. sapiens* with a Neandertal-like brow ridge. Archaic Chinese fossils with Neandertal-like features have been found at Maba and Dali. Neandertals themselves have been found in central Europe and the Middle East. For example, Neandertal fossils found in Israel and northern Iraq date to around 60,000 B.P. (Shreeve 1992).

In 2007 Svante Pääbo and his colleagues at Germany's Max Planck Institute for Evolutionary Anthropology announced their identification of Neandertal mitochondrial DNA (mtDNA) in bones found at two sites in central Asia and Siberia. One of them, Teshik Tash, in Uzbekistan, previously had been seen as the easternmost limit of Neandertal territory. However, bones from the second site, the Okladnikov cave in the Altai Mountains, place the Neandertals much farther (1,250 miles) east, in southern Siberia. The mtDNA sequence at these sites differs only slightly from that of European Neandertals. The Neandertals may have reached these areas around 127,000 years ago, when a warm period made Siberia more accessible than it is today (see Wade 2007).

## Cold-Adapted Neandertals

By 75,000 B.P., after an interglacial interlude, western Europe's hominins (Neandertals, by then) again faced extreme cold as the Würm glacial began. To deal with this environment, they wore clothes, made more elaborate tools (see the photo at the right), and hunted reindeer, mammoths, and woolly rhinos (see Conard 2011).

The Neandertals were stocky, with large trunks relative to limb length—a phenotype that minimizes surface area and thus conserves heat. Another adaptation to extreme cold was the Neandertal face,

which has been likened to an *H. erectus* face that has been pulled forward by the nose. Illustrating Thomson's rule, this extension increased the distance between outside air and the arteries that carry blood to the brain and was adaptive in a cold climate. The brain is sensitive to temperature changes and must be kept warm. The massive nasal cavities of Neandertal fossils suggest long, broad noses. This would expand the area for warming and moistening air.

Neandertal characteristics also include huge front teeth, broad faces, large brow ridges, and ruggedness of the skeleton and musculature. What activities were associated with these anatomical traits? Neandertal teeth probably did many jobs later done by tools. The front teeth show heavy wear, suggesting that they were used for varied purposes, including chewing animal hides to make soft winter clothing out of them. The massive Neandertal face showed the stresses of constantly using the front teeth for holding and pulling.

Neandertal technology, a Middle Paleolithic tradition called **Mousterian,** improved considerably on what had come before. Mousterian technology included at least 14 categories of tools designed for different jobs. The Neandertals elaborated on a revolutionary technique of flake-tool manufacture (the *Levallois* technique) invented in southern Africa around 200,000 years ago, which spread widely throughout the Old World. Uniform flakes were chipped off a specially prepared core of rock. Additional work on the flakes produced the special-purpose tools shown in Figure 9.5. Scrapers were used to prepare animal hides for clothing. Larger points

**Mousterian**
Middle Paleolithic tool-making tradition associated with Neandertals.

Tools representing Neandertal technology, the Middle Paleolithic tradition called Mousterian. These Mousterian flake tools come from Gorham's Cave, Gibraltar.

**FIGURE 9.5** Examples of Mousterian Tools: (a) Scraper, (b) Point, (c) Scraper, (d) Point, (e) Hand Ax.

The Neandertals manufacture of diverse tool types for special purposes confirms Neandertal sophistication.

SOURCE: From John Relethford, *The Human Species: An Introduction to Biological Anthropology*, 9th ed., p. 303. Copyright © 2013 by McGraw-Hill Education, LLC. Reprinted with permission.

were attached to spears. Other special tools were designed for sawing, gouging, and piercing (Binford and Binford 1979; Conard 2011).

## The Neandertals and Modern People

Generations of scientists have debated whether and to what extent the Neandertals were ancestral to anatomically modern humans (AMHs), especially those of the Middle East and Europe, where fossils of both groups have been found. The current prevailing view proposes that *H. erectus* split into separate groups: one ancestral to the Neandertals, the other ancestral to AMHs, who first reached Europe around 45,000 B.P. Current evidence leaves little doubt that modern humans evolved in Africa and eventually colonized Europe, displacing, or at least replacing, the Neandertals there.

Consider the contrasts between the Neandertals and AMHs. Like *H. erectus* before them, the Neandertals had heavy brow ridges and slanting foreheads. However, average Neandertal cranial capacity (more than 1,400 cm$^3$) surpassed the modern average. Neandertal jaws were large, providing support for huge front teeth, and their faces were massive. The bones and skull were generally more rugged and had greater sexual dimorphism—particularly in the face and skull—than do those of AMHs. In some western European fossils, these contrasts between Neandertals

Reconstruction of a Neandertal woman from skull and skeletal evidence found at Tabun in Israel.

and AMHs are accentuated—giving a stereotyped, or *classic Neandertal*, appearance. The interpretation of one fossil in particular helped create the popular stereotype of the slouching cave dweller. This was the complete human skeleton discovered in 1908 at La Chapelle-aux-Saints in southwestern France, in a layer containing the characteristic Mousterian tools made by Neandertals. It was the first Neandertal to be discovered with the whole skull, including the face, preserved.

The La Chapelle skeleton was given for study to the French paleontologist Marcellin Boule. His analysis helped create an inaccurate stereotype of Neandertals as brutes who had trouble walking upright. Boule suggested that the Neandertal head was slung forward like an ape's. To round out the primitive image, Boule proclaimed that the Neandertals were incapable of straightening their legs for fully erect locomotion. However, later fossil finds show that the La Chapelle fossil wasn't a typical Neandertal but an extreme one. Also, this much-publicized "classic" Neandertal turned out to be an aging man whose skeleton had been distorted by osteoarthritis. Hominins, after all, have been erect bipeds for millions of years. European Neandertals were a variable population. Other Neandertal finds lack La Chapelle's combination of extreme features.

Based on his reconstruction (announced in 2010) of the complete Neandertal genome, Svante Pääbo and his colleagues concluded that modern humans and Neandertals descend from common ancestors that lived 600,000 years ago. They also found between 1 and 4 percent of the Neandertal genome incorporated within the DNA of living Europeans and Asians (but not Africans). This

A cast of the anatomically extreme classic Neandertal skull found at La Chapelle-aux-Saints, France.

finding suggests that Neandertals did some interbreeding with AMHs soon after the latter left Africa.

## Life as a Neandertal

In their intriguing book *How to Think Like a Neanderthal* (2011), Thomas Wynn, an anthropological archaeologist, and Frederick L. Coolidge, a psychologist, offer a speculative reconstruction of Neandertal life. How did they live, feel, think, and cope? What were their strengths and weaknesses?

Neandertals, Wynn and Coolidge suggest, were strongly attached to their families and local communities (while suspicious of outsiders—whom they occasionally ate!). Capable of feelings like empathy and sympathy, they cared for the disabled and buried their dead, whether symbolically, as an expression of grief, or practically, as a way to dispose of a decaying body. They used some form of language, maybe tones or whistles (see Viegas 2013), which allowed them to communicate, coordinate, and plan ahead.

They were very strong and had excellent mechanical skills. If alive today, they might work effectively as commercial fishermen or mechanics, Wynn and Coolidge speculate. One illustration of their mechanical skills is the Levallois spear head, an intricately faceted point that could maim or kill an animal as large as a mammoth. The Neandertals learned how to fasten this point securely to a wooden shaft, so that it would not dislodge. They may have used bitumen as an adhesive or lashed the point to the spear. But they lacked the spear thrower, an artificial extension of the hunter's arm invented by AMHs, which put human hunters farther from their prey. Neandertal hunting was close range, dangerous, and sometimes lethal—a pursuit that left behind few elders.

At times they even hunted down their own kind. Important remains of 50,000-year-old Neandertal bones and stone tools discovered in El Sidrón Cave, a rich Neandertal site in northern Spain, have given scientists a glimpse of ancient social structure and behavior—including cannibalism. This discovery illustrates how anthropologists combine fossil, archaeological, and DNA evidence to reconstruct the hominin past. More than 1,800 Neandertal bone fragments have been found in the "Tunnel of the Bones" at El Sidrón; scientists were able to extract snippets of DNA from some of them (Zimmer 2010).

The remains appear to represent a dozen members of an extended family. How did they die? When the discovery team closely examined the bones, they found cut marks—signs that the stone blades had been used to slice muscle from bone. The long bones had been snapped open, presumably to get at their marrow. The scientists concluded that the El Sidrón Neandertals were victims of cannibalism. This find almost certainly predates the arrival of AMHs in this area, supporting the conclusion that, on occasion, Neandertals ate members of their own species.

The shape of the bones allowed the scientists to estimate the age and sex of the victims. The bones came from three men, three women, three teenage boys, and three children, including one infant. DNA analysis helped confirm the conclusions based on the bones. From four specimens, scientists extracted a Y chromosome, confirming their initial assessment that those four were males. El Sidrón turned out to be an excellent storehouse for ancient DNA because of its cold, dark, and damp environment. DNA even provided a clue about physical appearance: Two individuals shared an allele (gene variant) that likely gave them red hair (Zimmer 2010).

The Neandertals moved about within a particular territory—their home range. Their contacts with outsiders were limited (and, as we just saw, potentially hostile). There is no evidence that Neandertals engaged in long-distance trade. By contrast, we know that AMHs living far inland in Europe used shells imported from the Mediterranean and Atlantic coasts. Unlike Neandertals, AMHs were tied into regional social networks; they had relatives, trade partners, in-laws, and allies in other groups. The expanded, regional network and the alliances and social support it offered were key differences between AMHs and Neandertals.

Wynn and Coolidge (2011) interpret the archaeological and fossil evidence as indicating that Neandertals were suspicious of both outsiders and change. Their limited imagination is shown in their unchanging tool designs. Their tools, found across Eurasia, varied little in form or function over thousands of years, and miles. As far as we know, Neandertals created no art in the form of painting or carving, beyond a few pierced and pigmented shells. Neandertals no doubt were eventually exposed to the far more effective spears and spear throwers made by their AMH contemporaries, but they borrowed none of those techniques.

Their unwillingness or inability to borrow or innovate put them at a disadvantage in competing with AMHs for shrinking resources in Ice Age Europe around 30,000 years ago. AMHs lived in larger, regionally connected communities (see "Appreciating Anthropology" in Chapter 10) that encouraged innovation, social thinking, and mental processing of complex information. Twin lacks—of allies and of innovation—helped doom the Neandertals.

## THE DENISOVANS

In late 2010 scientists identified the Denisovan hominin group as distant cousins to Neandertals (Callaway 2011; Zimmer 2010). Once again, the ancient DNA research was led by Svante Pääbo, who earlier that year had published a complete Neandertal genome.

The Denisovans get their name from Denisova, a cave in southern Siberia where their traces (so far only a finger fragment and a wisdom tooth) were found. The Denisovans apparently lived in Asia from roughly 400,000 to 50,000 years ago. Remarkably, scientists have managed to extract the entire Denisovan genome from the finger and the tooth (see "Appreciating Diversity" in Chapter 4). The DNA suggests that the split between ancestral Neandertals and Denisovans happened around 400,000 years ago. The Neandertals spread to the west, eventually reaching the Middle East and Europe. The Denisovans headed east (while AMHs remained for a time in Africa).

The distinctive Denisovan wisdom tooth resembles the teeth of neither AMHs nor Neandertals. It has bulging sides and large, flaring roots. Only when someone finds the same kind of tooth in a fossil skull, or perhaps even a complete skeleton, will we be able to see what the Denisovans really looked like. The genome sequencing done of a Denisovan girl does, however, suggest that the phenotype included brown skin, hair, and eyes.

Comparison of the Denisovan genome with modern humans revealed a striking relationship. Melanesians, who inhabit Papua New Guinea and islands northeast of Australia, have inherited about 5 percent of their DNA from the Denisovans. This suggests that after the ancestors of today's Papuans split from other AMHs and migrated east, they interbred with Denisovans (see Callaway 2011). Precisely when and where is unclear. The oldest AMH remains in Southeast Asia, from a cave in northern Laos, date to at least 46,000 years ago (Demeter et al. 2012). If the Denisovan range extended from Siberia to Southeast Asia, they must have been a very successful kind of hominin. Based on the current fossil record, they may well have invented the world's first, and most durable, invisibility cloak!

## HOMO FLORESIENSIS

A decade ago, news reports trumpeted the discovery of bones and tools of a group of tiny humans who inhabited Flores, an Indonesian island 370 miles east of Bali, until fairly recent times (see Roach 2007; Wade 2004). Early in hominin evolution, as we saw in the last chapter, it wasn't unusual for different species, even genera, of hominins, to live at the same time. But until the 2003–2004 discoveries on Flores, few scientists imagined that a different human species had survived through 12,000 B.P., and possibly even later. These tiny people lived, hunted, and gathered on Flores from about 95,000 B.P. until at least 13,000 B.P. One of their most surprising features is a very small skull, about 370 cm$^3$—slightly smaller than the chimpanzee average.

A skull and several skeletons of these miniature people were found in a limestone cave on Flores by a team of Australian and Indonesian archaeologists, who assigned them to a new human species, *H. floresiensis*. (Additional specimens have been found

The skull of *Homo floresiensis* (left; modern human, right), a miniature hominin that inhabited Middle Earth, or at least the Indonesian island of Flores, between 95,000 and 13,000 years ago.

and described subsequently.) The discovery of *H. floresiensis*, described as a downsized version of *H. erectus*, shows that archaic humans survived much later than had been thought. Before modern people reached Flores, which is very isolated, the island was inhabited only by a select group of animals that had managed to reach it. These animals, including *H. floresiensis*, faced unusual evolutionary forces that pushed some toward gigantism and some toward dwarfism. The carnivorous lizards that reached Flores, perhaps on natural rafts, became giants. These Komodo dragons now are confined mainly to the nearby island of Komodo. Elephants, which are excellent swimmers, reached Flores, where they evolved to a dwarf form the size of an ox.

Previous excavations by Michael Morwood, one of the discoverers of *H. floresiensis*, estimated that *H. erectus* had reached Flores by 840,000 years ago, based on crude stone tools found there. This *H. erectus* population and its descendants are assumed to have been influenced by the same evolutionary forces that reduced the size of the elephants. The first specimen of *H. floresiensis*, an adult female, was uncovered in 2003 from a cave floor. Paleoanthropologists identified her as a very small but otherwise normal individual—a diminutive version of *H. erectus*. Because the downsizing was so extreme, smaller than that in modern human pygmies, she and her fellows were assigned to a new species. Her skeleton is estimated to date back some 18,000 years. Remains of six additional individuals found in the cave date from 95,000 to 13,000 B.P. The cave also has yielded bones of giant lizards, giant rats, pygmy elephants, fish, and birds.

*H. floresiensis* apparently controlled fire, and the stone tools found with them are more sophisticated than any known to have been made by *H. erectus*. Among the tools were small blades that might have been mounted on wooden shafts. Hunting elephants—probably cooperatively—and making complex tools, the Floresians may (or may not) have had some form of language. The suggestion of such cultural abilities is surprising for a hominin with a chimplike brain. The small cranium has raised some doubt that *H. floresiensis* actually made the tools. The ancestors of the anatomically modern people who colonized Australia might have traveled through this area, and it is possible that they made the stone tools. On the other hand, there is no evidence that modern humans reached Flores prior to 11,000 years ago.

This *H. floresiensis* population appears to have been wiped out by a volcanic eruption around 12,000 B.P., but they may have survived until much later elsewhere on Flores. The Ngadha people of central Flores and the Manggarai people of west Flores still tell stories about little people who lived in caves until the arrival of the Dutch traders in the 16th century (Wade 2004).

As reported in 2009, an analysis of the lower limbs and especially an almost complete left foot and parts of the right foot shows that *H. floresiensis* walked upright but possessed apelike features (Wilford 2009*b*). The big toe, for example, was stubby, like a chimp's. The feet were large, more than 7.5 inches long, out of proportion to the short lower limbs. These proportions, similar to those of some African apes, have never before been seen in hominins. The feet were flat. The bone that helps form the arch in modern human feet was more apelike than human. Without a strong arch, *H. floresiensis* could have walked but not run like humans (see Wilford 2009*b*).

# for REVIEW

**summary**

1. Compared with late *Australopithecus,* dental, facial, and cranial robustness was reduced in early *Homo*—*habilis* (1.9–1.44 m.y.a.) and *erectus* (1.9?–0.3? m.y.a.). *H. erectus* extended the hominin food quest to the hunting of large animals. *H. erectus,* with a much larger body, had smaller back teeth than *Australopithecus* but larger front teeth and supporting structures, including a massive eyebrow ridge. The Lower Paleolithic Acheulean tradition provided *H. erectus* with better tools. *H. erectus*'s average cranial capacity doubled the australopithecine average. Tool complexity and archaeological evidence for cooperative hunting suggest a long period of enculturation and learning. *H. erectus* extended the hominin range beyond Africa to Asia and Europe.

2. Ancient *H. erectus* skulls have been found in Kenya and Georgia (in Eurasia), dating back some 1.77–1.6 million years. *H. erectus* persisted for more than a million years, evolving into archaic *H. sapiens* by the Middle Pleistocene epoch, some 300,000 years ago. Fire allowed *H. erectus* to expand into cooler areas, to cook, and to live in caves.

3. The Neandertals, who inhabited western Europe during the early part of the Würm glacial, were among the first hominin fossils found. With no examples of *Australopithecus* or *H. erectus* yet discovered, the differences between them and modern humans were accentuated. The last common ancestors of Neandertals and modern humans (AMHs, or anatomically modern humans) lived about 600,000 years ago.

4. The Neandertals adapted physically and culturally to bitter cold. Their tool kits were more complex than those of preceding humans. Their front teeth were among the largest to appear in human evolution. The Neandertals manufactured Mousterian flake tools. Neandertals may have persisted in western Europe, where they did some interbreeding with AMHs, through 28,000 B.P. Compared with AMHs, Neandertals were suspicious of outsiders and reluctant to innovate. Their narrow social networks, lack of regional alliances, and limited imaginations help explain their eventual extinction.

5. The Denisovans were cousins of the Neandertals who lived in Asia between about 400,000 and 50,000 years ago. After their split around 400,000 B.P., the ancestral Neandertals spread westward, to the Middle East and Europe, while the Denisovans headed east.

6. *H. floresiensis* is the name of a species of tiny humans that lived on the isolated island of Flores in Indonesia. A probable descendant of *H. erectus,* which had settled Flores by 840,000 B.P., *H. floresiensis* is marked by the unusually small size of its body and its chimp-sized skull. There is debate about whether *H. floresiensis* was smart enough to have made the stone tools found in association with the skeletal remains, though there is no evidence that AMHs reached Flores before 11,000 B.P. The *H. floresiensis* remains have been assigned dates ranging from 95,000 to 13,000 B.P.

# critical thinking

1. As anatomically modern humans, we make up a variable population, yet we are all one species. When looking at the fossil record, how have scientists confronted the issue of variability and speciation? Consider the Neandertals and AMHs. Remembering the definition of species given in Chapter 5, should these hominins be placed in the same or different species?

2. *H. erectus* persisted for more than a million years. What were its key adaptation strategies? In particular, what do its toolmaking abilities suggest about its evolving cognitive capacities?

3. The Neandertals, who inhabited western Europe during the early part of the Würm glacial, were among the first hominin fossils found. Why did scientists have trouble interpreting these early discoveries? How have early misinterpretations of Neandertals persisted in our culture? Do these persistent misinterpretations matter?

4. Paleoanthropology is an exciting and constantly changing field! Pick 21st-century fossil finds discussed in this chapter and explain their significance.

# The Origin and Spread of Modern Humans

▶ When and where did modern human anatomy and behavior originate?

▶ What major changes took place in human lifestyles and adaptive strategies as the Ice Age ended?

▶ When and how did modern humans settle Australia, the Americas, and the Pacific?

Animal murals in Chauvet Cave at Vallon Pont-d'Arc in southern France date back 20,000 years.

# understanding OURSELVES

**O**ur choices about how, and to whom, we display aspects of ourselves say something about us not only as individuals but also as social and cultural beings. Think about your appearance right now. What does your clothing say about you—implicitly or explicitly, intentionally or unintentionally? Does your cap, shirt, or jacket display the name of your school, a brand, or a favorite sports team? Why do or don't you have tattoos or piercings? What does facial hair, or its absence, say about you or someone else? Why is your hair long or short? Why did you choose any makeup you are wearing? How about any jewelry? If you're male, why are you, or are you not, circumcised? The way that we present our bodies reflects both on (1) who and what we're trying to look like and (2) what sort of person we're trying *not* to resemble.

Body decoration is a cultural universal, as are other forms of creative expression, including the arts and language, and all say something about us. Expressive culture rests on symbolic thought. As is true generally of symbols (remember Chapter 2), the relation between a symbol and what it stands for is arbitrary.

Intrinsically, Nike shoes are no more swoosh-like than Adidas are. Michigan Wolverines are no more like wolverines than Florida Gators are, and

vice versa. For archaeologists, evidence for symbolic thought, as manifested materially in patterned or decorated artifacts, strongly suggests modern behavior. Consider the pigment red ocher, a natural iron oxide that modern hunter-gatherers use to create body paint for ritual occasions. Archaeologists are pretty sure that ocher was used similarly in the past. Evidence for the manufacture of red ocher dates back 100,000 years, at South Africa's Blombos Cave. An artifact also discovered in that cave has a carved cross-hatch design—three straight lines with another set of three at a diagonal to them—offering the world's earliest evidence for intentional patterning with symbolic meaning. There is abundant evidence for expressive culture, including art and music, in Europe by 35,000 years ago. At that point, humans were decorating themselves with paints and jewelry and making flutes and figurines. They would not have done all that without language. Linguist Merritt Ruhlen (1994) speculates that all the world's languages descend from a common one spoken 40,000 to 50,000 years ago by anatomically modern humans who originated in Africa. Did a "creative" gene emerge in Africa and fuel human colonization of the rest of the world? Although anthropologists don't have a definitive answer to this question, we do agree about the key role that expressive culture plays in human life.

## MODERN HUMANS

Anatomically modern humans (AMHs) evolved from an archaic *H. sapiens* African ancestor. Eventually, AMHs spread to other areas, including Europe, where they replaced the Neandertals, whose robust traits eventually disappeared (see Barton et al. 2011).

## Out of Africa: AMH Edition

### Recent Fossil and Archaeological Evidence

Fossil and archaeological evidence has been accumulating to support the African origin of AMHs. A major find was announced in 2003: the 1997 discovery in an Ethiopian valley of three anatomically modern skulls—those of two adults and a child. When found, the fossils had been fragmented so badly that their reconstruction took several years. Tim White and Berhane Asfaw were coleaders of the international team that made the find near the village of Herto, 140 miles northeast of Addis Ababa. All three skulls were missing the lower jaw. The skulls showed evidence of cutting and handling, suggesting they had been detached from their bodies and used—perhaps ritually—after death. A few teeth, but no other bones, were found with the skulls, again suggesting their deliberate removal from the body. Layers of volcanic ash allowed geologists to date them to 154,000–160,000 B.P. The people represented by the skulls lived on the shore of an ancient lake, where they hunted and fished. The skulls were found along with hippopotamus and antelope bones and some 600 tools, including blades and hand axes.

Except for a few archaic characteristics, the **Herto** skulls are anatomically modern—long with broad midfaces, featuring tall, narrow nasal bones. The cranial vaults are high, falling within modern dimensions. These finds offered important support for the view that modern humans originated in Africa.

Omo Kibish is one of several sites along the Omo River in southwestern Ethiopia. Between 1967 and 1974, Richard Leakey and his colleagues from the Kenya National Museum recovered AMH remains originally considered to be about 125,000 years old. The specimens now appear to be much older. Indeed, with an estimated date of 195,000 B.P., they appear to be the earliest AMH fossils yet found (McDougall, Brown, and Fleagle 2005). The Omo remains include two partial skulls (Omo 1 and Omo 2), four jaws, a leg bone, about 200 teeth, and several other parts. One site, Omo Kibish I, contained a nearly complete skeleton of an adult male. Middle Stone Age tools have been found in the same stratigraphic layers. The Omo 1 skull and the skeleton are modern overall, with a few primitive features. The Omo 2 skull is more archaic. (See the illustration on p. 169 for cranial contrasts between *H. erectus*, archaic *H. sapiens*, Neandertals, and AMHs.)

From sites in South Africa comes further evidence of early African AMHs. At Border Cave, a remote rock shelter in South Africa, fossil remains dating back perhaps 150,000 years are believed to be those of early modern humans. The remains of at least five AMHs have been discovered, including the nearly complete skeleton of a 4- to 6-month-old infant buried in a shallow grave. Excavations at Border Cave also have produced some 70,000 stone tools, along with the remains of several mammal species, including elephants, believed to have been hunted by the ancient people who lived there. Middle Stone Age tools and considerable evidence for behavioral modernity have been found at two other South African caves:

Pinnacle Point (164,000 B.P.) and Blombos Cave (100,000 B.P.).

A complex of South African caves near the Klasies River Mouth was occupied by a group of hunter-gatherers some 120,000 years ago. Fragmentary bones suggest how those people looked. A forehead fragment has a modern brow ridge. There is a thin-boned cranial fragment and a piece of jaw with a modern chin. The archaeological evidence suggests that these cave dwellers did coastal gathering and used Middle Stone Age stone tools.

Anatomically modern specimens, including the skull shown in Figure 10.1, have been found at Skhūl, a site on Mount Carmel in Israel. The Skhūl fossils date to 100,000 B.P. Other modern-looking and similarly dated (92,000 B.P.) skulls come from the Israeli site of Qafzeh. All these skulls have a modern shape; their braincases are higher and rounder than those of Neandertals. There is a more filled-out forehead region, which rises more vertically above the brows. A marked chin is another modern feature (see the photo on p. 168 of the original Cro Magnon find). (Early AMHs in western Europe often are called **Cro Magnons,** after the earliest fossil find of an anatomically modern human, in France's Les Eyzies region, Dordogne Valley, in 1868.)

Given these early dates from Israel, AMHs may have inhabited the Middle East before the Neandertals

**Herto**
Very early (160,000–154,000 B.P.) AMHs found in Ethiopia.

**Cro Magnon**
The first fossil find (1868) of an AMH, from France's Dordogne Valley.

**FIGURE 10.1**   Skhūl V.
This anatomically modern human with some archaic features dates to 100,000 B.P. This is one of several fossils found at Skhūl, Israel.

did. Ofer Bar-Yosef (1987) has suggested that during the last (Würm) glacial period, which began around 75,000 years ago, western European Neandertals spread into the Middle East as part of a general southward expansion of cold-adapted fauna. AMHs, in turn, may have followed warmer-climate fauna south into Africa, returning to the Middle East once the Würm ended.

## Genetic Evidence for the Spread of AMHs Out of Africa

In 1987 a group of molecular geneticists at the University of California at Berkeley offered support for the idea that modern humans (AMHs) arose fairly recently in Africa, then spread out and colonized the world. Rebecca Cann, Mark Stoneking, and Allan C. Wilson (1987) analyzed genetic markers in placentas donated by 147 women whose ancestors came from Africa, Europe, the Middle East, Asia, New Guinea, and Australia.

The researchers focused on mitochondrial DNA (mtDNA). This genetic material is located in the cytoplasm (the outer part, rather than the nucleus) of cells. Ordinary DNA, which makes up the genes that determine most physical traits, is found in the nucleus and comes from both parents. But only the mother contributes mitochondrial DNA to the fertilized egg. The father plays no part in mtDNA transmission, just as the mother has nothing to do with the transmission of the Y chromosome, which comes from the father and determines the sex of the child.

To establish a "genetic clock," the Berkeley researchers measured the variation in mtDNA in their 147 tissue samples. They cut each sample into segments to compare with the others. By estimating the number of mutations that had taken place in each sample since its common origin with the 146 others, the researchers drew an evolutionary tree with the help of a computer.

That tree started in Africa and then branched in two. One group remained in Africa, while the other one split off, carrying its mtDNA to the rest of the world. The variation in mtDNA was greatest among Africans. This suggests they have been evolving the longest. The Berkeley researchers concluded that everyone alive today has mtDNA that descends from a woman (dubbed "Eve") who lived in sub-Saharan Africa around 200,000 years ago. Eve was not the only woman alive then; she was just the only one whose descendants have included a daughter in each generation up to the present. Because mtDNA passes exclusively through females, mtDNA lines disappear whenever a woman has no children or has only sons. The details of the Eve theory suggest that her descendants left Africa no more than 135,000 years ago. They eventually displaced the Neandertals in Europe and went on to colonize the rest of the world.

Cro Magnon I, the skull of a 45-year-old anatomically modern human, discovered in 1868 near Les Eyzies in France's Dordogne region. Note the distinct chin.

The Cro Magnon rock shelter near Les Eyzies, Dordogne, France. Remains of anatomically modern humans, such as the famous fossil found here in 1868, have been found in rock shelters from France to South Africa. The Cro Magnon people lived here around 31,000 years ago.

In 1997, Svante Pääbo extracted ancient DNA from one of the Neandertal bones originally found in Germany's Neander Valley in 1856. He then compared this DNA, from an upper arm bone (humerus), with the DNA of modern humans. The kinds of matches we find in closely related humans did not occur. Thus, there were 27 differences between the Neandertal DNA and a reference sample of modern DNA. By contrast, samples of DNA from modern populations worldwide show only five to eight differences with the reference sample. This was the first time that DNA of a premodern human had been recovered.

The Neandertals may (or may not) have coexisted with modern humans in the Middle East for thousands of years. The overlap in Europe apparently spanned the period between 45,000 B.P. and Neandertal extinction around 28,000 B.P. The recent redatings of a piece of modern jawbone with three teeth from England and of two baby teeth from Italy provide the oldest known skeletal evidence for AMHs in Europe (Wilford 2011a). The baby teeth from Italy were dated at 43,000 to 45,000 years old (Benazzi et al. 2011). The jawbone, from Kents Cavern in Devon, was 41,500 to 44,200 years old—the oldest known AMH fossil from northwestern Europe. Also significant is the fact that the English jawbone was found in cave layers associated with Upper Paleolithic tools (Higham et al. 2011). Prior to these dates, the earliest reliably dated European AMH came from Romania (42,000–37,800 B.P.).

The English jawbone might represent an early dispersal of AMHs through central Europe that crossed into Britain on a land bridge where the North Sea now stands. The southern Italian remains might represent an even earlier migration along the southern European coasts (Wilford 2011a).

## The Red Deer Cave People

Hominin fossils found in two Chinese caves are notable because of their recent date (14,300–11,500 B.P.) and their unexpected blend of very primitive and modern features. The fossils, representing at least four individuals, consist of partial skulls and other bone fragments (Sample 2012). Specifically, they come from two caves in southwestern China—Longlin Cave and Maludong, or "Red Deer," Cave. The fossils have been labeled the "Red Deer Cave people" based on the cave name and on evidence that they cooked giant red deer (now extinct) there. The Longlin Cave fossils, unearthed in 1979, lay unnoticed in the basement of a Chinese scientific institute for 30 years until their rediscovery. The Red Deer Cave fossils, discovered 10 years later, also remained barely studied in another Chinese institute. Darren Curnoe and Ji Xueping began their study and analysis of both sets of fossils in 2008 (see Curnoe et al. 2012).

The Red Deer Cave people are the most recent human remains found anywhere in the world that do not closely resemble modern humans. The skulls differ from modern humans in their jutting jaws, large molar teeth, prominent brows, thick skulls, broad noses, flat faces, and lack of a chin. Scientists currently are debating their evolutionary status. Do they belong to a different and hitherto unknown species, or are they merely variable members of *H. sapiens*? Could they be late

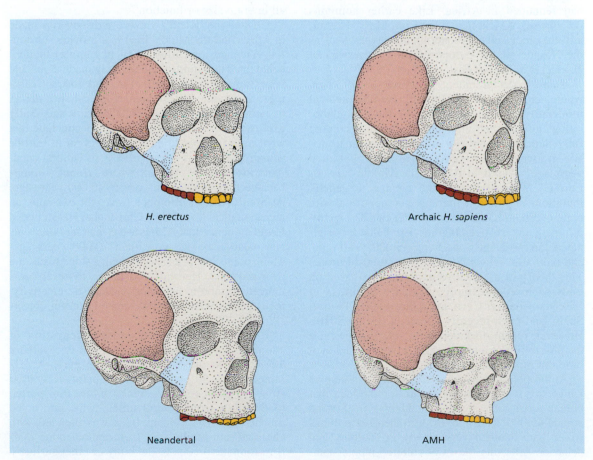

*H. erectus*

Archaic *H. sapiens*

Neandertal

AMH

Compare these drawings of *H. erectus*, archaic *H. sapiens*, Neandertal, and AMH. What are the main differences you notice? Is the Neandertal more like *H. erectus* or AMH?

Denisovans, or maybe a product of interbreeding between Denisovans and AMHs? Confirmation awaits the eventual analysis of DNA extracted from the Red Deer Cave bones—a task that so far has been unsuccessful.

The Red Deer Cave fossils also help fill a geographic gap: Very few post–Ice Age human fossils from Asia have been well described and reliably dated (Sample 2012). Our picture of recent human evolutionary history in Asia has grown more complex. We know now that multiple human populations lived in the area, perhaps representing different evolutionary lines (see, for example, the discussion of *H. floresiensis* in Chapter 9).

# THE ADVENT OF BEHAVIORAL MODERNITY

Scientists agree that (1) around six million years ago, our hominin ancestors originated in Africa, and as apelike creatures they became habitual bipeds; (2) by 2.6 million years ago, still in Africa, hominins were making crude stone tools; (3) by 1.7 million years ago, hominins had spread from Africa to Asia and eventually Europe; and (4) sometime around 200,000 years ago, anatomically modern humans (AMHs) evolved from ancestors who had remained in Africa. Like earlier hominins (*H. erectus*), AMHs spread out from Africa. Eventually, they replaced nonmodern human types, such as the Neandertals in Europe and the successors of *H. erectus* in the Far East.

There is disagreement, however, about when, where, and how early AMHs achieved **behavioral modernity**—relying on symbolic thought, elaborating cultural creativity, and as a result becoming fully human in behavior as well as in anatomy. Was it as much as 165,000 or as little as 45,000 years ago? Was it in Africa, the Middle East, or Europe? What triggered the change: a genetic mutation, population increase, competition with nonmodern humans, or some other cause? The traditional view has been that modern behavior originated fairly recently, perhaps 45,000 years ago, and only after *Homo sapiens* pushed into Europe. This theory of a "creative explosion" is based on finds such as the impressive cave paintings at Lascaux, Chauvet Cave, and other sites in France, Spain, and most recently Romania (Balter 2010). However, recent discoveries outside Europe raise the possibility of a much older, more gradual evolution of modern behavior.

Anthropologist Richard G. Klein of Stanford University is a leading advocate for the idea that human creativity dawned suddenly, in Europe around 45,000 years ago. Prior to then Klein thinks *Homo* had changed very slowly in anatomy and behavior. After this "dawn of culture," human anatomy changed little, but behavior started changing dramatically (Klein with Edgar 2002). Indeed, by 40,000 years ago, AMHs in Europe were making varied tools that display a pattern of abstract and symbolic thought. Their modern behavior included burying their dead with ceremonies, adorning their bodies with paints and jewelry, and making musical instruments and figurine images of fertile females. Their cave paintings displayed images from their minds, as they remembered the hunt, and events and symbols associated with it.

To explain such a flowering of creativity, Klein proposes a neurological hypothesis. Perhaps around 50,000 years ago, he thinks, a genetic mutation acted to rewire the human brain, possibly allowing for an advance in language. Improved communication, in Klein's view, could have given people "the fully modern ability to invent and manipulate culture" (quoted in Wilford 2002*b*). Klein thinks this genetic change probably happened in Africa and then allowed "human populations to colonize new and challenging environments" (quoted in Wilford 2002*b*). Reaching Europe, the rewired modern humans met and replaced the resident Neandertals. Klein recognizes that his genetic hypothesis "fails one important measure of a proper scientific hypothesis—it cannot be tested or falsified by experiment or by examination of relevant human fossils" (quoted in Wilford 2002*b*). AMH skulls from the time period in question show no change at all in brain size or function.

Challenging Klein's views are discoveries made in Africa and the Middle East that provide substantial evidence for earlier (than in Europe) modern behavior. These finds include finely made stone and bone tools, self-ornamentation, and abstract carvings. Surveying African archaeological sites dating to between 300,000 and 30,000 years ago, Sally McBrearty and Alison Brooks (2000) conclude that what might appear to be a sudden event in Europe actually rested on a slow process of cultural accumulation within Africa, where *Homo sapiens* became fully human long before 45,000 years ago. At South Africa's Blombos Cave, for example, an archaeological team led by Christopher Henshilwood found evidence that AMHs were making bone awls and weapon points more than 70,000 years ago. Three points had been shaped with a stone blade and then polished. Henshilwood thinks these artifacts indicate symbolic behavior and artistic creativity; their makers were trying to create beautiful objects (Wilford 2002*b*).

Representing an even earlier occupation of Blombos Cave, Henshilwood's team excavated a 100,000-year-old workshop where early AMHs mixed the world's earliest known paint. They used stones to grind colorful chunks of dirt, transported to Blombos from several miles away, into a red powder, known as ocher. This was blended with charcoal and binding fat from animal bone marrow, to make it stick to the body or other surfaces. The Blombos people mixed their ocher in large abalone shells, where they liquefied and stirred it,

An engraved stone fragment of red ocher from Blombos Cave, South Africa. The fragment, which is 77,000 years old, suggests early human creativity and symbolic thought.

then scooped it out as paint using a bone spatula (Wilford 2011b). They may have applied the mixture to their skin, perhaps as decoration for some special event.

What, if anything special, did the color red mean to these ancient people? Did they associate it with blood as a sign or life or death, or with menstruation as a sign of fertility? Could they have used red ocher to inspire anger in others? The ocher makers apparently used Blombos Cave only as a work site. Archaeologists found no associated evidence of living quarters,

such as hearths (Wilford 2011b). What they did the rest of the time remains a mystery. Surely, they hunted, gathered, and fished, most likely eating the abalone and other sea products whose shells also could be used as tools.

Excavations in Congo's Katanda region have uncovered bone harpoon points dating back 90,000 to 80,000 years (Yellen, Brooks, and Cornelissen 1995). Anthropologists Brooks and John Yellen contend that these ancient people "not only possessed considerable technological capabilities at this time, but also incorporated symbolic or stylistic content into their projectile forms" (quoted in Wilford 2002b).

In 2007 anthropologists reported the discovery of even earlier evidence (dating back to 164,000 B.P.) for behavioral modernity in a cave site at Pinnacle Point, South Africa. The cave yielded small stone bladelets, which could be attached to wood to make spears, as well as red ocher. Also significant is the ancient diet revealed by remains from this seaside site. For the first time, we see early representatives of *H. sapiens* subsisting on a variety of shellfish and other marine resources. According to paleoanthropologist Curtis Marean (Marean et al. 2007), who led the discovery team, once early humans knew how to make a living from the sea, they could use coastlines as productive home ranges and move long distances (see

Body ornamentation is a sign of behavioral modernity. On the left is a decorated Munjika man from Papua New Guinea. The photo on the right also shows body piercing and a necklace, plus distinctive eyeglasses and body tattoos. What are the social functions of such ornamentation?

# appreciating ANTHROPOLOGY

## In with the Old: The Evolutionary Importance of Grandparents

How do people transmit their knowledge, memories, and personal experience to others? Today we rely on the cloud of cyberspace (how often do you post on Instragram?) and the growing arsenal of audiovisual and digital means of storing, processing, and transmitting information orally, visually, and in writing. Before the advent of writing (which has been around only 6,000 years), humans could pass on their experience through enculturation (the process by which culture is learned and transmitted across the generations), but oral tradition preserves knowledge less effectively than writing does. Inevitably, and still today, information is lost, social bonds are severed, and people become mere memories whenever someone dies.

The extent of information transfer between generations increased during hominin evolution, particularly in Upper Paleolithic times, when human behavioral modernity began to flower. People started living longer. They couldn't write down lessons of the past, but they could share their memories orally over a longer lifespan and with more people, including their grandchildren. An evolutionary leap forward occurred when humans started benefiting from the coresidence and consistent association of three generations. In this situation, adults interacted with their beloved parents longer, and their children could thrive in a larger kinship network that included grandparents.

Experience counts in child rearing. Among nonhuman primates, infant survival rates are higher when the mother is experienced (Hrdy 2009; Rilling 2013). Among baboons, for example, infants of experienced mothers had a 63 percent survival rate, versus only 29 percent for infants of first-time mothers (Altmann, Hausfater,

and Altmann 1988). Having a grandmother around means that experience is available, and greater infant survival is one likely reason for the population burst associated with the Upper Paleolithic.

Underlying the cultural advances of the Upper Paleolithic was a fundamental change in human biology—the lengthening of the human lifespan. We have evidence for this change in hard materials that fossilize, specifically in teeth; the older you are, the more dental wear you exhibit. Biological anthropologists Rachel Caspari and Sang-Hee Lee (2004) examined the teeth of 768 hominins representing four fossil groups: later australopithecines (including gracile and robusts); Early and Middle Pleistocene *Homo* (including *erectus* and archaic *H. sapiens*, but not *habilis* or *rudolfensis*); Neandertals; and AMHs—early Upper Paleolithic Europeans. These groups were chosen because they provided large samples, whose teeth could be studied for wear and age estimation.

Caspari and Lee classified their specimens as older or younger adults based on patterns of molar eruption and degree of wear on the teeth. Any individual whose wisdom teeth (third molars) had come in was classified as an adult. More dental wear thereafter indicated greater age. The appearance of wisdom teeth is associated with physiological maturation, including reproductive maturity, in primates. For their sample, Caspari and Lee assumed that wisdom teeth appeared at age 15, and that it would be at this age that females could become mothers. (Age 15 is not unusual for current-day first-time mothers among the Inuit and some Australian populations.) A woman could become a grandmother by age 30 if she and her daughter both had had their first child at 15.

Using their sample of 768 specimens, Caspari and Lee calculated a ratio of older (age 30 and

older) to younger (age 15–29) adults (the OY ratio) in each of the four hominin groups. They found a steady increase in that ratio during human evolution—rising from late australopithecines, through early *Homo* and the Neandertals, to a real leap after 45,000 years ago, with the advent of the Upper Paleolithic. With that jump, for the first time in human history more adults—and significantly more—were dying after age 30 than before it.

This increase in lifespan created a reliable three-generation social structure, which had substantial evolutionary impact. Social groups with three generations could store, process, and transmit more information and experience. The increase in the number of older people facilitated the transmission of specialized knowledge, illustrated by the sophisticated tools and art of the Upper Paleolithic, compared with what came before, when elders were scarce.

Increased longevity also favored population growth, for two reasons. First, someone who lives longer (up to a point) can have more children. Second, elders typically assist their children's families. Having supportive grandparents enhances child survival (see Strassmann and Garrard 2011), which also favors population growth. Population increase likely spurred the many advances known through archaeology to have occurred during the Upper Paleolithic. Among those advances were increased mobility, long-distance trade (including of ornamental objects), and new forms of cooperation and competition between groups (Caspari and Lee 2004). All things considered, Caspari and Lee (2004) reasonably conclude that the extended human lifespan may be the most important biological factor underlying the flowering of behavioral modernity.

also Guyot and Hughes 2007; McBrearty and Stringer 2007).

Cultural advances would have facilitated the spread of AMHs out of Africa. Such advances had reached the Middle East by 43,000 years ago, where,

in Turkey and Lebanon, Steven Kuhn, Mary Stiner, and David Reese (2001) found evidence that coastal people made and wore beads and shell ornaments (see also Mayell 2004). Some of the shells were rare varieties, white or brightly colored. These

The Venus of Willendorf (left), carved from limestone, was discovered in Austria and is displayed in Vienna's Natural History Museum. It dates to about 25,000 years ago. The roughly contemporaneous Venus of Lespurge (right), carved from tusk ivory, was discovered in the foothills of the French Pyrenees and now resides at the Musée de l'Homme in Paris. Notice the apparent fertility symbolism in both figures.

authors suggest that population increase could have caused changes in the living conditions of these AMHs—putting pressure on their resources and forcing experimentation with new strategies for survival (Kuhn et al. 2001).

Even a modest increase in the population growth rate could double or triple the numbers and populations of small AMH bands (see this chapter's "Appreciating Anthropology"). People would be living nearer to one another with more opportunities to interact. Body ornaments could have been part of a system of communication, signaling group identity and social status. Such communication through ornamentation implies "the existence of certain [modern] cognitive capacities" (Stiner and Kuhn, quoted in Wilford 2002b; Kuhn et al. 2001).

Clive Gamble attributes the rise of modern human behavior more to increasing social competition than to population increase. Competition with neighboring populations, including the Neandertals, could have produced new subsistence strategies along with new ways of sharing ideas and organizing society. Such innovations would have advantaged AMH bands as they occupied new lands and faced new circumstances (see Barton et al. 2011).

According to archaeologist Randall White, early personal adornment in Africa and the Middle East shows that a creative capacity existed among AMHs long before they reached Europe (Wilford 2002b). Facing new circumstances, including competition, AMHs honed their cultural abilities, which enabled them to maintain a common identity, communicate ideas, and organize their societies into "stable, enduring regional groups" (quoted in Wilford 2002b). Symbolic thought and cultural advances, expressed most enduringly in artifacts, ornamentation, and art, gave them the edge over the Neandertals, whom they eventually replaced in Europe.

The origin of behavioral modernity continues to be debated. We see, however, that archaeological work in many world areas suggests strongly that neither anatomical modernity nor behavioral modernity was a European invention. Africa's role in the origin and development of humanity has been prominent for millions of years of hominin evolution (see also Stringer 2012a and Wilford 2012b; for a contrary view, see Klein 2013).

## ADVANCES IN TECHNOLOGY

In Europe, Upper Paleolithic toolmaking is associated with AMHs. In Africa, earlier AMHs made varied tools. The terms *Lower*, *Middle*, and *Upper*

*Paleolithic* are applied to stone tools from Europe. The terms *Early, Middle,* and *Late Stone Age* are applied to tools from Africa. The AMHs who lived at the Klasies River Mouth cave sites in South Africa made Middle Stone Age tools. However, some of the early tool finds at Blombos Cave and elsewhere in Africa are reminiscent of the European Upper Paleolithic. AMHs in Europe made tools in a variety of traditions, collectively known as Upper Paleolithic because of the tools' location in the upper, or more recent, layers of sedimentary deposits. Some European cave deposits have Middle Paleolithic Mousterian tools (made by Neandertals) at lower levels and increasing numbers of Upper Paleolithic tools at higher levels (Hublin 2012).

The **Upper Paleolithic** traditions all emphasized **blade tools.** Blades were hammered off a prepared core, as in Mousterian technology, but a blade is longer than a Mousterian flake—its length is more than twice its width. Blades were chipped off cores 4 to 6 inches (10 to 15 centimeters) high by hitting a punch made of bone or antler with a hammerstone (Figure 10.2). Blades were then modified to produce a variety of special-purpose implements. Some were composite tools that were made by joining reworked blades to other materials.

The blade-core method was faster than the Mousterian and produced 15 times as much cutting edge from the same amount of material. More efficient tool production might have been especially valued by people whose economy depended on cooperative hunting of mammoths, woolly rhinoceroses, bison, wild horses, bears, wild cattle, wild boars, and—principally—reindeer. It has been estimated that approximately 90 percent of the meat eaten by western Europeans between 25,000 and 15,000 B.P. came from reindeer.

We see certain trends when we compare Upper Paleolithic tools with the earlier Mousterian tradition. First, the number of distinct tool types increased. This trend reflected functional specialization—the manufacture of special tools for particular jobs. A second trend was increasing standardization in tool manufacture. The form and inventory of tools reflect several factors: the jobs tools are intended to perform, the physical properties of the raw materials, and distinctive cultural traditions about how to make tools (Isaac 1972).

Other trends include growth in *Homo*'s total population and geographic range and increasing local cultural diversity as people specialized in particular economic activities. Illustrating increasing economic diversity are the varied special-purpose tools made by Upper Paleolithic people. Scrapers were used to hollow out wood and bone, scrape animal hides, and remove bark from trees. Burins, the first chisels, were used to make slots in bone and wood and to engrave designs on bone. Awls, which were drills with sharp points, were used to make holes in wood, bone, shell, and skin.

Upper Paleolithic bone tools included knives, pins, needles with eyes, and fishhooks. The needles suggest clothing sewn with thread, probably from the sinews of animals. Fishhooks and harpoons confirm an increased emphasis on fishing. (As described by Marean et al. [2007], South Africa's Pinnacle Point Cave provides the earliest evidence, at 164,000 B.P., for a diet based on marine resources, along with small stone blade tools.)

Different tool groups (assemblages) may represent culturally distinct populations, or they may reflect different activities carried out by a single population for particular purposes. Some sites, for example, are obviously butchering stations, where prehistoric people hunted, made their kills, and carved them up. Others are residential sites, where a wider range of activities was carried out.

With increasing technological differentiation, specialization, and efficiency, humans have become increasingly adaptable. Through heavy reliance on cultural means of adaptation, *Homo* has become (in numbers and range) the most successful primate by far. The hominin range expanded significantly in Upper Paleolithic times (see "Focus on Globalization").

## GLACIAL RETREAT

Consider now one regional example, western Europe, of the consequences of glacial retreat. The Würm glacial ended in Europe between 17,000 and 12,000 years ago, with the melting of the ice sheet in northern Europe (Scotland, Scandinavia,

**Upper Paleolithic**
Blade-toolmaking traditions of early AMHs.

**blade tool**
Basic Upper Paleolithic tool, hammered off a prepared core.

**FIGURE 10.2** Upper Paleolithic Blade-Toolmaking. Blades are flakes that are detached from a specially prepared core. A punch (usually a piece of bone or antler) and a hammerstone (not shown here) were used to knock the blade off the core.

northern Germany, and Russia). As the ice retreated, the tundra and steppe vegetation grazed by reindeer and other large herbivores gradually moved north. Some people moved north, too, following their prey.

Shrubs, forests, and more solitary animals appeared in southwestern Europe. With most of the big-game animals gone, western Europeans were forced to use a greater variety of foods. To replace specialized economies based on big game, more generalized adaptations developed during the 5,000 years of glacial retreat.

As water flowed from melting glacial ice, sea levels all over the world started rising. Today, off most coasts, there is a shallow-water zone called the *continental shelf,* over which the sea gradually deepens until the abrupt fall to deep water, which is known as the *continental slope.* During the Ice Ages, so much water was frozen in glaciers that most continental shelves were exposed. Dry land extended right up to the slope's edge. The waters right offshore were deep, cold, and dark. Few species of marine life could thrive in this environment.

As the sea level rose, conditions became more favorable to marine life in the shallower, warmer offshore waters. The quantity and variety of edible species increased tremendously in waters over the shelf. Furthermore, because rivers now flowed more gently into the oceans, fish such as salmon could ascend rivers to spawn. Flocks of birds that nested in seaside marshes migrated across Europe during the winter. Even inland Europeans could take advantage of new resources, such as migratory birds and springtime fish runs.

Although hunting remained important, southwestern European economies became less specialized. A wider range, or broader spectrum, of plant and animal life was being hunted, gathered, collected, caught, and fished. This was the beginning of what anthropologist Kent Flannery (1969) has called the *broad-spectrum revolution.* It was revolutionary because, in the Middle East, it led to human control over the reproduction of plants and animals, a "Neolithic Revolution" to be examined in Chapter 11. In a mere 10,000 years—after millions of years during which hominins had subsisted by foraging for natural resources—plant cultivation and animal domestication replaced hunting and gathering in most areas.

## CAVE ART

It isn't the tools or the skeletons of Upper Paleolithic people but their art that has made them most familiar to us. Most extraordinary are the cave paintings, the earliest of which dates back some 36,000 years. More than a hundred cave painting sites are known, mainly from a limited area of southwestern France and adjacent northeastern

## focus on GLOBALIZATION

### Giant Steps toward Globalization

Among academic disciplines, anthropology is uniquely qualified to study the succession of necessary giant steps along the road to globalization. Those prerequisites to globalization may be summarized as follows: (1) settlement of the six continents by anatomically modern humans; (2) the Neolithic Revolution, which fueled the growth and expansion of human populations; (3) the rise of cities, states, civilizations, and empires; (4) the European Age of Discovery, which established the Columbian exchange and gave rise to (5) the world capitalist economy, the Industrial Revolution, and the modern world system.

For a global system to form, humans needed to settle all the habitable continents, and the hemispheres needed to be linked. The latter didn't happen until 1492, when Columbus reached the Americas. But global forces—most notably an early form of global climate change known as the Ice Age—did influence the human migrations that led to the settlement of the six continents. The Ice Age, with its ebb and flow of continental glaciers, had a strong impact on Paleolithic humans, influencing their livelihoods, settlement patterns, and opportunities to spread out. During the major glacial phases, with so much water frozen in ice, land bridges over areas that now are under water aided human colonization of vast new areas, especially Australia and North America.

Scientists can follow human migrations of the past by constructing global phylogenetic trees (as well as through fossil and archaeological evidence). Branches of such trees—human genetic lineages, or haplogroups—show how the peoples of today's world are related to one another. One key global genetic tree is based on mtDNA—mitochondrial DNA, which is transmitted only through the female line. (A son cannot transmit his mother's mtDNA; only daughters can.) Another tree, based on the Y chromosome tree, is based on transmission from fathers to sons. Only sons receive their father's Y chromosome and pass it on. (Girls get their dad's X chromosome.) The global phylogenetic tree based on mtDNA and the one based on the Y chromosome have known branches whose global distribution can be plotted to show relationships and human migratory paths. Certain branches, for example, are known to be associated with the spread of modern humans out of Africa between 70,000 and 50,000 B.P. Other (smaller) branches show that the Americas were settled not by a single ancestral population but by multiple haplogroups. In other words, there were waves of migration into North, and eventually South, America.

This chapter examines the human settlement of most of the globe, as anatomically modern humans spread from Africa into Australia, Europe, Asia, the Americas, and the Pacific. Chapter 11 focuses on a major economic transformation—the emergence of food production (i.e., farming and animal domestication)—sometimes called the Neolithic Revolution. Neolithic economies spread rapidly, because they were more productive and reliable than Paleolithic economies based on hunting, gathering, and collecting. The eventual rise of ancient cities and states was fueled by the population growth and economic complexity associated with food production. For thousands of years after the first cities and states appeared (see Chapter 12), empires rose and fell. None of them, however, was an empire on which "the sun never set." What was necessary before such an empire (of which the British empire is the best-known example) could form?

Vivid Upper Paleolithic cave paintings from Lascaux, Dordogne, France. How might you explain what you see depicted here?

Spain. The most famous site is Lascaux, found in 1940 in southwestern France by a dog and his young human companions.

The paintings adorn limestone walls of caves located deep in the Earth. Over time, the paintings have been absorbed by the limestone and thus preserved. Prehistoric big-game hunters painted their prey: woolly mammoths, wild cattle and horses, deer, and reindeer. The largest animal image is 18 feet (5.5 meters) long.

Most interpretations associate cave painting with magic and ritual surrounding the hunt. For example, because animals sometimes are depicted with spears in their bodies, the paintings might have been attempts to ensure success in hunting. Artists might have believed that by capturing the animal's image in paint and predicting the kill, they could influence the hunt's outcome.

Another interpretation sees cave painting as a magical human attempt to control animal reproduction. Something analogous was done by Native Australian (Australian aboriginal) hunters and gatherers, who held annual *ceremonies of increase* to honor and to promote, magically, the fertility of the plants and animals that shared their homeland. Australians believed that ceremonies were necessary to perpetuate the species on which humans depended. Similarly, cave paintings might have been part of annual ceremonies of increase. Some of the animals in the cave murals are pregnant, and some are copulating. Did Upper Paleolithic people believe they could influence the mating behavior and reproduction of their prey by drawing them? Or

did they perhaps think that animals would return each year to the place where their souls had been captured pictorially?

Paintings often occur in clusters. In some caves, as many as three paintings have been drawn over the original, yet next to these superimposed paintings stand blank walls never used for painting. It seems reasonable to speculate that an event in the outside world sometimes reinforced a painter's choice of a given spot. Perhaps there was an especially successful hunt soon after the painting had been done. Perhaps members of a social subdivision significant in Upper Paleolithic society customarily used a given area of wall for their drawings.

Cave paintings also might have been a kind of pictorial history. Perhaps Upper Paleolithic people, through their drawings, were reenacting the hunt after it took place, as hunters of the Kalahari Desert in southern Africa still do today. Designs and markings on animal bones may indicate that Upper Paleolithic people had developed a calendar based on the phases of the moon (Marshack 1972). If this is so, it seems possible that Upper Paleolithic hunters, who were certainly as intelligent as we are, would have been interested in recording important events in their lives.

It is worth noting that the *late* Upper Paleolithic, when many of the most spectacular multicolored cave paintings were done and Paleolithic artistic techniques were perfected, coincides with the period of glacial retreat. An intensification of cave painting for any of the reasons connected with hunting magic could have been caused by concern about decreases in herds as the open lands of southwestern Europe were being replaced by forests.

## SETTLING AUSTRALIA

As continental glaciers ebbed and flowed, modern humans took advantage of global climate change to expand their range. During the major glacial phases, with so much water frozen in ice, land bridges formed, aiding human colonization of new areas.

People spread from Africa into Europe and Asia, eventually reaching Australia and, much later, the Americas and the Pacific islands.

When and how was Australia settled? At times of major glacial advance, such as 50,000 years ago, dry land connected Australia, New Guinea, and Tasmania. *Sahul* is the name for the larger continent thus formed (O'Connell and Allen 2004). At its largest, Sahul was separated from Asia only by narrow straits (Figure 10.3). Humans somehow made the crossing, perhaps in primitive watercraft, from Asia

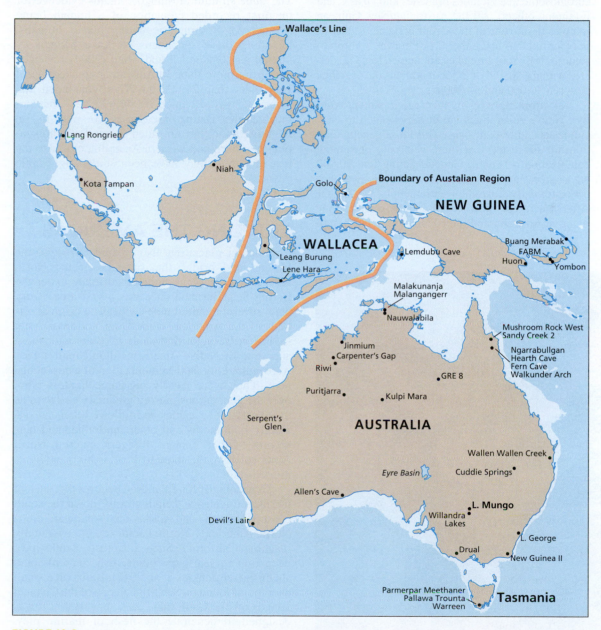

**FIGURE 10.3**

At times of major glacial advance, such as 50,000 years ago, dry land connected Australia, New Guinea, and Tasmania. *Sahul* is the name for the larger continent thus formed. At its largest, Sahul was separated from Asia only by narrow straits. Shaded on this map is the continent formed by a 650-foot (200-meter) fall in sea level. Wallacea is a transitional zoogeographic zone between Asia and Australia. The map also locates major archaeological sites, including Lake Mungo.

SOURCE: Reprinted from *Journal of Archaeological Science*, Vol. 31, No. 6, O'Connell, J. F., and J. Allen, "Dating the Colonization of Sahul (Pleistocene Australia–New Guinea): A Review of Recent Research," pp. 835–853, copyright 2004, with permission from Elsevier. http://www.journals.elsevier.com/journal-of-archaeological-science

into Sahul, perhaps around 50,000 B.P. Genetic markers, fossils, and archaeological sites help us understand that settlement process.

Georgi Hudjashov and his colleagues (2007) analyzed genetic samples from Native Australians and New Guineans/Melanesians. They looked at both mitochondrial DNA (mtDNA) (n = 172 samples) and Y chromosomes (n = 522). They compared those samples with known branches of global phylogenetic trees. The global mtDNA tree includes branches known as M and N (among others). The Y chromosome tree includes branches known as C and F (among others). All the Australian/New Guinean samples fit into one of those four branches (either M or N for mtDNA and either C or F for the Y chromosome). Those four branches are known to be associated with the spread of modern humans out of Africa between 70,000 and 50,000 B.P.

Not surprisingly (given their geographic proximity), Native Australians are closely related to New Guineans and Melanesians. This close genetic relationship suggested that there was only one initial colonization of Sahul. Genetic dating (ca. 50,000 B.P.) agrees more or less with archaeological evidence for early Australian settlement by 46,000 B.P. After that, gene flow continued between people living in Australia and the islands to the north until the land bridge connecting those areas was submerged around 8000 B.P.

In terms of the fossil record, Australia has given us a few of the oldest (ca. 46,000 B.P.) modern human skeletons known outside Africa. The earliest Australian skeletons come from Lake Mungo in New South Wales (Figure 10.3). One of these finds (Mungo III) is of the world's oldest ritual ocher burial. The body was intentionally buried and decorated with ocher (Bowler et al. 2003). The world's oldest AMH mtDNA was extracted from this fossil. The same stratum at Mungo contains evidence for the first recorded cremation of a human being (Mungo I). Radiometric dating places humans, including these specimens, at Lake Mungo by 46,000 B.P. O'Connell and Allen (2004) reviewed data from more than 30 Australian archaeological sites older than 20,000 B.P. They concluded that Australia was occupied by 46,000 B.P.—but not much earlier. Dating based on genetic markers, on the other hand, has not ruled out earlier colonization. Northern and western Australia, closer to the rest of Sahul, may have been settled by 50,000 years ago.

## SETTLING THE AMERICAS

Continental glaciation also created *Beringia,* the Bering land bridge that once connected North America and Siberia. Submerged today under the Bering Sea, Beringia once was a vast area of dry land, several hundred miles wide. The original settlers of the Americas came from northeast Asia. Living in Beringia thousands of years ago, these ancestors of Native Americans didn't realize they were embarking on the colonization of a new continent. They were merely big-game hunters who, over the generations, moved gradually eastward as they spread their camps and followed their prey—woolly mammoths and other tundra-adapted herbivores. Other ancient foragers entered North America along the shore by boat, fishing and hunting sea animals.

Archaeologist Jon Erlandson believes that ancient mariners traveled a "kelp highway" down the south coast of Beringia and Alaska, then southward down North America's North Pacific coast, eventually reaching California. Such a "forest" would have been rich in seals, sea otters, fish, seabirds, and shellfish (see Jenkins et al. 2012). Barbs on a small chert point found on San Miguel, one of the Channel Islands off the California coast, suggest that it was designed to penetrate the flesh of marine prey. Erlandson has collected dozens of these points on San Miguel, which people had reached, based on radiocarbon dating, by 12,000 B.P. Similar points have been found along the North Pacific rim. The oldest such implement, from coastal Japan, dates to 15,600 B.P. To Erlandson, these artifacts reveal a trail left by ancient mariners who journeyed coastwise

The earliest Australian skeletons, including the one being excavated here in 1974, come from Lake Mungo in New South Wales. The world's oldest human mtDNA (dating back 46,000 years) has been extracted from one of these Lake Mungo finds. When was Australia first settled?

from Japan to the Americas during the last Ice Age (see Pringle 2008).

Whatever their origin, this was truly a "new world" to its earliest colonists, as it would be to the European voyagers who rediscovered it thousands of years later. Its natural resources, particularly its big game, never before had been exploited by humans. Although ice sheets covered most of what is now Canada, colonization gradually penetrated the heartland of what is now the United States. Representing those who chose the inland route, successive generations of hunters followed game through unglaciated corridors, breaks in the continental ice sheets (see Figure 10.4).

On North America's grasslands, early American Indians, *Paleoindians*, hunted horses, camels, bison, elephants, mammoths, and giant sloths. The **Clovis** tradition—a sophisticated stone technology based on a point that was fastened to the end of a hunting spear (Figure 10.5)—flourished, widely but very briefly, in the Central Plains, on their western margins, and in what is now the eastern United States (Green 2006; Largent 2007a, 2007b). Non-Clovis sites dating to the Clovis period also exist, in both North and South America.

Using C[14] (radiocarbon) dates, where available, for all known Clovis sites, Michael Waters and Thomas Stafford (2007) concluded that the Clovis tradition lasted no more than 450 years (13,250–12,800 B.P.). During this short time span, Clovis technology originated and spread throughout North America. Unknown is whether its spread involved the actual movement of big-game hunters or the very rapid diffusion of a superior technology from group to group (Largent 2007b). Waters and Stafford (2007) also calculate that it would have taken from 600 to 1,000 years for the first Americans and their descendants to spread by land from the southern part of the Canadian ice-free corridor to Tierra del Fuego at the southern tip of South America—a distance of more than 8,680 miles (14,000 km). At least four sites in southern South America have C[14] dates that are roughly the same as the Clovis C[14] dates.

Waters and Stafford conclude there must have been people in the Americas before Clovis. Indeed, an emerging archaeological record supports a pre-Clovis occupation of the New World. One pre-Clovis find is a bone projectile point found embedded in a mastodon rib at the Manis site in Washington State, dated to 13,800 B.P. (Waters et al. 2011). Non-Clovis tools and butchered mammoth remains dating to 13,500 B.P. and 12,500 B.P. have been found at sites in Wisconsin. The oldest pre-Clovis site is in South America, at the northern Patagonia settlement of Monte Verde, Chile, dating to 14,800 B.P.

In Oregon's Paisley Caves, scientists have uncovered 13,200-year-old tools (Western Stemmed projectile points) and human *coprolites* (fossilized feces), from which DNA has been extracted (Jenkins et al. 2012). These non-Clovis points date to a time

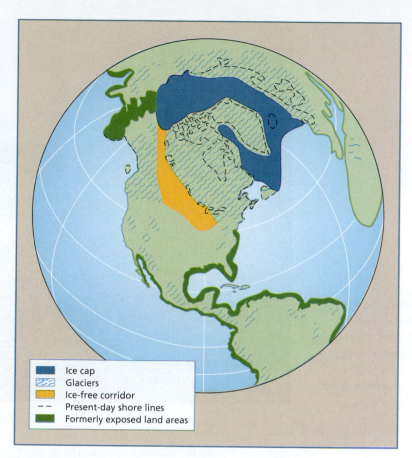

| | |
|---|---|
| ▓ (blue) | Ice cap |
| ▨ (light blue) | Glaciers |
| ▓ (orange) | Ice-free corridor |
| – – | Present-day shore lines |
| ▓ (green) | Formerly exposed land areas |

**FIGURE 10.4** The Ancestors of Native Americans Came to North America as Migrants from Asia.

They followed big-game herds across Beringia, an immense stretch of land exposed during the Ice Ages. Was their settlement of the Americas intentional? When did it probably happen? Other migrants reached North America along the shore by boat, fishing and hunting sea animals.

**Clovis**

Early American tool tradition; projectile point attached to hunting spear.

**FIGURE 10.5** A Clovis Spear Point.

Such points were attached to spears used by Paleoindians of the North American plains between 13,250 and 12,800 B.P. Are there sites with comparable ages or older elsewhere in the Americas?

Woolly-mammoth hunters in Beringia, the vast stretch of land between Siberia and North America that was exposed during the Ice Ages.

during or before the Clovis tradition. The Western Stemmed tradition appears to have developed separately from Clovis, which may have arisen in the southeastern United States and moved west. The Western Stemmed tradition began, perhaps earlier, in the West and moved east.

The DNA from the Paisley corprolites provides the oldest direct evidence for humans in the Americas. It represents haplogroup A, which is common in Siberia and found, along with haplogroup B, in contemporary Native Americans (see Jenkins et al. 2012). A haplogroup is a lineage marked by one or more specific genetic mutations. Analysis of DNA—bolstered, some anthropologists believe, by anatomical evidence—suggests that the Americas were settled by more than one haplogroup. The Clovis people were not the first or only early settlers of the Americas. Migration(s) of people into the Americas may date back as far as 18,000 years. Those early settlers came at different times and by different routes (see Wade 2012)

## PEOPLING THE PACIFIC

Who settled the vast Pacific? Today, when archaeologists dig in Australia, Papua New Guinea, and the neighboring islands of the southwest Pacific (consult the map in Figure 10.6 throughout this discussion), they find traces of humankind more than 30,000 years old. People may have reached Sahul by 50,000 years ago; others had journeyed

as far east as the Solomon Islands by 30,000 B.P. (Terrell 1998).

And there they stayed, apparently for thousands of years before sailing farther eastward on the open sea. Until 3000 B.P., the Solomon Islands formed the eastern edge of the inhabited Pacific. The deep-sea crossings and colonization that began around 3000 B.P. were linked to the rapid spread of the earliest pottery found in Oceania, an ornately decorated ware with geometric designs called Lapita.

The first Lapita potsherds were excavated in 1952. The name comes from the discovery site on the Melanesian island of New Caledonia. (Locate New Caledonia on the map in Figure 10.6.) Many scholars see this ornate ware as the creation of a distinct ethnic group (the Lapita people) and think this Lapita "cultural complex" was carried across the Pacific by a migration of newcomers from Asia.

No one knows why people with Lapita pottery left home and risked sailing in deeper waters. Was it for reasons of wanderlust, a pioneering spirit, or improvements in canoe building and navigation? Some experts think the domestication of certain plants and animals thought to be of Asian origin—such as dogs, pigs, and chickens—fueled Lapita's expansion (Terrell 1998). The resource base of the early Lapita pottery makers included diverse foods, some wild and some domesticated (e.g., yams, taro, pigs, chickens).

Archaeologist David Burley uncovered early Lapita shards (potsherds) at Fanga'uta Lagoon on

**FIGURE 10.6** Oceania.
Polynesian islands are shaded khaki. Other Central Pacific languages outside of Polynesia are spoken in the area shaded orange, which includes Fiji.

**Central Pacific Languages**

| | | |
|---|---|---|
| 1-Nuclear Western | 13-Southeast Vanua Levu | 25-Tongareva |
| 2-Nadroga | 14-Tongan | 26-Rapa |
| 3-Namosi-Naitasiri-Serua | 15-Niue | 27-Austral |
| 4-Southeast Viti Levu | 16-Samoan | 28-Cook Islands Maori |
| 5-Northeast Viti Levu | 17-Niuafo'ou | 29-Minihiki-Rakahanga |
| 6-Lomaiviti | 18-Tokelau | 30-Pa'umotu |
| 7-Kadavu | 19-Tuvalu | 31-New Zealand Maori |
| 8-Lau | 20-East Uvea | 32-Moriori |
| 9-Western Vanua Levu | 21-East Futuna | 33-Mangareva |
| 10-Gonedau | 22-Pukapuka | 34-North Marquesas |
| 11-Central Vanua Levu | 23-Easter Island | 35-South Marquesas |
| 12-Northeast Vanua Levu | 24-Tahitian | 36-Hawaiian |

the island of Tongatapu in the Polynesian kingdom of Tonga. Early outrigger canoes reached that lagoon after traveling hundreds, and perhaps more than a thousand, miles from the west. Radiocarbon dating of charcoal among the shards showed that seafarers reached Tonga between 2,950 and 2,850 years ago. *This is the earliest known settlement in Polynesia.* Burley thinks that Tongatapu "probably served as the initial staging point for population expansion" to other islands of Tonga, then to

On the left, an archaeologist holding a freshly scrubbed piece of Lapita pottery from the Teouma Lapita site, Republic of Vanuatu. On the right, a newly reconstructed stamped Lapita pot displayed in a Vanuatu museum.

This print from 1811 shows a traditional (New Zealand) Maori war canoe. Earlier, the Lapita people had reached and colonized vast areas of the Pacific, including New Zealand, in their outrigger canoes.

Samoa, and then on to the rest of Polynesia (quoted in Wilford 2002a).

Improvements in their outrigger canoes allowed Lapita navigators to sail across large stretches of open sea, thus propelling the Polynesian diaspora. The larger canoes could have carried dozens of people, plus pigs and other cargo. Polynesian seafarers eventually reached Tahiti to the east, as well as Hawaii—located more than 2,500 miles northeast of Tonga and Samoa. Later voyages carried the Polynesian diaspora south to New Zealand and farther east to Easter Island. Covering one-fourth of the Pacific, Polynesia became the last large area of the world to be settled by humans.

The Lapita pottery found at Tongatapu offered clues about where the seafarers originated. Analyzing bits of the shards, William Dickinson, a University of Arizona geologist, found sandy minerals from outside Tonga. Some of the pots had been brought there from elsewhere. It turned out that the artifacts were made of minerals found only on the Santa Cruz Islands in Melanesia, some 1,200 miles to the west of Tonga and just east of the Solomon Islands (Burley and Dickinson 2001). The shards from Tongatapu provided the first physical evidence linking the voyages of the Lapita people between the western and eastern parts of the Pacific. This evidence may mean that Tonga was first settled by people who had come directly from central Melanesia (Wilford 2002a).

Anthropologists from all four subfields—archaeologists and biological, cultural, and linguistic anthropologists—have considered questions about Polynesian origins. Who made Lapita pottery, along with the distinctive stone tools, beads, rings, and shell ornaments often found with it? Did the Lapita complex originate with indigenous dark-skinned Melanesians, assumed to have descended from the first settlers of the Pacific? Or was it introduced by new, lighter-skinned arrivals from Southeast Asia? Did lighter- and darker-skinned groups intermarry in Melanesia, forming a hybrid population that created the Lapita complex and eventually colonized Polynesia?

In the 18th century, the explorer Captain James Cook was struck by how similar were the appearance and customs of light-skinned Polynesians living on islands thousands of miles apart, such as Tonga, Hawaii, New Zealand, and Easter Island. Cook thought that the Polynesians originally had come from Malaysia. French navigators stressed the physical and cultural differences between the Polynesians and the darker-skinned Melanesians who lived near New Guinea, and who resembled the indigenous peoples of Papua New Guinea.

Until recently, anthropologists supposed that the ancestors of the Polynesians originated in mainland China and/or Taiwan, which they left between 3,600 and 6,000 years ago. They were seen as spreading rapidly through the Pacific, largely bypassing Melanesia. This would explain why the Polynesians are not dark-skinned and why they speak Austronesian languages, rooted in Taiwan, rather than Papuan languages, spoken in parts of Melanesia. This view now seems discredited by the fact that nothing resembling Lapita pottery has ever been found in Taiwan or southern China. Lapita features first show up in Melanesia, on islands of the Bismarck Archipelago. Recent genetic studies also suggest that ancestral Polynesians stopped off in Melanesia. Interbreeding between early Polynesians and Melanesians has left clear genetic markers in today's Polynesians. The debate now focuses on where the interbreeding took place and how extensive it was.

DNA evidence has convinced Mark Stoneking, a molecular anthropologist, that the ancestors of the Polynesians were indeed Austronesians. (The Austronesian, or Malayo-Polynesian, language family covers a large area of the world. Austronesian languages are the main languages of Polynesia [e.g., Hawaiian], Indonesia, and Malaysia and even of Madagascar, located just off the African coast.) Stoneking thinks that the ancestral Polynesians left Southeast Asia and sailed to, then expanded along, the coast of New Guinea. They intermingled with Melanesians there and then started voyaging eastward into the Pacific. Interacting with other human groups, ancestral Polynesians exchanged genes and cultural traits (Gibbons 2001; Wilford 2002a).

Excavating in Melanesia's Bismarck Archipelago, archaeologist Patrick Kirch found evidence that newcomers from the islands of Southeast Asia had reached Melanesia by 3500 B.P. They built their homes on stilts, as in houses still found in Southeast Asia. They sailed in outrigger canoes and took agricultural plants along with them. There was mixing between the newcomers and the Melanesians. *Out of their contact and interaction emerged the Lapita pottery style* (see Kirch 2000).

Why don't Polynesians resemble their presumed Melanesian cousins? How can we explain the physical differences between Polynesians and Melanesians? Might the Polynesian population have originated in what geneticists call a *founder effect*? In such an event, just a few people, whose physical traits do not randomly sample the larger population from which they came, happen to give rise to a very large diaspora. A very small number of people—say, a few canoeloads—reaching Tonga's Fanga'uta Lagoon, may have given rise to

On the left, a Polynesian woman from Tahiti, Society Islands, French Polynesia. On the right, a Melanesian woman from Madang, Papua New Guinea. What differences and similarities do you notice between these two women?

the entire, geographically dispersed Polynesian population. The physical traits of such a small founding group could not fully represent the population from which they had come. Whatever traits the founders happened to have, such as light skin color, would be transmitted to their descendants. This may explain why the Polynesians look so different from Melanesians, even though they have DNA in common.

By 2000 B.P., according to Patrick Kirch (2000), the people of Tonga had developed a significant new technology: the double-hull sailing canoe. Even though they could not spot other islands on the distant horizon, as their ancestors had been able to do in the southwestern Pacific, the notion that the ocean was full of islands endured. Once they could more securely travel long distances—with the new canoe—they set forth. These weren't all accidental voyages and discoveries, as once was thought. These ancient sailors tacked against the prevailing east-to-west winds, knowing that, if necessary, they could ride a following wind back home.

Long ago, the anthropologist Alexander Lesser disputed what he saw as the "myth of the primitive isolate" (quoted in Terrell 1998)—the idea that ancient peoples lived in closed societies, each one out of contact with others. It is doubtful that the human world has ever been one of distinct societies, sealed cultures, or isolated ethnic groups. Even on the small islands and atolls of the vast Pacific Ocean lived societies that contradicted the "primitive isolate." The adventurous and interconnected peoples of the Pacific and their prehistoric past reveal that human diversity is as much a product of contact as of isolation (Terrell 1998).

## summary

1. The ancestors of AMHs (anatomically modern humans) were archaic *H. sapiens* groups in Africa. The earliest AMH fossil finds include Herto (160,000–154,000 B.P.), Omo Kibish (195,000 B.P.), and various South African sites, along with Skhūl (100,000 B.P.) and Qafzeh (92,000 B.P.). The Neandertals (130,000–28,000 B.P.) and AMHs were contemporaries, rather than ancestor and descendant. AMHs made Upper Paleolithic blade tools in Europe and Middle and Late Stone Age flake tools in Africa.

2. Scientists continue to debate whether human behavioral modernity originated in Africa as early as 100,000 years ago or in Europe around 45,000 years ago. Mounting evidence now tends to favor an African origin. As glacial ice melted and the Upper Paleolithic ended, foraging patterns became generalized. Fish, fowl, and plant foods supplemented, then replaced, the diminishing big-game supply. The beginning of a broad-spectrum economy in western Europe coincided with an intensification of Upper Paleolithic cave art. On limestone cave walls, prehistoric hunters painted images of animals important in their lives. Explanations of cave paintings (a prime example of human behavioral modernity) link them to hunting magic, ceremonies of increase, and initiation rites.

3. During the major glacial advances, land bridges formed, aiding human colonization of new areas, including Australia and the Americas. Around 50,000 years ago, dry land connected Australia, New Guinea, and Tasmania, forming the large continent of Sahul, separated from Asia only by narrow straits, which humans somehow crossed. The close genetic relationship between Native Australians, New Guineans, and Melanesians suggests a single initial colonization of Sahul from Asia. Genetic dating (ca. 50,000 B.P.) agrees more or less with archaeological evidence for early Australian settlement by 46,000 B.P. Australia has yielded a few of the oldest (ca. 46,000 B.P.) modern human skeletons known outside Africa, including the Lake Mungo finds.

4. Humans probably entered the Americas no more than 18,000 years ago. Pursuing big game or moving by boat along the North Pacific coast, they gradually settled the Americas. Adapting to different environments, Native Americans developed a variety of cultures.

5. Papua New Guinea and the neighboring islands of the southwestern Pacific have been settled for at least 30,000 years. Only around 3000 B.P. did people start sailing farther eastward, carrying the earliest Oceanian pottery, called Lapita. Seafarers reached Tonga between 2,950 and 2,850 years ago—the earliest known settlement in Polynesia. Tonga appears to have served as the initial point of expansion, via outrigger canoe, to Samoa and eventually to Tahiti, Hawaii, New Zealand, and Easter Island. The ancestral Polynesians probably left Southeast Asia, sailed to, and then expanded along the coast of New Guinea. They intermingled with Melanesians there, then started voyaging eastward. The light skin color of Polynesians, which contrasts with the darker skin color of Melanesians, may have originated as an instance of the founder effect.

**key terms**

**critical thinking**

1. In 1997, ancient DNA was extracted from one of the Neandertal bones originally found in Germany in 1856. This was the first time that DNA of a premodern human had been recovered. What does the analysis of this DNA suggest about Neandertals' relation to AMHs? What other evidence have scientists presented regarding Neandertals' place in the modern human's evolutionary line?

2. What does *behavioral modernity* mean? What are the competing theories that attempt to explain the advent of behavioral modernity in AMHs? Is behavioral modernity a quality of individual humans or of humans as part of a social group? (Perhaps the answer is not one or the other but an interaction between the two, which some anthropologists might argue are inseparable.)

3. What cultural advances facilitated the spread of AMHs out of Africa?

4. What cultural changes accompanied glacial retreat in Europe during the late Upper Paleolithic?

5. It isn't the tools or the skeletons of Upper Paleolithic people but their art that has made them most familiar to us. What are some of the interpretations of cave art that researchers have proposed?

# The First Farmers

▶ When and where did the Neolithic originate, and what were its main features?

▶ What similarities and differences marked the Neolithic economies of the Old World and the New World?

▶ What costs and benefits are associated with food production?

A farmer holds rice stalks on Mindanao Island, the Philippines. Rice was domesticated in China more than 8,000 years ago.

# understanding OURSELVES

**W**hat could be more American than McDonald's, hamburgers, hot dogs, or apple pie—more American, in other words, than a now global fast-food chain, a sandwich and sausage named for German cities, or a fruit first grown in the Middle East baked in a pastry crust from wheat, domesticated there as well. What we think of as truly American usually has foreign roots. Consider just McDonald's Big Mac as a world system in miniature. It consists of two all-beef patties (from cattle, an Old World domesticate), special sauce (similar to mayonnaise, invented in France), lettuce (Egypt), cheese (from cow's milk—Old World), pickles (India), and onions (Iran and West Pakistan), and it comes on a sesame-seed (India) bun (wheat—the Middle East). The Breakfast Egg McMuffin is only slightly less cosmopolitan. Eggs are from chickens, domesticated in Southeast Asia. Cheese comes from cow's milk (cows were domesticated in India, the Middle East, and Africa's eastern Sahara). Canadian bacon is from pork (western Asia), and the muffin is made of wheat (the Middle East). If you crave "real American" food—that is, food of New World origin—have some turkey or beans on a taco or tortilla (from maize or corn) and chocolate for dessert.

The domestication of plants and animals for food occurred, independently, in both the Old World and the Americas around 11,000 years ago.

Animals and crops thrived together in the Middle East, Africa, Europe, and Asia. Not so in the Americas, where wild oxen, horses, pigs, and camels went extinct long before crops were ever cultivated. Key differences in early food production between the hemispheres help us understand their subsequent histories. A mutually supportive relationship developed between farming and herding in the Old World, where crops sustained sheep, goats, and eventually cattle, pigs, horses, and donkeys.

What, again deceptively, could be more American than the habit of using your own wheels to get to your favorite restaurant? Wheels? Only in Old World prehistory were animals harnessed to wheeled vehicles. Ancient Mexicans did also invent the wheel, but only for toys. Their homeland lacked the appropriate animals to pull plows, oxcarts, chariots, and carriages. How could a dog, turkey, or duck match a horse, a donkey, or an ox as a beast of burden? The absence of large-animal domestication in ancient Mexico is a key factor in world history, helping us understand the divergent development of societies on different sides of the oceans. Wheels fueled the growth of transport, trade, and travel in the Old World. Thousands of years after the origin of food production, advantages in transport would fuel an "Age of Discovery" and enable the European conquest of the Americas. Again, a key feature of contemporary American life turns out to have foreign roots.

As the Ice Age ended and glaciers retreated in Europe, foragers pursued a more generalized economy, focusing less on large animals. This was the beginning of what Kent Flannery (1969) has called the **broad-spectrum revolution.** This refers to the period beginning around 15,000 B.P. in the Middle East and 12,000 B.P. in Europe, during which a wider range, or broader spectrum, of plant and animal life was hunted, gathered, collected, caught, and fished. It was revolutionary because in the Middle East it led to food production—human control over the reproduction of plants and animals.

# THE MESOLITHIC

The broad-spectrum revolution in Europe includes the late Upper Paleolithic and the **Mesolithic,** which followed it. Again, because of the long history of European archaeology, our knowledge of the Mesolithic (particularly in southwestern Europe and the British Isles) is extensive. The Mesolithic had a characteristic tool type—the *microlith* (Greek for "small stone"). Of interest to us is what an abundant inventory of small and delicately shaped tools can tell us about the total economy and way of life of the people who made them (see Bailey and Spikins 2008).

By 10,000 B.P. the glaciers had retreated to such an extent that foragers now lived in the formerly glaciated British Isles and Scandinavia. People still hunted, but their prey were solitary forest animals, such as the roe deer, wild ox, and wild pig, rather than herd species. This led to new hunting techniques: solitary stalking and trapping. The coasts and lakes of Europe, the Middle East, and Japan were fished intensively. Some important Mesolithic sites are Scandinavian shell mounds—the garbage dumps of prehistoric oyster collectors. Microliths were used as fishhooks and in harpoons. Dugout canoes facilitated fishing and travel. For woodworking, Mesolithic carpenters used new kinds of axes, chisels, and gouges. The process of preserving meat and fish by smoking and salting grew increasingly important. (Meat preservation had been less of an issue when the climate was colder, because winter snow and ice, often on the ground nine months of the year, offered convenient refrigeration.) The bow and arrow became essential for hunting waterfowl in swamps and marshes. Dogs were used as retrievers (Champion and Gamble 1984). (Recent evidence for much earlier canine domestication [before 30,000 B.P.] comes from sites in the Czech Republic (at 33,000 B.P.), Siberia (at 33,000), and Belgium (at 36,000)[Rice 2012]).

Broad-spectrum economies lasted about 5,000 years longer in Europe than in the Middle East. Whereas Middle Easterners had begun to cultivate plants and breed animals by 10,000 B.P., farming and herding reached western Europe only around 5000 B.P. (3000 B.C.E.) and northern Europe 500 years later.

As the big-game supply dwindled after 15,000 B.P., foragers had to pursue new resources. Their attention shifted from large-bodied, slow reproducers (such as mammoths) to species such as fish, mollusks, and rabbits, which reproduce quickly and prolifically. This happened with the European Mesolithic. It also happened at the Japanese site of Nittano (Akazawa 1980), located on an inlet near Tokyo. Nittano was occupied several times between 6000 and 5000 B.P. by members of the *Jomon* culture (16,000–2500 B.P.), for which more than 30,000 sites are known in Japan. The Jomon people made stone and bone tools, and some of the world's

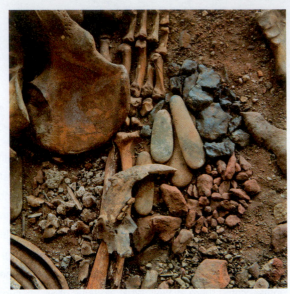

Evidence of the Mesolithic occupation of Italy. Displayed here are a beaver jaw, ocher, stone tools, and assorted bones, just as they were found (in situ) at a Mesolithic cave burial in Arene Candide grotto, near Savona, Italian Riviera.

earliest pottery—beginning as early as 15,500 B.P. They hunted deer, pigs, bears, and antelope, gathered plants and nuts, and ate fish and shellfish. Their sites have yielded the remains of more than 300 species of shellfish and 180 species of edible plants, including berries, nuts, and tubers (Akazawa and Aikens 1986; Habu et al. 2011).

Jomon foragers used their pottery to cook and serve stews of salmon and shellfish. In burnt fragments of clay pots dating back 15,300 years, scientists have found traces of fat from marine and freshwater fish and shellfish (Craig 2013; Subbaraman 2013). Whether in the form of a family meal, a potluck dinner, or a lavish feast, eating tends to be a social activity, just as it appears to have been in the Jomon culture. Not only did the Jomon people stew their fish, they feasted on it in groups. Their large clay pots weren't just utilitarian cooking vessels; they also brought people together to socialize (Craig 2013; Subbaraman 2013).

Even earlier than Jomon, the world's oldest known pottery has been found recently in Jiangxi Province, southern China (Wu et al. 2012). Dated to 20,000 B.P., these pots were simple vessels used for cooking food. It appears that pottery making began in China 20,000 years ago and never stopped. The Chinese kitchen always has been based on cooking and steaming, which ceramics facilitate. Unlike other parts of Asia and the Middle East, breads never have been prominent in Chinese cuisine. According to Harvard professor Ofer Bar-Yosef, a member of the discovery team, these early Chinese pots were made by a group of mobile hunter-gatherers (*Harvard Magazine* 2012). Plant cultivation did not reach China for another 10,000 years.

In the Middle East, the first pottery appeared 3,000–2,000 years after, rather than before, the turn to farming. Bar-Yosef suggests that the earliest farmers/herders in the Middle East had a diet based on barbecued meats and pita breads and didn't need pottery. In their cooking style, one simply grinds the seeds, mixes them with water, then cooks the dough right on the fire. Chinese cooking, by contrast, needed pots to cook and steam foods thousands of years earlier (*Harvard Magazine* 2012).

## THE NEOLITHIC

The Neolithic Revolution, sometimes called the Agricultural Revolution, was the widespread transition, beginning about 12,000 years ago, of human societies from lifestyles based on foraging to lifestyles based on farming and herding. The **Neolithic** is considered revolutionary because, in just a few thousand years—after millions of years of foraging as the sole human subsistence strategy—it would transform small, mobile groups into societies living in permanent settlements—villages, towns, and eventually cities.

The transition from Mesolithic to Neolithic occurs when groups become dependent on domesticated foods for more than 50 percent of their diet. Usually, this happens after a very long period of experimenting with and using domesticates (plants and animals used for consumption) as supplements to broad-spectrum foraging (see Bellwood 2005; Simmons 2007). More productive and reliable than foraging, Neolithic economies fueled population growth and expansion, as well as the settlement of new environments.

The archaeological signature of Neolithic cultures (which are called *Formative* in the Americas)

*Neolithic* was coined to refer to techniques of grinding and polishing stone tools, such as this hammer head and two polished axes, found in England. Was the new toolmaking style the most significant thing about the Neolithic?

includes dependence on cultivation, sedentary (settled) life, and the use of ceramic vessels. The term *Neolithic* originally was coined to refer to new techniques of grinding and polishing stone tools (see Saville 2012). However, the primary significance of the Neolithic was the new total economy rather than just its characteristic artifacts (see Simmons 2007).

## THE FIRST FARMERS AND HERDERS IN THE MIDDLE EAST

Early economies based on food production were associated with substantial changes in human lifestyles. By 12,000 B.P., the shift toward the Neolithic was under way in the Middle East (Turkey, Iraq, Iran, Syria, Jordan, and Israel). People started intervening in the reproductive cycles of plants and animals. No longer simply hunting, gathering, and fishing, people started modifying the biological characteristics of plants and animals as they began to grow their own food. By 10,000 B.P., domesticated plants and animals were part of the broad spectrum of resources used by Middle Easterners. By 7500 B.P., most Middle Easterners had abandoned broad-spectrum foraging for more specialized, Neolithic economies based on fewer species, which were domesticates (Bellwood 2005; Simmons 2007). They had become committed farmers and herders.

Kent Flannery (1969) laid out a series of eras during which the Middle Eastern transition to farming and herding took place. The era of seminomadic hunting and gathering (12,000–10,000 B.P.) encompasses the last stages of broad-spectrum foraging. This was the period just before the first domesticated plants (wheat and barley) and animals (goats and sheep) were added to the diet. Next came the era of early dry farming (of wheat and barley) and caprine domestication (10,000–7500 B.P.). *Dry farming* refers to farming without irrigation; such farming depended on rainfall. *Caprine* (from *capra,* Latin for "goat") refers to goats and sheep, which were domesticated during this era.

During the era of increased specialization in food production (7500–5500 B.P.), new crops were added to the diet, along with more productive varieties of wheat and barley. Cattle and pigs were domesticated (Simmons 2007). By 5500 B.P., agriculture had extended to the alluvial plain of the Tigris and Euphrates Rivers (Figure 11.1), where early Mesopotamians lived in walled towns, some of which grew into cities. (Recap 11.1 highlights these stages, or eras, in the transition to food production in the ancient Middle East.) After two million years of stone-toolmaking, *H. sapiens* was living in the Bronze Age, when metallurgy and the wheel were invented.

**Neolithic**
Term used to describe economies based on food production (cultivated crops and domesticated animals).

**FIGURE 11.1** *The Vertical Economy of the Ancient Middle East.*
Geographically close but contrasting environments were linked by seasonal movements and trade among broad-spectrum foragers. As people traveled and traded, they removed plants from the zones where they grew wild in the hilly flanks into adjacent zones where humans became agents of selection. Food production emerged on the margins of the hilly flanks, at places such as Ali Kosh, rather than within that area, at places such as Jarmo.

**sedentism**
Settled (sedentary) life.

**Natufians**
Widespread Middle Eastern foraging culture (12,800–10,200 B.P.).

**hilly flanks**
Woodland zone just north of Tigris and Euphrates Rivers.

Today, we know that although the world's first civilization (Mesopotamian) did indeed develop in this arid zone, irrigation, a late invention (7000 B.P.), was necessary to farm the alluvial desert. Plant cultivation and animal domestication started not in the dry river zone but in areas with reliable rainfall.

The archaeologist Robert J. Braidwood (1975) proposed instead that food production started in the hilly flanks, or subtropical woodland zone, where wild wheat and barley would have been most abundant (see Figure 11.1). In 1948, a team headed by Braidwood started excavations at Jarmo, an early farming village inhabited between 9000 and 8500 B.P., located in the hilly flanks. We now know that there were farming villages earlier than Jarmo in zones adjacent to the hilly flanks. One example is Ali Kosh (see Figure 11.1), a village in the foothills (piedmont steppe) of the Zagros Mountains. By 9000 B.P., the people of Ali Kosh were herding goats, intensively collecting various wild plants, and harvesting wheat during the late winter and early spring (Hole, Flannery, and Neely 1969).

Climate change played a role in the origin of food production (Bellwood 2005; Smith 1995). Lewis Binford (1968) proposed that in certain areas of the Middle East (such as the hilly flanks), local environments were so rich in resources that foragers could adopt **sedentism**—sedentary (settled) life in villages. Binford's prime example is the widespread Natufian culture (12,800–10,200 B.P.), based on broad-spectrum foraging. The **Natufians,** who collected wild cereals and hunted gazelles, had year-round villages. They could stay in the same place (early villages) because they could harvest nearby wild cereals for six months (see Simmons 2007).

The climate became warmer and more humid just before the Natufian period (Henry 1995). This expanded the altitude range of wild wheat and barley, thus enlarging the available foraging area and allowing a longer harvest season. Wheat and barley ripened in the spring at low altitudes, in the summer at middle altitudes, and in the fall at high altitudes. As locations for their villages, the Natufians chose central places where they could harvest wild cereals in all three zones.

Around 11,000 B.P., this favorable foraging pattern was threatened by a shift to drier conditions. Many wild cereal habitats dried up, and the optimal zone for foraging shrank. Natufian villages were now restricted to areas with permanent water. As

Middle Eastern food production arose in the context of four environmental zones. From highest to lowest, they are high plateau (5,000 feet, or 1,500 meters), hilly flanks, piedmont steppe (treeless plain), and alluvial desert. The last zone is the area watered by the Tigris and Euphrates Rivers (100–500 feet, or 30–150 meters). The **hilly flanks** is a subtropical woodland zone that flanks those rivers to the north (see Figure 11.1).

It once was speculated that food production might have begun in oases in the alluvial desert, places where water would have been available for humans, plants, and animals. (*Alluvial* describes rich, fertile soil deposited by rivers and streams.)

| **RECAP 11.1** | The Transition to Food Production in the Middle East |
| --- | --- |

| ERA | DATES |
| --- | --- |
| Origin of state (Sumer) | 5500 B.P. |
| Increased specialization in food production | 7500–5500 B.P. |
| Early dry farming and caprine domestication | 10,000–7500 B.P. |
| Seminomadic hunting and gathering (e.g., Natufians) | 12,000–10,000 B.P. |

population continued to grow, some Natufians attempted to maintain productivity by transferring wild cereals to well-watered areas, where they started cultivating those cereals.

In the view of many scholars, the people most likely to adopt a new subsistence strategy, such as cultivation, would be those having the most trouble in following their traditional subsistence strategy (Binford 1968; Flannery 1973; Wenke and Olszewski 2007). Thus, those ancient Middle Easterners living outside the area where wild foods were most abundant would be the most likely to experiment and to adopt new subsistence strategies. Recent archaeological finds support this hypothesis that food production began in *marginal areas,* such as the piedmont steppe, rather than in the optimal zones, such as the hilly flanks, where traditional foods were most abundant.

Wild wheat still grows so densely in areas of the hilly flanks that one person working just an hour with Neolithic tools can easily harvest a kilogram of wheat (Harlan and Zohary 1966). People would have had no reason to invent cultivation when wild grain was ample to feed them. Wild wheat ripens rapidly and can be harvested over a three-week period. According to Flannery, over that time period, a family of experienced plant collectors could harvest enough grain—2,200 pounds (1,000 kilograms)—to feed themselves for a year. But after harvesting all that wheat, they'd need a place to put it. They could no longer maintain a nomadic lifestyle: They'd need to stay close to their wheat.

Sedentary village life thus developed before farming and herding in the Middle East. The Natufians and other hilly flanks foragers had no choice but to build villages near the densest stands of wild grains. They needed a place to keep their grain. Furthermore, sheep and goats came to graze on the stubble that remained after humans had harvested the grain. The fact that basic plants and animals were available in the same area also favored village life. Hilly flanks foragers built houses, dug storage pits for grain, and made ovens to roast it.

Natufian settlements, occupied year round, show permanent architectural features and evidence for the processing and storage of wild grains. One such site is Abu Hureyra, Syria (see Figure 11.1), which was initially occupied by Natufian foragers around 11,000 to 10,500 B.P. Then it was abandoned—to be reoccupied later by farmer-herders, between 9500 and 8000 B.P.

Prior to domestication, the favored hilly flanks zone had the densest human population. Approaching *carrying capacity* (the maximum number of people who could be supported by a given subsistence base), that population began to spill over into adjacent, more marginal areas. Colonists from the flanks tried to maintain their traditional broad-spectrum foraging in these marginal zones. But with sparser wild foods available, they had to experiment with new subsistence strategies, including cultivation

(Binford 1968; Bocquet-Appel and Bar-Yosef 2008; Flannery 1969). *Early cultivation began as an attempt to copy, in a less favorable environment, the dense stands of wheat and barley that grew wild in the hilly flanks.*

The Middle East, along with certain other world areas where food production originated, is a region that for thousands of years has had a *vertical economy.* (Other examples include Peru and **Mesoamerica**—Middle America, including Mexico, Guatemala, and Belize.) A vertical economy exploits environmental zones that, although close together in space, contrast with one another in altitude, rainfall, overall climate, and vegetation (see Figure 11.1). Such a close juxtaposition of varied environments allowed broad-spectrum foragers to use different resources in different seasons.

Early seminomadic foragers in the Middle East had followed game from zone to zone. In winter they hunted in the piedmont steppe region, which had winter rains rather than snow and provided winter pasture for game animals 12,000 years ago. (Indeed, it still is used for winter grazing by herders today.) When winter ended, the steppe dried up. Game moved up to the hilly flanks and high plateau country as the snow melted. Pastureland became available at higher elevations. Foragers gathered as they climbed, harvesting wild grains that ripened later at higher altitudes. Sheep and goats followed the stubble in the wheat and barley fields after people had harvested the grain.

The four Middle Eastern environmental zones shown in Figure 11.1 also were tied together through trade. Certain resources were confined to specific zones. Asphalt, used as an adhesive in the manufacture of sickles, came from the steppe. Copper and turquoise sources were located in the high plateau. Contrasting environments were linked in two ways: by foragers' seasonal migration and by trade.

The movement of people, animals, and products between zones—plus population increase supported by highly productive broad-spectrum foraging—was a precondition for the emergence of food production (Bocquet-Appel and Bar-Yosef 2008). As they traveled between zones, people carried seeds into new habitats. Mutations, genetic recombinations, and human selection led to new kinds of wheat and barley. Some of the new varieties were better adapted to the steppe and, eventually, the alluvial desert than the wild forms had been.

## Genetic Changes and Domestication

What are the main differences between wild and domesticated plants? The seeds of domesticated cereals, and often the entire plant, are larger. Compared with wild plants, crops produce a higher yield per unit of area. Domesticated plants also lose their natural seed-dispersal mechanisms. Cultivated beans, for example, have pods that hold together,

**Mesoamerica**
Middle America, including Mexico, Guatemala, and Belize.

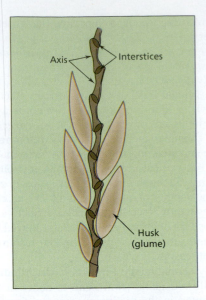

**FIGURE 11.2**   A Head of Wheat or Barley.
In the wild, the axis comes apart as its parts fall off one by one. The connecting parts (interstices) are tough and don't come apart in domesticated grains. In wild grains, the husks are hard. In domestic plants, they are brittle, which permits easy access to the grain. How did people deal with hard husks before domestication?

rather than shattering as they do in the wild. Domesticated cereals have tougher connective tissue holding the seedpods to the stem.

Grains of wheat, barley, and other cereals occur in bunches at the end of a stalk (Figure 11.2). The grains are attached to the stalk by an *axis* (plural, *axes*). In wild cereals, this axis is brittle. Sections of the axis break off one by one, and a seed attached to each section falls to the ground. This is how wild cereals spread their seeds and propagate their species. But a brittle axis is a problem for people. Imagine the annoyance experienced by broad-spectrum foragers as they tried to harvest wild wheat, only to have the grain fall off or be blown away.

In very dry weather, wild wheat and barley ripen—their axes totally disintegrating—in just three days (Flannery 1973). The brittle axis must have been even more irritating to people who planted the seeds and waited for the harvest. But fortunately, certain stalks of wild wheat and barley happened to have tough axes. These were the ones whose seeds people saved to plant the following year.

Another problem with wild cereals is that the edible portion is enclosed in a tough husk. This husk was too tough to remove with a pounding stone. Foragers had to roast the grain to make the husk brittle enough to come off. However, some wild plants happened to have genes for brittle husks. Humans chose the seeds of these plants (which would have germinated prematurely in nature), because they could be more effectively prepared for eating.

People also selected certain features in animals (Miller, Zeder, and Arter 2009; Smith 1995). Some time after sheep were domesticated, advantageous new phenotypes arose. Wild sheep aren't woolly; wool coats were products of domestication. Although it's hard to imagine, a wool coat offers protection against extreme heat. Skin temperatures of sheep living in very hot areas are much lower than temperatures on the surface of their wool. Woolly sheep, but not their wild ancestors, could survive in hot, dry alluvial lowlands.

What are some of the differences between wild and domesticated animals? Plants got larger with domestication, while animals got smaller, probably because smaller animals are easier to control. Middle Eastern sites document changes in the horns of domesticated goats. Such change may have been genetically linked to some other desirable trait that has left no skeletal evidence behind.

Archaeological evidence for herd management (from Iraq and Iran) predates anatomical evidence (e.g., in size or horns) for full animal domestication. For example, certain sites show a focus on killing 2- to 3-year-old males. This suggests a concern with preserving female breeding stock. Those ancient herd managers realized that a steady stream of young immigrant males from surrounding territories would replace slaughtered local males. Herd management also involved moving animals (goats, sheep, cattle, and pigs) from their natural habitats to lower altitudes, where they adapted to hotter, drier climates by becoming smaller. By managing (e.g., selectively

Between 12,000 and 10,000 years ago, foragers in the Middle East followed the availability of plants and animals from lower to higher zones. This pattern evolved into the nomadic herding of domesticated sheep and goats. Here we see a contemporary (2013) herder, a shepherd in Rajasthan, India.

culling) wild animal populations, ancient Middle Easterners were gradually converting their prey animals into herd animals. In doing so, in a process that lasted more than a thousand years, they also were transforming themselves from hunters into herders (Zeder 2008).

## Food Production and the State

The shift from foraging to food production was gradual (see Pandika 2013). The knowledge of how to grow crops and breed livestock didn't immediately convert Middle Easterners into full-time farmers and herders. Domesticated plants and animals began as minor parts of a broad-spectrum economy. Foraging for fruits, nuts, grasses, grains, snails, and insects continued (see Simmons 2007).

Over time, Middle Eastern economies grew more specialized, geared more exclusively toward crops and herds. The former marginal zones became centers of the new economy and of population increase and emigration. Some of the increasing population spilled back into the hilly flanks, where people eventually had to intensify production by cultivating. Domesticated crops could now provide a bigger harvest than could the grains that grew wild there. Thus, in the hilly flanks, too, farming eventually replaced foraging as the economic mainstay.

Farming colonies spread down into drier areas. By 7000 B.P., simple irrigation systems had developed, tapping springs in the foothills. By 6000 B.P., more complex irrigation techniques made agriculture possible in the arid lowlands of southern Mesopotamia. In the alluvial desert plain of the Tigris and Euphrates Rivers, a new economy based on irrigation and trade fueled the growth of an entirely new form of society. This was the *state,* a social and political unit featuring a central government, extreme contrasts of wealth, and social classes.

We now understand why the first farmers lived neither in the alluvial lowlands, where the Mesopotamian state arose around 5500 B.P., nor in the hilly flanks,

Simple irrigation systems, like this one in rural Bangladesh, were being used in the Middle East by 7000 B.P. More complex systems were supporting irrigated agriculture in the arid lowlands of southern Mesopotamia by 6000 B.P.

where wild plants and animals abounded. Food production began in marginal zones, such as the piedmont steppe, where people experimented at reproducing, artificially, the dense grain stands that grew wild in the hilly flanks. As seeds were taken to new environments, new phenotypes were favored by a combination of natural and human selection. The spread of cereal grains outside their natural habitats was part of a system of migration and trade between zones, which had developed in the Middle East during the broad-spectrum period. Food production also owed its origin to the need to intensify production to feed an increasing human population—the legacy of thousands of years of productive foraging (see Bocquet-Appel and Bar-Yosef 2008).

## OTHER OLD WORLD FOOD PRODUCERS

The path from foraging to food production was one that people followed independently in at least seven world areas. At least three were in the Americas, and at least four were in the Old World. In each of these centers, people independently invented domestication, although of different sets of crops and animals.

Food production also spread out from the Middle East. This happened through trade; through the diffusion of plants, animals, products, and information; and through the actual migration of farmers. Middle Eastern domesticates spread westward to northern Africa, including Egypt's Nile Valley, and eventually into Europe (Zeder 2008). Trade also extended eastward to India and Pakistan. In Egypt, an agricultural economy based on plants and animals originally domesticated in the Middle East led to a pharaonic civilization.

## The African Neolithic

Excavations in southern Egypt have revealed considerable complexity in its Neolithic economy and social system, along with very early pottery and cattle, which may have been domesticated locally. Located in southern Egypt, Nabta Playa is a basin in the eastern Sahara Desert that, during prehistoric summers, filled with water. Over several millennia this temporary lake attracted people, who used it for social and ceremonial activities (Wendorf and Schild 2000). Nabta Playa was first occupied around 12,000 B.P., as Africa's summer rains moved northward, providing moisture for grasses, trees, bushes, hares, and gazelle, along with humans. The earliest settlements (11,000–9300 B.P.) at Nabta were small, seasonal camps of herders of domesticated cattle. (Note the very early, and perhaps independent, domestication of cattle here.) According to Wendorf and Schild (2000), Nabta Playa provides early evidence for what anthropologists have called the "African cattle complex," in which cattle are used economically for their milk and blood, rather than killed for their meat (except on ceremonial occasions). Nabta was occupied only seasonally, as people came over from the Nile or from better-watered areas to the south. They returned to those areas in the fall.

By 9000 B.P. people were living at Nabta Playa year round. To survive in the desert, they dug large, deep wells and lived in well-organized villages, with small huts arranged in straight lines. Plant remains show they collected sorghum, millet, legumes (peas and beans), tubers, and fruits. These were wild plants, and so the economy was not fully Neolithic. By 8800 B.P. these people were making their own pottery, possibly the earliest pottery in Egypt. By 8100 B.P. sheep and goats had arrived from the Middle East.

Around 7500 B.P. new settlers occupied Nabta, whose previous inhabitants had been forced away by a major drought. The newcomers brought a more sophisticated social and ceremonial system. They sacrificed young cattle, which they buried in clay-lined chambers covered with stone slabs. They also built Egypt's earliest astronomical measuring device: a "calendar circle" used to mark the summer solstice. Nabta Playa had become a regional ceremonial center: a place where various groups gathered seasonally or occasionally to conduct ceremonies and to socialize. The existence of such centers, as well as their religious, political, and social functions, is familiar to ethnographers who have worked in Africa.

Nabta's role as a regional ceremonial center is also suggested by an alignment of nine large, upright stone slabs near the place where people gathered. This formation, probably dating between 7500 and 5500 B.P., recalls similar large stone alignments, such as Stonehenge, found in western Europe, that were built during the late Neolithic and early Bronze Age.

Construction of such large, complex megalithic structures requires well-organized work parties and a major effort. This suggests that some authority (religious or civil) may have been managing resources and human labor over time. The findings at Nabta Playa represent an elaborate and previously unsuspected ceremonialism, as well as social complexity, during the African Neolithic (see also Sadig 2010).

## The Neolithic in Europe

What about Europe? For generations, scholars have wondered how the Neolithic spread to that continent. Did Middle Eastern farmers colonize Europe, or did their ideas and techniques spread there without any actual migration? Scandinavian scientists recently have found evidence for the actual migration of farmers. They compared DNA from two sets of Swedish burials, both 5,000 years old. One burial

represented a hunter-gatherer group; the other, a farmer group about 400 kilometers away. The ancient hunter-gatherer DNA linked them to living northern Europeans, especially Finns, while the farmer genome resembled that of contemporary southeastern Europeans. The researchers concluded that migrating farmers spread their crops and technology across Europe from the Mediterranean beginning around 8,500 years ago. It took them about 3,000 years to reach northwestern Europe (Skoglund et al. 2012).

New excavations on Cyprus show that the island had been colonized by 10,600 B.P.—the early Neolithic—with village life and farming well underway. This confirms that migration from the mainland began—by boat—shortly after the beginning of farming in the Middle East (Vigne et al. 2012).

Sailing 60 kilometers from the mainland to Cyprus, Neolithic colonists carried with them all four major livestock species (sheep, goats, cattle, and pigs). To Cyprus they introduced the full Neolithic package: farming and herding, technologies, and, most likely, the social networks and belief systems they brought from their original homeland. Rather than an isolated event, the colonization of Cyprus can serve as a model of how the Neolithic spread across the rest of the Mediterranean basin—by boat and seafaring colonists (Zeder 2008).

The Mediterranean basin witnessed a diaspora—slowly at first, then more rapidly—of Neolithic people and their lifestyle westward from the Middle East and Cyprus to the shores of the Atlantic (Zeder 2008). Expansion from Cyprus to the Aegean may have taken as long as 2,000 years. Thereafter, only 500 years were required for seafaring colonists to reach Italy, then just 500–600 years to travel the much greater distance from Italy to the Atlantic. To be more specific, by 8000 B.P., farming villages had been established in Greece and on the Italian coast, first in the southeast and then, by 7800–7600 B.P., the northwest. Soon thereafter, seafaring migrants from Italy began to settle southern France, where a site, dated to 7700–7600 B.P., has yielded pottery, domestic sheep, and wheat. After the Neolithic reached its shores, southern France experienced a marked geographic, ecological, and cultural break between its interior Mesolithic settlements and its coastal Neolithic colonies. Rather than entirely replacing indigenous European foraging populations, the Neolithic colonists seem to have been confined to scattered Mediterranean coastal farming communities (Zeder 2008). By 6000 B.P., however, Europe had thousands of farming villages, from as far east as Russia to as far west as northern France (see Bogaard 2004).

## The Neolithic in Asia

Archaeological research confirms the early (8000 B.P.) presence of domesticated goats, sheep, cattle, wheat, and barley in Pakistan. In that country's Indus River

Valley, ancient cities (Harappa and Mohenjo-daro) emerged slightly later than did the first Mesopotamian city-states. Domestication and state formation in the Indus Valley were influenced by developments in, and trade with, the Middle East.

China was also one of the first world areas to develop farming, based on millet and rice. Millet is a tall, coarse cereal grass still grown in northern China. This grain, which today feeds a third of the world's population, is used in contemporary North America mainly as birdseed. By 7500 B.P., two varieties of millet supported early farming communities in northern China, along the Yellow River. Millet cultivation paved the way for widespread village life and eventually for Shang dynasty civilization, based on irrigated agriculture, between 3600 and 3100 B.P. The northern Chinese also had domesticated dogs, pigs, and possibly cattle, goats, and sheep by 7000 B.P. (Chang 1977).

Discoveries by Chinese archaeologists suggest that rice was domesticated in the Yangtze River corridor of southern China as early as 8400 B.P. (Jiao 2007; Smith 1995). Other early rice comes from the 7,000-year-old site Hemudu, on Lake Dongting in southern China. The people of Hemudu used both wild and domesticated rice, along with domesticated water buffalo, dogs, and pigs. They also hunted wild game (Jolly and White 1995).

China seems to have been the scene of two independent transitions to food production, based on different crops grown in strikingly different climates. Southern Chinese farming was rice aquaculture in rich subtropical wetlands. Southern winters were mild and summer rains reliable. Northern China, by contrast, had harsh winters, with unreliable rainfall during the summer growing season. This was an area of

Nepalese women harvest in a millet field at sunset. Millet was grown in China's Hwang-He (Yellow River) Valley by 7000 B.P. This grain supported early farming communities in northern China. What was being grown in southern China at the same time?

grasslands and temperate forests. Still, in both areas by 7500 B.P., food production supported large and stable villages. Based on the archaeological evidence, early Chinese villagers lived in substantial houses, made elaborate ceramic vessels, and had rich burials.

It appears that food production arose independently at least seven times in different world areas. Figure 11.3 is a map highlighting those seven areas: the Middle East, northern China, southern China, sub-Saharan Africa, central Mexico, the south central Andes, and the

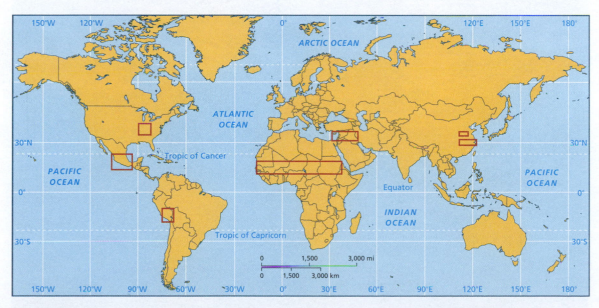

**FIGURE 11.3** *Seven World Areas Where Food Production Was Independently Invented.*
Do any of these areas surprise you?

SOURCE: Bruce D. Smith, *The Emergence of Agriculture* (New York: Scientific American Library, 1995), p. 12. Reprinted by permission of the author. smith.bruce@nmnh.si.edu

Chapter 11  The First Farmers    195

| WORLD AREA | MAJOR DOMESTICATED PLANTS/ANIMALS | EARLIEST DATE (B.P.) |
|---|---|---|
| Middle East | Wheat, barley<br>Sheep, goats, cattle, pigs | 10,000 |
| Andean region | Squash, potato, quinoa, beans<br>Camelids (llama, alpaca), guinea pigs | 10,000–5000 |
| Southern China<br>(Yangtze River corridor) | Rice<br>Water buffalo, dogs, pigs | 8500–6500 |
| Mesoamerica | Maize, beans, squash<br>Dogs, turkeys | 8000–4700 |
| Northern China<br>(Yellow River) | Millet<br>Dogs, pigs, chickens | 7500 |
| Sub-Saharan Africa | Sorghum, pearl millet, African rice | 4000 |
| Eastern United States | Goosefoot, marsh elder, sunflower, squash | 4500 |

SOURCE: Data compiled from Bruce D. Smith, *The Emergence of Agriculture* (New York: Scientific American Library, W. H. Freeman, 1995).

eastern United States. A different set of major foods was domesticated, at different times, in each area, as is shown in Recap 11.2. Some grains, such as millet and rice, were domesticated more than once. Millet grows wild in China and Africa, where it became an important food crop, as well as in Mexico, where it did not. Indigenous African rice, grown only in West Africa, belongs to the same genus as Asian rice. Pigs and probably cattle were independently domesticated in the Middle East, China, and sub-Saharan Africa. Independent domestication of the dog was virtually a worldwide phenomenon, including the Western Hemisphere. We turn now to archaeological sequences in the Americas.

## THE FIRST AMERICAN FARMERS

Benefiting from an abundance of game, human foragers gradually occupied the Americas, learning to cope with a great diversity of environments. Their descendants would eventually turn to farming, paving the way for the emergence of states based on agriculture and trade in Mexico and Peru.

The most significant contrast between Old and New World food production involved animal domestication, which was much more important in the Old World. The animals that had been hunted during the

Early Peruvians and Bolivians ate llama meat, harnessed llamas as beasts of burden, and used llama dung to fertilize their fields. What was the largest animal domesticated in the New World?

early American big-game tradition either became extinct before people could domesticate them or were not domesticable. The largest animal ever tamed in the New World (in Peru, around 4500 B.P.) was the llama. Ancient Peruvians and Bolivians ate llama meat and used that animal as a beast of burden (Flannery, Marcus, and Reynolds 1989). They bred the llama's relative, the alpaca, for its wool. Peruvians also added animal protein to their diet by raising and eating guinea pigs and ducks.

The turkey was domesticated in Mesoamerica and in the southwestern United States. Lowland South Americans domesticated a type of duck. The dog is the only animal that was domesticated throughout the New World. There were no cattle, sheep, or goats in the areas of the Americas where farming arose. Neither herding nor the kinds of relationships that linked Old World farmers and herders developed in the precolonial Americas.

Three key caloric staples, major sources of carbohydrates, were domesticated by Native Americans. **Maize,** or corn, first domesticated in the tropical lowlands of southwestern Mexico, became the caloric staple in Mesoamerica and Central America and eventually reached coastal Peru. The other two staples were root crops: white ("Irish") potatoes, first domesticated in the Andes,

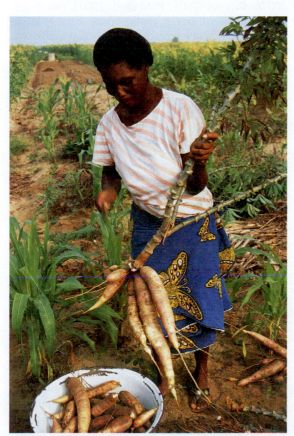

Spreading across oceans and continents, manioc or cassava, originally domesticated in lowland South America, has become a caloric staple throughout the tropics, including Ghana, shown here.

and **manioc,** or cassava, a tuber first cultivated in the South American lowlands, where other root crops such as yams and sweet potatoes also were important. Other crops added variety to New World diets and made them nutritious. Beans and squash provided essential proteins, vitamins, and minerals. Maize, beans, and squash were the basis of the Mesoamerican diet. Anthropologists recently have confirmed that the earliest domesticates in the Americas are about as early as the first Old World domesticates.

Food production was independently invented in at least three areas of the Americas: Mesoamerica, the eastern United States, and the south central Andes. (Mesoamerica is discussed in detail below.) Food plants known as goosefoot and marsh elder, along with the sunflower and a squash, had been domesticated in the eastern United States by 4500 B.P. Those crops supplemented a diet based mainly on hunting and gathering. They never became caloric staples like maize, wheat, rice, millet, manioc, and potatoes. Eventually, maize diffused from Mesoamerica into what is now the United States, reaching both the Southwest and the eastern area just mentioned. Maize provided a more reliable caloric staple for native North American farming. Domestication of several food species was under way in the south central Andes of Peru and Bolivia by 5000 B.P. They were the potato, quinoa (a cereal grain), beans, llamas, alpacas, and guinea pigs (Smith 1995). Anthropologists also have confirmed the (very early) domestication of squash, cotton, and peanuts in Peru.

## The Tropical Origins of New World Domestication

Based on current evidence, New World farming began in the South American lowlands, spreading eventually to Central America, Mexico, and the Caribbean Islands. Archaeologists and botanists have recovered and analyzed microscopic evidence from pollens, starch grains, and phytoliths (plant crystals) (Bryant 2003, 2007a). This evidence has forced revision of the old assumption that New World farming originated in upland areas, such as the highlands of Mexico and Peru. Domesticated squash seeds from Peru date back 10,000 years. Although found in the highlands (western Andes), those seeds, along with other early domesticates from the same site, were not domesticated there originally. Domestication must have occurred even earlier, most probably in South America's tropical lowlands.

Dolores Piperno and Karen Stothert (2003) found that phytoliths from cultivated squashes and gourds are substantially larger than those from wild species. They then used phytolith size to confirm that domesticated squash and gourds (*Cucurbita*) were grown in coastal Ecuador between 9,000 and 10,000 years ago.

manioc
Cassava; tuber domesticated in the South American lowlands.

maize
Corn; first domesticated in tropical southwestern Mexico around 8000 B.P.

Farming in the tropical lowlands of Central and South America started at about the same time as in the Middle East—around 10,000 years ago (Piperno and Pearsall 1998). By that time, people in Panama, Peru, Ecuador, and Colombia were cultivating plants in garden plots near their homes. Between 9000 and 8000 B.P., changes in seed form and phytolith size suggest that farmers were selecting certain characteristics in their cultivated plants. By 7,000 years ago, farmers had expanded their plots into nearby forests, which they cleared using slash-and-burn techniques. By that time, early farming ideas and techniques were diffusing from tropical lowlands into drier regions at higher elevations (Bryant 1999, 2003; Piperno and Pearsall 1998).

What about maize (corn), a major New World crop, long thought to have been domesticated in the Mexican highlands? Recent molecular and genetic studies indicate that maize domestication actually took place in the lowlands of southwestern Mexico. The wild ancestor of maize is a species of **teosinte** (a wild grain) native to the Rio Balsas watershed of tropical southwestern Mexico (Holst, Moreno, and Piperno 2007). Evidence for the evolution of maize

**teosinte**
Wild ancestor of maize; grows wild in southwestern Mexico.

from its wild ancestor has yet to be found in that poorly studied region. Still, we can infer some of the likely steps in maize domestication.

Such a process would have included increases in the number of kernels per cob, the cob size, and the number of cobs per stalk. These changes would make it increasingly profitable to collect wild teosinte and eventually to plant maize. Once people started harvesting wild maize intensively, they became selective agents, taking back to camp a greater proportion of plants with tough axes and cobs. These were the plants most likely to hold together during harvesting and least likely to disintegrate on the way back home. Eventually, teosinte became dependent on humans for its survival, because maize lacks a natural means of dispersal—a brittle axis or cob. If humans chose plants with tough axes inadvertently, their selection of plants with soft husks must have been intentional, as was their selection of larger cobs, more kernels per cob, and more cobs per plant.

A phytolith analysis of sediments from the Mexican state of Tabasco confirms the spread of maize cultivation eastward to the tropical Mexican Gulf Coast by 7300 B.P. Data from many sites now confirm that maize spread rapidly from its domestication cradle in tropical southwestern Mexico during the eighth millennium B.P. (8000–7000) (Bryant 2007*b*; Piperno 2001; Pohl et al. 2007). For example, analysis of starch grains from stone tools in Panama's tropical lowlands confirms that maize was grown there by 7800–7000 B.P. (Dickau, Ranere, and Cooke 2007).

During the last century, for reasons enumerated by Vaughn Bryant (2003), archaeologists tended to seek evidence for early farming in the highlands of Mexico and Peru. These upland areas had caves and rock shelters with preserved plant remains and were located near the centers of civilizations that eventually developed in the Mexican highlands. Decades ago, excavations in the Mexican Valleys of Tehuacan and Oaxaca (see the next section) yielded well-preserved seeds and fruits, along with maize kernels and cobs. Few archaeologists sought the origin of domestication in lowland and jungle regions, which were wrongly assumed to be infertile and where plants did not preserve well (Bryant 2003). Today, the microscopic evidence says otherwise and reveals the key role of tropical lowland regions in early New World farming.

## The Mexican Highlands

Long before Mexican highlanders developed a taste for maize, beans, and squash, they hunted as part of a pattern of broad-spectrum foraging. Mammoth remains dated to 11,000 B.P. have been found along with spear points in the basin that surrounds Mexico City. However, small animals were more important than big game, as were the grains, pods, fruits, and leaves of wild plants.

Two different types of corn (maize) from among the many varieties grown in Oaxaca, Mexico, where archaeologists have studied early highland maize cultivation. Do the earliest Mesoamerican domesticates come from the Mexican highlands?

In the Valley of Oaxaca, in Mexico's southern highlands, between 10,000 and 4000 B.P., foragers concentrated on certain wild animals—deer and rabbits—and plants—cactus leaves and fruits and tree pods, especially mesquite (Flannery 1986). Those early Oaxacans dispersed to hunt and gather in fall and winter. But they came together in late spring and summer, forming larger groups to harvest seasonally available plants. Cactus fruits appeared in the spring. Since summer rains would reduce the fruits to mush and since birds, bats, and rodents competed for them, cactus collection required hard work by large groups of people. The edible pods of the mesquite, available in June, also required intensive gathering.

Eventually, people started planting maize in the alluvial soils of valley floors. This was the zone where foragers traditionally had congregated for the annual spring/summer harvest of cactus fruits and mesquite pods. By 4000 B.P., a type of maize was available that provided more food than the mesquite pods did. Once that happened, people started cutting down mesquite trees and replacing them with cornfields.

By 3500 B.P. in the Valley of Oaxaca, where winter frosts are absent, simple irrigation permitted the establishment of permanent villages based on maize farming. Water close to the surface allowed early farmers to dig wells right in their cornfields. Using pots, they dipped water out of these wells and poured it on their growing plants, a technique known as pot irrigation. Early permanent villages supported by farming appeared in areas of Mesoamerica where there was reliable rainfall, pot irrigation, or access to humid river bottomlands.

The spread of maize farming resulted in further genetic changes, higher yields, higher human populations, and more intensive farming. Pressures to intensify cultivation led to improvements in water-control systems. New varieties of fast-growing maize eventually appeared, expanding the range of areas that could be cultivated. Increasing population and irrigation also helped spread maize farming. The advent of intensive cultivation laid the foundation for the emergence of the state in Mesoamerica—some 3,000 years later than in the Middle East.

## EXPLAINING THE NEOLITHIC

This section focuses on the factors that influenced the origin and spread of Neolithic economies in various world areas. (Much of this section is based on observations in Chapters 8 through 10 of Jared Diamond's influential book *Guns, Germs, and Steel: The Fates of Human Societies* [2005].)

Several factors had to converge to make domestication happen and to promote its spread. Most plants, and especially animals, aren't easy—or particularly valuable—to domesticate. Thus, of some

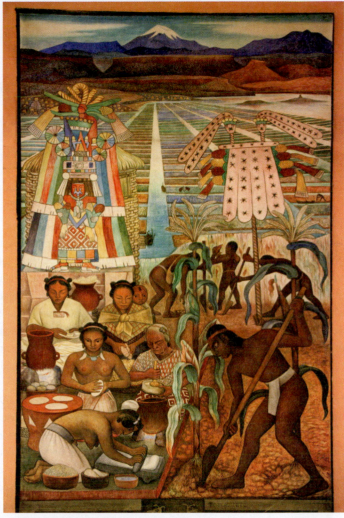

As maize cultivation spread, genetic changes led to higher yields and more productive farming, eventually supporting state-level societies, such as that of the Aztecs. This mural in the National Palace, Mexico City, depicts everyday Aztec life, including growing corn and making flour and bread.

148 large animal species that seem potentially domesticable, only 14 actually have been domesticated. And a mere dozen among 200,000 known plant species account for 80 percent of the world's farm production. Those 12 caloric staples are wheat, corn (maize), rice, barley, sorghum (millet), soybeans, potatoes, cassava (manioc), sweet potatoes, sugarcane, sugar beets, and bananas.

Domestication rested on a combination of conditions and resources that had not come together previously. The development of a full-fledged Neolithic economy required settling down. Sedentism, such as that adopted by ancient Natufian hunter-gatherers, was especially attractive when several species of plants and animals were available locally for foraging and eventual domestication. The Fertile Crescent area of the Middle East had such species, along with a Mediterranean climate favorable to the origin and spread of the Neolithic economy. Among those species were several self-pollinating plants, the easiest

# Global Climate Change and Political Threats to Sites

Global climate change (GCC) involves not only global warming, but also the fact that weather patterns are becoming more extreme and less predictable. GCC threatens archaeological sites, and Andrew Curry (2009) highlights some of those threats, which are summarized here, in locales as diverse as coastal Peru, Greenland, the Eurasian steppes, California's Channel Islands, and Africa's Sahara Desert.

*Coastal Peru.* When Spanish conquistadors arrived in Peru, they noticed a weather phenomenon that occasionally occurred around Christmas. They called it El Niño, or little boy, after the Christ child. El Niño occurs every 3 to 10 years, as currents in the Pacific Ocean shift, changing global weather patterns. In Peru, El Niño brings warmer water and heavy rainfall along the coast. Peru's deserts typically get just over an inch of rain annually. In 1998, a particularly severe El Niño season, the region was seriously flooded with 120 inches of rain. Excess water can threaten archaeological sites, many of which are located along rivers or on easily eroded slopes (Curry 2009). Severe flooding in 2010 closed Machu Picchu, Peru's most famous ancient site, to tourism. If GCC leads to more frequent El Niño years, Peru's archaeological treasures may be further damaged.

*Greenland.* Violent wave action linked to GCC is destroying early coastal sites. Traditionally in summer, Greenland's coasts have been surrounded by an ice belt 30 to 40 miles wide. This drifting ice serves as a shock absorber, dampening the strength of the North Atlantic. In the past decade, however, this ice shield has virtually vanished, and Greenland's coasts are being pounded by huge waves. Most threatened are sites associated with the Thule culture, likely ancestors of the Inuit, whose members reached Greenland about 2,000 years ago. Supported by hunting and fishing, Thule villages were built close to the shore. Today, their ancient homes are disappearing, along with buried tools and artifacts (Curry 2009).

*Scythian Tombs.* Between 3,000 and 2,200 years ago, Scythian nomads dominated the Eurasian steppes from the Black Sea in the west to China in the east. Huge Scythian burial mounds, called kurgans, have been rich resources for archaeologists. Found from Ukraine to Kazakhstan, some of the best-preserved kurgans are located in the Altai Mountains, near Siberian permafrost, where the cold has protected the graves for millennia. The tombs have yielded well-preserved mummies, often with clothing, burial goods,

horses, and even stomach contents intact. With GCC, as the mountains warm up and the permafrost melts, the tombs are in danger of thawing and rotting away (Curry 2009).

*California's Channel Islands.* Some of the early settlers of the Americas came by boat, island-hopping from Siberia down to the California coast. Some of the best evidence for this comes from the Channel Islands, which were occupied at least 13,000 years ago by settlers who hunted pygmy mammoths, elephant seals, and sea lions. Human bones found on Santa Rosa Island, radiocarbon-dated to 13,000 B.P., are the oldest human bones yet found in the Americas. At that time, the world was much colder, and the oceans much lower, than today. Rising sea levels now threaten shell middens and coastal rock shelters. As well, coastal winds, waves, storm surges, and even seals can damage coastal sites. GCC now threatens to wipe out clues about how early humans settled the Americas just as researchers have begun to focus on the likelihood of coastal migration (Curry 2009).

*Desertification in Sudan.* Encroaching desert sands increasingly threaten historic artwork at Musawwarat es-Sufra, Sudan. More than 2,000 years ago, the rulers of Meroe—a desert kingdom

---

wild plants to domesticate, including wheat, which required few genetic changes for domestication. We've seen that the Natufians adopted sedentism prior to farming. They lived off abundant wild grain and the animals attracted to the stubble left after the harvest. Eventually, with climate change, population growth, and the need for people to sustain themselves in the marginal zones, hunter-gatherers started cultivating (see Bocquet-Appel and Bar-Yosef 2008). (See this chapter's "Appreciating Anthropology" for a discussion of contemporary climate change and some of the dangers it poses to archaeological sites.)

Compared with other world areas, the Fertile Crescent region had the largest area with a Mediterranean climate, with the highest species diversity. As we saw previously, this was an area of vertical economy and closely packed microenvironments. Such

diverse terrains and habitats concentrated in a limited area offered a multiplicity of plant species, as well as goats, sheep, pigs, and cattle. As in Mesoamerica, where corn (supplying carbohydrate) was supplemented by squash and beans (supplying protein), the Middle Eastern diet combined caloric staples such as wheat and barley with protein-rich pulses such as lentils, peas, and chickpeas (garbanzo beans).

Anthropologists once thought, erroneously, that domestication would happen almost automatically once people gained sufficient knowledge of plants and animals and their reproductive habits to figure out how to make domestication work. Anthropologists now realize that foragers have an excellent knowledge of plant and animal reproduction, and that some other trigger is needed to start and sustain the process of domestication. A full-fledged Neolithic linked to ancient Egypt—constructed a temple complex and pilgrimage site 20 miles east of the Nile. Built of soft yellow sandstone, the walls and columns of the complex featured hieroglyphs and elaborate painted reliefs. Dominating the site was the 50-foot-long Temple of the Lion God, decorated with reliefs dedicated to the Meroitic god of fertility. Rising temperatures and overuse have killed off the area's vegetation, and Saharan sands creep ever closer. The reliefs suffer heavily from wind erosion, because the soft sandstone abrades easily (Curry 2009).

GCC is not, of course, the only current threat to archaeological sites and research. Political events also pose risks. In 2001 in Afghanistan, the Taliban destroyed a series of pre-Islamic figures, including two monumental stone Buddhas, in an attempt to stop the worship of false idols. In 2013, a group of ancient Islamic manuscripts in Mali's historic city of Timbuktu were threatened by a fire caused by fighting between Islamist militants and French troops.

Politics and regime change also can limit archaeological research. Iran and Iraq have been dangerous or off limits for decades. For on-site investigation of emerging food production and state formation in the Middle East, archaeologists turned increasingly to Syria and Turkey. The former country, too, now is off limits because of po-

The Peruvian village of Aguas Calientes is flooded by the Vilcanota River in January 2010. Heavy rains and mudslides that year blocked the train route to the nearby ancient Inca citadel of Machu Picchu, leaving nearly 2,000 tourists stranded.

litical unrest. Fortunately, previously assembled museum collections of human and animal remains outside those countries allow continuing analysis and new insights (e.g., Zeder 2008), even when national borders are closed to new fieldwork. However, archaeologists who manage museum collections increasingly must deal with nations and cultural groups who wish to repatriate remains collected, often a century ago or more and sometimes without proper legal authorization. Can you think of other threats to archaeological sites and research?

economy requires a minimal set of nutritious domesticates. Some world areas—for example, North America (north of Mesoamerica)—managed independently to invent domestication, but the inventory of available plants and animals was too meager to sustain a Neolithic economy. The early North American domesticates—squash, sunflower, marsh elder, and goosefoot—had to be supplemented by hunting and gathering. A full Neolithic economy and sedentism did not develop in the east, southeast, and southwest of what is now the United States until maize diffused in from Mesoamerica. This happened more than 3,000 years after the first domestication of other plants in the eastern United States.

We've seen how the presence or absence of domesticable animals helps explain the divergent trajectories of the Eastern and Western Hemispheres

in that the mixed economies that developed in Eurasia and Africa never emerged in Mesoamerica. Of the world's 14 large, (over 100 pounds) successful domesticated animal species, 13 are from Eurasia, and only one (the llama) is from South America. Ancient Mexicans domesticated dogs and turkeys and created toy wheels, but they lacked sheep, goats, and pigs as well as the oxen or horses needed to make the wheel a viable transport option. Once the big five Eurasian animal domesticates (cow, sheep, goat, pig, horse) were introduced into Africa and the Americas, they spread rapidly.

We've seen that detailed knowledge of plant reproduction is not a sufficient condition for domestication to occur. Similarly, the knowledge that animals can be tamed or kept as pets isn't enough to produce animal domestication, because not all tamed animals can

**FIGURE 11.4** Major Axes of the Continents.

Note the breadth of the east–west axis in Eurasia, compared with the much narrower east–west spreads in Africa, North America, and South America. Those three continents have north–south as their major axes.

SOURCE: Jared M. Diamond, *Guns, Germs, and Steel: The Fates of Human Societies* (New York: W. W. Norton, 1997), p. 177.

be domesticated. Just as some plants (e.g., self-pollinating annuals) are easier to domesticate than others are, so are some animals. Cattle, dogs, and pigs were so easy to domesticate that they were domesticated independently in multiple world areas.

A key factor in domestication is animal social structure. The easiest wild animals to domesticate live in hierarchical herds. Accustomed to dominance relations, they allow humans to assume superior positions in the hierarchy. Herd animals are easier to domesticate than solitary ones are. Among the latter, only cats and ferrets have been domesticated, and there's some question about the completeness of domestication of those animals (hence the expression "It's like herding cats").

## Geography and the Spread of Food Production

As Jared Diamond (2005, Chapter 10) observes convincingly, the geography of the Old World facilitated the diffusion of plants, animals, technology (e.g., wheels and vehicles), and information (e.g., writing) (see also Ramachandran and Rosenberg 2011). Most crops in Eurasia were domesticated just once and spread rapidly in an east–west direction. The first domesticates spread from the Middle East to Egypt, northern Africa, Europe, India, and eventually China (which, however, also had its own domesticates, as we have seen). By contrast, there was less diffusion of American domesticates.

Figure 11.4 shows that Eurasia has a much broader east–west spread than does Africa or either of the Americas, which are arranged north–south. This is important because climates are more likely to be similar moving across thousands of miles east–west than doing so north–south. In Eurasia, plants and animals could spread more easily east–west than north–south because of common day lengths and similar seasonal variations. More radical climatic contrasts have hindered north–south diffusion. In the Americas, for example, although the distance between the cool Mexican highlands and the South American highlands is just 1,200 miles, those two similar zones are separated by a low, hot, tropical region, which supports very different plant species than the highlands. Such environmental barriers to diffusion kept the Neolithic societies of Mesoamerica and South America more separate and independent than they were in Eurasia. It took some 3,000 years for maize to reach what is now the United States, where productive Neolithic economies eventually did develop. They were based on the cultivation of new varieties of maize adapted to a colder climate and different day lengths.

In the Old World, the spread of Middle Eastern crops southward into Africa eventually was halted by climatic contrasts as well. Certain tropical crops did spread west–east in Africa, but they did not reach southern Africa because of climatic barriers. Again and again, the geographic and climatic barriers posed by high mountains and broad deserts have slowed the spread of domesticates. In what is now the United States, for example, the east–west spread of farming from the Southeast to the Southwest was slowed by the dry climates of Texas and the southern Great Plains.

This section has examined the factors that favored or retarded the origin and spread of Neolithic economies in various world areas. Several factors combined to promote early domestication in the ancient Middle East. The first domesticates spread rapidly across Eurasia, facilitated by climatic similarities across a broad territorial expanse. In the Americas, food production spread less rapidly because of north–south contrasts. Another factor that slowed the Neolithic transition in the Americas was the lack of large animals suitable for domestication. Factors that explain the origin and diffusion of food production involve climate, economic adaptation, demography, and the specific attributes of plants and animals.

## COSTS AND BENEFITS

Food production brought advantages and disadvantages. Among the advantages were discoveries and inventions. People eventually learned to spin and weave; to make pottery, bricks, and arched masonry; and to smelt and cast metals. They developed trade and commerce by land and sea. By 5500 B.P., Middle Easterners were living in vibrant cities with markets, streets, temples, and palaces. They created sculpture, mural art, writing systems, weights, measures, mathematics, and new forms of political and social organization.

Because it increased economic production and led to new social, scientific, and creative forms, food production often is considered an evolutionary advance. But the new economy also brought hardships. For example, food producers typically work harder than foragers do—and for a less adequate diet. Because of their extensive leisure time, foragers have been characterized as living in "the original affluent society" (Sahlins 1972). Certain foragers have survived into recent times and have been studied by anthropologists. Among foragers living in the Kalahari Desert of southern Africa, for example, only part of the group needed to hunt and gather, maybe 20 hours a week, to provide an adequate diet for the entire group. Women gathered, and adult men hunted. Their labor supported older people and children. Early retirement from the food quest was possible, and forced child labor was unknown.

With food production, yields are more reliable, but people work much harder. Herds, fields, and irrigation systems need care. Weeding can require hours of arduous bending. No one has to worry about where to keep a giraffe or a gazelle, but pens and corrals are built and maintained for livestock. Trade takes men, and sometimes women, away from home, leaving burdens for those who stay behind. For several reasons, food producers tend to have more children than foragers do. This means greater child care demands, but child labor also tends to be more needed and valued than it is among foragers.

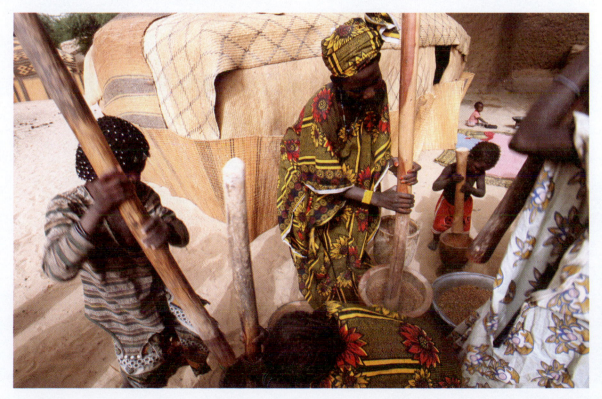

The labor demands of food production far exceed those associated with foraging. Here, in Timbuktu, Mali, a Songhai family pounds grain. Such processing of food is just one step in getting the grain from the fields into people's mouths. What are some of the other steps?

Many tasks in farming and herding can be done by children. The division of economic labor grows more complex, so that children and older people have assigned economic roles.

And public health declines. Diets based on crops and dairy products tend to be less varied, less nutritious, and less healthful than foragers' diets, which usually are higher in proteins and lower in fats and carbohydrates. With the shift to food production, the physical well-being of the population often declines. Communicable diseases, protein deficiency, and dental caries increase (Cohen and Armelagos 1984). Greater exposure to pathogens comes with food production.

Compared with a seminomadic foraging band, food producers tend to be sedentary. Their populations are denser, which makes it easier to transmit and maintain diseases. Malaria, sickle-cell anemia, and smallpox all spread along with food production. Population concentrations, especially cities, are breeding grounds for epidemic diseases. People live nearer to other people and animals and their wastes, which also affect public health (Diamond 2005). Compared with farmers, herders, and city dwellers, foragers were relatively disease free, stress free, and well nourished.

Other hardships and stresses accompanied food production and the state. Social inequality and poverty increased. Elaborate systems of social stratification eventually replaced the egalitarianism of the past. Resources were no longer common goods, open to all, as they tend to be among foragers. Property distinctions proliferated. Slavery and other forms of human bondage eventually were invented.

Crime, war, and human sacrifice became widespread.

The rate at which human beings degraded their environments also increased with food production. The environmental degradation in today's world, including air and water pollution and deforestation, is on a much larger scale, compared with early villages and cities, but modern trends are foreshadowed. After food production, population increase and the need to expand farming led to deforestation in the Middle East. Even today, many farmers think of trees as giant weeds to be cut down to make way for productive fields. Previously, we saw how early Mesoamerican farmers cut down mesquite trees for maize cultivation in the Valley of Oaxaca.

Many farmers and herders burn trees, brush, and pasture. Farmers burn to remove weeds; they also use the ashes for fertilizer. Herders burn to promote the growth of new, tender shoots for their livestock. But such practices do have environmental costs, including air pollution. Smelting and other chemical processes basic to the manufacture of metal tools also have environmental costs. As modern industrial pollution has harmful effluents, early chemical processes had by-products that polluted air, soils, and waters. Salts, chemicals, and microorganisms accumulate in irrigated fields. Pathogens and pollutants that were non-issues during the Paleolithic endanger growing human populations. To be sure, food production had benefits. But its costs are just as evident. Recap 11.3 summarizes the costs and benefits of food production. We see that *progress* is much too optimistic a word to describe food production, the state, and many other aspects of the evolution of society.

| RECAP 11.3 | The Benefits and Costs of Food Production (Compared with Foraging) |
|---|---|

| | DO THE COSTS OUTWEIGH THE BENEFITS? |
|---|---|
| **BENEFITS** | **COSTS** |
| Discoveries and inventions | Harder work |
| New social, political, scientific, and creative forms (e.g., spinning, weaving, pottery, bricks, metallurgy) | Less nutritious diets |
| | Child labor and child care demands |
| Monumental architecture, arched masonry, and sculpture | Taxes and military drafts |
| Writing | Public health declines (e.g., more exposure to pathogens, including communicable and epidemic diseases) |
| Mathematics, weights, and measures | Rise in protein deficiency and dental caries |
| Trade and markets | Greater stress |
| Urban life | Social inequality and poverty |
| Increased economic production | Slavery and other forms of human bondage |
| More reliable crop yields | Rise in crime, war, and human sacrifice |
| | Increased environmental degradation (e.g., air and water pollution, deforestation) |

summary

1. By 10,000 B.P., people were pursuing broad-spectrum economies in western Europe. Tool kits adapted to a forested environment included small, delicately shaped stone tools called microliths. The Mesolithic had begun. The broad-spectrum revolution, based on a wide variety of dietary resources, began in the Middle East somewhat earlier than in Europe. It culminated in the first food-producing economies in the Middle East around 10,000 B.P.

2. By 10,000 B.P., domesticated plants and animals were part of a broad spectrum of resources used by Middle Easterners. By 7500 B.P., most Middle Easterners were moving away from broad-spectrum foraging toward more specialized food-producing economies. *Neolithic* refers to the period when the first signs of domestication appeared.

3. Braidwood proposed that food production started in the hilly flanks zone, where wheat and barley grew wild. Others questioned this: The wild grain supply in that zone already provided an excellent diet for the Natufians and other ancient Middle Easterners. There would have been no incentive to domesticate. Other scholars view the origin of food production in the context of increasing population and climate changes.

4. Ancient Middle Eastern foragers migrated seasonally in pursuit of game. They also collected wild plant foods as the plants ripened at different altitudes. As they moved about, these foragers took grains from the hilly flanks zone, where they grew wild, to adjacent areas. Population spilled over from the hilly flanks into areas like the piedmont steppe. In such marginal zones, people started cultivating plants. They were trying to duplicate the dense wild grains of the hilly flanks.

5. After the harvest, sheep and goats fed off the stubble of these wild plants. Animal domestication occurred as people started selecting certain features and behavior and guiding the reproduction of goats, sheep, cattle, and pigs. Gradually, food production spread into the hilly flanks. Later, with irrigation it spread down into Mesopotamia's alluvial desert, where the first cities, states, and civilizations developed by 5500 B.P. Food production then spread west from the Middle East into North Africa and Europe and east to India and Pakistan.

6. There were at least seven independent inventions of food production: in the Middle East, sub-Saharan Africa, northern and southern China, Mesoamerica, the south central Andes, and the eastern United States. Millet was domesticated by 7000 B.P. in northern China; rice, by 8000 B.P. in southern China.

7. In the New World the most important domesticates were maize, potatoes, and manioc. The llama of the central Andes was the largest animal domesticated in the New World, where herding traditions analogous to those of the Old World did not develop. Economic similarities between the hemispheres must be sought in foraging and farming.

8. New World farming started in the lowlands of South America, then spread to Central America, Mexico, and the Caribbean Islands. Tropical lowland cultivation in Central and South America began at about the same time as food production arose in the Middle East—around 10,000 years ago. By 7000 B.P., farming was diffusing from tropical lowlands into drier regions at higher elevations. The ancestor of maize, teosinte, grows wild in tropical southwestern Mexico, where maize probably was domesticated around 8000 B.P. At Oaxaca, in Mexico's southern highlands, maize was gradually added to a broad-spectrum diet by 4000 B.P.

9. Several factors, including a diversity of useful plant and animal species and early sedentism, combined to promote domestication in the ancient Middle East. Domesticates spread rapidly across Eurasia, facilitated by climatic similarities across a broad territorial expanse. In the Americas, food production spread less rapidly because of north–south contrasts.

Another factor that slowed the Neolithic transition in the Americas was the lack of large animals suitable for domestication. Factors that explain the origin and diffusion of food production involve climate, economic adaptation, demography, and the specific attributes of plants and animals.

10. Food production and the social and political system it supported brought advantages and disadvantages. The advantages included discoveries and inventions. The disadvantages included harder work, poorer health, crime, war, social inequality, and environmental degradation.

# key terms

broad-spectrum revolution 187

hilly flanks 190

maize 197

manioc 197

Mesoamerica 191

Mesolithic 188

Natufians 190

Neolithic 189

sedentism 190

teosinte 198

# critical thinking

1. What is revolutionary about what Kent Flannery (1969) called the "broad-spectrum revolution"? What other more recent events in history do you consider revolutionary? Why?

2. Why is the lack of animal domestication in Mesoamerica considered a key factor in world history?

3. Previously, anthropologists had believed that Old World (Middle Eastern) farming predated the earliest cultivation in the Americas by three or four millennia. How have new dating techniques pushed back the origin of domestication in the New World?

4. In this chapter, what are some examples of the role geography plays in key events in human history? Geography also affects how we come to know about the past. How so?

5. Was the origin of food production good or bad? Why?

# The First Cities and States

▶ When, where, and why did early states originate, and what were their key attributes?

▶ How do archaeologists distinguish between chiefdoms and states?

▶ What similarities and differences marked the origin of early states in the Old World and the New World?

Overview of terraced royal Inca ruins at Machu Picchu, Peru, which has been designated one of the seven wonders of today's world.

# understanding OURSELVES

"You're not the boss of me": Have you ever heard or uttered those words? Who might say them to whom? Certainly, you would not be likely to say this to an employer, or to a police officer who had just pulled you over, or to someone judging you in a court of law. We resent it when our siblings, cousins, or friends tell us what to do. But we learn to call judges "Your Honor"; police officers "Officer," "Detective," "Lieutenant," "Captain," or "Chief"; and employers "Ms." or "Mr." (as in "Mr. Trump"). Such titles (honorifics) mark differences in status and authority. Generally, we learn to respect and obey such people ("the authorities"). That is, we follow their orders or instructions, as people in the military routinely do with their superiors.

Marked contrasts in status, power, wealth, and privilege distinguish cities and states from the societies that came before them. Everyone reading this book lives in a state-organized society. Our lives differ dramatically from those of our Paleolithic ancestors, or those of more recent foragers. The state has a lot to do with these differences. The demand for labor (human, animal, etc.) increased in Neolithic economies compared with Paleolithic times. This trend continued in states, whose economies and political systems have placed even greater demands on ordinary people.

Perhaps you've seen a museum display depicting an early state society (e.g., Egypt, Mesopotamia, Maya). Such exhibits tend to highlight the artistic, architectural, literary, and scientific achievements of those civilizations. Ancient Sumerians (in Mesopotamia), Egyptians, Mexicans, and Peruvians had their artists, architects, mathematicians, astronomers, priests, and rulers—just as we do. However (but depicted more rarely), their ordinary citizens had to sweat in the fields to grow food for landlords, specialists, and elites. Unlike hunter-gatherers, residents of states must deal with bosses, despots, and commanders. The elites of ancient states could summon involuntary labor to build temples and pyramids, and to move stone for enduring monuments. In all states, people must pay taxes; in many states, citizens are drafted for work or war. Ordinary people no longer set their own priorities.

How do modern state-organized societies mirror those of the past? Ordinary people no longer may be drafted for work or war, but we do have to work to pay the taxes that pay for wars and public works. Our society is still stratified. Perks still go with wealth, fame, and power. Most of us still work much harder (usually for bosses) than foragers ever did. It's a myth that leisure time has increased with civilization. For a few, there is leisure and privilege; for most, there is work and obligation. And that's not because of human nature; it's because of the state.

## THE ORIGIN OF THE STATE

As Neolithic economies spread, diversified, and became more productive, new political entities, or **polities** (singular, *polity*), developed to manage them. The major new political forms were chiefdoms and states. A **chiefdom** is a polity with hereditary leaders and a permanent political structure. Its people are ranked relative to one another and have differential access to resources: Some have more and some have less. They are not, however, divided into clearly defined social classes. Often in chiefdoms, individuals are ranked in terms of their genealogical distance from the chief. The closer one is to the chief the greater one's social importance.

A **state** is a polity that has a formal, central government and *social stratification*—a division of society into classes. The first states had developed in Mesopotamia by 5500 B.P. and in Mesoamerica about 3,000 years later. Chiefdoms were precursors to states, with privileged and effective leaders—chiefs—but lacking the sharp class divisions that characterize states. By 7000 B.P. in the Middle East and 3200 B.P. in Mesoamerica, there is evidence for what archaeologists call the *elite level* of social and political organization, indicating a chiefdom or a state.

How and why did these new polities originate? The development and spread of Neolithic economies fueled population growth and established large group settlements. New tasks, activities, and functions emerged in the larger and denser populations. Systems of political authority and control typically develop to handle regulatory problems that arise as the population grows, social groups proliferate, and the economy increases in scale and diversity.

**Primary states** are states that arose on their own, not through contact with other state societies (Wright 1994). Also called archaic states or first-generation states, primary states emerged from competition among chiefdoms, as one chiefdom managed to conquer its neighbors and make them part of a larger political unit (Stanish and Levine 2011). Scholars have documented the process of state formation in at least six areas where first-generation states are known to have developed: Egypt, Mesopotamia, the Indus River Valley, northern China, Mesoamerica, and the Andes (Millaire 2010).

A systemic, regional perspective is necessary to understand any case of state formation. Primary states emerge from a regional process that requires a long period (generations) of interaction among competing polities (Stanish and Levine 2011). Furthermore, multiple factors always contribute to state formation, with the effects of one magnifying those of the others.

## Hydraulic Systems

One factor favoring state formation has been the need to regulate hydraulic (water-based) agricultural economies (Wittfogel 1957). In arid areas, such as ancient Egypt and Mesopotamia, a key role of state officials was to manage systems of irrigation, drainage, and flood control. Hydraulic agriculture spurs state formation because it has certain implications. Because it can feed more people, while requiring more labor, irrigated agriculture sustains and fuels population growth, which in turn promotes expansion of the system. With larger and denser concentrations of people, the potential grows for conflict over access to water and irrigated land.

Political authorities typically arise to regulate production, as well as to manage interpersonal and intergroup relations. Regulators protect the economy by mobilizing crews to maintain and repair the hydraulic system, and they settle disputes about access to water. These life-and-death functions enhance the authority of state officials. Thus, growth in hydraulic systems is often (as in Mesopotamia, Egypt, and the Valley of Mexico) but not always associated with state formation.

## Regional Trade

Charles Stanish and Abigail Levine (2011) emphasize regional trade as another key factor in primary state formation. States may arise to control and regulate key nodes in regional trade networks. Examples include crossroads of caravan routes and places (e.g., mountain passes and river narrows) situated to threaten trade between centers. Long-distance trade has been important in the formation of many states, including those of Mesopotamia, Mesoamerica, and Peru (Hirth and Pillsbury 2013). Long-distance trade also exists, however, in areas where no primary states developed, such as in Papua New Guinea.

## Population, War, and Circumscription

Robert Carneiro (1970) saw three key factors interacting to produce state formation. Those factors are environmental circumscription, increasing population, and warfare (see Figure 12.1). Environmental circumscription may be either physical or social. Physically circumscribed environments include small islands and, in arid areas, river plains, oases, and valleys with streams—areas surrounded by some boundary. Social circumscription exists when neighboring societies block expansion, emigration, or access to resources. When strategic resources are concentrated in limited areas—even when no obstacles to migration exist—the effects are similar to those of circumscription.

Coastal Peru, usually one of the world's most arid areas, illustrates the interaction of environmental circumscription, warfare, and population increase. The earliest cultivation there was limited to valleys with springs. Each valley was circumscribed by the Andes Mountains to the east, the Pacific Ocean to the west, and desert regions to the north and south (see Millaire 2010). The advent of food production triggered population increase, leading to bigger villages in each valley. Colonists split off from the old villages and founded new ones. With more villages and people, a scarcity of land developed. Rivalries and raiding developed among villages in the same valley.

Because the valleys were circumscribed, when one village conquered another, the losers had to submit to the winners—they had nowhere else to go. Conquered villagers were allowed to keep their land

**polity**
Political entity, such as a chiefdom or state.

**chiefdom**
Society with permanent political structure, hereditary leaders, and social ranking but lacking class divisions.

**state**
Society with central government, administrative specialization, and social classes.

**primary states**
States arising through competition among chiefdoms.

Victors create large empires

↑

Intervalley warfare between states

↑

Valley states form as one chiefdom conquers all others

↑

Interchiefdom warfare

↑

Larger political units (chiefdoms) form

↑

Warfare intensifies

↑

Population increase continues

↑

More intensive agricultural techniques

↑

Some villages conquered, pay tribute

↑

Intravalley conflict over land

↑

Further population increase

↑

Intervillage, intravalley warfare

↑

New settlements spring up

↑

Population increase

↑

Cultivation begins in river valleys

**FIGURE 12.1** Carneiro's Approach to the Origin of the State as Applied to Coastal Peru.
In this very arid area, food production developed in narrow river valleys where water for cultivation was available (resource concentration). With cultivation, the population increased. Population pressure on land led to warfare, and some villages conquered others. Physical circumscription meant that the losers had no way to escape. The process accelerated as the population grew and as warfare and cultivation intensified. Chiefdoms, states, and empires eventually developed.

only by paying tribute to their conquerors. To do this, they had to intensify production, using new techniques to produce more food. By working harder, they managed to pay tribute while meeting their own subsistence needs. Villagers brought new areas under cultivation by means of irrigation and terracing.

Those early Peruvians didn't work harder because they chose to do so. They were forced to pay tribute,

accept political domination, and intensify production by factors beyond their control. Once established, all these trends accelerated. Population continued to grow, warfare intensified, and villages eventually were united in chiefdoms. The first states developed when one chiefdom in a valley conquered the others (Carneiro 1990; Stanish and Levine 2011). Eventually, different valleys began to fight. The winners brought the losers into growing states and empires, which eventually expanded from the coast to the highlands. (An **empire** is a mature state that is large, multiethnic, militaristic, and expansive.) By the 16th century, from their capital, Cuzco, in the high Andes, the Inca ruled one of the major empires of the tropics.

Sometimes, however, the coexistence of population increase, warfare, and circumscription is insufficient to spur state formation. In highland Papua New Guinea, for example, valleys that were socially or physically circumscribed had population densities close to those of many states. Warfare also was present, but no states emerged. Whether states would have formed eventually will never be known, because European conquest truncated autonomous development there.

In any case of state formation, interacting causes (often comparable ones) magnified each other's effects. Key ingredients in state formation are changes in patterns of control over resources, resulting in social stratification, and increasing regulatory concerns, fostering management by state machinery. Different agencies arise to handle particular functions. We must remember, too, that chiefdoms and states don't inevitably arise from food production. Many societies with Neolithic economies never developed chiefdoms or states. Similarly, there are chiefdoms that never developed into states, just as certain foragers never adopted food production, even when they knew about it.

# THE URBAN REVOLUTION

It was V. Gordon Childe (1951), one of the most influential archaeologists of the 20th century, who coined the phrase "Neolithic Revolution" to describe the origin and impact of food production. He chose the term *revolution* deliberately, because he wanted to compare the major social transformations of prehistory (food production and the state) to the Industrial Revolution (Smith 2009). Childe used the phrase "Urban Revolution" (1950) to describe the major transformation of human life and social institutions examined in this chapter. A key feature was that institutions of government, including rulers with real power, emerged for the first time, along with social stratification. As a result of the Urban Revolution, economic activity of all sorts expanded greatly, and the first cities were built. On the downside, former freedoms and independence were replaced by servitude, taxes, rules, and regulations (Smith 2009).

Childe listed 10 key attributes of early cities and states—all supported by archaeological evidence. They may be paraphrased as follows:

1. The first cities were larger and more densely populated than previous settlements.

2. Within the city were full-time specialist craftsmen, transport workers, merchants, officials, and priests.

3. Each primary producer (e.g., farmer) had to pay a tithe or tax to a deity or a divine king; those contributions were stored in a central place, such as a temple or treasury.

4. Monumental buildings distinguished cities from villages while also symbolizing the right of rulers to draw on the treasury and to command a labor force.

5. Supported by the treasury, priests, civil officials, and military leaders made up a ruling class.

6. Writing was used for record keeping.

7. Predictive sciences developed, including arithmetic, geometry, and astronomy.

8. Sophisticated art styles developed, expressed in sculpture, painting, and architecture.

9. There was long-distance and foreign trade.

10. Society was reorganized on the basis of territorial divisions (where one lived) rather than kinship groups.

Cities and writing were key features of Childe's Urban Revolution (1950). In and after the 1960s, however, anthropologists shifted to such phrases as "the origin of the state" and "state formation" for this process. Use of such terms, which continues today, recognizes that some instances of state formation lack writing and significant urbanism (see Peregrine, Ember, and Ember 2007; Spencer and Redmond 2004).

## ATTRIBUTES OF STATES

Childe's list of 10 defining attributes of the Urban Revolution aptly describes the first states in Mesopotamia and Egypt. Something a bit less specific, however, is needed to characterize all states, including those without writing. Most anthropologists today probably would agree that the following attributes (some shared with Childe's list) distinguished states from earlier forms of society:

1. A state controls a specific regional territory, such as the Nile Valley or the Valley of Mexico. The regional expanse of a state contrasts with the much smaller territories controlled by kin groups and villages in prestate societies. Early states were expansionist; they arose from competition among chiefdoms, as the most powerful chiefdom conquered others, extended its rule over a larger territory, and managed to hold on to, and rule, the land and people acquired through conquest.

Early states had hereditary rulers and a military, with the rulers often playing a military role. Rulers stayed in power by combining personal ability, religious authority, economic control, and the privileged use of force. Shown here is a detail from the painted casket of Egypt's Tutankhamun, the famous "King Tut," who ruled between 1347 and 1337 B.C.E.

# focus on GLOBALIZATION

## The Seven Wonders of the World

States are precursors to empires, which are precursors to the world system and globalization. The state is an expansive form of human social organization that wields considerable power. Many states have developed into empires that cover huge territories and rule large numbers of people. Some historic examples include the Persian empire, the empire created by Alexander the Great, the Roman and Byzantine empires, the Ottoman empire, and most recently the British and French empires. The Inca (Peru) and Aztec (Mexico) empires are New World examples.

States clearly mark their environments. They build; they create a "built environment"—architecture that lasts and that archaeologists can study to determine the spread and influence of ancient states. Early states erected imposing public buildings and monumental architecture, including temples, palaces, and storehouses.

Occasionally, a feature of a state's "built environment" is impressive enough to earn it the status of "wonder of the world." The "Seven Wonders of the Ancient World" were renowned among ancient Greeks and other Mediterranean tourists, particularly in the first and second centuries B.C.E. Those sites worth seeing were close to, or on, the eastern rim of the Mediterranean Sea. Of them, only the Great Pyramid of Giza, the oldest of the seven wonders, is still standing after all those years.

Listed in order from oldest to youngest, the seven wonders of the ancient world are as follows: the Great Pyramid of Giza (constructed by ancient Egyptians), the Hanging Gardens of Babylon (Babylonians), the Temple of Artemis at Ephesus (Lydians, Persians, Greeks), the Statue of Zeus at Olympia (Greeks), the Mausoleum of Halicarnassus (Carians, Persians, Greeks), the Colossus of Rhodes (Greeks), and the Lighthouse of Alexandria (Ptolemaic Egyptians, Greeks).

Today's world has its own seven wonders, selected through a worldwide popular vote and announced in 2007. The New Seven Wonders of the World (2001–2007) was an initiative launched in 2001 by a Swiss corporation to choose new wonders from a selection of 200 existing monuments through a popularity poll. The winners—from oldest to youngest, based on when construction began—were Petra (Jordan), the Great Wall of China (Beijing), the Colosseum (Rome, Italy), Chichén Itzá (Yucatan, Mexico), Machu Picchu (Peru), the Taj Mahal (Agra, India), and the Christ the Redeemer statue (Corcovado) (Rio de Janeiro, Brazil). Common to all these wonders—ancient and modern—is that they were erected by states, often for political or religious reasons, and eventually they became sites that people wanted to visit to marvel at these creations. Sightseeing tourism certainly existed in the ancient world, but on a much more limited scale than today. Nowadays, in the context of global tourism, the world's most popular attractions still include monuments named for people (e.g., Washington, Lincoln, Eiffel, Disney) and structures built for religious reasons (e.g., St. Peter's in Rome, Notre Dame de Paris, Hagia Sofia in Istanbul). No doubt the seven wonders of today's world are "must sees" for anyone doing tourism in a given country. I've seen five of the seven. How about you?

The Taj Mahal, in Agra, India, is considered one of the seven wonders of today's world.

2. Early states had productive farming economies, supporting dense populations, often in cities. The agricultural economies of early states usually involved some form of water control or irrigation.

3. Early states used tribute and taxation to accumulate, at a central place, resources needed to support hundreds, or thousands, of specialists. These states had rulers, a military, and control over human labor.

4. States are stratified into social classes. In the first states, the non-food-producing population consisted of a tiny elite, plus artisans, officials, priests, and other specialists. Most people were commoners. Slaves and prisoners constituted the lowest rung of the social ladder. Rulers stayed in power by combining personal ability, religious authority, economic control, and force.

5. Early states had imposing public buildings and monumental architecture, including temples, palaces, and storehouses. (See this chapter's "Focus on Globalization" for some of the most impressive examples of monumental architecture.)

6. Early states developed some form of record-keeping system, usually a written script (Fagan 1996).

# STATE FORMATION IN THE MIDDLE EAST

In the last chapter we saw that Neolithic economies emerged in the ancient Middle East around 10,000 B.P. In the ensuing process of change, the center of population growth shifted from the zone where wheat and barley grew wild to adjacent areas where those grains were first domesticated. By 6000 B.P., population was increasing most rapidly in the alluvial plain of southern Mesopotamia. (**Mesopotamia** refers to the area between the Tigris and Euphrates Rivers in what is now southern Iraq and southwestern Iran.) This growing population supported itself through irrigation and intensive river valley agriculture. By 5500 B.P. towns had grown into cities (Gates 2003). The earliest city-states were Sumer (southern Iraq) and Elam (southwestern Iran), with their capitals at Uruk (Warka) and Susa, respectively.

## Urban Life

The first towns arose around 10,000 years ago in the Middle East. Over the generations, houses of mud brick were built and rebuilt in the same place. Substantial *tells,* or mounds, arose from the debris of a

The world's earliest known town is Jericho, located in what now is Israel. Jericho was first settled by Natufian foragers around 11,000 B.P. The round tower in this photo dates back 8,000 years.

succession of such houses. These sites have yielded remains of ancient community life, including streets, buildings, terraces, courtyards, wells, and other artifacts. The earliest known town was Jericho, located in what is now Israel, at a well-watered oasis near the Dead Sea (Figure 12.2). From the lowest (oldest) level, we know that around 11,000 years ago Jericho was first settled by Natufian foragers. Occupation continued thereafter, through and beyond biblical times, when "Joshua fit the battle of Jericho, and the walls came tumbling down" (Laughlin 2006).

**Mesopotamia**
Area where earliest states developed, between Tigris and Euphrates Rivers.

**FIGURE 12.2** Sites in Middle Eastern State Formation.

During the phase just after the Natufians, the earliest known town appeared. It was an unplanned, densely populated settlement with round houses and about 2,000 people. The town was surrounded by a sturdy wall with a massive tower. The wall may have been built initially as a flood barrier rather than for defense. Around 9000 B.P. Jericho was destroyed, to be rebuilt later. The new occupants lived in square houses with finished plaster floors. They buried their dead beneath their homes, a pattern seen at other sites, such as Çatalhöyük in Turkey (see the following paragraph). Pottery reached Jericho around 8000 B.P. (Gowlett 1993).

**Halafian**
Early (7500–6500 B.P.), widespread Mesopotamian pottery style.

Long-distance trade, especially of obsidian, a volcanic glass used to make tools and ornaments, became important in the Middle East between 9500 and 7000 B.P. One town that prospered from this trade was Çatalhöyük in Anatolia, Turkey (Fowler 2011; Hodder 2006). A grassy mound 65 feet high holds the remains of this 9,000-year-old town, probably the largest settlement of the Neolithic age. Çatalhöyük was located on a river, which deposited rich soil for crops, created a lush environment for animals, and was harnessed for irrigation by 7000 B.P. Over the mound's 32 acres (12.9 hectares), up to 10,000 people once lived in crowded mud-brick houses packed so tightly that residents entered from their roofs.

Shielded by a defensive wall, Çatalhöyük flourished between 8000 and 7000 B.P. Its mud-brick dwellings, rarely larger than an American bedroom, had separate areas reserved for ritual and secular uses. In a given house, the ritual images (wall paintings) were placed along the walls that faced north, east, or west, but never south. That area was reserved for cooking and other domestic tasks.

The ritual spaces were decorated with wall paintings, sculpted ox heads, bull horns, and relief models of bulls and rams. The paintings showed bulls surrounded by stick figures running, dancing, and sometimes throwing stones. Vultures attacked headless humans. One frieze had human handprints painted below mounted bull horns. These images and their placement are reminiscent of Paleolithic cave art. The dwellings at Çatalhöyük were entered through the roof, and people had to crawl through holes from room to room, somewhat like moving between chambers in a cave. The deeper down one went, the richer the art became. The town's spiritual life seems to have revolved around a preoccupation with animals, danger, and death, perhaps related to the site's hunter-gatherer past.

Two or three generations of a family were buried beneath their homes. In one dwelling, archaeologists found remains of 17 individuals, mostly children. After two or three generations of family burials, the dwelling was burned. The site was then covered with fine dirt and a floor laid for a new dwelling.

Çatalhöyük's residents, although they lived in a town, acted independently in family groups without any apparent control by a priestly or political elite. The town never became a full-fledged city with centralized organization. Just as it lacked priests, Çatalhöyük never had leaders who controlled or managed trade and production. Food was stored and processed not collectively but on a smaller, domestic scale (DeMarco 1997; Fowler 2011; Hodder 2006).

## The Elite Level

The first Middle Eastern pottery dates back a bit more than 8,000 years, when it first reached Jericho. By 7000 B.P., pottery had become widespread in the Middle East. Archaeologists consider pottery shape, finishing, decoration, and type of clay as features used for dating. The geographic distribution of a given pottery style may indicate trade or an alliance spanning a large area at a particular time.

An early and widespread pottery style, the **Halafian,** was first found at Tell Halaf in the mountains of northern Syria. *Halafian* (7500–6500 B.P.) refers to a delicate ceramic style. It also describes the period during which the elite level and the first chiefdoms emerged (by 7000 B.P.). The low number of Halafian ceramics suggests they were luxury goods associated with a social hierarchy.

The Ubaid period (7000–6000 B.P.) is named for a southern Mesopotamian pottery type first discovered at a small site, Tell el-Ubaid, located near the major city of Ur in southern Iraq. Similar pottery has been discovered in the deep levels of the Mesopotamian cities of Ur, Uruk, and Eridu. Ubaid pottery is associated with advanced chiefdoms and perhaps the earliest states. It diffused rapidly over a large area, becoming more widespread than earlier ceramic styles such as the Halafian.

Archaeological research focusing on the Ubaid period farther north, in northern Syria, has found evidence for emerging urbanism dating back more than 6,000 years. In two seasons (2008, 2009) of preliminary surveying and digging at a site known as Tell Zeidan, American and Syrian investigators uncovered an array of artifacts from an early town on the upper Euphrates River. People occupied this site for two millennia, until 6000 B.P. The site, dominated by three large mounds, featured houses with mud-brick walls, floors with hearths, painted pottery, stone seals, kilns, and obsidian blades. There also is evidence suggesting the emergence of irrigated agriculture, long-distance trade, political leadership, and social differentiation (Wilford 2010).

Blocked by war from Iraq (with its prime sites of Mesopotamian antiquity), archaeologists, including the Tell Zeidan researchers, could still work in Syria. They turned their attention to the upper river valleys, across the border from Iraq in Syria and southern Turkey (see Hodder 2006; Wilford 2010). Unfortunately, recent political unrest in Syria has impeded continuation of archaeological research there, leaving Turkey as today's prime locus for research on Neolithic transformations and the emergence of social complexity in the Middle East (see Özdoğan, Başgelen, and Kuniholm 2011).

## Social Ranking and Chiefdoms

It's easy for archaeologists to identify early states. Evidence for state organization includes monumental architecture, central storehouses, irrigation systems, and written records. In Mesoamerica, even chiefdoms are easy to detect archaeologically. Ancient Mexican chiefdoms left behind stone works, such as temple complexes and the huge carved Olmec heads (see p. 221). Mesoamericans also had a penchant for distinguishing their elites with durable ornaments and prestige goods, including those buried with chiefs and their families. Early Middle Eastern chiefs, by contrast, were less ostentatious in their use of material markers of prestige, making their chiefdoms somewhat harder to detect archaeologically (Flannery 1999).

Considering the degrees of status differentiation within a society, the anthropologist Morton Fried (1960) divided societies into three types: egalitarian, ranked, and stratified. An **egalitarian society,** most typically found among foragers, lacks status distinctions except for those based on age, gender, and individual talents or achievements. Thus, depending on the society, adult men, elder women, talented musicians, or ritual specialists might receive special respect for their activities or knowledge. In egalitarian societies, status distinctions are not usually inherited. The child of a respected person will not receive special recognition because of his or her parent but must earn such respect.

**Ranked societies,** in contrast, do have hereditary inequality. But they lack **stratification** (sharp social divisions—*strata*—based on unequal access to wealth and power) into noble and commoner classes. In ranked societies, individuals tend to be ranked in terms of their genealogical distance from the chief. Closer relatives of the chief have higher rank or social status than more distant ones do. But there is a continuum of status, with many individuals and kin groups ranked about equally, which can lead to competition for positions of leadership. Recap 12.1 lists key features and examples of egalitarian, ranked, and stratified societies.

Not all ranked societies are chiefdoms. Robert Carneiro (1991) has distinguished between two kinds of ranked societies, only the second of which is a chiefdom. In the first type, exemplified by some Native Americans of the Pacific Northwest, there were hereditary differences in rank among individuals, but villages were independent of one another and not ranked in relation to one another. Exemplifying the second type were the Cauca of Colombia and the Natchez of

**ranked society**
Society with hereditary inequality but lacking social stratification.

**stratification**
Presence of social divisions—*strata*—with unequal wealth and power.

**egalitarian society**
Society with rudimentary status distinctions.

Unlike states such as Cameroon, whose Sultan Njoya is shown here, egalitarian societies lack inherited wealth and status and succession to political office. How are inherited status distinctions marked in your society?

| KIND OF STATUS DISTINCTION | NATURE OF STATUS | COMMON FORM OF SUBSISTENCE ECONOMY | COMMON FORMS OF SOCIAL ORGANIZATION | EXAMPLES |
| --- | --- | --- | --- | --- |
| Egalitarian | Status differences are not inherited. All status is based on age, gender, and individual qualities, talents, and achievements. | Foraging | Bands and tribes | Inuit, Ju/'hoansi San, and Yanomami |
| Ranked | Status differences are inherited and distributed along a continuum from the highest-ranking member (chief) to the lowest without any breaks. | Horticulture, pastoralism, and some foraging groups | Chiefdoms and some tribes | Native American groups of the Pacific Northwest (e.g., Salish and Kwakiutl), Natchez, Halaf and Ubaid period polities, Olmec |
| Stratified | Status differences are inherited and divided sharply between distinct noble and commoner classes. | Agriculture | States | Teotihuacán, Uruk period states, Inca, Shang dynasty, Rome, United States, Great Britain |

the eastern United States. These ranked societies had become chiefdoms, societies in which relations among villages as well as among individuals were unequal. The smaller villages had lost their autonomy and were under the authority of leaders who lived at larger villages. According to Kent Flannery (1999), *only those ranked societies with such loss of village autonomy should be called chiefdoms.* In chiefdoms, there is always inequality—differences in rank—among both individuals and communities.

Archaeological evidence for chiefdoms in Mesoamerica dates back more than 3,000 years. Mesoamerican chiefdoms are easy to detect archaeologically because they were flamboyant in the way they marked their aristocracy. High-status families

In chiefdoms and states, high-status families often bury their dead with distinctive symbols and grave goods. Jewelry is among the items buried with this Celtic woman in an Iron Age (200–400 C.E.) grave in Denmark.

distinguished their infants by deforming their heads. When they died, high-status infants were buried with special symbols and great goods. In burials, prestige goods show a continuum in numbers of precious minerals, such as jade and turquoise, from graves—some have many; some, fewer; and some, none at all (Flannery 1999).

The first Middle Eastern states developed between 6000 and 5500 B.P. The first societies based on rank, including the first chiefdoms, emerged during the preceding 1,500 years. In the Middle East, the archaeological record after 7300 B.P. reveals behavior typical of chiefdoms, including exotic goods used as markers of status, along with raiding and political instability. Early chiefdoms included both the Halafian culture of northern Iraq and the Ubaid culture of southern Iraq, which spread north.

As in Mesoamerica, ancient Middle Eastern chiefdoms had cemeteries where high-status people were buried with distinctive items: vessels, statuettes, necklaces, and high-quality ceramics. Such goods were buried with children too young to have earned prestige on their own, who happened to be born into elite families. In the ancient village of Tell es-Sawwan, infant graves show a continuum of richness from six statuettes, to three statuettes, to one statuette, to none. Such signs of slight gradations in social status are exactly what one expects in ranked societies (Flannery 1999).

Such burials convince Flannery (1999) that hereditary status differences were present in the Middle East by 7000 B.P. But had the leaders of large villages extended their authority to the smaller villages nearby? Is there evidence for the loss of village autonomy, converting simple ranked societies into chiefdoms? One clue that villages were linked in political units is the use of a common canal to irrigate several villages. This suggests a way of resolving disputes among farmers over access to water, for example, by appeal to a strong leader. By later Halafian times in northern Mesopotamia, there is evidence for such multivillage alliances (Flannery 1999). Another clue to the loss of village autonomy is the emergence of a two-tier settlement hierarchy, with small villages clustering around a large village, especially one with public buildings. There is evidence for this pattern in northern Mesopotamia during the Halafian.

## Advanced Chiefdoms

In northeastern Syria, near the border with Iraq, archaeologists have excavated an ancient settlement that once lay on a major trade route. This large site, Tell Hamoukar, dates back more than 5,500 years (Wilford 2000). Its remains suggest that advanced chiefdoms arose in northern areas of the Middle East independently of the better-known city-states of southern Mesopotamia, in southern Iraq (Wilford 2000).

By 5700 B.P. Tell Hamoukar was a prosperous town of 32 acres, enclosed by a defensive wall. The site had fine pottery and large ovens—evidence of food preparation on an institutional scale. The site has yielded pieces of large cooking pots, animal bones, and traces of wheat, barley, and oats for baking and brewing. The archaeologist McGuire Gibson, one of the excavators, believes that food preparation on this scale is evidence of a ranked society in which elites were organizing people and resources (Wilford 2000). Most likely they were hosting and entertaining in a chiefly manner.

Providing further evidence for social ranking are the seals used to mark containers of food and other goods. Some of the seals are small, with only simple incisions or cross-hatching. Others are larger and more elaborate, presumably for higher officials to stamp more valuable goods. Gibson suspects the larger seals with figurative scenes were held by the few people who had greater authority. The smaller, simply incised seals were used by many more people with less authority (Wilford 2000). (Visit the Tell Hamoukar project website at https://oi.uchicago.edu/research/projects/ham/.)

## The Rise of the State

In southern Mesopotamia at this time (5700 B.P.), an expanding population and increased food production from irrigation were changing the social landscape even more drastically than in the north. Irrigation had allowed Ubaid communities to spread along the Euphrates River. Travel and trade were expanding, with water serving as the highway system. Such raw materials as hardwood and stone, which southern Mesopotamia lacked, were imported via river routes. Social and economic networks now linked communities on the rivers in the south and in the foothills to the north. Social differentials also increased. Priests and political leaders joined expert potters and other specialists. These non-food-producers were supported by the larger population of farmers and herders (Gilmore-Lehne 2000).

Economies were being managed by central leadership. Agricultural villages had grown into cities, some of which were ruled by local kings. The Uruk period (6000–5200 B.P.), which succeeded the Ubaid period, takes its name from a prominent southern city-state located more than 400 miles south of Tell Hamoukar. The Uruk period established Mesopotamia as "the cradle of civilization" (see Pollock 1999). Recap 12.2 highlights archaeological periods in the process of state formation in the ancient Middle East.

There is no evidence of Uruk influence at Tell Hamoukar in Syria until 5200 B.P., when some Uruk pottery showed up. When southern Mesopotamians expanded north, they found advanced chiefdoms, which were not yet states. The fact that writing

| RECAP 12.2 | Archaeological Periods in Middle Eastern State Formation | |
|---|---|---|
| **DATES** | **PERIOD** | **AGE** |
| 3000–2539 B.P. | Neo-Babylonian | Iron Age |
| 3600–3000 B.P. | Kassite | |
| 4000–3600 B.P. | Old Babylonian | Bronze Age |
| 4150–4000 B.P. | Third Dynasty of Ur | |
| 4350–4150 B.P. | Akkadian | |
| 4600–4350 B.P. | Early Dynastic III | |
| 4750–4600 B.P. | Early Dynastic II | |
| 5000–4750 B.P. | Early Dynastic I | |
| 5200–5000 B.P. | Jemdet Nasr | |
| 6000–5200 B.P. | Uruk | Chalcolithic (Copper/Stone) |
| 7500–6000 B.P. | Ubaid (southern Mesopotamia)–Halaf (northern Mesopotamia) | |
| 10,000–7000 B.P. | | Neolithic |

Pictographic writing on a Mesopotamian clay tablet, inscribed between 3100 and 2900 B.C.E. The earliest such tablets represent the work of administrators, perhaps of large temple institutions.

originated in Sumer, in southern Mesopotamia, indicates a more advanced, state-organized society there. The first writing presumably developed to handle record keeping for a centralized economy.

Initially, writing was used to keep accounts, reflecting the needs of trade. Rulers, nobles, priests, and merchants were the first to benefit from it. Writing had reached Egypt by 5200 B.P., probably from Mesopotamia. The earliest writing was pictographic, for example, with pictorial symbols of horses used to represent them.

Early Mesopotamian scribes used a stylus (writing implement) to scrawl symbols on raw clay. This writing, called **cuneiform** writing, from the Latin word for "wedge," left a wedge-shaped impression on the clay. Both the Sumerian (southern Mesopotamia) and the Akkadian (northern Mesopotamia) languages were written in cuneiform (Gowlett 1993).

Writing and temples played key roles in the Mesopotamian economy. For the historic period after 5600 B.P., when writing was invented, there are temple records of economic activities. States can exist without writing, but literacy facilitates the flow and storage of information. We know that Mesopotamian priests managed herding, farming, manufacture, and trade. Temple officials allotted fodder and pastureland for cattle and donkeys, which were used as plow and cart animals. As the economy expanded, trade, manufacture, and grain storage were centrally managed. Temples collected and distributed meat, dairy products, crops, fish, clothing, tools, and trade items. Potters, metalworkers, weavers, sculptors, and other artisans perfected their crafts.

Prior to the invention of **metallurgy** (knowledge of the properties of metals, including their extraction and processing and the manufacture of metal tools), raw copper was shaped by hammering. If copper is hammered too long, it hardens and becomes brittle, with a risk of cracking. But once heated (annealed) in a fire, copper becomes malleable again. Such annealing of copper was an early form of metallurgy. A vital step for metallurgy was the discovery of **smelting,** the high-temperature process by which pure metal is produced from an ore. Ores, including copper ore, have a much wider distribution than does native copper, which was initially traded as a luxury good because of its rarity (Gowlett 1993).

When and how smelting was discovered is unknown. But after 5000 B.P., metallurgy evolved rapidly. The Bronze Age began when alloys of arsenic and copper, or tin and copper (in both cases known as **bronze**), became common and greatly extended the use of metals. Bronze flows more easily than copper does when heated to a similar temperature, so bronze was more convenient for metal casting. Early molds were carved in stone, as shaped depressions to be filled with molten metal. A copper ax cast from such a mold has been found in northern Mesopotamia and predates 5000 B.P. Thereafter, other metals came into common use. By 4500 B.P., golden objects were found in royal burials at Ur.

Iron ore is distributed more widely than is copper ore. Iron, when smelted, can be used on its own; there is no need for tin or arsenic to make a metal alloy (bronze). The Iron Age began once high-temperature iron smelting was mastered. In the Old World after 3200 B.P., iron spread rapidly. Formerly valued as highly as gold, iron crashed in value when it became plentiful (Gowlett 1993).

The Mesopotamian economy, based on intensive agriculture, craft production, and trade, spurred population growth and increased urbanism. Sumerian cities were protected by a fortress wall and surrounded by a farming area. By 4800 B.P., Uruk, the largest early Mesopotamian city, had a population of 50,000. As irrigation and the population expanded,

In *cuneiform*, another early Mesopotamian script, a stylus was used to scrawl wedge-shaped symbols on raw clay. What languages were written in cuneiform?

communities fought over water. People sought protection in the fortified cities (Adams 1981, 2008) when neighbors or invaders threatened.

By 4600 B.P., secular authority had replaced temple rule. The office of military coordinator developed into kingship. This change shows up architecturally in palaces and royal tombs. The palace raised armies and supplied them with armor, chariots, and metal armaments. At Ur's royal cemetery, by 4600 B.P. monarchs were being buried with soldiers, charioteers, and ladies in waiting. These subordinates were killed at the time of a royal burial to accompany the monarch to the afterworld.

Agricultural intensification made it possible for the number of people supported by a given area to increase. Population pressure on irrigated fields helped create a stratified society. Land became private property that was bought and sold. The wealth of people with large estates set them off from ordinary farmers. Those landlords joined the urban elite, while sharecroppers and serfs toiled in the fields. By 4600 B.P., Mesopotamia had a well-defined class structure, with complex stratification into nobles, commoners, and slaves.

This ziggurat, or temple tower, at Ur, Iraq, dates back to 4100 B.P. (2100 B.C.E.). Temples and their officials played key roles in the Mesopotamian economy. Who handles such duties in our society?

## OTHER EARLY STATES

In northwestern India and adjacent Pakistan, the Indus River Valley (*Harappan*) state, with major cities at Harappa and Mohenjo-daro, takes its name from the river valley along which it extended. (Figure 12.3 maps the four great early river valley states of the Old World: Mesopotamia, Egypt, India/Pakistan, and northern China.) Trade and the spread of writing from Mesopotamia may have played a role in the emergence of the Harappan state around 4600 B.P. Located in Pakistan's Punjab Province, the ruins of Harappa were the first to be identified as part of the Indus River Valley civilization. At its peak, the Indus River Valley state incorporated 1,000 cities, towns, and villages, spanning 280,000 square miles (725,000 square kilometers). This state, which flourished between 4600 and 3900 B.P., featured urban planning, social stratification, and an early

**FIGURE 12.3** The Four Great Early River Valley States of the Old World.

By approximately 4000 B.P., urban life had been established along the Tigris and Euphrates Rivers in Mesopotamia, the Nile River in Egypt, the Indus and Ganges Rivers in India/Pakistan, and the Yellow River in China.

SOURCE: Based on Map 1-1 from Craig, Albert M.; Graham, William A.; Kagan, Donald; Ozment, Steven; Turner, Frank M., *Heritage of World Civilizations: Volume I to 1650*, 4th ed. © 1997. Reprinted and electronically reproduced by permission of Pearson Education, Inc., Upper Saddle River, New Jersey.

writing system, which remains undeciphered. The Harappans maintained a uniform system of weights. Their cities had carefully planned residential areas with waste-water systems. An array of products from sophisticated craft industries included ceramic vessels made on potter's wheels (Meadow and Kenoyer 2000).

The Indus River Valley state collapsed, apparently through warfare, around 3900 B.P. Its cities were destroyed and abandoned. Skeletons of massacre victims have been found in the streets of Mohenjo-daro. Harappa continued to be occupied, but on a much smaller scale than previously (Meadow and Kenoyer 2000). (For more on the Harappa Archaeological Research Project, visit http://www.harappa.com.)

The first Chinese state, dating to 3750 B.P., was that of the Shang dynasty. It arose in the Huang He (Yellow) River area of northern China, with wheat as its dietary staple. This state was characterized by urbanism, palatial (as well as domestic) architecture, human sacrifice, and a sharp division between social classes. Burials of the aristocracy were marked by ornaments of stone, including jade. The Shang had bronze metallurgy and an elaborate writing system. In warfare they used chariots and took prisoners (Gowlett 1993).

Like Mesopotamia and China, many early civilizations came to rely on metallurgy. At Nok Nok Tha in northern Thailand, metalworking goes back 6,000 years. In Peru's Andes, metalworking appeared around 4000 B.P. Ancient Andeans were skilled in working with bronze, copper, and gold. They are well known, too, for their techniques of pottery manufacture. Their arts, crafts, and agricultural knowledge compared well with those of Mesoamerica at its height, to which we turn after a discussion of African states. Note that both Mesoamerican and Andean state formation were truncated by Spanish conquest. The Aztecs of Mexico were conquered in 1519 C.E., and the Inca of Peru in 1532 C.E.

## African States

Egypt, a major ancient civilization, developed in northern Africa, as one of the world's first states (Morkot 2005). Egyptian influence extended southward along the Nile into what is now Sudan. Sub-Saharan Africa witnessed the emergence of several states, only a few of which will be described here.

As in the states just discussed, metallurgy (especially iron and gold) played a role in the eventual rise of African states (Connah 2004). About 2,000 years ago, iron smelting began to diffuse rapidly throughout Africa. That spread was aided by the migrations of Bantu speakers. (Bantu is Africa's largest linguistic family.) The Bantu migrations, launched from north central Africa around 2100 B.P., continued for more than a thousand years. Bantu speakers migrated south into the rain forests of the Congo River and east into the African highlands. Along with their language and iron-smelting techniques, they also spread

farming, particularly of high-yielding crops such as yams, bananas, and plantains.

One crowning achievement of the Bantu migrations was the Mwenemutapa empire. The southeast-moving ancestors of the Mwenemutapa took iron smelting and farming to the region called Zimbabwe, south of the Zambezi River and located within the contemporary nation of the same name. This area was rich in gold, which the Mwenemutapa mined and traded with cities on the Indian Ocean, starting around 1000 C.E. (1000 B.P.). The Mwenemutapa developed a powerful kingdom based on trade. The first centralized state there was Great Zimbabwe (*zimbabwe* means "stone enclosure"—the capital was protected by huge stone walls), which arose around 1300 C.E. By 1500, Great Zimbabwe dominated the Zambezi Valley militarily and commercially as the seat of the Mwenemutapa empire.

Another African region where states arose, also abetted by trade, was the Sahel, the area just south of the Sahara in western Africa. Farming towns started appearing in the Sahel around 2600 B.P. One such town, Kumbi Saleh, eventually became the capital of the ancient kingdom of Ghana. West

A 16th-century bronze statue of a royal messenger from Benin. An important precolonial state in what is now southern Nigeria, Benin, which thrived in the 15th–16th centuries C.E., is known for its artistic creativity. Benin art became one of the most influential African art traditions.

Africa was rich in gold, precious metals, ivory, and other resources, which after 750 C.E. (1250 B.P.) were traded (thanks to the camel) across the Sahara to North Africa, Egypt, and the Middle East. Cities in the Sahel served as southern terminal points for the trans-Saharan trade (e.g., of gold for salt). Several kingdoms developed in this area: Ghana, Mali, Songhay, and Kanem-Bornu, together known as the Sahelian kingdoms, of which Ghana was the first. By 1000 B.P. Ghana's economic vitality, based on the trans-Saharan trade, was supporting an empire formed through the conquest of local chiefdoms, from which tribute was extracted.

States also arose in the forested region of western Africa south of the Sahel. Between 1000 and 1500 C.E., local farming villages started consolidating into larger units, which eventually became centralized states. The largest and most enduring of these states was Benin, in what is now southern Nigeria. Benin, which thrived in the 15th century C.E. (600–500 B.P.), is known for its artistic creativity, expressed in terra-cotta, ivory, and brass sculpture. Benin art became one of the most influential African art traditions.

## STATE FORMATION IN MESOAMERICA

In the last chapter we examined the independent inventions of farming in the Middle East and Mesoamerica. The processes of state formation that took place in these areas were also comparable, beginning with ranked societies and chiefdoms, and ending with fully formed states and empires.

The first monumental buildings (temple complexes) in the Western Hemisphere were constructed by Mesoamerican chiefdoms in many areas, from the Valley of Mexico to Guatemala. Those chiefdoms influenced one another as they traded materials, such as obsidian, shells, jade, and pottery. (Figure 12.4 maps major sites in the emergence of Mesoamerican food production, chiefdoms, and states.)

### Early Chiefdoms and Elites

The Olmec built a series of ritual centers on Mexico's southern Gulf Coast between 3,200 and 2,500 years ago. Three of these centers, each from a different century, are known. Earthen mounds were grouped into plaza complexes, presumably for religious use. Such centers show that Olmec chiefs could marshal human labor to construct such mounds. The Olmec were also master sculptors; they carved massive stone heads, perhaps as images of their chiefs or their ancestors.

There is evidence, too, that trade routes linked the Olmec with other parts of Mesoamerica, such as the Oaxaca Valley in the southern highlands and the Valley of Mexico (see Figure 12.4). By 3000 B.P. (1000 B.C.E.—formerly B.C.), a ruling elite had

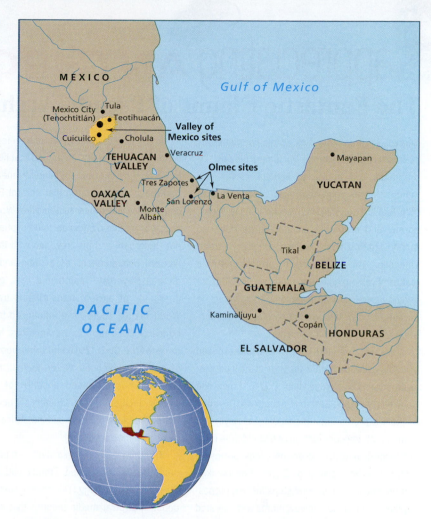

**FIGURE 12.4** Major Sites in the Emergence of Food Production and the State in Mesoamerica.

SOURCE: From Clifford J. Jolly and Fred Plog, *Physical Anthropology and Archaeology*, 4th ed., p. 115. Copyright © 1986 by The McGraw-Hill Companies, Inc. Reprinted with permission.

emerged in Oaxaca. The items traded at that time between Oaxaca and the Olmec were for elite consumption. High-status Oaxacans wore mussel-shell ornaments from the coast. In return the Olmec elites got mirrors and jade made by Oaxacan artisans.

A colossal Olmec head, carved from basalt, is displayed at the Jalapa Museum of Archaeology in Veracruz, Mexico, in a setting designed to recall its original site. Such heads, often weighing many tons, are thought to represent individual chiefs.

# appreciating ANTHROPOLOGY

## The Fantastic Claims of Pseudo-Archaeology

Interest in prehistory has spawned numerous popular-culture creations, including movies, TV programs, and books. In fictional works, the anthropologists don't bear much resemblance to their real-life counterparts. Unlike Indiana Jones, normal and reputable archaeologists don't go around fighting Nazis, lashing whips, or seizing antiquities. The archaeologist's profession isn't a matter of raiding lost arks, going on crusades, or finding crystal skulls but rather of reconstructing ancient lifeways through the careful and systematic analysis of material remains.

Over the generations, the media have exposed us to the pseudoscientific theories of such popular writers as Thor Heyerdahl (1971), Erich von Däniken (1971), and Graham Hancock (2011)—none of them a professional archaeologist. Heyerdahl argued that developments in one world area (e.g., Mesoamerica) were based on ideas borrowed from somewhere else (e.g., Egypt). Von Daniken carried diffusionism several steps further, proposing that major human achievements were created or assisted by extraterrestrials. These writers share a degree of contempt for human inventiveness. They assume that major features of the ancient human landscape were beyond the capabilities of people actually living in the places where the achievements occurred.

In *The Ra Expeditions,* world traveler and adventurer Heyerdahl (1971) argued that his voyage in a papyrus boat from the Mediterranean to the Caribbean demonstrated that ancient Egyptians could have navigated to the New World. (The boat was modeled on an ancient Egyptian vessel, but Heyerdahl and his crew had with them such modern conveniences as a radio and canned goods.) Heyerdahl maintained that, given the possibility of ancient trans-Atlantic travel, Old World people could have influenced the emergence of civilization in the Americas. In *Fingerprints of the Gods* (2011) and other books aimed at popular audiences, writer–journalist Graham Hancock has advanced a series of fantastic claims, including that Africans influenced the Olmec (because of, in his opinion, African-looking faces in Olmec sculpture).

The University of Michigan offers a popular undergraduate class titled Frauds and Fantastic Claims in Archaeology. The course examines and debunks popular media theories that archaeologists view as fringe, or "pseudoscientific." Especially problematic are claims that cultural achievements by indigenous peoples result from contact with superior beings. The course exposes the logical flaws and questionable evidence used to support such claims. The course textbook is Kenneth L. Feder's *Frauds, Myths, and Mysteries: Science and Pseudoscience in Archaeology* (2013)—a must for any reader wanting to pursue this topic further.

Pseudo-archaeologists often have trouble with chronology. We've seen in this chapter that around 2,000 years ago states fully comparable to those of Mesopotamia and Egypt began to rise and fall in the Mexican highlands. This occurred about 1,500 years after the major period of Egyptian pyramid building. If Egypt did contribute to Mesoamerican civilization, we would expect this influence to have been exerted during Egypt's heyday as an ancient power—not 1,500 years later. There is, however, no archaeological evidence for trans-Atlantic contact at either time.

There is, on the other hand, abundant archaeological evidence for the gradual emergence of food production and the state in the Middle East, in Mesoamerica, and in Peru. This evidence effectively counters the diffusionist theories and other fantastic claims about how and why human achievements, including farming and the state, began. Popular theories to the contrary, changes, advances, and setbacks in ancient American social life were the products of the ideas and activities of Native Americans themselves.

---

Chiefdoms in Oaxaca developed canal and well irrigation, exported magnetite mirrors, and were precocious in their use of adobes (mud bricks), stucco, stone masonry, and architecture. Chiefdoms in the Olmec area farmed river levees, built mounds of earth, and carved those colossal stone heads. Other early Mexican chiefdoms also had skilled artists and builders, using adobes and lime plaster and constructing stone buildings, precisely oriented 8 degrees north of east.

The period between 3200 and 3000 B.P. (1200–1000 B.C.E.) was one of rapid social change. Mesoamerica's many chiefdoms were linked by trade and exchange. Chiefly centers were concentrating labor power, intensifying agriculture, exchanging trade goods, and borrowing ideas, including art motifs and styles, from each other. Archaeologists now believe it was the *intensity of competitive interaction*—rather than the supremacy of any one chiefdom—that made social change so rapid. The social and political landscape of Mexico around 3000 B.P. (1000 B.C.E.) was one in which 25 or so chiefly centers were (1) sufficiently separate and autonomous to adapt to local zones and conditions and (2) sufficiently interactive and competitive to borrow and incorporate new ideas and innovations as they arose in other regions (Flannery and Marcus 2000).

It used to be thought that a single chiefdom could become a state on its own. Archaeologists know now that state formation involves one chiefdom's incorporating several others into the emerging state it controls, and making changes in its

Neither Mexico nor Peru has yielded a shred of accepted archaeological evidence for Old World interference prior to the European Age of Discovery, which began late in the 15th century. Francisco Pizarro conquered Peru's Inca state in 1532, 11 years after its Mesoamerican counterpart, Tenochtitlán, the Aztec capital, fell to Spanish conquistadores. (We do have abundant archaeological, as well as written, evidence for this contact between Europeans and Native Americans.)

The archaeological record also casts doubt on contentions that the advances of earthlings came with extraterrestrial help. Abundant, well-analyzed

Sarajevo-born American Semir Osmanagic claims to have discovered a giant pyramid built by an ancient civilization under Visocica Hill, Bosnia. Most scientists doubt his claim.

archaeological data from the Middle East, Mesoamerica, and Peru tell a clear story. Food production and the state were not brilliant secrets, discoveries, or inventions that humans needed to learn or borrow from outsiders. They were long-term developments, gradual processes with down-to-earth causes and effects. They required thousands of years of orderly change, not a chance meeting in the high Andes between an ancient Inca chief and a beneficent Johnny Appleseed from Aldebaran.

Occasionally, fantastic claims about prehistory exaggerate, rather than deny, the abilities of ancient humans. One example is when pseudo-archaeologists claim that Paleolithic societies could have constructed monumental structures. Graham Hancock, for example, has suggested that an Upper Paleolithic civilization, rather than ancient Egyptians, built Egypt's great Sphinx, some 7,000 years earlier than its actual construction date (Hancock and Bauval 1996).

Semir Osmanagic is a Bosnian amateur archaeologist who has been dubbed the Indiana Jones of the Balkans because of his favored flat-crowned Navajo hat. Osmanagic claims to have identified in Bosnia

the world's largest ancient pyramid, which he thinks is "older than the last ice age" (Smith 2006). Archaeologists and geologists, however, say that his "pyramid" is actually a large, symmetrical hill formed by buckling of the Earth's crust millions of years ago. Zilka Kujundzic-Vejzagic, a trained prehistoric archaeologist at Bosnia's National Museum, points out the lack of any evidence for a Paleolithic civilization in Bosnia. (Were there Paleolithic civilizations anywhere in the world?) Indeed, archaeologists working in Bosnia have found little more than flint tools from the end of the last Ice Age and only simple Neolithic settlements that appeared thousands of years after that. The country's most substantial ancient monument is a modest stone city in southern Bosnia built during the third century B.C.E. Nevertheless, uncritical media coverage has popularized Osmanagic's theories, and volunteers have flocked to the site to help him excavate (Smith 2006). Responding to his claims, the European Association of Archaeologists issued an official statement signed by the heads of the official archaeological organizations of seven European countries (Parzinger et al. 2006). Their statement called Osmanagic's so-called pyramid project "a cruel hoax on an unsuspecting public" that "has no place in the world of genuine science" (Parzinger et al. 2006). When and where have you heard a fantastic claim about prehistory?

own infrastructure as it acquires and holds on to new territories, followers, and goods. Waging warfare and attracting followers are two key elements in state formation. (This chapter's "Appreciating Anthropology" debunks popular pseudo-archaeological theories about the origin of Mesoamerican civilization.)

Many chiefdoms had dense populations, intensive agriculture, and settlement hierarchies that included hamlets, villages, and perhaps towns. These factors paved the way for greater social and political complexity. Political leaders emerged, and military success often solidified their position. Such figures attracted lots of followers, loyal to their leader. Conquest warfare brought in new territories and subjects. States, in contrast to chiefdoms, can

acquire labor and land and hold on to them. States have armies, warfare, developed political hierarchies, law codes, and military force, which can be used in fact or as a threat.

Olmec and Oaxaca were just two among many flamboyant early Mexican chiefdoms that once thrived in the area from the Valley of Mexico to Guatemala. Oaxaca went on to develop a state a bit earlier than the Teotihuacán state of the Valley of Mexico. Oaxaca and other highland areas came to overshadow the Olmec area and the Mesoamerican lowlands in general. By 2500 B.P. (500 B.C.E.), Oaxaca's Zapotec people had developed a distinctive art style, perfected at their capital city of Monte Albán (see Blanton 1999; Marcus and Flannery 1996).

Three of more than 300 carved stones depicting slain war captives at the important archaeological site of Monte Albán, Oaxaca, Mexico. Dated to 500–400 B.C.E., these images originally were set in the Prisoner Gallery of Monte Albán's Building L. This huge display of slain enemies was a form of political and military propaganda. The carved stones warned potential rivals what would happen if they defied Monte Albán.

## Warfare and State Formation: The Zapotec Case

**Zapotec state**
First Mesoamerican state, in the Valley of Oaxaca.

As has been noted previously, warfare played a key role in primary state formation. The first Meso-american state, the **Zapotec state,** had developed in Mexico's Valley of Oaxaca by the start of the Common Era (C.E.—formerly A.D.). The city of Monte Albán served as capital of this Zapotec polity for *1,200 years,* between 500 B.C.E. and 700 C.E. (The Zapotec polity was a chiefdom from ca. 500 B.C.E. to 100 B.C.E., and after that a state.) Kent Flannery and Joyce Marcus (2003*b*) describe the archaeological evidence for changing warfare patterns in Oaxaca—from early raiding among seden-tary villages to warfare aimed at conquest between 330 and 20 B.C.E.

A monument from the Oaxacan site of San José Mogote, erected no later than 500 B.C.E., is the earli-est reliably dated monument with writing in Meso-america. It depicts a named, sacrificed captive, likely a rival chief and a probable victim of intervil-lage raiding. Armed conflict in Oaxaca began as raiding, with killing, burning, and captive taking but no permanent acquisition of territory (Flannery and Marcus 2003*b*). As Charles Spencer (2003) notes, the first evidence for Oaxacan conquest warfare occurs simultaneously with evidence for emerging state organization. This co-occurrence supports the idea of a causal link between conquest warfare and state formation.

Long ago, Henry Wright (1977) described the state as a society with not only a centralized but also an internally specialized, administrative organization—a bureaucracy. Chiefdoms, by con-trast, lack administrative specialization. States have at least four levels of decision making (Wright 1977). The center, or capital, establishes subsidiary administrative centers (Elson 2007). The result is a nested structure of secondary, tertiary, and even quaternary centers. Population size tends to follow this administrative structure: States typically have at least a four-level hierarchy of settlements according to both administrative functions and population size. Chiefdoms have no more than three levels (Spencer 2003).

To expand, a state must send delegates, such as soldiers, governors, and other officials, to subjugate and rule in distant territories. Lacking a group of bureaucrats, chiefdoms can't do this, which means that the geographic range of chiefly authority is smaller than in a state. According to Spencer (2003), the limit of a chiefdom's range is half a day's travel from its center. States, however, can transcend such limits and carry out long-distance conquests. Archae-ological evidence for conquest warfare includes burned and abandoned villages, specialized forts and administrative outposts, and forced changes in the economic, social, and religious behaviors of subjugated peoples.

Expansion through conquest can play a key role in the formation of a primary state by building the administrative hierarchy. Subjugation of polities in other regions, coupled with regularized tribute exaction, can bring about a transition from chief-dom to state (Spencer 2003). For such a strategy to succeed (especially when the conquered polities lie more than a half-day's trip away), the leadership has to dispatch agents to the conquered areas. Gen-erals and bureaucrats are needed not only to carry out the subjugation but also to maintain long-term control and to manage tribute collection. Given its need to rely on distant representatives, the central leadership promotes internal administrative spe-cialization and loyalty. Tribute provides new resources to support this administrative transforma-tion. The conquest of distant polities and bureau-cratic growth were integral parts of the process of Zapotec state formation.

Typically, state bureaucracies occupy a group of administrative buildings, especially at the capital. Surrounding the Main Plaza at Monte Albán were specialized buildings, including palaces, temples, and ball courts. Hieroglyphs on one building in Monte Albán's Main Plaza record how outlying areas were acquired. We learn that Monte Albán did not expand its rule in a concentric fashion. Although it had managed to subjugate distant regions to the north, west, and southwest by approximately 300 B.C.E., certain areas to the east and south managed to resist for centuries. For example, Monte Albán burned its chief rival, San Martín Tilcajete, a day's travel to the south, around 330 B.C.E., but its people refused to capitulate. They rebuilt their community and constructed defensive walls at a higher location. They continued to resist Monte Albán until roughly 20 B.C.E., when they finally succumbed.

Evidence for co-occurrence of Monte Albán's conquest strategy with the emerging Zapotec state offers strong support for an expansionist model of primary state formation (see also Stanish and Levine 2011). The Zapotec state had formed by 30–20 B.C.E., with a four-tier settlement hierarchy (see Elson 2007). After centuries of dominating the region, Monte Albán eventually lost its central role as capital, as other Zapotec centers successfully challenged its authority. After 700 C.E. (formerly A.D. 700), the Zapotec state fragmented into a series of smaller centers, or principalities, alternately vying for supremacy through continued warfare and peaceful alliances through marriage (Flannery and Marcus 2003a; Marcus 1989).

Teotihuacán is one of the most important archaeological sites in the Americas. In the photo we see the Pyramid of the Sun (back left), Teotihuacán's largest structure, along with the Avenue of the Dead (foreground leading back). At its height around 500 C.E., Teotihuacán was larger than imperial Rome. The mobilization of manual labor to build such a city is one of the costs of state organization.

## States in the Valley of Mexico

During the first century C.E., the Valley (Basin) of Mexico, located in the highlands where Mexico City now stands, rose to prominence in Mesoamerican state formation. In this large valley, **Teotihuacán** flourished between 100 and 700 C.E.

A large basin surrounded by mountains, the valley has rich volcanic soils, but rainfall isn't always reliable. The northern valley, where the huge city and state of Teotihuacán eventually arose, is colder and drier than the south. Frosts limited farming in the northern valley until quick-growing varieties of maize were developed. Until 500 B.C.E., most people lived in the warmer and wetter southern part of the valley, where rainfall made farming possible. After 500 B.C.E., new maize varieties and small-scale irrigation appeared. The population increased and began to spread north.

By 1 C.E. Teotihuacán was a town of 10,000 people. It governed a territory of a few thousand square kilometers and perhaps 50,000 people (Parsons 1974). Teotihuacán's growth reflected its agricultural potential. Perpetual springs permitted irrigation of a large alluvial plain. Rural farmers supplied food for the growing urban population (Clayton 2013).

By this time, a clear **settlement hierarchy** had emerged. This is a ranked series of communities that differ in size, function, and building types. The settlements at the top of the hierarchy were political and religious centers. Those at the bottom were rural villages. We have seen that a four-level settlement hierarchy provides archaeological evidence for state organization.

Along with state organization at Teotihuacán went large-scale irrigation, status differentiation, and complex architecture. Teotihuacán thrived between 100 and 700 C.E. It grew as a planned city built on a grid pattern, with the Pyramid of the Sun at its center. By 500 C.E. the population of Teotihuacán may have reached 125,000, making it larger than imperial Rome. Farmers were one of its diverse specialized groups, along with artisans, merchants, and political, religious, and military personnel (see Clayton 2013; Cowgill 2008).

After 700 C.E. Teotihuacán declined in size and power. By 900 C.E. its population had shrunk to 30,000. Between 900 and 1200 C.E., the Toltec period, the population scattered, and small cities and towns sprang up throughout the valley (see Cowgill 2013). People also left the Valley of Mexico to live in larger cities—like Tula, the Toltec capital—on its edge (see Figure 12.4).

Population increase (including immigration by the ancestors of the Aztecs) and urban growth returned to the Valley of Mexico between 1200 and 1520 C.E. During the **Aztec** period (1325–1520 C.E.) there were several cities, the largest of which—Tenochtitlán, the capital—may have surpassed Teotihuacán at its height (Rojas and Smith 2012). A dozen Aztec towns had more than 10,000 people. Fueling this population growth was intensification of agriculture, particularly in the southern part of the valley, where the drainage of lake bottoms and swamps added new cultivable land (see Berdan 2013).

Another factor in the renaissance of the Valley of Mexico was trade. Local manufacture created products for a series of markets. The major towns and markets were located on the lakeshores, with easy access to canoe traffic. The Aztec capital stood on an island in the lake. In Tenochtitlán, the production of luxury goods was more prestigious and more highly

**Teotihuacán**
First Valley of Mexico state (100–700 C.E.); earliest Mesoamerican empire.

**Aztec**
Last independent Valley of Mexico state (thrived between 1325 and the Spanish Conquest in 1520).

**settlement hierarchy**
Communities with varying size, function, and building types.

organized than that of pottery making, basket making, and weaving. Luxury producers, such as stone workers, feather workers, and gold- and silversmiths, occupied a special position in Aztec society. The manufacture of luxury goods for export was an important part of the economy of the Aztec capital (see Garraty 2013).

## WHY STATES COLLAPSE

States can disintegrate along the same cleavage lines (e.g., regional political units) that were originally forged together to form the state. Various factors, such as invasion, disease, famine, or prolonged drought, can threaten their economies and political institutions. Citizens might degrade the environment, usually with economic costs. For example, farmers and smelters might cut down trees. Such deforestation promotes erosion and leads to a decline in the water supply. Overuse of land may deplete the soil of the nutrients needed to grow crops.

If factors such as irrigation help create states to begin with, does their decline or failure explain the fall of the state? Irrigation does have costs as well as benefits. In ancient Mesopotamia, irrigation water came from the Tigris and Euphrates Rivers. Because sediment (silt) had accumulated in those rivers, their beds were higher than the alluvial plain and fields they irrigated. Canals channeled river water as it

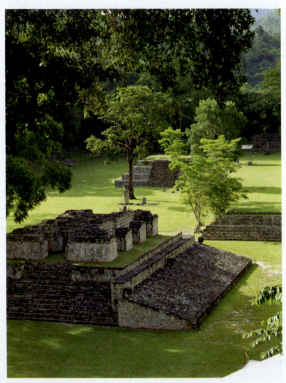

Ruins at Copán, a center of classic Maya royalty in western Honduras.

flowed down into the fields by gravity. As the water evaporated, water-borne mineral salts remained in the fields. This accumulation eventually created a poisonous environment for crops, forcing abandonment of the fields.

## The Maya Decline

Generations of scholars have debated the decline of classic Maya civilization around 900 C.E. Classic Maya culture, featuring several competing states, flourished between 300 and 900 C.E. in parts of what are now Mexico, Honduras, El Salvador, Guatemala, and Belize. The ancient Maya are known for their monuments (temples and pyramids), calendars, mathematics, and hieroglyphic writing.

Archaeological clues to Maya decline have been found at Copán, in western Honduras. This classic Maya royal center, the largest site in the southeastern part of the Maya area, covered 29 acres (11.7 hectares). It was built on an artificial terrace overlooking the Copán River. Its rulers inscribed their monuments with accounts of their coronation, their lineage history, and reports of important battles. The Maya dated their monuments with the names of kings and the dates of their reign. One monument at Copán was intended to be the ruler's throne platform, but only one side had been finished. The monument bears a date, 822 C.E., in a section of unfinished text. Copán has no monuments with later dates. The site probably had been abandoned by 830 C.E.

The environmental factors behind Copán's collapse may have included deforestation, erosion, and soil exhaustion due to overpopulation and overfarming. Hillside farmhouses, in particular, had debris from erosion—probably caused by overfarming of the hillsides. This erosion began as early as 750 C.E.—until these farm sites were abandoned, with some eventually buried by erosion debris.

Food stress and malnutrition were clearly present at Copán, where 80 percent of the buried skeletons display signs of anemia, due to iron deficiency. One skull shows anemia severe enough to have been the cause of death. Even the nobility were malnourished. One noble skull, known to be such from its carved teeth and cosmetic deformation, also has telltale signs of anemia: spongy areas at its rear (Annenberg/CPB Exhibits 2000).

Just as the origins of states, and their causes, are diverse, so are the reasons for state decline. The Maya state was not as powerful as was once assumed; it was fragile and vulnerable. Increased warfare and political competition destabilized many of its dynasties and governments. Archaeologists now stress the role of warfare in Maya state decline. Hieroglyphic texts document increased warfare among many Maya cities. From the period just before the collapse, there is archaeological evidence for increased concern with fortifications and relocation to defensible locations. Archaeologists have evidence of the burning of structures, the projectile points from spears, and some of the bodies of those killed. Some sites were abandoned, with the people fleeing into the forests to occupy perishable huts. (Copán, as we have seen, was depopulated after 822 C.E.) Archaeologists now believe that social, political, and military upheaval and competition had as much as or more to do with the Maya decline and abandonment of cities as did natural environmental factors (Marcus, personal communication).

Formerly, archaeologists tended to explain state origin and decline mainly in terms of natural environmental factors, such as climate change, habitat destruction, and demographic pressure (see Weiss 2005). Archaeologists now see state origins and declines more fully—in social and political terms—because they can read the texts. And the Maya texts document competition and warfare between dynasties jockeying for position and power. Warfare was indeed a creator and a destroyer of ancient chiefdoms and states. What is its role in our own?

# for REVIEW

summary

1. States develop to handle regulatory problems as the population grows, social groups proliferate, and the economy gets more complex. Important factors that contribute to state formation include irrigation, warfare, and regional trade. Coastal Peru, a very arid area, illustrates how environmental circumscription, population growth, and warfare may contribute to state formation.

2. A state is a society with a formal, central government and a division of society into classes. The first cities and states, supported by irrigated farming, developed in southern Mesopotamia between 6000 and 5500 B.P. Evidence for early state organization includes monumental architecture, central storehouses, irrigation systems, and written records.

3. The first Middle Eastern towns grew up 10,000 to 9,000 years ago. The first pottery dates back just over 8,000 years. Halafian (7500–6500 B.P.) is a pottery style and the period when the first chiefdoms emerged. Ubaid pottery (7000–6000 B.P.) is associated with advanced chiefdoms and perhaps the earliest states. Most state formation occurred during the Uruk period (6100–5100 B.P.).

4. Based on the status distinctions they include, societies may be divided into egalitarian, ranked, and stratified types. In egalitarian societies, status distinctions are not usually inherited. Ranked societies have hereditary inequality, but they lack stratification. Stratified societies have sharp social divisions—social classes, or *strata*—based on unequal access to wealth and power. Ranked societies with loss of village autonomy are chiefdoms.

5. Mesopotamia's economy was based on craft production, trade, and intensive agriculture. Writing, invented by 5600 B.P., was first used to keep accounts for trade. With the invention of smelting, the Bronze Age began just after 5000 B.P.

6. In northwestern India and Pakistan, the Indus River Valley state flourished from 4600 to 3900 B.P. The first Chinese state, dating to 3750 B.P., was that of the Shang dynasty in northern China. Various states developed in sub-Saharan Africa. The major early states of the Western Hemisphere were in Mesoamerica and Peru.

7. Between 3200 and 3000 B.P. (1200–1000 B.C.E.—formerly B.C.), intense competitive interaction among many chiefdoms in Mesoamerica fueled rapid social change. Some chiefdoms would develop into states (e.g., Oaxaca, Valley of Mexico). Others (e.g., Olmec) would not. In the Valley of Oaxaca, changing military patterns—from village raiding to conquest warfare—played a prominent role in the formation of Mesoamerica's earliest state, the Zapotec state, whose capital was Monte Albán. This city served as the Zapotec capital for 1,200 years, from 500 B.C.E. to 700 C.E. (formerly A.D.). After that, the Zapotec state continued, but in the form of small principalities that fought among themselves until Spanish conquest in the early 16th century C.E. By 1 C.E., the Valley of Mexico had come to prominence. In this large valley in the highlands, Teotihuacán thrived between 100 and 700 C.E. Tenochtitlán, the capital of the Aztec state (1325–1520 C.E.), may have surpassed Teotihuacán at its height.

**8.** Early states faced various threats: invasion, disease, famine, drought, soil exhaustion, erosion, and the buildup of irrigation salts. States may collapse when they fail to keep social and economic order or to protect themselves against outsiders. The Maya state fell in the face of increased warfare among competing dynasties.

## key terms

Aztec 225

bronze 218

chiefdom 208

cuneiform 218

egalitarian society 215

empire 210

Halafian 214

Mesopotamia 213

metallurgy 218

polity 208

primary states 209

ranked society 215

settlement hierarchy 225

smelting 218

state 209

stratification 215

Teotihuacán 225

Zapotec state 224

## critical thinking

1. This chapter describes Robert Carneiro's (1970) theory of state formation. Summarize that theory. How is it representative of a systemic perspective?

2. Imagine yourself an archaeologist trying to identify ancient chiefdoms in the Middle East after excavating Mesoamerican chiefdom sites. What similar and different lines of evidence for ranking and political alliance might you find in the two contexts?

3. How could reviewing the history of state formation prompt us to reexamine our assumptions about what is natural or universal about social organization?

4. Only those ranked societies with loss of village autonomy should be called chiefdoms. What kinds of evidence could archaeologists search for as clues of this loss of autonomy?

5. Based on the evidence from coastal Peru (near the beginning of this chapter) and Oaxaca (near the end of this chapter), what role did warfare play in early state formation?

## CHAPTER 13

# Method and Theory in Cultural Anthropology

- ▶ Where and how do cultural anthropologists do fieldwork?

- ▶ What are some ways of studying modern societies?

- ▶ What theories have guided anthropologists over the years?

A French anthropologist (left) converses with villagers in the Aru Islands, eastern Indonesia.

# understanding OURSELVES

To many, the word "anthropology" may evoke an image of archaeological digs. Remember, however, that anthropology has four subfields, only two of which (archaeology and biological anthropology) require much digging—in the ground, at least. To be sure, cultural anthropologists "dig out" information about lifestyles, just as linguistic anthropologists do about the features of unwritten languages. Traditionally, cultural anthropologists have done a variant on the *Star Trek* theme of seeking out if not new, at least different "life" and "civilizations," sometimes boldly going where no scientist has gone before.

Despite globalization, the cultural diversity under anthropological scrutiny right now may be as great as ever before, because the anthropological universe has expanded to modern nations. Today's cultural anthropologists are as likely to be studying artists in Miami or bankers in Beirut as Trobriand sailors in the South Pacific. Still, we can't forget that anthropology did originate in non-Western, nonindustrial societies. Its research techniques, especially those subsumed under the label "ethnography," were developed to deal with small populations. Even when working in modern nations, anthropologists still consider ethnography with small groups to be an excellent way of learning about how people live their lives and make decisions.

For the general public, biological anthropologists and archaeologists tend to be better known than cultural anthropologists because of what they study. One cultural anthropologist was an extremely important public figure when (and before and after) I was in college. Margaret Mead, famed for her work on teen sexuality in Samoa and gender roles in New Guinea, may well be the most famous anthropologist who ever lived. Mead, one of my own professors at Columbia University, appeared regularly on NBC's *The Tonight Show*. In all her venues, including teaching, museum work, TV, anthropological films, popular books, and magazines, Mead helped Americans appreciate the relevance of anthropology to understanding their daily lives. Her work is featured here and elsewhere in this book.

## ETHNOGRAPHY: ANTHROPOLOGY'S DISTINCTIVE STRATEGY

Anthropology emerged as a distinctive field of inquiry as its early scholars focused on Native Americans or traveled to distant lands to study small groups of foragers (hunters and gatherers) and cultivators. Traditionally, the process of becoming a cultural anthropologist has required a field experience in another society. Early ethnographers studied small-scale, relatively isolated societies with simple technologies and economies.

Ethnography thus emerged as a research strategy in societies with less social differentiation than is found in large, modern, industrial nations (see Moore 2009). Traditionally, ethnographers have tried to understand the whole of a particular culture (or, more realistically, as much as they can, given limitations of time and perception). To pursue this goal, ethnographers adopt a free-ranging strategy. The ethnographer moves from setting to setting, place to place, and subject to subject to discover the totality and interconnectedness of social life. Ethnographers draw on varied techniques to piece together a picture of otherwise alien lifestyles. Anthropologists usually employ several (but rarely all) of the techniques discussed next (see also Bernard 2011; Wolcott 2010).

# ETHNOGRAPHIC TECHNIQUES

The characteristic *field techniques* of the ethnographer include the following:

1. Direct, firsthand observation of behavior, including *participant observation.*

2. Conversation with varying degrees of formality, from the daily chitchat that helps maintain rapport and provides knowledge about what is going on to prolonged *interviews,* which can be unstructured or structured.

3. The *genealogical method.*

4. Detailed work with *key consultants,* or *informants,* about particular areas of community life.

5. In-depth interviewing, often leading to the collection of *life histories* of particular people (narrators).

6. Problem-oriented research of many sorts.

7. Longitudinal research—the continuous long-term study of an area or a site.

8. Team research—coordinated research by multiple ethnographers.

## Observation and Participant Observation

Ethnographers must pay attention to hundreds of details of daily life, seasonal events, and unusual happenings. They should record what they see as they see it. Things never again will seem quite as strange as they do during the first few weeks in the field. Often anthropologists experience culture shock—a creepy and profound feeling of alienation—on arrival at a new field site. Although anthropologists study human diversity, the actual field experience of diversity takes some getting used to, as we see in this chapter's "Appreciating Diversity." The ethnographer eventually grows accustomed to, and accepts as normal, cultural patterns that initially were alien. Staying a bit more than a year in the field allows the ethnographer to repeat the season of his or her arrival, when certain events and processes may have been missed because of initial unfamiliarity and culture shock.

Many ethnographers record their impressions in a personal *diary,* which is kept separate from more formal *field notes.* Later, this record of early impressions will help point out some of the most basic aspects of cultural diversity. Such aspects include distinctive smells, noises people make, how they cover their mouths when they eat, and how they gaze at others. These patterns, which are so basic as to seem almost trivial, are part of what Bronislaw Malinowski called "the imponderabilia of native life

and of typical behavior" (Malinowski 1922/1961, p. 20). These aspects of culture are so fundamental that natives take them for granted. They are too basic even to talk about, but the unaccustomed eye of the fledgling ethnographer picks them up. Thereafter, becoming familiar, they fade to the edge of consciousness. I mention my initial impressions of some such imponderabilia of northeastern Brazilian culture in this chapter's "Appreciating Diversity."

Ethnographers strive to establish *rapport,* a good, friendly working relationship based on personal contact, with their hosts. One of ethnography's most characteristic procedures is participant observation, which means that we take part in community life as we study it. As human beings living among others, we cannot be totally impartial and detached observers. We take part in many events and processes we are observing and trying to comprehend. By participating, we may learn why people find such events meaningful, as we see how they are organized and conducted.

In Arembepe, Brazil, I learned about fishing by sailing on the Atlantic with local fishers. I gave Jeep rides to malnourished babies, to pregnant mothers, and once to a teenage girl possessed by a spirit. All those people needed to consult specialists outside the village. I danced on Arembepe's festive occasions, drank libations commemorating new births, and became a godfather to a village girl. Most anthropologists have similar field experiences. The common humanity of the student and the studied, the ethnographer and the research community, makes participant observation inevitable.

## Conversation, Interviewing, and Interview Schedules

Participating in local life means that ethnographers constantly talk to people and ask questions. As their knowledge of the local language and culture increases, they understand more. There are several stages in learning a field language. First is the naming phase—asking name after name of the objects around us. Later we are able to pose more complex questions and understand the replies. We begin to understand simple conversations between two villagers. If our language expertise proceeds far enough, we eventually become able to comprehend rapid-fire public discussions and group conversations.

One data-gathering technique I have used in both Arembepe and Madagascar involves an ethnographic survey that includes an interview schedule. During my second summer of fieldwork in Arembepe, my fellow field workers and I attempted to complete an interview schedule in each of that community's 160 households. We entered almost every household (fewer than 5 percent refused to participate) to ask a set of questions on a printed form. Our results provided us with a census and basic information about the village. We wrote down the name, age, and

# appreciating DIVERSITY

## Even Anthropologists Get Culture Shock

My first field experience in Arembepe (Brazil) took place between my junior and senior years at New York City's Columbia College, where I was majoring in anthropology. I went to Arembepe as a participant in a now defunct program designed to provide undergraduates with experience doing ethnography—firsthand study of an alien society's culture and social life.

Brought up in one culture, intensely curious about others, anthropologists nevertheless experience culture shock, particularly on their first field trip. *Culture shock* refers to the whole set of feelings about being in an alien setting, and the ensuing reactions. It is a chilly, creepy feeling of alienation, of being without some of the most ordinary, trivial (and therefore basic) cues of one's culture of origin.

As I planned my departure for Brazil that year, I could not know just how naked I would feel without the cloak of my own language and culture. My sojourn in Arembepe would be my first trip outside the United States. I was an urban boy who had grown up in Atlanta, Georgia, and New York City. I had little experience with rural life in my own country, none with Latin America, and I had received only minimal training in the Portuguese language.

New York City direct to Salvador, Bahia, Brazil. Just a brief stopover in Rio de Janeiro; a longer

visit would be a reward at the end of fieldwork. As our prop jet approached tropical Salvador, I couldn't believe the whiteness of the sand. "That's not snow, is it?" I remarked to a fellow field team member. . . .

My first impressions of Bahia were of smells—alien odors of ripe and decaying mangoes,

bananas, and passion fruit—and of swatting the ubiquitous fruit flies I had never seen before, although I had read extensively about their reproductive behavior in genetics classes. There were strange concoctions of rice, black beans, and gelatinous gobs of unidentifiable meats and floating pieces of skin. Coffee was strong and sugar crude,

**FIGURE 13.1** Location of Arembepe, Bahia, Brazil.

gender of each household member. We gathered data on family type, religion, present and previous jobs, income, expenditures, diet, possessions, and many other items on our eight-page form.

Although we were doing a survey, our approach differed from the survey research done by sociologists and other social scientists working in large, industrial nations. That survey research, discussed on pp. 237–238, involves *sampling* (choosing a small, manageable study group from a larger population). We did not select a partial sample from Arembepe's total population. Instead, we tried to interview in all households (i.e., to have a total sample). We used an interview schedule rather than a questionnaire. With the **interview schedule,** the eth-

nographer talks face-to-face with people, asks the questions, and writes down the answers. **Questionnaire** procedures tend to be more impersonal; often the respondent fills in the form.

Our goal of getting a total sample allowed us to meet almost everyone in the village and helped us establish rapport. Decades later, Arembepeiros still talk warmly about how we were interested enough in them to visit their homes and ask them questions. We stood in sharp contrast to the other outsiders the villagers had known, who considered them too poor and backward to be taken seriously.

Like other survey research, however, our interview schedule did gather comparable quantifiable information. It gave us a basis for assessing patterns and every tabletop had containers for toothpicks and for manioc (cassava) flour to sprinkle, like Parmesan cheese, on anything one might eat. I remember oatmeal soup and a slimy stew of beef tongue in tomatoes. At one meal a disintegrating fish head, eyes still attached, but barely, stared up at me as the rest of its body floated in a bowl of bright orange palm oil. . . .

I only vaguely remember my first day in Arembepe [Figure 13.1]. Unlike ethnographers who have studied remote tribes in the tropical forests of interior South America or the highlands of Papua New Guinea, I did not have to hike or ride a canoe for days to arrive at my field site. Arembepe was not isolated relative to such places, only relative to every other place I had ever been. . . .

I do recall what happened when we arrived. There was no formal road into the village. Entering through southern Arembepe, vehicles simply threaded their way around coconut trees, following tracks left by automobiles that had passed previously. A crowd of children had heard us coming, and they pursued our car through the village streets until we parked in front of our house, near the central square. Our first few days in Arembepe were spent with children following us everywhere. For weeks we had few moments of privacy. Children watched our every move through our living room window. Occasionally one made an incomprehensible remark. Usually they just stood there. . . .

The sounds, sensations, sights, smells, and tastes of life in northeastern Brazil, and in Arembepe, slowly grew familiar. . . . I grew accustomed to this world without Kleenex, in which globs of mucus habitually drooped from the noses of village children whenever a cold passed through Arembepe. A world where, seemingly without effort, women . . . carried 18-liter kerosene cans of water on their heads, where boys sailed kites and sported at catching houseflies in their bare hands, where old women smoked pipes, storekeepers offered cachaça (common rum) at nine in the morning, and men played dominoes on lazy afternoons when there was no fishing. I was visiting a world where human life was oriented toward water—the sea, where men fished, and the lagoon, where women communally washed clothing, dishes, and their own bodies.

Conrad Kottak, with his Brazilian nephew, Guilherme Roxo, on a revisit to Arembepe in 2004.

This description is adapted from my ethnographic study *Assault on Paradise: The Globalization of a Little Community in Brazil*, 4th ed. (New York: McGraw-Hill, 2006).

and exceptions in village life. Our schedules included a core set of questions that were posed to everyone. However, some interesting side issues often came up during the interview, which we would pursue then or later. We followed such leads into many dimensions of village life. One woman, for instance, a midwife, became the key cultural consultant we sought out later when we wanted detailed information about local childbirth. Another woman had done an internship in an Afro-Brazilian cult (*candomblé*) in the city. She still went there regularly to study, dance, and get possessed. She became our candomblé expert.

Thus, our interview schedule provided a structure that *directed but did not confine* us as researchers.

It enabled our ethnography to be both quantitative and qualitative. The quantitative part consisted of the basic information we gathered and later analyzed statistically. The qualitative dimension came from our follow-up questions, open-ended discussions, pauses for gossip, and work with key consultants.

## The Genealogical Method

Many of us learn about our ancestry and relatives by tracing our genealogies. Computer programs and websites allow us to fill in our "family trees." The **genealogical method** is a well-established ethnographic technique. Extended kinship is a prominent

**genealogical method**
Using diagrams and symbols to record kin connections.

Kinship and descent are vital social building blocks in nonindustrial cultures. Without writing, genealogical information may be preserved in material culture, such as this totem pole being raised in Metlakatla, Alaska.

organizing such societies, because strategic marriages between villages, tribes, and clans create political alliances.

## Key Cultural Consultants

The term **cultural consultants,** or *informants,* refers to individuals the ethnographer gets to know in the field, the people who teach him or her about their culture. Every community has people who by accident, experience, talent, or training can provide the most complete or useful information about particular aspects of life. These people are **key cultural consultants,** also called *key informants.* In Ivato, the Betsileo village in Madagascar where I spent most of my time, a man named Rakoto was particularly knowledgeable about village history. However, when I asked him to work with me on a genealogy of the 50 to 60 people buried in the village tomb, he called in his cousin Tuesdaysfather, who knew more about that subject. Tuesdaysfather had survived an epidemic of influenza that ravaged Madagascar, along with much of the world, around 1919. Immune to the disease himself, Tuesdaysfather had the grim job of burying his kin as they died. He kept track of everyone buried in the tomb. Tuesdaysfather helped me with the tomb genealogy. Rakoto joined him in telling me personal details about the deceased villagers.

**cultural consultants**
People who teach an ethnographer about their culture.

**key cultural consultants**
Experts on a particular aspect of local life.

**life history**
Of a key consultant; a personal portrait of someone's life in a culture.

building block in the social organization of nonindustrial societies, where people live and work each day with their close kin. Anthropologists need to collect genealogical data to understand current social relations and to reconstruct history. In many nonindustrial societies, links through kinship and marriage form the core of social life. Anthropologists even call such cultures "kin-based societies." Everyone is related and spends most of his or her time with relatives. Rules of behavior associated with particular kin relations are basic to everyday life (see Carsten 2004). Marriage also is crucial in

## Life Histories

In nonindustrial societies as in our own, individual personalities, interests, and abilities vary. Some villagers prove to be more interested in the ethnographer's work and are more helpful, interesting, and pleasant than others are. Anthropologists develop likes and dislikes in the field as we do at home. Often, when we find someone unusually interesting, we collect his or her **life history.** This recollection of a lifetime of experiences provides a more intimate and personal cultural portrait than would be possible otherwise. Life histories, which may be recorded or videoed for later review and analysis, reveal how specific people perceive, react to, and contribute to changes that affect their lives. Such accounts can illustrate diversity, which exists within any community, because the focus is on how different people interpret and deal with some of the same problems. Many ethnographers include the collection of life histories as an important part of their research strategy.

## Problem-Oriented Ethnography

Although anthropologists are interested in the whole context of human behavior, it is impossible to study everything. Most ethnographers now enter the field with a specific problem to investigate, and they collect data relevant to that problem (see Murchison 2010; Sunstein and Chiseri-Strater 2012). Local people's answers to questions are not the only data source.

Anthropologists such as Christie Kiefer typically form personal relationships with their cultural consultants, such as this Guatemalan weaver.

Anthropologists also gather information on factors such as population density, climate, diet, and land use. Sometimes this involves direct measurement—of rainfall, temperature, fields, yields, dietary quantities, or time allocation. Often it means that we consult government records or archives.

The information of interest to ethnographers is not limited to what local people can and do tell us. In an increasingly interconnected and complicated world, local people lack knowledge about many factors that affect their lives. Our local consultants may be as mystified as we are by the exercise of power from regional, national, and international centers.

## Longitudinal Research

Geography limits anthropologists less now than in the past, when it could take months to reach a field site and return visits were rare. New systems of transportation allow anthropologists to widen the area of their research and to return repeatedly. Ethnographic reports now routinely include data from two or more field stays. **Longitudinal research** is the long-term study of a community, region, society, culture, or other unit.

One example of such research is the ongoing study of Gwembe District, Zambia (see Figure 13.2). This study, planned in 1956 as a longitudinal project by Elizabeth Colson and Thayer Scudder, continues with Colson, Scudder, and their associates of various nationalities. Thus, as is often the case with longitudinal research, the Gwembe study also illustrates team research—coordinated research by multiple ethnographers (Colson and Scudder 1975; Scudder and Colson 1980). The researchers have studied four villages, in different areas, for over 50 years. Periodic village censuses provide basic data on population, economy, kinship, and religious behavior. Censused people who have moved are traced and interviewed to see how their lives compare with those of people who have stayed in the villages.

Over time new research questions have emerged, although basic data on communities and individuals continue to be collected. The first focus of study was the impact of a large hydroelectric dam, which subjected the Gwembe people to forced resettlement. The dam also spurred road building and other activities that brought the people of Gwembe more closely in touch with the rest of Zambia. In subsequent research Scudder and Colson (1980) examined how education provided access to new opportunities as it also widened a social gap between people with different educational levels. A third study examined a change in brewing and drinking patterns, including a rise in alcoholism, in relation to changing markets, transportation, and exposure to town values (Colson and Scudder 1988). Retired from the University of California at Berkeley, where she holds the title of Professor Emerita, Colson, now in her nineties, currently resides in Gwembe district, where the project continues.

**FIGURE 13.2** Location of Gwembe in Zambia.

## Team Research

As mentioned, longitudinal research often is team research. My own field site of Arembepe, Brazil, for example, first entered the world of anthropology as a field-team village in the 1960s. It was one of four sites for the now defunct Columbia-Cornell-Harvard-Illinois Summer Field Studies Program in Anthropology. For at least three years, that program sent a total of about 20 undergraduates annually, the author included, to do summer research abroad. We were stationed in rural communities in four countries: Brazil, Ecuador, Mexico, and Peru. See this chapter's "Appreciating Diversity" on pp. 232–233 for information on how a novice undergraduate ethnographer perceived Arembepe.

Since my wife, Isabel Wagley Kottak, and I first studied it in the 1960s, Arembepe has become a longitudinal field site. Multiple researchers have monitored various aspects of change and development there. Arembepe, now a small city, illustrates the process of globalization at the local level. Its

**longitudinal research**

Long-term study, usually based on repeated visits.

economy, religion, and social life have been transformed (see Kottak 2006).

Brazilian and American researchers worked with us on team research projects during the 1980s (on television's impact) and the 1990s (on ecological awareness and environmental risk perception). Students from various universities have drawn on our baseline information from the 1960s in their recent studies in Arembepe. Their topics have included standards of physical attractiveness, family planning and changing female reproductive strategies, conversion to Protestantism, and changing food habits in relation to globalization. Arembepe is thus a site where various field workers have worked as members of a longitudinal, multigenerational team. The more recent researchers have built on prior contacts and findings to increase knowledge about how local people meet and manage new circumstances. As of this writing (2013), new researchers are at work in Arembepe and other Brazilian communities, updating our study of media, which began during the 1980s.

# ETHNOGRAPHIC PERSPECTIVES

## Emic and Etic

One goal of ethnography is to discover local (native) views, beliefs, and perceptions, which may be compared with the ethnographer's own observations and conclusions. In the field, ethnographers typically combine two perspectives, the emic (native-oriented) and the etic (scientist-oriented). These terms, derived from linguistics, have been applied to ethnography by various anthropologists. Marvin Harris (1968/2001b) popularized the following meanings of the terms: An **emic** perspective is concerned with how local people think. How do they perceive, categorize, and explain things? What are their rules for behavior?

Janet Dunn, one of many anthropologists who have worked in Arembepe. Her study focused on family planning and female reproductive strategies. Where is Arembepe, and what kinds of research have been done there?

What has meaning for them? The ethnographer seeks to understand the "native viewpoint," relying on local people to explain things and to say whether something is significant or not.

With the **etic** perspective, the focus shifts from local observations, categories, explanations, and interpretations to those of the anthropologist. Members of a culture often are too involved in what they are doing to interpret their culture impartially. Operating etically, the ethnographer emphasizes what he or she (the observer) notices and considers important. As a trained scientist, the ethnographer should try to bring an objective and comprehensive viewpoint to the study of other cultures. Of course, the ethnographer, like any other scientist, is also a human being with cultural blinders that prevent complete objectivity. As in other sciences, proper training can reduce, but not totally eliminate, the observer's bias. But anthropologists do have special training to compare behavior in different societies.

What are some examples of emic versus etic perspectives? Consider our holidays. For North Americans, Thanksgiving Day has special significance. In our view (emically) it is a unique cultural celebration that commemorates particular historical themes. But a wider, etic, perspective sees Thanksgiving as just one more example of the postharvest festivals held in many societies. Another example: Local people (including many Americans) may believe that chills and drafts cause colds, which scientists know are caused by germs. In cultures that lack the germ theory of disease, illnesses are emically explained by various causes, ranging from spirits to ancestors to witches. *Illness* refers to a culture's (emic) perception and explanation of bad health, whereas *disease* refers to the scientific (etic) explanation of poor health, involving known pathogens.

Ethnographers typically combine emic and etic perspectives in their fieldwork. The statements, perceptions, categories, and opinions of local people help ethnographers understand how cultures work. Local beliefs also are interesting and valuable in themselves. However, people often fail to admit, or even recognize, certain causes and consequences of their behavior. This is as true of North Americans as it is of people in other societies.

## Expansion in Analytic Scale

The previous sections on longitudinal and team research illustrate an important shift in cultural anthropology. Traditional ethnographic research focused on a single community or "culture," which was treated as more or less isolated and unique in time and space. The shift has been toward a wider and larger scale of analysis that includes flows (now global in scope) of people, technology, images, and information. The study of such flows and linkages is now an important part of anthropological analysis. And reflecting today's world—in which people, images, and information move about as never

**etic**
Research strategy emphasizing the ethnographer's explanations and categories.

**emic**
Research strategy focusing on local explanations and meanings.

before—fieldwork must be more flexible and on a larger scale. Ethnography is increasingly multitimed and multisited. Malinowski could focus on Trobriand culture and spend most of his field time in a particular community. Nowadays we cannot afford to ignore, as Malinowski did, the "outsiders" who increasingly impinge on the places we study (e.g., migrants, refugees, terrorists, warriors, tourists, developers). Integral to our analyses now are the external organizations and forces (e.g., governments, businesses, nongovernmental organizations) laying claim to land, people, and resources throughout the world.

Anthropologists increasingly study people in motion. Examples include people living on or near national borders, nomads, seasonal migrants, homeless and displaced people, immigrants, and refugees (see Lugo 1997). As fieldwork changes, with less and less of a spatially set field, what can we take from traditional ethnography? Gupta and Ferguson correctly cite the "characteristically anthropological emphasis on daily routine and lived experience" (1997a, p. 5). The treatment of communities as discrete entities may be a thing of the past. However, "anthropology's traditional attention to the close observation of particular lives in particular places" has an enduring importance (Gupta and Ferguson, eds., 1997b, p. 25). The method of close observation helps distinguish cultural anthropology from sociology and survey research (see pp. 237–238).

## Online Ethnography

The relatively recent creation of virtual worlds has attracted contemporary ethnographers to venture into online communities. Tom Boellstorff, Bonnie Nardi, Celia Pearce, and T. L. Taylor offer a handbook for fieldwork in virtual worlds (Boellstorff et al. 2012). All four have researched gaming-oriented online environments, including *Second Life, World of Warcraft, Dreamscape, There.com,* and *Myst Online: Uru Live.* Various techniques have been used to study these virtual worlds. Most important is participant observation; the ethnographic researchers became skilled players as they observed the online environment and the interactions within it. Each virtual world has developed its own culture, which includes rules and governance, customary practices and events, social roles and modes of interaction, and power differentials. When *Uru Live* was discontinued in 2008, Uru refugees moved on to other virtual worlds, where they have created and retain a strong ethnic Uru identity. Although virtual environments are created by software designers, those who enter and thrive in these worlds can innovate within the constraints set by "the system"—either the software program or other participants. Within these worlds, the online ethnographers have observed and described various forms of play, performance, creativity, and ritual.

Virtual worlds have been heavily influenced by works of science fiction and fantasy. Early games

A teen plays computer games in his bedroom. To what extent is this kind of gaming a social experience?

owed a debt to the imaginary world of Middle Earth created by J. R. R. Tolkien, of *The Hobbit* and *The Lord of the Rings* fame. Online worlds are sophisticated places of imagination with their own species, artifacts, characters, and customs. The avatar is the representation of self in a virtual world. People in cyberspace can have multiple identities, which often contrast—in gender, for example—with their real-world identities. A person's multiple avatars are known as alts—alternative identities or personalities.

The online ethnographer sometimes moves offline to visit players in their real-world setting (e.g., a home or an Internet café). In some cases, ethnographers have traveled abroad to see how a given game is played in different countries and how real-world culture influences participation in the virtual world. There are virtual world fan conventions, which the ethnographer may attend. Interviews can be conducted either or both on- and offline in a participant's virtual or real-world home. Informal conversations online reveal what players are thinking about as they play. To understand the social organization of their virtual field site, ethnographers may draw diagrams of social relations, similar to genealogies drawn during real-world fieldwork. Timelines are useful for understanding the succession of virtual events such as dances, festivals, or auctions. Brief site drop-ins can be used to respond to instant messages, keep up with announcements, and find out when players typically log in. Virtual research offers various means of record keeping, note taking, and recording typical of the online environment. These include chat logs and screenshots, as well as audio and video recording.

This section has summarized some features of online research as discussed by Boellstorff and his coauthors (2012). Readers interested in doing virtual world fieldwork should consult that handbook.

## SURVEY RESEARCH

As anthropologists work increasingly in large-scale societies, they have developed innovative ways of blending ethnography and survey research

(Fricke 1994). Before examining such combinations of field methods, let's consider survey research and the main differences between survey research and ethnography. Working mainly in large, populous nations, sociologists, political scientists, and economists have developed and refined the **survey research** design, which involves sampling, impersonal data collection, and statistical analysis. Survey research usually draws a **sample** (a manageable study group) from a much larger population. By studying a properly selected and representative sample, social scientists can make accurate inferences, or at least good guesses, about the larger population.

In smaller-scale societies and communities, ethnographers get to know most of the people. Given the greater size and complexity of nations, survey research can't help being more impersonal. Survey researchers call the people they study *respondents*. These are people who respond to questions during a survey. Sometimes survey researchers interview their respondents directly—in person or by phone. Respondents may be asked to fill out a questionnaire, written or online. A survey may be mailed or e-mailed to randomly selected sample members. In a **random sample,** all members of the population have an equal statistical chance of being chosen for inclusion. A random sample is selected by randomizing procedures, such as tables of random numbers, which are found in many statistics textbooks.

Probably the most familiar example of sampling is political polling. An ever increasing number of organizations now gather information designed to estimate outcomes and to determine what kinds of people voted for which candidates. During sampling, researchers gather information about age, gender, religion, occupation, income, and political party preference. These characteristics (**variables**—attributes that vary among members of a sample or population) are known to influence political decisions.

Many more variables affect social identities, experiences, and activities in a modern nation than in the small communities where ethnography grew up. In contemporary North America, hundreds of factors influence our behavior and attitudes. These social predictors include our religion; where we grew up; and our parents' professions, ethnic origins, political leanings, and income levels.

Ethnography can be used to supplement and fine-tune survey research. Anthropologists can transfer the personal, firsthand techniques of ethnography to virtually any setting. A combination of survey research and ethnography can provide new perspectives on life in **complex societies** (large and populous societies with social stratification and central governments). Preliminary ethnography also can help develop culturally appropriate questions for inclusion in surveys. Recap 13.1 contrasts traditional ethnography with elements of survey research.

In any complex society, many predictor variables (*social indicators*) influence behavior and opinions. Because we must be able to detect, measure, and compare the influence of social indicators, many contemporary anthropological studies have a statistical foundation. Even in rural fieldwork, anthropologists increasingly use samples, gather quantitative data, and use statistics to interpret them (see Bernard 1998, 2011). Quantifiable information may permit a more precise assessment of similarities and differences among communities. Statistical analysis can support and round out an ethnographic account of local social life.

However, in the best studies, the hallmark of ethnography remains: Anthropologists enter the community and get to know the people. They participate in local activities, networks, and associations. They watch the effects of national and international policies on local life. The ethnographic method and the emphasis on personal relationships in social research are valuable gifts that cultural anthropology brings to the study of any society.

## DOING ANTHROPOLOGY RIGHT AND WRONG: ETHICAL ISSUES

The anthropologist Clyde Kluckhohn (1944) saw a key public service role for anthropology. It could provide a "scientific basis for dealing with the crucial dilemma of the world today: how can peoples of different appearance, mutually unintelligible languages, and dissimilar ways of life get along peaceably together?" Many anthropologists never would have

On November 1, 2010, in China's Shandong Province, census takers gathered personal information from a family during the Sixth National Population Census. From November 1 to November 10, more than six million census takers visited over 400 million households across the country.

| ETHNOGRAPHY (TRADITIONAL) | SURVEY RESEARCH |
|---|---|
| Studies whole, functioning communities | Studies a small sample of a larger population |
| Usually is based on firsthand fieldwork, during which information is collected after rapport, based on personal contact, is established between researcher and hosts | Often is conducted with little or no personal contact between study subjects and researchers, as interviews are frequently conducted by assistants over the phone or in printed form |
| Traditionally is interested in all aspects of local life (holistic) | Usually focuses on a small number of variables (e.g., factors that influence voting) rather than on the totality of people's lives |
| Traditionally has been conducted in nonindustrial, small-scale societies, where people often do not read and write | Normally is carried out in modern nations, where most people are literate, permitting respondents to fill in their own questionnaires |
| Makes little use of statistics, because the communities being studied tend to be small, with little diversity besides that based on age, gender, and individual personality variation | Depends heavily on statistical analyses to make inferences regarding a large and diverse population, based on data collected from a small subset of that population |

chosen their profession had they doubted that anthropology had the capacity to enhance human welfare. Because we live in a world full of failed states, unrest, war, and terrorism, we must consider the proper role of anthropologists in studying such phenomena.

Anthropologists can't study things simply because they happen to be interesting or of value to science—or even because they may benefit the public. Ethical issues must also be a prime consideration. Working internationally and in the context of cultural diversity, different ethical codes and value systems will meet, and often challenge one another (see Whiteford and Trotter 2008).

Anthropologists must be sensitive to cultural differences and aware of procedures and standards in the host country (the place where the research takes place). Researchers must inform officials and colleagues about the purpose, funding, and likely results, products, and impacts of their research. **Informed consent** should be obtained from anyone who provides information or who might be affected by the research.

Anthropologists should try to (1) include host country colleagues in their research planning, (2) establish collaborative relationships with host country institutions, (3) include host country colleagues in dissemination, including publication, of the research results, and (4) ensure that something is "given back" to the host country. For example, research equipment stays in the host country, or funding is sought for host country colleagues to do research, attend international meetings, or visit foreign institutions.

## The Code of Ethics

The Code of Ethics of the American Anthropological Association (AAA) recognizes that anthropologists have obligations to their scholarly field, to the wider society, and to the human species, other

species, and the environment. The anthropologist's primary obligation is to *do no harm* to the people being studied. The stated aim of the AAA code is to offer guidelines and to promote discussion and education, rather than to investigate possible misconduct. Some of the code's main points may be reviewed.

Anthropologists should inform all parties affected by their research about its nature, goals, procedures, potential impacts, and source(s) of funding. Researchers should establish proper relationships with the countries and communities where they work. The full AAA Code of Ethics, as revised in 2012, can be found at the following website: http://ethics.aaanet.org/category/statement/.

## Anthropologists and Terrorism

The AAA has deemed it of "paramount importance" that anthropologists study the roots of terrorism and violence. How should such studies be conducted? What ethical issues might arise?

Consider a Pentagon program, Project Minerva, initiated late in the (George W.) Bush administration, designed to draw on social science expertise in dealing with national security threats. Project Minerva sought scholars to translate original documents captured in Iraq, study political shifts in China, and explain the resurgence of the Taliban in Afghanistan (Cohen 2008). Project Minerva and related programs raised concerns that governments might use anthropological knowledge in ethically problematic ways. Government policies and military operations have the potential to harm the people anthropologists study.

More recently, anthropologists have been especially critical of the Pentagon's Human Terrain System (HTS) program. Launched in February 2007, HTS has embedded anthropologists and other social scientists in military teams in Iraq and Afghanistan.

**informed consent** Agreement to take part in research—after having been informed about its purpose, nature, procedures, and possible impacts.

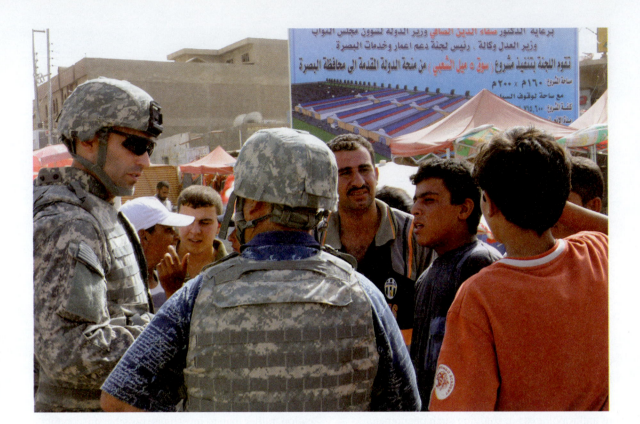

A member of a U.S. Army Human Terrain Team, left, talks (through an interpreter) to local people at a market in Basra, Iraq, in June 2009. What's problematic about anthropologists' participation in such projects?

On October 31, 2007, the AAA Executive Board issued a statement of disapproval of HTS—outlining how HTS violates the AAA Code of Ethics. (See http://www.aaanet.org/about/policies/statements/human-terrain-system-statement.cfm.) The board noted that HTS places anthropologists, as contractors with the U.S. military, in war zones, where they are charged with collecting cultural and social data for use by the military. The ethical concerns raised by these activities include the following:

1. It may be impossible for anthropologists in war zones to identify themselves as anthropologists, as distinct from military personnel. This constrains their ethical responsibility as anthropologists to disclose who they are and what they are doing.

2. HTS anthropologists are asked to negotiate relations among several groups, including local populations and the military units in which they are embedded. Their responsibilities to their units may conflict with their obligations to the local people they study or consult. This may interfere with the obligation, stipulated in the AAA Code of Ethics, to do no harm.

3. In an active war zone, it is difficult for local people to give informed consent without feeling coerced to provide information. As a result, "voluntary informed consent" (as stipulated in the AAA Code of Ethics) is compromised.

4. Information supplied by HTS anthropologists to military field commanders could help target specific groups for military action. Such use of fieldwork-derived information would violate the AAA Code of Ethics stipulation to do no harm to people.

5. The identification of anthropology and anthropologists with the U.S. military may indirectly (through suspicion of guilt by association) endanger the research, and even the personal safety, of other anthropologists and their consultants throughout the world.

What do you think about anthropologists' proper role in studying terrorism and war?

## THEORY IN ANTHROPOLOGY OVER TIME

Anthropology has various fathers and mothers. The fathers include Lewis Henry Morgan, Sir Edward Burnett Tylor, Franz Boas, and Bronislaw Malinowski. The mothers include Ruth Benedict and Margaret Mead. Some of the fathers might be classified better as grandfathers, since one, Franz Boas, was the intellectual father of Mead and Benedict, and since what is known now as Boasian anthropology arose mainly in opposition to the 19th-century evolutionism of Morgan and Tylor.

My goal in the remainder of this chapter is to survey the major theoretical perspectives that have characterized anthropology since its emergence in the second half of the 19th century (see also Erickson and Murphy 2013; McGee and Warms 2012; Moore

2009). Evolutionary perspectives, especially those associated with Morgan and Tylor, dominated 19th-century anthropology. The early 20th century witnessed various reactions to 19th-century evolutionism. In Great Britain, functionalists such as Malinowski and Alfred Reginald Radcliffe-Brown abandoned the speculative historicism of the evolutionists and instead did studies of living societies. In the United States, Boas and his followers rejected the search for evolutionary stages in favor of a historical approach that traced borrowing and the spread of culture traits across geographic areas. Functionalists and Boasians alike saw cultures as integrated and patterned.

## Unilinear Evolutionism

Let's begin this survey of anthropology's history with Tylor and Morgan, both of whom wrote classic books during the 19th century. Tylor (1871/1958) offered a definition of culture and proposed it as a topic that could be studied scientifically. Morgan's influential books included *Ancient Society* (1877/1963), *League of the Ho-dé-no-sau-nee or Iroquois* (1851/1966), and *Systems of Consanguinity and Affinity of the Human Family* (1870/1997). The first was a key work in cultural evolution. The second was an early ethnography. The third was the first systematic compendium of cross-cultural data on systems of kinship terminology.

*Ancient Society* is a key example of 19th-century evolutionism applied to society. Morgan assumed that human society had evolved through a series of stages, which he called savagery, barbarism, and civilization. He subdivided savagery and barbarism into three sub-stages each: lower, middle, and upper savagery and lower, middle, and upper barbarism. In Morgan's scheme, the earliest humans lived in lower savagery, with a subsistence based on fruits and nuts. In middle savagery people started fishing and gained control over fire. The invention of the bow and arrow ushered in upper savagery. Lower barbarism began when humans started making pottery. Middle barbarism in the Old World depended on the domestication of plants and animals, and in the Americas on irrigated agriculture. Iron smelting and the use of iron tools ushered in upper barbarism. Civilization, finally, came about with the invention of writing.

Morgan's evolutionism is known as **unilinear evolutionism,** because he assumed there was one line or path through which all societies evolved. Any society in upper barbarism, for example, had to include in its history, in order, periods of lower, middle, and upper savagery, and then lower and middle barbarism. Furthermore, Morgan believed that the societies of his time could be placed in the various stages. Some had not advanced beyond upper savagery. Others had made it to middle barbarism, while others had attained civilization.

Morgan's critics have disputed various elements of his scheme, including such loaded terms as "savagery" and "barbarism," and the particular criteria he used for

The early American anthropologist Lewis Henry Morgan described lacrosse (shown here) as one of the six games played by the tribes of the Iroquois nation, whose League he described in a famous book (1851).

each stage. Also, Morgan erred in assuming that societies could follow only one evolutionary path. In fact, societies have followed multiple developmental paths.

In his book *Primitive Culture* (1871/1958), Tylor took an evolutionary approach to the anthropology of religion. Like Morgan, Tylor proposed a unilinear path—from animism to polytheism, then monotheism, and finally science. In Tylor's view, religion would retreat when science provided better explanations. Both Tylor and Morgan were interested in *survivals,* practices that survive in contemporary society from earlier evolutionary stages. The belief in ghosts today, for example, would represent a survival from the stage of animism—the belief in spiritual beings. Survivals were taken as evidence that a particular society had passed through earlier evolutionary stages.

Morgan is well known also for *The League of the Iroquois,* anthropology's earliest ethnography. It was based on occasional rather than protracted fieldwork. Morgan, although one of anthropology's founders, was not himself a professionally trained anthropologist. He was a lawyer in upper New York State who was fond of visiting a nearby Seneca reservation and learning about their history and customs. The Seneca were one of six Iroquois tribes. Through his fieldwork, and his friendship with Ely Parker, an educated Iroquois man, Morgan was able to describe the social, political, religious, and economic principles of Iroquois life, including the history of their confederation. He laid out the structural principles on which Iroquois society was based. Morgan also used his skills as a lawyer to help the Iroquois in their fight with the Ogden Land Company, which was attempting to seize their lands.

**unilinear evolutionism**
Idea (19th-century) of a single line or path of cultural development.

# Historical Particularism

Franz Boas is the founder of American four-field anthropology. His book *Race, Language, and Culture* (1940/1966) is a collection of essays on those key topics. Boas contributed to cultural, biological, and linguistic anthropology. His biological studies of European immigrants to the United States revealed and measured phenotypical plasticity. The children of immigrants differed physically from their parents not because of genetic change but because they had grown up in a different environment. Boas showed that human biology was plastic. It could be changed by the environment, including cultural forces. Boas and his students worked hard to demonstrate that biology (including race) did not determine culture. In an important book, Ruth Benedict (1940) stressed the idea that people of many races have contributed to major historical advances.

In his fieldwork, Boas studied language and culture among Native Americans, most notably the Kwakiutl of the North Pacific coast of North America. Boas and his many influential students at New York's Columbia University took issue with 19th-century evolutionism on many counts, including the idea of a single, preordained evolutionary path. The Boasians argued that a given cultural feature, for example, totemism, did not follow a single path of development but could arise for many reasons. Their position was one of **historical particularism.** Because the particular histories of totemism in societies A, B, and C had all been different, those forms of totemism had different causes, which made them incomparable. They might seem to have been the same, but they were really different, because they had different histories. Any cultural form, from totemism to clans, could develop, they

believed, for all sorts of reasons. Boasian historical particularism rejected what those scholars called the *comparative method,* which was associated not only with Morgan and Tylor but with any anthropologist interested in cross-cultural comparison. The evolutionists had compared societies in attempting to reconstruct human evolutionary history. Later anthropologists, such as Émile Durkheim and Claude Lévi-Strauss (see pp. 247–248), also compared societies in attempting to explain cultural phenomena such as totemism. Indeed, cross-cultural comparison is alive and well in contemporary anthropology.

To explain *cultural generalities* (cultural traits that are shared by some but not all societies), the evolutionists had stressed independent invention: Eventually people in many areas had come up with the same cultural solution to a common problem. Agriculture, for example, was invented several times. The Boasians, while not denying independent invention, stressed the importance of diffusion, or borrowing, among cultures. The analytic units they used to study diffusion were the culture trait, the trait complex, and the culture area. A culture trait was something like a bow and arrow. A trait complex was the hunting pattern that went along with it. A culture area was based on the diffusion of traits and trait complexes across a particular geographic area, such as the Plains, the Southwest, or the North Pacific coast. Such areas usually had environmental boundaries that could limit the spread of culture traits outside that area. For the Boasians, historical particularism and diffusion were complementary. As culture traits diffused, they developed their particular histories as they entered and moved through particular societies. Boasians such as Alfred Kroeber, Clark Wissler, and Melville Herskovits

Franz Boas, founder of American four-field anthropology, studied the Kwakwaka'wakw, or Kwakiutl, in British Columbia (BC), Canada. The photo above shows Boas posing for a museum model of a Kwakiutl dancer. The photo on the right is a still from a film by anthropologist Aaron Glass titled *In Search of the Hamat'sa: A Tale of Headhunting* (DER distributor). It shows a real Kwakiutl dancer, Marcus Alfred, performing the same Hamat'sa (or "Cannibal Dance"), which is a vital part of an important Kwakiutl ceremony. The U'mista Cultural Centre in Alert Bay, BC (www.umista.org) owns the rights to the video clip of the Hamat'sa featuring Marcus Alfred.

studied the distribution of traits and developed culture area classifications for Native North America (Wissler and Kroeber) and Africa (Herskovits).

Historical particularism was based on the idea that each element of culture, such as the culture trait or trait complex, had its own distinctive history and that social forms (such as totemism in different societies) that might look similar were far from identical because of their different histories. Historical particularism rejected comparison and generalization in favor of an individuating historical approach. In this rejection, historical particularism stands in contrast to most of the approaches that have followed it.

## Functionalism

Another challenge to evolutionism (as well as to historical particularism) came from Great Britain. *Functionalism* postponed the search for origins (whether through evolution or through diffusion) and instead focused on the role of culture traits and practices in contemporary society. The two main strands of **functionalism** are associated respectively with Alfred Reginald Radcliffe-Brown and Bronislaw Malinowski, a Polish anthropologist who taught mainly in Great Britain.

### Malinowski

Both Malinowski and Radcliffe-Brown focused on the present rather than on historical reconstruction. Malinowski did pioneering fieldwork among living people. Usually considered the father of ethnography by virtue of his years of fieldwork in the Trobriand Islands, Malinowski was a functionalist in two senses. In the first, rooted in his ethnography, he believed that all customs and institutions in society were integrated and interrelated, so that if one changed, others would change as well. Each, then, was a *function* of the others. A corollary of this belief was that an ethnographer could begin anywhere and eventually get at the rest of the culture. Thus, a study of Trobriand fishing eventually would lead the ethnographer to study the entire economic system, the role of magic and religion, myth, trade, and kinship. The second strand of Malinowski's functionalism is known as *needs functionalism*. Malinowski (1944) believed that humans had a set of universal biological needs, and that customs developed to fulfill those needs. The function of any practice was the role it played in satisfying those universal biological needs, such as the need for food, sex, shelter, and so on.

### Radcliffe-Brown

According to Radcliffe-Brown (1962/1965), although history is important, social anthropology could never hope to discover the histories of people without writing. (*Social anthropology* is what cultural anthropology is called in Great Britain.) He trusted neither evolutionary nor diffusionist reconstructions. Viewing all historical statements about nonliterate peoples as merely conjectural, Radcliffe-Brown urged

Bronislaw Malinowski (1884–1942), who was born in Poland but spent most of his professional life in England, did fieldwork in the Trobriand Islands from 1914 to 1918. Malinowski is generally considered to be the father of ethnography. Does this photo suggest anything about his relationship with Trobriand villagers?

anthropologists to focus on the role that particular practices play in the life of societies today. In a famous essay Radcliffe-Brown (1962/1965) examined the prominent role of the mother's brother among the Ba Thonga of Mozambique. An evolutionist priest previously had explained the special role of the mother's brother in this patrilineal society as a survival from a time when the descent rule had been matrilineal. (In a patrilineal society, people belong to their father's group, whereas in a matrilineal society they belong to their mother's group. The unilinear evolutionists believed all human societies had passed through a matrilineal stage before becoming patrilineal.) Because Radcliffe-Brown believed that the history of the Ba Thonga could only be conjectural, he explained the special role of the mother's brother with reference to the institutions of present rather than past Ba Thonga society. Radcliffe-Brown advocated that social anthropology be a **synchronic** rather than a **diachronic** science, that is, that it study societies as they exist today (synchronic, at one time) rather than across time (diachronic).

### Structural Functionalism

The term *structural functionalism* is associated with Radcliffe-Brown and Edward Evan Evans-Pritchard, another prominent British social anthropologist. The latter is famous for many books, including *The Nuer* (1940), an ethnographic classic that laid out very clearly the structural principles that organized Nuer society in what is now South Sudan. According to functionalism and structural functionalism, customs (social practices) function to preserve the social structure. In Radcliffe-Brown's view, the *function* of any practice is the role it plays in maintaining the system of which it is a part. That system has a structure whose parts work (function) to maintain the whole. Radcliffe-Brown saw social systems

**functionalism**
Approach focusing on the role (function) of sociocultural practices in social systems.

**synchronic**
(Studying societies) at one time.

**diachronic**
(Studying societies) across time.

as comparable to anatomical and physiological systems. The function of organs and physiological processes is their role in keeping the body running smoothly. So, too, he thought, did customs, practices, social roles, and behavior function to keep the social system running smoothly. Given this suggestion of harmony, some functionalist models have been criticized as Panglossian, after Dr. Pangloss, a character in Voltaire's *Candide* who was fond of proclaiming this "the best of all possible worlds." Panglossian functionalism means a tendency to see things as functioning not just to maintain the system but to do so in the most optimal way possible, so that any deviation from the norm would only damage the system.

**configurationalism**
View of culture as integrated and patterned.

### The Manchester School

A group of British social anthropologists working at the University of Manchester, dubbed the Manchester school, are well known for their research in African societies and their departure from a Panglossian view of social harmony. Manchester anthropologists Max Gluckman and Victor Turner made conflict an important part of their analysis, such as when Gluckman wrote about rituals of rebellion. However, the Manchester school did not abandon functionalism totally. Its members examined how rebellion and conflict were regulated and dissipated, thus maintaining the system.

### Contemporary Functionalism

A form of functionalism persists today in the widely accepted view that there are social and cultural systems and that their elements, or constituent parts, are functionally related (are functions of each other) so that they covary: When one part changes, others also change. Also enduring is the idea that some elements—often the economic ones—are more important than others are. Few would deny, for example, that significant economic changes, such as the increasing cash employment of women, have led to changes in family and household organization and in related variables such as age at marriage and frequency of divorce. Changes in work and family arrangements then affect other variables, such as frequency of church attendance, which has declined in the United States and Canada.

## Configurationalism

Two of Boas's students, Benedict and Mead, developed an approach to culture that has been called **configurationalism.** This is related to functionalism in the sense that culture is seen as integrated. We've seen that the Boasians traced the geographic distribution of culture traits. But Boas recognized that diffusion wasn't automatic. Traits might not spread if they met environmental barriers, or if they were not accepted by a particular culture. There had to be a fit between the culture and the trait diffusing in, and borrowed traits would be *indigenized*—modified to fit the culture adopting them. Although traits can diffuse in from various directions, Benedict stressed that culture traits—indeed, whole cultures—are uniquely patterned or integrated. Her best-selling book *Patterns of Culture* (1934/1959) described such culture patterns.

Mead also found patterns in the cultures she studied, including Samoa, Bali, and Papua New Guinea. Mead was particularly interested in how cultures varied in their patterns of enculturation. Stressing the plasticity of human nature, she saw culture as a powerful force that created almost endless possibilities. Even among neighboring societies, different enculturation patterns could produce very different personality types and cultural configurations. Mead's best-known—albeit controversial—book is *Coming of Age in Samoa* (1928/1961). She traveled to Samoa to study female adolescence there in order to compare it with the same period of life in the United States. Suspicious of biologically determined universals, she assumed that Samoan adolescence would differ from the same period in the United States and that this would affect adult personality. Using her Samoan ethnographic findings, Mead contrasted the apparent sexual freedom there with the repression of adolescent sexuality in the United States. Her findings supported the Boasian view that culture, not biology, determines variation in human behavior and personality. Mead's later fieldwork among the Arapesh, Mundugumor, and Tchambuli of New Guinea resulted in *Sex and Temperament in Three Primitive Societies* (1935/1950). That book documented variation in male and female personality traits and behavior across cultures. She offered it as further support for cultural determinism. Like Benedict, Mead was more interested in describing how cultures were uniquely patterned or configured than in explaining how they got to be that way.

Max Gluckman, one of the founders of anthropology's "Manchester school," taught at the University of Manchester (shown here in a more recent shot) from 1949 until his death in 1975.

Two U.S. stamps commemorating anthropologists. The 46-cent stamp, issued in 1995, honors Ruth Fulton Benedict (1887–1948), best known for her widely read book *Patterns of Culture*. In 1998, the U.S. Postal Service issued this 32-cent Margaret Mead (1901–1978) stamp as part of its "Celebrate the Century" commemorative series. The stamp shows a young Dr. Mead against a Samoan background.

## Neoevolutionism

Around 1950, with the end of World War II and a growing anticolonial movement, anthropologists renewed their interest in culture change and even evolution. The American anthropologists Leslie White and Julian Steward complained that the Boasians had thrown the baby (evolution) out with the bath water (the particular flaws of 19th-century evolutionary schemes). There was a need, the neo-evolutionists contended, to reintroduce within the study of culture a powerful concept—evolution itself. This concept, after all, remains basic to biology. Why should it not apply to culture as well?

In his book *The Evolution of Culture* (1959), White claimed to be returning to the same concept of cultural evolution used by Tylor and Morgan, but now better informed by a century of archaeological discoveries and a much larger ethnographic record. White's approach has been called *general evolution,* the idea that over time and through the archaeological, historical, and ethnographic records, we can see the evolution of culture as a whole. For example, human economies have evolved from Paleolithic foraging, through early farming and herding, to intensive forms of agriculture, to industrialism. Sociopolitically, too, there has been evolution, from bands and tribes to chiefdoms and states. There can be no doubt, White argued, that culture has evolved. But unlike the unilinear evolutionists of the 19th century, White realized that particular cultures might not evolve in the same direction.

Julian Steward, in his influential book *Theory of Culture Change* (1955), proposed a different evolutionary model, which he called *multilinear evolution.* He showed how cultures have followed several different evolutionary paths. For example, he recognized different paths to statehood (e.g., those followed by irrigated versus nonirrigated societies). Steward was also a pioneer in a field of anthropology he called *cultural ecology,* today generally known as *ecological anthropology,* which considers the relationships between cultures and environmental variables.

Unlike Mead and Benedict, who were not interested in causes, White and Steward were. For White, energy capture was the main measure and cause of cultural advance: Cultures advanced in proportion to the amount of energy harnessed per capita per year. In this view, the United States is one of the world's

Margaret Mead in the field in Bali, Indonesia, in 1957.

Marvin Harris (1927–2001), chief advocate of the approach known as cultural materialism. Harris taught anthropology at Columbia University and the University of Florida.

which uncovers relations of cause and effect; and that the role of science is to discover causes, to find determinants. One of White's two influential books was *The Science of Culture* (1949). Malinowski set forth his theory of needs functionalism in a book titled *A Scientific Theory of Culture and Other Essays* (1944). Mead viewed anthropology as a humanistic science of unique value in understanding and improving the human condition.

Like Harris, White, and Steward, all of whom looked to infrastructural factors as determinants, Mead was a determinist, but of a very different sort. Mead's cultural determinism viewed human nature as more or less a blank slate on which culture could write almost any lesson. Culture was so powerful that it could change drastically the expression of a biological stage—adolescence—in Samoa and the United States. Mead stressed the role of culture rather than economy, environment, or material factors in this difference.

most advanced societies because of all the energy it harnesses and uses. White's formulation is ironic in viewing societies that deplete nature's bounty as being more advanced than those that conserve it.

Steward was equally interested in causality, and he looked to technology and the environment as the main causes of culture change. The environment and the technology available to exploit it were seen as part of what he called the *culture core*—the combination of environmental and economic factors that determined the overall configuration of any culture.

## Cultural Materialism

**cultural materialism**
Idea (Harris) that cultural infrastructure determines structure and superstructure.

In proposing **cultural materialism** as a theoretical paradigm, Marvin Harris drew on models of determinism associated with White and Steward. For Harris (1979/2001*a*) all societies had an *infrastructure,* corresponding to Steward's culture core, consisting of technology, economics, and demography—the systems of production and reproduction without which societies could not survive. Growing out of infrastructure was *structure*—social relations, forms of kinship and descent, patterns of distribution and consumption. The third layer was *superstructure:* religion, ideology, play—aspects of culture farthest away from the meat and bones that enable cultures to survive. Harris's key belief, shared with White, Steward, and Karl Marx, was that in the final analysis infrastructure determines structure and superstructure. Harris therefore took issue with theorists (he called them "idealists"), such as Max Weber, who argued for the prominent role of religion in changing society.

## Science and Determinism

**superorganic**
(Kroeber) The special domain of culture, beyond the organic and inorganic realms.

Harris's influential books include *The Rise of Anthropological Theory* (1968/2001*b*) and *Cultural Materialism: The Struggle for a Science of Culture* (1979/2001*a*). Like most of the anthropologists discussed so far, Harris insisted that anthropology is a *science;* that science is based on explanation,

## Culture versus the Individual
### White's Culturology
Interestingly, Leslie White, the avowed evolutionist and champion of energy as a measure of cultural progress, was, like Mead, a strong advocate of the importance of culture. White saw cultural anthropology as a science, and he named that science *culturology.* Cultural forces, which rested on the unique human capacity for symbolic thought, were so powerful, White believed, that individuals made little difference. White disputed what was then called the "great man theory of history," the idea that particular individuals were responsible for great discoveries and epochal changes. White looked instead to the constellation of cultural forces that produced great individuals. During certain historical periods, such as the Renaissance, conditions were right for the expression of creativity and greatness, and individual genius blossomed. At other times and places, there may have been just as many great minds, but the culture did not encourage their expression. As proof of this theory, White pointed to the simultaneity of discovery. Several times in human history, when culture was ready, people working independently in different places have come up with the same revolutionary idea or achievement at the same time. Examples include the formulation of the theory of evolution through natural selection by Charles Darwin and Alfred Russel Wallace, the independent rediscovery of Mendelian genetics by three scientists in 1917, and the independent invention of flight by the Wright brothers in the United States and Santos Dumont in Brazil.

### Kroeber's Superorganic
Much of the history of anthropology has been about the roles and relative prominence of culture and the individual. Like Mead and White, the prolific Boasian anthropologist Alfred Kroeber stressed the power of culture. Kroeber (1952/1987) described the realm of culture as **superorganic.** Its study, he thought, was

just as important as the study of the organic (life—without which there could be no superorganic) and the inorganic (chemistry and physics—the basis of the organic). Like White (and long before him Tylor, who first proposed a science of culture), Kroeber saw culture as the basis of a new science, which became cultural anthropology. Kroeber (1923) laid out the basis of this science in anthropology's first textbook. He attempted to demonstrate the power of culture over the individual by focusing on the rise and fall of particular styles and fashions, such as those involving women's hem lengths. Kroeber (1944) thought that individuals had little choice but to follow the trends of their times. Unlike White, Steward, and Harris, however, Kroeber did not attempt to explain cultural forces; he simply used them to show the power of culture over the individual. Like Mead, he was a cultural determinist.

### Durkheim's *Conscience Collectif*

In France, Émile Durkheim had taken a similar approach, calling for a new social science to be based in what he called, in French, the *conscience collectif.* The usual translation of this as "collective consciousness" does not convey adequately the similarity of this notion to Kroeber's superorganic and White's culturology. This new science, Durkheim proposed, would be based on the study of *social facts,* which were analytically distinct from facts about individuals. Psychologists study individuals; anthropologists study individuals as representative of something more. It is those larger systems, which consist of social positions—statuses and roles—and which are perpetuated across the generations through enculturation, that anthropologists should study.

Of course, sociologists also study such social systems, and Durkheim was a prominent early figure in both anthropology and sociology. Durkheim wrote of religion in Native Australia as readily as of suicide rates in modern societies. As analyzed by Durkheim, suicide rates (1897/1951) and religion (1912/2001) are collective phenomena. Individuals commit suicide for all sorts of reasons, but the variation in rates (which apply only to collectivities) can and should be linked to social phenomena, such as a sense of anomie, malaise, or alienation at particular times and in particular places.

## Symbolic and Interpretive Anthropology

Victor Turner was a colleague of Max Gluckman in the Department of Social Anthropology at the University of Manchester, and thus a member of the Manchester school, previously described, before moving to the United States, where he taught at the University of Chicago and the University of Virginia. Turner wrote several important works on ritual and symbols. *The Forest of Symbols* (1967) is a collection of essays about symbols and rituals among the Nbembu of Zambia, where Turner did his major fieldwork. In

*The Forest of Symbols,* Turner examines how symbols and rituals are used to regulate, anticipate, and avoid conflict. He also examines a hierarchy of meanings of symbols, from their social meanings and functions to their internalization within individuals.

Turner recognized links between **symbolic anthropology** (the study of symbols in their social and cultural context), a school he pioneered along with Mary Douglas (1970*a*), and such other fields as social psychology, psychology, and psychoanalysis. The study of symbols is all-important in psychoanalysis, whose founder, Sigmund Freud, also recognized a hierarchy of symbols, from potentially universal ones to those that had meaning for particular individuals and emerged during the analysis and interpretation of their dreams. Turner's symbolic anthropology flourished at the University of Chicago, where another major advocate, David Schneider (1968), developed a symbolic approach to American culture in his book *American Kinship: A Cultural Account* (1968).

Related to symbolic anthropology, and associated with the University of Chicago (and later with Princeton University), is **interpretive anthropology.** A primary advocate of this approach was Clifford Geertz, who defined culture as ideas based on cultural learning and symbols. During enculturation, individuals internalize a previously established system of meanings and symbols. They use this cultural system to define their world, express their feelings, and make their judgments.

Interpretive anthropology (Geertz 1973, 1983) approaches cultures as texts whose meanings must be deciphered in particular cultural and historical settings. Geertz's approach recalls Malinowski's belief that the ethnographer's primary task is "to grasp the native's point of view, his relation to life, to realize *his* vision of *his* world" (1922/1961, p. 25—Malinowski's italics). Since the 1970s, interpretive anthropology has considered the task of describing and interpreting that which is meaningful to natives. According to Geertz (1973), anthropologists may choose anything in a culture that interests or engages them (such as a Balinese cockfight he interprets

**symbolic anthropology**
The study of symbols in their social and cultural context.

**interpretive anthropology**
(Geertz) The study of a culture as a system of meaning.

Mary Douglas (1921–2007), a prominent symbolic anthropologist, who taught at University College, London, England, and Northwestern University, Evanston, Illinois. This photo shows her at an awards ceremony celebrating her receipt in 2003 of an honorary degree from Oxford.

in a famous essay), fill in details, and elaborate to inform their readers about meanings in that culture. Meanings are carried by public symbolic forms, including words, rituals, and customs.

## Structuralism

In anthropology, structuralism mainly is associated with Claude Lévi-Strauss, a renowned and prolific French anthropologist, who died in 2009 at the age of 100. Lévi-Strauss's structuralism evolved over time, from his early interest in the structures of kinship and marriage systems to his later interest in the structure of the human mind. In this latter sense, Lévi-Straussian structuralism (1967) aims not at explaining relations, themes, and connections among aspects of culture but at discovering them.

Structuralism rests on Lévi-Strauss's belief that human minds have certain universal characteristics, which originate in common features of the *Homo sapiens* brain. These common mental structures lead people everywhere to think similarly regardless of their society or cultural background. Among these universal mental characteristics are the need to classify: to impose order on aspects of nature, on people's relation to nature, and on relations between people.

According to Lévi-Strauss, a universal aspect of classification is opposition, or contrast. Although many phenomena are continuous rather than discrete, the mind, because of its need to impose order, treats them as being more different than they are. One of the most common means of classifying is by using binary opposition. Good and evil, white and black, old and young, high and low are oppositions that, according to Lévi-Strauss, reflect the universal human need to convert differences of degree into differences of kind.

Lévi-Strauss applied his assumptions about classification and binary opposition to myths and folk tales. He showed that these narratives have simple building blocks—elementary structures or "mythemes." Examining the myths of different cultures, Lévi-Strauss shows that one tale can be converted into another through a series of simple operations—for example, by doing the following:

1. Converting the positive element of a myth into its negative.

2. Reversing the order of the elements.

3. Replacing a male hero with a female hero.

4. Preserving or repeating certain key elements.

Through such operations, two apparently dissimilar myths can be shown to be variations on a common structure—that is, to be transformations of each other. One example is Lévi-Strauss's (1967) analysis of "Cinderella," a widespread tale whose elements vary between neighboring cultures. Through reversals, oppositions, and negations, as the tale is told, retold, diffused, and incorporated within the traditions of successive societies, "Cinderella" becomes "Ash Boy," along with a series of other oppositions (e.g., stepfather versus stepmother) related to the change in gender from female to male.

## Processual Approaches

### Agency

Anthropologists traditionally have viewed culture as a kind of social glue transmitted across the generations, binding people through their common past. More recently, anthropologists have come to see culture as something continually created and reworked in the present. Contemporary anthropologists now emphasize how day-to-day action, practice, or resistance can make and remake culture (Gupta and Ferguson 1997). **Agency** refers to the actions that individuals take, both alone and in groups, in forming and transforming culture.

### Practice Theory

The approach to culture known as *practice theory* (Ortner 1984) recognizes that individuals within a society vary in their motives and intentions and in the amount of power and influence they have. Such contrasts may be associated with gender, age, ethnicity, class, and other social variables. Practice theory focuses on how these varied individuals—through their actions and practices—influence and

**agency**
The actions of individuals, alone and in groups, that create and transform culture.

(a) Three books by the prominent and prolific anthropologist Clifford Geertz (1926–2006): *The Interpretation of Cultures* (the book that established the field of interpretive anthropology); *After the Fact: Two Countries, Four Decades, One Anthropologist;* and *Islam Observed: Religious Development in Morocco and Indonesia.* (b) Geertz himself in 1998.

(a)

(b)

transform the world they live in. Practice theory appropriately recognizes a reciprocal relation between culture and the individual. Culture shapes how individuals experience and respond to events, but individuals also play an active role in how society functions and changes. Practice theory recognizes both constraints on individuals and the flexibility and changeability of cultures and social systems. Well-known practice theorists include Sherry Ortner, an American anthropologist, and Pierre Bourdieu and Anthony Giddens, French and British social theorists, respectively.

### Leach

Some of the germs of practice theory, sometimes also called action theory (Vincent 1990), can be traced to the British anthropologist Edmund Leach, who wrote the influential book *Political Systems of Highland Burma* (1954/1970). Leach focused on how individuals work to achieve power and how their actions can transform society. In the Kachin Hills of Burma, now Myanmar, Leach identified three forms of sociopolitical organization, which he called *gumlao, gumsa,* and Shan. Leach made a tremendously important point by taking a regional rather than a local perspective. The Kachins participated in a regional system that included all three forms of organization. Leach showed how the three coexist and interact, as forms and possibilities known to everyone, in the same region. He also showed how Kachins creatively use power struggles—for example, to convert *gumlao* into *gumsa* organization—and how they negotiate their own identities within the regional system. Leach brought process into the formal models of structural functionalism. By focusing on power and how individuals get and use it, he showed the creative role of the individual in transforming culture.

## World-System Theory and Political Economy

Leach's regional perspective was not all that different from another development at the same time. Julian Steward, discussed previously as a neoevolutionist, joined the faculty of Columbia University in 1946, where he worked with several graduate students, including Eric Wolf and Sidney Mintz. Steward, Mintz, Wolf, and others planned and conducted a team research project in Puerto Rico, described in Steward's volume *The People of Puerto Rico* (1956). This project exemplified a post–World War II turn of anthropology away from "primitive" and nonindustrial societies, assumed to be somewhat isolated and autonomous, to contemporary societies recognized as forged by colonialism and participating fully in the modern world system. The team studied communities in different parts of Puerto Rico. The field sites were chosen to sample major events and adaptations, such as the sugar plantation, in the

island's history. The approach emphasized economics, politics, and history.

Wolf and Mintz retained their interest in history throughout their careers. Wolf wrote the modern classic *Europe and the People without History* (1982), which viewed local people, such as Native Americans, in the context of world-system events, such as the fur trade. Wolf focused on how such "people without history"—that is, nonliterate people, those who lacked written histories of their own—participated in and were transformed by the world system and the spread of capitalism. Mintz's *Sweetness and Power* (1985) is another example of historical anthropology that focuses on **political economy** (the web of interrelated economic and power relations). Mintz traces the domestication and spread of sugar, its transformative role in England, and its impact on the New World, where it became the basis for slave-based plantation economies in the Caribbean and Brazil. Such works in political economy illustrate a movement of anthropology toward interdisciplinarity, drawing on other academic fields, such as history and sociology. Such approaches have been criticized, however, for overstressing the influence of outsiders, and for paying insufficient attention to the transformative actions of "the people without history" themselves. Recap 13.2 summarizes anthropology's major theoretical perspectives and key works associated with them.

## Culture, History, Power

More recent approaches in historical anthropology, while sharing an interest in power with the world-system theorists, have focused more on local agency, the transformative actions of individuals and groups within colonized societies. Archival work has been prominent in recent historical anthropology, particularly in areas, such as Indonesia, for which colonial and postcolonial archives contain valuable information on relations between colonizers and colonized. Studies of culture, history, and power have drawn heavily on the work of European social theorists such as Antonio Gramsci and Michel Foucault.

Gramsci (1971) developed the concept of *hegemony* for a stratified social order in which subordinates comply with domination by internalizing their rulers' values and accepting domination as "natural." Both Pierre Bourdieu (1977) and Foucault (1979) contend that it is easier to dominate people in their minds than to try to control their bodies. Contemporary societies have devised various forms of social control in addition to physical violence. These include techniques of persuading, coercing, and managing people and of monitoring and recording their beliefs, behavior, movements, and contacts. Anthropologists interested in culture, history, and power, such as Ann Stoler (1995, 2002), have examined systems of power, domination, accommodation, and resistance in various contexts, including colonies, postcolonies, and other stratified contexts.

**political economy**
The web of interrelated economic and power relations in society.

| THEORETICAL APPROACH | KEY AUTHORS AND WORKS |
| --- | --- |
| Culture, history, power | Ann Stoler, *Carnal Knowledge and Imperial Power* (2002); Frederick Cooper and Ann Stoler, *Tensions of Empire* (1997) |
| Crisis of representation/ postmodernism | Jean-François Lyotard, *The Postmodern Explained* (1993); George Marcus and Michael Fischer, *Anthropology as Cultural Critique* (1986) |
| Practice theory | Sherry Ortner, "Theory in Anthropology Since the Sixties" (1984); Pierre Bourdieu, *Outline of a Theory of Practice* (1977) |
| World-system theory/ political economy | Sidney Mintz, *Sweetness and Power* (1985); Eric Wolf, *Europe and the People without History* (1982) |
| Feminist anthropology (see the chapter "Gender") | Rayna Reiter, *Toward an Anthropology of Women* (1975); Michelle Rosaldo and Louise Lamphere, *Women, Culture, and Society* (1974) |
| Cultural materialism | Marvin Harris, *Cultural Materialism* (1979), *The Rise of Anthropological Theory* (1968) |
| Interpretive anthropology | Clifford Geertz, *The Interpretation of Cultures* (1973)* |
| Symbolic anthropology | Mary Douglas, *Purity and Danger* (1970b); Victor Turner, *The Forest of Symbols* (1967)* |
| Structuralism | Claude Lévi-Strauss, *Structural Anthropology* (1967)* |
| Neoevolutionism | Leslie White, *The Evolution of Culture* (1959); Julian Steward, *Theory of Culture Change* (1955) |
| Manchester school and Leach | Victor Turner, *Schism and Continuity in an African Society* (1957); Edmund Leach, *Political Systems of Highland Burma* (1954) |
| Culturology | Leslie White, *The Science of Culture* (1949)* |
| Configurationalism | Alfred Kroeber, *Configurations of Cultural Growth* (1944); Margaret Mead, *Sex and Temperament in Three Primitive Societies* (1935); Ruth Benedict, *Patterns of Culture* (1934) |
| Structural functionalism | A. R. Radcliffe-Brown, *Structure and Function in Primitive Society* (1962)*; E. E. Evans-Pritchard, *The Nuer* (1940) |
| Functionalism | Bronislaw Malinowski, *A Scientific Theory of Culture* (1944)*, *Argonauts of the Western Pacific* (1922) |
| Historical particularism | Franz Boas, *Race, Language, and Culture* (1940)* |
| Unilinear evolutionism | Lewis Henry Morgan, *Ancient Society* (1877); Sir Edward Burnett Tylor, *Primitive Culture* (1871) |

*Includes essays written at earlier dates.

# ANTHROPOLOGY TODAY

Early American anthropologists, such as Morgan, Boas, and Kroeber, were interested in, and made contributions to, more than a single subfield. If there has been a single dominant trend in anthropology since the 1960s, it has been one of increasing specialization. During the 1960s, when this author attended graduate school at Columbia University, one had to study and take qualifying exams in all four subfields. This has changed. There are still strong four-field anthropology departments, but many excellent departments lack one or more of the subfields. Four-field departments such as the University of Michigan's still require courses and teaching expertise across the subfields, but graduate students are expected to specialize in a particular subfield. In Boasian anthropology, all four subfields shared a single theoretical assumption about human plasticity. Today, following specialization, the theories that guide the subfields differ. Evolutionary paradigms of various sorts still dominate biological anthropology and remain strong in archaeology as well. Within cultural anthropology, it has been many decades since evolutionary approaches dominated.

Ethnography, too, has grown more specialized. Cultural anthropologists now head for the field with a specific problem in mind, rather than with the goal of producing a holistic ethnography—a complete account of a given culture—as Morgan and Malinowski intended when they studied, respectively, the Iroquois and the Trobriand Islanders.

Boas, Malinowski, and Mead went somewhere and stayed there for a while, studying the local culture. Today "the field" that anthropologists study has expanded—inevitably and appropriately—to include regional and national systems and the movement of people, such as immigrants and diasporas, across national boundaries. Border theory (Lugo 1997) is an emerging field that examines social relations at the margins of a society, contexts in which members of different groups increasingly meet and interact. Border research can occur on the boundaries of nation-states, such as the U.S.–Mexican border, as well as in places within a nation where diverse groups come into regular contact. Many anthropologists now follow the flows of people, information, finance, and media to multiple sites. Such movement—and the anthropologist's ability to study it—has been made possible by advances in transportation and communication.

Reflecting the trend toward specialization, the American Anthropological Association (AAA) now has all sorts of active and vital subgroups. In its early years, there were just anthropologists within the AAA. Now there are groups based on specialization in biological anthropology, archaeology, and linguistic, cultural, and applied anthropology. The AAA includes dozens of groups formed around particular interests (e.g., psychological anthropology, urban anthropology, culture and agriculture) and identities (e.g., midwestern or southeastern anthropologists, anthropologists in community colleges or small programs). The AAA also includes units representing senior anthropologists, LGBT anthropologists, Latino/a anthropologists, and so on.

Anthropology also has witnessed a crisis in representation, including questions about the ethnographer's impartiality and the validity of ethnographic accounts. Science itself may be challenged, because all scientists come from particular individual and cultural backgrounds that prevent complete and absolute objectivity. What are we to do if we, as I do, continue to share Margaret Mead's view of anthropology as a humanistic science of unique value in understanding and improving the human condition? We must try, I think, to stay aware of our biases and our inability totally to escape them. The best scientific choice would seem to be to combine the perpetual goal of objectivity with skepticism about our capacity to achieve it.

# for REVIEW

## summary

1. Ethnographic methods include observation, rapport building, participant observation, interviewing, genealogies, work with key consultants, life histories, and longitudinal research. Ethnographers do not systematically manipulate their subjects or conduct experiments. Rather, they work in actual communities and form personal relationships with local people as they study their lives.

2. An interview schedule is a form that an ethnographer completes as he or she visits a series of households. The schedule organizes and guides each interview, ensuring that comparable information is collected from everyone. Key cultural consultants teach about particular areas of local life. Life histories dramatize the fact that culture bearers are individuals. Such case studies document personal experiences with culture and culture change. Genealogical information is particularly useful in societies in which principles of kinship and marriage organize social and political life. Emic approaches focus on native perceptions and explanations. Etic approaches give priority to the ethnographer's own observations and conclusions. Longitudinal research is the systematic study of an area or a site over time. Anthropological research may be done by teams and at multiple sites. Outsiders, flows, linkages, and people in motion are now included in ethnographic analyses. Anthropologists also have developed techniques of doing online ethnography in studying virtual worlds.

3. Traditionally, anthropologists worked in small-scale societies; sociologists, in modern nations. Different techniques were developed to study such different kinds of societies. Social scientists working in complex societies use survey research to sample variation. Anthropologists do their fieldwork in communities and study the totality of social life. Sociologists study samples to make inferences about a larger population. The diversity of social life in modern nations and cities requires social survey procedures. However, anthropologists add the intimacy and direct investigation characteristic of ethnography.

4. Because science exists in society, and in the context of law and ethics, anthropologists can't study things simply because they happen to be interesting or of scientific value. Anthropologists have obligations to their scholarly field, to the wider society and culture (including that of the host country), and to the human species, other species, and the environment. The AAA Code of Ethics offers ethical guidelines for anthropologists. Ethical problems often arise when anthropologists work for governments, especially the military.

5. Evolutionary perspectives, especially those of Morgan and Tylor, dominated early anthropology, which emerged during the latter half of the 19th century. The early 20th century witnessed various reactions to 19th-century evolutionism. In the United States, Boas and his followers rejected the search for evolutionary stages in favor of a historical approach that traced borrowing between cultures and the spread of culture traits across geographic areas. In Great Britain, functionalists such as Malinowski and Radcliffe-Brown abandoned conjectural history in favor of studies of present-day living societies. Functionalists and Boasians alike saw cultures as integrated and patterned. The functionalists especially viewed societies as systems in which various parts worked together to maintain the whole. A form of functionalism persists in the widely accepted view that there are social and cultural systems whose constituent parts are functionally related, so that when one part changes, others change as well.

6. In the mid-20th century, following World War II and as colonialism was ending, there was a revived interest in change, including new evolutionary approaches. Some anthropologists developed symbolic and interpretive approaches to uncover patterned symbols and meanings within cultures. By the 1980s, anthropologists had grown more interested in the relation between culture and the individual, as well as the role of human action (agency) in transforming culture. There also was a resurgence of historical approaches, including those that viewed local cultures in relation to colonialism and the world system.

7. Contemporary anthropology is marked by increasing specialization, based on special topics and identities. Reflecting this specialization, some universities have moved away from the holistic, biocultural view of anthropology that is reflected in this book. However, this Boasian view of anthropology as a four-subfield discipline—including biological, archaeological, cultural, and linguistic anthropology—continues to thrive at many universities as well.

## key terms

agency 248

complex societies 238

configurationalism 244

cultural materialism 246

cultural consultants 234

diachronic 243

emic 236

etic 236

functionalism 243

genealogical method 233

historical particularism 242

informed consent 239

interpretive anthropology 247

interview schedule 232

key cultural consultants 234

life history 234

longitudinal research 235

political economy 249

questionnaire 232

random sample 238

sample 238

superorganic 246

survey research 238

symbolic anthropology 247

synchronic 243

unilinear evolutionism 241

variables 238

## critical thinking

1. What do you see as the strengths and weaknesses of ethnography compared with survey research? Which provides more accurate data? Might one be better for finding questions, while the other is better for finding answers? Or does it depend on the context of research?

2. In what sense is anthropological research comparative? How have anthropologists approached the issue of comparison? What do they compare (what are their units of analysis)?

3. In your view, is anthropology a science? How have anthropologists historically addressed this question? Should anthropology be a science?

4. Historically, how have anthropologists studied culture? What are some contemporary trends in the study of culture, and how have they changed the way anthropologists carry out their research?

5. Do the theories examined in this chapter relate to ones you have studied in other courses? Which courses and theories? Are those theories more scientific or humanistic, or somewhere in between?

# Language and Communication

- ▶ What makes language different from other forms of communication?

- ▶ How do anthropologists and linguists study language in general and specific languages in particular?

- ▶ How does language change over short and long time periods?

Schoolgirls wearing traditional Punjabi attire laugh as they wait to take part in a national celebration in the northern Indian city of Amritsar. Republic Day, celebrated annually on January 26, commemorates the transition of India from British domination to a republic on January 26, 1950.

# understanding OURSELVES

**C**an you appreciate anything distinctive or unusual in the way you talk? If you're from Canada, Virginia, or Savannah, you may say "oot" instead of "out." A southerner may request a "soft drink" rather than the New Yorker's "soda." How might a "Valley girl" or "surfer dude" talk? Usually when we pay attention to how we talk, it's because someone comments on our speech. It may be only when students move from one state or region to another that they appreciate how much of a regional accent they have. I moved as a teenager from Atlanta to New York City. Previously I hadn't realized I had a southern accent, but teachers in my new high school did. They put me in a speech class, pointing out linguistic flaws I never knew I had. One was my "dull s," particularly in terminal consonant clusters, as in the words "tusks" and "breakfasts." Apparently I didn't pronounce all three consonants at the ends of those words. Later it occurred to me that these weren't words I used very often. As far as I know, I've never conversed about tusks or proclaimed, "I ate seven breakfasts last week."

Unlike grammarians, linguists and anthropologists are interested in what people do say, rather than what they should say. Speech differences are associated with, and tell us a lot about, social variation, such as region, education, ethnic background, and gender. Men and women talk differently. I'm sure you can think of examples based on your own experience, although you probably never realized that women tend to peripheralize their vowels (think of "aiiee"), whereas men tend to centralize them (think of "uh"). Men are more likely to speak "ungrammatically" than women are. Men and women also show differences in their sports and color terminologies. Men typically know more terms related to sports, make more distinctions among them (e.g., "runs" versus "points"), and try to use the terms more precisely than women do.

Correspondingly, women use more color terms and attempt to use them more specifically than men do. To make this point when I lecture, I bring an off-purple shirt to class. Holding it up, I first ask women to say aloud what color the shirt is. The women rarely answer with a uniform voice, as they try to distinguish the actual shade (mauve, lilac, lavender, wisteria, or some other purplish hue). I then ask the men, who consistently answer as one, "PURPLE." Rare is the man who on the spur of the moment can imagine the difference between fuchsia and magenta or grape and aubergine.

## WHAT IS LANGUAGE?

**Language,** which may be spoken (*speech*) or written (*writing*), is our primary means of communication. Writing has existed for less than 6,000 years. Language originated thousands of years before that, but no one can say exactly when. Like culture in general, of which language is a part, language is transmitted through learning, as part of enculturation. Language is based on arbitrary, learned associations between words and the things for which they stand. The complexity of language—absent in the communication systems of other animals—allows humans to conjure up elaborate images, to discuss the past and the future, to share our experiences with others, and to benefit from their experiences.

Anthropologists study language in its social and cultural context (see Bonvillain 2012; Salzmann, Stanlaw, and Adachi 2012). Linguistic anthropology illustrates anthropology's characteristic interest in comparison, variation, and change—but here the focus is on language (see Duranti 2009; Salzmann

2012). A key feature of language is that it is always changing. Some linguistic anthropologists reconstruct ancient languages by comparing their contemporary descendants and in so doing make discoveries about history. Others study linguistic differences to discover the varied worldviews and patterns of thought in a multitude of cultures. Sociolinguists examine linguistic diversity in nation-states, ranging from multilingualism to the varied dialects and styles used in a single language, to show how speech reflects social differences (Fasold and Connor-Linton 2006; Labov 1972a, 2006). Linguistic anthropologists also explore the role of language in colonization and in the expansion of the world economy (Geis 1987; Trudgill 2010).

Apes, such as these chimpanzees, use call systems to communicate in the wild. Their vocal systems consist of a limited number of sounds—*calls*—that are produced only when particular environmental stimuli are encountered. What might they be signaling here?

# NONHUMAN PRIMATE COMMUNICATION

## Call Systems

Only humans speak. No other animal has anything approaching the complexity of language. The natural communication systems of other primates (monkeys and apes) are **call systems.** These vocal systems consist of a limited number of sounds—*calls*—that are produced only when particular environmental stimuli are encountered. Such calls may be varied in intensity and duration, but they are much less flexible than language because they are automatic and can't be combined. When primates encounter food and danger simultaneously, they can make only one call. They can't combine the calls for food and danger into a single utterance, indicating that both are present. At some point in human evolution, however, our ancestors began to combine calls and to understand the combinations. The number of calls also expanded, eventually becoming too great to be transmitted even partly through the genes. Communication came to rely almost totally on learning.

Although wild primates use call systems, the vocal tract of apes is not suitable for speech. Until the 1960s, attempts to teach spoken language to apes suggested that they lack linguistic abilities. In the 1950s, a couple raised a chimpanzee, Viki, as a member of their family and systematically tried to teach her to speak. However, Viki learned only four words ("mama," "papa," "up," and "cup").

## Sign Language

More recent experiments have shown that apes can learn to use, if not speak, true language. Several apes have learned to converse with people through means other than speech. One such communication system is American Sign Language, or ASL, which is widely used by hearing-impaired Americans. ASL employs a limited number of basic gesture units that are analogous to sounds in spoken language. These units combine to form words and larger units of meaning.

The first chimpanzee to learn ASL was Washoe, a female who died in 2007 at the age of 42. Captured in West Africa, Washoe was acquired by R. Allen Gardner and Beatrice Gardner, scientists at the University of Nevada in Reno, in 1966, when she was a year old. Four years later, she moved to Norman, Oklahoma, to a converted farm that had become the Institute for Primate Studies. Washoe revolutionized the discussion of the language-learning abilities of apes (Carey 2007). At first she lived in a trailer and heard no spoken language. The researchers always used ASL to communicate with each other in her presence. The chimp gradually acquired a vocabulary of more than 100 signs representing English words (Gardner, Gardner, and Van Cantfort 1989). At the age of 2, Washoe began to combine as many as five signs into rudimentary sentences such as "you, me, go out, hurry."

The second chimp to learn ASL was Lucy, Washoe's junior by one year. Lucy died, or was murdered by poachers, in 1986, after having been introduced to "the wild" in Africa in 1979 (Carter 1988). From her second day of life until her move to Africa, Lucy lived with a family in Norman, Oklahoma. Roger Fouts, a researcher from the nearby Institute for Primate Studies, came two days a week to test and improve Lucy's knowledge of ASL. During the rest of the week, Lucy used ASL to converse with her foster parents. After acquiring language, Washoe and Lucy exhibited several human traits: swearing, joking, telling lies, and trying to teach language to others (Fouts 1997).

When irritated, Washoe called her monkey neighbors at the institute "dirty monkeys." Lucy insulted her "dirty cat." On arrival at Lucy's place, Fouts once found a pile of excrement on the floor. When he asked the chimp what it was, she replied, "dirty, dirty," her expression for feces. Asked whose "dirty, dirty" it was, Lucy named Fouts's coworker, Sue. When Fouts refused to believe her about Sue, the chimp blamed the excrement on Fouts himself.

**language**
Primary means of human communication, spoken and written.

**call systems**
Communication systems of nonhuman primates.

| HUMAN LANGUAGE | PRIMATE CALL SYSTEMS |
|---|---|
| Has the capacity to speak of things and events that are not present (displacement) | Are stimuli-dependent; the food call will be made only in the presence of food; it cannot be faked |
| Has the capacity to generate new expressions by combining other expressions (productivity) | Consist of a limited number of calls that cannot be combined to produce new calls |
| Is group specific in that all humans have the capacity for language, but each linguistic community has its own language, which is culturally transmitted | Tend to be species specific, with little variation among communities of the same species for each call |

**cultural transmission**
Transmission through learning, basic to language.

**productivity**
Creating new expressions that are comprehensible to other speakers.

**displacement**
Describing things and events that are not present; basic to language.

**Cultural transmission** of a communication system through learning is a fundamental attribute of language. Washoe, Lucy, and other chimps have tried to teach ASL to other animals. Washoe taught gestures to other institute chimps, including her son Sequoia, who died in infancy (Gardner, Gardner, and Van Cantfort 1989).

Because of their size and strength as adults, gorillas are less likely subjects than chimps for such experiments. Lean adult male gorillas in the wild weigh 400 pounds (180 kilograms), and full-grown females can easily reach 250 pounds (110 kilograms). Because of this, psychologist Penny Patterson's work with gorillas at Stanford University seems more daring than the chimp experiments. Patterson raised the now full-grown female gorilla, Koko, in a trailer next to a Stanford museum. Koko's vocabulary surpasses that of any chimp. She regularly employs 400 ASL signs and has used about 700 at least once.

Koko and the chimps also show that apes share still another linguistic ability with humans: **productivity.** Speakers routinely use the rules of their language to produce entirely new expressions that are comprehensible to other native speakers. I can, for example, create "baboonlet" to refer to a baboon infant. I do this by analogy with English words in which the suffix *-let* designates the young of a species. Anyone who speaks English immediately understands the meaning of my new word. Koko, Washoe, Lucy, and others have shown that apes also are able to use language productively. Lucy used gestures she already knew to create "drinkfruit" for watermelon. Washoe, seeing a swan for the first time, coined "waterbird." Koko, who knew the gestures for "finger" and "bracelet," formed "finger bracelet" when she was given a ring.

Chimps and gorillas have a rudimentary capacity for language. They may never have invented a meaningful gesture system in the wild. However, given such a system, they can learn and use it. Of course, language use by apes is a product of human intervention and teaching. The experiments mentioned here do not suggest that apes can invent language (nor are human children ever faced with that task). However, young apes have managed to learn the basics of gestural language. They can employ it productively and creatively, although not with the sophistication of human ASL users.

Apes also have demonstrated linguistic **displacement.** Absent in call systems, this is a key ingredient in language. Normally, a call is tied to a particular environmental stimulus and is uttered only when that stimulus is present. Displacement means that humans can talk about things that are not present. We can discuss the past and future, share our experiences with others, and benefit from theirs.

Patterson has described several examples of Koko's capacity for displacement (Patterson 1978, 1999). The gorilla once expressed sorrow about having bitten Penny three days earlier. Koko has used the sign "later" to postpone doing things she doesn't want to do. Recap 14.1 summarizes the contrasts between language, whether sign or spoken, and the call systems that primates use in the wild.

Certain scholars doubt the linguistic abilities of chimps and gorillas (Hess 2008; Sebeok and Umiker-Sebeok 1980; Terrace 1979). These people contend that Koko and the chimps are comparable to trained circus animals and don't really have

Kanzi, a male bonobo, identifies an object he has just heard named through headphone speakers. At a young age, Kanzi learned to understand simple human speech and to communicate by using lexigrams, abstract symbols that represent objects and actions. A keyboard of lexigrams is pictured in the background.

linguistic ability. However, in defense of Patterson and the other researchers (Hill 1978; Van Cantfort and Rimpau 1982), only one of their critics has worked with an ape. This was Herbert Terrace, whose experience teaching a chimp sign language lacked the continuity and personal involvement that have contributed so much to Patterson's success with Koko. (For more on Terrace and his ill-fated chimp, Nim Chimpsky, see Hess [2008] and the acclaimed 2011 documentary film *Project Nim*.)

No one denies the huge difference between human language and gorilla signs. There is a major gap between the ability to write a book or say a prayer and the few hundred gestures employed by a well-trained chimp. Apes aren't people, but they aren't just animals, either. Let Koko express it: When asked by a reporter whether she was a person or an animal, Koko chose neither. Instead, she signed "fine animal gorilla" (Patterson 1978).

## The Origin of Language

Although the capacity to remember and combine linguistic symbols may be latent in the apes, human evolution was needed for this seed to flower into language. A mutated gene known as *FOXP2* helps explain why humans speak and chimps don't (Paulson 2005). The key role of *FOXP2* in speech came to light in a study of a British family, identified only as KE, half of whose members had an inherited, severe deficit in speech (Trivedi 2001). The same variant form of *FOXP2* that is found in chimpanzees causes this disorder. Those who have the nonspeech version of the gene cannot make the fine tongue and lip movements that are necessary for clear speech, and their speech is unintelligible—even to other members of the KE family (Trivedi 2001). Chimps

have the same (genetic) sequence as the KE family members with the speech deficit. Comparing chimp and human genomes, it appears that the speech-friendly form of *FOXP2* took hold in humans around 150,000 years ago. This mutation conferred selective advantages (linguistic and cultural abilities) that allowed those who had it to spread at the expense of those who did not (Paulson 2005).

Language offered a tremendous adaptive advantage to *Homo sapiens*. Language permits the information stored by a human society to exceed by far that of any nonhuman group. Language is a uniquely effective vehicle for learning. Because we can speak of things we have never experienced, we can anticipate responses before we encounter the stimuli. Adaptation can occur more rapidly in *Homo* than in the other primates because our adaptive means are much more flexible.

## NONVERBAL COMMUNICATION

Language is our principal means of communicating, but it isn't the only one we use. We communicate when we transmit information about ourselves to others and receive such information from them. Our facial expressions, bodily stances, gestures, and movements, even if unconscious, convey information. Deborah Tannen (1990) discusses differences in the communication styles of American men and women. She notes that American girls and women tend to look directly at each other when they talk, whereas American boys and men do not. Males are more likely to look straight ahead rather than turn and make eye contact with someone, especially another man, seated beside them. Also, in conversational

Compare the communication style of these women in a café with that of these men in a fishing boat. Do you think the men would use the same communication style as the women if they were in a café setting?

groups, American men tend to relax and sprawl out. American women may adopt a similar relaxed posture in all-female groups, but when they are with men, they tend to draw in their limbs and adopt a tighter stance.

**Kinesics** is the study of communication through body movements, stances, gestures, and facial expressions. Linguists pay attention not only to what is said but to how it is said, and to features besides language itself that convey meaning. A speaker's enthusiasm is conveyed not only through words but also through facial expressions, gestures, and other signs of animation. We use gestures, such as a jab of the hand, for emphasis. We use verbal and nonverbal ways of communicating our moods: enthusiasm, sadness, joy, regret. We vary our intonation and the pitch or loudness of our voices. We communicate through strategic pauses, and even by being silent. An effective communication strategy may be to alter pitch, voice level, and grammatical forms, such as declaratives ("I am . . ."), imperatives ("Go forth . . ."), and questions ("Are you . . . ?"). Culture teaches us that certain manners and styles should accompany certain kinds of speech. Our demeanor, verbal and nonverbal, when our favorite team is winning would be out of place at a funeral.

Much of what we communicate is nonverbal and reflects our emotional states and intentions. This can create problems when we use contemporary means of communication such as texting and online messaging. People can use emoticons (☺, ☹, :~/ [confused], :~0 ["hah!" no way!]) and abbreviations (lol—laugh out loud; lmao—laugh my a** off; wtf—what the f**; omg—oh my gosh) to fill in what would otherwise be communicated by tone of voice, laughter, and facial expression (see Baron 2009; Tannen and Trester 2012).

Culture always plays a role in shaping how people communicate. Cross-culturally, nodding does not always mean affirmative, nor does head shaking from side to side always mean negative. Brazilians wag a finger to mean no. Americans say "uh huh" to affirm; in Madagascar a similar sound is used to deny. Americans point with their fingers; the people of Madagascar point with their lips.

Body movements communicate social differences. In Japan, bowing is a regular part of social interaction, but different bows are used depending on the social status of the people who are interacting. In Madagascar and Polynesia, people of lower status should not hold their heads above those of people of higher status. When one approaches someone older or of higher status, one bends one's knees and lowers one's head as a sign of respect. In Madagascar, one always does this, for politeness, when passing between two people. Although our gestures, facial expressions, and body stances have roots in our primate heritage, they have not escaped cultural shaping. Language, which is so highly dependent on the use of symbols, is the domain of communication, in which culture plays the strongest role.

# THE STRUCTURE OF LANGUAGE

The scientific study of a spoken language (*descriptive linguistics*) involves several interrelated areas of analysis: phonology, morphology, lexicon, and syntax. **Phonology,** the study of speech sounds, considers which sounds are present and significant in a given language. **Morphology** studies how sounds combine to form *morphemes*—words and their meaningful parts. Thus, the word *cats* would be analyzed as containing two morphemes: *cat*, the name for a kind of animal, and *-s,* a morpheme indicating plurality. A language's **lexicon** is a dictionary containing all its morphemes and their meanings. **Syntax** refers to the arrangement and order of words in phrases and sentences. Syntactic questions include whether nouns usually come before or after verbs, and whether adjectives normally precede or follow the nouns they modify.

## Speech Sounds

From the movies and TV, and from actually meeting foreigners, we know something about foreign accents and mispronunciations. We know that someone with a marked French accent doesn't pronounce *r* the same way an American does. But at least someone from France can distinguish between "craw" and "claw," which someone from Japan may not be able to do. The difference between *r* and *l* makes a difference in English and in French, but it doesn't in Japanese. In linguistics, we say that the difference between *r* and *l* is *phonemic* in English and French but not in Japanese; that is, *r* and *l* are phonemes in English and French but not in Japanese. A **phoneme** is a sound contrast that makes a difference, that differentiates meaning.

We find the phonemes in a given language by comparing *minimal pairs,* words that resemble each other in all but one sound. The words have totally different meanings, but they differ in just one sound. The contrasting sounds are therefore phonemes in that language. An example in English is the minimal pair *pit/bit*. These two words are distinguished by a single sound contrast between /p/ and /b/ (we enclose phonemes in slashes). Thus /p/ and /b/ are phonemes in English. Another example is the different vowel sounds of *bit* and *beat* (see Figure 14.1). This contrast serves to distinguish these two words and the two vowel phonemes written /I/ and /i/ in English.

Standard (American) English (SE), the "region-free" dialect of TV network newscasters, has about 35 phonemes: at least 11 vowels and 24 consonants. The number of phonemes varies from language to language—from 15 to 60, averaging between 30 and 40. The number of phonemes also varies between dialects of a given language. In American English, for example, vowel phonemes vary noticeably from dialect to dialect. Readers should pronounce

---

**kinesics**
Study of communication through body movements and facial expressions.

**phonology**
Study of sounds used in speech in a particular language.

**morphology**
(Linguistic) study of morphemes and word construction.

**lexicon**
Vocabulary; all the morphemes in a language and their meanings.

**syntax**
Arrangement and order of words in phrases and sentences.

**phoneme**
Smallest sound contrast that distinguishes meaning.

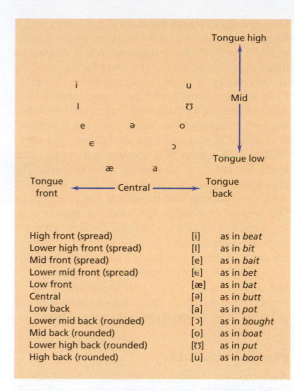

| High front (spread) | [i] | as in *beat* |
| Lower high front (spread) | [I] | as in *bit* |
| Mid front (spread) | [e] | as in *bait* |
| Lower mid front (spread) | [ɛ] | as in *bet* |
| Low front | [æ] | as in *bat* |
| Central | [ə] | as in *butt* |
| Low back | [a] | as in *pot* |
| Lower mid back (rounded) | [ɔ] | as in *bought* |
| Mid back (rounded) | [o] | as in *boat* |
| Lower high back (rounded) | [ʊ] | as in *put* |
| High back (rounded) | [u] | as in *boot* |

**FIGURE 14.1** Vowel Phonemes in Standard American English.

The phonemes are shown according to height of tongue and tongue position at front, center, or back of mouth. Phonetic symbols are identified by English words that include them; note that most are minimal pairs.

SOURCE: Adaptation of excerpt and Figure 2-1 from Dwight Bolinger and Donald A. Sears, *Aspects of Language*, 3rd ed. © 1981 Heinle/Arts & Sciences, a part of Cengage Learning, Inc. Reproduced by permission. www.cengage.com/permissions

the words in Figure 14.1, paying attention to (or asking someone else) whether they distinguish each of the vowel sounds. Most Americans don't pronounce them all.

**Phonetics** is the study of speech sounds in general, what people actually say in various languages. **Phonemics** studies only the *significant* sound contrasts (phonemes) of a given language. In English, like /r/ and /l/ (remember *craw* and *claw*), /b/ and /v/ are also phonemes, occurring in minimal pairs like *bat* and *vat*. In Spanish, however, the contrast between [b] and [v] doesn't distinguish meaning, and they therefore are not phonemes (we enclose sounds that are not phonemic in brackets). Spanish speakers normally use the [b] sound to pronounce words spelled with either *b* or *v*.

In any language, a given phoneme extends over a phonetic range. In English, the phoneme /p/ ignores the phonetic contrast between the [pʰ] in *pin* and the [p] in *spin*. Most English speakers don't even notice that there is a phonetic difference: [pʰ] is aspirated, so that a puff of air follows the [p]; the [p] in *spin* is not. (To see the difference, light a match, hold it in front of your mouth, and watch the flame as you pronounce the two words.) The contrast between

[pʰ] and [p] is phonemic in some languages, such as Hindi (spoken in India). That is, there are words whose meaning is distinguished only by the contrast between an aspirated and an unaspirated [p].

Native speakers vary in their pronunciation of certain phonemes. This variation is important in the evolution of language. With no shifts in pronunciation, there can be no linguistic change. The section on sociolinguistics below considers phonetic variation and its relationship to social divisions and the evolution of language.

## LANGUAGE, THOUGHT, AND CULTURE

The well-known linguist Noam Chomsky (1955) has argued that the human brain contains a limited set of rules for organizing language, so that all languages have a common structural basis. (Chomsky calls this set of rules *universal grammar*.) The fact that people can learn foreign languages and that words and ideas can be translated from one language into another tends to support Chomsky's position that all humans have similar linguistic abilities and thought processes. Another line of support comes from creole languages. Such languages develop from pidgins, languages that form in situations of acculturation, when different societies come into contact and must devise a system of communication. Pidgins based on English and native languages developed in the context of trade and colonialism in China, Papua New Guinea, and West Africa (see Gu 2012). Eventually, after generations of being spoken, pidgins may develop into *creole languages*. These are more mature languages, with developed grammatical rules and native speakers (i.e., people who learn the language as their primary means of communication during enculturation). Creoles are spoken in several Caribbean societies. Gullah, which is spoken by African Americans on coastal islands in South Carolina and Georgia, is a creole language. Supporting the idea that creoles are based on universal grammar is the fact that they all share certain features. Syntactically, all creole languages use particles (e.g., will, was) to form future and past tenses and multiple negation to deny or negate (e.g., he don't got none). Also, all form questions by changing inflection rather than by changing word order—for example, "You're going home for the holidays?" (with a rising tone at the end) rather than "Are you going home for the holidays?"

### The Sapir-Whorf Hypothesis

Other linguists and anthropologists take a different approach to the relation between language and thought. Rather than seeking universal linguistic structures and processes, they believe that different languages produce different ways of thinking. This

**phonetics**
Study of speech sounds—what people actually say.

**phonemics**
Study of significant sound contrasts (phonemes) in a language.

At the top, Lee Wayne Lomayestewa of the Hopi Cultural Preservation Office points out the site of the ancient Tutuveni petroglyphs near Tuba City, Arizona. This site, whose name means "newspaper rock," contains some 5,000 petroglyphs of Hopi clan symbols. The photo on the bottom shows the petroglyphs (rock engravings) up close.

Hopi speakers to think about time and reality in different ways than English speakers do. A similar example comes from Portuguese, which employs a future subjunctive verb form, introducing a degree of uncertainty into discussions of the future. In English, we routinely use the future tense to talk about something we think will happen. We don't feel the need to qualify "The sun'll come out tomorrow" by adding "if it doesn't go supernova." We don't hesitate to proclaim "I'll see you next year," even when we can't be absolutely sure we will. The Portuguese future subjunctive qualifies the future event, recognizing that the future can't be certain. Our way of expressing the future as certain is so ingrained that we don't even think about it, just as the Hopi don't see the need to distinguish between present and past, both of which are real, while the future remains hypothetical. It would seem, however, that language does not tightly restrict thought, because cultural changes can produce changes in thought and in language, as we shall see in the next section.

## Focal Vocabulary

A *lexicon* (vocabulary) is a language's dictionary, its set of names for things, events, actions, and qualities. Lexicon influences perception. Thus, Eskimos recognize, and have several distinct words for, types of snow that in English are all called *snow*. Most English speakers never notice the differences between these types of snow and might have trouble seeing them even if someone pointed them out. Similarly, the Nuer of South Sudan have an elaborate vocabulary to describe cattle. Eskimos have several words for snow and Nuer have dozens for cattle because of their particular histories, economies, and environments (Robson 2013). When the need arises, English speakers also can elaborate their snow and cattle vocabularies. For example, skiers name varieties of snow with words that are missing from the

position is sometimes known as the **Sapir-Whorf hypothesis** after Edward Sapir (1931) and his student Benjamin Lee Whorf (1956), its prominent early advocates. Sapir and Whorf argued that the grammatical categories of different languages lead their speakers to think about things in particular ways. For example, the third-person singular pronouns of English (*he, she; him, her; his, hers*) distinguish gender, whereas those of the Palaung, a small tribe in Burma, do not (Burling 1970). Gender exists in English, although a fully developed noun-gender and adjective-agreement system, as in French and other Romance languages (*la belle fille, le beau fils*), does not. The Sapir-Whorf hypothesis therefore might suggest that English speakers can't help paying more attention to differences between males and females than do the Palaung and less than do French or Spanish speakers.

English divides time into past, present, and future. Hopi, a language of the Pueblo region of the Native American Southwest, does not. Rather, Hopi distinguishes between events that exist or have existed (what we use present and past to discuss) and those that don't or don't yet (our future events, along with imaginary and hypothetical events). Whorf argued that this difference causes

Spices galore, but what kinds? Merchants at this spice market in Istanbul, Turkey, have a much more elaborate focal vocabulary for what they sell than you or I do.

lexicons of Florida retirees. Similarly, the cattle vocabulary of a Texas rancher is much ampler than that of a salesperson in a New York City department store. Such specialized sets of terms and distinctions that are particularly important to certain groups (those with particular foci of experience or activity) are known as **focal vocabulary.**

Vocabulary is the area of language that changes most readily. New words and distinctions, when needed, appear and spread. For example, who would have texted or e-mailed anything a generation ago? Names for items get simpler as they become common and important. A television has become a *TV,* an automobile a *car,* and a digital video disc a *DVD.*

Language, culture, and thought are interrelated. However, and in opposition to the Sapir-Whorf hypothesis, it might be more reasonable to say that changes in culture produce changes in language and thought than the reverse. Consider differences between female and male Americans in regard to the color terms they use (Lakoff 2004). Distinctions implied by such terms as *salmon, rust, peach, beige, teal, mauve, cranberry,* and *dusky orange* aren't in the vocabularies of most American men. However, many of them weren't even in American women's lexicons 70 years ago. Color terms and distinctions have increased with the growth of the fashion and cosmetic industries. A similar contrast (and growth) in Americans' lexicons shows up in football, basketball, and hockey vocabularies. Sports fans, more often males than females, use more terms in reference to, and make more elaborate distinctions between, the games they watch, such as hockey (see Table 14.1). Thus, cultural contrasts and changes affect lexical distinctions (for instance, "peach" versus "salmon") within semantic domains (for instance, color terminology). **Semantics** refers to a language's meaning system.

## Meaning

Speakers of particular languages use sets of terms to organize, or categorize, their experiences and perceptions. Linguistic terms and contrasts encode

**TABLE 14.1** Focal Vocabulary for Hockey

*Insiders have special terms for the major elements of the game.*

| ELEMENT OF HOCKEY | INSIDERS' TERM |
|---|---|
| puck | biscuit |
| goal/net | pipes |
| penalty box | sin bin |
| hockey stick | twig |
| helmet | bucket |
| space between a goalie's leg pads | five hole |

In the final game of the 2013 Stanley Cup playoffs, the Chicago Blackhawks won the Cup by scoring a pair of goals in the final minutes. How might an avid fan describe this photo?

(embody) differences in meaning that people perceive. **Ethnosemantics** studies such classification systems in various languages. Well-studied ethnosemantic *domains* (sets of related things, perceptions, or concepts named in a language) include kinship terminology and color terminology. When we study such domains, we are examining how those people perceive and distinguish between kin relationships or colors. Other such domains include ethnomedicine—the terminology for the causes, symptoms, and cures of disease; ethnobotany—native classification of plant life; and ethnoastronomy.

Anthropologists have discovered that certain lexical domains and vocabulary items evolve in a determined order. For example, after studying color terminology in more than 100 languages, Berlin and Kay (1991, 1999) discovered 10 basic color terms: *white, black, red, yellow, blue, green, brown, pink, orange,* and *purple* (they evolved in more or less that order). The number of terms varied with cultural complexity. Representing one extreme were Papua New Guinea cultivators and Australian hunters and gatherers, who used only two basic terms, which translate as *black* and *white* or *dark* and *light.* At the other end of the continuum were European and Asian languages with all the color terms. Color terminology was most developed in areas with a history of using dyes and artificial coloring.

## SOCIOLINGUISTICS

No language is a uniform system in which everyone talks just like everyone else. Linguistic *performance* (what people actually say) is the concern of sociolinguists. The field of sociolinguistics investigates relationships between social and linguistic variation, or language in its social context. How do different speakers use a given language? How do linguistic features correlate with social stratification, including

**focal vocabulary**
Set of words describing particular domains (foci) of experience.

**ethnosemantics**
Study of lexical (vocabulary) categories and contrasts.

**semantics**
A language's meaning system.

# appreciating DIVERSITY

## Googling Locally

Despite globalization, linguistic diversity is alive, well, and thriving in many countries, including India, as described here. Despite that nation's colonial history, only about a tenth of the Indian population speaks English. However, even many of those English speakers appreciate being able to read, and to seek out Internet content in, their own regional languages. In this account we see how local entrepreneurs and global companies, including Google, Yahoo, and Microsoft, are rushing to meet the demand for web content in local languages. This example illustrates one of the main lessons of applied anthropology, that external inputs, including global brands, fit in best when they are tailored properly to local settings.

Asia already has [three times] as many Internet users as North America. . . . More than half of the search queries on Google come from outside the United States.

The globalization of the Web has inspired entrepreneurs like Ram Prakash Hanumanthappa, an engineer from outside Bangalore, India. Mr. Ram Prakash learned English as a teenager, but he still prefers to express himself to friends and family members in his native Kannada. But using Kannada on the Web involves computer keyboard maps that even Mr. Ram Prakash finds challenging to learn.

So in 2006 he developed Quillpad, an online service for typing in 10 South Asian languages. Users spell out words of local languages phonetically in Roman letters, and Quillpad's predictive engine converts them into local-language script. Bloggers and authors rave about the service, which has attracted interest from the cellphone maker Nokia and the attention of Google Inc., which has since introduced its own transliteration tool.

Mr. Ram Prakash said Western technology companies have misunderstood the linguistic landscape of India, where English is spoken proficiently by only about a tenth of the population and even many college-educated Indians prefer the contours of their native tongues for everyday speech. "You've got to give them an opportunity to express themselves correctly, rather than make a fool out of themselves and forcing them to use English," he said. Only there is a shortage of non-English content and applications. So, American technology giants are spending hundreds of millions of dollars each year to build and develop foreign-language Web sites and services—before local companies like Quillpad beat them to the punch and the profits. . . .

Nowhere are the obstacles, or the potential rewards, more apparent than in India. . . . Indians may speak one language to their boss, another to their spouse and a third to a parent. In casual speech, words can be drawn from a grab bag of tongues. . . .

Yahoo and Google have introduced more than a dozen services to encourage India's Web users to search, blog, chat and learn in their mother tongues. Microsoft has built its Windows Live bundle of online consumer services in seven Indian languages. Facebook has enlisted hundreds of volunteers to translate its social networking site into Hindi and other regional languages, and Wikipedia now has more entries in Indian local languages than in Korean. Google's search service has lagged behind the local competition in China, and that has made providing locally flavored services a priority for the company in India. Google's initiatives in India are aimed at opening the country's historically slow-growing personal computer market, and at developing expertise that Google will be able to apply to building services for emerging markets worldwide.

class, ethnic, and gender differences (McConnell-Ginet 2010; Tannen 1990, 1993)? How is language used to gain, express, reinforce, or resist power (Geis 1987; Mooney 2011; Trudgill 2010)?

Sociolinguists don't deny that the people who speak a given language share knowledge of its basic rules. Such common knowledge is the basis of mutually intelligible communication. However, sociolinguists focus on features that vary systematically with social position and situation. To study variation, sociolinguists must observe, define, and measure variable use of language in real-world situations. To show that linguistic features correlate with social, economic, and political differences, the social attributes of speakers also must be measured and related to speech (Fasold and Connor-Linton 2006; Labov 2006; Trudgill 2010).

Variation within a language at a given time is historic change in progress. The same forces that, working gradually, have produced large-scale linguistic change over the centuries are still at work today. Linguistic change occurs not in a vacuum but in society. When new ways of speaking are associated with social factors, they are imitated, and they spread. In this way, a language changes.

## Linguistic Diversity

As an illustration of the linguistic variation that is encountered in all nations, consider the contemporary United States. Ethnic diversity is revealed by the fact that millions of Americans learn first languages other than English. Spanish is the most common. Most of those people eventually become

"India is a microcosm of the world," said Dr. Prasad Bhaarat Ram, Google India's head of research and development. "Having 22 languages creates a new level of complexity in which you can't take the same approach that you would if you had one predominant language and applied it 22 times."

Global businesses are spending hundreds of millions of dollars a year working their way down a list of languages into which to translate their Web sites. . . .

English simply will not suffice for connecting with India's growing online market, a lesson already learned by Western television producers and consumer products makers. . . .

Even among the largely English-speaking base of around 50 million Web users in India today, nearly three-quarters prefer to read in a local language, according to a survey by JuxtConsult, an Indian market research company. . . .

A Microsoft initiative, Project Bhasha, coordinates the efforts of Indian academics, local businesses and solo software developers to expand computing in regional languages. The project's Web site, which counts thousands of registered members, refers to language as "one of the main contributors to the digital divide" in India. The company is also seeing growing demand from Indian government agencies and companies creating online public services in local languages.

"As many of these companies want to push their services into rural India or tier-two towns or smaller towns, then it becomes essential they communicate with their customers in the local language," said Pradeep Parappil, a Microsoft program manager. "Localization is the key to success in countries like India," said Gopal Krishna, who oversees consumer services at Yahoo India.

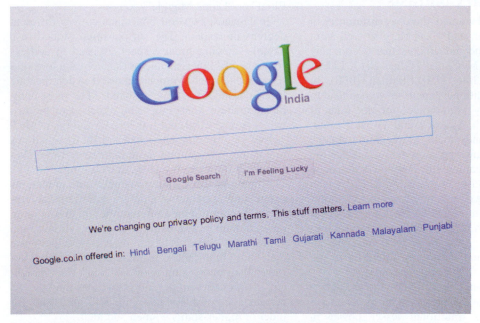

Google has been expanding in India, where it offers searches in multiple languages, including Hindi, Gujarati, Tamil, and several others.

bilinguals, adding English as a second language. In many multilingual (including colonized) nations, people use two languages on different occasions: one in the home, for example, and the other on the job or in public. This chapter's "Appreciating Diversity" focuses on India, a multilingual, formerly colonized nation. Only about one-tenth of India's population speaks English, the colonial language. In "Appreciating Diversity" we see how even those English speakers appreciate being able to read, and to find Internet content in, their own regional languages.

Whether bilingual or not, we all vary our speech in different contexts; we engage in **style shifts** (see Eckert and Rickford 2001). In certain parts of Europe, people regularly switch dialects. This phenomenon, known as **diglossia,** applies to "high" and "low" variants of the same language, for example, in German and Flemish (spoken in Belgium). People employ the "high" variant at universities and in writing, professions, and the mass media. They use the "low" variant for ordinary conversation with family members and friends.

Just as social situations influence our speech, so do geographic, cultural, and socioeconomic differences. Many dialects coexist in the United States with Standard (American) English (SE). SE itself is a dialect that differs, say, from "BBC English," which is the preferred dialect in Great Britain. According to the principle of *linguistic relativity*, all dialects are equally effective as systems of communication, which is language's main job. Our tendency to think of particular dialects as cruder or more sophisticated than others is a social rather than

**style shifts**
Varying one's speech in different social contexts.

**diglossia**
Language with "high" (formal) and "low" (informal, familial) dialects.

a linguistic judgment. We rank certain speech patterns as better or worse because we recognize that they are used by groups that we also rank. People who say *dese, dem,* and *dere* instead of *these, them,* and *there* communicate perfectly well with anyone who recognizes that the *d* sound systematically replaces the *th* sound in their speech. However, this form of speech is stigmatized; it has become an indicator of low social rank. We call it, like the use of *ain't,* "uneducated speech." The use of *dem, dese,* and *dere* is one of many phonological differences that Americans recognize and look down on (see Labov 2012).

## Gender Speech Contrasts

Comparing men and women, there are differences in phonology, grammar, and vocabulary as well as in the body stances and movements that accompany speech (Eckert and McConnell-Ginet 2013; Lakoff 2004; McConnell-Ginet 2010; Tannen 1990). In public contexts, traditional Japanese women tend to adopt an artificially high voice, for the sake of politeness. In North America and Great Britain, women's speech tends to be more similar to the standard dialect than men's speech. Consider the data in Table 14.2, gathered in Detroit. In all social classes, but particularly in the working class, men were more apt to use double negatives (e.g., "I don't want none"). Women tend to be more careful about "uneducated speech." Men may adopt working-class speech because they associate it with masculinity. Perhaps women pay more attention to the media, where standard dialects are employed.

According to Robin Lakoff (2004), the use of certain types of words and expressions has been associated with women's traditional lesser power in American society (see also Tannen 1990). For example, *Oh dear, Oh fudge,* and *Goodness!* are less forceful than *Hell* and *Damn.* Watch the lips of a disgruntled player in a football game. What's the likelihood he's saying "Phooey on you"? Women are more likely to use such adjectives as *adorable, charming, sweet, cute, lovely,* and *divine* than men are.

## Language and Status Position

**honorifics**
Terms of respect; used to honor people.

**Honorifics** are terms used with people, often by being added to their names, to "honor" them. Such terms may convey or imply a status difference between the speaker and the person being referred to ("the good doctor") or addressed ("Professor Dumbledore"). Although Americans tend to be less formal than other nationalities, American English still has its honorifics. They include such terms as *Mr., Mrs., Ms., Dr., Professor, Dean, Senator, Reverend, Honorable,* and *President.* Often these terms are attached to names, as in "Dr. Wilson," "President Obama," and "Senator Feinstein," but some of them can be used to address someone without using his or her name, such as "Dr.," "Mr. President," "Senator," and "Miss." The British have a more developed set of honorifics, corresponding to status distinctions based in class, nobility (e.g., Lord and Lady Trumble), and special recognition (e.g., knighthood—"Sir Elton" or "Dame Maggie").

In Japanese, several honorifics convey different degrees of respect. The suffix *-sama* (added to a name), showing great respect, is used to address someone of higher social status, such as a lord or a respected teacher. Women can use it to demonstrate love or respect for their husbands. The most common Japanese honorific, *-san,* attached to the last name, is respectful, but it is less formal than "Mr.," "Mrs.," or "Ms." in American English. Attached to a first name, *-san* denotes more familiarity (*Free Dictionary* 2004; Loveday 1986, 2001).

Kin terms, too, can be associated with gradations in age, rank, and status. *Dad* is a more familiar, less formal kin term than *Father,* but it still shows more respect than would using the father's first name. Outranking their children, parents routinely use their kids' first names, nicknames, or baby names, rather than addressing them as "son" and "daughter." Southerners up to (and sometimes long past) a certain age routinely use "ma'am" and "sir" for older or higher-status women and men.

## Stratification

We use and evaluate speech in the context of *extralinguistic* forces—social, political, and economic. Mainstream Americans evaluate the speech of low-status groups negatively, calling it "uneducated." This is not because these ways of speaking are bad in themselves but because they have come to symbolize low status. Consider variation in the pronunciation of *r.* In some parts of the United States, *r* is regularly pronounced, and in other (*r*less) areas, it is not. Originally, American *r*less speech was modeled on the

**TABLE 14.2**  Multiple Negation ("I don't want none") According to Gender and Class (in Percentages)

|  | UPPER MIDDLE CLASS | LOWER MIDDLE CLASS | UPPER WORKING CLASS | LOWER WORKING CLASS |
|---|---|---|---|---|
| Male | 6.3 | 32.4 | 40.0 | 90.1 |
| Female | 0.0 | 1.4 | 35.6 | 58.9 |

SOURCE: Peter Trudgill, *Sociolinguistics: An Introduction to Language and Society,* 5th ed. (London: Penguin Books, 1974, revised editions 1983, 1995, 2000), p. 70. Copyright © Peter Trudgill, 1974, 1983, 1995, 2000, 2010. Reproduced by permission of Penguin Books Ltd.

fashionable speech of England. Because of its prestige, *r*lessness was adopted in many areas and continues as the norm around Boston and in the South.

New Yorkers sought prestige by dropping their *r*'s in the 19th century, after having pronounced them in the 18th. However, contemporary New Yorkers are going back to the 18th-century pattern of pronouncing *r*'s. What matters, and what governs linguistic change, is not the reverberation of a strong midwestern *r* but *social* evaluation, whether *r*'s happen to be "in" or "out."

Studies of *r* pronunciation in New York City have clarified the mechanisms of phonological change. William Labov (1972*b*) focused on whether *r* was pronounced after vowels in such words as *car, floor, card,* and *fourth.* To get data on how this linguistic variation correlated with social class, he used a series of rapid encounters with employees in three New York City department stores, each of whose prices and locations attracted a different socioeconomic group. Saks Fifth Avenue (68 encounters) catered to the upper middle class, Macy's (125) attracted middle-class shoppers, and S. Klein's (71) had predominantly lower-middle-class and working-class customers. The class origins of store personnel tended to reflect those of their customers.

Having already determined that a certain department was on the fourth floor, Labov approached ground-floor salespeople and asked where that department was. After the salesperson had answered, "Fourth floor," Labov repeated his "Where?" in order to get a second response. The second reply was more formal and emphatic, the salesperson presumably thinking that Labov hadn't heard or understood the first answer. For each salesperson, therefore, Labov had two samples of /r/ pronunciation in two words.

Labov calculated the percentages of workers who pronounced /r/ at least once during the interview. These were 62 percent at Saks, 51 percent at Macy's, but only 20 percent at S. Klein's. He also found that personnel on upper floors, where he asked "What floor is this?" (and where more expensive items were sold), pronounced /r/ more often than ground-floor salespeople did (see also Labov 2006).

In Labov's study, summarized in Table 14.3, /r/ pronunciation was clearly associated with prestige. Certainly the job interviewers who had hired the salespeople never counted *r*'s before offering employment. However, they did use speech evaluations to make judgments about how effective certain people would be in selling particular kinds of merchandise. In other words, they practiced sociolinguistic discrimination, using linguistic features in deciding who got certain jobs.

Americans have stereotypes about how people from certain regions talk, and some stereotypes are more widespread than others are (see this chapter's "Appreciating Anthropology" on pp. 266–267 for stereotypes about, and the reality of, California speech patterns). Most Americans think they can imitate a "southern accent," and southern speech tends to be devalued outside the South. Americans also stereotype, without necessarily stigmatizing, speech in New York City (the pronunciation of *coffee,* for example), Boston ("I pahked the kah in Hahvahd Yahd"), and Canada ("oot" for "out").

It's sometimes asserted that midwestern Americans don't have accents. This belief stems from the fact that midwestern dialects don't have many stigmatized linguistic variants—speech patterns that people in other regions recognize and look down on, such as *r*lessness and *dem, dese,* and *dere* (instead of *them, these,* and *there*).

Far from having no accents, midwesterners, even in the same high school, exhibit linguistic diversity (see Eckert 1989, 2000). One of the best examples of variable midwestern speech, involving vowels, is pronunciation of the *e* sound (the /e/ phoneme) in such words as *ten, rent, section, lecture, effect, best,* and *test.* In southeastern Michigan, there are four different ways of pronouncing this *e* sound. Speakers of African American English (see below) and immigrants from Appalachia often pronounce *ten* as "tin," just as southerners

**TABLE 14.3** Pronunciation of *r* in New York City Department Stores

| STORE | NUMBER OF ENCOUNTERS | % *r* PRONUNCIATION |
|---|---|---|
| Saks Fifth Avenue | 68 | 62 |
| Macy's | 125 | 51 |
| S. Klein's | 71 | 20 |

Certain dialects are stigmatized, not because of actual linguistic deficiencies but because of a symbolic association between a certain way of talking and low social status. In this scene from the movie *My Fair Lady,* Professor Henry Higgins (Rex Harrison) teaches Eliza Doolittle (Audrey Hepburn), formerly a Cockney flower girl, how to speak "proper English."

# appreciating ANTHROPOLOGY

## I Wish They All Could Be California Vowels

Is there a "California accent"? Popular stereotypes of how Californians talk reflect exposure to media images of blond surfer boys who say things like "dude" and "gnarly" and white Valley girls who intone "Like, totally!" and "Gag me with a spoon!" Such stereotypes have some accuracy, as we'll see. Just as striking, however, is the linguistic diversity that also marks contemporary California.

To document this diversity, Professor Penelope Eckert, a sociolinguist at Stanford University, and her graduate students are engaged in an ongoing, multiyear research project called Voices of California (see http://www.stanford.edu/dept/linguistics/VoCal/). Eckert's team of 10–15 researchers visits a new site each fall, spending about 10 days interviewing residents who grew up in the area. Recently, their focus has been on inland California, which has been less studied than have the main coastal cities. In previous years, the group visited Merced and Redding; in 2012, they focused on Bakersfield. The researchers always test certain words that elicit specific pronunciations. These words include *wash,* sometimes pronounced "warsh," *greasy* ("greezy"), and *pin* and *pen,* which some people pronounce the same. Interviews in Merced and Shasta Counties have revealed ways that Depression-era migrants from

Oklahoma's Dust Bowl left their mark on California speech, such as their pronunciation of *wash* and *greasy* (see King 2012).

We see, then, that one factor in determining how people speak is where their ancestors came from. Another factor is their own attitudes and feelings about the people around them and about the outside world. For example, in California's Central Valley, which is economically depressed, young people must choose whether to stay put or to move elsewhere, seeking work. When people are, and want to stay, involved in their home community, they tend to talk like locals. A desire not to be perceived as being from a particular place also affects how people talk (King 2012).

I know this feeling well, having abandoned my original southern accent when I was an adolescent. In fact, my own speech shift wasn't totally voluntary: as mentioned previously, I was placed in a speech class when I moved from Atlanta to New York City at the age of 13. The same thing happened to my college roommate, from Baton Rouge, Louisiana, when he enrolled at Columbia University in New York City. By then, my own speech had become sufficiently accent free to avoid further speech indoctrination.

In addition to regional diversity, the speech of Californians also reflects ethnic contrasts. Non-

Hispanic whites now represent under 40 percent of the state's total population, while Latinos (Hispanics) constitute 38 percent. California also has a large and diverse Asian American population and a sizable group of African Americans.

Representing California's largest minority, as well as its earliest nonindigenous settlers, Chicanos (Mexican Americans) display interesting speech patterns. California's Mexican-derived populations can claim the longest continuous (nonindigenous) linguistic history in the state, including Spanish/English bilingualism and the source of most important place names. So strong is the Spanish heritage that Spanish-like vowels even influence the way English is spoken by Hispanics who learn English as their first, or native, language. For example, among Chicano speakers in northern California the vowel in the second syllable of *nothing* has come to resemble the Spanish "ee" sound. Not all innovations in Chicano English come from Spanish. One widespread speech innovation in Los Angeles has been the lowering of the vowel in the first syllable of *elevator,* so that it rhymes with the first syllable of *alligator*. That shift owes nothing to Spanish (see Eckert and Mendoza-Denton 2002).

Despite the well-documented diversity in California speech, linguists have detected trends

habitually do. Some Michiganders say "ten," the correct pronunciation in Standard English. However, two other pronunciations also are common. Instead of "ten," many Michiganders say "tan," or "tun" (as though they were using the word *ton,* a unit of weight).

My students often astound me with their pronunciation. One day I met a Michigan-raised graduate student instructor in the hall. She was deliriously happy. When I asked why, she replied, "I've just had the best suction."

"What?" I said.

She finally spoke more precisely. "I've just had the best saction." She considered this a clearer pronunciation of the word *section.*

In another example of such speech, one of my students lamented, after an exam, that she had not done her "bust on the tust" (i.e., best on the test). The truth is, regional patterns affect the way we all speak.

Our speech habits help determine how others evaluate us and thus our access to employment and other material resources. Because of this, "proper language" itself becomes a strategic resource—and a path to wealth, prestige, and power (Gal 1989; Mooney 2011). Illustrating this, many ethnographers have described the importance of verbal skill and oratory in politics (Beeman 1986; Brenneis 1988; Geis 1987). Ronald Reagan, known as a "great communicator," toward uniformity as well, particularly among coastal whites. Since the 1940s, a distinctive "California accent" has been developing, and some of its features were indeed highlighted in Moon Unit Zappa's 1982 recording of "Valley Girl."

The accent is most evident in vowels, as we see in the following examples. First, the vowels in *hock* and *hawk,* or *cot* and *caught,* are pronounced the same, so that *awesome* rhymes with *possum*. Second, the vowel sound in *boot* and *dude* has shifted and now is pronounced as in *pure* or *cute* (thus, *boot* becomes "beaut," and *dude* becomes "dewed," rather than "dood"). Third, the vowel sound in *but* and *cut* is shifting, so that those words sound more like *bet* and *ket*. Finally, *black* is being pronounced more like *block;* and *bet,* like *bat* (see Eckert and Mendoza-Denton 2002).

Such coordinated phonological changes are known as chain shifts. The most extreme versions of these chain-shifted vowel sounds are found in the speech of young white Californians. Young people tend to be leaders in speech innovations, which is why linguists spend a lot of time studying them. California's communities bring together adolescents from varied backgrounds. Their linguistic styles, like their clothing and behavioral styles, influence one another. Hostility may cause people to differentiate and diversify their styles, while curiosity or admiration may cause people to copy, or adopt elements from, other styles. Whose styles, linguistic or otherwise, might you have copied—or avoided?

Stereotypes about regional speech styles show up in mass media, which then reinforce and help spread those stereotypes. Linguistic stereotypes abound in the movies, *Clueless* and *Bill and Ted's Excellent Adventure.*

dominated American society in the 1980s as a two-term president. Another twice-elected president, Bill Clinton, despite his southern accent, is known for his verbal skills. Communications flaws may have helped doom the presidencies of Gerald Ford, Jimmy Carter, and George Bush (the elder). How do you evaluate the linguistic skills of the current leader of your country?

The French anthropologist Pierre Bourdieu views linguistic practices as *symbolic capital* that people, if trained properly, can convert into economic and social capital. The value of a dialect—its standing in a "linguistic market"— depends on the extent to which it provides access to desired positions in society. In turn, this reflects its legitimation by formal institutions: educational institutions, state, church, and prestige media. Even people who don't use the prestige dialect accept its authority and correctness, its "symbolic domination" (Bourdieu 1982, 1984; Labov 2012). Thus, linguistic forms, which lack power in themselves, take on the power of the groups they symbolize. The education system, however (defending its own worth), denies linguistic relativity, misrepresenting prestige speech as being inherently better. The linguistic insecurity often felt by lower-class and minority speakers is a result of this symbolic domination.

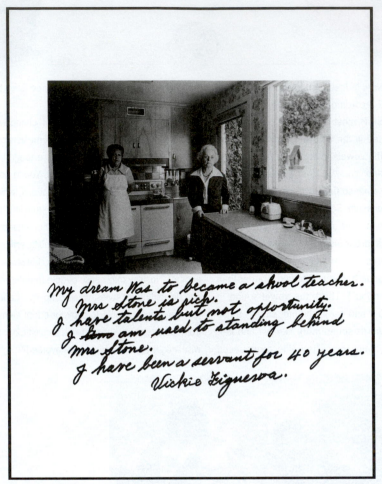

My dream Was to became a skvol teacher.
Mrs Stone is rich.
I have talents but not opportunity.
I here am used to standing behind
Mrs Stone.
I have been a servant for 40 years.
Vickie Figueroa.

"Proper language" is a strategic resource, correlated with wealth, prestige, and power. How is linguistic (and social) stratification illustrated in the photo above, including the handwritten comments below it?

## African American Vernacular English (AAVE)

**African American Vernacular English (AAVE)**

Rule-governed dialect spoken by some African Americans.

No one pays much attention when someone says "saction" instead of "section." But some nonstandard speech carries more of a stigma. Sometimes stigmatized speech is linked to region, class, or educational background; sometimes it is associated with ethnicity or "race."

Sociolinguists have conducted detailed studies of what they call **African American Vernacular English (AAVE).** (*Vernacular* means ordinary, casual speech.) AAVE is the "relatively uniform dialect spoken by the majority of black youth in most parts of the United States . . . , especially in the inner city areas of New York, Boston, Detroit, Philadelphia, Washington, Cleveland, . . . and other urban centers. It is also spoken in most rural areas and used in the casual, intimate speech of many adults" (Labov 1972a, p. xiii). This does not imply that all, or even most, African Americans speak AAVE.

AAVE may be a nonstandard dialect, but it is not an ungrammatical hodgepodge. Rather, AAVE is a complex linguistic system with its own rules, which linguists have described. The phonology and syntax of AAVE are similar to those of southern dialects. This reflects generations of contact between southern whites and blacks, with mutual influence on each other's speech patterns. Many features that distinguish AAVE from SE (Standard English) also show up in southern white speech, but less frequently than in AAVE.

Linguists disagree about exactly how AAVE originated (Rickford 1997; Rickford and Rickford 2000). Smitherman (1986) notes certain structural similarities between West African languages and AAVE. African linguistic backgrounds no doubt influenced how early African Americans learned English. Did they restructure English to fit African linguistic patterns? Or, possibly, in acquiring English, did African slaves fuse English with African languages to make a pidgin or creole, which influenced the subsequent development of AAVE? Creole speech may have been brought to the American colonies by the many slaves who were brought in from the Caribbean during the 17th and 18th centuries (Rickford 1997).

Origins aside, there are phonological and grammatical differences between AAVE and SE. One phonological difference is that AAVE speakers are less likely to pronounce *r* than SE speakers are. Actually, many SE speakers don't pronounce *r*'s that come right before a consonant (ca*r*d) or at the end of a word (ca*r*). But SE speakers do usually pronounce an *r* that comes right before a vowel, either at the end of a word (fou*r* o'clock) or within a word (Ca*r*ol). AAVE speakers, by contrast, are much more likely to omit such intervocalic (between vowels) *r*'s. The result is that speakers of the two dialects have different *homonyms* (words that sound the same but have different meanings). AAVE speakers who don't pronounce intervocalic *r*'s have the following homonyms: Carol/Cal; Paris/pass.

Observing different phonological rules, AAVE speakers pronounce certain words differently than SE speakers do. Particularly in the elementary school context, the homonyms of AAVE-speaking students typically differ from those of their SE-speaking teachers. To evaluate reading accuracy, teachers should determine whether students are recognizing the different meanings of such AAVE homonyms as *passed, past,* and *pass.* Teachers need to make sure students understand what they are reading, which is probably more important than whether they are pronouncing words correctly according to the SE norm.

The phonological contrasts between AAVE and SE speakers often have grammatical consequences. One of these involves *copula deletion,* which means the absence of SE forms of the copula—the verb *to be.* SE habitually uses contractions, as in "you're tired" instead of "you are tired." Where SE shortens with contractions, AAVE goes one step further and deletes the copular altogether—thus "you tired." AAVE's copula deletion is a grammatical result of its phonological rules, which dictate that *r*'s (as in *you're, we're,* and *they're*) and word-final *s*'s (as in *he's*) be dropped. However, AAVE speakers do pronounce *m,* so that the AAVE first-person singular is "I'm tired," just as in SE. In its deletion of the present tense of the verb *to be,* AAVE is similar to many languages, including Russian, Hungarian, and Hebrew.

| SE | SE CONTRACTION | AAVE |
|---|---|---|
| you are tired | you're tired | you tired |
| he is tired | he's tired | he tired |
| we are tired | we're tired | we tired |
| they are tired | they're tired | they tired |

Also, phonological rules may lead AAVE speakers to omit *-ed* as a past-tense marker and *-s* as a marker of plurality. However, other speech contexts demonstrate that AAVE speakers do understand the difference between past and present verbs, and between singular and plural nouns. Confirming this are irregular verbs (e.g., *tell, told*) and irregular plurals (e.g., *child, children*), in which AAVE works the same as SE.

SE is not superior to AAVE as a linguistic system, but it does happen to be the prestige dialect—the one used in the mass media, in writing, and in most public and professional contexts. SE is the dialect that has the most "symbolic capital." In areas of Germany where there is diglossia, speakers of Plattdeusch (Low German) learn the High German dialect to communicate appropriately in the national context. Similarly, upwardly mobile AAVE-speaking students learn SE.

## HISTORICAL LINGUISTICS

Sociolinguists study contemporary variation in speech—language change in progress. **Historical linguistics** deals with longer-term change. Language changes over time. It evolves—varies, spreads, divides into dialects and eventually into **subgroups** (languages within a taxonomy of related languages that are most closely related). Historical linguists can reconstruct many features of past languages by studying contemporary **daughter languages.** These are languages that descend from the same parent language and that have been changing for hundreds or even thousands of years. We call the original language from which they diverge the **protolanguage.** Romance languages such as

Rappers Taboo, will.i.am, and apl.de.ap perform in February, 2013 in Hollywood, California. How does contemporary music reflect and express ideas about race, ethnicity, and gender?

French and Spanish, for example, are daughter languages of Latin, their common protolanguage. German, English, Dutch, and the Scandinavian languages are daughter languages of proto-Germanic. Latin and proto-Germanic were both Indo-European (IE) languages (see Figure 14.2). The common protolanguage of Latin, proto-Germanic, and many other ancient languages is known as proto-Indo-European (PIE).

According to one theory, PIE was the language of chariot-driving pastoralists who spread out from the Eurasian steppes above the Black Sea about 4,000 years ago and conquered Europe and Asia (see Wade 2012). The main line of evidence for this view is linguistic: PIE had a vocabulary for chariots and wagons that included words for "wheel," "axle," "harness-pole," and "to go or convey in a vehicle." These PIE words (as reconstructed by historical linguists) have recognizable descendant words in many IE languages. This suggests that wheeled vehicles must have been invented before PIE started diverging (Wade 2012). The earliest such vehicles date to 3500 B.C.E.

The main rival theory, first proposed by archaeologist Colin Renfrew (1987), is that PIE was spoken and spread by peaceful farmers who lived in Anatolia, now Turkey, about 9,000 years ago. Recent studies by the evolutionary biologist Quentin Atkinson and his colleagues in New Zealand support the Anatolian origin of PIE (see Bouckaert et al. 2012). Atkinson's team focused on a set of vocabulary items known to be resistant to linguistic change. These include pronouns, parts of the body, and family relations. For 103 IE languages, the researchers

**historical linguistics**
Study of languages over time.

**subgroups**
(Linguistic) closely related languages.

**daughter languages**
Languages sharing a common parent language, e.g., Latin.

**protolanguage**
Language ancestral to several daughter languages.

**FIGURE 14.2** PIE Family Tree.

This is a family tree of the Indo-European languages. All can be traced back to a protolanguage, Proto-Indo-European (PIE). PIE split into dialects that eventually evolved into separate daughter languages, which, in turn, evolved into granddaughter languages such as Latin and proto-Germanic, which are ancestral to dozens of modern languages.

compared those words with the PIE ancestral word (as reconstructed by historical linguists). Words that clearly descend from the same ancestral word are known as *cognates*. For example, "mother" (English) is cognate with all these words for the same relative: "mutter" (German), "mat" (Russian), "madar" (Persian), "matka" (Polish) and "mater" (Latin). All are descendants of the PIE word "mehter."

For each language, when the word was a cognate the researchers scored it 1; when it was not (having been replaced by an unrelated word), it was scored 0. With each language represented by a string of 1s and 0s, the researchers could establish a family tree showing the relationships among the 103 languages. Based on those relationships and the geographic areas where the daughter languages are spoken, the computer determined the likeliest routes of movement from an origin. The calculation pointed to Anatolia,

southern Turkey. This is precisely the region originally proposed by Renfrew, because it was the area from which farming spread to Europe. Atkinson also ran a computer simulation on a grammar-based IE tree—once again finding Anatolia to be the most likely origin point for PIE (Wade 2012). Although many linguists still support the chariot/steppe origin theory, several lines of biological and archaeological evidence now indicate that the Neolithic economy spread more through the actual migration of farmers than through the diffusion of crops and ideas. This would seem to offer support to the Renfrew–Atkinson model of PIE origin and dispersal of Neolithic farmers.

Historically oriented linguists suspect that a very remote protolanguage, spoken perhaps 50,000 years ago in Africa, gave rise to all contemporary languages. Murray Gell-Mann and Merritt Ruhlen (2011), who co-direct the Program on the Evolution

Modern technology can be a valuable tool for language preservation. Two centuries after a Cherokee silversmith named Sequoyah developed a system of symbols for Cherokee syllables, students at the Cherokee Nation Immersion School in Oklahoma use computers, tablets, iPhones, and iPods to learn to read and write the Cherokee language.

of Human Languages at the Sante Fe Institute, have reconstructed the syntax (word ordering) of this ancient protolanguage. Their study focused on how subject (S), object (O), and verb (V) are arranged in phrases and sentences in some 2,000 contemporary languages. There are six possible word orders: SOV, SVO, OSV, OVS, VSO, and VOS. Most common is SOV ("I you like," e.g., Latin), present in more than half of all languages. Next comes SVO ("I like you," e.g., English). Much rarer are OSV, OVS, VOS, and VSO. Gell-Mann and Ruhlen constructed a family tree of relationships among 2,000 contemporary languages. The directions of change involving the six word orders were clear. All the languages that were SVO, OVS, and OSV derived from SOV languages—never the other way around. Furthermore, any language with VSO or VOS word order always came from an SVO language (see Figure 14.3). The fact that SVO always comes from SOV confirms SOV as the original, ancestral word order.

## Language, Culture, and History

A close relationship between languages does not necessarily mean that their speakers are closely related biologically or culturally, because people can adopt new languages. In the equatorial forests of Africa, "pygmy" hunters have discarded their ancestral languages and now speak those of the cultivators who have migrated to the area. Immigrants to the United

States and Canada spoke many different languages on arrival, but their descendants now speak fluent English.

Knowledge of linguistic relationships is often valuable to anthropologists interested in history, particularly events during the past 5,000 years. Cultural features may (or may not) correlate with the distribution of language families. Groups that speak related languages may (or may not) be more culturally similar to each other than they are to groups whose speech derives from different linguistic ancestors. Of course, cultural similarities aren't limited to speakers of related languages. Even groups whose members speak unrelated languages have contact through trade, intermarriage, and warfare. Ideas and inventions diffuse widely among human groups. Many

**FIGURE 14.3** Evolution of Word Order from Original SVO (Subject, Verb, Object) in Ancient Ancestral Protolanguage.

items of vocabulary in contemporary English come from French. Even without written documentation of France's influence after the Norman Conquest of England in 1066, linguistic evidence in contemporary English would reveal a long period of important first-hand contact with France. Similar linguistic evidence may confirm cultural contact and borrowing when written history is lacking. By considering which words have been borrowed, we also can make inferences about the nature of the contact.

## Language Loss

One aspect of linguistic history is language loss. When languages disappear, cultural diversity is reduced as well. According to linguist K. David Harrison, "When we lose a language, we lose centuries of thinking about time, seasons, sea creatures, reindeer, edible flowers, mathematics, landscapes, myths, music, the unknown and the everyday" (quoted in Maugh 2007). Harrison's book *When Languages Die* (2007), notes that an indigenous language goes extinct every two weeks, as its last speakers die. The world's linguistic diversity has been cut in half (measured by number of distinct languages) in the past 500 years, and half of the remaining languages are predicted to disappear during this century. Colonial languages (e.g., English, Spanish, Portuguese, French, Dutch, Russian) have expanded at the expense of indigenous ones. Of approximately 7,000 remaining languages, about 20 percent are endangered, compared with 18 percent of mammals, 8 percent of plants, and 5 percent of birds (Harrison 2010; Maugh 2007). National Geographic's Enduring Voices Project (http://national-geographic.com/travel/enduring-voices/ strives to preserve endangered languages by identifying the geographic areas with unique, poorly understood, or threatened languages and by documenting those languages and cultures. The website shows various language hot spots where the endangerment rate ranges from low to severe. The rate is high in an area encompassing Oklahoma, Texas, and New Mexico, where 40 Native American languages are at risk. The top hot spot is northern Australia, where 153 Aboriginal languages are endangered (Maugh 2007). Other hot spots are in central South America, the Pacific Northwest of North America, and eastern Siberia. In all these areas indigenous tongues have yielded, either voluntarily or through coercion, to a colonial language (see Harrison 2010).

## for REVIEW

## summary

1. Wild primates use call systems to communicate. Environmental stimuli trigger calls, which cannot be combined when multiple stimuli are present. Contrasts between language and call systems include displacement, productivity, and cultural transmission. Over time, our ancestral call systems grew too complex for genetic transmission, and hominid communication began to rely on learning. Humans still use nonverbal communication, such as facial expressions, gestures, and body stances and movements. But language is the main system humans use to communicate. Chimps and gorillas can understand and manipulate nonverbal symbols based on language.

2. No language uses all the sounds the human vocal tract can make. Phonology—the study of speech sounds—focuses on sound contrasts (phonemes) that distinguish meaning. The grammars and lexicons of particular languages can lead their speakers to perceive and think in certain ways. Studies of domains such as kinship, color terminologies, and pronouns show that speakers of different languages categorize their experiences differently.

3. Linguistic anthropologists share anthropology's general interest in diversity in time and space. Sociolinguistics investigates relationships between social and linguistic variation by focusing on the actual use of language. Only when features of speech acquire social meaning are they imitated. If they are valued, they will spread. People vary their speech, shifting styles, dialects, and languages. As linguistic systems, all languages and dialects are equally complex, rule-governed, and effective for communication. However, speech is used, is evaluated, and changes in the context of political, economic, and social forces. Often the linguistic traits of a low-status group are negatively evaluated. This devaluation is not because of *linguistic* features per se. Rather, it reflects the association of such features with low *social* status. One dialect, supported by the dominant institutions of the state, exercises symbolic domination over the others.

4. Historical linguistics is useful for anthropologists interested in historic relationships among populations. Cultural similarities and differences often correlate with linguistic ones. Linguistic clues can

suggest past contacts between cultures. Related languages—members of the same language family—descend from an original protolanguage. Relationships between languages don't necessarily mean that there are biological ties between their speakers, because people can learn new languages.

5. One aspect of linguistic history is language loss. The world's linguistic diversity has been cut in half in the past 500 years, and half of the remaining 7,000 languages are predicted to disappear during this century.

**critical thinking**

1. What dialects and languages do you speak? Do you tend to use different dialects, languages, or speech styles in different contexts? Why or why not?

2. Culture always plays a role in shaping what we understand as "natural." What does this mean? Provide three examples of the relevance of this fact in the context of human language and communication.

3. Consider how changing technologies are altering the ways you communicate with family, friends, and even strangers. Suppose your best friend decides to study sociolinguistics in graduate school. What ideas about the relationship between changing technologies, language, and social relations could you suggest to him or her as worth studying?

4. List some stereotypes about how different people speak. Are those real differences, or just stereotypes? Are the stereotypes positive or negative? Why do you think those stereotypes exist?

5. What is language loss? Why are some researchers and communities worldwide so concerned by this growing phenomenon?

CHAPTER 15

# Ethnicity and Race

▶ What is social status, and how does it relate to ethnicity?

▶ How are race and ethnicity socially constructed in various societies?

▶ What are the positive and negative aspects of ethnicity?

Racial/ethnic diversity in today's United States. Might this photo have been taken in your neighborhood? Is baseball more ethnically diverse than other sports?

# understanding OURSELVES

When asked "Who are you?" what first comes to mind? Think of the last person you met, or the person sitting nearest you. What labels pop into your head to describe that person? What kinds of identity cues and clues do people use to figure out the kinds of people they are dealing with, and how to act in various social situations? Part of human adaptive flexibility is our ability to shift self-presentation in response to context. Italians, for example, maintain separate sets of clothing to be worn inside and outside the home. They invest much more in their outside wardrobe (thus supporting a vibrant Italian fashion industry)—and what it says about their public persona—than in indoor garb, which is for family and intimates to see. Identities and behavior change with context: "I may be a Neandertal at the office, but I'm all *Homo sapiens* at home." Many of the social statuses we occupy, the "hats" we wear, depend on the situation. A person can be both black and Hispanic, or both a father and a ballplayer. One identity is claimed or perceived in certain settings, another in different ones. Among African Americans a "Hispanic" baseball player might be black; among Hispanics, Hispanic.

When our claimed or perceived identity varies depending on the context, this is called the *situational negotiation of social identity*. Depending on the situation, the same woman might declare: "I'm Jimmy's mother." "I'm your boss." "I'm African American." "I'm your professor." In face-to-face encounters, other people see who we are—actually, who they perceive us to be. They may expect us to think and act in certain (stereotypical) ways based on their perception of our identity (e.g., Latina woman, older white male golfer). Although we can't know which aspect of identity they'll focus on (e.g., ethnicity, gender, age, or political affiliation), face to face it's hard to be anonymous or to be someone else entirely. That's what masks, costumes, disguises, and hiding are for. Who's that little man behind the curtain?

Unlike our early ancestors, people today don't just interact face to face. We routinely give our money and our trust to individuals and institutions we've never laid eyes on. We phone, write, and—more than ever—use the Internet, where we must choose which aspects of ourselves to reveal. The Internet allows myriad forms of cybersocial interaction, and people can create new personas by using different "handles," including fictitious names and identities. In anonymous regions of cyberspace, people can manipulate ("lie about") their ages, genders, and physical attributes and create their own cyberfantasies. In psychology, multiple personalities are abnormal, but for anthropologists, multiple identities are more and more the norm.

Ethnicity is based on cultural similarities (with members of the same ethnic group) and differences (between that group and others) in a society or nation. Ethnic groups must deal with other such groups in the nation or region they inhabit. Interethnic relations are important in the study of any nation or region, especially because of contemporary and recent international migration. (Table 15.1 lists American ethnic groups, based on 2012 figures.)

**TABLE 15.1** Racial/Ethnic Identification in the United States, 2012

| CLAIMED IDENTITY | NUMBER (MILLIONS) | PERCENTAGE |
|---|---|---|
| White (non-Hispanic) | 195.1 | 62.8% |
| Hispanic | 53.1 | 17.1 |
| Black | 40.1 | 12.9 |
| Asian | 16.4 | 5.3 |
| Other | 5.9 | 1.9 |
| Total population | 310.6 | 100.0% |

SOURCE: C. DeNavas-Walt, B. D. Proctor, and J. C. Smith, 2013, Income, Poverty, and Health Insurance Coverage in the United States: U.S. Census Bureau, Current Population Reports, P60-245. http://www.census.gov/prod/2013pubs/p60-245.pdf

# ETHNIC GROUPS AND ETHNICITY

**ethnic group**
One among several culturally distinct groups in a society or region.

**ethnicity**
Identification with an ethnic group.

**status**
Any position that determines where someone fits in society.

**ascribed status**
Social status based on little or no choice.

**achieved status**
Social status based on choices or accomplishments.

As with any cultural identity, members of an **ethnic group** *share* certain beliefs, values, habits, customs, and norms because of their common background. They define themselves as different and special because of cultural features. This distinction may arise from language, religion, historical experience, geographic placement, kinship, or "race" (see Spickard 2004, 2012). Markers of an ethnic group may include a collective name, belief in common descent, a sense of solidarity, and an association with a specific territory, which the group may or may not hold (Ryan 1990, pp. xiii, xiv).

According to Fredrik Barth (1969), ethnicity can be said to exist when people claim a certain ethnic identity for themselves and are defined by others as having that identity. **Ethnicity** means identification with, and feeling part of, an ethnic group and exclusion from certain other groups because of this affiliation. But issues of ethnicity can be complex. Ethnic feelings and associated behavior vary in intensity within ethnic groups and countries and over time. A change in the degree of importance attached to an ethnic identity may reflect political changes (Soviet rule ends—ethnic feeling rises) or individual life-cycle changes (old people relinquish, or young people reclaim, an ethnic background).

## Status Shifting

Ethnicity is only one basis for group identity. Cultural differences also are associated with class, region, religion, and other social variables. Individuals often have more than one group identity. People may be loyal (depending on circumstances) to their neighborhood, school, town, state or province, region, nation, continent, religion, ethnic group, or interest group (Ryan 1990, p. xxii). In a complex society such as the United States or Canada, people constantly negotiate their social identities. All of us "wear different hats," presenting ourselves sometimes as one thing, sometimes as another.

These different social identities are known as statuses. In daily conversation, we hear the term *status* used as a synonym for *prestige*. In this context, "She's got a lot of status" means she's got a lot of prestige; people look up to her. Among social scientists, that's not the primary meaning of *status*. Social scientists use *status* more neutrally—for any position, no matter what the prestige, that someone occupies in society. In this sense, **status** encompasses the various positions that people occupy in society. Parent is a social status. So are professor, student, factory worker, Republican, salesperson, homeless person, labor leader, ethnic-group member, and thousands of others. People always occupy multiple statuses (e.g., Hispanic, Catholic, infant, brother). Among the statuses we occupy, particular ones dominate in particular settings, such as son or daughter at home and student in the classroom.

Some statuses are **ascribed:** People have little or no choice about occupying them. Age is an ascribed status; we can't choose not to age. Race and gender usually are ascribed; people are born members of a certain group and remain so all their lives. **Achieved statuses,** by contrast, aren't automatic; they come through choices, actions, efforts, talents, or accomplishments and may be positive or negative (Figure 15.1). Examples of achieved statuses include physician, senator, convicted felon, salesperson, union member, father, and college student (see Figure 15.1).

Sometimes our identities or social statuses, particularly ascribed ones, are mutually exclusive. It's hard to bridge the gap between black and white, or male and female. Sometimes, taking a status or joining a group requires a conversion experience, acquiring a new and overwhelming primary identity, such as becoming a "born again" Christian.

Some statuses aren't mutually exclusive, but contextual. People can be both black and Hispanic or both a mother and a senator. One identity is used in certain settings, another in different ones. We call this the *situational negotiation of social identity* (Leman 2001).

It is not uncommon for members of an ethnic group to shift their ethnic identities. Hispanics, for

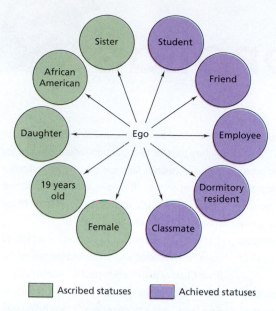

**FIGURE 15.1**  Social Statuses.
The person in this figure—"ego," or "I"—occupies many social statuses. The green circles indicate ascribed statuses; the purple circles represent achieved statuses.

example, may use different ethnic labels (e.g., "Cuban" or "Latino") to describe themselves depending on context. In a recent study, half (51 percent) of American Hispanics surveyed preferred to identify using their family's country of origin (as in "Mexican," "Cuban," or "Dominican") rather than "Hispanic" or "Latino." Just one-quarter (24 percent) chose one of those two pan-ethnic terms, while 21 percent said they use the term "American" most often (Taylor et al. 2012).

Latinos of different national origins may, however, mobilize to promote general Hispanic issues (e.g., opposition to "English-only" laws), while acting as separate interest groups in other contexts. Among Hispanics, Cuban Americans are richer on average than Mexican Americans and Puerto Ricans, and their class interests and voting patterns differ. Cuban Americans are more likely to vote

Republican than Puerto Ricans and Mexican Americans are. Some Mexican Americans whose families have lived in the United States for generations have little in common with new Hispanic immigrants, such as those from Central America.

Hispanics represent the fastest-growing ethnic group in the United States, increasing by 50 percent between 2000 and 2012—from 35.3 million to 53.1 million. "Hispanic" is a category based mainly on language. It includes whites, blacks, and "racially" mixed Spanish speakers and their ethnically conscious descendants. (There also are Native American and even Asian Hispanics.) The label "Hispanic" lumps together people of diverse geographic origin—Puerto Rico, Mexico, Cuba, El Salvador, Guatemala, the Dominican Republic, and other Spanish-speaking countries of Central and South America and the Caribbean. "Latino" is a broader category, which also can include Brazilians (who speak Portuguese). The national origins of Hispanics/Latinos in the contemporary U.S. population are shown in Table 15.2.

## Minority Groups and Stratification

In many societies an ascribed status is associated with a position in the social-political hierarchy. Certain groups, called *minority groups,* are subordinate. They have inferior power and less secure access to resources than do *majority groups* (which are superordinate, dominant, or controlling). Often ethnic groups are minorities.

Minority groups are obvious features of stratification in the United States. The 2012 poverty rate was 9.7 percent for non-Hispanic whites, 11.7 percent for Asian Americans, 25.6 percent for Hispanics, and 27.2 percent for African Americans (DeNavas-Walt, Proctor, and Smith 2013). Inequality shows up consistently in unemployment figures and in median household income. Median household incomes in 2012 were as follows: $68,636 for Asian Americans, $57,009 for non-Hispanic whites, $39,005 for Hispanics, and $33,321 for African Americans (DeNavas-Walt et al. 2013). The median wealth of

**TABLE 15.2**  National Origins of American Hispanics, Latinos, 2012

| NATIONAL ORIGIN | PERCENTAGE |
|---|---|
| Mexican American | 62% |
| Puerto Rican | 9 |
| Cuban | 4 |
| Dominican | 3 |
| Central and South American | 19 |
| Other Hispanic/Latino origin | 3 |
| Total | 100.0% |

SOURCE: P. Taylor, M. H. Lopez, J. H. Martínez, and G. Velasco, "When Labels Don't Fit: Hispanics and Their Views of Identity," Pew Research Hispanic Center, April 4, 2012. http://www.pewhispanic.org/2012/04/04/when-labels-dont-fit-hispanics-and-their-views-of-identity

# What's Wrong with Race?

Anthropologists have a lot to say about the race concept. There is considerable public confusion about the meaning and relevance of "race," and false claims about biological differences among "races" continue to be advanced. Stemming from previous actions by the American Anthropological Association (AAA) designed to address public misconceptions about race and intelligence, the need was apparent for a clear AAA statement on the biology and politics of race that would be educational and informational (see also http://www.understandingrace.org/).

The following statement was adopted by the AAA Executive Board, based on a draft prepared by a committee of representative anthropologists. This statement represents the thinking and scholarly positions of most anthropologists, including me—your textbook author.

In the United States both scholars and the general public have been conditioned to viewing human races as natural and separate divisions within the human species based on visible physical differences. With the vast expansion of scientific knowledge in this century, however, it has become clear that human populations are not unambiguous, clearly demarcated, biologically distinct groups. Evidence from the analysis of genetics (e.g., DNA) indicates that most physical variation, about 94%, lies within so-called racial groups. Conventional geographic "racial" groupings differ from one another only in about 6% of their genes. This means that there is greater variation within "racial" groups than between them. In neighboring populations there is much overlapping of genes and their phenotypic (physical) expressions. Throughout history whenever different groups have come into contact, they have interbred. The continued sharing of genetic materials has maintained all of humankind as a single species.

Physical variations in any given trait tend to occur gradually rather than abruptly over geographic areas. And because physical traits are inherited independently of one another, knowing the range of one trait does not predict the presence of others. For example, skin color varies largely from light in the temperate areas in the north to dark in the tropical areas in the south; its intensity is not related to nose shape or hair texture. Dark skin may be associated with frizzy or kinky hair or curly or wavy or straight hair, all of which are found among different indigenous peoples in tropical regions. These facts render any attempt to establish lines of division among biological populations both arbitrary and subjective.

Historical research has shown that the idea of "race" has always carried more meanings than mere physical differences; indeed, physical variations in the human species have no meaning except the social ones that humans put on them. Today scholars in many fields argue that "race" as it is understood in the United States of America was a social mechanism invented during the 18th century to refer to those populations brought together in colonial America: the English and other European settlers, the conquered Indian (Native American) peoples, and those peoples of Africa brought in to provide slave labor.

From its inception, this modern concept of "race" was modeled after an ancient theorem of the Great Chain of Being, which posited natural categories on a hierarchy established by God or nature. Thus "race" was a mode of classification linked specifically to peoples in the colonial situation. It subsumed a growing ideology of inequality devised to rationalize European attitudes and treatment of the conquered and enslaved peoples. Proponents of slavery in particular during the 19th century used "race" to justify the retention of slavery. The ideology magnified the differences among Europeans, Africans, and Indians (Native Americans), established a rigid hierarchy of socially exclusive categories, underscored and bolstered unequal rank and status differences, and provided the rationalization that the inequality was natural or God-given. The different physical traits of African-Americans and Indians (Native Americans) became markers or symbols of their status differences.

As they were constructing US society, leaders among European-Americans fabricated the cultural/behavioral characteristics associated with each "race," linking superior traits with Europeans and negative and inferior ones to blacks and Indians

white households is 20 times that of black households and 18 times that of Hispanic households (Kochhar, Fry, and Taylor 2011).

## RACE AND ETHNICITY

When an ethnic group is assumed to have a biological basis (distinctively shared "blood" or genes), it is called a **race.** Discrimination against such a group is called **racism** (Gotkowitz 2011; Kuper 2006; Scupin 2012). However, race, like ethnicity in general, actually is a *cultural* category rather than a biological reality. That is, "races" are defined through contrasts perceived and perpetuated in particular societies, rather than from scientific classifications based on common genes (see Wade 2002).

This chapter's "Appreciating Anthropology" is a statement on race issued by the American Anthropological Association (AAA). It discusses how races have been socially constructed, for example under colonialism. The AAA statement also stresses that inequalities among "racial" groups are not consequences of their biological inheritance but products of social, economic, educational, and political circumstances.

**race**
Ethnic group assumed to have a biological basis.

**racism**
Discrimination against an ethnic group assumed to have a biological basis.

(Native Americans). Numerous arbitrary and fictitious beliefs about the different peoples were institutionalized and deeply embedded in American thought. . . .

Ultimately "race" as an ideology about human differences was subsequently spread to other areas of the world. It became a strategy for dividing, ranking, and controlling colonized people used by colonial powers everywhere. But it was not limited to the colonial situation. In the latter part of the 19th century it was employed by Europeans to rank one another and to justify social, economic, and political inequalities among their peoples. During World War II, the Nazis under Adolf Hitler enjoined the expanded ideology of "race" and "racial" differences and took them to a logical end: the extermination of 11 million people of "inferior races" (e.g., Jews, Gypsies, Africans, homosexuals, and so forth) and other unspeakable brutalities of the Holocaust.

"Race" thus evolved as a world view, a body of prejudgments that distorts our ideas about human differences and group behavior. Racial beliefs constitute myths about the diversity in the human species and about the abilities and behavior of people homogenized into "racial" categories. The myths fused behavior and physical features together in the public mind, impeding our comprehension of both biological variations and cultural behavior, implying that both are genetically determined. Racial myths bear no relationship to the reality of human capabilities or behavior. . . .

We now understand that human cultural behavior is learned, conditioned into infants beginning at birth, and always subject to modification. No human is born with a built-in culture or language. Our temperaments, dispositions, and personalities, regardless of genetic propensities, are developed within sets of meanings and values that we call "culture." . . .

This photo, taken near Bucharest, Romania, shows a Rom (Gypsy) woman standing in front of another woman as she holds her baby daughter. Gypsies (Rom or Roma) have faced discrimination in many nations. During World War II, the Nazis led by Adolf Hitler murdered 11 million Jews, Gypsies, Africans, homosexuals, and others.

It is a basic tenet of anthropological knowledge that all normal human beings have the capacity to learn any cultural behavior. The American experience with immigrants from hundreds of different language and cultural backgrounds who have acquired some version of American culture traits and behavior is the clearest evidence of this fact. Moreover, people of all physical variations have learned different cultural behaviors and continue to do so as modern transportation moves millions of immigrants around the world.

How people have been accepted and treated within the context of a given society or culture has a direct impact on how they perform in that society. The "racial" world view was invented to assign some groups to perpetual low status, while others were permitted access to privilege, power, and wealth. The tragedy in the United States has been that the policies and practices stemming from this world view succeeded all too well in constructing unequal populations among Europeans, Native Americans, and peoples of African descent. Given what we know about the capacity of normal humans to achieve and function within any culture, we conclude that present-day inequalities between so-called "racial" groups are not consequences of their biological inheritance but products of historical and contemporary social, economic, educational, and political circumstances.

SOURCE: From the American Anthropological Association (AAA) Statement on "Race" (May 1998). http://www.aaanet.org/stmts/racepp.htm. Reprinted with permission of the American Anthropological Association.

In American culture, we hear the words *ethnicity* and *race* frequently, without clear distinctions made between them. Consider a *New York Times* article published on May 29, 1992. Discussing the changing ethnic composition of the United States, the article explained (correctly) that Hispanics "can be of any race" (Barringer 1992, p. A12). In other words, "Hispanic" is an ethnic category that crosscuts racial contrasts such as that between "black" and "white." However, another *Times* article published the same day reported that during Los Angeles riots in spring 1992, "hundreds of Hispanic residents were interrogated about their immigration status on the basis of their *race* alone [emphasis added]" (Mydans 1992*a*, p. A8). Use of "race" here seems inappropriate because "Hispanic" usually is perceived as referring to a linguistically based (Spanish-speaking) ethnic group, rather than a biologically based race. Since these Los Angeles residents were being interrogated because they were Hispanic, the article is actually reporting on ethnic, not racial, discrimination.

In a more recent case, consider a speech delivered by then appeals court judge Sonia Sotomayor, newly nominated (in May 2009; confirmed in August 2009) for the U.S. Supreme Court by President Barack Obama. In a 2001 lecture titled "A

"Hispanic" and "Latino" are ethnic categories that crosscut "racial" contrasts such as that between "black" and "white." Note the physical diversity among these multiracial schoolchildren in Havana, Cuba.

Latina Judge's Voice," delivered at the University of California, Berkeley, School of Law, Sotomayor declared (as part of a much longer speech):

> I would hope that a wise Latina woman with the richness of her experiences would more often than not reach a better conclusion than a white male who hasn't lived that life. (Sotomayor 2001/2009)

Conservatives, including Newt Gingrich and radio talk show host Rush Limbaugh, seized on this declaration as evidence that Sotomayor was a "racist" or a "reverse racist." Again, however, "Latina" is an ethnic (and gendered-female) rather than a racial category. I suspect that Sotomayor also was using "white male" as an ethnic-gender category, to refer to nonminority men. These examples illustrate the difficulty in drawing a precise distinction between race and ethnicity.

## THE SOCIAL CONSTRUCTION OF RACE

Most Americans believe (incorrectly) that their population includes *biologically based* races to which various labels are applied. Such *racial terms* include "white," "black," "yellow," "red," "Caucasoid," "Negroid," "Mongoloid," "Amerindian," "Euro-American," "African American," "Asian American," and "Native American."

We have seen that races, while assumed to have a biological basis, actually are socially constructed in particular societies. Let's consider now several examples of the social construction of race, beginning with the United States.

## Hypodescent: Race in the United States

Americans acquire their racial identity at birth, as an ascribed status, but race isn't based on biology or on simple ancestry. Take the case of the child of a "racially mixed" marriage involving one black and one white parent. We know that 50 percent of the child's genes come from one parent and 50 percent from the other. Still, American culture overlooks heredity and classifies this child as black. This classificatory rule is arbitrary. On the basis of genotype (genetic composition), it would be just as logical to classify the child as white. Operating here is a rule of **descent** (it assigns social identity on the basis of ancestry), but of a sort that is rare outside the contemporary United States. It is called **hypodescent** (Harris and Kottak 1963) because it automatically places children of mixed unions in the group of their minority parent (*hypo* means "lower"). Hypodescent divides American society into groups that have been unequal in their access to wealth, power, and prestige.

**descent**
Social identity based on ancestry.

**hypodescent**
Children of mixed unions assigned to the same group as their minority parent.

The hypodescent rule may be arbitrary, but it is very strong. How else can we explain the common assertion that Barack Obama is the first black president, rather than the first biracial president, of the United States? American rules for assigning racial status can be even more arbitrary. In some states, anyone known to have any black ancestor, no matter how remote, can be classified as a member of the black race. The following case from Louisiana is an excellent illustration of the arbitrariness of the hypodescent rule and of the role that governments (federal or, in this case, state) play in legalizing, inventing, or eradicating race and ethnicity (see Mullaney 2011; B. Williams 1989). Susie Guillory Phipps, a light-skinned woman with Caucasian features and straight black hair, discovered as an adult that she was black. When Phipps ordered a copy of her birth certificate, she found her race listed as "colored." Since she had been "brought up white and married white twice," Phipps challenged a 1970 Louisiana law declaring anyone with at least one-thirty-second "Negro blood" to be legally black. Although the state's lawyer admitted that Phipps "looks like a white person," the state of Louisiana insisted that her racial classification was proper (Yetman 1991, pp. 3–4).

Cases like Phipps's are rare because racial identity usually is ascribed at birth and doesn't change. The rule of hypodescent affects blacks, Asians, Native Americans, and Hispanics differently (see Hunter 2005). It's easier to negotiate Native American or Hispanic identity than black identity. The ascription rule isn't as definite, and the assumption of a biological basis isn't as strong.

To be considered Native American, one ancestor out of eight (great-grandparents) or out of four (grandparents) may suffice. This depends on whether the assignment is by federal or state law or by a Native American tribal council. The child of a Hispanic may (or may not, depending on context) claim Hispanic identity. Many Americans with a Native American or Latino grandparent consider themselves white and lay no claim to minority group status.

## Race in the Census

The U.S. Census Bureau has gathered data by race since 1790. Figure 15.2 shows that the 2010 census asked about both race and Hispanic origin. What do you think of the racial categories included?

Racial classification in the census is a political issue involving access to resources, including jobs, voting districts, and programs aimed at minorities. The hypodescent rule results in all the population growth being attributed to the minority category. Attempts to add a "multiracial" category to

A biracial American, Halle Berry, with her mother. What is Halle Berry's race?

**5.** **Is this person of Hispanic, Latino, or Spanish origin?**

☐ No, not of Hispanic, Latino, or Spanish origin
☐ Yes, Mexican, Mexican Am., Chicano
☐ Yes, Puerto Rican
☐ Yes, Cuban
☐ Yes, another Hispanic, Latino, or Spanish origin — *Print origin, for example, Argentinean, Colombian, Dominican, Nicaraguan, Salvadoran, Spaniard, and so on.* ↗

☐☐☐☐☐☐☐☐☐☐☐☐☐☐☐☐

**6.** **What is this person's race?** *Mark* ☒ *one or more boxes.*

☐ White
☐ Black, African Am., or Negro
☐ American Indian or Alaska Native — *Print name of enrolled or principal tribe.* ↗

☐☐☐☐☐☐☐☐☐☐☐☐☐☐☐☐

☐ Asian Indian     ☐ Japanese        ☐ Native Hawaiian
☐ Chinese          ☐ Korean          ☐ Guamanian or Chamorro
☐ Filipino         ☐ Vietnamese      ☐ Samoan
☐ Other Asian — *Print race, for example, Hmong, Laotian, Thai, Pakistani, Cambodian, and so on.* ↗     ☐ Other Pacific Islander — *Print race, for example, Fijian, Tongan, and so on.* ↗

☐☐☐☐☐☐☐☐☐☐☐☐☐☐☐☐

☐ Some other race — *Print race.* ↗

☐☐☐☐☐☐☐☐☐☐☐☐☐☐☐☐

**FIGURE 15.2** Reproduction of Questions on Race and Hispanic Origin from Census 2010.

SOURCE: U.S. Census Bureau, Census 2010 questionnaire.

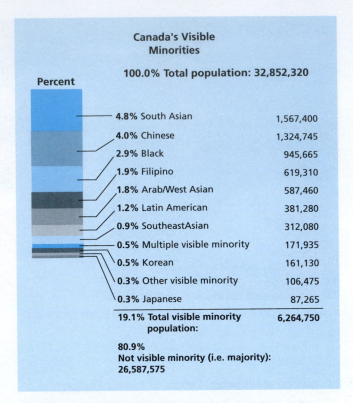

## Canada's Visible Minorities

**100.0% Total population: 32,852,320**

Percent

| | | |
|---|---|---|
| 4.8% | South Asian | 1,567,400 |
| 4.0% | Chinese | 1,324,745 |
| 2.9% | Black | 945,665 |
| 1.9% | Filipino | 619,310 |
| 1.8% | Arab/West Asian | 587,460 |
| 1.2% | Latin American | 381,280 |
| 0.9% | SoutheastAsian | 312,080 |
| 0.5% | Multiple visible minority | 171,935 |
| 0.5% | Korean | 161,130 |
| 0.3% | Other visible minority | 106,475 |
| 0.3% | Japanese | 87,265 |
| **19.1%** | **Total visible minority population:** | **6,264,750** |

**80.9%
Not visible minority (i.e. majority):
26,587,575**

**FIGURE 15.3** Visible Minority Population of Canada, 2011 National Household Survey.

SOURCE: From Statistics Canada, 2011 National Household Survey. http://www12.statcan.gc.ca/nhs-enm/2011/as-sa/99-010-x/99-010-x2011001-eng.cfm#a4

colour" (Statistics Canada 2001). "South Asian" and "Chinese" are Canada's largest visible minorities (see Figure 15.3). Canada's visible minority population of 19.1 percent in 2011 (up from 11.2 percent in 1996) contrasts with a figure of 38 percent for the United States in 2012 (up from 25 percent in 2000).

As in the United States, Canada's visible minority population has been growing much faster than the country's overall population. In 1981, visible minorities accounted for just 4.7 percent of the Canadian population, versus 19.1 percent in 2011 (the most recent data available as of this writing). Between 2006 and 2011, Canada's total population increased 5 percent, while visible minorities rose 24 percent. If recent immigration trends continue, by 2031 visible minorities will comprise almost one-third (31 percent) of the Canadian population (Statistics Canada 2010).

## Not Us: Race in Japan

Japan is commonly viewed as a nation that is homogeneous in race, ethnicity, language, and culture—an image the Japanese themselves cultivate. Thus, in 1986 then Prime Minister Nakasone created an international furor by contrasting his country's supposed homogeneity (responsible, he suggested, for Japan's success at that time in international business) with the ethnically mixed United States.

Although less diverse than most countries, Japan is hardly the uniform entity Nakasone described. About 10 percent of its population consists of minorities. These include aboriginal Ainu, annexed Okinawans, outcast *burakumin*, children of mixed marriages, and immigrant nationalities, especially Koreans, who number more than 700,000 (Lie 2001; Ryang and Lie 2009).

To describe racial attitudes in Japan, Jennifer Robertson (1992) uses Kwame Anthony Appiah's (1990) term "intrinsic racism"—the belief that a (perceived) racial difference is a sufficient reason to value one person less than another. In Japan the valued group is majority ("pure") Japanese, who are believed to share "the same blood." Thus, the caption to a printed photo of a Japanese American model reads: "She was born in Japan but raised in Hawaii. Her nationality is American but no foreign blood flows in her veins" (Robertson 1992, p. 5). Something like hypodescent also operates in Japan, but less precisely than in the United States, where mixed offspring automatically become members of the minority group. The children of mixed marriages between majority Japanese and others (including Euro-Americans) may not get the same "racial" label as their minority parent, but they are still stigmatized for their non-Japanese ancestry (De Vos and Wagatsuma 1966).

How is race culturally constructed in Japan? The (majority) Japanese define themselves by opposition to others, whether minority groups in their own nation or outsiders—anyone who is "not us." The

the U.S. Census have been opposed by the National Association for the Advancement of Colored People (NAACP) and the National Council of La Raza (a Hispanic advocacy group). Minorities fear their political clout will decline if their numbers go down.

But things are changing. Choice of "some other race" in the U.S. Census tripled from 1980 (6.8 million) to 2010 (over 19 million)—suggesting imprecision in and dissatisfaction with the existing categories. In the 2000 census, 2.4 percent of Americans chose a first-ever option of identifying themselves as belonging to more than one race. That figure rose to 2.9 percent in the 2010 census. The number of interracial marriages and children is increasing, with implications for the traditional system of American racial classification. "Interracial," "biracial," or "multiracial" children undoubtedly identify with qualities of both parents. It is troubling for many of them to have so important an identity as race dictated by the arbitrary rule of hypodescent. It may be especially discordant when racial identity doesn't parallel gender identity, for instance, a boy with a white father and a black mother, or a girl with a white mother and a black father.

Rather than race, the Canadian census asks about "visible minorities." That country's Employment Equity Act defines such groups as "persons, other than Aboriginal peoples [First Nations in Canada], who are non-Caucasian in race or non-white in "not us" should stay that way; assimilation generally is discouraged. Cultural mechanisms, especially residential segregation and taboos on "interracial" marriage, work to keep minorities "in their place."

In its construction of race, Japanese culture regards certain ethnic groups as having a biological basis, when there is no evidence that they do. The best example is the burakumin, a stigmatized group of at least 4 million outcasts, sometimes compared to India's untouchables. The burakumin are physically and genetically indistinguishable from other Japanese. Many of them "pass" as (and marry) majority Japanese, but a deceptive marriage can end in divorce if burakumin identity is discovered (Aoki and Dardess 1981).

Burakumin are perceived as standing apart from majority Japanese. Based on their ancestry (and thus, it is assumed, their "blood," or genetics), burakumin are considered "not us." Majority Japanese try to keep their lineage pure by discouraging mixing. The burakumin are residentially segregated in neighborhoods (rural or urban) called *buraku,* from which the racial label is derived. Compared with majority Japanese, the burakumin are less likely to attend high school and college. When burakumin attend the same schools as majority Japanese, they face discrimination. Majority children and teachers may refuse to eat with them because burakumin are considered unclean.

In applying for university admission or a job and in dealing with the government, Japanese must list their address, which becomes part of a household or family registry. This list makes residence in a buraku, and likely burakumin social status, evident. Schools and companies use this information to discriminate. (The best way to pass is to move so often that the buraku address eventually disappears from the registry.) Majority Japanese also limit "race" mixture by hiring marriage mediators to check out the family histories of prospective spouses. They are especially careful to check for burakumin ancestry (De Vos, Wetherall, and Stearman 1983).

The origin of the burakumin lies in a historical tiered system of stratification (from the Tokugawa period, 1603–1868). The top four ranked categories were warrior-administrators (*samurai*), farmers, artisans, and merchants. The ancestors of the burakumin were below this hierarchy. They did "unclean" jobs such as animal slaughter and disposal of the dead. Burakumin still do similar jobs, including work with leather and other animal products. They are more likely than majority Japanese to do manual labor (including farm work) and to belong to the national lower class. Burakumin and other Japanese minorities also are more likely to have careers in crime, prostitution, entertainment, and sports (De Vos et al. 1983).

Like blacks in the United States, the burakumin are internally **stratified.** In other words, there are class contrasts within the group. Because certain jobs are reserved for the burakumin, people who

Japan's stigmatized burakumin are physically and genetically indistinguishable from other Japanese. In response to burakumin political mobilization, Japan has dismantled the legal structure of discrimination against burakumin. This Sports Day for burakumin children is one kind of mobilization.

are successful in those occupations (e.g., shoe factory owners) can be wealthy. Burakumin also have found jobs as government bureaucrats. Financially successful burakumin can temporarily escape their stigmatized status by travel, including foreign travel.

Discrimination against the burakumin is strikingly like the discrimination that blacks have experienced in the United States. The burakumin often live in villages and neighborhoods with poor housing and sanitation. They have limited access to education, jobs, amenities, and health facilities. In response to burakumin political mobilization, Japan has dismantled the legal structure of discrimination against burakumin and has worked to improve conditions in the buraku. (The website http://blhrri.org/index_e.htm is sponsored by the Buraku Liberation and Human Rights Research Institute and includes the most recent information about the burakumin liberation movement.) However, discrimination against nonmajority Japanese is still the rule in companies. Some employers say that hiring burakumin would give their company an unclean image and thus create a disadvantage in competing with other businesses (De Vos et al. 1983).

## Phenotype and Fluidity: Race in Brazil

There are more flexible, less exclusionary ways of socially constructing race than those used in the United States and Japan. Consider Brazil, which shares a history of slavery with the United States but lacks the hypodescent rule. Nor does Brazil have racial aversion of the sort found in Japan.

**stratified**
Class-structured, with differences in wealth, prestige, and power.

Brazilians use many more racial labels—over 500 were once reported (Harris 1970)—than Americans or Japanese do. In northeastern Brazil, I found 40 different racial terms in use in Arembepe, a village of only 750 people (Kottak 2006). Through their traditional classification system, Brazilians recognize and attempt to describe the physical variation that exists within their population. The system used in the United States, by recognizing relatively few races, blinds Americans to an equivalent range of evident physical contrasts. The system Brazilians use to construct social race has other special features. In the United States one's race is an ascribed status; it is assigned automatically by hypodescent and usually doesn't change. In Brazil racial identity is more flexible, more of an achieved status.

Brazilian racial classification pays attention to **phenotype.** Scientists distinguish between *genotype,* or hereditary makeup, and *phenotype*—expressed physical characteristics. Genotype is what you are genetically; phenotype is what you appear as. Identical twins and clones have the same genotype, but their phenotypes vary if they have been raised in different environments. *Phenotype* describes an organism's evident traits, its "manifest biology"— physiology and anatomy, including skin color, hair form, facial features, and eye color. A Brazilian's phenotype and racial label may change because of environmental factors, such as the tanning rays of the sun or the effects of humidity on the hair.

A Brazilian can change his or her "race" (say from "Indian" to "mixed") by changing his or her manner of dress, language, location (e.g., rural to urban), and even attitude (e.g., by adopting urban behavior). Two racial/ethnic labels used in Brazil are *indio* (indigenous, Native American) and *cabô-clo* (someone who "looks *indio*" but wears modern clothing and participates in Brazilian culture, rather than living in an indigenous community). Similar shifts in racial/ethnic classification occur in other parts of Latin America, for example, Guatemala (see Wade 2010). The perception of biological race is influenced not just by the physical phenotype but by how one dresses and behaves.

Furthermore, racial differences in Brazil may be so insignificant in structuring community life that people may forget the terms they have applied to others. Sometimes they even forget the ones they've used for themselves. In Arembepe, I made it a habit to ask the same person on different days to tell me the races of others in the village (and my own). In the United States I am always "white" or "Euro-American," but in Arembepe I got lots of terms besides *branco* ("white"). I could be *claro* ("light"),

**phenotype**
Expressed physical characteristics of an organism.

These photos, taken in Brazil by the author, give just a glimpse of the spectrum of phenotypical diversity encountered among contemporary Brazilians.

*louro* ("blond"), *sarará* ("light-skinned redhead"), *mulato claro* ("light mulatto"), or *mulato* ("mulatto"). The racial term used to describe me or anyone else varied from person to person, week to week, even day to day. My best informant, a man with very dark skin color, changed the term he used for himself all the time—from *escuro* ("dark") to *preto* ("black") to *moreno escuro* ("dark brunet").

For centuries the United States and Brazil have had mixed populations, with ancestors from Native America, Europe, Africa, and Asia. Although races have mixed in both countries, Brazilian and American cultures have constructed the results differently. The historical reasons for this contrast lie mainly in the different characteristics of the settlers of the two countries. The mainly English early settlers of the United States came as women, men, and families, but Brazil's Portuguese colonizers were mainly men—merchants and adventurers. Many of these Portuguese men married indigenous women and recognized their racially mixed children as their heirs. Like their North American counterparts, Brazilian plantation owners had sexual relations with their slaves. But the Brazilian landlords more often freed the children that resulted. (Sometimes these were their only children.) Freed offspring became plantation overseers and foremen and filled many intermediate positions in the emerging Brazilian economy. They were not classed with the slaves but were allowed to join a new intermediate category. No hypodescent rule developed in Brazil to ensure that whites and blacks remained separate (see Degler 1970; Harris 1964).

In today's world system, Brazil's system of racial classification is changing in the context of international identity politics and rights movements. Just as more and more Brazilians claim indigenous identities, an increasing number now assert their blackness and self-conscious membership in the African diaspora. Particularly in such northeastern Brazilian states as Bahia, where African demographic and cultural influence is strong, public universities have instituted affirmative action programs aimed at indigenous peoples and especially at blacks. Racial identities firm up in the context of international (e.g., pan-African and pan–Native American) mobilization and access to strategic resources based on race.

## ETHNIC GROUPS, NATIONS, AND NATIONALITIES

The term **nation** once was synonymous with *tribe* or *ethnic group*. All three of these terms have been used to refer to a single culture sharing a single language, religion, history, territory, ancestry, and kinship. Thus, one could speak interchangeably of the Seneca (Native American) nation, tribe, or ethnic group. Now *nation* has come to mean **state**—an independent, centrally organized political unit, or a government. *Nation* and *state* have become synonymous. Combined in **nation-state** they refer to an autonomous political entity, a country—like the United States, "one nation, indivisible" (see Farner 2004; Gellner 1997).

Because of migration, conquest, and colonialism, most nation-states aren't ethnically homogeneous. A 2003 study by James Fearon found that about 70 percent of all countries have an ethnic group that forms an absolute majority of the population; the average population share of such a group is 65 percent. The average size of the second-largest group, or largest ethnic minority, is 17 percent. Only 18 percent of all countries, including Brazil and Japan, have a single ethnic group accounting for 90 percent or more of the population.

There is substantial regional variation in countries' ethnic structures. Strong states, particularly in Europe (e.g., France), have deliberately and actively worked to homogenize their diverse premodern populations to a common national identity and culture (see Beriss 2004; Gellner 1983). Although countries with no ethnic majority are fairly rare in the rest of the world, this is the norm in Africa. The average African country has a plurality group of about 22 percent, with the second largest slightly less than this. Rwanda, Burundi, Lesotho, Swaziland, and Zimbabwe are exceptions; each has a large majority group and a minority that makes up almost all the rest of the population. Botswana has a large majority (the Tswana) and a set of smaller minorities (Fearon 2003).

Most Latin American and Caribbean countries have a majority group (speaking a European language, such as Portuguese in Brazil, Spanish in Argentina) and a single minority group—"indigenous peoples." The latter is a catch-all category encompassing several small Native American tribes or remnants. Exceptions are Guatemala and the Andean countries of Bolivia, Peru, and Ecuador, with large indigenous populations (see Gotkowitz 2011; Wade 2010).

Most countries in Asia and the Middle East/North Africa have ethnic majorities. The Asian countries of Myanmar, Laos, Vietnam, and Thailand contain a large lowland majority edged by more fragmented mountain folk. Several oil-producing countries in the Middle East, including Saudi Arabia, Bahrain, United Arab Emirates, Oman, and Kuwait, contain an ethnically homogeneous group of citizens who form either a plurality or a bare majority; the rest of the population consists of ethnically diverse noncitizen workers. Other countries in the Middle East/North Africa contain two principal ethnic or ethnoreligious groups: Arabs and Berbers in Morocco, Algeria, Libya, and Tunisia; Muslims and Copts in Egypt; Turks and Kurds in Turkey; Greeks and Turks in Cyprus; and Palestinians and Transjordan Arabs in Jordan (Fearon 2003).

**nation-state**
An autonomous political entity; a country.

**nation**
Society sharing a language, religion, history, territory, ancestry, and kinship.

**state**
Stratified society with formal, central government.

## Nationalities and Imagined Communities

Ethnic groups that once had, or wish to have or regain, autonomous political status (their own country) are called **nationalities.** In the words of Benedict Anderson (1991/2006), they are "imagined communities." Even when they become nation-states, they remain imagined communities because most of their members, though feeling comradeship, will never meet (Anderson 1991, pp. 6–10). They can only imagine they all participate in the same unit.

Anderson traces Western European nationalism, which arose in imperial powers such as England, France, and Spain, back to the 18th century. He stresses that language and print played a crucial role in the growth of European national consciousness. The novel and the newspaper were "two forms of imagining" communities (consisting of all the people who read the same sources and thus witnessed the same events) that flowered in the 18th century (Anderson 1991, pp. 24–25).

Over time, political upheavals, wars, and migration have divided many imagined national communities that arose in the 18th and 19th centuries. The German and Korean homelands were artificially divided after wars, according to communist and capitalist ideologies. World War I split the Kurds, who remain an imagined community, forming a majority in no state. Kurds are a minority group in Turkey, Iran, Iraq, and Syria.

In creating multitribal and multiethnic states, **colonialism,** the foreign domination of a territory, often erected boundaries that corresponded poorly with preexisting cultural divisions. But colonial institutions also helped create new "imagined communities" beyond nations. A good example is the idea of *négritude* ("black identity") developed by African intellectuals in Francophone (French-speaking) West Africa. Négritude can be traced to the association and common experience in colonial times of youths from Guinea, Mali, the Ivory Coast, and Senegal at the William Ponty School in Dakar, Senegal (Anderson 1991, pp. 123–124).

# ETHNIC TOLERANCE AND ACCOMMODATION

Ethnic diversity may be associated with either positive group interaction and coexistence or with conflict (to be discussed shortly). There are nation-states in which multiple ethnic groups live together in reasonable harmony, including some less-developed countries.

## Assimilation

**Assimilation** describes the process of change that a minority ethnic group may experience when it moves to a country where another culture dominates.

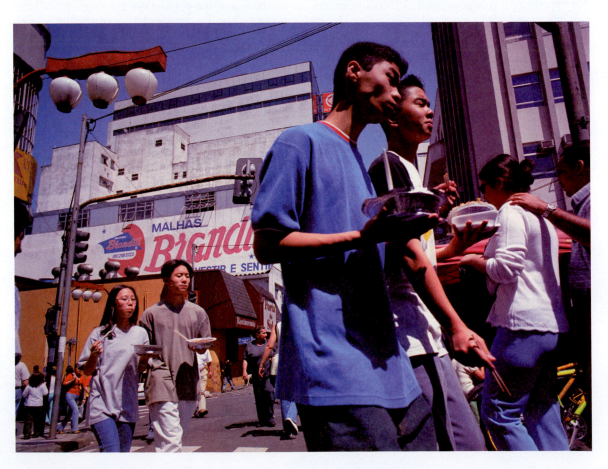

German, Italian, Japanese, Middle Eastern, and Eastern European immigrants have assimilated, culturally and linguistically, to a common Brazilian culture. More than 220,000 people of Japanese descent live in Brazil, mostly in and around the city of São Paulo, Brazil's largest. Shown here, a Sunday morning street scene in São Paulo's Liberdade district, home to many of that city's assimilated Japanese Brazilians.

By assimilating, the minority adopts the patterns and norms of its host culture. It is incorporated into the dominant culture to the point that it no longer exists as a separate cultural unit. Some countries, such as Brazil, are more assimilationist than others. Germans, Italians, Japanese, Middle Easterners, and Eastern Europeans started migrating to Brazil late in the 19th century. These immigrants have assimilated to a common Brazilian culture, which has Portuguese, African, and Native American roots. The descendants of these immigrants speak the national language (Portuguese) and participate in the national culture. (During World War II, Brazil, which was on the Allied side, forced assimilation by banning instruction in any language other than Portuguese—especially in German.)

## The Plural Society

Assimilation isn't inevitable, and there can be ethnic harmony without it. Ethnic distinctions can persist despite generations of interethnic contact. Through a study of three ethnic groups in Swat, Pakistan, Fredrik Barth (1958/1968) challenged an old idea that interaction always leads to assimilation. He showed that ethnic groups can be in contact for generations without assimilating and can live in peaceful coexistence.

Barth (1958/1968, p. 324) defines **plural society** (an idea he extended from Pakistan to the entire Middle East) as a society combining ethnic contrasts, ecological specialization (i.e., use of different environmental resources by each ethnic group), and the economic interdependence of those groups. In Barth's view, ethnic boundaries are most stable and enduring when the groups occupy different ecological niches. That is, they make their living in different ways and don't compete. Ideally, they should depend on one another's activities and exchange with one another. When different ethnic groups exploit the *same* ecological niche, the militarily more powerful group usually will replace the weaker one. If they exploit more or less the same niche, but the weaker group is better able to use marginal environments, they also may coexist (Barth 1958/1968, p. 331). Given niche specialization, ethnic boundaries and interdependence can be maintained, although the specific cultural features of each group may change. By shifting the analytic focus from individual cultures or ethnic groups to *relationships* between cultures or ethnic groups, Barth (1958/1968, 1969) has made important contributions to ethnic studies (see also Kamrava 2011).

## Multiculturalism

The view of cultural diversity in a country as something good and desirable is called **multiculturalism** (see Kottak and Kozaitis 2012). The multicultural model is the opposite of the assimilationist model, in which minorities are expected to abandon their cultural traditions and values, replacing them with those of the majority population. The multicultural view encourages the practice of cultural–ethnic traditions. A multicultural society socializes individuals not only into the dominant (national) culture but also into an ethnic culture. Thus, in the United States millions of people speak both English and another language, eat both "American" (apple pie, steak, hamburgers) and "ethnic" foods, and celebrate both national (July 4, Thanksgiving) and ethnic–religious holidays.

Multiculturalism seeks ways for people to understand and interact that depend not on sameness but rather on respect for differences. Multiculturalism stresses the interaction of ethnic groups and their contribution to the country. It assumes that each group has something to offer to and learn from the others. Several forces have propelled North America away from the assimilationist model toward multiculturalism. First, multiculturalism reflects the fact of recent large-scale migration, particularly from the "less-developed" countries to the "developed" nations of North America and Western Europe. The global scale of modern migration introduces unparalleled ethnic variety to host nations. Multiculturalism is related to globalization: People use modern means of transportation to migrate to nations whose lifestyles they learn about through the media and from tourists who increasingly visit their own countries.

Migration also is fueled by rapid population growth, coupled with insufficient jobs (for both educated and uneducated people), in the less-developed countries. As traditional rural economies decline or mechanize, displaced farmers move to cities, where they and their children often are unable to find jobs. As people in the less-developed countries get better educations, they seek more skilled employment. They hope to partake of an international culture of consumption that includes such modern amenities as refrigerators, televisions, computers, and automobiles (Ahmed 2004).

## Changing Demographics

In the United States and Canada multiculturalism is of growing importance. This reflects an awareness that the number and size of ethnic groups have grown dramatically in recent years. As this trend continues, the ethnic composition of the United States will change dramatically (see Figure 15.4).

In October 2006, the population of the United States reached 300 million people, just 39 years after reaching 200 million (in 1967) and 91 years after reaching the 100 million mark (in 1915). The country's ethnic composition has changed dramatically in the past 40 years. The 1970 census, the first to attempt an official count of Hispanics, found they represented no more than 4.7 percent of the American population. By 2012 this figure had risen to 17.1 percent—over 53 million Hispanics. The

**plural society**
Society with economically interdependent ethnic groups.

**multiculturalism**
View of cultural diversity as valuable and worth maintaining.

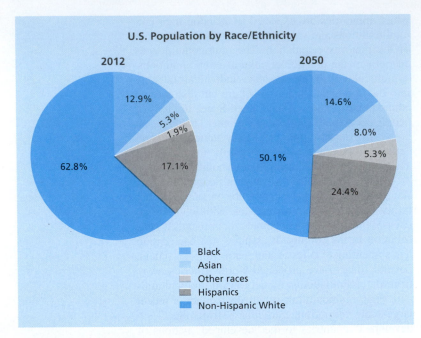

## U.S. Population by Race/Ethnicity

**2012**

- 12.9%
- 5.3%
- 1.9%
- 62.8%
- 17.1%

**2050**

- 14.6%
- 8.0%
- 5.3%
- 50.1%
- 24.4%

■ Black
■ Asian
■ Other races
■ Hispanics
■ Non-Hispanic White

**FIGURE 15.4** Ethnic Composition of the United States.

The proportion of the American population that is white and non-Hispanic is declining. The projection for 2050 shown here comes from a 2008 U.S. Census Bureau report. Note especially the dramatic rise in the Hispanic portion of the American population between 2012 and 2050.

SOURCE: 2012 data from C. DeNavas-Walt, B. D. Proctor, and J. C. Smith, 2013, Income, Poverty, and Health Insurance Coverage in the United States: U.S. Census Bureau, Current Population Reports, P60-245. http://www.census.gov/prod/2013pubs/p60-245.pdf; 2050 projection from a 2008 projection by the U.S. Census Bureau, http://www.census.gov/population/www/projections/analytical-document09.pdf, Table 1, p. 17.

In the United States, Canada, and western Europe, multiculturalism is of growing importance, as is suggested by this contemporary scene from London, England. Can you find evidence for both multiculturalism and globalization in this photo?

number of African Americans grew from 11.1 percent in 1967 to 12.9 percent in 2012, while (non-Hispanic) whites ("Anglos") declined from 83 to 62.8 percent (DeNavas-Walt et al. 2013). In 1967 fewer than 10 million people in the United States (5 percent of the population) had been born elsewhere, compared with more than 38 million foreign born today (12.5 percent) (all data from U.S. Census Bureau). In 2011, for the first time in American history, minorities (including Hispanics, blacks, Asians, Native Americans, and those of mixed race) accounted for more than half (50.4 percent) of all births in the United States (Tavernise 2012). Figure 15.4 projects that minorities will constitute half the population of the United States by 2050.

In 1973, 78 percent of the students in American public schools were white, and 22 percent were minorities. By 2004, only 57 percent of public school students were white. If current trends continue, minority students will outnumber (non-Hispanic) white students by 2015. They already do in California, Hawaii, Mississippi, New Mexico, and Texas. (See this chapter's "Focus on Globalization.")

Immigration, mainly from southern and eastern Europe, had a similar effect on classroom diversity, at least in the largest American cities, a century ago. A study of American public schools in 1908–1909 found that only 42 percent of urban students were native born, while 58 percent were immigrants. In a very different context (multicultural now versus assimilationist then), today's American public school classrooms have regained the ethnic diversity they contained in the early 1900s, when my German-speaking Austro-Hungarian-born father and grandparents migrated to the United States.

In a world with growing rural–urban and transnational migration, ethnic identities are used increasingly to form self-help organizations focused on enhancing a group's economic competitiveness (Williams 1989). People claim and express ethnic identities for political and economic reasons. Michel Laguerre's (1984, 1998) studies of Haitian immigrants in the United States show that they mobilize to deal with the discriminatory structure (racist in this case, since Haitians tend to be black) of American society. Ethnicity (their common Haitian French creole language and cultural background) is a basis for their mobilization. Haitian ethnicity helps distinguish them from African Americans and other ethnic groups.

In the face of globalization, much of the world, including the entire "democratic West," is experiencing an "ethnic revival." The new assertiveness of long-resident ethnic groups extends to the Welsh and Scots in the United Kingdom, Bretons and Corsicans in France, and Basques and Catalans in Spain. The United States and Canada are becoming increasingly multicultural, focusing on their internal diversity (see Laguerre 1999). Rather than as "melting pots," they are better described as ethnic "salads" (each ingredient remains distinct, although in the same bowl, with the same dressing).

# focus on GLOBALIZATION

## The Gray and the Brown

International migration, a key feature of globalization, has transformed the demographic composition of the United States, Canada, and Western Europe. Drawing on a 2010 Brookings Institution report titled "State of Metropolitan America: On the Front Lines of Demographic Transformation," Ronald Brownstein (2010) analyzes an intensifying confrontation between groups he describes as "the gray and the brown." Brownstein and demographer William Frey, an author of the Brookings report, focus on two key U.S. demographic trends:

(1) Ethnic/racial diversity is increasing, especially among the young, with minorities now constituting 45 percent of all American children under 18. (2) The country is aging, and about 80% of the senior population is white.

The under-18 share of the U.S. population is projected eventually to stabilize at around 23 percent, as the senior share rises steadily from about 12 percent today to 20 percent by 2040. The U.S. working-age population is projected to shrink from about 63 percent today to 57 percent in two to three decades. Frey (in Brookings Institution 2010, pp. 26, 63) sees these trends as creating a "cultural generation gap"—a sharp contrast in the attitudes, priorities, and political leanings of younger and older Americans. Whites now constitute 80 percent of older Americans, but only 56 percent of children—a 24-point spread, versus just 14 points in 1980.

Politically the two groups—the gray (older) and the brown (younger)—are poles apart. Older whites oppose taxes and public spending, while younger people and minorities value government support of education, health, and social welfare. In the 2008 and 2012 elections, young people, especially minorities, strongly supported Democrat Barack Obama. Seniors, especially white ones, voted solidly for Republicans John McCain and Mitt Romney. These differences persisted post-election in measures of approval for President Obama's job performance—consistently highest among nonwhites and young people.

The gray and the brown are actually more interdependent economically than either usually realizes. If minority children benefit disproportionately from public education today, minority workers will pay a growing share of the payroll taxes needed to sustain Social Security and Medicare—programs that most directly benefit older white people.

The history of national immigration policy helps us understand how the gap between the gray and the brown arose. Federal policies established in the 1920s had severely curtailed immigration from areas other than northern Europe. In 1965, Congress loosened restrictions—resulting in an eventual influx of immigrants from southern Europe, Asia, Africa, the Caribbean, and Latin America (see Vigil 2012).

Non-Hispanic whites comprised the overwhelming majority of Americans through the mid–20th century, including the post–World War II baby boom (1946–1964). Most baby boomers grew up and have lived much of their lives in white suburbs, residentially isolated from minorities (Brownstein 2010). As they age and retire, many older white Americans are reconstituting such communities in racially homogeneous enclaves in the Southeast and Southwest.

In such communities, except for their yard and construction workers and house cleaners, older white Americans live apart from the minorities who represent a growing share of the national population. Since 1965, expanded immigration and higher fertility rates among minorities have transformed American society. As recently as 1980, minorities made up only 20 percent of the total population (versus 38 percent today), and 25 percent of children under 18 (versus 45 percent today). Similar trends are evident in Western Europe and are everyday expressions of globalization.

# ROOTS OF ETHNIC CONFLICT

**discrimination**
Policies and practices that harm a group and its members.

Ethnicity, based on perceived cultural similarities and differences in a society or nation, can be expressed in peaceful multiculturalism or in discrimination or violent interethnic confrontation. Culture can be both adaptive and maladaptive. The perception of cultural differences can have disastrous effects on social interaction.

The roots of ethnic differentiation—and therefore, potentially, of ethnic conflict—can be political, economic, religious, linguistic, cultural, or racial (see Kuper 2006). Why do ethnic differences often lead to conflict and violence? The causes include economic and political competition; reaction to discrimination, prejudice, and other expressions of devalued identity; and resentment about actual or perceived inequality or political favoritism (see Donham 2011; Friedman 2003; Ryan 1990).

In Iraq, under the dictator Saddam Hussein, there was discrimination by one Muslim group (Sunnis) against others (Shiites and Kurds). Sunnis, although a numeric minority within Iraq's population, enjoyed privileged access to power, prestige, and position. After the elections of 2005, which many Sunnis chose to boycott, Shiites gained political control. A civil war soon developed out of "sectarian violence" (conflicts among sects of the same religion) as Sunnis (and their foreign supporters) fueled an insurgency against the new government and its foreign supporters, including the United States. Shiites retaliated against Sunni attacks and a history of Sunni privilege and perceived discrimination against Shiites. Sectarian tension in Iraq remains unresolved as of this writing.

Syrian President Bashar al-Assad, like his father and predecessor in office, Hafez al-Assad (who ruled from 1971 to 2000), has favored his own minority Muslim group (Alawites) over his country's Sunni majority. Should Assad lose power, Sunni reprisals are likely against Alawites and other religious minorities, including Christians and Shiite Muslims (see Adams 2012).

## Prejudice and Discrimination

Ethnic conflict often arises in reaction to prejudice (attitudes and judgments) or discrimination (action). **Prejudice** means devaluing (looking down on) a group because of its assumed behavior, values, capabilities, or attributes. People are prejudiced when they hold stereotypes about groups and apply them to individuals. (**Stereotypes** are fixed ideas—often unfavorable—about what the members of a group are like.) Prejudiced people assume that members of the group will act as they are "supposed to act" (according to the stereotype) and interpret a wide range of individual behaviors as evidence of the stereotype. They use this behavior

**prejudice**
Devaluing a group because of its assumed attributes.

**stereotypes**
Fixed ideas—often unfavorable—about what members of a group are like.

to confirm their stereotype (and low opinion) of the group.

**Discrimination** refers to policies and practices that harm a group and its members. Discrimination may be *de facto* (practiced, but not legally sanctioned) or *de jure* (part of the law). An example of de facto discrimination is the harsher treatment that American minorities (compared with other Americans) tend to get from the police and the judicial system. This unequal treatment isn't legal, but it happens anyway. Segregation in the southern United States and *apartheid* in South Africa provide two historical examples of de jure discrimination. In both systems, by law, blacks and whites once had different rights and privileges. Also, their social interaction ("mixing") was legally curtailed.

## Chips in the Mosaic

Although the multicultural model is increasingly prominent in North America, ethnic competition and conflict also are evident. There is conflict between newer arrivals, for instance, Central Americans and Koreans, and longer-established ethnic groups, such as African Americans. Ethnic antagonism flared in South-Central Los Angeles in spring 1992 in rioting that followed the acquittal of four white police officers who were tried for the videotaped beating of Rodney King (see Abelmann and Lie 1995).

Attacks against whites, Koreans, and Latinos expressed frustration by African Americans about their prospects in an increasingly multicultural society. A poll done just after the Los Angeles riots found that blacks had a bleaker outlook than whites about the effects of immigration on their lives. Only 23 percent of blacks felt they had more opportunities than recent immigrants, compared with twice that many whites (Toner 1992).

Korean stores were hard hit during the 1992 riots, and more than a third of the businesses destroyed were Latino owned. A third of those who died in the riots were Latinos. These mainly recent migrants lacked deep roots to the neighborhood and, as Spanish speakers, faced language barriers (Newman 1992). Many Koreans also had trouble with English.

Koreans interviewed on ABC's *Nightline* on May 6, 1992, recognized that blacks resented them and considered them unfriendly. One man explained, "It's not part of our culture to smile." African Americans interviewed on the same program did complain about Korean unfriendliness: "They come into our neighborhoods and treat us like dirt." These comments suggest a shortcoming of the multicultural perspective: Ethnic groups (blacks here) expect other ethnic groups in the same nation-state to assimilate to some extent to a shared (national) culture. The African Americans' comments invoked

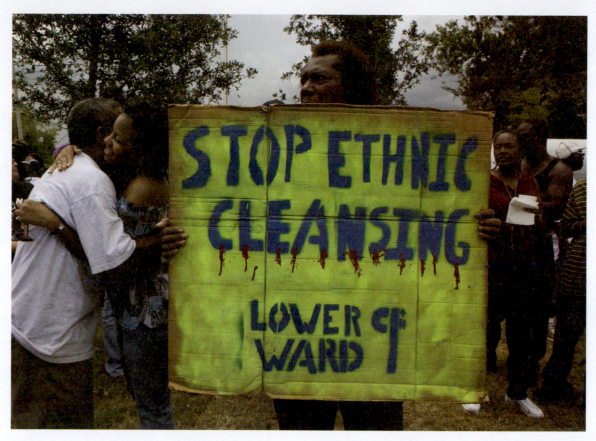

*Discrimination* refers to policies and practices that harm a group and its members. This protest sign, hoisted in New Orleans's Lower Ninth Ward, shows that at least some community residents see ethnic and racial bias in the fact that African Americans in that city bore the brunt of Hurricane Katrina's devastation.

a general American value system that includes friendliness, openness, mutual respect, community participation, and "fair play." Los Angeles blacks wanted their Korean neighbors to act more like generalized Americans—and good neighbors.

## Aftermaths of Oppression

Forms of discrimination against ethnic groups include genocide, ethnocide, forced assimilation, and cultural colonialism. The most extreme form is **genocide,** the deliberate elimination of a group (such as Jews in Nazi Germany, Muslims in Bosnia, or Tutsi in Rwanda) through mass murder (see Hinton and O'Neill 2009). A dominant group may try to destroy the cultures of certain ethnic groups (**ethnocide**) or force them to adopt the dominant culture (*forced assimilation*). Many countries have penalized or banned the language and customs of an ethnic group (including its religious observances). One example of forced assimilation is the anti-Basque campaign that the dictator Francisco Franco (who ruled between 1939 and 1975) waged in Spain. Franco banned Basque books, journals, newspapers, signs, sermons, and tombstones and imposed fines for using the Basque language in schools. His policies led to the formation of a Basque terrorist group and spurred strong nationalist sentiment in the

Basque region (Ryan 1990). A policy of *ethnic expulsion* aims at removing groups who are culturally different from a country. There are many examples, including Bosnia-Herzegovina in the 1990s. Uganda expelled 74,000 Asians in 1972. The neo-fascist parties of contemporary Western Europe advocate repatriation (expulsion) of immigrant workers, such as Algerians in France and Turks in Germany (see Friedman 2003; Ryan 1990, p. 9). Expulsion may create **refugees**—people who have been forced (involuntary refugees) or who have chosen (voluntary refugees) to flee a country, to escape persecution or war.

In many countries, colonial nation building left ethnic strife in its wake. Thus, over a million Hindus and Muslims were killed in the violence that accompanied the division of the Indian subcontinent into India and Pakistan. Problems between Arabs and Jews in Palestine began during the British mandate period (see Kamrava 2011).

Multiculturalism may be growing in the United States and Canada, but the opposite is happening in the former Soviet Union, where ethnic groups (nationalities) want their own nation-states. The flowering of ethnic feeling and conflict as the Soviet empire disintegrated illustrates that years of political repression and ideology provide insufficient common ground for lasting unity. **Cultural colonialism**

**genocide**
Deliberate elimination of a group through mass murder.

**refugees**
People who flee a country to escape persecution or war.

**ethnocide**
Destruction of cultures of certain ethnic groups.

**cultural colonialism**
Internal domination by one group and its culture or ideology over others.

In the Darfur region of western Sudan (shown here), government-supported Arab militias, called the *Janjaweed,* have forced black Africans off their land. The militias are accused of genocide, of killing up to 30,000 darker-skinned Africans. In this photo, a group of new refugees arrive by truck at a camp.

refers to internal domination by one group and its culture or ideology over others. One example is the domination over the former Soviet empire by Russian people, language, and culture and by communist ideology. The dominant culture makes itself the official culture. This is reflected in schools, the media, and public interaction. Under Soviet rule ethnic minorities had very limited self-rule in republics and regions controlled by Moscow. All the republics

and their peoples were to be united by the oneness of "socialist internationalism." One common technique in cultural colonialism is to flood ethnic areas with members of the dominant ethnic group. Thus, in the former Soviet Union, ethnic Russian colonists were sent to many areas, to diminish the cohesion and clout of the local people.

For example, when Ukraine was a part of the Soviet Union, a policy of Russian in-migration and

Faces of ethnic difference in the former Soviet empire. The propaganda poster on the left depicts a happy mix of nationalities representing the populace of Kyrgyzstan, Central Asia. The photo on the right, taken in March 2014 in eastern Ukraine, shows a rally by ethnic Russians protesting the ouster of Ukraine's pro-Russian president.

| TYPE | NATURE OF INTERACTION | EXAMPLES |
|---|---|---|
| **POSITIVE** | | |
| Assimilation | Ethnic groups absorbed within dominant culture | Brazil; United States in early, mid-20th century |
| Plural society | Society or region contains economically interdependent ethnic groups | Areas of Middle East with farmers/herders; Swat, Pakistan |
| Multiculturalism | Cultural diversity valued; ethnic cultures coexist with dominant culture | Canada; United States in 21st century |
| **NEGATIVE** | | |
| Prejudice | Devaluing a group based on assumed attributes | Worldwide |
| Discrimination de jure | Legal policies and practices harm ethnic group | South African apartheid; former segregation in southern U.S. |
| Discrimination de facto | Not legally sanctioned but practiced | Worldwide |
| Genocide | Deliberate elimination of ethnic group through mass murder | Nazi Germany; Bosnia; Rwanda; Cambodia; Darfur |
| Ethnocide | Cultural practices attacked by dominant culture or colonial power | Spanish Basques under Franco |
| Ethnic expulsion | Forcing ethnic group(s) out of a country or region | Ugandan Asians; Serbia; Bosnia; Kosovo |

Ukrainian out-migration was in effect, and ethnic Ukrainians' share of the population in Ukraine declined from 77 percent in 1959 to 73 percent in 1991. That trend reversed after Ukraine gained independence, so that, by the turn of the 21st century, ethnic Ukrainians made up more than three-fourths of the population. Russians still constitute Ukraine's largest minority, but they now represent less than one-fifth of the population. The remainder of the population includes Belarusians, Moldovans, Bulgarians, Poles, Hungarians, Romanians, Roma (Gypsies), and other groups (http://www.britannica.com/EBchecked/topic/612921/Ukraine/30110/Government-and-society?anchor=ref404764).

Within the former Soviet Union, ethnic groups (nationalities) have sought, and continue to seek, to forge separate and viable nation-states. This celebration of ethnic autonomy is part of an ethnic florescence that—as surely as globalization and transnationalism—is a trend of the late 20th and early 21st centuries.

Recap 15.1 summarizes the various types of ethnic interaction—positive and negative—that have been discussed.

# for **REVIEW**

**summary**

1. *Ethnic group* refers to members of a particular culture in a nation or region that contains others. Ethnicity is based on cultural similarities (among members of the same ethnic group) and differences (between that group and others). A race is an ethnic group assumed to have a biological basis.

2. Human races are cultural (rather than biological) categories that derive from contrasts perceived in particular societies. Racial labels such as "white" and "black" designate socially constructed races—categories defined by American culture. In American racial classification, governed by the rule of

hypodescent, children of mixed unions, no matter what their appearance, are classified with the minority group parent.

3. Racial attitudes in Japan illustrate intrinsic racism—the belief that a perceived racial difference is a sufficient reason to value one person less than another. The valued group is majority (pure) Japanese, who define themselves in opposition to others, anyone who is "not us." In Brazil, racial identity is more of an achieved status, which can change during someone's lifetime, reflecting phenotypical changes.

4. The term *nation,* which once was synonymous with *ethnic group,* now means a state—a centrally organized political unit. Most nation-states are not ethnically homogeneous. Ethnic groups that seek autonomous political status are nationalities.

5. An ethnic group may undergo assimilation when it moves to a country where another culture dominates. It adopts the patterns and norms of its host culture. A plural society combines ethnic contrasts and economic interdependence between ethnic groups. Multiculturalism socializes individuals not only into the dominant (national) culture but also into an ethnic one.

6. Ethnic conflict often arises in reaction to prejudice (attitudes and judgments) or discrimination (action). The most extreme form of ethnic discrimination is genocide, the deliberate elimination of a group through mass murder. A dominant group may try to destroy certain ethnic practices (ethnocide), or to force ethnic group members to adopt the dominant culture (forced assimilation). *Cultural colonialism* refers to internal domination by one group and its culture or ideology over others.

## key terms

achieved status 276
ascribed status 276
assimilation 286
colonialism 286
cultural colonialism 291
descent 280
discrimination 290
ethnic group 276
ethnicity 276
ethnocide 291
genocide 291
hypodescent 280
multiculturalism 287

nation 285
nationalities 286
nation-state 285
phenotype 284
plural society 287
prejudice 290
race 278
racism 278
refugees 291
state 285
status 276
stereotypes 290
stratified 283

## critical thinking

1. What's the difference between a culture and an ethnic group? In what culture(s) do you participate? To what ethnic group(s) do you belong? What is the basis of your primary cultural identity? Do others readily recognize this basis and identity? Why or why not?

2. Name five social statuses you currently occupy. Which of those statuses are ascribed, and which ones are achieved? Are any of these statuses mutually exclusive? Which are contextual?

3. In describing the recent history of the census in the United States, this chapter notes how the National Association for the Advancement of Colored People and the National Council of La Raza (a Hispanic advocacy group) have opposed adding a "multiracial" census category. What does this suggest about racial categories?

4. If "race" is a discredited concept when applied to humans, what has replaced it?

5. This chapter describes different types of ethnic interaction. What are they? Are they positive or negative? Anthropologists have made and continue to make important contributions to understanding past and ongoing cases of ethnic conflict. What are some examples of this?

# Making a Living

- ▶ How do people make a living in different types of society?

- ▶ What is an economy, and what is economizing behavior?

- ▶ What principles regulate the exchange of goods and services in various societies?

Thailand's Damnoen Saduak floating market, located about 100 kilometers (62 miles) south of Bangkok. What's being sold here, and by whom?

# understanding OURSELVES

The necessities of work, marriage, and raising children are fundamental. However, in the non-Western societies where the study of anthropology originated, the need to balance work (economy) and family (society) wasn't as stark as it is for us. In traditional societies, one's workmates usually were also one's kin. There was no need for a "take your child to work" day, because most women did that every day. People didn't work with strangers. Home and office, society and economy, were intertwined.

The fact that subsistence and sociality are both basic human needs creates conflicts in modern society. People have to make choices about allocating their time and energy between work and family. Parents in dual-earner and single-parent households always have faced a work–family time bind, and the number of Americans living in such households has almost doubled in recent decades. Fewer than one-third of American wives worked outside the home in 1960, compared with about two-thirds today. The same year, only one-fifth of married women with children under age 6 were in the workforce, versus three-fifths today. With women increasingly able to make it "on their own," the economic importance of marriage has declined. In 2007, for the first time ever, the percentage of adult American women who were unmarried exceeded 50.

Think about the choices your parents have made in terms of economic versus social goals. Have their decisions maximized their incomes, their lifestyles, their individual happiness, family benefits, or what? What about you? What factors motivated you when you chose to apply to and attend college? Did you want to stay close to home, to attend college with friends, or to maintain a romantic attachment (all social reasons)? Did you seek the lowest tuition and college costs—or get a generous scholarship (economic decisions)? Did you choose prestige, or perhaps the likelihood that one day you would earn more money because of the reputation of your alma mater (maximizing prestige and future wealth)? Economists tend to assume that the profit motive rules in contemporary society. However, different individuals, like different cultures, may choose to pursue goals other than monetary gain.

Studies show that most American women now expect to join the paid labor force, just as men do. But the family remains attractive. Most young women also plan to stay home with small children and return to the workforce once their children enter school. How about you? If you have definite career plans, how do you imagine your work will fit in with your future family life—if you have one planned? What do your parents want most for you—a successful career or a happy family life with children? Probably both. Will it be easy to fulfill such expectations?

In today's globalizing world, communities and societies are being incorporated, at an accelerating rate, into larger systems. The first major acceleration in the growth of human social systems can be traced back to around 12,000–10,000 years ago, when humans started intervening in the reproductive cycles of plants and animals. *Food production* refers to human control over the reproduction of plants and animals, and it contrasts with the foraging economies that preceded it and that still persist in some parts of the world today. To make their living, foragers hunt, gather, and collect what nature has to offer. Foragers may harvest, but they don't plant. They may hunt animals, but (except for the dog) they don't domesticate them. Only food producers systematically select and breed for desirable traits in plants and animals. With the advent of **food production,** which includes plant cultivation and animal domestication, people, rather than nature, become selective agents. Human selection replaces natural selection as food collectors become food producers.

The origin and spread of food production (plant cultivation and animal domestication) accelerated human population growth and led to the formation of larger and more powerful social and political systems. The pace of cultural transformation increased enormously. This chapter provides a framework for understanding a variety of human adaptive strategies and economic systems.

## ADAPTIVE STRATEGIES

The anthropologist Yehudi Cohen (1974) used the term **adaptive strategy** to describe a group's main system of economic production. Cohen argued that the most important reason for similarities between two (or more) unrelated societies is their possession of a similar adaptive strategy. For example, there are clear similarities among societies that have a foraging (hunting-and-gathering) strategy. Cohen developed a typology of societies based on correlations between their economies and their social features. His typology includes these five adaptive strategies: foraging, horticulture, agriculture, pastoralism, and industrialism. This chapter focuses on the first four adaptive strategies.

## FORAGING

Until about 12,000 years ago all humans were foragers (see Barnard 2004). However, environmental differences did create substantial contrasts among the world's foragers. Some, like the people who lived in Europe during the Ice Ages, were big-game hunters. Today, hunters in the Arctic still focus on large animals; they have much less vegetation and variety in their diets than do tropical foragers. Moving from colder to hotter areas, the number of species increases. The tropics contain tremendous biodiversity, and tropical foragers typically hunt and gather a wide range of plant and animal species. The same may be true in temperate areas. For example, on the North Pacific Coast of North America, foragers could draw on varied sea, river, and land species, such as salmon and other fish, sea mammals, berries, and mountain goats. Despite differences caused by such environmental variation, all foraging economies have shared one essential feature: People rely on nature to make their living. They don't grow crops or breed and or tend animals.

Animal domestication (initially of sheep and goats) and plant cultivation (of wheat and barley) began 12,000 to 10,000 years ago in the Middle East. Cultivation based on different crops, such as corn (maize), manioc (cassava), and potatoes, arose independently in the Americas. In both hemispheres most societies eventually turned from foraging to food production. Today most foragers have at least some dependence on food production or on food producers (Kent 1992, 2002).

The foraging way of life survived into modern times in certain forests, deserts, islands, and very cold areas—places where cultivation was not practicable with simple technology (see Lee and Daly 1999). In many areas, foragers knew about food production but never adopted it because their own economies provided a perfectly satisfactory lifestyle and an adequate and nutritious diet. In some places, people reverted to foraging after trying food production and abandoning it.

All contemporary foragers live in nation-states and are influenced by national policies. Typically, they are in contact with food-producing neighbors as well as with missionaries and other outsiders. We should not view contemporary foragers as isolated or pristine survivors of the Stone Age. Modern foragers are influenced by national and international policies and political and economic events in the world system.

## Geographic Distribution of Foragers

In Africa we can identify two broad belts of contemporary or recent foraging. One is the Kalahari Desert of southern Africa. This is the home of the San ("Bushmen"), who include the Ju/'hoansi (see Kent 1996; Lee 2003, 2012). The other main African foraging area is the equatorial forest of central and eastern Africa, home of the Mbuti, Efe, and other "pygmies" (Bailey et al. 1989; Turnbull 1965).

People still do, or until recently did, subsistence foraging in certain remote forests in Madagascar, South and Southeast Asia, Malaysia, and the Philippines and on certain islands off the Indian coast. Some of the best-known recent foragers are the aborigines of Australia. Those Native Australians lived on their island continent for perhaps 50,000 years without developing food production.

The Western Hemisphere also had recent foragers. The Eskimos, or Inuit, of Alaska and Canada are well-known hunters. These (and other) northern foragers now use modern technology, including rifles and snowmobiles, in their subsistence activities. The native populations of California, Oregon, Washington, and British Columbia all were foragers, as were those of inland subarctic Canada and the Great Lakes. For many Native Americans, fishing, hunting, and gathering remain important subsistence (and sometimes commercial) activities.

Coastal foragers also lived near the southern tip of South America, in Patagonia. On the grassy plains of Argentina, southern Brazil, Uruguay, and Paraguay, there were other hunter-gatherers. The contemporary Aché of Paraguay usually are called

**food production**
Plant cultivation and animal domestication.

**adaptive strategy**
Means of making a living; productive system.

In southwestern Madagascar, Vezo children (members of a maritime ethnic group) play in a lagoon. Is fishing a form of foraging?

"hunter-gatherers" although they now get just a third of their livelihood from foraging. The Aché also grow crops, have domesticated animals, and live in or near mission posts, where they receive food from missionaries (Hawkes, O'Connell, and Hill 1982; Hill et al. 2011).

Jana Fortier (2009) summarizes key attributes of foragers in South Asia, which today is home to more full- and part-time hunter-gatherers than any other world area. In India, Nepal, and Sri Lanka, about 40 societies and an estimated 150,000 people continue to derive their subsistence from full- or part-time foraging. Hill Kharias and Yanadis are the largest contemporary South Asian (SA) foraging populations, with about 20,000 members each. Several other ethnic groups are highly endangered, with fewer than 350 members still doing subsistence foraging.

Surviving South Asian foraging societies are those whose members, despite having lost many of their natural resources to deforestation and spreading farming populations, have been unwilling to adopt food cultivation and its cultural correlates. These hunter-gatherers share features with other foragers worldwide: small social groups, mobile settlement patterns, sharing of resources, immediate food consumption, egalitarianism, and decision making by mutual consent (Fortier 2009).

As is true elsewhere, specific foraging techniques reflect variations in environment and resource distribution. Hill and mountain SA foragers favor focused hunting of medium-sized prey (langur monkey, macaque, porcupine). Other groups pursue several small species or practice broad-spectrum foraging of bats, porcupines, and deer. Larger groups use communal hunting techniques, such as spreading nets over large fig trees to entangle sleeping bats. Some South Indian foragers focus on such wild plant resources as yams, palms, and taro, in addition to 100+ locally available plants. Harvesting honey and beeswax has been prominent in many SA foraging societies (Fortier 2009).

Their members cherish their identities as people who forage for a living in biologically rich and diverse environments. They stress their need for ongoing access to rich forest resources to continue their lifestyles, yet many have been evicted from their traditional habitats. Their best chances for cultural survival depend on national governments that maintain healthy forests, allow foragers access to their traditional natural resources, and foster cultural survival rather than assimilation (Fortier 2009).

Throughout the world, foraging survived in environments that posed major obstacles to food production. The difficulties of cultivating at the North Pole are obvious. In southern Africa the Dobe Ju/'hoansi San area studied by Richard Lee and others is surrounded by a waterless belt 43 to 124 miles (70 to 200 kilometers) in breadth (Solway and Lee 1990). Figure 16.1 presents a partial distribution of recent hunter-gatherers. Their niches tend to have one thing in common—their marginality. Their environments were not of immediate interest to farmers, herders, or colonialists.

As the modern world system spreads, however, the number of foragers continues to decline. Each year more and more foragers come under the control of nation-states and are influenced by forces of globalization. As described by Motseta (2006), for example, between 1997 and 2002, the government of Botswana in southern Africa relocated

**FIGURE 16.1** Worldwide Distribution of Selected Hunter-Gatherers.

Robert L Kelly, *The Foraging Spectrum: Diversity in Hunter-Gatherer Lifeways,* fig. 1.1. Copyright 2007 by Eliot Werner Publications, Inc. Reprinted by permission of the publisher.

On December 13, 2006, San men and women celebrated outside court in Lobatse, Botswana. The court had just ruled that the plaintiffs could return to live and hunt on their ancestral lands, which had been enclosed within a game reserve.

about 3,000 Basarwa San Bushmen outside their ancestral territory, which was converted into a reserve for wildlife protection. Botswana's High Court eventually ruled that the Basarwa had been wrongly evicted from the "Central Kalahari Game Reserve" and issued a court order allowing them to return, but under conditions likely to prevent most of them from doing so. Only the 189 people who actually filed the lawsuit were granted automatic right of return with their children, compared with some 2,000 Basarwa wishing to go back. The others would have to apply for special permits. Returning Basarwa would be allowed to build only temporary structures and to use enough water for subsistence needs. Water would be a major obstacle, since the government had shut the main well. Furthermore, anyone wishing to hunt would have to apply for a permit. So goes the foraging way of life in today's world.

## Correlates of Foraging

Typologies, such as Cohen's adaptive strategies, are useful because they suggest **correlations**—that is, association or covariation between two or more variables. (Correlated variables are factors that are linked and interrelated, such as food intake and body weight, such that when one increases or decreases, the other changes as well.) Ethnographic studies in hundreds of societies have revealed many correlations between the economy and social life. Associated (correlated) with each adaptive strategy is a bundle of particular sociocultural features. Correlations, however, rarely are perfect. Some foragers lack cultural features usually associated with foraging, and some of those features are found in groups with other adaptive strategies.

What, then, are some correlates of foraging? People who subsisted by hunting and gathering often, but not always, lived in band-organized societies. Their basic social unit, the **band,** was a small group of fewer than a hundred people, all related by kinship or marriage. Among some foragers, band size stayed about the same year-round. In others, the band split up for part of the year. Families left to gather resources that were better exploited by just a few people. Later, they regrouped for cooperative work and ceremonies.

Typical characteristics of the foraging life are flexibility and mobility. In many San groups, as among the Mbuti of Congo, people shifted band membership several times in a lifetime. One might be born, for example, in a band in which one's mother had kin. Later, one's family might move to a band in which the father had relatives. Because bands were exogamous (people married outside their own band), one's parents came from two different bands, and one's grandparents might have come from four. People could join any band to which they had kin or marital links. A couple could live in, or shift between, the husband's band and the wife's band.

**band**
Basic social unit among foragers; fewer than 100 people; may split up seasonally.

**correlation**
Association; when one variable changes, another does, too.

Many foraging societies make distinctions based on age. Old people may receive respect as guardians of myths, legends, stories, and traditions. Younger people may value the elders' special knowledge of ritual and practical matters. In general, foraging societies tend to be *egalitarian,* with only minor contrasts in prestige and no significant contrasts in wealth and power.

When considering issues of "human nature," we should remember that the egalitarian society associated with the foraging strategy of adaptation was a basic form of human social life for most of our history. Food production has existed less than 1 percent of the time *Homo* has spent on Earth. However, it has produced huge social differences. We now consider the main economic features of food-producing strategies.

**horticulture**
Nonindustrial plant cultivation with fallowing.

**agriculture**
Cultivation using land and labor continuously and intensively.

# ADAPTIVE STRATEGIES BASED ON FOOD PRODUCTION

In Cohen's typology, the three adaptive strategies based on food production in nonindustrial societies are horticulture, agriculture, and pastoralism. With horticulture and agriculture, plant cultivation is the mainstay of the economy, while with pastoralism, herding is key. All three strategies originated in nonindustrial societies, although they may persist as ways of making a living even after some degree of industrialization reaches the nation-states that include them. In fully industrial societies, such as the United States and Canada, most cultivation has become large-scale, commercial, mechanized, agrochemical-dependent farming. Rather than simple pastoralism, industrial societies use technologically sophisticated systems of ranch and livestock management.

Just as they do in the United States and Canada, people in nonindustrial societies carry out a variety of economic activities. In Cohen's typology, each adaptive strategy refers to the main economic activity. Pastoralists (herders), for example, consume milk, butter, blood, and meat from their animals as mainstays of their diet. However, they also add grain to their diet by doing some cultivating or by trading with neighbors.

## Horticulture

The two types of plant cultivation found in nonindustrial societies are **horticulture** (nonintensive, shifting cultivation) and **agriculture** (intensive, continuous cultivation). Both differ from the commercially oriented farming systems of industrial nations, which use large land areas and rely on machinery and petrochemicals.

Horticulturalists use simple tools such as hoes and digging sticks to grow their crops. Horticulturalists preserve their ecosystems by allowing their fields to lie fallow for varying lengths of time. Often, horticulturalists employ *slash-and-burn* techniques; they clear land by cutting down (slashing) and burning forest or bush or by setting fire to the grass covering the plot. The vegetation is broken down, pests are killed, and the ashes remain to fertilize the soil. Crops then are sown, tended, and harvested. Use of the plot is not continuous. Often it is cultivated only for a year or two.

When horticulturalists abandon a plot, they clear another piece of land, and the original plot reverts to forest. After several years of fallowing (the duration varies in different societies), the cultivator returns to farm the original plot again. Horticulture is also called *shifting cultivation*. Such shifts from plot to plot do not mean that whole villages must move when plots are abandoned. Horticulture can support large, permanent villages. Among the Kuikuru of the South American tropical forest, for example, one village of 150 people remained in the same place for 90 years (Carneiro 1956). Kuikuru houses are large and well made. Because the work involved in building them is great, the Kuikuru would rather walk farther to their fields than construct a new village. They shift their plots rather than their settlements. On the other hand, horticulturalists in the montaña (Andean foothills) of Peru live in small villages of about thirty people (Carneiro 1961/1968). Their houses are small and simple. After a few years in one place, these people build new villages near virgin land. Because their houses are so simple, they prefer rebuilding to walking even a half-mile to their fields.

## Agriculture

The greater labor demands associated with agriculture, as compared with horticulture, reflect its common use of domesticated animals, irrigation, or terracing.

### Domesticated Animals

Many agriculturalists use animals as means of production—for transport, as cultivating machines, and for their manure. Asian farmers typically

In slash-and-burn horticulture, the land is cleared by cutting down (slashing) and burning trees and bush, using simple technology. After such clearing, digging sticks are used to plant mountain rice in Madagascar.

incorporate cattle and/or water buffalo into agricultural economies based on rice production. Rice farmers may use cattle to trample pretilled flooded fields, thus mixing soil and water, prior to transplanting. Many agriculturalists attach animals to plows and harrows for field preparation before planting or transplanting. Also, agriculturalists typically collect manure from their animals, using it to fertilize their plots, thus increasing yields. Animals are attached to carts for transport as well as to implements of cultivation.

## Irrigation

While horticulturalists must await the rainy season, agriculturalists can schedule their planting in advance, because they control water. Like other irrigation experts in the Philippines, the Ifugao (Figure 16.2) irrigate their fields with canals from rivers, streams, springs, and ponds. Irrigation makes it possible to cultivate a plot year after year. Irrigation enriches the soil, because the irrigated field is a unique ecosystem with several species of plants and animals, many of them minute organisms, whose wastes fertilize the land.

An irrigated field is a capital investment that usually increases in value. It takes time for a field to start yielding; it reaches full productivity only after several years of cultivation. The Ifugao, like other irrigators, have farmed the same fields for generations. In some agricultural areas, including the Middle East, however, salts carried in the irrigation water can make fields unusable after 50 or 60 years.

## Terracing

Terracing is another agricultural technique the Ifugao have mastered. Their homeland has small valleys separated by steep hillsides. Because the population is dense, people need to farm the hills. However, if they simply planted on the steep hillsides, fertile soil and crops would be washed away during the rainy season. To prevent this, the Ifugao cut into the hillside and build stage after stage of terraced fields rising above the valley floor. Springs located above the terraces supply their irrigation water. The labor necessary to build and maintain a system of terraces is great. Terrace walls crumble each year and must be partially rebuilt. The canals that bring water down through the terraces also demand attention.

## Costs and Benefits of Agriculture

Agriculture requires human labor to build and maintain irrigation systems, terraces, and other works. People must feed, water, and care for their animals. Given sufficient labor input and management, agricultural land can yield one or two crops annually for years or even generations. An agricultural field does not necessarily produce a higher single-year yield than does a horticultural plot. The first crop grown by horticulturalists on long-idle land may be larger than that from an agricultural plot of the same size. Furthermore, because agriculturalists have to work more hours than horticulturalists do, agriculture's

**FIGURE 16.2** Location of the Ifugao.

yield relative to the labor time invested also is lower. Agriculture's main advantage is that the long-term yield per area is far greater and more dependable. Because a single field sustains its owners year after year, there is no need to maintain a reserve of uncultivated land as horticulturalists do. This is why agricultural societies tend to be more densely populated than are horticultural ones.

Agriculture requires longer hours than horticulture does and uses land intensively and continuously. Labor demands associated with agriculture reflect its use of domesticated animals, irrigation, and terracing. Shown here, irrigated terraces surround the Ifugao village of Banaue on Luzon Island in the Philippines.

## The Cultivation Continuum

**cultivation continuum**
Continuum of land and labor use.

Because nonindustrial economies can have features of both horticulture and agriculture, it is useful to discuss cultivators as being arranged along a **cultivation continuum.** Horticultural systems stand at one end—the "low-labor, shifting-plot" end. Agriculturalists are at the other—the "labor-intensive, permanent-plot" end.

We speak of a continuum because there are intermediate economies, combining horticultural and agricultural features—more intensive than annually shifting horticulture but less intensive than agriculture. Unlike nonintensive horticulturalists, who farm a plot just once before fallowing it, the South American Kuikuru grow two or three crops of *manioc,* or cassava—an edible tuber—before abandoning their plots. Cultivation is even more intense in certain densely populated areas of Papua New Guinea, where plots are planted for two or three years, allowed to rest for three to five, and then recultivated. After several of these cycles, the plots are abandoned for a longer fallow period. Such a pattern is called *sectorial fallowing* (Wolf 1966). Besides Papua New Guinea, such systems occur in places as distant as West Africa and highland Mexico. Sectorial fallowing is associated with denser populations than is simple horticulture.

The key difference between horticulture and agriculture is that *horticulture always has a fallow period,* whereas agriculture does not. The earliest cultivators in the Middle East and in Mexico were rainfall-dependent horticulturalists. Until recently, horticulture was the main form of cultivation in several areas, including parts of Africa, Southeast Asia, the Pacific islands, Mexico, Central America, and the South American tropical forest.

## Intensification: People and the Environment

The range of environments available for cultivation has widened as people have increased their control over nature. Agriculturalists have been able to colonize many areas that are too arid for nonirrigators or too hilly for nonterracers. Agriculture's increased labor intensity and permanent land use have major demographic, social, political, and environmental consequences.

**pastoralists**
Herders of domesticated animals.

Thus, because of their permanent fields, agriculturalists tend to be sedentary. People live in larger and more permanent communities located closer to other settlements. Growth in population size and density increases contact between individuals and groups. There is more need to regulate interpersonal relations, including conflicts of interest. Economies that support more people usually require more coordination in the use of land, labor, and other resources.

Intensive agriculture has significant environmental effects. Irrigation ditches and paddies (fields with irrigated rice) become repositories for organic wastes, chemicals (such as salts), and disease microorganisms. Intensive agriculture typically spreads at the expense of trees and forests, which are cut down to be replaced by fields. Accompanying such deforestation is loss of environmental diversity (see Srivastava, Smith, and Forno 1999). Compared with horticulture, agricultural economies are specialized. They focus on one or a few caloric staples, such as rice, and on the animals that are raised and tended to aid the agricultural economy. Because tropical horticulturalists typically cultivate dozens of plant species simultaneously, a horticultural plot tends to mirror the botanical diversity that is found in a tropical forest. Agricultural plots, by contrast, reduce ecological diversity by cutting down trees and concentrating on just a few staple foods.

Agriculturalists attempt to reduce risk by favoring stability in the form of a reliable annual harvest and long-term production. Tropical foragers and horticulturalists, by contrast, attempt to reduce risk by relying on multiple species and benefiting from ecological diversity. The agricultural strategy is to put all one's eggs in one big and dependable basket. Of course, even with agriculture, there is a possibility that the single staple crop may fail, and famine may result. The strategy of horticulturalists is to have several, smaller baskets, a few of which may fail without endangering subsistence. The agricultural strategy makes sense when there are lots of children to raise and adults to be fed. Horticulture, like foraging, is associated with smaller, sparser, and more mobile populations.

Many indigenous groups, especially foragers and horticulturalists, have done a reasonable job of managing their resources and preserving their ecosystems (see also Menzies 2006). Such societies had traditional ways of categorizing resources and regulating their use. Increasingly, however, these traditional management systems have been challenged by national and international incentives to exploit and degrade the environment (see Dove, Sajise, and Doolittle 2011).

## Pastoralism

Herders, or **pastoralists,** are people whose activities focus on such domesticated animals as cattle, sheep, goats, camels, yak, and reindeer. They live in North and sub-Saharan Africa, the Middle East, Europe, and Asia. East African pastoralists, like many others, live in symbiosis with their herds. (*Symbiosis* is an obligatory interaction between groups—here, humans and animals—that is beneficial to each.) Herders attempt to protect their animals and to ensure their reproduction in return for food (dairy products and meat) and other products, such as leather.

People use livestock in various ways. Natives of North America's Great Plains, for example, didn't eat, but only rode, their horses. (They got those horses after Europeans reintroduced them to the Western Hemisphere; the native American horse had become extinct thousands of years earlier.) For Plains Indians, horses served as "tools of the trade," means of production used to hunt buffalo, the main target of their economies. So the Plains Indians were not true pastoralists but hunters who used horses—as many agriculturalists use animals—as means of production.

Pastoralists, by contrast, typically use their herds for food. They consume their meat, blood, and milk, from which they make yogurt, butter, and cheese. Although some pastoralists rely on their herds more completely than others do, it is impossible to base subsistence solely on animals. Most pastoralists therefore supplement their diet by hunting, gathering, fishing, cultivating, or trading.

The Samis (also known as Lapps or Laplanders) of Norway, Sweden, and Finland domesticated the reindeer, which their ancestors once hunted, in the 16th century. Like other herders, they follow their animals as they make an annual trek, in this case from coast to interior. Today's Samis use modern technology, such as snowmobiles and four-wheel-drive vehicles, to accompany their herds on their annual nomadic trek. Some of them probably use reindeer management software on their laptops, tablets, PDAs, or smartphones. Although their environment is harsher, the Samis, like other herders, live in nation-states and must deal with outsiders, including government officials, as they follow their herds and make their living through animal husbandry, trade, and sales (Hoge 2001; Paine 2009).

Unlike foraging and cultivation, which existed throughout the world before the Industrial Revolution, herding was confined almost totally to the Old World. Before European conquest, the only herders in the Americas lived in the Andean region of South America. They used their llamas and alpacas for food and wool and in agriculture and transport. Much more recently, Navajo of the southwestern United States developed a pastoral economy based on sheep, which were brought to North America by Europeans. The populous

Navajo became the major pastoral population in the Western Hemisphere.

Two patterns of movement occur with pastoralism: nomadism and transhumance. Both are based on the fact that herds must move to use pasture available in particular places in different seasons. In **pastoral nomadism,** the entire group—women, men, and children—moves with the animals throughout the year. The Middle East and North Africa provide numerous examples of pastoral nomads (see Salzman 2008). In Iran, for example, the Basseri and the Qashqai ethnic groups traditionally followed a nomadic route more than 300 miles (480 kilometers) long (see Salzman 2004).

**nomadism (pastoral)**
Annual movement of entire pastoral group with herds.

Pastoralists may be nomadic or transhumant, but they don't typically live off their herds alone. They either trade or cultivate. Above, a nomadic Afghan Koochi (also spelled Kuchi) woman, with her herd and belongings, returns to Afghanistan from a tribal area of neighboring Pakistan. Nomadic caravans like this one have followed this route for thousands of years. Below, in spring 2011, a transhumant shepherd guides sheep along a country road in Altlandsberg, Germany.

| ADAPTIVE STRATEGY | ALSO KNOWN AS | KEY FEATURES/VARIETIES |
|---|---|---|
| Foraging | Hunting-gathering | Mobility, use of nature's resources |
| Horticulture | Slash-and-burn, shifting cultivation, swiddening, dry farming | Fallow period |
| Agriculture | Intensive farming | Continuous use of land, intensive use of labor |
| Pastoralism | Herding | Nomadism and transhumance |
| Industrialism | Industrial production | Factory production, capitalism, socialist production |

**transhumance**
System in which only part of population moves seasonally with herds.

With **transhumance,** part of the group moves with the herds, but most people stay in the home village. There are examples from Europe and Africa. In Europe's Alps it is just the shepherds and goatherds—not the whole hamlet, village, or town—who accompany the flocks to highland meadows in summer. Among the Turkana of Uganda, men and boys take the herds to distant pastures, while much of the village stays put and does some horticultural farming. During their annual trek, pastoral nomads trade for crops and other products with more sedentary people. Transhumants don't have to trade for crops. Because only part of the population accompanies the herds, transhumants can maintain year-round villages and grow their own crops. (Recap 16.1 summarizes the major adaptive strategies.)

## MODES OF PRODUCTION

**economy**
System of resource production, distribution, and consumption.

An **economy** is a system of production, distribution, and consumption of resources; *economics* is the study of such systems. Economists focus on modern nations and capitalist systems. Anthropologists have broadened understanding of economic principles by gathering data on nonindustrial economies. *Economic anthropology* brings a comparative perspective to the study of economics (see Chibnik 2011; Hann and Hart 2011; Sahlins 2004; Wilk and Cliggett 2007).

**mode of production**
Specific set of social relations that organizes labor.

A **mode of production** is a way of organizing production—"a set of social relations through which labor is deployed to wrest energy from nature by means of tools, skills, organization, and knowledge" (Wolf 1982, p. 75). In the *capitalist* mode of production, money buys labor power, and there is a social gap between the people (bosses and workers) involved in the production process. By contrast, in nonindustrial societies, labor is not usually bought but is given as a social obligation. In such a *kin-based* mode of production, mutual aid in production is one among many expressions of a larger web of social relations.

Societies representing each of the adaptive strategies just discussed (e.g., foraging) tend to have roughly similar modes of production. Differences in the mode of production within a given strategy may reflect differences in environments, target resources, or cultural traditions. Thus, a foraging mode of production may be based on individual hunters or teams, depending on whether the game is a solitary or a herd or flocking animal. Gathering is usually more individualistic than hunting, although collecting teams may assemble when abundant resources ripen and must be harvested quickly. Fishing may be done alone (as in ice fishing or spearfishing) or in crews (as with open-sea fishing and hunting of sea mammals).

## Production in Nonindustrial Societies

Although some kind of division of economic labor related to age and gender is a cultural universal, the specific tasks assigned to each gender and to people of different ages vary. Many horticultural societies assign a major productive role to women, but some make men's work primary. Similarly, among pastoralists, men generally tend large animals, but in some cultures women do the milking. Jobs accomplished through teamwork in some cultivating societies are done by smaller groups or individuals working over a longer period of time in others.

The Betsileo of Madagascar have two stages of teamwork in rice cultivation: transplanting and harvesting. Team size varies with the size of the field. Both transplanting and harvesting feature a traditional division of labor by age and gender that is well known to all Betsileo and is repeated across the generations. The first job in transplanting is the trampling of a previously tilled flooded field by young men driving cattle, in order to mix earth and water. They bring cattle to trample the fields just before transplanting. The young men yell at and beat the cattle, striving to drive them into a frenzy, so that they will trample the fields properly. Trampling breaks up clumps of earth and mixes irrigation water with soil to form a smooth mud, into which women transplant seedlings. Once the tramplers leave the field, older men arrive. With their spades, they break up the clumps that the cattle missed. Meanwhile, the owner and other adults uproot rice seedlings and take them to the field.

At harvest time, four or five months later, young men cut the rice off the stalks. Young women carry it to the clearing above the field. Older women arrange and stack it. The oldest men and women then stand on the stack, stomping and compacting it. Three days later, young men thresh the rice, beating the stalks against a rock to remove the grain. Older men then attack the stalks with sticks to make sure all the grains have fallen off.

Most of the other tasks in Betsileo rice cultivation are done by individual owners and their immediate families. All household members help weed the rice field. It's a man's job to till the fields with a spade or a plow. Individual men repair the irrigation and drainage systems and the earth walls that separate one plot from the next. Among other agriculturalists, however, repairing the irrigation system is a task involving teamwork and communal labor.

## Means of Production

In nonindustrial societies, there is a more intimate relationship between the worker and the means of production than there is in industrial nations. **Means, or factors, of production** include land (territory), labor, technology, and capital.

### Land

Among foragers, ties between people and land were less permanent than among food producers. Although many bands had territories, the boundaries usually were not marked, and there was no way they could be enforced. The hunter's stake in an animal being stalked or hit with a poisoned arrow was more important than where the animal finally died. A person acquired the rights to use a band's territory by being born in the band or by joining it through a tie of kinship, marriage, or fictive kinship. In Botswana in southern Africa, Ju/'hoansi San women, whose work provided over half the food, habitually used specific tracts of berry-bearing trees. However, when a woman changed bands, she immediately acquired a new gathering area.

Among food producers, rights to the means of production also come through kinship and marriage. Descent groups (groups whose members claim common ancestry) are common among nonindustrial food producers, and those who descend from the founder share the group's territory and resources. If the adaptive strategy is horticulture, the estate includes garden and fallow land for shifting cultivation. As members of a descent group, pastoralists have access to animals to start their own herds, to grazing land, to garden land, and to other means of production.

### Labor, Tools, and Specialization

Like land, labor is a means of production. In nonindustrial societies, access to both land and labor comes through social links such as kinship, marriage, and descent. Mutual aid in production is

Betsileo women transplant rice seedlings in south central Madagascar. Transplanting and weeding are arduous tasks that especially strain the back.

merely one aspect of ongoing social relations that are expressed on many other occasions.

Nonindustrial societies contrast with industrial nations in regard to another means of production: technology. Manufacturing is often linked to age and gender. Women may weave and men may make pottery or vice versa. Most people of a particular age and gender share the technical knowledge associated with that age and gender. If married women customarily make baskets, all or most married women know how to make baskets. Neither technology nor technical knowledge is as specialized as it is in states.

However, some tribal societies do promote specialization. Among the Yanomami of Venezuela and Brazil (Figure 16.3), for instance, certain villages manufacture clay pots and others make hammocks. They don't specialize, as one might suppose, because certain raw materials happen to be available near particular villages. Clay suitable for pots is widely available. Everyone knows how to make pots, but not everybody does so. Craft specialization reflects the social and political environment rather than the natural environment. Such specialization promotes trade, which is the first step in creating an alliance with enemy villages (Chagnon 1997). Specialization contributes to keeping the peace, although it has not prevented intervillage warfare.

## Alienation in Industrial Economies

There are some significant contrasts between industrial and nonindustrial economies. When factory workers produce for sale and for their employer's profit, rather than for their own use, they may be alienated from the items they make. Such alienation means they don't feel strong pride in or personal

**means (factors) of production** Major productive resources, e.g., land, labor, technology, capital.

**FIGURE 16.3** Location of the Yanomami.

identification with their products. They see their product as belonging to someone else, not to the man or woman whose labor actually produced it. In nonindustrial societies, by contrast, people usually see their work through from start to finish and have a sense of accomplishment in the product. The fruits

In a garment factory in Hlaing Tharyar, Myanmar, Burmese women stitch sports clothing for a Taiwanese company. Their average wage is less than one American dollar per day. Throughout Southeast Asia, hundreds of thousands of young women from peasant families now work in factories. Chances are good that you own one of their products.

of their labor are their own, rather than someone else's. (This chapter's "Focus on Globalization" describes the increasingly impersonal nature of today's global economy.)

In nonindustrial societies, the economic relation between coworkers is just one aspect of a more general social relation. They aren't just coworkers but kin, in-laws, or celebrants in the same ritual. In industrial nations, people don't usually work with relatives and neighbors. If coworkers are friends, the personal relationship usually develops out of their common employment rather than being based on a previous association.

Thus, industrial workers have impersonal relations with their products, coworkers, and employers. People sell their labor for cash, and the economic domain stands apart from ordinary social life. Work is separate from family. In nonindustrial societies, however, the relations of production, distribution, and consumption are *social relations with economic aspects*. Economy is not a separate entity but is *embedded* in the society.

## A Case of Industrial Alienation

For decades, the government of Malaysia has promoted export-oriented industry, allowing transnational companies to install labor-intensive manufacturing operations in rural Malaysia. The industrialization of Malaysia is part of a global strategy. In search of cheaper labor, corporations headquartered in Japan, Western Europe, and the United States have been moving labor-intensive factories to developing countries. Malaysia has hundreds of Japanese and American subsidiaries, which produce mainly garments, foodstuffs, and electronics components. In electronics plants in rural Malaysia, thousands of young women from peasant families now assemble microchips and microcomponents for transistors and capacitors. Aihwa Ong (1987, 2010) did a study of electronics assembly workers in an area where 85 percent of the workers were young, unmarried females from nearby villages.

Ong found that, unlike village women, female factory workers had to cope with a rigid work routine and constant supervision by men. The discipline that factories value was being taught in local schools, where uniforms helped prepare girls for the factory dress code. Village women wore loose, flowing tunics, sarongs, and sandals, but factory workers had to don tight overalls and heavy rubber gloves, in which they felt constrained. Assembling electronics components requires precise, concentrated labor. Demanding and depleting, labor in these factories illustrates the separation of intellectual and manual activity—the alienation that Karl Marx considered the defining feature of industrial work. One woman said about her bosses, "They exhaust us very much, as if they do not think that we too are human beings" (Ong 1987, p. 202). Nor does factory work bring women a substantial financial reward, given low wages, job uncertainty, and family claims on wages. Young women typically

## Our Global Economy

Economic systems are based on production, distribution, and consumption. All these processes now have global, and increasingly impersonal, dimensions. The products, images, and information we consume each day can come from anywhere. How likely is it that the item you last bought from a website, an outlet, or a retail store was made in the United States, rather than Canada, Mexico, Peru, or China?

The national has become international. Consider a few familiar "American" brands: Good Humor, French's mustard, Frigidaire, Adidas, Caribou Coffee, Church's Chicken, Trader Joe's, Holiday Inn, Dial soap, T-Mobile, and Toll House Cookies. All of them have foreign ownership. As well, the following iconic brands have been bought by foreign companies: Budweiser, Alka-Selzer, Hellmann's, IBM ThinkPad, Ben and Jerry's, 7-Eleven, Popsicle, Woman's Day, Purina, Gerber, Vaseline, Lucky Strike, Firestone, and Car and Driver Magazine.

Also foreign owned are such American architectural icons as New York's Plaza Hotel, Flatiron Building, and Chrysler Building, along with the Indiana Toll Road and the Chicago Skyway. A Brazilian billionaire now owns a significant share in Burger King, a whopper of a chain with over 12,000 outlets worldwide.

Much of America, including half our national debt, now belongs to outsiders. Already by the mid-1980s, 75 percent of the buildings in downtown Los Angeles were owned at least in part by foreign capital (Rouse 1991). According to Bruce Bartlett (2010), the share of the U.S. national debt owned by foreigners has swollen since the 1970s, when it was only 5 percent. Since the 1970s, oil-producing countries have invested their profits in U.S. Treasury securities because of their liquidity and safety. By 1975 the foreign share of U.S. national debt had reached 17 percent, where it remained through the 1990s, when China started buying large amounts of Treasury bills. By 2009, foreigners were financing almost half the total publicly held U.S. national debt.

The Internet is a vital organ in our 21st-century global economy. All kinds of products—music, movies, clothing, appliances, this book, you name it—are produced, distributed, and consumed via the Internet. Economic functions that are spatially dispersed (perhaps continents apart) are coordinated online in real time. Activities that once involved face-to-face contact are now conducted impersonally, often across vast distances. When you order something via the Internet, the only human being you might speak to is the delivery driver (Smith and Doyle 2002). The computers that take and process your order from Amazon can be on different continents. The products you order can come from a warehouse anywhere in the world.

Transnational finance has shifted the economic control of local life to outsiders (see Kennedy 2010). Greeks blame Germans for their austerity. The European debt crisis that recently has occupied so much of the world's attention shows the fragility of the economic ties created through consolidation (of the European Union and the euro) and globalization.

How different is today's global economy from British poet Henry Wadsworth Longfellow's vision of production—noble, local, and autonomous:

Under a spreading chestnut-tree
The village smithy stands. . . .

Toiling—rejoicing—sorrowing,

Onward through life he goes;

Each morning sees some task begin,

Each evening sees it close.

(Longfellow, "The Village Blacksmith," 1839)

A scene from an Amazon warehouse on Cyber Monday, December 5, 2011, the busiest day of the year for online shoppers. This warehouse could be in a lot of places, but it happens to be in Great Britain.

work just a few years. Production quotas, three daily shifts, overtime, and surveillance take their toll in mental and physical exhaustion.

One response to factory relations of production has been spirit possession (factory women are possessed by spirits). Ong interprets this phenomenon as the women's unconscious protest against labor discipline and male control of the industrial setting. Sometimes possession takes the form of mass hysteria. Spirits have simultaneously invaded as many as 120 factory workers. Weretigers (the Malay equivalent of the werewolf) arrive to avenge the construction of a factory on aboriginal burial grounds. Disturbed earth and grave spirits swarm on the shop floor. First the women see the spirits; then their bodies are invaded. The women become violent and scream abuses. The weretigers send the women into sobbing, laughing, and shrieking fits.

## Scarcity and the Betsileo

In the realm of cultural diversity, perceptions and motivations can change substantially over time. Consider some changes I've observed among the Betsileo of Madagascar during the decades I've been studying them. Initially, compared with modern consumers, the Betsileo had little perception of scarcity. Now, with population increase and the spread of a cash-oriented economy, perceived wants and needs have increased relative to means. Motivations have changed, too, as people increasingly seek profits, even if it means stealing from their neighbors or destroying ancestral farms.

In the late 1960s my wife and I lived among the Betsileo people of Madagascar, studying their economy and social life (Kottak 1980, 2004). Soon after our arrival we met two well-educated schoolteachers (first cousins) who were interested in our research. The woman's father was a congressional representative who became a cabinet minister during our stay. Their family came from a historically important and typical Betsileo village called Ivato, which they invited us to visit with them.

We had traveled to many other Betsileo villages, where often we were displeased with our reception. As we drove up, children would run away screaming. Women would hurry inside. Men would retreat to doorways, where they lurked bashfully. This behavior expressed the Betsileo's great fear of the mpakafo. Believed to cut out and devour his victim's heart and liver, the mpakafo is

the Malagasy vampire. These cannibals are said to have fair skin and to be very tall. Because I have light skin and stand well over 6 feet tall, I was a natural suspect. The fact that such creatures were not known to travel with their wives offered a bit of assurance that I wasn't really a mpakafo.

When we visited Ivato, its people were different—friendly and hospitable. Our very first day there we did a brief census and found out who lived in which households. We learned people's names and their relationships to our schoolteacher friends and to each other. We met an excellent informant who knew all about the local history. In a few afternoons I learned much more than I had in the other villages in several sessions.

Ivatans were so willing to talk because we had powerful sponsors, village natives who had made it in the outside world, people the Ivatans knew would protect them. The schoolteachers vouched for us, but even more significant was the cabinet minister, who was like a grandfather and benefactor to everyone in town. The Ivatans had no reason to fear us because their more influential native son had asked them to answer our questions.

Once we moved to Ivato, the elders established a pattern of visiting us every evening. They came to talk, attracted by the inquisitive foreigners but also by the wine, tobacco, and food we offered. I asked questions about their customs and beliefs. I eventually developed interview schedules about various subjects,

including rice production. I used these forms in Ivato and in two other villages I was studying less intensively. Never have I interviewed as easily as I did in Ivato.

As our stay neared its end, our Ivatan friends lamented, saying, "We'll miss you. When you leave, there won't be any more cigarettes, any more wine, or any more questions." They wondered what it would be like for us back in the United States. They knew we had an automobile and that we could afford to buy products they never would have. They commented, "When you go back to your country, you'll need a lot of money for things like cars, clothes, and food. We don't need to buy those things. We make almost everything we use. We don't need as much money as you, because we produce for ourselves."

The Betsileo weren't unusual for nonindustrial people. Strange as it may seem to an American consumer, those rice farmers actually believed they had all they needed. The lesson from the Betsileo of the 1960s is that scarcity, which economists view as universal, is variable. Although shortages do arise in nonindustrial societies, the concept of scarcity (insufficient means) is much less developed in stable subsistence-oriented societies than in the societies characterized by industrialism, particularly as the reliance on consumer goods increases.

But with globalization over the past few decades, significant changes have affected the

---

To deal with possession, factories employ local medicine men, who sacrifice chickens and goats to fend off the spirits. This solution works only some of the time; possession still goes on. Factory women continue to act as vehicles to express their own frustrations and the anger of avenging ghosts.

Ong argues that spirit possession expresses anguish at, and resistance to, capitalist relations of production. By engaging in this form of rebellion, however, factory women avoid a direct confrontation with the source of their distress. Ong concludes that spirit possession, while expressing repressed resentment, doesn't do much to modify factory conditions. (Other tactics, such as unionization, would

do more.) Spirit possession may even help maintain the current system by operating as a safety valve for accumulated tensions.

## ECONOMIZING AND MAXIMIZATION

Economic anthropologists have been concerned with two main questions:

1. How are production, distribution, and consumption organized in different societies? This question focuses on *systems* of human behavior and their organization.

Betsileo—and most nonindustrial peoples. On my last visit to Ivato, in 2006, the effects of cash and of rapid population increase were evident there—and throughout Madagascar—where the national growth rate has been about 3 percent per year. Madagascar's population doubled between 1966 and 1991—from 6 to 12 million people. Today it exceeds 22 million—almost four times as many people to feed as when I first did fieldwork there. One result of population pressure has been agricultural intensification. In Ivato, farmers who formerly had grown only rice in their rice fields now were using the same land for cash crops, such as carrots, after the annual rice harvest. Another change affecting Ivato in recent years has been the breakdown of social and political order, fueled by increasing demand for cash.

Cattle rustling is a growing threat. Cattle thieves (sometimes from neighboring villages) have terrorized peasants who previously felt secure in their villages. Some of the rustled cattle are driven to the coasts for commercial export to nearby islands. Prominent among the rustlers are relatively well-educated young men who have studied long enough to be comfortable negotiating with outsiders but who have been unable to find formal work and are unwilling to work the rice fields as their peasant ancestors did. The formal education system has familiarized them with external institutions and norms, including the need for cash. The concepts of scarcity, commerce, and negative reciprocity now thrive among the Betsileo.

I've witnessed other striking evidence of the new addiction to cash during my most recent visits to Betsileo country. Near Ivato's county seat, people now sell semiprecious stones—tourmalines, which originally were found by chance in local rice fields. We saw an amazing sight: dozens of villagers destroying an ancestral resource, digging up a large rice field, seeking tourmalines—clear evidence of the encroachment of cash on the local subsistence economy. You can't eat gemstones.

Throughout the Betsileo homeland, population growth and density are propelling emigration. Locally, land, jobs, and money are all scarce. One woman with ancestors from Ivato, herself now a resident of the national capital (Antananarivo), remarked that half the children of Ivato now lived in that city. Although she was exaggerating, a census of all the descendants of Ivato reveals a substantial emigrant and urban population.

Ivato's recent history is one of increasing participation in a cash economy. That history, combined with the pressure of a growing population on local resources, has made scarcity not just a concept but a reality for Ivatans and their neighbors.

Women hull rice in a Betsileo village. In the village of Ivato, farmers who traditionally grew only rice in their rice fields now use the same land for commercial crops, such as carrots, after the annual rice harvest.

2. What *motivates* people in different cultures to produce, distribute or exchange, and consume? Here the focus is not on systems of behavior but on the motives of the *individuals* who participate in those systems.

Anthropologists view both economic systems and motivations in a cross-cultural perspective. Motivation is a concern of psychologists, but it also has been, implicitly or explicitly, a concern of economists and anthropologists. Economists tend to assume that producers and distributors make decisions rationally by using the *profit motive,* as do consumers when they shop around for the best value. Although anthropologists know that the profit motive is not universal, the assumption that individuals try to maximize profits is basic to the capitalist world economy and to much of Western economic theory. In fact, the subject matter of economics is often defined as **economizing,** or the rational allocation of scarce means (resources) to alternative ends (uses) (see Chibnik 2011).

What does that mean? Classical economic theory assumes that our wants are infinite and that our means are limited. Since means are limited, people must make choices about how to use their scarce resources: their time, labor, money, and capital. (This chapter's "Appreciating Diversity" disputes

**economizing**
Allocation of scarce means (resources) among alternative ends.

the idea that people always make economic choices based on scarcity.) Economists assume that when confronted with choices and decisions, people tend to make the one that maximizes profit. This is assumed to be the most rational (reasonable) choice.

The idea that individuals choose to maximize profit was a basic assumption of the classical economists of the 19th century and is one that is held by many contemporary economists. However, certain economists now recognize that individuals in Western cultures, as in others, may be motivated by many other goals. Depending on the society and the situation, people may try to maximize profit, wealth, prestige, pleasure, comfort, or social harmony. Individuals may want to realize their personal or family ambitions or those of another group to which they belong (see Chibnik 2011; Sahlins 2004).

## Alternative Ends

To what uses do people in various societies put their scarce resources? Throughout the world, people devote some of their time and energy to building up a *subsistence fund* (Wolf 1966). In other words, they have to work to eat, to replace the calories they use in their daily activity. People also must invest in a *replacement fund*. They must maintain their technology and other items essential to production. If a hoe or plow breaks, they must repair or replace it. They also must obtain and replace items that are essential not to production but to everyday life, such as clothing and shelter.

People also have to invest in a *social fund*. They have to help their friends, relatives, in-laws, and neighbors. It is useful to distinguish between a social fund and a *ceremonial fund*. The latter term refers to expenditures on ceremonies or rituals. To prepare a festival honoring one's ancestors, for example, requires time and the outlay of wealth.

Citizens of nation-states also must allocate scarce resources to a *rent fund*. We think of rent as payment for the use of property. However, "rent fund" has a wider meaning. It refers to resources that people must render to an individual or agency that is superior politically or economically. Tenant farmers and sharecroppers, for example, either pay rent or give some of their produce to their landlords, as peasants did under feudalism.

**Peasants** are small-scale agriculturalists who live in nonindustrial states and have rent fund obligations (see Kearney 1996). They produce to feed themselves, to sell their produce, and to pay rent. All peasants have two things in common:

1. They live in state-organized societies.

2. They produce food without the elaborate technology—chemical fertilizers, tractors, airplanes to spray crops, and so on—of modern farming or agribusiness.

In addition to paying rent to landlords, peasants must satisfy government obligations, paying taxes in the form of money, produce, or labor. The rent fund is not simply an *additional* obligation for peasants. Often it becomes their foremost and unavoidable duty. Sometimes, to meet the obligation to pay rent, their own diets suffer. The demands of paying rent may divert resources from subsistence, replacement, social, and ceremonial funds.

Motivations vary from society to society, and people often lack freedom of choice in allocating their resources. Because of obligations to pay rent, peasants may allocate their scarce means toward ends that are not their own but those of government officials. Thus, even in societies where there is a profit motive, people are often prevented from rationally maximizing self-interest by factors beyond their control.

## DISTRIBUTION, EXCHANGE

The economist Karl Polanyi (1968) stimulated the comparative study of exchange, and several anthropologists followed his lead. To study exchange cross-culturally, Polanyi defined three principles orienting exchanges: the market principle, redistribution, and reciprocity. These principles can all be present in the same society, but in that case they govern different kinds of transactions. In any society, one of them usually dominates. The principle of exchange that dominates in a given society is the one that allocates the means of production (see Chibnik 2011; Hann and Hart 2011).

## The Market Principle

In today's world capitalist economy, the **market principle** dominates. It governs the distribution of the means of production: land, labor, natural resources, technology, knowledge, and capital. "Market exchange refers to the organizational process of purchase and sale at money price" (Dalton 1967; see also Hann and Hart 2009; Madra 2004). With market exchange, items are bought and sold, using money, with an eye to maximizing profit, and value is determined by the *law of supply and demand* (things cost more the scarcer they are and the more people want them).

Bargaining is characteristic of market-principle exchanges. The buyer and seller strive to maximize—to get their "money's worth." In bargaining, buyers and sellers don't need to meet personally. But their offers and counteroffers do need to be open for negotiation over a fairly short time period.

## Redistribution

**Redistribution** operates when goods, services, or their equivalent move from the local level to a center. The center may be a capital, a regional collection point, or a storehouse near a chief's residence. Products often move through a hierarchy of officials

**market principle**
Buying, selling, and valuation based on supply and demand.

**peasant**
Small-scale farmer with rent fund obligations.

**redistribution**
Flow of goods from local level into center, then back out; characteristic of chiefdoms.

for storage at the center. Along the way, officials and their dependents may consume some of them, but the exchange principle here is *re*distribution. The flow of goods eventually reverses direction—out from the center, down through the hierarchy, and back to the common people.

One example of a redistributive system comes from the Cherokee, the original owners of the Tennessee Valley. The Cherokee were productive cultivators of maize, beans, and squash, which they supplemented by hunting and fishing. They also had chiefs. Each of their main villages had a central plaza, where meetings of the chief's council took place, and where redistributive feasts were held. According to Cherokee custom, each family farm had an area where the family set aside a portion of its annual harvest for the chief. This supply of corn was used to feed the needy, as well as travelers and warriors journeying through friendly territory. This store of food was available to all who needed it, with the understanding that it "belonged" to the chief and was dispersed through his generosity. The chief also hosted the redistributive feasts held in the main settlements (Harris 1978).

## Reciprocity

**Reciprocity** is exchange between social equals, who are normally related by kinship, marriage, or another close personal tie. Because it occurs between social equals, it is dominant in the more egalitarian societies—among foragers, cultivators, and pastoralists. There are three degrees of reciprocity: generalized, balanced, and negative (Sahlins 1968, 2004; Service 1966). These may be imagined as areas of a continuum defined by these questions:

1. How closely related are the parties to the exchange?

2. How quickly and unselfishly are gifts reciprocated?

*Generalized reciprocity,* the purest form of reciprocity, is characteristic of exchanges between closely related people. In *balanced reciprocity,* social distance increases, as does the need to reciprocate. In *negative reciprocity,* social distance is greatest and reciprocation is most calculated. This range, from generalized to negative, is called the **reciprocity continuum.**

With **generalized reciprocity,** someone gives to another person and expects nothing concrete or immediate in return. Such exchanges (including parental gift giving in contemporary North America) are not primarily economic transactions but expressions of personal relationships. Most parents don't keep accounts of every penny they spend on their children. They merely hope that the children will respect their culture's customs involving love, honor, loyalty, and other obligations to parents.

**FIGURE 16.4** Location of the San, Including Ju/'hoansi.

Among foragers, generalized reciprocity has usually governed exchanges. People routinely share with other band members. A study of the Ju/'hoansi San (Figure 16.4) found that 40 percent of the population contributed little to the food supply (Lee 1968/1974). Children, teenagers, and people over 60 depended on other people for their food. Despite the high proportion of dependents, the average worker hunted or gathered less than half as much (12 to 19 hours a week) as the average American works. Nonetheless, there was always food because different people worked on different days.

So strong is the ethic of reciprocal sharing that most foragers have lacked an expression for "thank you." To offer thanks would be impolite because it would imply that a particular act of sharing, which is the keystone of egalitarian society, was unusual. Among the Semai, foragers of central Malaysia (Dentan 1979, 2008), to express gratitude would suggest surprise at the hunter's generosity or success.

**Balanced reciprocity** applies to exchanges between people who are more distantly related than are members of the same band or household. In a horticultural society, for example, a man presents a gift to someone in another village. The recipient

**reciprocity**
Principle governing exchanges among social equals.

**reciprocity continuum**
A continuum running from generalized reciprocity (closely related/deferred return) to negative reciprocity (strangers/immediate return).

**generalized reciprocity**
Exchanges among closely related individuals.

**balanced reciprocity**
Midpoint on *reciprocity continuum,* between generalized and negative reciprocity.

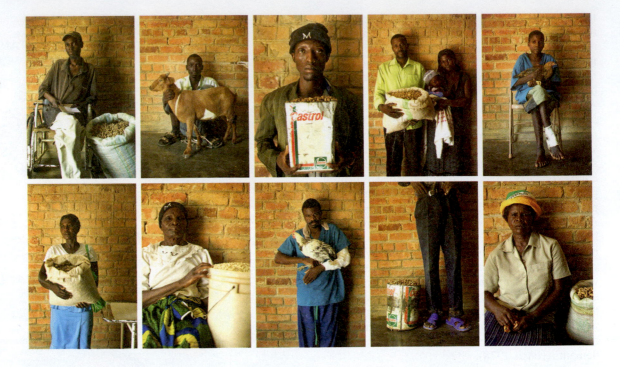

At Zimbabwe's Chidamoyo Hospital, patients often barter farm products for medical treatment. How does barter fit with the exchange principles discussed here?

may be a cousin, a trading partner, or a brother's fictive kinsman. The giver expects something in return. This may not come immediately, but the social relationship will be strained if there is no reciprocation.

Exchanges in nonindustrial societies also may illustrate **negative reciprocity,** mainly in dealing with people outside or on the fringes of their social systems. To people who live in a world of close personal relations, exchanges with outsiders are full of ambiguity and distrust. Exchange is one way of establishing friendly relations with outsiders, but especially when trade begins, the relationship is still tentative. Often, the initial exchange is close to being purely economic; people want to get something back immediately. Just as in market economies, but without using money, they try to get the best possible immediate return for their investment (see Clark 2010; Hann and Hart 2009).

Generalized and balanced reciprocity are based on trust and a social tie. But negative reciprocity involves the attempt to get something for as little as possible, even if it means being cagey or deceitful or cheating. Among the most extreme and "negative" examples of negative reciprocity was 19th-century horse thievery by North American Plains Indians. Men would sneak into camps and villages of neighboring tribes to steal horses. Such thefts were likely to be reciprocated. A similar pattern of cattle raiding continues today in East Africa, among tribes such as the Kuria (Fleisher 2000). In these cases, the party that starts the raiding can expect reciprocity—a raid on their own village—or worse. The Kuria hunt down cattle thieves and kill them. It's still reciprocity, governed by "Do unto others as they have done unto you."

One way of reducing the tension in situations of potential negative reciprocity is to engage in "silent trade." One example is the silent trade of the Mbuti "pygmy" foragers of the African equatorial forest and their neighboring horticultural villagers. There is no personal contact during their exchanges. A Mbuti hunter leaves game, honey, or another forest product at a customary site. Villagers collect it and leave crops in exchange. The parties can bargain silently. If one feels the return is insufficient, he or she simply leaves it at the trading site. If the other party wants to continue trade, it will be increased.

## Coexistence of Exchange Principles

In today's North America, the market principle governs most exchanges, from the sale of the means of production to the sale of consumer goods. We also have redistribution. Some of our tax money goes to support the government, but some of it also comes back to us in the form of social services, education, health care, and road building. We also have reciprocal exchanges. Generalized reciprocity characterizes the relationship between parents and children. However, even here the dominant market mentality surfaces in comments about the high cost of raising children and in the stereotypical statement of the disappointed parent: "We gave you everything money could buy."

Exchanges of gifts, cards, and invitations exemplify reciprocity, usually balanced. Everyone has heard remarks like "They invited us to their daughter's wedding, so when ours gets married, we'll have to invite them" and "They've been here for dinner three times and haven't invited us yet. I don't think we should ask them back until they do." Such precise balancing of reciprocity would be out of place in a foraging band, where resources are communal (common to all) and daily sharing based on generalized reciprocity is an essential ingredient of social life and survival.

## POTLATCHING

One of the most thoroughly studied cultural practices known to ethnography is the **potlatch,** a festive event within a regional exchange system among tribes of the North Pacific Coast of North America, including the Salish and Kwakiutl of Washington and British Columbia and the Tsimshian of Alaska (Figure 16.5). At each such event, assisted by members of their communities, potlatch sponsors traditionally gave away food, blankets, pieces of copper, or other items. In return for this, they got prestige. To give a potlatch enhanced one's reputation. Prestige increased with the lavishness of the potlatch, the value of the goods given away in it. Some tribes still practice the potlatch, sometimes as a memorial to the dead (Kan 1986, 1989).

The potlatching tribes were foragers, but atypical ones. They were sedentary and had chiefs. They had access to a wide variety of land and sea resources. Among their most important foods were salmon, herring, candlefish, berries, mountain goats, seals, and porpoises (Piddocke 1969).

According to classical economic theory, the profit motive is universal, with the goal of maximizing material benefits. How, then, does one explain the potlatch, in which substantial wealth is given away (and even destroyed)? Christian missionaries considered potlatching to be wasteful and antithetical to the Protestant work ethic. By 1885, under pressure from Indian agents, missionaries, and Indian converts to Christianity, both Canada and the United States had outlawed potlatching. Between 1885 and 1951, the custom went underground. By 1951 both countries had discreetly dropped the antipotlatching laws from the books (Miller n.d.).

The economist and social commentator Thorstein Veblen cited potlatching as an example of conspicuous consumption in his influential book *The Theory of the Leisure Class* (1934), claiming that potlatching was based on an economically irrational drive for prestige. This interpretation stressed the lavishness and supposed wastefulness, especially of the Kwakiutl displays, to support the contention that in some societies people strive to maximize prestige at the expense of their material well-being. This interpretation has been challenged.

Ecological anthropology, also known as *cultural ecology,* is a theoretical school in anthropology that attempts to interpret cultural practices, such as the potlatch, in terms of their possible long-term role in helping humans adapt to their environments. The ecological anthropologists Wayne Suttles (1960) and Andrew Vayda (1961/1968) viewed potlatching

**FIGURE 16.5** Location of Potlatching Groups.

not in terms of its apparent wastefulness but in terms of its long-term role as a cultural adaptive mechanism. This view not only helps us understand potlatching; it also helps explain similar patterns of lavish feasting in many other parts of the world. Here is the ecological interpretation: *Customs like the potlatch are cultural adaptations to alternating periods of local abundance and shortage.*

How does this work? The overall natural environment of the North Pacific Coast is favorable, but resources fluctuate from year to year and place to place. Salmon and herring aren't equally abundant every year in a given locality. One village can have a good year while another is experiencing a bad one. Later their fortunes reverse. In this context, the potlatch cycle of the Kwakiutl and Salish had adaptive value; the potlatch was not a competitive display that brought no material benefit.

A village enjoying an especially good year had a surplus of subsistence items, which it could trade for more durable wealth items, such as blankets, canoes, or pieces of copper. Wealth, in turn, by being distributed, could be converted into prestige. Members of several villages were invited to any potlatch

**potlatch**
Competitive feast on North Pacific Coast of North America.

The potlatch then and now. The historic (1904) photo above shows potlatch dancers at the Haida village of Klinkwan, Alaska. In the photo below, taken in 2004, Tlingit clan members in Sitka, Alaska, celebrate the 100th anniversary of "The Last Potlatch," held in 1904.

and got to take home the resources that were given away. In this way, potlatching linked villages together in a regional economy—an exchange system that distributed food and wealth from wealthy to needy communities. In return, the potlatch sponsors and their villages got prestige. The decision to potlatch was determined by the health of the local econ-omy. If there had been subsistence surpluses, and thus a buildup of wealth over several good years, a village could afford a potlatch to convert its food and wealth into prestige.

The long-term adaptive value of intercommunity feasting becomes clear when we consider what happened when a formerly prosperous village had a run of bad luck. Its people started accepting invitations to potlatches in villages that were doing better. The tables were turned as the temporarily rich became temporarily poor and vice versa. The newly needy accepted food and wealth items. They were willing to receive rather than bestow gifts and thus to relinquish some of their stored-up prestige. They hoped their luck would eventually improve, so that resources could be recouped and prestige regained.

The potlatch linked local groups along the North Pacific Coast into a regional alliance and exchange network. Potlatching and intervillage exchange had adaptive functions, regardless of the motivations of the individual participants. The anthropologists who stressed rivalry for prestige were not wrong. They were merely emphasizing *motivations* at the expense of an analysis of economic and ecological *systems*.

The use of feasts to enhance individual and community reputations and to redistribute wealth is not peculiar to populations of the North Pacific Coast. Competitive feasting is widely characteristic of non-industrial food producers. But among most foragers, who live, remember, in marginal areas, resources are too meager to support feasting on such a level. In such societies, sharing rather than competition prevails.

Like many other cultural practices that have attracted considerable anthropological attention, the potlatch does not, and did not, exist apart from larger world events. For example, within the spreading world capitalist economy of the 19th century, the potlatching tribes, particularly the Kwakiutl, began to trade with Europeans (fur for blankets, for example). Their wealth increased as a result. Simultaneously, a huge proportion of the Kwakiutl population died from diseases brought by the Europeans. The increased wealth from trade flowed into a drastically reduced population. With many of the traditional sponsors dead (such as chiefs and their families), the Kwakiutl extended the right to give a potlatch to everyone. This stimulated intense competition for prestige. Given trade, increased wealth, and a decreased population, the Kwakiutl also started converting wealth into prestige by destroying wealth items such as blankets, pieces of copper, and houses (Vayda 1961/1968). Blankets and houses could be burned, and pieces of copper could be buried at sea. Being rich enough to destroy wealth conveyed prestige. Kwakiutl potlatching changed its nature. It became much more destructive than it had been previously and than potlatching continued to be among tribes that were less affected by trade and disease.

In any case, note that potlatching also prevented the development of socioeconomic stratification, a system of social classes. Wealth relinquished or destroyed was converted into a nonmaterial item: prestige. Under capitalism, we reinvest our profits (rather than burning our cash), with the hope of making an additional profit. However, the potlatching tribes were content to relinquish their surpluses rather than use them to widen the social distance between themselves and their fellow tribe members.

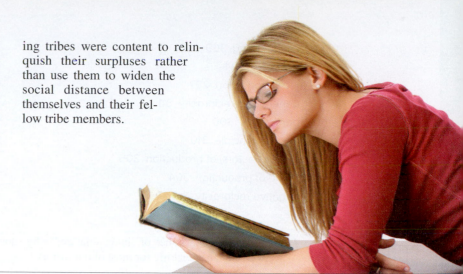

# for REVIEW

summary

1. Cohen's adaptive strategies include foraging (hunting and gathering), horticulture, agriculture, pastoralism, and industrialism. Foraging was the only human adaptive strategy until the advent of food production (farming and herding) 12,000–10,000 years ago. Food production eventually replaced foraging in most places. Almost all modern foragers have at least some dependence on food production or food producers.

2. Horticulture and agriculture stand at opposite ends of a continuum based on labor intensity and continuity of land use. Horticulture doesn't use land or labor intensively. Horticulturalists cultivate a plot for one or two years and then abandon it. Farther along the continuum, horticulture becomes more intensive, but there is always a fallow period. Agriculturalists farm the same plot of land continuously and use labor intensively. They use one or more of the following: irrigation, terracing, and domesticated animals as means of production and manuring.

3. The pastoral strategy is mixed. Nomadic pastoralists trade with cultivators. Part of a transhumant pastoral population cultivates while another part takes the herds to pasture. Except for some Peruvians and the Navajo, who are recent herders, the New World lacks native pastoralists.

4. Economic anthropology is the cross-cultural study of systems of production, distribution, and consumption. In nonindustrial societies, a kin-based mode of production prevails. One acquires rights to resources and labor through membership in social groups, not impersonally through purchase and sale. Work is just one aspect of social relations expressed in varied contexts.

5. Economics has been defined as the science of allocating scarce means to alternative ends. Western economists assume that the notion of scarcity is universal—which it isn't—and that in making choices, people strive to maximize personal profit. In nonindustrial societies, indeed as in our own, people often maximize values other than individual profit.

6. In nonindustrial societies, people invest in subsistence, replacement, social, and ceremonial funds. States add a rent fund: People must share their output with social superiors. In states, the obligation to pay rent often becomes primary.

7. In addition to studying production, economic anthropologists study and compare exchange systems. The three principles of exchange are the market principle, redistribution, and reciprocity. The market principle, based on supply and demand and the profit motive, dominates in states. With redistribution, goods are collected at a central place, but some of them are eventually given back, or redistributed, to the people. Reciprocity governs exchanges between social equals. It is the characteristic mode of exchange among foragers and horticulturalists. Reciprocity, redistribution, and the market principle may coexist in a society, but the primary exchange mode is the one that allocates the means of production.

8. Patterns of feasting and exchanges of wealth among villages are common among nonindustrial food producers, as well as among the potlatching cultures of North America's North Pacific Coast. Such systems help even out the availability of resources over time.

key terms

adaptive strategy 297

agriculture 300

balanced reciprocity 311

band 299

correlation 299

cultivation continuum 302

## critical thinking

1. When considering issues of "human nature," why should we remember that the egalitarian band was a basic form of human social life for most of our history?
2. Intensive agriculture has significant effects on social and environmental relations. What are some of these effects? Are they good or bad?
3. What does it mean when anthropologists describe nonindustrial economic systems as "embedded" in society?
4. What are your scarce means? How do you make decisions about allocating them?
5. Give examples from your own exchanges of different degrees of reciprocity. Why are anthropologists interested in studying exchange across cultures?

# Political Systems

- ▶ What kinds of political systems have existed worldwide, and what are their social and economic correlates?

- ▶ How does the state differ from other forms of political organization?

- ▶ What is social control, and how is it established and maintained in various societies?

State-organized societies have formal governmental institutions, such as the German Reichstag (Parliament) in Berlin, shown here on a typical workday.

# understanding OURSELVES

Y ou've probably heard the expression "Big Man on Campus" (BMOC) used to describe a collegian who is very well known and/or popular. BMOC status might be the result of having a large network of friends, a trendy car or way of dressing, good looks, a nice smile, a sports connection, and a sense of humor. "Big man" has a different but related meaning in anthropology. Many indigenous cultures of the South Pacific had a kind of political figure that anthropologists call the "big man." Such a leader achieved his status through hard work, amassing wealth in the form of pigs and other native riches. Characteristics that distinguished the big man from his fellows, enabling him to attract loyal supporters (a large network of friends), included wealth, generosity, eloquence, physical fitness, bravery, and supernatural powers. Those who became big men did so because of their personalities rather than by inheriting their wealth or position. Do any of the factors that make for a successful big man (or BMOC, for that matter) contribute to political success in a modern nation such as the United States? Although American politicians often use their own wealth, inherited or created, to finance campaigns, they also solicit labor and monetary contributions (rather than pigs) from supporters. And like big men, successful American politicians try to be generous with their supporters. Payback may take the form of a night in the Lincoln bedroom, an invitation to a strategic dinner, an ambassadorship, or largesse to a particular area of the country. Tribal big men amass wealth and then give away pigs. Successful American politicians also dish out "pork."

As with the big man, eloquence and communication skills contribute to political success (e.g., Barack Obama, Bill Clinton, and Ronald Reagan), although lack of such skills isn't necessarily fatal (e.g., either President Bush). What about physical fitness? Hair, height, health (and even a nice smile) are certainly political advantages. Bravery, as demonstrated through distinguished military service, may help political careers, but it certainly isn't required. Nor does it guarantee success. Just ask John McCain, or John Kerry. Supernatural powers? Candidates who proclaim themselves atheists are as rare as self-identified witches—or not witches. Almost all political candidates claim to belong to a mainstream religion. Some even present their candidacies or policies as promoting God's will. However, contemporary politics isn't just about personality, as big man systems are. We live in a state-organized, stratified society with inherited wealth, power, and privilege, all of which have political implications. As is typical of states, inheritance and kin connections play a role in political success. Just think of Kennedys, Bushes, and Clintons.

Anthropologists share with political scientists an interest in political systems, power, and politics. Here again, however, the anthropological approach is global and comparative and includes nonstates, while political scientists tend to focus on contemporary and recent nation-states (see Kamrava 2008). Anthropological studies have revealed substantial variation in power, authority, and legal systems in different societies. (**Power** is the ability to exercise one's will over others; *authority* is the formal, socially approved use of power, e.g., by government officials.) (See Kurtz 2001; Lewellen 2003; Nugent and Vincent 2004; Schwartz, Turner, and Tuden 2011; Wolf with Silverman 2001.)

## WHAT IS "THE POLITICAL"?

Morton Fried offered the following definition of political organization:

> Political organization comprises those portions of social organization that specifically relate to the individuals or groups that manage the affairs of public policy or seek to control the appointment or activities of those individuals or groups. (Fried 1967, pp. 20–21)

This definition certainly fits contemporary North America. Under "individuals or groups that manage the affairs of public policy" come various agencies and levels of government. Those who seek to influence public policy include political parties, unions, corporations, lobbyists, activists, political action committees (including superpacs), religious groups, and nongovernmental organizations (NGOs).

Fried's definition is less applicable to nonstates, where it's often difficult to detect any "public policy." For this reason, I prefer to speak of *socio*political organization in discussing the exercise of power and the regulation of relations among groups and their representatives. Political regulation includes such processes as decision making, dispute management, and conflict resolution. The study of political regulation draws our attention to those who make decisions and resolve conflicts (are there formal leaders?).

## TYPES AND TRENDS

Ethnographic and archaeological studies in hundreds of places have revealed many correlations between the economy and social and political organization. Decades ago, the anthropologist Elman Service (1962) listed four types, or levels, of political organization: band, tribe, chiefdom, and state. Today, none of the first three types can be studied as a self-contained form of political organization, because all now exist within nation-states and are subject to state control (see Ferguson 2003). There is archaeological evidence for early bands, tribes, and chiefdoms that existed before the first states appeared. However, because anthropology came into being long after the origin of the state, anthropologists never have been able to observe "in the flesh" a band, tribe, or chiefdom outside the influence of some state. There still may be local political leaders (e.g., village heads) and regional figures (e.g., chiefs) of the sort discussed in this chapter, but all now exist and function within the context of state organization.

A *band* is a small, kin-based group (all its members are related by kinship or marriage) found among foragers. **Tribes** have economies based on horticulture and pastoralism. Living in villages and organized into kin groups based on common descent (clans and lineages), tribes have no formal government and no reliable means of enforcing political

Participants in a labor rally hold up signs and posters in Santa Fe, New Mexico. As anthropologist Margaret Mead once observed about political mobilization, small groups of committed citizens have the capacity to change the world.

decisions. *Chiefdom* refers to a form of sociopolitical organization intermediate between the tribe and the state. In chiefdoms, social relations were based mainly on kinship, marriage, descent, age, generation, and gender—just as in bands and tribes. However, although chiefdoms were kin based, they featured **differential access** to resources (some people had more wealth, prestige, and power than others did) and a permanent political structure. The *state* is a form of sociopolitical organization based on a formal government structure and socioeconomic stratification.

The four labels in Service's typology are much too simple to account for the full range of political diversity and complexity known to archaeology and ethnography. We'll see, for instance, that tribes have varied widely in their political systems and institutions. Nevertheless, Service's typology does highlight some significant contrasts in political organization, especially those between states and nonstates. For example, in bands and tribes—unlike states, which have clearly visible governments—political organization did not stand out as separate and distinct from the total social order. In bands and tribes, it was difficult to characterize an act or event as political rather than merely social.

Service's labels "band," "tribe," "chiefdom," and "state" are categories or types within a *sociopolitical typology*. These types are associated with particular adaptive strategies or economic systems. Thus, foragers (an economic type) tended to have band organization (a sociopolitical type). Similarly, many horticulturalists and pastoralists lived in tribes. Although most chiefdoms had farming

**power**
The ability to exercise one's will over others.

**differential access**
Favored access to resources by superordinates over subordinates.

**tribe**
Food-producing society with rudimentary political structure.

economies, herding was important in some Middle Eastern chiefdoms. Nonindustrial states usually had an agricultural base.

Food production led to larger, denser populations and more complex economies than was the case among foragers. Many sociopolitical trends reflect the increased regulatory demands associated with cultivation and herding. Archaeologists have studied these trends through time, and cultural anthropologists have observed them among more recent, including contemporary, groups (see Shore, Wright, and Però 2011).

## BANDS AND TRIBES

This chapter discusses a series of societies, as case studies with different political systems. A common set of questions will be addressed for each one. What kinds of social groups does the society have? How do those groups represent themselves to each other? How are their internal and external relations regulated?

## Foraging Bands

Modern hunter-gatherers are today's remnants of foraging band societies. The strong ties they now maintain with sociopolitical groups outside the band make them markedly different from Stone Age hunter-gatherers. Modern foragers live in nation-states and an interlinked world. The pygmies of Congo, for example, have for generations shared a social world and economic exchanges with their neighbors who are cultivators. All foragers now trade with food producers. In addition, most contemporary hunter-gatherers rely on governments and on missionaries for at least part of what they consume.

### The San

San speakers ("Bushmen") of southern Africa have been influenced by Bantu speakers (farmers and herders) for 2,000 years and by Europeans for centuries. Edwin Wilmsen (1989) contends that many San descend from herders who were pushed into the desert by poverty or oppression. He sees the San today as a rural underclass in a larger political and economic system dominated by Europeans and Bantu food producers. Within this system, many San now tend cattle for wealthier Bantu rather than foraging independently. San also have their own domesticated animals, further illustrating their movement away from a foraging lifestyle.

Susan Kent (1992, 1996, 2002) noted a tendency to stereotype foragers, to treat them all as alike. They used to be stereotyped as isolated, primitive survivors of the Stone Age. A new, and more accurate, view of contemporary foragers sees them as groups forced into marginal environments by states, colonialism, and world events.

Kent (1996, 2002) focused on variation among foragers, describing considerable diversity in time and space among the San. The nature of San life has changed considerably since the 1950s and 1960s, when a series of anthropologists from Harvard University, including Richard B. Lee, embarked on a systematic study of their lives. Studying the San over time, Lee and others have documented many changes (see Lee 1979, 1984, 2003, 2012; Silberbauer 1981; Tanaka 1980). Such longitudinal research monitors variation in time, while fieldwork in many San areas has revealed variation in space. One of the most important contrasts is between settled (sedentary) and nomadic groups (Kent and Vierich 1989). Although sedentism has increased substantially in recent years, some San groups (along rivers) have been sedentary for generations. Others, including the Dobe Ju/'hoansi San studied by Lee (1984, 2003) and the Kutse San whom Kent studied, have retained more of the hunter-gatherer lifestyle.

To the extent that foraging continues to be their subsistence base, groups like the San can illustrate links between a foraging economy and other aspects of life in bands. For example, San groups that still are mobile, or that were so until recently, emphasize social, political, and gender equality, which are traditional band characteristics. A social system based on kinship, reciprocity, and sharing is appropriate for an economy with few people and limited resources. People have to share meat when they get it; otherwise, it rots. The nomadic pursuit of wild plants and animals tends to discourage permanent settlement, wealth accumulation, and status distinctions.

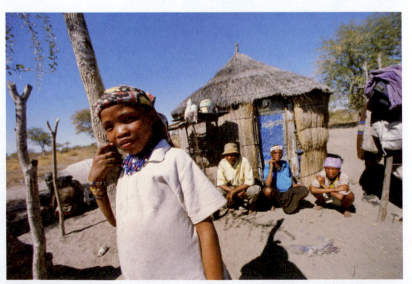

Among tropical foragers, women make an important economic contribution through gathering, as is true among the San shown here in Namibia. What evidence do you see in this photo that contemporary foragers participate in the modern world system?

**FIGURE 17.1** Location of the Inuit.

In the past, foraging bands—small nomadic or seminomadic social units—formed seasonally when component nuclear families got together. The particular families might vary from year to year. Marriage and kinship created ties between members of different bands. Trade and visiting also linked them. Band leaders were leaders in name only. In such an *egalitarian* society, they were first among equals (see Solway 2006). Sometimes they gave advice or made decisions, but they had no way to enforce those decisions. Because of the spread of states and globalization, it is increasingly difficult for ethnographers to find and observe such patterns of band organization.

### The Inuit

The aboriginal Inuit (Hoebel 1954, 1954/1968), another group of foragers, provide a classic example of methods of settling disputes—**conflict resolution**—in stateless societies. All societies have ways of settling disputes (of variable effectiveness) along with cultural rules or norms about proper and improper behavior. *Norms* are cultural standards or guidelines that enable individuals to distinguish between appropriate and inappropriate behavior in a given society (N. C. Kottak 2002). While rules and norms are cultural universals, only state societies, those with established governments, have laws that are formulated, proclaimed, and enforced (see Donovan 2007).

Foragers lacked formal **law** in the sense of a legal code with trial and enforcement, but they did have methods of social control and dispute settlement. The absence of law did not mean total anarchy. As described by E. A. Hoebel (1954) in a classic ethnographic study of conflict resolution, a sparse population of some 20,000 Inuit spanned 6,000 miles (9,500 kilometers) of the Arctic region (Figure 17.1). The most significant social groups were the nuclear family and the band. Personal relationships linked the families and bands. Some bands had headmen. There also were shamans (part-time religious specialists). However, these positions conferred little power on those who occupied them.

**law**
Legal code of a state society, with trial and enforcement.

**conflict resolution**
Means of settling disputes.

Hunting and fishing by men were the primary Inuit subsistence activities. The diverse and abundant plant foods available in warmer areas, where female labor in gathering is important, were absent in the Arctic. Traveling on land and sea in a bitter environment, Inuit men faced more dangers than women did. The traditional male role took its toll in lives, so that adult women outnumbered men. This permitted some men to have two or three wives. The ability to support more than one wife conferred a certain amount of prestige, but it also encouraged envy. (*Prestige* is social esteem, respect, or approval.) If a man seemed to be taking additional wives just to enhance his reputation, a rival was likely to steal one of them. Most Inuit disputes were between men and originated over women, caused by wife stealing or adultery.

A jilted husband had several options. He could try to kill the wife stealer. However, if he succeeded, one of his rival's kinsmen surely would try to kill him in retaliation. One dispute might escalate into several deaths as relatives avenged a succession of murders. No government existed to intervene and stop such a *blood feud* (a murderous feud between families). However, one also could challenge a rival to a song battle. In a public setting, contestants made up insulting songs about each other. At the end of the match, the audience proclaimed the winner. However, if the winner was the man whose wife had been stolen, there was no guarantee she would return. Often she stayed with her abductor.

Thefts are common in societies with marked property differentials, like our own, but thefts are uncommon among foragers. Each Inuit had access to the resources he or she needed to sustain life. Every man could hunt, fish, and make the tools necessary for subsistence. Every woman could obtain the materials needed to make clothing, prepare food, and do domestic work. Inuit men could even hunt and fish in the territories of other local groups. There was no notion of private ownership of territory or animals.

## Tribal Cultivators

As is true of foraging bands, there are no totally autonomous tribes in today's world. Still, there are societies, for example, in Papua New Guinea and in South America's tropical forests, in which tribal principles continue to operate. Tribes typically have a horticultural or pastoral economy and are organized into villages and/or *descent groups* (kin groups whose members trace descent from a common ancestor). Tribes lack socioeconomic stratification (i.e., a class structure) and a formal government of their own. A few tribes still conduct small-scale warfare, in the form of intervillage raiding. Tribes have more effective regulatory mechanisms than foragers do, but tribal societies have no sure means of enforcing political decisions. The main regulatory officials are village heads, "big men," descent-group

leaders, village councils, and leaders of pantribal associations. All these figures and groups have limited authority.

Like foragers, horticulturalists tend to be egalitarian, although some have marked *gender stratification*: an unequal distribution of resources, power, prestige, and personal freedom between men and women. Horticultural villages usually are small, with low population density and open access to strategic resources. Age, gender, and personal traits determine how much respect people receive and how much support they get from others. Egalitarianism diminishes, however, as village size and population density increase. Horticultural villages usually have headmen—rarely, if ever, headwomen.

## The Village Head

The Yanomami (Chagnon 1997, 2013; Ferguson 1995; Ramos 1995) are Native Americans who live in southern Venezuela and the adjacent part of Brazil. When anthropologists first studied them, they numbered about 26,000 people, living in 200 to 250 widely scattered villages, each with a population between 40 and 250. The Yanomami are horticulturalists who also hunt and gather. Their staple crops are bananas and plantains (a banana-like crop). There are more significant social groups among the Yanomami than exist in a foraging society. The Yanomami have families, villages, and descent groups. Their descent groups, which span more than one village, are patrilineal (ancestry is traced back through males only) and exogamous (people must marry outside their own descent group). However, branches of two different descent groups may live in the same village and intermarry.

Traditionally among the Yanomami the only leadership position has been that of **village head** (always a man). His authority, like that of a foraging band's leader, is severely limited. If a headman wants something done, he must lead by example and persuasion. The headman lacks the right to issue orders. He can only persuade, harangue, and try to influence public opinion. For example, if he wants people to clean up the central plaza in preparation for a feast, he must start sweeping it himself, hoping his covillagers will take the hint and relieve him.

When conflict erupts within the village, the headman may be called on as a mediator who listens to both sides. He will give an opinion and advice. If a disputant is unsatisfied, the headman has no power to back his decisions and no way to impose punishments. Like the band leader, he is first among equals.

A Yanomami village headman also must lead in generosity. Expected to be more generous than any other villager, he cultivates more land. His garden provides much of the food consumed when his village hosts a feast for another village. The headman represents the village in its dealings with outsiders, including Venezuelan and Brazilian government agents.

**village head**
Local tribal leader with limited authority.

The way someone acts as headman depends on his personal traits and the number of supporters he can muster. Napoleon Chagnon (1997) describes how one village headman, Kaobawa, guaranteed safety to a delegation from a village with which a covillager of his wanted to start a war. Kaobawa was a particularly effective headman. He had demonstrated his fierceness in battle, but he also knew how to use diplomacy to avoid offending other villagers. No one in his village had a better personality for the headmanship. Nor (because Kaobawa had many brothers) did anyone have more supporters. Among the Yanomami, when a village is dissatisfied with its headman, its members can leave and found a new village. This happens from time to time and is called *village fissioning*.

With its many villages and descent groups, Yanomami sociopolitical organization is more complicated than that of a band-organized society. The Yanomami face more problems in regulating relations between groups and individuals. Although a headman sometimes can prevent a specific violent act, intervillage raiding has been a feature of some areas of Yanomami territory, particularly those studied by Chagnon (1997, 2013).

It's important to recognize as well that the Yanomami are not isolated from outside events. They live in two nation-states, Venezuela and Brazil, and attacks by outsiders, especially Brazilian ranchers and miners, have plagued them (Chagnon 1997; *Cultural Survival Quarterly* 1989; Ferguson 1995). During a Brazilian gold rush between 1987 and 1991, one Yanomami died each day, on average, from such attacks. By 1991, there were some 40,000 miners in the Brazilian Yanomami homeland. Some Yanomami were killed outright. The miners introduced new diseases, and the swollen population ensured that old diseases became epidemic. In 1991, the American Anthropological Association reported on the plight of the Yanomami (*Anthropology Newsletter*, September 1991). Brazilian Yanomami were dying at a rate of 10 percent annually, and their fertility rate had dropped to zero. Since then, one Brazilian president has declared a huge Yanomami territory off limits to outsiders. Unfortunately, local politicians, miners, and ranchers have managed to evade the ban. The future of the Yanomami remains uncertain (see Romero 2008).

## The "Big Man"

Many societies of the South Pacific, particularly on the Melanesian Islands and in Papua New Guinea, had a kind of political leader that we call the big man. The **big man** (almost always a male) was an elaborate version of the village head, but with one significant difference. Unlike the village head, whose leadership was limited to one village, the big man had supporters in several villages. The big man thus was a regulator of regional political organization.

**FIGURE 17.2** Location of the Kapauku.

Consider the Kapauku Papuans, inhabitants of Irian Jaya, Indonesia (located on the island of New Guinea) (see Figure 17.2.). Anthropologist Leopold Pospisil (1963) studied the Kapauku (then 45,000 people), who grew crops (with the sweet potato as their staple) and raised pigs. Their cultivation system was too labor-intensive to be described as simple horticulture. It required mutual aid in turning the soil before planting. The digging of long drainage ditches, which a big man often helped organize, was even more complex. Kapauku cultivation supported a larger and denser population than does the simpler horticulture of the Yanomami. The Kapauku economy required collective cultivation and political regulation of the more complex tasks.

The key political figure among the Kapauku was the big man. Known as a *tonowi*, he achieved his status through hard work, amassing wealth in the form of pigs and other native riches. The achieved status of big man rested on certain characteristics that distinguished him from his fellows. Key attributes included wealth, generosity, eloquence, physical fitness, bravery, supernatural powers, and the ability to gain the support and loyalty of others. Men became big men because they had certain personalities; they did not inherit their status but created

**big man**
Generous tribal entrepreneur with multivillage support.

The "big man," like this one from highland Papua New Guinea, persuades people to organize feasts, which distribute pork and wealth. Big men owe their status to their individual personalities rather than to inherited wealth or position. Does our society have equivalents of big men?

it through hard work and good judgment. Wealth resulted from successful pig breeding and trading. As a man's pig herd and prestige grew, he attracted supporters. He sponsored pig feasts in which pork (provided by the big man and his supporters) was distributed to guests, bringing him more prestige and widening his network of support.

The big man's supporters, recognizing his past favors and anticipating future rewards, recognized him as a leader and accepted his decisions as binding. The *tonowi* was an important regulator of regional events in Kapauku life. He helped determine the dates for feasts and markets. He initiated economic projects requiring the cooperation of a regional community.

The Kapauku big man again exemplifies a generalization about leadership in tribal societies: If someone achieves wealth and widespread respect and support, he or she must be generous. The big man worked hard not to hoard wealth but to be able to give away the fruits of his labor, to convert wealth into prestige and gratitude. A stingy big man would lose his support. Selfish and greedy big men sometimes were murdered by their fellows (Zimmer-Tamakoshi 1997).

## Pantribal Sodalities

Big men could forge regional political organization, albeit temporarily, by mobilizing supporters from several villages. Other principles in tribal societies—such as a belief in common ancestry, kinship, or descent—could be used to link local groups within a region. The same descent group, for example, might span several villages, and its dispersed members might recognize the same leader.

Principles other than kinship also can link local groups, especially in modern societies. People who live in different parts of the same nation may belong to the same labor union, sorority or fraternity, political party, or religious denomination. In tribes, nonkin groups called *associations* or *sodalities* may serve a similar linking function. Often, sodalities are based on common age or gender, with all-male sodalities more common than all-female ones.

**Pantribal sodalities** are groups that extend across the whole tribe, spanning several villages. Such sodalities were especially likely to develop in situations of warfare with a neighboring tribe. Mobilizing their members from multiple villages within the same tribe, pantribal sodalities could assemble a force to attack or retaliate against another tribe.

The best examples of pantribal sodalities come from the Central Plains of North America and from tropical Africa. During the 18th and 19th centuries, Native American populations of the Great Plains of the United States and Canada experienced a rapid growth of pantribal sodalities. This development reflected an economic change that followed the spread of horses, which had been reintroduced to the Americas by the Spanish, to the area between the Rocky Mountains and the Mississippi River. Many Plains Indian societies changed their adaptive strategies because of the horse. At first they had been foragers who hunted bison (buffalo) on foot. Later they adopted a mixed economy based on hunting, gathering, and horticulture. Finally, they changed to a much more specialized economy based on horseback hunting of bison (eventually with rifles).

As the Plains tribes were undergoing these changes, other tribes also adopted horseback hunting and moved into the Plains. Attempting to occupy the same area, groups came into conflict. A pattern of warfare developed in which the members of one tribe raided another, usually for horses. The economy demanded that people follow the movement of the bison herds. During the winter, when the bison dispersed, a tribe fragmented into small bands and families. In the summer, when huge herds assembled on the Plains, the tribe reunited. They camped together for social, political, and religious activities, but mainly for communal bison hunting.

Two activities demanded strong leadership: organizing and carrying out raids on enemy camps (to capture horses) and managing the summer bison hunt. All the Plains societies developed pantribal sodalities, and leadership roles within them, to police the summer hunt. Leaders coordinated hunting efforts, making sure that people did not cause a stampede with an early shot or an ill-advised action. Leaders imposed severe penalties, including seizure of a culprit's wealth, for disobedience.

Many tribes that adopted this Plains strategy of adaptation had once been foragers for whom hunting and gathering had been individual or small-group affairs. They never had come together previously as a single social unit. Age and gender were available as social principles that could quickly and

Natives of the Great Plains of North America originally hunted bison (buffalo) on foot, using the bow and arrow. The introduction of horses and rifles fueled a pattern of horse raiding and warfare. How far had the change gone, as depicted in this painting?

efficiently forge unrelated people into pantribal sodalities.

Raiding of one tribe by another, this time for cattle rather than horses, also was common in eastern and southeastern Africa, where pantribal sodalities also developed. Among the pastoral Masai of Kenya, men born during the same four-year period were circumcised together and belonged to the same named group, an *age set,* throughout their lives. The sets moved through *age grades,* the most important of which was the warrior grade. Members of a set felt a strong allegiance to one another. Masai women lacked comparable set organization, but they also passed through culturally recognized age grades: the initiate, the married woman, and the female elder.

In certain parts of western and central Africa, pantribal sodalities are secret societies, made up exclusively of men or women. Like our college fraternities and sororities, these associations have secret initiation ceremonies. Among the Mende of Sierra Leone, men's and women's secret societies were very influential. The men's group, the Poro, trained boys in social conduct, ethics, and religion and it supervised political and economic activities. Leadership roles in the Poro often overshadowed village headship and played an important part in social control, dispute management, and tribal political regulation. Age, gender, and ritual can link members of different local groups into a single social collectivity in a tribe and thus create a sense of ethnic identity, of belonging to the same cultural tradition.

## Nomadic Politics

Herders have varied political systems. Unlike the Masai (just discussed) and other tribal herders, some pastoralists have chiefs and live in nation-states. The scope of political authority among pastoralists expands considerably as regulatory problems increase in densely populated regions (see Salzman 2008). Consider two Iranian pastoral nomadic

Among the Masai of Kenya and Tanzania, men born during the same four-year period belonged to the same named group, an age set, throughout their lives. The sets moved through grades, of which the most important was the warrior grade. Shown here is the *eunoto* ceremony in which young men become senior warriors and are allowed to choose wives.

**FIGURE 17.3**   Location of the Basseri and Qashqai.

tribes—the Basseri and the Qashqai (Salzman 1974). Starting each year from a plateau near the coast, these groups took their animals to grazing land 17,000 feet (5,400 meters) above sea level (see Figure 17.3).

The Basseri and the Qashqai shared this route with each other and with several other ethnic groups. Use of the same pastureland at different times of year was carefully scheduled. Ethnic-group movements were tightly coordinated. Expressing this schedule is *il-rah,* a concept common to all Iranian nomads. A group's *il-rah* is its customary path in time and space. It is the schedule, different for each group, of when specific areas can be used in the annual trek.

Each tribe had its own leader, known as the *khan* or *il-khan.* The Basseri *khan,* because he dealt with a smaller population, faced fewer problems in coordinating its movements than did the leaders of the Qashqai. Correspondingly, his rights, privileges, duties, and authority were weaker. Nevertheless, his authority exceeded that of any political figure discussed so far. The *khan*'s authority still came from his personal traits rather than from his office. That is, the Basseri followed a particular *khan* not because of a political position he happened to fill but because of their personal allegiance and loyalty to him as a man. The *khan* relied on the support of the heads of the descent groups into which Basseri society was divided.

Among the Qashqai, however, allegiance shifted from the person to the office. The Qashqai had multiple levels of authority and more powerful chiefs or *khans.* Managing 400,000 people required a complex hierarchy. Heading it was the *il-khan,* helped by a deputy, under whom were the heads of constituent tribes, under each of whom were descent-group heads.

A case illustrates just how developed the Qashqai authority structure was. A hailstorm prevented some nomads from joining the annual migration at the appointed time. Although all the nomads recognized

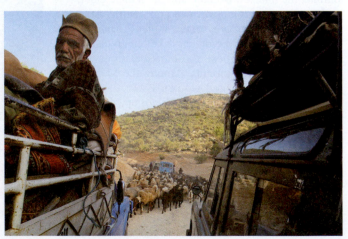

The Qashqai are pastoral nomads who traditionally trekked about 300 miles (480 kilometers) from highland summer pastures to lowland winter pastures near the Persian Gulf. The traditional migration is shown on the left; the modern trek, incorporating motor vehicles, on the right.

that they were not responsible for their delay, the *il-khan* assigned them less favorable grazing land, for that year only, in place of their usual pasture. The tardy herders and other Qashqai considered the judgment fair and didn't question it. Thus, Qashqai authorities regulated the annual migration. They also adjudicated disputes between people, tribes, and descent groups.

These Iranian cases illustrate the fact that pastoralism often is just one among many specialized economic activities within a nation-state. As part of a larger whole, pastoral tribes are constantly pitted against other ethnic groups. In these nations, the state becomes a final authority, a higher-level regulator that attempts to limit conflict between ethnic groups. State organization arose not just to manage agricultural economies but also to regulate the activities of ethnic groups within expanding social and economic systems (see Das and Poole 2004).

# CHIEFDOMS

The first states emerged in the Old World around 5,500 years ago. The first chiefdoms had developed perhaps a thousand years earlier, but few survive today. In many parts of the world, the chiefdom was a transitional form of organization that emerged during the evolution of tribes into states. State formation began in Mesopotamia (currently Iran and Iraq). It next occurred in Egypt, the Indus Valley of Pakistan and India, and northern China. A few thousand years later states arose in two parts of the Western Hemisphere—Mesoamerica (Mexico, Guatemala, Belize) and the central Andes (Peru and Bolivia). Early states are known as archaic, or nonindustrial, states, in contrast to modern industrial nation-states. Robert Carneiro defines the state as "an autonomous

political unit encompassing many communities within its territory, having a centralized government with the power to collect taxes, draft men for work or war, and decree and enforce laws" (1970, p. 733).

The chiefdom and the state, like many categories used by social scientists, are ideal types. That is, they are labels that make social contrasts seem sharper than they really are. In reality there is a continuum from tribe to chiefdom to state. Some societies had many attributes of chiefdoms but retained tribal features. Some advanced chiefdoms had many attributes of archaic states and thus are difficult to assign to either category. Recognizing this "continuous change" (Johnson and Earle 2000), some anthropologists speak of "complex chiefdoms" (Earle 1987, 1997), which are almost states.

## Political and Economic Systems

Geographic areas where chiefdoms existed included the circum-Caribbean (e.g., Caribbean islands, Panama, Colombia), lowland Amazonia, what is now the southeastern United States, and Polynesia. Chiefdoms created the megalithic cultures of Europe, including the one that built Stonehenge. Bear in mind that chiefdoms and states can fall (disintegrate) as well as rise. Before Rome's expansion, much of Europe was organized at the chiefdom level, to which it reverted for centuries after the fall of Rome in the fifth century C.E. Much of our ethnographic knowledge about chiefdoms comes from Polynesia (Kirch 2000), where they were common at the time of European exploration. In chiefdoms, social relations are mainly based on kinship, marriage, descent, age, generation, and gender—as they are in bands and tribes. This is a basic difference between chiefdoms and states. States bring nonrelatives together and oblige them to pledge allegiance to a government.

Unlike bands and tribes, however, chiefdoms administer a clear-cut and permanent regional political system. Chiefdoms may include thousands of people living in many villages or hamlets. Regulation is carried out by the chief and his or her assistants, who occupy political offices. An **office** is a permanent position, which must be refilled when it is vacated by death or retirement. Because official vacancies are filled systematically, the political system that is the chiefdom endures across the generations, thus ensuring permanent political regulation.

Polynesian chiefs were full-time specialists whose duties included managing the economy. They regulated production by commanding or prohibiting (using religious taboos) the cultivation of certain lands and crops. Chiefs also regulated distribution and consumption. At certain seasons—often on a ritual occasion, such as a first-fruit ceremony—people would offer part of their harvest to the chief through his or her representatives. Products moved up

**office**
Permanent political position.

Chiefdoms as widespread as Mexico's Olmecs, England's Stonehenge, and Polynesia's Easter Island (Rapanui) are famed for their major works in stone. The statues shown here are Easter Island's major tourist attraction.

the hierarchy, eventually reaching the chief. Conversely, illustrating obligatory sharing with kin, chiefs sponsored feasts at which they gave back some of what they had received. Unlike big men, chiefs were exempt from ordinary work and had rights and privileges unavailable to the masses. Like big men, however, they still returned a portion of the wealth they took in.

Such a flow of resources to and then from a central place is known as *chiefly redistribution,* which offers economic advantages. If different parts of the chiefdom specialized in particular products, chiefly redistribution made those products available to the entire society. Chiefly redistribution also helped stimulate production beyond the basic subsistence level and provided a central storehouse for goods that might become scarce in times of famine (Earle 1987, 1997).

## Status Systems

Social status in chiefdoms was based on seniority of descent. Polynesian chiefs kept extremely long genealogies. Some chiefs (without writing) managed to trace their ancestry back dozens of generations. All the people in the chiefdom were thought to be related to one another. Presumably, all were descended from a group of founding ancestors.

An outdoor portrait of a Maori chief at the Polynesian Cultural Center in Hawaii. Both Hawaii and New Zealand, where the Maori live, were sites of traditional Polynesian chiefdoms. How do chiefs differ from ordinary people?

**wealth**
All a person's material assets; basis of economic status.

The status of chief was ascribed, based on seniority of descent. The chief would be the oldest child (usually son) of the oldest child of the oldest child, and so on. Degrees of seniority were calculated so intricately on some islands that there were as many ranks as people. For example, the third son would rank below the second, who in turn would rank below the first. The children of an eldest brother, however, would all rank above the children of the next brother, whose children in turn would outrank those of younger brothers. However, even the lowest-ranking man or woman in a chiefdom was still the chief's relative. In such a kin-based context, everyone, even a chief, had to share with his or her relatives. Because everyone had a slightly different status, it was difficult to draw a line between elites and common people. Other chiefdoms calculated seniority differently and had shorter genealogies than did those in Polynesia. Still, the concern for seniority and the lack of sharp gaps between elites and commoners are features of all chiefdoms.

The status systems of chiefdoms, as of states, were associated with differential access to resources. Some men and women had privileged access to power, prestige, and wealth. They controlled strategic resources, such as land and water. Earle characterizes chiefs as "an incipient aristocracy with advantages in wealth and lifestyle" (1987, p. 290).

Compared with chiefdoms, archaic states drew a much firmer line between elites and masses, distinguishing at least between nobles and commoners. Kinship ties did not extend from the nobles to the commoners because of stratum endogamy—marriage within one's own group. Commoners married commoners; elites married elites.

## The Emergence of Stratification

The status system of a chiefdom differed from that of a state because of the chiefdom's kinship basis. In the context of differential wealth and power, the chiefly type of status system didn't last very long. Chiefs would start acting like kings and try to erode the kinship basis of the chiefdom. In Madagascar they would do this by demoting their more distant relatives to commoner status and banning marriage between nobles and commoners (Kottak 1980). Such moves, if accepted by the society, created separate social strata—unrelated groups that differ in their access to wealth, prestige, and power. (A *stratum* is one of two or more groups that contrast in social status and access to strategic resources. Each stratum includes people of both genders and all ages.) The creation of separate social strata is called *stratification,* and its emergence signified the transition from chiefdom to state. The presence of stratification is one of the key distinguishing features of a state.

The influential sociologist Max Weber (1922/1968) defined three related dimensions of social stratification: (1) Economic status, or **wealth,** encompasses

## TABLE 17.1 Max Weber's Three Dimensions of Stratification

| | | |
|---|---|---|
| wealth | => | economic status |
| power | => | political status |
| prestige | => | social status |

all a person's material assets, including income, land, and other types of property. (2) *Power*, the ability to exercise one's will over others—to get what one wants—is the basis of political status. (3) **Prestige**—the basis of social status—refers to esteem, respect, or approval for acts, deeds, or qualities considered exemplary. Prestige, or "cultural capital" (Bourdieu 1984), gives people a sense of worth and respect, which they may often convert into economic advantage (Table 17.1).

In archaic states—for the first time in human evolution—there were contrasts in wealth, power, and prestige between entire groups (social strata) of men and women. Each stratum included people of both genders and all ages. The **superordinate** (higher or elite) stratum had privileged access to valued resources. Access to those resources by members of the **subordinate** (lower or underprivileged) stratum was limited by the privileged group.

## STATE SYSTEMS

Recap 17.1 summarizes the information presented so far on bands, tribes, chiefdoms, and states. States, remember, are autonomous political units with social strata and a formal government. States tend to be large and populous, and certain statuses, systems, and subsystems with specialized functions are found in all states (see Sharma and Gupta 2006). They include the following:

1. Population control: fixing of boundaries, establishment of citizenship categories, and censusing.
2. Judiciary: laws, legal procedure, and judges.

This 2013 Spanish lottery winner celebrates a first place prize. Do lottery winners usually gain prestige, or merely money, as a result of their luck?

3. Enforcement: permanent military and police forces.
4. Fiscal support: taxation.

In archaic states, these subsystems were integrated by a ruling system or government composed of civil, military, and religious officials (Fried 1960). Let's look at the four subsystems one by one.

## Population Control

To keep track of whom they govern, states conduct censuses. A state demarcates boundaries to separate that state from other societies. Customs agents, immigration officers, navies, and coast guards patrol frontiers. States also regulate population through administrative subdivision: provinces, districts, "states," counties, subcounties, and parishes. Lower-level officials manage the populations and territories of the subdivisions.

States often promote geographic mobility and resettlement, severing longstanding ties among people, land, and kin (Smith 2003). Population displacements have increased with globalization and as war, famine, and job seeking churn up migratory currents. People in states come to identify themselves by new

**prestige**
Esteem, respect, or approval.

**superordinate**
Upper, privileged group in a stratified society.

**subordinate**
Lower, underprivileged group in a stratified society.

## RECAP 17.1 Economic Basis of and Political Regulation in Bands, Tribes, Chiefdoms, and States

| SOCIOPOLITICAL TYPE | ECONOMIC TYPE | EXAMPLES | TYPE OF REGULATION |
|---|---|---|---|
| Band | Foraging | Inuit, San | Local |
| Tribe | Horticulture, pastoralism | Yanomami, Kapauku, Masai | Local, temporary regional |
| Chiefdom | Productive horticulture, pastoral nomadism, agriculture | Qashqal, Polynesia, Cherokee | Permanent regional |
| State | Agriculture, industrialism | Ancient Mesopotamia, contemporary United States and Canada | Permanent regional |

statuses, both ascribed and achieved—including residence, ethnicity, occupation, political party, religion, and team or club affiliation—rather than only as members of a descent group or an extended family.

States also manage their populations by granting different rights and obligations to citizens and noncitizens. Status distinctions among citizens also are common. Archaic states granted different rights to nobles, commoners, and slaves. In American history prior to the Emancipation Proclamation, there were different laws for enslaved and free people. In European colonies, separate courts judged cases involving only natives and cases involving Europeans. In contemporary America, a military judiciary coexists alongside the civil system.

## Judiciary

All states have laws based on precedent and legislative proclamations. Without writing, laws may be preserved in oral tradition. Crimes are violations of the legal code ("breaking the law"), with specified types of punishment. To handle crimes and disputes, all states have courts and judges (see Donovan 2007).

A striking contrast between states and nonstates is intervention in family affairs. Governments step in to halt blood feuds and regulate previously private disputes. States attempt to curb internal conflict, but they aren't always successful. About 85 percent of the world's armed conflicts since 1945 have begun within states—in efforts to overthrow a ruling regime or as disputes over ethnic, religious, or human rights issues (see Barnaby 1984; Chatterjee 2004; Nordstrom 2004; Tishkov 2004).

**fiscal**
Pertaining to finances and taxation.

To handle disputes and crimes, all states, including Bermuda, shown here, have courts and judges. Does this photo say anything about cultural diffusion and/or colonialism?

## Enforcement

All states have agents to enforce judicial decisions, for example, to impose punishments and collect fines. Confinement requires jailers. If there is a death penalty, executioners are needed. Government officials have the power to collect fines and confiscate property. The government attempts to suppress internal disorder (with police) and to guard against external threats (with the military and border officials). As described in this chapter's "Focus on Globalization," censorship is another tool that governments may employ to secure their authority.

Armies help states subdue and conquer neighboring nonstates, but this isn't the only reason state organization has spread. Although states impose hardships, they also offer advantages (see this chapter's "Appreciating Diversity" on p. 332 for some benefits government offers to peasants in rural Thailand). States have formal mechanisms designed to protect against external threats and to preserve internal order. When they are successful in promoting internal peace, states enhance production. Their economies can support massive, dense populations, which supply armies and colonists to promote expansion.

## Fiscal Support

States need financial, or **fiscal,** mechanisms (e.g., taxation) to support government officials and numerous other specialists. As in the chiefdom, the state intervenes in production, distribution, and consumption. The state may require a certain area to produce specific things, or ban certain activities in particular places. Like chiefdoms, states have redistribution ("spreading the wealth around"), but less of what comes in from the people actually goes back to the people.

In nonstates, people customarily share with their relatives, but citizens also have to turn over a substantial portion of what they produce to the state. Markets and trade usually are under at least some state oversight, with officials overseeing distribution and exchange, standardizing weights and measures, and collecting taxes on goods passing into or through the state. Of the revenues the state collects, it reallocates part for the general good and keeps another part (often larger) for itself—its agents and agencies. State organization doesn't bring more freedom or leisure to the common people, who may be conscripted to build monumental public works. Some projects, such as dams and irrigation systems, may be economically necessary, but residents of archaic states also had to build temples, palaces, and tombs for the elites. Those elites reveled in the consumption of sumptuary goods—jewelry, exotic food and drink, and stylish clothing reserved for, or affordable only by, the rich. Peasants' diets suffered as they struggled to meet government demands.

# focus on GLOBALIZATION

## The Political Role of New Media

Global forces often face roadblocks to their international spread. Although the Internet makes possible the instantaneous global transmission of information, many countries censor the Internet and other mass media for political or moral reasons. Cuba makes all unauthorized Internet surfing illegal. Many countries limit access to porn sites. China has a sophisticated censorship system—sometimes called the "Great Firewall of China." China's local search engine, Baidu, which observes Chinese censorship rules, dwarfs Google, Bing, and Yahoo in the Chinese market. As of 2013, despite censorship, China had almost twice the number of Internet users as the United States.

Censorship can be a barrier to international business. The World Trade Organization (WTO) favors freedom of access to the Internet for commercial reasons: to allow free trade. WTO rules allow member nations to restrict trade to protect public morals or ensure public order, but with the understanding that such restrictions will disrupt trade as little as possible.

If the Internet and other media are used to promote free trade, how about free thought? The media have the capacity to enlighten by providing users with unfamiliar information and viewpoints and by offering a forum for dissident voices. On the other hand, the media also spread and reinforce stereotypes and misinformation, and, in doing so, close people's minds to complexity.

The media also promote fear, which often is manipulated for political reasons. Waves of internationally transmitted images and information can reinforce the perception that the world is a dangerous place, with threats to security and order everywhere. Facebook, Twitter, YouTube, cell-phone and digital cameras, and cable/satellite TV link people across the globe. Constant and instantaneous reporting has blurred the distinction between the international, the national, and the local. Geographic distance is obscured, and risk perception is magnified, by the barrage of "bad news" received daily from so many places. Many people have no idea how far away the disasters and threats really are. Was that suspicious package found in Paris or Pasadena? Did that bomb go off in Mumbai or Michigan? Votes in Athens, Greece, or Rome, Italy, can affect the American stock market more than votes in Athens or Rome, Georgia.

The political manipulation of media is not new. (Think of book banning and burning, for example. See http://www.adlerbooks.com/banned.html for a list of books that have been banned at some time in the United States.) Would-be guardians of morality and authoritarian regimes always have sought to silence dissident voices. What is new is the potentially instantaneous and global reach of the voices that question authority. New media, including cell phones, Twitter, and YouTube, have been used to muster public opinion against authority figures in places as distant as Cairo, Egypt; Istanbul, Turkey; and Davis, California. Can you think of examples of how new media have been used to question authority?

---

Commoners perished in territorial wars that had little relevance to their own needs. Are any of these observations true of contemporary states?

## SOCIAL CONTROL

In studying political systems, anthropologists pay attention not only to the formal institutions but to other forms of social control as well. The concept of social control is broader than "the political." **Social control** refers to "those fields of the social system (beliefs, practices, and institutions) that are most actively involved in the maintenance of any norms and the regulation of any conflict" (N. C. Kottak 2002, p. 290). Norms are cultural standards or guidelines that enable individuals to distinguish between appropriate and inappropriate behavior.

Previous sections of this chapter have focused more on formal political organization than on sociopolitical process. We've seen how the scale and strength of political systems have expanded in relation to economic changes. We've examined means of conflict resolution, or their absence, in various types of society. We've looked at political decision making, including leaders and their limits. We've also recognized that all contemporary humans have been affected by states, colonialism, and the spread of the world system (see Shore, et al. 2011).

*Sociopolitical* was introduced as a key concept at the beginning of this chapter. So far, we've focused mainly on the political part of sociopolitical; now we focus on the social part. In this section we'll see that political systems have their informal, social, and subtle aspects along with their formal, governmental, and public dimensions.

## Hegemony and Resistance

Antonio Gramsci (1971) developed the concept of **hegemony** for a stratified social order in which subordinates comply with domination by internalizing their rulers' values and accepting the "naturalness" of domination (this is the way things were meant to be). According to Pierre Bourdieu (1977, p. 164), every social order tries to make its own arbitrariness (including its mechanisms of control and domination) seem natural and in everyone's

**social control**
Maintaining social norms and regulating conflict.

**hegemony**
Stratified social order in which subordinates accept hierarchy as "natural."

# appreciating DIVERSITY

## Globalization Spreads Political Power to the Countryside

The following news story discusses local-level politics in rural Thailand, which through globalization has experienced a dramatic social, economic, and political transformation. In July 2011, Thailand's empowered rural electorate played a key role in the landslide election of Yingluck Shinawatra as that country's first female prime minister. A series of opposition-led protests, mainly in urban areas, marked the years after her election. On May 7, 2014, Shinawatra was removed from office by Thailand's Constitutional Court after serving less than three years as Prime Minister. The stated reason for her dismissal was that she had unlawfully transferred a top security official soon after taking office. Although Ms. Shinawatra's political future remains uncertain, the rural-urban contrast in political preferences described here remains as strong as ever.

BAAN NONG TUN, Thailand—Smiling farmers knee deep in emerald rice paddies and shirtless children riding on the backs of mud-caked water buffalo. These are the romantic images of the Thai countryside. There is one problem with it, says Udom Thapsuri, a farmer here. . . . It does not exist anymore. . . .

As campaigning for the national election . . . entered its final days, there was broad consensus that rural votes would be crucial in deciding the outcome. But no one is quite sure what rural means anymore. Villagers here complain of slow Internet download speeds. . . . Residents tell of work stints in Taiwan, Singapore, Israel and Saudi Arabia. . . .

Villagers are now better educated, more mobile, less deferential and ultimately more politically demanding. . . . The old social contract, whereby power flowed from Bangkok and the political establishment could count on quiet acquiescence in the Thai countryside, has broken down.

Charles Keyes, . . . who first studied village life here nearly five decades ago, describes a transformation from "peasants to cosmopolitan villagers."

"There is a sense in Thai society that the social contract is being renegotiated," said Mr. Keyes, a professor emeritus of anthropology at the Univer-

U.S. President Barack Obama, left, and Thai Prime Minister Yingluck Shinawatra listen to national anthems during a welcome ceremony at the government house in Bangkok, Thailand on November 18, 2012.

sity of Washington. The convulsive changes to village life and the breakdown of a national political consensus are not just relevant to Thailand, but are a cautionary tale for other countries in Asia that are developing so rapidly, Mr. Keyes says. . . .

In the 1990s, as part of an effort to decentralize power, the government introduced a system of local councils, known as township administrative organizations.

The councils gave villagers a sense that they could control their own political destiny, said Mr. Udom. . . . The system has come with its disappointments—council budgets are strained and have shrunk in recent years—but the system has brought a greater sense of political intimacy than elections for the national Parliament in Bangkok. . . . "We have a lot more expectations," Mr. Udom said.

Those expectations were partly answered after the election a decade ago of the populist prime minister, Thaksin Shinawatra, whose power base was in rural areas. . . . Mr. Thaksin, a billionaire tycoon and thus a seemingly unlikely champion of the peasant class, managed to cement his popularity by introducing universal health care and funneling government funds into villages, where local officials decided how to distribute it.

When Mr. Thaksin's party was re-elected in 2005 by a wide margin, Mr. Keyes . . . remembers a villager's elation. "It used to be that the elite decided who was in power," Mr. Keyes remembers the villager saying. "Today we decide." But Mr. Thaksin's concentration of power—his critics would say his abuse of power—alienated many voters, especially the elite.

Mr. Thaksin faced large-scale street demonstrations in Bangkok against his rule and was overthrown in a military coup in 2006, polarizing the country. . . .

Mr. Thaksin's allies are trying once again to win power in the election Sunday with the tycoon's sister, Yingluck Shinawatra, as the candidate for prime minister. Ms. Yingluck, who is leading in the polls, is up against the party of Abhisit Vejjajiva, the current prime minister, who is allied with the military leadership and the Bangkok establishment. . . .

More than two-thirds of Thailand's population lives in rural areas. . . . But migrations in recent decades have blurred the distinction between countryside and city. . . .

Technology has brought great changes to many parts of the world in recent decades, but the pace of change has been particularly breathless in the Thai countryside.

Five decades ago, Mr. Keyes . . . witnessed isolated, self-sufficient villages where farmers grew their own food and rarely used money because they counted on their neighbors to help with farm work. . . . There was no electricity, piped water or telephone service. . . .

Today, Baan Nong Tun is plugged into the rest of Thailand by television, radio and the Internet. . . .

The generation gap—from peasant to cosmopolitan villager—is evident in villagers' hands. Mr. Udom's calloused fingers are swollen by years of farm work. Younger people have the soft, thin fingers of city dwellers. . . .

interest. Often promises are made (things will get better if you're patient).

Both Bourdieu (1977) and Michel Foucault (1979) argue that it is easier and more effective to dominate people in their minds than to try to control their bodies. Besides, and often replacing, physical coercion are more insidious forms of social control. These include various techniques of persuading and managing people and of monitoring and recording their beliefs, activities, and contacts.

Hegemony, the internalization of a dominant ideology, is one way in which elites curb resistance and maintain power. Another way is to make subordinates believe they eventually will gain power—as young people usually foresee when they let their elders dominate them. Another way of curbing resistance is to separate or isolate people while supervising them closely, as is done in prisons (Foucault 1979).

Popular resistance is most likely to be expressed openly when people are allowed to assemble. The oppressed may draw courage from their common sentiments and the anonymity of the crowd. Sensing danger, the elites often discourage public gatherings. They try to limit and control holidays, funerals, dances, festivals, and other occasions that might unite the oppressed. For example, in the American South before the Civil War, gatherings of five or more slaves were prohibited unless a white person was present.

Factors that interfere with community formation—such as geographic, linguistic, and ethnic separation—also work to curb resistance. Consequently, Southern U.S. plantation owners sought slaves with diverse cultural and linguistic backgrounds. Despite the measures used to divide them, the slaves resisted, developing their own popular culture, linguistic codes, and religious vision. The masters stressed portions of the Bible that emphasized compliance (e.g., the book of Job). The slaves, however, preferred the story of Moses and deliverance. The cornerstone of slave religion became the idea of a reversal in the conditions of whites and blacks. Slaves also resisted directly, through sabotage and flight. In many New World areas, slaves managed to establish free communities in the hills and other isolated areas (Price 1973).

## Weapons of the Weak

The study of sociopolitical systems also should consider the sentiments and activity that may lurk beneath the surface of evident, public behavior. In public, the oppressed may seem to accept their own domination, even as they question it in private. James Scott (1990) uses the phrase "public transcript" to describe the open, public interactions between superordinates and subordinates—the outer shell of power relations. He uses "hidden transcript" to describe the critique of power that proceeds out of sight of the powerholders. In public, the elites and the oppressed may observe the etiquette of

power relations. The dominants act like masters while their subordinates show humility and defer.

Often, situations that seem to be hegemonic do have active resistance, but it is individual and disguised rather than collective and defiant. James Scott (1985) uses Malay peasants, among whom he did fieldwork, to illustrate small-scale acts of resistance—which he calls "weapons of the weak." The Malay peasants used an indirect strategy to resist an Islamic tithe (religious tax). Peasants were expected to pay the tithe, usually in the form of rice, which was sent to the provincial capital. In theory, the tithe would come back as charity, but it never did. Peasants didn't resist the tithe by rioting, demonstrating, or protesting. Instead, they used a "nibbling" strategy, based on small acts of resistance. For example, they failed to declare their land or lied about the amount they farmed. They underpaid, or they delivered rice contaminated with water, rocks, or mud to add weight. Because of this resistance, only 15 percent of what was due actually was paid (Scott 1990, p. 89).

Hidden transcripts tend to be expressed publicly at certain times (festivals and Carnavals) and in certain places (e.g., markets). Because of its costumed anonymity, Carnaval (Mardi Gras in New Orleans) is an excellent arena for expressing normally suppressed feelings. Carnavals celebrate freedom through immodesty, dancing, gluttony, and sexuality (DaMatta 1991). Carnaval may begin as a playful outlet for frustrations built up during the year. Over time, it may evolve into a powerful annual critique of stratification and domination and thus a threat to the established order (Gilmore 1987). (Recognizing that ceremonial license could turn into political defiance, the Spanish dictator Francisco Franco outlawed Carnaval.)

## Shame and Gossip

Many anthropologists have noted the importance of "informal" processes of social control, such as fear, stigma, shame, and gossip, especially in small-scale societies (see Freilich, Raybeck, and Savishinsky 1991). Gossip, which can lead to shame, sometimes is used when a direct or formal sanction is risky or impossible (Herskovits 1937). Margaret Mead (1937) and Ruth Benedict (1946) distinguished between shame as an external sanction (i.e., forces set in motion by others) and guilt as an internal sanction, psychologically generated by the individual. They regarded shame as a more prominent form of social control in non-Western societies and guilt as a more dominant emotional sanction in Western societies. Of course, to be effective as a sanction, the prospect of being shamed or of shaming oneself must be internalized by the individual. In small-scale societies, in a social environment where everyone knows everyone else, most people try to avoid behavior that might spoil their reputations and alienate them from their social network.

"Schwellkoepp," or "Swollen Heads," caricature local characters during a Carnaval parade in Mainz, Germany. Because of its costumed anonymity, Carnaval is an excellent arena for expressing normally suppressed speech. Is there anything like Carnaval in your society?

**FIGURE 17.4** Location of the Makua and the Village of Nicane in Northern Mozambique.

The Province of Nampula shown here is Makua territory.

Nicholas Kottak (2002) studied political systems, and social control more generally, among the rural Makua of northern Mozambique (Figure 17.4). Social control mechanisms among the Makua extended well beyond the formal political system, as revealed in conversations about social norms and crimes. The Makua talk easily about norm violations, conflicts, and the sanctions that can follow them. Jail, sorcery, and shame are the main sanctions anticipated by the rural Makua.

Makua ideas about social control emerged most clearly in discussions about what would happen to someone who stole his or her neighbor's chicken. Most Makua villagers have a makeshift chicken coop in a corner of their home. Chickens leave the coop before sunrise each day and wander around, looking for scraps. Villagers may be tempted to steal a chicken when its owner seems oblivious to its whereabouts. The Makua have few material possessions and a meat-poor diet, making free-ranging chickens a real temptation. Their discussions about unsupervised chickens and the occasional chicken theft as community problems clarified their ideas about social control—about why people did *not* steal their neighbor's chickens.

The Makua perceived three main disincentives or sanctions: jail (*cadeia*), sorcery attack (*enretthe*), and shame (*ehaya*). (As used here, a *sanction* refers to a kind of punishment that follows a norm violation.) The main sanctions—sorcery and, above all, shame—came from society rather than from the formal political system. First, sorcery: Once someone discovered his chicken had been stolen, he would, the Makua thought, ask a traditional healer to launch a sorcery attack on his behalf. This would either kill the thief or make him very ill.

According to Nicholas Kottak (2002), the Makua constantly mention the existence of sorcerers and sorcery, although they aren't explicit about who the sorcerers are. They see sorcery as based on malice, which everyone feels at some point. Having felt malice themselves, individual Makua probably experience moments of self-doubt about their own potential status as a sorcerer. They recognize that others have similar feelings. Local theories see sickness, social misfortune, and death as caused by malicious sorcery. Life expectancy is short and infant mortality high in a Makua village. Health, life, and existence are far more problematic than they are for most Westerners. Such uncertainty heightens fears relating to sorcery. Any conflict or norm violation is dangerous because it might trigger a sorcery attack. In particular, the Makua see the chicken thief as the inevitable target of a vengeance sorcery attack.

Makua fear sorcery, but they overwhelmingly mentioned shame as the main reason not to steal a neighbor's chicken. The chicken thief, having been discovered, would have to attend a formal, publicly organized village meeting, which would determine the appropriate punishment and compensation. The Makua were concerned not so much with a potential

Nicholas Kottak (back center) attends a village meeting among the Makua of northern Mozambique. Two chiefs have called the meeting to renegotiate the boundaries of their political jurisdictions.

fine as with the intense and enduring shame or embarrassment they would feel as a confirmed chicken thief.

Rural Makua tend to live in one community for their entire lives. Such communities typically have fewer than a thousand people, so that residents can easily keep track of one another's identities and reputations. Tight clustering of homes, markets, and schools facilitates the monitoring process. In this social environment, people try to avoid behavior that might spoil their reputations and alienate them from society.

Shame can be a very powerful sanction. Bronislaw Malinowski (1927) described how Trobriand Islanders might climb to the top of a palm tree and dive to their deaths because they couldn't tolerate the shame associated with public knowledge of some stigmatizing action. Makua villagers tell the story of a man rumored to have fathered a child with his stepdaughter. The political authorities imposed no formal sanctions (e.g., a fine or jail time) on this man, but gossip about the affair circulated widely. The gossip crystallized in the lyrics of a song that groups of young women would perform. After the man heard his name and behavior mentioned in that song, he hanged himself by the neck from a tree (N. C. Kottak 2002). (Previously we saw the role of song in the social control system of the Inuit. We'll see it again in the case of the Igbo women's war, discussed in the next section.)

We see from this discussion that people aren't just citizens of governments; they are also members of society, and social sanctions exist alongside governmental ones. Such sanctions also exemplify other "weapons of the weak," because they often are wielded most effectively by people—for example,

women or young people—who have limited access to the formal authority structure, as in the Igbo case, to which we now turn.

## The Igbo Women's War

Shame and ridicule, used by women against men, played a decisive role in a protest movement in southeastern Nigeria in 1929. This is remembered as the "Aba Women's Riots of 1929" in British colonial history and as the "Women's War" in Igbo history (see Dorward 1983; Martin 1988; Mba 1982; Oriji 2000; Van Allen 1971). During this two-month "war," at least 25,000 Igbo women joined protests against British officials, their agents, and their colonial policies. This massive revolt touched off the most serious challenge to British rule in the history of what was then the British colony of Nigeria.

In 1914, the British had implemented a policy of indirect rule by appointing local Nigerian men as their agents—known as "warrant chiefs." These chiefs became increasingly oppressive, seizing property, imposing arbitrary regulations, and imprisoning people who criticized them. Colonial administrators further stoked local outrage when they announced plans to impose taxes on Igbo market women. These women were key suppliers of food for Nigeria's growing urban population; they feared being forced out of business by the new tax. Market women were key organizers of the protests.

After hearing about the tax, thousands of Igbo women assembled in various towns to protest both the warrant chiefs and the taxes on market women. They used a traditional practice of censoring and shaming men through all-night song-and-dance ridicule (called "sitting on a man"). This process

In Nigeria, contemporary Igbo women collect water from a well standpipe. Political action by organized groups of Igbo women posed the first major challenge to British authority in Nigeria and in West Africa more generally during the colonial period.

entailed constant singing and dancing around the houses and offices of the warrant chiefs. The women also followed the chiefs' every move, forcing the men to pay attention by invading their space. Wives of the warrant chiefs also urged their husbands to listen to the protesters' demands.

The protests were remarkably effective. The tax was abandoned, and many of the warrant chiefs resigned, some to be replaced by women. Other women were appointed to the Native courts as judges. The position of women improved in Nigeria, where market women especially remain a powerful political force to this day. Many Nigerian political events in the 1930s, 1940s, and 1950s were inspired by the Women's War, including additional tax protests. This Women's War inspired many other protests in regions all over Africa. The Igbo uprising is seen as the first major challenge to British authority in Nigeria and West Africa during the colonial period. This case shows how women effectively used their social power (through song, dance, noise, and "in-your-face" behavior) to subvert the formal authority structure and, in so doing, gained greater influence within that structure. Can you think of other, perhaps recent, examples?

## Resistance via Social Media: A Case Study

As we saw in this chapter's "Focus on Globalization," new media, including Facebook, Twitter, and smartphones, have been used prominently during uprisings in Turkey, Egypt, and other countries. Anthropologists have done research on the role of social media in various places, including Brazil.

What some have dubbed Brazil's "Facebook Revolution" took place between June and September 2013. In cities large and small, Brazilians took to the streets (and cyberspace) to protest against the government and its public services policies. The movement began in São Paulo with small-scale demonstrations against bus fare increases. It exploded when images of police brutality—many recorded on cell-phone cameras—flooded first the Internet and then television broadcasts. These raw images recalled memories of the military dictatorship (1964–1985) for the older generation. Younger Brazilians were shocked at scenes of violent repression by agents of the government. The startling image of a young journalist's disfigured eye, caused by a riot police rubber bullet, was a particularly powerful visual shown repeatedly.

Media-borne calls for public action were spurred by citizens' concerns about the direction of Brazil's economic and political policies. The use of Facebook was vital in planning the demonstrations and recruiting protesters. Television news joined in, broadcasting the time and location of protests and then airing the ensuing encounters for nightly viewing. The protesters were overwhelmingly middle-class urbanites. The demonstrations accelerated during the international Confederation's Cup soccer games, which Brazil was hosting, focusing on the government's lavish spending—on stadiums for that competition and for the upcoming World Cup (2014) and Olympic Games (2016)—while ignoring the health, education, and transportation needs of most Brazilians.

While this civil unrest was evolving and expanding, a team of ethnographers from American and Brazilian universities was conducting research on the use and impact of electronic media in five Brazilian communities. (Anthropologist Richard Pace and I are coprincipal investigators in this research project conducted in various parts of Brazil, which is sponsored by the U.S. National Science Foundation.) As the protests intensified, our research team was observing how local Brazilians used media to understand the manifestations of these actions and, in some cases, to plan their own parallel protests. How did local Brazilians learn about, interpret, and participate in the discontent being played out at the national level?

Local interest and participation were greatest in Ibirama, a town of almost 15,000 people in Santa Catarina state, southern Brazil. In that community, project researcher Cynthia Pace (University of South Florida) observed extensive use of Facebook and television to both follow and participate in the protests. Ibirama is a tightly knit community founded in the late 19th century by German, Polish, and Russian migrants. Overwhelmingly middle class, it has had quality access to the Internet for at least a decade. Facebook is the preferred form of communication, with people posting daily, and even hourly, to signal people's comings and goings, issue invitations to local events, and advertise local businesses. (Cynthia Pace was chided one week for being invited to only five events instead of the normal 10 or more. She was told she needed more Facebook friends.)

As the protests spread in June 2013, Cynthia Pace's housemate, Pedro, an engineering student, used Facebook to post his plans to protest government corruption and the policies of President Dilma Rousseff. Pedro's Facebook network included thousands of people in Ibirama, and the resulting demonstration attracted hundreds. Cynthia Pace filmed the protest, and Pedro posted the footage on his Facebook page, from which a regional TV station obtained it for the evening news broadcast. The protest focused squarely on political and economic mismanagement by the federal government. Participants felt certain their actions would combine with others across the nation and bring down the Rousseff presidency. (As of this writing President Rousseff remains in power. In September 2013 President Rousseff used her opening address to the United Nations to decry American surveillance of Brazilians' personal data on the Internet, including her own e-mail.)

Far from our other research sites is Gurupá, a community of 9,500 people located on the Amazon River in the state of Pará. Its inhabitants are poor by national standards, but the community has benefited greatly from government programs for poverty alleviation, as well as a recent boom in the export of açaí (a tropical fruit). Gurupá has a history of social activism and protest and strongly supports President Rousseff's

Workers' Party. In town, local access to the Internet is unreliable, slow, and regularly interrupted. In Gurupá's rural areas, access is nonexistent. Cell phones (available only since 2011) are used to access Facebook when service allows. Local people watched the distant street protests mainly on television, given the issues with Internet access. According to researcher Monte Hendrickson (Vanderbilt University), the people of Gurupá tended to see the manifestations as political venting by urban residents far removed from the realities of the Amazon. Eventually, a local protest event was planned and posted on Facebook, although the real organization was accomplished by face-to-face interactions. The event, which drew about 100 people, was photographed and placed on Facebook by its organizers. Framed as a protest against the Rousseff presidency, the real focus of the event became local politics, with participants from the opposition party.

Another community studied by our research team is Turedjam, population 500, which is located in the Kayapó Indigenous Territories near the Brazilian town of Ourilândia do Norte, Pará. The village was established in 2010. Unlike most other Kayapó villages, it has electricity, television, and cell-phone service. Although the community lacks Internet access, some villagers have gone online in nearby Brazilian towns, and a few even have Facebook pages. According to researcher Glenn Shepard (Goeldi Museum, Belem, Brazil), the villagers watched the

On Rio de Janeiro's Copacabana beach, protesters agitate for political reform and better public services and against PEC37, a proposed law that would have deprived independent public prosecutors of the right to probe crimes and political corruption. (The law was not passed.)

demonstrations on television. With limited proficiency in the Portuguese language, however, many Kayapó had trouble following the details of the protest movement. They interpreted the distant street protests as manifestations of general discontent among "whites" with their own government. Opportunistically, the Kayapó seized the national events as an opening to pursue their own longstanding grievances. Local men painted their bodies solid black (a sign of war-footing among these Native Americans) and maintained constant contact with other villages via short-wave radio and cell phones. Their plan was to block traffic on the Transamazon Highway, in an attempt to force concessions from the Rousseff government. Their main concerns included demarcation of Kayapó lands and a potentially destructive regional dam project. The proposed highway blockage eventually was abandoned in favor of direct talks with government officials.

From these case studies we see that urban events, when broadcast nationally via television, cell phones, and the Internet, also affect people living in small towns and villages far from those urban centers. But the effects are varied, reflecting the particular local context, including its class status and degree of media access. The national "mediascape" gets fragmented locally. For a few months in Brazil in 2013, nationwide knowledge of urban discontent created a momentary imagined solidarity—most strongly among urban, middle-class Brazilians. The protests expressed a general discontent with Brazil's direction, but the goals of political action were unclear and diffuse, and there was no real common enemy (e.g., a brutal dictator). This political action, this form of resistance, may have mobilized people but, as of this writing, it has not led to significant political change. Although the media can disseminate political goals and spur action, social media cannot in themselves guarantee political change.

# for REVIEW

## summary

1. Although no ethnographer has been able to observe a sociopolitical system uninfluenced by some state, many anthropologists use a typology that classifies societies as bands, tribes, chiefdoms, or states. Foragers tended to live in egalitarian, band-organized societies. Personal networks linked individuals, families, and bands. Band leaders were first among equals, with no sure way to enforce decisions. Disputes rarely arose over strategic resources, which were open to all.

2. Political authority increased with growth in population size and density and in the scale of regulatory problems. More people mean more relations among individuals and groups to regulate. Increasingly complex economies pose further regulatory problems.

3. Heads of horticultural villages are local leaders with limited authority. They lead by example and persuasion. Big men have support and authority beyond a single village. They are regional regulators, but temporary ones. In organizing a feast, they mobilize labor from several villages. Sponsoring such events leaves them with little wealth but with prestige and a reputation for generosity.

4. Age and gender also can be used for regional political integration. Among North America's Plains Indians, men's associations (pantribal sodalities) organized raiding and buffalo hunting. Such sodalities provide offense and defense when there is intertribal raiding for animals. Among pastoralists, the degree of authority and political organization reflects population size and density, interethnic relations, and pressure on resources.

5. The state is an autonomous political unit that encompasses many communities. Its government collects taxes, drafts people for work and war, and decrees and enforces laws. The state is a form of sociopolitical organization based on central government and social stratification. Early states are known as archaic, or nonindustrial, states, in contrast to modern industrial nation-states.

6. Unlike tribes, but like states, chiefdoms had permanent regional regulation and differential access to resources. But chiefdoms lacked stratification. Unlike states, but like bands and tribes, chiefdoms were organized by kinship, descent, and marriage. Chiefdoms emerged in several areas, including the circum-Caribbean, lowland Amazonia, the southeastern United States, and Polynesia.

7. Weber's three dimensions of stratification are wealth, power, and prestige. In early states—for the first time in human history—contrasts in wealth, power, and prestige between entire groups

of men and women came into being. A socioeconomic stratum includes people of both genders and all ages. The superordinate—higher or elite—stratum enjoys privileged access to resources.

8. Certain systems are found in all states: population control, judiciary, enforcement, and fiscal. These are integrated by a ruling system or government composed of civil, military, and religious officials. States conduct censuses and demarcate boundaries. Laws are based on precedent and legislative proclamations. Courts and judges handle disputes and crimes. A police force maintains internal order, as a military defends against external threats. A financial, or fiscal, system supports rulers, officials, judges, and other specialists and government agencies.

9. *Hegemony* describes a stratified social order in which subordinates comply with domination by internalizing its values and accepting its "naturalness." Situations that appear hegemonic may have resistance that is individual and disguised rather than collective and defiant. "Public transcript" refers to the open, public interactions between the dominators and the oppressed. "Hidden transcript" describes the critique of power that goes on where the powerholders can't see it. Discontent also may be expressed in public rituals such as Carnaval.

10. Broader than the political is the concept of social control—those fields of the social system most actively involved in the maintenance of norms and the regulation of conflict. Sanctions are social as well as governmental. Shame and gossip can be effective social sanctions. In the Igbo women's war, women effectively used their social power (through song, dance, noise, and "in-your-face" behavior) to subvert the formal authority structure and, in so doing, gained greater influence within that structure. Urban events, when broadcast nationally via TV, cell phones, and the Internet, also affect people far from those urban centers. Such effects, however, are varied, reflecting the particular local context. Although the media can disseminate political goals and spur action, social media cannot in themselves guarantee political change.

## key terms

big man 323

conflict resolution 321

differential access 319

fiscal 330

hegemony 331

law 321

office 327

pantribal sodalities 324

power 318

prestige 329

social control 331

subordinate 329

superordinate 329

tribe 319

village head 322

wealth 328

## critical thinking

1. This chapter notes that the labels "band," "tribe," "chiefdom," and "state" are too simple to account for the full range of political diversity and complexity known to archaeologists and ethnographers. Why not get rid of this typology altogether if it does not accurately describe reality? What is the value, if any, of researchers retaining the use of ideal types to study society?

2. Why shouldn't modern hunter-gatherers be seen as representative of Stone Age peoples? What are some of the stereotypes associated with foragers?

3. What are sodalities? Does your society have them? Do you belong to any? Why or why not?

4. What conclusions do you draw from this chapter about the relationship between population density and political hierarchy?

5. This chapter describes population control as one of the specialized functions found in all states. What are examples of population control? Have you had direct experiences with these controls? (Think of the last time you traveled abroad, registered to vote, paid taxes, or applied for a driver's license.) Do you think these controls are good or bad for society?

## CHAPTER 18

# Gender

▶ How are biology and culture expressed in human sex/gender systems?

▶ How do gender, gender roles, and gender stratification correlate with other social, economic, and political variables?

▶ What is sexual orientation, and how do sexual practices vary cross-culturally?

Gender-neutral "emotion dolls" using in teaching at "Egalia," a preschool in Stockholm, Sweden. The school's staff avoid words like "him" or "her" and address the children as "friends" rather than "girls" and "boys." This public preschool exemplifies Sweden's efforts to engineer lifelong gender equality.

# understanding OURSELVES

A table (18.1) in this chapter lists activities that are generally done by the men in a society, generally done by the women in a society, or done by either men or women (swing). In this table, you will see some "male" activities familiar to our own culture, such as hunting, butchering, and building houses, along with activities that we consider typically female, such as doing the laundry and cooking. This list may bring to mind as many exceptions as followers of these "rules." Although it is not typical, it certainly is not unheard of for an American woman to hunt large game or an American man to cook (think of any male celebrity chef). Celebrities aside, women in our culture increasingly work outside the home in a wide variety of jobs—doctor, lawyer, accountant, professor—traditionally considered men's work. It is not true, however, that women have achieved equity in all types of employment. As of this writing, only 20 out of 100 United States senators are women. Only four women have ever served on the United States Supreme Court.

Ideas about proper gender behavior are changing just as inconsistently as are the employment patterns of men and women. Today's TV shows may feature characters who display non-traditional gender behavior and sexual behavior, while old beliefs, cultural expectations, and gender stereotypes linger. The American expectation that proper female behavior should be polite, restrained, or meek poses a challenge for women, because American culture also values decisiveness and "standing up for your beliefs." When American men and women display similar behavior—speaking their minds, for example—they are judged differently. A man's assertive behavior may be admired and rewarded, but similar behavior by a woman may be labeled "aggressive"—or worse.

Both men and women are constrained by their cultural training, stereotypes, and expectations. For example, American culture stigmatizes male crying. It's okay for little boys to cry, but becoming a man often means giving up this natural expression of joy and sadness. Why shouldn't "big lugs" cry when they feel emotions? American men are trained as well to make decisions and stick to them. In our stereotypes, changing one's mind is more associated with women than with men and may be perceived as a sign of weakness. Politicians routinely criticize their opponents for being indecisive, for waffling or "flip-flopping" on issues. What a strange idea—that people shouldn't change their positions if they've discovered there's a better way. Males, females, and humanity may be equally victimized by aspects of cultural training.

## SEX AND GENDER

Questions about nature and nurture emerge in the discussion of human sex-gender roles and sexuality. Men and women differ genetically. Women have two X chromosomes, and men have an X and a Y. The father determines a baby's sex because only he has the Y chromosome to transmit. The mother always provides an X chromosome.

The chromosomal difference is expressed in hormonal and physiological contrasts.

Because anthropologists study biology, society, and culture, they are in a unique position to comment on nature (biological predispositions) and nurture (environment) as determinants of human behavior. Human attitudes, values, and behavior are limited not only by our genetic predispositions—which often are difficult to identify—but also by our experiences during enculturation. Our attributes as adults are determined both by our genes and by our environment during growth and development.

The realm of cultural diversity contains richly different social constructions and expressions of gender roles, as is illustrated by this Wodaabe man at the annual Gerewol male beauty contest in Niger.

**sexual dimorphism**
Marked differences in male and female biology, beyond breasts and genitals.

**gender**
The cultural construction of whether one is female, male, or something else.

**gender roles**
The tasks and activities that a culture assigns to each sex.

**gender stereotypes**
Oversimplified, strongly held views about the characteristics of males and females.

**gender stratification**
Unequal distribution of social resources between men and women.

Humans are sexually dimorphic, more so than some primates, such as gibbons (small, tree-living Asiatic apes), and less so than others, such as gorillas and orangutans. **Sexual dimorphism** refers to differences in male and female biology besides the contrasts in breasts and genitals. Women and men differ not just in primary (genitalia and reproductive organs) and secondary (breasts, voice, hair distribution) sexual characteristics but in average weight, height, strength, and longevity. Women tend to live longer than men and have excellent endurance capabilities. In a given population, men tend to be taller and to weigh more than women do. Of course, there is a considerable overlap between the sexes in terms of height, weight, and physical strength, and there has been a pronounced reduction in sexual dimorphism during human evolution.

Just how far, however, do such genetically and physiologically determined differences go? What effects do they have on the way men and women act and are treated in different societies? Anthropologists have discovered both similarities and differences in the roles of men and women in different cultures. The predominant anthropological position on sex-gender roles and biology may be stated as follows:

The biological nature of men and women [should be seen] not as a narrow enclosure limiting the human organism, but rather as a broad base upon which a variety of structures can be built. (Friedl 1975, p. 6)

Although in most societies men tend to be somewhat more aggressive than women are, many of the behavioral and attitudinal differences between the sexes emerge from culture rather than biology. Sex differences are biological, but gender encompasses all the traits that a culture assigns to and inculcates in males and females. **Gender,** in other words, refers to the cultural construction of whether one is female, male, or something else.

Given the "rich and various constructions of gender" within the realm of cultural diversity, Susan Bourque and Kay Warren (1987) note that the same images of masculinity and femininity do not always apply. Margaret Mead did an early ethnographic study of variation in gender roles. Her book *Sex and Temperament in Three Primitive Societies* (1935/1950) was based on fieldwork in three societies in Papua New Guinea: the Arapesh, Mundugumor, and Tchambuli. The extent of personality variation in men and women among those three societies on the same island amazed Mead. She found that Arapesh men and women both acted as Americans traditionally have expected women to act: in a mild, parental, responsive way. Mundugumor men and women both, in contrast, acted as she believed we expect men to act: fiercely and aggressively. Finally, Tchambuli men were "catty," wore curls, and went shopping, but Tchambuli women were energetic and managerial and placed less emphasis on personal adornment than did the men. (Drawing on their case study of the Tchambuli, whom they call the Chambri, Errington and Gewertz [1987], while recognizing gender malleability, have disputed the specifics of Mead's account.)

There is a well-established field of feminist scholarship within anthropology (Di Leonardo 1991; Rosaldo 1980b; Strathern 1988). Anthropologists have gathered systematic ethnographic data about similarities and differences involving gender in many cultural settings (Bonvillain 2007; Brettell and Sargent 2012; Mascia-Lees 2010; Stimpson and Herdt 2014; Ward and Edelstein 2013). Anthropologists can detect recurrent themes and patterns involving gender differences. They also can observe that gender roles vary with environment, economy, adaptive strategy, and type of political system. Before we examine the cross-cultural data, some definitions are in order.

**Gender roles** are the tasks and activities a culture assigns by gender. Related to gender roles are **gender stereotypes,** which are oversimplified but strongly held ideas about the characteristics of males and females. **Gender stratification** describes an unequal distribution of rewards (socially valued resources, power, prestige, human rights, and personal freedom) between men and women, reflecting their different positions in a social hierarchy. According to Ann Stoler (1977), the "economic determinants of gender status" include freedom or autonomy (in disposing of one's labor and its fruits) and social power (control over the lives, labor, and produce of others).

In stateless societies, gender stratification often is more obvious in regard to prestige than it is in regard to wealth. In her study of the Ilongots of northern

**FIGURE 18.1** *Location of Ilongots in the Philippines.*

Luzon in the Philippines (Figure 18.1), Michelle Rosaldo (1980a) described gender differences related to the positive cultural value placed on adventure, travel, and knowledge of the external world. More often than women, Ilongot men, as headhunters, visited distant places. They acquired knowledge of the external world, amassed experiences there, and returned to express their knowledge, adventures, and feelings in public oratory. They received acclaim as a result. Ilongot women had inferior prestige because they lacked external experiences on which to base knowledge and dramatic expression. On the basis of Rosaldo's study and findings in other stateless societies, Ong (1989) argues that we must distinguish between prestige systems and actual power in a given society. High male prestige does not necessarily entail economic or political power held by men over their families. (For more on Rosaldo's contributions to gender studies, see Lugo and Maurer 2000.)

## RECURRENT GENDER PATTERNS

Ethnologists compare ethnographic data from several cultures (i.e., cross-cultural data) to discover and explain differences and similarities. Data relevant to the cross-cultural study of gender can be drawn from the domains of economics, politics, domestic activity, kinship, and marriage. Review

Table 18.1 (on p. 344) for cross-cultural data from 185 randomly selected societies on the division of labor by gender.

The findings in Table 18.1 illustrate cultural generalities rather than absolute cultural universals. That is, among the societies known to ethnography, there is a general, indeed a very strong, tendency for men to build boats, but there are exceptions. One was the Hidatsa, a Native American group in which the women made the boats used to cross the Missouri River. (Traditionally, the Hidatsa were village farmers and bison hunters on the North American Plains; they now live in North Dakota.) Another exception is that Pawnee women worked wood; this is the only Native American group that assigned this activity to women. (The Pawnee, also traditionally Plains farmers and bison hunters, originally lived in what is now central Nebraska and central Kansas; they now live on a reservation in north central Oklahoma.) Among the Mbuti "pygmies" of Africa's Ituri forest, women hunt—by catching small, slow animals, using their hands or a net (Murdock and Provost 1973).

Exceptions to cross-cultural generalizations may involve societies or individuals. That is, a society like the Hidatsa can contradict the cross-cultural generalization that men build boats by assigning that task to women. Or in a society where the cultural expectation is that men build boats, a particular woman or women can contradict that expectation by doing the male activity. Table 18.1 shows that in a sample of 185 societies, certain activities ("swing activities") are assigned to either or both men and women. Among the most important of such activities are planting, tending, and harvesting crops. Some societies customarily assign more farming chores to women, whereas others make men the primary farmers. Among the tasks almost always assigned to men (Table 18.1), some (e.g., hunting large animals on land and sea) seem clearly related to the greater average size and strength of males. Others, such as working wood and making musical instruments, seem more culturally arbitrary. And women, of course, are not exempt from arduous and time-consuming physical labor, such as gathering firewood and fetching water. In Arembepe, Bahia, Brazil, for example, women used to transport water in 5-gallon tins, balanced on their heads, from wells and lagoons located at long distances from their homes.

Notice that Table 18.1 includes no mention of trade and market activity, in which either men or women, or both, are active. Is Table 18.1 somewhat androcentric in detailing more tasks for men than for women? More than men, women do child care, but the study on which Table 18.1 is based does not break down domestic activities to the same extent that it details work done outside the home. Think about Table 18.1 in terms of today's home and job roles and with respect to the activities done by contemporary women and men. Men still do most of the

**TABLE 18.1** Generalities in the Division of Labor by Gender, Based on Data from 185 Societies

| GENERALLY MALE ACTIVITIES | SWING (MALE OR FEMALE) ACTIVITIES | GENERALLY FEMALE ACTIVITIES |
|---|---|---|
| Hunting large aquatic animals (e.g., whales, walrus) | Making fire | Gathering fuel (e.g., firewood) |
| Smelting ores | Body mutilation | Making drinks |
| Metalworking | Preparing skins | Gathering wild vegetal foods |
| Lumbering | Gathering small land animals | Dairy production (e.g., churning) |
| Hunting large land animals | Planting crops | Spinning |
| Working wood | Making leather products | Doing the laundry |
| Hunting fowl | Harvesting | Fetching water |
| Making musical instruments | Tending crops | Cooking |
| Trapping | Milking | Preparing food (e.g., processing cereal grains) |
| Building boats | Making baskets | |
| Working stone | Caring for small animals | |
| Working bone, horn, and shell | Preserving meat and fish | |
| Mining and quarrying | Loom weaving | |
| Setting bones | Gathering small aquatic animals | |
| Butchering* | Clothing manufacture | |
| Collecting wild honey | Making pottery | |
| Clearing land | | |
| Fishing | | |
| Tending large herd animals | | |
| Building houses | | |
| Preparing the soil | | |
| Making nets | | |
| Carrying burdens | | |
| Making mats | | |
| Making rope | | |

*All the activities above "butchering" are almost always done by men; those from "butchering" through "making rope" usually are done by men.

SOURCE: Adapted from G. P. Murdock and C. Provost, "Factors in the Division of Labor by Sex: A Cross-Cultural Analysis," *Ethnology* 12(2): 202–225.

hunting; either gender can collect the honey from a supermarket, even as most baby-bottom wiping (part of child care and not included in Table 18.1) continues to be in female hands.

Cross-culturally the subsistence contributions of men and women are roughly equal (Table 18.2). But in domestic activities and child care, female labor clearly predominates, as we see in Tables 18.3 and 18.4. Table 18.3 shows that in about half the societies studied, men did virtually no domestic work. Even in societies where men did domestic chores, the bulk of such work was done by women. Adding together their subsistence activities and their domestic work, women tend to work more hours than men do. Has this changed in the contemporary world?

What about child care? Women tend to be the main caregivers in most societies, but men often play a role. Again there are exceptions, both within and between societies. Table 18.4 uses cross-cultural data to answer the question "Who—men or women—is primarily responsible for the care, handling, and discipline of children younger than 4 years?" Women have primary responsibility for young children in two-thirds of the societies, but there are exceptions. In the United States and Canada today, some men are primary caregivers despite the cultural fact that the female role in child care remains more prominent. Given the critical role of breast-feeding in ensuring infant survival, it makes sense, for infants especially, for the mother to be the primary caregiver.

There are differences in male and female reproductive strategies. Women give birth, breast-feed, and assume primary responsibility for infant care. Women ensure that their progeny will survive by establishing a close bond with each baby. It's also

**TABLE 18.2**  Time and Effort Expended on Subsistence Activities by Men and Women*

| | |
|---|---|
| More by men | 16 |
| Roughly equal | 61 |
| More by women | 23 |

*Percentage of 88 randomly selected societies for which information was available on this variable.

SOURCE: M. F. Whyte, "Cross-Cultural Codes Dealing with the Relative Status of Women," *Ethnology* 17(2):211–239.

**TABLE 18.3**  Who Does the Domestic Work?*

| | |
|---|---|
| Males do virtually none | 51 |
| Males do some, but females do most | 49 |

*Percentage of 92 randomly selected societies for which information was available on this variable.

SOURCE: M. F. Whyte, "Cross-Cultural Codes Dealing with the Relative Status of Women," *Ethnology* 17(2):211–239.

**TABLE 18.4**  Who Is Primarily Responsible for the Care, Handling, and Discipline of Infant Children (under 4 Years Old)?*

| | |
|---|---|
| Males have more say | 18 |
| Roughly equal | 16 |
| Females have more say | 66 |

*Percentage of 67 randomly selected societies for which information was available on this variable.

SOURCE: M. F. Whyte, "Cross-Cultural Codes Dealing with the Relative Status of Women," *Ethnology* 17(2):211–239.

**TABLE 18.5**  Does the Society Allow Multiple Spouses?*

| | |
|---|---|
| Only for males | 77 |
| For both, but more commonly for males | 4 |
| For neither | 16 |
| For both, but more commonly for females | 2 |

*Percentage of 92 randomly selected societies.

SOURCE: M. F. Whyte, "Cross-Cultural Codes Dealing with the Relative Status of Women," *Ethnology* 17(2):211–239.

**TABLE 18.6**  Is There a Double Standard with Respect to PREMARITAL Sex?*

| | |
|---|---|
| Yes—females are more restricted | 44 |
| No—equal restrictions on males and females | 56 |

*Percentage of 73 randomly selected societies for which information was available on this variable.

SOURCE: M. F. Whyte, "Cross-Cultural Codes Dealing with the Relative Status of Women," *Ethnology* 17(2):211–239.

**TABLE 18.7**  Is There a Double Standard with Respect to EXTRAMARITAL Sex?*

| | |
|---|---|
| Yes—females are more restricted | 43 |
| Equal restrictions on males and females | 55 |
| Males punished more severely for transgression | 3 |

*Percentage of 73 randomly selected societies for which information was available on this variable.

SOURCE: M. F. Whyte, "Cross-Cultural Codes Dealing with the Relative Status of Women," *Ethnology* 17(2):211–239.

advantageous for a woman to have a reliable mate to ease the child-rearing process and help ensure the survival of her children. Women can have only so many babies during the course of their reproductive years, which begin after menarche (the advent of menstruation) and end with menopause (cessation of menstruation). Men have a longer reproductive period, which can last into the elder years. If they choose to do so, men can enhance their reproductive success by impregnating several women over a longer time span. Cross-culturally, men are much more likely to have multiple mates than women are (see Tables 18.5, 18.6, and 18.7). Among the societies known to ethnography, polygyny (multiple wives) is much more common than polyandry (multiple husbands) (see Table 18.5).

Men mate, within and outside marriage, more than women do. Table 18.6 shows cross-cultural data on premarital sex, and Table 18.7 summarizes the data on extramarital sex. In both cases men are

In many societies women (and children) routinely do hard physical labor, as is illustrated by these stone factory workers in Kathmandu, Nepal.

Among foragers, gender stratification tends to increase when men contribute much more to the diet than women do—as has been true among the Inuit and other northern hunters and fishers. Shown here, in Foxe Basin, Nunavut (in Canada's Northwest Territories), Inuit hunters load walrus onto their boats.

**domestic–public dichotomy**
Work at home versus more valued work outside the home.

less restricted than women are, although the restrictions are equal in about half the societies studied. Double standards that restrict women more than men are one illustration of gender stratification, which we now examine more systematically.

## GENDER ROLES AND GENDER STRATIFICATION

Economic roles affect gender stratification. In one cross-cultural study, Sanday (1974) found that gender stratification decreased when men and women

Many jobs that men do in some societies are done by women in others, and vice versa. In West Africa, women play a prominent role in trade and marketing. In Togo, shown here, women dominate textile sales. Is there a textile shop near you? Who runs it?

made roughly equal contributions to subsistence. She found that gender stratification was greatest when the women contributed either much more or much less than the men did.

In foraging societies, gender stratification was most marked when men contributed much more to the diet than women did. This was true among the Inuit and other northern hunters and fishers. Among tropical and semitropical foragers, by contrast, gathering usually provides more food than hunting and fishing do. Gathering generally is women's work. Men usually hunt and fish, and there is no culture in which women are the primary hunters. However, women also do some fishing and may hunt small animals, as is true among the Agta of the Philippines (Griffin and Estioko-Griffin 1985). When gathering is prominent, gender status tends to be more equal than it is when hunting and fishing are the main subsistence activities.

Gender status also is more equal when the domestic and public spheres aren't sharply separated. (*Domestic* means within or pertaining to the home.) Strong differentiation between the home and the outside world is called the **domestic–public dichotomy** or the *private–public contrast*. The outside world can include politics, trade, warfare, or work. Often when domestic and public spheres are clearly separated, public activities have greater prestige than domestic ones do. This can promote gender stratification, because men are more likely to be active in the public domain than women are. Cross-culturally, women's activities tend to be closer to home than men's are. Another reason hunter-gatherers have less gender stratification than farmers and herders do is that the domestic–public dichotomy is less developed among foragers.

We've seen that certain gender roles are more sex-linked than others. Men are the usual hunters and warriors. Given such tools and weapons as spears, knives, and bows, men make better hunters and fighters because they are bigger and stronger on the average than are women in the same population (Divale and Harris 1976). The male hunter-fighter role also reflects a tendency toward greater male mobility.

In foraging societies, women are either pregnant or lactating during most of their childbearing period. Late in pregnancy and after childbirth, carrying a baby limits a woman's movements, even her gathering. However, among the Agta of the Philippines (Griffin and Estioko-Griffin 1985), women not only gather; they also hunt with dogs while carrying their babies with them. Still, given the effects of pregnancy and breast-feeding on mobility, it would be problematic for women to be the primary hunters (Friedl 1975). Warfare, which also requires mobility, is not typical of foraging societies, nor is interregional trade well developed. Warfare and trade are two public arenas that can contribute to status inequality of males and females among food producers.

## Reduced Gender Stratification—Matrilineal-Matrilocal Societies

Cross-cultural variation in gender status is related to rules of descent and postmarital residence. Many horticultural societies have **matrilineal descent** (descent traced through females only) and *matrilocality* (residence after marriage with the wife's relatives). In such societies, female status tends to be high. Matriliny and matrilocality disperse related males, rather than consolidating them. By contrast, patriliny and patrilocality keep male relatives together, which is advantageous when warfare is present. Matrilineal-matrilocal systems tend to occur in societies where population pressure on strategic resources is minimal and warfare is infrequent.

Women tend to have high status in matrilineal-matrilocal societies for several reasons. Descent-group membership, succession to political positions, allocation of land, and overall social identity all come through female links. In Negeri Sembilan, Malaysia (Peletz 1988), matriliny gave women sole inheritance of ancestral rice fields. Matrilocality created solidary clusters of female kin. Women had considerable influence beyond the household. In such matrilineal contexts, women are the basis of the entire social structure. Although public authority may be (or may appear to be) assigned to the men, much of the power and decision making may actually belong to the senior women.

## Matriarchy

Cross-culturally, anthropologists have described tremendous variation in the roles of men and women, and the power differentials between them. If a *patriarchy* is a political system ruled by men, is a matriarchy necessarily a political system ruled by women? Or might we apply the term *matriarchy*, as anthropologist Peggy Reeves Sanday (2002) does, to a political system in which women play a much more prominent role than men do in social and political organization? One example would be the Minangkabau of West Sumatra, Indonesia, whom Sanday has studied for decades.

Sanday considers the Minangkabau a matriarchy because women are the center, origin, and foundation of the social order. Senior women are associated with the central pillar of the traditional house, the oldest one in the village. The oldest village in a cluster is called the "mother village." In ceremonies, women are addressed by the term used for their mythical Queen Mother. Women control land inheritance, and couples reside matrilocally. In the wedding ceremony, the wife collects her husband from his household and, with her female kin, escorts him to hers. If there is a divorce, the husband simply takes his things and leaves. Yet despite the special position of women, the Minangkabau matriarchy is not the equivalent of female rule, given the Minangkabau belief that all decision making should be by consensus.

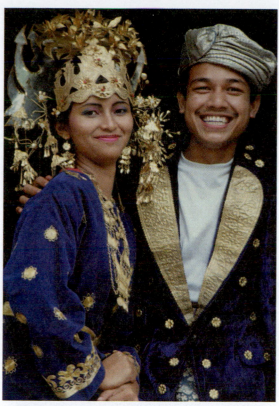

A Minangkabau bride and groom in West Sumatra, Indonesia, where anthropologist Peggy Reeves Sanday has conducted several years of ethnographic fieldwork.

**matrilineal descent**
Descent traced through women only.

## Increased Gender Stratification—Patrilineal-Patrilocal Societies

Martin and Voorhies (1975) link the decline of matriliny and the spread of the **patrilineal-patrilocal complex** (consisting of patrilineality, patrilocality, warfare, and male supremacy) to pressure on resources. (Societies with **patrilineal descent** trace descent through males only. In *patrilocal* societies a woman moves to her husband's village after marriage.) Faced with scarce resources, patrilineal-patrilocal cultivators such as the Yanomami often wage warfare against other villages. This favors patrilocality and patriliny, customs that keep related men together in the same village, where they make strong allies in battle. Such societies tend to have a sharp domestic–public dichotomy, and men tend to dominate the prestige hierarchy. Men may use their public roles in warfare and trade and their greater prestige to symbolize and reinforce the devaluation or oppression of women.

The patrilineal-patrilocal complex characterizes many societies in highland Papua New Guinea. Women work hard growing and processing subsistence crops, raising and tending pigs (the main domesticated animal and a favorite food), and doing domestic cooking, but they are isolated from the public domain, which men control. Men grow and distribute prestige crops, prepare food for feasts,

**patrilineal-patrilocal complex**
Male supremacy based on patrilineality, patrilocality, and warfare.

**patrilineal descent**
Descent traced through men only.

In some parts of Papua New Guinea, the patrilineal-patrilocal complex has extreme social repercussions. Regarding females as dangerous and polluting, men may segregate themselves in men's houses (such as this one, located near the Sepik River), where they hide their precious ritual objects from women. Are there places like this in your society?

and arrange marriages. The men even get to trade the pigs and control their use in ritual.

In densely populated areas of the Papua New Guinea highlands, male–female avoidance is associated with strong pressure on resources (Lindenbaum 1972). Men fear all female contacts, including sexual acts. They think that sexual contact with women

In many societies, especially patriarchal ones, women experience, and fear, intimidation as they increasingly enter the public sphere, especially in impersonal, urban settings. "Ladies Only" lines like this one at the Golden Temple in Amritsar, Punjab, India, are designed to help women move unmolested through public space.

will weaken them. Indeed, men see everything female as dangerous and polluting. They segregate themselves in men's houses and hide their precious ritual objects from women. They delay marriage, and some never marry.

By contrast, the sparsely populated areas of Papua New Guinea, such as recently settled areas, lack taboos on male–female contacts. The image of woman as polluter fades, male–female intercourse is valued, men and women live together, and reproductive rates are high.

# Patriarchy and Violence

**Patriarchy** describes a political system ruled by men in which women have inferior social and political status, including basic human rights. Barbara Miller (1997), in a study of systematic neglect of females, describes women in rural northern India as "the endangered sex." Societies that feature a full-fledged patrilineal-patrilocal complex, replete with warfare and intervillage raiding, also typify patriarchy. Such practices as dowry murders, female infanticide, and clitoridectomy (removal of the clitoris) exemplify patriarchy, which extends from tribal societies such as the Yanomami to state societies such as India and Pakistan.

Although more prevalent in certain social settings than in others, family violence and domestic abuse of women are worldwide problems. Domestic violence certainly occurs in nuclear family settings, such as Canada and the United States. Cities, with their impersonality and isolation from extended kin networks, are breeding grounds for domestic violence, as also may be rural areas in which women lead isolated lives.

We've seen that gender stratification typically is reduced in societies in which women have prominent roles in the economy and social life. When a woman lives in her own village, she has kin nearby to protect her interests. Even in patrilocal polygynous (multiple wives) settings, women often count on the support of their cowives and sons in disputes with potentially abusive husbands. Such settings, which can provide a safe haven for women, are retracting rather than expanding in today's world. Isolated families and patrilineal social forms have spread at the expense of matriliny. Many nations have declared polygyny illegal. More and more women, and men, find themselves cut off from their families and extended kin.

With the spread of the women's rights movement and the human rights movement, attention to domestic violence and abuse of women has increased. Laws have been passed, and mediating institutions established. Brazil's female-run police stations for battered women provide an example, as do shelters for victims of domestic abuse in the United States and Canada. A series of "Ladies only" facilities, including trains and entry lines, can be found throughout India. But patriarchal institutions do persist in what should be a more enlightened world.

# GENDER IN INDUSTRIAL SOCIETIES

The domestic–public dichotomy also influences gender stratification in industrial societies, including Canada and the United States, where gender roles have been changing rapidly. The "traditional" idea that "a woman's place is in the home" developed among middle- and upper-class Americans as industrialism spread after 1900. Earlier, pioneer women in the Midwest and West were recognized as fully productive workers in farming and home industry. Under industrialism, attitudes about gendered work came to vary with class and region. In early industrial Europe, men, women, and children flocked to factories as wage laborers. Enslaved Americans of both sexes toiled in cotton fields. After abolition, southern African American women continued working as field hands and domestics. Poor white women labored in the South's early cotton mills. In the 1890s, more than one million American women held menial, repetitious, and unskilled factory positions. In the early 20th century, a wave of European immigration provided a male labor force willing to work for wages lower than those of American-born men. Immigrant men were hired for factory jobs that previously would have gone to women. As machine tools and mass production further reduced the need for female labor, the notion gained ground that women were biologically unfit for factory work.

Maxine Margolis (2000) describes how gendered work, attitudes, and beliefs have varied in response to American economic needs. For example, wartime shortages of men have promoted the idea that work outside the home is women's patriotic duty. During the world wars, the notion that women are biologically unfit for hard physical labor faded. Inflation and the culture of consumption also have spurred female employment. When demand and/or prices rise, multiple paychecks help maintain family living standards.

The increase in female paid employment in the United States since World War II also reflects the baby boom and industrial expansion. American culture traditionally has defined clerical work, public school teaching, and nursing as female occupations. With rapid population growth and business expansion after World War II, the demand for women to fill such jobs grew steadily. Employers also found that they could increase their profits by paying women lower wages than they would have to pay to returning male war veterans.

Economic changes paved the way for the contemporary women's movement, which also was spurred by the publication of Betty Friedan's book *The Feminine Mystique* in 1963 and the founding of NOW, the National Organization for Women, in 1966. The movement in turn promoted expanded work opportunities for women, including the goal (as yet unrealized) of equal pay for equal work. Between 1970 and 2011, the female percentage of the American workforce rose from 38 to 46 percent. Over 71 million women now have paid employment, compared with 83 million men. Women fill more than half (52 percent) of all management and professional jobs (*Proquest Statistical Abstract of the United States 2013*, Table 662). And it's not mainly single women working, as once was the case. Table 18.8 presents figures on the increasing cash employment of American wives and mothers, including those with children under 6 years old.

Note in Table 18.8 that the cash employment of American married men has been falling while that of American married women has been rising. There has been a dramatic change in behavior and attitudes since 1960, when 89 percent of all married men worked, compared with just 32 percent of married women. The comparable figures in 2011 were 75 percent and 60 percent. The median income of American women working full-time, year-round, in 2012 was 77 percent of that of a comparably employed male. This ratio of female-to-male earnings was only 68 percent in 1989. By 2002 it had risen to 77 percent, where it has remained for a decade (Entmacher et al. 2013).

As women increasingly work outside the home, ideas about the gender roles of males and females have changed. Compare your grandparents and your parents. Chances are you have an employed mother, but your grandmother was more likely a stay-at-home

---

**TABLE 18.8**  Cash Employment of American Mothers, Wives, and Husbands, 1960–2011*

| YEAR | PERCENTAGE OF MARRIED WOMEN, HUSBAND PRESENT WITH CHILDREN UNDER AGE 6 | PERCENTAGE OF ALL MARRIED WOMEN† | PERCENTAGE OF ALL MARRIED MEN‡ |
|---|---|---|---|
| 1960 | 19 | 32 | 89 |
| 1970 | 30 | 40 | 86 |
| 1980 | 45 | 50 | 81 |
| 1990 | 59 | 58 | 79 |
| 2011 | 62 | 60 | 75 |

*Civilian population 16 years of age and older.
†Husband present.
‡Wife present.

SOURCE: *Proquest Statistical Abstract of the United States 2013*, Table 607, p. 396; Table 609, p. 397.

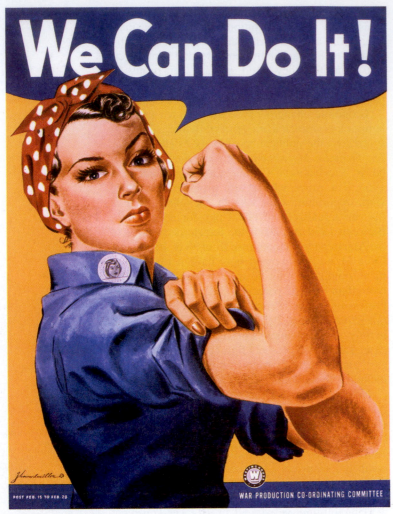

During the world wars, the notion that women were biologically unfit for hard physical labor faded. World War II's Rosie the Riveter—a strong, competent woman dressed in overalls and a bandana—was introduced as a symbol of patriotic womanhood. Is there a comparable poster woman today? What does her image say about modern gender roles?

mom. Your grandfather is more likely than your father to have worked in manufacturing and to have belonged to a union. Your father is more likely than your grandfather to have shared child-care and domestic responsibilities. Age at marriage has been delayed for both men and women. College educations and professional degrees have increased. What other changes do you associate with the increase in female employment outside the home?

Today's jobs aren't especially demanding in terms of physical labor. With machines to do the heavy work, the smaller average body size and lesser average strength of women are no longer impediments to blue-collar employment. The main reason we don't see more modern-day Rosies working alongside male riveters is that the U.S. workforce itself has been abandoning heavy-goods manufacture. In the 1950s, two-thirds of American jobs were blue-collar, compared with less than 15 percent today. The location of those jobs has shifted within the world capitalist economy. Third World countries, with their cheaper labor costs, produce steel, automobiles, and other heavy goods less expensively than the United States can, but the United States excels at services. The American mass education system has many inadequacies, but it does train millions of people for service and information-oriented jobs.

## The Feminization of Poverty

Alongside the economic gains of many American women stands an opposite extreme: the feminization of poverty. This refers to the increasing representation of women (and their children) among America's poorest people. Women head over half of U.S. households with incomes below the poverty line. Table 18.9 shows that the average income of married-couple families is more than twice that of families maintained by a single woman. The median female-headed one-earner family had an annual

**TABLE 18.9**  Median Annual Income of U.S. Households, by Household Type, 2010

| | NUMBER OF HOUSEHOLDS (1,000s) | MEDIAN ANNUAL INCOME (DOLLARS) | PERCENTAGE OF MEDIAN EARNINGS COMPARED WITH MARRIED-COUPLE HOUSEHOLDS |
|---|---|---|---|
| All households | 118,682 | 49,445 | 70 |
| *Family households* | 78,613 | 61,544 | 85 |
| Married-couple households | 58,036 | 72,751 | 100 |
| Male earner, no wife | 5,559 | 49,718 | 68 |
| Female earner, no husband | 15,019 | 32,031 | 44 |
| *Nonfamily households* | 38,705 | 29,730 | 41 |
| Single male | 18,835 | 35,627 | 50 |
| Single female | 21,234 | 25,456 | 35 |

SOURCE: *Proquest Statistical Abstract of the United States 2013,* Table 706, p. 470.

income of $32,031 in 2010, compared with $72,751 for a married-couple household.

The feminization of poverty isn't just a North American phenomenon. The percentage of single-parent (usually female-headed) households has been increasing worldwide. The figure ranges from about 10 percent in Japan, to below 20 percent in certain South Asian and Southeast Asian countries, to almost 50 percent in certain African countries and the Caribbean. The percentage of single-parent households rose in every nation listed in Table 18.10 between 1980–81 and 2009. The United States maintains the largest percentage of single-parent households (29.5 percent), followed by the United Kingdom (25 percent), Canada (24.6 percent), Ireland (22.6 percent), and Denmark (21.7 percent). The rate of increase in single-parent households over the past 30 years has been highest in Ireland, where it tripled, from 7.2 to 22.6 percent. Globally, households headed by women tend to be poorer than those headed by men. In the United States in 2012, the poverty rate for female-headed families with children was 41 percent, compared with 23 percent for male-headed families with children, and 9 percent for families with children headed by a married couple. More than half the poor children in the United States live in families headed by women (Entmacher et al. 2013).

It is widely believed that one way to improve the situation of poor women is to encourage them to organize. New women's groups can in some cases revive or replace traditional forms of social organization that have been disrupted. Membership in a group can help women to mobilize resources, to rationalize

**TABLE 18.10** Percentage of Single-Parent Households, Selected Countries, 1980–81 and 2009

| COUNTRY | 1980–81 | 2009 |
|---|---|---|
| United States | 19.5 | 29.5 |
| United Kingdom | 13.9 | 25.0 |
| Canada | 12.7 | 24.6 |
| Ireland | 7.2 | 22.6 |
| Denmark | 13.4 | 21.7 |
| France | 10.2 | 19.8 |
| Japan | 4.9 | 10.2 |

SOURCE: *Proquest Statistical Abstract of the United States 2013,* Table 1353, p. 869.

production, and to reduce the risks and costs associated with credit (Dunham 2009). Organization also allows women to develop self-confidence and to decrease dependence on others. This chapter's "Focus on Globalization" on p. 352 describes an index designed to measure, country by country, gender-based disparities and to track progress in reducing them.

## Work and Happiness

Table 18.11 shows female labor force participation in various countries—condensed from 30 countries for which data were available—in 2011. The United States, with 61.7 percent of its women employed or looking for work that year, ranked 13th, while Canada (74.4 percent) ranked seventh.

**TABLE 18.11** Female Labor Force Participation by Country, 2011

| COUNTRY | PERCENTAGE OF WOMEN IN LABOR FORCE | RANK AMONG WORLD'S 15 "HAPPIEST COUNTRIES" |
|---|---|---|
| Switzerland | 82.2 | 7 |
| Iceland | 81.6 | * |
| Sweden | 79.0 | 9 |
| Norway | 77.5 | 3 |
| Denmark | 75.7 | 1 |
| New Zealand | 74.9 | 8 |
| Canada | 74.5 | 6 |
| Finland | 73.6 | 2 |
| Netherlands | 72.8 | 4 |
| Germany | 72.5 | * |
| Australia | 72.3 | 11 |
| United Kingdom | 70.8 | * |
| United States | 61.7 | 12 |
| Turkey (lowest in table) | 31.8 | * |

*These countries were not among the 15 "happiest countries."

SOURCE: *Proquest Statistical Abstract of the United States 2013,* Table 1383, p. 887; Huffington Post, http://www.huffingtonpost.com/2010/07/03/worlds-happiest-countries_n_633814.html#s109416title=Denmark_77.

## The Global Gender Gap Index

The World Economic Forum, based in Switzerland, began publishing its annual Global Gender Gap Index in 2006 (see Hausmann, Tyson, and Zahidi 2012). This index assesses gender inequality, and progress in reducing it, in 135 countries. For each country, the index measures the gap between males and females in four major categories: economic opportunity and participation, educational achievement, health and survival, and political empowerment.

Most of the indexed countries, representing over 90 percent of the world's population, have reduced their gender gaps. Worldwide, 96 percent of the gender gap in health has been closed, along with 93 percent in education. Only 60 percent of the economic gap, however, and a paltry 20 percent of the political gap between men and women have been closed.

Worldwide, only about 20 women serve as elected heads of government. In 2012, *Forbes* magazine ranked Angela Merkel, Germany's chancellor, the world's second most powerful person (after President Barack Obama). Merkel, however, was the only woman in the top 10 and was 1 of only 3 women in the top 20 most powerful people in the world (see http://www.forbes.com/powerful-people/). In ministries, parliaments, and houses of congress the global average is less than 20 percent female.

North America has been the world's most successful region in terms of correcting gender-based inequality. Next come Europe and Central Asia, followed by Latin America, Asia, and Africa. The Middle East/North Africa comes in last.

Four Nordic countries consistently have held the top four positions in the index: Iceland, Finland, Norway, and Sweden. (Consider how this might relate to the happiness index discussed in this chapter.) Although no country has yet achieved full gender equality, those four countries have closed over 80 percent of their gender gaps, considering all criteria. The lowest-ranking country, Yemen, has closed only about half of its gender gap.

The United States ranked 22nd overall in the Global Gender Gap Index in 2012. There was no gender gap in educational attainment. U.S. literacy rates are high for both genders, and male and female rates of enrollment are comparable at all educational levels. The United States fared less well in terms of economics and politics. While ranking eighth in economic participation and opportunity, the U.S. was only 61st in terms of equal pay for equal work. The United States did rise somewhat in political empowerment—from 66th place in 2006 to 55th place in 2012.

To summarize: By 2012, 20 percent of the global political empowerment gap had been closed, versus 14 percent in 2006. In economic participation, 60 percent of the global gap had been closed, versus 56 percent in 2006. In 2012, 93 percent of the educational gap had been closed, up a bit from 92 percent

in 2006. In terms of health, however, there was a small decline between 2006 and 2012, from 97 percent to 96 percent.

These rates of improvement strike me as being rather slow. There's still a lot of progress to be made. A country's gender equality is correlated with its overall economic development and its global competitiveness. Because women represent about half of any national talent base, a country's long-run competitiveness depends significantly on the opportunities it offers its women. How might your country act to reduce its gender gap?

German Chancellor Angela Merkel holds a press conference prior to attending the annual EU summit meeting in Brussels, Belgium, in March 2014. Merkel has been called the world's most powerful woman.

Denmark, which has a high rate of workplace women, a rising birthrate, and readily available child care, is rated the world's happiest country. The genetics researcher shown here is the mother of a toddler.

Switzerland topped the list, with 82.2 percent of its women in the workforce. Turkey was lowest; only 31.8 percent of its women were employed.

In 2010 Gallup conducted a survey of the world's 132 happiest countries, based on various measures, including the percentages of people in that country who were thriving, and suffering. Respondents also were asked to rate their own lives on a scale from zero (worst possible) to 10 (best possible). Denmark was the world's happiest nation; Canada came in sixth; and the United States, 12th.

We see in Table 18.11 that of the 13 countries with greatest female labor force participation, 10 ranked among the world's happiest (see Levy 2010). Why, as more women work outside the home, might a country's population achieve a greater sense of well-being? Note that many of the countries listed as among the world's happiest not only have more employed women but also have a higher living standard and a more secure government safety net. Can you think of other factors that might explain a relationship between happiness and work outside the home?

## BEYOND MALE AND FEMALE

Gender is socially constructed, and societies may recognize more than two genders. The contemporary United States, for example, includes individuals who self-identify using such labels as "transgender," "intersex," "third gender," and "transsexual." Such persons contradict dominant male/female gender distinctions by being part male and part female, or neither male nor female. Because people who self-identify as "transgender" or "gender creative" are increasingly visible, we must be careful about seeing "masculine" and "feminine" as absolute and binary categories.

Sex, we have seen, is biological, whereas gender is socially constructed. Transgender is a social category that includes individuals who *may or may not* contrast biologically with ordinary males and females. Within the transgender category, intersex people (see below) usually contrast biologically with ordinary males and females, but *transgender also includes people whose gender identity has no apparent biological roots*. The term **intersex** encompasses a group of conditions involving a discrepancy between the external genitals (penis, vagina, etc.) and the internal genitals (testes, ovaries, etc.). The older term for this condition, *hermaphroditism,* combined the names of a Greek god and goddess. Hermes was a god of male sexuality (among other things) and Aphrodite a goddess of female sexuality, love, and beauty.

The causes of intersex are varied and complex (Kaneshiro 2009): (1) An XX intersex person has the chromosomes of a woman (XX) and normal ovaries, uterus, and fallopian tubes, but the external genitals appear male. Usually, this results from a female fetus having been exposed to an excess of male hormones before birth. (2) An XY intersex

**intersex**
Pertaining to a group of conditions reflecting a discrepancy between external and internal genitals.

South Africa's Caster Semenya celebrates her gold medal run in the final of the Women's 800 meters during the World Athletics Championships in Berlin in August 2009. Following that victory, questions were raised about her gender, and she was subjected to gender testing. She was sidelined for 11 months while the tests were reviewed before being cleared to run again in 2010.

person has the chromosomes of a man (XY), but the external genitals are incompletely formed, ambiguous, or female. The testes may be normal, malformed, or absent. (3) A true gonadal intersex person has both ovarian and testicular tissue. The external genitals may be ambiguous or may appear to be female or male. (4) Intersex also can result from an unusual chromosome combination, such as X0 (only one X chromosome), XXY, XYY, and XXX. In the last three cases there is an extra sex chromosome, either an X or a Y. These chromosomal combinations don't typically produce a discrepancy between internal and external genitalia, but there may be problems with sex hormone levels and overall sexual development.

The XXY configuration, known as *Klinefelter's syndrome,* is the most common of these combinations and the second most common condition (after Down syndrome) caused by the presence of extra chromosomes in humans. Effects of Klinefelter's syndrome occur in about 1 of every 1,000 males. One in every 500 males has an extra X chromosome but lacks the main symptoms—small testicles and reduced fertility. With XXX, also known as *triple X syndrome,* there is an extra X chromosome in each cell of a human female. Triple X occurs in about 1 of every 1,000 female births. There usually is no physically distinguishable difference between triple X women and other women. The same is true of XYY compared with other males. *Turner syndrome* encompasses several conditions, of which 0X (absence of one sex chromosome) is most common. In this case, all or part of one of the sex chromosomes is absent. Girls with Turner syndrome typically are sterile because of nonworking ovaries and amenorrhea (absence of a menstrual cycle).

Biology, remember, isn't destiny; people construct their identities in society. Many individuals affected by one of the biological conditions just described see themselves simply as male or female, rather than transgender. Self-identified **transgender** people tend to be individuals whose gender identity contradicts their biological sex at birth and the gender identity that society assigned to them in infancy. Feeling that their previous gender assignment was incorrect, they assert or seek to achieve a new one. The transgender category is diverse. Some transgender individuals lean toward male; some, female; and some toward neither of the dominant genders.

The anthropological record attests that gender diversity beyond male and female exists in many societies and has taken many forms across societies and cultures. Consider, for example, the eunuch, or "perfect servant" (a castrated man who served as a safe attendant to harems in Byzantium [Tougher 2008]). Hijras, who live mainly in northern India, are culturally defined as "neither men nor women," or as men who become women by undergoing castration and adopting women's dress and behavior. Hijras identify with the Indian mother goddess and are believed to channel her power. They are known for their ritualized performances at births and marriages, where they dance and sing, conferring the mother goddess's blessing on the child or the married couple. Although culturally defined as celibate, some hijras now engage in prostitution, in which their role is as women with men (Nanda 1996, 1998). Hijra social movements have campaigned for recognition as a third gender, and in 2005, Indian passport application forms were updated with three gender options: M, F, and E (for male, female, and eunuch [i.e., hijra], respectively) (*Telegraph* 2005).

Roscoe (1991, 1998) writes of the "Zuni manwoman," or berdache, in the 19th century. A berdache was a male who adopted social roles traditionally assigned to women and, through performance of a third gender, contributed to the social and spiritual well-being of the community. Some Balkan societies included "sworn virgins," born females who assumed male gender roles and activities to meet societal needs when there was a shortage of men (Gremaux 1993).

Among the Gheg tribes of North Albania, "virginal transvestites" were biologically female, but locals consider them "honorary men" (Shryock 1988). Some Albanian adolescent girls have chosen to become men, remain celibate, and live among men, with the support of their families and villagers (Young 2000). And consider Polynesia. In

**transgender**
Describes individuals whose gender identity contradicts their biological sex at birth and the gender identity assigned to them in infancy.

Neither men nor women, hijras constitute India's third gender. Many hijras get their income from performing at ceremonies, begging, or prostitution. The beauty contest shown here was organized by an AIDS prevention and relief organization that works with the local hijra community.

Tonga the term *fakaleitis* describes males who behave as women do, thereby contrasting with mainstream Tongan men. Similar to Tonga's *fakaleitis,* Samoan *fa'afafine* and Hawaiian *mahu* are men who adopt feminine attributes, behaviors, and visual markers.

This chapter's "Appreciating Anthropology" on pp. 356–357 describes how *transvestites* (men dressing as women) form a third gender in relation to Brazil's polarized male–female identity scale. Transvestites, not uncommon in Brazil, are members of one gender (usually males) who dress as another (female). At the time of the case described in "Appreciating Anthropology," a Brazilian man who wished to have gender reassignment surgery could not obtain the operation in Brazil. Some men, including Roberta Close, as described in "Appreciating Anthropology," traveled to Europe for the procedure. In France, transvestites regardless of nationality commonly are referred to as "Brésiliennes" (the feminine form of the French word for *Brazilian*), so common are Brazilians among the transvestites in Europe. In Brazil many men do have sexual relations with transvestites, with little stigma attached, as described in "Appreciating Anthropology."

The category transgender encompasses varied individuals whose gender performance and identity enlarge an otherwise binary gender structure. In recent years, the lesbian and gay rights movement has expanded to include bisexual and transgender individuals. This Lesbian, Gay, Bisexual, and Transgender (LGBT) community in the United States works to promote government policies and social practices that protect its members' civil and human rights. In recent years, the LGBT movement and its supporters have achieved many successes, including the repeal of the Defense of Marriage Act (DOMA), legalization of same-sex marriage in several states, and the repeal of the "Don't Ask Don't Tell" (DADT) policy of the U.S. armed services.

## SEXUAL ORIENTATION

**Gender identity** refers to whether a person feels, and is regarded as, male, female, or something else. One's gender identity does not dictate one's sexual orientation. Men who have no doubt about their masculinity can be sexually attracted to women or to other men. Ditto women with regard to female gender identity and variable sexual attraction. **Sexual orientation** refers to a person's habitual sexual attraction to, and sexual activities with, persons of the opposite sex, *heterosexuality;* the same sex, *homosexuality;* or both sexes, *bisexuality. Asexuality,* indifference toward or lack of attraction to either sex, also is a sexual orientation. All four of these forms are found throughout the world. But each type of desire and experience holds different meanings for individuals and groups. For example, male–male sexual activity may be a private affair in Mexico, rather than public, socially sanctioned, and encouraged as it was among the Etoro of Papua New Guinea (see pp. 356–357).

In any society, individuals will differ in the nature, range, and intensity of their sexual interests and urges (see Blackwood 2010; Herdt and Polen 2013; Kottak and Kozaitis 2012; Lancaster and Di Leonardo 1997; Nanda 2000). No one knows for sure why such individual sexual differences exist. Part of the answer appears to be biological, reflecting genes or hormones. Another part may have to do with experiences during growth and development. But whatever the reasons for individual variation, culture always plays a role in molding individual sexual urges toward a collective norm. And such sexual norms vary from culture to culture.

What do we know about variation in sexual norms from society to society, and over time? A classic cross-cultural study (Ford and Beach 1951) found wide variation in attitudes about forms of sexual activity. Even in a single society, such as the United States, attitudes about sex differ over time and with socioeconomic status, region, and rural versus urban residence. However, even in the 1950s, prior to the "age of sexual permissiveness" (the pre-HIV period from the mid-1960s through the 1970s), research showed that almost all American men (92 percent) and more than half of American women (54 percent) admitted to masturbation. In the famous Kinsey report (Kinsey, Pomeroy, and Martin 1948), 37 percent of the men surveyed admitted having had at least one sexual experience leading to orgasm with another male. In a later study of 1,200 unmarried women, 26 percent reported same-sex sexual activities. (Because Kinsey's research relied on nonrandom samples, it should be considered merely illustrative, rather than a statistically accurate representation, of sexual behavior at the time.)

In almost two-thirds (63 percent) of the 76 societies in the Ford and Beach study, various forms of same-sex sexual activity were acceptable. Occasionally sexual relations between people of the same sex involved transvestism on the part of one of the partners (see Kulick 1998). Transvestism did not characterize male–male sex among the Sudanese Azande, who valued the warrior role (Evans-Pritchard 1970). Prospective warriors—young men aged 12 to 20—left their families and shared quarters with adult fighting men, who had sex with them. The younger men were considered temporary brides of the older men and did the domestic duties of women. Upon reaching warrior status, these young men took their own younger male brides. Later, retiring from the warrior role, Azande men married women. Flexible in their sexual expression, Azande males had no difficulty shifting from sex with older men (as male brides), to sex with younger men (as warriors), to

**gender identity**
A person's identification by self and others as male, female, or something else.

**sexual orientation**
Sexual attraction to persons of the opposite sex, same sex, or both sexes.

# Hidden Women, Public Men—Public Women, Hidden Men

Generations of anthropologists have applied their field's comparative, cross-cultural, and biocultural approaches to the study of sex and gender. To some extent at least, gender, sexual preferences, and even sexual orientation are culturally constructed. Here I describe a case in which popular culture and comments by ordinary Brazilians about beauty and sex led me to an analysis of some striking gender differences between Brazil and the United States.

For several years, one of Brazil's top sex symbols was Roberta Close, whom I first saw in a furniture commercial. Roberta ended her pitch with an admonition to prospective furniture buyers to accept no substitute for the advertised product. "Things," she warned, "are not always what they seem."

Nor was Roberta. This petite and incredibly feminine creature was actually a man. Nevertheless, despite the fact that he—or she (speaking as Brazilians do)—is a man posing as a woman, Roberta won a secure place in Brazilian mass culture. Her photos decorated magazines. She was a pan-

elist on a TV variety show and starred in a stage play in Rio with an actor known for his super-macho image. Roberta even inspired a well-known, and apparently heterosexual, pop singer to make a video honoring her. In it, she pranced around Rio's Ipanema Beach in a bikini, showing off her ample hips and buttocks.

The video depicted the widespread male appreciation of Roberta's beauty. As confirmation, one heterosexual man told me he had recently been on the same plane as Roberta and had been struck by her looks. Another man said he wanted to have sex with her. These comments, it seemed to me, illustrated striking cultural contrasts about gender and sexuality. In Brazil, a Latin American country noted for its machismo, heterosexual men did not feel that attraction toward a transvestite blemished their masculine identities.

Roberta Close can be understood in relation to a gender-identity scale that jumps from extreme femininity to extreme masculinity, with little in between. Masculinity is stereotyped as active and

public, femininity as passive and domestic. The male–female contrast in rights and behavior is much stronger in Brazil than it is in North America. Brazilians confront a more rigidly defined masculine role than North Americans do.

The active–passive dichotomy also provides a stereotypical model for male–male sexual relations. One man is supposed to be the active, masculine (inserting) partner, whereas the other is the passive, effeminate one. The latter man is derided as a bicha (intestinal worm), but little stigma attaches to the inserter. Indeed, many "active" (and married) Brazilian men like to have sex with transvestite prostitutes, who are biological males.

If a Brazilian man is unhappy pursuing either active masculinity or passive effeminacy, there is one other choice—active femininity. For Roberta Close and others like her, the cultural demand of ultramasculinity has yielded to a performance of ultrafemininity. These men–women form a third gender in relation to Brazil's polarized male–female identity scale.

sex with women (as husbands) (see Murray and Roscoe 1998).

An extreme example of tension involving male–female sexual relations in Papua New Guinea is provided by the Etoro (Kelly 1976), a group of 400 people who subsist by hunting and horticulture in the Trans-Fly region (Figure 18.2, p. 358). The Etoro illustrate the power of culture in molding human sexuality. The following account, based on ethnographic fieldwork by Raymond C. Kelly in the late 1960s, applies only to Etoro males and their beliefs. Etoro cultural norms prevented the male anthropologist who studied them from gathering comparable information about female attitudes and behavior. Note, also, that the activities described have been discouraged by missionaries. Since there has been no restudy of the Etoro specifically focusing on these activities, the extent to which these practices continue today is unknown. For this reason, I'll use the past tense in describing them.

Etoro opinions about sexuality were linked to their beliefs about the cycle of birth, physical

growth, maturity, old age, and death. Etoro culture promoted the idea that semen was necessary to give life force to a fetus, which, they believed, was implanted in a woman by an ancestral spirit. Sexual intercourse during pregnancy nourished the growing fetus. The Etoro believed that men had a limited lifetime supply of semen. Any sex act leading to ejaculation was seen as draining that supply, and as sapping a man's virility and vitality. The birth of children, nurtured by semen, symbolized a necessary sacrifice that would lead to the husband's eventual death. Male–female intercourse, required only for reproduction, was discouraged. Women who wanted too much sex were viewed as witches, hazardous to their husbands' health. Etoro culture allowed male–female intercourse only about 100 days a year. The rest of the time it was tabooed. Seasonal birth clustering shows the taboo was respected.

So objectionable was male–female sex that it was removed from community life. It could occur neither in sleeping quarters nor in the fields. Coitus

Transvestites like Roberta are particularly prominent in Rio de Janeiro's annual Carnaval, when an ambience of inversion rules the city. In the culturally accurate words of the American popular novelist Gregory McDonald, who sets one of his books in Brazil at Carnaval time:

> Everything goes topsy-turvy. . . . Men become women; women become men; grown-ups become children; rich people pretend they're poor; poor people, rich; sober people become drunkards; thieves become generous. Very topsy-turvy. (McDonald 1984, p. 154)

Most notable in this costumed inversion (DaMatta 1991), men dress as women. Carnaval reveals and expresses normally hidden tensions and conflicts as social life is turned upside down. Reality is illuminated through a dramatic presentation of its opposite.

This is the final key to Roberta's cultural meaning. She emerged in a setting in which male–female inversion is part of the year's most popular festival. Transvestites are the pièces de résistance at Rio's Carnaval balls, where they dress as scantily as the real women do. They wear postage-stamp bikinis, sometimes with no tops. Photos of real women and transformed ones vie for space in the magazines. It is often impossible to tell the born women from the hidden men. Roberta Close

Roberta Close, photographed in 1999, at age 35. In 1989, Close underwent sex reassignment surgery in England. Subsequently she was voted the "Most Beautiful Woman in Brazil."

is a permanent incarnation of Carnaval—a year-round reminder of the spirit of Carnavals past, present, and yet to come.

Roberta emerged from a Latin culture whose gender roles contrast strongly with those of the United States. From small village to massive city, Brazilian males are public and Brazilian females are private creatures. Streets, beaches, and bars belong to the men. Although bikinis adorn Rio's beaches on weekends and holidays, there are many more men than women there on weekdays. The men revel in their ostentatiously sexual displays. As they sun themselves and play soccer and volleyball, they regularly stroke their genitals to keep them firm. They are living publicly, assertively, and sexually in a world of men.

Brazilian men must work hard at this public image, constantly acting out their culture's definition of masculine behavior. Public life is a play whose strong roles go to men. Roberta Close, of course, was a public figure. Given that Brazilian culture defines the public world as male, we can perhaps better understand now why a popular Brazilian sex symbol could be a man who excels at performing in public as a woman.

could happen only in the woods, where it was risky because poisonous snakes, the Etoro believed, were attracted by the sounds and smells of male–female sex.

Although coitus was discouraged, sex acts between males were viewed as essential. Etoro believed that boys could not produce semen on their own. To grow into men and eventually give life force to their children, boys had to acquire semen orally from older men. No taboos were attached to this. This oral insemination could proceed in the sleeping area or garden. Every three years, young men around the age of 20 were formally initiated into manhood. They went to a secluded mountain lodge, where they were visited and inseminated by several older men.

Male–male sex among the Etoro was governed by a code of propriety. Although sexual relations between older and younger males were considered culturally essential, those between boys of the same age were discouraged. A boy who took semen from other youths was believed to be sapping their life force and stunting their growth. A boy's rapid physical development might suggest that he was getting semen from other boys. Like a sex-hungry wife, he might be shunned as a witch.

The sexual practices just described rested not on hormones or genes but on cultural beliefs and traditions. The Etoro shared a cultural pattern, which Gilbert Herdt (ed. 1984, 2006) calls "ritualized homosexuality," with some 50 other tribes in a region of Papua New Guinea. These societies illustrate one extreme of a male–female avoidance pattern that has been widespread in Papua New Guinea, and patrilineal-patrilocal societies more generally.

Flexibility in sexual expression seems to be an aspect of our primate heritage. Both masturbation and same-sex sexual activity exist among chimpanzees and other primates. Male bonobos (pygmy chimps) regularly engage in a form of mutual masturbation that has been called "penis fencing." Female bonobos get sexual pleasure from rubbing their genitals against those of other females (de Waal 1997). Our primate

**FIGURE 18.2**  The Location of the Etoro, Kaluli, and Sambia in Papua New Guinea.
The western part of the island of New Guinea is part of Indonesia. The eastern part of the island is the independent nation of Papua New Guinea, home of the Etoro, Kaluli, and Sambia.

sexual potential is molded by culture, the environment, and reproductive necessity. Male–female coitus is practiced in all human societies—which, after all, must reproduce themselves—but alternatives also are widespread (Rathus, Nevid, and Fichner-Rathus 2014). Like our gender roles, the sexual component of human identity—just how we express our "natural," or biological, sexual urges—is a matter that culture and environment influence and limit.

# for REVIEW

## summary

1.  *Gender roles* are the tasks and activities that a culture assigns to each sex. *Gender stereotypes* are oversimplified ideas about attributes of males and females. *Gender stratification* describes an unequal distribution of rewards by gender, reflecting different positions in a social hierarchy. Cross-cultural

comparison reveals some recurrent patterns involving the division of labor by gender and gender-based differences in reproductive strategies. Gender roles and gender stratification also vary with environment, economy, adaptive strategy, level of social complexity, and degree of participation in the world economy.

2. When gathering is prominent, gender status is more equal than it is when hunting or fishing dominates the foraging economy. Gender status is more equal when the domestic and public spheres aren't sharply separated. Foragers lack two public arenas that contribute to higher male status among food producers: warfare and organized interregional trade.

3. Gender stratification also is linked to descent and residence. Women's status in matrilineal societies tends to be high because overall social identity comes through female links. Women in many societies, especially matrilineal ones, wield power and make decisions. Scarcity of resources promotes intervillage warfare, patriliny, and patrilocality. The localization of related males is adaptive for military solidarity. Men may use their warrior role to symbolize and reinforce the social devaluation and oppression of women. *Patriarchy* describes a political system ruled by men in which women have inferior social and political status, including basic human rights.

4. Americans' attitudes toward gender vary with class and region. When the need for female labor declines, the idea that women are unfit for many jobs increases, and vice versa. Factors such as war, falling wages, and inflation help explain female cash employment and Americans' attitudes toward it. Countering the economic gains of many American women is the feminization of poverty. This has become a global phenomenon, as impoverished female-headed households have increased worldwide.

5. Societies may recognize more than two genders. The term *intersex* describes a group of conditions, including chromosomal configurations, that may produce a discrepancy between external and internal genitals. Transgender individuals may or may not contrast biologically with ordinary males and females. Self-identified transgender people tend to be individuals whose gender identity contradicts their biological sex at birth and the gender identity that society assigned to them in infancy.

6. *Gender identity* refers to whether a person feels, and is regarded as, male, female, or something else. One's gender identity does not dictate one's sexual orientation. Sexual orientation stands for a person's habitual sexual attraction to, and activities with, persons of the opposite sex (heterosexuality), the same sex (homosexuality), or both sexes (bisexuality). Sexual norms and practices vary widely from culture to culture.

**key terms**

domestic–public dichotomy  346
gender  342
gender identity  355
gender roles  342
gender stereotypes  342
gender stratification  342
intersex  353

matrilineal descent  347
patriarchy  348
patrilineal descent  347
patrilineal-patrilocal complex  347
sexual dimorphism  342
sexual orientation  355
transgender  354

**critical thinking**

1. How are sexuality, sex, and gender related to one another? What are the differences between these three concepts? Provide an argument about why anthropologists are uniquely positioned to study the relationships between sexuality, sex, and gender in society.

2. Using your own society, give an example of a gender role, a gender stereotype, and gender stratification.

3. What is the feminization of poverty? Where is this trend occurring, and what are some of its causes?

4. Is intersex the same as transgender? If not, how do they differ? How might biological, cultural, and personal factors influence gender identity?

5. This chapter describes Raymond Kelly's research among the Etoro of Papua New Guinea. What were his findings regarding Etoro male–female sexual relations? How did Kelly's own gender affect some of the content and extent of his study? Can you think of other research projects where the ethnographer's gender would have an impact?

# CHAPTER 19

# Families, Kinship, and Descent

A family reunion celebrating the Chinese Lunar New Year outside a cave dwelling in central China's Henan Province.

▶ Why and how do anthropologists study kinship?

▶ How do families and descent groups differ, and what are their social correlates?

▶ How is kinship calculated, and how are relatives classified, in various societies?

# understanding OURSELVES

Although it still is something of an ideal in our culture, the nuclear family (mother, father, and biological children) now accounts for barely one-fifth of all American households. Such phrases as "marriage and the family" and "mom and pop" no longer apply to a majority of American households. What kind of family raised you? Perhaps it was a nuclear family. Or maybe you were raised by a single parent, with or without the help of extended kin. Perhaps your extended kin acted as your parents. Or maybe you had a stepparent and/or step- or half-siblings in a blended family. Your own family may match none of these descriptions, or it may have had different descriptions at different times.

Although contemporary American families may seem amazingly diverse, other cultures offer family alternatives that Americans might have trouble understanding. Imagine a society in which someone doesn't know for sure, and doesn't care much about, who his actual mother was. Consider Joseph Rabe, a Betsileo man who was my field assistant in Madagascar. Rabe, who had been raised by his aunt—his father's sister—told me about two sisters, one of whom was his mother and the other his mother's sister. He knew their names, but he didn't know which was which. Illustrating an adoptive pattern common among the Betsileo, Rabe was given as a toddler to his childless aunt. His mother and her sister lived far away and died in his childhood (as did his father), so he didn't really know them. But he was very close to his father's sister, for whom he used the term for mother. Indeed, he had to call her that because the Betsileo have only one kin term, *reny*, for mother, mother's sister, and father's sister. (They also use a single term, *ray*, for father and all uncles.) The difference between "real" (biologically based) and socially constructed kinship didn't matter to Rabe.

Contrast this Betsileo case with Americans' attitudes about kinship and adoption. On family-oriented radio talk shows, I've heard hosts distinguish between "birth mothers" and adoptive mothers, and between "sperm daddies" and "daddies of the heart." The latter may be adoptive fathers or stepfathers who have "been like fathers" to someone. American culture tends to promote the idea that kinship is, and should be, biological. It's increasingly common for adopted children to seek out their birth parents (which used to be discouraged as disruptive), even after a perfectly satisfactory upbringing in an adoptive family. The American emphasis on biology for kinship is seen also in the recent proliferation of DNA testing. Viewing our beliefs through the lens of cross-cultural comparison helps us appreciate that kinship and biology don't always converge, nor do they need to.

## FAMILIES

The kinds of societies anthropologists have studied traditionally, including many examples considered in this chapter, have stimulated a strong interest in families, along with larger systems of kinship, descent, and marriage. Cross-culturally, the social construction of kinship illustrates considerable diversity. Understanding kinship systems has become an essential part of anthropology because of the importance of those systems to the people we study. We are ready to take a closer look at the systems of kinship and descent that have organized human life during much of our history.

Ethnographers quickly recognize social divisions—groups—within any society they study. During fieldwork, they learn about significant groups by observing their activities and composition. People often live in the same village or neighborhood, or work, pray, or celebrate together because they are related in some way. To understand the social structure,

**family of orientation**
Nuclear family in which one is born and grows up.

**family of procreation**
Nuclear family established when one marries and has children.

**descent group**
Group based on belief in shared ancestry.

an ethnographer must investigate such kin ties. For example, the most significant local groups may consist of descendants of the same grandfather. These people may live in neighboring houses, farm adjoining fields, and help each other in everyday tasks. Other sorts of groups, based on different or more distant kin links, get together less often.

The nuclear family is one kind of kin group that is widespread in human societies. The nuclear family consists of parents and children, normally living together in the same household. Other kin groups include extended families (families consisting of three or more generations) and descent groups—lineages and clans. Such groups are not usually residentially based, as the nuclear family is. Extended family members get together from time to time, but they don't necessarily live together. Branches of a given descent group may reside in several villages and rarely assemble for common activity. **Descent groups,** which are composed of people claiming common ancestry, are basic units in the social organization of nonindustrial farmers and herders.

## Nuclear and Extended Families

A nuclear family lasts only as long as the parents and children remain together. Most people belong to at least two nuclear families at different times in their lives. They are born into a family consisting of their parents and siblings. Reaching adulthood, they may establish a nuclear family that includes their spouse

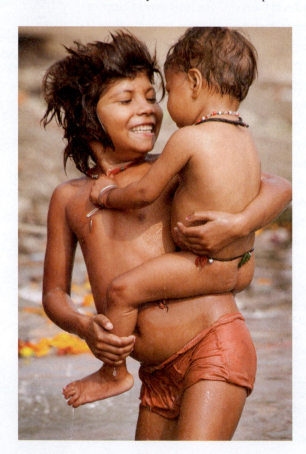

A big sister has been bathing her little brother in India's Ganges River. Siblings play a prominent role in child rearing in many societies. Do your siblings belong to your family of orientation or procreation?

(or domestic partner) and eventually their children. Some people establish more than one family through successive marriages or domestic partnerships.

Anthropologists distinguish between the **family of orientation** (the family in which one is born and grows up) and the **family of procreation** (formed when one has children). From the individual's point of view, the critical relationships are with parents and siblings in the family of orientation and with spouse (or domestic partner) and children in the family of procreation.

In most societies, relations with nuclear family members (parents, siblings, and children) take precedence over relations with other kin. Nuclear family organization is very widespread but not universal, and its significance in society differs greatly from one place to another. In a few societies, such as the classic Nayar case (described below), nuclear families are rare or nonexistent. In others, the nuclear family plays no special role in social life. Other social units—most notably descent groups and extended families—can assume many of the functions otherwise associated with the nuclear family.

Consider an example from the former Yugoslavia. Traditionally, among the Muslims of western Bosnia (Lockwood 1975), nuclear families lacked autonomy. Several such families were embedded in an extended family household called a *zadruga*. The *zadruga* was headed by a male household head and his wife, the senior woman. It also included married sons and their wives and children, as well as unmarried sons and daughters. Each nuclear family had a sleeping room, decorated and partly furnished from the bride's trousseau. However, possessions—even clothing items—were freely shared by *zadruga* members. Even trousseau items could be appropriated for use by other *zadruga* members. Such a residential unit is known as a *patrilocal* extended family, because each couple resides in the husband's father's household after marriage.

The *zadruga* took precedence over its component units. Social interaction was more usual among women, men, or children than between spouses or between parents and children. Larger households ate at three successive settings: for men, women, and children. Traditionally, all children over 12 slept together in boys' or girls' rooms. When a woman wished to visit another village, she sought the permission of the male *zadruga* head. Although men usually felt closer to their own children than to those of their brothers, they were obliged to treat them equally. Children were disciplined by any adult in the household. When a nuclear family broke up, children under 7 went with the mother. Older children could choose between their parents. Children were considered part of the household where they were born even if their mother left. One widow who remarried had to leave her five children, all over 7, in their father's *zadruga,* headed by his brother.

Another example of an alternative to the nuclear family is provided by the Nayars (or Nair), a large and powerful caste on the Malabar Coast of southern

India (Figure 19.1). Their traditional kinship system was matrilineal (descent traced only through females). Nayar lived in matrilineal extended family compounds called *tarawads*. The *tarawad* was a residential complex with several buildings, its own temple, granary, water well, orchards, gardens, and landholdings. Headed by a senior woman, assisted by her brother, the *tarawad* housed her siblings, her sisters' children, and other matrikin—matrilineal relatives (Gough 1959; Shivaram 1996).

Traditional Nayar marriage seems to have been hardly more than a formality—a kind of coming-of-age ritual. A young woman would go through a marriage ceremony with a man, after which they might spend a few days together at her *tarawad*. Then the man would return to his own *tarawad*, where he lived with his sisters, mother, aunts, and other matrikin. Nayar men belonged to a warrior class, who left home regularly for military expeditions, returning permanently to their *tarawad* on retirement. Nayar women could have multiple sexual partners. Children became members of the mother's *tarawad*; they were not considered to be relatives of their biological father. Indeed, many Nayar children didn't even know who their genitor was. Child care was the responsibility of the *tarawad*. Nayar society therefore reproduced itself biologically without the nuclear family.

# Industrialism and Family Organization

For many North Americans, the nuclear family is the only well-defined kin group. Family isolation arises from geographic mobility, which is associated with industrialism. Born into a family of orientation, we leave home for work or college, and the break with parents is under way. Eventually, most North Americans will enter a marriage or domestic partnership and establish a family of procreation. Because only about 2 percent of the U.S. population now farms, most people aren't tied to the land. We can move to places where jobs are available.

Married couples often live hundreds of miles from their parents. Their jobs have determined where they live (see Descartes and Kottak 2009). Such a post-marital residence pattern is called **neolocality:** Married couples establish a new place of residence—a "home of their own." Among middle-class North Americans, neolocal residence is both a cultural preference and a statistical norm. Most middle-class Americans eventually do establish households and nuclear families of their own.

Within stratified nations, value systems vary to some extent from class to class, and so does kinship. There are significant differences between middle-class and poorer North Americans. For example, in the lower class the incidence of *expanded family households* (those that include nonnuclear relatives) is greater than it is in the middle class. When an expanded family household includes three or more generations, it is an **extended family household,**

**FIGURE 19.1** Location of the Nayars in India's Kerala province.

**neolocality**
Living situation in which a couple establishes new residence.

**extended family household**
Household with three or more generations.

A just-married Khasi couple in India's northeastern city of Shillong. The Khasis are matrilineal, tracing descent through women and taking their maternal ancestors' surnames. Women choose their husbands, family incomes are pooled, and extended family households are managed by older women.

## Social Security, Kinship Style

In all societies, people care for others. Sometimes, as in our own state-organized society, social security is a function of government as well as of the individual and the family. In other societies, such as Arembepe, as described here, social security is part of systems of kinship, marriage, and fictive kinship.

My book *Assault on Paradise,* 4th edition (Kottak 2006), describes social relations in Arembepe, the Brazilian fishing community I've studied for many years. When I first studied Arembepe, I was struck by how similar its social relations were to those in the egalitarian, kin-based societies anthropologists have studied traditionally. The twin assertions "We're all equal here" and "We're all relatives here" were offered repeatedly as Arembepeiros' summaries of the nature and basis of local life. Like members of a clan (who claim to share common ancestry but who can't say exactly how they are related), most villagers couldn't trace precise genealogical links to their distant kin. "What difference does it make, as long as we know we're relatives?"

As in most nonindustrial societies, close personal relations were either based or modeled on kinship. A degree of community solidarity was promoted, for example, by the myth that everyone was kin. However, social solidarity was actually much less developed in Arembepe than in societies with clans and lineages—which use genealogy to include some people, and exclude others from membership, in a given descent group. Intense social solidarity demands that some people be excluded. By asserting they all were related—that is, by excluding no one—Arembepeiros were actually weakening kinship's potential strength in creating and maintaining group solidarity.

Rights and obligations always are associated with kinship and marriage. In Arembepe, the closer the kin connection and the more formal the marital tie, the greater the rights and obligations. Couples could be married formally or informally. The most common union was a stable common-law marriage. Less common, but with more prestige, was legal (civil) marriage, performed by a justice of the peace and conferring inheritance rights. The union with the most prestige combined legal validity with a church ceremony.

The rights and obligations associated with kinship and marriage constituted the local social security system, but people had to weigh the benefits of the system against its costs. The most obvious cost was this: Villagers had to share in proportion to their success. As people (usually ambitious men) climbed the local ladder of success, they got more dependents. To maintain their standing in public opinion, and to guarantee that they could depend on others in old age, they had to share. However, sharing was a powerful leveling mechanism. It drained surplus wealth and restricted upward mobility.

How, specifically, did this leveling work? As is often true in stratified nations, Brazilian national cultural norms are set by the upper classes. Middle- and upper-class Brazilians usually marry legally and in church. Even Arembepeiros knew this was the only "proper" way to marry. The most successful and ambitious local men copied the behavior of elite Brazilians. By doing so, they hoped to acquire some of their prestige.

An extended family of *cocoteros,* workers on a coconut plantation in the rural town of Barigua in eastern Cuba. Try to guess the relationships among them.

such as the *zadruga.* Another type of expanded family is the *collateral household,* which includes siblings and their spouses and children.

The higher proportion of expanded family households among poorer Americans has been explained as an adaptation to poverty (Stack 1975). Unable to survive economically as nuclear family units, relatives band together in an expanded household and pool their resources. Adaptation to poverty causes kinship values and attitudes to diverge from middle-class norms (see Hansen 2005). Thus, when North Americans raised in poverty achieve financial success, they often feel obligated to provide financial help to a wide circle of less fortunate relatives. (This chapter's "Appreciating Diversity" shows how poor Brazilians use kinship, marriage, and fictive kinship as a form of social security.)

### Changes in North American Kinship

The nuclear family may remain a cultural ideal for many Americans, but, as we see in Table 19.1 and

However, legal marriage drained individual wealth, for example, by creating a responsibility to help one's in-laws financially. Such obligations could be regular and costly. Obligations to kids also increased with income, because successful people tended to have more living children. Children were valued as companions and as an eventual economic benefit to their parents. Boys especially were prized because their economic prospects were so much brighter than those of girls.

Children's chances of survival surged dramatically in wealthier households with better diets. The normal household diet included fish—usually in a stew with tomatoes, onions, palm oil, vinegar, and lemon. Dried beef replaced fish once a week. Roasted manioc flour was the main source of calories and was eaten at all meals. Other daily staples included coffee, sugar, and salt. Fruits and vegetables were eaten in season. Diet was one of the main contrasts between households. The poorest people didn't eat fish regularly; often, they subsisted on manioc flour, coffee, and sugar. Better-off households supplemented the staples with milk, butter, eggs, rice,

beans, and more ample portions of fresh fish, fruits, and vegetables.

Adequate incomes bought improved diets and provided the means and confidence to seek out better medical attention than was locally available. Most of the children born in the wealthier households survived. But this meant more mouths to feed, and (since the heads of such households usually wanted a better education for their children) it meant increased expenditures on schooling. The correlation between economic success and large families was a siphoner of wealth that restricted individual economic advance. Tomé, a fishing entrepreneur, envisioned a life of constant hard work if he was to feed, clothe, and educate his growing family. Tomé and his wife had never lost a child. But he recognized that his growing family would, in the short run, be a drain on his resources. "But in the end, I'll have successful sons to help their mother and me, if we need it, in our old age."

Arembepeiros knew who could afford to share with others; success can't be concealed in a small community. Villagers based their expectations of others on this knowledge. Successful people had

to share with more kin and in-laws, and with more distant kin, than did poorer people. Successful captains and boat owners were expected to buy beer for ordinary fishermen; store owners had to sell on credit. As in bands and tribes, any well-off person was expected to exhibit a corresponding generosity. With increasing wealth, people also were asked more frequently to enter ritual kin relationships. Through baptism—which took place twice a year when a priest visited, or which could be done outside—a child acquired two godparents. These people became the coparents (compadres) of the baby's parents. The fact that ritual kinship obligations increased with wealth was another factor limiting individual economic advance.

We see that kinship, marriage, and ritual kinship in Arembepe had costs and benefits. The costs were limits on the economic advance of individuals. The primary benefit was social security—guaranteed help from kin, in-laws, and ritual kin in times of need. Benefits, however, came only after costs had been paid—that is, only to those who had lived "proper" lives, not deviating too noticeably from local norms, especially those about sharing.

**TABLE 19.1** Changes in Family and Household Organization in the United States, 2012 Compared with 1970

|  | 2012 | 1970 |
|---|---|---|
| *Numbers* | | |
| Total number of households | 122 million | 63 million |
| Number of people per household | 2.6 | 3.1 |
| *Percentages of households* | | |
| Married couples with children | 20% | 40% |
| Married couples without children | 29% | 30% |
| Family households | 66% | 81% |
| Five or more people | 10% | 21% |
| People living alone | 27% | 17% |
| Single-mother family households | 13% | 5% |
| Single-father family households | 5% | 0% |
| Children under 18 | 29% | 45% |

SOURCE: Jonathan Vespa, Jamie M. Lewis, and Rose M. Kreider, 2013, "America's Families and Living Arrangements: 2012," Current Population Reports, P20-570, U.S. Census Bureau, Washington, DC. https://www.census.gov/prod/2013pubs/p20-570.pdf

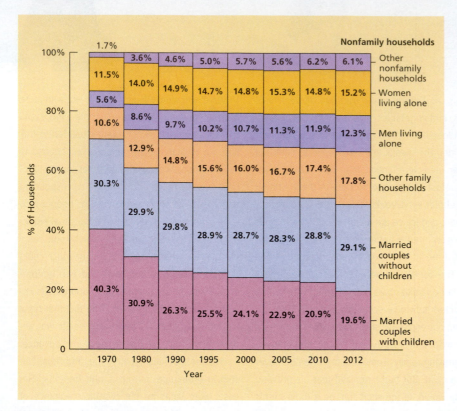

**FIGURE 19.2** Households by Type: Selected Years, 1970 to 2012 (Percent Distribution).

SOURCES: Jonathan Vespa, Jamie M. Lewis, and Rose M. Kreider, 2013, "America's Families and Living Arrangements: 2012," Current Population Reports, P20-570, U.S. Census Bureau, Washington, DC. https://www.census.gov/prod/2013pubs/p20-570.pdf

increased sixfold, from 4.3 million to 28 million. (Note, however, that each divorce creates two divorced people.) Table 19.2 shows the ratio of divorces to marriages in the United States for selected years between 1950 and 2011. The divorce rate jumped between 1960 and 1980 as the ratio of divorces to marriages doubled. Thereafter, between 1980 and 2000, the ratio hovered around 50 percent. That is, each year there were about half as many new divorces as there were new marriages. Since 2000 the rate has drifted up slightly, to 53 percent in 2011.

The growth of single-parent households also has outstripped population growth, almost tripling from fewer than 4 million in 1970 to 11.2 million in 2012. (The overall American population in 2012 was about 1.5 times its size in 1970.) The percentage (24 percent) of children living in fatherless households (mother-headed, no resident dad) in 2012 was more than twice the 1970 rate, while the percentage (4 percent) in motherless homes (father-headed, no resident mom) increased fivefold.

Fewer than half (46 percent) of American women lived with a husband in 2012, compared with 65 percent in 1950 and 51 percent in 2000 (Roberts et al. 2007; Vespa et al. 2013). The proportion of one-person households rose by 10 percentage points between 1970 and 2012, from 17 percent to 27 percent (Vespa et al. 2013).

Table 19.3 documents comparable declines in the size of families and households in the United States and Canada since 1980. The trend toward smaller families and living units also is detectable in Western Europe and other industrial nations. To be sure, contemporary Americans maintain social lives through work, friendship, sports, clubs, religion, and organized social activities. However, the growing isolation from kin that these figures suggest may well be unprecedented in human history.

The entire range of kin attachments is narrower for North Americans, particularly those in the middle class, than it is for nonindustrial peoples. Although we recognize ties to grandparents, uncles, aunts, and cousins, we have less contact with, and depend less on, those relatives than people in other cultures do. We see this when we answer a few questions: Do we know exactly how we are related to all our cousins? How much do we know about our ancestors, such as their full names and where they

Figure 19.2, nuclear families now account for barely one-fifth of American households. Other domestic arrangements now outnumber the "traditional" American household five to one. There are several reasons for this changing household composition. Women increasingly have joined men in the cash workforce. Often, this removes them from their family of orientation while making it economically feasible to delay (or even forgo) marriage. Often, job demands compete with romantic attachments. The median age at first marriage for American women rose from 21 years in 1970 to 27 in 2012. For men the comparable ages were 23 and 29. More than a third (36 percent) of American men and 30 percent of American women had never married as of 2012 (Vespa, Lewis, and Kreider 2013).

The divorce rate also has risen. Between 1970 and 2012, the number of divorced Americans

**TABLE 19.2** Ratio of Divorces to Marriages per 1,000 U.S. Population, Selected Years, 1950–2011

| 1950 | 1960 | 1970 | 1980 | 1990 | 2000 | 2010 |
|------|------|------|------|------|------|------|
| 23%  | 26%  | 33%  | 50%  | 48%  | 50%  | 53%  |

SOURCE: *Statistical Abstract of the United States 2012*, Table 132, http://www.census.gov/prod/2011pubs/12statab/pop.pdf; http://www.cdc.gov/nchs/nvss/marriage_divorce_tables.htm.

**TABLE 19.3** Household and Family Size in the United States and Canada, 1980 versus 2010

|  | 1980 | 2011 |
|---|---|---|
| *Average family size* |  |  |
| United States | 3.3 | 3.1 |
| Canada | 3.4 | 3.1 |
| *Average household size* |  |  |
| United States | 2.9 | 2.6 |
| Canada | 2.9 | 2.5 |

SOURCES: J. M. Fields, "America's Families and Living Arrangements: 2003," Current Population Reports, P20-553, November 2004, http://www.census.gov/prod/2004pubs/p20-553.pdf, pp. 3–4; *Statistics Canada, 2011 Census of Canada*, http://www.statcan.gc.ca/tables-tableaux/sum-som/l01/cst01/famil53a-eng.htm; J. Vespa, J. M. Lewis, and R. M. Kreider, 2013, "America's Families and Living Arrangements: 2012," Current Population Reports, P20-570, U.S. Census Bureau, Washington, D.C.

One among many kinds of American family: A single mother (by choice) bakes cupcakes with her twin daughters at their home in Brooklyn, New York. What do you see as the main differences between nuclear families and single-parent families?

lived? How many of the people with whom we associate regularly are our relatives?

Differences in the answers to these questions by people from industrial and those from nonindustrial societies confirm the declining importance of kinship in contemporary nations. Immigrants are often shocked by what they perceive as weak kinship bonds and lack of proper respect for family in contemporary North America. In fact, most of the people whom middle-class North Americans see every day are either nonrelatives or members of the nuclear family (see also Willie and Reddick 2009).

Interestingly, a recent study (Qian 2013) found that the traditional American nuclear family was best represented among recent immigrants. Sociologist Zhenchao Qian describes several differences involving marriage and the family between recent immigrants and native-born Americans. By 2010, the end point of Qian's 10-year study, immigrants comprised 13 percent of the U.S. population. They brought customs of their cultures of origin with them to the United States. One such pattern was marital stability, although brides tended to be significantly younger than their grooms. Among immigrants in their mid- to late twenties, 62 percent of women were married, compared with just 43 percent of men. At every age, however, the immigrant marriage rate was greater than that of native-born Americans, including those of their own ethnicity. Asian immigrants, for example, were twice as likely to marry as were U.S.-born Asians. Compared with native-born marriages, those of immigrants also tended to be more ethnically homogeneous and less prone to divorce. In 2010, about 30 percent of immigrant children lived in homes with a male breadwinner and a stay-at-home mother. This was nine percentage points higher than the figure for native-born Americans, which helps explain why immigrant couples were more likely to be among the working poor than native-born families. In general, dual-income families make more than single-income ones.

What does "family" mean in different cultures? Consider a striking contrast between the United States and Brazil, the two most populous nations of the Western Hemisphere, in the meaning of "family." Contemporary North American adults usually define their families as consisting of their spouse (or domestic partner) and their children. However, when Brazilians talk about their families, they mean their parents, siblings, aunts, uncles, grandparents, and cousins. Later they add their children, but rarely the spouse, who has his or her own family. The children are shared by the two families. Because middle-class Americans lack an extended family support system, marriage assumes more importance. The spousal relationship is supposed to take precedence over either spouse's relationship with his or her own parents. This places a significant strain on American marriages (see this chapter's "Appreciating Anthropology" on p. 368 for a study of American family life in the 21st century).

Living in a less mobile society, Brazilians stay in closer contact with their relatives, including members of the extended family, than North Americans do. Residents of Rio de Janeiro and São Paulo, two of South America's largest cities, are reluctant to leave those urban centers to live away from family and friends. Brazilians find it hard to imagine, and unpleasant to live in, social worlds without relatives. Contrast this with a characteristic American theme: learning to live with strangers.

## The Family among Foragers

Populations with foraging economies are far removed from industrial societies in terms of social complexity, but they do feature geographic mobility,

# appreciating ANTHROPOLOGY

## American Family Life in the 21st Century

Anthropologists today increasingly study daily life in the United States, including that of middle-class families. An excellent example is *Life at Home in the Twenty-First Century: 32 Families Open Their Doors* (Arnold et al. 2012), a study of home life in 32 middle-class, dual-income families in Los Angeles, focusing on physical surroundings and material culture, the items owned and used in daily life. The book's authors are three UCLA anthropologists—Jeanne Arnold, Anthony Graesch, and Elinor Ochs—and Italian photographer Enzo Ragazzini. All did research through UCLA's Center on Everyday Lives of Families (CELF), which was founded in 2001 and is directed by Ochs.

The families selected for, and agreeing to participate in, the study on which *Life at Home* was based were all middle-class and owned or were buying their homes. They varied in ethnicity, income level, and neighborhood. Same-sex couples were included. The authors took a systematic approach to their subjects. They videotaped the activities of family members, tracked their movements using positioning devices, measured their stress levels through saliva samples, and took almost 20,000 photographs (approximately 600 per family) of homes, yards, and activities. The researchers also asked family members to narrate tours of their homes and videotaped them as they did so. Over a 4-year period, the project generated 47 hours of family-narrated video home tours and 1,540 hours of videotaped family interactions and interviews (see Arnold et al. 2012; Feuer 2012; Sullivan 2012).

A key finding of the study was the extent of clutter in those homes, a manifestation of a high degree of consumerism among dual-income American families. Never in human history, the researchers conclude, have families accumulated so many personal possessions. Hypothesizing that dealing with so much clutter would have psychological effects, the researchers collected saliva samples from the subjects in order to measure diurnal cortisol, an indicator of stress. Mothers' saliva, it turned out, contained more diurnal cortisol than did fathers'. The

researchers also noticed that, in their video tours, mothers often used words like "mess" and "chaotic" to describe their homes, while fathers rarely mentioned messiness. Author Anthony Graesch reasons that clutter bothers moms so much because it challenges deeply ingrained notions that homes should be tidy and well managed (see Feuer 2012). The role of domestic manager, of course, is traditionally a female one. For dads and kids, more than for moms, possessions appeared to be a source of pleasure, pride, and contentment rather than stress (Arnold et al. 2012; Feuer 2012).

Another finding was that children rarely went outside, despite the overall mild weather in Los Angeles. They used their possessions indoors, resulting in more clutter, including whole walls devoted to displays of dolls and toys. More than half of the 32 households had special rooms designed for work or schoolwork, but even in home offices kids' stuff tended to crowd parental items. The researchers speculate that guilt motivates dual-income parents to overbuy for their children. The parents in the study managed to spend, on an average weekday, no more than four hours with

their kids, perhaps leading them to overcompensate with toys, clothes, and other possessions (Graesch quoted in Feuer 2012).

The study found that the kitchen was the center of home life. In this space, family members met, interacted, exchanged information, and socialized with their children. And in the kitchen, the refrigerator played a key role. Stuck on its doors and sides were pictures, displays of children's achievements, reminders, addresses, and phone lists (including many outdated ones). The typical refrigerator front panel held 52 objects. The most crowded refrigerator had 166 stick-ons. The refrigerator served as a compact representation of that family's history and activities (Feuer 2012; Sullivan 2012).

Researchers found a correlation between the number of objects on the refrigerator and the overall clutter in a home. The refrigerator thus served not only as a chronicler of family life but also as a measure of its degree of consumerism—and perhaps of stress. We might hypothesize that a high number of refrigerator stick-ons indicates that someone in the household needs to take up meditation to lower his or her blood pressure.

As studied by anthropologists in greater Los Angeles, the clutter that typifies many middle-class American homes reflects a high degree of consumerism, especially among dual-income families. Never in human history have non-elite families owned so many possessions.

which is associated with nomadic or seminomadic hunting and gathering. Here again the nuclear family is often the most significant kin group, although in no foraging society is the nuclear family the only group based on kinship. The two basic social units of traditional foraging societies are the nuclear family and the band.

Unlike middle-class couples in industrial nations, foragers don't usually reside neolocally. Instead, they join a band in which either the husband or the wife has relatives. However, couples and families may move from one band to another several times (see Hill et al. 2011). Although nuclear families are ultimately as impermanent among foragers as they are in any other society, they are usually more stable than bands are.

Many foraging societies lacked year-round band organization. The Native American Shoshoni of the Great Basin in Utah and Nevada (Figure 19.3) provide an example. The resources available to the Shoshoni were so meager that for most of the year families traveled alone through the countryside, hunting and gathering. In certain seasons families assembled to hunt cooperatively as a band; after just a few months together, they dispersed (see Fowler and Fowler 2008).

In neither industrial nor foraging societies are people tied permanently to the land. The mobility and the emphasis on small, economically self-sufficient family units promote the nuclear family as a basic kin group in both types of societies.

## DESCENT

We've seen that the nuclear family is important in industrial nations and among foragers. The analogous group among nonindustrial farmers and herders is the descent group, a permanent social unit whose members say they have ancestors in common. Descent-group members believe they share, and descend from, those common ancestors. The group endures even though its membership changes, as members are born and die, move in and move out. Often, descent-group membership is determined at birth and is lifelong. In this case, it is an ascribed status.

### Descent Groups

Descent groups frequently are exogamous (members must seek their mates from other descent groups). Two common rules admit certain people as descent-group members while excluding others. With a rule of *matrilineal descent*, people join the mother's group automatically at birth and stay members throughout life. With *patrilineal descent*, people automatically have lifetime membership in the father's group. (In Figures 19.4 and 19.5, which show matrilineal and patrilineal descent groups, respectively, the triangles stand for males and the

**FIGURE 19.3**  Location of the Shoshoni.

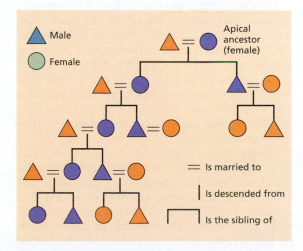

**FIGURE 19.4**  A Matrilineage Five Generations Deep.

Matrilineages are based on demonstrated descent from a female ancestor. Only the children of the group's women (blue) belong to the matrilineage. The children of the group's men are excluded; they belong to their mother's matrilineage.

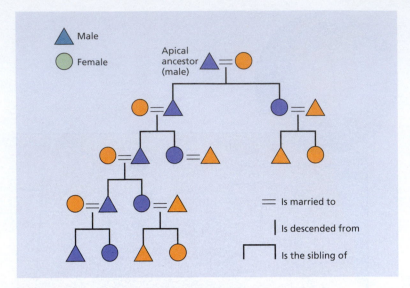

△ Male

○ Female

Apical
ancestor
(male)

══ Is married to

| Is descended from

⌐⌐ Is the sibling of

**FIGURE 19.5** A Patrilineage Five Generations Deep.

Lineages are based on demonstrated descent from a common ancestor. With patrilineal descent, children of the group's men (blue) are included as descent-group members. Children of the group's female members are excluded; they belong to their father's patrilineage.

**unilineal descent**
Matrilineal or patrilineal descent.

**lineage**
Unilineal descent group based on demonstrated descent.

**clan**
Unilineal descent group based on stipulated descent.

**ambilineal descent**
Flexible descent rule, neither patrilineal nor matrilineal.

circles for females.) Matrilineal and patrilineal descent are types of **unilineal descent.** This means the descent rule uses one line only, either the male or the female line.

Descent groups may be **lineages** or **clans.** Common to both is the belief that members descend from the same *apical ancestor.* That person stands at the apex, or top, of the common genealogy. For example, Adam and Eve, according to the Bible, are the apical ancestors of all humanity. Since Eve is said to have come from Adam's rib, Adam stands as the original apical ancestor for the patrilineal genealogies laid out in the Bible.

How do lineages and clans differ? A lineage uses *demonstrated descent.* Members can name their forebears in each generation from the apical ancestor through the present. (This doesn't mean the genealogy is accurate, only that lineage members think it is.) In the Bible the litany of men who "begat" other men is a demonstration of descent for a large patrilineage that ultimately includes Jews and Arabs (who share Abraham as their last common apical ancestor).

Unlike lineages, clans use *stipulated descent.* Clan members merely say they descend from the apical ancestor. They don't try to trace the actual genealogical links between themselves and that ancestor. The Betsileo of Madagascar have both clans and lineages. Descent may be demonstrated for the most recent 8 to 10 generations, then stipulated for the more remote past—sometimes with mermaids and vaguely defined foreign royalty mentioned among the founders (Kottak 1980). Like the Betsileo, many societies have both lineages and clans. In such a case, clans have more members and cover a larger geographic area than lineages do.

Sometimes a clan's apical ancestor is not a human at all but an animal or a plant (called a *totem*). Whether human or not, the ancestor symbolizes the social unity and identity of the members, distinguishing them from other groups.

The economic types that usually have descent-group organization are horticulture, pastoralism, and agriculture. A given society usually has multiple descent groups. Any one of them may be confined to a single village, but they usually span more than one village. Any branch of a descent group that lives in one place is a *local descent group.* Two or more local branches of different descent groups may live in the same village. Descent groups in the same village or different villages may establish alliances through frequent intermarriage.

## Lineages, Clans, and Residence Rules

As we've seen, descent groups, unlike nuclear families, are permanent units, with new members gained and lost in each generation. Members have access to the lineage estate, where some of them must live, in order to benefit from and manage that estate across the generations. To endure, descent groups need to keep at least some of their members at home. An easy way to do this is to have a rule about who belongs to the descent group and where they should live after they get married. Patrilineal and matrilineal descent, and the postmarital residence rules that usually accompany them, ensure that about half the people born in each generation will live out their lives on the ancestral estate. Neolocal residence, which is the rule for most middle-class Americans, isn't very common outside modern North America, Western Europe, and the European-derived cultures of Latin America and modern Australia and New Zealand.

Much more common is *patrilocality:* A married couple moves to the husband's father's community, so that the children will grow up in their father's village. Patrilocality is associated with patrilineal descent. This makes sense. If the group's male members are expected to exercise their rights in the ancestral estate, it's a good idea to raise them on that estate and to keep them there after they marry.

A less common postmarital residence rule, associated with matrilineal descent, is *matrilocality:* Married couples live in the wife's mother's community, and their children grow up in their mother's village. Together, patrilocality and matrilocality are known as *unilocal* rules of postmarital residence.

## Ambilineal Descent

The descent rules examined so far admit certain people as members while excluding others. A unilineal rule uses one line only, either the female or the male. Besides the unilineal rules, there is another descent rule called nonunilineal or **ambilineal** descent. As in any descent group, membership comes through descent from a common ancestor. However, ambilineal groups differ from unilineal groups in that they do not *automatically* exclude either the children of sons or those of daughters. People can choose the descent group they join (e.g., that of their father's father, father's mother, mother's father, or mother's mother). People also can change their descent-group membership, or belong to two or more groups at the same time.

Unilineal descent is a matter of ascribed status; ambilineal descent illustrates achieved status. With unilineal descent, membership is automatic; no choice is permitted. People are born members of their father's group in a patrilineal society or of their mother's group in a matrilineal society. They are members of that group for life. Ambilineal descent permits more flexibility in descent-group affiliation.

Before 1950, descent groups were generally described simply as patrilineal or matrilineal. If the society tended toward patrilineality, the anthropologist classified it as a patrilineal rather than an ambilineal group. The treatment of ambilineal descent as a separate category was a formal recognition that many descent systems are flexible—some more so than others.

## Family versus Descent

There are rights, duties, and obligations associated with kinship and descent. Many societies have both families and descent groups. Obligations to one may conflict with obligations to the other—more so in matrilineal than in patrilineal societies. In the latter, a woman typically leaves home when she marries and raises her children in her husband's community. After leaving home, she has no primary or substantial obligations to her own descent group. She can invest fully in her children, who will become members of her husband's group. In a matrilineal society things are different. A man has strong obligations both to his family of procreation (his wife and children) and to his closest matrikin (his sisters and their children). The continuity of his descent group depends on his sisters and their children, since descent is carried by females, and he has descent-based obligations to look out for their welfare. He also has obligations to his wife and children. If a man is sure his wife's children are his own, he has more incentive to invest in them than is the case if he has doubts.

Compared with patrilineal systems, matrilineal societies tend to have higher divorce rates and greater female promiscuity (Schneider and Gough 1961). According to Nicholas Kottak (2002), among the matrilineal Makua of northern Mozambique, a husband is concerned about his wife's potential promiscuity. A man's sister also takes an interest in her brother's wife's fidelity; she doesn't want her brother wasting time on children who may not be his, thus diminishing his investment as an uncle

Most societies have a prevailing opinion about where couples should live after they marry; this is called a postmarital residence rule. A common rule is patrilocality: The couple lives with the husband's relatives, so that children grow up in their father's community. The top image shows a young Muslim bride (veiled in pink) in the West African country of Guinea Bissau. On the last day of her three-day wedding ceremony, she will collect laundry from her husband's family, wash it with her friends, and be taken to his village on a bicycle. In the bottom image, in the village of Olympos, on the Greek island of Karpathos, dowry is transported as part of a traditional wedding.

(mother's brother) in her children. A confessional ritual that is part of the Makua birthing process demonstrates the sister's allegiance to her brother. When a wife is deep in labor, the husband's sister, who attends her, must ask, "Who is the real father of this child?" If the wife lies, the Makua believe the birth will be difficult, often ending in the death of the woman and/or the baby. This ritual serves as an important social paternity test. It is in both the husband's and his sister's interest to ensure that his wife's children are indeed his own.

# KINSHIP CALCULATION

In addition to studying kin groups, anthropologists are interested in **kinship calculation**: the system by which people in a society reckon kin relationships. To study kinship calculation, an ethnographer must first determine the word or words for different types of "relatives" used in a particular language and then ask questions such as "Who are your relatives?" Like race and gender, kinship is culturally constructed. This means that some genealogical kin are considered to be relatives, whereas others are not. It also means that even people who aren't genealogical relatives can be constructed socially as kin.

Cultures maintain varied beliefs about biological processes involving kinship, including the role of insemination in creating human life. We know that fertilization of an ovum by a single sperm is responsible for conception. Other cultures have different ideas about procreation. In some societies it is believed that spirits, rather than men, place babies in women's wombs. In others, people think that a fetus must be nourished by continuing insemination during pregnancy. People in many cultures believe that several acts of intercourse are needed to make a baby (see Beckerman and Valentine 2002). The Barí of Venezuela and their neighbors, for example, believe that multiple men can create the same fetus. When a Barí child is born, the mother publicly announces the names of the one or more men she believes to be the father(s). If those men accept paternity, they must provide care for the mother and child. Barí children with more than one official father turn out to be advantaged compared with those who have just one. Anthropologists report that 80 percent of Barí children with multiple dads survived to adulthood, compared with just 64 percent who had just one (Beckerman and Valentine 2002).

Ethnographers strive to discover, in a given society, the specific genealogical relationships between "relatives" and the person who has named them—the **ego**. *Ego* means *I* (or *me*) in Latin. It's who you, the reader, are in the kin charts that follow. It's your perspective looking out on your kin. By posing the same questions to several local people, the ethnographer learns about the extent and direction of kinship calculation in that society. The ethnographer also begins to understand the relationship between kinship calculation and kin groups: how people use kinship to create and maintain personal ties and to join social groups. In the kinship charts that follow, the gray square labeled "ego" identifies the person whose kinship calculation is being examined.

## Genealogical Kin Types and Kin Terms

At this point, we may distinguish between *kin terms* (the words used for different relatives in a particular language) and *genealogical kin types*. We designate genealogical kin types with the letters and symbols

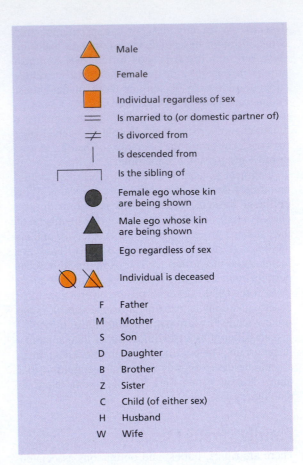

**FIGURE 19.6** Kinship Symbols and Genealogical Kin Type Notation.

shown in Figure 19.6. *Genealogical kin type* refers to an actual genealogical relationship (e.g., father's brother) as opposed to a kin term (e.g., *uncle*).

Kin terms reflect the social construction of kinship in a given culture. A kin term may (and usually does) lump together several genealogical relationships. In English, for instance, we use *father* primarily for one kin type: the genealogical father. However, *father* can be extended to an adoptive father or stepfather—and even to a priest. *Grandfather* includes mother's father and father's father. The term *cousin* lumps together several kin types. Even the more specific *first cousin* includes mother's brother's son (MBS), mother's brother's daughter (MBD), mother's sister's son (MZS), mother's sister's daughter (MZD), father's brother's son (FBS), father's brother's daughter (FBD), father's sister's son (FZS), and father's sister's daughter (FZD). *First cousin* thus lumps together at least eight genealogical kin types.

*Uncle* encompasses mother's and father's brothers, and *aunt* includes mother's and father's sisters. We also use *uncle* and *aunt* for the spouses of our "blood" aunts and uncles. We use the same term for mother's brother and father's brother because we perceive them as being the same sort of relative. Calling them *uncles,* we distinguish between them and another kin type, F, whom we call *Father, Dad, or Pop*. In many societies, however, it is common to call a father and a father's brother by the same term. Later we'll see why.

In the United States and Canada, the nuclear family continues to be the most important group based on kinship. This is true despite an increased incidence of single parenthood, divorce, and remarriage. The nuclear family's relative isolation from other kin groups in modern nations reflects geographic mobility within an industrial economy with sale of labor for cash.

It's reasonable for North Americans to distinguish between relatives who belong to their nuclear families and those who don't. We are more likely to grow up with our parents than with our aunts and uncles. We tend to see our parents more often than we see our uncles and aunts, who may live in different towns and cities. We often inherit from our parents, but our cousins have first claim to inherit from our aunts and uncles. If our marriage is stable, we see our children daily as long as they remain at home. They are our heirs. We feel closer to them than to our nieces and nephews.

American kinship calculation and kin terminology reflect these social features. Thus, the term *uncle* distinguishes between the kin types MB and FB on the one hand and the kin type F on the other. However, this term also lumps kin types together. We use the same term for MB and FB, two different kin types. We do this because American kinship calculation is **bilateral**—traced equally through males and females, for example, father and mother. Both kinds of uncle are brothers of one of our parents. We think of both as roughly the same kind of relative.

"No," you may object, "I'm closer to my mother's brother than to my father's brother." That may be. However, in a representative sample of Americans, we would find a split, with some favoring one side and some favoring the other. We'd actually expect a bit of *matrilateral skewing*—a preference for relatives on the mother's side. This occurs for many reasons. When contemporary children are raised by just one parent, it's much more likely to be the mother than the father. Also, even with intact marriages, the wife tends to play a more active role in managing family affairs, including family visits, reunions, holidays, and extended family relations, than the husband does. This would tend to reinforce her kin network over his and thus favor matrilateral skewing.

*Bilateral kinship* means that people tend to perceive kin links through males and females as being similar or equivalent. This bilaterality is expressed in interaction with, living with or near, and rights to inherit from relatives. We don't usually inherit from uncles, but if we do, there's about as much chance that we'll inherit from the father's brother as from the mother's brother. We usually don't live with an aunt, but if we do, it might be either the mother's sister or the father's sister.

A neolocal American nuclear family in front of their home. The nuclear family's relative isolation from other kin groups in modern nations reflects geographic mobility within an industrial economy with sale of labor for cash.

## KINSHIP TERMINOLOGY

People perceive and define kin relations differently in different societies. In any culture, kinship terminology is a classification system, a taxonomy or typology. It is a *native taxonomy,* developed over generations by the people who live in a particular society. A native classification system is based on how people perceive similarities and differences in the things being classified.

However, anthropologists have discovered that there are a limited number of patterns in which people classify their kin. People who speak very different languages may use exactly the same system of kinship terminology. This section examines the four main ways of classifying kin on the parental generation: lineal, bifurcate merging, generational, and bifurcate collateral. We also consider the social correlates of these classification systems. (Note that each of the systems described here applies to the parental generation. There also are differences in kin terminology on ego's generation. These systems involve the classification of siblings and cousins. There are six such systems, called Eskimo, Iroquois, Hawaiian, Crow, Omaha, and Sudanese cousin terminology, after societies that traditionally used them. You can see them diagrammed and discussed at the following websites: http://anthro.palomar.edu/kinship/kinship_5.htm; http://anthro.palomar.edu/kinship/kinship_6.htm; http://www.umanitoba.ca/faculties/arts/departments/anthropology/tutor/kinterms/termsys.html.)

**bilateral kinship calculation**
Kin ties calculated equally through both sexes.

**functional explanation**
One based on correlation or co-occurrence of social variables.

**lineal kinship terminology**
Four parental kin terms: M, F, FB=MB, and MZ=FZ.

**lineal relatives**
Ego's direct ancestors and descendants.

**collateral relative**
Relative outside ego's direct line, e.g., B, Z, FB, MZ.

**affinals**
Relatives by marriage.

**bifurcate merging kinship terminology**
Four parental kin terms: M=MZ, F=FB, MB, and FZ each stand alone.

A **functional explanation** will be offered for each system of kinship terminology, such as lineal, bifurcate merging, and generational terminology. Functional explanations attempt to relate particular customs (such as the use of kin terms) to other features of a society, such as rules of descent and postmarital residence. Certain aspects of a culture are *functions* of others. That is, they are correlated variables, so that when one of them changes, the others inevitably change too. For certain terminologies, the social correlates are very clear.

Kin terms provide useful information about social patterns. If two relatives are designated by the same term, we can assume that they are perceived as sharing socially significant attributes. Several factors influence the way people interact with, perceive, and classify relatives. For instance, do certain kinds of relatives customarily live together or apart? How far apart? What benefits do they derive from each other, and what are their obligations? Are they members of the same descent group or of different descent groups? With these questions in mind, let's examine systems of kinship terminology.

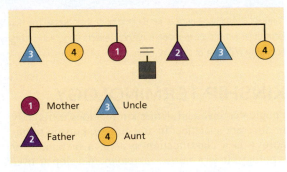

**FIGURE 19.7**  Lineal Kinship Terminology

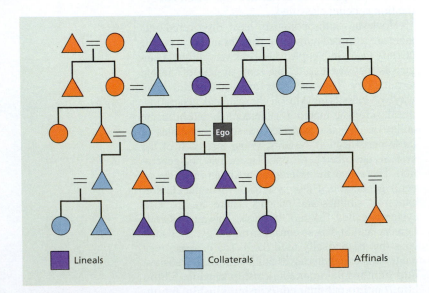

**FIGURE 19.8**  The Distinctions among Lineals, Collaterals, and Affinals as Perceived by Ego.

## Lineal Terminology

Our own system of kinship classification is called the *lineal system* (Figure 19.7). The number 3 and the color light blue stand for the term *uncle*, which we apply both to FB and to MB. **Lineal kinship terminology** is found in societies such as the United States and Canada in which the nuclear family is the most important group based on kinship.

Lineal kinship terminology has absolutely nothing to do with lineages, which are found in very different social contexts. (What contexts are those?) Lineal kinship terminology gets its name from the fact that it distinguishes lineal relatives from collateral relatives. What does that mean? A **lineal relative** is an ancestor or a descendant, anyone on the direct *line* of descent that leads to and from ego (Figure 19.8). Thus, lineal relatives are one's parents, grandparents, great-grandparents, and other direct forebears. Lineal relatives also include children, grandchildren, and great-grandchildren. **Collateral relatives** are all other kin. They include siblings, nieces and nephews, aunts and uncles, and cousins (Figure 19.8). **Affinals** are relatives by marriage, whether of lineals (e.g., son's wife) or of collaterals (sister's husband).

## Bifurcate Merging Terminology

**Bifurcate merging kinship terminology** (Figure 19.9) *bifurcates,* or splits, the mother's side and the father's side. But it also *merges* same-sex siblings of each parent. Thus, mother and mother's sister are merged under the same term (1), while father and father's brother also get a common term (2). There are different terms for mother's brother (3) and father's sister (4).

People use this system in societies with unilineal (patrilineal and matrilineal) descent rules and unilocal (patrilocal and matrilocal) postmarital residence rules. When the society is unilineal and unilocal, the logic of bifurcate merging terminology is fairly clear. In a patrilineal society, for example, father and father's brother belong to the same descent group, gender, and generation. Since patrilineal societies usually have patrilocal residence, the father and his

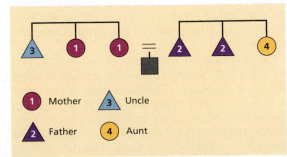

**FIGURE 19.9**  Bifurcate Merging Kinship Terminology.

brother live in the same local group. Because they share so many attributes that are socially relevant, ego regards them as social equivalents and calls them by the same kinship term—2. However, the mother's brother belongs to a different descent group, lives elsewhere, and has a different kin term—3.

What about mother and mother's sister in a patrilineal society? They belong to the same descent group, the same gender, and the same generation. Often they marry men from the same village and go to live there. These social similarities help explain the use of the same term—1—for both.

Similar observations apply to matrilineal societies. Consider a society with two matrilineal clans, the Ravens and the Wolves. Ego is a member of his mother's clan, the Raven clan. Ego's father is a member of the Wolf clan. His mother and her sister are female Ravens of the same generation. If there is matrilocal residence, as there often is in matrilineal societies, they will live in the same village. Because they are so similar socially, ego calls them by the same kin term—1.

The father's sister, however, belongs to a different group, the Wolves; lives elsewhere; and has a different kin term—4. Ego's father and father's brother are male Wolves of the same generation. If they marry women of the same clan and live in the same village, this creates additional social similarities that reinforce this usage.

## Generational Terminology

Like bifurcate merging kinship terminology, **generational kinship terminology** uses the same term for parents and their siblings, but the lumping is more complete (Figure 19.10). With generational terminology, there are only two terms for the parental *generation*. We may translate them as "father" and "mother," but more accurate translations would be "male member of the parental generation" and "female member of the parental generation."

Generational kinship terminology does not distinguish between the mother's and father's sides. It does not bifurcate, but it certainly does merge. It uses just one term for father, father's brother, and mother's brother. In a unilineal society, these three kin types would never belong to the same descent group. Generational kinship terminology also uses a single term for mother, mother's sister, and father's sister. Nor, in a unilineal society, would these three ever be members of the same group.

Nevertheless, generational terminology suggests closeness between ego and his or her aunts and uncles—much more closeness than exists between Americans and these kin types. How likely would you be to call your uncle "Dad" or your aunt "Mom"? We'd expect to find generational terminology in societies in which extended kinship is much more important than it is in our own but in which there is no rigid distinction between the father's side and the mother's side.

It's logical, then, that generational kin terminology is found in societies with ambilineal descent, where descent-group membership is not automatic. People may choose the group they join, change their descent-group membership, or belong to two or more descent groups simultaneously. Generational terminology fits these conditions. The use of intimate kin terms signals that people have close personal relations with all their relatives of the parental generation. People exhibit similar behavior toward their aunts, uncles, and parents. Someday they'll have to choose a descent group to join. Furthermore, in ambilineal societies, postmarital residence is usually ambilocal. This means that the married couple can live with either the husband's or the wife's group.

Significantly, generational terminology also characterizes certain foraging bands, including Kalahari San groups and several native societies of North America. Use of this terminology reflects certain similarities between foraging bands and ambilineal descent groups. In both societies, people have a choice about their kin-group affiliation. Foragers always live with kin, but they often shift band affiliation and so may be members of several different bands during their lifetimes. Just as in food-producing societies with ambilineal descent, generational terminology among foragers helps maintain close personal relationships with several parental-generation relatives, whom ego may eventually use as a point of entry into different groups.

**generational kinship terminology** Just two parental kin terms: M=MZ=FZ and F=FB=MB.

## Bifurcate Collateral Terminology

Of the four kin classification systems, **bifurcate collateral kinship terminology** is the most specific. It has separate terms for each of the six kin types of the parental generation (Figure 19.11). Bifurcate collateral terminology isn't as common as the other types. Many of the societies that use it are in North Africa and the Middle East, and many of them are offshoots of the same ancestral group.

Bifurcate collateral terminology also may be used when a child has parents of different ethnic backgrounds and uses terms for aunts and uncles derived from different languages. Thus, if you have a mother who is Latina and a father who is Anglo, you may call your aunts and uncles on your mother's side "tia" and

**bifurcate collateral kinship terminology** Six separate parental kin terms: M, F, MB, MZ, FB, and FZ.

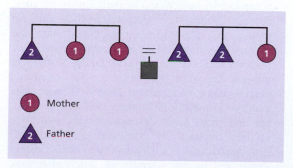

**FIGURE 19.10**  *Generational Kinship Terminology.*

1  Mother

2  Father

| KINSHIP TERMINOLOGY | KIN GROUP | RESIDENCE RULE | ECONOMY |
|---|---|---|---|
| Lineal | Nuclear family | Neolocal | Industrialism, foraging |
| Bifurcate merging | Unilineal descent group—patrilineal or matrilineal | Unilocal—patrilocal or matrilocal | Horticulture, pastoralism, agriculture |
| Generational | Ambilineal descent group, band | Ambilocal | Agriculture, horticulture, foraging |
| Bifurcate collateral | Varies | Varies | Varies |

"tio," while calling those on your father's side "aunt" and "uncle." And your mother and father may be "Mom" and "Pop." That's a modern form of bifurcate collateral kinship terminology. Recap 19.1 lists the types of kin group, the postmarital residence rule, and the economy associated with the four types of kinship terminology.

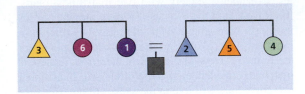

**FIGURE 19.11** Bifurcate Collateral Kinship Terminology.

# for REVIEW

## summary

1. In nonindustrial societies, kinship, descent, and marriage organize social and political life. In studying kinship, we must distinguish between kin groups, whose composition and activities can be observed, and kinship calculation—how people identify and designate their relatives.

2. One widespread kin group is the nuclear family, consisting of a married couple and their children. There are functional alternatives to the nuclear family. That is, other groups may assume functions usually associated with the nuclear family. Nuclear families tend to be especially important in foraging and industrial societies. Among farmers and herders, other kinds of kin groups often overshadow the nuclear family.

3. In contemporary North America, the nuclear family is a characteristic kin group for the middle class. Expanded households and sharing with extended family kin occur more frequently among the poor, who may pool their resources in dealing with poverty. Today, however, even in the American middle class, nuclear family households are declining as single-person households and other domestic arrangements increase.

4. The descent group is a basic kin group among nonindustrial farmers and herders. Unlike families, descent groups have perpetuity—they last for generations. Descent-group members share and manage a common estate: land, animals, and other resources. There are several kinds of descent groups. Lineages are based on demonstrated descent; clans, on stipulated descent. Descent rules may be unilineal or ambilineal. Unilineal (patrilineal and matrilineal) descent is associated with unilocal (respectively, patrilocal and matrilocal) postmarital residence. Obligations to one's descent group and to one's family of procreation may conflict, especially in matrilineal societies.

**5.** A kinship terminology is a classification of relatives based on perceived differences and similarities. Comparative research has revealed a limited number of ways of classifying kin. Because there are correlations between kinship terminology and other social practices, we often can predict kinship terminology from other aspects of culture. The four basic kinship terminologies for the parental generation are lineal, bifurcate merging, generational, and bifurcate collateral. Many foraging and industrial societies use lineal terminology, which is associated with nuclear family organization. Cultures with unilocal residence and unilineal descent tend to have bifurcate merging terminology. Generational terminology correlates with ambilineal descent and ambilocal residence.

## key terms

affinals  374

ambilineal descent  370

bifurcate collateral kinship terminology  375

bifurcate merging kinship terminology  374

bilateral kinship calculation  373

clan  370

collateral relative  374

descent group  362

ego  372

extended family household  363

family of orientation  362

family of procreation  362

functional explanation  374

generational kinship terminology  375

kinship calculation  372

lineage  370

lineal kinship terminology  374

lineal relatives  374

neolocality  363

unilineal descent  370

## critical thinking

**1.** Why is kinship so important to anthropologists? How might the study of kinship be useful for research in fields of anthropology other than cultural anthropology?

**2.** What are some examples of alternatives to nuclear family arrangements considered in this chapter? What may be the impact of new (and increasingly accessible) reproductive technologies on domestic arrangements?

**3.** Although the nuclear family remains the cultural ideal for many Americans, other domestic arrangements now outnumber the "traditional" American household about five to one. What are some reasons for this? Do you think this trend is good or bad? Why?

**4.** To what sorts of family or families do you belong? Have you belonged to other kinds of families? How do the kin terms you use compare with the four classification systems discussed in this chapter?

**5.** Cultures with unilocal residence and unilineal descent tend to have bifurcate merging terminology, while ambilineal descent and ambilocal residence correlate with generational terminology. Why does this make sense? What are some examples of each case?

CHAPTER 20

# Marriage

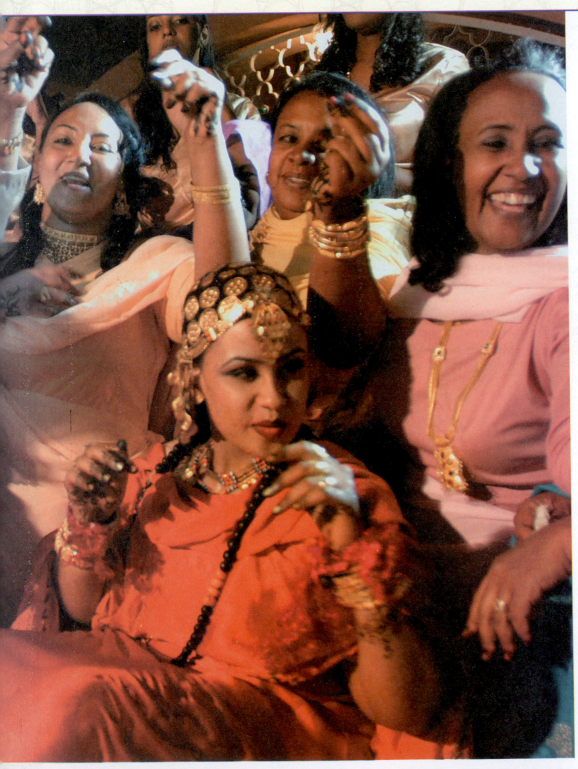

How is marriage defined and regulated, and what rights does it convey?

What role does marriage play in creating and maintaining group alliances?

What forms of marriage exist cross-culturally, and what are their social correlates?

Part of a wedding ceremony in Khartoum, Sudan. On women's night, friends gather and an older woman anoints the bride with oil.

# understanding OURSELVES

According to the radio talk show psychologist (and undergraduate anthropology major) Dr. Joy Browne, parents' job is to give their kids "roots and wings." Roots, she says, are the easier part. In other words, it's easier to raise children than to let them go. Has that been true of your parents with respect to you? I've heard comments about today's "helicopter parents" hovering over even their college-aged kids, using cell phones, e-mail, and texting to follow their progeny more closely than in prior generations. Do you have any experience with such a pattern?

It can be difficult to make the transition between the family that raised us (our family of orientation) and the family we form if we have children (our family of procreation). In contemporary America, we usually get a head start by "leaving home" long before we establish a family of procreation. We go off to college or find a job that enables us to support ourselves, so that we can live independently or with roommates. In nonindustrial societies people, especially women, may leave home abruptly when they marry. Often, a woman must leave her home village and her own kin and move in with her husband and his relatives. This can be an unpleasant and alienating transition. Many women complain about feeling isolated, or being mistreated, in their husband's village.

In contemporary North America, although neither women nor men typically have to adjust to in-laws living nearby full-time, conflicts with in-laws aren't at all uncommon. Just read "Dear Abby" or listen to Dr. Joy Browne (cited previously) for a week. Even more of a challenge is learning to live with a spouse. Marriage always raises issues of accommodation and adjustment. Initially, the married couple is just that, unless there are children from a previous marriage. If there are, adjustment issues will involve step-parenthood—and a prior spouse—as well as the new marital relationship. Once a couple has its own child, the family-of-procreation mentality takes over. In the United States, family loyalty shifts, but not completely, from the family of orientation to the family that includes spouse and child(ren). Given our bilateral kinship system, we maintain relations with our sons and daughters after they marry, and grandchildren theoretically are as close to one set of grandparents as to the other set. In practice, grandchildren tend to be a bit closer to their mother's than to their father's families. Can you speculate about why that might be? How is it for you? Are you closer to your paternal or maternal grandparents? How about your uncles and aunts on one side or the other? Why is that?

## WHAT IS MARRIAGE?

"Love and marriage," "marriage and the family": These familiar phrases show how we link the romantic love of two individuals to marriage and how we link marriage to reproduction and family creation. But marriage is an institution with significant roles and functions in addition to reproduction. What is marriage, anyway?

No definition of marriage is broad enough to apply easily to all societies and situations.

A commonly quoted definition comes from *Notes and Queries on Anthropology:*

> Marriage is a union between a man and a woman such that the children born to the woman are recognized as legitimate offspring of both partners. (Royal Anthropological Institute 1951, p. 111)

This definition isn't universally valid for several reasons. In many societies, marriages unite more than two spouses. Here we speak of *plural marriages,* as when a man weds two (or more) women, or a woman weds a group of brothers—an arrangement called *fraternal polyandry* that is characteristic of certain Himalayan cultures. In the Brazilian community of Arembepe, people can choose among various forms of marital union. Most people live in long-term "common-law" domestic partnerships that are not legally sanctioned. Some have civil marriages, which are licensed and legalized by a justice of the peace. Still others go through religious ceremonies, so that they are united in "holy matrimony," although not legally. And some have both civil and religious ties. The different forms of union permit someone to have multiple spouses (e.g., one common-law, one civil, one religious) without ever getting divorced.

Some societies recognize various kinds of same-sex marriages. In South Sudan, a Nuer woman can marry a woman if her father has only daughters but no male heirs, who are necessary if his patrilineage is to survive. He may ask his daughter to stand as a son in order to take a bride. This daughter will become the socially recognized husband of another woman (the wife). This is a symbolic and social relationship rather than a sexual one. The "wife" has sex with a man or men (whom her female "husband" must approve) until she gets pregnant. The children born to the wife are accepted as the offspring of both the female husband and the wife. Although the female husband is not the actual **genitor,** the biological father, of the children, she is their **pater,** or socially recognized father. What's important in this Nuer case is *social* rather than *biological paternity.* We see again how kinship is socially constructed. The bride's children are considered the legitimate offspring of her female "husband," who is biologically a woman but socially a man, and the descent line continues.

## INCEST AND EXOGAMY

In nonindustrial societies, a person's social world includes two main categories—friends and strangers. Strangers are potential or actual enemies. Marriage is one of the primary ways of converting strangers into friends, of creating and maintaining personal and political alliances. **Exogamy,** the custom and practice of seeking a mate outside one's own group, has adaptive value, because it links people into a wider social network that nurtures, helps, and protects them in times of need. Incest restrictions (prohibitions on sex with relatives) reinforce exogamy by pushing people to seek their mates outside the local group. Most societies discourage sexual contact involving close relatives, especially members of the same nuclear family.

**Incest** refers to sexual contact with a relative, but cultures define their kin, and thus incest, differently. In other words, incest, like kinship, is socially constructed. Marriage entails sex, so one can marry only someone with whom sex is permitted. Besides kinship, other factors that restrict sexual access include age and the range of sexual acts that are socially tolerated. In the United States the age of consent for sexual activity varies by state between 16 and 18. It is 16 in Canada and 14 in Italy. Cultures and governments routinely try to regulate sexual activity. Until 2003, when the Supreme Court struck them down, several states had sodomy laws, used mainly against gay men who engaged in nonreproductive sex. Most people probably don't know what is legal and what isn't in a given state or country and can get in trouble as a result (e.g., when an 18-year-old has sex with a 17-year-old).

Sex is contested. That is, people in the same culture can disagree and argue about the definition and propriety of particular sexual acts. President Bill Clinton famously asserted, "I did not have sexual relations with that women. . . ." Should sexual practices other than heterosexual coitus (oral sex, for example) be considered "sexual relations"? With respect to incest restrictions, what, if any, kind of sexual contact is permissible between a teenager and his or her cousin of comparable age? How about step-siblings, half-siblings, and siblings? Some U.S. states permit marriage, and therefore sex, with first cousins, while others ban it. The social construction of kinship, and of incest, is far from simple.

For example, is a first cousin always a relative? Many societies distinguish between two kinds of first cousins: cross cousins and parallel cousins. The children of two brothers or two sisters are **parallel cousins.** The children of a brother and a sister are **cross cousins.** Your mother's sister's children and your father's brother's children are your parallel cousins. Your father's sister's children and your mother's brother's children are your cross cousins.

The American kin term *cousin* doesn't distinguish between cross and parallel cousins, but in many societies, especially those with unilineal descent, the distinction is essential. As an example, consider a community with only two descent groups. This exemplifies what is known as *moiety* organization—from the French *moitié,* which means "half." Descent bifurcates the community so that everyone belongs to one half or the other. Some societies have patrilineal moieties; others have matrilineal moieties.

In Figures 20.1 and 20.2, notice that cross cousins always are members of the opposite moiety and parallel cousins always belong to your (ego's) own moiety. With patrilineal descent (Figure 20.1), people take the father's descent-group affiliation; in a matrilineal society (Figure 20.2), they take the mother's affiliation. You can see from these diagrams that your mother's sister's children (MZC) and your father's brother's children (FBC) always belong to your group. Your cross cousins—that is, FZC and MBC—belong to the other moiety.

Parallel cousins belong to the same generation and the same descent group as ego does, and they

---

**genitor**
A child's biological father.

**pater**
One's socially recognized father; not necessarily the genitor.

**parallel cousins**
Children of two brothers or two sisters.

**cross cousins**
Children of a brother and a sister.

**exogamy**
Marriage outside one's own group.

**incest**
Sexual relations with a close relative.

are like ego's brothers and sisters. They are called by the same kin terms as brothers and sisters are. Defined as close relatives, parallel cousins, like siblings, are excluded as potential mates; cross cousins are not.

In societies with unilineal moieties, cross cousins always belong to the opposite group. Sex with cross cousins isn't incestuous, because they aren't considered relatives. In fact, in many unilineal societies, people must marry either a cross cousin or someone from the same descent group as a cross cousin. A unilineal descent rule ensures that the cross cousin's descent group is never one's own. With moiety exogamy, spouses must belong to different moieties.

Among the Yanomami of Venezuela and Brazil (Chagnon 1997), boys anticipate eventual marriage to a cross cousin by calling her "wife." They call their male cross cousins "brother-in-law." Yanomami girls call their male cross cousins "husband" and their female cross cousins "sister-in-law." Here, as in many other societies with unilineal descent, sex with cross cousins is proper but sex with parallel cousins is incestuous.

If cousins can be classified as nonrelatives, how about even closer biological kin types? When unilineal descent is very strongly developed, the parent who belongs to a different descent group than your own isn't considered a relative. Thus, with strict patrilineality, the mother is not a relative but a kind of in-law who has married a member of your own group—your father. With strict matrilineality, the father isn't a relative because he belongs to a different descent group.

The Lakher of Southeast Asia (Figure 20.3) are strictly patrilineal (Leach 1961). Using the male ego (the reference point, the person in question) in Figure 20.4, let's suppose that ego's father and mother get divorced. Each remarries and has a daughter by a second marriage. A Lakher always belongs to his or her father's group, all of whose members (one's *agnates,* or *patrikin*) are considered relatives, because they belong to the same descent group. Ego can't have sex with or marry his father's daughter by the second marriage, just as in contemporary North America it's illegal for half-siblings to have sex and marry. However, unlike our society, where all half-siblings are restricted, sex between our Lakher ego and his maternal half-sister would be nonincestuous. She isn't ego's relative because she belongs to her own father's descent group rather than ego's. The Lakher illustrate very well that definitions of relatives, and therefore of incest, vary from culture to culture.

# INCEST AND ITS AVOIDANCE

We know from primate research that adolescent males (among monkeys) or females (among apes) often move away from the group in which they were born (see Rodseth et al. 1991 and this chapter's

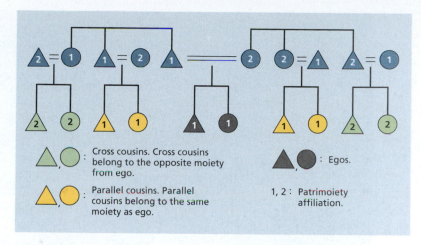

**FIGURE 20.1** Parallel and Cross Cousins and Patrilineal Moiety Organization.

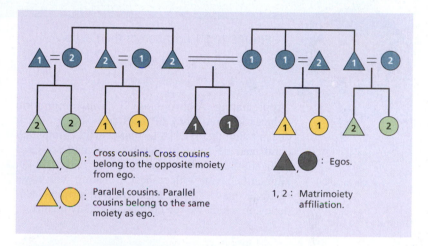

**FIGURE 20.2** Matrilineal Moiety Organization.

Among the Yanomami of Brazil and Venezuela (shown here), sex with (and marriage to) cross cousins is proper, but sex with parallel cousins is considered incestuous. With unilineal descent, sex with cross cousins isn't incestuous because cross cousins never belong to ego's descent group.

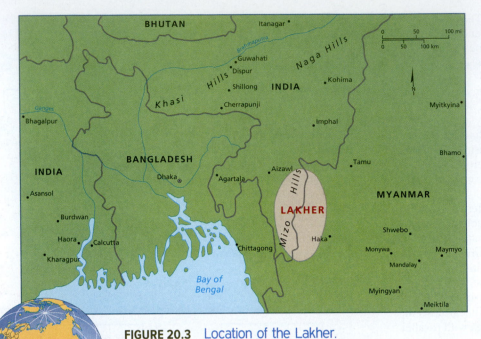

FIGURE 20.3  Location of the Lakher.

A cross-cultural study of 87 societies (Meigs and Barlow 2002) suggested that incest occurred in several of them. It's not clear, however, whether the authors of the study controlled for the social construction of incest. They report, for example, that incest occurs among the Yanomami, but they may be considering cross-cousin marriage to be incestuous, when it is not so considered by the Yanomami. Another society in their sample is the Ashanti, for whom the ethnographer Meyer Fortes reports, "In the old days it [incest] was punished by death. Nowadays the culprits are heavily fined" (Fortes 1950, p. 257). This suggests that there really were violations of Ashanti incest restrictions, and that such violations were, and still are, punished. More strikingly, among 24 Ojibwa individuals from whom he obtained information about incest, A. Irving Hallowell found 8 cases of parent–child incest and 10 cases of brother–sister incest (Hallowell 1955, pp. 294–95). Because reported cases of actual parent–child and sibling incest are very rare in the ethnographic literature, questions about the possibility of social construction arise here too. In many cultures, including the Ojibwa, people use the same terms for their mother and their aunt, their father and their uncle, and their cousins and siblings. Could the siblings in the Ojibwa case actually have been cousins, and the parents and children, uncles and nieces?

"Appreciating Anthropology"). This emigration reduces the frequency of incestuous unions, but it doesn't stop them. DNA testing of wild chimps has confirmed incestuous unions between adult sons and their mothers, which reside in the same group. Human behavior with respect to mating with close relatives may express a generalized primate tendency, in which we see both urges and avoidance.

In ancient Egypt, sibling marriage apparently was allowed for both royalty and commoners, in some districts at least. Based on official census records from Roman Egypt (first to third centuries C.E.), 24 percent of all documented marriages in the Arsinoites district were between "brothers" and "sisters." The rates were 37 percent for the city of Arsinoe and 19 percent for the surrounding villages. These figures are much higher than any other documented levels of inbreeding among humans (Scheidel 1997). Again one wonders if the relatives involved were actually as close biologically as the kin terms would imply.

According to Anna Meigs and Kathleen Barlow (2002), for Western societies with nuclear family organization, "father–daughter incest" is much more common with stepfathers than with biological fathers. But is it really incest if they aren't biological relatives? American culture is unclear on this matter. Incest also happens with biological fathers, especially those who were absent or did little caretaking of their daughters in childhood (Williams and Finkelhor 1995). In a carefully designed study, Linda M. Williams and David Finkelhor (1995) found father–daughter incest to

FIGURE 20.4  Patrilineal Descent-Group Identity and Incest among the Lakher.

Ego

Incestuous union

Nonincestuous union

●, ▲ : Ego's patrilineage

●, ▲ : Ego's mother's second husband's patrilineage

● : Ego's mother's patrilineage

● : Ego's father's second wife's patrilineage

≠ : Separation or divorce.
FD by second marriage is a comember of ego's descent group and is included within the incest taboo.
MD by second marriage is not a comember of ego's descent group and is not tabooed.

# appreciating ANTHROPOLOGY

## Come Join My Band, Baby

Based on data from 32 recent foraging societies, anthropologists suggest how early hominin society might have diverged from protochimpanzee society. Key developments in early human evolution would have been (1) formation of an enduring pair bond between a male and a female and (2) the possibility of both male and female dispersal and movement between bands. Humans uniquely recognize their relatives through both males and females. Recognition of kin in different bands would have enhanced cooperation between bands. As people moved from band to band, they would have shared ideas and inventions through social learning. Although few anthropologists would doubt the central role of cooperation and social learning in human evolution, many would question the use of contemporary and recent hunter-gatherers as models for early hominin social organization.

Anthropologists studying living hunter-gatherers have radically revised their view of how early human societies were structured, a shift that yields new insights into how humans evolved away from apes.

Early human groups, according to the new view, would have been more cooperative and willing to learn from one another than . . . chimpanzees. . . . The advantages of cooperation and social learning then propelled the incipient human groups along a different evolutionary path. . . .

A team of anthropologists led by Kim R. Hill of Arizona State University and Robert S. Walker of the University of Missouri analyzed data from 32 living hunter-gatherer peoples. . . .

Michael Tomasello, a psychologist at the Max Planck Institute for Evolutionary Anthropology in Germany, said the survey provided a strong foundation for the view that cooperative behavior, as distinct from the fierce aggression between chimp groups, was the turning point that shaped human evolution. . . .

The finding corroborates an influential new view of early human origins advanced by Bernard Chapais, a primatologist at the University of Montreal, in his book *Primeval Kinship* (2008). Dr. Chapais showed how a simple development, the emergence of a pair bond between male and female, would have allowed people to recognize their relatives, something chimps can do only to a limited extent. When family members dispersed to other bands, they would be recognized and neighboring bands would cooperate instead of fighting to the death as chimp groups do.

In chimpanzee societies, males stay where they are born and females disperse at puberty to neighboring groups, thus avoiding incest. . . .

Dr. Hill and Dr. Walker find that though it is the daughters who move in many hunter-gatherer societies, the sons leave the home community in many others. In fact, the human pattern of residency is so variable that it counts as a pattern in itself, one that the researchers say is not known for any species of ape or monkey. Dr. Chapais calls this social pattern "bilocality."

Modern humans have lived as hunter-gatherers for more than 90 percent of their existence as a species. If living hunter-gatherers are typical of ancient ones, the new data about their social pattern has considerable bearing on early human evolution. . . .

The new data . . . furnishes the context in which two distinctive human behaviors emerged, those of cooperation and social learning, Dr. Hill said. A male chimp may know in his lifetime just 12 other males, all from his own group. But a hunter-gatherer, because of cooperation between bands, may interact with a thousand individuals in his tribe. Because humans are unusually adept at social learning, including copying useful activities from others, a large social network is particularly effective at spreading and accumulating knowledge.

Knowledge can in fact be lost by hunter-gatherers if a social network gets too small. One group of the Ache people of Paraguay, cut off from its home territory, had lost use of fire when first contacted. Tasmanians apparently forgot various fishing techniques after rising sea levels broke their contact with the Australian mainland 10,000 years ago.

Dr. Chapais said that the new findings "validate and enrich" the model of human social evolution proposed in his book. "If you take the promiscuity that is the main feature of chimp society, and replace it with pair bonding, you get many of the most important features of human society," he said.

Recognition of relatives promoted cooperation between neighboring bands, in his view, allowing people to move freely from one to another. Both sons and daughters could disperse from the home group, unlike chimp society, where only females can disperse. . . .

be least likely when there was substantial paternal parenting of daughters. This experience enhanced the father's parenting skills and his feelings of nurturance, protectiveness, and identification with his daughter, thus reducing the chance of incest.

A century ago, early anthropologists speculated that incest restrictions reflect an instinctive horror of mating with close relatives (Hobhouse 1915; Lowie 1920/1961). But why, one wonders, if humans really do have an instinctive aversion to incest, would formal restrictions be necessary? No one would want to

Discovered in Egypt's Valley of the Kings, a gold and silver inlaid throne from the tomb of Tutankhamun is now on display in Cairo's Egyptian Museum. Sibling marriage was allowed not only for ancient Egyptian royalty but also for commoners in some regions.

**endogamy**
Marriage of people from the same social group.

have sexual contact with a relative. Yet as social workers, judges, psychiatrists, and psychologists are well aware, incest is more common than we might suppose.

## Incest Avoidance

Why do societies discourage incest? Is it because incestuous unions tend to produce abnormal offspring, as the early anthropologist Lewis Henry Morgan (1877/1963) suggested? Laboratory experiments with animals that reproduce faster than humans do (such as mice and fruit flies) have been used to investigate the effects of inbreeding: A decline in survival and fertility does accompany brother–sister mating across several generations. However, despite the potentially harmful biological results of systematic inbreeding, human marriage patterns are based on specific cultural beliefs rather than universal concerns about fertility decline several generations in the future. Biological concerns certainly cannot explain why so many societies promote marriage of cross cousins but not of parallel cousins.

In most societies, people avoid incest by following rules of exogamy, which force them to mate and marry outside their kin group (Lévi-Strauss 1949/1969; Tylor 1889; White 1959). Exogamy is adaptively advantageous because it creates new social ties and alliances. Marrying a close relative, with whom one already is on peaceful terms, would be counterproductive. There is more to gain by extending peaceful relations to a wider network of groups (see "Appreciating Anthropology"). Marriage within the group would isolate that group from its neighbors and their

resources and social networks, and might ultimately lead to the group's extinction. Exogamy helps explain human adaptive success. Besides its sociopolitical function, exogamy also ensures genetic mixture between groups and thus maintains a successful human species.

## ENDOGAMY

The practice of exogamy pushes social organization outward, establishing and preserving alliances among groups. In contrast, rules of **endogamy** dictate mating or marriage within a group to which one belongs. Formal endogamic rules are less common but are still familiar to anthropologists. Indeed, most societies *are* endogamous units, although they usually don't need a formal rule requiring people to marry someone from their own society. In our own society, classes and ethnic groups are quasi-endogamous groups. Members of an ethnic or religious group often want their children to marry within that group, although many of them do not do so. The outmarriage rate varies among such groups, with some more committed to endogamy than others are.

How many fingers do this Indian woman and her child have? Such genetically determined traits as polydactylism (extra fingers) may show up when there is a high incidence of endogamy. Despite the biological effects of inbreeding, marriage preferences and prohibitions are based on specific cultural beliefs rather than universal concerns about future biological degeneration.

*Homogamy* means to marry someone similar, as when members of the same social class intermarry. In modern societies, there's a correlation between socio-economic status (SES) and education. People with similar SES tend to have similar educational aspirations, to attend similar schools, and to pursue similar careers. For example, people who meet at an elite private university are likely to have similar backgrounds and career prospects. Homogamous marriage can work to concentrate wealth in social classes and to reinforce the system of social stratification. In the United States, for example, the rise in female employment, especially in professional careers, when coupled with homogamy, has dramatically increased household incomes in the upper classes. This pattern has been one factor in sharpening the contrast in household income between the richest and poorest quintiles (top and bottom 20 percent) of Americans.

## Caste

An extreme example of endogamy is India's caste system, which was formally abolished in 1949, although its structure and effects linger. Castes are stratified groups in which membership is ascribed at birth and is lifelong. Indian castes are grouped into five major categories, or *varna.* Each is ranked relative to the other four, and these categories extend throughout India. Each *varna* includes a large number of subcastes (*jati*), each of which includes people within a region who may intermarry. All the *jati* in a single *varna* in a given region are ranked, just as the *varnas* themselves are ranked.

Occupational specialization often sets off one caste from another. A community may include castes of agricultural workers, merchants, artisans, priests, and sweepers. The untouchable *varna,* found throughout India, includes subcastes whose ancestry, ritual status, and occupations are considered so impure that higher-caste people consider even casual contact with untouchables to be defiling.

The belief that intercaste sexual unions lead to ritual impurity for the higher-caste partner has been important in maintaining endogamy. A man who has sex with a lower-caste woman can restore his purity with a bath and a prayer. However, a woman who has intercourse with a man of a lower caste has no such recourse. Her defilement cannot be undone. Because the women have the babies, these differences protect the purity of the caste line, ensuring the pure ancestry of high-caste children. Although Indian castes are endogamous groups, many of them are internally subdivided into exogamous lineages. Traditionally, this meant that Indians had to marry a member of another descent group from the same caste.

## Royal Endogamy

Royal endogamy, based in a few societies on brother–sister marriage, is similar to caste endogamy. Inca Peru, ancient Egypt, and traditional

An extreme example of endogamy is India's caste system, which was formally abolished in 1949, although its structure and effects linger. Shown here, a member of the Dalit, or untouchable caste, cleans a sewer drain in a market in Jodhpur, India. The work of sweepers and tanners has been considered so smelly and dirty that they have been segregated residentially.

Hawaii all allowed royal brother–sister marriages. In ancient Peru and Hawaii, such marriages were permitted despite the restrictions on sibling incest that applied to commoners in those societies.

### Manifest and Latent Functions

To understand royal brother–sister marriage, it is useful to distinguish between the manifest and latent functions of customs and behavior. The *manifest function* of a custom refers to the reasons people in that society give for it. Its *latent function* is an effect the custom has on the society that its members don't mention or may not even recognize.

Royal endogamy illustrates this distinction. Hawaiians and other Polynesians believed in an impersonal force called *mana.* Mana could exist in things or people, in the latter case marking them off from other people and making them sacred. The Hawaiians believed that no one had as much mana as the ruler. Mana depended on genealogy. The person whose own mana was exceeded only by the king's was his sibling. The most appropriate wife for a king was his own full sister. Notice that the brother–sister marriage also meant that royal heirs would be as manaful, or sacred, as possible. The manifest function of royal endogamy in ancient Hawaii was part of that culture's beliefs about mana and sacredness.

Royal endogamy also had latent functions—political repercussions. The ruler and his wife had the same parents. Since mana was believed to be inherited, they were almost equally sacred. When the king and his sister married, their children indisputably had the most mana in the land. No one could question their right to rule. But if the king had taken as a wife someone with less mana than his sister, his sister's children eventually could cause problems. Both sets of children could assert their sacredness and right to rule. Royal sibling marriage therefore limited conflicts about succession by reducing the number of people with claims to rule. The same result would be true in ancient Egypt and Peru.

Other kingdoms, including European royalty, also have practiced endogamy, but based on cousin marriage rather than sibling marriage. In many cases, as in Great Britain, it is specified that the eldest child (usually the son) of the reigning monarch should succeed. This custom is called *primogeniture*. Commonly, rulers have banished or killed claimants who rival the chosen heir.

Royal endogamy also had a latent economic function. By limiting the number of heirs, marriage of relatives helped keep estates intact. Power often rests on wealth, and royal endogamy tended to ensure that royal wealth remained concentrated in the same line.

## MARITAL RIGHTS AND SAME-SEX MARRIAGE

The British anthropologist Edmund Leach (1955) observed that, depending on the society, several different kinds of rights are allocated by marriage. According to Leach, marriage can, but doesn't always, accomplish the following:

1. Establish legal parentage.

2. Give either or both spouses a monopoly on the sexuality of the other.

3. Give either or both spouses rights to the labor of the other.

4. Give either or both spouses rights over the other's property.

5. Establish a joint fund of property—a partnership—for the benefit of the children.

6. Establish a socially significant "relationship of affinity" between spouses and their relatives.

The discussion of same-sex marriage that follows will illustrate the six rights just listed by seeing what happens in their absence. What if same-sex marriage, which remains illegal in most of the United States, were legal? Could a same-sex marriage establish legal parentage of children born to one or both partners after the partnership is formed? In the case of a different-sex marriage, children born to the wife after the marriage takes place usually are legally defined as her husband's regardless of whether he is the genitor.

Nowadays, of course, DNA testing makes it possible to establish paternity, just as modern reproductive technology makes it possible for a lesbian couple to have one or both partners artificially inseminated. When same-sex marriages are legal, the social construction of kinship easily makes both partners parents. Just as a Nuer woman married to a woman can be the pater of a child she did not father, a lesbian can be the **mater** (socially recognized mother) of a child she did not bear. Furthermore, if a married different-sex couple can adopt a child who becomes theirs through the social and legal construction of kinship, the same logic could be applied to a same-sex couple.

Continuing with Leach's list of the rights transmitted by marriage, same-sex marriage can certainly give each spouse rights to the sexuality of the other. When unable to marry legally, gay men and lesbians have used various devices, such as mock weddings, to declare their commitment and desire for a monogamous sexual relationship. In April 2000, Vermont passed a bill allowing same-sex couples to unite legally, with virtually all the benefits of marriage. In June 2003, a court ruling established same-sex marriages as legal in the province of Ontario, Canada. On June 28, 2005, Canada's House of Commons voted to guarantee full marriage rights to same-sex couples throughout that nation. In the United States 17 states—California, Connecticut, Delaware, Hawaii, Illinois, Iowa, Maine, Maryland, Massachusetts, Minnesota, New Hampshire, New Jersey, New Mexico, New York, Rhode Island, Vermont, and Washington—allowed same-sex marriage as of this writing. These rights have come despite efforts at the federal and state level to discourage same-sex marriage. In 1996 the U.S. Congress approved the Defense of Marriage

This photo shows the May 2008 wedding, in Windsor, Ontario, Canada, of a lesbian couple from New York. At that time, Massachusetts was the only U.S. state where same-sex marriage was legal, compared with 17 states and the District of Columbia as of this writing.

**mater**
Socially recognized mother of a child.

Act (DOMA), which denied federal recognition and benefits to same-sex couples. Voters in at least 29 U.S. states have approved measures in their state constitutions defining marriage as an exclusively heterosexual union. In November 2008, Californians voted 52 percent to 48 percent for Proposition 8, banning same-sex marriage, which the courts had approved earlier that year. In 2012, California's 9th Circuit Court struck down that ban as unconstitutional.

Public and legal opinions about same-sex marriage have been changing rapidly. On June 26, 2013, the U. S. Supreme Court, striking down a key part of DOMA, declared that same-sex couples who are legally married deserve equal rights to the benefits under federal law that go to all other married couples. In August 2013, the California Supreme Court rejected an attempt to revive the state's ban on same-sex marriage. Any adult in California can now marry the partner of his or her choice and receive all federal benefits available to any legally married couple.

Legal same-sex marriages can give each spouse rights to the other spouse's labor and its products. Some societies have allowed marriage between members of the same biological sex, who may, however, be considered to belong to a different, socially constructed gender. Several Native American groups had figures known as *berdaches,* representing a third gender (Murray and Roscoe 1998). These were biological men who assumed many of the mannerisms, behavior patterns, and tasks of women. Sometimes *berdaches* married men, who shared the products of their labor from hunting and filled traditional male roles, as the *berdache* fulfilled the traditional wifely role. Also, in some Native American cultures, a marriage of a "manly hearted woman" (a third or fourth gender) to another woman brought the traditional male–female division of labor to their household. The manly woman hunted and did other male tasks, while the wife played the traditional female role.

Regarding property, in many of the United States, the same inheritance rights that apply to male–female couples don't apply to same-sex couples. For instance, even in the absence of a will, property can pass to a widow or a widower without going through probate. The wife or husband pays no inheritance tax. This benefit is unavailable for gay men and lesbians in most states. Concerning Leach's fifth right (establishing a joint fund of property to benefit the children), same-sex couples again have been disadvantaged. Without legal marriage, property must be passed on separately, rather than jointly.

Finally, there is the matter of establishing a socially significant "relationship of affinity" between spouses and their relatives. In many societies, one of the main roles of marriage is to establish an alliance between groups, in addition to the individual bond. *Affinals* are relatives through marriage, such as a brother-in-law or mother-in-law. For same-sex couples in contemporary North America, affinal relations can be problematic. In an unofficial union, terms like "daughter-in-law" and "mother-in-law" may sound strange. Many parents are suspicious of their children's sexuality and lifestyle choices and may not recognize a relationship of affinity with a child's partner of the same sex.

In Lagos, Nigeria, women work with green vegetables in a bayside market. In parts of Nigeria, prominent market women may take a wife. Such marriage allows wealthy women to strengthen their social status and the economic importance of their households.

This discussion of same-sex marriage has been intended to illustrate the different kinds of rights that typically accompany marriage by seeing what can happen when there is a permanent pair-bond without legal sanction. In only 17 of the United States are same-sex unions fully legal. As we have seen, same-sex marriages have been recognized in many different historical and cultural settings. In certain African cultures, including the Igbo of Nigeria and the Lovedu of South Africa, women have been permitted to marry other women. In situations in which women, such as prominent market women in West Africa, are able to amass property and other forms of wealth, they may take a wife. Such marriage allows the prominent woman to strengthen her social status and the economic importance of her household (Amadiume 1987).

## MARRIAGE AS GROUP ALLIANCE

Outside industrial societies, marriage often is more a relationship between groups than one between individuals. We think of marriage as an individual matter. Although the bride and groom usually seek their parents' approval, the final choice (to live together, to marry, to divorce) lies with the couple. Contemporary Western societies stress the notion that romantic love is necessary for a good marriage. Increasingly, this idea characterizes other cultures as well. The mass media and migration spread to other societies Western ideas about the importance of love for marriage.

Just how widespread is romantic love, and what role should it play in marriage? A study by anthropologists William Jankowiak and Edward Fischer (1992) found romantic ardor to be very common cross-culturally. Previously, anthropologists had tended to ignore evidence for romantic love in other cultures, probably because arranged marriages were so common. Surveying ethnographic data from 166 cultures, Jankowiak and Fischer (1992) found evidence for romantic love in 147 of them—89 percent (see also Jankowiak 1995, 2008).

Furthermore, recent diffusion of Western ideas about the importance of love for marriage has influenced marital decisions in other cultures. Among villagers in the Kangra valley of northern India, as reported by anthropologist Kirin Narayan (quoted in Goleman 1992), even in the traditional arranged marriages, the partners might eventually fall in love. In that area today, however, the media have spread the idea that young people should choose their own spouse based on romantic love, and elopements now rival arranged marriages.

The same trend away from arranged marriages toward love matches has been noted among Native Australians. Traditionally in the Australian Outback, marriages were arranged when children were very young. Missionaries disrupted that pattern, urging that marriage be postponed to adolescence. Before the missionaries, according to anthropologist Victoria Burbank, all girls married before puberty, some as early as age 9; nowadays the average female age at marriage is 17 years (see Burbank 1988). Parents still prefer the traditional arrangement in which a girl's mother chooses a boy from the appropriate kin group. But more and more girls now choose to elope and get pregnant, thus forcing a marriage to someone they love. In the group Burbank studied, most marriages now are love matches (see Burbank 1988; Goleman 1992).

Whether or not they are cemented by passion, marriages in nonindustrial societies remain the concern of social groups rather than mere individuals. The scope of marriage extends from the social to the political. Strategic marriages are tried-and-true ways of establishing alliances between groups.

### Gifts at Marriage

In societies with descent groups, people enter marriage not alone but with the help of the descent group. Often, it is customary for a substantial gift to be given before, at, or after the marriage by the husband and his kin to the wife and her kin. The BaThonga of Mozambique call such a gift *lobola,* and the custom of giving something like **lobola** is very widespread in patrilineal societies (Radcliffe-Brown 1924/1952). This gift compensates the bride's group for the loss of her companionship and labor. More important, it makes the children born to the woman full members of her husband's descent group. In matrilineal societies, children are members of the mother's group, and there is no reason for a lobola-like gift.

Another kind of marital gift, **dowry,** occurs when the bride's family or kin group provides substantial

**lobola**

A substantial marital gift from the husband and his kin to the wife and her kin.

**dowry**

Substantial gifts to the husband's family from the wife's group.

This "I love you" wall is on display in an open area of Monmartre, Paris, France. It shows how to say "I love you" in various languages. Is romantic love a cultural universal?

gifts when their daughter marries. For rural Greece, Ernestine Friedl (1962) has described a form of dowry in which the bride gets a wealth transfer from her mother, to serve as a kind of trust fund during her marriage. Usually, however, the dowry goes to the husband's family, and the custom is correlated with low female status. In this form of dowry, best known from India, women are perceived as burdens. When a man and his family take a wife, they expect to be compensated for the added responsibility.

Lobola-like gifts exist in many more cultures than dowry does, but the nature and quantity of transferred items differ. Among the BaThonga of Mozambique, whose name—lobola—I am using for this widespread custom, the gift consists of cattle. Use of livestock (usually cattle in Africa, pigs in Papua New Guinea) for lobola is common, but the number of animals given varies from society to society. We can generalize, however, that the larger the gift, the more stable the marriage. Lobola is insurance against divorce.

Imagine a patrilineal society in which a marriage requires the transfer of about 25 cattle from the groom's descent group to the bride's. Michael, a member of descent group A, marries Sarah from group B. His relatives help him assemble the lobola. He gets the most help from his close agnates (patrilineal relatives): his older brother, father, father's brother, and closest patrilineal cousins.

The distribution of the cattle once they reach Sarah's group mirrors the manner in which they were assembled. Sarah's father, or her oldest brother if the father is dead, receives her lobola. He keeps most of the cattle to use as lobola for his sons' marriages. However, a share also goes to everyone who will be expected to help when Sarah's brothers marry.

When Sarah's brother David gets married, many of the cattle go to a third group: C, which is David's wife's group. Thereafter, they may serve as lobola to still other groups. Men constantly use their sisters' lobola cattle to acquire their own wives. In a decade, the cattle given when Michael married Sarah will have been exchanged widely.

In such societies, marriage entails an agreement between descent groups. If Sarah and Michael try to make their marriage succeed but fail to do so, both groups may conclude that the marriage can't last. Here it becomes especially obvious that such marriages are relationships between groups as well as between individuals. If Sarah has a younger sister or niece (her older brother's daughter, for example), the concerned parties may agree to Sarah's replacement by a kinswoman.

However, incompatibility isn't the main problem that threatens marriage in societies with lobola customs. Infertility is a more important concern. If Sarah has no children, she and her group have not fulfilled their part of the marriage agreement. If the relationship is to endure, Sarah's group must furnish another woman, perhaps her younger sister, who can have children. If this happens, Sarah may choose to stay with her husband. Perhaps she will someday have a child. If she does stay on, her husband will have established a plural marriage.

Many nonindustrial societies allow **plural marriages,** or *polygamy* (see Zeitzen 2008). There are

**plural marriage**
More than two spouses simultaneously; polygamy.

A bride and groom are escorted back to the bride's home after their wedding ceremony in a village in southwest China's Guizhou province. Having observed traditional wedding customs of their Miao ethnic group, they are congratulated by fellow villagers and tourists.

This photo, taken in South Africa, shows the lobola cattle presented at the 2010 wedding of Mandla Mandela (grandson of former South African president Nelson Mandela) and his French wife, Anais Grimaud.

**polygyny**
Man has more than one wife at the same time.

**polyandry**
Woman has more than one husband at the same time.

**levirate**
Widow marries brother of her deceased husband.

**sororate**
Widower marries sister of his deceased wife.

two varieties; one is common, and the other is very rare. The more common variant is **polygyny,** in which a man has more than one wife at the same time. The rare variant is **polyandry,** in which a woman has more than one husband at the same time. If the infertile wife remains married to her husband after he has taken a substitute wife provided by her descent group, this is polygyny. Reasons for polygyny other than infertility will be discussed shortly.

## Durable Alliances

It is possible to exemplify the group-alliance nature of marriage by examining still another common practice: continuation of marital alliances when one spouse dies.

### Sororate

What happens if Sarah dies young? Michael's group will ask Sarah's group for a substitute, often her sister. This custom is known as the **sororate** (Figure 20.5). If Sarah has no sister or if all her sisters are already married, another woman from her group may be available. Michael marries her, there is no need to return the lobola, and the alliance continues. The sororate exists in both matrilineal and patrilineal societies. In a matrilineal society with matrilocal postmarital residence, a widower may remain with his wife's group by marrying her sister or another female member of her matrilineage.

### Levirate

What happens if the husband dies? In many societies, the widow may marry his brother. This custom is known as the **levirate.** Like the sororate, it is a continuation marriage that maintains the alliance between descent groups, in this case by replacing the husband with another member of his group. The implications of the levirate vary with age. One study found that in African societies, the levirate, though widely permitted, rarely involves cohabitation of the

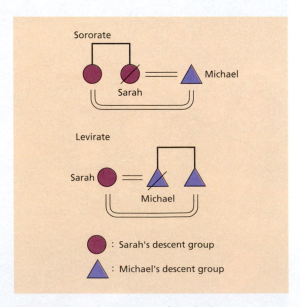

**FIGURE 20.5** Sororate and Levirate.

widow and her new husband. Furthermore, widows don't automatically marry the husband's brother just because they are allowed to. Often, they prefer to make other arrangements (Potash 1986).

# DIVORCE

Ease of divorce varies across cultures. What factors work for and against divorce? As we've seen, marriages that are political alliances between groups are more difficult to dissolve than are marriages that are more individual affairs, of concern mainly to the married couple and their children. We've seen that a substantial lobola gift may decrease the divorce rate for individuals and that replacement marriages (levirate and sororate) also work to preserve group alliances. Divorce tends to be more common in matrilineal than in patrilineal societies. When residence is matrilocal (in the wife's place), the wife may simply send off a man with whom she's incompatible.

Among the Hopi of the American Southwest, houses were owned by matrilineal clans, with matrilocal postmarital residence. The household head was the senior woman of that household, which also included her daughters and their husbands and children. A son-in-law had no important role there; he returned to his own mother's home for his clan's social and religious activities. In this matrilineal society, women were socially and economically secure, and the divorce rate was high. Consider the Hopi of Oraibi (Orayvi) pueblo, northeastern Arizona (Levy with Pepper 1992; Titiev 1992). In a study of the marital histories of 423 Oraibi women, Mischa Titiev found that 35 percent had been divorced at least once. Jerome Levy found that 31 percent of 147 adult women had been divorced and remarried at least once. For comparison, of all ever-married women in the United States, only 4 percent had been divorced in 1960, 10.7 percent in 1980, and 13.7 percent in 2010. Titiev characterizes Hopi marriages as unstable. Part of this brittleness was due to conflicting loyalties to matrikin versus spouse. Most Hopi divorces appear to have been matters of personal choice. Levy generalizes that, cross-culturally, high divorce rates are correlated with a secure female economic position. In Hopi society, women were secure in their home and land ownership and in the custody of their children. In addition, there were no formal barriers to divorce.

Divorce is harder in a patrilineal society, especially when substantial lobola would have to be reassembled and repaid if the marriage failed. A woman residing patrilocally (in her husband's household and community) might be reluctant to leave him. Unlike the Hopi, who let the kids stay with the mother, in patrilineal-patrilocal societies, the children of divorce would be expected to remain with their father, as members of his patrilineage. From the women's perspective this is a strong impediment to divorce.

Political and economic factors complicate the divorce process. Among foragers, different factors tend to favor and oppose divorce. What factors work against durable marriages? Since foragers tend to lack descent groups, the political alliance functions of marriage are less important to them than they are to food producers. Foragers also tend to have minimal material possessions. The process of dissolving a joint fund of property is less complicated when spouses do not hold substantial resources in common. What factors favor marital stability among foragers? In societies where the family is an important year-round unit with a gender-based division of labor, ties between spouses tend to be durable. Also, sparse populations mean few alternative spouses if a marriage doesn't work out. But in band-organized societies, foragers can always find a band to join or rejoin if a marriage doesn't work. And food producers can always draw on their descent-group estate if a marriage fails. With patriliny, a woman often can return home, albeit without her children, and with matriliny, a man can do the same. Descent-group estates are not transferred through marriages, although movable resources such as lobola cattle certainly are.

In contemporary Western societies, when romance fails, so may the marriage. Or it may not fail, if the other rights associated with marriage are compelling.

Hopi piki bread maker Rebecca Namingha mixes blue corn meal and ashes with water. She'll cook the batter on a hot stone. Traditionally among the matrilineal-matrilocal Hopi, women were socially and economically secure, and the divorce rate was high.

Economic ties and obligations to kids, along with other factors, such as concern about public opinion, or simple inertia, may keep marriages intact after sex, romance, and/or companionship fade. Also, even in modern societies, royalty, leaders, and other elites may have political marriages similar to the arranged marriages of nonindustrial societies.

In the United States, divorce figures have been kept since 1860. Divorces tend to increase after wars and to decrease when times are bad economically. But with more women working outside the home, economic dependence on the husband as breadwinner is weaker, which no doubt facilitates a decision to divorce when a marriage has major problems.

Table 20.1 is based on two measures of the divorce rate through 2010. The second column shows the rate per 1,000 people per year in the overall population. The third column shows the annual rate per 1,000 married women aged 15 and older, which is the best measure of divorce. The most notable rate rise in the American divorce rate occurred between 1960 and 1980. Since then the rate has declined.

Among nations, the United States has one of the world's highest divorce rates. There are several probable causes: economic, cultural, and religious among them. Economically, the United States has a large percentage of gainfully employed women. Work outside the home provides a cash basis for independence, as it also places strains on marriage and social life for both partners. Culturally, Americans tend to value independence and its modern form, self-actualization. Also, Protestantism (in its various guises) is the most common form of religion in the United States. Of the two major religions in the United States and Canada (where Catholicism predominates), Protestantism has been less stringent in denouncing divorce than has Catholicism.

## PLURAL MARRIAGES

In contemporary North America, where divorce is fairly easy and common, polygamy (marriage to more than one spouse at the same time) is against the law. Marriage in industrial nations joins individuals, and relationships between individuals can be severed more easily than can those between groups. As divorce grows more common, North Americans practice *serial monogamy:* Individuals have more than one spouse but never, legally, more than one at the same time. As stated earlier, the two forms of polygamy are polygyny and polyandry. Polyandry is practiced in only a few cultures, notably among certain groups in Tibet, Nepal, and India. Polygyny is much more common.

### Polygyny

We must distinguish between the social approval of plural marriage and its actual frequency in a particular society. Many cultures approve of a man's having more than one wife. However, even when polygyny is encouraged, most men are monogamous, and polygyny characterizes only a fraction of the marriages. Why is this true?

One reason is equal sex ratios. In the United States, about 105 males are born for every 100 females. In adulthood, the ratio of men to women equalizes, and eventually it reverses. The average North American woman outlives the average man. In many nonindustrial societies as well, the male-biased sex ratio among children reverses in adulthood.

The custom of men marrying later than women promotes polygyny. Among the Kanuri people of Bornu, Nigeria, men got married between the ages of 18 and 30; women, between 12 and 14 (Cohen 1967). The age difference between spouses meant that there were more widows than widowers. Most of the widows remarried, some in polygynous unions. Among the Kanuri and in other polygynous societies, widows made up a large number of the women involved in plural marriages (Hart, Pilling, and Goodale 1988). In many societies, including the Kanuri, the number of wives is an indicator of a man's household productivity, prestige, and social position. The more wives, the more workers. Increased productivity means more wealth. This wealth in turn attracts additional wives to the household. Wealth and wives bring greater prestige to the household and its head.

If a plural marriage is to work, there needs to be some agreement among the existing spouses when another one is to be added, especially if they are to share the same household. In certain societies, the first wife requests a second wife to help with household chores. The second wife's status is lower than that of the first; they are senior and junior wives. The senior wife sometimes chooses the junior one from

**TABLE 20.1**  Changing Divorce Rates (Number per Year) in the United States, 1940 through 2010

| YEAR | DIVORCE RATE PER 1,000 POPULATION | DIVORCE RATE PER 1,000 WOMEN AGED 15 AND OLDER |
|---|---|---|
| 1940 | 2.0 | 8.8 |
| 1950 | 2.6 | 10.3 |
| 1960 | 2.2 | 9.2 |
| 1970 | 3.5 | 14.9 |
| 1980 | 5.2 | 22.6 |
| 1990 | 4.7 | 20.9 |
| 2000 | 4.2 | 19.5 |
| 2010 | 3.5 | 13.7 |

SOURCE: S. C. Clarke, "Advance Report of Final Divorce Statistics, 1989 and 1990," *Monthly Vital Statistics Report* 43(8, 9), Hyattsville, MD: National Center for Health Statistics; R. Hughes, Jr., "Demographics of Divorce," 1996, http://www.hec.ohiostate.edu/famlife/divorce/demo.htm; *National Vital Statistics Reports* 54(12), 2006, http://www.cdc.gov/nchs/data/nvsr/nvsr54/nvsr54_12.pdf; *Statistical Abstract of the United States* 2012, Tables 56, 78, and 132.

Modern-day polygyny is illustrated by this photo (left) of South African President Joseph Zuma and his three wives. In the United States as in South Africa, powerful men often have multiple wives, but not legally at the same time. The three marriages of former House Speaker Newt Gingrich (shown here with his third wife Callista) illustrate serial monogamy.

among her close kinswomen. Among the Betsileo of Madagascar, the different wives always lived in different villages. A man's first and senior wife, called "Big Wife," lived in the village where he cultivated his best rice field and spent most of his time. High-status men with several rice fields and multiple wives had households near each field. They spent most of their time with the senior wife but visited the others throughout the year.

Plural wives can play important political roles in nonindustrial states. The king of the Merina, a populous society in the highlands of Madagascar, had palaces for each of his 12 wives in different provinces. He stayed with them when he traveled through the kingdom. They were his local agents, overseeing and reporting on provincial matters. The king of Buganda, the major precolonial state of Uganda, took hundreds of wives, representing all the clans in his nation. Everyone in the kingdom became the king's in-law, and all the clans had a chance to provide the next ruler. This was a way of giving the common people a stake in the government.

These examples show that there is no single explanation for polygyny. Its context and function vary from society to society and even within the same society. Some men are polygynous because they have inherited a widow from a brother (the levirate). Others have plural wives because they seek prestige or want to increase household productivity. Still others use marriage as a political tool or a means of economic advancement. Men and women with political and economic ambitions cultivate marital alliances that serve their aims. In many societies, including the Betsileo of Madagascar and the Igbo of Nigeria, women arrange the marriages.

Like all institutions studied by anthropologists, customs involving plural marriage are changing in the contemporary world and in the context of nation-states and globalization. In Turkey, for example, polygyny has been allowed for men who could afford multiple wives and many children. Polygyny now is outlawed, but it still is practiced. Because polygynous unions have lost legal status, secondary wives are at much

greater risk now than previously if their husband mistreats, neglects, or leaves them (Bilefsky 2006).

## Polyandry

Polyandry is rare and is practiced under very specific conditions. Most of the world's polyandrous peoples live in South Asia—Tibet, Nepal, India, and Sri Lanka. In some of these areas, polyandry seems to be a cultural adaptation to mobility associated with customary male travel for trade, commerce, and military operations. Polyandry ensures there will be at least one man at home to accomplish male activities within a gender-based division of labor. Fraternal polyandry is also an effective strategy when resources are scarce. Brothers with limited resources (in land) pool their resources in expanded (polyandrous) households. They take just one wife. Polyandry restricts the number of wives and heirs. Less competition among heirs means that land can be transmitted with minimal fragmentation.

## THE ONLINE MARRIAGE MARKET

People today shop for everything, including romantic relationships, in what has been labeled the "marriage market." There are huge differences in the marriage markets of industrial versus nonindustrial societies. In some of the latter, potential spouses may be limited to cross cousins or members of the other moiety (see Figures 20.1 and 20.2). Sometimes there are set rules of exogamy, such that, for example, women of descent group A have to marry men from descent group B, while men from A must marry women from C. Often, marriages are arranged by relatives. In almost all cases, however, there is some kind of preexisting social relationship between any two individuals who marry and their kin groups.

Potential mates still meet in person in modern nations. Sometimes friends—more rarely relatives—help arrange such meetings. Besides friends of friends, the marriage market includes the workplace, bars, clubs, parties, churches, and hobby groups. Add the Internet, which in contemporary societies has become a new place to seek out and develop "virtual" relationships, including romantic ones that may lead eventually to a face-to-face meeting. As part of the "Me, My Spouse, and the Internet" project at the University of Oxford, Bernie Hogan, Nai Li, and William Dutton (2011) surveyed cohabiting couples in 18 countries (Table 20.2 lists those countries and the sample size for each). This study (conducted online) sampled 12,600 couples (25,200 individuals aged 18 and older), all with home Internet access. Respondents were asked about how they met their partners, their dating strategies, how they maintain their current relationships and social networks, and how they use the Internet.

The Oxford survey found that online dating (through both dating sites and social network sites) has become a significant part of the marriage market. The role of the Internet has been complementary, rather than a substitution, for offline partner shopping. That is, people still seek and find partners in the old, familiar places, but they look online as well. One-third of the respondents in the study had some

## TABLE 20.2 Countries Sampled in the Oxford Internet Institute Project "Me, My Spouse, and the Internet"

| COUNTRY | SAMPLE SIZE | PERCENT |
|---|---|---|
| Italy | 3,515 | 13.9 |
| France | 2,970 | 11.8 |
| Spain | 2,673 | 10.6 |
| Germany | 2,638 | 10.5 |
| UK | 2,552 | 10.1 |
| Brazil | 2,438 | 9.7 |
| Japan | 2,084 | 8.3 |
| Netherlands | 1,491 | 5.9 |
| Belgium | 1,124 | 4.5 |
| Sweden | 794 | 3.1 |
| Portugal | 603 | 2.4 |
| Finland | 508 | 2.0 |
| Ireland | 368 | 1.5 |
| Norway | 317 | 1.3 |
| Austria | 309 | 1.2 |
| Greece | 297 | 1.2 |
| Switzerland | 278 | 1.1 |
| Denmark | 241 | 1.0 |
| Total | 25,200 | 100.0 |

SOURCE: Bernie Hogan, Nai Li, and William H. Dutton, *A Global Shift in the Social Relationships of Networked Individuals: Meeting and Dating Online Comes of Age* (February 14, 2011, Table 1.1, p. 5). Oxford Internet Institute, University of Oxford. http://ssrn.com/abstract=1763884 or http://dx.doi.org/10.2139/ssrn.1763884. Reprinted with permission.

experience with online dating, and about 15 percent were in a relationship that had started online. Use of the Internet for partner shopping began to soar in 1997, when Web 2.0 technologies introduced dynamic websites based on databases rather than static html pages. By 2009, over 30 percent of Internet-enabled couples were meeting through online dating (Hogan et al. 2011).

Online dating is socially shaped: One's offline social connections influence one's opinions and use of online dating. People who know someone who dates online are themselves more likely to date online and to approve of online dating. Like online banking and online shopping, Internet dating is an "experience technology" (Hogan et al. 2011): One's attitudes about that technology reflect one's experiences with it. The more one is exposed to online dating, the more one approves of it. People don't even need to have been successful at online dating to feel positive about it. Simply trying it enhances their view of the experience.

Who benefits most from the new technology? Is it young, tech-savvy people who go online for almost everything? Or might it be people who are socially isolated in the offline world, including divorced, older, and widowed people and others who feel alone in their local community? Interestingly, the Oxford researchers found that older people were more likely than younger ones to use online dating to find their current partner. About 36 percent of people over 40 had done so, versus 23 percent of younger adults.

A country's degree of media exposure influences its citizens' Internet access and use of online resources. In Europe, the media-saturated nations of Northern Europe were most likely to use online dating, which benefits from a critical mass of Internet connectivity (the more people online, the larger the pool of potential contacts). On the other hand, online Brazilians (who tend to be gregarious both on- and offline) were most likely to know someone who either began a relationship online or married someone first met online. Personal knowledge of an online romantic relationship was reported by 81 percent of the Brazilians in the sample versus less than 40 percent of Germans. Brazilians were most, while Britons and Austrians were least, likely to know someone whose partner had been met online.

The Internet reconfigures access to people in general. More of the respondents in the Oxford study reported making online friends or work connections than romantic liaisons. More than half (55 percent) of respondents (considering all 18 countries) had met someone new online (Hogan et al. 2011). The 2,438 Brazilians in the sample were the most likely to move from an online to a face-to-face contact. Fully 83 percent of Internet-enabled Brazilians reported meeting someone face-to-face after first meeting him or her online. Japanese respondents were least likely to meet in person after an online acquaintance. They also were least likely to engage in online dating.

In some countries, Internet penetration is almost total, and social network sites have rapidly diffused. In others, social networking and personal sites are less pervasive. With advanced Internet penetration, the online and offline worlds begin to merge. People grow less suspicious. They include more of their "real-world" contacts in their online network, and they reveal more about themselves. In countries (and regions) with less Internet access, online contacts remain more impersonal and disguised. They tend to take place on websites where icons, pseudonyms, and handles, rather than personal data and pictures, predominate. In this setting, the online world is more separate and foreign—a place where one goes to meet people who may be (and remain) otherwise inaccessible.

The Internet enhances our opportunities to meet people and to form personal relationships. It lets us connect with old friends, new friends, groups, and individuals. But this accessibility also can be disruptive. It can spur jealousy, for example, when a partner makes new friends or reconnects to old ones—and with good reason. The Oxford researchers found that many people disclosed intimate personal details in online settings with someone other than their spouse or partner (Hogan et al. 2011).

In a later analysis of the same sample, researchers tested the hypothesis that the more social media channels one uses and the more often one uses them, the stronger one's relationship ties. On the contrary, Hogan and associates (see Oxford 2013) found that heavy media use did not necessarily enhance—and might even decrease—marital satisfaction. At a certain point, the complexity of maintaining many distinct communication threads (e.g., Facebook, e-mails, texts, and instant messages) may start undermining relationship ties (Oxford 2013).

# for REVIEW

**summary**

1. Marriage, which usually is a form of domestic partnership, is hard to define. Human behavior with respect to mating with close relatives may express generalized primate tendencies, but types, risks, and avoidance of incest also reflect specific kinship structures. The avoidance of incest promotes exogamy, which widens social networks.

2. Endogamic rules are common in stratified societies. One extreme example is India, where castes are the endogamous units. Certain ancient kingdoms encouraged royal incest while prohibiting incest by commoners.

3. The discussion of same-sex marriage illustrates the various rights that go along with different-sex marriages. Marriage establishes legal parentage, and it gives each spouse rights to the sexuality, labor, and property of the other. Marriage also establishes a "relationship of affinity" between each spouse and the other spouse's relatives.

4. In societies with descent groups, marriages are relationships between groups as well as between spouses.

In patrilineal societies, the groom and his relatives often transfer wealth to the bride and her relatives. As the value of that transfer increases, the divorce rate declines. Examples of how marital customs create and maintain group alliances include the sororate and the levirate.

5. The ease and frequency of divorce vary across cultures. Political, economic, social, cultural, and religious factors affect the divorce rate. When marriage is a matter of intergroup alliance, divorce is less common. A large fund of joint property also complicates divorce.

6. Many societies permit plural marriages. The two kinds of polygamy are polygyny and polyandry. The former (and more common) involves multiple wives; the latter, multiple husbands.

7. The Internet, which reconfigures social relations and networks more generally, is an important addition to the marriage market in contemporary nations.

**key terms**

cross cousins  380

dowry  388

endogamy  384

exogamy  380

genitor  380

incest  380

levirate  390

lobola  388

## critical thinking

1. What is homogamy? In countries such as the United States, what are the social and economic implications of homogamy (especially when coupled with other trends such as the rise of female employment)?

2. What is dowry? What customs involving gift giving typically occur with marriage in patrilineal societies? Do you have comparable customs in your society? Why or why not?

3. According to Edmund Leach (1955), depending on the society, several different kinds of rights are allocated by marriage. What are these rights? Which among these rights do you consider more fundamental than others in your definition of marriage? Which ones can you do without? Why?

4. Outside industrial societies, marriage is often more a relationship between groups than one between individuals. What does this mean? What are some examples of this?

5. Divorce tends to be more common in matrilineal than in patrilineal societies. Why?

# Religion

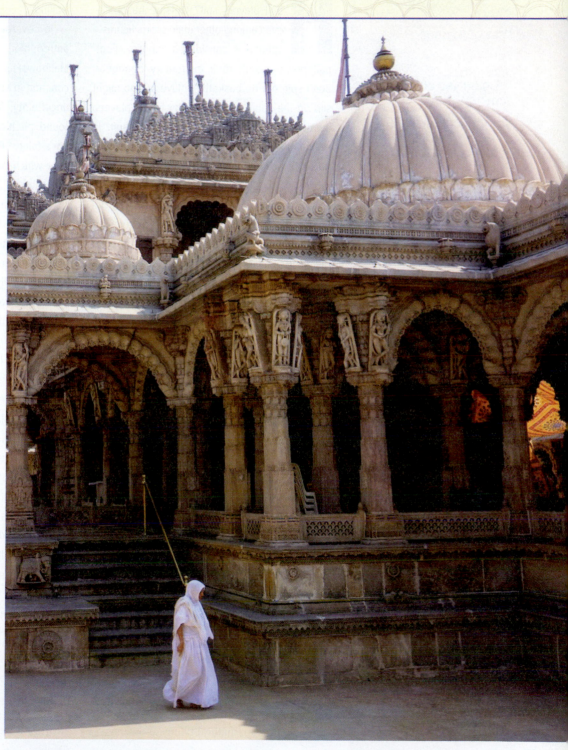

▶ What is religion, and what are its various forms, social correlates, and functions?

▶ What is ritual, and what are its various forms and expressions?

▶ What role does religion play in maintaining and changing societies?

The Hathee Singh Jain temple in Ahmedabad, Gujarat, India.

# understanding OURSELVES

Have you ever noticed how much base-ball players spit? Outside baseball—even among other male sports figures—spitting is considered impolite. Football players, with their customary headgear, don't spit, nor do basketball players, who might slip on the court. No spitting by tennis players, gymnasts, or swimmers, not even Mark Spitz (a swimmer turned dentist). But watch any baseball game for a few innings and you'll see spitting galore. Since pitchers appear to be the spitting champions, the custom likely originated on the mound. It continues today as a carryover from the days when pitchers routinely chewed tobacco, believing that nicotine enhanced their concentration and effectiveness. The spitting custom spread to other players, who unabashedly spew saliva from the outfield to the dugout steps.

For the student of custom, ritual, and magic, baseball is an especially interesting game, to which lessons from anthropology are easily applied. The pioneering anthropologist Bronislaw Malinowski, writing about Pacific Islanders rather than baseball players, noted they had developed all sorts of magic to use in sailing, a hazardous activity. He proposed that when people face conditions they can't control (e.g., wind and weather), they turn to magic. Magic, in the form of rituals, taboos, and sacred objects, is particularly evident in baseball. Like sailing magic, baseball magic reduces psychological stress, creating an illusion of control when real control is lacking.

In several publications about baseball, the anthropologist George Gmelch makes use of Malinowski's observation that magic is most common in situations dominated by chance and uncertainty. All sorts of magical behaviors surround pitching and batting, which are full of uncertainty. There are fewer rituals for fielding, over which players have more control. (Batting averages of .350 or higher are very rare after a full season, but a fielding percentage below .900 is a disgrace.) Especially obvious are the rituals (like the spitting) of pitchers, who may tug their cap between pitches, spit in a particular direction, magically manipulate the resin bag, talk to the ball, or wash their hands after giving up a run. Batters have their rituals, too. It isn't uncommon to see Milwaukee Brewer outfielder Carlos Gomez kiss his bat, which he likes to talk to, smell, threaten—and reward when he gets a hit. Another batter routinely would spit, then ritually touch his gob with his bat, to enhance his success at the plate.

Humans use tools to accomplish a lot, but technology still doesn't let us "have it all." To keep hope alive in situations of uncertainty, and for outcomes we can't control, all societies draw on magic and religion as sources of nonmaterial comfort, explanation, and control. What are your rituals?

## WHAT IS RELIGION?

Given the varied nature and worldwide scope of beliefs and behavior labeled "religious," anthropologists know how difficult it is to define **religion.** In his book *Religion: An Anthropological View,* Anthony F. C. Wallace offered this definition: "belief and ritual concerned with supernatural beings, powers, and forces" (1966, p. 5). By "supernatural" he referred to a nonmaterial realm beyond (but believed to impinge on) the observable world. This realm cannot be verified or falsified empirically and is inexplicable in ordinary terms. It must be accepted "on faith." Supernatural beings (e.g., deities, ghosts, demons, souls, spirits) dwell outside our material world, which they may visit from time to time. There also are supernatural or sacred forces, some of them wielded by deities and spirits, others that simply exist. In many societies, people believe they can benefit from, become imbued with, or manipulate such forces (see Bowen 2011; Bowie 2006; Crapo 2003; Hicks 2010; Lambek 2008; Stein and Stein 2011; Warms, Garber, and McGee 2009).

Wallace's definition of religion focuses on presumably universal categories (beings, powers, and forces) within the supernatural realm. For Émile Durkheim (1912/2001), one of the founders of the anthropology of religion, the key distinction was between the sacred and the profane. Like the supernatural for Wallace, Durkheim's "sacred" was the domain set off from the ordinary, or the mundane (he used the word *profane*). For Durkheim, every society had its sacred, but that domain varied from society to society. Durkheim focused on Native Australian societies, which he believed had preserved the most elementary, or basic, forms of religion. He noted that their most sacred objects, including plants and animals that served as totems, were not supernatural at all. Rather, they were "real-world" entities (e.g., kangaroos, grubs) that, over the generations, had acquired special meaning for the social groups that had made them sacred and continued to "worship" them.

Many definitions of religion focus on groups of people who gather together regularly for worship (see Reese 1999). These congregants or adherents internalize common beliefs and a shared system of meaning. They accept a set of doctrines involving the relationship between the individual and divinity, the sacred, or whatever is taken to be the ultimate nature of reality. Anthropologists like Durkheim have stressed the collective, social, shared, and enacted nature of religion, the emotions it generates, and the meanings it embodies. As Michael Lambek (2008, p. 5) remarks, "good anthropology understands that religious worlds are real, vivid, and significant to those who construct and inhabit them." Durkheim (1912/2001) highlighted religious effervescence, the bubbling up of collective emotional intensity generated by worship. Victor Turner (1969/1995) updated Durkheim's notion, using the term **communitas,** an intense community spirit, a feeling of great social solidarity, equality, and togetherness.

The word *religion* derives from the Latin *religare*— "to tie, to bind"—but it is not necessary for all members of a given religion to meet together as a common body. Subgroups meet regularly at local congregation sites. They may attend occasional meetings with adherents representing a wider region. And they may form an imagined community with people of similar faith throughout the world.

In studying religion cross-culturally, anthropologists pay attention to religion as a social phenomenon as well as to the meanings of religious doctrines, settings, acts, and events. Verbal manifestations of religious beliefs include prayers, chants, myths,

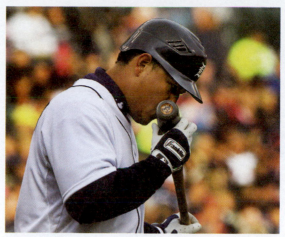

Detroit Tiger third baseman Miguel Cabrera kisses his maple bat before hitting his 42nd home run of 2012 at Comerica Park. Sometimes baseball magic works: Cabrera went on that year to achieve baseball's Triple Crown and win the American League's MVP award. He repeated as AL batting champion and MVP in 2013.

texts, and statements about, including rules of, ethics and morality (see Hicks 2010; Klass 2003; Moro and Meyers 2012; Stein and Stein 2011). The anthropological study of religion also encompasses notions about purity and pollution (including taboos involving diet and physical contact), sacrifice, initiation, rites of passage, vision quests, pilgrimages, spirit possession, prophecy, study, devotion, and moral actions (Lambek 2008, p. 9).

Like ethnicity and language, religion both unites and divides. Participation in common rites can affirm, and thus maintain, the solidarity of a group of adherents. Religious differences also can be associated with bitter enmity. Contacts and confrontations have increased between so-called world religions, such as Christianity and Islam, and the more localized forms of religion that missionaries typically lump together under the disparaging term "paganism." Increasingly, ethnic, regional, and class conflicts come to be framed in religious terms. Recent and contemporary examples of religion as a social and political force include the Iranian revolution, the rise of the religious right in the United States, and the worldwide spread of Pentecostalism.

Long ago, Edward Sapir (1928/1956) argued for a distinction between "a religion" and "religion." The former term would apply only to a formally organized religion, such as the world religions just mentioned. The latter—religion—is universal; it refers to religious beliefs and behavior, which exist in all societies, even if they don't stand out as a separate and clearly demarcated sphere. Indeed, many anthropologists (e.g., Asad 1983/2008) argue that such categories as "religion," "politics," and "the economy" are arbitrary constructs that apply best, and perhaps only, to Western, Christian, and modern societies. In such contexts religion can be seen as a

**religion**
Belief and ritual concerned with supernatural beings, powers, and forces.

**communitas**
Intense feeling of social solidarity.

Illustrating polytheism, this section of the East Frieze of the Parthenon (Athens, Greece) shows Poseidon, Apollo, and Artemis. The frieze dates to ca. 447–432 B.C.E.

**animism**
Belief in souls, or doubles.

**polytheism**
Belief in multiple deities, who control aspects of nature.

**monotheism**
Belief in a single all-powerful deity.

**mana**
Sacred, impersonal force, so named in Melanesia and Polynesia.

specific domain, separate from politics and the economy. By contrast, in nonindustrial societies, religion typically is more embedded in society. Religious beliefs can help regulate the economy (e.g., astrologers determine when to plant) or permeate politics (e.g., divine right of kings).

Anthropologists agree that religion exists in all human societies; it is a cultural universal. However, we'll see that it isn't always easy to distinguish the sacred from the profane and that different societies conceptualize divinity, the sacred, the supernatural, and ultimate realities very differently.

## EXPRESSIONS OF RELIGION

When did religion begin? No one knows for sure. There are suggestions of religion in Neandertal burials and on European cave walls, where painted stick figures may represent shamans, early religious specialists. Nevertheless, any statement about when, where, why, and how religion arose, or any description of its original nature, can only be speculative. Although such speculations are inconclusive, many have revealed important functions and effects of religious behavior. Several theories will be examined now.

### Spiritual Beings

Another founder of the anthropology of religion was the Englishman Sir Edward Burnett Tylor (1871/1958). Religion arose, Tylor thought, as people tried to understand conditions and events they could not explain by reference to daily experience. Tylor believed that ancient humans—and contemporary

nonindustrial peoples—were particularly intrigued with death, dreaming, and trance. People see images they remember when they wake up or come out of a trance state. Tylor concluded that attempts to explain dreams and trances led early humans to believe that two entities inhabit the body. One is active during the day, and the other—a double, or soul—is active during sleep and trance states. Although they never meet, they are vital to each other. When the double permanently leaves the body, the person dies. Death is departure of the soul. From the Latin for soul, *anima,* Tylor named this belief animism. The soul was one sort of spiritual entity; people remembered various images from their dreams and trances— other spirits. For Tylor, **animism,** the earliest form of religion, was a belief in spiritual beings.

Tylor proposed that religion evolved through stages, beginning with animism. **Polytheism** (the belief in multiple gods) and then **monotheism** (the belief in a single, all-powerful deity) developed later. Because religion originated to explain things, Tylor thought it would decline as science offered better explanations. To an extent, he was right. We now have scientific explanations for many things that religion once elucidated. Nevertheless, because religion persists, it must do something more than explain. It must, and does, have other functions and meanings.

### Powers and Forces

In addition to animism—and sometimes coexisting with it in the same society—is a view of the supernatural as a domain of impersonal power, or force, which people can control under certain conditions. (You'd be right to think of *Star Wars.*) Such a conception has been particularly prominent in Melanesia, the area of the South Pacific that includes Papua New Guinea and adjacent islands. Melanesians traditionally believed in **mana,** a sacred, impersonal force existing in the universe. Mana could reside in people, animals, plants, and objects.

Melanesian mana was similar to our notion of good luck. Objects with mana could change someone's luck. For example, a charm or an amulet belonging to a successful hunter could transmit the hunter's mana to the next person who held or wore it. A woman could put a rock in her garden, see her yields improve, and attribute the change to the force contained in the rock.

Beliefs in manalike forces have been widespread, although the specifics of the religious doctrines have varied. Consider the contrast between mana in Melanesia and mana in Polynesia (the islands included in a triangular area marked by Hawaii to the north, Easter Island to the east, and New Zealand to the southwest). In Melanesia, anyone could acquire mana by chance, or by working hard to get it. In Polynesia, however, mana was attached to political offices. Chiefs and nobles had more mana than ordinary people did.

So charged with mana were the highest chiefs that contact with them was dangerous to commoners. The mana of chiefs flowed out of their bodies. It could infect the ground, making it dangerous for others to walk in the chief's footsteps. It could permeate the containers and utensils chiefs used in eating. Because high chiefs had so much mana, their bodies and possessions were **taboo** (set apart as sacred and off-limits to ordinary people). Because ordinary people couldn't bear as much sacred current as royalty could, when commoners were accidentally exposed, purification rites were necessary.

One function of religion is to explain. As Horton (1993) and Lambek (2008) point out, there are universals in human thought and experience, common conditions and situations that call out for explanation. What happens in sleep and trance, and with death? The soul leaves the body. Why do some people prosper, while others fail? Blame it on such nonmaterial factors as luck, mana, sorcery, or being one of "God's chosen."

The beliefs in spiritual beings (e.g., animism) and supernatural forces (e.g., mana) fit within Wallace's definition of religion, given at the beginning of this chapter. Most religions include both spirits and impersonal forces. Likewise, the supernatural beliefs of contemporary North Americans can include beings (gods, saints, souls, demons) and forces (charms, talismans, crystals, and sacred objects).

## Magic and Religion

**Magic** refers to supernatural techniques intended to accomplish specific aims. These techniques include magical actions, offerings, spells, formulas, and incantations. Magicians employ *imitative magic* to produce a desired effect by imitating it. If magicians wish to harm someone, they can imitate that effect on an image of the victim—for instance, by sticking pins in "voodoo dolls." With *contagious magic*, whatever is done to an object is believed to affect a person who once had contact with it. Sometimes practitioners of contagious magic use body products from prospective victims—their nails or hair, for example. The spell performed on the body product is believed eventually to reach the person (see Stein and Stein 2011). Magic exists in societies with diverse religious beliefs, including animism, mana, polytheism, and monotheism.

## Uncertainty, Anxiety, Solace

Religion and magic don't just explain things and help people accomplish goals. They also enter the realm of human feelings. In other words, they serve emotional needs as well as cognitive (e.g., explanatory) ones. For example, supernatural beliefs and practices can help reduce anxiety. Magical techniques can dispel doubts that arise when outcomes are beyond human control. Similarly, religion helps people face death and endure life crises.

Although all societies have techniques to deal with everyday matters, there are certain aspects of people's lives over which they lack control. When people face uncertainty and danger, according to Malinowski, they turn to magic.

> [H]owever much knowledge and science help man in allowing him to obtain what he wants, they are unable completely to control chance, to eliminate accidents, to foresee the unexpected turn of natural events, or to make human handiwork reliable and adequate to all practical requirements. (Malinowski 1931/1978, p. 39)

As was discussed in this chapter's "Understanding Ourselves," Malinowski found that the Trobriand Islanders used a variety of magical practices when they went on sailing expeditions, a hazardous activity. He proposed that because people can't control matters such as wind, weather, and the fish supply, they turn to magic. People may call on magic when they come to a gap in their knowledge or powers of practical control yet have to continue in a pursuit (Malinowski 1931/1978).

Malinowski noted that it was only when confronted by situations they could not control that Trobrianders, out of psychological stress, turned from technology to magic. Despite our improving technical skills, we can't control every outcome, and magic persists in contemporary societies. As was discussed in "Understanding Ourselves," magic is particularly evident in baseball, where George Gmelch (1978, 2001, 2006) describes a series of rituals, taboos, and sacred objects. Like Trobriand

**taboo**
Sacred and forbidden; prohibition backed by supernatural sanctions.

**magic**
Use of supernatural techniques to accomplish specific ends.

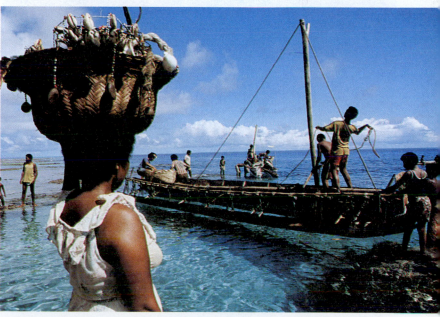

Trobriand Islanders prepare a traditional trading canoe for use in the Kula, which is a regional exchange system. The women bring trade goods in a basket, while the men prepare the long canoe to set sail. Magic is often associated with uncertainty, such as sailing in unpredictable waters.

**ritual**
Formal, repetitive, stereotyped behavior; based on a liturgical order.

**rites of passage**
Rites marking transitions between places or stages of life.

sailing magic, these behaviors reduce psychological stress, creating an illusion of magical control when real control is lacking. Baseball magic is especially prevalent in pitching and batting.

According to Malinowski, magic is used to establish control, but religion "is born out of . . . the real tragedies of human life" (1931/1978, p. 45). Religion offers emotional comfort, particularly when people face a crisis. Malinowski saw tribal religions as concerned mainly with organizing, commemorating, and helping people get through such life events as birth, puberty, marriage, and death.

## Rituals

Several features distinguish **ritual** behavior from other kinds of behavior (Rappaport 1974, 1999). Rituals are formal—stylized, repetitive, and stereotyped. People perform them in special (sacred) places and at set times. Rituals include liturgical orders—sequences of words and actions invented prior to the current performance of the ritual in which they occur. Rituals convey information about the participants and their traditions. Repeated year after year, generation after generation, rituals translate enduring messages, values, and sentiments into action.

Rituals are social acts. Inevitably, some participants are more committed than others are to the beliefs that lie behind the rites. However, just by taking part in a joint public act, the performers signal that they accept a common social and moral order, one that transcends their status as individuals.

## Rites of Passage

Magic and religion, as Malinowski noted, can reduce anxiety and allay fears. Ironically, beliefs and rituals also can create anxiety and a sense of insecurity and danger (Radcliffe-Brown 1962/1965). Anxiety can arise because a rite exists. Indeed, participation in a collective ritual (e.g., circumcision of early teen boys, common among East African pastoralists) can produce stress, whose common reduction, once the ritual is completed, enhances the solidarity of the participants.

Rites of passage can be individual or collective. Traditional Native American vision quests illustrate individual **rites of passage** (customs associated with the transition from one place or stage of life to another). To move from boyhood to manhood, a youth would temporarily separate from his community. After a period of isolation in the wilderness, often featuring fasting and drug consumption, the young man would see a vision, which would become his guardian spirit. He would return then to his community as a socially recognized adult.

Contemporary rites of passage include confirmations, baptisms, bar and bat mitzvahs, initiations, weddings, and application for Social Security and Medicare. Passage rites involve changes in social status, such as from boyhood to manhood and from nonmember to sorority sister. More generally, a rite of passage can mark any change in place, condition, social position, or age.

All rites of passage have three phases: separation, liminality, and incorporation. In the first phase, people withdraw from ordinary society. In the third phase, they reenter society, having completed a rite that changes their status. The second, or liminal, phase is the most interesting. It is the limbo, or "time-out," during which people have left one status but haven't yet entered or joined the next (Turner 1969/1995).

Passage rites are often collective. A group—such as these initiates in Togo or these Navy trainees in San Diego—passes through the rites as a unit. Such liminal people experience the same treatment and conditions and must act alike. They share communitas, an intense community spirit, a feeling of great social solidarity or togetherness.

| LIMINALITY | NORMAL SOCIAL STRUCTURE |
|---|---|
| Transition | State |
| Homogeneity | Heterogeneity |
| Communitas | Structure |
| Equality | Inequality |
| Anonymity | Names |
| Absence of property | Property |
| Absence of status | Status |
| Nakedness or uniform dress | Dress distinctions |
| Sexual continence or excess | Sexuality |
| Minimization of sex distinctions | Maximization of sex distinctions |
| Absence of rank | Rank |
| Humility | Pride |
| Disregard of personal appearance | Care for personal appearance |
| Unselfishness | Selfishness |
| Total obedience | Obedience only to superior rank |
| Sacredness | Secularity |
| Sacred instruction | Technical knowledge |
| Silence | Speech |
| Simplicity | Complexity |
| Acceptance of pain and suffering | Avoidance of pain and suffering |

SOURCE: Victor W. Turner, The Ritual Process: Structure and Anti-Structure (Chicago: Aldine de Gruyter, 1969), pp. 106–107. Reproduced with permission of Aldine Transaction via Copyright Clearance Center.

**Liminality** always has certain characteristics. Liminal people exist apart from ordinary distinctions and expectations; they are living in a time out of time. A series of contrasts demarcate liminality from normal social life. For example, among the Ndembu of Zambia, a chief underwent a rite of passage prior to taking office. During the liminal period, his past and future positions in society were ignored, even reversed. He was subjected to a variety of insults, orders, and humiliations.

Passage rites often are collective. Several individuals—boys being circumcised, fraternity or sorority initiates, men at military boot camps, football players in summer training camps, women becoming nuns—pass through the rites together as a group. Recap 21.1 summarizes the contrasts, or oppositions, between liminality and normal social life. Most notable is the social aspect of collective liminality called communitas (Turner 1967). Liminal people experience the same treatment and conditions and must act alike. Liminality can be marked ritually and symbolically by reversals of ordinary behavior. For example, sexual taboos may be intensified; conversely, sexual excess may be encouraged. Liminal symbols, such as special clothing or body paint, mark the condition as extraordinary—beyond ordinary society and everyday life.

Liminality is basic to all passage rites. Furthermore, in certain societies, including our own, liminal symbols can be used to set off one (religious) group from another—and from society as a whole. Such "permanent liminal groups" (e.g., sects, brotherhoods, and cults) are found most characteristically in nation-states. Such liminal features as humility, poverty, equality, obedience, sexual abstinence, and silence (see Recap 21.1) may be required for all sect or cult members. Those who join such a group agree to its rules. As if they were undergoing a passage rite—but in this case a never-ending one—they may have to abandon their previous possessions and social ties, including those with family members. Is liminality compatible with Facebook?

Members of a sect or cult often wear uniform clothing. Often they adopt a common hairstyle (shaved head, short hair, or long hair). Liminal groups submerge the individual in the collective. This may be one reason Americans, whose core values include individuality and individualism, are so fearful and suspicious of "cults."

Not all collective rites are rites of passage. Most societies have occasions on which people come together to worship or celebrate and, in doing so, affirm and reinforce their solidarity. Rituals such as the totemic ceremonies described in the next section

**liminality**
The in-between phase of a rite of passage.

are *rites of intensification:* They intensify social solidarity. The ritual creates communitas and produces emotions (the collective spiritual effervescence described by Durkheim 1912/2001) that enhance social solidarity.

## Totemism

Totemism was a key ingredient in the religions of the Native Australians. **Totems** could be animals, plants, or geographic features. In each tribe, groups of people had particular totems. Members of each totemic group believed themselves to be descendants of their totem. They customarily neither killed nor ate it, but this taboo was lifted once a year, when people assembled for ceremonies dedicated to the totem. These annual rites were believed to be necessary for the totem's survival and reproduction.

Totemism uses nature as a model for society. The totems usually are animals and plants, which are part of nature. People relate to nature through their totemic association with natural species. Because each group has a different totem, social differences mirror natural contrasts. Diversity in the natural order becomes a model for diversity in the social order. However, although totemic plants and animals occupy different niches in nature, on another level they are united because they all are part of nature. The unity of the human social order is enhanced by symbolic association with and imitation of the natural order (Durkheim 1912/2001; Lévi-Strauss 1963; Radcliffe-Brown 1962/1965).

Totemism is one form of **cosmology**—a system, in this case a religious one, for imagining and understanding the universe. Claude Lévi-Strauss, a prolific French anthropologist and a key figure in the anthropology of religion, is well known for his studies of myth, folklore, totemism, and cosmology. Lévi-Strauss believed that one role of religious rites and beliefs is to affirm, and thus maintain, the solidarity of a religion's adherents. Totems are sacred emblems symbolizing common identity. This is true not just among Native Australians but also among Native American groups of the North Pacific Coast of North America, whose totem poles are well known. Their totemic carvings, which commemorated and told visual stories about ancestors, animals, and spirits, were also associated with ceremonies. In totemic rites, people gather together to honor their totem. In so doing, they use ritual to maintain the social oneness that the totem symbolizes.

Totemic principles continue to demarcate groups, including clubs, teams, and universities, in modern societies. Badgers and Wolverines are animals, and (it is said in Michigan) Buckeyes are some kind of nut (more precisely, buckeye nuts come from the buckeye tree). Differences between natural species (e.g., Lions, and Tigers, and Bears) distinguish sports teams, and even political parties (donkeys and elephants). Although the modern context is more secular, one can still witness, in intense college football rivalries, some of the effervescence Durkheim noted in Australian totemic religion and other rites of intensification.

## RELIGION AND CULTURAL ECOLOGY

Another domain in which religion plays a role is cultural ecology. Behavior motivated by beliefs in supernatural beings, powers, and forces can help people survive in their material environment. Beliefs and rituals can function as part of a group's cultural adaptation to its environment.

## Sacred Cattle in India

The people of India revere zebu cattle, which are protected by the Hindu doctrine of *ahimsa,* a principle of nonviolence that forbids the killing of animals generally. Western economic development agents occasionally (and erroneously) cite the Hindu cattle taboo to illustrate the idea that religious beliefs can stand in the way of rational economic decisions. Hindus might seem to be irrationally ignoring a valuable food (beef) because of their cultural or religious traditions. Development agents also have asserted that Indians don't know how to raise proper cattle. They point to the scraggly zebus that wander around town and country. Western techniques of animal husbandry grow bigger cattle that produce more beef and milk. Western planners lament that Hindus are set in their ways. Bound by culture and tradition, they refuse to develop rationally.

Cows freely walk the streets of any Indian city, including Ahmedabad, Gujarat, shown here. India's zebu cattle are protected by the doctrine of *ahimsa,* a principle of nonviolence that forbids the killing of animals generally.

However, these assumptions are both ethnocentric and wrong. Sacred cattle actually play an important adaptive role in an Indian ecosystem that has evolved over thousands of years (Harris 1974, 1978). Peasants' use of cattle to pull plows and carts is part of the technology of Indian agriculture. Indian peasants have no need for large, hungry cattle of the sort that Westerners prefer. Scrawny animals pull plows and carts well enough but don't eat their owners out of house and home. How could peasants with limited land and marginal diets feed super-steers without taking food away from themselves?

Indians use cattle manure to fertilize their fields. Not all the manure is collected, because peasants don't spend much time watching their cattle, which wander and graze at will during certain seasons. In the rainy season, some of the manure that cattle deposit on the hillsides washes down to the fields. In this way, cattle also fertilize the fields indirectly. Furthermore, in a country where fossil fuels are scarce, dry cattle dung, which burns slowly and evenly, is a basic cooking fuel.

Sacred cattle are essential to Indian cultural adaptation. Biologically adapted to poor pasture land and a marginal environment, the scraggly zebu provides fertilizer and fuel, is indispensable in farming, and is affordable for peasants. The Hindu doctrine of *ahimsa* puts the full power of organized religion behind the command not to destroy a valuable resource, even in times of extreme need.

## SOCIAL CONTROL

Religion means a lot to people. It helps them cope with uncertainty, adversity, fear, and tragedy. It offers hope that things will get better. Lives can be transformed through spiritual healing. Sinners can repent and be saved—or they can go on sinning and be damned. If the faithful truly internalize a system of religious rewards and punishments, their religion becomes a powerful influence on their attitudes and behavior, as well as what they teach their children.

Many people engage in religious activity because it works for them. Prayers get answered. Native Americans in southwestern Oklahoma use faith healers at high monetary costs, not just because it makes them feel better about the uncertain, but because they think it works (Lassiter 1998). Each year legions of Brazilians visit a church, Nosso Senhor do Bonfim, in the city of Salvador, Bahia. They vow to repay "Our Lord" (Nosso Senhor) if healing happens. Showing that the vows work, and are repaid, are the thousands of *ex votos,* plastic impressions of every conceivable body part, that adorn the church, along with photos of people who have been cured.

Religion can work by getting inside people and mobilizing their emotions—their joy, their wrath, their righteousness. Adherents can feel a deep sense of shared joy, meaning, experience, communion, belonging, and commitment to their religion. The power of religion affects action. When religions meet, they can coexist peacefully, or their differences can be a basis for enmity and disharmony, even battle. Religious fervor has inspired Christians on crusades against the infidel and has led Muslims to wage holy wars against non-Islamic peoples. Throughout history, political leaders have used religion to promote and justify their views and policies.

How can leaders mobilize communities to support their own policies? One way is by persuasion; another is by hatred or fear. Consider witchcraft accusations. Witch hunts can be powerful means of social control by creating a climate of danger and insecurity that affects everyone. No one wants to seem deviant, to be accused of being a witch. Witch hunts often aim at socially marginal people who can be accused and punished with least chance of retaliation. During the great European witch craze, during the 15th, 16th, and 17th centuries (Harris 1974), most accusations and convictions were against poor women with little social support.

To ensure proper behavior, religions offer rewards (e.g., the fellowship of the religious community) and punishments (e.g., the threat of being cast out, or excommunicated). Religions, especially the formal, organized ones found in state societies, often prescribe a code of ethics and morality to guide behavior. Moral codes are ways of maintaining

The Right Reverend Kay Goldsworthy during her consecration service and ordination as Australia's first female Anglican bishop at St. George's Cathedral in Perth, Australia.

order and stability that are constantly reinforced in sermons, catechisms, and the like. They become internalized psychologically. They guide behavior and produce regret, guilt, shame, and the need for forgiveness, expiation, and absolution when they are not followed.

## KINDS OF RELIGION

Although religion is a cultural universal, religions exist in particular societies, and cultural differences show up systematically in religious beliefs and practices. For example, the religions of stratified, state societies differ from those of societies with less marked social contrasts—societies without kings, lords, and subjects. What can a given society afford in terms of religion? Churches, temples, and other full-time religious establishments, with their monumental structures and hierarchies of officials, must be supported in some consistent way, such as by tithes and taxes. What kinds of societies can support such hierarchies and architecture?

All societies have religious figures—those believed capable of mediating between humans and the supernatural. More generally, all societies have medico-magico-religious specialists. Modern societies can support both priesthoods and health care professionals. Lacking the resources for such specialization, foraging societies typically have only part-time specialists, who often have both religious and healing roles. **Shaman** is the general term encompassing curers ("witch doctors"), mediums, spiritualists, astrologers, palm readers, and other independent diviners. In foraging societies, shamans usually are part-time; that is, they also hunt or gather.

Societies with productive economies (based on agriculture and trade) and large, dense populations—that is, nation-states—can support full-time religious specialists—professional priesthoods. Like the state itself, priesthoods are hierarchically and bureaucratically organized. Anthony Wallace (1966) describes the religions of such stratified societies as "ecclesiastical" (pertaining to an established church and its hierarchy of officials) and Olympian, after Mount Olympus, home of the classical Greek gods. In such religions, powerful anthropomorphic gods have specialized functions, for example, gods of love, war, the sea, and death. Such *pantheons* (collections of deities) were prominent in the religions of many nonindustrial nation-states, including the Aztecs of Mexico, several African and Asian kingdoms, and classical Greece and Rome.

Greco-Roman religions were polytheistic, featuring many deities. In monotheism, all supernatural phenomena are believed to be manifestations of, or under the control of, a single eternal, omniscient, omnipotent, and omnipresent being. In the ecclesiastical monotheistic religion known as Christianity, a single supreme being is manifest in a trinity. Robert

Bellah (1978) viewed most forms of Christianity as examples of "world-rejecting religion." According to Bellah, the first world-rejecting religions arose in ancient civilizations, along with literacy and a specialized priesthood. These religions are so named because of their tendency to reject the natural (mundane, ordinary, material, secular) world and to focus instead on a higher (sacred, transcendent) realm of reality. The divine is a domain of exalted morality to which humans can only aspire. Salvation through fusion with the supernatural is the main goal of such religions.

## Protestant Values and Capitalism

Notions of salvation and the afterlife dominate Christian ideologies. However, most varieties of Protestantism lack the hierarchical structure of earlier monotheistic religions, including Roman Catholicism. With a diminished role for the priest (minister), salvation is directly available to individuals. Regardless of their social status, Protestants have unmediated access to the supernatural. The individualistic focus of Protestantism offers a close fit with capitalism and with American culture.

In his influential book *The Protestant Ethic and the Spirit of Capitalism* (1904/1958), the social theorist Max Weber linked the spread of capitalism to the values preached by early Protestant leaders. Weber saw European Protestants (and eventually their American descendants) as more successful financially than Catholics. He attributed this difference to the values stressed by their religions. Weber saw Catholics as more concerned with immediate happiness and security. Protestants were more ascetic, entrepreneurial, and future oriented, he thought.

Capitalism, said Weber, required that the traditional attitudes of Catholic peasants be replaced by values befitting an industrial economy based on capital accumulation. Protestantism placed a premium on hard work, an ascetic life, and profit seeking. Early Protestants saw success on Earth as a sign of divine favor and probable salvation. According to some Protestant credos, individuals could gain favor with God through good works. Other sects stressed predestination, the idea that only a few mortals have been selected for eternal life and that people cannot change their fates. However, material success, achieved through hard work, could be a strong clue that someone was predestined to be saved.

Weber also argued that rational business organization required the removal of industrial production from the home, its setting in peasant societies. Protestantism made such a separation possible by emphasizing individualism: Individuals, not families or households, would be saved or not. Interestingly, given the connection that is usually made with morality and religion in contemporary American discourse about family values, the family was a secondary matter for Weber's early Protestants. God and the individual reigned supreme.

**shaman**
Part-time medico-magico-religious practitioner.

Today, of course, in North America, as throughout the world, people of many religions and with diverse worldviews are successful capitalists. Furthermore, traditional Protestant values often have little to do with today's economic maneuvering. Still, there is no denying that the individualistic focus of Protestantism was compatible with the severance of ties to land and kin that industrialism demanded. These values remain prominent in the religious background of many of the people of the United States.

## WORLD RELIGIONS

Information on the world's major religions as of 2010 is provided in Figure 21.1, based on a recent comprehensive study by the Pew Research Center (2012). Considering data from more than 230 countries, that study estimated that the world contains about 5.8 billion religiously affiliated people—84 percent of its population of 6.9 billion in 2010.

That study found 2.2 billion Christians (32 percent of the global population), 1.6 billion Muslims (23 percent), 1 billion Hindus (15 percent), nearly 500 million Buddhists (7 percent), and 14 million Jews (0.2 percent). In addition, more than 400 million people (6 percent) practice folk or traditional religions of various sorts. Some 58 million people, a bit less than 1 percent of the world's population, belong to other religions, including Baha'i, Jainism, Sikhism, Shintoism, Taoism, Tenrikyo, Wicca, and Zoroastrianism.

The same study found that about 1.1 billion people—16 percent of the world's population—lacked any religious affiliation. The unaffiliated therefore constitute the third-largest group worldwide with respect to religious affiliation, behind Christians and Muslims. There are about as many unaffiliated people as Roman Catholics in the world. Many of the unaffiliated actually hold some religious or spiritual beliefs, even if they don't identify with a particular religion (Pew Research Center 2012).

Worldwide, Islam is growing at a rate of about 2.9 percent annually, compared with 2.3 percent for Christianity. Within Christianity, the growth rate varies. There were an estimated 680 million "born-again" Christians (e.g., Evangelicals/Pentecostals) in the world in 2001, with an estimated annual worldwide growth rate of 7 percent, versus just 2.3 percent for Christianity overall. (This would translate into 1.6 billion Pentecostals and Evangelicals by 2014.) The global growth rate of Roman Catholics has been estimated at only 1.3 percent, compared with an overall Protestant growth rate of 3.3 percent per year (Winter 2001).

## RELIGION AND CHANGE

Like political organization, religion helps maintain social order. And like political mobilization, religious energy can be harnessed not just for change but also for revolution. Reacting to conquest or to actual or perceived foreign domination, for instance, religious leaders may seek to alter or revitalize their society.

### Cargo Cults

**Revitalization movements** are social movements that occur in times of change, in which religious

**revitalization movements**
Social movements aimed at altering or revitalizing a society.

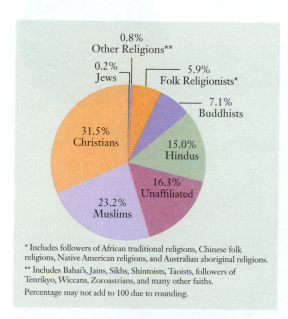

**FIGURE 21.1** Major World Religions by Percentage of World Population, 2010.

0.8% Other Religions**
0.2% Jews
5.9% Folk Religionists*
7.1% Buddhists
31.5% Christians
15.0% Hindus
16.3% Unaffiliated
23.2% Muslims

* Includes followers of African traditional religions, Chinese folk religions, Native American religions, and Australian aboriginal religions.
** Includes Baha'is, Jains, Sikhs, Shintoists, Taoists, followers of Tenrikyo, Wiccans, Zoroastrians, and many other faiths.
Percentage may not add to 100 due to rounding.

SOURCE: Pew Research Center. The Global Religious Landscape: A Report on the Size and Distribution of the World's Major Religious Groups as of 2010, Analysis, December 18, 2012. http://www.pewforum.org/global-religious-landscape-exec.aspx#src=global-footer. Reprinted by permission.

On the island of Tanna, in Vanuatu, Melanesia, members of the John Frum cargo cult stage a military parade. The young men, who carry fake guns and have "USA" painted on their bodies, see themselves as an elite force within the American army.

leaders emerge and undertake to alter or revitalize a society. Christianity originated as a revitalization movement. Jesus was one of several prophets who preached new religious doctrines while the Middle East was under Roman rule. It was a time of social unrest, when a foreign power ruled the land. Jesus inspired a new, enduring, and major religion. His contemporaries were not so successful.

**cargo cults**
Postcolonial, acculturative religious movements in Melanesia.

Revitalization movements known as **cargo cults** have arisen in colonial situations in which local people have regular contact with outsiders but lack their wealth, technology, and living standards. Cargo cults attempt to explain European domination and wealth and to achieve similar success magically by mimicking European behavior and manipulating symbols of the desired lifestyle. The cargo cults of Melanesia and Papua New Guinea (see Figure 21.2) are hybrid creations that weave Christian doctrine with aboriginal beliefs. They take their name from their focus on cargo—European goods of the sort natives have seen unloaded from the cargo holds of ships and airplanes.

**syncretisms**
Cultural, especially religious, mixes, emerging from acculturation.

In one early cult, members believed that the spirits of the dead would arrive in a ship. These ghosts would bring manufactured goods for the natives and would kill all the whites. More recent cults replaced ships with airplanes (Worsley 1959/1985). Many cults have used elements of European culture as sacred objects. The rationale is that Europeans use these objects, have wealth, and therefore must know the "secret of cargo." By mimicking how Europeans use or treat objects, natives hope also to come upon the secret knowledge needed to gain cargo.

For example, having seen Europeans' reverent treatment of flags and flagpoles, the members of one cult began to worship flagpoles. They believed the flagpoles were sacred towers that could transmit messages between the living and the dead. Other natives built airstrips to entice planes bearing canned goods, portable radios, clothing, wristwatches, and motorcycles.

Some cargo cult prophets proclaimed that success would come through a reversal of European domination and native subjugation. The day was near, they preached, when natives, aided by God, Jesus, or native ancestors, would turn the tables. Native skins would turn white, and those of Europeans would turn brown; Europeans would die or be killed.

**Syncretisms** are cultural, especially religious, mixes that emerge from acculturation. Cargo cults are syncretisms that blend aboriginal and Christian beliefs. Melanesian myths told of ancestors shedding their skins and changing into powerful beings and of dead people returning to life. Christian missionaries also preached resurrection. The cults' preoccupation with cargo is related to traditional Melanesian big man systems. A Melanesian big man was expected to be generous. People worked for the big man, helping him amass wealth, but eventually he had to host a feast and give away all that wealth.

Because of their experience with big man systems, Melanesians believed that all wealthy people

**FIGURE 21.2** Location of Melanesia.

eventually had to give their wealth away. For decades, they had attended Christian missions and worked on plantations. All the while they expected Europeans to return the fruits of their labor as their own big men did. When the Europeans refused to distribute the wealth or even to let natives know the secret of its production and distribution, cargo cults developed.

Like arrogant big men, Europeans would be put in their place or leveled, by death if necessary. However, natives lacked the physical means of doing what their traditions said they should do. Thwarted by well-armed colonial forces, natives resorted to magical leveling. They called on supernatural beings to intercede, to kill or otherwise deflate the European big men and redistribute their wealth.

Cargo cults are religious responses to the expansion of the world capitalist economy. However, this religious mobilization had political and economic results. Cult participation gave Melanesians a basis for common interests and activities and thus helped pave the way for political parties and economic interest organizations. Previously separated by geography, language, and customs, Melanesians started forming larger groups as members of the same cults and followers of the same prophets. The cargo cults paved the way for political action through which the indigenous peoples eventually regained their autonomy.

## New and Alternative Religious Movements

Providing recent evidence for the evolution of religious practice in the United States is a study published by the Pew Research Center in 2012. That study found that between 1990 and 2010, the number of Americans giving no religious preference increased from 7 to 16 percent. In Canada the comparable figure doubled from 12 to 24 percent between 1991 and 2011 (Statistics Canada 2011). Of course, people who lack a religious preference aren't necessarily atheists. Many of them are believers who don't belong to a church. According to the most recent available U.S. Census Bureau figures, 3.6 million Americans (just over 1 percent of the population) self-identified as atheists or agnostics.

Contemporary industrial societies also feature new religious trends and forms of spiritualism. The New Age movement, which emerged in the 1980s, draws on and blends cultural elements from multiple traditions. It advocates change through individual personal transformation. In the United States and Australia, respectively, some people who are not Native Americans or Native Australians have appropriated the symbols, settings, and purported religious practices of Native Americans and Native

Australians for New Age religions. Native American activists decry the appropriation and commercialization of their spiritual beliefs and rituals, as when "sweat lodge" ceremonies are held on cruise ships, with wine and cheese served. They see the appropriation of their ceremonies and traditions as theft. This chapter's "Appreciating Diversity" on pp. 410–411 shows how some Hindus feel similarly about the popularization of yoga.

New religious movements have varied origins. Some have been influenced by Christianity, others by Eastern (Asian) religions, still others by mysticism and spiritualism. Religion also evolves in tandem with science and technology. For example, the Raelian movement, a religious group centered in Switzerland and Montreal, promotes cloning as a way of achieving eternal life (Palmer 2001).

Many contemporary nations contain unofficial religions. One example is "Yoruba religion," a term applied to perhaps 15 million adherents in Africa as well as to millions of practitioners of syncretic, or blended, religions (with elements of Catholicism and spiritism) in the Western Hemisphere. Forms of Yoruba religion include *santeria* (in the Spanish Caribbean and the United States), *candomblé* (in Brazil), and *vodoun* (in the French Caribbean). Yoruba religion, with roots in precolonial nation-states of West Africa, has spread far beyond its religion of origin, as part of the African diaspora. It remains an influential, identifiable religion today, despite suppression, such as by Cuba's communist government. There are perhaps 3 million practitioners of santeria in Cuba, plus another 800,000 in the United States. At least 1 million Brazilians participate in candomblé, also known as macumba. Voodoo (*vodoun*) has between 2.8 and 3.2 million practitioners (Ontario Consultants 2011), many (perhaps most) of whom would name something else, such as Catholicism, as their religion.

## RELIGION AND CULTURAL GLOBALIZATION

### Evangelical Protestantism and Pentecostalism

The rapid spread of Evangelical Protestantism, which originated in Europe and North America, constitutes a highly successful form of contemporary cultural globalization. A century ago, more than 90 percent of the then approximately 80 million Evangelicals in the world lived in Europe and North America (Pew Research Center 2011). Today, estimates of the number of Evangelicals worldwide range from 400 million to well over 1 billion, with most living outside Europe and North America—in sub-Saharan Africa, the Middle East and North Africa, Latin America, and Asia.

# appreciating DIVERSITY

## Hinduism Takes Back Yoga

As long as *Homo sapiens* has existed, shamans have played both religious and healing roles. The spillover of religion into health continues today. Fitness is a major industry in contemporary North America and Western Europe. Yoga classes are routine offerings in gyms and fitness centers. But what of yoga's origins, its religious underpinnings? Here we learn of a growing movement, abetted by print media and the Internet, to foster awareness of yoga's roots in Hinduism. Raised here are issues of commercialism and IPR (intellectual property rights): Who has the right to the yoga "brand"?

Yoga is practiced by about 15 million people in the United States, for reasons almost as numerous—from the physical benefits mapped in brain scans to the less tangible rewards that New Age journals call spiritual centering. Religion, for the most part, has nothing to do with it.

But a group of Indian-Americans has ignited a surprisingly fierce debate in the gentle world of yoga by mounting a campaign to acquaint Westerners with the faith that it says underlies every single yoga style: Hinduism.

The campaign, labeled "Take Back Yoga," does not ask yoga devotees to become Hindu, or instructors to teach more about Hinduism. The . . . group behind it, the Hindu American Foundation, suggests only that people become more aware of yoga's debt to the faith's ancient traditions.

That suggestion . . . has drawn a flurry of strong reactions from figures far apart on the religious spectrum. Dr. Deepak Chopra, the New Age writer, has dismissed the campaign as a jumble of faulty history and Hindu nationalism. R. Albert Mohler Jr., president of the Southern Baptist Theological Seminary, . . . agrees that yoga is Hindu—and cited that as evidence that the practice imperiled the souls of Christians who engage in it.

The question at the core of the debate—who owns yoga?—has become an enduring topic of chatter in yoga Web forums, Hindu American newspapers and journals catering to the many consumers of what is now a multibillion-dollar yoga industry. . . .

Organizers of the Take Back Yoga effort point out that the philosophy of yoga was first described in Hinduism's seminal texts and remains at the core of Hindu teaching. Yet, because the religion has been stereotyped in the West as a polytheistic faith of "castes, cows and curry," they say, most Americans prefer to see yoga as the legacy of a more timeless, spiritual "Indian wisdom."

"In a way," said Dr. Aseem Shukla, the foundation's co-founder, "our issue is that yoga has thrived, but Hinduism has lost control of the brand."

For many practitioners, including Debbie Desmond, 27, a yoga instructor in Williamsburg, Brooklyn, the talk of branding and ownership is bewildering. "Nobody owns yoga," she said, sitting cross-legged in her studio, Namaste Yoga. . . . "Yoga is not a religion. It is a way of life, a method of becoming. We were taught that the roots of yoga go back further than Hinduism itself."

Like Dr. Chopra and some religious historians, Ms. Desmond believes that yoga originated in the Vedic culture of Indo-Europeans who settled in India in the third millennium B.C., long before the

---

The growth of Evangelical Protestantism has been particularly explosive in Brazil—traditionally (and still) the world's most Catholic country. In 1980, when Pope John Paul II visited the country, 89 percent of Brazil's population claimed to be Roman Catholic. Since then, Evangelical Protestantism has spread like wildfire. Having made small inroads during the first half of the 20th century, Evangelical Protestantism grew exponentially in Brazil during the second half. Protestants accounted for less than 5 percent of the population through the 1960s. By 2000, Evangelical Protestants comprised more than 15 percent of Brazilians affiliated with a church. The current estimate of the Evangelical share of Brazil's population is between 20 and 25 percent and growing. Evangelical Protestantism's penetration of Brazil has been mainly at the expense of Catholicism. Among the factors that have worked against Catholicism are these: a declining priesthood overly dependent on foreigners, sharply contrasting political agendas of many

of its clerics, and its reputation as mainly a women's religion.

Evangelical Protestantism stresses conservative morality, biblical authority, and a personal ("born-again") conversion experience. Most Brazilian Evangelicals are Pentecostals, who additionally embrace glossolalia (speaking in tongues) and beliefs in faith healing, spirits, exorcism, and miracles. São Paulo, Brazil's largest city, has been called the Pentecostal world capital, with over 4 million adherents.

Like members of a sect marked by liminal attributes, converts to Pentecostalism are expected to separate themselves both from their pasts and from the secular social world that surrounds them. In Arembepe, Brazil, for example, the *crentes* ("true believers," as members of the local Pentecostal community are called) set themselves apart by their beliefs, behavior, and lifestyle (Kottak 2006). They worship, chant, and pray. They dress simply and forgo such worldly temptations (seen as vices) as tobacco, alcohol, gambling, and extramarital tradition now called Hinduism emerged. Other historians trace the first written description of yoga to the Bhagavad Gita, the sacred Hindu scripture believed to have been written between the fifth and second centuries B.C.

The effort to "take back" yoga began . . . with a scholarly essay . . . on the Web site of the Hindu American Foundation, a Minneapolis-based group that promotes human rights for Hindu minorities worldwide. The essay lamented a perceived snub in modern yoga culture, saying that yoga magazines and studios had assiduously decoupled the practice "from the Hinduism that gave forth this immense contribution to humanity."

Dr. Shukla put a sharper point on his case . . . in a column on the On Faith blog of *The Washington Post*. Hinduism, he wrote, had become a victim of "overt intellectual property theft," made possible by generations of Hindu yoga teachers who had "offered up a religion's spiritual wealth at the altar of crass commercialism."

That drew the attention of Dr. Chopra, an Indian-American who has done much to popularize Indian traditions like alternative medicine and yoga. He posted a reply saying that Hinduism was

Yoga is performed on the river bank stairs at Varanasi, India. Yoga is rooted in Hinduism, the religion of this practitioner in the land of its origin.

too "tribal" and "self-enclosed" to claim ownership of yoga. . . .

The debate . . . raised important issues about a spectrum of Hindu concepts permeating American culture, including meditation, belief in karma and reincarnation, and even cremation. . . . The effort [to "take back yoga"] has been received most favorably by Indian-American community leaders

like Dr. Uma V. Mysorekar, the president of the Hindu Temple Society of North America, in Flushing, Queens, which helps groups across the country build temples.

A naturalized immigrant, she said Take Back Yoga represented a coming-of-age for Indians in the United States. "My generation was too busy establishing itself in business and the professions," she said. "Now, the second and third generation is looking around and finding its voice, saying, 'Our civilization has made contributions to the world, and these should be acknowledged.'"

In the basement of the society's Ganesha Temple, an hourlong yoga class ended one recent Sunday morning with a long exhalation of the sacred syllable "om." Via the lung power of 60 students, it sounded as deeply as a blast from the organ at St. Patrick's Cathedral.

sexuality, along with dancing, movies, and other forms of popular culture. Wherever Pentecostalism exists, the converted observe an ascetic moral code and view the surrounding social world as a realm governed by Satan (Robbins 2004).

Pentecostalism strengthens family and household through a moral code that enjoins respect for marriage and prohibits adultery, gambling, drinking, and fighting. These activities were valued mainly by men in preconversion culture. Pentecostalism has appeal for men, however, because it does not publicly question their authority and even solidifies it within the household. Although Pentecostal ideology is strongly patriarchal, with women expected to subordinate themselves to men, women tend to be more active church members than men are. Pentecostalism promotes services and prayer groups by and for women. In such settings women develop leadership skills, as they also extend their social-support network beyond family and kin (Burdick 1998).

In São Paulo, Brazil, evangelicals pray inside the Bola de Neve Church. Popular with youths, this church sponsors activities, including surfing, skating, and rock 'n' roll and reggae music with religious lyrics.

In its focus on ecstatic and exuberant worship, Pentecostalism has been heavily influenced by—and shares features with—African American Protestantism. In Brazil it shares features with candomblé, which also features chanting and spirit possession. Pentecostalism's habitual ritual engagement with spirits distinguishes it from other forms of Christianity (Casanova 2001; Meyer 1999).

Peter Berger (2010) suggests that modern Pentecostalism may be the fastest-growing religion in human history and focuses on its social dimensions to explain why. According to Berger, Pentecostalism promotes strong communities while offering practical and psychological support to people whose circumstances are changing. My own experience in Brazil supports Berger's hypothesis; most new Pentecostals I encountered came from underprivileged, poor, and otherwise marginalized groups in areas undergoing rapid social change.

The British sociologist David Martin (1990) argues that Pentecostalism is spreading so rapidly because its adherents embody Max Weber's Protestant ethic—valuing self-discipline, hard work, and thrift. Others see Pentecostalism as a kind of cargo cult, built on the belief that magic and ritual activity can promote material success (Freston 2008; Meyer 1999). Berger (2010) suggests that today's Pentecostals probably include both types—Weberian Protestants working to produce material wealth as a sign of their salvation along with people who believe that magic and ritual will bring them good fortune.

## Homogenization, Indigenization, or Hybridization?

Any cultural form that spreads from one society to another—be it a Starbucks or a form of religion—has to fit into the country and culture it enters. We can use the rapid spread of Pentecostalism as a case study of the process of adaptation of foreign cultural forms to local settings.

Joel Robbins (2004) has examined the extent to which what he calls Pentecostal/charismatic Christianity preserves its basic form and core beliefs as it spreads and adapts to various national and local cultures. Pentecostalism is a Western invention: Its beliefs, doctrines, organizational features, and rituals originated in the United States, following the European rise and spread of Protestantism. The core doctrines of acceptance of Jesus as one's savior, baptism with the Holy Spirit, faith healing, and belief in the second coming of Jesus have spread across nations and cultures without losing their basic shape.

Scholars have argued about whether the global spread of Pentecostalism is best understood as (1) a process of Western cultural domination and homogenization (perhaps supported by a right-wing political agenda) or (2) a process in which diffused cultural forms respond to local needs and are differentiated and indigenized. Joel Robbins (2004) takes a middle-ground position, viewing the spread of Pentecostalism as a form of cultural hybridization. Robbins (2004) argues that global and local features appear with equal intensity within these Pentecostal cultures. Churches retain certain core Pentecostal beliefs and behaviors while responding to the local culture and being organized at the local level.

Reviewing the literature, Robbins (2004) finds little evidence that a Western political agenda is propelling the global spread of Pentecostalism. It is true that foreigners (including American pastors and televangelists) have helped introduce Pentecostalism to countries outside North America. There is little evidence, however, that overseas churches are largely funded and ideologically shaped from North America. Pentecostal churches typically are staffed from top to bottom with locals, who run them as organizations that are attentive and responsive to local situations. Conversion is typically a key feature of that agenda. Once converted, a Pentecostal is expected to be an active Evangelist, seeking to bring in new members. This Evangelization is one of the most important activities in Pentecostal culture and certainly aids its expansion.

Pentecostalism spreads as other forces of globalization displace people and disrupt local lives (Martin 1990). To people who feel socially adrift, Pentecostal evangelists offer tightly knit communities and a weblike structure of personal connections within and between Pentecostal communities. Such networks can facilitate access to health care, job placement, educational services, and other resources.

Unlike Catholicism, which is hierarchical, Pentecostalism is egalitarian. Adherents need no special education—only spiritual inspiration—to preach or to run a church. Based on his research in Brazil, John Burdick (1993) notes that many Afro-Brazilians are drawn to the Pentecostal community because others who are socially and racially like them are in the congregation, some serving as preachers. Opportunities for participation and leadership are abundant, for example, as lay preachers, deacons, and leaders of various men's, women's, and youth groups. The churches fund outreach to the needy and other locally relevant social services.

## Antimodernism and Fundamentalism

**Antimodernism** is the rejection of the modern (including secular forces of globalization) in favor of what is perceived as an earlier, purer, and better way of life. This viewpoint arose out of disillusionment with the Industrial Revolution and with subsequent developments in science, technology, and consumption patterns. Antimodernists typically consider the use of modern technology to be misguided or think technology should have a lower priority than religious and cultural values. (A related

**antimodernism**
Rejecting the modern for a presumed earlier, purer, better way of life.

example would be the avoidance of many machines by the Old Order Amish or Pennsylvania Dutch in the United States.)

Religious **fundamentalism** describes antimodernist movements in various religions, including Christianity, Islam, and Judaism. Ironically, religious fundamentalism itself is a modern phenomenon, based on its adherents' strong feelings of alienation from the perceived secularism of the surrounding (modern) culture. Fundamentalists separate from a larger religious group, whose founding principles, they believe, have been corrupted or abandoned. Fundamentalists advocate return and strict fidelity to the "true" (fundamental) religious principles of the larger religion.

Fundamentalists also seek to rescue religion from absorption into modern, Western culture, which they see as having corrupted mainstream religions. In Christianity, fundamentalists are "born-again Christians" as opposed to "mainline Protestants." In Islam they are jama'at (in Arabic, enclaves based on close fellowship) engaged in jihad (struggle) against a Western culture hostile to Islam and the God-given (shariah) way of life. In Judaism they are Haredi, "Torah-true" Jews. All such groups see a sharp divide between themselves and other religions, as well as between a "sacred" view of life and the "secular" world (see Antoun 2008).

Both Pentecostalism and Christian fundamentalism preach ascetic morality, the duty to convert others, and respect for the Bible. Fundamentalists, however, tend to cite their success in living a moral life as proof of their salvation, whereas Pentecostals find assurance of their salvation in exuberant, ecstatic experience. Fundamentalists also seek to remake the political sphere along religious lines, whereas Pentecostals tend to have less interest in politics (Robbins 2004).

## The Spread of Islam

Islam—whose 1.6 billion followers constitute over a fifth of the world's population—is another rapidly spreading global religion that can be used to illustrate cultural globalization. The globalization of Islam also illustrates cultural hybridization. Islam has adapted successfully to the many nations and cultures it has entered, adopting architectural styles, linguistic practices, and even religious beliefs from host cultures.

For example, while Mosques (Islamic houses of worship) all share certain characteristics (e.g., they face Mecca and have some common architectural features), they also incorporate architectural and decorative elements from their national setting. Although Arabic is Islam's liturgical language, used for prayer, most Muslims' discussion of their faith occurs in their local language. In China, Islamic concepts have been influenced by Confucianism. In India and Bangladesh, the Islamic idea of the prophet has blended with the Hindu notion of the

Indonesian Muslims pray at the Sunda Kelapa port in Jakarta on August 19, 2012. Muslims around the world were celebrating the end of Ramadan, the Muslim calendar's ninth and holiest month.

avatar, a deity who takes mortal form and descends to Earth to fight evil and guide the righteous. Islam entered Indonesia by means of Muslim merchants who devised devotional exercises that fit in with preexisting religions—Hinduism and Buddhism in Java and Sumatra and animism in the eastern islands, which eventually became Christian. In Bali, Hinduism survived as the dominant religion. Both Pentecostalism and Islam, we have learned, hybridize and become locally relevant as they spread globally. Although certain core features endure, local people always assign their own meanings to the messages and social forms they receive from outside, including religion. Such meanings reflect their cultural backgrounds, experiences, and prior belief systems. We must consider the processes of hybridization and indigenization in examining and understanding any form of cultural diffusion or globalization.

**fundamentalism**
Advocating strict fidelity to a religion's presumed founding principles.

## SECULAR RITUALS

In concluding this chapter on religion, we can recognize some problems with the definition of religion given at the beginning of this chapter. The first problem: If we define religion with reference to supernatural beings, powers, and forces, how do we classify ritual-like behavior that occurs in secular contexts? Some anthropologists believe there are both sacred and secular rituals. Secular rituals include formal, invariant, stereotyped, earnest, repetitive behavior and rites of passage that take place in nonreligious settings.

A second problem: If the distinction between the supernatural and the natural is not consistently made in a society, how can we tell what is religion and what isn't? The Betsileo of Madagascar, for example, view witches and dead ancestors as real people who play roles in ordinary life. However, their occult powers are not empirically demonstrable.

On August 27, 2011, this flashmob meditation session was held in London's (England) Trafalgar Square. Does this performance illustrate secular religion?

grown up in their presence. For example, identities and loyalties based on fandom, football, baseball, and soccer can be powerful, indeed. Rock stars and bands can mobilize many. A World Series win led to celebrations across a "Red Sox nation." Italians and Brazilians are rarely, if ever, as nationally focused and emotionally unified as they are when their teams are competing in the World Cup. The collective effervescence that Durkheim found so characteristic of religion can equally well describe what Brazilians experience when their country wins a World Cup.

In the context of comparative religion, the idea that the secular can become sacred isn't surprising. Long ago, Durkheim (1912/2001) pointed out that almost everything, from the sublime to the ridiculous, has in some societies been treated as sacred. The distinction between sacred and profane doesn't depend on the intrinsic qualities of the sacred symbol. In Australian totemic religion, for example, sacred beings include such humble creatures as ducks, frogs, rabbits, and grubs, whose inherent qualities could hardly have given rise to the religious sentiment they inspire.

Many Americans believe that recreation and religion are separate domains. From my fieldwork in Brazil and Madagascar and my reading about other societies, I believe that this separation is both ethnocentric and false. Madagascar's tomb-centered ceremonies are times when the living and the dead are joyously reunited, when people get drunk, gorge themselves, and enjoy sexual license. Perhaps the gray, sober, ascetic, and moralistic aspects of many religious events in the United States, in taking the "fun" out of religion, force us to find our religion in fun.

A third problem: The behavior considered appropriate for religious occasions varies tremendously from culture to culture. One society may consider drunken frenzy the surest sign of faith, whereas another may encourage quiet reverence among the faithful. Who is to say which is "more religious"?

It is possible for apparently secular settings, things, and events to acquire intense meaning for individuals who have

## for REVIEW

### summary

1. Religion, a cultural universal, consists of belief and behavior concerned with supernatural beings, powers, and forces. Religion also encompasses the feelings, meanings, and congregations associated with such beliefs and behavior. Anthropological studies have revealed many aspects and functions of religion.

2. Tylor considered animism—the belief in spirits or souls—to be religion's earliest and most basic form. He focused on religion's explanatory role, arguing that religion would eventually disappear as science provided better explanations. Besides animism, yet another view of the supernatural also occurs in nonindustrial societies. This sees

the supernatural as a domain of raw, impersonal power or force (called mana in Polynesia and Melanesia). People can manipulate and control mana under certain conditions.

3. When ordinary technical and rational means of doing things fail, people may turn to magic. Often they use magic when they lack control over outcomes. Religion offers comfort and psychological security at times of crisis. However, rites also can create anxiety. Rituals are formal, invariant, stylized, earnest acts in which people subordinate their particular beliefs to a social collectivity. Rites of passage have three stages: separation, liminality, and incorporation. Such rites can mark any change in social status, age, place, or social condition. Collective rites often are cemented by communitas, a feeling of intense solidarity.

4. Besides their psychological and social functions, religious beliefs and practices play a role in the adaptation of human populations to their environments. The Hindu doctrine of *ahimsa,* which prohibits harm to living things, makes cattle sacred and beef a tabooed food. The taboo's force stops peasants from killing their draft cattle, even in times of extreme need.

5. Religion establishes and maintains social control through a series of moral and ethical beliefs, and real and imagined rewards and punishments, internalized in individuals. Religion also achieves social control by mobilizing its members for collective action. Religion helps maintain social order, but it also can promote change. Revitalization movements blend old and new beliefs and have helped people adapt to changing conditions.

6. Protestant values have been important in the United States, as they were in the rise and spread of capitalism in Europe. The world's major religions vary in their growth rates, with Islam expanding more rapidly than Christianity. There is growing religious diversity in the United States and Canada. Fundamentalists are antimodernists who claim an identity separate from the larger religious group from which they arose; they advocate strict fidelity to the "true" religious principles on which the larger religion was founded. Religious trends in contemporary North America include rising secularism and new religions, some inspired by science and technology, some by spiritism. There are secular as well as religious rituals.

7. The spread of Evangelical/Pentecostal Protestantism worldwide illustrates contemporary cultural globalization. Evangelical Protestantism stresses conservative morality, the authority of the Bible, and a personal ("born-again") conversion experience. To people who feel socially adrift, Pentecostalism offers tightly knit communities and a weblike structure of personal connections. Antimodernism is the rejection of the modern, including globalization, in favor of what is perceived as an earlier, purer, and better way of life. Religious fundamentalism describes antimodernist movements in Christianity, Islam, and Judaism. The rapid spread of Islam also illustrates cultural globalization and hybridization. Although certain core features endure, local people always assign their own meanings to the messages and social forms they receive from outside, including religion. The processes of hybridization and indigenization are always associated with cultural diffusion and globalization.

## key terms

animism 400

antimodernism 412

cargo cults 408

communitas 399

cosmology 404

fundamentalism 413

liminality 403

magic 401

mana 400

monotheism 400

polytheism 400

religion 398

revitalization movements 407

rites of passage 402

ritual 402

shaman 406

syncretisms 408

taboo 401

totem 404

## critical thinking

1. How did anthropologist Anthony Wallace define religion? After reading this chapter, what problems do you think there are with his definition?

2. Describe a rite of passage you (or a friend) have been through. How did it fit the three-stage model given in the text?

3. From the news or your own knowledge, can you provide additional examples of revitalization movements, new religions, or liminal cults?

4. Religion is a cultural universal. But religions are parts of particular cultures, and cultural differences show up systematically in religious beliefs and practices. How so?

5. This chapter notes that many Americans see recreation and religion as separate domains. Based on my fieldwork in Brazil and Madagascar and my reading about other societies, I believe that this separation is both ethnocentric and false. Do you agree with this? What has been your own experience?

# Arts, Media, and Sports

▶ What are the arts, and how have they varied historically and cross-culturally?

▶ How does culture influence the media, and vice versa?

▶ How are culture and cultural contrasts expressed in sports?

The Olympics unite arts, media, and sports. This ArcelorMittal Orbit Sculpture was constructed for London's Olympic Park. The sculpture, made mostly of recycled steel, stands 376 feet (114.5 meters) high. Can you see the five Olympic rings within it?

# understanding OURSELVES

Imagine a TV broadcast attracting over 70 percent of a nation's viewers. That has happened repeatedly in Brazil as a popular telenovela draws to a close. (Telenovelas are prime-time serial melodramas that run for about 150 episodes.) It happened in the United States in 1953, when 72 percent of all sets were tuned to *I Love Lucy* as Lucy Ricardo went to the hospital to give birth to Little Ricky. It happened even more impressively in 1956, when 83 percent of all sets tuned to *The Ed Sullivan Show* to watch Elvis Presley's TV debut. A single broadcast's largest audience share in more recent years occurred in 1983, when 106 million viewers and 77 percent of all sets watched the final episode of *M\*A\*S\*H*. In the 21st century, five successive Super Bowls (2010, 2011, 2012, 2013, and 2014) topped the viewership, but not nearly the audience share, of the *M\*A\*S\*H* finale. The 2014 Super Bowl set a record, with 111.5 million viewers, but the half-time show that year, which featured Bruno Mars and the Red Hot Chili Peppers, did even better, attracting 115.3 million viewers.

One notable development in the United States over the past few decades has been a shift from mass culture to segmented cultures. An increasingly differentiated nation recognizes, even celebrates, diversity. The mass media join—and intensify—this trend, measuring and catering to various "demographics." Products and messages are aimed less at the masses than at particular segments—target audiences.

As one example, consider the evolution of sports coverage. From 1961 to 1998, ABC offered a weekly sports anthology titled *Wide World of Sports*. On a given Saturday afternoon Americans might see bowling, track and field, skating, college wrestling, gymnastics, curling, swimming, diving, or another of many sports. It was like having a mini-Olympics running throughout the year. Today, dozens of specialized (often pay-for-view) sports channels cater to every taste, including Major League Baseball, the National Football League, and international soccer. Think of the choices now available through cable and satellite, websites, smartphones, tablets, Netflix, DVDs, DVRs, and the remote control. Target audiences now have access to a multiplicity of channels, featuring all kinds of music, sports, games, news, comedy, science fiction, soaps, movies, cartoons, old TV sitcoms, programs in Spanish and various other languages, nature shows, travel shows, adventure shows, histories, biographies, and home shopping. News channels (e.g., Fox News or MSNBC) even cater to particular political interests.

It seems likely there is a connection between these media developments and the "special interests" about which politicians perpetually complain. Do you think people might agree more—and Americans be less polarized—if everyone still watched the same TV programs?

## WHAT IS ART?

The **arts** include music, performance arts, visual arts, and storytelling and literature (oral and written). These manifestations of human creativity sometimes are called **expressive culture.** People express themselves in dance, music, song, painting, sculpture, pottery, cloth, storytelling, verse, prose, drama, and comedy. Many cultures lack terms that can be translated easily as "art" or "the arts." Yet even without a word for art, people everywhere do associate an aesthetic experience—a sense of beauty, appreciation, harmony, pleasure—with sounds, patterns, objects, and events that have certain qualities. Among the Yoruba of Nigeria, the word for art, *ona,* encompasses the designs made on objects, the art objects themselves, and the profession of the creators of those works. For two Yoruba lineages of leather workers, Otunisona and Osiisona, the suffix *-ona* in their names denotes art (Adepegba 1991).

A dictionary defines **art** as "the quality, production, expression, or realm of what is beautiful or of more than ordinary significance; the class of objects subject to aesthetic criteria" (*Random House College Dictionary* 1982, p. 76). According to the same dictionary, **aesthetics** involves "the qualities perceived in works of art . . . ; the . . . mind and emotions in relation to the sense of beauty" (p. 22). A more recent definition sees art as "something that is created with imagination and skill and that is beautiful or that expresses important ideas or feelings" (Merriam-Webster 2013). We know, however, that a work of art can attract attention, have special significance, and demonstrate imagination and skill without being considered beautiful. Pablo Picasso's *Guernica,* a famous painting of the Spanish Civil War, comes to mind as a scene that, while not beautiful, is indisputably moving and thus a work of art.

In many societies, art isn't viewed as a separate, special activity. But this doesn't stop individuals from being moved by sounds, patterns, objects, and events in a way that we would call aesthetic. Our own society does provide a fairly well-defined role for the connoisseur of the arts. We also have sanctuaries—concert halls, theaters, museums—where people can go to be aesthetically pleased and emotionally moved by objects and performances.

Western culture tends to compartmentalize art as something apart from everyday life. This reflects a more general modern separation of institutions like government and the economy from the rest of society. All these fields are considered distinct domains and have their own academic specialists. In non-Western societies, however, the production and appreciation of art are part of everyday life, just as popular culture is in our own society.

This chapter will not attempt to do a systematic survey of all the arts. Rather, the general approach will be to examine topics and issues that apply to expressive culture generally. The term *art* will be used to encompass all the arts, including print and film narratives. In other words, the observations to be made about art are intended to apply to music, theater, film, television, books, stories, and lore, as well as to painting and sculpture. Expressive culture also encompasses such creative forms as jokes, storytelling, dance, children's play, games, and festivals, and anthropologists have written about all of these.

That which is aesthetically pleasing is perceived with the senses. Usually, when we think of art, we have in mind something that can be seen or heard. But others might define art more broadly to include things that can be smelled (scents, fragrances), tasted (recipes), or touched (cloth textures). How enduring must art be? Visual works and written works, including musical compositions, may last for centuries. Can a single noteworthy event, such as a feast, which is not in the least eternal, except in memory, be a work of art?

## Art and Religion

Some of the issues raised in the discussion of religion also apply to art. Definitions of both art and religion mention the "more than ordinary" or the "extraordinary." Religious scholars may distinguish between the sacred (religious) and the profane (secular). Similarly, art scholars may distinguish between the artistic and the ordinary.

If we adopt a special attitude or demeanor when confronting a sacred object, do we display something similar when experiencing a work of art? According to the anthropologist Jacques Maquet (1986), an artwork is something that stimulates and sustains contemplation. It compels attention and reflection. Maquet stresses the importance of the object's form in producing such contemplation. But other scholars stress feeling and meaning in addition to form. The experience of art involves feelings, such as being moved, as well as appreciation of form, such as balance or harmony.

Such an artistic attitude can be combined with and used to bolster a religious attitude. Many of the high points of Western art and music had religious inspiration, or were done in the service of religion, as a visit to a church or a large museum will surely illustrate. Bach and Handel are as well known for their church music as Michelangelo is for his religious painting and sculpture. The buildings (churches and cathedrals) in which religious music is played and in which visual art is displayed may themselves be works of art. Some of the major

Many of the high points of Western art had religious inspiration or were done in the service of religion. Consider *The Creation of Adam* (and other frescoes painted from 1508 to 1512) by Michelangelo, on the ceiling of the Sistine Chapel in Vatican City, Rome, Italy.

architectural achievements of Western art are religious structures.

Art may be created, performed, or displayed outdoors in public or in special indoor settings. Just as churches demarcate religion, museums and theaters set art off from the ordinary world, making it special, while inviting spectators in. Buildings dedicated to the arts help create the artistic atmosphere. Architecture may accentuate the setting as a place for works of art to be presented.

The settings of rites and ceremonies, and of art, may be temporary or permanent. State societies have permanent religious structures: churches and temples. So, too, may state societies have buildings and structures dedicated to the arts. Nonstate societies tend to lack such permanently demarcated settings. Both art and religion are more "out there" in society. Still, in bands and tribes, religious settings can be created without churches. Similarly, an artistic atmosphere can be created without museums. At particular times of the year, ordinary space can be set aside for a visual art display or a musical performance. Such special occasions parallel the times set aside for religious ceremonies. In fact, in tribal performances, the arts and religion often mix. For example, masked and costumed performers may imitate spirits. Rites of passage often feature special music, dance, song, bodily adornment, and other manifestations of expressive culture.

Among tribes of the North Pacific Coast of North America, various art forms combined to create a ceremonial atmosphere (Gunther 1971). Masked and costumed dancers reenacted spirit encounters with human beings, which are part of the origin myths of villages, clans, and lineages. Sometimes, dancers devised intricate patterns of choreography. Their esteem was measured by the number of people who followed them when they danced.

Non-Western art is often, but wrongly, assumed to have an inevitable connection to ritual (Schildkrout and Keim 1990). In fact, non-Western societies have art for art's sake, just as Western societies do. Even when acting in the service of religion, there is room for individual creative expression (see Osborne and Tanner 2007). In the oral arts, for example, the audience is much more interested in the delivery and performance of the artist than in the particular god for whom the performer may be speaking.

## Locating Art

Aesthetic value is one way of distinguishing art. Another way is to consider placement. If something is displayed in a museum, someone must think it's art. Although tribal societies lack museums, they may have special areas where artistic expression takes place. The Tiwi of North Australia, for example, traditionally commissioned the manufacture of commemorative burial poles after a death. The pole artists were sequestered in a work area near the grave. That area was taboo to everyone else. The artists were

The French artist known as JR specializes in transforming urban space into art. The image shown here is part of a large-scale 2008–2009 art project, titled "Women Are Heroes," in Rio de Janeiro, Brazil. Here we see a woman's face on steep steps in Rio's Favela Morro da Providência. (See http://www.jr-art.net/projects/women-are-heroes-brazil for more images.)

freed temporarily from the daily food quest. Other community members served as their patrons, supplying the artists with the hard-to-get materials needed for their work (Goodale and Koss 1971).

The boundary between what's art and what's not isn't always sharp. The American artist Andy Warhol is famous for transforming Campbell's soup cans, Brillo pads, and images of Marilyn Monroe into art. Many recent artists (see photo above) have tried to erase the distinction between art and ordinary life by converting the everyday into a work of art. Objects never intended as art, such as the Valentine Olivetti typewriter, may be transformed into art by being placed in a museum, such as New York's Museum of Modern Art. Jacques Maquet (1986) distinguishes such "art by transformation" from art created and intended to be art, which he calls "art by destination."

In state societies, we have come to rely on critics, judges, and experts to tell us what's art and what isn't. A play titled *Art* is about conflict that arises among three friends when one of them buys an all-white painting. They disagree, as people often do, about the definition and value of a work of art. Such variation in art appreciation is especially common in contemporary society, with its professional artists and critics and great cultural diversity. We'd expect more uniform standards and agreement in less diverse, less stratified societies.

To be culturally relativistic, we need to avoid applying our own standards about what art is to the products of other cultures. Sculpture is art, right?

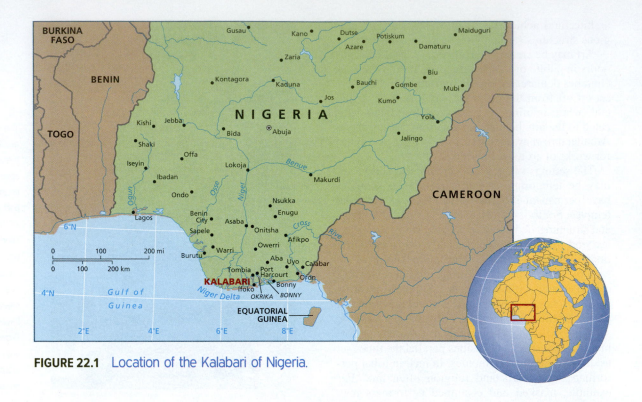

**FIGURE 22.1** Location of the Kalabari of Nigeria.

Not necessarily. Previously, we challenged the view that non-Western art always has some kind of connection to religion. The Kalabari case to be discussed now makes the opposite point: that religious sculpture is not always art.

The Kalabari of southern Nigeria (Figure 22.1) carve wooden sculptures not for aesthetic reasons but to serve as "houses" for spirits (Horton 1963). The Kalabari place these sculptures, and thus localize the spirits, in a cult house. Here, sculpture is done not for art's sake but as a means of manipulating spiritual forces. The Kalabari do have standards for the carvings, but beauty isn't one of them. A sculpture must be sufficiently complete to represent its spirit, and carvers must base their work on past models. Each spirit has a known image associated with it, and it's risky to deviate too much from that image. Offended spirits may retaliate. As long as they observe these standards of completeness and established images, carvers are free to express themselves. But these images are considered repulsive rather than beautiful. And they are not manufactured for artistic but for religious reasons.

## Art and Individuality

Those who work with non-Western art have been criticized for ignoring the individual and focusing too much on the social nature and context of art. When art objects from Africa or Papua New Guinea are displayed in museums, often only the name of the tribe and of the Western donor are given, rather than that of the individual artist. It's as though skilled individuals don't exist in non-Western societies. The impression is that art is collectively produced. Sometimes it is; sometimes it isn't.

To some extent, there *is* more collective production of art in non-Western societies than in the United States and Canada. According to Hackett (1996), African artworks (sculpted figures, textiles, paintings, and pots) generally are enjoyed, critiqued, and used by communities or groups. The artist may receive more feedback during the creative process than the individual artist typically gets in our own society. Here, the feedback often comes too late, after the product is complete, rather than during production, when it can still be changed.

During his fieldwork among Nigeria's Tiv people, Paul Bohannan (1971) concluded that the proper study of art there should pay less attention to artists and more attention to art critics and products. There were few skilled Tiv artists, and such people avoided doing their art publicly. However, mediocre artists would work in public, where they routinely got comments from onlookers (critics). Based on suggestions, an artist often changed a design, such as a carving, in progress. There was yet another way in which Tiv artists worked socially rather than individually. Sometimes, when artists put their work aside, someone else would pick it up and start working on it. The Tiv clearly didn't recognize the same kind of connection between individuals and their art that we do.

In Western societies, artists of many sorts (e.g., writers, painters, sculptors, actors, musicians) have reputations for being iconoclastic and antisocial. Social acceptance may be more important in non-Western societies. Still, there are well-known individual artists in non-Western societies. They are recognized as such by other community members, perhaps by outsiders as well. Their artistic labor may even be conscripted for special displays and performances, including ceremonies, or palace arts and events.

To what extent can a work of art stand apart from its creator? Haapala (1998) argues that artists and their works are inseparable: "By creating works of art a person creates an artistic identity for himself. He creates himself quite literally into the pieces he puts into his art. He exists in the works he has created." In this view, Picasso created many Picassos, and he continues to exist in and through those works.

Sometimes little is known or recognized about the individual artist responsible for an enduring artwork. We are more likely to know the name of the recording artist than that of the writer of familiar songs. Sometimes we fail to acknowledge art individually because the artwork was collectively created. To whom should we attribute a pyramid or a cathedral? Should it be the architect, the ruler or leader who commissioned the work, or the master builder who implemented the design?

## The Work of Art

The word *opera* is the plural of *opus,* which means a work. For the artist, at least, art is work, albeit creative work. In nonstate societies, artists may have to hunt, gather, herd, fish, or farm in order to eat, but they still manage to find time to work on their art. In state societies, at least, artists have been defined as specialists—professionals who have chosen careers as artists, musicians, writers, or actors. If they manage to support themselves from their art, they may be full-time professionals. If not, they do their art part-time while earning a living from another activity. Sometimes artists associate in professional groups, such as medieval guilds or contemporary unions. Actors Equity in New York, a labor union, is a modern guild, designed to protect the interests of its artist members.

Just how much work is needed to make a work of art? In the early days of French impressionism, many experts viewed the paintings of Claude Monet and his colleagues as too sketchy and spontaneous to be true art. Established artists and critics were accustomed to more formal and classic studio styles. The French impressionists got their name from their sketches—*impressions* in French—of natural and social settings. They took advantage of technological innovations, particularly the availability of oil paints in tubes, to take their palettes, easels, and canvases into the field. There they made the pictures of changing light and color that hang today in so many museums, where they are now fully recognized as art. But before impressionism became an officially recognized "school" of art, its works were perceived by its critics as crude and unfinished. In terms of community standards, the first impressionist paintings were evaluated as harshly as were the crude and incomplete Kalabari wood carvings of spirits.

For familiar genres, such as painting or music, societies tend to have standards by which they judge whether an artwork is complete or fully realized. Most people would doubt, for instance, that an all-white painting could be a work of art. Standards may be maintained informally in society, or by specialists, such as art critics. It may be difficult for unorthodox or renegade artists to innovate. But like the impressionists, they may eventually succeed. Some societies tend to reward conformity, an artist's skill with traditional models and techniques. Others encourage breaks with the past, innovation.

# ART, SOCIETY, AND CULTURE

Around 100,000 years ago, some of the world's first artists occupied Blombos Cave, located on a high cliff facing the Indian Ocean at the tip of what is now South Africa. They hunted game and ate fish from the waters below them. In terms of body and brain size, these ancient Africans were anatomically modern humans. They also were turning animal bones into finely worked tools and weapon points. Furthermore, they were engraving artifacts with symbolic marks—manifestations of abstract and creative thought and, presumably, communication through language (Wilford 2002*b*).

A group led by Christopher Henshilwood of South Africa has analyzed bone tools and other artifacts from Blombos Cave, along with the mineral ocher that may have been used for body painting. The most impressive bone tools are three sharp instruments. The bone appears first to have been shaped with a stone blade, then finished into a symmetrical shape and polished for hours. According to Henshilwood (quoted in Wilford 2002*b*), "It's actually unnecessary for projectile points to be so carefully made. It suggests to us that this is an expression of symbolic thinking. The people said, 'Let's make a really beautiful object. . . .' Symbolic thinking means that people are using something to mean something else. The tools do not have to have only a practical purpose. And the ocher might be used to decorate their equipment, perhaps themselves."

In Europe, art goes back more than 30,000 years, to the Upper Paleolithic period in western Europe. Cave paintings, the best-known examples of Upper Paleolithic art, were painted in true caves, located deep in the bowels of the Earth. They may have been painted as part of some kind of rite of passage involving retreat from society. Portable art objects carved in stone, bone, and ivory, along with musical whistles and flutes, also confirm artistic expression throughout the Upper Paleolithic (see Lesure 2011). Art usually is more public than the cave paintings.

This musician living in the Central African Republic carved this instrument himself.

Typically, it is exhibited, evaluated, performed, and appreciated in society. It has spectators or audiences. It isn't just for the artist.

## Ethnomusicology

**Ethnomusicology** is the comparative study of the musics of the world and of music as an aspect of culture and society. The field of ethnomusicology thus unites music and anthropology. The music side involves the study and analysis of the music itself and the instruments used to create it. The anthropology side views music as a way to explore a culture, to determine the role that music plays in that society, and the specific social and cultural features that influence how music is created and performed.

Ethnomusicology studies non-Western music, traditional and folk music, and even contemporary popular music from a cultural perspective. To do this there has to be fieldwork—firsthand study of particular forms of music, their social functions and cultural meanings, within particular societies. Ethnomusicologists talk with local musicians, make recordings in the field, and learn about the place of musical instruments, performances, and performers in a given society (Kirman 1997). Nowadays, given globalization, diverse cultures and musical styles easily meet and mix. Music that draws on a wide range of cultural instruments and styles is called World Fusion, World Beat, or World Music—another topic within contemporary ethnomusicology.

Because music is a cultural universal, and because musical abilities seem to run in families, it has been suggested that a predisposition for music may have a genetic basis (Crenson 2000). Could a "music gene" that arose tens, or hundreds, of thousands of years ago have conferred an evolutionary advantage on those early humans who possessed it? The fact that music has existed in all known cultures suggests that it arose early in human history. Providing direct evidence for music's antiquity is an ancient carved bone flute from a cave in Slovenia. This "Divje babe flute," the world's oldest known musical instrument, dates back more than 43,000 years.

Exploring the possible biological roots of music, Sandra Trehub (2001) notes striking similarities in the way mothers worldwide sing to their children—with a high pitch, a slow tempo, and a distinctive tone. All cultures have lullabies, which sound so much alike they cannot be mistaken for anything else (Crenson 2000). Trehub speculates that music might have been adaptive in human evolution because musically talented mothers had an easier time calming their babies. Calm babies who fell asleep easily and rarely made a fuss might have been more likely to survive to adulthood. Their cries would not attract predators; they and their mothers would get more rest; and they would be less likely to be mistreated. If a gene conferring musical ability appeared early in human evolution, given a selective advantage, musical adults would pass their genes to their children.

Music is among the most social of the arts, because it typically unites people in groups, such as choirs, symphonies, ensembles, and bands. Could it be that early humans with a biological penchant for music were able to live more effectively in social groups—another possible adaptive advantage?

Originally coined for European peasants, **folk** art, music, and lore are the expressive culture of ordinary people, as contrasted with the "high" art, or "classic" art, of the European elites. When folk music is performed (see photo on p. 423), the combination of costumes, music, and often song and dance is supposed to say something about local culture and about tradition. Tourists and other outsiders often perceive rural and folk life mainly in terms of such performances. Community residents themselves often use such performances to display and enact their local culture and traditions for outsiders.

In Planinica, a Muslim village in (prewar) Bosnia, Yvonne Lockwood (1983) studied folksong, which could be heard there day or night. The most active singers were unmarried females aged 16 to 26 (maidens). The social transition from girl to maiden (marriageable female) was signaled by active participation in public song and dance. Adolescent girls were urged to sing along with women and performing maidens. This was part of a rite of passage by which a little girl (*dite*) became a maiden (*cura*). Marriage, in contrast, moved most women from the public to the private sphere; public singing generally stopped. Married women sang in their own homes or among other women. Only occasionally would they join maidens in public song. After age 50, wives tended to stop singing, even in private. For

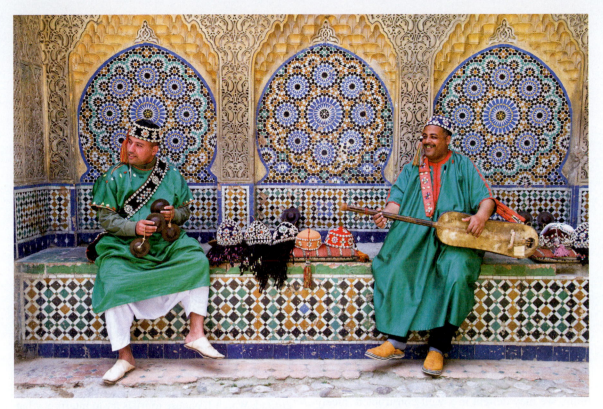

In this 2011 photo, musicians play carcaba (iron castanets) and gambri (guitar) in the Kasbah, Tangier, Morocco. For whose pleasure do you suppose this performance is being given? Nowadays, such performances attract tourists as well as local people.

women, singing thus signaled a series of transitions between age grades: girl to maiden (public singing), maiden to wife (private singing), and wife to elder (no more singing).

Singing and dancing were common at Bosnian *prelos* attended by males and females. In Planinica the Serbo-Croatian word *prelo,* usually defined as "spinning bee," meant any occasion for visiting. *Prelos* were especially common in winter. During the summer, villagers worked long hours, and *prelos* were few. The *prelo* offered a context for play, relaxation, song, and dance. All gatherings of maidens, especially *prelos,* were occasions for song. Married women encouraged them to sing, often suggesting specific songs. If males were also present, a singing duel might occur, in which maidens and young men teased each other. A successful *prelo* was well attended, with much singing and dancing.

Public singing was traditional in many other contexts among prewar Bosnian Muslims. After a day of cutting hay on mountain slopes, parties of village men would congregate at a specific place on the trail above the village. They formed lines according to their singing ability, with the best singers in front and the less talented ones behind. They proceeded to stroll down to the village together, singing as they went, until they reached the village center, where they dispersed. According to Lockwood, whenever an activity brought together a group of maidens or young men, it usually would end with public singing. The inspiration for parts of *Snow White* and *Shrek* (the movies) can be traced back to such customs of the European countryside.

## Representations of Art and Culture

The creative products and images of folk, rural, and non-Western cultures are increasingly spread—and commercialized—by the media and tourism. A result is that many Westerners have come to think of "culture" in terms of colorful customs, music, dancing, and adornments: clothing, jewelry, and hairstyles. A bias toward the arts and religion, rather than the more mundane economic and social aspects of culture, shows up on TV's Discovery Channel, and even in many anthropological films (see Grimshaw and Ravetz 2009). Many ethnographic films start off with music, often drumbeats: "Bonga, bonga, bonga, bonga. Here in [supply place name], the people are very religious." Such presentations just reinforce the previously critiqued assumption that the arts of nonindustrial societies are always linked to religion. This may create a false impression that non-Western peoples spend much of their time wearing colorful clothes, singing, dancing, and practicing religious rituals. Taken to an extreme, such images portray culture as recreational and ultimately not serious, rather than as something that ordinary people live every day of their lives—not just when they have festivals.

## Art and Communication

Art also functions as a form of communication between artist and community or audience. Sometimes, however, there are intermediaries between the artist and the audience. Actors, for example, translate the works and ideas of other artists (writers and directors) into performances. Musicians play and sing compositions of other people along with music they themselves have composed. Using music written by others, choreographers plan and direct patterns of dance, which dancers then execute for audiences.

How does art communicate? We need to know what the artist intends to communicate and how the audience reacts. Often, the audience communicates right back to the artist. Live performers, for instance, get immediate feedback, as may writers and directors by viewing a performance of their own work. In contemporary societies, with increasing diversity in the audience, uniform reactions are rare. Contemporary artists, like businesspeople, are well aware that they have target audiences. Certain segments of the population are more likely to appreciate certain forms of art than other segments are.

Art can transmit several kinds of messages. It can convey a moral lesson or tell a cautionary tale. It can teach lessons the artist, or society, wants told. Like the rites that induce, then dispel, anxiety, the tension and resolution of drama can lead to **catharsis,** intense emotional release, in the audience. Art can move emotions, make us laugh, cry, feel up or down. Art appeals to the intellect as well as to the emotions. We may delight in a well-constructed, nicely balanced, well-realized work of art.

Often, art is meant to commemorate and to last, to carry an enduring message. Like a ceremony, art may serve a mnemonic function, making people remember. Art may be designed to make people remember either individuals or events, such as the AIDS epidemic that has proved so lethal in many world areas or the cataclysmic events of September 11, 2001.

**catharsis**
Intense emotional release.

## Art and Politics

To what extent should art serve society? Art can be self-consciously prosocial. It can be used to either express or challenge community sentiment and standards. Decisions about what counts as a work of art, or about how to display art, may be political and controversial. Museums have to balance concern over community standards with a wish to be as creative and innovative as the artists and works they display.

Much art that is valued today was received with revulsion in its own time. Children were prohibited from seeing paintings by Matisse, Braque, and Picasso when those works first were displayed in New York in the Armory Show of 1913. Almost a century later, the City of New York and then mayor Rudolph Giuliani took the Brooklyn Museum to court over its 1999–2000 "Sensation" exhibit. After religious groups protested Chris Ofili's *Holy Virgin Mary,* a collage that included elephant dung, Giuliani deemed the work sacrilegious. At the ensuing court trial, art advocates spoke out against the mayor's actions. The museum won the case, but Ofili's work again came under attack when a man smuggled paint inside the Brooklyn exhibition and tried to smear it on the *Virgin* (University of Virginia, n.d.). According to art professor Michael Davis, Ofili's collage is "shocking," because it deliberately provokes and intends to jolt viewers into an expanded frame of reference. The mayor's reactions may have been based on the narrow definition that art must be beautiful and an equally limited stereotype of a Virgin Mary as depicted in Italian Renaissance paintings (Mount Holyoke College 1999).

Today, no museum director can mount an exhibit without worrying that it will offend some politically organized segment of society. In the United States there has been an ongoing battle between liberals and conservatives involving the National Endowment for the Arts. Artists have been criticized as being aloof from society, as creating only for themselves and for elites, as being out of touch with conventional and traditional aesthetic values, and even as mocking the values of ordinary people.

## The Cultural Transmission of the Arts

Appreciation of the arts reflects one's cultural background. Watch Japanese tourists try to interpret what they are seeing in a Western art museum. Conversely, the form and meaning of a Japanese tea

Art appreciation must be learned, the earlier the better. How does the placement of art in museums, such as this one, affect art appreciation?

**FIGURE 22.2** Location of the Navajo.

ceremony, or a demonstration of origami (Japanese paper folding), will be alien to a foreign observer. Appreciation of the arts is learned, in particular cultural settings (Layton 1991).

For example, music with certain tonalities and rhythm patterns pleases some people but alienates others. In a study of Navajo music, McAllester (1954) found that it reflected the overall culture of that time in three main ways. First, individualism was a key Navajo cultural value: It was up to the individual to decide what to do with his or her songs. Second, the Navajo saw foreign music as dangerous and rejected it. (This second point is no longer true; there are now Navajo rock bands.) Third, a general stress on proper form applied to music. There was, in Navajo belief, a right way to sing every kind of song (see Figure 22.2 for the location of the Navajo).

People learn to appreciate certain kinds of music and other art forms, just as they learn to hear and decipher a foreign language. Unlike Londoners and New Yorkers, Parisians don't flock to musicals. Despite its multiple French origins, even the musical *Les Misérables,* a huge hit in London, New York, and dozens of cities worldwide, bombed in Paris. Humor, too, a form of verbal art, depends on cultural background and setting. What's funny in one culture may not translate as funny in another. When a joke doesn't work, an American may say, "Well, you had to be there at the time." Jokes, like aesthetic judgments, depend on context.

Anthropology's approach to the arts contrasts with the traditional humanities' focus on "fine arts," as in art history, "Great Books," and classical music. Anthropology has extended the definition of "cultured" well beyond the elitist meaning of "high" art and culture. For anthropologists, everyone acquires culture through enculturation. In academia today, growing acceptance of the anthropological definition of culture has helped broaden the study of the humanities from fine art and elite art to "folk" and non-Western arts, as well as the creative expressions of popular culture.

Using examples from popular culture, this chapter's "Appreciating Anthropology" on pp. 426–427 shows that techniques anthropologists use to analyze myths and folktales can be extended to two fantasy films that most of you have seen: *The Wizard of Oz* and *Star Wars.* "Appreciating Anthropology" also highlights the contributions of the French anthropologist Claude Lévi-Strauss (1967) along with the neo-Freudian psychoanalyst Bruno Bettelheim (1975). Both have made important contributions to the study of myths and fairy tales.

## I'll Get You, My Pretty, and Your Little R2

Techniques that anthropologists have used to analyze myths and folktales can be extended to two fantasy films that most of you have seen. *The Wizard of Oz* has been telecast regularly for decades. The original *Star Wars* remains one of the most popular films of all time. Both are familiar and significant cultural products with obvious mythic qualities. The contributions of the French structuralist anthropologist Claude Lévi-Strauss (1967) and the neo-Freudian psychoanalyst Bruno Bettelheim (1975) to the study of myths and fairy tales permit the following analysis of visual fairy tales that contemporary Americans know well.

Examining the myths and tales of different cultures, Lévi-Strauss determined that one tale could be converted into another through a series of simple operations—for example, by doing the following:

1. Converting the positive element of a myth into its negative.
2. Reversing the order of the elements.
3. Replacing a male hero with a female hero.
4. Preserving or repeating certain key elements.

Through such operations, two apparently dissimilar myths can be shown to be variations on a common structure—that is, to be transformations of each other.

We'll see that *Star Wars* is a systematic structural transformation of *The Wizard of Oz*. We may speculate about how many of the resemblances were conscious and how many simply reflect a process of enculturation that *Star Wars* writer and director George Lucas shares with other Americans.

*The Wizard of Oz* and *Star Wars* both begin in arid country, the first in Kansas and the second on the desert planet Tatooine. (Recap 22.1 lists the similarities discussed here.) *Star Wars* converts *The Wizard's* female hero, Dorothy, into a boy, Luke Skywalker. Fairy-tale heroes usually have short, common first names and second names that describe their origin or activity. Thus, Luke, who travels aboard spaceships, is a Skywalker, while Dorothy Gale is swept off to Oz by a cyclone (a gale of wind). Dorothy leaves home with her dog, Toto, which is pursued by and has managed to escape from a woman who in Oz becomes the Wicked Witch of the West. Luke follows his "Two-Two" (R2D2), who is fleeing Darth Vader, the witch's structural equivalent.

Dorothy and Luke each start out living with an uncle and an aunt. However, because of the gender change of the hero, the primary relationship is reversed and inverted. Thus, Dorothy's relationship with her aunt is primary, warm, and loving, whereas Luke's relationship with his uncle, though primary, is strained and distant. Aunt and uncle are in the tales for the same reason. They represent home (the nuclear family of orientation), which children (according to American culture norms) must eventually leave to make it on their own. As Bettelheim (1975) points out, fairy tales often disguise parents as uncle and aunt, and this establishes social distance. The child can deal with the hero's separation from aunt and uncle (in *The Wizard of Oz*) or the aunt's and uncle's deaths (in *Star Wars*) more easily than with the separation from or death of real parents. Furthermore, this permits the child's strong feelings toward his or her real parents to be represented in different, more central characters, such as the Wicked Witch of the West and Darth Vader. Both films focus on the child's relationship with the parent of the same sex, dividing that parent into three parts. In *The Wizard,* the mother is split into two parts bad and one part good. They are the Wicked Witch of the East, dead at the beginning of the movie; the Wicked Witch of the West, dead at the end; and Glinda, the good mother, who survives. The original *Star Wars* reversed the proportion of good and bad, giving Luke a good father (his own), the Jedi knight who is proclaimed dead at the film's beginning. There is another good father, Ben Kenobi, who is ambiguously dead when the movie ends. Third is the evil father figure, Darth Vader. As the good-mother third survives *The Wizard of Oz,* the bad-father third lives on after *Star Wars,* to strike back in the sequel.

The child's relationship with the parent of the opposite sex also is represented in the two films. Dorothy's father figure is the Wizard of Oz, an initially terrifying figure who later is proved to be a fake. Bettelheim notes that the typical fairy-tale father is disguised as a monster or giant. Or else, when preserved as a human, he is weak, distant, or ineffective. Dorothy counts on the wizard to save her but finds that he makes seemingly impossible demands and in the end is just an ordinary man. She succeeds on her own, no longer relying on a father who offers no more than she herself possesses.

In *Star Wars* (although not in the later films), Luke's mother figure is Princess Leia. Bettelheim notes that boys commonly fantasize their mothers to be unwilling captives of their fathers. Fairy tales often disguise mothers as princesses whose freedom the boy-hero must obtain. In graphic Freudian imagery, Darth Vader threatens Princess Leia with a needle the size of the witch's broomstick. By the end of the film, Luke has freed Leia and defeated Vader.

There are other striking parallels in the structure of the two films. Fairy-tale heroes often are accompanied on their adventures by secondary characters who personify the virtues needed in a successful quest. Such characters often come in

| RECAP 22.1 | *Star Wars* as a Structural Transformation of *The Wizard of Oz* |
|---|---|

| STAR WARS | THE WIZARD OF OZ |
|---|---|
| Male hero (Luke Skywalker) | Female hero (Dorothy Gale) |
| Arid Tatooine | Arid Kansas |
| Luke follows R2D2:<br>  R2D2 flees Vader | Dorothy follows Toto:<br>  Toto flees witch |
| Luke lives with uncle and aunt:<br>  Primary relationship with uncle<br>  (same sex as hero)<br>  Strained, distant relationship with uncle | Dorothy lives with uncle and aunt:<br>  Primary relationship with aunt<br>  (same sex as hero)<br>  Warm, close relationship with aunt |
| Tripartite division of same-sex parent:<br>  2 parts good, 1 part bad father<br>  Good father dead at beginning<br>  Good father dead (?) at end<br>  Bad father survives | Tripartite division of same-sex parent:<br>  2 parts bad, 1 part good mother<br>  Bad mother dead at beginning<br>  Bad mother dead at end<br>  Good mother survives |
| Relationship with parent of opposite sex<br>    (Princess Leia Organa):<br>  Princess is unwilling captive<br>  Needle<br>  Princess is freed | Relationship with parent of opposite sex<br>    (Wizard of Oz):<br>  Wizard makes impossible demands<br>  Broomstick<br>  Wizard turns out to be sham |
| Trio of companions:<br>  Han Solo, C3PO, Chewbacca | Trio of companions:<br>  Scarecrow, Tin Woodman, Cowardly Lion |
| Minor characters:<br>  Jawas<br>  Sand People<br>  Stormtroopers | Minor characters:<br>  Munchkins<br>  Apple Trees<br>  Flying Monkeys |
| Settings:<br>  Death Star<br>  Verdant Tikal (rebel base) | Settings:<br>  Witch's castle<br>  Emerald City |
| Conclusion:<br>  Luke uses magic to accomplish goal<br>  (destroy Death Star) | Conclusion:<br>  Dorothy uses magic to accomplish goal<br>  (return to Kansas) |

threes. Dorothy takes along wisdom (the Scarecrow), love (the Tin Woodman), and courage (the Lion). *Star Wars* includes a structurally equivalent trio—Han Solo, C3PO, and Chewbacca—but their association with particular qualities isn't as precise. The minor characters also are structurally parallel: Munchkins and Jawas, Apple Trees and Sand People, Flying Monkeys and Stormtroop-

ers. And compare settings—the witch's castle and the Death Star, the Emerald City and the rebel base. The endings also are parallel. Luke accomplishes his objective on his own, using the Force (mana, magical power). Dorothy's goal is to return to Kansas. She does that by tapping her shoes together and drawing on the Force in her ruby slippers.

All successful cultural products blend old and new, drawing on familiar themes. They may rearrange them in novel ways and thus win a lasting place in the imaginations of the culture that creates or accepts them. *Star Wars* successfully used old cultural themes in novel ways. It did that by drawing on the American fairy tale, one that had been available in book form since the turn of the 20th century.

Schoolchildren play violins in an orchestra. Does this scene illustrate education, enculturation, or both?

A traditional musician and story teller performs with local children in Panama's Tusipono Embera Community. Are there comparable figures in your society? Does this scene illustrate education, enculturation, or both?

In many societies, myths, legends, tales, and the art of storytelling play important roles in the transmission of culture. Oral traditions may preserve details of history and genealogy, as in many parts of West Africa. Storytelling and music may be combined for drama and emphasis (see lower photo above), much as they are in films and theater.

At what age do children start learning the arts? In some cultures, they start early. Contrast the photo of the violin class (upper photo above) with the photo of the Tusipono Embera Community gathering (lower photo above). The violin scene shows formal instruction. Teachers take the lead in showing students how to play the violin. The lower photo shows a more informal local scene in which children are learning about the arts as part of their overall enculturation. Many of the violin students are learning the

arts because their parents want them to, rather than because they have an artistic temperament they are eager to express. In the United States, performance, often associated with schools, has a strong social, and usually competitive, component. Kids perform with their peers. In the process, they learn to compete, whether for a first-place finish in a sports event or for a first chair in the school orchestra or band.

## Continuity and Change

The arts go on changing, although certain art forms have survived for thousands of years. The Upper Paleolithic cave art that has survived for more than 30,000 years was itself a highly developed manifestation of human creativity and symbolism, with a long evolutionary history. Monumental architecture, along with sculpture, ornamental pottery, and written music, literature, and drama, have survived from early civilizations.

Countries and cultures are known for particular contributions, including the arts. The Balinese are known for dance; the Navajo for sand paintings, jewelry, and weaving; and the French for making cuisine an art form. We still read Greek tragedies and comedies in college, as we also read Shakespeare and Milton and view the works of Michelangelo. Greek theater is among the most enduring of the arts. The words of Aeschylus, Sophocles, Euripides, and Aristophanes have been captured in writing and live on. Who knows how many great preliterate creations and performances have been lost?

Classic Greek theater survives throughout the world. It is read in college courses and performed on stages from Athens to New York. In today's world, the dramatic arts are part of a huge "arts and leisure" industry, which links Western and non-Western art forms in a global network that has both aesthetic and commercial dimensions (see Marcus and Myers 1995; Root 1996). Non-Western musical traditions and instruments have joined this network. Folk musicians routinely perform for outsiders, including tourists who increasingly visit their villages. And "tribal" instruments such as the Native Australian didgeridoo, a very long, wooden wind instrument, are now exported worldwide. At least one shop in Amsterdam, the Netherlands, sells only didgeridoos. Stores in any world capital hawk "traditional" arts, including musical instruments, from a hundred Third World countries.

Although American culture values experimentation and innovation, creativity also can be expressed in variations on a traditional form. We see this in "Appreciating Anthropology," in which *Star Wars,* despite its specific story and innovative special effects, is shown to share its structure with a previous narrative. Thanks to globalization, ingredients and flavors from all over the world now combine in modern cuisine. So, too, are elements from many cultures and epochs woven into our contemporary arts and expressive culture, including in modern media.

# MEDIA AND CULTURE

Today's mass culture, or popular culture, features cultural forms that have appeared and spread rapidly because of major changes in the material conditions of contemporary life—particularly work organization, transportation, and communication, including the media. Sports, movies, TV shows, video games, digital media, amusement parks, and fast-food restaurants have become powerful elements of national (and international) culture. They offer a framework of common expectations, experiences, and behavior overriding differences in region, class, formal religious affiliation, political sentiment, gender, ethnic group, and place of residence.

## Using the Media

Any media-borne image or message can be analyzed in terms of its nature, including its symbolism, and its effects. It also can be analyzed as a **text**—something that can be received, processed, interpreted, and assigned meaning by anyone exposed to it. In this sense, a text doesn't have to be written. The term may refer to a film, an image, or an event. "Readers"—users of the text—make their own interpretations and derive their own feelings from it. "Readers" of media messages constantly produce their own meanings.

According to the media scholar John Fiske (1989, 2011), any individual's use of popular culture is a personal creative act (an original "reading" of a "text"). A particular celebrity, movie, game, or TV show means something different to each fan. Fiske argues that the personal meanings one finds in popular culture are most pleasurable when they relate directly and practically to that person's everyday life (Fiske 1989, 2011; see also Fiske and Hartley 2003).

Consumers actively select, evaluate, and interpret media in ways that make sense to them. People use media for all sorts of reasons: to validate beliefs, to indulge fantasies, to find messages unavailable in the local setting, to locate information, to make social comparisons, to relieve frustrations, to chart social courses, and to formulate life plans. Popular culture (from hip-hop to comedy) can be used to express discontent and resistance by groups that are or feel powerless or oppressed.

In Ibirama, a town in southern Brazil, anthropologist Alberto Costa found that women and young adults of both sexes were particularly attracted to telenovelas, melodramatic nightly programs often compared to American soap operas, usually featuring sophisticated urban settings (see Kottak 2009). Women and young men in Ibirama used the (socially more liberal) content of telenovelas to challenge conservative local norms. In Brazil, elites, intellectuals, educators, the clergy, and older men have tended to be more suspicious and dismissive of mass media than are less powerful people. Often, these groups view media messages as threatening or subverting

In an ancient amphitheater at Syracuse, Sicily, ancient Greek theater (*Medea*) is being performed for a contemporary audience. Theater is typically a multimedia experience, with visual, aural, and often musical attributes.

A synthesis of new and old theater techniques, including puppetry, is used in this production of the stage play *War Horse* at London's Olivier Theatre.

their traditional authority as guardians of power or cultural capital.

During our fieldwork in a middle-class Michigan town, Lara Descartes and I found that parents selected media messages that supported and reinforced their own opinions and life choices (Descartes and Kottak 2009). Media images of work and family gave parents the chance to identify, or contrast themselves, with media figures. Townfolk compared themselves with people and situations from the

**text**
Cultural product that is processed and assigned meaning by anyone exposed to it.

media as well as with people in their own lives. We also found, as in Brazil, that some people (traditionalists) were much more dismissive of, distrustful of, or hostile to media than others were.

When people seek certain messages and can't easily find them in their home communities, they are likely to look somewhere else. The media, especially modern social media, allow local people to link in to a rich web of connections that can provide contact, information, entertainment, and potential social validation. In Brazil, we've found that greater use of all media is part of an external orientation, a general wish for information, contacts, models, and support beyond those that are locally and routinely available. For some of the parents (especially mothers) in our Michigan study, media offered a welcome gateway to a wider world. Others, however, were comfortable with, and even sought to enhance, their isolation, limiting both media exposure and the outside social contacts of themselves and their children.

Connection to a wider world, real or imagined, on- or offline, is a way to move beyond local standards and expectations, even if the escape is only temporary and vicarious. David Ignatius (2007) describes the escapist value of 19th-century English novels, whose strong heroines pursued "free thought and personal freedom," rejecting the "easy comforts and arranged marriages of their class" in a quest for something more. Despite (and/or because of) their independent or rebellious temperaments, characters such as Elizabeth Bennett in Jane Austen's *Pride and Prejudice* almost always found a happy ending. Nineteenth-century readers found such a heroine's success "deeply satisfying," because there were so few opportunities in real life (the local community) to see such behavior and choices (all quotes from Ignatius 2007, p. A21).

Another role of the media is to provide social cement—a basis for sharing—as families or friends watch favorite programs or attend events together. The media also can provide common ground for much larger groups, nationally and internationally. Brazilians and Italians can be just as excited, at the same moment but with radically different emotions, by a soccer goal scored in a World Cup match. And they can remember the same winning goal for decades. The common information and knowledge that people acquire through exposure to the same media illustrate *culture* in the anthropological sense (see also Askew and Wilk 2002; Ginsburg, Abu-Lughod, and Larkin 2002).

## Assessing the Effects of Television

My co-researchers and I first got the idea that TV might be influencing family planning in Brazil from a brief article in the *New York Times*. Based on interviews with Brazilians, that report suggested that TV (along with other factors) was influencing Brazilians to have smaller families. Fortunately, our research project on media impact in rural Brazil had provided us with the quantitative data we needed to test that hypothesis.

Our findings already had confirmed many other studies showing that the strongest predictor of (smaller) family size is a woman's educational level. However, it turned out that two television variables—current viewing level and especially the number of years of TV presence in the home—were better predictors of (smaller) family size than were many other potential predictors, including income, class, and religiosity.

In the four towns in our study with the longest exposure to television, the average woman had had a TV set in her home for 15 years and had had 2.3 pregnancies. In the three communities where TV had arrived most recently, the average woman had had a home set for 4 years and had had 5 pregnancies. Thus, length of site exposure was a useful predictor of reproductive histories. Of course, television exposure at a site is an aspect of that site's increasing overall access to external systems and resources, which usually include improved methods of contraception. But the impact of longer home TV exposure showed up not only when we compared sites but also within sites, within age cohorts, and among individual women in our total sample.

What social mechanisms were behind these correlations? Family planning opportunities (including contraception) are greater in Brazil now than they used to be. However, experience in Africa, Asia, and Latin America has shown that mere access to contraception does not ensure family planning (Manoff 1994). Rather, popular demand for contraception must be created. Often, as in India (see photo on p. 431), this is done through "social marketing," including planned multimedia campaigns. In Brazil, however, there has been little direct use of TV to get people to limit their offspring. How, then, has television influenced Brazilians to plan smaller families?

We noticed that Brazilian TV families tend to have fewer children than traditional small-town Brazilians do. Narrative form and production costs limit the number of players in each telenovela (nightly soap opera) to about 50 characters. Telenovelas usually are gender-balanced and include three-generation extended families of different social classes, so that some of the main characters can "rise in life" by marrying up. These narrative conventions limit the number of young children per TV family. We concluded that people's ideas about proper family size are influenced as they see, day after day, nuclear families smaller than the traditional ones in their towns. Furthermore, the aim of commercial television is to sell products and lifestyles. Brazilian TV families routinely are shown enjoying consumer goods and lives of leisure, to which viewers learn to aspire. Telenovelas may convey the idea that viewers can achieve such lifestyles by emulating the apparent family planning of TV characters. The effect of Brazilian television on family planning seems to

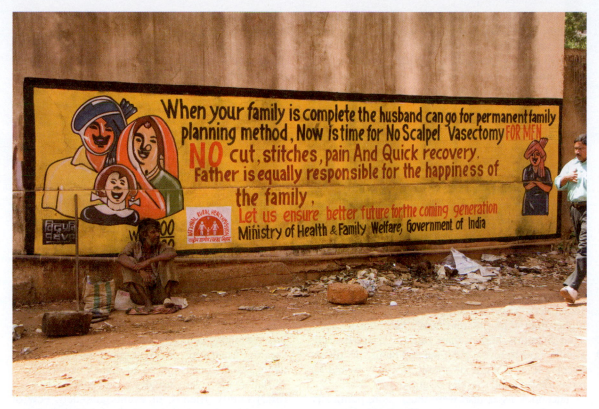

When your family is complete the husband can go for permanent family planning method, Now is time for No Scalpel Vasectomy FOR MEN NO cut, stitches, pain And Quick recovery. Father is equally responsible for the happiness of the family, Let us ensure better future for the coming generation Ministry of Health & Family Welfare, Government of India

In some countries, popular demand for birth control has been created through multimedia campaigns, illustrated by this poster in Panaji, Goa, India. In Brazil, there has been little direct use of TV to get people to limit their offspring. How, then, has television influenced Brazilians to plan smaller families?

be a corollary of a more general, TV-influenced shift from traditional toward more liberal social attitudes. Anthropologist Janet Dunn's (2000) further fieldwork in Brazil has demonstrated how TV exposure actually works to influence reproductive choice and family planning.

## Networking and Sociability On- and Offline

For generations, anthropologists have stressed the linking social functions (alliance creation) of such ages-old institutions as marriage and trade. Today's world offers some radically new ways to connect socially. Aaron Sorkin chose *The Social Network* as the title for his movie about the founding of Facebook, which (like LinkedIn) is precisely that—a social networking site (SNS), where people go to get linked in cyberspace. We already have seen (p. 430) that modern media allow local people access to connections that provide contact, information, entertainment, and potential social validation. Among Brazilians, we saw that extensive media use reflects an external orientation, a general wish for connections—a social network—beyond what is locally and routinely available.

Brazil is rapidly increasing its Internet access and its use of social media. During the last decade, as the Brazilian middle class has grown, Internet access has spread across the country, although it remains unreliable in small communities along the Amazon and rural areas in general. About 40 percent of Brazilians are now online, compared with about 80 percent of Americans. Most of those online Brazilians (68 million of about 78 million) use Facebook, which has been free on cell phones since 2010 (Richard Pace, personal communication). Brazil is now second in the world in number of Facebook, Twitter, and YouTube users (Holmes 2013). As of 2013, 35 percent of all Brazilians were on Facebook, compared with 51 percent of all Americans. Facebook's recent growth rate in Brazil has been phenomenal, with 30 million new users added between 2012 and 2013 (Richard Pace, personal communication). Offline, Brazilians are inherently social people, and they seem to be transferring this sociability to the online world. As in the United States, SNSs reinforce family connections while establishing and maintaining contacts in a wider world of nonrelatives.

Research in the United States provides additional evidence that SNSs enhance social connectivity, rather than (as some have feared) isolating people and truncating their social relationships. Through survey research, the Pew Research Center's ongoing Internet & American Life Project has investigated how the use of SNSs is related to trust, social support, and political engagement (see Hampton et al. 2011). In a 2010–2011 Pew study, 79 percent of American adults (aged 18 and over) said they used the Internet, and 59 percent of those users participated in at least one SNS. Facebook was dominant, attracting 92 percent of SNS users, compared with

18 percent for LinkedIn, and 13 percent for Twitter. Slightly more than half the Facebook users were daily users of that site, where the typical visitor was most likely (in this order) to "like" another user's post, comment on a post or status, comment on a posted photo, update his or her own status, or send a private message.

In the Pew study, as SNS use increased, so did measures of trust, sociability, and political engagement. Internet users overall were twice as likely as nonusers to say people can be trusted, with Facebookers especially trusting and socially oriented. Those who visited Facebook multiple times each day (heavy Facebook users) were 43 percent more likely than other Internet users (and three times as likely as non-Internet users) to say most people can be trusted. The average heavy Facebook user also identified more "close ties" in his or her overall social network than did other Internet users. In terms of support and companionship provided by their social networks, Internet users scored 3 to 6 points higher than nonusers, and heavy Facebookers averaged 5 points higher than Internet users overall. People have to reveal personal and family details on Facebook, so it's not surprising that they would be more trusting and socially oriented.

Facebook users also were much more politically engaged than most Americans. The Pew survey was conducted over the November 2010 elections. At that time, 10 percent of respondents had attended a political rally, 23 percent had tried to convince someone to vote for a specific candidate, and 66 percent had

voted or intended to vote. Internet users were significantly more likely than offliners to attend political meetings, to vote, and to try to influence someone else's vote. Here again, heavy Facebook users stood out as even more likely than the average Internet user to do those things.

What kind of relationships does Facebook support and reinforce? In this order, one's Facebook "friends" are likely to be a high school friend, an extended family member, a coworker, a college friend, an immediate family member, a member of one's club or group, and, finally, a neighbor. Only 7 percent of Facebook friends are people whom users have never met in person (Hampton et al. 2011).

In another Pew Internet study, Kate Purcell (2013) describes how Americans increasingly are sharing action images of their lives and social connections. The percentage (31 percent) of American adult Internet users posting video online doubled between 2009 and 2013. Of American adults who use SNSs, 71 percent have displayed a video. As is true of Internet use generally, online video use is greatest among younger, better-educated, and higher-earning Americans, with younger users twice as likely as older ones to post and share videos online.

Self-made videos usually are personal, showing (off?) family, friends, or events attended. Few of these videos have been carefully staged or scripted. More than twice as many (78 percent) watch as post (31 percent). People now get their entertainment online, as well as from TV and movies. Comedy and educational videos are most popular, along with how-to and music videos. People aged 18–29 are twice as likely as those 50 and older to watch music videos or animation. Men are more likely than women to view videos featuring sports (49 versus 23 percent), politics (40–30 percent), and adult content (25–8 percent).

While Internet use thrives among the young, educated, and affluent (in the United States and worldwide), a significant chunk (15–20 percent) of the populace remains cut off from the connectivity available online (Zickuhr 2013). In a few (mainly rural) areas of the United States, access remains unavailable or limited. Cost (e.g., of computer and broadband) is another limitation. Forty-four percent of Americans aged 65 and older lack connectivity, versus only 2 percent of those aged 18–29. Of Americans who never finished high school, 41 percent lack Internet access, compared with only 4 percent of college graduates (Ortutay 2013). Millions of Americans, therefore, remain isolated offline because of their advanced age or limited educations. One-third of the offliners claim to be uninterested in using the Internet, to be unwilling to try it, or to not need the Internet. The remainder cite various obstacles to going online, including affordability and availability (Zickuhr 2013). In an increasingly interconnected world, these obstacles and excuses will surely diminish, as an ever greater percentage of the U.S. and the world goes online.

Indonesians use their mobile devices to access Facebook in Jakarta—suggesting the extent to which the use of social media has become a global phenomenon.

## SPORTS AND CULTURE

We now turn to the cultural context of sports and the cultural values expressed in them. Because so much of what we know about sports comes from the media, this section also extends our consideration of the pervasive role of the mass media in contemporary life. This section mainly describes how sports and the media *reflect* culture. Sports and the media *influence* culture as well, as we saw in the discussion of how Brazilian television modifies social attitudes and family planning. Does it surprise you that the influence of media (and sports) on culture and vice versa are reciprocal?

## American Football

On fall Saturdays, millions of Americans travel to and from college football games. Smaller congregations meet in high school stadiums. Millions of Americans watch televised football. Indeed, nearly half the adult population of the United States watches the Super Bowl, which attracts people of diverse ages, ethnic backgrounds, regions, religions, political parties, jobs, social statuses, levels of wealth, and genders.

The popularity of football, particularly professional football, depends directly on the mass media. Is football, with its territorial incursion, hard hitting, and violence, popular because Americans are violent people? Are football spectators vicariously realizing their own hostile and aggressive tendencies? The anthropologist W. Arens (1981) has discounted this interpretation, arguing that if football were a particularly effective channel for expressing aggression, it would have spread (like soccer and baseball) to many other countries, where people have as many aggressive tendencies and hostile feelings as Americans do. He concludes reasonably that the explanation for football's popularity must lie elsewhere.

Arens contends that football is popular because it symbolizes certain key aspects of American life. In particular, it features teamwork based on division of labor, which is a pervasive feature of contemporary life. Susan Montague and Robert Morais (1981) take the analysis a step further. They link football's values, particularly teamwork, to those associated with business. Like corporate workers, the ideal players are diligent and dedicated to the team. Within corporations, however, decision making is complicated, and workers aren't always rewarded for their dedication and good job performance. Decisions are simpler and rewards are more consistent in football, these anthropologists contend, and this helps explain its popularity. Even if we can't figure out how ExxonMobil or Microsoft runs, any fan can become an expert on football's rules, teams, scores, statistics, and patterns of play. Even more important, football suggests that the values stressed by business really do pay off. Teams whose members work the hardest, show the most spirit, and best develop and coordinate their talents can be expected to win more often than other teams do.

## What Determines International Sports Success?

Why do countries excel at particular sports? Why do certain nations pile up dozens of Olympic medals, while others win only a handful? It isn't simply a matter of rich and poor, developed and underdeveloped, or even governmental or other institutional support of promising athletes. It isn't even a question of a "national will to win," for although certain nations stress winning even more than Americans do, a cultural focus on winning doesn't necessarily lead to the desired result.

Cultural values, social forces, and the media influence international sports success. We can see this by contrasting the United States and Brazil, two countries with continental proportions and large, physically and ethnically diverse populations. Although each is its continent's major economic power, they offer revealing contrasts in Olympic success: In the 2012 London Summer Olympics, the United States won 104 medals, including 46 gold medals, compared with 17 and 3 respectively for Brazil.

Americans' interest in sports has been honed over the years by an ever-growing media establishment, which provides a steady stream of games, matches, playoffs, championships, and analyses. Cable and satellite TV offer almost constant sports coverage, including packages for every major sport and season. The Super Bowl is a national event. The Olympic games get extensive coverage and attract significant audiences. Brazilian television, by contrast, traditionally has offered less sports coverage, with no nationally televised annual event comparable to the Super Bowl. The World (soccer) Cup, held every 4 years, is the only sports event that consistently draws huge national audiences.

In international competition, a win by a Brazilian team or the occasional nationally known individual athlete is felt to bring respect to the entire nation, but the Brazilian media are strikingly intolerant of losers. When the now legendary swimmer Ricardo Prado swam for his silver medal in the finals of the 400 Individual Medley (IM), during prime time on national TV in 1984, one newsmagazine observed that "it was as though he was the country with a swimsuit on, jumping in the pool in a collective search for success" (*Isto É* 1984). Prado's own feelings confirmed the magazine, "When I was on the stands, I thought of just one thing: what they'll think of the result in Brazil." After beating his old world record by 1.33 seconds, in a second-place finish, Prado told a fellow team member, "I think I did everything right. I feel like a winner, but will they think I'm a loser in Brazil?" Prado contrasted the situations of Brazilian and American athletes. The United States has, he said, so many athletes that no single one has to summarize the country's hopes (*Veja* 1984*a*). Fortunately, Brazil did seem to value Prado's performance, which was responsible for "Brazil's best result ever in Olympic swimming" (*Veja* 1984*a*). Labeling Prado "the man of silver," the media never tired of characterizing his main event, the 400 IM, in which he once had held the world record, as the most challenging event in swimming. However, the kind words for Ricardo Prado did not extend to the rest of the Brazilian team. The press lamented their "succession of failures" (*Veja* 1984*a*). (Brazil finally got swimming gold at the 2008 games in Beijing, with César Cielo Filho winning the 50-meter freestyle race.)

Because Brazilian athletes are viewed as stand-ins for their entire country, and because team sports are emphasized, the Brazilian media focus too exclusively on winning. Winning, of course, is also an American cultural value, particularly for team sports, as in Brazil. American football coaches are famous for comments like "Winning isn't everything; it's the only thing" and "Show me a good loser and I'll show you a loser." However, and particularly for sports such as running, swimming, diving, gymnastics, and skating, which focus on the individual, and in which American athletes usually do well, American culture also admires "moral victories," "personal bests," "comeback athletes," and "Special Olympics" and commends those who run good races without finishing first. In amateur and individual sports, American culture tells us that hard work and personal improvement can be as important as winning.

Americans are so accustomed to being told their culture overemphasizes winning that they may find it hard to believe other cultures value it even more. Brazil certainly does. Brazilian sports enthusiasts are preoccupied with world records, probably because only a win (as in soccer) or a best time (as in swimming) can make Brazil indisputably, even if temporarily, the best in the world at something. Prado's former world record in the 400 IM was mentioned constantly in the press prior to his Olympic swim. Such a best-time standard also provides Brazilians with a ready basis to fault a swimmer or runner for not going fast enough, when he or she doesn't make previous times. One might predict, accurately, that sports with more subjective standards would not be very popular in Brazil. Brazilians like to assign blame to athletes who fail them, and negative comments about gymnasts or divers are more difficult, because grace and execution can't be quantified as easily as time can.

Brazilians, I think, value winning so much because it is rare. In the United States, resources are more abundant, chances to achieve more numerous, and poverty less pervasive. American society has room for many winners. Brazilian society is more stratified; together the middle class and the small elite group at the top comprise just about half of the national population. Brazilian sports echo lessons from the larger society: Victories are scarce and usually reserved for the privileged few.

## Being versus Doing

The factors believed to contribute to sports success belong to a larger context of cultural values. Particularly relevant is the contrast between ascribed and achieved status. Individuals have little control over their ascribed statuses (e.g., age, gender); these depend on what one *is* rather than what one *does*. On the other hand, people have more control over their achieved statuses (e.g., student, golfer, tennis player). American culture emphasizes achieved over ascribed status: We are supposed to make of our lives what we will and can. Success comes through achievement. An American's identity emerges as a result of what he or she does.

In Brazil, on the other hand, identity rests not so much on doing as on being, on what one is from the start—a strand in a web of personal connections, originating in social class and the extended family. Social position and network membership contribute substantially to individual fortune, and all social life is hierarchical. High-status Brazilians don't stand patiently in line as Americans do. Important people expect their business to be attended to immediately, and social inferiors readily yield. The final resort in any conversation is "Do you know who you're talking to?" The American opposite, reflecting our democratic and egalitarian ethos, is "Who do you think you are?" (DaMatta 1991).

The following description of a Brazilian judo medalist (as reported by *Veja* magazine) illustrates the importance of ascribed status and privilege.

> Walter Carmona began judo at age six and became a São Paulo champion at twelve. . . . Carmona . . . is fully supported by his father, a factory owner. Walter Carmona's life has been comfortable—he has been able to study and dedicate himself to judo without worries. (*Veja* 1984*b*, p. 61)

Faced with an athlete from a well-off family, American reporters, by contrast, rarely conclude that privilege is the main reason for success. American media almost always focus on some aspect of doing, some special personal triumph or achievement. Often, this involves the athlete's struggle with adversity (illness, injury, pain, or the death of a parent, sibling, friend, or coach). The featured athlete is presented as not only successful but noble and self-sacrificing as well.

Given the Brazilian focus on ascribed status, the guiding assumption is that one cannot do more than what one is. One year the Brazilian Olympic Committee sent no female swimmers to the Summer Olympics, because none had made arbitrarily established cutoff times. This excluded a South American record holder, while swimmers with slower times were attending from other countries. No one seemed

At the 2012 London Summer Olympics, Brazilian judoist Maria Suelen Altheman celebrates her victory over Gulzhan Issanova of Kazakstan. This win advanced Altheman to the bronze medal judo match in her weight category.

Athletes internalize these values. Brazilians assume that if you go into an event with a top seed time, as Ricardo Prado did, you've got a chance to win a medal. Prado's second-place finish made perfect sense back home, because his former world record had been bettered before the race began.

Given the overwhelming value American culture places on work, it might seem surprising that our media devote so much attention to unforeseen results and so little to the years of training, preparation, and competition that underlie Olympic performance. It probably is assumed that hard work is so obvious and fundamental that it goes without saying. Or perhaps the assumption is that by the time athletes actually enter Olympic competition all are so similar (the American value of equality) that only mysterious and chance factors can explain variable success. The American focus on the unexpected applies to losses as well as wins. Such concepts as chance, fate, mystery, and uncertainty are viewed as legitimate reasons for defeat. Runners and skaters fall; ligaments tear; a gymnast "inexplicably" falls off the pommel horse.

Brazilians place more responsibility on the individual. Less is attributed to factors beyond human control. When individuals who should have performed well don't do so, they are blamed for their failures. It is, however, culturally appropriate in Brazil to use poor health as an excuse for losing. The American media, by contrast, talk much more about the injuries and illnesses of the victors than those of the losers.

to imagine that Olympic excitement might spur swimmers to extraordinary efforts.

American culture, supposedly so practical and realistic, has a remarkable faith in the possibility of coming from behind. These values are those of an achievement-oriented society where (ideally) "anything is possible" compared with an ascribed-status society in which it's over before it's begun. In American sports coverage, underdogs and unexpected results, virtually ignored by the Brazilian media, provide some of the "brightest" moments. Brazilian culture has little interest in the unexpected.

## The Fall from Grace: Golf and the Celebrity Scandal

We consider now another example of the sports–media intersection—the world of golf and of celebrity within it. Golf's popularity has been growing, not only in the United States but also in Europe,

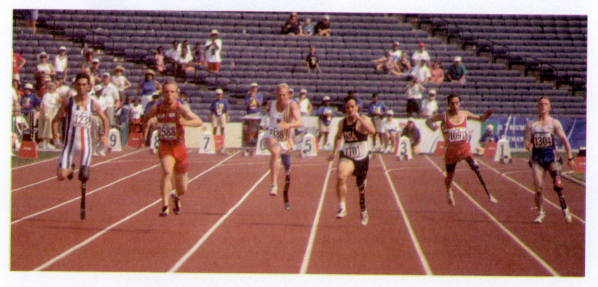

Reflecting larger cultural values, Americans usually do well in sports that emphasize individual achievement. "Special Olympics" and Paralympics, which is shown here in Atlanta, Georgia, commend people who run good races without being the best in the world.

Asia, and Australia. More than 20 million Americans play golf, an industry that also supports about 400,000 workers (Starn 2011). For decades, golf has been the preferred sport of business tycoons and politicians. President Dwight D. Eisenhower (1953–1960), whose love for golf was well known, etched a lasting (and accurate) image of golf as a Republican sport (despite the fact that Presidents Bill Clinton and Barack Obama also play the game). A recent survey found that only 2 of the top 125 PGA touring pros identified as Democrats (Starn 2011).

A glance at golfers in any televised game reveals a remarkable lack of variation in skin color. Although golf was the last major sport to desegregate, minorities traditionally have played supporting roles in American golf. Until the motorized golf cart replaced them, African Americans had significant opportunities to observe and learn the game by caddying. Indeed, there once was a tradition of African American caddies becoming excellent golfers. In terms of diversity, the sport has regressed since the 1970s, when 11 African Americans played on the PGA tour. If we consider multiracial players to be African American, there currently is only 1 African American (Tiger Woods) among the 125 top players on the PGA tour (Starn 2011).

Economic factors play a key role in limiting minority access. Prospective golfers need money for instruction, equipment, access to top-notch courses, and travel to tournaments (Starn 2011). Asian Americans, who enjoy a relatively high socioeconomic status, are the only minority group in the United States with a growing representation in golf, for both men and women.

Remarkable in this mainly white, affluent, Republican sport has been a single exceptional individual—a true champion called Tiger Woods. The Woods image rested not only on his success in golf but also on his reputation as a devoted family man, first as the ambitious and achieving son of an Asian mother and an African American father, second as husband and father to his Scandinavian wife and two children. Tiger Woods became one of the most admired men in America. It even has been suggested that his reputation as a successful and trustworthy multiracial African American man helped pave the way for Barack Obama's 2008 election as president of the United States (Starn 2011). In his 2011 book *The Passion of Tiger Woods: An Anthropologist Reports on Golf, Race, and Celebrity Scandal*, Orin Starn offers an anthropological take on the rise and fall of Tiger Woods.

On the upside of an achievement-oriented society is major success—rising to the top, becoming a star; on the downside is failure—a fall from grace. The American expression "the bigger they are, the harder they fall" applies easily to American celebrities, ranging from sports and entertainment figures to

politicians. Increasingly familiar to all Americans (because of the growth and ubiquity of the media) is the celebrity scandal and its stages. First, a transgression of some sort (usually involving sex) becomes publicly known, and a media frenzy follows. After a period of public humiliation and ridicule, the celebrity issues a well-publicized apology, ideally with an aggrieved loved one close at hand. Various other acts of atonement are expected to follow, but they aren't always publicly known. If the apology and atonement are accepted by the public, the scandal begins to fade. If there is no repeat transgression, the celebrity can find eventual redemption through rehabilitation, reform, or a lifestyle change.

Americans have witnessed this process several times in recent years—most often with politicians. Examples include President Bill Clinton, Idaho senator Larry Craig, Louisiana senator David Vitter, New York governor Eliot Spitzer, and vice presidential candidate John Edwards. Former South Carolina governor (and now South Carolina congressman) Mark Sanford famously claimed a fictitious hike on the Appalachian Trail to conceal a visit to Buenos Aires and his Argentinian lover. Serial sexter and former congressman Anthony Weiner has gone through the process (at least) twice. His first fall from grace led to his resignation from the United States Congress. His second round of infractions derailed his 2013 candidacy for mayor of New York City. Initially perceived as appropriately repentant and reformed, Weiner's reputation sank again as media reports revealed more recent (and postrepentance) sexting episodes.

Celebrities who fall in this way almost always are men. Female celebrity scandals (e.g., Lindsay Lohan, Miley Cyrus) typically feature media reports

Brandon Keeler, age 18 in this 2008 photo, worked then as a caddy at the Detroit Golf Club in Detroit, Michigan. Keeler, now a biomedical engineer, graduated from Yale University in 2012. Although, there once was a tradition of African-American caddies becoming excellent golfers, there currently is only one top-tier African-American golfer.

of serial erratic and/or unlawful behavior, changes in body image (such as noticeable weight gain or loss), and accusations of being out of control, followed by healing via some form of seclusion and/or rehabilitation. In the luckiest cases, redemption leads to career rejuvenation.

In sports, the most celebrated scandal in recent years features Tiger Woods as its central figure (see Starn 2011). The fall from grace began late in 2009, with media reports of his post-Thanksgiving, post-midnight car crash into a fire hydrant and his wife's use of a golf club to shatter a window of the vehicle. Preceding that crash, a tabloid story had accused the golfer of an extramarital tryst. A media frenzy built up after the crash, as additional extramarital affairs were reported and it became apparent that Tiger Woods was a serial philanderer. His fall was particularly steep, because the golfer had been so successful and admired, and because he had managed his image so carefully and effectively.

That image was one of an unusually talented nonwhite player in a sport traditionally dominated by whites. The golfer's transgression and ensuing public humiliation and trial by media were followed by the inevitable apology and period of atonement (although his marriage did not survive), leading to Wood's gradual reintegration into the world of golf. Signifying his reintegration, he received the 2013 PGA (Professional Golfers' Association) Tour Player of the Year Award. He had won 5 of the 16 tournaments he played in that year and placed in the top 10 in 3 others. Tiger Woods may be back, but he is no longer the untarnished alpha golf champion of yesteryear. This fall from grace, for now at least, seems to have run its course.

# for REVIEW

## summary

1. Even if they lack a word for "art," people everywhere do associate an aesthetic experience with objects and events having certain qualities. The arts, sometimes called "expressive culture," include the visual arts, literature (written and oral), music, and theater arts. Some issues raised about religion also apply to art. If we adopt a special attitude or demeanor when confronting a sacred object, do we display something similar with art? Much art has been done in association with religion. In tribal performances, the arts and religion often mix. But non-Western art isn't always linked to religion.

2. The special places where we find art include museums, concert halls, opera houses, and theaters. However, the boundary between what's art and what's not may be blurred. Variation in art appreciation is especially common in contemporary society, with its professional artists and critics and great cultural diversity.

3. Those who work with non-Western art have been criticized for ignoring individual artists and for focusing too much on the social context and collective artistic production. Art is work, albeit creative work. In state societies, some people manage to support themselves as full-time artists. In nonstates, artists are normally part-time. Community standards judge the mastery and completion displayed in a work of art. Typically, the arts are exhibited, evaluated, performed, and appreciated in society. Music, which often is performed in groups, is among the most social of the arts. Folk art, music, and lore are the expressive culture of ordinary, usually rural, people.

4. Art can stand for tradition, even when traditional art is removed from its original context. Art can express community sentiment, with political goals used to call attention to social issues. Often, art is meant to commemorate and to last. Growing acceptance of the anthropological definition of culture has guided the humanities beyond fine art, elite art, and Western art to the creative expressions of the masses and of many cultures. Myths, legends, tales, and the art of storytelling often play important roles in the transmission of culture.

5. The arts go on changing, although certain art forms have survived for thousands of years. Countries and cultures are known for particular contributions. Today, a huge "arts and leisure" industry links Western and non-Western art forms in an international network with both aesthetic and commercial dimensions.

6. Any media-borne message can be analyzed as a text, something that can be "read"—that is, processed, interpreted, and assigned meaning by

anyone exposed to it. People use media to validate beliefs, indulge fantasies, seek out messages, make social comparisons, relieve frustrations, chart social courses, and resist unequal power relations. The media can provide common ground for social groups. Length of home TV exposure is a useful measure of the impact of television on values, attitudes, and beliefs. The effect of Brazilian television on family planning seems to be a corollary of a more general TV-influenced shift from traditional toward more liberal social attitudes. Use of online social networking sites (SNSs) correlates with overall social connectivity and sociability, including measures of trust, companionship, and political involvement.

7. Much of what we know about sports comes from the media. Both sports and the media reflect and influence culture. Football symbolizes and simplifies certain key aspects of American life and values (e.g., hard work and teamwork). Cultural values, social forces, and the media influence international sports success. In amateur and individual sports, American culture tells us that hard work and personal improvement can be as important as winning. Other cultures, such as Brazil, may value winning even more than Americans do. The factors believed to contribute to sports success belong to a larger context of cultural values. Particularly relevant is the contrast between ascribed and achieved status: being versus doing. An American's identity emerges as a result of what he or she does. In Brazil, by contrast, identity rests on being: what one is from the start—a strand in a web of personal connections, originating in social class and the extended family. The media-driven celebrity scandal, whether in politics, entertainment, or sports, can be analyzed as a social drama with four known stages: breech, public reaction, atonement, and reintegration.

## key terms

aesthetics 418

art 418

arts 417

catharsis 424

ethnomusicology 422

expressive culture 417

folk 422

text 429

## critical thinking

1. Recall the last time you were in an art museum. What did you like, and why? How much of your aesthetic tastes can you attribute to your education, to your culture? How much do you think responds to your own individual tastes? How can you make the distinction?

2. Think of a musical composition or performance you consider to be art, but whose status as such is debatable. How would you convince someone else that it is art? What kinds of arguments against your position would you expect to hear?

3. Can you think of a political dispute involving art or the arts? What were the different positions being debated?

4. Media consumers actively select, evaluate, and interpret media in ways that make sense to them. People use media for all sorts of reasons. What are some examples? Which are most relevant to the way you consume, and maybe even creatively alter and produce, media?

5. This chapter describes how sports and the media *reflect* culture. Can you come up with examples of how sports and media *influence* culture?

# The World System and Colonialism

▶ When and why did the world system develop, and what is it like today?

▶ When and how did European colonialism develop, and how is its legacy expressed in postcolonial studies?

▶ How do colonialism, neoliberalism, development, and industrialization exemplify intervention philosophies?

In Kebili, Tunisia, two Bedouin men use a laptop in the desert. Might they be uploading a photo of their camel to Instagram?

# understanding OURSELVES

In our 21st-century world system, people are linked as never before by modern means of transportation and communication. Descendants of villages that hosted ethnographers a generation ago now live transnational lives. For me, some of the most vivid illustrations of this new transnationalism come from Madagascar. They begin in Ambalavao, a town in southern Betsileo country, where I rented a small house in 1966–1967.

By 1966, Madagascar had gained independence from France, but its towns still had foreigners to remind them of colonialism. Besides my wife and me, Ambalavao had at least a dozen world-system agents, including an Indian cloth merchant, Chinese grocers, and a few French people. Two young men in the French equivalent of the Peace Corps were there teaching school. One of them, Noel, lived across the street from a prominent local family. Since Noel often spoke disparagingly of the Malagasy, I was surprised to see him courting a young woman from this family. She was Lenore, the sister of Leon, a schoolteacher who became my good friend.

My next trip to Madagascar was a brief visit in February 1981. I had to spend a few days in Antananarivo, the capital. There I was confined each evening to the newly built Hilton hotel by a curfew imposed after a civil insurrection. I shared the hotel with a group of Russian military pilots,

there to teach the Malagasy to defend their island, strategically placed in the Indian Ocean, against imagined enemies. Later, I went down to Betsileo country to visit Leon, my schoolteacher friend from Ambalavao, who had become a prominent politician. Unfortunately for me, he was in Moscow, participating in a 3-month exchange program.

During my next visit to Madagascar, in summer 1990, I met Emily, the 22-year-old daughter of Noel and Lenore, whose courtship I had witnessed in 1967. One of her aunts brought Emily to meet me at my hotel in Antananarivo. Emily was about to visit several cities in the United States, where she planned to study marketing. I met her again just a few months later in Gainesville, Florida. She asked me about her father, whom she had never met. She had sent several letters to France, but Noel had never responded.

Descendants of Ambalavao are dispersed globally. Emily, a child of colonialism, had aunts in France (Malagasy women married to French men) and another in Switzerland (a retired diplomat). Members of her family, which is not especially wealthy, have traveled to Russia, Canada, the United States, France, Germany, and West Africa. How many of your classmates, including perhaps you, yourself, have recent transnational roots? A descendant of a Kenyan village (although not born there himself) is a twice-elected president of the United States.

Although fieldwork in small communities is anthropology's hallmark, isolated groups are impossible to find today. Truly isolated human societies probably never have existed. For thousands of years, human groups have been in contact with one another. Local societies always have participated in a larger system, which today has global dimensions. We call it the *modern world system,* by which we mean a world in which nations are economically and politically interdependent.

# THE WORLD SYSTEM

The world system and the relations among the countries within it are shaped by the capitalist world economy (see White 2009). A huge increase in international trade during and after the 15th century led to the **capitalist world economy** (Wallerstein 2004; Wallerstein et al. 2013), a single world system committed to production for sale or exchange, with the object of maximizing profits rather than supplying domestic needs. **Capital** refers to wealth or resources invested in business, with the intent of using the means of production to make a profit.

World-system theory can be traced to the French social historian Fernand Braudel. In his three-volume work *Civilization and Capitalism, 15th–18th Century* (1981, 1982, 1992), Braudel argued that society consists of interrelated parts assembled into a system. Societies are subsystems of larger systems, with the world system the largest. The key claim of **world-system theory** is that an identifiable social system, featuring wealth and power differentials, extends beyond individual countries. That system has been formed by a set of economic and political relations that has characterized much of the globe since the 16th century, when the Old World established regular contact with the Americas (see Bodley 2003).

According to Wallerstein (1982, 2004), countries within the world system occupy three different positions of economic and political power: core, periphery, and semiperiphery (see also Wallerstein, Rojas, and Lemert 2012). The **core,** the dominant position, includes the strongest and most powerful nations. In core nations, "the complexity of economic activities and the level of capital accumulation is the greatest" (Thompson 1983, p. 12). With its sophisticated technologies and mechanized production, the core churns out products that flow mainly to other core countries. Some also go to the periphery and semiperiphery. According to Arrighi (2010), the core monopolizes the most profitable activities, especially the control of world finance.

The **semiperiphery** is intermediate between the core and the periphery. Contemporary nations of the semiperiphery are industrialized. Like core nations, they export both industrial goods and commodities, but they lack the power and economic dominance of core nations. Thus, Brazil, a semiperiphery nation, exports automobiles to Nigeria (a periphery nation) and auto engines, orange juice extract, coffee, and shrimp to the United States (a core nation). The **periphery** includes the world's least privileged and powerful countries. Economic activities there are less mechanized than are those in the semiperiphery, although some degree of industrialization has reached even periphery nations. The periphery produces raw materials, agricultural commodities, and, increasingly, human labor for export to the core and the semiperiphery (Shannon 1996).

In the United States and Western Europe today, immigration—legal and illegal—from the periphery and semiperiphery supplies cheap labor for agriculture. U.S. states as distant as California, Michigan, and South Carolina make significant use of farm labor from Mexico. The availability of relatively cheap workers from noncore nations such as Mexico (in the United States) and Turkey (in Germany) benefits farmers and business owners in core countries while supplying remittances to families in the semiperiphery and periphery. As a result of 21st-century telecommunications technology, cheap labor doesn't even need to migrate to the United States. Thousands of families in India are being supported as American companies "outsource" jobs—from telephone assistance to software engineering—to nations outside the core (see this chapter's "Focus on Globalization" on p. 448).

## The Emergence of the World System

By the 15th century, Europeans were profiting from a transoceanic trade-oriented economy, and people worldwide entered Europe's sphere of influence. What was new was the trans-Atlantic component of a long history of Old World sailing and commerce. As early as 600 B.C.E., the Phoenicians/Carthaginians sailed around Britain on regular trade routes and circumnavigated Africa. Likewise, Indonesia and Africa have been linked in Indian Ocean trade for at least 2,000 years. In the 15th century, Europe established regular contact with Asia, Africa, and eventually the New World (the Caribbean and the Americas). Christopher Columbus's first voyage from Spain to the Bahamas and the Caribbean in 1492 was soon followed by additional voyages. These journeys opened the way for a major exchange of people, resources, products, ideas, and diseases, as the Old and New Worlds were forever linked (Crosby 2003; Diamond 1997; Mann 2011). Led by Spain and Portugal, Europeans extracted silver and gold, conquered the natives (taking some as slaves), and colonized their lands.

The frequency and nature of conflict, violence, and warfare vary among the world's cultures. This chapter's "Appreciating Diversity" on pp. 442–443 examines a debate about the origin and characteristics of warfare among Native Americans. Did European contact play a role in fostering increased violence? The *Columbian exchange* is the term for the spread of people, resources, products, ideas, and diseases between Eastern and Western Hemispheres after contact. As you read "Appreciating Diversity," consider the impact of trade, disease, and slave raiding on Native Americans, including conflict and warfare.

Previously in Europe as throughout the world, rural people had produced mainly for their own

---

**capitalist world economy**
Profit-oriented global economy based on production for sale or exchange.

**capital**
Wealth invested with the intent of producing profit.

**world-system theory**
Idea that a discernible social system, based on wealth and power differentials, transcends individual countries.

**core**
Dominant position in the world system; nations with advanced systems of production.

**semiperiphery**
Position in the world system intermediate between core and periphery.

**periphery**
Weakest structural and economic position in the world system.

# appreciating DIVERSITY

## Bones Reveal Some Truth in "Noble Savage" Myth

Conflict and violence are variable aspects of human diversity. Here we examine an anthropological debate about the origin and nature of warfare and the role of European contact in fostering conflicts among indigenous peoples in the Americas. Violence among Native Americans did increase after contact. As the article begins, it suggests, mistakenly, that Native Americans lived in prehistory and lacked "civilization." In fact, Native Americans developed states and "civilizations" (e.g., Aztec, Maya, Inca) comparable to those of the Old World (e.g., ancient Mesopotamia and Egypt). Native Americans, most notably the Maya, also developed writing, which they used to record their history—rendering the label "prehistory" inaccurate. As you read, to understand why violence increased after contact, pay attention to the role of trade, disease, and slave raiding.

A romantic-sounding notion dating back more than 200 years has it that people in prehistory, such as Native Americans, lived in peace and harmony.

Then "civilization" showed up, sowing violence and discord. Some see this claim as naive. It even has a derisive nickname, the "noble savage myth." But new research seems to suggest the "myth" contains at least some truth. Researchers examined thousands of Native American skeletons and found that those from after Christopher Columbus landed in the New World showed a rate of traumatic injuries more than 50 percent higher than those from before the Europeans arrived.

"Traumatic injuries do increase really significantly," said Phillip L. Walker, an anthropology professor at the University of California at Santa Barbara, who conducted the study with Richard H. Steckel of Ohio State University.

The findings suggest "Native Americans were involved in more violence after the Europeans arrived than before," Walker said. But he emphasized there was also widespread violence before the Europeans came. Nevertheless, he said, "probably we're just seeing the tip of the iceberg" as far as the difference between violence levels before and after. That's because as many as half of bullet wounds miss the skeleton. Thus, the study couldn't detect much firearm violence, though some tribes wiped each other out using European-supplied guns.

The findings shed light on a controversy that has stirred not only living room discussions, but also an intense, sometimes ugly debate among anthropologists.

It involves two opposing views of human nature: Are we hard-wired for violence, or pushed into it?

Anthropologists who believe the latter seized on the findings as evidence for their view. "What it all says to me is that humans aren't demonic. Human

The encounter between Hernán Cortés (1485–1547) and Montezuma II (1466–1520) is the subject of this 1820 painting by Gallo Gallina of Milan, Italy. Cortés went on to conquer Montezuma's Aztec empire.

needs, growing their own food and making clothing, furniture, and tools from local products. People produced beyond their immediate needs in order to pay taxes and to purchase trade items, such as salt and iron. As late as 1650 the English diet, like diets in most of the world today, was based on locally grown starches (Mintz 1985). In the 200 years that followed, however, the English became extraordinary consumers of imported goods. One of the earliest and most popular of those goods was sugar (Mintz 1985).

Sugarcane, originally domesticated in Papua New Guinea, was first processed in India. Reaching Europe via the eastern Mediterranean, it was carried to the Americas by Columbus (Mintz 1985, 2007). The climate of Brazil and the Caribbean proved ideal for growing sugarcane, and Europeans built plantations there to supply the growing demand for sugar. This led to the development in the 17th century of a plantation economy based on a single cash crop—a system known as *monocrop* production.

The demand for sugar in a growing international market spurred the development of the trans-Atlantic slave trade and New World plantation economies based on slave labor. By the 18th century, an increased English demand for raw cotton had led to rapid settlement of what is now the southeastern males don't have an ingrained propensity for war. . . . They can learn to be very peaceful, or terribly violent," said R. Brian Ferguson, a professor of anthropology at Rutgers University in Newark. Ferguson contends that before about 10,000 years ago, war was virtually nonexistent. But experts on the opposing side also said the findings fit their views.

"A 50 percent increase is the equivalent of moving from a suburb to the city, in terms of violence," said Charles Stanish, a professor of anthropology at the University of California at Los Angeles. "This shows the Native Americans were like us. Under stress, they fought more." Both sides called the study, which was presented Friday at the annual meeting of the American Association of Physical Anthropologists in Buffalo, a valuable contribution. . . .

Walker and colleagues examined the skeletons of 3,375 pre-Columbian and 1,165 post-Columbian Native Americans, from archaeological sites throughout North and Central America.

The North Americans came mostly from the coasts and the Great Lakes region, Walker said.

Pre-Columbian skeletons showed an 11 percent incidence of traumatic injuries, he said, compared with almost 17 percent for the post-Columbians.

Walker said his findings surprised him. "I wasn't really expecting it," he said. Yet it undeniably suggests violence, he added. Most of the increase consisted of head injuries in young males, "which conforms pretty closely to the pattern you see today in homicides." The researchers defined "traumatic injury" as anything leaving a mark on the skeleton, such as a skull fracture, a healed broken arm, or an embedded arrow point or bullet.

Walker said that although part of the increased injury rate doubtless stems from violence by whites themselves, it probably reflects mostly native-on-native violence. "In a lot of cases, such as in California, there weren't that many Europeans around—just a few priests, and thousands of Indians," he said.

Walker said the higher injury rate could have many explanations. Increased violence is normally associated with more densely populated, settled life, which Native Americans experienced in modernity, he said. Disease could also touch off war, he said.

"Here in California, there was a lot of inter-village warfare associated with the introduction of European diseases. People would attribute the disease to evil shamanic activity in another village," he said. Ferguson cited other factors. The Europeans often drew natives into their imperial wars, he said.

"Sometimes, the Europeans would enable someone to pursue a preexisting fight more aggressively, by backing one side," he added. Other times, he said, Europeans got natives to conduct slave raids on one another. Natives also fought over control of areas around trading outposts, to become middlemen, he said. "Sometimes that was a life-or-death matter, since it meant the difference between who would get guns or not." Stanish agreed. "Obviously, having an expanding imperial power coming at you is going to exacerbate tensions," he said. . . . They're going to push you somewhere—into other groups."

"You're also going to get competition over access to the Europeans, who are a form of wealth," he added. Native Americans fought over areas rich in fur, which the whites would buy.

Yet Native American warfare was widespread long before that, Stanish said. . . .

Keith F. Otterbein, an anthropology professor at the State University of New York at Buffalo, said the skeleton findings contribute to a balanced, middle-of-the-road view.

"The folks who are saying there was no early warfare—they're wrong, too. There is, in fact, a myth of the peaceful savage," he said. Otterbein said the controversy won't end here; both sides are too ideologically entrenched.

"Underlying the 'noble savage' myth," Stanish said, "is a political agenda by both the far right and far left. The right tries to turn the 'savages' into our little brown brothers, who need to be pulled up. . . . On the left, they have another agenda, that the Western world is bad."

SOURCE: Jack Lucentini, "Bones Reveal Some Truth in 'Noble Savage Myth,'" *Washington Post*, April 15, 2002. Reprinted by permission of Jack Lucentini.

United States and the emergence there of another slave-based monocrop production system. Like sugar, cotton was a key trade item that fueled the growth of the world system.

## INDUSTRIALIZATION

By the 18th century the stage had been set for the **Industrial Revolution**—the historical transformation (in Europe, after 1750) of "traditional" into "modern" societies through industrialization. The seeds of industrial society had been planted well before the 18th century (Gimpel 1988). For example, a knitting machine invented in England in 1589 was so far ahead of its time that it played a profitable role in factories two and three centuries later. The appearance of cloth mills late in the Middle Ages foreshadowed the search for new sources of wind and water power that characterized the Industrial Revolution.

Industrialization required capital for investment. The established system of transoceanic commerce supplied that capital from the enormous profits it generated. As wealthy people invested in machines and engines to drive machines, capital and scientific innovation fueled invention. Industrialization increased production in both farming and manufacturing.

**Industrial Revolution**
In Europe, after 1750, socioeconomic transformation through industrialization.

From producer to consumer, in the modern world system. The top photo, taken in the Caribbean nation of Dominica, shows the hard labor required to extract sugar using a manual press. In the bottom photo, an English middle-class family enjoys afternoon tea, sweetened with imported sugar. Which of the ingredients in your breakfast today were imported?

European industrialization developed from, and eventually replaced, the *domestic system* of manufacture (home-handicraft system). In this system, an organizer-entrepreneur supplied the raw materials to workers in their homes and collected the finished products from them. The entrepreneur, whose sphere of operations might span several villages, owned the materials, paid for the work, and arranged the marketing.

## Causes of the Industrial Revolution

The Industrial Revolution began with cotton products, iron, and pottery. These were widely used items whose manufacture could be broken down into simple routine motions that machines could perform. When manufacturing moved from homes to factories, where machinery replaced handwork, agrarian societies evolved into industrial ones. As factories produced cheap staple goods, the Industrial Revolution led to a dramatic increase in production. Industrialization fueled urban growth and created a new kind of city, with factories crowded together in places where coal and labor were cheap.

The Industrial Revolution began in England, rather than in France (Figure 23.1, p. 446). Why? Unlike the English, the French didn't have to transform their domestic manufacturing system by industrializing. Faced with an increased need for products, with a late-18th-century population at least twice that of Great Britain, France could simply enlarge its domestic system of production by drawing in new homes. Thus, the French were able to increase production *without innovating*—they could grow the existing system rather than having to adopt a new one. To meet mounting demand for staples—at home and in its colonies—England had to industrialize.

As its industrialization proceeded, Britain's population began to increase dramatically. It doubled during the 18th century (especially after 1750) and did so again between 1800 and 1850. This demographic explosion fueled consumption, but British entrepreneurs couldn't meet the increased demand with the traditional production methods. This spurred experimentation, innovation, and rapid technological change.

English industrialization drew on national advantages in natural resources. Britain was rich in coal and iron ore and had navigable coasts and waterways. It was a seafaring island-nation located at the crossroads of international trade. These features gave Britain a favored position for importing raw materials and exporting manufactured goods. Another factor in England's industrial growth was the fact that much of its 18th-century colonial empire was occupied by English settler families, who looked to the mother country as they tried to replicate European civilization abroad. These colonies bought large quantities of English staples.

It also has been argued that particular cultural values and religion contributed to industrialization. Many members of the emerging English middle class were Protestant nonconformists. Their beliefs and values encouraged industry, thrift, the dissemination of new knowledge, inventiveness, and willingness to accept change (Weber 1904/1958).

## SOCIOECONOMIC EFFECTS OF INDUSTRIALIZATION

The socioeconomic effects of industrialization were mixed. English national income tripled between 1700 and 1815 and increased 30 times more by 1939. Standards of comfort rose, but prosperity was uneven. At first, factory workers got wages higher than those available in the domestic system. Later, however, owners started recruiting labor in places where living standards were low and labor (including that of women and children) was cheap. Filth and smoke polluted 19th-century cities. Housing was crowded and unsanitary. People experienced rampant disease and rising death rates. This was the world of Ebenezer Scrooge, Bob Cratchit, Tiny Tim—and Karl Marx.

## Industrial Stratification

The social theorists Karl Marx and Max Weber focused on the stratification systems associated with industrialization. From his observations in England and his analysis of 19th-century industrial capitalism, Marx (Marx and Engels 1848/1976) saw socioeconomic stratification as a sharp and simple division between two opposed classes: the bourgeoisie (capitalists) and the proletariat (propertyless workers). The bourgeoisie traced its origins to overseas ventures and the world capitalist economy, which had transformed the social structure of northwestern Europe, creating a wealthy commercial class (White 2009).

Industrialization shifted production from farms and cottages to mills and factories, where mechanical power was available and where workers could be assembled to operate heavy machinery. The **bourgeoisie** owned the factories, mines, estates,

*The Art of Stocking-Frame-Work-Knitting.*

*Engrav'd for the Universal Magazine 1750 for J. Hinton at the Kings Arms in St. Pauls Church Yard LONDON.*

In the home-handicraft, or domestic, system of production, an organizer supplied raw materials to workers in their homes and collected their products. Family life and work were intertwined, as in this English scene. Is there a modern equivalent to the domestic system of production?

and other means of production. Members of the **working class,** or **proletariat,** had to sell their labor to survive.

**bourgeoisie**
Owners of the means of production.

**working class (proletariat)**
People who must sell their labor to survive.

Large paintings of Karl Marx (1818–1883) on display in Tiananmen Square, Beijing, China.

**FIGURE 23.1** Location of England (United Kingdom) and France.

Industrialization and the rural-to-urban migration it fueled hastened the process of *proletarianization*—the separation of workers from the means of production. Bourgeoisie domination extended to the means of communication, the schools, and other key institutions. *Class consciousness* (recognition of collective interests and personal identification with one's economic group) was a vital part of Marx's view of class. He saw bourgeoisie and proletariat as socioeconomic divisions with radically opposed interests. Marx viewed classes as powerful collective forces that could mobilize human energies to influence the course of history. On the basis of their common experience, workers, he thought, would develop class consciousness, which could lead to revolutionary change. Although no proletarian revolution was to occur in England, workers did develop organizations to protect

their interests and increase their share of industrial profits. During the 19th century, trade unions and socialist parties emerged to express a rising anticapitalist spirit. The concerns of the English labor movement were to remove young children from factories and limit the hours during which women and children could work. The profile of stratification in industrial core nations gradually took shape. Capitalists controlled production, but labor was organizing for better wages and working conditions. By 1900 many governments had factory legislation and social-welfare programs. Mass living standards in core nations rose as population grew.

Today, the existence of publicly traded companies complicates the division between capitalists and workers. Through pension plans and personal investments, some workers have become part-owners

**TABLE 23.1**  U.S. National Income by Quintile, 2012

| | PERCENT SHARE OF NATIONAL INCOME | MEAN HOUSEHOLD INCOME |
|---|---|---|
| Top 20 percent | 51.0 | $181,905 |
| Second 20 percent | 23.0 | 82,098 |
| Third 20 percent | 14.4 | 51,179 |
| Fourth 20 percent | 8.3 | 29,696 |
| Bottom 20 percent | 3.2 | 11,490 |
| Top 5 percent | 22.3 | 318,052 |

SOURCE: J. Martel, "Income Analysis Shows Widening Gap," Bankrate.com, December 10, 2013. http://www.bankrate.com/finance/economics/income-gap-widening-1.aspx

rather than propertyless workers. Today's key capitalist isn't the factory owner, who may have been replaced by stockholders, but the CEO or the chair of the board of directors, neither of whom may actually own the corporation.

## Modern Stratification Systems

Modern stratification systems aren't simple and dichotomous. They include (particularly in core and semiperiphery nations) a middle class of skilled and professional workers. Gerhard Lenski (1966) argued that social equality tends to increase in advanced industrial societies. The masses improve their access to economic benefits and political power. In Lenski's scheme, the shift of political power to the masses reflects the growth of the middle class, which reduces the polarization between owning and working classes. The proliferation of middle-class occupations creates opportunities for social mobility and a more complex stratification system (Giddens 1981).

Most contemporary Americans claim to belong to the middle class, which they tend to perceive as a vast, undifferentiated group. There are, however, significant, and growing, socioeconomic contrasts within the middle class, and especially between the richest and the poorest Americans. Table 23.1 shows how income varied from the top to the bottom fifth (quintile) of American earners in 2012. In the table, we see that the top fifth earned more than half of all income generated in the United States, 16 times the share of the bottom fifth. This 2012 ratio of 16:1 compares with 14:1 in 2000 and 11:1 in 1970. Furthermore, by 2012 even the top 10 percent of American earners took home more than half of the country's total income. The top 1 percent alone had over one-fifth of national income, one of the highest shares ever recorded in the United States (Lowrey 2013).

Although incomes for the top 1 percent dropped sharply (about 36 percent) during the Great Recession of 2007–2009, by 2012 those incomes had rebounded by 31 percent. The incomes of the other 99 percent, which dropped 12 percent during the recession, have recovered by less than 1 percent. The top 1 percent has received about 95 percent of

the income gains since the recession ended. Higher stock prices, home values, and corporate profits propelled the recovery among affluent Americans, while blue- and white-collar workers continued to feel the effects of high unemployment and stagnant wages (Lowrey 2013).

When we consider wealth (investments, property, possessions, etc.) rather than income, the contrast is even more striking: The top 1 percent of American households hold over one-third (35 percent) of the nation's wealth (Allegretto 2011; Economic Policy Institute 2012). Their net worth was 288 times greater than the median, or typical, household's net worth (Figure 23.2). This is the highest ratio on record. Between 1983 and 2010, 74 percent of U.S.

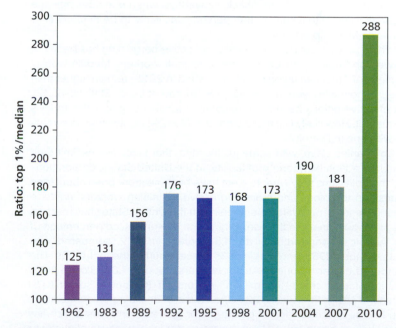

**FIGURE 23.2**  The Ratio of the Wealthiest 1 Percent to Median Wealth in the United States.

SOURCE: S. A. Allegretto, "The State of Working America's Wealth, 2011," Briefing Paper no. 292, Economic Policy Institute, March 23, 2011. http://www.epi.org/page/-/BriefingPaper292.pdf; Economic Policy Institute, "The State of Working America: Key Numbers," 2012. http://stateofworkingamerica.org/files/book/factsheets/wealth.pdf

# focus on GLOBALIZATION

## Where in the World Are the Jobs?

Throughout the world, young people are abandoning traditional subsistence pursuits and seeking cash. A once popular song asked, "How're you gonna keep 'em down on the farm after they've seen Paree?" Nowadays, most people have seen Paree (Paris, that is), along with other world capitals—maybe not in person but in print or on-screen images. Young people today are better educated and wiser in the ways of the world than ever before. Increasingly, they are exposed to the material and cultural promises of a better life away from the farm. They seek paying jobs, but work is scarce, spurring migration within and across national boundaries. If they can't get cash legally, they seek it illegally.

For the past few years, work also has been scarce in the industrial world, including the United States and Western Europe. As ordinary Americans were struggling to recover from the "Great Recession" of 2007–2009, the U.S. stock market (Dow Jones Industrial Average [DJIA]) was skyrocketing. From its low of 6,457 in March 2009, the DJIA surpassed 15,000 for the first time ever in May 2013. During much of that time, however, corporations held on to their rising profits, rather than hiring new workers. The goal of capitalism, after all, is profitability, and paying good wages to fellow citizens isn't necessarily the best way to maximize profits. To reduce labor costs, jobs continue to be outsourced, and machines continue to replace people. Increasingly, corporations offer their customers incentives to bypass humans. Through the Internet we can buy plane tickets (bye bye, travel agents), print boarding passes, reserve hotel rooms, move money, and pay bills. Amazon.com dominates not only "mom and pop" stores but even once powerful chains like Barnes and Noble, Sears, and Radio Shack. Nowadays, when one does manage to speak to an actual human, that person is as likely to be in Mumbai or Manila as Minneapolis or Miami.

What can workers do? Historically, collective bargaining has been the answer, and unions still bring benefits to their workers. Median weekly earnings of American union members—$943 in 2012—remain higher than those of nonunion workers—$742 (U.S. Bureau of Labor Statistics 2012). But effective unions have been national or local—not global like today's job market. How likely is it that a worker in Mumbai would strike in sympathy with one in Detroit?

Companies claim, with some justification, that labor unions limit their flexibility, adaptability, and profitability. In the United States, corporations and the politicians they work to elect have become more open about their opposition to unions and more aggressive in limiting workers' rights to organize and recruit. Union membership in the United States has reached its lowest point in more than seventy years. The unionized percentage of the American workforce fell to 11.3 percent in 2012, compared with 20.1 percent in 1983, and a high of 35 percent during the mid-1950s. The number of unionized private-sector workers stood at 7.0 million in 2012, versus a larger share—7.3 million workers—in the public sector (U.S. Bureau of Labor Statistics 2012). One cause of declining union membership has been a reduction in public-sector (government) jobs (which are more likely to be unionized than private-sector jobs) because of austerity measures imposed by politicians. From the United States to Greece to the United Kingdom, such austerity measures have been spreading internationally, reducing employment and workers' benefits.

wealth growth went to the top 5 percent, while the bottom 60 percent of Americans actually lost wealth (Economic Policy Institute 2012). Recognition of such disparities, and that the rich have been getting richer and the poor, poorer, led to the Occupy movement of 2011. That movement began on Wall Street in New York City and quickly spread to many other cities in an attempt to draw attention to the lack of economic recovery for 99 percent of Americans.

Max Weber faulted Karl Marx for an overly simple and exclusively economic view of stratification. Weber (1922/1968) looked beyond class and identified three (separate but correlated) dimensions of social stratification: wealth, power, and prestige. Weber also believed that social identities based on nationality, ethnicity, and religion could take priority over class (social identity based on economic status). In fact, the modern world system *is* cross-cut by collective identities based on nationality, ethnicity, and religion. Class conflicts tend to occur within nations, and nationalism has impeded global class solidarity, particularly of proletarians (see "Focus on Globalization").

Although the capitalist class dominates politically in most countries, growing wealth has made it easier for core nations to benefit their workers (Hopkins and Wallerstein 1982). However, the improvement in core workers' living standards wouldn't have occurred without the world system. The wealth that flows from periphery and semiperiphery to core has helped core capitalists maintain

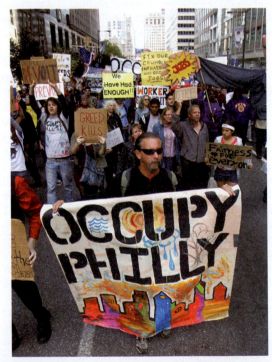

This October 15, 2011, demonstration in Philadelphia was one of many that were held in the United States and Canada in support of the Occupy Wall Street demonstration in New York City.

Max Weber (1864–1920). Did Weber improve on Marx's view of stratification?

their profits while satisfying the demands of core workers. In the periphery and semiperiphery, wages and living standards are lower. The current *world stratification system* features a substantial contrast between both capitalists and workers in the core nations, on the one hand, and workers on the periphery on the other.

## COLONIALISM

The major forces influencing cultural interactions during the past 500 years have been commercial expansion, industrial capitalism, and the dominance of colonial and core nations (Wallerstein 2004; Wolf 1982). As state formation had done previously, industrialization accelerated local participation in larger networks. According to Bodley (2012), perpetual expansion is a distinguishing feature of industrial economic systems.

During the 19th century, European business interests initiated a concerted search for markets. This process led to European imperialism in Africa, Asia, and Oceania. **Imperialism** refers to a policy of extending the rule of a country or an empire over foreign nations and of taking and holding foreign colonies (see Burbank and Cooper 2010). Imperialism goes back to early states, including Egypt in the Old World and the Incas in the New. A Greek empire was forged by Alexander the Great, and Julius Caesar and his successors spread the Roman empire. More recent examples include the British, French, and Soviet empires (see Burbank and Cooper 2010).

During the second half of the 19th century, European imperial expansion was aided by improved transportation, which facilitated the colonization of vast areas of sparsely settled lands in Australia and the interior of North and South America. The new colonies purchased goods from the industrial centers and shipped back wheat, cotton, wool, mutton, beef, and leather. The first phase of European colonialism had been the exploration and exploitation of the Americas and the Caribbean after Columbus. A second phase began as European nations competed for colonies between 1875 and 1914.

**Colonialism** is the political, social, economic, and cultural domination of a territory and its people by a foreign power for an extended time (see Bremen and Shimizu 1999; Stoler, McGranahan, and Perdue 2007). If imperialism is almost as old as the state, colonialism can be traced back to the Phoenicians, who established colonies along the eastern Mediterranean 3,000 years ago. The ancient Greeks and Romans were avid colonizers as well as empire builders.

The first phase of modern colonialism began with the European "Age of Discovery"—of the Americas and of a sea route to the Far East. After 1492, the Spanish, the original conquerors of the Aztecs and the Incas, explored and colonized widely in the Caribbean, Mexico, the southern portions of what was to become the United States, and Central and South America. In the Pacific, Spain extended its rule to the Philippines and Guam. The Portuguese empire included Brazil, South America's largest colonial territory; Angola and Mozambique in Africa; and Goa in South Asia. Rebellions and wars aimed at independence ended the first phase of European colonialism by the early 19th century. Brazil declared independence from Portugal in 1822. By 1825 most of Spain's colonies were politically independent. Spain held on to Cuba and the Philippines until 1898 but otherwise withdrew from the colonial field. During the first phase of colonialism, Spain and Portugal, along with Britain and France, were major colonizing nations. The last two (Britain and France) dominated the second phase.

### British Colonialism

At its peak about 1914, the British empire covered a fifth of the world's land surface and ruled a fourth of its population (see Figure 23.3). Like several other European nations, Britain had two stages of colonialism. The first began with the Elizabethan voyages of the 16th century. During the 17th century, Britain acquired most of the eastern coast of North America, Canada's St. Lawrence basin, islands in the Caribbean, slave stations in Africa, and interests in India.

The British shared the exploration of the New World with the Spanish, Portuguese, French, and Dutch. The British by and large left Mexico, along with Central and South America, to the Spanish and the Portuguese. The end of the Seven Years' War in 1763 forced a French retreat from most of Canada

**colonialism**
Long-term foreign control of a territory and its people.

**imperialism**
Policy aimed at seizing and ruling foreign territory and peoples.

**FIGURE 23.3** Map of British Empire in 1765 and 1914.

SOURCE: From the *Academic American Encyclopedia*, Vol. 3, p. 496. 1998 Edition. Copyright © 1998 by Grolier Incorporated. Reprinted with permission.

and India, where France previously had competed with Britain (Cody 1998).

The American Revolution ended the first stage of British colonialism. A second colonial empire, on which the "sun never set," rose from the ashes of the first. Beginning in 1788, but intensifying after 1815, the British settled Australia. Britain had acquired Dutch South Africa by 1815. By 1819 Singapore anchored a British trade network that extended to much of South Asia and along the coast of China. By this time, the empires of Britain's traditional rivals,

particularly Spain, had been severely diminished in scope. Britain's position as imperial power and the world's leading industrial nation was unchallenged.

During the Victorian Era (1837–1901), as Britain's colonial expansion continued, Prime Minister Benjamin Disraeli implemented a foreign policy justified by a view of imperialism as shouldering "the white man's burden"—a phrase coined by the poet Rudyard Kipling. People in the empire were seen as incapable of governing themselves, so British guidance was needed to civilize and Christianize them. This paternalistic and racist doctrine was used to legitimize Britain's acquisition and control of parts of central Africa and Asia (Cody 1998; Cooper 2014).

After World War II, the British empire began to fall apart, with nationalist movements for independence. India became independent in 1947, as did the Republic of Ireland in 1949. Decolonization in Africa and Asia accelerated during the late 1950s. Today, the ties that remain between Britain and its former colonies are mainly linguistic or cultural rather than political (Cody 1998).

## French Colonialism

French colonialism also had two phases. The first began with the explorations of the early 1600s. Prior to the French Revolution in 1789, missionaries, explorers, and traders carved out niches for France in Canada, the Louisiana Territory, several Caribbean islands, and parts of India, which were lost along with Canada to Great Britain in 1763 (Harvey 1980).

The foundations of the second French empire were established between 1830 and 1870. In Great Britain the drive for profit led expansion, but French colonialism was spurred more by the state, church,

On January 1, 1900, a British officer in India receives a pedicure from a servant. What does this photo say to you about colonialism? Who gives pedicures in your society?

**FIGURE 23.4** Map of the French Empire at Its Height around 1914.

SOURCE: From the *Academic American Encyclopedia*, Vol. 8, p. 309. 1998 Edition. Copyright © 1998 by Grolier Incorporated. Reprinted with permission.

and armed forces than by pure business interests. France acquired Algeria and part of what eventually became Indochina (Cambodia, Laos, and Vietnam). By 1914 the French empire covered 4 million square miles and included some 60 million people (see Figure 23.4). By 1893 French rule had been fully established in Indochina. Tunisia and Morocco became French protectorates in 1883 and 1912, respectively (Harvey 1980).

To be sure, the French, like the British, had substantial business interests in their colonies, but they also sought, again like the British, international glory and prestige. The French promulgated a *mission civilisatrice,* their equivalent of Britain's "white man's burden." The goal was to implant French culture, language, and religion (Roman Catholicism), throughout the colonies (Harvey 1980).

The French used two forms of colonial rule: *indirect rule,* governing through native leaders and established political structures, in areas with long histories of state organization, such as Morocco and Tunisia; and *direct rule* by French officials in many areas of Africa, where the French imposed new government structures to control diverse societies, many of them previously stateless. Like the British empire, the French empire began to disintegrate after World War II. France fought long—and ultimately futile—wars to keep its empire intact in Indochina and Algeria (Harvey 1980).

## Colonialism and Identity

Many geopolitical labels in the news today had no equivalent meaning before colonialism. Whole countries, along with social groups and divisions within them, were colonial inventions. In West Africa, for example, by geographic logic, several adjacent countries could be one (Togo, Ghana, Ivory Coast [Côte d'Ivoire], Guinea, Guinea-Bissau, Sierra Leone, Liberia). Instead, they are separated by linguistic, political, and economic contrasts promoted under colonialism (Figure 23.5).

Hundreds of ethnic groups and "tribes" are colonial constructions (see Ranger 1996). The Sukuma of Tanzania, for instance, were first registered as a single tribe by the colonial administration. Then missionaries standardized a series of dialects into a single Sukuma language, into which they translated the Bible and other religious texts. Thereafter, those texts were taught in missionary schools and to European foreigners and other non-Sukuma speakers. Over time this standardized the Sukuma language and ethnicity (Finnstrom 1997).

As in most of East Africa, in Rwanda and Burundi farmers and herders live in the same areas and speak the same language. Historically, they have shared the same social world, although their social organization is "extremely hierarchical," almost "caste-like" (Malkki 1995, p. 24). There has been a tendency to see the pastoral Tutsis as superior to the agricultural Hutus. Tutsis have been presented as nobles, Hutus as commoners. Yet when distributing identity cards in Rwanda, the Belgian colonizers simply identified all people with more than 10 head of cattle as Tutsi. Owners of fewer cattle were registered as Hutus (Bjuremalm 1997). Years later, these arbitrary colonial registers were used systematically for "ethnic" identification during the mass killings (genocide) that took place in Rwanda in 1994 (as portrayed vividly in the film *Hotel Rwanda*).

**FIGURE 23.5** Small West African Nations Created by Colonialism.

## Postcolonial Studies

**postcolonial**

Describes relations between European nations and areas they colonized and once ruled.

In anthropology, history, and literature, the field of postcolonial studies has gained prominence since the 1970s (see Ashcroft, Griffiths, and Tiffin 2013; Cooper and Stoler 1997). **Postcolonial** refers to the study of the interactions between European nations and the societies they colonized (mainly after 1800). In 1914, European empires, which broke up after World War II, ruled more than 85 percent of the world (Petraglia-Bahri 1996). The term *postcolonial* also has been used to describe the second half of the 20th century in general, the period succeeding colonialism. Even more generically, *postcolonial* may be used to signify a position against imperialism and Eurocentrism (Petraglia-Bahri 1996).

The former colonies (*postcolonies*) can be divided into settler, nonsettler, and mixed (Petraglia-Bahri 1996). The settler countries, with large numbers of European colonists and sparser native populations, include Australia and Canada. Examples of nonsettler countries include India, Pakistan, Bangladesh, Sri Lanka, Malaysia, Indonesia, Nigeria, Senegal, and Madagascar. All these had substantial native populations and relatively few European settlers. Mixed countries include South Africa, Zimbabwe, Kenya, and Algeria. Such countries had

significant European settlement despite having sizable native populations.

Given the varied experiences of such countries, *postcolonial* has to be a loose term. The United States, for instance, was colonized by Europeans and fought a war for independence from Britain. Is the United States a postcolony? It usually isn't perceived as such, given its current world power position, its treatment of Native Americans (sometimes called internal colonization), and its annexation of other parts of the world (Petraglia-Bahri 1996). Research in postcolonial studies is growing, permitting a wide-ranging investigation of power relations in varied contexts. Broad topics in the field include the formation of an empire, the impact of colonization, and the state of the postcolony today (Petraglia-Bahri 1996).

## DEVELOPMENT

During the Industrial Revolution, a strong current of thought viewed industrialization as a beneficial process of organic development and progress. Many economists still assume that industrialization increases production and income. They seek to create in Third World ("developing") countries a process like the one that first occurred spontaneously in 18th-century Great Britain.

We have seen that Britain used the notion of a white man's burden to justify its imperialist expansion and that France claimed to be engaged in a *mission civilisatrice,* a civilizing mission, in its colonies. Both these ideas illustrate an **intervention philosophy,** an ideological justification for outsiders to guide native peoples in specific directions. Economic development plans also have intervention philosophies. John Bodley (2012) argues that the basic belief behind interventions—whether by colonialists, missionaries, governments, or development planners—has been the same for more than 100 years. This belief is that industrialization, modernization, Westernization, and individualism are desirable evolutionary advances and that development schemes that promote them will bring long-term benefits to local people.

Black workers wash the hair of white customers at a hair salon in Johannesburg's (South Africa) exclusive Hyde Park shopping center. What story does the photo tell you?

## Neoliberalism

One currently prominent intervention philosophy is neoliberalism, which encompasses a set of assumptions that have become widespread during the last 30 years. Neoliberal policies are being implemented in developing nations, including postsocialist societies (e.g., those of the former Soviet Union). **Neoliberalism** is the current form of the classic economic liberalism laid out in Adam Smith's famous capitalist manifesto *The Wealth of Nations,* published in 1776, soon after the Industrial Revolution. Smith advocated laissez-faire (hands-off) economics as the basis of capitalism: The government should stay out of its nation's economic affairs. Free trade, Smith argued, is the best way for a nation's economy to develop. There should be no restrictions on manufacturing, no barriers to commerce, and no tariffs. This philosophy is called "liberalism" because it aimed at liberating or freeing the economy from government controls. Economic liberalism encouraged "free" enterprise and competition, with the goal of generating profits. (Ironically, Adam Smith's liberalism is today's capitalist "conservatism.")

Economic liberalism prevailed in the United States until President Franklin Roosevelt's New Deal during the 1930s. The Great Depression produced a turn to Keynesian economics, which challenged liberalism. John Maynard Keynes (1927, 1936) insisted that full employment was necessary for capitalism to grow, that governments and central banks should intervene to increase employment, and that government should promote the common good.

Especially since the fall of Communism (1989–1991), there has been a revival of neoliberalism, which has been spreading globally. Around the world, neoliberal policies have been imposed by powerful financial institutions such as the International Monetary Fund (IMF), the World Bank, and the Inter-American Development Bank (see Edelman and Haugerud 2005). Neoliberalism entails open (tariff- and barrier-free) international trade and investment. Profits are sought through the lowering of costs, whether through improving productivity, laying off workers, or seeking workers who accept lower wages. In exchange for loans, the governments of postsocialist and developing nations have been required to accept the neoliberal premise that deregulation leads to economic growth, which will eventually benefit everyone through a process sometimes called "trickle down." Accompanying the belief in free markets and the idea of cutting costs is a tendency to impose austerity measures that cut government expenses. This can entail reduced public spending

**intervention philosophy**
Ideological justification for outsiders to guide or rule native peoples.

**neoliberalism**
Principle that governments shouldn't regulate private enterprise; free market forces should rule.

The face of the Scottish economist Adam Smith aptly appears on this English 20-pound banknote. In his famed capitalist manifesto, *The Wealth of Nations,* published in 1776, Smith advocated "free" enterprise and competition, with the goal of generating profits.

on education, health care, and other social services, as has happened recently with imposed austerity in Greece.

## NAFTA's Economic Refugees

In recent decades, many of the migrants seeking work in the United States have come from Mexico. Most Americans are aware of this large-scale

On the top, farmers harvest native corn in Oaxaca, Mexico. These are some of the many varieties that were first cultivated in Mesoamerica around 8,000 years ago. On the bottom, demonstrators in Mexico City protest NAFTA's removal of import tariffs on farm goods entering Mexico from the United States and Canada.

Mexican immigration, often of undocumented workers. Most Americans are unaware, however, of the extent to which international forces, including new technologies and the neoliberal North American Free Trade Agreement (NAFTA), are responsible for this migration. Ana Aurelia López (2011) shows how such forces have destroyed traditional Mexican farming systems, degraded agricultural land, and displaced Mexican farmers and small-business people—thereby fueling the migration of millions of undocumented Mexicans to the United States. The following account is a synopsis of her findings.

To understand what is happening in North America today, we need to be aware of an agricultural tradition that began at least 7,000 years ago. For thousands of years, Mexican farmers have grown corn (maize) in a sustainable manner. For all those millennia, Mexican farmers planted corn, beans, and squash (known as "the three sisters") together. This polyculture (cultivation of multiple crops) results in corn yields higher than those obtained when corn is cultivated by itself (monoculture). To preserve the fertility of the soil, a "three sisters" plot was allowed to "rest" for five years after being cultivated for two.

Over the generations, Mexican farmers selected diverse strains of corn well adapted to a huge variety of specific microclimates. Mexico became a repository of corn genetic diversity for the world. When corn grown elsewhere developed disease or pest susceptibility or was of poor quality, Mexico could provide other countries with genetically superior plants.

Prior to NAFTA, Mexico supported its farmers by buying a portion of their harvest each year at an elevated cost through price supports. This corn went to a countrywide chain of successful CONASUPO (Compañía Nacional de Subsistencias Populares) stores, which sold corn and other staple foodstuffs below market price to the urban and rural poor. Border tariffs protected Mexican farmers from the entrance of foreign corn, such as that grown in the United States.

The first assault on Mexico's sustainable farming culture began in the 1940s when "Green Revolution" technologies were introduced, including seeds that require chemical inputs (e.g., fertilizer). The Mexican government encouraged farmers to replace their traditional, genetically diverse maíz crillo ("creole corn") with the genetically homogenized maíz mejorado ("improved corn"), a hybrid from the United States. Agrochemical companies initially supplied the required chemical inputs free of charge.

Company representatives visited rural villages and offered free samples of seeds and agrochemicals to a few farmers. As news of unusually large first-year crops spread, other farmers abandoned their traditional corn strains for the "improved," chemically dependent corn. As the transition accelerated, the price of both the new seeds and associated inputs rose gradually. Eventually, farmers no longer could afford either the seeds or the required agrochemicals. When cash-strapped farmers tried to return to planting their former maíz criollo seeds, the plants would grow but corn would not appear. Only the hybrid seeds from the United States would produce corn on the chemically altered soils. Today over 60 percent of Mexico's farmland is degraded due to the spread of agrochemicals—chemical fertilizers and pesticides. (This chapter's "Appreciating Anthropology" on pp. 456–457 describes another case of environmental degradation due to chemical pollution, with mining as the culprit.)

The second major assault on traditional Mexican farming came when NAFTA went into effect in 1994. The World Bank granted Mexico a loan to restructure its economy to fit the neoliberal "free trade" agreement. The loan required Mexico to end corn price supports for its small-scale corn farmers. Also ended were Mexico's CONASUPO food stores, which had benefited the rural and urban poor.

While small-scale Mexican farmers have suffered, American agricultural industries have profited from NAFTA. The U.S. government continues to subsidize its own corn farmers, who otherwise would go out of business. Prior to NAFTA, Mexico's border tariffs made the sale of U.S. corn in Mexico unprofitable. Under NAFTA, Mexican corn tariffs were supposed to be phased out over 15 years, providing time for small farmers to adjust to the NAFTA economy. In fact, the Mexican corn tariffs mysteriously disappeared after only 30 months. Corn from the United States began flooding the Mexican markets.

The NAFTA economy offers Mexico's small-scale corn farmers few options: (1) stay in rural Mexico and suffer, (2) look for work in a Mexican city, or (3) migrate to the United States in search of work. NAFTA did not create a common labor market (i.e., the ability of Mexicans, Americans, and Canadians to move freely across each country's borders and work legally anywhere in North America). Nor did NAFTA make provisions for the predicted 15 million Mexican corn farmers who would be forced off the land as a result of the trade agreement. As could have been expected (and planned for), millions of Mexicans migrated to the United States.

Because of NAFTA and neoliberalism, Mexico's 7,000-year-old traditional farming culture is disappearing. Corn farmers have fled the countryside, and U.S.-subsidized corn has flooded the Mexican market. A declining number of traditional farmers remain to plant and conserve Mexico's unique corn varieties. Between one-third and one-half of Mexico's corn now is imported from the United States, much of it by U.S.-based Archer-Daniels-Midland, the world's largest corporate corn exporter. NAFTA also has facilitated the entrance of other giant U.S. corporations into Mexico: Walmart, Dow Agribusiness, Monsanto, Marlboro cigarettes, and Coca-Cola. These multinationals, in turn, have displaced many small Mexican businesses, creating yet another wave of immigrants—former shopkeepers and their employees—to the United States.

In this summary of Ana Aurelia López's (2011) insightful analysis, we see how farmers and small-business men and women have been forced, by decisions beyond their control, to leave Mexico for the United States. In migrating, these millions of economic refugees continue to face daunting challenges, including separation from their families and homeland, dangerous border crossings, and the ever-present possibility of deportation from the United States.

Within today's world system, comparable effects of neoliberal policies extend well beyond Mexico. As forces of globalization transform rural landscapes throughout the world, rural–urban and transnational migration have become global phenomena. Over and over again, Green Revolution technologies have transformed subsistence into cash economies, fueling a need for money to acquire foreign inputs while hooking the land on chemicals, reducing genetic diversity and sustainability, and forcing the poorest farmers off the land. Few Americans are aware, specifically, of NAFTA's role in ending a 7,000-year-old sustainable farming culture and displacing millions of Mexicans and, more generally, that comparable developments are happening all over the world.

## THE SECOND WORLD

The labels "First World," "Second World," and "Third World" represent a common, although ethnocentric, way of categorizing nations. The *First World* refers to the "democratic West"—traditionally conceived in opposition to a "Second World" ruled by "Communism." The *Second World* refers to the former Soviet Union and the socialist and once-socialist countries of Eastern Europe and Asia. Proceeding with this classification, the "less developed countries," or "developing nations," make up the *Third World*.

## Communism

The two meanings of communism involve how it is written, whether with a lowercase (small) or an uppercase (large) *c*. Small-*c* **communism** is a social system in which property is owned by the community and in which people work for the common good. Large-*C* **Communism** was a political movement and doctrine seeking to overthrow capitalism and to establish a form of communism such as that

**communism**
Political system in which property is owned by the community and people work for the common good.

**Communism**
Political movement aimed at replacing capitalism with Soviet-style communism.

# appreciating ANTHROPOLOGY

## Is Mining Sustainable?

How can anthropologists help the people they study? The spread of industrialization, illustrated by the mining described here, has contributed to the destruction of indigenous economies, ecologies, and populations. Today multinational conglomerates, along with nations such as Papua New Guinea, are repeating—at an accelerated rate—the process of resource depletion that started in Europe and the United States during the Industrial Revolution. Fortunately, however, today's world has some environmental watchdogs, including anthropologists, that did not exist during the first centuries of the Industrial Revolution. Described here is a conundrum confronting a major university. Is a firm whose operations have destroyed the landscapes and livelihoods of indigenous peoples a proper adviser for an institute devoted to ecological sustainability?

In the 1990s, the giant mining company now known as BHP Billiton drew worldwide condemnation for the environmental damage caused by its copper and gold mine in Papua New Guinea. Its mining practices destroyed the way of life of thousands of farming and fishing families who lived along and subsisted on the rivers polluted by the mine, and it was only after being sued in a landmark class-action case that the company agreed to compensate them.

Today several activists and academics who work on behalf of indigenous people around the world say the company continues to dodge responsibility for the problems its mines create. . . .

Yet at the University of Michigan at Ann Arbor, BHP Billiton . . . [became] one of 14 corporate members of an External Advisory Board for the university's new Graham Environmental Sustainability Institute.

Critics at and outside the university contend that Michigan's decision to enlist BHP Billiton as an adviser to an institute devoted to sustainability reflects badly on the institution and allows the company to claim [an undeserved] mantle of environmental and social responsibility. . . .

The arguments echo the discussions about corporate "greenwashing" that have arisen at Stanford University and the University of California at Berkeley over major research grants from ExxonMobil and BP, respectively. . . .

For one BHP Billiton critic at Michigan, the issue is personal. Stuart Kirsch, an associate professor of anthropology, has spent most of his academic career documenting the damage caused by BHP Billiton's Ok Tedi mine in Papua New Guinea. . . .

Mr. Kirsch, who first visited some of the affected communities as a young ethnographer in 1987, became involved in the class-action lawsuit brought against the company and helped villagers participate in the 1996 legal settlement. "I put my career on hold while being an activist," he says.

He subsequently published several papers related to his work with the Yonggom people as they fought for recognition and compensation from mine operators—scholarship that helped him win tenure. . . . He remains involved with the network of activists and academics who follow mining and its impact on undeveloped communities around the world. . . .

The company's practices polluted the Ok Tedi and Fly Rivers and caused thousands of people to leave their homes because the mining-induced flooding made it impossible for them to grow food to feed themselves, says Mr. Kirsch.

BHP Billiton, based in Australia, later acknowledged that the mine was "not compatible with our environmental values," and spun it off to an independent company that pays all of its mining royalties to the government of Papua New Guinea.

But Mr. Kirsch says that in doing so, the company skirted responsibility for ameliorating the damage it caused. BHP Billiton says it would have preferred to close the mine, but the Papua New Guinea government, in need of the mine revenues, pressed to keep it open. The deal freed BHP Billiton from any future liabilities for environmental damage. . . .

Illtud Harri, a BHP Billiton spokesman, says the company regrets its past with Ok Tedi but considers its pullout from the mine "a responsible exit" that left in place a system that supports educational, agricultural, and social programs for the people of the community. . . .

---

which prevailed in the Soviet Union (USSR) from 1917 to 1991. The heyday of Communism was a 40-year period from 1949 to 1989, when more Communist regimes existed than at any time before or after. Today only five Communist states remain—China, Cuba, Laos, North Korea, and Vietnam, compared with 23 in 1985.

Communism, which originated with Russia's Bolshevik Revolution in 1917 and took its inspiration from Karl Marx and Friedrich Engels, was not uniform over time or among countries. All Communist systems were *authoritarian* (promoting obedience to authority rather than individual freedom). Many were *totalitarian* (banning rival parties and demanding total submission of the individual to the state). The Communist Party monopolized power in every Communist state, and relations within the party were highly centralized and strictly disciplined. Communist nations had state ownership, rather than private ownership, of the means of production. Finally, all Communist regimes, with the goal of advancing communism, cultivated a

Mr. Talbot, the interim director of the two-year-old sustainability institute, says . . . "We intentionally selected a cross-sector group of organizations" for the advisory board from a list of about 140 nominees, . . . and several companies that "weren't making any serious efforts" toward sustainability were rejected. . . . BHP Billiton, a company formed from the 2001 merger of the Australian mining enterprise Broken Hill Proprietary Company with London-based Billiton, is now the world's largest mining company, with more than 100 operations in 25 countries. . . . The BHP Billiton charter includes a statement that the company has "an overriding commitment to health,

safety, environmental responsibility, and sustainable development." But its critics say the company continues to play a key role in mining projects with questionable records on environmental and human rights, even though in many of those cases, it is not directly responsible. . . . BHP Billiton has the resources to present itself as the "golden boy," but, says Mr. Kirsch, "it's much harder to see the people on the Ok Tedi and Fly rivers."

A forum could help to right that imbalance, he says. "Let the students and faculty decide whether this is an appropriate company to advise the University of Michigan," says Mr. Kirsch. "It would be an educational process for everyone involved."

**Update:** As of this writing (2014), BHP Billiton no longer is listed as a member of the advisory board of Michigan's Graham Institute. And in Papua New Guinea, after BHP Billiton transferred its ownership of the mine to Ok Tedi Mining Limited, that independent company has spent more than a billion dollars on environmental remediation. The 1996 settlement decreed that BHP would be spared future legal claims in return for giving all its shares to the people of PNG. Those shares are now held in trust (valued at over $1 billion, and growing) in a Singapore-based entity, PNG Sustainable Development Program Limited. The mission of that trust is to promote development in PNG's Western Province, where the mine is located, and across PNG. Today, the provincial and national governments of PNG and the PNG Sustainable Development Program are the only shareholders of Ok Tedi Mining Limited, which pays all its royalties to the PNG government. For hundreds of miles down the Fly River, fishers and farmers still complain about the destruction of their habitat, even as the Ok Tedi mine supplies 16 percent of PNG's national revenue.

Ecological devastation caused by the Ok Tedi copper mine in Papua New Guinea.

SOURCE OF STORY: Goldie Blumenstyk, "Mining Company Involved in Environmental Disaster Now Advises Sustainability Institute at U. of Michigan," *Chronicle of Higher Education,* Vol. 54, Issue 15 (December 7, 2007), p. A22. Copyright 2007, The Chronicle of Higher Education. Reprinted with permission. SOURCES OF UPDATE: http://www.radioaustralia.net.au/pacific/radio/program/pacific-beat/documentary-special-ok-tedi/1069558 and Stuart Kirsch (personal communication).

sense of belonging to an international movement (Brown 2001).

Social scientists have tended to refer to such societies as socialist rather than Communist. Today research by anthropologists is thriving in *postsocialist* societies—those that once emphasized bureaucratic redistribution of wealth according to a central plan (Verdery 1997, 2001). In the postsocialist period, states that once featured planned economies have been following the neoliberal agenda, by divesting themselves of state-

owned resources in favor of privatization and marketization. Some of them have moved toward formal liberal democracy, with political parties, elections, and a balance of powers.

## Postsocialist Transitions

Neoliberal economists assumed that dismantling the Soviet Union's planned economy would raise gross domestic product (GDP) and living standards. The goal was to enhance production by

Before and after Communism. Above: on May Day (May 1, 1975), large photos of Politburo members (Communist Party leaders) adorn buildings in Moscow. Below: in 2010, a Burger King outlet opens at a shopping mall in Moscow. Burger King started opening its outlets in Russia nearly two decades after McDonald's, looking to capitalize on new markets' growing appetite for fast food.

substituting a free market system and providing incentives through privatization. In October 1991, Boris Yeltsin, who had been elected president of Russia that June, announced a program of radical market-oriented reform, pursuing a changeover to capitalism. Yeltsin's program of "shock therapy" cut subsidies to farms and industries and ended price controls. During the 1990s, postsocialist Russia endured a series of disruptions, leading to declines in its GDP, average life expectancy, and birthrate, as well as increased poverty. In 2008–2009, Russia shared in the global recession after 10 years of economic growth, but its economy recuperated rapidly and was growing again by 2010, as were its birthrate and average life expectancy. The poverty rate has fallen substantially since the late 1990s but recently has been on the rise—even as Moscow is home to more billionaires than New York City or London (Rapoza 2012). The 2012 Russian poverty rate of 13 percent was below the American rate of 16 percent the same year.

## THE WORLD SYSTEM TODAY

The spread of industrialization continues today, although nations have shifted their positions within the world system. Recap 23.1 summarizes those shifts. By 1900, the United States had become a core nation within the world system and had overtaken Great Britain in iron, coal, and cotton production. In a few decades (1868–1900), Japan had changed from a medieval handicraft economy to an industrial one, joining the semiperiphery by 1900 and moving to the core between 1945 and 1970. India and China have joined Brazil as leaders of the semiperiphery. Figure 23.6 is a map showing the modern world system.

Twentieth-century industrialization added hundreds of new industries and millions of new jobs. Production increased, often beyond immediate demand, spurring strategies, such as advertising, to sell everything industry could churn out. Mass production gave rise to a culture of consumption, which valued acquisitiveness and conspicuous consumption. That culture has become global in scope.

| RECAP 23.1 | Ascent and Decline of Nations within the World System | |
| --- | --- | --- |
| **PERIPHERY TO SEMIPERIPHERY** | **SEMIPERIPHERY TO CORE** | **CORE TO SEMIPERIPHERY** |
| United States (1800–1860) | United States (1860–1900) | Spain (1620–1700) |
| Japan (1868–1900) | Japan (1945–1970) | |
| Taiwan (1949–1980) | Germany (1870–1900) | |
| S. Korea (1953–1980) | | |

SOURCE: Thomas R. Shannon, *An Introduction to the World-System Perspective,* 2nd ed., p. 147. Copyright © 1989, 1996 by Westview Press, Inc. Reprinted by permission of Westview Press, a member of the Perseus Books Group.

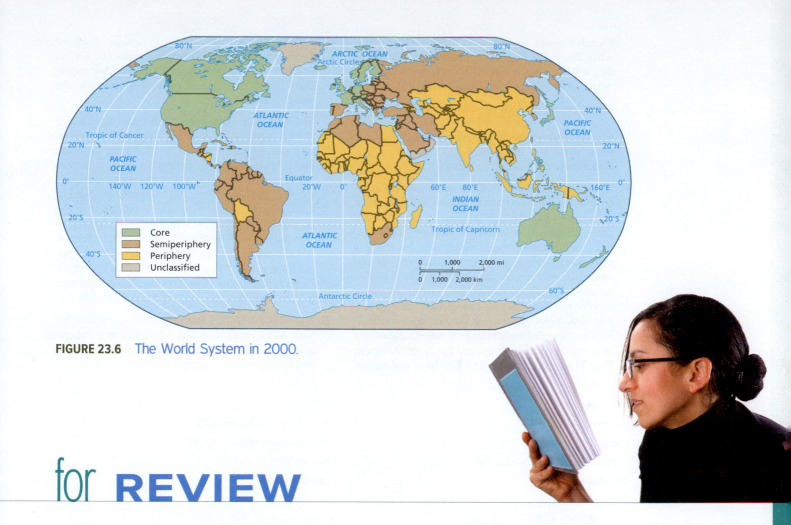

**FIGURE 23.6** The World System in 2000.

Map legend:
- Core
- Semiperiphery
- Periphery
- Unclassified

# for REVIEW

1. Local societies increasingly participate in wider systems—regional, national, and global. The capitalist world economy depends on production for sale, with the goal of maximizing profits. The key claim of world-system theory is that an identifiable social system, based on wealth and power differentials, extends beyond individual countries. That system is formed by a set of economic and political relations that has characterized much of the globe since the 16th century. World capitalism has political and economic specialization at the core, semiperiphery, and periphery.

2. Columbus's voyages opened the way for a major exchange between the Old and New Worlds. Seventeenth-century plantation economies in the Caribbean and Brazil were based on sugar. In the 18th century, plantation economies based on cotton arose in the southeastern United States.

3. The Industrial Revolution began in England around 1750. Transoceanic commerce supplied capital for industrial investment. Industrialization hastened the separation of workers from the means of production. Marx saw a sharp division between the bourgeoisie and the proletariat. Class consciousness was a key feature of Marx's view of this stratification. Weber believed that social solidarity based on ethnicity, religion, race, or nationality could take priority over class. Today's capitalist world economy maintains the contrast between those who own the means of production and those who don't, but the division is now worldwide. There is a substantial contrast between not only capitalists but also workers in the core nations versus workers on the periphery.

4. Imperialism is the policy of extending the rule of a nation or an empire over other nations and of taking and holding foreign colonies. Colonialism is the domination of a territory and its people by a foreign power for an extended time. European colonialism had two main phases. The first started in 1492 and lasted through 1825. For Britain this phase ended with the American Revolution. For France it ended when Britain won the Seven Years' War, forcing the French to abandon Canada and India. For Spain it ended with Latin American independence. The second phase of European colonialism extended approximately from 1850 to 1950. The British and

French empires were at their height around 1914, when European empires controlled 85 percent of the world. Britain and France had colonies in Africa, Asia, Oceania, and the New World.

5. Many geopolitical labels and identities that were created under colonialism had little or nothing to do with existing social demarcations. The new ethnic or national divisions were colonial inventions, sometimes aggravating conflicts.

6. Like colonialism, economic development has an intervention philosophy that provides a justification for outsiders to guide native peoples toward particular goals. Development usually is justified by the idea that industrialization and modernization are desirable evolutionary advances. Neoliberalism revives and extends classic economic liberalism: the idea that governments should not regulate private enterprise and that free market forces should rule. This intervention philosophy currently dominates aid agreements with postsocialist and developing nations. Neoliberal policies, new technologies, and the North American Free Trade Agreement (NAFTA) have endangered traditional Mexican farming systems, degraded agricultural land, and displaced Mexican farmers and small-business people—thereby fueling the migration of millions of undocumented Mexicans to the United States.

7. Spelled with a lowercase *c*, communism is a social system in which property is owned by the community and in which people work for the common good. Spelled with an uppercase *C,* Communism indicates a political movement and doctrine seeking to overthrow capitalism and to establish a form of communism such as that which prevailed in the Soviet Union from 1917 to 1991. The heyday of Communism was between 1949 and 1989. The fall of Communism can be traced to 1989–1990 in eastern Europe and 1991 in the Soviet Union. Postsocialist states have followed the neoliberal agenda, through privatization, deregulation, and democratization.

8. By 1900 the United States had become a core nation. Mass production had given rise to a culture, now global in scope, that valued acquisitiveness and conspicuous consumption.

## key terms

bourgeoisie  445

capital  441

capitalist world economy  441

colonialism  449

communism  455

Communism  455

core  441

imperialism  449

Industrial Revolution  443

intervention philosophy  453

neoliberalism  453

periphery  441

postcolonial  452

semiperiphery  441

working class (proletariat)  445

world-system theory  441

## critical thinking

1. According to world-system theory, societies are subsystems of bigger systems, with the world system as the largest. What are the various systems, at different levels, in which you participate?

2. How does world-system theory help explain why companies hire thousands of workers in India while laying off an equivalent number in Europe and the United States?

3. What were the causes of the Industrial Revolution? Why did it begin in England rather than France? How might this knowledge be relevant for an anthropologist interested in investigating the dynamics of industrialization today?

4. Think of a recent case in which a core nation has intervened in the affairs of another nation. What was the intervention philosophy used to justify the action?

5. This chapter describes the labels "First World," "Second World," and "Third World" as a common, although ethnocentric, way of categorizing nations. Why is it ethnocentric? Do you think there is any reason to keep using these labels, despite their problems? Why or why not?

# Anthropology's Role in a Globalizing World

▶ What is global climate change, and how can anthropologists study it, along with other environmental threats?

▶ What is cultural imperialism, and what forces work to favor and oppose it?

▶ What are indigenous peoples, and how and why has their importance increased in recent years?

Perito Moreno glacier, in Patagonia, Argentina. Portions of this massive glacier have been collapsing since winter 2009, as a likely reflection of global climate change.

# understanding OURSELVES

What's your favorite science fiction movie or TV show? What imagined images of other planets, or of a future Earth, stand out in your memory? Can you visualize *Star Wars*'s Death Star, poor old Alderan, the two suns of Tatooine? How about *Avatar*'s Pandora? Such images may be as familiar to you as those of real planets. Think, too, about how extraterrestrials have been portrayed in movies. On the one hand are *ET*'s harmless plant collectors and *Avatar*'s endangered Na'vi. More typical are Earth's would-be conquerors, as shown in *Independence Day, Starship Troopers, V,* and a hundred others. Still other films, most notably *The Day the Earth Stood Still* (either the 1951 or the 2008 version), feature omnipotent, omniscient guardians of interplanetary affairs.

If some of our most vivid perceptions of other planets are based in fiction, modern technology makes it easier than ever for us to perceive the Earth as both a planet and our world. Anthropologists can use Google Earth to locate communities they have studied in remote corners of the world. My colleagues and I have even used space images to choose communities to study on Earth. Interested in the causes of deforestation in Madagascar, we examined a series of satellite images taken in successive years to determine areas where the forest cover had diminished

significantly. Then we traveled to Madagascar to study those areas on the ground. It's interesting to imagine what an alien might "see" in similar images. If these aliens were (as the more benevolent science fiction movies imagine) interested in studying life on Earth, rather than conquering, controlling, or even eating its inhabitants, they would have a lot to interpret. In my work abroad, I've been impressed by two major global trends: population increase and the shift from subsistence to cash economies. These trends have led to agricultural intensification, resource depletion (including deforestation), and emigration and have made it increasingly harder to not think globally when asking ourselves who we are.

I'm struck by the growing number of young people worldwide who have abandoned traditional subsistence pursuits. They seek jobs for cash, but work is scarce, spurring migration within and across national boundaries. In turn, transnational migration increases cultural diversity in the United States, Canada, and Western European countries. Even small towns in the South and Midwest have Chinese restaurants. Pizza and tacos are as American as apple pie. Every day we encounter people whose ancestral countries and cultures have been studied by anthropologists for generations—making cultural anthropology all the more relevant to our daily lives in an increasingly interconnected world.

This chapter applies an anthropological perspective to contemporary global issues. Let's begin by reviewing two different meanings of the term *globalization:* (1) Globalization as fact: the spread and connectedness of production, distribution, consumption, communication, and technologies across the world. This is the primary meaning of globalization used throughout this book. (2) Globalization as contested ideology and policy: efforts by the International Monetary Fund (IMF), the World Bank, the World Trade Organization (WTO), and other international financial powers to create a global free market for goods and services. This second meaning is political and continues to generate considerable opposition.

The fact that certain practices and risks have global implications warrants a discussion of energy consumption and environmental degradation, including climate change, or global warming. Also considered are the threats that deforestation and emerging diseases pose to global biodiversity and human life. The second half of this chapter turns from ecology to the contemporary flows of people, technology, finance, information, messages, images, and ideology that contribute to a global culture of consumption. Globalization promotes intercultural communication, through the media, travel, and migration, which bring people from different societies into direct contact. Finally, we'll consider how such contacts and external linkages affect indigenous peoples, as well as how those groups have organized to confront and deal with national and global issues.

It would be impossible in a single chapter to do a complete review of all the global issues that are salient today and that anthropologists have studied. Many such issues (e.g., war, displacement, terrorism, NGOs, the media) have been considered in previous chapters, and a series of boxes have "focused on globalization" throughout this book. For timely anthropological analysis of a range of global issues, see recent books by John Bodley (2008, 2012) and Richard Robbins (2011).

## ENERGY CONSUMPTION AND INDUSTRIAL DEGRADATION

Industrialization entailed a shift from reliance on renewable resources to the use of fossil fuels. Earth's supply of oil, gas, and coal is being depleted to support a previously unknown level of consumption. Americans are the world's foremost consumers of nonrenewable energy. The average American consumes about 35 times more energy than the average forager or tribesperson (Bodley 2008).

Table 24.1 compares energy consumption, per capita and total, in the United States and selected other countries. Overall the United States represents 18.6 percent of the world's annual energy consumption, compared with China's 21.5 percent, but the average American consumes almost 4 times the energy used by the average Chinese and 16 times the energy used by the average inhabitant of India. Consumption has been rising in China and India, while declining a bit in the United States and Canada, and more dramatically in Europe.

Industrialization has spread to Asia, Latin America, Africa, and the Pacific. One result of industrial expansion has been the destruction of indigenous economies, ecologies, and populations. Two centuries ago, as industrialization was developing, 50 million people still lived in politically independent bands, tribes, and

**TABLE 24.1** Total Energy Consumption, 2011–2012, by Country, Top Ten Countries (in quadrillion BTUs)

|  | TOTAL | PER CAPITA |
|---|---|---|
| World | 510.6* | 74.4[†] |
| China | 109.6 | 82.0 |
| United States | 95.1 | 312.8 |
| Russia | 32.8 | 229.9 |
| India | 23.6 | 19.9 |
| Japan | 20.2 | 163.6 |
| Canada | 13.6 | 396.6 |
| Germany | 13.2 | 160.6 |
| Brazil | 11.7 | 59.0 |
| South Korea | 11.3 | 228.9 |
| France | 10.6 | 165.1 |

*510.6 quadrillion (510,600,000,000,000,000) BTUs

[†]74.4 million BTUs

SOURCE: U.S. Energy Information Administration, International Energy Statistics. http://www.eia.gov/cfapps/ipdbproject/IEDIndex3.cfm?tid=44&pid=44&aid=2

chiefdoms. Occupying vast areas, those nonstate societies, although not totally isolated, were only marginally affected by nation-states and the world capitalist economy. In 1800, bands, tribes, and chiefdoms controlled half the globe and 20 percent of its population (Bodley 2008). Industrialization tipped the balance in favor of states (see Hornborg and Crumley 2007).

Many contemporary nations are repeating—at an accelerated rate—the process of resource depletion that started in Europe and the United States during the Industrial Revolution. Fortunately, however, today's world has some environmental watchdogs that did not exist during the Industrial Revolution. Given national and international cooperation and sanctions, the modern world may benefit from the lessons of the past (see Hornborg, McNeill, and Martinez-Alier 2007).

A key component of globalization is the globalization of risk (Smith and Doyle 2002). Hazards linked to industrial production, emerging diseases, or a cyber attack can spread quickly beyond their point of origin. Climate risks have become globalized, as each consumer of fossil fuels makes his or her individual contribution (the consumer's "carbon footprint") to global climate change, to which we now turn.

## GLOBAL CLIMATE CHANGE

Globally, the year 2010 tied 2005 as the hottest ever recorded by NASA's Goddard Institute for Space Studies (GISS) (2011 was the second hottest). For the United States (but not the globe), 2012 was the hottest year since record keeping began in 1895

# appreciating DIVERSITY

## The Plight of Climate Refugees

The United Nations Intergovernmental Panel on Climate Change estimates that 150 million people worldwide could become environmental refugees by 2050 (York 2009). The Alaskan villagers described here are among the first climate change refugees in the United States. During the past 50 years, the state of Alaska has warmed at more than twice the rate of the rest of the United States (York 2009). Residents of Newtok, Alaska, belong to a federally recognized American Indian tribe. Decades ago, the U.S. government mandated that they (and other Alaskan natives) abandon a nomadic life based on hunting and fishing and settle down in what used to be a winter camp. What obligations does government have to local people whose lives have been disrupted not only by government decree but also by climate change?

NEWTOK, Alaska . . . The earth beneath much of Alaska is not what it used to be. The permanently frozen subsoil, known as permafrost, upon which Newtok and so many other Native Alaskan villages rest is melting, yielding to warming air temperatures and a warming ocean. Sea ice that would normally protect coastal villages is forming later in the year, allowing fall storms to pound away at the shoreline.

Erosion has made Newtok an island, caught between the ever widening Ninglick River and a slough to the north. The village is below sea level, and sinking. Boardwalks squish into the spring muck. Human waste, collected in "honey buckets" that many residents use for toilets, is often dumped within eyeshot in a village where no point is more than a five-minute walk from any other. The ragged wooden houses have to be adjusted regularly to level them on the shifting soil.

Studies say Newtok could be washed away within a decade. Along with the villages of Shishmaref and Kivalina farther to the north, it has been the hardest hit of about 180 Alaska villages that suffer some degree of erosion. Some villages plan to hunker down behind sea walls built or planned by the Army Corps of Engineers, at least for now. Others, like Newtok, have no choice but to abandon their patch of tundra. The corps has estimated that to move Newtok could cost $130 million because of its remoteness, climate and topography. That comes to almost $413,000 for each of the 315 residents. . . .

Newtok's leaders say the corps' relocation estimates are inflated, that they intend to move piecemeal rather than in one collective migration, which they say will save money. But they say government should pay, no matter the cost—if only there were a government agency charged with doing so. There is not a formal process by which a village can apply to the government to relocate.

"They grossly overestimate it, and that's why federal and state agencies are afraid to step in," said Stanley Tom, the current tribal administrator. . . . "They don't want to spend that much money." Still, Newtok has made far more progress toward moving than other villages, piecing together its move grant by grant. Through a land swap with the United States Fish and Wildlife Service, it has secured a new site, on Nelson Island, nine miles south. It is safe from the waves on a windy rise above the Ninglick River. They call it Mertarvik, which means "getting water from the spring." They tell their children they will grow up in a place where *E. coli* does not thrive in every puddle, the way it does here.

With the help of state agencies, it won a grant of about $1 million to build a barge landing at the new site. Bids go out this summer, and construction could be complete next year, providing a platform to unload equipment for building roads, water and sewer systems, houses and a new landing strip. . . .

The administrative leaders of Newtok are mostly men in their 40s, nearly all of them related. They are widely praised by outsiders for their initiative and determination to relocate.

---

**anthropogenic**
Caused by humans and their activities.

**greenhouse effect**
Warming caused by trapped atmospheric gases.

(Gillis 2013; Zaborenko 2012). Earth's surface temperatures have risen about 1.48°F (0.78°C) since the early 20th century (see Johansen 2008). (This chapter's "Appreciating Diversity" discusses how this rise has affected an indigenous group in Alaska.) About two-thirds of this increase has been since 1978 (Figure 24.1). Global warming is not due to increased solar radiation. The causes are mainly **anthropogenic**—caused by humans and their activities. Who can reasonably deny that 7 billion people, along with their animals, crops, machines, and increasing use of fossil fuels, have a greater environmental impact than the 5 million or so pre-Neolithic hunter-gatherers estimated to have lived on our planet 12,000 years ago?

The **greenhouse effect** is a natural phenomenon that keeps the Earth's surface warm. Without greenhouse gases—water vapor ($H_2O$), carbon dioxide ($CO_2$), methane ($CH_4$), nitrous oxide ($N_2O$),

**FIGURE 24.1** Global Temperature Change.
Global annual-mean surface air temperature derived from measurements at meteorological stations has increased by 1.4°F (0.7°C) since the early 20th century, with about 0.9°F (0.5°C) of the increase occurring since 1978.

SOURCE: National Academies, Washington, D.C., Understanding and Responding to Climate Change: Highlights of National Academies Reports, 2008 edition. http://www.tribesandclimatechange.org/documents/nccc/nccc20110504_229.pdf

Yet nearly any place would seem an improvement over Newtok as it exists today, and not all of its problems are rooted in climate change. Some are almost universal to Alaskan villages, which have struggled for decades to reconcile their culture of subsistence hunting and fishing with the expectations and temptations of the world outside.

Excrement dumped from honey buckets is piled on the banks of the slow-flowing Newtok River, not far from wooden shacks where residents take nightly steam baths. An elderly man drains kerosene into a puddle of snowmelt. Children pedal past a walrus skull left to rot, tusks intact, in the mud beside a boardwalk that serves as

a main thoroughfare. There are no cars here, just snow machines, boats and all-terrain vehicles that tear up the tundra. Village elders speak their native Yupik more often than they speak English. They remember when the village was a collection of families who moved with the seasons, making houses from sod, fishing from Nelson Island in the summer, hunting caribou far away in the winter.

Many men still travel with the seasons to hunt and fish. Some will take boats into Bristol Bay this summer to catch salmon alongside commercial fishermen from out of state. But the waterproof jacket sewn from seal gut that Stanley Tom once wore is now stuffed inside a display case at Newtok School next to other relics.

Now Mr. Tom puts on a puffy parka to walk the few hundred feet he travels to work. He checks his e-mail messages to see if there is news from the corps . . . while his brother, Nick, sketches out a budget proposal for a nonprofit corporation to help manage the relocation, presuming the money arrives. [The projected move to the new site described in this story is proceeding as of 2014.]

SOURCE: William Yardley, "Engulfed by Climate Change, Town Seeks Lifeline." From *The New York Times*, May 27, 2007. © 2007 The New York Times. All rights reserved. Used by permission and protected by the Copyright Laws of the United States. The printing, copying, redistribution, or retransmission of this Content without express written permission is prohibited. www.nytimes.com

Thousands of indigenous people living on the Alaskan tundra derive 90 percent or more of what they eat annually from the land, the rivers, and the Bering Sea. Among them are Stanley and Elizabeth Tom and their children, shown here standing beside the Newtok River in Newtok, Alaska. The local and regional effects of climate change have made the Toms and their fellow villagers climate change refugees.

halocarbons, and ozone ($O_3$)—life as we know it wouldn't exist. Like a greenhouse window, such gases allow sunlight to enter and then trap heat from escaping the atmosphere. All those gases have increased since the Industrial Revolution. In fact, the atmospheric concentration of greenhouse gases is now at its highest level in 400,000 years. It will continue to rise, as will global temperatures, without actions to slow it down (National Academy of Sciences 2008; National Research Council 2011).

Scientists prefer the term **climate change** to *global warming*. The former term points out that, beyond rising temperatures, there have been changes in sea levels, storm patterns, and ecosystem effects. The precise effects of climate change on regional weather patterns have yet to be fully determined. Land areas are predicted to warm more than oceans, with the greatest warming in higher latitudes, such as Canada, the northern United States, and northern

**climate change**
Global warming, plus changing sea levels, precipitation, storms, and ecosystem effects.

Methane ($CH_4$) is a greenhouse gas whose atmospheric concentration has risen due to an increase in various human activities, including livestock raising. Shown here, cattle feeding in Lubbock, Texas. How do cattle produce methane?

| WARMING | |
|---|---|
| Carbon dioxide ($CO_2$) | Has natural and human sources; levels increasing due to burning of fossil fuels. |
| Methane ($CH_4$) | Has risen due to an increase in human activities, including livestock raising, rice growing, landfill use, and the extraction, handling, and transport of natural gas. |
| Ozone ($O_3$) | Has natural sources, especially in the stratosphere, where chemicals have depleted the ozone layer; ozone also produced in the troposphere (lower part of the atmosphere) when hydrocarbons and nitrogen oxide pollutants react. |
| Nitrous oxide ($N_2O$) | Has been rising from agricultural and industrial sources. |
| Halocarbons | Include chlorofluorocarbons (CFCs), which remain from refrigerants in appliances made before CFC ban. |
| Aerosols | Some airborne particles and droplets warm the planet; black carbon particles (soot) produced when fossil fuels or vegetation are burned; generally have a warming effect by absorbing solar radiation. |
| **COOLING** | |
| Aerosols | Some cool the planet; sulfate ($SO_4$) aerosols from burning fossil fuels reflect sunlight back to space. |
| Volcanic eruptions | Emit gaseous $SO_2$, which, once in the atmosphere, forms sulfate aerosol and ash; both reflect sunlight back to space. |
| Sea ice | Reflects sunlight back to space. |
| Tundra | Reflects sunlight back to space. |
| **WARMING/COOLING** | |
| Forests | Deforestation creates land areas that reflect more sunlight back to space (cooling); it also removes trees that absorb $CO_2$ (warming). |

Europe. Climate change may benefit these areas, offering milder winters and extended growing seasons. However, many more people worldwide probably will be harmed (see Cribb 2010). Already we know that in the Arctic temperatures have risen almost twice as much as the global average. Arctic landscapes and ecosystems are changing rapidly and perceptibly, as this chapter's "Appreciating Diversity" illustrates. Coastal communities worldwide can anticipate increased flooding and more severe storms and surges. At risk are people, animals, plants, freshwater supplies, and such industries as tourism and farming (Crate and Nuttall 2008; National Academy of Sciences 2008). (Recap 24.1 summarizes the major factors that work to heat and to cool Earth.)

Global energy demand is the single greatest obstacle to slowing down climate change. Worldwide, energy consumption continues to grow with economic and population expansion. China and India, in particular, are rapidly increasing their use of energy, mainly from fossil fuels, and consequently their emissions. China now accounts for over 21 percent of world energy consumption, compared with 9 percent in 2000. The U.S. share fell from 25 percent in 2000 to 19 percent in 2012 (U.S. Energy Information Administration 2013). (See Table 24.1.) Among the alternatives to fossil fuels are nuclear power and such renewable energy technologies as solar, wind, and biomass generators.

# ENVIRONMENTAL ANTHROPOLOGY

Anthropology always has been concerned with how environmental forces influence humans and how human activities affect the environment. The 1950s–1970s witnessed the emergence of an area of study known as cultural ecology, or **ecological anthropology** (see Haenn and Wilk 2006). That field initially focused on how cultural beliefs and practices helped human populations adapt to their environments, as well as how people used elements of their culture to maintain their ecosystems. Ecological anthropologists showed that many indigenous groups

**ecological anthropology**
Study of cultural adaptations to environments.

did a reasonable job of managing their resources and preserving their ecosystems (see Menzies 2006). Such groups had traditional ways of categorizing resources and using them sustainably. The term **ethnoecology** describes a society's set of environmental perceptions and practices.

Given national and international incentives to exploit and degrade, ethnoecological systems that once preserved local and regional environments increasingly are ineffective or irrelevant (see Dove, Sajise, and Doolittle 2011). Anthropologists routinely witness threats to the people they study and their environments. Among such threats are commercial logging, industrial pollution, and the imposition of external management systems on local ecosystems (see Johnston 2009). Today's ecological anthropology, *environmental anthropology,* attempts not only to understand but also to find solutions to environmental problems. As aspects of the globalization of risk, such problems must be tackled at the national and international levels.

Local people and their landscapes, ideas, values, and traditional management systems face attacks from all sides (see Hornborg, Clark, and Hermele 2011). Outsiders attempt to remake native landscapes and cultures in their own image. The aim of many agricultural development projects, for example, seems to be to make the world as much like a midwestern American agricultural state as possible. Often, there is an attempt to impose mechanized farming and nuclear family ownership, even though these institutions may be inappropriate in areas far removed from the midwestern United States. Anthropologists know that development projects usually fail when they try to replace indigenous institutions with culturally alien concepts (Kottak 1990*b*).

## Global Assaults on Local Autonomy

A clash of cultures related to environmental change may occur when development threatens indigenous peoples and their environments (as we saw in the previous chapter's "Appreciating Anthropology"). A second clash of cultures related to environmental change may occur when external regulation aimed at conservation confronts indigenous peoples and their ethnoecologies. Like development projects, conservation schemes may ask people to change their ways in order to satisfy planners' goals rather than local goals. In places as different as Madagascar, Brazil, and the Pacific Northwest of the United States, people have been asked, told, or forced to abandon basic economic activities because to do so is good for "nature" or "the globe." "Good for the globe" doesn't play very well in Brazil, whose Amazon has been a focus of international environmentalist attention. Brazilians complain that outsiders (e.g., Europeans

The world's most populous nations, China and India, are rapidly increasing their use of energy, mainly from fossil fuels, and consequently their emissions of $CO_2$. Pictured here are crowds of cars and buses moving slowly during a serious Beijing traffic jam.

and North Americans) promote "global needs" and "saving the Amazon" after having destroyed their own forests for economic growth. Well-intentioned conservation plans can be as insensitive as development schemes that promote radical changes without involving local people in planning and carrying out the policies that affect them. When people are asked to give up the basis of their livelihood, they usually resist.

Consider the case of a Tanosy man living on the edge of the Andohahela reserve of southeastern Madagascar. For years he has relied on rice fields and grazing land inside that reserve. Now external agencies are telling him to abandon that land for the sake of conservation. This man is a wealthy *ombiasa* (traditional sorcerer-healer). With four wives, a dozen children, and 20 head of cattle, he is an ambitious, hardworking, and productive peasant. With money, social support, and supernatural authority, he has mounted effective resistance against the park ranger who has been trying to get him to abandon his fields. The *ombiasa* claims he has already relinquished some of his fields, but he is waiting for compensatory land. His most effective resistance has been supernatural. The death of the ranger's young son was attributed to the *ombiasa*'s magic. After that, the ranger became less vigilant in his enforcement efforts.

The spread of environmentalism may reveal radically different notions about the "rights" and value of plants and animals versus humans. In Madagascar, many intellectuals and officials complain that

**ethnoecology**

A culture's set of environmental perceptions and practices.

A scene from the "great red island" of Madagascar. On that island, the effects of deforestation, water runoff, and soil erosion are visible to the naked eye.

Madagascar's population is growing at a rate of 3 percent annually, doubling every generation. Population pressure leads to migration, including rural–urban migration. Madagascar's capital, Antananarivo, had just 100,000 people in 1967. The population stands at about 2 million today. Urban growth promotes deforestation if city dwellers rely on fuel wood from the countryside, as is true in Madagascar. As forested watersheds disappear, crop productivity declines. Madagascar is known as the "great red island," after the color of its soil. On that island, the effects of soil erosion and water runoff are visible to the naked eye. From the look of its rivers, Madagascar appears to be bleeding to death. Increasing runoff of water no longer trapped by trees causes erosion of low-lying rice fields near swollen rivers as well as siltation in irrigation canals (Kottak 2007).

Globally, other causes of deforestation include commercial logging, road building, cash cropping, and clearing and burning associated with livestock and grazing. The fact that forest loss has several causes has a policy implication: Different deforestation scenarios require different conservation strategies.

What can be done? On this question applied anthropology weighs in, spurring policy makers to think about new conservation strategies. The traditional approach has been to restrict access to forested areas designated as parks, then employ park guards and punish violators. Modern strategies are more likely to consider the needs, wishes, and abilities of the people (often impoverished) living in and near the forest. Because effective conservation depends on the cooperation of the local people, their concerns must be addressed in devising conservation strategies.

Reasons to change behavior must make sense to local people (see Sillitoe 2007). In Madagascar, the economic value of the forest for agriculture (as an anti-erosion mechanism and a reservoir of potential irrigation water) provides a much more powerful incentive against forest degradation than do such global goals as "preserving biodiversity." Most Malagasy have no idea that lemurs and other endemic species exist only in Madagascar. Nor would such knowledge provide much of an incentive for them to conserve the forests if doing so jeopardized their livelihoods.

To curb the global deforestation threat, we need conservation strategies that work. Laws and enforcement may help reduce commercially driven deforestation caused by burning and clear-cutting. But local people also use and abuse forested lands. A challenge for the environmentally oriented applied anthropologist is to find ways to make forest preservation attractive to local people and ensure their cooperation. Applied anthropologists must work to make "good for the globe" good for the people.

foreigners seem more concerned about lemurs and other endangered species than about the people of Madagascar (the Malagasy). As a geographer there remarked to me, "The next time you come to Madagascar, there'll be no more Malagasy. All the people will have starved to death, and a lemur will have to meet you at the airport." Most Malagasy perceive human poverty as a more pressing problem than animal and plant survival.

Still, who can doubt that conservation, including the preservation of biodiversity, is a worthy goal? The challenge for applied ecological anthropology is to devise culturally appropriate strategies for achieving biodiversity conservation in the face of unrelenting population growth and commercial expansion. How does one get people to support conservation measures that may—in the short run, at least—diminish their access to resources? Like development plans in general, the most effective conservation strategies pay attention to the needs and wishes of the local people.

## Deforestation

Anthropologists know that food producers (farmers and herders) typically do more to degrade the environment than foragers do. Population increase and the need to expand farming caused deforestation in many parts of the ancient Middle East and Mesoamerica (see Hornborg and Crumley 2007). Even today, many farmers think of trees as giant weeds to be removed and replaced with productive fields.

Often, deforestation is demographically driven—caused by population pressure. For example,

## Emerging Diseases

When humans modify or destroy environments and ecosystems, nature has a way of striking back. Most or all infectious diseases that have emerged in the

Applied anthropology uses anthropological perspectives to identify and solve contemporary problems that affect humans. Deforestation is one such problem. Here, women take part in a reforestation project in coastal Tanzania near Dar es Salaam.

last few decades are due to human encroachment on wild lands, particularly forests, and to changes in demography (human population increase and changing settlement patterns). In the Amazon, one study showed that an increase in deforestation of just 4 percent produced a 50 percent increase in the incidence of malaria. This is because mosquitoes, which transmit malaria, thrive in the right mix of sunlight and water in recently deforested areas (Robbins 2012; see also Livingstone 1969). The recent emergence and spread of infectious diseases like HIV/AIDS, Ebola, West Nile, SARS (severe acute respiratory syndrome), and Lyme disease are all the result of things people have done to their environments.

The spread of disease from wild to domesticated animals and then to humans has been going on since the Neolithic, when animals first were domesticated. Diseases that spread from animals to humans are known as *zoonotic* diseases, and they pose a huge threat today because of human population increase and forces of globalization. Emerging diseases kill more than two million people annually, and 60 percent of those diseases originate in animals (Robbins 2012).

Especially since the Neolithic, infectious diseases, including malaria and plague, have moved from woods and wildlife to humans, often through their domesticated animals. One such disease, the Nipah virus, began its migration from fruit bats to humans in South Asia. Because fruit bats have co-evolved with the Nipah virus for millions of years, it

does little damage to their health. When the virus moves from bats into other species, however, it can be lethal. Fruit bats eat the pulp of fruit and spit out the residue. In rural Malaysia in 1999, an infected bat appears to have dropped a piece of chewed fruit into the food supply of a swine herd (a scenario depicted in the movie *Contagion*). The virus then spread from those pigs to humans. Of 276 people infected in Malaysia, 106 died. Eleven more people died in Signapore, when the virus was exported there via live pigs. South Asia has experienced a dozen smaller Nipah outbreaks in recent years.

Spillovers from wildlife to humans have quadrupled in the last half-century, reflecting increasing human encroachment on disease hotspots, especially in the tropics (Robbins 2012). Wildlife trafficking and modern air travel contribute to the potential for a serious outbreak or pandemic among humans. (A *pandemic* is an epidemic with global scope.) The zero patient for the HIV/AIDS pandemic (in North America, at least) is reputed to have been a flight attendant who flew internationally. HIV/AIDS originally jumped from chimpanzees to humans through bush-meat hunters in Africa, who kill and butcher chimps.

The threat posed by zoonotic diseases has been recognized by biologists and doctors. One international project, called PREDICT, funds teams of veterinarians, conservation biologists, medical doctors, and epidemiologists to identify disease-causing organisms in wildlife before they spread to humans (see http://www.vetmed.ucdavis.edu/ohi/

On the left, microbiologists at Atlanta's Centers for Disease Control suit up before entering the CDC's Biosafety Level-4 (BSL-4) laboratory. CDC's Special Pathogens Branch focuses on such emerging disease viruses as Ebola, hantavirus, Nipah, and tickborne encephalitis. On the right, a scientist in Nigeria pursues bats, to test for zoonotic diseases.

**Westernization**
The acculturative influence of Western expansion on local cultures worldwide.

predict/index.cfm). PREDICT, which is financed by the United States Agency for International Development (USAID), attempts to "predict," spot, and prevent the spread of zoonotic diseases in global geographic hotspots with high potential for disease transmission. At least 24 countries in Africa, Latin America, and Asia participate in the program. PREDICT scientists monitor areas where deadly viruses are known to exist and where humans are encroaching. One such locale is a new highway being built to link the Atlantic and Pacific Oceans in South America, traversing Brazil and the Peruvian Andes.

PREDICT scientists also gather blood, saliva, and other samples from high-risk wildlife species to create a "library" of viruses, in order to facilitate identification when a threat is imminent. This library focuses on the animals most likely to carry diseases that affect people, such as primates, rats, and bats. PREDICT scientists also study ways of preventing disease spillovers and the pandemics that might follow. Sometimes solutions can be remarkably simple. In Bangladesh, for example, outbreaks of the Nipah virus were contained by placing bamboo screens (which cost 8 cents each) over the containers used to collect date palm sap (Robbins 2012). Because human groups create the conditions that allow zoonotic pathogens to jump species and to spread, anthropologists have a key role to play in studying the cultural (including economic) causes of environmental encroachment and in suggesting culturally appropriate and workable solutions.

## INTERETHNIC CONTACT

Since at least the 1920s, anthropologists have studied the changes that arise from contact between industrial and nonindustrial societies. *Acculturation* refers to changes that result when groups come into continuous firsthand contact—changes in the cultural patterns of either or both groups (Redfield, Linton, and Herskovits 1936, p. 149).

Acculturation differs from diffusion, or cultural borrowing, which can occur without firsthand contact. For example, most North Americans who eat hot dogs ("frankfurters") have never been to Frankfurt, Germany, nor have most North American Toyota owners or sushi eaters ever visited Japan. Although *acculturation* can be applied to any case of cultural contact and change, the term most often has described **Westernization**—the influence of Western expansion on indigenous peoples and their cultures. Thus, local people who wear store-bought clothes, learn Indo-European languages, and otherwise adopt Western customs are called "acculturated." Acculturation may be voluntary or forced, and there may be considerable resistance to the process.

Different degrees of destruction, domination, resistance, survival, adaptation, and modification of native cultures may follow interethnic contact. In the most destructive encounters, native and subordinate cultures face obliteration. When contact with powerful outsiders seriously threatens an indigenous culture, a "shock phase" often follows the initial encounter (Bodley 2012). Outsiders may attack or exploit the native people. Such exploitation may increase mortality, disrupt subsistence, fragment kin groups, damage social support systems, and inspire new religious movements. During the shock phase, there may be civil repression backed by military force. Such factors may lead to the group's cultural collapse (*ethnocide*) or physical extinction (*genocide*).

## Cultural Imperialism and Indigenization

**Cultural imperialism** refers to the spread or advance of one culture at the expense of others, or its imposition on other cultures, which it modifies, replaces, or destroys—usually because of differential economic or political influence. Thus, children in the French colonial empire learned French history, language, and culture from standard textbooks also used in France. Tahitians, Malagasy, Vietnamese, and Senegalese learned the French language by reciting from books about "our ancestors the Gauls."

Some commentators think that modern technology, international brands, and the mass media are erasing cultural differences, as homogeneous products reach more people worldwide. But others see a role for modern technology in allowing social groups (local cultures) to express themselves and to survive (Marcus and Fischer 1999). For example, radio, TV, film, digital media, and increasingly the Internet (e.g., YouTube) constantly bring local happenings to the attention of a larger public. Susan Boyle's rendition of "I Dreamed a Dream" on a British TV show soon became an Internet sensation and made her a global star. Without YouTube, appreciation of Boyle's voice might have been confined to the United Kingdom. Contemporary media play a role in stimulating and organizing local and community activities of many sorts. Think of ways in which this is done by YouTube, Facebook, and Twitter—global networks all.

In Brazil, local practices, celebrations, and performances have changed in the context of outside forces, including the mass media and tourism. In the town of Arembepe, Brazil (Kottak 2006), TV coverage stimulated increased participation in a traditional annual performance, the Chegança. This is a danceplay that reenacts the Portuguese discovery of Brazil. Arembepeiros have traveled to the state capital to perform the Chegança before television cameras, for a TV program featuring traditional performances from many rural communities, and cameras have gone to Arembepe to record it.

In several towns along the Amazon River, annual folk ceremonies now are staged more lavishly for TV and video cameras. In the Amazon town of Parantíns, for example, boatloads of tourists arriving any time of year are shown a video recording of the town's annual Bumba Meu Boi festival. This is a costumed performance mimicking bullfighting, parts of which have been shown on national TV. This pattern, in which local communities preserve, revive, and intensify the scale of traditional ceremonies to perform for the media and tourists, is expanding. To see whether I could, I just managed to watch snippets of these annual events in Arembepe and Parantíns on YouTube!

**cultural imperialism** Spread or advance of one (dominant) culture at the expense of others.

In San Gimignano, Italy, boys and young men don medieval costumes and beat drums in a parade through the streets during one of the town's many pageants. Increasingly, local communities perform "traditional" ceremonies for TV and tourists.

Brazilian TV also has aided the national spread of Carnaval beyond its traditional urban centers (Kottak 2009). Still, local reactions to the nationwide broadcasting of Carnaval and its trappings (elaborate parades, costumes, and frenzied dancing) are not simple or uniform responses to external stimuli. Rather than direct adoption of Carnaval, local Brazilians respond in various ways. Often, they don't take up Carnaval itself but modify their local festivities to fit Carnaval images. Others actively spurn Carnaval. One example is Arembepe, where Carnaval has never been important, probably because of its calendrical closeness to the main local festival, which is held in February to honor Saint Francis of Assisi. In the past, villagers couldn't afford to celebrate both occasions. Now, not only do the people of Arembepe reject Carnaval; they also are increasingly hostile to their own main festival. Arembepeiros resent the fact that the Saint Francis festival has become "an outsiders' event," because it draws thousands of tourists to Arembepe each year. The villagers think that commercial interests and outsiders have appropriated their festival for Saint Francis.

Arembepeiros now prefer the traditional June festivals honoring Saint John, Saint Peter, and Saint Anthony. Formerly, these were observed on a much smaller scale than was the Saint Francis celebration. Arembepeiros observe them now with a new vigor and enthusiasm, as they react to outsiders and their celebrations, real and televised. The national or the global can become that only if the local populace cooperates.

People constantly make and remake culture as they assign their own meanings to the information, images, and products they get from outside. **Indigenization** refers to the process by which people modify borrowed forms to make them fit into their local culture. Indigenization occurs in cultural domains as different as fast food, music, movies, social media, housing styles, science, terrorism, celebrations, religion, and political ideas and institutions (Fiske 2011; Wilk 2006; Wilk and Barbosa 2012).

## A Global System of Images

With globalization, more people in many more places imagine "a wider set of 'possible' lives than they ever did before. One important source of this change is the mass media . . ." (Appadurai 1991, p. 197). The United States as a global media center has been joined by Canada, Japan, Western Europe, Brazil, Mexico, Nigeria, Egypt, India, and Hong Kong.

Like print (see Anderson 2006), modern media can diffuse the cultures of countries within (and often beyond) their borders. Millions of Brazilians, for example, used to be cut off (by geographic isolation or illiteracy) from urban, national, and international events and information; they now participate in a larger "mediascape" (Appadurai 1991) through mass media and the Internet (Kottak 1990a, 2009).

Brazil's most popular network (Rede Globo) relies heavily on its own productions, especially telenovelas (nightly serial programs often compared to American soap operas). Globo plays each night to the world's largest and most devoted audience (perhaps 80 million viewers throughout the nation and beyond—via satellite TV). The programs that attract this horde are made by Brazilians, for Brazilians.

The mass media and the Internet also play a prominent role in maintaining ethnic and national identities among people who lead transnational lives. Arabic-speaking Muslims, including migrants in several countries, follow the TV network Al Jazeera, based in Qatar, which helps reinforce ethnic and religious identities. As groups move, they can stay linked to each other and to their homeland through global media. **Diasporas** (people who have spread out from an original, ancestral homeland) have enlarged the markets for media, communication, brands, and travel services targeted at specific ethnic, national, or religious groups who now live in various parts of the world. This market growth in depth and breadth is evidenced by the launching of Al Jazeera America in 2013, with a stated mission of "rebalancing global media by respecting the diversity and humanity of the world."

## A Global Culture of Consumption

Besides the electronic media, other key global forces are production, commerce, and finance. As Arjun Appadurai (1991, p. 194) puts it, "money,

Illustrating both globalization and indigenization, McDonald's now routinely tries to tailor its offerings to specific cultural appetites. Shown here in downtown Fort de France, Martinique (French West Indies), is a billboard advertising a hamburger topped with Italian cheese (Parmigiano-Reggiano).

commodities, and persons unendingly chase each other around the world." Residents of many Latin American communities now depend on outside cash, remitted from international labor migration. Also, the economy of the United States is increasingly influenced by foreign investment, especially from Britain, Canada, Germany, the Netherlands, Japan, and China. The American economy also has increased its dependence on foreign labor—through both the immigration of laborers and the export of jobs.

Business, technology, and the media have increased the craving for commodities and images throughout the world. This has forced nation-states to open to a global culture of consumption. In the Middle East, for example, social media use exploded during the Arab Spring of 2011. In cyberspace Middle Easterners found something missing from their ordinary, offline worlds: platforms permitting social connectivity and the collective airing of grievances. Since then, social media have entered the region commercially, promoting and selling digital advertising (Hamdan 2013). In 2012 the number of Twitter users tripled in the Arab world, growing fastest in Saudi Arabia, Egypt, Kuwait, and the United Arab Emirates. Arabic has become Twitter's fastest-growing language. Facebook's Middle Eastern user base grew from 16 million in 2010 to 45 million in 2012. LinkedIn (a professional social networking and job search site) has five million Middle Eastern users. (This region has one of the highest youth unemployment rates in the world.) This rapidly rising Middle Eastern Internet presence is occurring in an area where 40 percent of the population (of 380 million) is younger than 30 years. The smartphone is another key element in the Middle Eastern marketing mediascape. A global survey by Google found that 93 percent of smartphone users notice mobile ads, and 39 percent of those follow up with an online purchase. Saudi Arabia's mobile phone penetration rate is 190 percent, meaning that everyone has almost two cell phones (Hamdan 2013). Media and marketing are the new It couple.

Almost everyone today participates in the global consumers' culture. Few people have never seen a T-shirt advertising a Western product. American and English rock stars' recordings blast through the streets of Rio de Janeiro, while taxi drivers from Toronto to Madagascar listen to Brazilian music. The popularity of Korean pop singers spreads internationally via the Internet. Peasants and tribal people participate in the modern world system not only because they have been hooked on cash but also because their products and images are appropriated by world capitalism (Root 1996). They are commercialized by others (like the Quileute nation in the *Twilight* series of books and movies). Furthermore, indigenous peoples also market their own images and products, through outlets like Cultural Survival.

Business and the media spur global demand for certain products and brands. This photo was taken in Yangon, Myanmar. What brands and products stand out in the photo?

## PEOPLE IN MOTION

The linkages created through globalization have both enlarged and erased old boundaries and distinctions. Arjun Appadurai (1990, p. 1) characterizes today's world as a "translocal" "interactive system" that is "strikingly new." Whether as refugees, migrants, tourists, pilgrims, proselytizers, laborers, businesspeople, development workers, politicians, terrorists, soldiers, sports figures, or media-borne images, people travel more than ever. The scale of human movement has expanded dramatically. So important is transnational migration that many Mexican villagers are as likely to have friends and relatives living hundreds or thousands of miles away as immediately around them. Migrants maintain their ties with home through social media, by phoning, texting, Skyping, e-mailing, Facebooking, and FaceTiming. Frequently, they send money home; when possible, they also visit. In a sense, they live multilocally—in different places at once. Dominicans in New York City, for example, have been characterized as living "between two islands": Manhattan and the Dominican Republic (Grasmuck and Pessar 1991).

With so many people "in motion," the unit of anthropological study expands from the local community to the diaspora—the offspring of an area who have spread to many lands. Anthropologists increasingly follow descendants of the villages we have studied as they move from rural to urban areas and across national boundaries. For an annual meeting of the American Anthropological Association held in Chicago, the anthropologist Robert Kemper organized a session of presentations about long-term ethnographic fieldwork. Kemper's own long-time research focus has been the Mexican village of

With so many people on the move, the unit of anthropological study has expanded from the local community to the diaspora, the offspring of an area who have spread to many lands, such as the owners of this falafel shop in Paris, France.

larger associations. There is a growing pan–Native American identity and an international pantribal movement as well. Thus, in June 1992, the World Conference of Indigenous Peoples met in Rio de Janeiro concurrently with UNCED (the United Nations Conference on the Environment and Development). Along with diplomats, journalists, and environmentalists came 300 representatives of the tribal diversity that survives under globalization—from Lapland to Mali (Brooke 1992; see also Maybury-Lewis 2002; Maybury-Lewis, Macdonald, and Maybury-Lewis 2009). The meeting itself was a global forum, sponsored by the United Nations, perhaps the closest thing Earth has to a planetary council.

## INDIGENOUS PEOPLES

All too often, conquest, annexation, and development have been associated with **genocide**—the deliberate extermination of a specific ethnic group. Examples include the Holocaust, Rwanda in 1994, and Bosnia in the early 1990s. Bodley (2008) estimates that an average of 250,000 indigenous people perished annually between 1800 and 1950. The causes included warfare, outright murder, introduced diseases, slavery, land grabbing, and other forms of dispossession and impoverishment.

The indigenous groups that have survived now live within nation-states. Often, they maintain a distinct ethnic identity, despite having lost their ancestral cultures to varying degrees. Many such groups aspire to autonomy. As the original inhabitants of their territories, they are called indigenous peoples (see Maybury-Lewis 2002).

The term *indigenous people* entered international law in 1982 with the creation of the United Nations Working Group on Indigenous Populations (WGIP). This group meets annually and has members from six continents. The UN General Assembly adopted its Declaration of Indigenous Rights in 2007. Convention 169, a document supporting cultural diversity and indigenous empowerment, was approved by the International Labor Organization (ILO) in 1989. Such documents, along with the global work of the WGIP, have influenced governments, NGOs, and international agencies to adopt policies favorable to indigenous peoples. Social movements worldwide now use *indigenous people* as a self-identifying label in their quests for social, cultural, and political rights (Brower and Johnston 2007; de la Peña 2005).

In Spanish-speaking Latin America, social scientists and politicians now favor the term *indígena* (indigenous person) over *indio* (Indian), the colonial term that European conquerors used for Native Americans (de la Peña 2005). Until the mid- to late 1980s, Latin American public policy emphasized assimilation. The past 30 years have witnessed a dramatic shift. The emphasis has shifted from

**genocide**
Deliberate elimination of a group through mass murder.

**postmodernity**
Time of questioning of established canons, identities, and standards.

**postmodern**
Marked by the breakdown of established canons, categories, distinctions, and boundaries.

**postmodernism**
Movement after modernism in architecture; now describes comparable developments in music, literature, and visual art.

Tzintzuntzan, which, with his mentor George Foster, he has studied for decades. However, their database now includes not just Tzintzuntzan but its descendants all over the world. Given the Tzintzuntzan diaspora, Kemper was even able to use some of his time in Chicago to visit people from Tzintzuntzan who had established a colony there. In today's world, as people move, they take their traditions and their anthropologists along with them.

**Postmodernity** describes our time and situation: today's world in flux, these people on the move who have learned to manage multiple identities depending on place and context. In its most general sense, **postmodern** refers to the blurring and breakdown of established canons (rules or standards), categories, distinctions, and boundaries. The word is taken from **postmodernism**—a style and movement in architecture that succeeded modernism, beginning in the 1970s. Postmodern architecture rejected the rules, geometric order, and austerity of modernism. Modernist buildings were expected to have a clear and functional design. Postmodern design is "messier" and more playful. It draws on a diversity of styles from different times and places—including popular, ethnic, and non-Western cultures. Postmodernism extends "value" well beyond classic, elite, and Western cultural forms. *Postmodern* is now used to describe comparable developments in music, literature, and visual art. From this origin, *postmodernity* describes a world in which traditional standards, contrasts, groups, boundaries, and identities are opening up, reaching out, and breaking down.

New kinds of political and ethnic units have emerged along with globalization. In some cases, cultures and ethnic groups have banded together in biological and cultural assimilation—*mestizaje*—to identities that value difference, especially as indigenous peoples.

In Ecuador, groups seen previously as Quichua-speaking peasants are classified now as indigenous communities with assigned territories. Other Andean "peasants" have experienced similar reindigenization as well. Brazil has recognized 30 new indigenous communities in the northeast, a region previously seen as having lost its indigenous population. In Guatemala, Nicaragua, Brazil, Colombia, Mexico, Paraguay, Ecuador, Argentina, Bolivia, Peru, and Venezuela, constitutional reforms have recognized those nations as multicultural (Jackson and Warren 2005). Several national constitutions now recognize the rights of indigenous peoples to cultural distinctiveness, sustainable development, political representation, and limited self-government (de la Peña 2005).

The indigenous rights movement exists in the context of globalization, including transnational movements focusing on human rights, women's rights, and environmentalism. Transnational organizations have helped indigenous peoples to influence legislation. Since the 1980s, there has been a general shift in Latin America from authoritarian to democratic rule. Still, inequality and discrimination persist, including assassinations of indigenous leaders and their supporters (Jackson and Warren 2005).

Ceuppens and Geschiere (2005) explore an upsurge, in several world areas, of the notion of *autochthony* (being native to, or formed in, the place where found), with an implicit call for excluding strangers. The terms *autochthony* and *indigenous* both go back to classical Greek history, with similar implications. *Autochthony* refers to self and soil. *Indigenous* literally means born inside, with the connotation in classical Greek of being born "inside the house." Both notions stress rights of first-comers to privileged status and protection versus later immigrants—legal or illegal (Ceuppens and Geschiere 2005; Hornborg et al. 2011).

During the 1990s, autochthony became an issue in many parts of Africa, inspiring violent efforts to exclude (European and Asian) "strangers." Simultaneously, autochthony became a key notion in debates about immigration and multiculturalism in Europe. European majority groups have claimed the label *autochthon*. This term highlights the prominence that the exclusion of strangers has assumed in day-to-day politics worldwide (Ceuppens and Geschiere 2005). One familiar example is the United States, as represented in debates over undocumented immigrants.

**Essentialism** describes the process of viewing an identity as innate, real, and frozen, thus ignoring the historical processes within which that identity developed. Identities, however, are not fixed; they are fluid and multiple. People draw on particular, sometimes competing, self-labels and identities. Some Peruvian groups, for instance, self-identify as *mestizos* but still see themselves as indigenous.

Mary Simat, with the Maasai Women for Education and Economic Development from Kenya, testifies at the Indigenous Peoples' Global Summit on Climate Change in Anchorage, Alaska, in April 2009. The five-day United Nations–affiliated conference attracted about 400 people from 80 nations.

Identity is a fluid, dynamic process, and there are multiple ways of being indigenous. Neither speaking an indigenous language nor wearing "native" clothing is required to self-identify as indigenous (Jackson and Warren 2005).

**essentialism**
Viewing identities that have developed historically as innate and unchanging.

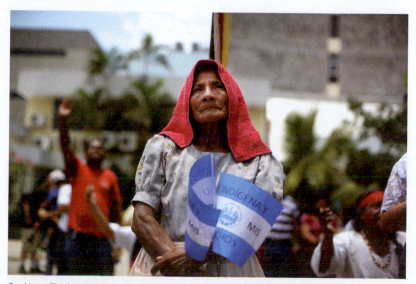

Seeking official recognition of El Salvador's indigenous peoples, a member of one such group, the Lenca, participates in a 2013 demonstration in the national capital, San Salvador. In 1932, dictator Maximiliano Hernández Martínez, suppressing a peasant uprising, massacred up to 30,000 natives. The survivors, as a result, stopped using their language and hid their traditional customs. Here, as throughout Latin America, things have been changing.

## ANTHROPOLOGY'S LESSONS

Anthropology teaches us that the adaptive responses of humans can be more flexible than those of other species, because our main adaptive means are sociocultural. However, in the face of globalization, the cultural institutions of the past always influence subsequent adaptation, producing continued diversity in the actions and reactions of different groups as they indigenize global inputs. In our globalizing world, anthropology offers a people-centered vision of social change. The existence of anthropology is itself a tribute to the continuing need to understand similarities and differences among human beings throughout the world.

Anthropology offers relevant, indeed powerful, ways of seeing how the world actually works. Lessons of the past can and should be applied to the present and future, hopefully to benefit humanity. Anthropologists know that civilizations and world powers rise and fall, and that social transformations typically follow major innovations, such as the Neolithic and the Industrial Revolution. There is no guarantee that the current world system and the power relations within it will last forever. What will happen if humans do survive and find themselves living in entirely new systems? Try to answer this question using your new knowledge of anthropology.

# for REVIEW

## summary

1. Fueling global warming are human population growth and increasing use of fossil fuels. The term *climate change* encompasses global warming along with changing sea levels, precipitation, storms, and ecosystem effects.

2. Anthropologists have studied how environmental forces influence humans and how human activities affect the Earth's atmosphere. An ethnoecology is a society's set of environmental practices and perceptions. Indigenous ethnoecologies increasingly are being challenged by global forces. A challenge for applied ecological anthropology is to devise culturally appropriate strategies for conservation in the face of population growth and commercial expansion.

3. Causes of deforestation include demographic pressure on subsistence economies, commercial logging, road building, cash cropping, urban expansion, and clearing and burning associated with livestock. Infectious diseases such as HIV/AIDS, Ebola, West Nile, and SARS have emerged and spread because of things that people have done to their environments. Cultural imperialism is the spread of one culture and its imposition on other cultures, which it modifies, replaces, or destroys—usually because of differential economic or political influence. Some critics worry that modern technology, including the mass media, is destroying traditional cultures. But others see an important role for new technology in allowing local cultures to express themselves.

4. As the forces of globalization spread, they are modified (indigenized) to fit into local cultures. Modern media can help diffuse a national culture within its own boundaries. The media also play a role in preserving ethnic and national identities among people who lead transnational lives.

5. People travel more than ever. But migrants also maintain ties with home, so they live multilocally. *Postmodernity* describes this world in flux, with people on the move who manage multiple social identities depending on place and context. New kinds of political and ethnic units are emerging as others break down or disappear.

6. Governments, NGOs, and international agencies have adopted policies designed to recognize and benefit indigenous peoples. Social movements worldwide have adopted this term as a self-identifying and political label based on past oppression but now signaling a search for social, cultural, and political rights. In Latin America, several national constitutions now recognize the rights of indigenous peoples. Identity is a fluid, dynamic process, and there are multiple ways of being indigenous.

1. What does it mean to apply an anthropological perspective to contemporary global issues? Can you come up with an anthropological research question that investigates such issues? Imagine you had a year (and the money!) to carry out this project. How would you spend your time and your resources?

2. The topic of global climate change has been hotly debated during the last few years. Why is there so much debate? Are you concerned about global climate change? Do you think everyone on the planet should be equally concerned and share the responsibility of doing something about it? Why or why not?

3. Consider majority and minority rights in the context of contemporary events involving religion, ethnicity, politics, and law. Should religion be an ascribed or an achieved status? How about ethnicity? Why?

4. Do you now live, or have you ever lived, multilocally? If so, how so?

5. What term do anthropologists use to describe the view that identities have developed historically as innate and unchanging? We know, however, that identities are not fixed; they are fluid and multiple. What does this mean? What implications does this have for understanding indigenous political movements?

# GLOSSARY

**absolute dating** Dating techniques that establish dates in numbers or ranges of numbers; examples include the radiometric methods of $^{14}$C, K/A, $^{238}$U, TL, and ESR dating.

**acculturation** The exchange of cultural features that results when groups come into continuous firsthand contact; the cultural patterns of either or both groups may be changed, but the groups remain distinct.

**Acheulean** Derived from the French village of St. Acheul, where these tools were first identified; Lower Paleolithic tool tradition associated with *H. erectus.*

**achieved status** Social status that comes through talents, choices, actions, and accomplishments, rather than ascription.

**adaptive** Favored by natural selection in a particular environment.

**adaptive strategy** Means of making a living; productive system.

**aesthetics** Appreciation of the qualities perceived in works of art; the mind and emotions in relation to a sense of beauty.

**affinals** Relatives by marriage.

**African American Vernacular English (AAVE)** Rule-governed dialect spoken by some African Americans.

**agency** The actions of individuals, alone and in groups, that create and transform culture.

**agriculture** Nonindustrial systems of plant cultivation characterized by continuous and intensive use of land and labor.

**allele** A biochemical variant of a particular gene.

**Allen's rule** Rule stating that the relative size of protruding body parts (such as ears, tails, bills, fingers, toes, and limbs) tends to increase in warmer climates.

**ambilineal descent** Principle of descent that does not automatically exclude the children of either sons or daughters.

**AMHs** See *anatomically modern humans.*

**analogies** Similarities arising as a result of similar selective forces; traits produced by convergent evolution.

**anatomically modern humans (AMHs)** Hominins including the Cro-Magnons of Europe (31,000 B.P.) and the older fossils from Skhūl (100,000), Qafzeh (92,000), Herto, and other sites; continue through the present; also known as *H. sapiens sapiens.*

**animism** Belief in souls, or doubles.

**anthropogenic** Caused by humans and their activities.

**anthropoids** Members of Anthropoidea, one of the two suborders of primates; monkeys, apes, and humans are anthropoids.

**anthropological archaeology** The study of human behavior through material remains.

**anthropology** The study of the human species and its immediate ancestors.

**anthropology and education** Anthropological research in classrooms, homes, and neighborhoods, viewing students as total cultural creatures whose enculturation and attitudes toward education belong to a larger context that includes family, peers, and society.

**anthropometry** The measurement of human body parts and dimensions, including skeletal parts (*osteometry*).

**antimodernism** The rejection of the modern in favor of what is perceived as an earlier, purer, and better way of life.

**applied anthropology** The application of anthropological data, perspectives, theory, and methods to identify, assess, and solve contemporary social problems.

**arboreal** Tree-dwelling; arboreal primates include gibbons, New World monkeys, and many Old World monkeys.

**archaic *H. sapiens*** Early *H. sapiens*, consisting of the Neandertals of Europe and the Middle East, the Neandertal-like hominids of Africa and Asia, and the immediate ancestors of all these hominids; lived from about 300,000 to 28,000 B.P.

***Ardipithecus*** Earliest recognized hominin genus (5.8–4.4 m.y.a), Ethiopia; species are *kadabba* (earlier) and *ramidus* (later).

**art** An object or event that evokes an aesthetic reaction—a sense of beauty, appreciation, harmony, and/or pleasure; the quality, production, expression, or realm of what is beautiful or of more than ordinary significance; the class of objects subject to aesthetic criteria.

**arts** The arts include the visual arts, literature (written and oral), music, and performance arts.

**ascribed status** Social status (e.g., race or gender) that people have little or no choice about occupying.

**assimilation** The process of change that a minority group may experience when it moves to a country where another culture dominates; the minority is incorporated into the dominant culture to the point that it no longer exists as a separate cultural unit.

**association** An observed relationship between two or more variables.

***Au. afarensis*** Early forms of *Australopithecus*, known from Hadar in Ethiopia ("Lucy") and Laetoli in Tanzania; the Hadar remains date to 3.3–3.0 m.y.a.; the Laetoli remains are older, dating to 3.8–3.6 m.y.a.; despite its many apelike features, *Au. afarensis* was an upright biped.

***Au. africanus*** Gracile *Australopithecus* species (3.0?–2.0? m.y.a.), South Africa; first australopithecine ever discovered.

***Au. anamensis*** Earliest known *Australopithecus* species (4.2–3.9 m.y.a.), from Kenya.

***Au. boisei*** Late, hyperrobust *Australopithecus* species (2.6?–1.2 m.y.a.), East Africa; coexisted with early *Homo.*

***Au. garhi*** Toolmaking *Australopithecus* species (2.6–2.5 m.y.a.); discovered in Ethiopia.

***Au. robustus*** *Paranthropus;* robust *Australopithecus* species (2.0?–1.0? m.y.a.), South Africa.

**australopithecines** Varied group of Pliocene–Pleistocene hominids. The term is derived from their former classification as members of a distinct subfamily, the Australopithecinae; now they are distinguished from *Homo* only at the genus level.

**Aztec** Last independent state in the Valley of Mexico; capital was Tenochtitlán; thrived between 1325 and the Spanish Conquest in 1520.

**balanced polymorphism** Two or more forms, such as alleles of the same gene, that maintain a constant frequency in a population from generation to generation.

**balanced reciprocity** See *generalized reciprocity*.

**band** Basic unit of social organization among foragers. A band includes fewer than 100 people; it often splits up seasonally.

**behavioral ecology** Study of the evolutionary basis of social behavior.

**behavioral modernity** Fully human behavior based on symbolic thought and cultural creativity.

**Bergmann's rule** Rule stating that the smaller of two bodies similar in shape has more surface area per unit of weight and therefore can dissipate heat more efficiently; hence, large bodies tend to be found in colder areas and small bodies in warmer ones.

**bifurcate collateral kinship terminology** Kinship terminology employing separate terms for M, F, MB, MZ, FB, and FZ.

**bifurcate merging kinship terminology** Kinship terminology in which M and MZ are called by the same term, F and FB are called by the same term, and MB and FZ are called by different terms.

**big man** Regional figure found among tribal horticulturalists and pastoralists. The big man occupies no office but creates his reputation through entrepreneurship and generosity to others. Neither his wealth nor his position passes to his heirs.

**bilateral kinship calculation** A system in which kinship ties are calculated equally through both sexes: mother and father, sister and brother, daughter and son, and so on.

**biocultural** Referring to the inclusion and combination (to solve a common problem) of both biological and cultural approaches—one of anthropology's hallmarks.

**biological anthropology** The study of human biological variation in time and space; includes evolution, genetics, growth and development, and primatology.

**bipedal** Upright, two-legged locomotion, the key feature distinguishing early hominins from the apes.

**blade tool** The basic Upper Paleolithic tool type, hammered off a prepared core.

**bone biology** The study of bone as a biological tissue, including its genetics; cell structure; growth, development, and decay; and patterns of movement (*biomechanics*).

**bourgeoisie** One of Marx's opposed classes; owners of the means of production (factories, mines, large farms, and other sources of subsistence).

**brachiation** Under-the-branch swinging.

**broad-spectrum revolution** Period beginning around 15,000 B.P. in the Middle East and 12,000 B.P. in Europe, during which a wider range, or broader spectrum, of plant and animal life was hunted, gathered, collected, caught, and fished; revolutionary because it led to food production.

**bronze** An alloy of arsenic and copper or tin and copper.

**call systems** Systems of communication among nonhuman primates, composed of a limited number of sounds that vary in intensity and duration. Tied to environmental stimuli.

**capital** Wealth or resources invested in business, with the intent of producing a profit.

**capitalist world economy** The single world system, which emerged in the 16th century, committed to production for sale, with the object of maximizing profits rather than supplying domestic needs.

**cargo cults** Postcolonial, acculturative religious movements, common in Melanesia, that attempt to explain European domination and wealth and to achieve similar success magically by mimicking European behavior.

**catharsis** Intense emotional release.

**chiefdom** Society with permanent political structure, hereditary leaders, and social ranking but lacking class divisions.

**chromosomes** Basic genetic units, occurring in matching (homologous) pairs; lengths of DNA made up of multiple genes.

**clan** Unilineal descent group based on stipulated descent.

**climate change** Global warming plus changing sea levels, precipitation, storms, and ecosystem effects.

**cline** A gradual shift in gene frequencies between neighboring populations.

**Clovis** Stone technology based on a projectile point that was fastened to the end of a hunting spear; it flourished between 12,000 and 11,000 B.P. in North America.

**collateral relative** A genealogical relative who is not in ego's direct line, such as B, Z, FB, or MZ.

**colonialism** The political, social, economic, and cultural domination of a territory and its people by a foreign power for an extended time.

**communism** Spelled with a lowercase *c*, describes a social system in which property is owned by the community and in which people work for the common good.

**Communism** Spelled with an uppercase *C*, a political movement and doctrine seeking to overthrow capitalism and to establish a form of communism such as that which prevailed in the Soviet Union from 1917 to 1991.

**communitas** Intense community spirit, a feeling of great social solidarity, equality, and togetherness; characteristic of people experiencing liminality together.

**complex societies** Nations; large and populous, with social stratification and central governments.

**configurationalism** View of culture as integrated and patterned.

**conflict resolution** Means of settling disputes.

**convergent evolution** Independent operation of similar selective forces; the process by which analogies are produced.

**core** Dominant structural position in the world system; consists of the strongest and most powerful states with advanced systems of production.

**core values** Key, basic, or central values that integrate a culture and help distinguish it from others.

**correlation** An association between two or more variables such that when one changes (varies), the other(s) also change(s) (covaries)—for example, temperature and sweating.

**cosmology** A system, often religious, for imagining and understanding the universe.

**Cro Magnon** The first fossil find (1868) of an AMH, from France's Dorlogne Valley.

**cross cousins** Children of a brother and a sister.

**crossing over** During meiosis, the process by which homologous chromosomes intertwine and exchange segments of their DNA.

**cultivation continuum** A continuum based on the comparative study of nonindustrial cultivating societies in which labor intensity increases and fallowing decreases.

**cultural anthropology** The study of human society and culture; describes, analyzes, interprets, and explains social and cultural similarities and differences.

**cultural colonialism** Internal domination by one group and its culture or ideology over others.

**cultural consultants** Subjects in ethnographic research; people the ethnographer gets to know in the field, who teach him or her about their culture.

**cultural imperialism** The rapid spread or advance of one culture at the expense of others, or its imposition on other cultures, which it modifies, replaces, or destroys—usually because of differential economic or political influence.

**cultural materialism** Idea (Harris) that cultural infrastructure determines structure and superstructure.

**cultural relativism** The position that the values and standards of cultures differ and deserve respect. Anthropology is characterized by methodological rather than moral relativism: In order to understand another culture fully, anthropologists try to understand its members' beliefs and motivations. Methodological relativism does not preclude making moral judgments or taking action.

**cultural resource management** The branch of applied archaeology aimed at preserving sites threatened by dams, highways, and other projects.

**cultural rights** Doctrine that certain rights are vested in identifiable groups, such as religious and ethnic minorities and indigenous societies. Cultural rights include a group's ability to preserve its culture, to raise its children in the ways of its forebears, to continue its language, and not to be deprived of its economic base by the nation-state in which it is located.

**cultural transmission** A basic feature of language; transmission through learning.

**culture** Distinctly human; transmitted through learning; traditions and customs that govern behavior and beliefs.

**cuneiform** Early Mesopotamian writing that used a stylus (writing implement) to write wedge-shaped impressions on raw clay; from the Latin word for "wedge."

**curer** Specialized role acquired through a culturally appropriate process of selection, training, certification, and acquisition of a professional image; the curer is consulted by patients, who believe in his or her special powers, and receives some form of special consideration; a cultural universal.

**daughter languages** Languages developing out of the same parent language; for example, French and Spanish are daughter languages of Latin.

**dendrochronology** Tree-ring dating: a method of absolute dating based on the study and comparison of patterns of tree-ring growth.

**descent** Rule assigning social identity on the basis of some aspect of one's ancestry.

**descent group** A permanent social unit whose members claim common ancestry; fundamental to tribal society.

**development anthropology** The branch of applied anthropology that focuses on social issues in—and the cultural dimension of—economic development.

**diachronic** (Studying societies) across time.

**diaspora** The offspring of an area who have spread to many lands.

**differential access** Unequal access to resources; basic attribute of chiefdoms and states. Superordinates have favored access to such resources, while the access of subordinates is limited by superordinates.

**diffusion** Borrowing of cultural traits between societies, either directly or through intermediaries.

**diglossia** The existence of "high" (formal) and "low" (informal, familial) dialects of a single language, such as German.

**discrimination** Policies and practices that harm a group and its members.

**disease** A scientifically identified health threat caused by a bacterium, virus, fungus, parasite, or other pathogen.

**displacement** A basic feature of language; the ability to speak of things and events that are not present.

**domestic–public dichotomy** Contrast between women's role in the home and men's role in public life, with a corresponding social devaluation of women's work and worth.

**dominant** Allele that masks another allele in a heterozygote.

**dowry** A marital exchange in which the wife's group provides substantial gifts to the husband's family.

**ecological anthropology** Study of cultural adaptations to environments.

**economizing** The rational allocation of scarce means (or resources) to alternative ends (or uses); often considered the subject matter of economics.

**economy** A population's system of production, distribution, and consumption of resources.

**egalitarian society** A type of society, most typically found among hunter-gatherers, that lacks status distinctions except those based on age, gender, and individual qualities, talents, and achievements.

**ego** Latin for I. In kinship charts, the point from which one views an egocentric genealogy.

**emic** The research strategy that focuses on local explanations and criteria of significance.

**empire** A mature, territorially large, and expansive state; empires are typically multiethnic, multilinguistic, and more militaristic, with a better-developed bureaucracy than earlier states.

**enculturation** The social process by which culture is learned and transmitted across the generations.

**endogamy** Rule or practice of marriage between people of the same social group.

**essentialism** The process of viewing an identity as established, real, and frozen to hide the historical processes and politics within which that identity developed.

**ethnic group** Group distinguished by cultural similarities (shared among members of that group) and differences (between that group and others); ethnic-group members share beliefs, customs, and norms and, often, a common language, religion, history, geography, and kinship.

**ethnicity** Identification with, and feeling part of, an ethnic group and exclusion from certain other groups because of this affiliation.

**ethnocentrism** The tendency to view one's own culture as best and to judge the behavior and beliefs of culturally different people by one's own standards.

**ethnocide** Destruction of cultures of certain ethnic groups.

**ethnoecology** Any society's set of environmental practices and perceptions; its cultural model of the environment and its relation to people and society.

**ethnography** Fieldwork in a particular cultural setting.

**ethnology** Cross-cultural comparison; the comparative study of ethnographic data, society, and culture.

**ethnomusicology** The comparative study of the musics of the world and of music as an aspect of culture and society.

**ethnosemantics** The study of lexical (vocabulary) contrasts and classifications in various languages.

**etic** The research strategy that emphasizes the ethnographer's rather than the locals' explanations, categories, and criteria of significance.

**evolution** Belief that species arose from others through a long and gradual process of transformation, or descent with modification.

**excavation** Digging through the layers of deposits that make up an archaeological or fossil site.

**exogamy** Rule requiring people to marry outside their own group.

**expressive culture** The arts; people express themselves creatively in dance, music, song, painting, sculpture, pottery, cloth, storytelling, verse, prose, drama, and comedy.

**extended family household** Expanded household including three or more generations.

**family of orientation** Nuclear family in which one is born and grows up.

**family of procreation** Nuclear family established when one marries and has children.

**fiscal** Pertaining to finances and taxation.

**focal vocabulary** A set of words and distinctions that are particularly important to certain groups (those with particular foci of experience or activity), such as types of snow to Eskimos or skiers.

**folk** Of the people; originally coined for European peasants; refers to the art, music, and lore of ordinary people, as contrasted with the "high" art, or "classic" art, of the European elites.

**food production** An economy based on cultivation of plants and domestication (stockbreeding) of animals; first developed 10,000 to 12,000 years ago.

**fossils** Remains (e.g., bones), traces, or impressions (e.g., footprints) of ancient life.

**functional explanation** Explanation that establishes a correlation or an interrelationship between social customs. When customs are functionally interrelated, if one changes, the others also change.

**functionalism** Approach focusing on the role (function) of sociocultural practices in social systems.

**fundamentalism** Describes antimodernist movements in various religions. Fundamentalists assert an identity separate from the larger religious group from which they arose; they advocate strict fidelity to the "true" religious principles on which the larger religion was founded.

**gender** The cultural construction of whether one is female, male, or something else.

**gender identity** A person's identification by self and others as male, female, or something else.

**gender roles** The tasks and activities that a culture assigns to each sex.

**gender stereotypes** Oversimplified but strongly held ideas about the characteristics of males and females.

**gender stratification** Unequal distribution of rewards (socially valued resources, power, prestige, and personal freedom) between men and women, reflecting their different positions in a social hierarchy.

**gene** Area in a chromosome pair that determines, wholly or partially, a particular biological trait, such as whether one's blood type is A, B, or O.

**genealogical method** Procedures by which ethnographers discover and record connections of kinship, descent, and marriage, using diagrams and symbols.

**gene flow** Exchange of genetic material between populations of the same species through direct or indirect interbreeding.

**gene pool** All the alleles, genes, chromosomes, and genotypes within a breeding population—the "pool" of genetic material available.

**general anthropology** The field of anthropology as a whole, consisting of cultural, archaeological, biological, and linguistic anthropology.

**generality** Culture pattern or trait that exists in some but not all societies.

**generalized reciprocity** Principle that characterizes exchanges between closely related individuals. As social distance increases, reciprocity becomes balanced and finally negative.

**generational kinship terminology** Kinship terminology with only two terms for the parental generation, one designating M, MZ, and FZ and the other designating F, FB, and MB.

**genetic evolution** Change in gene frequency within a breeding population.

**genitor** Biological father of a child.

**genocide** Deliberate elimination of a group through mass murder.

**genotype** An organism's hereditary makeup.

**gibbons** The smallest apes, natives of Asia; arboreal.

**glacials** The four or five major advances of continental ice sheets in northern Europe and North America.

**globalization** The accelerating interdependence of nations in a world system linked economically and through mass media and modern transportation systems.

**gracile** Opposite of robust; "gracile" indicates that members of *Au. africanus* were a bit smaller and slighter, less robust, than members of *Au. robustus*.

**greenhouse effect** Warming from trapped atmospheric gases.

**Halafian** An early (7500–6500 B.P.) and widespread Mesopotamian pottery style, first found in northern Syria; refers to a delicate ceramic style and to the period when the first chiefdoms emerged.

**haplogroup** A lineage marked by one or more specific genetic mutations.

**health care systems** Beliefs, customs, and specialists concerned with ensuring health and preventing and curing illness; a cultural universal.

**hegemony** As used by Antonio Gramsci, a stratified social order in which subordinates comply with domination by internalizing its values and accepting its "naturalness."

**Herto** Very early (160,000–154,000 B.P.) AMHs found in Ethiopia.

**heterozygous** Having dissimilar alleles of a given gene.

**hilly flanks** Woodland zone that flanks the Tigris and Euphrates Rivers to the north; zone of wild wheat and barley and of sedentism (settled, nonmigratory life) preceding food production.

**historical linguistics** Subdivision of linguistics that studies languages over time.

**historical particularism** Idea (Boas) that histories are not comparable; diverse paths can lead to the same cultural result.

**holistic** Interested in the whole of the human condition: past, present, and future; biology, society, language, and culture.

**hominid** A member of the taxonomic family that includes humans and the African apes and their immediate ancestors.

**hominins** Members of the human lineage after its split from ancestral chimps; the term *hominin* is used to describe all the human species that ever have existed, including the extinct ones, and excluding chimps and gorillas.

**hominoid** Member of the superfamily including extinct and living humans and all the apes.

**Homo habilis** Term coined by L. S. B. and Mary Leakey; immediate ancestor of *H. erectus;* lived from about 2.4 to 1.4 m.y.a.

**homologies** Traits that organisms have jointly inherited from a common ancestor.

**homozygous** Possessing identical alleles of a particular gene.

**honorific** A term, such as "Mr." or "Lord," used with people, often by being added to their names, to "honor" them.

**horticulture** Nonindustrial system of plant cultivation in which plots lie fallow for varying lengths of time.

**human rights** Doctrine that invokes a realm of justice and morality beyond and superior to particular countries, cultures, and religions. Human rights, usually seen as vested in individuals, would include the right to speak freely, to hold religious beliefs without persecution, and not to be murdered, injured, enslaved, or imprisoned without charge.

**hypodescent** Rule that automatically places the children of a union or mating between members of different socioeconomic groups in the less privileged group.

**hypothesis** A suggested but as yet unverified explanation.

**illness** A condition of poor health perceived or felt by an individual.

**imperialism** A policy of extending the rule of a nation or an empire over foreign nations or of taking and holding foreign colonies.

**incest** Sexual relations with a close relative.

**increased equity** A reduction in absolute poverty and a fairer (more even) distribution of wealth.

**independent assortment** Mendel's law of; chromosomes are inherited independently of one another.

**independent invention** Development of the same cultural trait or pattern in separate cultures as a result of comparable needs, circumstances, and solutions.

**indigenization** Process by which borrowed forms are modified to fit the local culture.

**Industrial Revolution** The historic transformation (in Europe, after 1750) of "traditional" into "modern" societies through industrialization of the economy.

**informed consent** Agreement to take part in research, after the people being studied have been told about that research's purpose, nature, procedures, and potential impact on them.

**interglacials** Extended warm periods between such major glacials as Riss and Würm.

**international culture** Cultural traditions that extend beyond national boundaries.

**interpretive anthropology** (Geertz) The study of a culture as a system of meaning.

**intersex** Pertaining to a group of conditions reflecting a discrepancy between the external genitals (penis, vagina, etc.) and the internal genitals (testes, ovaries, etc.).

**intervention philosophy** Guiding principle of colonialism, conquest, missionization, or development; an ideological justification for outsiders to guide native peoples in specific directions.

**interview schedule** Ethnographic tool for structuring a formal interview. A prepared form (usually printed or mimeographed) that guides interviews with households or individuals being compared systematically. Contrasts with a *questionnaire* because the researcher has personal contact with the local people and records their answers.

**IPR** Intellectual property rights, consisting of each society's cultural base—its core beliefs and principles. IPR are claimed as a group right—a cultural right—allowing indigenous groups to control who may know and use their collective knowledge and its applications.

**key cultural consultants** Persons who are experts on a particular aspect of local life.

**kinesics** The study of communication through body movements, stances, gestures, and facial expressions.

**kinship calculation** The system by which people in a particular society reckon kin relationships.

**language** Human beings' primary means of communication; may be spoken or written; features productivity and displacement and is culturally transmitted.

**law** A legal code, including trial and enforcement; characteristic of state-organized societies.

**levirate** Custom by which a widow marries the brother of her deceased husband.

**lexicon** Vocabulary; a dictionary containing all the morphemes in a language and their meanings.

**life history** Gathered by an ethnographer, an account of the life of a key consultant or narrator; provides a personal cultural portrait of existence or change in a culture.

**liminality** The critically important marginal or in-between phase of a rite of passage.

**lineage** Unilineal descent group based on demonstrated descent.

**lineal kinship terminology** Parental generation kin terminology with four terms: one for M, one for F, one for FB and MB, and one for MZ and FZ.

**lineal relatives** Any of ego's ancestors or descendants (e.g., parents, grandparents, children, grandchildren) on the direct line of descent that leads to and from ego.

**linguistic anthropology** The descriptive, comparative, and historical study of language and of linguistic similarities and differences in time, space, and society.

**lobola** A substantial marital gift from the husband and his kin to the wife and her kin.

**longitudinal research** Long-term study of a community, region, society, culture, or other unit, usually based on repeated visits.

**magic** Use of supernatural techniques to accomplish specific aims.

**maize** Corn; first domesticated in tropical southwestern Mexico around 8000 B.P.

**mana** Sacred impersonal force in Melanesian and Polynesian religions.

**manioc** Cassava; a tuber domesticated in the South American lowlands.

**market principle** Profit-oriented principle of exchange that dominates in states, particularly industrial states. Goods and services are bought and sold, and values are determined by supply and demand.

**mater** Socially recognized mother of a child.

**matrilineal descent** Unilineal descent rule in which people join the mother's group automatically at birth and stay members throughout life.

**means (factors) of production** Land, labor, technology, and capital—major productive resources.

**medical anthropology** Unites biological and cultural anthropologists in the study of disease, health problems, health care systems, and theories about illness in different cultures and ethnic groups.

**meiosis** Special process by which sex cells are produced; four cells are produced from one, each with half the genetic material of the original cell.

**melanin** Substance manufactured in specialized cells in the lower layers of the epidermis (outer skin layer); melanin cells in dark skin produce more melanin than do those in light skin.

**Mesoamerica** Middle America, including Mexico, Guatemala, and Belize.

**Mesolithic** Middle Stone Age, whose characteristic tool type was the microlith; broad-spectrum economy.

**Mesopotamia** The area between the Tigris and Euphrates Rivers in what is now southern Iraq and southwestern Iran; location of the first cities and states.

**metallurgy** Knowledge of the properties of metals, including their extraction and processing and the manufacture of metal tools.

**mitosis** Ordinary cell division; DNA molecules copy themselves, creating two identical cells out of one.

**mode of production** Way of organizing production—a set of social relations through which labor is deployed to wrest energy from nature by means of tools, skills, and knowledge.

**molecular anthropology** Genetic analysis, involving comparison of DNA sequences, to determine evolutionary links and distances among species and among ancient and modern populations.

**monotheism** Belief in a single all-powerful deity.

**morphology** The study of form; used in linguistics (the study of morphemes and word construction) and for form in general—for example, biomorphology relates to physical form.

**Mousterian** Middle Paleolithic toolmaking tradition associated with Neandertals.

**multiculturalism** The view of cultural diversity in a country as something good and desirable; a multicultural society socializes individuals not only into the dominant (national) culture but also into an ethnic culture.

**mutation** Change in the DNA molecules of which genes and chromosomes are built.

**m.y.a.** Million years ago.

**nation** Once a synonym for "ethnic group," designating a single culture sharing a language, religion, history, territory, ancestry, and kinship; now usually a synonym for *state* or *nation-state*.

**national culture** Cultural experiences, beliefs, learned behavior patterns, and values shared by citizens of the same nation.

**nationalities** Ethnic groups that once had, or wish to have or regain, autonomous political status (their own country).

**nation-state** An autonomous political entity; a country such as the United States or Canada.

**Natufians** Widespread Middle Eastern culture, dated to between 12,500 and 10,200 B.P.; subsisted on intensive wild cereal collecting and gazelle hunting and had year-round villages.

**natural selection** The process by which the forms most fit to survive and reproduce in a given environment do so in greater numbers than others in the same population; more than survival of the fittest, natural selection is differential reproductive success.

**Neandertals** *H. sapiens neanderthalensis*, representing an archaic *H. sapiens* group that lived in Europe and the Middle East between 130,000 and 28,000 B.P.

**negative reciprocity** See *generalized reciprocity*.

**neoliberalism** Revival of Adam Smith's classic economic liberalism, the idea that governments should not regulate private enterprise and that free market forces should rule; a currently dominant intervention philosophy.

**Neolithic** Term used to describe economies based on food production (cultivated crops and domesticated animals).

**neolocality** Postmarital residence pattern in which a couple establishes a new place of residence rather than living with or near either set of parents.

**nomadism (pastoral)** Movement throughout the year by the whole pastoral group (men, women, and children) with their animals; more generally, nomadism is movement throughout the year in pursuit of strategic resources.

**office** Permanent political position.

**Oldowan** Earliest (2.6 to 1.2 m.y.a.) stone tools; sharp flakes struck from cores (choppers).

**opposable thumb** A thumb that can touch all the other fingers.

**overinnovation** Characteristic of projects that require major changes in natives' daily lives, especially ones that interfere with customary subsistence pursuits.

**paleoanthropology** Study of hominid and human life through the fossil record.

**Paleolithic** Old Stone Age (from Greek roots meaning "old" and "stone"); divided into Lower (early), Middle, and Upper (late).

**paleontology** Study of ancient life through the fossil record.

**paleopathology** Study of disease and injury in skeletons from archaeological sites.

**pantribal sodalities** Non-kin-based groups that exist throughout a tribe, spanning several villages.

**parallel cousins** Children of two brothers or two sisters.

**particularity** Distinctive or unique culture trait, pattern, or integration.

**pastoralists** People who use a food-producing strategy of adaptation based on care of herds of domesticated animals.

**pastoral nomadism** See *nomadism (pastoral)*.

**pater** Socially recognized father of a child; not necessarily the genitor.

**patriarchy** Political system ruled by men in which women have inferior social and political status, including basic human rights.

**patrilineal descent** Unilineal descent rule in which people join the father's group automatically at birth and stay members throughout life.

**patrilineal-patrilocal complex** An interrelated constellation of patrilineality, patrilocality, warfare, and male supremacy.

**peasant** Small-scale agriculturalist living in a state with rent fund obligations.

**periphery** Weakest structural position in the world system.

**phenotype** An organism's evident traits, its "manifest biology"—anatomy and physiology.

**phenotypical adaptation** Adaptive biological changes that occur during the individual's lifetime, made possible by biological plasticity.

**phoneme** Significant sound contrast in a language that serves to distinguish meaning, as in minimal pairs.

**phonemics** The study of significant sound contrasts (phonemes) of a particular language.

**phonetics** The study of speech sounds in general; what people actually say in various languages.

**phonology** The study of sounds used in speech in a particular language.

**physical anthropology** See *biological anthropology*.

**Pleistocene** Epoch of *Homo*'s appearance and evolution; began 1.8 million years ago; divided into Lower, Middle, and Upper.

**plural marriage** Any marriage with more than two spouses; polygamy.

**plural society** A society that combines ethnic contrasts and economic interdependence of the ethnic groups.

**political economy** The web of interrelated economic and power relations in society.

**polity** Political entity, such as a chiefdom or state.

**polyandry** Variety of plural marriage in which a woman has more than one husband at the same time.

**polygyny** Variety of plural marriage in which a man has more than one wife at the same time.

**polytheism** Belief in several deities who control aspects of nature.

**population genetics** Field that studies causes of genetic variation, maintenance, and change in breeding populations.

**postcolonial** Referring to interactions between European nations and the societies they colonized (mainly after 1800);

more generally, "postcolonial" may be used to signify a position against imperialism and Eurocentrism.

**postmodern** In its most general sense, describes the blurring and breakdown of established canons (rules, standards), categories, distinctions, and boundaries.

**postmodernism** A style and movement in architecture that succeeded modernism. Compared with modernism, post-modernism is less geometric, less functional, less austere, more playful, and more willing to include elements from diverse times and cultures; *postmodern* now describes comparable developments in music, literature, visual art, and anthropology.

**postmodernity** Condition of a world in flux, with people on the move, in which established groups, boundaries, identities, contrasts, and standards are reaching out and breaking down.

**potlatch** Competitive feast among Indians on the North Pacific Coast of North America.

**power** The ability to exercise one's will over others—to do what one wants; the basis of political status.

**prejudice** Devaluing (looking down on) a group because of its assumed behavior, values, capabilities, attitudes, or other attributes.

**prestige** Esteem, respect, or approval for acts, deeds, or qualities considered exemplary.

**primary states** States that arise on their own (through competition among chiefdoms), not through contact with other state societies.

**primatology** The study of fossil and living apes, monkeys, and prosimians, including their behavior and social life.

**productivity** A basic feature of language; the ability to use the rules of one's language to create new expressions comprehensible to other speakers.

**prosimians** The primate suborder that includes lemurs, lorises, and tarsiers.

**protolanguage** Language ancestral to several daughter languages.

**public anthropology** Efforts to extend anthropology's visibility beyond academia and to demonstrate its public policy relevance.

**punctuated equilibrium** Evolutionary theory that long periods of stasis (stability), during which species change little, are interrupted (punctuated) by evolutionary leaps.

**questionnaire** Form (usually printed) used by sociologists to obtain comparable information from respondents. Often mailed to and filled in by research subjects rather than by the researcher.

**race** An ethnic group assumed to have a biological basis.

**racial classification** The attempt to assign humans to discrete categories (purportedly) based on common ancestry.

**racism** Discrimination against an ethnic group assumed to have a biological basis.

**random genetic drift** Change in gene frequency that results not from natural selection but from chance; most evident in small populations.

**random sample** A sample in which all members of the population have an equal statistical chance of being included.

**ranked society** A type of society with hereditary inequality but not social stratification; individuals are ranked in terms of their genealogical closeness to the chief, but there is a continuum of status, with many individuals and kin groups ranked about equally.

**recessive** Genetic trait masked by a dominant trait.

**reciprocity** One of the three principles of exchange; governs exchange between social equals; major exchange mode in band and tribal societies.

**reciprocity continuum** A continuum running from generalized (closely related/deferred return) to negative (strangers/immediate return) reciprocity.

**redistribution** Major exchange mode of chiefdoms, many archaic states, and some states with managed economies.

**refugees** People who have been forced (involuntary refugees) or who have chosen (voluntary refugees) to flee a country, to escape persecution or war.

**relative dating** Dating technique, for example, stratigraphy, that establishes a time frame in relation to other strata or materials, rather than absolute dates in numbers.

**religion** Belief and ritual concerned with supernatural beings, powers, and forces.

**remote sensing** Use of aerial photos and satellite images to locate sites on the ground.

**revitalization movements** Social movements that occur in times of change, in which religious leaders emerge and undertake to alter or revitalize a society.

**rickets** Nutritional disease caused by a shortage of vitamin D; interferes with the absorption of calcium and causes softening and deformation of the bones.

**rites of passage** Culturally defined activities associated with the transition from one place or stage of life to another.

**ritual** Behavior that is formal, stylized, repetitive, and stereotyped, performed earnestly as a social act; rituals are held at set times and places and have liturgical orders.

**robust** Large, strong, sturdy; said of skull, skeleton, muscle, and teeth; opposite of gracile.

**sample** A smaller study group chosen to represent a larger population.

**Sapir-Whorf hypothesis** Theory that different languages produce different ways of thinking.

**science** A systematic field of study or body of knowledge that aims, through experiment, observation, and deduction, to produce reliable explanations of phenomena, with reference to the material and physical world.

**scientific medicine** As distinguished from Western medicine, a health care system based on scientific knowledge and procedures, encompassing such fields as pathology, microbiology, biochemistry, surgery, diagnostic technology, and applications.

**sedentism** Settled (sedentary) life; preceded food production in the Old World and followed it in the New World.

**semantics** A language's meaning system.

**semiperiphery** Structural position in the world system intermediate between core and periphery.

**settlement hierarchy** A ranked series of communities differing in size, function, and type of building; a three-level settlement hierarchy indicates state organization.

**sexual dimorphism** Marked differences in male and female biology besides the contrasts in breasts and genitals.

**sexual orientation** A person's habitual sexual attraction to, and activities with, persons of the opposite sex, heterosexuality; the same sex, homosexuality; or both sexes, bisexuality.

**sexual selection** Based on differential success in mating, the process in which certain traits of one sex (e.g., color in male birds) are selected because of advantages they confer in winning mates.

**shaman** A part-time religious practitioner who mediates between ordinary people and supernatural beings and forces.

**smelting** The high-temperature process by which pure metal is produced from an ore.

**social control** Those fields of the social system (beliefs, practices, and institutions) that are most actively involved in the maintenance of norms and the regulation of conflict.

**sociolinguistics** Investigates relationships between social and linguistic variations.

**sororate** Custom by which a widower marries the sister of his deceased wife.

**speciation** Formation of new species; occurs when subgroups of the same species are separated for a sufficient length of time.

**species** Population whose members can interbreed to produce offspring that can live and reproduce.

**state** Sociopolitical organization based on central government and socioeconomic stratification—a division of society into classes.

**state (nation-state)** Complex sociopolitical system that administers a territory and populace with substantial contrasts in occupation, wealth, prestige, and power. An independent, centrally organized political unit; a government. A form of social and political organization with a formal, central government and a division of society into classes.

**status** Any position that determines where someone fits in society; may be ascribed or achieved.

**stereotypes** Fixed ideas—often unfavorable—about what the members of a group are like.

**stratification** Characteristic of a system with socioeconomic strata—groups that contrast in regard to social status and access to strategic resources. Each stratum includes people of both sexes and all ages.

**stratified** Class-structured; stratified societies have marked differences in wealth, prestige, and power between social classes.

**stratigraphy** Science that examines the ways in which earth sediments are deposited in demarcated layers known as *strata* (singular, *stratum*).

**style shifts** Variations in speech in different contexts.

**subcultures** Different cultural traditions associated with subgroups in the same complex society.

**subgroups** Languages within a taxonomy of related languages that are most closely related.

**subordinate** The lower, or underprivileged, group in a stratified system.

**superordinate** The upper, or privileged, group in a stratified system.

**superorganic** (Kroeber) The special domain of culture, beyond the organic and inorganic realms.

**survey research** Characteristic research procedure among social scientists other than anthropologists. Studies society through sampling, statistical analysis, and impersonal data collection.

**symbol** Something, verbal or nonverbal, that arbitrarily and by convention stands for something else, with which it has no necessary or natural connection.

**symbolic anthropology** The study of symbols in their social and cultural context.

**synchronic** (Studying societies) at one time.

**syncretisms** Cultural mixes, including religious blends, that emerge from acculturation—the exchange of cultural features when cultures come into continuous firsthand contact.

**syntax** The arrangement and order of words in phrases and sentences.

**systematic survey** Information gathered on patterns of settlement over a large area; provides a regional perspective on the archaeological record.

**taboo** Set apart as sacred and off-limits to ordinary people; prohibition backed by supernatural sanctions.

**taphonomy** The study of the processes that affect the remains of dead animals, such as their scattering by carnivores and scavengers, their distortion by various forces, and their possible fossilization.

**taxonomy** Classification scheme; assignment to categories (*taxa;* singular, *taxon*).

**teosinte** Or teocentli, a wild grass; apparent ancestor of maize.

**Teotihuacán** C.E. 100 to 700; first state in the Valley of Mexico and earliest major Mesoamerican empire.

**terrestrial** Ground-dwelling; baboons, macaques, and humans are terrestrial primates; gorillas spend most of their time on the ground.

**text** Any cultural product that can be "read"—that is, processed, interpreted, and assigned meaning by anyone (any "reader") exposed to it.

**theory** A set of ideas formulated (by reasoning from known facts) to explain something. The main value of a theory is to promote new understanding. A theory suggests patterns, connections, and relationships that may be confirmed by new research.

**Thomson's nose rule** Rule stating that the average nose tends to be longer in areas with lower mean annual temperatures; based on the geographic distribution of nose length among human populations.

**totem** An animal, a plant, or a geographic feature associated with a specific social group, to which that totem is sacred or symbolically important.

**transgender** A category of varied individuals whose gender identity contradicts their biological sex at birth and the gender identity that society assigned to them in infancy.

**transhumance** One of two variants of pastoralism; part of the population moves seasonally with the herds while the other part remains in home villages.

**tribe** Form of sociopolitical organization usually based on horticulture or pastoralism. Socioeconomic stratification and centralized rule are absent in tribes, and there is no means of enforcing political decisions.

**tropics** Geographic belt extending about 23 degrees north and south of the equator, between the Tropic of Cancer (north) and the Tropic of Capricorn (south).

**underdifferentiation** Planning fallacy of viewing less-developed countries as an undifferentiated group; ignoring cultural diversity and adopting a uniform approach (often ethnocentric) for very different types of project beneficiaries.

**uniformitarianism** Belief that explanations for past events should be sought in ordinary forces that continue to work today.

**unilineal descent** Matrilineal or patrilineal descent.

**unilinear evolutionism** Idea (19th century) of a single line or path of cultural development—a series of stages through which all societies must evolve.

**universal** Something that exists in every culture.

**Upper Paleolithic** Blade-toolmaking traditions associated with early *H. sapiens sapiens;* named from their location in upper, or more recent, layers of sedimentary deposits.

**urban anthropology** Anthropological study of cities and urban life.

**variables** Attributes (e.g., sex, age, height, weight) that differ from one person or case to the next.

**village head** A local leader in a tribal society who has limited authority, leads by example and persuasion, and must be generous.

**wealth** All a person's material assets, including income, land, and other types of property; the basis of economic status.

**Westernization** The acculturative influence of Western expansion on native cultures.

**working class (proletariat)** Those who must sell their labor to survive; the antithesis of the bourgeoisie in Marx's class analysis.

**world-system theory** Idea that a discernible social system, based on wealth and power differentials, transcends individual countries.

**Zapotec state** First Mesoamerican state, in the Valley of Oaxaca.

# BIBLIOGRAPHY

Abelmann, N., and J. Lie
    1995   *Blue Dreams: Korean Americans and the Los Angeles Riots.* Cambridge, MA: Harvard University Press.

Adams, R. M.
    1981   *Heartland of Cities.* Chicago: Aldine.
    2008   An Interdisciplinary Overview of a Mesopotamian City and Its Hinterlands, *Cuneiform Digital Library Journal,* http://cdli.ucla.edu/pubs/cdlj/2008/cdlj2008_001.

Adams, S.
    2012   The World's Next Genocide. *New York Times,* November 15. www.nytimes.com.

Adepegba, C. O.
    1991   The Yoruba Concept of Art and Its Significance in the Holistic View of Art as Applied to African Art. *African Notes* 15: 1–6.

Ahmed, A. S.
    2004   *Postmodernism and Islam: Predicament and Promise,* rev. ed. New York: Routledge.

Aiello, L., and M. Collard
    2001   Our Newest Oldest Ancestor? *Nature* 410: 526–527.

Akazawa, T.
    1980   *The Japanese Paleolithic: A Techno-Typological Study.* Tokyo: Rippo Shobo.fiske.

Akazawa, T., and C. M. Aikens, eds.
    1986   *Prehistoric Hunter-Gatherers in Japan: New Research Methods.* Tokyo: University of Tokyo Press.

Allegretto, S. A.
    2011   The State of Working America's Wealth, Briefing Paper no. 292, Economic Policy Institute, March 23. http://www.epi.org/page/-/BriefingPaper292.pdf.

Altmann, J., G. Hausfater, and S. Altmann
    1988   Determinants of Reproductive Success in Savannah Baboons, *Papio cynocephalus.* In *Reproductive Success: Studies of Individual Variation in Contrasting Breeding Systems,* T. H. Clutton-Brock, ed., pp. 403–418. Chicago: University of Chicago Press.

Amadiume, I.
    1987   *Male Daughters, Female Husbands.* Atlantic Highlands, NJ: Zed.

American Psychiatric Association
    2013   *Diagnostic and Statistical Manual of Mental Disorders: DSM-5,* 5th ed. Washington, DC: American Psychiatric Association.

Anderson, B.
    2006   (orig. 1991) *Imagined Communities: Reflections on the Origin and Spread of Nationalism,* rev. ed. New York: Verso.

Anderson-Levitt, K. M., ed.
    2012   *Anthropologies of Education: A Global Guide to Ethnographic Studies of Learning and Schooling.* New York: Berghahn Books.

Anemone, R. L.
    2011   *Race and Human Diversity: A Biocultural Approach.* Upper Saddle River, NJ: Prentice Hall/Pearson.

Annenberg/CPB Exhibits
    2000   Collapse, Why Do Civilizations Fall? http://www.learner.org/exhibits/collapse/.

Anthropology Newsletter
    n.d.   Arlington, VA: American Anthropological Association. Published nine times annually.

Antoun, R. T.
    2008   *Understanding Fundamentalism: Christian, Islamic, and Jewish Movements,* 2nd ed. Lanham, MD: AltaMira.

Aoki, M. Y., and M. B. Dardess, eds.
    1981   *As the Japanese See It: Past and Present.* Honolulu: University of Hawaii Press.

Appadurai, A.
    1990   Disjuncture and Difference in the Global Cultural Economy. *Public Culture* 2(2): 1–24.
    1991   Global Ethnoscapes: Notes and Queries for a Transnational Anthropology. In *Recapturing Anthropology: Working in the Present,* R. G. Fox, ed. pp. 191–210. Santa Fe: School of American Research Advanced Seminar Series.

Appadurai, A., ed.
    2001   *Globalization.* Durham, NC: Duke University Press.

Appiah, K. A.
    1990   Racisms. In *Anatomy of Racism,* David Theo Goldberg, ed. pp. 3–17. Minneapolis: University of Minnesota Press.

Arens, W.
    1981   Professional Football: An American Symbol and Ritual. In *The American Dimension: Cultural Myths and Social Realities,* 2nd ed., W. Arens and S. P. Montague, eds. pp. 1–10. Sherman Oaks, CA: Alfred.

Arensberg, C.
    1987   Theoretical Contributions of Industrial and Development Studies. In *Applied Anthropology in America,* E. M. Eddy and W. L. Partridge, eds. New York: Columbia University Press.

Arnold, J. E., et al.
    2012   *Life at Home in the Twenty-First Century: 32 Families Open Their Doors.* Los Angeles: Cotsen Institute of Archaeology Press.

Arrighi, G.
    2010   *The Long Twentieth Century: Money, Power, and the Origins of Our Times,* new and updated ed. New York: Verso.

Asad, T.
    2008   (orig. 1983) The Construction of Religion as an Anthropological Category. In *A Reader in the Anthropology of Religion,* M. Lambek, ed., pp. 110–226. Malden, MA: Blackwell.

Asfaw, B., T. White, and O. Lovejoy
    1999   *Australopithecus garhi:* A New Species of Early Hominid from Ethiopia. *Science* 284: 629.

Ashcroft, B., G. Griffiths, and H. Tiffin
    2013   *Postcolonial Studies: The Key Concepts,* 3rd ed. New York: Routledge, Taylor and Francis.

Askew, K. M., and R. R. Wilk, eds.
    2002   *The Anthropology of Media: A Reader.* Malden, MA: Oxford, Blackwell.

Avert.org
    2010   Global HIV and AIDS Epidemic. http://www.avert.org/global-hiv-aids-epidemic.htm.

Baer, H. A., M. Singer, and I. Susser
    2013   *Medical Anthropology and the World System,* 3rd ed. Santa Barbara, CA: Praeger.

Bailey, G., and P. Spikins, eds.
    2008   *Mesolithic Europe.* New York: Cambridge University Press.

Bailey, R. C., G. Head, M. Jenike, B. Owen, R. Rechtman, and E. Zechenter
    1989   Hunting and Gathering in Tropical Rain Forests: Is It Possible? *American Anthropologist* 91: 59–82.

Balter, M.
    2010   Romanian Cave Art May Boast Central Europe's Oldest Cave Art. *Science Now,* June 21. http://news.sciencemag.org/sciencenow/2010/06/romanian-cave-may-boast-central.html.

Banks, C. G.
    1992   "Culture" in Culture-Bound Syndromes: The Case of Anorexia Nervosa. *Social Science and Medicine* 34(8): 867–884.

Barnaby, F., ed.
    1984   *Future War: Armed Conflict in the Next Decade.* London: M. Joseph.

Barnard, A., ed.
    2004   *Hunter-Gatherers in History, Archaeology and Anthropology.* New York: Oxford University Press.

Barnes, E.
    2005   *Diseases and Human Evolution.* Albuquerque: University of New Mexico Press.

Baro, M., and T. F. Deubel
    2006    Persistent Hunger: Perspectives on Vulnerability,
    Famine, and Food Security in Sub-Saharan Africa. *Annual
    Review of Anthropology* 35: 521–538.
Baron, D. E.
    2009    *A Better Pencil: Readers, Writers, and the Digital
    Revolution.* New York: Oxford University Press.
Barringer, F.
    1992    New Census Data Show More Children Living in
    Poverty. *New York Times,* May 29, pp. A1, A12–A13.
Barth, F.
    1968    (orig. 1958) Ecologic Relations of Ethnic Groups in
    Swat, North Pakistan. In *Man in Adaptation: The Cultural
    Present,* Yehudi Cohen, ed., pp. 324–331. Chicago: Aldine.
    1969    *Ethnic Groups and Boundaries: The Social Organization
    of Cultural Difference.* London: Allen and Unwin.
Bartlett, B.
    2010    America's Foreign Owned National Debt. *Forbes,*
    March 12. http://www.forbes.com/2010/03/11/treasury-securities-
    national-debt-chinatrade-opinions-columnists-bruce-Bartlett_
    print.html.
Barton, C. M., et al.
    2011    Modeling Human Ecodynamics and Biocultural
    Interactions in the Late Pleistocene of Western Eurasia.
    *Human Ecology.* doi:10.1007/s10745-011-9433-8.
Bar-Yosef, O.
    1987    Pleistocene Connections between Africa and Southwest
    Asia: An Archaeological Perspective. *African Archaeological
    Review* 5: 29–38.
Beck, S., and C. A. Maida, eds.
    2013    *Toward Engaged Anthropology.* New York: Berghahn
    Books.
Beckerman, S., and P. Valentine
    2002    *Cultures of Multiple Fathers: The Theory and Practice
    of Partible Paternity in Lowland South America.* Gainesville:
    University of Florida Press.
Beeman, W.
    1986    *Language, Status, and Power in Iran.* Bloomington:
    Indiana University Press.
Bellah, R. N.
    1978    Religious Evolution. In *Reader in Comparative Religion:
    An Anthropological Approach,* 4th ed., W. A. Lessa and E. Z.
    Vogt, eds., pp. 36–50. New York: Harper & Row.
Bellwood, P. S.
    2005    *The First Farmers: Origins of Agricultural Societies.*
    Malden, MA: Blackwell.
Benazzi, S., et al.
    2011    Early Dispersal of Modern Humans in Europe and
    Implications for Neanderthal Behaviour. *Nature* 479
    (November 24): 525–528. doi:10.1038/nature10617.
Benedict, R.
    1940    *Race, Science and Politics.* New York: Modern Age Books.
    1946    *The Chrysanthemum and the Sword.* Boston: Houghton
    Mifflin.
    1959    (orig. 1934) *Patterns of Culture.* New York: New
    American Library.
Bennett, J. W.
    1969    *Northern Plainsmen: Adaptive Strategy and Agrarian
    Life.* Chicago: Aldine.
Berdan, F. F.
    2013    *Aztec Archaeology and Ethnohistory.* New York:
    Cambridge University Press.
Berger, P.
    2010    Pentecostalism—Protestant Ethic or Cargo Cult? Peter
    Berger's blog, July 29. http://blogs.the-american-interest.com/
    berger/2010/07/29/pentecostalism-%E2%80%93-protestant-
    ethic-or-cargo-cult/.
Beriss, D.
    2004    *Black Skins, French Voices: Caribbean Ethnicity and
    Activism in Urban France.* Boulder, CO: Westview Press.
*Berkeleyan*
    1999    Berkeley Researchers Head Team That Discovers New
    Species of Human Ancestor: Earliest Evidence of Meat-Eating,
    Early Beings Has Been Unearthed in Ethiopia. April 28–May 4,

pp. 27, 32. http://www. berkeley.edu/news/berkeleyan/1999/
0428/species.html.
Berlin, B. D., and P. Kay
    1991    *Basic Color Terms: Their Universality and Evolution,*
    2nd ed. Berkeley: University of California Press.
    1999    *Basic Color Terms: Their Universality and Evolution.*
    Stanford, CA: Center for the Study of Language and Information.
Berna, F., et al.
    2012    Microstratigraphic Evidence of in Situ Fire in the
    Acheulean Strata of Wonderwerk Cave, Northern Cape
    Province, South Africa. *Proceedings of the National Academy
    of Sciences.* doi:10.1073/pnas.1117620109.
Bernard, H. R.
    2011    *Research Methods in Anthropology: Qualitative and
    Quantitative Methods,* 5th ed. Lanham, MD: AltaMira.
Bernard, H. R., ed.
    1998    *Handbook of Methods in Cultural Anthropology.* Walnut
    Creek, CA: AltaMira.
Bettelheim, B.
    1975    *The Uses of Enchantment: The Meaning and Importance
    of Fairy Tales.* New York: Vintage.
Bilefsky, D.
    2006    Polygamy Fosters Culture Clashes (and Regrets) in
    Turkey. *New York Times,* July 10.
Binford, L. R.
    1968    Post-Pleistocene Adaptations. In *New Perspectives
    in Archeology,* S. R. Binford and L. R. Binford, eds.,
    pp. 313–341. Chicago: Aldine.
Binford, L. R., and S. R. Binford
    1979    Stone Tools and Human Behavior. In *Human Ancestors,
    Readings from Scientific American,* G. L. Isaac and R. E. F.
    Leakey, eds., pp. 92–101. San Francisco: W. H. Freeman.
Bjuremalm, H.
    1997    Rättvisa kan skipas i Rwanda: Folkmordet 1994 går att
    förklara och analysera på samma sätt som förintelsen av judarna.
    *Dagens Nyheter* [06-03-1997, p. B3].
Blackwood, E.
    2010    *Falling into the Lesbi World: Desire and Difference in
    Indonesia.* Honolulu: University of Hawaii Press.
Blanton, R. E.
    1999    *Ancient Oaxaca: The Monte Alban State.* New York:
    Cambridge University Press.
Blum, H. F.
    1961    Does the Melanin Pigment of Human Skin Have
    Adaptive Value? *Quarterly Review of Biology* 36: 50–63.
Boas, F.
    1966    (orig. 1940) *Race, Language, and Culture.* New York:
    Free Press.
Boaz, N. T., and R. L. Ciochon
    2004    Headstrong Hominids. *Natural History* 113(1): 28–34.
Bocquet-Appel, J.-P., and O. Bar-Yosef
    2008    *The Neolithic Demographic Transition and Its
    Consequences.* New York: Springer.
Bodley, J. H.
    2003    *The Power of Scale: A Global History Approach.*
    Armonk, NY: M. E. Sharpe.
    2008    *Victims of Progress,* 5th ed. Lanham, MD: AltaMira.
    2012    *Anthropology and Contemporary Human Problems,*
    6th ed. Lanham, MD: AltaMira.
Boellstorff, T., B. Nardi, C. Pearce, and T. L. Taylor
    2012    *Ethnography and Virtual Worlds: A Handbook of
    Method.* Princeton, NJ: Princeton University Press.
Bogaard, A.
    2004    *Neolithic Farming in Central Europe: An Archaeobotani-
    cal Study of Crop Husbandry Practices.* New York: Routledge.
Bogin, B.
    2001    *The Growth of Humanity.* New York: Wiley-Liss.
Bohannan, P.
    1971    Artist and Critic in an African Society. In *Anthropology
    and Art: Readings in Cross-Cultural Aesthetics,* C. Otten, ed.,
    pp. 172–181. Austin: University of Texas Press.
Bono
    2011    A Decade of Progress on AIDS. *New York Times,*
    November 30, p. 39. http://www.nytimes.com/2011/12/01/

opinion/a-decade-of-progress-on-aids.html?scp=1&sq=bono%20world%20aids%20day&st=cse.

Bonvillain, N.
2007 *Women and Men: Cultural Constructs of Gender,* 4th ed. Upper Saddle River, NJ: Prentice Hall.
2012 *Language, Culture, and Communication: The Meaning of Messages,* 7th ed. Boston: Pearson Prentice Hall.

Borofsky, R.
2000 Public Anthropology: Where To? What Next? *Anthropology Newsletter* 41(5): 9–10.

Bouckaert, R., et al.
2012 Mapping the Origins and Expansion of the Indo-European Language Family. *Science* 337(6097): 957–960.

Bourdieu, P.
1977 *Outline of a Theory of Practice.* Translated by Richard Nice. Cambridge, UK: Cambridge University Press.
1982 *Ce Que Parler Veut Dire.* Paris: Fayard.
1984 *Distinction: A Social Critique of the Judgment of Taste.* Translated by R. Nice. Cambridge, MA: Harvard University Press.

Bourque, S. C., and K. B. Warren
1987 Technology, Gender and Development. *Daedalus* 116(4): 173–197.

Bowen, J. R.
2011 *Religion in Practice: An Approach to Anthropology of Religion,* 5th ed. Boston: Pearson/Allyn and Bacon.

Bower, B.
2013 Fossils Point to Ancient Ape-Monkey Split. *Science News* 183(12): 9, May 15. http://www.sciencenews.org/view/generic/id/350410/description/Fossils_point_to_ancient_ape-monkey_split.

Bowie, F.
2006 *The Anthropology of Religion: An Introduction.* Malden, MA: Blackwell.

Bowler, J. M., H. Johnston, J. M. Olley, J. R. Prescott, R. G. Roberts, W. Shawcross, and N. A. Spooner
2003 New Ages for Human Occupation and Climatic Change at Lake Mungo, Australia. *Nature* 421: 837–840.

Brace, C. L.
2005 *"Race" Is a Four-Letter Word: The Genesis of the Concept.* New York: Oxford University Press.

Bradley, B. J., D. M. Doran-Sheehy, D. Lukas, C. Boesch, and L. Vigilant
2004 Dispersed Male Networks in Western Gorillas. *Current Biology* 14: 510–513.

Braidwood, R. J.
1975 *Prehistoric Men,* 8th ed. Glenview, IL: Scott, Foresman.

Braudel, F.
1981 *Civilization and Capitalism, 15th–18th Century.* Volume I: *The Structure of Everyday Life: The Limits.* Translated by S. Reynolds. New York: Harper & Row.
1982 *Civilization and Capitalism, 15th–18th Century.* Volume II: *The Wheels of Commerce.* New York: HarperCollins.
1992 *Civilization and Capitalism, 15th–18th Century.* Volume III: *The Perspective of the World.* Berkeley: University of California Press.

Bremen, J. V., and A. Shimizu, eds.
1999 *Anthropology and Colonialism in Asia and Oceania.* London: Curzon.

Brenneis, D.
1988 Language and Disputing. *Annual Review of Anthropology* 17: 221–237.

Brettell, C. B., and C. F. Sargent, eds.
2012 *Gender in Cross-Cultural Perspective,* 6th ed. Upper Saddle River, NJ: Pearson/Prentice Hall.

Briggs, C. L.
2005 Communicability, Racial Discourse, and Disease. *Annual Review of Anthropology* 34: 269–291.

Brooke, J.
1992 Rio's New Day in Sun Leaves Laplander Limp. *New York Times,* June 1, p. A7.

Brookings Institution
2010 *State of Metropolitan America: On the Front Lines of Demographic Transition.* The Brookings Institution Metropolitan Policy Program. http://www.brookings.edu/~/media/Files/Programs/Metro/state_of_metro_america/metro_america_report1.pdf.

Brower, B., and B. R. Johnston
2007 *Disappearing Peoples? Indigenous Groups and Ethnic Minorities in South and Central Asia.* Walnut Creek, CA: Left Coast Press.

Brown, A.
2001 Communism. *International Encyclopedia of the Social & Behavioral Sciences,* pp. 2323–2326. New York: Elsevier.

Brown, D.
1991 *Human Universals.* New York: McGraw-Hill.

Brown, M. F.
2003 *Who Owns Native Culture?* Cambridge, MA: Harvard University Press.

Brown, P. J., and R. L. Barrett
2010 *Understanding and Applying Medical Anthropology,* 2nd ed. New York: McGraw-Hill.

Brownstein, R.
2010 The Gray and the Brown: The Generational Mismatch. *National Journal,* July 24. http://www.nationaljournal.com/njmagazines/cs_20100724_3946php.

Bryant, V. M.
1999 Review of Piperno, D. R., and D. M. Pearsall, *The Origins of Agriculture in the Lowland Neotropics* (1998), *North American Archaeologist* 26: 245–246.
2003 Invisible Clues to New World Domestication. *Science* February 14, 299(5609): 1029–1030.
2007a Artifact: Maize Pollen. *Archaeology* 60(4). www.archaeology.org/0707/etc/artifact.html.
2007b Little Things Mean a Lot: The Search for Starch Grains at Archaeological Sites. *Mammoth Trumpet* 22(4): 3–4, 16.
2013 Please Don't Wash the Artifacts. *General Anthropology* 20(2): 1–7.

Buikstra, J. E., and L. A. Beck
2006 *Bioarchaeology: The Contextual Analysis of Human Remains.* New York: Academic Press.

Burawoy, M.
2000 Introduction. *Global Ethnography: Forces, Connections, and Imaginations in a Postmodern World.* Berkeley: University of California Press.

Burbank, J., and F. Cooper
2010 *Empires in World History: Power and the Politics of Difference.* Princeton, NJ: Princeton University Press.

Burbank, V. K.
1988 *Aboriginal Adolescence: Maidenhood in an Australian Community.* New Brunswick, NJ: Rutgers University Press.

Burdick, J.
1993 *Looking for God in Brazil: The Progressive Catholic Church in Urban Brazil's Religious Arena.* Berkeley: University of California Press
1998 *Blessed Anastácia: Women, Race, and Popular Christianity in Brazil.* New York: Routledge.

Burger, J., M. Kirchner, B. Bramanti, W. Haak, and M. G. Thomas
2007 Absence of the Lactase-Persistence Associated Allele in Early Neolithic Europeans. *Proceedings of the National Academy of Sciences* 104(10): 3736–3741.

Burke, H., et al., eds.
2008 *Kennewick Man: Perspectives on the Ancient One.* Walnut Creek, CA: Left Coast Press.

Burley, D. V., and W. R. Dickinson
2001 Origin and Significance of a Founding Settlement in Polynesia. *Proceedings of the National Academy of Sciences* 98: 11829–11831.

Burling, R.
1970 *Man's Many Voices: Language in Its Cultural Context.* New York: Harcourt Brace Jovanovich.

Byers, S. N.
2011 *Introduction to Forensic Anthropology,* 4th ed. Boston: Prentice Hall.

Callaway, E.
2011 Ancient DNA Reveals Secrets of Human History. *Nature* 476: 136–137.

Campbell, C. J., ed.
2011 *Primates in Perspective,* 2nd ed. New York: Oxford University Press.

Cann, R. L., M. Stoneking, and A. C. Wilson
1987 Mitochondrial DNA and Human Evolution. *Nature* 325: 31–36.

Carey, B.
2007 Washoe, a Chimp of Many Words Dies at 42. *New York Times,* November 1. http:// www.nytimes.com.

Carneiro, R. L.
1956 Slash-and-Burn Agriculture: A Closer Look at Its Implications for Settlement Patterns. In *Men and Cultures,* Selected Papers of the Fifth International Congress of Anthropological and Ethnological Sciences, pp. 229–234. Philadelphia: University of Pennsylvania Press.
1968 (orig. 1961) Slash-and-Burn Cultivation among the Kuikuru and Its Implications for Cultural Development in the Amazon Basin. In *Man in Adaptation: The Cultural Present,* Y. A. Cohen, ed., pp. 131–145. Chicago: Aldine.
1970 A Theory of the Origin of the State. *Science* 69: 733–738.
1990 Chiefdom-Level Warfare as Exemplified in Fiji and the Cauca Valley. In *The Anthropology of War,* J. Haas, ed., pp. 190–211. Cambridge, UK: Cambridge University Press.
1991 The Nature of the Chiefdom as Revealed by Evidence from the Cauca Valley of Colombia. In *Profiles in Cultural Evolution,* A. T. Rambo and K. Gillogly, eds., *Anthropological Papers* 85, pp. 167–190. Ann Arbor: University of Michigan Museum of Anthropology.

Carsten, J.
2004 *After Kinship.* New York: Cambridge University Press.

Carter, J.
1988 Freed from Keepers and Cages, Chimps Come of Age on Baboon Island. *Smithsonian,* June, pp. 36–48.

Casanova, J.
2001 Religion, the New Millennium, and Globalization. *Sociology of Religion* 62: 415–441.

Caspari, R., and S.-H. Lee
2004 Older Age Becomes Common Late in Human Evolution. *Proceedings of the National Academy of Sciences* July 27, 101(30): 10895–10900.

Castells, M.
2001 Information Technology and Global Capitalism. In *On the Edge. Living with Global Capitalism,* W. Hutton and A. Giddens, eds. London: Vintage.

Caulkins, D., and A. T. Jordan
2013 *A Companion to Organizational Anthropology.* Malden, MA: Wiley-Blackwell.

Cefkin, M., ed.
2009 *Ethnography and the Corporate Encounter: Reflections on Research in and of Corporations.* New York: Berghahn Books.

Cernea, M. M., ed.
1991 *Putting People First: Sociological Variables in Rural Development,* 2nd ed. New York: Oxford University Press (published for the World Bank).

Ceuppens, B., and P. Geschiere
2005 Autochthony: Local or Global? New Modes in the Struggle over Citizenship and Belonging in Africa and Europe. *Annual Review of Anthropology* 34: 385–407.

Chagnon, N. A.
1997 *Yanomamö,* 5th ed. Fort Worth: Harcourt Brace.
2013 *Noble Savages: My Life among Two Dangerous Tribes— the Yanomamo and the Anthropologists.* New York: Simon and Schuster.

Chambers, E.
1987 Applied Anthropology in the Post-Vietnam Era: Anticipations and Ironies. *Annual Review of Anthropology* 16: 309–337.

Champion, T., and C. Gamble, eds.
1984 *Prehistoric Europe.* New York: Academic Press.

Chang, K. C.
1977 *The Archaeology of Ancient China.* New Haven, CT: Yale University Press.

Chapais, B.
2008 *Primeval Kinship: How Pair Bonding Gave Birth to Human Society.* Cambridge, MA: Harvard University Press.

Chatterjee, P.
2004 *The Politics of the Governed: Reflections on Popular Politics in Most of the World.* New York: Columbia University Press.

Cheney, D. L., and R. M. Seyfarth
1990 In the Minds of Monkeys: What Do They Know and How Do They Know It? *Natural History,* September, pp. 38–46.

Chibnik, M.
2011 *Anthropology, Economics, and Choice.* Austin: University of Texas Press.

Childe, V. G.
1950 The Urban Revolution, *Town Planning Review* 21: 3–17.
1951 *Man Makes Himself.* New York: New American Library.

Choi, C. Q.
2011 Savanna, Not Forest, Was Human Ancestors' Proving Ground. *Live Science,* August 3. http://www.livescience. com/15377-savannas-human-ancestors-evolution.html.
2012 Ancient Foot Suggests How Man Gave Up Treehouses. *Live Science,* March 28. http://www.livescience.com/19333- hominin-foot-humanity-bipedalism.html.

Chomsky, N.
1955 *Syntactic Structures.* The Hague: Mouton.

Ciochon, R. L., and J. G. Fleagle, eds.
2012 *Primate Evolution and Human Origin.* New Brunswick, NJ: Transaction.

Ciochon, R. L., J. Olsen, and J. James
1990 *Other Origins: The Search for the Giant Ape in Human Prehistory.* New York: Bantam Books.

Clark, G.
2010 *African Market Women: Seven Life Stories from Ghana.* Indianapolis: Indiana University Press.

Clayton, S. C.
2013 Measuring the Long Arm of the State: Teotihuacan's Relations in the Basin of Mexico. *Ancient Mesoamerica* 24(1): 87–105.

Coburn, N.
2011 *Bazaar Politics: Power and Pottery in an Afghan Market Town.* Stanford, CA: Stanford University Press.

Cody, D.
1998 British Empire. http://www.victorianweb.org/.

Cohen, M. N., and G. J. Armelagos, eds.
1984 *Paleopathology at the Origins of Agriculture.* New York: Academic Press.
2013 *Paleopathology at the Origins of Agriculture,* 2nd ed. Gainesville: University of Florida Press.

Cohen, P.
2008 The Pentagon Enlists Social Scientists to Study Security Issues. *New York Times,* June 18.

Cohen, R.
1967 *The Kanuri of Bornu.* New York: Harcourt Brace Jovanovich.

Cohen, Y. A.
1974 Culture as Adaptation. In *Man in Adaptation: The Cultural Present,* 2nd ed., Y. A. Cohen, ed., pp. 45–68. Chicago: Aldine.

Colson, E., and T. Scudder
1975 New Economic Relationships between the Gwembe Valley and the Line of Rail. In *Town and Country in Central and Eastern Africa,* David Parkin, ed., pp. 190–210. London: Oxford University Press.
1988 *For Prayer and Profit: The Ritual, Economic, and Social Importance of Beer in Gwembe District, Zambia, 1950–1982.* Stanford, CA: Stanford University Press.

Conard, N. J.
2011 *Neanderthal Lifeways, Subsistence, and Technology.* New York: Springer.

Connah, G.
2004 *Forgotten Africa: An Introduction to Its Archaeology.* New York: Routledge.

Cooper, F.
2014 *Africa in the World: Capitalism, Empire, Nation-State.* Cambridge, MA: Harvard University Press.

Cooper, F., and A. L. Stoler, eds.
1997 *Tensions of Empire: Colonial Cultures in a Bourgeois World.* Berkeley: University of California Press.

Cowgill, G. L.

2008   Teotihuacan as an Urban Place. In *Urbanism in Meso-america,* vol. 2, R. H. Cobean, A. G. Mastache, Á. C. Cook, and K. G. Hirth, eds., pp. 85–112. University Park: Pennsylvania State University.

2013   Possible Migrations and Shifting Identities in the Central Mexican Epiclassic. *Ancient Mesoamerica* 24(1): 131–149.

Craig, O.

2013   Earliest Evidence for the Use of Pottery. *Nature* 496: 351–354, April 18. http://www.nature.com/nature/journal/v496/n7445/full/nature12109.html.

Crapo, R. H.

2003   *Anthropology of Religion: The Unity and Diversity of Religions.* New York: McGraw-Hill.

Crate, S. A., and M. Nuttall

2008   *Anthropology and Climate Change: From Encounters to Actions.* Walnut Creek, CA: Left Coast Press.

Crenson, M.

2000   Music—from the Heart or from the Genes. http://www.cis.vt.edu/modernworld/d/musicgenes.html.

Cresswell, T.

2006   *On the Move: Mobility in the Modern West.* New York: Routledge.

Crewe, E., and R. Axelby

2013   *Anthropology and Development: Culture, Morality and Politics in a Globalised World.* Cambridge, UK: Cambridge University Press.

Cribb, J.

2010   *The Coming Famine: The Global Food Crisis and What We Can Do to Avoid It.* Berkeley: University of California Press.

Crick, F. H. C.

1968   (orig. 1962) The Genetic Code. In *The Molecular Basis of Life: An Introduction to Molecular Biology, Readings from Scientific American,* pp. 198–205. San Francisco: W. H. Freeman.

Crosby, A. W., Jr.

2003   *The Columbian Exchange: Biological and Cultural Consequences of 1492.* Westport, CT: Praeger.

*Cultural Survival Quarterly*

1989   Quarterly journal. Cambridge, MA: Cultural Survival.

Curnoe, D., et al.

2012   Human Remains from the Pleistocene-Holocene Transition of Southwest China Suggest a Complex Evolutionary History for East Asians. *Plos One Online,* March 14. http://www.plosone.org/article/info%3Adoi%2F10.1371%2Fjournal.pone.0031918.

Curry, A.

2009   Climate Change: Sites in Peril. *Archaeology* 62(2). http://archive.archaeology.org/0903/etc/climate_change.html.

Dalton, G., ed.

1967   *Tribal and Peasant Economies.* Garden City, NY: Natural History Press.

Dalton, R.

2006   Ethiopia: Awash with Fossils. http://www.nature.com/news/2006/060102/full/439014a.html.

DaMatta, R.

1991   *Carnivals, Rogues, and Heroes: An Interpretation of the Brazilian Dilemma.* Translated from the Portuguese by John Drury. Notre Dame, IN: University of Notre Dame Press.

D'Andrade, R.

1984   Cultural Meaning Systems. In *Culture Theory: Essays on Mind, Self, and Emotion,* R. A. Shweder and R. A. Levine, eds., pp. 88–119. Cambridge, UK: Cambridge University Press.

Darwin, C.

2009   (orig. 1859) *On the Origin of Species.* Alachua, FL: Bridge-Logos.

Das, V., and D. Poole, eds.

2004   *Anthropology in the Margins of the State.* Santa Fe, NM: School of American Research Press.

Degler, C.

1970   *Neither Black nor White: Slavery and Race Relations in Brazil and the United States.* New York: Macmillan.

de la Peña, G.

2005   Social and Cultural Policies toward Indigenous Peoples: Perspectives from Latin America. *Annual Review of Anthropology* 34: 717–739.

deLumley, H.

1976   (orig. 1969) A Paleolithic Camp at Nice. In *Avenues to Antiquity, Readings from Scientific American,* B. M. Fagan, ed., pp. 36–44. San Francisco: W. H. Freeman.

DeMarco, E.

1997   New Dig at 9,000-Year-Old City Is Changing Views on Ancient Life. *New York Times,* November 11. http://www.nytimes.com.

Dembski, W. A.

2004   *The Design Revolution: Answering the Toughest Questions about Intelligent Design.* Downers Grove, IL: InterVarsity Press.

Demeter, F., et al.

2012   Anatomically Modern Humans in Southeast Asia (Laos) by 46 ka. *Proceedings of the National Academy of Sciences,* 109(36): 14375–14380, September 4.

DeNavas-Walt, C., B. D. Proctor, and J. C. Smith

2013   *Income, Poverty, and Health Insurance Coverage in the United States: 2012.* U.S. Census Bureau, Current Population Reports, P60-245. Washington, DC: U.S. Government Printing Office. http://www.census.gov/prod/2010pubs/p60-245.pdf.

Dentan, R. K.

1979   *The Semai: A Nonviolent People of Malaya,* fieldwork edition. New York: Harcourt Brace.

2008   *Overwhelming Terror: Love, Fear, Peace and Violence among the Semai of Malaysia.* Lanham, MD: Rowman & Littlefield.

Descartes, L., and C. P. Kottak

2009   *Media and Middle-Class Moms.* New York: Routledge.

De Vos, G. A., and H. Wagatsuma

1966   *Japan's Invisible Race: Caste in Culture and Personality.* Berkeley: University of California Press.

De Vos, G. A., W. O. Wetherall, and K. Stearman

1983   *Japan's Minorities: Burakumin, Koreans, Ainu and Okinawans.* Report no. 3. London: Minority Rights Group.

de Waal, F. B. M.

1995   Bonobo Sex and Society: The Behavior of a Close Relative Challenges Assumptions about Male Supremacy in Human Evolution. *Scientific American,* March, pp. 82–88.

1997   *Bonobo: The Forgotten Ape.* Berkeley: University of California Press.

1998   *Chimpanzee Politics: Power and Sex among Apes.* Baltimore: Johns Hopkins Universty Press.

Diamond, J. M.

1990   A Pox upon Our Genes. *Natural History,* February, pp. 26–30.

1997   *Guns, Germs, and Steel: The Fates of Human Societies.* New York: W. W. Norton.

2005   (orig. 1997) *Guns, Germs, and Steel: The Fates of Human Societies.* New York: W. W. Norton.

Dickau, R. A. J. Ranere, and R. G. Cooke

2007   Starch Grain Evidence for the Preceramic Dispersals of Maize and Root Crops into Tropical Dry and Humid Forests of Panama. *Proceedings of the National Academy of Sciences of the United States of America* 104(9): 3651–3656. http://www.pnas.org/cgi/content/full/104/9/3651.

Di Leonardo, M., ed.

1991   *Gender at the Crossroads of Knowledge: Feminist Anthropology in the Postmodern Era.* Berkeley: University of California Press.

Divale, W. T., and M. Harris

1976   Population, Warfare, and the Male Supremacist Complex. *American Anthropologist* 78: 521–538.

Donham, D. L.

2011   *Violence in a Time of Liberation: Murder and Ethnicity at a South African Gold Mine, 1994.* Durham, NC: Duke University Press.

Donovan, J. M.

2007   *Legal Anthropology: An Introduction.* Lanham, MD: Rowman & Littlefield.

Dorward, D. C., ed.

1983   *The Igbo "Women's War" of 1929: Documents Relating to the Aba Riots in Eastern Nigeria.* Wakefield, UK: East Ardsley.

Douglas, M.

1970a   *Natural Symbols: Explorations in Cosmology.* London: Barrie and Rockliff, The Crescent Press.

1970b  *Purity and Danger: An Analysis of Concepts of Pollution and Taboo.* Harmondsworth, UK: Penguin.

Dove, M. R., P. E. Sajise, and A. A. Doolittle, eds.
2011  *Beyond the Sacred Forest: Complicating Conservation in Southeast Asia.* Durham, NC: Duke University Press.

Dressler, W. W., K. S. Oths, and C. C. Gravlee
2005  Race and Ethnicity in Public Health Research. *Annual Review of Anthropology* 34: 231–252.

Duffield, M., and V. Hewitt, eds.
2009  *Empire, Development, and Colonialism: The Past in the Present.* Rochester, NY: James Currey.

Dunham, S. A.
2009  *Surviving Against the Odds: Village Industry in Indonesia.* Durham, NC: Duke University Press.

Dunn, J. S.
2000  *The Impact of Media on Reproductive Behavior in Northeastern Brazil.* Ph.D. dissertation, Department of Anthropology, University of Michigan, Ann Arbor.

Duranti, A., ed.
2009  *Linguistic Anthropology: A Reader.* Malden, MA: Wiley Blackwell.

Durkheim, E.
1951  (orig. 1897) *Suicide: A Study in Sociology.* Glencoe, IL: Free Press.
2001  (orig. 1912) *The Elementary Forms of the Religious Life.* Translated by Carol Cosman. Abridged with an introduction and notes by Mark S. Cladis. New York: Oxford University Press.

Dürr, E., and R. Jaffe, eds.
2010  *Urban Pollution: Cultural Meanings, Social Practices.* New York: Berghahn Books.

Earle, T. K.
1987  Chiefdoms in Archaeological and Ethnohistorical Perspective. *Annual Review of Anthropology* 16: 279–308.
1997  *How Chiefs Come to Power: The Political Economy in Prehistory.* Stanford, CA: Stanford University Press.

Eckert, P.
1989  *Jocks and Burnouts: Social Categories and Identity in the High School.* New York: Teachers College Press, Columbia University.
2000  *Linguistic Variation as Social Practice: The Linguistic Construction of Identity in Belten High.* Malden, MA: Blackwell.

Eckert, P., and S. McConnell-Ginet
2013  *Language and Gender,* 2nd ed. Cambridge, UK: Cambridge University Press.

Eckert, P., and N. Mendoza-Denton
2002  Getting Real in the Golden State. *Language,* March 29. http://www.pbs.org/speak/seatosea/americanvarieties/californian/.

Eckert, P., and J. R. Rickford, eds.
2001  *Style and Sociolinguistic Variation.* New York: Cambridge University Press.

Economic Policy Institute
2012  The State of Working America: Key Numbers. http://stateofworkingamerica.org/files/book/factsheets/wealth.pdf.

Edelman, M., and A. Haugerud
2005  *The Anthropology of Development and Globalization: From Classical Political Economy to Contemporary Neoliberalism.* Malden, MA: Blackwell.

Edgar, H. J. H., and K. L. Hunley
2009  Race Reconciled: How Biological Anthropologists View Human Variation. *American Journal of Physical Anthropology* 139(1): 1–4.

Egan, T.
2005  A Skeleton Moves from the Courts to the Laboratory. *New York Times,* July 19.

Eldredge, N.
1985  *Time Frames: The Rethinking of Darwinian Evolution and the Theory of Punctuated Equilibria.* New York: Simon & Schuster.

Eldredge, N., and S. Pearson
2010  *Charles Darwin and the Mystery of Mysteries.* New York: Rb Flash Point/Roaring Brook Press.

Elson, C.
2007  *Excavations at Cerro Tilcajete: A Monte Alban II Administrative Center in the Valley of Oaxaca.* Memoir 42 of the Museum of Anthropology, University of Michigan, Ann Arbor.

Ember, M., and C. R. Ember
1997  Science in Anthropology. In *The Teaching of Anthropology: Problems, Issues, and Decisions,* C. P. Kottak, J. J. White, R. H. Furlow, and P. C. Rice, eds., pp. 29–33. Mountain View, CA: Mayfield.

Entmacher, J., K. G. Robbins, J. Vogtman, and L. Frohlich
2013  *Insecure and Unequal: Poverty and Income among Women and Families 2000–2012.* Washington, DC: National Women's Law Center. http://www.nwlc.org/resource/insecure-unequal-poverty-among-women-and-families-2000-2012.

Erickson, P. A., and L. D. Murphy
2013  *A History of Anthropological Theory,* 4th ed. Toronto: University of Toronto Press.

Errington, F., and D. Gewertz
1987  *Cultural Alternatives and a Feminist Anthropology: An Analysis of Culturally Constructed Gender Interests in Papua New Guinea.* New York: Cambridge University Press.

Ervin, A. M.
2005  *Applied Anthropology: Tools and Perspectives for Contemporary Practice,* 2nd ed. Boston: Pearson/Allyn & Bacon.

Escobar, A.
1991  Anthropology and the Development Encounter: The Making and Marketing of Development Anthropology. *American Ethnologist* 18: 658–682.
1995  *Encountering Development: The Making and Unmaking of the Third World.* Princeton, NJ: Princeton University Press.

Evans-Pritchard, E. E.
1940  *The Nuer: A Description of the Modes of Livelihood and Political Institutions of a Nilotic People.* Oxford: Clarendon Press.
1970  Sexual Inversion among the Azande. *American Anthropologist* 72: 1428–1433.

Ezekiel, E.
2011  Foreign Aid Is Not a Rathole. *New York Times,* November 30, 2011. www.nytimes.com. http://opinionator.blogs.nytimes.com/2011/11/30/foreign-aid-is-not-a-rathole/?scp=3&sq=ezekiel%20emanuel%20december%201&st=cse.

Fagan, B. M.
1996  *World Prehistory: A Brief Introduction,* 3rd ed. New York: HarperCollins.

Farner, R. F., ed.,
2004  *Nationalism, Ethnicity, and Identity: Cross-national and Comparative Perspectives.* New Brunswick, NJ: Transaction.

Fasold, R. W., and J. Connor-Linton
2006  *An Introduction to Language and Linguistics.* New York: Cambridge University Press.

Fearon, J. D.
2003  Ethnic and Cultural Diversity by Country. *Journal of Economic Growth* 8(2): 195–222.

Feder, K. L.
2013  *Frauds, Myths, and Mysteries: Science and Pseudoscience in Archaeology,* 8th ed. New York: McGraw-Hill.

Ferguson, R. B.
1995  *Yanomami Warfare: A Political History.* Santa Fe, NM: School of American Research Press.
2003  *The State, Identity, and Violence: Political Disintegration in the Post–Cold War Era.* New York: Routledge.

Ferraro, G. P.
2010  *The Cultural Dimension of International Business,* 6th ed. Upper Saddle River, NJ: Prentice Hall.

Ferraro, J. V., et al.
2013  Earliest Archaeological Evidence of Persistent Hominin Carnivory. *Plos One Online,* April 5, 2013. http://www.plosone.org/article/info%3Adoi%2F10.1371%2Fjournal.pone.0062174.

Feuer, J.
2012  The Clutter Culture, *UCLA Magazine Online,* July 1, 2012. http://magazine.ucla.edu/features/the-clutter-culture/.

Finnstrom, S.
1997  Postcoloniality and the Postcolony: Theories of the Global and the Local. http://www.postcolonialweb.org/.

Fiske, J.
1989  *Understanding Popular Culture.* Boston: Unwin Hyman.
2011  *Reading the Popular,* 2nd ed. New York: Routledge.

Fiske, J., and J. Hartley
2003  *Reading Television,* 2nd ed. New York: Routledge.

Flannery, K. V.

1969 Origins and Ecological Effects of Early Domestication in Iran and the Near East. In *The Domestication and Exploitation of Plants and Animals,* P. J. Ucko and G. W. Dimbleby, eds., pp. 73–100. Chicago: Aldine.

1973 The Origins of Agriculture. *Annual Review of Anthropology* 2: 271–310.

1986 *Guila Naquitz: Archaic Foraging and Early Agriculture in Oaxaca, Mexico.* Orlando, FL: Academic Press.

1999 Chiefdoms in the Early Near East: Why It's So Hard to Identify Them. In *The Iranian World: Essays on Iranian Art and Archaeology,* A. Alizadeh, Y. Majidzadeh, and S. M. Shahmirzadi, eds. Tehran: Iran University Press.

Flannery, K. V., and J. Marcus

2000 Formative Mexican Chiefdoms and the Myth of the "Mother Culture." *Journal of Anthropological Archaeology* 19: 1–37.

2003a *The Cloud People: Divergent Evolution of the Zapotec and Mixtec Civilizations.* Clinton Corners, NY: Percheron Press.

2003b The Origin of War: New 14C Dates from Ancient Mexico. *Proceedings of the National Academy of Sciences of the United States of America,* 100(20): 11801–11805.

Flannery, K. V., J. Marcus, and R. G. Reynolds

1989 *The Flocks of the Wamani: A Study of Llama Herders on the Punas of Ayacucho, Peru.* San Diego: Academic Press.

Fleisher, M. L.

2000 *Kuria Cattle Raiders: Violence and Vigilantism on the Tanzania/Kenya Frontier.* Ann Arbor: University of Michigan Press.

Ford, C. S., and F. A. Beach

1951 *Patterns of Sexual Behavior.* New York: Harper Torchbooks.

Fortes, M.

1950 Kinship and Marriage among the Ashanti. In *African Systems of Kinship and Marriage,* A. R. Radcliffe-Brown and D. Forde, eds., pp. 252–284. London: Oxford University Press.

Fortier, J.

2009 The Ethnography of South Asian Foragers. *Annual Review of Anthropology* 39: 99–114.

Fossey, D.

1983 *Gorillas in the Mist.* Boston: Houghton Mifflin.

Foster, G. M., and B. G. Anderson

1978 *Medical Anthropology.* New York: McGraw-Hill.

Foucault, M.

1979 *Discipline and Punish: The Birth of the Prison.* Translated by Alan Sheridan. New York: Vintage Books, University Press.

1990 *The History of Sexuality,* vol. 2, *The Use of Pleasure.* Translated by R. Hurley. New York: Vintage.

Fouts, R.

1997 *Next of Kin: What Chimpanzees Have Taught Me about Who We Are.* New York: William Morrow.

Fowler, C. S., and D. D. Fowler, eds.

2008 *The Great Basin: People and Place in Ancient Times.* Santa Fe, NM: School for Advanced Research Press.

Fowler, S.

2011 Into the Stone Age with a Scalpel: A Dig with Clues on Early Urban Life. *New York Times,* September 7. http://www.nytimes.com/2011/09/08/world/europe/08iht-M08C-TURKEY-DIG.html?pagewanted=all.

*Free Dictionary*

2004 Honorific. http://encyclopedia.thefreedictionary.com/Honorific.

Freilich, M., D. Raybeck, and J. Savishinsky

1991 *Deviance: Anthropological Perspectives.* Westport, CT: Bergin and Garvey.

Freston, P., ed.

2008 *Evangelical Christianity and Democracy in Latin America.* New York: Oxford University Press.

Fricke, T.

1994 *Himalayan Households: Tamang Demography and Domestic Processes,* 2nd ed. New York: Columbia University Press.

Fried, M. H.

1960 On the Evolution of Social Stratification and the State. In *Culture in History,* S. Diamond, ed., pp. 713–731. New York: Columbia University Press.

1967 *The Evolution of Political Society: An Essay in Political Anthropology.* New York: McGraw-Hill.

Friedan, B.

1963 *The Feminine Mystique.* New York: W. W. Norton.

Friedl, E.

1962 *Vasilika: A Village in Modern Greece:* New York: Holt, Rinehart, and Winston.

1975 *Women and Men: An Anthropologist's View.* New York: Harcourt Brace Jovanovich.

Friedman, J., ed.

2003 *Globalization, the State, and Violence.* Walnut Creek, CA: AltaMira.

Friedman, K. E., and J. Friedman

2008 *The Anthropology of Global Systems.* Lanham, MD: AltaMira.

Frisancho, A. R.

1993 *Human Adaptation and Accommodation.* Ann Arbor: University of Michigan Press.

Furuichi, R., and J. Thompson, eds.

2008 *The Bonobos: Behavior, Ecology, and Conservation.* New York: Springer.

Gal, S.

1989 Language and Political Economy. *Annual Review of Anthropology* 18: 345–367.

Galdikas, B. M.

2007 The Vanishing Man of the Forest. *International Herald Tribune,* January 7. http://www.nytimes.com/2007/01/07/opinion/07iht-edgald.4127210.html?_r=1&scp=1&sq=orangutan%20endangered&st=cse.

Gardner, R. A., B. T. Gardner, and T. E. Van Cantfort, eds.

1989 *Teaching Sign Language to Chimpanzees.* Albany: State University of New York Press.

Garraty, C. P.

2013 Market Development and Pottery Exchange under Aztec and Spanish Rule in Cerro Portezuelo. *Ancient Mesoamerica* 24(1): 151–176.

Gates, C.

2003 *Ancient Cities: The Archaeology of Urban Life in the Ancient Near East, Egypt, Greece, and Rome.* New York: Routledge.

Geertz, C.

1973 *The Interpretation of Cultures.* New York: Basic Books.

1983 *Local Knowledge.* New York: Basic Books.

Geis, M. L.

1987 *The Language of Politics.* New York: Springer-Verlag.

Gell-Mann, M., and M. Ruhlen

2011 The Origin and Evolution of Word Order. *Proceedings of the National Academy of Sciences* 108(42): 17290–17295. http://www.pnas.org/content/early/2011/10/04/1113716108.

Gellner, E.

1983 *Nations and Nationalism.* Ithaca, NY: Cornell University Press.

1997 *Nationalism.* New York: New York University Press.

Gibbons, A.

2001 The Peopling of the Pacific. *Science* 291: 1735. http://www.familytreedna.com/pdf/Gibbons_Science2001.pdf.

2012 A New Face Reveals Multiple Lineages Alive at the Dawn of Our Genus *Homo. Science* 337(August 10): 635.

Giddens, A.

1981 *The Class Structure of the Advanced Societies,* 2nd ed. London: Hutchinson.

Gijswijt-Hofstra, M., H. Oosterhuis, J. Vijselaar, and H. Freeman, eds.

2005 *Psychiatric Cultures Compared: Psychiatry and Mental Health Care in the Twentieth Century.* Amsterdam, Netherlands: Amsterdam University Press.

Gillespie, J. H.

2004 *Population Genetics: A Concise Guide,* 2nd ed. Baltimore: Johns Hopkins University Press.

Gillis, J.

2013　It's Official: 2012 Was Hottest Year Ever in U.S. *New York Times,* January 8. http://www.nytimes.com/2013/01/09/science/earth/2012-was-hottest-year-ever-in-us.html?hp&_r=0.

Gilmore, D. D.

1987　*Aggression and Community: Paradoxes of Andalusian Culture.* New Haven, CT: Yale University Press.

Gilmore-Lehne, W. J.

2000　Pre-Sumerian Cultures: Natufian through Ubaid Eras: 10,500–3500 B.C.E. http://loki.stockton.edu/~gilmorew/consorti/1bnear.htm.

Gimpel, J.

1988　*The Medieval Machine: The Industrial Revolution of the Middle Ages,* 2nd ed. Aldershot, Hants, UK: Wildwood House.

Ginsburg, F. D., L. Abu-Lughod, and B. Larkin, eds.

2002　*Media Worlds: Anthropology on New Terrain.* Berkeley: University of California Press.

Gmelch, G.

1978　Baseball Magic. *Human Nature* 1(8): 32–40.

2001　*Inside Pitch: Life in Professional Baseball.* Washington, DC: Smithsonian Institution Press.

2006　*Inside Pitch: Life in Professional Baseball.* Lincoln: University of Nebraska Press.

Gmelch, G., R. V. Kemper, and W. Zenner, eds.

2010　*Urban Life: Readings in the Anthropology of the City,* 5th ed. Long Grove, IL: Waveland.

Goleman, D.

1992　Anthropology Goes Looking for Love in All the Old Places. *New York Times,* November 24, 1992, p. B1.

1995　Making Room on the Couch for Culture. *New York Times,* December 5. http://www.nytimes.com/1995/12/05/science/making-room-on-the-couch-for-culture. html?pagewanted=all&src=pm.

Goodale, J., and J. D. Koss

1971　The Cultural Context of Creativity among Tiwi. In *Anthropology and Art: Readings in Cross-Cultural Aesthetics,* C. Otten, ed., pp. 182–203. Austin: University of Texas Press.

Goodall, J.

1996　*My Life with the Chimpanzees.* New York: Pocket Books.

2009　*Jane Goodall: 50 Years at Gombe, a Tribute to Five Decades of Wildlife Research, Education, and Conservation.* New York: Stewart, Tabori, and Chang.

2010　*In the Shadow of Man,* new ed. Boston: Mariner Books.

Goodman, A. H., et al.

2013　*Race: Are We So Different?* Malden, MA: Wiley-Blackwell.

Gotkowitz, L., ed.

2011　*Histories of Race and Racism: The Andes and Mesoamerica from Colonial Times to the Present.* Durham, NC: Duke University Press.

Gough, E. K.

1959　The Nayars and the Definition of Marriage. *Journal of Royal Anthropological Institute* 89: 23–34.

Gould, S. J.

2007　*Punctuated Equilibrium.* Cambridge, MA: Belknap Press of Harvard University Press.

Gowlett, J. A. J.

1993　*Ascent to Civilization: The Archaeology of Early Humans.* New York: McGraw-Hill.

Gramsci, A.

1971　*Selections from the Prison Notebooks.* Edited and translated by Quenten Hoare and Geoffrey Nowell Smith. London: Wishart.

Grasmuck, S., and P. Pessar

1991　*Between Two Islands: Dominican International Migration.* Berkeley: University of California Press.

Gravlee, C.

2009　How Race Becomes Biology: Embodiment of Social Inequality. *American Journal of Physical Anthropology* 139(1): 47–57.

Greaves, T. C.

1995　Problems Facing Anthropologists: Cultural Rights and Ethnography. *General Anthropology* 1(2): 1, 3–6.

Green, G. M., and R. W. Sussman

1990　Deforestation History of the Eastern Rain Forests of Madagascar from Satellite Images. *Science* 248: 212–215.

Green, T.

2006　Archaeologist Makes the Case for Burying Dominant Theory of First Americans. Austin: University of Texas Research. http://www.utexas.edu/research/impact/collins.html.

Greiner, T. M.

2003　What Is the Difference between Hominin and Hominid When Classifying Humans? MadSci Network: Evolution. http://www.madsci.org/posts/archives/Apr2003/1050350684.Ev.r.html.

Gremaux, R.

1993　Woman Becomes Man in the Balkans. In *Third Sex Third Gender: Beyond Sexual Dimorphism in Culture and History,* G. Herdt, ed. Cambridge: MIT Press.

Griffin, P. B., and A. Estioko-Griffin, eds.

1985　*The Agta of Northeastern Luzon: Recent Studies.* Cebu City, Philippines: University of San Carlos.

Grimshaw, A., and A. Ravetz

2009　*Observational Cinema: Anthropology, Film, and the Exploration of Social Life.* Bloomington: Indiana University Press.

Gu, S.

2012　*Language and Culture in the Growth of Imperialism.* Jefferson, NC: McFarland.

Gugliotta, G.

2002　Earliest Human Ancestor? Skull Dates to When Apes, Humans Split. *Washington Post,* July 11, p. A01.

2005　Tools Found in Britain Show Much Earlier Human Existence. *Washington Post,* December 15, p. A-24.

Gunther, E.

1971　Northwest Coast Indian Art. In *Anthropology and Art: Readings in Cross-Cultural Aesthetics,* C. Otten, ed., pp. 318–340. Austin: University of Texas Press.

Gupta, A., and J. Ferguson

1997　Beyond "Culture": Space, Identity, and the Politics of Difference. In *Culture, Power, Place: Explorations in Critical Anthropology,* A. Gupta and J. Ferguson, eds., pp. 33–51. Durham, NC: Duke University Press.

Gupta, A., and J. Ferguson, eds.

1997a　*Anthropological Locations: Boundaries and Grounds of a Field Science.* Berkeley: University of California Press.

1997b　*Culture, Power, Place: Explorations in Critical Anthropology.* Durham, NC: Duke University Press.

Guyot, J., and C. Hughes

2007　Researchers Find Earliest Evidence for Modern Human Behavior. *Arizona State University Research Magazine.* http://researchmag.asu.edu/2008/02/researchers_find_earliest_evid.html.

Haapala, A.

1998　Literature: Invention of the Self. *Canadian Aesthetics Journal* 2. http://www.uqtr.ca/AE/vol_2/haapala.html.

Habu, J., A. Matsui, N. Yamamoto, and T. Kanno

2011　Shell Midden Archaeology in Japan: Aquatic Food Acquisition and Long-term Change in the Jomon Culture. *Quaternary International* 239(1-2): 19–27.

Hackett, R. I. J.

1996　*Art and Religion in Africa.* London: Cassell.

Haenn, N., and R. R. Wilk, eds.

2006　*The Environment in Anthropology: A Reader in Ecology, Culture, and Sustainable Living.* New York: New York University Press.

Hallowell, A. I.

1955　*Culture and Experience.* Philadelphia: University of Pennsylvania Press.

Hamdan, S.

2013　Social Media Firms Move to Capitalize on Popularity in Middle East. *New York Times,* February 6. http://www.nytimes.com/2013/02/07/world/middleeast/social-media-firms-move-to-capitalize-on-popularity-in-middle-east.html?pagewanted=print.

Hamilton, M. B.

2009　*Population Genetics.* Hoboken, NJ: Wiley-Blackwell.

Hampton, K., L. S. Goulet, L. Rainie, and K. Purcell

2011　Social Networking Sites and Our Lives. Pew Research Center, Internet and American Life Project, June 16.

http://www.pewinternet.org/~/media//Files/Reports/2011/PIP percent20- percent20Social percent20networking percent20sites percent20and percent20our percent20lives.pdf.

Hancock, G.
2011    *Fingerprints of the Gods.* New York: MJF Books.

Hancock, G., and R. Bauval
1996    *Message of the Sphinx: A Quest for the Hidden Legacy of Mankind.* New York: Three Rivers Press.

Handwerk, B.
2008    Half of Humanity Will Live in Cities by Year's End. *National Geographic News,* March 13. www.nationalgeographic.com/news/pf30472163.html.

Hann, C., and K. Hart
2011    *Economic Anthropology: History, Ethnography, Critique.* Malden, MA: Polity Press.

Hann, C., and K. Hart, eds.
2009    *Market and Society: The Great Transformation Today.* New York: Cambridge University Press.

Hansen, K. V.
2005    *Not-So-Nuclear Families: Class, Gender, and Networks of Care.* New Brunswick, NJ: Rutgers University Press.

Harlan, J. R., and D. Zohary
1966    Distribution of Wild Wheats and Barley. *Science* 153: 1074–1080.

Harlow, H. F.
1971    *Learning to Love.* San Francisco: Albion.

Harris, M.
1964    *Patterns of Race in the Americas.* New York: Walker.
1970    Referential Ambiguity in the Calculus of Brazilian Racial Identity. *Southwestern Journal of Anthropology* 26(1): 1–14.
1974    *Cows, Pigs, Wars, and Witches: The Riddles of Culture.* New York: Random House.
1978    *Cannibals and Kings.* New York: Vintage.
2001*a*    (orig. 1979) *Cultural Materialism: The Struggle for a Science of Culture.* Walnut Creek, CA: AltaMira.
2001*b*    (orig. 1968) *The Rise of Anthropological Theory.* Walnut Creek, CA: AltaMira.

Harris, M., and C. P. Kottak
1963    The Structural Significance of Brazilian Racial Categories. *Sociologia* 25: 203–209.

Harrison, G. G., W. L. Rathje, and W. W. Hughes
1994    Food Waste Behavior in an Urban Population. In *Applying Anthropology: An Introductory Reader,* 3rd ed., A. Podolefsky and P. J. Brown, eds., pp. 107–112. Mountain View, CA: Mayfield.

Harrison, K. D.
2007    *When Languages Die: The Extinction of the World's Languages and the Erosion of Human Knowledge.* New York: Oxford University Press.
2010    *The Last Speakers: The Quest to Save the World's Most Endangered Languages.* Washington, DC: National Geographic.

Hart, C. W. M., A. R. Pilling, and J. C. Goodale
1988    *The Tiwi of North Australia,* 3rd ed. Fort Worth: Harcourt Brace.

Hartigan, J., ed.
2013    *Anthropology of Race: Genes, Biology, and Culture.* Santa Fe, NM: School for Advanced Research Press.

Hartl, D. L.
2014    *Essential Genetics: A Genomics Perspective,* 6th ed. Burlington, MA: Jones and Bartlett.

*Harvard Magazine*
2012    Pottery Predates Agriculture. *Harvard Magazine,* June 19. http://harvardmagazine.com/2012/06/pottery-20000-years-old.

Harvey, D. J.
1980    French Empire. *Academic American Encyclopedia,* vol. 8, pp. 309–310. Princeton, NJ: Arete.

Haugerud, A., M. P. Stone, and P. D. Little, eds.
2011    *Commodities and Globalization: Anthropological Perspectives.* Lanham, MD: Rowman & Littlefield.

Hausfater, G., and S. Hrdy, eds.
2008    *Infanticide: Comparative and Evolutionary Perspectives.* New Brunswick, NJ: Aldine.

Hausmann, R., L. D. Tyson, and S. Zahidi
2012    *The Global Gender Gap Report 2012.* Geneva: World Economic Forum.

Hawkes, K., J. O'Connell, and K. Hill
1982    Why Hunters Gather: Optimal Foraging and the Aché of Eastern Paraguay. *American Ethnologist* 9: 379–398.

Helman, C.
2007    *Culture, Health, and Illness,* 5th ed. New York: Oxford University Press.

Henry, D. O.
1995    *Prehistoric Cultural Ecology and Evolution: Insights from Southern Jordan.* New York: Plenum Press.

Henry, J.
1955    Docility, or Giving Teacher What She Wants. *Journal of Social Issues* 2: 33–41.

Herdt, G.
2006    *The Sambia: Ritual, Sexuality, and Change in Papua New Guinea.* Belmont, CA: Thomson/Wadsworth.

Herdt, G. H., ed.
1984    *Ritualized Homosexuality in Melanesia.* Berkeley: University of California Press.

Herdt, G. H., and N. Polen
2013    *Sexual Literacy: Sexuality in Human Nature, Culture and Society.* New York: McGraw-Hill.

Herskovits, M.
1937    *Life in a Haitian Valley.* New York: Knopf.

Hess, E.
2008    *Nim Chimsky: The Chimp Who Would Be Human.* New York: Bantam Books.

Heyerdahl, T.
1971    *The Ra Expeditions.* Translated by P. Crampton. Garden City, NY: Doubleday.

Hicks, D., ed.
2010    *Ritual and Belief: Readings in the Anthropology of Religion,* 3rd ed. Boston: McGraw-Hill.

Higham, T., et al.
2011    The Earliest Evidence for Anatomically Modern Humans in Northwestern Europe. *Nature* 479(November 24): 521–524. doi:10.1038/nature10484.

Hill, J. H.
1978    Apes and Language. *Annual Review of Anthropology* 7: 89–112.

Hill, K. R., et al.
2011    Co-residence Patterns in Hunter-Gatherer Societies Show Unique Human Social Structure. *Science* 11(March): 1286–1289. doi:10.1126/science.1199071.

Hill-Burnett, J.
1978    Developing Anthropological Knowledge through Application. In *Applied Anthropology in America,* E. M. Eddy and W. L. Partridge, eds., pp. 112–128. New York: Columbia University Press.

Hinton, A. L., and K. L. O'Neill, eds.
2009    *Genocide: Truth, Memory, and Representation.* Durham, NC: Duke University Press.

Hirth, K. G., and J. Pillsbury, eds.
2013    *Merchants, Markets, and Exchange in the Pre-Columbian World.* Washington, DC: Dumbarton Oaks Research Library and Collection.

Hobhouse, L. T.
1915    *Morals in Evolution,* rev. ed. New York: Holt.

Hodder, I.
2006    *The Leopard's Tale: Revealing the Mysteries of Çatalhöyük.* New York: Thames and Hudson.

Hoebel, E. A.
1954    *The Law of Primitive Man.* Cambridge, MA: Harvard University Press.
1968    (orig. 1954) The Eskimo: Rudimentary Law in a Primitive Anarchy. In *Studies in Social and Cultural Anthropology,* J. Middleton, ed., pp. 93–127. New York: Crowell.

Hogan, B., N. Li, and W. H. Dutton
2011    *A Global Shift in the Social Relationships of Networked Individuals: Meeting and Dating Online Comes of Age* (February 14). Oxford Internet Institute, University of Oxford. http://ssrn.com/abstract=1763884 or http://dx.doi.org/10.2139/ssrn.1763884.

Hoge, W.
    2001    Kautekeino Journal: Reindeer Herders, at Home on a (Very Cold) Range. *New York Times,* March 26, late ed. final, sec. A, p. 4.
Holden, A.
    2005    *Tourism Studies and the Social Sciences.* New York: Routledge.
Hole, F., K. V. Flannery, and J. A. Neely
    1969    *The Prehistory and Human Ecology of the Deh Luran Plain.* Memoir no. 1. Ann Arbor: University of Michigan Museum of Anthropology.
Holmes, R.
    2013    The Future of Social Media? Forget about The U.S., Look to Brazil. *Forbes,* September 12. http://www.forbes.com/sites/ciocentral/2013/09/12/the-future-of-social-media-forget-about-the-u-s-look-to-brazil.
Holst, I., J. E. Moreno, and D. R. Piperno
    2007    The Identification of Teosinte, Maize, and *Tripsacum* in Mesoamerica by Using Pollen, Starch Grains, and Phytoliths. *Proceedings of the National Academy of Sciences USA* 104: 17608–17613.
Hopkins, T., and I. Wallerstein
    1982    Patterns of Development of the Modern World System. In *World System Analysis: Theory and Methodology,* by T. Hopkins, I. Wallerstein, R. Bach, C. Chase-Dunn, and R. Mukherjee, pp. 121–141. Thousand Oaks, CA: Sage.
Hornborg, A., B. Clark, and K. Hermele, eds.
    2011    *Ecology and Power: Struggles over Land and Material Resources in the Past, Present and Future.* New York; Routledge.
Hornborg, A., and C. L. Crumley, eds.
    2007    *The World System and the Earth System: Global Socio-environmental Change and Sustainability since the Neolithic.* Walnut Creek, CA: Left Coast Press.
Hornborg, A., J. R. McNeill, and J. Martinez-Alier, eds.
    2007    *Rethinking Environmental History: World-System History and Global Environmental Change.* Lanham, MD: AltaMira.
Horton, R.
    1963    The Kalabari Ekine Society: A Borderland of Religion and Art. *Africa* 33: 94–113.
    1993    *Patterns of Thought in Africa and the West: Essays on Magic, Religion, and Science.* New York: Cambridge University Press.
Hrdy, S. B.
    2009    *Mothers and Others.* Cambridge, MA: Harvard University Press.
Hublin, J.-J.
    2012    The Earliest Modern Human Colonization of Europe. *Proceedings of the National Academy of Sciences* 109 (34) 13471–13472. http://www.pnas.org/content/109/34/13471.full.
Hudjashov, G., T. Kivisilda, P. A. Underhill, P. Endicott, J. J. Sanchez, A. A. Lin, P. Shen, P. Oefner, C. Renfrew, R. Villems, and P. Forster
    2007    Revealing the Prehistoric Settlement of Australia by Y Chromosome and mtDNA Analysis. *Proceedings of the National Academy of Sciences* 104(21): 8726–8730.
Hunter, M. L.
    2005    *Race, Gender, and the Politics of Skin Tone.* New York: Routledge.
Hurtado. A. M., C. A. Lambourne, P. James, K. Hill, K. Cheman, and K. Baca
    2005    Human Rights, Biomedical Science, and Infectious Diseases among South American Indigenous Groups. *Annual Review of Anthropology* 34: 639–665.
Ignatius, D.
    2007    Summer's Escape Artists. *Washington Post,* July 26. http://www.washingtonpost.com/wp-dyn/content/article/2007/07/25/AR2007072501879.html.
Inhorn, M. C., and P. J. Brown
    1990    The Anthropology of Infectious Disease. *Annual Review of Anthropology* 19: 89–117.
Inhorn, M. C., and E. A. Wentzell, eds.
    2012    *Medical Anthropology at the Intersections: Histories, Activisms, and Futures.* Durham, NC: Duke University Press.

Iqbal, S.
    2002    A New Light on Skin Color. *National Geographic Online Extra.* http://magma.nationalgeographic.com/ngm/0211/feature2/online_extra.html.
Isaac, G. L.
    1972    Early Phases of Human Behavior: Models in Lower Paleolithic Archaeology. In *Models in Archaeology,* D. L. Clarke, ed., pp. 167–199. London: Methuen.
Isaacson, A.
    2012    A Mini-Eden for Endangered Orangutans. *New York Times,* January 6.
Isto É
    1984    *Olimpíiadas,* August 8.
Jablonski, N. G.
    2006    *Skin: A Natural History.* Berkeley: University of California Press.
    2012    *Living Color: The Biological and Social Meaning of Skin Color.* Berkeley: University of California Press.
Jablonski, N. G., and Chaplin, G.
    2000    The Evolution of Human Skin Coloration. *Journal of Human Evolution* 39: 57–106.
Jackson, J., and K. B. Warren
    2005    Indigenous Movements in Latin America, 1992–2004: Controversies, Ironies, New Directions. *Annual Review of Anthropology* 34: 549–573.
Jankowiak, W. R., ed.
    1995    *Romantic Passion: A Universal Experience?* New York: Columbia University Press.
    2008    *Intimacies: Love and Sex across Cultures.* New York: Columbia University Press.
Jankowiak, W. R., and E. F. Fischer
    1992    A Cross-Cultural Perspective on Romantic Love. *Ethnology* 31(2): 149–156.
Jenkins, D. L., et al.
    2012    Clovis Age Western Stemmed Projectile Points and Human Coprolites at the Paisley Caves. *Science* 13(July): 223–228. doi: 10.1126/science.1218443.
Jenks, C.
    2005    *Culture,* 2nd ed. New York: Routledge.
Jiao, T.
    2007    *The Neolithic of Southeast China: Cultural Transformation and Regional Interaction on the Coast.* Youngstown, NY: Cambria Press.
Johansen, B. E.
    2008    *Global Warming 101.* Westport, CT: Greenwood.
Johanson, D. C., and T. D. White
    1979    A Systematic Assessment of Early African Hominids. *Science* 203: 321–330.
Johnson, A. W., and T. Earle
    2000    *The Evolution of Human Societies: From Foraging Group to Agrarian State,* 2nd ed. Stanford, CA: Stanford University Press.
Johnston, B. R.
    2005    Chixoy Dam Legacy Issues Study. http://www.centerforpoliticalecology.org/chixoy.html.
    2009    *Life and Death Matters: Human Rights, Environment and Social Justice,* 2nd ed. Walnut Creek, CA: Left Coast Press.
Jolly, C. J., and R. White
    1995    *Physical Anthropology and Archaeology,* 5th ed. New York: McGraw-Hill.
Joralemon, D.
    2010    *Exploring Medical Anthropology,* 3rd ed. Boston: Pearson.
Jordan, B., ed.
    2013    *Advancing Ethnography in Corporate Environments: Challenges and Emerging Opportunities.* Walnut Creek, CA: Left Coast Press.
Kamrava, M.
    2008    *Understanding Comparative Politics: A Framework for Analysis,* 2nd ed. New York: Routledge.
    2011    *The Modern Middle East: A Political History since the First World War,* 2nd ed. Berkeley: University of California Press.
Kan, S.
    1986    The 19th-Century Tlingit Potlatch: A New Perspective. *American Ethnologist* 13: 191–212.

1989  *Symbolic Immortality: The Tlingit Potlatch of the Nineteenth Century.* Washington, DC: Smithsonian Institution Press.

Kaneshiro, N. K.
2009  Intersex. *Medline Plus.* National Institutes of Health, U.S. National Library of Medicine. http://www.nlm.nih.gov/medlineplus/ency/article/001669.htm.

Kaufman, S. R., and L. M. Morgan
2005  The Anthropology of the Beginnings and Ends of Life. *Annual Review of Anthropology* 34: 317–341.

Kearney, M.
1996  *Reconceptualizing the Peasantry: Anthropology in Global Perspective.* Boulder, CO: Westview Press.

Kelly, R. C.
1976  Witchcraft and Sexual Relations: An Exploration in the Social and Semantic Implications of the Structure of Belief. In *Man and Woman in the New Guinea Highlands,* P. Brown and G. Buchbinder, eds., pp. 36–53. Special Publication, no. 8. Washington, DC: American Anthropological Association.

Kennedy, P.
2010  *Local Lives and Global Transformations: Towards a World Society.* New York: Palgrave Macmillan.

Kent, S.
1992  The Current Forager Controversy: Real versus Ideal Views of Hunter-Gatherers. *Man* 27: 45–70.
1996  *Cultural Diversity among Twentieth-Century Foragers: An African Perspective.* New York: Cambridge University Press.
1998  *Gender in African Prehistory.* Walnut Creek, CA: AltaMira.

Kent, S., ed.
2002  *Ethnicity, Hunter-Gatherers, and the "Other": Association or Assimilation in Africa.* Washington, D.C.: Smithsonian Institution Press.

Kent, S., and H. Vierich
1989  The Myth of Ecological Determinism: Anticipated Mobility and Site Organization of Space. In *Farmers as Hunters: The Implications of Sedentism,* S. Kent, ed., pp. 96–130. New York: Cambridge University Press.

Keppel, K. G., J. N. Pearch, and D. K. Wagener
2002  Trends in Racial and Ethnic-Specific Rates for the Health Status Indicators: United States 1990–98. *Healthy People Statistical Notes No. 23.* Hyattsville, MD: National Center for Health Statistics.

Keynes, J. M.
1927  *The End of Laissez-Faire.* London: L. and Virginia Woolf.
1936  *General Theory of Employment, Interest, and Money.* New York: Harcourt Brace.

Kimmel, M. S., and M. A. Messner, eds.
2013  *Men's Lives,* 9th ed. Boston: Allyn & Bacon.

King, E.
2012  Stanford Linguists Seek to Identify the Elusive California Accent. *Stanford Report,* August 6. http://news.stanford.edu/news/2012/august/california-dialect-linguistics-080612.html.

King, T. F., ed.
2011  *A Companion to Cultural Resource Management.* Malden, MA: Wiley-Blackwell.

Kinsey, A. C., W. B. Pomeroy, and C. E. Martin
1948  *Sexual Behavior in the Human Male.* Philadelphia: W. B. Saunders.

Kirch, P. V.
2000  *On the Road of the Winds: An Archaeological History of the Pacific Islands before European Contact.* Berkeley: University of California Press.

Kirman, P.
1997  An Introduction to Ethnomusicology. http://www.inside-worldmusic.com/library/weekly/aa101797.htm.

Kjaerulff, J.
2010  *Internet and Change: An Ethnography of Knowledge and Flexible Work.* Walnut Creek, CA: Left Coast Press.

Klass, M.
2003  *Mind over Mind: The Anthropology and Psychology of Spirit Possession.* Lanham, MD: Rowman & Littlefield.

Klein, N.
2000  *No Logo: Taking Aim at the Brand Bullies.* New York: Picador.

Klein, R. G.
2013  Modern Human Origins. *General Anthropology* 20(1): 1–4.

Klein, R. G., with B. Edgar
2002  *The Dawn of Human Culture.* New York: Wiley.

Kleinman, A.
1991  *Rethinking Psychiatry: From Cultural Category to Personal Experience.* New York: Free Press.

Kluckhohn, C.
1944  *Mirror for Man: A Survey of Human Behavior and Social Attitudes.* Greenwich, CT: Fawcett.

Kochhar, R., R. Fry, and P. Taylor
2011  Wealth Gaps Rise to Record Highs between Whites, Blacks, Hispanics. Pew Research Center. *Pew Social and Economic Trends.* http://www.pewsocialtrends.org/2011/07/26/wealth-gaps-rise-to-record-highs-between-whites-blacks-hispanics/.

Kottak, C. P.
1980  *The Past in the Present: History, Ecology, and Social Organization in Highland Madagascar.* Ann Arbor: University of Michigan Press.
1990a  *Prime-Time Society: An Anthropological Analysis of Television and Culture.* Belmont, CA: Wadsworth.
1990b  Culture and Economic Development. *American Anthropologist* 92(3): 723–731.
1991  When People Don't Come First: Some Lessons from Completed Projects. In *Putting People First: Sociological Variables in Rural Development,* 2nd ed., ed. M. Cernea, pp. 429–464. New York: Oxford University Press.
2004  An Anthropological Take on Sustainable Development: A Comparative Study of Change. *Human Organization* 63(4): 501–510.
2006  *Assault on Paradise: The Globalization of a Little Community in Brazil,* 4th ed. New York: McGraw-Hill.
2007  Return to Madagascar: A Forty Year Retrospective. *General Anthropology: Bulletin of the General Anthropology Division of the American Anthropological Association* 14(2): 1–10.
2009  *Prime-Time Society: An Anthropological Analysis of Television and Culture,* updated ed. Walnut Creek, CA: Left Coast Press.

Kottak, C. P., L. L. Gezon, and G. Green
1994  Deforestation and Biodiversity Preservation in Madagascar: The View from Above and Below. CIESIN Human Dimensions Kiosk. http://www.ciesin.com.

Kottak, C. P., and K. A. Kozaitis
2012  *On Being Different: Diversity and Multiculturalism in the North American Mainstream,* 4th ed. New York: McGraw-Hill.

Kottak, N. C.
2002  *Stealing the Neighbor's Chicken: Social Control in Northern Mozambique.* Ph.D. dissertation. Department of Anthropology, Emory University, Atlanta, GA.

Kretchmer, N.
1975  (orig. 1972) Lactose and Lactase. In *Biological Anthropology, Readings from Scientific American,* S. H. Katz, ed., pp. 310–318. San Francisco: W. H. Freeman.

Kroeber, A. L.
1923  *Anthropology.* New York: Harcourt, Brace.
1944  *Configurations of Cultural Growth.* Berkeley: University of California Press.
1987  (orig. 1952) *The Nature of Culture.* Chicago: University of Chicago Press.

Kronenfeld, D., G. Bennardo, V. C. de Munck, and M. D. Fischer, eds.
2011  *A Companion to Cognitive Anthropology.* Malden, MA: Wiley-Blackwell.

Kuhn, S. L., M. C. Stiner, and D. S. Reese
2001  Ornaments of the Earliest Upper Paleolithic: New Insights from the Levant. *Proceedings of the National Academy of Sciences of the United States of America* 98(13): 7641–7646.

Kulick, D.
1998  *Travesti: Sex, Gender, and Culture among Brazilian Transgendered Prostitutes.* Chicago: University of Chicago Press.

Kuniholm, P. I.
2004 Home page of the Malcolm and Carolyn Wiener Laboratory for Aegean and Near Eastern Dendrochronology at Cornell University. http://www.arts.cornell.edu/dendro/.

Kuper, L.
2006 *Race, Class, and Power: Ideology and Revolutionary Change in Plural Societies.* New Brunswick, NJ: Transaction.

Kurtz, D. V.
2001 *Political Anthropology: Power and Paradigms.* Boulder, CO: Westview Press.

Labov, W.
1972a *Language in the Inner City: Studies in the Black English Vernacular.* Philadelphia: University of Pennsylvania Press.
1972b *Sociolinguistic Patterns.* Philadelphia: University of Pennsylvania Press.
2006 *The Social Stratification of English in New York City.* New York: Cambridge University Press.
2012 *Dialect Diversity in America: The Politics of Language Change.* Charlottesville: University of Virginia Press.

Laguerre, M. S.
1984 *American Odyssey: Haitians in New York.* Ithaca, NY: Cornell University Press.
1998 *Diasporic Citizenship: Haitian Americans in Transnational America.* New York: St. Martin's Press.
1999 *The Global Ethnopolis: Chinatown, Japantown, and Manilatown in American Society.* New York: St. Martin's Press.

Lakoff, R. T.
2004 *Language and Woman's Place.* New York: Harper & Row.

Lambek, M., ed.
2008 *A Reader in the Anthropology of Religion.* Malden, MA: Blackwell.

Lancaster, R. N., and M. Di Leonardo, eds.
1997 *The Gender/Sexuality Reader: Culture, History, Political Economy.* New York: Routledge.

Landes, D.
1999 *The Wealth and Poverty of Nations. Why Some Are So Rich and Some Are So Poor.* London: Abacus.

Lange, M.
2009 *Lineages of Despotism and Development: British Colonialism and State Power.* Chicago: University of Chicago Press.

Largent, F.
2007a Clovis Dethroned: A New Perspective on the First Americans, Part 1. *Mammoth Trumpet* 22(3): 1–3, 20.
2007b Clovis Dethroned: A New Perspective on the First Americans, Part 2. *Mammoth Trumpet* 22(4): 1–2, 13.

Larsen, C. S.
2000 *Skeletons in Our Closet: Revealing Our Past through Bioarchaeology.* Princeton, NJ: Princeton University Press.
2011 *Our Origins: Discovering Physical Anthropology.* New York: W. W. Norton.

Lassiter, L. E.
1998 *The Power of Kiowa Song: A Collaborative Ethnography.* Tucson: University of Arizona Press.

Laughlin, J. C. H.
2006 *Fifty Major Cities of the Bible.* New York: Routledge.

Layton, R.
1991 *The Anthropology of Art,* 2nd ed. New York: Cambridge University Press.

Leach, E. R.
1955 Polyandry, Inheritance and the Definition of Marriage. *Man* 55: 182–186.
1961 *Rethinking Anthropology.* London: Athlone Press.
1970 (orig. 1954) *Political Systems of Highland Burma: A Study of Kachin Social Structure.* London: Athlone Press.

Leadbeater, C.
1999 *Europe's New Economy.* London: Centre for European Reform.

Leakey, M. G., C. S. Feibel, I. McDougall, and A. Walker
1995 New Four-Million-Year-Old Hominid Species from Kanapoi and Allia Bay, Kenya. *Nature* 376: 565–571.

Leakey, M. G., et al.
2012 New fossils from Koobi Fora in Northern Kenya Confirm Taxonomic Diversity in Early *Homo. Nature* 488 (August 9): 201–204.

Lee, R. B.
1974 (orig. 1968) What Hunters Do for a Living, or, How to Make Out on Scarce Resources. In *Man in Adaptation: The Cultural Present,* 2nd ed., Y. A. Cohen, ed., pp. 87–100. Chicago: Aldine.
1979 *The !Kung San: Men, Women, and Work in a Foraging Society.* New York: Cambridge University Press.
1984 *The Dobe !Kung.* New York: Holt, Rinehart and Winston.
2003 *The Dobe Ju/'hoansi,* 3rd ed. Belmont, CA: Wadsworth.
2012 The !Kung and I: Reflections on My Life and Times with the Ju/'hoansi. *General Anthropology* 19(1): 1–4.

Lee, R. B., and R. H. Daly
1999 *The Cambridge Encyclopedia of Hunters and Gatherers.* New York: Cambridge University Press.

Leman, J.
2001 *The Dynamics of Emerging Ethnicities: Immigrant and Indigenous Ethnogenesis in Confrontation.* New York: Peter Lang.

Lemonick, M. D., and A. Dorfman
1999 Up from the Apes: Remarkable New Evidence Is Filling In the Story of How We Became Human. *Time* 154(8): 5–58.

Lenski, G.
1966 *Power and Privilege: A Theory of Social Stratification.* New York: McGraw-Hill.

Lesure, R. G.
2011 *Interpreting Ancient Figurines: Context, Comparison, and Prehistoric Art.* New York: Cambridge University Press.

LeVine, R. A., ed.
2010 *A Reader on Self in Culture.* Malden, MA: Wiley-Blackwell.

Levinson, B. A. U., and M. Pollock, eds.
2011 *A Companion to the Anthropology of Education.* Malden, MA: Blackwell.

Lévi-Strauss, C.
1963 *Totemism.* Translated by R. Needham. Boston: Beacon Press.
1967 *Structural Anthropology.* New York: Doubleday.
1969 (orig. 1949) *The Elementary Structures of Kinship.* Boston: Beacon Press.

Levy, F.
2010 The World's Happiest Countries. *Forbes,* July 14. http://www.forbes.com/2010/07/14/world-happiest-countries-lifestyle-realestate-gallup.html.

Levy, J. E., with B. Pepper
1992 *Orayvi Revisited: Social Stratification in an "Egalitarian" Society.* Santa Fe, NM: School of American Research Press; Seattle: University of Washington Press.

Lewellen, T. C.
2003 *Political Anthropology: An Introduction,* 3rd ed. Westport, CT: Praeger.
2010 Groping toward Globalization: In Search of Anthropology without Boundaries. *Reviews in Anthropology* 31(1): 73–89.

Lewontin, R. C.
1981 Evolution/Creation Debate: A Time for Truth. *Bioscience* 31, 559.

Lie, J.
2001 *Multiethnic Japan.* Cambridge, MA: Harvard University Press.

Lindenbaum, S.
1972 Sorcerers, Ghosts, and Polluting Women: An Analysis of Religious Belief and Population Control. *Ethnology* 11: 241–253.

Livingstone, F. B.
1969 Gene Frequency Clines of the *b* Hemoglobin Locus in Various Human Populations and Their Similarities by Models Involving Differential Selection. *Human Biology* 41: 223–236.

Lockwood, W. G.
1975 *European Moslems: Economy and Ethnicity in Western Bosnia.* New York: Academic Press.

Lockwood, Y. R.
1983 *Text and Context: Folksong in a Bosnian Muslim Village.* Columbus, OH: Slavica.

Loomis, W. F.
   1967   Skin-Pigmented Regulation of Vitamin-D Biosynthesis
   in Man. *Science* 157: 501–506.
Lopez, A. A.
   2011   New Questions in the Immigration Debate. *Anthropology
   Now* 3(1): 47–53.
Loveday, L.
   1986   Japanese Sociolinguistics: An Introductory Survey.
   *Journal of Pragmatics* 10: 287–326.
   2001   *Explorations in Japanese Sociolinguistics.* Philadelphia:
   J. Benjamins.
Lowie, R. H.
   1961   (orig. 1920) *Primitive Society.* New York: Harper &
   Brothers.
Lowrey, A.
   2013   The Rich Get Richer through the Recovery. *New York
   Times,* September 13. http://economix.blogs.nytimes.com/
   2013/09/10/the-rich-get-richer-through-the-recovery/?_r=0.
Lugo, A.
   1997   Reflections on Border Theory, Culture, and the Nation.
   In *Border Theory: The Limits of Cultural Politics,* S. Michaelsen
   and D. Johnson, eds., pp. 43–67. Minneapolis: University of
   Minnesota Press.
Lugo, A., and B. Maurer
   2000   *Gender Matters: Rereading Michelle Z. Rosaldo.* Ann
   Arbor: University of Michigan Press.
Lukas, D., and T. H. Clutton-Brock
   2013   The Evolution of Social Monogamy in Mammals.
   *Science* 341(6145): 526–530. http://www.sciencemag.org/
   content/341/6145/526.
Lupton, D.
   2012   *Medicine as Culture: Illness, Disease, and the Body,*
   3rd ed. Los Angeles: SAGE.
Lyell, C.
   1969   (orig. 1830–37) *Principles of Geology.* New York: Johnson.
Lyotard, J-F.
   1993   *The Postmodern Explained.* Translated by J. Pefanis,
   M. Thomas, and D. Barry. Minneapolis: University of Minnesota
   Press.
Madra, Y. M.
   2004   Karl Polanyi: Freedom in a Complex Society.
   *Econ-Atrocity Bulletin: In the History of Thought.*
   http://www.fguide.org/Bulletin/polanyi.htm.
Malinowski, B.
   1927   *Sex and Repression in Savage Society.* London and
   New York: International Library of Psychology, Philosophy
   and Scientific Method.
   1929   Practical Anthropology. *Africa* 2: 23–38.
   1944   *A Scientific Theory of Culture and Other Essays.*
   Chapel Hill: University of North Carolina Press.
   1961   (orig. 1922) *Argonauts of the Western Pacific.*
   New York: Dutton.
   1978   (orig. 1931) The Role of Magic and Religion. In *Reader
   in Comparative Religion: An Anthropological Approach,* 4th
   ed., W. A. Lessa and E. Z. Vogt, eds., pp. 37–46. New York:
   Harper & Row.
Malkki, L. H.
   1995   *Purity and Exile: Violence, Memory, and National
   Cosmology among Hutu Refugees in Tanzania.* Chicago:
   University of Chicago Press.
Mann, C. C.
   2011   *1493: Uncovering the New World Columbus Created.*
   New York: Knopf.
Manoff, R. K.
   1994   How Family Planning Came to Bangladesh. Letter to the
   Editor. *New York Times,* Sunday, January 16, pp. 4–16.
Maquet, J.
   1964   Objectivity in Anthropology. *Current Anthropology* 5: 47–55.
   1986   *The Aesthetic Experience: An Anthropologist Looks at
   the Visual Arts.* New Haven, CT: Yale University Press.
Marcus, G. E., and M. M. J. Fischer
   1986   *Anthropology as Cultural Critique: An Experimental
   Moment in the Human Sciences.* Chicago: University of Chicago
   Press.

   1999   *Anthropology as Cultural Critique: An Experimental
   Moment in the Human Sciences,* 2nd ed. Chicago: University of
   Chicago Press.
Marcus, G. E., and F. R. Myers, eds.
   1995   *The Traffic in Culture: Refiguring Art and Anthropology.*
   Berkeley: University of California Press.
Marcus, J.
   1989   From Centralized Systems to City-States: Possible
   Models for the Epiclassic. In *Mesoamerica after the Decline of
   Teotihuacan: A.D. 700–900,* R. A. Diehl and J. C. Berlo, eds.,
   pp. 201–208. Washington, DC: Dumbarton Oaks.
Marcus, J., and K. V. Flannery
   1996   *Zapotec Civilization: How Urban Society Evolved
   in Mexico's Oaxaca Valley.* New York: Thames and Hudson.
Marean, C. W., et al.
   2007   Early Human Use of Marine Resources and Pigment
   in South Africa during the Middle Pleistocene. *Nature*
   449(October 18): 905–908. doi:10.1038/nature06204.
Margolis, M.
   2000   *True to Her Nature: Changing Advice to American
   Women.* Prospect Heights, IL: Waveland.
Marshack, A.
   1972   *Roots of Civilization.* New York: McGraw-Hill.
Martin, D.
   1990   *Tongues of Fire: The Explosion of Protestantism in Latin
   America.* Cambridge, MA: Blackwell.
Martin, D. L., R. P. Harrod, and V. R. Perez
   2013   *Bioarchaeology: An Integrated Approach to Working
   with Human Remains.* New York: Springer.
Martin, K., and B. Voorhies
   1975   *Female of the Species.* New York: Columbia University
   Press.
Martin, S. M.
   1988   *Palm Oil and Protest: An Economic History of the
   Ngwa Region, South-Eastern Nigeria, 1800–1980.* New York:
   Cambridge University Press.
Marx, K., and F. Engels
   1976   (orig. 1848) *Communist Manifesto.* New York:
   Pantheon.
Mascia-Lees, F.
   2010   *Gender & Difference in a Globalizing World: Twenty-
   First Century Anthropology.* Long Grove, IL: Waveland.
Matsuzawa, T., ed.
   2011   *The Chimpanzees of Bossou and Nimba.* New York:
   Springer.
Maugh, T. H., III
   2007   One Language Disappears Every 14 Days; about Half of
   the World's Distinct Tongues Could Vanish This Century,
   Researchers Say. *Los Angeles Times,* September 19.
Maybury-Lewis, D.
   2002   *Indigenous Peoples, Ethnic Groups, and the State,* 2nd
   ed. Boston: Allyn & Bacon.
Maybury-Lewis, D., T. Macdonald, and B. Maybury-Lewis, eds.
   2009   *Manifest Destinies and Indigenous Peoples.* Cambridge,
   MA: David Rockefeller Center for Latin American Studies and
   Harvard University Press.
Mayell, H.
   2003   Orangutans Show Signs of Culture, Study Says. *National
   Geographic News,* January 3. http://news.nationalgeographic.
   com/news/2002/12/1220_021226_orangutan.html.
   2004   Is Bead Find Proof Modern Thought Began in Africa?
   *National Geographic News,* March 31. http://news.nationalgeo-
   graphic.com/news/2004/03/0331_040331_ostrichman.html.
Mayr, E.
   2001   *What Evolution Is.* New York: Basic Books.
Mazzeo, J., A. Rödlach, and B. P. Brenton
   2011   Introduction: Anthropologists Confront HIV/AIDS
   and Food Insecurity in Sub-Saharan Africa. American Anthropological Association, *Annals of Anthropological Practice*
   35 (1–7).
Mba, N. E.
   1982   *Nigerian Women Mobilized: Women's Political Activity
   in Southern Nigeria, 1900–1965.* Berkeley: University of
   California Press, 1982.

McAllester, D. P.
1954 *Enemy Way Music: A Study of Social and Esthetic Values as Seen in Navaho Music.* Cambridge, MA: Peabody Museum of American Archaeology and Ethnology, Papers 41(3).

McBrearty, S., and A. S. Brooks
2000 The Revolution That Wasn't: A New Interpretation of the Origin of Modern Human Behavior. *Journal of Human Evolution* 39: 453–563.

McBrearty, S., and C. Stringer
2007 The Coast in Colour. *Nature* 449: 793–794.

McConnell-Ginet, S.
2010 *Gender, Sexuality, and Meaning: Linguistic Practice and Politics.* New York: Oxford University Press.

McDonald, G.
1984 *Carioca Fletch.* New York: Warner Books.

McDougall, I., F. H. Brown, and J. G. Fleagle
2005 Stratigraphic Placement and Age of Modern Humans from Kibish, Ethiopia. *Nature* 433: 733–736.

McElroy, A., and P. K. Townsend
2009 *Medical Anthropology in Ecological Perspective,* 5th ed. Boulder, CO: Westview Press.

McGee, R. J., and R. L. Warms
2012 *Anthropological Theory: An Introductory History,* 5th ed. New York: McGraw-Hill.

Mead, M.
1937 *Cooperation and Competition among Primitive Peoples.* New York: McGraw-Hill.
1950 (orig. 1935) *Sex and Temperament in Three Primitive Societies.* New York: New American Library.
1961 (orig. 1928) *Coming of Age in Samoa.* New York: Morrow Quill.
1977 Applied Anthropology: The State of the Art. In *Perspectives on Anthropology, 1976.* Washington, DC: American Anthropological Association.

Meadow, R. H., and J. M. Kenoyer
2000 The Indus Valley Mystery: One of the World's First Great Civilizations Is Still a Puzzle. *Discovering Archaeology,* April, pp. 38–43.

Meigs, A., and K. Barlow
2002 Beyond the Taboo: Imagining Incest. *American Anthropologist* 104(1): 38–49.

Menzies, C. R., ed.
2006 *Traditional Ecological Knowledge and Natural Resource Management.* Lincoln: University of Nebraska Press.

Mercader, J., M. Panger, and C. Boesch
2002 Excavation of a Chimpanzee Stone Tool Site in the African Rainforest. *Science* 296: 1452–1455.

Merriam-Webster
2013 Art (definition of). http://www.merriam-webster.com/dictionary/art.

Meyer, B.
1999 *Translating the Devil: Religion and Modernity among the Ewe in Ghana.* Trenton, NJ: Africa World Press.

Mielke, J. H., L. W. Konigsberg, and J. H. Relethford
2011 *Human Biological Variation,* 2nd ed. New York: Oxford University Press.

Millaire, J. F.
2010 Primary State Formation in the Viru Valley, North Coast of Peru. *Proceedings of the National Academy of Sciences of the United States of America* 107(14): 6186–6191. http://www.pnas.org/content/107/14/6186.abstract.

Miller, B. D.
1997 *The Endangered Sex: Neglect of Female Children in Rural North India.* New York: Oxford University Press.

Miller, J.
n.d. Alaskan Tlingit and Tsimtsian. Seattle: University of Washington Libraries, Digital Collections. http://content.lib.washington.edu/aipnw/miller1.html.

Miller, L.
2004 The Ancient Bristlecone Pine, Dendrochronology. http://www.sonic.net/bristlecone/dendro.html.

Miller, N. F., M. A. Zeder, and S. R. Arter
2009 From Food and Fuel to Farms and Flocks: The Integration of Plant and Animal Remains in the Study of Ancient Agro-Pastoral Economies. *Current Anthropology* 50: 915–924.

Mintz, S. W.
1985 *Sweetness and Power: The Place of Sugar in Modern History.* New York: Viking Penguin.
2007 *Caribbean Transformations.* New Brunswick, NJ: Aldine Transaction.

Mitani, J. C., J. Call, P. M. Kappeler, R. A. Palombit, and J. B. Silk, eds.
2012 *The Evolution of Primate Societies.* Chicago: University of Chicago Press.

Mitani, J. C., and D. P. Watts
1999 Demographic Influences on the Hunting Behavior of Chimpanzees. *American Journal of Physical Anthropology* 109: 439–454.

Montague, S., and R. Morais
1981 Football Games and Rock Concerts: The Ritual Enactment. In *The American Dimension: Cultural Myths and Social Realities,* 2nd ed., W. Arens and S. B. Montague, eds., pp. 33–52. Sherman Oaks, CA: Alfred.

Montgomery, H.
2008 *An Introduction to Childhood: Anthropological Perspectives on Children's Lives.* Oxford: Blackwell.

Mooney, A.
2011 *Language, Society, and Power.* New York: Routledge.

Moore, J. D.
2009 *Visions of Culture: An Introduction to Anthropological Theories and Theorists,* 3rd ed. Lanham, MD: AltaMira.

Moran, L.
1993 Evolution Is a Fact and a Theory. *The Talk Origins Archive.* http://www.talkorigins.org/faqs/evolution-fact.html.

Morgan, L. H.
1963 (orig. 1877) *Ancient Society.* Cleveland: World Publishing.
1966 (orig. 1851) *League of the Ho-dé-no-sau-nee or Iroquois.* New York: B. Franklin.
1997 (orig. 1870) *Systems of Consanguinity and Affinity of the Human Family.* Lincoln: University of Nebraska Press.

Morkot, R.
2005 *The Egyptians: An Introduction.* New York: Routledge.

Moro, P. A., and J. E. Myers
2012 *Magic, Witchcraft, and Religion: A Reader in the Anthropology of Religion,* 9th ed. New York: McGraw-Hill.

Mosse, D., ed.
2011 *Adventures in Aidland: The Anthropology of Professionals in International Development.* New York: Berghahn Books.

Motseta, S.
2006 Botswana Gives Bushmen Tough Conditions. *Washington Post,* December 14. http://www.washingtonpost.com/wp-dyn/content/article/2006/12/14/AR2006121401008.html.

Mounier, A., S. Condemi, and G. Manzi
2011 The Stem Species of Our Species: A Place for the Archaic Human Cranium from Ceprano, Italy. *PLoS ONE* 6(4): e18821. doi:10.1371/journal.pone.0018821.

Mount Holyoke College
1999 Dung-Covered Madonna Sparks Controversy; Art Professor Michael Davis Takes a Look. *College Street Journal* 13(6), October 8. http://www.mtholyoke.edu/offices/comm/csj/991008/madonna.html.

Moyà-Solà, S., et al.
2004 *Pierolapithecus catalaunicus:* A New Middle Miocene Great Ape from Spain. *Science* 306(5700): 1339–1344.

Mukhopadhyay, C. C., R. Henze, and Y. T. Moses
2007 *How Real Is Race? A Sourcebook on Race, Culture, and Biology.* Lanham, MD: AltaMira.

Mullaney, T.
2011 *Coming to Terms with the Nation: Ethnic Classification in Modern China.* Berkeley: University of California Press.

Munoz, R., A. Primm, J. Ananth, and P. Ruiz
2007 *Life in Color: Culture in American Psychiatry.* Chicago: Hilton.

Murchison, J. M.
2010 *Ethnography Essentials: Designing, Conducting, and Presenting Your Research.* San Francisco: Jossey Bass.

Murdock, G. P., and C. Provost

1973  Factors in the Division of Labor by Sex: A Cross-Cultural Analysis. *Ethnology* 12(2): 203–225.

Murray, S. O., and W. Roscoe, eds.

1998  *Boy-Wives and Female Husbands: Studies in African Homosexualities.* New York: St. Martin's Press.

Mydans, S.

1992a  Criticism Grows over Aliens Seized during Riots. *New York Times,* May 29, p. A8.

1992b  Judge Dismisses Case in Shooting by Officer. *New York Times,* June 4, p. A8.

Nanda, S.

1996  Hijras: An Alternative Sex and Gender Role in India. In *Third Sex Third Gender: Beyond Sexual Dimorphism in Culture and History,* G. Herdt, ed., pp. 373–418. New York: Zone Books.

1998  *Neither Man nor Woman: The Hijras of India.* Belmont, CA: Thomson/Wadsworth.

2000  *Gender Diversity: Crosscultural Variations.* Prospect Heights, IL: Waveland.

National Academy of Sciences

2008  Understanding and Responding to Climate Change: Highlights of National Academies Reports. http://dels.nas.edu/dels/rpt_briefs/climate_change_2008_final.pdf.

National Research Council

2011  America's Climate Choices. http://nas-sites.org/americasclimatechoices/sample-page/panel-reports/americas-climate-choices-final-report/.

Newman, M.

1992  Riots Bring Attention to Growing Hispanic Presence in South-Central Area. *New York Times,* May 11, p. A10.

*New York Times*

2005  Intelligent Design Derailed. Editorial Desk, December 22. http://www.nytimes.com/2005/12/22/opinion/22thur1.html?ex=1292907600&en=af56b21719a9dd8f&ei=5090&partner=rssuserland&emc=rss.

Ni, X., et al.

2013  The Oldest Known Primate Skeleton and Early Haplorhine Evolution. *Nature* 498, 60–64.

Nishida, T.

2012  *Chimpanzees at the Lakeshore: Natural History and Culture at Mahale.* New York: Cambridge University Press.

Nolan, R. W.

2002  *Development Anthropology: Encounters in the Real World.* Boulder, CO: Westview Press.

Nordstrom, C.

2004  *Shadows of War: Violence, Power, and International Profiteering in the Twenty-First Century.* Berkeley: University of California Press.

Nugent, D., and J. Vincent, eds.

2004  *A Companion to the Anthropology of Politics.* Malden, MA: Blackwell.

Nunn, N., and N. Qian

2010  The Columbian Exchange: A History of Disease, Food, and Ideas. *Journal of Economic Perspectives* 24(2): 163–188.

Nystrom, P., and P. Ashmore

2008  *The Life of Primates.* Upper Saddle River, NJ: Pearson Prentice Hall.

O'Connell, J. F., and J. Allen

2004  Dating the Colonization of Sahul (Pleistocene Australia–New Guinea): A Review of Recent Research. *Journal of Archaeological Science* 31: 835–853.

Omohundro, J. T.

2001  *Careers in Anthropology,* 2nd ed. New York: McGraw-Hill.

Ong, A.

1987  *Spirits of Resistance and Capitalist Discipline: Factory Women in Malaysia.* Albany: State University of New York Press.

1989  Center, Periphery, and Hierarchy: Gender in Southeast Asia. In *Gender and Anthropology: Critical Reviews for Research and Teaching,* S. Morgen, ed., pp. 294–312. Washington, DC: American Anthropological Association.

2010  *Spirits of Resistance and Capitalist Discipline: Factory Women in Malaysia,* 2nd ed. Albany: State University of New York Press.

Ong, A., and S. J. Collier, eds.

2005  *Global Assemblages: Technology, Politics, and Ethics as Anthropological Problems.* Malden, MA: Blackwell.

Ontario Consultants on Religious Tolerance

2011  Religions of the World: Number of Adherents of Major Religions, Their Geographical Distribution, Date Founded, and Sacred Texts. http://www.religioustolerance.org/worldrel.htm.

Opie, C., et al.

2013  Male Infanticide Leads to Social Monogamy in Primates. *Proceedings of the National Academy of Sciences* 110(33): 13328–13332.

Oriji, J. N.

2000  Igbo Women from 1929–1960. *West Africa Review* 2: 1.

Ortner, S. B.

1984  Theory in Anthropology since the Sixties. *Comparative Studies in Society and History* 126(1): 126–166.

Ortutay, B.

2013  Survey: 15% of Americans Not Online. *Post and Courier,* September 26.

Osborne, R., and J. Tanner, eds.

2007  *Art's Agency and Art History.* Malden, MA: Blackwell.

Ottaviani, J., and D. Meconis

2007  *Wire Mothers: Harry Harlow and the Science of Love.* Ann Arbor, MI: G. T. Labs.

Owen, J.

2006  "Lucy's Baby"—World's Oldest Child—Found by Fossil Hunters. *National Geographic News,* September 20. http://news.nationalgeographic.com/news/2006/09/060920-lucys-baby.html.

2012  "Lucy's Baby" a Born Climber, Hinting Human Ancestors Lingered in Trees. *National Geographic News,* October 26. http://news.nationalgeographic.com/news/2012/10/121026-australopithecus-afarensis-human-evolution-lucy-scapula-science/.

Oxford, University of

2013  Social Media: The Perils and Pleasures. http://www.ox.ac.uk/media/news_stories/2013/130411_1.html.

Özdoğan, M., N. Başgelen, and P. Kuniholm

2011  *The Neolithic in Turkey: New Excavations and New Research.* Galatasaray, Istanbul: Archaeology and Art Publications.

Paine, R.

2009  *Camps of the Tundra: Politics through Reindeer among Saami Pastoralists.* Oslo: Instituttet for sammenlignende kulturforskning.

Palmer, S.

2001  The Rael Deal. *Religion in the News* 4: 2. Hartford, CT: Trinity College. The Leonard E. Greenberg Center for the Study of Religion in Public Life. http://www.trincoll.edu/depts/csrpl/PJNVol4No2/Rael.htm.

Pandika, M.

2013  Agriculture Arose in Many Parts of the Fertile Crescent at Once. *Los Angeles Times,* July 5. latimes.com/news/science/sciencenow/la-sci-sn-agriculture-fertile-crescent-iran-20130705,0,5657443.story.

Pardo, I., and G. B. Prato, eds.

2012  *Anthropology in the City: Methodology and Theory.* Burlington, VT: Ashgate.

Parsons, J. R.

1974  The Development of a Prehistoric Complex Society: A Regional Perspective from the Valley of Mexico. *Journal of Field Archaeology* 1: 81–108.

Parzinger, H., et al.

2006  Declaration (on the Bosnia Pyramid Hoax). *The European Archaeologist,* December 11. http://www.e-a-a.org/statement.pdf.

Patterson, F.

1978  Conversations with a Gorilla. *National Geographic,* October, pp. 438–465.

1999  *Koko-love! Conversations with a Signing Gorilla.* New York: Dutton.

Paul, R.

1989  Psychoanalytic Anthropology. *Annual Review of Anthropology* 18: 177–202.

Paulson, T. E.

2005  Chimp, Human DNA Comparison Finds Vast Similarities, Key Differences. *Seattle Post-Intelligencer Reporter,* September 1. http://seattlepi.nwsource.com/local/238852_chimp01.html.

Peletz, M.
  1988 *A Share of the Harvest: Kinship, Property, and Social History among the Malays of Rembau.* Berkeley: University of California Press.

Pelto, P. J.
  2013 *Applied Anthropology: Guidelines for Field Research.* Walnut Creek, CA: Left Coast Press.

Peregrine, P. N., C. R. Ember, and M. Ember
  2007 Modeling State Origins Using Cross-Cultural Data. *Cross-Cultural Research* 41: 75–86.

Petraglia-Bahri, D.
  1996 Introduction to Postcolonial Studies. http://www.emory.edu/ENGLISH/Bahri/.

Pew Research Center
  2011 The Pew Forum on Religion and Public Life. http://www.pewforum.org/uploadedFiles/Topics/Religious_Affiliation/Christian/Evangelical_Protestant_Churches/Global%20Survey%20of%20Evan.%20Prot.%20Leaders.pdf.
  2012 *The Global Religious Landscape: A Report on the Size and Distribution of the World's Major Religious Groups as of 2010, Analysis,* December 18. http://www.pewforum.org/global-religious-landscape-exec.aspx#src=global-footer.

Piddocke, S.
  1969 The Potlatch System of the Southern Kwakiutl: A New Perspective. In *Environment and Cultural Behavior,* A. P. Vayda, ed., pp. 130–156. Garden City, NY: Natural History Press.

Piperno, D. R.
  2001 On Maize and the Sunflower. *Science* 292(5525): 2260–2261.

Piperno, D. R., and D. M. Pearsall
  1998 *The Origins of Agriculture in the Lowland Neotropics.* San Diego: Academic Press.

Piperno, D. R., and K. E. Stothert
  2003 Phytolith Evidence for Early Holocene *Cucurbita* Domestication in Southwest Ecuador. *Science* 299(5609): 1054–1057.

Podolefsky, A., and P. J. Brown, eds.
  1992 *Applying Anthropology: An Introductory Reader,* 2nd ed. Mountain View, CA: Mayfield.

Pohl, M. E. D., D. R. Piperno, K. O. Pope, and J. G. Jones
  2007 Microfossil Evidence for Pre-Columbian Maize Dispersals in the Neotropics from San Andrés, Tabasco, Mexico. *Proceedings of the National Academy of Sciences of the United States of America* 104(29): 11874–11881. doi:10.1073/pnas.0701425104.

Polanyi, K.
  1968 *Primitive, Archaic and Modern Economies: Essays of Karl Polanyi.* G. Dalton, ed. Garden City, NY: Anchor Books.

Pollock, S.
  1999 *Ancient Mesopotamia: The Eden That Never Was.* Cambridge, UK: Cambridge University Press.

Pospisil, L.
  1963 *The Kapauku Papuans of West New Guinea.* New York: Harcourt Brace Jovanovich.

Potash, B., ed.
  1986 *Widows in African Societies: Choices and Constraints.* Stanford, CA: Stanford University Press.

Price, D.
  2000 Anthropologists as Spies. *Nation,* November 20, 24–27.

Price, R., ed.
  1973 *Maroon Societies.* New York: Anchor Press, Doubleday.

Pringle, H.
  2008 Did Humans Colonize the World by Boat? Research Suggests Our Ancestors Traveled the Oceans 70,000 Years Ago. *Discover,* May 20. http://discovermagazine.com/2008/jun/20-did-humans-colonize-the-world-by-boat.

Purcell, K.
  2013 New Data Show a Large Increase in the Percent of Online Adults Who Post Videos Online. Pew Research Center, Internet and American Life Project, October 10. http://www.pewinternet.org/Press-Releases/2013/Online-Video-2013.aspx.

Qian, Z.
  2013 Divergent Paths of American Families. September 11. Brown University, US2010. http://www.s4.brown.edu/us2010/Data/Report/report09112013.pdf.

Radcliffe-Brown, A. R.
  1952 (orig. 1924) The Mother's Brother in South Africa. In A. R. Radcliffe-Brown, *Structure and Function in Primitive Society,* pp. 15–31. London: Routledge & Kegan Paul.
  1965 (orig. 1962) *Structure and Function in Primitive Society.* New York: Free Press.

Raffaele, P.
  2010 *Among the Great Apes: Adventures on the Trail of Our Closest Relatives.* New York: Smithsonian, Harper.

Ramachandran, S., and N. Rosenberg
  2011 A Test of the Influence of Continental Axes of Orientation on Patterns of Human Gene Flow. *Journal of Physical Anthropology* 146(4): 515–529.

Ramos, A. R.
  1995 *Sanumá Memories : Yanomami Ethnography in Times of Crisis.* Madison: University of Wisconsin Press.

*Random House College Dictionary*
  1982, revised ed. New York: Random House.

Ranger, T. O.
  1996 Postscript. In *Postcolonial Identities,* R. Werbner and T. O. Ranger, eds. London: Zed.

Rapoza, K.
  2012 Disturbing Trend for Putin, Russian Poverty Rising. *Forbes.* April 12. http://www.forbes.com/sites/kenrapoza/2012/04/12/disturbing-trend-for-putin-russian-poverty-rising/.

Rappaport, R. A.
  1974 Obvious Aspects of Ritual. *Cambridge Anthropology* 2: 2–60.
  1999 *Holiness and Humanity: Ritual in the Making of Religious Life.* New York: Cambridge University Press.

Rathje, W. L., and C. Murphy
  2001 *Rubbish!: The Archaeology of Garbage.* Tucson: University of Arizona Press.

Rathus, S. A., J. S. Nevid, and J. Fichner-Rathus
  2014 *Human Sexuality in a World of Diversity,* 9th ed. Boston: Allyn & Bacon.

Redfield, R., R. Linton, and M. Herskovits
  1936 Memorandum on the Study of Acculturation. *American Anthropologist* 38: 149–152.

Reese, W. L.
  1999 *Dictionary of Philosophy and Religion: Eastern and Western Thought.* Amherst, NY: Humanities Books.

Reiter, R., ed.
  1975 *Toward an Anthropology of Women.* New York: Monthly Review Press.

Relethford, J. H.
  2009 Race and Global Patterns of Phenotypic Variation. *American Journal of Physical Anthropology* 139(1): 16–22.
  2013 *Human Population Genetics.* Hoboken, NJ: Wiley-Blackwell.

Renfrew, C.
  1987 *Archaeology and Language: The Puzzle of Indo-European Origin.* London: Pimlico.

Renfrew, C., and P. Bahn, eds.
  2005 *Archaeology: The Key Concepts,* New York: Routledge.

Rice, P. C.
  2002 Paleoanthropology 2001—Part 2. *General Anthropology* 8(2): 11–14.
  2012 Paleoanthropology 2012—Part 2. *General Anthropology* 19(2): 10.

Rickford, J. R.
  1997 Suite for Ebony and Phonics. http://www.stanford.edu/~rickford/papers/SuiteForEbonyandPhonics.html (also published in *Discover,* December 1997).

Rickford, J. R., and R. J. Rickford
  2000 *Spoken Soul: The Story of Black English.* New York: Wiley.

Rilling, J. K.
  2013 The Neural and Hormonal Bases of Human Parental Care. *Neuropsychologia* 51: 731–747.

Roach, J.
  2007 "Hobbit" Human Was Unique Species, Wrist Bones Suggest. *National Geographic News,* September 20. http://news.nationalgeographic.com/news/pf/65255655.html.

Robbins, J.

2004    The Globalization of Pentecostal and Charismatic Christianity. *Annual Review of Anthropology* 33: 17–143.

2012    The Ecology of Disease. *New York Times,* July 14. http://www.nytimes.com/2012/07/15/sunday-review/the-ecology-of-disease.html?pagewanted=all.

Robbins, R.

2011    *Global Problems and the Culture of Capitalism,* 5th ed. Boston: Pearson/Allyn & Bacon.

Roberts, D. F.

1953    Body Weight, Race and Climate. *American Journal of Physical Anthropology* 11: 533–558.

Roberts, S., A. Sabar, B. Goodman, and M. Balleza

2007    51% of Women Are Now Living without Spouse. *New York Times,* January 16. http://www.nytimes.com.

Robertson, J.

1992    Koreans in Japan. Paper presented at the University of Michigan Department of Anthropology, Martin Luther King Jr. Day Panel, January. Ann Arbor: University of Michigan Department of Anthropology (unpublished).

Robson, D.

2013    There Really Are 50 Eskimo Words for Snow. *Washington Post,* January 14. http://articles.washingtonpost.com/2013-01-14/national/36344037_1_eskimo-words-snow-inuit.

Rodseth, L., R. W. Wrangham, A. M. Harrigan, and B. Smuts

1991    The Human Community as a Primate Society. *Current Anthropology* 32: 221–254.

Rojas, J. L., and M. E. Smith

2012    *Tenochtitlan: Capital of the Aztec Empire.* Gainesville: University Press of Florida.

Romero, S.

2008    Rain Forest Tribe's Charge of Neglect Is Shrouded by Religion and Politics. *New York Times,* October 7. http://www.nytimes.com.

Root, D.

1996    *Cannibal Culture: Art, Appropriation, and the Commodification of Difference.* Boulder, CO: Westview Press.

Rosaldo, M. Z.

1980a    *Knowledge and Passion: Notions of Self and Social Life.* Stanford, CA: Stanford University Press.

1980b    The Use and Abuse of Anthropology: Reflections on Feminism and Cross-Cultural Understanding. *Signs* 5(3): 389–417.

Rosaldo, M. Z., and L. Lamphere, eds.

1974    *Woman, Culture, and Society.* Stanford, CA: Stanford University Press.

Roscoe, W.

1991    *The Zuni Man-Woman.* Albuquerque: University of New Mexico Press.

1998    *Changing Ones: Third and Fourth Genders in Native North America.* New York: St. Martin's Press.

Rosenberg, K. R., and W. R. Trevathan

2001    The Evolution of Human Birth. *Scientific American* 285(5): 60–65.

Rothman, J. M., D. Raubenheimer, and C. A. Chapman

2011    Nutritional Geometry: Gorillas Prioritize Non-protein Energy While Consuming Surplus Protein. *Biology Letters* 7: 847–849. London: The Royal Society. sbi.royalsocietypublishing.org.

Rothstein, E.

2006    Protection for Indian Patrimony That Leads to a Paradox. *New York Times,* March 29.

Rouse, R.

1991    Mexican Migration and the Social Space of Postmodernism. *Diaspora* 1(1): 8–23.

Ruhlen, M.

1994    *The Origin of Language: Tracing the Evolution of the Mother Tongue.* New York: Wiley.

Ryan, S.

1990    *Ethnic Conflict and International Relations.* Brookfield, MA: Dartmouth.

Ryang, S., and J. Lie

2009    *Diaspora without Homeland: Being Korean in Japan.* Berkeley: University of California Press.

Rylko-Bauer, B., M. Singer, and J. Van Willigen

2006    Reclaiming Applied Anthropology: Its Past, Present, and Future. *American Anthropologist* 108(1): 178–190.

Sabloff, J. A.

2008    *Archaeology Matters: Action Archaeology in the Modern World.* Walnut Creek, CA: Left Coast Press.

Sack, K.

2011    In Tough Times, a Boom in Cremations as a Way to Save Money. *New York Times,* December 8. http://www.nytimes.com/2011/12/09/us/in-economic-downturn-survivors-turning-to-cremations-over-burials.html?scp=1&sq=cremations&st=cse.

Sadig, A. M.

2010    *The Neolithic of the Middle Nile Region: An Archeology of Central Sudan and Nubia.* East Lansing: Michigan State University Press.

Sahlins, M. D.

1968    *Tribesmen.* Englewood Cliffs, NJ: Prentice Hall.

1972    *Stone Age Economics.* Chicago: Aldine-Atherton.

2004    (orig. 1972) *Stone Age Economics.* New York: Routledge.

Salzman, P. C.

1974    Political Organization among Nomadic Peoples. In *Man in Adaptation: The Cultural Present,* 2nd ed., Y. A. Cohen, ed., pp. 267–284. Chicago: Aldine.

2004    *Pastoralists: Equality, Hierarchy, and the State.* Boulder, CO: Westview Press.

2008    *Culture and Conflict in the Middle East.* Amherst, NY: Humanity Books.

Salzmann, Z.

2012    *Linguistic Anthropology: A Short Introduction.* Prague, Czech Republic: Nezavisle centrum pro studium politiky.

Salzmann, Z., J. M. Stanlaw, and N. Adachi

2012    *Language, Culture, and Society: An Introduction to Linguistic Anthropology,* 5th ed. Boulder, CO: Westview Press.

Sample, I.

2012    "Red Deer Cave People" May Be New Species of Human. *The Guardian,* March 14. http://www.guardian.co.uk/science/2012/mar/14/red-deer-cave-people-species-human.

Sanday, P. R.

1974    Female Status in the Public Domain. In *Woman, Culture, and Society,* M. Z. Rosaldo and L. Lamphere, eds., pp. 189–206. Stanford, CA: Stanford University Press.

2002    *Women at the Center: Life in a Modern Matriarchy.* Ithaca, NY: Cornell University Press.

2003    Public Interest Anthropology: A Model for Engaged Social Science. http://www.sas.upenn.edu/anthro/CPIA/PAPERS/SARdiscussion%20paper.65.html.

Sanjek, R.

2004    Going Public: Responsibilities and Strategies in the Aftermath of Ethnography. *Human Organization* 63(4): 444–456.

Sapir, E.

1931    Conceptual Categories in Primitive Languages. *Science* 74: 578–584.

1956    (orig. 1928) The Meaning of Religion. In E. Sapir, *Culture, Language and Personality: Selected Essays.* Berkeley: University of California Press.

Saville, A., ed.

2012    *Flint and Stone in the Neolithic Period.* Oakville, CT: Oxbow Books.

Schaefer, R.

2013    *Race and Ethnicity in the United States,* 7th ed. Upper Saddle River, NJ: Prentice Hall.

Schaik, C. V.

2004    *Among Orangutans: Red Apes and the Rise of Human Culture.* Tucson: University of Arizona Press.

Scheidel, W.

1997    Brother-Sister Marriage in Roman Egypt. *Journal of Biosocial Science* 29(3): 361–371.

Schildkrout, E., and C. A. Keim

1990    *African Reflections: Art from Northeastern Zaire.* Seattle: University of Washington Press.

Schneider, D. M.
    1968    *American Kinship: A Cultural Account.* Englewood Cliffs, NJ: Prentice Hall.

Schneider, D. M., and K. Gough, eds.
    1961    *Matrilineal Kinship.* Berkeley: University of California Press.

Scholte, J. A.
    2000    *Globalization: A Critical Introduction.* New York: St. Martin's Press.

Schultz, S., C. Opie, and Q. D. Atkinson
    2011    Stepwise Evolution of Stable Sociality in Primates. *Nature* 479: 229–222, November 11. http://www.nature.com/nature/journal/v479/n7372/full/nature10601.html.

Schwartz, M. J., V. W. Turner, and A. Tuden, eds.
    2011    *Political Anthropology.* New Brunswick, NJ: Aldine Transaction.

Schweingruber, F. H.
    2007    *Wood Structure and Environment.* New York: Springer.

Scott, Janny
    2011    *A Singular Woman: The Untold Story of Barack Obama's Mother.* New York: Riverhead Books.

Scott, Jim
    2002    Prehistoric Human Footpaths Lure Archaeologists Back to Costa Rica. University of Colorado Press Release, May 20. http://www.eurekalert.org/pub_releases/2002-05/uoca-phf052002.php.

Scott, J. C.
    1985    *Weapons of the Weak.* New Haven, CT: Yale University Press.
    1990    *Domination and the Arts of Resistance.* New Haven, CT: Yale University Press.

Scott, S., and C. Duncan
    2004    *Return of the Black Death: The World's Greatest Serial Killer.* Hoboken, NJ: Wiley.

Scudder, T., and E. Colson
    1980    *Secondary Education and the Formation of an Elite: The Impact of Education on Gwembe District, Zambia.* London: Academic Press.

Scupin, R.
    2012    *Race and Ethnicity: The United States and the World,* 2nd ed. Upper Saddle River, NJ: Prentice Hall.

Sebeok, T. A., and J. Umiker-Sebeok, eds.
    1980    *Speaking of Apes: A Critical Anthropology of Two-Way Communication with Man.* New York: Plenum Press.

Senut, B., M. Pickford, D. Gommery, P. Mein, K. Cheboi, and Y. Coppens
    2001    First Hominid from the Miocene (Lukeino Formation, Kenya). *Comptes Rendus de l'Academie des Sciences, Series IIA—Earth and Planetary Science* 332(30): 137–144.

Service, E. R.
    1962    *Primitive Social Organization: An Evolutionary Perspective.* New York: McGraw-Hill.
    1966    *The Hunters.* Englewood Cliffs, NJ: Prentice Hall.

Shannon, T. R.
    1996    *An Introduction to the World-System Perspective,* 2nd ed. Boulder, CO: Westview Press.

Sharma, A., and A. Gupta, eds.
    2006    *The Anthropology of the State: A Reader.* Malden, MA: Blackwell.

Sheets, P. D.
    2006    *The Ceren Site: An Ancient Village Buried by Volcanic Ash.* Belmont, CA: Thomson Higher Education.

Shermer, M.
    2011    *In Darwin's Shadow: The Life and Science of Alfred Russel Wallace: A Biographical Study on the Psychology of History.* New York: Oxford University Press.

Shivaram, C.
    1996    Where Women Wore the Crown: Kerala's Dissolving Matriarchies Leave a Rich Legacy of Compassionate Family Culture. *Hinduism Today* 96(2). http://www.hinduism-today.com/archives/1996/2/1996-2-03.shtml.

Shore, B.
    1996    *Culture in Mind: Meaning, Construction, and Cultural Cognition.* New York: Oxford University Press.

Shore, C., S. Wright, and D. Però, eds.
    2011    *Policy Worlds: Anthropology and the Analysis of Contemporary Power.* New York: Berghahn Books.

Shreeve, J.
    1992    The Dating Game: How Old Is the Human Race? *Discover* 13(9): 76–83.

Shryock, A.
    1988    Autonomy, Entanglement, and the Feud: Prestige Structures and Gender Values in Highland Albania. *Anthropological Quarterly* 61(3): 113–118.

Silberbauer, G.
    1981    *Hunter and Habitat in the Central Kalahari Desert.* New York: Cambridge University Press.

Sillitoe, P., ed.
    2007    *Local Science versus Global Science: Approaches to Indigenous Knowledge in International Development.* New York: Berghahn Books.

Simmons, A. H.
    2007    *The Neolithic Revolution in the Near East: Transforming the Human Landscape.* Tucson: University of Arizona Press.

Simons, E. L., and P. C. Ettel
    1970    *Gigantopithecus. Scientific American,* January, pp. 77–85.

Singer, M.
    2008    *Drugging the Poor: Legal and Illegal Drugs and Social Inequality.* Long Grove, IL: Waveland.

Singer, M., and H. Baer
    2012    *Introducing Medical Anthropology: A Discipline in Action,* 2nd ed. Lanham, MD: AltaMira.

Singer, M., and P. I. Erickson, eds.
    2011    *A Companion to Medical Anthropology.* Malden, MA: Wiley-Blackwell.

Skoglund, P., et al.
    2012    Origins and Genetic Legacy of Neolithic Farmers and Hunter-Gatherers in Europe. *Science* 27(April): 336, 6080: 466–469. doi: 10.1126/science.1216304. http://www.sciencemag.org/content/336/6080/466.

Smith, A. T.
    2003    *The Political Landscape: Constellations of Authority in Early Complex Polities.* Westport, CT: Praeger.

Smith, B. D.
    1995    *The Emergence of Agriculture.* New York: Scientific American Library, W. H. Freeman.

Smith, C. H., and G. Beccaloni, eds.
    2010    *Natural Selection and Beyond: The Intellectual Legacy of Alfred Russel Wallace.* New York: Oxford University Press.

Smith, C. S.
    2006    Some See a "Pyramid" to Hone Bosnia's Image. Others See a Big Hill. *New York Times,* May 15.

Smith, M. E.
    2009    V. Gordon Childe and the Urban Revolution: A Historical Perspective on a Revolution in Urban Studies. *Town Planning Review* 80(1): 2–29.

Smith, M. K., and M. E. Doyle
    2002    "Globalization," *The Encyclopedia of Informal Education.* http://www.infed.org/biblio/globalization.

Smitherman, G.
    1986    *Talkin and Testifyin: The Language of Black America.* Detroit: Wayne State University Press.

Solway, J., ed.
    2006    *The Politics of Egalitarianism.* New York: Berghahn Books.

Solway, J., and R. Lee
    1990    Foragers, Genuine and Spurious: Situating the Kalahari San in History (with CA treatment). *Current Anthropology* 31(2): 109–146.

Sotomayor, S.
    2009    (orig. 2001) A Latina Judge's Voice. The Judge Mario G. Olmos Memorial Lecture, delivered at the University of California, Berkeley, School of Law in 2001; published in the spring 2002 issue of the *Berkeley La Raza Law Journal,* republished by the *New York Times* on May 14, 2009.

Speer, J. H.
    2010    *Fundamentals of Tree-Ring Research.* Tucson: University of Arizona Press.

Spencer, C. S.
    2003    War and Early State Formation in Oaxaca, Mexico. *Proceedings of the National Academy of Sciences of the United States of America* 100(20): 11185–11187. http://www.pnas.org/cgi.doi/10.1073/pnas.2034992100.

Spencer, C. S., and E. M. Redmond
    2004    Primary State Formation in Mesoamerica. *Annual Review of Anthropology* 33: 173–179.

Spickard, P., ed.
    2004    *Race and Nation: Ethnic Systems in the Modern World.* New York: Routledge.
    2012    *Race and Immigration in the United States: New Histories.* New York: Routledge.

Spindler, G. D., and L. Hammond, eds.
    2006    *Innovations in Educational Ethnography: Theory, Methods, and Results.* Mahwah, NJ: L. Erlbaum Associates.

Spoor, F., M. G. Leakey, P. N. Gathongo, F. H. Brown, S. C. Anton, I. McDougall, C. Kiarie, F. K. Manthi, and L. N. Leakey
    2007    Implications of New Early Homo Fossils from Ileret, East of Lake Turkana, Kenya. *Nature* 448(7154): 688–691. http://news.nature.com//news/2007/070806/070806-5.html.

Srivastava, J., N. J. H. Smith, and D. A. Forno
    1999    *Integrating Biodiversity in Agricultural Intensification: Toward Sound Practices.* Washington, DC: World Bank.

Stack, C. B.
    1975    *All Our Kin: Strategies for Survival in a Black Community.* New York: Harper Torchbooks.

Stanish, C., and A. Levine
    2011    War and Early State Formation in the Northern Titicaca Basin, Peru. *Proceedings of the National Academy of Sciences* 108(34): 13901–13906.

Starn, Orin
    2011    *The Passion of Tiger Woods: An Anthropologist Reports on Golf, Race, and Celebrity Scandal.* Durham, NC: Duke University Press.

Statistics Canada
    2001    1996 Census. Nation Tables. http://www.statcan.ca/english/census96/nation.htm.
    2010    Study: Projections of the Diversity of the Canadian Population. http://www.statcan.gc.ca/daily-quotidien/100309/dq100309a-eng.htm
    2011    Census of Canada. http://www.statcan.gc.ca/tables-tableaux/sum-som/l01/cst01/famil53a-eng.htm.

Steegmann, A. T., Jr.
    1975    Human Adaptation to Cold. In *Physiological Anthropology,* A. Damon, ed., pp. 130–166. New York: Oxford University Press.

Stefoff, R.
    2011    *Forensic Anthropology.* New York: Marshall Cavendish Benchmark.

Stein, R. L., and P. L. Stein, eds.
    2011    *The Anthropology of Religion, Magic, and Witchcraft,* 3rd ed. Upper Saddle River, NJ: Pearson Prentice Hall.

Stephens, W. R.
    2002    *Careers in Anthropology: What an Anthropology Degree Can Do for You.* Boston: Allyn and Bacon.

Stevens, N. J., et al.
    2013    Palaeontological Evidence for an Oligocene Divergence between Old World Monkeys and Apes. *Nature* 497: 611–614, May 30. http://www.nature.com/nature/journal/v497/n7451/full/nature12161.html.

Steward, J. H.
    1955    *Theory of Culture Change.* Urbana: University of Illinois Press.
    1956    *The People of Puerto Rico: A Study in Social Anthropology.* Urbana: University of Illinois Press.

Stimpson, C. R., and G.H. Herdt
    2014    *Critical Terms for the Study of Gender.* Chicago: University of Chicago Press.

Stodder, A. L. W., and A. M. Palkovich, eds.
    2012    *The Bioarchaeology of Individuals.* Gainesville: University of Florida Press.

Stoffel, M., et al., eds.
    2010    *Tree Rings and Natural Hazards: A State-of-the-Art.* New York: Springer.

Stoler, A.
    1977    Class Structure and Female Autonomy in Rural Java. *Signs* 3: 74–89.

Stoler, A. L.
    1995    *Race and the Education of Desire: Foucault's History of Sexuality and the Colonial Order of Things.* Durham, NC: Duke University Press.
    2002    *Carnal Knowledge and Imperial Power: Race and the Intimate in Colonial Rule.* Berkeley: University of California Press.

Stoler, A. L., C. McGranahan, and P. C. Perdue, eds.
    2007    *Imperial Formations.* Santa Fe, NM: School for Advanced Research Press.

Strachan, T., and A. P. Read
    2011    *Human Molecular Genetics,* 4th ed. New York: Garland Press.

Strassmann, B. I., and W. M. Garrard
    2011    Alternatives to the Grandmother Hypothesis: A Meta-Analysis of the Association between Grandparental and Grandchild Survival in Patrilineal Populations. *Human Nature* 22: 201–222.

Strathern, A., and P. J. Stewart
    2010    *Kinship in Action: Self and Group.* Boston: Prentice Hall.

Strathern, M.
    1988    *Dealing with Inequality: Analysing Gender Relations in Melanesia and Beyond: Essays by Members of the 1983/1984 Anthropological Research Group at the Research School of Pacific Studies, the Australian National University.* New York: Cambridge University Press.

Stringer, C.
    2012a  *Lone Survivors: How We Came to Be the Only Humans on Earth.* New York: Henry Holt.
    2012b  Palaeontology: The 100-Year Mystery of Piltdown Man. *Nature* 492(December 12): 177–179.

Subbaraman, N.
    2013    Earliest Fish Stews Were Cooked in Japan during Last Ice Age, Experts Say. *NBC News.* June 22, 2013. http://science.nbcnews.com/_news/2013/04/10/17687754-earliest-fish-stews-were-cooked-in-japan-during-last-ice-age-experts-say?lite.

Sudbery, P., and I. Sudbery
    2009    *Human Molecular Genetics,* 7th ed. Boston: Pearson Prentice Hall.

Sullivan, M.
    2012    Trouble in Paradise: UCLA Book Enumerates Challenges Faced by Middle-Class L.A. Families, June 19. http://newsroom.ucla.edu/portal/ucla/trouble-in-paradise-new-ucla-book.aspx.

Sunderland, P. L., and R. M. Denny
    2007    *Doing Anthropology in Consumer Research.* Walnut Creek, CA: Left Coast Press.

Sunstein, B. S., and E. Chiseri-Strater
    2012    *Fieldworking: Reading and Writing Research,* 4th ed. Boston: Bedford/St. Martin's.

Suttles, W.
    1960    Affinal Ties, Subsistence, and Prestige among the Coast Salish. *American Anthropologist* 62: 296–395.

Tague, R. G., and C. O. Lovejoy
    1986    The Obstetric Pelvis of A. L. 288-1 (Lucy). *Journal of Human Evolution* 15: 237–255.

Tanaka, J.
    1980    *The San Hunter-Gatherers of the Kalahari.* Tokyo: University of Tokyo Press.

Tannen, D.
    1990    *You Just Don't Understand: Women and Men in Conversation.* New York: Ballantine.

Tannen, D., ed.
    1993    *Gender and Conversational Interaction.* New York: Oxford University Press.

Tannen, D., and A. M. Trester, eds.
    2012    *Discourse 2.0: Language and New Media.* Washington, DC: Georgetown University Press.

Tattersall, I., and R. DeSalle
    2011    *Race? Debunking a Scientific Myth.* College Station: Texas A&M University Press.

Tavernise, S.
2012   Whites Account for under Half of Births in U.S. *New York Times,* May 17. http://www.nytimes.com/2012/05/17/us/whites-account-for-under-half-of-births-in-us.html?pagewanted=all&_r=0.

Taylor, C.
1987   Anthropologist-in-Residence. In *Applied Anthropology in America,* 2nd ed., E. M. Eddy and W. L. Partridge, eds. New York: Columbia University Press.

Taylor, P., M. H. Lopez, J. H. Martínez, and G. Velasco
2012   "When Labels Don't Fit: Hispanics and Their Views of Identity," Pew Research Hispanic Center, April 4. http://www.pewhispanic.org/2012/04/04/when-labels-dont-fit-hispanics-and-their-views-of-identity/.

*Telegraph*
2005   Third Sex Finds a Place on Indian Passport Forms. *The Telegraph,* March 10. http://infochangeindia.org/humanrights/news/third-sex-finds-a-place-on-indianpassport-forms.html.

Terrace, H. S.
1979   *Nim.* New York: Knopf.

Terrell, J. E.
1998   The Prehistoric Pacific. *Archaeology* 51(6). Archaeological Institute of America. http://www.archaeology.org/ 9811/abstracts/pacific.html.

Tersigni-Tarrant, M. T. A., and N. R. Shirley, eds.
2012   *Forensic Anthropology: An Introduction.* Boca Raton, FL: CRC Press.

Than, K.
2012   Human Ancestors Ate Bark—Food in Teeth Hints at Chimplike Origins. *National Geographic News,* June 12. http://news.nationalgeographic.com/news/2012/06/120627-sediba-teeth-fossils-bark-human-evolution-max-planck-nature/.

Thompson, W.
1983   Introduction: World System with and without the Hyphen. In *Contending Approaches to World System Analysis,* W. Thompson, ed., pp. 7–26. Thousand Oaks, CA: Sage.

Thomson, A., and L. H. D. Buxton
1923   Man's Nasal Index in Relation to Certain Climatic Conditions. *Journal of the Royal Anthropological Institute* 53: 92–112.

Tice, K.
1997   Reflections on Teaching Anthropology for Use in the Public and Private Sector. In *The Teaching of Anthropology: Problems, Issues, and Decisions,* C. P. Kottak, J. J. White, R. H. Furlow, and P. C. Rice, eds., pp. 273–284. Mountain View, CA: Mayfield.

Tishkoff, S. A., et al.
2007   Convergent Adaptation of Human Lactase Persistence in Africa and Europe. *Nature Genetics* 39(1): 31–40.

Tishkov, V. A.
2004   *Chechnya: Life in a War-Torn Society.* Berkeley: University of California Press.

Titiev, M.
1992   *Old Oraibi: A Study of the Hopi Indians of Third Mesa.* Albuquerque: University of New Mexico Press.

Toner, R.
1992   Los Angeles Riots Are a Warning, Americans Fear. *New York Times,* May 11, pp. A1, A11.

Toth, N.
1985   The Oldowan Reassessed: A Close Look at Early Stone Artifacts. *Journal of Archaelogical Science* 2: 101–120.

Tougher, S.
2008   *The Eunuch in Byzantine History and Society.* New York: Routledge.

Trehub, S. E.
2001   Musical Predispositions in Infancy. *Annals of the New York Academy of Sciences* 930(1): 1–16.

Trevathan, W. R., E. O. Smith, and J. McKenna
2008   *Evolutionary Medicine and Health.* New York: Oxford University Press.

Trivedi, B. P.
2001   Scientists Identify a Language Gene. *National Geographic News,* October 4. http://news.nationalgeographic.com/news/2001/10/1004_TVlanguagegene.html.

Trudgill, P.
2010   *Investigations in Sociohistorical Linguistics: Stories of Colonisation and Contact.* New York: Cambridge University Press.

Turnbull, C.
1965   *Wayward Servants: The Two Worlds of the African Pygmies.* Garden City, NY: Natural History Press.

Turner, V. W.
1967   *The Forest of Symbols: Aspects of Ndembu Ritual.* Ithaca, NY: Cornell University Press.
1995   (orig. 1969) *The Ritual Process.* Hawthorne, NY: Aldine.
1996   (orig. 1957) *Schism and Continuity in an African Society: A Study of Ndembu Village Life.* Washington, DC: Berg.

Tylor, E. B.
1889   On a Method of Investigating the Development of Institutions: Applied to Laws of Marriage and Descent. *Journal of the Royal Anthropological Institute* 18: 245–269.
1958   (orig. 1871) *Primitive Culture.* New York: Harper Torchbooks.

Ulijaszek, S. J., and H. Lofink
2006   Obesity in Biocultural Perspective. *Annual Review of Anthropology* 35: 337–360.

University of Virginia
n.d. American Studies Program, Armory Show of 1913. http://xroads.virginia.edu/~MUSEUM/Armory/ofili.html.

U.S. Bureau of Labor Statistics
2012   *National Compensation Survey.* Washington, DC: U.S. Department of Labor. http://www.bls.gov/ncs/.

U.S. Energy Information Administration
2013   International Energy Statistics. http://www.eia.gov/cfapps/ipdbproject/IEDIndex3.cfm?tid=44&pid=44&aid=2.

Van Allen, J.
1971   "Aba Riots" or "Women's War"?: British Ideology and Eastern Nigerian Women's Political Activism. Waltham, MA: African Studies Association.

Van Cantfort, T. E., and J. B. Rimpau
1982   Sign Language Studies with Children and Chimpanzees. *Sign Language Studies* 34: 15–72.

Vayda, A. P.
1968   (orig. 1961) Economic Systems in Ecological Perspective: The Case of the Northwest Coast. In *Readings in Anthropology,* 2nd ed., vol. 2, M. H. Fried, ed., pp. 172–178. New York: Crowell.

Veblen, T.
1934   *The Theory of the Leisure Class: An Economic Study of Institutions.* New York: The Modern Library.

*Veja*
1984a   Olimpíadas, August 8, pp. 36–50.
1984b   Vitórias no Tatame. August 15, p. 61.

Vekua, A., D. Lordkipanidze, and G. P. Rightmire
2002   A Skull of Early Homo from Dmanisi, Georgia. *Science,* July 5, pp. 85–89.

Ventkatesan, S., and T. Yarrow, eds.
2012   *Differentiating Development: Beyond an Anthropology of Critique.* New York: Berghahn Books.

Verdery, K.
1997   *What Was Socialism and What Comes Next?* Princeton, NJ: Princeton University Press.
2001   Socialist Societies: Anthropological Aspects. *International Encyclopedia of the Social & Behavioral Sciences,* pp. 14496–14500. New York: Elsevier.

Vespa, J., J. M. Lewis, and R. M. Kreider
2013   *America's Families and Living Arrangements: 2012,* Current Population Reports, P20-570. Washington, DC: U.S. Census Bureau.

Vidal, J.
2003   Every Third Person Will Be a Slum Dweller Within 30 Years, UN Agency Warns: Biggest Study of World's Cities Finds 940 Million Already Living in Squalor. *The Guardian,* October 4. http://www.theguardian.com/world/2003/oct/04/population.johnvidal.

Viegas, J.
   2013   Scientists Say Our Languages Might Preserve Neanderthal Talk. NBC News, July 11. http://www.nbcnews.com/science/scientists-say-our-languages-might-preserve-neanderthal-talk-6C10604072.
Vigil, J. D.
   2003   Urban Violence and Street Gangs. *Annual Review of Anthropology* 32: 225–242.
   2010   *Gang Redux: A Balanced Anti-gang Strategy.* Long Grove, IL: Waveland.
   2012   *From Indians to Chicanos: The Dynamics of Mexican-American Culture,* 3rd ed. Boulder, CO: Westview Press.
Vigne, J.-D., et al.
   2012   First Wave of Cultivators Spread to Cyprus at Least 10,600 Years Ago. *Proceedings of the National Academy of Sciences* 109(22): 8445–8449.
Vincent, J.
   1990   *Anthropology and Politics: Visions, Traditions, and Trends.* Tucson: University of Arizona Press.
von Cramon-Taubadel, N.
   2011   Global Human Mandibular Variation Reflects Differences in Agricultural and Hunter-Gatherer Subsistence Strategies. *Proceedings of the National Academy of Sciences* 108(49): 19546–19551.
von Däniken, E.
   1971   *Chariots of the Gods: Unsolved Mysteries of the Past.* New York: Bantam.
Wade, N.
   2004   New Species Revealed: Tiny Cousins of Humans. *New York Times,* October 28, national edition, pp. A1, A6.
   2007   Fossil DNA Expands Neanderthal Range. *New York Times,* October 2. www.nytimes.com.
   2012   Family Tree of Languages Has Roots in Anatolia, Biologists Say. *New York Times,* August 23.
Wade, P.
   2002   *Race, Nature, and Culture: An Anthropological Perspective.* Sterling, VA: Pluto Press.
   2010   *Race and Ethnicity in Latin America,* 2nd ed. New York: Pluto Press.
Walker, S. M., and D. W. Owsley
   2012   *Their Skeletons Speak: Kennewick Man and the Paleoamerican World.* Minneapolis, MN: Carolrhoda Books.
Wallace, A. F. C.
   1966   *Religion: An Anthropological View.* New York: McGraw-Hill.
Wallerstein, I. M.
   1982   The Rise and Future Demise of the World Capitalist System: Concepts for Comparative Analysis. In *Introduction to the Sociology of "Developing Societies,"* H. Alavi and T. Shanin, eds., pp. 29–53. New York: Monthly Review Press.
   2004   *World-Systems Analysis: An Introduction.* Durham, NC: Duke University Press.
Wallerstein, I. M., et al.
   2013   *Does Capitalism Have a Future?* New York: Oxford University Press.
Wallerstein, I. M., C. A. G. Rojas, and C Lemert
   2012   *Uncertain Worlds: World-Systems Analysis in Changing Times.* Boulder, CO: Paradigm.
Ward, C. V., W. H. Kimbel, and D. C. Johanson
   2011   Complete Fourth Metatarsal and Arches in the Foot of *Australopithecus afarensis. Science* 331(6018): 750–753.
Ward, M. C., and M. Edelstein
   2013   *A World Full of Women,* 6th ed. Upper Saddle River, NJ: Pearson.
Warms, R., J. Garber, and R. J. McGee, eds.
   2009   *Sacred Realms: Readings in the Anthropology of Religion,* 2nd ed. New York: Oxford University Press.
Wasson, C., M. O. Butler, and J. Copeland-Carson, eds.
   2012   *Applying Anthropology in the Global Village.* Walnut Creek, CA: Left Coast Press.
Waters, M. R., and T. W. Stafford, Jr.
   2007   Redefining the Age of Clovis: Implications for the Peopling of the Americas. *Science* 315(February 23): 1122–1126. doi: 10.1126/science.1137166.

Waters, M. R., et al.
   2011   Pre-Clovis Mastodon Hunting 13,800 Years Ago at the Manis Site, Washington. *Science* 334(6054): 351–353. doi:10.1126/science.1207663.
Watson, J. D.
   1970   *Molecular Biology of the Gene.* New York: Benjamin.
Watters, E.
   2010   The Americanization of Mental Illness. *New York Times,* January 8. http://www.nytimes.com/2010/01/10/magazine/10psyche-t.html?pagewanted=all.
Watzman, H.
   2006   The Echoes of Ancient Humans. *Chronicle of Higher Education,* January 27. http://chronicle.com/weekly/v52/i21/21a01601.htm.
Weber, M.
   1958   (orig. 1904) *The Protestant Ethic and the Spirit of Capitalism.* New York: Scribner.
   1968   (orig. 1922) *Economy and Society.* Translated by E. Fischoff et al. New York: Bedminster Press.
*Webster's New World Encyclopedia*
   1993   College Edition. Englewood Cliffs, NJ: Prentice Hall.
Weiner, J. S.
   1954   Nose Shape and Climate. *American Journal of Physical Anthropology* 12: 1–4.
   2003   *The Piltdown Forgery.* New York: Oxford University Press.
Weiss, H.
   2005   *Collapse.* New York: Routledge.
Wendorf, F., and R. Schild
   2000   Late Neolithic Megalithic Structures at Nabta Playa (Sahara), Southwestern Egypt. http://www.comp-archaeology.org/WendorfSAA98.html.
Wenke, R. J., and D. I. Olszewski
   2007   *Patterns in Prehistory: Mankind's First Three Million Years,* 5th ed. New York: Oxford University Press.
White, L. A.
   1949   *The Science of Culture: A Study of Man and Civilization.* New York: Farrar, Strauss.
   1959   *The Evolution of Culture: The Development of Civilization to the Fall of Rome.* New York: McGraw-Hill.
   2009   *Modern Capitalist Culture,* abridged ed. Walnut Creek, CA: Left Coast Press.
White, T. D., M. T. Black, and P. A. Folkens
   2012   *Human Osteology,* 3rd ed. San Diego: Academic Press.
Whiteford, L. M., and R. T. Trotter II
   2008   *Ethics for Anthropological Research and Practice.* Long Grove, IL: Waveland.
Whiting, J. M.
   1964   Effects of Climate on Certain Cultural Practices. In *Explorations in Cultural Anthropology: Essays in Honor of George Peter Murdock,* ed. W. H. Goodenough, pp. 511–544. New York: McGraw-Hill.
Whorf, B. L.
   1956   A Linguistic Consideration of Thinking in Primitive Communities. In *Language, Thought, and Reality: Selected Writings of Benjamin Lee Whorf,* J. B. Carroll, ed., pp. 65–86. Cambridge, MA: MIT Press.
Wiley, A. S., and J. S. Allen
   2013   *Medical Anthropology: A Biocultural Approach,* 2nd ed. New York: Oxford University Press.
Wilford, J. N.
   2000   Ruins Alter Ideas of How Civilization Spread. *New York Times,* May 23. http://www.nytimes.com.
   2002a   Seeking Polynesia's Beginnings in an Archipelago of Shards. *New York Times,* January 8, Science Desk.
   2002b   When Humans Became Human. *New York Times,* February 26, late edition, final, section F, p. 1. http://www.nytimes.com.
   2007a   Fossils in Kenya Challenge Linear Evolution. *New York Times,* August 9, p. A6.
   2007b   Fossils Reveal Clues on Human Ancestors. *New York Times,* September 20. www.nytimes.com.
   2009a   Fossil Skeleton from Africa Predates Lucy. *New York Times,* October 2, pp. A1, A6.

2009b    Feet Offer Clue about Tiny Hominid. *New York Times,* May 9. http://www.nytimes.com.

2010    In Syria, a Prologue for Cities. *New York Times,* April 6. http://www.nytimes.com/2010/04/06/science/06archeo.html?_r=0&pagewanted=print.

2011a    Fossil Teeth Put Humans in Europe Earlier Than Thought. *New York Times,* November 3, p. A4.

2011b    In African Cave, Signs of an Ancient Paint Factory. *New York Times,* October 13, p. A14.

2011c    Earliest Signs of Advanced Tools Found. *New York Times,* August 31. http://www.nytimes.com.

2012    Artifacts Revive Debate on Transformation of Human Behavior. *New York Times,* July 30. http://www.nytimes.com/2012/07/31/science/cave-findings-revive-debate-on-human-behavior.html?_r=0.

2013    Palm-Size Fossil Resets Primates' Clock, Scientists Say. *New York Times,* June 5. http://www.nytimes.com/2013/06/06/science/palm-size-fossil-resets-primates-clock-scientists-say.html?pagewanted=all&_r=0.

Wilk, R. R.
2006    *Fast Food/Slow Food: The Cultural Economy of the Global Food System.* Lanham, MD: AltaMira.

Wilk, R. R., and L. Barbosa
2012    *Rice and Beans: A Unique Dish in a Hundred Places.* New York: Berg.

Wilk, R. R., and L. Cliggett
2007    *Economies and Culture: Foundations of Economic Anthropology.* Boulder, CO: Westview Press.

Williams, B.
1989    A Class Act: Anthropology and the Race to Nation across Ethnic Terrain. *Annual Review of Anthropology* 18: 401–444.

Williams, L. M., and D. Finkelhor
1995    Paternal Caregiving and Incest: Test of a Biosocial Model. *American Journal of Orthopsychiatry* 65(1): 101–113.

Willie, C. V., and R. J. Reddick
2009    *A New Look at Black Families,* 6th ed. Lanham, MD: Rowman & Littlefield.

Wilmsen, E. N.
1989    *Land Filled with Flies: A Political Economy of the Kalahari.* Chicago: University of Chicago Press.

Wilson, D. S.
2002    *Darwin's Cathedral: Evolution, Religion, and the Nature of Society.* Chicago: University of Chicago Press.

Wilson, M. L., and R. W. Wrangham
2003    Intergroup Relations in Chimpanzees. *Annual Review of Anthropology* 32: 363–392.

Winter, R.
2001    Religions of the World: Number of Adherents; Names of Houses of Worship; Names of Leaders; Rates of Growth. http://www.religioustolerance.org/worldrel.htm.

Wittfogel, K. A.
1957    *Oriental Despotism: A Comparative Study of Total Power.* New Haven, CT: Yale University Press.

Wolcott, H. F.
2010    *Ethnography Lessons: A Primer.* Walnut Creek, CA: Left Coast Press.

Wolf, E. R.
1966    *Peasants.* Englewood Cliffs, NJ: Prentice Hall.
1982    *Europe and the People without History.* Berkeley: University of California Press.

Wolf, E. R., with S. Silverman
2001    *Pathways of Power: Building an Anthropology of the Modern World.* Berkeley: University of California Press.

Wolpoff, M. H.
1999    *Paleoanthropology,* 2nd ed. New York: McGraw-Hill.

Wood, B., ed.
2011    *Wiley-Blackwell Encyclopedia of Human Evolution.* Hoboken, NJ: Wiley-Blackwell.

Worsley, P.
1985    (orig. 1959) Cargo Cults. In *Readings in Anthropology* 85/86. Guilford, CT: Dushkin.

Wrangham, R., W. McGrew, F. de Waal, and P. Heltne, eds.
1994    *Chimpanzee Cultures.* Cambridge, MA: Harvard University Press.

Wright, H. T.
1977    Recent Research on the Origin of the State. *Annual Review of Anthropology* 6: 379–397.
1994    Prestate Political Formations. In *Chiefdoms and Early States in the Near East: The Organizational Dynamics of Complexity,* ed. G. Stein and M. S. Rothman, *Monographs in World Archaeology* 18: 67–84. Madison, WI: Prehistory Press.

Wu, X., et al.
2012    Early Pottery at 20,000 Years Ago in Xianrendong Cave, China. *Science* 336(6089): 1696.

Wynn, T., and F. L. Coolidge
2011    *How to Think Like a Neanderthal.* New York: Oxford University Press.

Yellen, J. E., A. S. Brooks, and E. Cornelissen
1995    A Middle Stone Age Worked Bone Industry from Katanda, Upper Semliki Valley, Zaire. *Science* 268: 553–556.

Yetman, N., ed.
1991    *Majority and Minority: The Dynamics of Race and Ethnicity in American Life,* 5th ed. Boston: Allyn & Bacon.

York, A.
2009    Alaskan Village Stands on Leading Edge of Climate Change, *Mother Nature Network,* August 19. http://news21.jomc.unc.edu/index.php/stories/alaska.html.

Young, A.
2000    *Women Who Become Men: Albanian Sworn Virgins.* New York: Berg.

Zaborenko, D.
2012    In U.S., 2012 So Far Is Hottest Year on Record. *Yahoo News.* http://news.yahoo.com/u-2012-far-hottest-record-192659729.html.

Zeder, M. A.
1997    The American Archaeologist: Results of the 1994 SAA Census. *SAA Bulletin* 15(2): 12–17.
2008    Domestication and Early Agriculture in the Mediterranean Basin: Origins, Diffusion, and Impact. *Proceedings of the National Academy of Sciences* 105(33): 11597–11604, August 12. http://www.pnas.org/content/early/2008/08/11/0801317105.

Zeitzen, M. K.
2008    *Polygamy: A Cross-Cultural Analysis.* New York: Berg.

Zickuhr, K.
2013    Home Broadband 2013. Pew Research Center, Internet and American Life Project, August 26. http://www.pewinternet.org/Press-Releases/2013/Home-Broadband-2013.aspx.

Zimmer, C.
2010    Siberian Fossils Were Neanderthals' Eastern Cousins, DNA Reveals. *New York Times,* December 22. http://www.nytimes.com/2010/12/23/science/23ancestor.html.
2013    Monogamy and Human Evolution. *New York Times,* August 2. http://www.nytimes.com/2013/08/02/science/monogamys-boost-to-human-evolution.html?

Zimmer-Tamakoshi, L.
1997    The Last Big Man: Development and Men's Discontents in the Papua New Guinea Highlands. *Oceania* 68(2):107–122.

Zimring, C. A., ed.
2012    *Encyclopedia of Consumption and Waste: The Social Science of Garbage.* Thousand Oaks, CA: Sage Reference.

# PHOTO CREDITS

## CONTENTS

Page vi: © Martin Roemers/Panos; p. vii(top): © Chel Beeson/ Photolibrary/Getty Images; p. vii(bottom): © Michael Stuparyk/ Toronto Star via Getty Images; p. viii(top): © Javier Trueba/Madrid Scientific Films/Science Source; p. viii(bottom): © Frans Lanting/ National Geographic Stock; p. ix(top): © Matt McClain for The Washington Post via Getty Images; p. ix(bottom): © Paul Souders/ Getty Images; p. x: © Alexander Joe/AFP/Getty Images; p. xi(top): © Frank Franklin II/AP Images; p. xi(bottom): © Arterra Picture Library/Alamy; p. xii(top): © Philippe Lissac/Godong/Corbis; p. xii(bottom): © Jeffrey Becom/Lonely Planet Images/Getty Images; p. xiii: © Jack Fields/Corbis; p. xiv(top): © Raminder Pal Singh/epa/Corbis; p. xiv(bottom): © David Grossman/ Alamy; p. xv(top): © Nicholas Pitt/Photodisc/Getty Images RF; p. xv(bottom): © Rudi Meisel/VISUM/The Image Works; p. xvi(top): © Scanpix Sweden, Fredrik Sandberg/AP Images; p. xvi (bottom): © Wang Song/Xinhua Press/Corbis; p. xvii(top): © Michael Freeman/Corbis; p. xvii(bottom): © Conrad P. Kottak; p. xviii: © Tim Hales/AP/Corbis; p. xix(top): © Philippe Lissac/ Godong/Corbis; p. xix(bottom): © Javier Etcheverry/Alamy.

## ABOUT THE AUTHOR

Page xxii: Courtesy of Conrad P. Kottak and Juliet K. Mavromatis.

## CHAPTER 1

Opener: © Martin Roemers/Panos; p. 4: © Punchstock/Brand X Pictures RF; p. 6: National Archives and Records Administration; p. 7: © Al Bello/Getty Images Sport/Getty Images; p. 10: © George H.H. Huey/Alamy; p. 13: © Riccardo De Luca/ MAXPPP/Newscom; p. 15: © Obama Presidential Campaign/AP Images; p. 16: © Ton Koene; p. 17: © BrazilPhotos.com/Alamy.

## CHAPTER 2

Opener: © Chel Beeson/Photolibrary/Getty Images; p. 23: © Ingram Publishing RF; p. 24(top): © William Gottlieb/Corbis; p. 24(bottom): © ERproductions Ltd/Blend Images RF; p. 26: © Kenneth Garrett/National Geographic Stock; p. 27(left): © Clive Bromhall/Oxford Scientific/Getty Images; p. 27(right): © Stan Osolinski/Oxford Scientific/Getty Images; p. 28(top): © Hideo Haga/ HAGA/The Image Works; p. 28(bottom): © Carl D. Walsh/ Aurora Photos; p. 30: © Elizabeth Dalziel/AP Images; p. 33(top and bottom): © Dan Levine/AFP Getty Images; p. 34(left): © J.D. Dallet/age fotostock; p. 34(right): © ZUMA Press, Inc./Alamy; p. 35: © Wu changqing - Imaginechina/AP Images; p. 36(top): © Travel Pictures/Alamy.

## CHAPTER 3

Opener: © Michael Stuparyk/Toronto Star via Getty Images; p. 41: © Will & Deni McIntyre/Corbis; p. 42: © Michael S. Yamashita/Corbis; p. 43: © Sean Sprague/The Image Works; p. 45: © Shah Marai/AFP/Getty Images; p. 46: © adrian arbib/ Alamy; p. 47: © PNC/Brand X Pictures/Getty Images RF; p. 49: © Joe Amon/The Denver Post/AP Images; p. 50: Courtesy Melville J. Herskovits Library of African Studies, Northwestern University; p. 51: © Carl D. Walsh/Aurora Photos; p. 52(top): © age fotostock/ Alamy; p. 52(bottom): © Charles Cherney/MCT/Newscom.

## CHAPTER 4

Opener: © Javier Trueba/Madrid Scientific Films/Science Source; p. 59(all): Courtesy of Dolores R. Piperno, National Museum of Natural History; p. 60: © Axel Fassio/Aurora/Getty Images; p. 62: © Kenneth Garrett/ National Geographic Stock; p. 63: © Jonathan Blair/Corbis; p. 64: Image courtesy of Prof Christopher Henshilwood; p. 65(left): © Nigel Pavitt/JWL/Aurora Photos; p. 65(right): © Charles V. Angelo/Science Source; p. 66: © Jim Sugar/Corbis; p. 68: © Eye of Science/Science Source; p. 69: © Francis Demange/Gamma-Rapho via Getty Images; p. 71: © Michael Gurven; p. 72(top left): © Kevin P. Casey/AP Images; p. 72 (top center left): © Elaine Thompson/AP Images; p. 72(top center right and top right): © Emmanuel Laurent/Science Source.

## CHAPTER 5

Opener: © Frans Lanting/National Geographic Stock; p. 75: © Graham Dunn/Alamy; p. 76: © Philadelphia Museum of Art/Corbis; p. 78: © The Natural History Museum/The Image Works; p. 80(top left): © Photo Inc/Photo Researchers/Getty Images; p. 80(top right): © Print Collector/Hulton Archive/Getty Images; p. 80(bottom): © Time & Life Pictures/Getty Images; p. 83: © Nathan Devery/Science Source; p. 85: © Brian Zak/ SIPA/Newscom; p. 87: © Holly Wilmeth/Aurora Photos; p. 88: © Eye of Science/Science Source.

## CHAPTER 6

Opener: © Matt McClain for The Washington Post via Getty Images; p. 95(top): © Paul Grebliunas/The Image Bank/Getty Images; p. 95(bottom): © Leonid Plotkin/Alamy; p. 96(left): © Conrad P. Kottak; p. 96(right): © Darrell Gulin/Corbis; p. 97: © Horizons WWP/Alamy; p. 98(top): © Jan Spieczny/Photolibrary/ Getty Images; p. 98(bottom): © Antony Jones/Julian Parker/ Mark Cuthbert/UK Press via Getty Images; p. 100: © Brent Frazee/Kansas City Star/MCT via Getty Images; p. 101(top): © Antonio Ciufo/Flickr Vision/Getty Images; p. 101(bottom): © Cindy Hopkins/Alamy; p. 103: © Claudia Lopez/Aurora Photos; p. 104(top): © Tony Camerano/AP Images; p. 104(bottom): NIH History of Medicine Division, U.S. National Library of Medicine.

## CHAPTER 7

Opener: © Paul Souders/Getty Images; p. 113(top): © All Rights Reserved, Image Archives, Denver Museum of Nature & Science; p. 113(bottom): © Tom McHugh/Science Source; p. 114(right): © Frans Lanting/Corbis; p. 115: © blickwinkel/Alamy; p. 117(top): © Holger Ehlers/Alamy; p. 117(bottom): © Irwin Fedriansyah/AP Images; p. 118: © Liam White/Alamy; p. 119: © Michael Nichols/ National Geographic/Getty Images; p. 120: © Purestock/Getty Images RF; p. 123(left): © Tom McHugh/Science Source; p. 123(right): © Arco Images GmbH/Alamy; p. 124: © Russell Ciochon, University of Iowa; p. 125(top): © Luis Gene/AFP/Getty Images.

## CHAPTER 8

Opener: © Alexander Joe/AFP/Getty Images; p. 129: © The Natural History Museum/Alamy; p. 131(left): © Patrick Robert/ Corbis; p. 131(right): © Acques Demarthon/AFP/Getty Images; p. 132: © Tim White; p. 133(top):© David L. Brill; p. 133(bottom): © Tim White; p. 134: © Kenneth Garrett/National Geographic Stock; p. 136: © John Reader/Science Photo Library/Science Source; p. 137: © Lionel Bret/Science Source; p. 141: © Alexander Joe/ Agence France-Presse/Getty Images; p. 142(left and right): © The Natural History Museum/Alamy; p. 143: © Des Bartlett/Science Source; p. 144: © Javier Trueba/MSF/Science Source.

p. 353(top): © Schoene/laif/Aurora Photos; p. 353(bottom): © David J. Phillip/AP Images; p. 354: © Maciej Dakowicz/Alamy; p. 357: © Ricardo Gomes/Globo via Getty Images.

## CHAPTER 19

Opener: © Wang Song/Xinhua Press/Corbis; p. 362: © April Maciborka/Lonely Planet Images/Getty Images; p. 363: © Reuters/Corbis; p. 364: © James Quine/Alamy; p. 367: © Katja Heinemann/Aurora Photos; p. 368: © The Washington Times/ZUMA Press, Inc./Newscom; p. 371(top): © Ami Vitale/Alamy; p. 371(bottom): © Voutsas/IML/age fotostock; p. 373: © Ariel Skelley/Blend Images LLC RF.

## CHAPTER 20

Opener: © Michael Freeman/Corbis; p. 381: © Universal Images Group/Getty Images; p. 384(top): © Kenneth Garrett/National Geographic Stock; p. 384(bottom): © DPA/The Image Works; p. 385: © Jake Norton/Alamy; p. 386: © Jim West/Alamy; p. 387: © James Marshall/The Image Works; p. 388: © Conrad P. Kottak; p. 389: © Qin Gang/Xinhua Press/Corbis; p. 390: © Bonile Bam/Gallo Images/Alamy; p. 391: ©Angel Wynn/DanitaDelimont.com "Danita Delimont Photography"/Newscom; p. 393(left): © Mike Hutchings/AP Images; p. 393(right): © John Bazemore/AP Images.

## CHAPTER 21

Opener: © Conrad P. Kottak; p. 399: © Stan Grossfeld/The Boston Globe via Getty Images; p. 400: © Gianni Dagli Orti/Corbis; p. 401: © Peter Essick/Aurora Photos; p. 402(top): © Thierry Secretan/Cosmos/Woodfin Camp and Associates; p. 402(bottom): © Joe McNally/Hulton Archive/Getty Images; p. 404: © Conrad P. Kottak; p. 405: © Paul Kane/Getty Images News/Getty Images; p. 407: © Thierry Falise/LightRocket via Getty Images; p. 411(top): © Ville Palonen/Alamy; p. 411(bottom): Caetano Barreira/X01990/Reuters/Corbis; p. 413: © Chicarito/AFP/Getty Images; p. 414(top): © Behzad/Demotix/Demotix/Corbis.

## CHAPTER 22

Opener: © Tim Hales/AP/Corbis; p. 418: © Alex Segre/Alamy; p. 419: © JR/Aurora Photos; p. 422: © John Moss/Science Source; p. 423: © Nico Tondini/Robert Harding World Imagery/Corbis; p. 424: © National Geographic Image Collection/Alamy RF; p. 428(top): © Richard Mittleman/Alamy RF; p. 428(bottom): © Kike Calvo/National Geographic Stock; p. 429 (top): © Ingolf Pompe/age fotostock; p. 429(bottom): © Elliott Franks/ArenaPal/The Image Works; p. 431: © Stuart Forster/Alamy; p. 432: © Bay Ismoyo/AFP/Getty Images; p. 435(top): © David Finch/Getty Images Sport/Getty Images; p. 435(bottom): © Robert W. Ginn/Alamy; p. 436: © Andre J. Jackson/MCT/Newscom.

## CHAPTER 23

Opener: © Philippe Lissac/Godong/Corbis; p. 442: © Gallo Gallina/The Bridgeman Art Library/Getty Images; p. 444(top): © Bruce Dale/National Geographic Stock; p. 444(bottom): © Henglein and Steets/Cultura/Getty Images RF; p. 445(top): © ARPL/Topham/The Image Works; p. 445(bottom): © Michael Nichols/National Geographic Stock; p. 448: © Alex Brandon/AP Images; p. 449: General Collections, Prints and Photographs Division, Library of Congress, LC-USZ62-74580; p. 450: © Hulton Archive/Getty Images; p. 453(top): © Gideon Mendel/Corbis; p. 453(bottom): © Chris Leslie Smith/PhotoEdit; p. 454(top): © Philippe Psaila/Science Source; p. 454(bottom): © Eduardo Verdugo/AP Images; p. 457: © Friedrich Stark/Alamy; p. 458(top): © Bettmann/Corbis; p. 458(bottom): © Misha Japaridze/AP Images.

## CHAPTER 24

Opener: © Javier Etcheverry/Alamy; p. 465(top): © Monica Almeida/New York Times Photo/Redux Pictures; p. 465(bottom): © Royalty-Free/Corbis; p. 467: © STR/AFP/Getty Images; p. 468: © UNEP-Topham/The Image Works; p. 469: © Edward Parker/Alamy; p. 470(left): James Gathany, CDC/Dr. Scott Smith; p. 470(right): © Ivan Kuzmin/Alamy; p. 471: © Paul Seheult/Eye Ubiquitous/Corbis; p. 472: © Guiziou Franck/hemis.fr/Getty Images; p. 473: © Sakchai Lalit/AP Images; p. 474: © Lionel Derimais/VISUM/The Image Works; p. 475(top): © Al Grillo/AP Images; p. 475(bottom): © Jose Cabezas/AFP/Getty Images.

# NAME INDEX

Names of all persons and of organizations cited as references are found herein. Page numbers followed by f indicate material in figures and illustrations and their captions; page numbers followed by t indicate material in tables and Recap boxes.

## A

Abelmann, N., 290
Abu-Lughod, L., 430
*Academic American Encyclopedia,*
    450f, 451f
Adachi, N., 254
Adams, R. M., 219
Adams, S., 290
Adepegba, C. O., 418
Aeschylus, 428
Ahmed, A. S., 287
Ahmed, Akbar, 44
Aiello, L., 132
Aikens, C. M., 188
Akazawa, T., 188
al-Assad, Bashar, 290
al-Assad, Hafez, 290
Aldenderfer, Mark, 102, 103
Alexander the Great, 212, 449
Alfred, Marcus, 242f
Allegretto, S. A., 447, 447f
Allen, J., 177, 177f, 178
Allen, J. A., 101
Allen, J. S., 49
Altheman, Maria Suelen, 435f
Altmann, J., 172
Altmann, S., 172
Amadiume, I., 388
American Anthropological Association
    (AAA), 279
American Psychiatric Association
    (APA), 12
Ananth, J., 12
Anderson, Barbara G., 49, 50, 51
Anderson, Benedict, 286, 472
Anderson, Gregory, 271f
Anderson-Levitt, K. M., 47
Anemone, R. L., 96
Annenberg/CPB Exhibits, 226
*Anthropology Newsletter,* 323
Anton, S. C., 143, 150
Antoun, R. T., 413
Antrosio, Jason, 54
Aoki, M. Y., 283
apl.de.ap, 269f
Appadurai, Arjun, 34, 472–473
Appiah, Kwame Anthony, 282
Arens, W., 433
Arensberg, C., 52
Aristophanes, 428
Armelagos, George J., 49, 68, 86,
    87, 204
Arnold, Jeanne E., 368
Arouet, François-Marie (Voltaire), 244
Arrighi, G., 441
Arter, S. R., 192
Asad, T., 399
Asfaw, Berhane, 132, 133f, 144, 167

Ashcroft, B., 452
Ashmore, P., 112
Askew, K. M., 430
Atkinson, Quentin D., 123, 269, 270
Austen, Jane, 430
Avert.org, 50
Axelby, R., 43

## B

Baca, K., 49
Bach, Johann Sebastian, 418
Baer, H. A., 49, 50
Bahn, P., 63
Bailey, G., 188
Bailey, R. C., 297
Balleza, M., 366
Balter, M., 170
Banks, C. G., 12
Barbosa, L., 472
Barfield, Thomas, 44, 45
Barlow, Kathleen, 382
Barnaby, F., 330
Barnard, A., 297
Barnes, E., 49
Baro, M., 50
Baron, D. E., 258
Barrett, R. L., 49, 52
Barringer, F., 279
Barry, Nancy, 14
Barth, Fredrik, 44, 276, 287
Bartlett, Bruce, 307
Barton, C. M., 166, 173
Bar-Yosef, Ofer, 168, 188, 189, 191,
    193, 200
Başgelen, N., 66, 214
Bauval, R., 223
Beach, F. A., 355
Beall, Cynthia, 102, 103
Beccaloni, G., 77
Beck, L. A., 59
Beck, S., 40
Beckerman, S., 372
Beeman, W., 266
Bellah, Robert N., 406
Bellwood, P. S., 189, 190
Beltré, Adrian, 8
Benazzi, S., 155, 169
Benedict, Ruth Fulton, 240, 242, 244,
    245, 245f, 250t, 333
Bennardo, G., 12
Bennett, J. W., 9
Berdan, F. F., 225
Berger, Lee R., 140, 141f
Berger, Matthew, 141f
Berger, Peter, 412
Bergmann, Karl Christian, 101
Beriss, D., 285
*Berkeleyan,* 144

Berlin, B. D., 261
Berna, F., 153
Bernard, H. R., 16, 230, 238
Bernstein, Paula, 85f
Berry, Halle, 281f
Best, Amy L., 5
Bettelheim, Bruno, 425, 426
Bilefsky, D., 393
Binford, Lewis R., 160, 190, 191
Binford, S. R., 160
Bingham, Hiram, 69
Bjuremalm, H., 451
Black, M. T., 68
Blackwood, E., 355
Blanton, R. E., 223
Blum, H. F., 99
Blumenstyk, Goldie, 457
Boas, Franz, 7, 34, 97, 240, 242, 242f,
    244, 250, 250t, 251
Boaz, Noel T., 152
Bocquet-Appel, J.-P., 191, 193, 200
Bodley, John H., 441, 449, 453, 463,
    470, 474
Boellstorff, Tom, 237
Boesch, C., 26, 115
Bogaard, A., 194
Bogin, B., 85, 105
Bohannan, Paul, 420
Bolinger, Dwight, 259f
Bono, 50
Bonvillain, N., 254, 342
Borofsky, R., 54
Bouckaert, R., 269
Boule, Marcellin, 160
Bourdieu, Pierre, 249, 250t, 267, 329,
    331, 333
Bourque, Susan C., 342
Bowen, J. R., 399
Bower, B., 124
Bowie, F., 399
Bowler, J. M., 178
Boyle, Susan, 471
Brace, C. L., 100, 101
Bradley, B. J., 115
Braidwood, Robert J., 190, 205
Bramanti, B., 105
Braque, Georges, 424
Braudel, F., 441
Bremen, J. V., 449
Brenneis, D., 266
Brenton, B. P., 50
Brettell, C. B., 342
Briggs, C. L., 51, 52
Brooke, J., 474
Brookings Institution, 289
Brooks, Alison S., 170, 171
Broom, Robert, 142f
Brower, B., 474

Lewontin, R. C., 79
Li, Nai, 394, 394t, 395
Lie, J., 282, 290
Lightfoot, John, 76
Limbaugh, Rush, 280
Lin, A. A., 178
Lindenbaum, S., 348
Lindholm, Charles, 44
Linnaeus, Carolus, 76, 91
Linton, R., 34, 470
Little, P. D., 34
Livingstone, F. B., 89, 469
Lockwood, W. G., 362
Lockwood, Yvonne R., 422, 423
Lofink, H., 49
Lohan, Lindsay, 436
Lomayestewa, Lee Wayne, 260f
Longfellow, Henry Wadsworth, 307
Loomis, W. F., 99
López, Ana Aurelia, 454, 455
Lopez, M. H., 277, 277t
Lordkipanidze, D., 155
Loveday, L., 264
Lovejoy, C. O., 138
Lovejoy, O., 144
Lowie, R. H., 383
Lowrey, A., 447
Lucas, George, 426
Lucentini, Jack, 443
Lugo, A., 36, 237, 251, 343
Lukas, D., 115, 145
Lupton, D., 49, 50
Lyell, Charles, 77
Lyotard, Jean-François, 250t

**M**

Macdonald, T., 474
Madeleine, Princess of Sweden, 98f
Madra, Y. M., 310
Maida, C. A., 40
Makhubele, Jane, 50
Malinowski, Bronislaw, 12, 41, 231, 237,
    240, 241, 243, 243f, 246, 247, 250,
    250t, 251, 335, 398, 401, 402
Malkki, L. H., 451
Mann, C. C., 441
Manoff, R. K., 430
Manthi, F. K., 143, 150
Manzi, G., 155, 157
Maquet, Jacques, 41, 418, 419
Marcus, George E., 5, 11, 250t, 428, 471
Marcus, Joyce, 197, 222, 223, 224
Marean, C. W., 171, 174
Margolis, Maxine L., 349
Mars, Bruno, 417
Marshack, A., 176
Martel, J., 447t
Martin, C. E., 355
Martin, D. L., 59
Martin, David, 412
Martin, K., 347
Martin, Robert, 111t
Martin, S. M., 335
Martínez, J. H., 277, 277t
Martinez-Alier, J., 463
Marx, Karl, 246, 306, 445, 445f, 446,
    448, 449f, 456, 459

Mascia-Lees, F., 342
Matisse, Henri, 424
Matsui, A., 188
Matsuzawa, T., 115, 118, 119
Maugh, T. H., III, 272
Maurer, B., 343
Maybury-Lewis, B., 474
Maybury-Lewis, D., 35, 474
Mayell, Hillary, 26, 103, 172
Mayr, E., 84
Mazzeo, J., 50
Mba, N. E., 335
McAllester, D. P., 425
McBrearty, Sally, 170, 172
McCain, John, 289
McCarty, Micah L., 32
McConnell-Ginet, S., 262, 264
McDonald, Gregory, 357
McDougall, I., 134, 143, 150, 167
McElroy, A., 51
McGee, R. J., 240, 399
McGranahan, C., 449
McGrew, W., 120
McKenna, J., 49
McNeill, J. R., 463
Mead, Margaret, 4, 12, 41, 230, 240, 244,
    245, 245f, 250t, 251, 319f, 333, 342
Meadow, R. H., 220
Meconis, D., 68
Meigs, Anna, 382
Mein, P., 132
Mendel, Gregor, 78, 80–82, 80f–82f, 84,
    90, 91
Mendoza-Denton, N., 266, 267
Menzies, C. R., 302, 467
Mercader, J., 26
Merkel, Angela, 352, 352f
Merriam-Webster, 418
Metcalf, Crysta, 52f
Meyer, B., 412
Meyer, Matthias, 67
Meyers, J. E., 399
Michelangelo, 418, 418f, 428
Middleton, Catherine, 8
Mielke, J. H., 105
Millaire, J. F., 209
Miller, Barbara D., 348
Miller, J., 313
Miller, L., 66
Miller, N. F., 192
Milton, John, 428
Mintz, Sidney W., 249, 250t, 442
Mitani, John C., 26, 116
Mohler, R. Albert, Jr., 410
Monet, Claude, 421
Monroe, Marilyn, 419
Montague, Susan, 433
Montezuma II, 442f
Montgomery, H., 12
Mooney, A., 262, 266
Moore, J. D., 230, 240
Morais, Robert, 433
Moran, L., 79
Moreno, J. E., 198
Morgan, L. M., 52
Morgan, Lewis Henry, 240, 241, 241f,
    242, 245, 250, 250t, 384

Morin, Monte, 141
Morkot, R., 220
Moro, P. A., 399
Morwood, Michael, 162
Moses, Y. T., 94
Mosse, D., 43
Motseta, S., 298
Mounier, A., 155, 157
Mount Holyoke College, 424
Moyà -Solà , S., 124
Mukhopadhyay, C. C., 94
Mullaney, T., 281
Munns, Bill, 124f
Munoz, R., 12
Murchison, J. M., 234
Murdock, G. P., 343, 344t
Murphy, C., 9
Murphy, L. D., 240
Murray, S. O., 356, 387
Mydans, S., 48, 279
Myers, F. R., 428
Mysorekar, Uma V., 411

**N**

Nakasone, Yasuhiro, 282
Namingha, Rebecca, 391f
Nanda, S., 354, 355
Narayan, Kirin, 388
Nardi, Bonnie, 237
National Academies, 464f
National Academy of Sciences, 465, 466
National Research Council, 465
*National Vital Statistics Reports,* 392t
Neely, J. A., 190
Nevid, J. S., 358
Newman, M., 290
*New York Times,* 79
Ngeneo, Bernard, 149
Ni, X., 122
Nishida, T., 115, 119, 120
Njoy, Sultan of Cameroon, 215f
Nolan, R. W., 43
Nordstrom, C., 330
Nugent, D., 318
Nunn, N., 105
Nuttall, M., 466
Nystrom, P., 112

**O**

Obama, Barack, 13, 14, 15f, 50, 279–280,
    281, 289, 352, 436
Obama, Barack, Sr., 14, 15f
Ochs, Elinor, 368
O'Connell, J., 298
O'Connell, J. F., 177, 177f, 178
Oefner, P., 178
Ofili, Chris, 424
Olley, J. M., 178
Olsen, J., 124
Olszewski, D. I., 191
Omohundro, J. T., 54
O'Neill, K. L., 291
Ong, Aihwa, 306, 307, 308, 343
Ontario Consultants on Religious
    Tolerance, 409
Oosterhuis, H., 12
Opie, C., 123, 145

# SUBJECT INDEX

Page numbers followed by f indicate material in figures and illustrations and their captions; page numbers followed by t indicate material in tables and Recap boxes. Names of persons discussed as subjects may be found in this index. Names of all persons, as well as organizations cited as references, may be found in the Name Index.

## A

AAA. *See* American Anthropological Association
AAVE (African American Vernacular English), 268f, 268–269, 269f
Aba Women's Riots of 1929, 335–336, 336f
ABO blood group, 102–104, 104f
aboriginals. *See* Native Australians
absolute dating methods
    dendrochronology, 65–66, 66t, 66f, 72
    radiometric techniques, 61, 64–65, 65f, 66t, 72
Abu Hureyra site, 191
academic (general) anthropology, 6f, 6–7, 19, 42
accommodation, 286–288
acculturation, 34, 470
Aché people, 297–298, 383
Acheulean tools, 150, 151, 153, 153f, 163
achieved statuses, 276, 277f
    ambilineal descent as, 371
    "big man" as, 323–324
action theory, 248–249
acute hypoxia, 102
adaptation, 3t, 3–5
    biological (*See* biological adaptation)
    cultural (*See* cultural adaptation)
    in foraging economy, 144
    to high altitudes, 3t, 3–4, 102–103, 103f
    music as, 422
    of religion to local culture, 412
    through learning, 129–130
adaptive advantage, 78
adaptive strategies, 300f, 300–304
    agriculture as, 300–301
    economic, 297
    foraging as (*See* foraging)
    of *Homo erectus,* 153f, 153–154
    horticulture as, 300, 300f, 302
    industrialism as, 315
    pastoralism as, 302–304, 303f, 304t
adaptive traits, 85
adaptivity of culture, 25
advertising, 36, 36f
Aegean dendrochronology project, 66
aerial photos, 60, 60f
aerosols, 466t
aesthetics, 417
affinials, 374, 374f, 387
Afghanistan, 44–45, 45f
*Afghanistan: A Cultural and Political History* (Barfield), 45
Afghan Koochi (Kuchi), 303f
Africa. *See also specific countries, peoples, and archaeological sites*
    artworks of, 420

contemporary foraging in, 297
ethnic structure of countries in, 286
expansion of AMHs from, 168–169
French colonization of, 451, 451f
Great Rift Valley, 65, 65f
HIV/AIDS pandemic in, 50, 50f
Neolithic farming in, 193–194
origin of AMHs in, 155, 166–168, 167f, 168f
state formation in, 220f, 220–221, 327
African Americans, 5, 290–291
African American Vernacular English (AAVE), 268f, 268–269, 269f
"African cattle complex," 194
*After the Fact: Two Countries, Four Decades, One Anthropologist* (Geertz), 248f
age, 300
age grades, 325, 325f
agency, 29, 248
agency theory, 248
Age of Discovery, 175
age sets, 325, 325f
agnates, 381, 389
agricultural economies, 209
agriculturalism, 310
Agricultural Revolution, 189
agriculture, 304t, 315
    agricultural traditions, 454f, 454–455
    costs and benefits of, 301
    in cultivation continuum, 302
    domesticated animals, 300–301, 301f
    effects on environment, 302
    irrigation used in, 301, 301f
    monocrop production, 442–443
    polyculture, 454
    terracing, 301, 301f
Agta people, 346
*ahimsa* doctrine, 404f, 404–405, 415
Ainu people, 282
Akkadian language, 218, 218f
Alaska
    climate change refugees in, 464–465, 465f
    potlatching in, 313, 313f, 314f
Alawite Muslims, 290
Algeria, 451, 451f
alienation, 232, 305–308, 306f
Ali Kosh, 190
Al Jazeera network, 472
alleles, 81, 81f
Allen's rule, 101, 101f
Allia Bay site, 134
allocation of resources. *See* resource(s)
alluvial desert, 190
Alps, 303f, 304
alternative religious movements, 409

altitude, adaptation to, 3t, 3–4, 102–103, 103f
Amazon.com, 307f, 448
Ambalavao, 440
ambilineal descent, 370–371
ambilineal societies, 375, 375f, 376t
American Anthropological Association (AAA), 42, 473–474
    Code of Ethics, 71–72, 239, 240, 252
    disapproval of HTS program, 240
    on plight of Yanomami, 323
    RACE Project of, 97
    statement on race, 278–279, 279f
    subgroups of, 251
American football, 433
*American Kinship: A Cultural Account* (Schneider), 247
American Psychiatric Association, 12
American Revolution, 450, 459
American Sign Language (ASL), 255–256
Americas
    British colonialism in, 449–450, 450f
    farming in, 196–199, 197f, 198f, 205
    Mexican highland farming, 198–199, 199f
    settlement of, 441, 459
    spread of humans to, 178–180, 179f, 180f, 184
    tropical origins of farming in, 197–198
AMHs. *See* anatomically modern humans
analogies, 111
analytic scale, 236–237
Anasazi site, 10f
Anatolia, origin of PIE in, 270
anatomically modern humans (AMHs), 137t, 151, 166–170, 184. *See also* humans
    advent of behavioral modernity in, 170–173, 171f, 173f
    African origin of, 166–168, 167f, 168f, 184
    chimpanzees compared, 137, 138f
    dentition, 136f
    distribution of fossils, 131t
    glacial retreat and, 174–175, 184
    Neandertals as contemporaries of, 168–169, 184
    Neandertals compared, 160f, 160–161, 169f
    origin in Africa, 155, 166–168, 167f, 168f
    Red Deer Cave people, 169–170
    spread out of Africa, 168–169
    technological advances by, 173–174, 174f
anatomic specialization, 114, 114f
anatomy, human, 58
*Ancient Society* (Morgan), 241

Ashanti society, 382
"Ash Boy," 248
Asia. *See also specific countries*
  ethnic structure of countries in, 286
  Neolithic farming in, 194–196, 195f, 196t
  primate evolution in, 122
ASL (American Sign Language), 255–256
*Assault on Paradise* (Kottak), 364
assimilation, 293t, 294
  discouraged in Japan, 283
  of ethnic groups, 286–287
  expectations of, 290–291
  forced, 291
  in Latin America, 474–475
associations, 14, 15
audience, art and, 424
Australia, 177f, 177–178, 178f, 184, 450
australopithecines, 130, 134–142, 137t, 156
  brain size of, 138–139, 142
  chewing muscles of, 140, 141f, 142
  chronology of, 134, 145–146
  dentition, 140, 142, 143f
  early *Homo* and, 142–143, 143f
  gracile and robust, 137t, 139–140, 141f, 142, 143f, 146
  hyperrobust, 139, 142
  sociality of, 139–140
  summary of data on, 137t
*Australopithecus aethiopicus,* 142
*Australopithecus afarensis* ("Lucy"), 129, 133, 134, 135–139, 136f–139f, 137t, 143f, 146
  as ancestor of *Homo habilis,* 142–143
  brain size, 142
  dentition, 136, 136f, 140
*Australopithecus africanus,* 134, 137t, 143
  skull of, 142, 142f, 143f
  sociality of, 134, 137t, 143
*Australopithecus anamensis,* 134–135, 135f, 137t
*Australopithecus boisei,* 134, 137t, 139, 143, 148
  chewing muscles of, 140, 141f
  extinction of, 144, 146
  palate of, 143f
  skull of, 142, 142f, 150f
*Australopithecus garhi,* 134, 144, 146
*Australopithecus robustus,* 134, 137t, 139, 143, 143f
  brain size of, 142
  chewing muscles of, 140, 141f, 142
*Australopithecus sediba,* 60, 134, 137t, 139, 140–141f
Austronesian languages, 183
authoritarian systems, 456
authority, political, 318, 338
autochthony, 475
*Avatar* (film), 462
avatars (alts), 237
axes of plant stalks, 192, 192f
Azande people, 355–356

Aztec civilization
  Aztec state, 225, 227
  everyday life among, 199f
  smallpox epidemics among, 105

## B

baboons, 114–115, 172
baby boomers, 289, 289f
Baganda people, 105
Baidu (search engine), 331
Bai people, 95f
balanced polymorphism, 86–87
balanced reciprocity, 311–312
bands, 319
  divorce in, 391
  economy and regulation in, 329t
  foragers, 299, 320–322
  movement between, 383
Bangladesh, Nipah virus in, 470
Bantu language, 220
bargaining, 310
Barí people, 372
bartering, 312f
baseball, 8, 398, 399f, 402, 414
base substitution mutation, 84
Basques, 291
Basseri people, 303, 325–326, 326f
Ba Thonga people, 243, 388, 389
"bathroom" habits, 24
bats, 469, 470f
*Bazaar Politics* (Coburn), 44
*Beagle* (ship), 77
beauty contests, male, 342f
beauty standards, 6–7, 7f
behavioral ecology, 120–121, 126
behavioral modernity
  advent of, 170–173, 171f, 173f, 184
  evidence of, 167
  increased lifespan and, 172
bejel (nonvenereal syphilis), 86
Benedict, Ruth, 244, 245f
Benin, 220f, 221
*berdache,* 354, 387
Bergmann's rule, 101, 101f
Beringia, 178, 179, 179f, 180f
Betsileo people, 28, 28f. *See also*
  Madagascar
  beliefs of, 413
  clans and lineages of, 370
  concept of scarcity, 308–309, 309f
  key cultural consultants of, 234
  kinships among, 361
  polygyny among, 393
  rice cultivation among, 304–305, 305f
Bhagavad Gita, 411
BHP Billiton, 456–457, 457f
bifurcate collateral kinship terminology, 375–376, 376t, 376f
bifurcate merging kinship terminology, 374f, 374–375, 376t
Bigfoot (Sasquatch), 124
"Big Man," 318, 322, 323f, 323–324, 324f, 338
big man systems, 408–409
bilateral kinship calculation, 373
bilharzia (liver flukes), 49–50, 51f

bilingual education, 47–48
*Bill and Ted's Excellent Adventure* (film), 267f
Billiton, 457
bilocality, 383
bioarchaeology, 59
biochemical genetics, 78, 82f, 82–84, 91
  cell division, 83, 83f
  crossing over, 83f, 83–84
  mutation, 84
biocultural perspective, 6–7, 7f, 70–71, 71f
biodiversity, 468
biological adaptation, 25, 97–106
  facial features, 100–101
  genes and disease, 101–106, 104f
  to high altitude, 3t, 4, 102–103, 103f
  lactose tolerance, 105–106
  size and body build, 101, 101f
  skin color as, 98f, 98–100, 99t, 100f
  tooth size, 100–101, 143f
biological anthropology, 6, 9–10, 10f, 19, 40, 242
  anthropometry, 68, 69f, 72–73
  bone biology, 68, 68f, 72
  primatology, 9, 10, 68–69, 69f
  research methods in, 59–63
biological diversity
  gender differences, 341–343, 342f, 343f
  human, 78, 79
biological plasticity, 9, 75, 85, 242, 257
biological taxonomy, 76, 91
biological universals, 27
biomedicine, 51, 52
bipedalism, 112
  *Au. sediba,* 140–141
  birthing process and, 58
  evidence of, 136
  in hominins, 129, 129f
  by nonhuman primates, 26f
  pelvis adapted to, 129, 138f
  significance of, 128
birthing process, 58
bisexuality, 355
bison, 324–325, 325f
"black skull," 142
blade tools, 174, 174f
Blombos Cave site, 166, 167
  engravings from, 421
  paint making, 170–171, 171f, 421
  tools, 174
blood feud, 322
blood types (groups), 82, 82f, 102–104, 104f
Boas, Franz, 242, 242f, 252
body build, 101, 101f
body image, 6–7, 7f
body mass, 68, 69f, 72–73
body ornamentation, 166, 171f, 173
body size
  adaptation of, 101, 101f
  of *H. floresiensis,* 162, 162f
  meat in diet and, 145
Bolshevik Revolution of 1917, 456
bone biology, 68, 68f, 72
*Bones* (TV series), 41f, 59, 68

bonobo *(Pan paniscus),* 116, 119, 120, 120f, 357
Border Cave site, 167
border theory, 251
"born-again Christians," 413
Bosnia, 362, 422–423, 474
Botswana, 285, 298–299, 299f
bourgeoisie, 445
brachiation, 115f, 115–117, 117f, 126, 128
brain complexity, 112, 170
brain size
    of australopithecines, 138–139, 142
    of *H. rudolfensis,* 149
    of hominins, 129
    of Neandertals, 148
Brazil. *See also* Arembepe
    assimilation in, 287
    Carnaval, 333, 357, 472
    development policies in, 47
    Evangelical Protestantism in, 410–411, 411f
    "Facebook Revolution" in, 336–338, 337f
    family planning in, 430–431
    fluid conception of race in, 283–285, 284f, 285f, 294
    folk ceremonies in, 471
    food and meal customs, 53
    importance of ascribed statuses, 434–435
    meaning of family in, 367
    nonverbal communication in, 257
    online dating in, 394
    Pentecostalism in, 410–411, 412
    sexual orientation in, 356–357, 357f
    sports in, 433–435, 435f, 438
    study of media in, 17f, 17–18
    telenovelas, 417, 429, 430, 472
    use of social media in, 431
    women's sports in, 6–7, 7f
"Brésiliennes," 355
bristlecone pine chronology, 66
British empire, 449–450, 450f, 459–460
broad-spectrum revolution, 175, 184, 187, 188, 205
Broken Hill Proprietary Company, 457
bronze, 218
Bronze Age, 189, 218, 227
Brooklyn Museum, 424
bubonic plague, 104
built environment, 212, 212f
Bumba Meu Boi festival, 471
Buraku Liberation and Human Rights Research Institute, 283
*burakumin,* 282, 283, 283f
bureaucracies, 224
burials
    cemeteries, 60, 216
    commemorative poles, 419
    cremation, 28, 178
    grave goods, 216, 216f
    ocher burials, 178
burins, 174
Burundi, 451

business
    applied anthropology in, 42, 52f, 52–54
    careers in, anthropology and, 54–55
    culturally appropriate marketing, 53
butchering, 144, 145, 174

## C

*cabôclos,* 284
"calendar circle," 194
call systems, 255, 255f, 256t, 272
Canada
    census categories in, 282, 282f
    same-sex marriage in, 386, 386f
    urban anthropology in, 48
cancer, 68
El Candelabro, 60f
*Candide* (Voltaire), 244
*candomblé,* 233, 409, 412
cannibalism, 161
capital, 441, 443
capitalism
    cargo cults and, 409
    global spread of, 36
    potlatching and, 314, 315
    Protestantism and, 406–407
capitalist mode of production, 304
capitalist world economy, 441, 459
Capoid race, 96
Caprine farming, 189
carbon-14 ($^{14}C$) dating technique, 64–65, 66t, 72
carbon dioxide, 466t
cargo cults, 407f, 407–409, 408f
Caribbean, 285, 450
Carnaval, 333, 357, 472
Carnivora, 111
carrying capacity of land, 191
cash, addiction to, 309
cash economies, 462
cassava (manioc), 59f, 197, 197f, 205, 302
caste systems, 362–363, 385, 385f
Çatalhöyük, 66, 214
catarrhines (Old World monkeys), 111t, 114f, 114–115, 126
catastrophism, 76f, 76–77
catharsis, 424
cattle
    "African cattle complex," 194
    methane produced by, 465f
    sacred, 404f, 404–405
    theft of, 309, 312
    use in agriculture, 301
Cauca people (Colombia), 215–216
cave art, 184, 421
    Chauvet Cave, 165f, 170
    Lascaux Cave, 175–177, 176f
*CCR5-Δ32* allele, 104–105
CDC (Centers for Disease Control and Prevention), 470f
Ceboidea, 110, 111t
celebrity scandals, 435–437, 436f, 438
CELF (Center on Everyday Lives of Families), 368
cell division, 83, 83f
cemeteries, 60
    Mesoamerican, 216

Cenozoic era, 121, 121f, 122–123, 123f, 126
censorship, 331
census(es)
    racial classifications, 281f, 281–282, 282f
    used in longitudinal research, 235
Center on Everyday Lives of Families (CELF), 368
Centers for Disease Control and Prevention (CDC), 470f
"Central Kalahari Game Reserve," 299
Ceprano site, 155, 157
Cercopithecoidea, 110, 111t, 115
ceremonial centers, 194
ceremonial fund, 310, 315
ceremonies of increase, 176
chain shifts, 267
Channel Islands, 200
Chauvet Cave, 165f, 170
Chegança danceplay, 471
Cherokee tribe, 311
chewing muscles, 140, 141f, 142, 151
Chicanos, 266
chief(s)
    as ascribed status, 328, 328f
    "Big Men," 318, 322, 323f, 323–324, 324f
    duties of, in Polynesia, 327–328
chiefdoms, 208–209, 319–320, 327–329, 338
    advanced, 217
    economy and regulation in, 329t
    emergence of stratification in, 328–329, 329t
    of Mesoamerica, 215, 216, 216f, 221f, 221–223
    monument building in, 327f
    political and economic systems, 327f, 327–328
    potlatching tribes, 313f, 313–315, 314f
    redistributive systems in, 311, 327–328
    social ranking in, 215f, 215–217, 216t, 216f
    status systems, 328, 328f
    stratification in, 328–329, 329t
chiefly redistribution, 328
child care, 344–345, 345t, 363
childhood dependency, 129, 139
child rearing, 172
chimpanzees *(Pan troglodytes),* 26f, 58, 109, 116, 119f, 119–120, 126, 137t
    brain size of, 142
    call systems of, 255, 255f
    compared with AMHs, 137, 138f
    dentition, 136f
    DNA in common with humans, 68
    hunting and tool use, 26
    learning studies with, 255, 256, 257
    linguistic capacities of, 256–257, 272
    sexual behavior of, 357
    social patterns among, 383
    tool use by, 26, 27f, 37
China
    censorship in, 331
    development of farming in, 195, 195f
    origin of pottery in, 188
    primary states in, 209, 227
    Shang dynasty, 219f, 220, 227

cholera, 49, 52
chopper, 144
Christianity, 406, 407, 407f
chromosomal differences, 341–342
chromosomal rearrangement, 84
chromosomes, 81, 81f
"Cinderella," analysis of, 248
circumcision, 31, 50
circumscription, 209–210, 210f
cities
    fortified, 219
    key attributes of, 210–211, 211f
    rise of, 175
    urban life, 213f, 213–214
citizenship, 330
*Civilization and Capitalism, 15th–18th Century* (Braudel), 441
clans, 370
class consciousness, 446
classical archaeology, 63
classification, 248. *See also* racial classification
climate change, 460f, 463t, 463–466, 464f, 466t, 476
    origin of food production and, 190t, 190–191
    refugees from, 464–465, 465f
    threats to archaeological sites from, 200–201, 201f
climatic variation
    food production and, 202f, 202–203
    ice ages, 156–157, 175, 184
    tree rings and, 66
clines, 94
clitoridectomy, 30, 348
Clixoy Dam, 43
Clovis tradition, 179f, 179–180
*Clueless* (film), 267f
clutter, in U.S. homes, 368, 368f
coastal areas, 200
Coca-Cola Company, 36, 36f, 40
*cocoteros,* 364f
Code of Ethics (AAA), 71–72, 239, 240, 252
codominance, 82
cognates, 270
cold adaptation
    body size and build, 101, 101f
    by Neandertals, 159f, 159–160, 160f, 163
collage, 424
collateral household, 364
collateral relatives, 374, 374f
collective phenomena, 247
college education, 54–55
colonial applied anthropology, 41
colonial archaeology, 63
colonialism, 440, 449–452, 459
    anticolonial movement, 245
    British empire, 449–450, 450f
    ethnic conflict and, 291
    ethnic identity and, 451, 452f
    French colonialism, 450–451, 451f
    health of indigenous peoples and, 49
    Igbo Women's War and, 335–336, 336f
    postcolonial studies, 452, 453f
colonial languages, 272

color terminology, 261
Columbia-Cornell-Harvard-Illinois Summer Field Studies Program in Anthropology, 235
Columbian exchange, 105, 441
*Coming of Age in Samoa* (Mead), 244
commemoration, art as, 419, 424
commercialization of art, 423
"common-law" partnerships, 380
communication
    among nonhuman primates, 255–257
    art as, 423–424
    call systems, 255, 255f, 256t, 272
    gender differences in, 257f, 257–258
    nonverbal, 257f, 257–258
    sign language, 255–257, 256f
    skill in, politics and, 318
    texting and online messaging, 258
Communism (political movement), 453, 455–457, 458f, 460
communism (social system), 455, 460
Communist Party, 456
communitas, 399, 402f, 403, 404
Compañía Nacional de Subsistencias Populares (CONASUPO) stores, 454, 455
comparative method, 242
competition, 173
competitive interaction, 222
complex societies
    settlement hierarchy in, 61–62
    social identity in, 276
    survey research in, 237, 238
CONASUPO (Compañía Nacional de Subsistencias Populares) stores, 454, 455
configurationalism, 244, 245f, 250t
conflict resolution, 321–322
conquest, 224
*conscience collectif,* 247
conscription, 330
conservation schemes, 467–468, 468f
*Contagion* (film), 105, 469
contagious magic, 401
contemporary functionalism, 244, 244f
contemporary life, study of, 9
continental shelf, 175
continental slope, 175
contraception, 430–431
contract archaeology, 63
Convention 169 (ILO), 474
convergent evolution, 111
conversation, 231–233, 237
cooking, 188–189
cooperation, 58
    among hunter-gatherers, 26–27
    emergence of, 383
    in hunting, 153–154, 369
cooperatives, 46, 46f
Copán, 226, 226f, 227
copper, annealing of, 218
coprolites, 179, 180
core nations, 441, 448–449, 458, 458f
core values of culture, 25
corn. *See* maize
correlations, 18, 299
cosmology, 404

*Cosmopolitan* magazine, 104f
cotton, 442–443
cousin marriage, 386
cousin terminology, 373, 380–381, 381f
covariations, 14, 299
Covenant on Civil and Political Rights, 31
Covenant on Economic, Social and Cultural Rights, 31
craft specialization, 305
craftspeople, 211
cranial capacity
    AMH v. Neandertal, 160, 160f
    of australopithecines, 138–139
    *H. erectus,* 150, 151, 153
    of hominins, 129
creationism, 76, 90
*The Creation of Adam* (Michelangelo), 418f
"creative explosion" theory, 170
creativity, "dawn" of, 170, 173
cremation, 28, 178
*crentes* ("true believers"), 410–411
"creole corn," 454
creole languages, 259, 268
Cricket World Cup, 8
crisis of representation, 250t
CRM (cultural resource management), 13, 42f, 42–43, 62, 63
Cro Magnons, 167, 168f
cross cousins, 380, 381f
cross-cultural expertise, 53–54
cross-cultural perspectives, 2, 3, 6
    of economic systems, 309
    of nonverbal communication, 257
    psychological anthropology, 12
    urban anthropology, 48
cross-cultural studies, 15–16, 16f, 355–356, 399
crossdating, 66
crossing over, 83f, 83–84
Cuba, 331, 364f
*Cucurbita,* 197
cult houses, art in, 420
cultivation continuum, 302, 315
cultivation of plants, 5
    manioc (cassava), 302
    millet, 195, 195f, 196
    rice, 300f, 301, 304–305, 305f
    shifting cultivation, 300, 300f, 302, 315
cults, 403
cultural adaptation, 5, 25, 37
    to environmental stresses, 76
    to high altitude, 3t, 4
    in India, sacred cattle essential to, 405
cultural advance, 245–246
cultural anthropology, 6, 7–8, 18, 19, 229–252, 242
    ethical issues in, 238–240
    ethnography used in, 230
    functionalism and, 243
    longitudinal research in, 231, 235f, 235–236, 236f, 251
    problem orientation in, 231, 234–235
    sociology and, 11, 18
    survey research in, 237–238, 238f, 239t, 251
    team research in, 231, 235–236
    theory, evolution of, 240–249

ethnic identity
    colonialism and, 451, 452f
    of indigenous peoples, 474–475, 475f
    multiculturalism and, 288
ethnic interaction, 293t
ethnicity, 276–278. *See also* race
    demographics of, 289, 289f
    ethnic conflict, 290–293
    in professional golf, 436
    race compared, 278–280, 280f
    racial/ethnic identification in U.S.,
        275, 276t
    in sports, 8
    status shifting, 276–277, 277t, 277f
    stratification and, 277–278
    tolerance and accommodation, 286–288
    types of ethnic interaction, 293t
ethnocentrism, 21, 37, 455
    culture and, 30–31, 37
    human rights and, 30–31, 34, 34f
ethnocide, 291, 293t, 294, 470–471
ethnoecology, 467, 476
ethnographic techniques, 231–236, 251
    conversation and interviewing,
        231–233, 237
    cultural consultants, 234, 234f
    genealogical method, 231, 233–234, 234f
    life histories, 231, 234, 251
    longitudinal research, 235f,
        235–236, 236f
    observation and participant
        observation, 11, 231, 237
    problem orientation, 234–235
    team research, 235–236
ethnography, 7–8, 9t, 11
    analytic scale, expansion of, 236–237
    in business, 52–53
    in cultural anthropology, 230
    emic and etic perspectives, 236, 251
    ethnographic method, 41
    online, 237, 237f, 251
    as research strategy, 230
    specialization in, 250–251, 252
    survey research contrasted, 238, 239t
    urban anthropology, 48
ethnology, 8, 9t, 13, 19, 343–346, 344t,
        345t, 345f
ethnomedicine, 31, 34f
ethnomusicology, 11, 422f, 422–423, 423f
ethnosemantic domains, 261
ethnosemantics, 261
etic perspective, 236, 251
Etoro people, 355, 356–357
EU (European Union), 35, 36
*Eulemur macao,* 123f
*eunoto* ceremony, 325f
eunuchs, 354
Europe
    "Age of Discovery," 449
    dendrochronology in, 66
    Neolithic farming in, 194
European Central Bank, 36
*Europe and the People without History*
        (Wolf), 249
European Union (EU), 35, 36
Evangelical Protestantism, 407, 409–412,
        411f, 415

"Eve," mtDNA from, 168
evolution, 9, 76f, 76–78
    as basis for culture, 25–27, 37
    chronology of, 130, 131t, 145–146
    convergent, 111
    dependence on mutation, 84
    fossil record of, 121
    importance of grandparents, 172
    "intelligent design" and, 77–78, 78f
    "modern synthesis" of, 89–90, 91
    multilinear, 245
    overall dental reduction and, 130
    punctuated equilibrium model of,
        90, 91
    theory and fact in, 77–78, 78f
evolutionary theory, 75–79, 78f, 240, 252
    intelligent design contrasted, 79
    uniformitarianism and, 77
    unilinear evolutionism, 241, 241f,
        243, 250t
evolutionary trees. *See* phylogenetic trees
evolutionism
    neoevolutionism, 245f, 245–246, 250t
    unilinear, 241, 241f, 243, 250t
*The Evolution of Culture* (White), 245
excavation, 62f, 62–63, 72
exchange, 310–313, 315
    coexistence of principles in, 312–313
    market principle, 310, 312
    reciprocity, 311f, 311–312, 312f
    redistribution, 310–311, 312
exogamy, 27
    in foraging bands, 299
    incest and, 380–381, 381f, 382f
    incest avoidance and, 384, 384f
    rules of, 393
expanded family households, 363
experimental archaeology, 63
explanations, 14
expressive culture, 166, 417, 418
extended families
    households, 363–364, 364f
    nuclear families compared,
        362f, 362–363, 363f
    as social unit, 46
extramarital sex, 345t, 345–346
*ex votos,* 405

# F

*fa'afafine,* 355
Facebook, 262, 431–432, 432f
"Facebook Revolution," 336–338, 337f
facial features, adaptation of, 100–101
factors of production, 305
fairy tales, visual, analysis of, 426–427, 427t
*fakaleitis,* 355
fallowing, 300, 302
family(ies), 361–369. *See also* marriage
    among foragers, 367, 369, 369f
    attitudes toward, 24, 24f
    changing, in North America, 364,
        365t–367t, 366f, 366–367, 367f
    daily life of, in U.S., 368, 368f
    declining size of, 366–367, 367t
    descent and, 371, 371f
    effects of industrialism on, 363–364, 364f
    extended (*See* extended families)

government intervention in, 330
    nuclear (*See* nuclear families)
    single-parent households, 351, 351t, 366
    size of, television and, 430
    as social security system, 364–365
family of orientation, 362, 379
family of procreation, 362, 371, 379
family planning, 430–431
Fanga'uta Lagoon site, 180–181, 183
farming, 186–205
    in Americas, 196–199, 197f, 198f
    costs and benefits of, 203–204, 204t
    domestication of plants and animals,
        191–193, 192f
    growth of state and, 193, 193f, 199f
    Mesolithic, 188f, 188–189
    in Middle East, 189–193, 190t, 190f
    Neolithic, 189, 189f, 193–196, 196t
    Neolithic economies and, 199–203
    Old World food producers, 193–196
    spread of infectious diseases and,
        101–102, 204
    state formation and, 225
farming economies, 212
father-daughter incest, 382–383
feet, 26f, 163
female genital mutilation (FGM), 30–31
female-headed households, 351, 351t, 359
female infanticide, 348
female-run police stations, 348
*The Feminine Mystique* (Friedan), 349
feminist anthropology, 250t
feminist theory, 342
feminization of poverty, 350t, 350–351,
        351t, 359
Fertile Crescent, 199–200
FGM (female genital mutilation), 30–31
field notes, 231
field techniques. *See* ethnographic
        techniques
FIFA World Cup, 8, 29, 414, 430, 433
films, comparison of, 426–427, 427t
financial globalization, 36
finches, 74f
*Fingerprints of the Gods* (Hancock), 222
fire, use by *H. erectus,* 153–154
fiscal support mechanisms, 330–331
fishing, 188, 304
fitness industry, 410–411, 411f
fixation, 89
Flores, 162, 162f
flotation technique, 63
fluorine absorption analysis, 64
focal vocabulary, 260–261, 261t, 261f
folate deficiency, 99t, 100
folk arts, 422
folklore, 11
folksong, 422–423
food preservation, 188
food production, 296–297
    adaptive strategies in, 300f, 300–304
    agriculture, 300–301
    animal domestication, 5, 191–193,
        192f, 205
    complex economies and, 320
    costs and benefits of, 203–204, 204t, 206
    cultivation (*See* cultivation of plants)

glaciation
  Ice Age, 156–157, 175, 184
  Mindel and Riss glacial periods, 158
  Würm glacial period, 157, 159, 168, 174
global economy, 307, 307f
Global Gender Gap Index, 352, 352f
globalization, 34–36, 35f, 37, 461–476
  climate change (*See* climate change)
  Columbian exchange, 105
  cultural generation gap, 289, 289f
  culture and, 34–36, 35f, 37
  effects of industrialization, 463, 463t
  global economy, 307, 307f
  Global Gender Gap Index, 352, 352f
  global-local linkages, 8
  HIV/AIDS pandemic, 50, 50f, 469
  local politics and, 332, 332f
  multiculturalism related to, 287
  prerequisites for, 175
  religion and, 409–413
  spread of disease and, 49–50, 86
  spread of Pentecostalism and, 412
  transnational migration and, 462,
    473–474, 474f
  of Western psychiatric disorders,
    12–13, 13f
  world events, 8
globalization of risk, 463
global warming. *See* climate change
glossolalia, 410
Goddard Institute for Space Studies
    (GISS), 463
golf, scandals in, 435–437, 436f
Gombe Stream National Park, 26, 119
Gona site, 144
Google Inc., 262–263, 263f
gorillas, 108f, 109, 116, 118f, 126
  cranial capacity of, 142
  linguistic capacities of, 256–257, 272
  sociality of, 118–119
gossip, 333–335, 334f, 335f
government(s)
  prohibition of same-sex marriage,
    386–387
  use of anthropology, ethics of,
    239–240, 240f
gracile australopithecines, 137t., 139–140,
    141f, 142, 143f, 146
Gran Dolina site, 57f, 157
grandparents, 172
grasping, 112
grave goods, 216, 216f
great apes. *See* chimpanzees; gorillas
Great Apes Conservation Act of 2000, 116
Great Apes Conservation Fund, 116
Great Britain. *See also* London
  applied anthropology (colonial), 41
  colonialism: British empire,
    449–450, 450f
  industrialization of, 78, 78f
  Industrial Revolution in, 444, 446f
  primogeniture in, 386
  royal family, global interest in, 8
  Stonehenge, 194, 327, 327f
Great Chain of Being theorem, 278
Great Depression of 1930s, 453
"great man theory of history," 246

Great Plague of 1665–1666, 104–105
Great Recession of 2007–2009, 447, 448
Great Rift Valley, 65, 65f
  formation of, 124
  fossil record of, 132, 135
Great Zimbabwe state, 220
Greco-Roman religions, 406
Greece, 194
Greek theater, 428, 429f
greenhouse effect, 464–465, 465f
Greenland, 200
Greenpeace, 33
"Green Revolution" technologies,
    454–455
"greenwashing," 456
grids, 62, 62f
gross domestic product (GDP), 457
group(s)
  cultural and ethnic associations, 474
  cultural rights of, 31
  culture as attribute of, 23
  disease rates and, 49
  totemism among, 404
group alliance, marriage as, 388–391
  gifts at marriage, 388f, 388–390,
    389f, 390f
  sororate and levirate marriage,
    390, 390f, 391
guenon, 114f
*Guernica* (Picasso), 418
guilds, 421
Gullah language, 259
*gumlao,* 249
*gumsa,* 249
*Guns, Germs, and Steel: The Fates of
    Human Societies* (Diamond), 199
Gurupá, 336–337
Guyana, 86
Gwembe District, 235, 235f

**H**
habitat destruction, 116, 118
Hadar site, 135
Haida tribe, 314f
Halafian era, 214, 216, 217, 227
Halafian pottery, 214
Hallmark Cards, 54
halocarbons, 466t
Hamat'sa ("Cannibal Dance"), 242f
hand ax (Acheulean), 153, 153f
hands, 26f, 112, 141
haplogroups, 68, 97, 180
happiness, work and, 351, 351t, 353, 353f
Harappa, 194–195
Harappan civilization, 219f, 219–220
Haredi (Jewish fundamentalists), 413
Harris, Marvin, 246, 246f
Hawaii, 182, 355, 385
health care systems, 51
hearing impairment, 75
hegemony, 249, 331, 333, 338–339
"Heidelberg man," 157
hemoglobin, 87–88, 88f, 91, 102
hemophilia, 75
Hemudu site, 195
herding, 192–193
hereditary inequality, 215

hermaphroditism, 353–354
Herto site, 166–167
heterosexuality, 355
heterozygous traits, 81, 81f, 87, 91
Hidatsa tribe, 343
"hidden transcripts," 333
high-altitude adaptation, 3t, 3–4,
    102–103, 103f
Hijras, 354, 354f
Hill Kharia people, 298
hilly flanks, farming on, 190
Himalayas, 2, 4
Hindu American Foundation, 410, 411
Hinduism, 404f, 404–405, 407, 407f
  *ahimsa* doctrine, 404f, 404–405, 415
  yoga and, 410–411, 411f
Hispanics, 47–48, 279
historical anthropology, 241, 249,
    250t, 252
historical archaeology, 63
historical linguistics, 10–11, 269–272,
    270f, 271f, 272–273
historical particularism, 242f,
    242–243, 250t
HIV (human immunodeficiency virus),
    104–105
HIV/AIDS pandemic, 50, 50f, 469
hoaxes, 64
*The Hobbit* (Tolkien), 237
hockey, focal vocabulary for, 261t
holistic science, 3, 11
Holocaust, 279, 279f, 474
Holocene epoch, 121f, 122
*Holy Virgin Mary* (Ofili), 424
holy water, 22–23
home-handicraft manufacture, 444, 445f
hominids, 128–129, 131t
hominins, 25, 37, 109, 127–146
  *Ardipithecus,* 129, 132f, 132–134,
    133f, 137t
  australopithecines
    (*See* australopithecines)
  bipedalism in, 129, 129f
  brain and cranial size, 129
  characteristics of, 128–130
  childhood dependency, 129
  chronology of evolution, 130, 131t,
    145–146
  dentition, 130
  fossils, 122, 130, 131t
  *Kenyanthropus platyops,* 134, 134f
  Oldowan tools, 143–144, 144f, 146,
    151, 153
  *Orrorin tugenensis,* 129, 132–133
  *Sahelanthropus tchadensis* ("Toumai"),
    129, 130, 131f, 132
  stone toolmaking, 26
  tool use in, 129–130
hominoids, 115, 126
  fossils, 122, 123–124, 131t
  homologies among, 111–112
  Miocene hominoids, 124f,
    124–125, 125f
*Homo,* 110, 146
  archaic (*See* archaic *Homo*)
  cranial capacity of, 142
  palate of, 143f

Pleistocene ice ages and, 156–157
timeline of species in, 156f
*Homo antecessor,* 157f, 157–158, 158f
*Homo erectus,* 142, 143, 146, 148, 156, 156f, 163
adaptive strategies of, 153f, 153–154
evolution and expansion of, 154f, 154–155, 155f, 157
*H. habilis* compared, 149–151
migration from Africa, 151f, 151–155
skulls of, 152, 152f, 153, 169f
toolmaking by, 151, 153, 153f, 157
*Homo floresiensis,* 162f, 162–163
homogamy, 385
homogenization of religion, 412
*Homo habilis,* 146
*H. erectus* compared, 149–151
*H. rudolfensis* compared, 149, 149f
origin of, 142–143
skull of, 150f, 163
toolmaking by, 144
*Homo heidelbergensis,* 157f, 157–158, 158f
homologies
mammals, 110t, 110–111
in taxonomies, 111t, 111–112, 112f
homophobia, 21
*Homo rudolfensis,* 149, 149f
*Homo sapiens*
archaic, 155–158, 156t, 156f, 169f
language and adaptation, 257
modern (*See* anatomically modern humans)
*Homo sapiens neanderthalensis.*
*See* Neandertals
homosexuality, 355–357
homozygous traits, 81, 81f, 87, 91
H1N1 virus, 86–87, 87f
Hong Kong, 12–13
"honorary men," 354
honorifics, 264
hoodia plant, 34f
Hopi Indians, 70, 391, 391f
Hopi language, 260
horse thievery, 312
horticulturalists, 322
horticulture, 300, 300f, 302, 315
Hostalets de Pierola site, 125
host countries, 69, 239
*Hotel Rwanda* (film), 451
household income
homogamy and, 385
by household type, 350t, 350–351
income gap, 447, 447t
of minority groups, 277–278
*How to Think Like a Neanderthal* (Wynn), 161
Huang He (Yellow) River, 219f, 220
hugging, 4f, 4–5
human diversity, 2–5, 94–106
adaptation, variation, and change, 3–5
biological, 78, 79
biological adaptation and (*See* biological adaptation)
cultural differences, 4f, 4–5
race (*See* race)
human ecology, 9

Humane Society of the United States, 32
human evolution, 9
human genetics, 9
human immunodeficiency virus (HIV), 50, 50f, 104–105, 469
humanistic science, 11
humanities, 11
*Human Nature* (journal), 71
"human nature," 24
human rights, 30–31, 34, 34f
humans. *See also* anatomically modern humans
biological diversity of, 78, 79
capacity for learning, 22
cave art by, 165f, 170, 175–177, 176f, 184, 421
differences from nonhuman primates, 26–27
place among primates, 110t, 110f, 110–111
similarity to apes, 25, 37
spread to Americas, 178–180, 179f, 180f
spread to Australia, 177f, 177–178, 178f, 184, 450
spread to Pacific, 180–183, 181f–183f
traits shared with nonhuman primates, 26, 26f, 27f
Human Terrain System (HTS) program, 239–240, 240f
Human Terrain Teams, 44
Humboldt's woolly monkey, 114f
hunter-gatherers. *See* foragers
hunting
of apes, 116
of bison, 324–325, 325f
by chimpanzees, 26
cooperative, 153–154, 369
of marine animals, 178–179
Mesolithic period, 188
reenaction of, 176
significance of, 150f, 150–151
techniques of foragers, 298
hunting and gathering. *See* foraging
husks of plants, 192, 192f
Hutu people, 451
hybrid forms, 80
hydraulic systems, 209
hyperrobust australopithecines, 139, 142
hypodescent, 280–281, 281f, 285, 293–294
hypotheses, 14, 16
hypoxia, acute, 102

**I**

Ibirama, 336–337, 429
IBM, 53
Ice Age (Pleistocene), 156–157, 175, 184
ice shield, 200
ID (intelligent design), 78f, 79
Idea Couture, 39f
ideal culture, 29
ideal types, 327
*Identical Strangers: A Memoir of Twins separated and Reunited* (Bernstein & Schein), 85f
identical twins, 84, 85f
"I Dreamed a Dream" (song), 471

IE (Indo-European) languages, 269–270
Igbo people, 105, 393
Igbo Women's War, 335–336, 336f, 339
market women of, 387f, 388
illness, 49. *See also* disease; infectious diseases
culturally specific syndromes, 12
as emic perception of bad health, 236
ILO (International Labor Organization), 474
Ilongot people, 342–343, 343f
*I Love Lucy* (TV series), 417
*il-rah,* 326
imagined communities, 286
IMF (International Monetary Fund), 35, 36, 453, 462–463
imitative magic, 401, 401f
immigration
to core nations, 441
"cultural generation gap" and, 289, 289f
of nuclear families, 367
imperialism, 449, 459
"improved corn," 454–455
Incas, 105
incest
avoidance of, 384, 384f, 395
exogamy and, 380–381, 381f, 382f
social construction of, 380, 381–384, 384f
inclusive fitness, 120–121
income. *See* household income
increased equity, 43
*Independence Day* (film), 462
independent assortment, 82, 83, 84, 91
independent invention, 34
India
caste system in, 362–363, 385, 385f
family planning in, 430, 431
Hijras, 354, 354f
"ladies only" facilities, 348
linguistic diversity in, 262–263, 263f
sacred cattle, 404f, 404–405
skin color in, 96, 96f
smallpox in, 103–104
violence against women in, 348, 348f
indigenization, 244
in cultural domains, 472, 472f, 476
reindigenization, 475
of religion, 412
indigenous peoples
disease and mortality rates, 49–51
effects of conservation schemes on, 467–468, 468f
effects of industrialization on, 463
ethnic identity of, 474–475, 475f, 476
Indigenous People's Global Summit on Climate Change, 475f
indigenous rights movement, 475
indigenous social models, 46–47
*indios,* 284
indirect diffusion, 34
indirect rule, 451
individual, culture and, 29–34, 246–247
individual fitness, 120
individualism, 21, 406–407

Klinefelter's syndrome, 354
knuckle-walking, 116, 125
Kob site, 59f
Kokiselei site, 150
Koko (gorilla), 256
Koobi Fora site, 149
Korea, 286
Koreans, 290–291
*koro*, 12
Koro language, 281f
Kraft Foods, 39f
Kroeber, Alfred, 246–247
Kuikuru people, 300, 302
Kurds, 285, 286, 290
kurgans (Scythian tombs), 200
Kuria people, 312
Kutse San people, 320
Kwabe site, 158f, 159
Kwakiutl tribe, 242, 242f, 313, 313f, 314
kwashiorkor, 15–16, 16f

**L**

labor. *See also* division of labor; work
    in agriculture, 301
    as factor of production, 305
    industrial workers, 306, 306f
labor unions
    collective bargaining by, 448
    trade unions, 446
La Chapelle-aux-Saints site,
        148, 160, 160f
lactose tolerance, 105–106
"ladies only" facilities, 348
Laetoli site, 135, 136
laissez-faire economics, 453
Lake Mungo site, 177f, 178, 178f
Lake Turkana site, 134, 142, 149
Lakher people, 381, 382f
land, 191, 209–210, 210f, 305
land bridges, 177, 184
landmasses, 122f
language. *See also* linguistic
        anthropology; *specific languages*
    biological origin of, 257
    cultural and historical aspects of,
        271–272
    cultural transmission of, 256
    development of, 259
    ethnic diversity and, 262–264
    focal vocabulary, 260–261, 261t, 261f
    historical linguistics, 269–272,
        270f, 271f
    learning, in ethnography, 231
    meaning in, 261
    nature of, 254–255
    of Neanderthal, 161
    pidgin and Creole, 34, 259, 268
    protolanguages, 269, 270–271, 273
    Sapir-Whorf hypothesis of,
        259–260, 260f
    sign language, 255–257, 256f
    sociolinguistics (*See* sociolinguistics)
    stratification and, 264–267, 265t, 267f
    structure of, 258–259
    symbolic, 22
    thought and culture related to, 259–260,
        260f, 261

language loss, 271f, 272, 273
Lantian site, 154f, 155
Lapita people, 180–182, 184
Lapita pottery, 180–181, 181f, 182, 184
La Raza, National Council of, 281–282
Lascaux Cave, 170, 175–177, 176f
latent function of customs, 385, 386
"A Latina Judge's Voice" (Sotomayor),
        279–280
Latin America, 47, 285, 474–475
Latinos, 277, 277t
law (legal code), 321
law enforcement, 329, 330, 348
law of independent assortment, 82, 83,
        84, 91
law of supply and demand, 310
laws, scientific, 15
lawsuits, 69–70
LDCs (less-developed countries), 46
Leach, Edmund, 249
*League of the Ho-dé-no-sau-nee or
    Iroquois* (Morgan), 241
learning
    adaptation through, 129–130
    capacity for, 22, 25
    by chimpanzees, 255, 256, 257
    cultural, 22, 36–37
    cultural transmission by, 3
    from grandparents, 172
    social learning, 383
lemurs, 111t, 113, 113f, 122, 123f, 125
Lenca people, 475f
Lesbian, Gay, Bisexual, and Transgender
        (LGBT) community, 355
lesbian and gay rights movement, 355
*Les Misérables* (play), 425
less-developed countries (LDCs), 46, 48
Levallois toolmaking technique,
        159, 160f, 161
levirate marriage, 390, 390f, 391
Lévi-Strauss, Claude, 248
lexicon, 258, 260, 272
LGBT (Lesbian, Gay, Bisexual, and
        Transgender) community, 355
"liberalism," 453
*Life at Home in the Twenty-First Century:
    32 Families Open Their Doors*
        (Arnold et al.), 368, 368f
life-cycle events, 28, 28f, 371
life histories, 231, 234, 251
lifespan, 172
limb proportions, 115f, 138f, 150
liminality, 402–403, 403t
lineages, 370, 376
lineal kinship terminology, 374, 374f,
        376t, 377
lineal relatives, 374, 374f
linguistic anthropology, 6, 10–11, 19, 41,
        242, 254, 272
linguistic diversity, 262–264
linguistic relativity, 263–264, 267
LinkedIn, 431, 432
Linnaean Society, 77
liver flukes (bilharzia), 49–50, 51f
Living Tongues Institute for Endangered
        Languages, 271f
llamas, 196f, 197, 205

lobola customs, 388, 389, 390, 391
local autonomy, 467–468, 468f
local culture, 412
local descent group, 370
locally based demand, 40
London, England
    Great Plague of 1665–1666, 104–105
    Summer Olympics (2012), 416f,
        433–434
longitudinal research
    in cultural anthropology, 231, 235f,
        235–236, 236f, 251
    on foraging bands, 320
    Internet & American Life Project,
        431–432
Longlin Cave site, 169
*The Lord of the Rings* (Tolkien), 237
lorises, 111t
Louisiana Territory, 450
Lovedu people, 387f, 388
Lucy (chimp), 255, 256
"Lucy." *See Australopithecus afarensis*
"Lucy's Baby," 135
Lyme disease, 469

**M**

Maasai Women for Education and
        Economic Development, 475f
Maba site, 158f, 159
macaques, 26, 114–115
Machu Picchu, 69, 200, 201f
macroevolution, 90, 91
Madagascar, 46–47, 122, 393, 440
    Betsileo people of (*See* Betsileo people)
    effects of environmentalism on,
        467–468, 468f
    foraging groups in, 297, 298f
    nonverbal communication in, 257
    "soul loss," 12, 51
    stratification in, 328
magic, belief in, 401, 401f, 409, 415
*mahu*, 355
maize (corn), 59f
    domestication of, 197, 198, 198f,
        199, 205
    Mexican polyculture, 454f, 454–455
majority groups, 277–278
Makah Indians, 32–33, 33f
Makua people, 334f, 334–335, 335f, 371
maladaptivity of culture, 25
Malagasy people, 46–47
malaria, 88, 88f. *See also* sickle-cell
        anemia
    adaptation to malarial environments,
        101
    spread to Europeans, 105, 106
Malaysia, 306–308, 333, 469
*mal de ojo* ("evil eye"), 12
Malinowski, Bronislaw, 243, 243f, 246
malnutrition, 226
Maludong Cave site, 169–170
mammals, 110t, 110–111
*mana*, 385, 400–401
Manchester school, 244, 244f, 247, 250t
mandrills, 115f
Manggarai people, 163
manifest functions, 385

manioc (cassava), 59f, 197, 197f, 205, 302
Manis Site, 179
"manly hearted woman," 387
man-made disasters, 8
manual dexterity, 112
Maori people, 182f, 328f
Mardi Gras, 333
marginal areas, 191
Marine Mammal Protection Act of 1972, 32–33
mariners, 178, 194
marketing, 53, 346f
market principle, 310, 312, 315
market women, 387f, 388
marriage, 27, 378–395. *See also* family(ies)
  age at marriage, 350, 366, 392
  arranged marriages, 388
  defined, 379–380
  divorce and, 391–392, 391f, 392t
  economic importance of, 296
  employment of married women, 349, 349t
  endogamy and, 384–386
  extramarital sex, 345t, 345–346
  gifts at marriage, 388f, 388–390, 389f, 390f
  as group alliance, 388–391
  incest and (*See* incest)
  in kin-based societies, 234
  online marriage market, 381f, 393–395, 394t
  plural marriage (*See* plural marriage)
  rates of, 367
  rights allocated by, 386–388
  same-sex marriage, 386f, 386–388, 387f, 395
  sibling marriage, 382, 384f, 385–386
  sororate and levirate, 390, 390f, 391
"marriage market," 393
Marx, Karl, 445f, 445–446, 448, 459
Masai (Maasai) people, 325, 325f, 475f
*M\*A\*S\*H* (TV series), 417
mass extinctions, 90
mass media. *See* media
matai system, 48
mater, 386
maternal care, 121, 126
mating, 27
matriarchies, 347, 347f
matrilateral skewing, 373
matrilineal descent rule, 369, 369f
matrilineal extended families, 362–363, 363f
matrilineal-matrilocal societies, 347, 347f, 359
matrilineal moieties, 381, 381f
matrilineal societies, 243
  cross cousins in, 380, 381f
  divorce in, 391, 391f
  kinship terminology, 374, 374f, 375
  sororate marriage in, 390, 390f
matrilocality, 347, 370
Mauer site, 157
Max Planck Institute for Evolutionary Anthropology, 67, 159, 383

Maya civilization, 226f, 226–227
Mbuti people, 297, 299, 312, 343
McDonald's, 53, 187, 472f
"Me, My Spouse, and the Internet" project, 394t, 394–395
Mead, Margaret, 244, 245f
meaning, 261, 429
means of production, 305
*Medea* (play), 429f
media. *See also* television
  anthropological blogs, 54
  commercialization of art, 423, 437–438
  globalization and, 35, 35f, 472
  interethnic contact and, 472
  political role of, 331
  in popular culture, 429–430
  role in sports, 417, 433, 434
  study of effects in Brazil, 17f, 17–18
mediation, 322
medical anthropology, 40, 49–52, 51f, 52f, 55
Mediterranean, 194
meiosis, 83, 83f
Melanesia
  belief in *mana*, 399
  cargo cults of, 407f, 408f, 408–409
  Lapita potsherds, 180–181, 181f, 183
Melanesian people, 162, 178, 183, 183f, 184
melanin, 98
men
  communication styles of, 257f, 257–258
  gender speech contrasts, 264, 264t
  male role among Inuit, 322
Mendel, Gregor, 78, 80f, 80–82, 90, 91
Mendelian genetics, 78, 80–82, 81f, 82f, 91
Mende people, 325
Merina state, 46–47, 393
Meroe, 200–201
Mesa Verde National Park, 10f
Mesoamerica
  chiefdoms in, 215, 216, 216f, 221f, 221–223
  collapse of Maya civilization, 226f, 226–227
  food production in, 197
  primary states in, 209
  state formation in, 221f, 221–226
  Valley of Mexico states, 221f, 225f, 225–226
  Zapotec state, 224f, 224–225
Mesolithic period, 188f, 188–189
Mesopotamia
  cities of, 213f, 213–214
  economy of, 218–219, 227
  origins of writing in, 217–218, 218f
  primary states in, 209, 213f, 213–219
Mesozoic era, 121, 122, 122f
*mestizos,* 475
metallurgy, 218, 220
methane, 465f, 466t
Mexican highlands, 198–199, 199f
Miao people, 389f
microenculturation, 52
microevolution, 90, 91

microliths, 188, 188f, 205
Microsoft, 262, 263
middle class, 447
Middle East
  early food production in, 189–193, 190t, 190f, 205, 297
  ethnic structure of countries in, 285
  social media in, 473
  spread of food production from, 193–196
  state formation in, 213–219, 227
midwives, 233
migrations
  globalization and, 175, 462, 473–474, 474f
  of *Homo erectus,* 151f, 151–155
  multiculturalism and, 287, 288f
military, 240, 330. *See also* warfare
millet cultivation, 195, 195f, 196
Minangkabau people, 347, 347f
Mindel glacial period, 158
minimal pairs (phonemes), 258
mining, 456–457, 457f
minority groups, 277–278, 436
Miocene epoch, 121, 121f, 122, 126
  apes of, 124, 124f
  appearance of humans in, 130
Miocene hominoids
  later Miocene apes, 124f, 124–125, 125f
  *Pierolapithecus catalaunicus,* 124–125, 125f
missionaries, Christian, 313
*mission civilisatrice,* 451, 453
mitochondrial DNA (mtDNA)
  of AMHs, 168
  of Neandertals, 159
  phylogenetic tree based on, 97, 175, 178
mitosis, 83
mixed countries, 452, 453f
modern humans. *See* humans
"modern synthesis," 89–90, 91
modern world system. *See* world system
modes of production, 304–308
  factors of production, 305
  industrial economies, 305–308, 306f
  in nonindustrial societies, 304–305, 305f
Mohenjo-daro, 194–195
moiety organization, 381
molecular anthropology, 66, 68
molecular genetics. *See* biochemical genetics
monkeys, 113–115, 114f. *See also specific species*
  call systems of, 255
  New World monkeys, 114, 114f
  Old World monkeys, 114f, 114–115
monocrop production, 442–443
monoculture, 454
monotheism, 400, 406
Monte Albán, 223, 224f, 224–225, 227
Monte Verde site, 179
monumental architecture, 212, 212f, 223, 224, 224f
monument building, 212, 212f, 327f
moral codes, 405–406, 410–411
morphemes, 258

morphology, 258
mosques, 413
mountain gorillas, 118, 118f
Mousterian toolmaking, 159f,
    159–160, 174
*movimento*, 48
moxibustion, 52f
mpakafo (Malagasy vampire), 308
mtDNA. *See* mitochondrial DNA
multiculturalism, 287, 293t, 294
multidisciplinary approaches, 59f, 59–61,
    60f, 72
multifactorial traits, 90
multilinear evolution, 245
multinational corporations, 36, 455,
    456–457, 457f
"multiplaced" people, 36
"multiracial" classification, 281f, 281–282
Mundugumor people, 342
Munjika people, 171f
muriqui (woolly spider monkey), 114f
Musawwarat es-Sufra, 200–201
museums
    lawsuits against, 69–70
    placement of art in, 424, 424f, 437
music, 428, 428f
    as communication, 424
    ethnomusicology, 11, 422f,
        422–423, 423f
    Navajo music, 425, 425f, 428
    religious, 418
Muslims, 290, 362
mutations, 82, 84
    incest and, 384, 384f
    linguistic abilities and, 257
Mwenemutapa empire, 220
m.y.a., 121
*My Fair Lady* (film), 265f
*Myst Online: Uru Live* (online game), 237
myth(s)
    comparison of, 425, 426–427, 427t
    "noble savage" myth, 442f, 442–443
"mythemes," 248
"myth of primitive isolate," 183

## N

NAACP (National Association for the
    Advancement of Colored People),
    281–282
Nabta Playa basin, 193–194
NAFTA (North American Free Trade
    Agreement), 454f, 454–455, 460
NAGPRA (Native American Graves
    Protection and Repatriation
    Act), 70
Nariokotome boy, 155
NASA (National Aeronautics and Space
    Administration), 463
Natchez people, 215–216
National Aeronautics and Space
    Administration (NASA), 463
National Association for the
    Advancement of Colored People
    (NAACP), 281–282
national culture(s), 21, 29, 30t
national development, 47
National Endowment for the Arts, 424

nationalism, 286
nationalities, 286
National Oceanic and Atmospheric
    Administration (NOAA), 32, 33
National Organization for Women
    (NOW), 349
nations, 285–286, 294
nation-states, 285–286
    foragers in, 297
    in former Soviet Union, 293
    of pastoralists, 325–326, 326f
    "permanent liminal groups" in, 403
    professional priesthoods in, 406
    rent funds, 310, 315
Native American Graves Protection and
    Repatriation Act (NAGPRA), 70
Native Americans, 6, 6f, 66, 94, 96. *See
    also* Plains Indians; *specific tribes*
    art forms of, 419
    depopulation of, slave trade and, 105
    faith healers of, 405
    as foragers, 297
    haplogroups, 68
    languages of, 272
    New Age religions and, 409
    "noble savage" myth, 442f, 442–443
    pantribal sodalities of, 324–325
    racial classification as, 281
    ranked societies among, 215
    socially constructed gender among,
        354, 387
    totemism among, 404
    vision quests, 402
Native Australians (aboriginals), 419
    arranged marriages among, 388
    ceremonies of increase, 176
    as foragers, 297
    haplogroup of, 69
    languages of, 272
    music of, 428
    related to Melanesians, 178
    tooth size of, 100–101
    totemism among, 404, 414
native taxonomy, 373
Natufian culture
    food production, 190–191, 199, 205
    settlement of Jericho, 213f, 213–214
natural disasters, 8, 291f, 466
naturalistic disease theories, 51
natural selection, 77–78, 78f, 84–88,
    85f, 91
    changes in tooth size, 151
    directional selection, 85
    as evolutionary mechanism, 77, 87
    sexual selection, 86
    skin color and, 98–100
    stabilizing selection, 86–88, 88f
natural settings, 68–69
natural threats, 24
nature, 24, 404
Navajo tribe, 303, 425, 425f, 428
Nayar (Nair) caste, 27, 362–363
Nazca lines, 60f
Nazi Germany, 279, 279f
Ndembu people, 247, 403
Neandertals, 147f, 156, 159–161,
    163, 169f

AMHs as contemporaries of,
    168–169, 184
AMHs compared to, 160f, 160–161, 169f
cold-adapted, 159f, 159–160, 160f
daily lives of, 161
discovery sites for, 148, 158, 158f,
    160, 160f
Neander Valley, 159
needs functionalism, 243
negative reciprocity, 312
Negeri Sembilan, 347
*négritude* ("black identity"), 286
neoevolutionism, 245f, 245–246, 250t
neoliberalism, 453f, 453–454, 455
Neolithic period, 199–203, 205
    archaeological sites, 66
    economies of, 209
    farming and, 199–203
    farming in, 189, 189f, 193–196, 196t
    spread of food production, 202f,
        202–203, 203f
"Neolithic Revolution," 175, 189, 210
neolocality, 363, 370, 373f
networking, 431–432, 432f
neural tube defects (NTDs), 99t, 100, 100f
New Age movement, 409
New Caledonia, 180, 181f
New Deal, 453
"New Seven Wonders of the World,"
    212, 212f
"newspaper rock," 260f
New World. *See* Americas
New World monkeys, 114, 114f, 123, 126
*New York Times*, 430
New Zealand, 182, 182f
Ngadha people, 163
NGOs (nongovernmental organizations),
    46f, 60
niche specialization, 287
*Nightline* (TV program), 290
Nilote people, 96, 100, 101f
Nim Chimpsky, 257
Nipah virus, 469, 470, 470f
nitrous oxide, 466t
Nittano site, 188
NOAA (National Oceanic and Atmospheric
    Administration), 32, 33
"noble savage" myth, 442f, 442–443
nocturnal life, 113, 113f
nomadism, 303, 303f
nomads, 325–327, 326f
nongovernmental organizations (NGOs),
    46f, 60
nonhuman primates
    birthing process, 58
    call systems of, 255, 255f, 256t, 272
    communication among, 255–257
    differences from humans, 26–27
    linguistic capacities of, 256
    traits shared with humans, 26, 26f, 27f
nonindustrial societies
    concept of scarcity, 308–309, 309f
    kinship and descent in, 376
    modes of production in, 304–305, 305f,
        306, 315
    plural marriage in, 389–390
nonsettler countries, 452

phylum, 110, 110f, 110t
physical anthropology. *See* biological
    anthropology
physiological adaptation, 3t, 3–4,
    102–103, 103f
phytolith ("plant stone"), 59f, 59–60, 198
pidgin languages, 34, 259, 268
piedmont steppes, 191
PIE (proto-Indo-European) languages,
    269–270, 270f
*Pierolapithecus catalaunicus,* 124–125,
    125f, 126
Piltdown man, 64
Pinnacle Point Cave site, 167, 171, 174
pinta, 87
Plains Indians
    bison hunting by, 324–325, 325f
    horse thievery among, 312
    pantribal sodalities of, 324–325, 338
    use of horses, 302–303, 324
*Planet of the Apes* films, 109, 116
planned social change, 55
plantation economies, 249
plants
    domestication of, 186f, 191–193, 192f
    hoodia, 34f
    husks of, 192, 192f
    maize (corn), 59f, 197, 198, 198f, 199,
        205, 454f, 454–455
    manioc (cassava), 59f, 197, 197f,
        205, 302
    microscopic evidence from, 59f, 59–60
    pea plants, 78, 80
    self-pollinating, 199–200
    taxonomy of, 76, 91
platyrrhines (New World monkeys), 111t,
    114, 114f, 126
Pleistocene epoch, 121f, 122, 130,
    156–157
Pliocene epoch, 121, 121f, 122
plural marriage, 379–380, 392–393, 395
    fraternal polyandry, 380, 393
    polyandry, 345, 345t, 390, 393
    polygyny, 345, 345t, 348, 390,
        392–393, 393f
plural societies, 287, 293t, 294
PNG Sustainable Development Program
    Limited, 457
political activism
    "Facebook Revolution," 336–338, 337f
    Igbo Women's War, 335–336,
        336f, 339
    in Japan, 283, 283f
political authority, 318, 338
political economy, 249, 250t
political engagement, 432
political organization, 319, 319f
political polling, 238
political systems, 317–339
    among nomads, 325–327, 326f
    in chiefdoms, 327–329
    fiscal mechanisms of, 330–331
    of foragers, 320–322
    judiciary of, 330, 330f
    law enforcement in, 330
    pantribal sodalities, 324–325, 325f
    political organization, 319, 319f

population control by, 329–330
    social control and, 331, 333–338
    state systems, 329t, 329–331
    types and trends in, 319–320
*Political Systems of Highland Burma*
    (Leach), 249
political use of race, 95
politics, 318, 436
    art and, 424
    exclusion of strangers in, 475
    fundamentalism and, 413
    importance of verbal skill in,
        266–267, 272
    at local level, globalization and,
        332, 332f
    research limited by, 201
    role of media in, 331
    role of polygyny in, 393
polities, 208
polyandry, 345, 345t, 390, 393
polyculture, 454f, 454–455
polydactyly, 384f
polygamy. *See* plural marriage
polygyny, 345, 345t, 348, 390,
    392–393, 393f
Polynesia
    belief in *mana,* 385, 400–401
    chiefdoms of, 327f, 327–328
    colonized by Lapita people,
        180–182, 184
    males behaving as women, 354–355
    nonverbal communication in, 257
    origin of peoples in, 182–183
    skin color in, 95–96, 96f, 182–183,
        183f, 184
    spread of humans to, 182, 184
polytheism, 400, 406
pongids, 111, 112f, 117
popular culture, 24, 429–432
    effects of television on, 430–431, 431f
    media in, 429–430
    networking and sociability,
        431–432, 432f
population(s), 22
population control, 329–330
population displacement, 329–330
population genetics, 78, 84–89, 91
    gene flow, 89, 89f, 91
    natural selection and, 84–88, 85f
    random genetic drift, 89, 91
population increase, 211
    deforestation and, 468, 468f
    industrialization and, 444
    as major global trend, 462
    state formation and, 209–210, 210f
    transnational migration and, 287
Portuguese language, 260
postcolonial studies, 452, 453f
postmarital residence rules, 371f
"postmodern," 474
postmodernism, 250t, 474
postmodernity, 474, 476
postsocialist era, 457–458, 458f
postsocialist societies, 457, 460
potassium-argon (K/A) dating technique,
    65, 65f, 66t, 72
potlatching, 313f, 313–315, 314f, 315

pottery
    Chinese origin of, 188
    of early states, 214
    Halafian, 214
    Jomon culture, 188
    Lapita pottery, 180–181, 181f, 182,
        183, 184
    of Nabta Playa basin, 194
    potsherds, 8–9
poverty
    expanded households and, 364
    feminization of, 350t, 350–351, 351t
power, 318
    language and, 262
    methods of domination, 249, 250t
    prestige distinguished from, 343
    in social stratification, 329, 329t, 338
practice theory, 29, 248–249, 250t
predictive sciences, 211
predictor variables, 14, 16, 238
PREDICT project, 469–470
prehensile tails, 114, 114f
prehistory, 9
prejudice, 290, 291f, 293t
*prelos,* 423
premarital sex, 345t, 345–346
prestige, 329f
    among Inuit, 322
    gender stratification and, 342–343
    in social stratification, 329, 329t, 338
    synonymous with status, 276
*Pride and Prejudice* (Austin), 430
primary groups, 117
primary states, 209
primates, generally, 108–126. *See also*
        nonhuman primates
    apes (*See* apes)
    behavioral ecology and fitness,
        120–121
    chronology of, 121f, 121–122
    of early Cenozoic, 122–123, 123f, 126
    evolution of, 121
    Miocene hominoids, 124f,
        124–125, 125f
    monkeys (*See* monkeys)
    Oligocene anthropoids, 123–124
    place of humans among, 110t, 110f,
        110–111
    prosimians, 113, 113f
    tendencies of, 112–113, 392
primatology, 9, 10, 68–69, 69f, 109
*Primeval Kinship* (Chapais), 383
*Primitive Culture* (Tylor), 21–22, 241
primogeniture, 386
*Principles of Geology* (Lyell), 77
private-public contrast, 346, 349
problem orientation, 231, 234–235
processual approaches, 248–249
*proconsul* species, 124
profane realm, 399
Professional Golfers' Association
    (PGA), 437
profit motive, 309
Program on the Evolution of Human
    Languages, 281
Project Bhasha (Microsoft), 263
Project Minerva (Pentagon), 239

*Project Nim* (film), 257
proletarianization, 446
proletariat (working class), 445
pronunciation, 264–266, 268
prosimians, 111t, 112, 113, 113f, 122, 125
prostitution, 50
*The Protestant Ethic and the Spirit of Capitalism* (Weber), 406
Protestantism, 392, 406–407
    Evangelical Protestantism, 407, 409–412, 411f, 415
    Pentecostalism, 407, 409–412, 411f, 415
protoapes, 124, 126
proto-Indo-European (PIE) languages, 269–270, 270f
protolanguages, 269, 270–271, 273
protomonkeys, 123
pseudo-archaeology, 222–223, 223f
psychological needs, 25, 401, 401f
psychology, 11–13, 13f, 19
public anthropology, 54
public archaeology, 13
public displays of affection (PDAs), 4f, 4–5
public health, 204
publicly traded companies, 446–447
public policy, 319
"public transcripts," 333
punctuated equilibrium model, 90
Punnett squares, 81, 81f
"pygmies," 297, 312
pygmy mouse lemur, 122
Pyramid of the Sun, 225, 225f

**Q**

Qafzeh site, 167, 184
Qashqai people
    nomadism of, 303
    political system of, 326f, 326–327
quadrupedalism, 129
Quaternary period, 121, 121f
Quechua people, 95f
questionnaires, 232–233
Quileute nation, 473
quinine, 105

**R**

race. *See also* ethnic groups; ethnicity
    biological similarities, 95–96
    census classifications, 281f, 281–282, 282f
    as concept, 278–279, 279f
    as discredited concept, 94–97, 95f–97f, 106
    ethnicity compared, 278–280, 280f
    fluidity in Brazil, 283–285, 284f, 285f, 294
    genetic v. phenotypic variation, 96–97
    homogeneity in Japan, 282–283, 283f
    hypodescent, 280–281, 281f
    racial/ethnic identification in U.S., 275, 276t
    social construction of, 278, 280–285, 293–294
*Race, Language, and Culture* (Boas), 242
RACE Are We So Different? program, 97

RACE Project (of AAA), 97
racial classification
    problems with, 94
    skin color used for, 95–96, 95f–97f
    tripartite scheme of, 95–96
    in U.S. census, 281f, 281–282, 282f
racial terms, 280, 284–285
racism, 282–283, 283f
Radcliffe-Brown, Alfred Reginald, 243–244
radiometric dating techniques, 61, 64–65, 65f, 66t, 72
Raelian movement, 409
*The Ra Expeditions* (Heyerdahl), 222
"rafts" of vegetation, 123
random genetic drift, 89, 91
random sample, 238
ranked societies, 215f, 215–217, 216t, 216f, 227
Rapanui (Easter Island), 182, 327f
rapport, establishing, 231
real culture, 29
Recent epoch, 130
recessive traits, 80
reciprocity, 311f, 311–312, 312f, 315
reciprocity continuum, 311
recombination, 82
recordkeeping, 211, 212, 237
Red Deer Cave people, 169–170
Rede Globo network, 472
Red Hot Chili Peppers, 417
redistribution
    in chiefdoms, 311, 327–328
    in exchange, 310–311, 312, 315
refugees
    from climate change, 464–465, 465f
    due to ethnic expulsion, 291, 292f
    economic, due to NAFTA, 454f, 454–455, 460
regional accents. *See* dialects
regional economies, 313–314
Reichstag, 317f
reindeer, 303
reindigenization, 475
relative dating, 64, 64f
religion, 397–415. *See also specific religions*
    adaptation to local culture, 412
    alternative religious movements, 409
    antimodernism, 412–413
    art and, 418f, 418–419, 420
    belief in spiritual beings, 400
    cargo cults, 407f, 407–409, 408f
    cultural globalization and, 409–413
    defined, 398–400
    ecological anthropology and, 404f, 404–405
    emotional needs and, 401–402, 405
    Evangelicals and Pentecostals, 407, 409–412, 411f, 415
    expressions of, 400–404
    fitness industry and, 410–411, 411f
    fundamentalism, 413
    industrialization and, 444
    intelligent design as religious view, 79
    kinds of, 406–407
    magic in, 401, 401f

powers and forces in, 400–401
rites of passage, 402f, 402–404, 403t
ritual in, 402
secular rituals and, 413–414, 414f
social change and, 407–409
social control through, 405f, 405–406
subcultural differences and, 30
totemism, 404
world religion statistics, 407, 407f
*Religion: An Anthropological View* (Wallace), 398
religious conflict, 399
remote sensing, 60f, 60–61
rent fund, 310, 315
replacement fund, 310, 315
reproductive isolation, 139
reproductive strategies, 345, 345t
research methods, 59–63
    excavation, 62f, 62–63, 72
    fossils, 61, 72
    multidisciplinary approaches, 59f, 59–61, 60f, 72
    survey, 61–62, 72
residence rules, 370
resistance to social control
    hegemony and, 331, 333
    Igbo Women's War, 335–336, 336f, 339
    shame and gossip as, 333–335, 334f, 335f
    by social media, 336–338, 337f
    "weapons of the weak," 333
resource(s)
    abundance and shortage, 313–314
    differential access to, 319, 328
    rational allocation of, 308–310
    uneven distribution of, 43, 43f
resource depletion
    due to mining, 456–457, 457f
    energy consumption and, 463, 463t
respondents, 238
revitalization movements, 407f, 407–409, 408f
rhinarium, 123
rice
    cultivation of, 300f, 301, 304–305, 305f
    domestication of, 186f, 195, 196
rickets, 99t, 99–100
*The Rise of Anthropological Theory* (Harris), 246
*Rise of the Planet of the Apes* (film), 116
risk, globalization of, 463
Riss glacial period, 158
rites of intensification, 403–404
rites of passage, 402f, 402–404, 403t
ritual(s)
    in baseball, 398, 399f, 402
    cave painting and, 176
    hugging as, 4f, 4–5
    life-cycle events and, 28, 28f, 371
    ocher burials, 178
    in religion, 402, 415
    sacred and secular, 413–414, 414f
ritual behavior, 402
ritual images, 214
ritual impurity, 385
"ritualized homosexuality," 355, 356–357

ritual kinship, 365
RNA, 82–83
robust australopithecines, 137t., 139–140,
    141f, 142, 143f, 146
Rodentia, 111
Roman Catholicism, 407, 410
    common culture of, 29, 30f
    symbols in, 22–23
romantic love, 388, 388f
Rosie the Riveter, 350, 350f
royal endogamy, 384f, 385–386
Rukwa Rift Basin, 123–124
ruling class, 211
Russia, 456, 457–458, 458f
Rwanda, 451, 474

## S
sacred realm, 399
Sahel, 220–221
*Sahelanthropus tchadensis* ("Toumai"),
    129, 130, 131f, 132, 145
Sahul, 177f, 177–178, 184
Salish tribe, 313, 313f
Samburu people, 98f
same-sex marriage, 386f, 386–388,
    387f, 395
Sami people, 303
sampling, 232, 238
sanctions, 334, 339
Sangiran 17 *(H. erectus)*, 155, 155f
"sanitary citizens," 51–52
San José Mogote, 224
San Martín Tilcajete, 225
San ("Bushmen") of Africa
    band membership among, 299
    foraging by, 297, 298
    generalized reciprocity among,
        311, 311f
    generational terminology, 375
    Ju/'hoansi people, 297, 298, 311,
        311f, 320
    political system of, 320f, 320–321
    relocated by Botswana, 298–299, 299f
    skin color of, 96
Santa Rosa Island, 200
*santeria,* 409
Sapir-Whorf hypothesis, 259–260, 260f
SARS (severe acute respiratory
    syndrome), 469
Sasquatch (Bigfoot), 124
Saudi Arabia, 473
scarcity, 308–309, 309f
schistosomiasis, 49–50, 51f
science, 11, 246
"Science in Anthropology" (Ember and
    Ember), 14
*The Science of Culture* (White), 246
scientific explanations, 78
scientific medicine, 51, 52
scientific method, 13–18, 16t, 19
*A Scientific Theory of Culture and Other
    Essays* (Malinowski), 246
Scythian tombs (kurgans), 200
SE (Standard [American] English),
    258–259, 263, 268–269
sea levels, rising, 175
*Sea Shepherd* (ship), 33f

*Second Life* (online game), 237
sectorial fallowing, 302
sects, 403
secular rituals, 413–414, 414f
sedentism
    among San groups, 320
    development of, 190t, 190–191
    food production and, 199–200, 204
segregation, 283, 290
self-help organizations, 288
Semai people, 311
semantics, 261
semiperiphery, 441, 458, 458f
Seneca tribe, 241
"Sensation" exhibit (Brooklyn
    Museum), 424
Serce Liman Bay, 63f
serial monogamy, 392, 393f
SES (socioeconomic status), 385
settlement hierarchy, 225
settlement patterns, 61
settler countries, 452
"Seven Wonders of the Ancient World," 212
Seven Years' War, 449–450, 459
severe acute respiratory syndrome
    (SARS), 469
*Sex and Temperament in Three Primitive
    Societies* (Mead), 244, 342
sex chromosomes, 83, 83f
sexual behavior, 120, 345t, 345–346,
    357, 386
sexual customs, diet and, 15–16, 16f
sexual dimorphism, 342
    in apes, 117, 118
    in *Au. afarensis,* 136
    in australopithecines, 140
    in chimpanzees, 119
    in *H. erectus,* 150
    in terrestrial primates, 114, 115f, 126
sexually transmitted diseases (STDs)
    AIDS, 50, 50f, 469
    syphilis, 86–87
sexual orientation, 355–358, 358f, 359
sexual selection, 86
sexual taboos, 14, 16
shamans, 51, 308, 321, 406
shame, 333–335, 334f, 335f, 339
Shang dynasty, 219f, 220, 227
Shan sociopolitical organization, 249
shared culture, 23
sheep, 192, 192f, 303, 303f
Sherpas, 103f
shifting cultivation (horticulture), 300,
    300f, 302, 315
Shiite Muslims, 290
shipbuilding, 181, 182, 182f, 183, 343
Shoshoni tribe, 369, 369f
*Shoshonius,* 113f
*Shrek* (film), 423
siamangs, 115, 126
sibling marriage, 382, 384f, 385–386
siblings, 362f
sickle-cell allele, 101, 106
sickle-cell anemia, 75, 84, 87–88, 88f, 91
El Sidrón site, 161
sign language, 255–257, 256f
"silent trade," 312

silverback gorillas, 108, 108f, 119
simultaneity of discovery, 246
single-parent households, 351, 351t,
    366, 367f
*A Singular Woman: The Untold Story
    of Barack Obama's Mother,*
    14–15, 15f
Sistine Chapel, 418f
situational negotiation of social identity,
    275, 276
skeletal (bone) biology, 68, 68f, 72
Skhūl site, 167, 167f, 184
skin cancer, 98–99, 99t
skin color
    as biological adaptation, 98f, 98–100,
        99t, 100f
    origin of Polynesian peoples and,
        182–183, 183f
    used for racial classification, 95–96,
        95f–97f
skulls
    "black skull," 142
    changes in form of, 97
    comparison of, 169f
    early *Homo* specimens, 149, 149f
    from Herto site, 167
    of *Homo erectus,* 152, 152f, 153, 169f
    human v. chimpanzee, 139f
    from Skhūl site, 167, 167f, 184
    stronger, natural selection and, 151
slash-and-burn horticulture, 300, 300f
slavery
    in Brazil, 283, 285
    plantation economies, 249, 442–443
    resistance to, 333
smallpox, 102–104, 104f
smell to sight shift, 112
smelting, 218
*Smilodectes,* 123f
*Smithsonian* magazine, 140
*Snow White* (film), 423
SNSs (social networking sites),
    431, 438
soccer (football)
    civil unrest over, 336
    global interest in, 8
    World Cup, 8, 29, 414, 430, 433
sociability, 431–432, 432f
social anthropology. *See* cultural
    anthropology
"social cement," 430
social change, 55, 222, 407–409
social classes, 212, 264, 272, 384
social complexity, 61–62, 194
social construction
    of gender, 353f, 353–355, 354f
    of incest, 380, 381–384, 384f
    of kinship, 361, 372–373, 380
    of religion, 399–400
social construction of race, 278, 280–285,
    293–294
    in Brazil, 283–285, 284f, 285f, 294
    hypodescent in U.S., 280–281, 281f
    in Japan, 282–283, 283f
    in U.S. census, 281f, 281–282, 282f
social contact, 58
social contract, 332

status in matriarchal societies, 347
violence against, 348, 348f
women's sports, 6–7, 7f
women in workforce, 296
effects on family, 366
female factory workers, 306f, 306–308
happiness and, 351, 351t, 353, 353f
industrial societies, 349, 349t, 350f
market women, 387f, 388
in trade, 346f
women's groups, 351
women's movement, 349
Wonderwerk Cave site, 153–154
Woods, Eldrick ("Tiger"), 436–437
woolly mammoth, 180f
woolly spider monkey (muriqui), 114f
word order (syntax), 258, 271, 271f
work
attitudes toward, 24, 24f
happiness and, 351, 351t, 353, 353f
industrial workers, 306, 306f
pursuit of, industrialization and, 448
by women (*See* women in workforce)
working class (proletariat), 445
Working Group on Indigenous
Populations (WGIP) of UN, 474
World Bank, 35, 36, 40, 453, 455, 462–463
World Conference of Indigenous
Peoples, 474
World Cup (FIFA), 8, 29, 414, 430, 433
World Economic Forum, 352, 352f

world events, 8
World fusion (music), 422
*World of Warcraft* (online game), 237
world religion statistics, 407, 407f
World Series (baseball), 8
world stratification system, 449
world system, 440
emergence of, 441–443
industrialization and, 443–444, 444f
"Second World" (*See* Soviet Union
[former])
world-system theory, 249, 250t, 441, 459
World Trade Organization (WTO), 35,
331, 462–463
World War II
Nazi Germany, 279, 279f
Rosie the Riveter, 350, 350f
study of Japanese and German culture,
41–42
*World War Z* (film), 105
writing. *See also* language
cuneiform, 218, 218f
origins of, 217–218, 218f
for recordkeeping, 211, 212
WTO (World Trade Organization), 35,
331, 462–463
Würm glacial period, 157, 159, 168, 174

**X**

X chromosome, 341
Xerox, 53

**Y**

Yanadi people, 298
Yanomami people, 305, 306f
kinship in, 380, 380f, 382
village headman of, 322–323
warfare waged by, 347
yaws, 86, 87
Y chromosome, 341
yeti, 124
yoga, 410–411, 411f
Yonggom people, 456
Yoruba people, 105, 418
"Yoruba religion," 409

**Z**

*zadruga*, 362, 364
Zapotec state, 223, 224f, 224–225
Zhoukoudian cave site, 154, 154f, 155
ziggurat, 219f
zoological taxonomy
homologies and analogies in, 111t,
111–112, 112f
place of humans in, 110t, 110f,
110–111
*Zoonomia* (E. Darwin), 77
zoonotic diseases, 469–470, 470f
"Zuni man-woman," 354
zygote, 83

# Important Theories

*Anthropology: Appreciating Human Diversity* provides comprehensive coverage of the major theoretical perspectives at the core of anthropological study. The list below indicates specific text chapters in which these concepts are discussed.

## GENERAL APPROACHES

Adaptation: *1, 2, 3, 5, 6, 7, 8, 9, 10, 15, 16, 17, 18, 19, 20, 21, 22, 23, 24*

Biocultural approaches: *1, 3, 5, 6, 7, 8, 9, 10, 16, 20, 21, 22, 23, 24*

Comparative approaches: *1, 2, 6, 7, 11, 12, 13, 15, 16, 17, 18, 19, 20, 21, 22, 23, 24*
  *Classification and typologies: 2, 6, 7, 8, 9, 10, 11, 12, 13, 16, 17, 18, 19, 20, 21, 22, 23, 24*
  *Systemic cross-cultural comparison: 2, 13, 18, 21, 22, 23*

Ethnography: *1, 2, 3, 13, 16, 17, 18, 19, 20, 21, 22, 23, 24*
  *Emic and etic approaches: 2, 3, 13, 16, 19, 21, 22, 23, 24*
  *Longitudinal and multi-sited approaches: 2, 13, 17, 18, 24*
  *Quantitative and qualitative approaches: 2, 13, 18, 21, 22*

Ethnological theory: *1, 2, 3, 13, 15, 18, 19, 20, 21, 22, 23, 24*

Evolutionary theory: *5, 6, 7, 8, 9, 10, 11, 12, 13, 16, 17, 21, 22, 23, 24*

Explanation: *1, 2, 3, 5, 6, 7, 8, 9, 10, 11, 12, 13, 15, 16, 17, 18, 19, 20, 21, 22, 23, 24*

Holism: *1, 3, 16, 22*

Scientific theory: *1, 2, 3, 5, 7, 8, 9, 10, 11, 12, 13, 16, 17, 18, 20, 21, 22, 23, 24*

Social theory: *1, 2, 3, 13, 21, 22, 23, 24*

## SPECIFIC APPROACHES

Colonialism and postcolonial studies: *2, 13, 15, 17, 21, 23, 24*

Configurationalism/cultural patterning: *2, 13, 16, 17, 21, 22, 23, 24*

Cultural studies and postmodernism: *24*

Ecological anthropology: *16, 17, 18, 21, 22, 23, 24*

Feminist theory: *3, 13, 18, 23*

Functional approaches: *13, 16, 17, 18, 19, 20, 21, 22, 23, 24*

Humanistic approaches: *1, 2, 13, 21, 22, 23, 24*

Integration and patterning: *2, 3, 13, 15, 17, 21, 22, 23, 24*

Interpretive approaches: *2, 13, 17, 21, 22, 24*

Political-economy and world-system approaches: *2, 3, 13, 15, 16, 17, 18, 21, 23, 24*

Political/legal anthropology and power: *2, 3, 12, 13, 15, 17, 18, 20, 21, 22, 23, 24*
  *Conflict: 3, 13, 15, 16, 17, 18, 21, 23, 24*
  *Rise and fall of state, theories for: 12, 16, 23*
  *Social control: 17, 21, 23, 24*

Practice theory: *2, 8, 13, 23, 24*
  *Culture as contested: 2, 3, 13, 15, 18, 21, 23, 24*
  *Public and private culture: 2, 17, 21, 22, 23, 24*
  *Resistance: 2, 3, 15, 17, 21, 23, 24*

Psychological approaches: *13, 16, 17, 21, 22, 23, 24*

Symbolic approaches: *2, 12, 13, 18, 21, 22, 24*

Systemic approaches: *2, 3, 11, 12, 13, 16, 17, 18, 19, 21, 23, 24*

Theories of social construction: *2, 6, 15, 18, 19, 20, 21, 22, 23, 24*
  *Identities: 15, 17, 18, 19, 20, 21, 22, 23, 24*
  *Native theories (folk classification): 2, 3, 13, 15, 17, 18, 19, 20, 21, 22*
  *Race and ethnicity: 2, 15, 17, 19, 21, 22, 23, 24*
  *Social status: 2, 15, 16, 17, 18, 19, 20, 21, 22, 23, 24*